to say our recieved canon
of scriptures is "the
only word of God," is
to be highly presumptious
— and possibility be putting
words into Gods mouth,
how revolting that would
be — a real herisy.
Jw

"ALL SCRIPTURES IS INSPIRED
BY GOD which is useful
for teaching..." 2 TIM 3:16

Careful we don't eliminate
real scripture! That is, that
which is God breathed.
Jw

THE
CANON
DEBATE

THE
CANON
DEBATE

LEE MARTIN McDONALD
JAMES A. SANDERS
EDITORS

HENDRICKSON
PUBLISHERS

Hendrickson Publishers, Inc.
P.O. Box 3473
Peabody, Massachusetts 01961–3473

Printed in the United States of America

Second printing — June 2004

Library of Congress Cataloging-in-Publication Data

The canon debate : on the origins and formation of the Bible   /   edited by
  Lee Martin McDonald and James A. Sanders.
      p. cm.
    Includes bibliographical references and index.
    ISBN 1–56563–517–5 (hardcover : alk. paper) ⋎
    1. Bible—Canon.   I. McDonald, Lee Martin, 1942–   II. Sanders, James A., 1927–
BS465 C335 2002
220.1′2—dc21
                                        2002015966

Contents

Part Three: The New/Second Testament Canon

Appendixes

Contributors

William Adler is professor of early Christianity and Judaism in the Department of Philosophy and Religion, North Carolina State University, Raleigh, North Carolina.

Peter Balla is professor of New Testament studies at the Faculty of Theology, Károli Gáspár Reformed University, Budapest.

John Barton is Oriel and Laing Professor of the Interpretation of Holy Scripture in the University of Oxford.

Joseph Blenkinsopp is John A. O'Brien Professor of Old Testament Studies emeritus at the University of Notre Dame, Indiana.

François Bovon is Frothingham Professor of the History of Religion at Harvard University, Cambridge, Massachusetts.

Kent D. Clarke is associate professor of New Testament at Trinity Western University, Langley, British Columbia.

Philip R. Davies is professor of biblical studies at the University of Sheffield and editorial director of Sheffield Academic Press.

James D. G. Dunn is Lightfoot Professor of Divinity in the University of Durham.

Eldon Jay Epp is Harkness Professor of Biblical Literature emeritus and Dean of Humanities and Social Sciences emeritus at Case Western Reserve University, Cleveland, Ohio, and currently resides in Lexington, Massachusetts.

Craig A. Evans is Payzant Distinguished Professor of New Testament at Acadia Divinity College, Wolfville, Nova Scotia.

The late **William R. Farmer** was professor of New Testament at the University of Dallas, Irving, Texas.

Everett Ferguson is distinguished scholar in residence at Abilene Christian University, Abilene, Texas.

Robert W. Funk is director of the Westar Institute in Santa Rosa, California.

Harry Y. Gamble is professor of religious studies and chair of the Department of Religious Studies at the University of Virginia, Charlottesville, Virginia.

Geoffrey Mark Hahneman is an Episcopal priest currently serving as interim rector at St. Andrew's Church, New London, New Hampshire.

Daniel J. Harrington, S.J., is professor of New Testament at Weston Jesuit School of Theology, Cambridge, Massachusetts.

Everett R. Kalin is professor emeritus of New Testament at Pacific Lutheran Theological Seminary, Berkeley, California.

Robert A. Kraft is the Moritz and Josephine Berg Professor in Religious Studies (early Judaism, early Christianity) at the University of Pennsylvania in Philadelphia, Pennsylvania.

Jack P. Lewis is professor emeritus of Bible at Harding University Graduate School of Bible and Religion, Memphis, Tennessee.

Jack N. Lightstone is professor of religion, provost, and vice-rector for research at Concordia University, Montreal, Quebec.

Steve Mason is professor of humanities (classics, religious studies, and graduate history) at York University, Toronto, Ontario.

Lee Martin McDonald is principal and professor of biblical studies at Acadia Divinity College, Acadia University, Wolfville, Nova Scotia.

Pheme Perkins is professor of New Testament at Boston College, Boston, Massachusetts.

James A. Sanders is president of the Ancient Biblical Manuscript Center and professor emeritus of biblical studies at the Claremont School of Theology and the Claremont Graduate University, Claremont, California.

Daryl D. Schmidt is professor of religion and chair of the Department of Religion at Texas Christian University, Fort Worth, Texas.

Albert C. Sundberg Jr. is professor emeritus of New Testament interpretation at Garrett-Evangelical Theological Seminary, Evanston, Illinois.

Emanuel Tov is J. L. Magnes Professor of Bible at the Hebrew University, Jerusalem.

Julio C. Trebolle Barrera is professor in the Department of Hebrew and Aramaic Studies at the Complutensian University, Madrid.

Eugene Ulrich is John A. O'Brien Professor of Hebrew Scriptures at the University of Notre Dame, Notre Dame, Indiana.

James C. VanderKam is John A. O'Brien Professor of Hebrew Scriptures at the University of Notre Dame, Notre Dame, Indiana.

Robert W. Wall is professor of the Christian Scriptures at Seattle Pacific University, Seattle, Washington.

Part One

Introduction

Introduction

Lee Martin McDonald and James A. Sanders

In the last forty years interest has been growing not only in the origins of the biblical canon but also in its development, continuing viability, and future as a fixed collection of sacred writings. Despite the stability of the various biblical canons over the last four hundred years, the twentieth century brought significantly increased interest in canon formation. Much of this interest began with the earlier works of H. E. Ryle, Alexander Souter, Heinrich Graetz, Moses Stuart, and Edward Reuss. A brief look at the variety as well as volume of recent literature in this field in the Select Bibliography at the end of this volume will illustrate this growing interest. More than a generation ago, Kurt Aland raised the question of reducing the biblical canon by omitting works that some scholars consider to be an embarrassment to the majority of the church, for example, the apocalyptic literature of the New Testament (2 Peter, Revelation, etc.) in order to promote Christian unity.[1] Not long after that Ernst Käsemann also asked whether there should be a "canon within the canon"—in essence, a reduction of the biblical text—in order to alleviate concerns over the diversity within the Bible.[2] James Sanders and Brevard Childs, for quite different reasons, in 1972 introduced "canonical criticism" or "canonical context" as distinct alternatives to the biblical theology movement.[3] More recently, some members of the Jesus Seminar have advocated both reducing the current biblical canon (especially eliminating the apocalyptic literature) and expanding the biblical canon to include such writings as the *Gospel of Thomas,* the *Gospel of Mary,* and the "Unknown Gospel" of the Egerton Papyri.[4] Robert Funk of the Jesus Seminar will address that issue and others below. Bruce

---

[1] Kurt Aland, *The Problem of the New Testament Canon* (London: Mowbray, 1962), 28–33.

[2] Ernst Käsemann, "The Canon of the New Testament Church and the Unity of the Church," *Essays on New Testament Themes* (London: SCM, 1968), 95–107. J. D. G. Dunn (*The Living Word* [Philadelphia: Fortress, 1987], 141–42, 161–74) also discusses the notion of a canon within the canon, albeit in a different sense, and, after describing four levels of canonical activity or four ways to view the canon, he concludes that the most important level of authority for exegesis and faith is the level of "final composition" (ibid., 172). See also his chapter in this volume.

[3] See J. A. Sanders, *Torah and Canon* (1972) and B. Childs, *Biblical Theology in Crisis* (1972).

[4] Jeffrey L. Sheler, "Cutting Loose the Holy Canon: A Controversial Re-examination of the Bible," *U.S. News & World Report* 15, no. 18 (Nov. 8, 1993): 75. The Jesus Seminar has recently created a "Canon Seminar" which hopes to create a "Scholar's Canon" that will, among other things, eliminate the book of Revelation and include the *Gospel of Thomas.* See also a new article by Kim Sue Lia Perkes, "Scripture Revision Won't Be a Bible," *Arizona Republic* (Sunday, Oct. 24, 1993, B1 and B4). See Jacob Milgrom, "An Amputated Bible, Peradventure?" *BR* 10, no. 4 (August 1994): 17,

Metzger contends that although in principle the Bible canon may be changed, in all practi-
cality any changes in the present Christian Bible would undoubtedly cause more, not less,
division in the church.[5]

1. Major Questions

Much of the recent discussion of canon formation has challenged well-known and
widely held views. Some popular positions that are now being challenged include: (1) the
view that the Hebrew scriptures achieved canonical acceptance among the Jews in a three-
stage development beginning ca. 400 B.C.E. for the Pentateuch, 200 B.C.E. for the Prophets,
and 90–100 C.E. for the Writings; (2) that the early Christians received from Jesus a closed
Old Testament canon; (3) that most of the New Testament canon was settled by the end of
the second century C.E.; and (4) that evidence of the latter is provided by a late second-century canonical list called the Muratorian Fragment.

Other emerging questions also call for a reasoned response. For example:

1. What precisely is a biblical canon and how sure are we that such a notion flour-
ished before, during, or immediately after the time of Jesus? As basic as this is, the reader
will see presently that even here there is no universally accepted position. In the next chapter, Eugene Ulrich has made some interesting observations on this matter and his discussion may advance a common understanding of what a biblical canon is. Some of the
ensuing papers, however, show disagreement with his effort to seek a universally agreed on
definition of the term "canon" as the final product of a canonical process. What complicates any discussion of canonicity in the various Judaisms of the first century of the common era and in early Christianity is the paucity of any clearly stated and universally
accepted definitions of what constitutes scripture and canon. Most definitions available
can be employed to show that there were more writings acknowledged as scripture in antiquity than those that were eventually included in the current biblical canon. Some
ancient literature functioned in scripture-like manner, that is, similar to other long-
accepted scriptures that were normative for a believing community, long before it was ever
called scripture and placed in a biblical canon. Similarly, some ancient literature functioned this way (normatively) earlier, but never made it into the biblical canon.[6]

55, for a critique of one recently reissued abridgment of the Bible. Milgrom argues for the relevance
of those very sections that were eliminated from the Hebrew scriptures as either boring or irrelevant
(e.g., the book of Leviticus).

[5] B. M. Metzger, *The Canon of the New Testament: Its Origin, Development, and Significance*
(Oxford: Clarendon, 1987), 275. We should note here that Professor Metzger was invited to participate in this volume but because of other commitments was unable to do so.

[6] Eugene Ulrich (*The Dead Sea Scrolls and the Origins of the Bible* [SDSSRL; Grand Rapids:
Eerdmans, 1999], 53–61) discusses the problem of definition and precision in current use of the
word "canon." He concludes that the term (1) should be used of a reflexive judgment on the scope of
the Bible, (2) that it denotes a closed list, and (3) that it pertains to biblical books and not the specific textual form of those books. In this sense, he concludes that Judaism had no biblical canon as
such at least until the middle of the second century C.E. and that the church had none until the
fourth century. James Sanders, following a different path, suggested the same ("Text and Canon: Old
Testament and New," in *Mélanges Dominique Barthélemy* [ed. P. Casseti et al.; Fribourg: Editions

2. Why were discussions about the scope of the Old Testament biblical canon going on in the church well into the fourth through the sixth centuries and even later if the matter was largely settled before the time of Jesus? And further, why did it take the church three to four hundred years to establish its twenty-seven book New Testament canon?

3. Whenever an ancient writer cites a source from an even more ancient text, does that cited text automatically become a part of the ancient writer's biblical canon?[7] More recently, one scholar has questioned whether the rabbinic sages of late antiquity ever discussed the issue of a closed biblical canon.[8]

4. What sources more accurately reflect the earliest strands of Christian faith? Again, some scholars today believe that other ancient sources relate the earliest traditions of Jesus more faithfully than the canonical gospels. In scholarly discussions these days it is not unusual to call for enlarging the traditional data base of knowledge of the historical Jesus to include, for example, the *Gospel of Thomas* and the "Unknown Gospel" discovered in the Egerton Papyri as well as several other noncanonical writings. (See Robert Funk's chapter in this volume.)

5. That issue leads us to the next question, namely, what of the agrapha (or sayings of Jesus not found in the canonical gospels)? Some scholars have suggested that these sayings, at least, can help us understand more clearly who Jesus was. This is not a new proposal,[9] and it continues to surface here and there. The agrapha served as an authoritative resource for the ancient Christians who cited them. If we can with some assurance determine which of the approximately 200 known noncanonical sayings of Jesus are genuine,[10] should they be added to the data base of information that informs us about Jesus?[11] Should they be added to the biblical canon?

---

universitaires, 1980], 373–94; and "Stability and Fluidity in Text and Canon," in *Tradition of the Text* [ed. G. Norton and S. Pisano; Göttingen: Vandenhoeck & Ruprecht, 1991], 201–17).

[7] Roger Beckwith ("Formation of the Hebrew Bible," in *Mikra: Text, Translation, Reading and Interpretation of the Hebrew Bible in Ancient Judaism and Early Christianity* [CRINT II/1; ed. M. J. Mulder; Assen/Maastricht: Van Gorcum; Philadelphia: Fortress, 1988], 46, 48–49) seems to imply as much when he simply accumulates a writer's references to earlier sources and calls that a biblical canon. (For more detail see L. M. McDonald, *Formation of the Christian Biblical Canon* [rev. and enl. ed.; Peabody, Mass.: Hendrickson, 1995], 27–28, 99, 101.) Caution is required in discerning what ancient writers concluded about the divine status of earlier literature that they cited. How certain are we that the notion of a fixed biblical canon was already current in the first century? What if we delay the notion of a closed or fixed scriptural canon until we see it discussed or clearly presented, as we do in the fourth to the sixth centuries? Perhaps the notion of an *unclosed* biblical canon is present even though the ancient writers did not yet have a term available to identify it, but see E. Ulrich for arguments against an "open canon" in the next chapter.

[8] Jacob Neusner, *Judaism and Christianity in the Age of Constantine* (Chicago: University of Chicago Press, 1987), 128–45. See also his *Midrash in Context: Exegesis in Formative Judaism* (Atlanta: Scholars Press, 1988), 1–22. He claims that the notion of Torah was expanded in the formative years of Judaism to include the Mishnah, Tosefta, the two Talmuds, and the various midrashim. A canon was constructed by defining Torah in a new way that encompassed all the literature that followed it. It was tied together through exegesis. The notion of a biblical canon, however, is not *prominent* in second-century rabbinic Judaism or even later.

[9] Metzger (*NT Canon,* 272 n. 11) notes that E. Platshoff-Lejeune ("Zur Problematik des biblischen Kanons," *Schweizerische theologische Umschau* 19 [1949]: 108–16) made just such a proposal.

[10] Scholars differ on the matter.

[11] Joachim Jeremias (*Unbekannte Jesuworte* [Zürich: Zwingli, 1947; 2d ed., Gütersloh: Bertelsmann, 1951; 3d ed., 1961]; ET: *The Unknown Sayings of Jesus* [London: SPCK, 1957; 2d ed., 1964])

6. And what of the biblical *text* itself? With the recent advances in the investigation of the Dead Sea Scrolls and the ancient Greek and Latin translations of the Bible, which text of the Bible is more authoritative for the church and for the Jewish community? Tov, Epp, and Schmidt in their respective chapters in this volume raise some important questions in that regard. It appears that the ancient communities of Christianity and Judaism did not set aside one particular text of the scriptures to be included in their Bible. If that is so, as the available evidence suggests, then how does one determine what the most appropriate scripture text should be? Which text of scripture should be authoritative for the church? Is the text in its original and earliest form the focus of authority and exegesis for the church, or rather the later canonical or "received" form of the biblical text? See a discussion of this in Kraft's, Epp's, and Sanders's papers below. The greater church admittedly has received many textual additions, some of which were intentional and others accidental. For instance, is the original form of Philippians canonical or authoritative, or the one that currently exists in the New Testament canon?[12] Does it make a difference in one's reading if the two parts are separated for study and preaching? Is John best read as it was written, namely, as a single gospel, or as the Fourth Gospel? Is the final form of Isaiah authoritative for preaching and teaching, or do we look for an earlier First, Second, or even Third Isaiah? Should we receive Mark 16:9–20, John 21, and Acts 8:37 as canonical, even though most scholars agree that they were later additions to the text? Further, should we accept as our scriptures only the earliest texts available today, reflecting the original hand of the author? Our choice in this matter may be guided by the early church, which grounded its theology in the witness of the apostolic community.[13]

7. Recent studies of the various surviving biblical manuscripts show that not until very recently did all of the current twenty-seven writings that make up the commonly received New Testament canon emerge in the same manuscript.[14] In other words, if all of

---

claims that of the 266 such sayings, some eighteen are genuine. If this is correct, what should be done with such sayings? The agrapha are introduced, listed, and discussed in the following works: W. D. Stroker (*Extracanonical Sayings of Jesus* [SBLRBS 18; Atlanta: Scholars, 1989]) offers the text of 266 of these sayings but does not sufficiently evaluate their contents nor pass judgment on their authenticity. They have been discussed more recently in detail in Otfried Hofius, "Isolated Sayings of Jesus," *New Testament Apocrypha* (2d ed., Wilhelm Schneemelcher, ed.; Louisville, Ky.: Westminster John Knox, 1991), 1:88ff. James H. Charlesworth and Craig A. Evans conveniently list and discuss the agrapha in "Jesus in the Agrapha and Apocryphal Gospels," in *Studying the Historical Jesus: Evaluations of the State of Current Research* (eds. Bruce Chilton and C. A. Evans; NTTS 19; Leiden: Brill, 1994). In this article, Evans contends that there is essentially nothing new in the agrapha that should cause concern or that would alter the understanding of Jesus that is found in the canonical gospels. See also Otfried Hofius, "Unknown Sayings of Jesus," *The Gospel and the Gospels* (ed. Peter Stuhlmacher; Grand Rapids, Mich.: Eerdmans, 1991), 336–60, and "Isolated Sayings of the Lord," *NT Apo* (2d ed.) 1:90.

[12] It is likely that the letter to the Philippians is a composite of Paul's writings on at least two separate occasions, namely, chapters 1:1–3:1 and chapters 3:2–4:23.

[13] Notice, for example, that Eusebius (*Hist. eccl.* 3.25.7) emphasizes both "apostolic style" and "orthodoxy" as criteria for genuineness, and even the *MF (Muratorian Fragment)* lines 73–80 excluded a work from consideration (Hermas) because it did not stem from the apostolic community. The rise of New Testament pseudepigraphy also demonstrates a desire to ground theology in the witness of the apostolic community. The early church anchored its life and faith in God's activity in Jesus. Writings that were believed to be closer in time to him and that reflected early tradition about him were passed on and became canon for the church.

[14] The reader should be aware that the common New Testament canon is not the only one that exists. The Ethiopian church, which parallels to some extent the Coptic New Testament canon,

the literature that comprises our current biblical canon was important to the Christians in antiquity, why do we not find many manuscripts containing them? Eldon Epp, Robert Kraft, and Daryl Schmidt, and to some extent Emanuel Tov for the Hebrew Bible, address this problem in this volume.

8. What criteria were employed to determine which writings would make up the Christian biblical canon? There is little doubt among canon scholars that authorship by an apostle was the most important factor considered by the church leaders of the fourth and following centuries. If it was believed that an apostle produced a particular writing, that writing was accepted and treated as scripture. This also helps to explain the large collection of literature pseudonymously attributed to the apostles, the so-called apocryphal New Testament writings. There is no doubt that several books of the New Testament were placed in the canon of scripture because the majority of the church fathers believed that they were written by members of the apostolic community if not by apostles themselves. All of these questions, of course, concern the viability and integrity of the current biblical canon. Most canonical literature is anonymous and a considerable amount of it became pseudepigraphic under hellenistic influence, that is, attributed to great personages of the past. In semitic culture in antiquity the focus was on a text's message, not its author, for its authenticity. This may have been the case for the Gospels and Acts. (See McDonald's discussion of this topic below.)

Kent Clarke makes an important contribution to the question of whether any pseudonymous writings exist in the Bible. What if the one to whom a biblical writing was attributed is not the author of that work? What do we do with it then? Most, but not all, biblical scholars have concluded that such literature does exist in the New Testament. Does it matter? These too are important questions that share in the complexity of canon formation. What has commonly been called the canonization of scripture was, according to some students, in reality a canonical process involving the various parts of the present Bible over a long period of time. The literature that made it into the Jewish and Christian scripture canons had to be multivalent and adaptable to the conditions and needs of numerous communities just to survive and be included in a biblical canon. Once that literature was placed in those canons, it has continued to be multivalent and adaptable for two thousand years. A canon's continuing adaptability or relevance to the lives of communities and of individuals is as salient a characteristic as its stability or "final shape."[15]

Discussion of the limits or scope of the New Testament canon of writings first occurs in the fourth century in the writings of Eusebius (*Hist. eccl.* 3.3). Many Christians had already made their decisions about the contents of their New Testament scriptures by then, but the churches were never fully agreed. The catalogues and collections listed in Appendix C demonstrate the variety of opinion present in the churches in the fourth century. Here we first see terms used to identify this literature. Although "Old Testament" and "New Testament" began to be used in some churches to designate their sacred writings in the late second century, it is only in the fourth century that they are referred to by Eusebius as

---

has a much larger New Testament canon than that commonly received, and may have earlier support for its decision in the matter. Besides the commonly received books, their New Testament canon includes the books of *Sinodos, Clement, The Book of the Covenant,* and *Didascalia.* For a discussion of this canon, see B. M. Metzger, *Canon,* 225–28.

[15] See J. A. Sanders, *Canon and Community* (Philadelphia: Fortress, 1984).

"encovenanted" and "recognized" writings (Eusebius, *Hist. eccl.* 3.3.1–6; 3.25.1–7; and 5.8.1). Further it is not until 367 that we first hear them referred to as "canon" (Athanasius, *Festal Letter* 39). Athanasius is the first to list the complete 27 books that most Christians now call the New Testament canon, but he did not settle the issue for many other churches, as we can see from the variety in the subsequent lists of New Testament scriptures in Appendix C. His Old Testament canon was broader than the current Protestant Old Testament canon, which contains the same books found in the Hebrew Bible though not in the same order. Kalin, Balla, Ferguson, and Hahneman have all made significant contributions in this volume to our understanding of this question.

2. The Notions of Scripture and Canon

As we introduce this volume, we offer some preliminary definitions of both "scripture" and "canon" that will enable the reader to follow the debate over these terms in this volume.

A. The Meaning of Scripture

Judaism, Christianity, and Islam are the primary world religions that have defined themselves in terms of a sacred written text. The development of a collection of scriptures in these traditions appears to be related to a common belief in the notion of a "heavenly book" which contains both divine knowledge and decrees from God. This heavenly book generally contains wisdom, destinies (or laws), a book of works, and a book of life.[16] W. Graham has argued that this notion goes back to ancient Mesopotamia and Egypt, where the heavenly book indicated the future plans of God and the destinies of human beings. An example can be found in Ps 139:15–16 which says, "My frame was not hidden from you, when I was being made in secret, intricately woven in the depths of the earth. Your eyes beheld my unformed substance. In your book were written all the days that were formed for me, when none of them as yet existed" (NRSV). This notion is also carried on in the New Testament in Rev 5:1, 3 and in the description of the opening of that book in 6:1–17 and 8:1–10:11. Books are opened before the great white throne of God and "another book was opened, the book of life. And the dead were judged according to their works, as recorded in the books . . . and anyone whose name was not found written in the book of life was thrown into the lake of fire" (Rev 20:12, 15, NRSV). In Exod 32:33 the Lord says that those who have sinned will be blotted out of his book. The same notion occurs in Phil 4:3, where Paul speaks of Clement and the rest of his colleagues in ministry "whose names are in the book of life." Graham claims that this belief gave rise to the notion in both Judaism and early Christianity that the repository of divine knowledge and heavenly decrees are contained in a divine book symbolized in written scriptures.[17] He also cites an example from the Qur'an which speaks of a divine book of destinies. Surah 57.22 reads: "No misfortune strikes on earth or in yourselves without its being [written] in a Book be-

---

[16] William A. Graham, *Beyond the Written Word: Oral Aspects of Scripture in the History of Religion* (Cambridge/New York: Cambridge University Press, 1987), 49–50.
[17] Ibid., 50–51.

fore we cause it to be. Truly, that is easy for God."[18] Graham goes on to argue that for Judaism, long before the notion of a biblical canon, the Torah was believed to have come directly from God. Moses proclaimed the words and ordinances of God (Exod 24:3) and was commissioned by God to write them (Exod 34:4, 27). It was believed that God was the writer of the Decalogue, or Ten Commandments (Exod 34:1 and Deut 4:13; 10:4) and this, according to Graham, gave rise to the notion that the law of God was written down in the form of scripture and played a significant role in the development of the idea of a revealed and authoritative scripture.[19]

For both Judaism and Christianity the final authority for faith is, of course, God, but especially in the later stages of the Old Testament the belief arose that the revelation and will of God were disclosed not only in mighty acts through which Yahweh invades history, for example, in the exodus, but also in written materials. See the Pentateuch for examples where the writing down of something was an important mark of revelation (Exod 24:12; 31:8; 32:15, 32; 34:1; Deut 4:13; 8:10; etc.). Just as Moses wrote down the commandments of the Lord in Exod 24:4; 34:27, so also does Joshua in Josh 24:26 and Samuel in 1 Sam 10:25. In the book of Deuteronomy, which was probably written toward the end of the Old Testament era, the king is called upon to write down for himself a copy of the law of God for reading all the days of his life to remind him of the statutes of God and to be humble in his dealings with his people (Deut 17:18–20). The people also were called upon to write the words of God on their door posts (Deut 6:9; 11:20). By way of contrast, the Gospels of the New Testament do not indicate that Jesus wrote anything down nor did he command others to write anything down. The only New Testament exception is found in the book of Revelation where Jesus commanded the angels of the churches to put his message in written form (Rev 2:1–3:14).[20]

James Barr has observed that in the Old Testament "the writers do not reckon with a written 'scripture' as a totally dominant, known and acknowledged factor and force in the life of Israel."[21] He goes on to argue that even the prophets who say, "Thus says the Lord," are not speaking on the basis of an already existing text. Almost nothing in the Old Testament suggests that there were sacred scriptures to turn to when guidance was needed.[22] Neither David, Solomon, nor Hezekiah had any focus or emphasis on any sacred books current and normative in the life of Israel. Rather, as Barr has observed, the Old Testament individuals related to God more through persons (priests, prophets) and institutions (tabernacle, temple) than through sacred writings.[23] This is not to suggest that there were no traditions that functioned authoritatively in the life of the ancient Jewish people. No religious community exists without canon (or rule), however it is expressed (scriptures,

---

[18] Ibid.

[19] Ibid., 51–52.

[20] Gottlob Schrenk, "*Graphē*," *TDNT* 1:744–56. The secondary text of John 7:53–58, even if genuine, would hardly qualify as a written document.

[21] Barr, *Holy Scripture: Canon, Authority, Criticism* (Philadelphia: Westminster, 1983), 5.

[22] Many of the Psalms, especially 19 and 119, which focus on the meditation on the word, law, precepts, and statutes of God, are almost certainly preexilic in origin, but most of these quite possibly do not date before the time of Josiah's finding of the book of the law (probably Deuteronomy) ca. 622–621 B.C.E. (compare 2 Kgs 18:20a with 22:3–13).

[23] Barr, *Scripture*, 5.

creeds, liturgies, traditions, etc.), and by its nature, that which is canon can be adapted to new circumstances of life or it ceases to be canonical.[24]

The religion of Israel came to be governed by or built upon the law probably not much before the reforms of Josiah (621 B.C.E.), but certainly no later than the reforms of Ezra (Neh 8:1–8; 9:1–3). The Deuteronomic movement in Israel in the eighth to the seventh centuries B.C.E. no doubt had a major role in effecting that change. See for example the admonition to obey the commandments of Yahweh and not to add to them nor take away from them (Deut 4:2). At any rate, when that which was written down in Israel began to be translated and explained to the people as having normative value in the life of their community (Neh 8:8–11), the notion of scriptures was clearly present in Judaism.

The belief that the revelation and will of God had been preserved in written documents was also shared by the earliest Christian community. The early church, by and large, believed that God had acted decisively in the life, death, and resurrection of Jesus, and that this had also been *foretold* in the normative literature of Judaism—the Hebrew scriptures. It also held that the proclamation of and about Jesus was passed on faithfully through the oral tradition of the church, much of which was written down and *later* (ca. 70 C.E.) also became widely recognized as normative literature in many of the churches. Many of the New Testament writings were recognized as authoritative and useful in various churches almost from the time of their production, but it is primarily in the second century that many of them began to function as scripture. Many Christians began to call them "scripture" near the end of the second century. The recognition of the New Testament writings as scripture can only be described as a growing process, which did not meet with unanimous or simultaneous acknowledgment in the ancient churches. The Christian books which eventually received this normative status were not the same for all the churches. Even when there was agreement, not all churches recognized the authority of the literature at the same time. This much can be seen in the differences in the "lists" of early Christian literature recommended or tabulated for church use in the fourth century and later.[25] The *recognition* of the inspiration and authority of the New Testament literature—that is, the recognition of its scriptural status—cannot be dated with any precision, but it seems certain that with one possible exception no part of that body of literature was so recognized in the first century. Only the book of Revelation (ca. 90–95 C.E.) claims for itself something close to the notion of inspiration and scripture (Rev 1:3, 10–11; 22:7–9, 18–19; cf. Deut 4:2). This is the only book in the New Testament that claims to be a revelation from God. The author of 2 Pet 3:15–16 (written ca. 120–150 C.E. and possibly as late as 180 C.E.) apparently recognized Paul's letters as "scripture," however, nowhere does Paul or any other author of the New Testament claim this special recognition for his own writings. Even the Gospels do not make the claim of final authority for their readers, and the many changes in these writings in subsequent centuries suggests that the recognition of their divine authority was not immediate even if they (especially Matthew) were popular within the churches early on. Such divine authority appears to be reserved for Jesus alone (Matt 28:19–20) even though the many Old Testament citations and allusions in the Gospels is

---

[24] For a further development of this thought, see Sanders, *Torah and Canon*.

[25] See Appendix C, which compares several important lists of Old Testament and New Testament books.

evidence of their authoritative status in the life and ministry of the early Christian communities. Although Paul was mindful that he was communicating the authoritative words of Jesus on occasion (1 Cor 7:10–11; 9:14; 11:23–26), he apparently was unaware of the divinely inspired status of his own advice (1 Cor 7:12, 25). He never wrote as if he himself were setting forth scripture, although he did acknowledge the superior authority of the words of Jesus in settling matters of Christian ethics. He likewise emphasized his own apostolic authority in resolving disputes in the churches he founded (for example, 1 Cor 4:14–5:5; 7:12; 2 Cor 13:10, etc.). Although Paul is the first New Testament writer to make a qualified claim to being inspired by the Spirit in regard to what he said, he still does not write "scripturally," that is, consciously aware that he is writing from a divinely inspired and therefore scripturally authoritative perspective. Even though his counsel to the Christians at Corinth about the marriage status of a woman whose husband has died is joined by the words "And I think that I too have the Spirit of God" (1 Cor 7:40, NRSV), this is a far cry from an acknowledgment by Paul of the scriptural status of his letter to the Corinthian community. This passage certainly suggests Paul's awareness that he is speaking by the power of the Spirit and he is thereby giving what he considers to be the will of God in the matter, but it is not a claim that he is consciously writing scripture.

B. The Meaning of "Canon"

The meaning of "canon" is not exactly equal to that of "scripture" even though there is considerable overlap in definition. Both terms refer to recognition of sacredness and authority within a believing community. Scripture has to do with the divine status of a written document that is authoritative in the life of a community of faith. Canon, while also referring to literature that is normative to a religious community and is employed in establishing its identity and mission, is moreover a fixed standard (or collection of writings) that defines the faith and identity of a particular religious community. In this sense, all scripture is canonical, but a biblical canon is more precisely a fixed collection of scriptures that comprise that authoritative witness for a religious body. The Greek *kanōn* is derived from *kanē*, a loanword from the Semitic *kaneh*, which means "measuring rod" or "measuring stick." By a process which will not be dealt with in detail here, the word canon came to mean among the Greeks and many other ancient residents of the Greco-Roman world, a standard or norm by which all things are judged or evaluated, whether the perfect form to follow in architecture or the infallible criterion *(kritērion)* by which things are to be measured.[26] The term was used in several areas with a similar meaning. In sculpture and architecture it denoted the perfect frame to be copied. In music the monochord was the canon by which all other tonal relationships were controlled. The term was also used in regard to grammar by the Alexandrians, who set forth a canon of writers whose Greek was used as a model. It was even employed in philosophy as the criterion by which one discovers what is true and

---

[26] See the helpful descriptions of the use of the term by Hermann Wolfgang Beyer ("*Kanōn*," *TDNT* 3:596–602) and Robert W. Funk (*Parables and Presence* [Philadelphia: Fortress, 1982], 151–53). A brief but careful theological and historical description of the use of the term in the church is found in Paul J. Achtemeier, *The Inspiration of Scripture* (Philadelphia: Westminster, 1980), 118–23. A more recent and excellent treatment of the term is also found in Metzger, *Canon*, 289–93.

false.[27] Beyer has shown that Epicurus himself argued that logic and method in thought stemmed from a canon *(kanōn)* or basis by which one could know what was true or false and was worth investigating or not.[28] This is not unlike the way the Jewish and Christian communities of faith have understood and employed the biblical scriptures.

At the end of the first century C.E., Clement of Rome called the Corinthians away from strife to the "glorious and venerable rule *(kanona)* of our tradition" (*1 Clem.* 7.2).[29] As will be shown later, Irenaeus used the term in reference to the rule of faith that defined orthodox Christianity at the end of the second century in Rome. In the late second century, Clement of Alexandria spoke of the *rule (kanōn)* of faith that was the truth of the church, but did not apply the term specifically to biblical literature.[30] From approximately the middle of the fourth century of the common era onward, *kanōn* was increasingly used of the collection of sacred writings of both the Old Testament and New Testament.[31] Eusebius is sometimes reckoned the first to use the term in reference to a collection of Christian scriptures, in his *Ecclesiastical History* 6.25.3 ca. 325 C.E. However, a careful study of his references to the scriptures of the church indicates that his favorite terms for this literature were "covenanted," or more accurately, "encovenanted" (Greek, *endiathēkē*),[32] and "recognized" (Greek, *homologoumenon*). The preferred term for describing a list of sacred scriptures is "catalogue" (Greek, *katalogos; Hist. eccl.* 3.25.6 and 4.26.13). When Eusebius uses the term *kanōn*, he is generally focusing on the church's traditions or its rule of faith. Of the ten times he used the term, only two are possible candidates for an exclusive list of sacred scriptures (*Hist. eccl.* 5.28.13 and 6.25.3). Although he provides the first datable list of the later recognized canonical books of the church in, *Hist. eccl.* 3.25.1–7, he does not use the term *kanōn* to refer to it, but rather "covenanted" (Greek, *endiathēkē; Hist. eccl.* 3.25.6). Setting forth what he claimed was Origen's canon of scriptures, Eusebius writes: "These things he inserts in the above mentioned treatise. But in the first of his [Commentaries] on the Gospel according to Matthew, defending the canon of the church *(ton ekklēsiastikon phylattōn kanona)*, he gives his testimony that he knows only four Gospels" (*Hist. eccl.* 6.25.3). The question here is whether the "canon of the church" refers to the rule of faith or to a body of sacred Christian literature, that is, a list or catalogue. The context suggests that he is talking about a collection or catalogue of writings. See also *Hist. eccl.* 6.25.1 where he cites Origen's "encovenanted books" *(endiathēkous biblous)*.

While Eusebius apparently uses *kanōn* (canon) in reference to the list of four gospels in *Hist. eccl.* 6.25.3, his typical term for a collection of sacred books remains not *kanōn* but

---

[27] Beyer, "*Kanōn*," 596–98.

[28] Ibid.

[29] The precise meaning of this phrase is difficult to determine. It could refer to the Christian message and its implications as passed on in the church, *or* to a common code of church ethics, *or* to a reference to the *Christian* use of the Old Testament scriptures. Probably the first of these is intended. If so, this is similar to Paul's use of *kanona* in Gal 6:16.

[30] See Clement of Alexandria, *Stromateis* 6.15.125, where *kanōn* is the harmony between the Law and the Prophets on the one side and the *covenant* instituted by the incarnation of the Lord on the other.

[31] Beyer, "*Kanōn*," *TDNT* 3:600–601. See also Hennecke, *NT Apo.*, 22–24, and G. W. H. Lampe, "The Early Church," in *Scripture and Tradition* (ed. F. W. Dillistone; London: Lutterworth, 1955), 24ff.

[32] Metzger (*Canon*, 292) translates this term "contained in the covenant" as opposed to "apocryphal literature."

"encovenanted." Athanasius, however, in his *Festal Letter* of 367 C.E., uses a verbal form of *kanōn* (*kanonizomenōn* = "canonized") in reference to a body of sacred literature. The earliest clear use of a form of the term *kanōn* for a collection of scriptures appears around the middle of the fourth century. We should be clear, however, that the current use of the term "canon" to refer to a collection of scripture books was introduced by David Ruhnken in 1768 in his *Historia critica oratorum graecorum* for lists of sacred scriptures. While it is tempting to think that such usage has its origins in antiquity in reference to a closed collection of scriptures, such is not the case.[33]

With such a long delay in the church's use of the term "canon" to describe a closed body of Christian scriptures, one may well ask why there was an emergence of "canon consciousness" in the church of the fourth century C.E. and little evidence of it before? A better understanding of the socio-historical conditions present in the fourth century C.E. may offer part of the answer. Again, we must consider how the Hellenistic understanding of canon influenced the Christian as well as Jewish communities in their establishment of biblical canons. To what extent was the Hellenistic idea of following that which is a perfect guide taken over into the religious thought of Judaism, Christianity, and later Islam? It may well be that interactions with "heretical" teachings and other factors (chs. 18, 20) led the church to propose a standard by which it could define authentic Christianity. This was done at first by the "rule of faith," which appears to have embodied the oral tradition about Jesus, but eventually also the rule of certain writings that were believed to transmit the tradition of Jesus faithfully.

The proposal of a standard "rule" eventually led to the formation of a *closed* canon of authoritative writings (scriptures) which, as A. C. Sundberg has argued, was unique in the Christian church, since it had not received a closed canon of scriptures from Judaism.[34] There appear to have been no rigid guidelines on what could or could not qualify as Christian scripture, though apostolicity and tradition (that is, long term use in the churches) were certainly prominent features. The church, then, inherited from Judaism the notion of sacred scripture, but not a closed canon of scriptures. This was a later development owing to a wide variety of influences.[35] According to Sundberg, there were three stages in the history of the New Testament canon: (1) the rise of the New Testament writings to the status of scripture; (2) the conscious groupings of such literature into closed collections—for example, the four gospels and the epistles of Paul; and (3) the formation of a closed list of authoritative literature.[36] Eusebius employs a threefold classification of the Christian lit-

---

[33] For a helpful discussion of the background on the use of the term for a collection of scriptures, see Gregory Allen Robbins, "Eusebius' Lexicon of 'Canonicity,'" *Studia Patristica* 25 (ed. Elizabeth A. Livingstone; Leuven: Peeters, 1993), 134–41. Robbins argues that Eusebius never used the term *kanōn* in the way in which it has been employed in more modern times in reference to the collection of sacred scriptures. He also agrees that the list that Eusebius provides of Origen's Old Testament canon is an invention by Eusebius since, in fact, Origen used the number twenty-two to refer only to the books of the Jewish scriptures, but not his own (ibid., 140).

[34] A. C. Sundberg, "The Making of the New Testament Canon," *The Interpreter's One-Volume Commentary on the Bible* (ed. Charles M. Laymon; New York: Abingdon, 1971), 1216. This will be discussed in chapter 3.

[35] These are discussed in McDonald, *Formation,* 170–90.

[36] Sundberg, "The Making of the New Testament Canon," 1217. A careful description of the canonical process is found in James A. Sanders, *Canon and Community* (Philadelphia: Fortress,

erature that indicated at least a category between authoritative and heretical for literature that was deemed profitable for teaching but not considered normative in the church. These distinctions will be discussed in considerable detail in Kalin's paper, but also to some extent in Balla's, Hahneman's, Ferguson's, and McDonald's papers below.

Another feature of early Christian views of scripture, unlike Judaism, included an eschatological feature. That is, they believed that the scriptures had their primary fulfillment in Jesus (e.g., Matt 2:5, 17, 23: 3:3; 4:14; Mark 14:49; 15:28; Luke 4:21; Acts 1:16; John 17:12; 19:24, 28). Although Paul adds that this fulfillment is also found in the Christian community (see Rom 4:23; 15:4; 16:26; 1 Cor 9:10; 10:11), Jesus the Christ was considered the primary norm for the understanding and use of the Old Testament scriptures by the early church.[37] However, the church still held that the Old Testament scriptures themselves were of unimpeachable authority (John 10:35; Matt 5:18). Schrenk notes that for primitive Christianity scripture is "the authoritative declaration of the divine will," but that it was "not valid apart from the 'I say unto you,'" of Jesus—that is, its christological fulfillment.[38] Childs is correct when he recognizes that "the Christian understanding of canon functions theologically in a very different way from Judaism. Although the church adopted from the synagogue a concept of scripture as an authoritative collection of sacred writings, its basic stance toward its canon was shaped by christology." He adds that "the Old Testament functioned as Christian scripture because it bore witness to Christ. The scriptures of the Old and New Testament were authoritative in so far as they pointed to God's redemptive intervention for the world in Jesus Christ."[39]

As the reader will see in the rest of this volume, there are no agreed upon definitions of canon in contemporary writing. Perhaps what we mean by scripture is covered by the notion of a scripture canon, namely, that which is written down and becomes normative for a religious community is essentially both scripture and canon. Other nuances will be seen later in this volume. There has been a growing awareness that there are two broad ways of understanding canon in the ancient world, namely, as a fluid authority within a religious community and also as a fixed body of literature to which nothing can be added or taken away. James Sanders was the first to identify these distinctions in his discussions of canon (1976, 1981, and more recently in 1992)[40] and subsequently Gerald Sheppard em-

---

1984), 21–45. Sanders's more recent work (*From Sacred Story to Sacred Text* [Philadelphia: Fortress, 1987], 127–47, 175–90) has an excellent discussion of the process of recognition of the authority and the stabilization of the Old Testament biblical text. He makes points which are applicable to both the Old Testament and New Testament canonical inquiry. See also his "Text and Canon: Old Testament and New," in *Mélanges Dominique Barthélemy: Etudes bibliques* (ed. Pierre Casetti, Othmar Keel, and Adrian Scheuber; Orbis biblicus et orientalis 38; Fribourg: Editions universitaires; Göttingen: Vandenhoeck & Ruprecht, 1981), 373–94.

[37] See especially 2 Cor. 3:12–16.

[38] Schrenk, "*Graphē*," *TDNT* 1:759–61. See also Barr, *Scripture,* 14–15, and Kümmel, *Introduction,* 335.

[39] Brevard Childs, *Biblical Theology of Old and New Testaments* (Minneapolis: Fortress, 1992), 64.

[40] See his "Adaptable for Life: The Nature and Function of Canon," in *Magnalia Dei: The Mighty Acts of God: Essays on the Bible and Archaeology in Memory of G. E. Wright* (New York: Doubleday, 1976), 531–60; idem, *Canon and Community: A Guide to Canonical Criticism* (Philadelphia: Fortress, 1984); idem, "Canon. Hebrew Bible," in *Anchor Bible Dictionary* (ed. D. N. Freedman; New York: Doubleday, 1992), 1:837–52; idem, "Text and Canon: Old Testament and New," in

ployed the terms "canon 1" and "canon 2" to describe this same reality (1987).[41] Both scholars recognize that canons are not always fixed, especially in their early history. Sanders underscores their adaptability to the life circumstances of believing communities. In the next chapter, Eugene Ulrich offers a more detailed discussion of the definitions of scripture and canon, especially in terms of the Hebrew scriptures (First Testament) and the Christian Old Testament, but much of what he says is also true of the New or Second Testament.

3. Summary

All of the contributors in this volume recognize in one way or another the remarkable diversity in the canons of Judaism and Christianity and how the same events and stories are sometimes told from quite different points of view with differing messages. This brings some students of canon to speak of the Bible as a dialogical literature providing its own built-in self-corrective apparatus. James Sanders made these observations early on and they are reflected in his paper in this volume. Efforts to resolve the tension made by such an observation lead some to seek a canon within the canon, and others to resist such a move. Others seek a kind of unity in the Bible's *kerygma* or overall message. Some suggest reliance on an abstracted or even external *regula fidei* ("rule of faith") by which to guide the perplexed, while still others resist that as well. One suggestion has been to view Jewish and Christian canons as paradigms for how dialogue can continue to take place between these ancient texts and the ever-changing communities of faith, as well as for learning how to conjugate the verbs and decline the nouns of ongoing encounters with the divine.

Four papers below (those of Epp, Schmidt, Gamble, and Sanders) note that the plethora of manuscripts for both Testaments now available may be as helpful in canon studies as ancient extracanonical lists. While some have supposed that the acceptance or rejection of certain ancient books from canon lists may have been politically motivated, we are no longer privy to such supposed ancient debates. As a result, examination of the surviving manuscripts of their sacred literature may offer important indicators of the positions of many churches as to the scope of their biblical canons and when they were stabilized. The related issues of how the apocryphal and pseudepigraphal literature factors into to this discussion are carefully discussed in the chapters by Daniel Harrington, William Adler, and Kent Clarke. We should also add that the papers produced by Emanuel Tov, James VanderKam, and Julio Trebolle Barrera offer valuable insights into the often over-looked relevance of the Dead Sea Scrolls for this whole discussion. Pheme Perkins makes an important contribution to our understanding of the influence of the gnostic community on the formation of the biblical canon. Her expertise in this field is widely known and well appreciated.

Before any new advances can be made in our understanding of the formation of the Bible, far more research is needed than has emerged so far. As we observed above, new

---

Mélanges Dominique Barthélemy: Etudes bibliques (ed. Pierre Casetti, Othmar Keel, and Adrian Scheuber; Orbis Biblicus et Orientalis 38; Fribourg: Editions Universitaires; Göttingen: Vandenhoeck & Ruprecht, 1981), 373–94.

[41] Gerald T. Sheppard, "Canon," in *The Encyclopedia of Religion* (ed. Mircea Eliade; New York: Macmillan Publishing Co., 1987), 3:62–69.

advances in canonical studies will undoubtedly affect our understanding of the long and highly complex canonical process. New advances have already prompted some scholars to reconsider the present scope of the biblical literature; some advocate ways to marginalize those parts of the biblical canon that no longer appear to be relevant to us or that offend us. This is what is known as seeking a "canon within the canon."

These and other questions will be considered in the remainder of this volume. We will begin our study with an examination of the problem of definition and then focus on some of the critical issues related to the formation of the Bible. Those who choose to pursue the topics of discussion in more detail may see important aids in the appendixes, including some of the most important primary, or ancient, sources for the study of canon formation and also a collection of some of the oldest lists of sacred scriptures. The Select Bibliography at the end is rather extensive and includes all of the most important contributions to the discussion of canon debate as well as many important but smaller and lesser known works. The bibliography is the product of the cumulative effort of many contributors to this volume and, though not exhaustive, is one of the most extensive bibliographies on canon available.

We are deeply grateful to the scholars who have contributed to this volume. The long effort to bring their many points together to form this collection has been rewarded many times over by their excellent contributions. In many cases the reader will find these chapters to be foundational for the discussion of the origins of the Bible, probably for some time to come. In most cases, the contributors to this volume are the most significant players in the world of canon research. They have made many significant advances in this volume. This collection of essays is something of a distillation of their previous work, but often it is also an advance over all previous work in canon studies. They have seen the importance of setting forth for student and scholar alike the issues surrounding the origins and development of the Bible. We are all in their debt for doing so. As a result, we can now see more clearly the contours of the significant debate that has emerged over the last 100 years or more in this field of inquiry.

Some of the discussions are quite familiar to canon students and have been pivotal in the investigation at significant junctures. For example, as we noted above, James Sanders, whose work on canon is well known and also foundational for most recent discussions of canon formation, argues that the Jews were able to adapt their authoritative scriptures to new and changing circumstances, and the very adaptability of those scriptures allowed them to continue as authoritative texts within the Jewish community.[42] He has observed that canons by their very nature are adaptable to the changing life of the believing communities that cherish them, and that is undoubtedly the reason why the current biblical canons for Judaism and Christianity continue to function as such in their synagogues and churches. Canons also change, most typically by expansion, though historically also by reduction: the *Shepherd of Hermas* and the *Epistle of Barnabas* eventually dropped out of sacred collections. As the Jewish communities developed, there came a time when they recognized more than the law of Moses as their sacred scriptures. They included the Prophets and eventually the Writings. As the church grew and developed, the early Chris-

---

[42] Sanders, *From Sacred Story to Sacred Text*, 9–39, but especially 23–30.

tians accepted the words of and about Jesus as their final norm. Craig Evans has a very useful chapter below on this matter.

As the church developed, however, it became obvious that written gospels and eventually the letters of Paul were also advantageous in the ongoing life of the community. When some writings ceased to be relevant to the religious needs of some Christian communities, they also ceased to be canon to those communities, and that is seen in the neglect of those texts or even the disappearance of complete books (for example, *Hermas, 1 Clement, Eldad and Modat*). Dunn has argued that the New Testament, for example, "decanonizes"[43] much of the Old or First Testament's emphasis on the law, especially its focus on clean and unclean foods or ritualistic cleansings, because such things were no longer deemed relevant to their faith. As you will see in his renewed and expanded discussion below, Dunn makes the point that the Old Testament can never function as canon for Christians in the same way that it does for the Jews. For the Christian, the New Testament always functions to some extent as *the* canon within the biblical canon.[44]

Finally, we want to offer a special word of appreciation to all of those who have helped bring this volume to its completion and to those who graciously contributed to it. We both express our appreciation to Peter Flint, who was significantly involved in the initial stages of the production of this volume and was very helpful in enlisting the participation of several scholars. Because of other important commitments he needed to withdraw from the project, but we recognize his significant labors and valuable contributions to this volume. Several other notable scholars were invited to participate, but for various reasons they were unable to join us in this venture, especially Bruce Metzger, Roger Beckwith, Earle Ellis, Brevard Childs, and Gerald Sheppard. Their works are frequently cited in the chapters that follow. Our goal was to include the most significant scholars in canon research in the world, and we are delighted that most of them have accepted our invitation to contribute to this volume. Their work makes important advances in our understanding of the origins and development of the biblical canons, and for that we are deeply grateful. The first editor of this volume would also like to express his sincere appreciation to James A. Sanders for his willingness to share the responsibilities as a co-editor after Peter Flint had to withdraw. Sanders has made many important suggestions along the way that have significantly improved the quality of this volume and added expertise that would otherwise have been absent. Finally, we both extend our special thanks to the editorial staff at Hendrickson Publishers.

Our goal in this project has been to advance the study of the origins of the biblical canon and to deal forthrightly with the significant issues raised by contemporary research. We have not tried to advocate a particular position, though each contributor has one, as the reader will soon see. We have wanted rather for the reader to see how diverse and complex the issues and positions on canon formation are. The hope, of course, is that the reader will be able to make use of the most current research on this question and further advance our understanding of the canonical process that produced the Bible.

---

[43] This is Dunn's expression in his *Living Word* (Philadelphia: Fortress, 1987), 156.
[44] Ibid., 156.

Part Two

The Old/First Testament Canon

2

The Notion and Definition of Canon

Eugene Ulrich

Plato may not seem to be the most apt starting point for a discussion of the biblical canon, but I suggest that he might be. Though his views were not always correct, he did manage to make several rather permanent advances in human civilization. Perhaps one of the most frequently applied—or forgotten with resultant peril—is his insistence that intelligent argument cannot safely proceed without a clear definition of terms.

> *Socrates:* However, when friendly people . . . want to converse with each other, one's reply must . . . not only be true, but must employ terms with which the questioner admits he is familiar. . . .
>
> I believe we rejected the type of answer that employs terms which are still in question and not yet agreed upon. . . .
>
> You say this and that about virtue, but what *is* it?
>
> . . . to define so-and-so, and thus to make plain whatever may be chosen as the topic for exposition. For example, take the definition given just now . . . , it was that which enabled our discourse to achieve lucidity and consistency.[1]

The purpose assigned to this chapter is to consider and attempt to clarify the notion and definition of "canon." It is an understatement to say that confusion currently surrounds the term and permeates recent discussions of the topic. Some scholars think that canon is a theological *terminus technicus* with a clear meaning, a specific denotation, and a long history of discussion, while others think that the term may be used more broadly to fit any of several aspects related to the collections of authoritative sacred texts of Judaism or Christianity. While the topic has at times been dormant, in this generation it has generated a great deal of interest due to the new and unexpected light that the discovery of the Dead Sea Scrolls contributes to the rather scant body of available evidence.

When topics are intermittently vigorous and dormant, continuity and valuable advances in the discussion sometimes get lost. It is quite predictable that the discovery of a cache of ancient manuscripts of books that came to form the Bible of Jews and Christians would excite both popular and scholarly hopes of sharpening our knowledge of the history

---

[1] Plato, *Meno* 75d and 79d, and *Phaedrus* 265d. The translations are by W. K. C. Guthrie and R. Hackforth, *The Collected Dialogues of Plato* (ed. E. Hamilton and J. Cairns; Princeton: Princeton University Press, 1961), 358, 362, and 511.

of the formation of the Bible. Indeed, great gains have been made in that knowledge. But many recent discussions bemoan the lack of clarity and agreement regarding terminology. So in this paper we will attempt to clarify the definition of canon and discuss some partially overlapping concepts. The specific histories of various aspects of the process leading to the Jewish and Christian canons will be dealt with in other chapters of this volume.[2] After some preliminary considerations, this chapter will turn to the definition of canon, surveying a spectrum of theological dictionaries, isolating the essential elements of the concept of canon, and distinguishing it from other related concepts that tend to cause confusion.

1. Preliminary Considerations

A. Etymology

Although much ink has been spilled discussing the etymology of "canon," the results are only mildly helpful, because the word as used in later theology or biblical studies does not exactly coincide with ancient usage. The word can be traced to the Sumerian *gi, gi-na,* meaning "reed" and then extended to mean "standard." Hebrew and other Semitic languages received these meanings, as did Greek, though the last multiplied additional metaphorical uses.[3]

For practical purposes regarding the canon of scripture, Bruce Metzger is correct that "the word 'canon' is Greek; its use in connection with the Bible belongs to Christian times; the idea of a canon of scripture originates in Judaism."[4] The term as used in relation to the Bible arose in Christian circles, though it was borrowed from the Hellenistic world. In Greek the term originally had a concrete meaning and then several metaphorical extensions. It meant a "rod" or "measuring stick" and acquired the figurative senses of "norm" or "ideal": in the realm of sculpture it meant the "perfect form of the human frame"; in philosophy, the "basis . . . by which to know what is true and false"; in law, "that which binds us, . . . specific ideals"; and also a "list" or "table."[5] A number of metaphorical uses also pervaded Latin and derivative languages and literatures.

Interestingly, no similar term is attested in Jewish writings, including the Septuagint, or in the Hebrew language until comparatively late. Although *qnh* ("reed, stalk") is used,

---

[2] For a discussion of the relation of the biblical Dead Sea Scrolls to the issue of canon, see Eugene Ulrich, "Canon," *Encyclopedia of the Dead Sea Scrolls* (ed. Lawrence H. Schiffman and James C. VanderKam; New York: Oxford University Press, 2000), 117–20. The scrolls preserved at Qumran are not "sectarian" but are characteristic of general Judaism at the time (see Ulrich, "The Qumran Biblical Scrolls—The Scriptures of Late Second Temple Judaism," in *The Dead Sea Scrolls in Their Historical Context* [ed. Timothy H. Lim et al.; Edinburgh: T&T Clark, 2000], 67–87). They demonstrate that the Jews clearly had books that were considered authoritative scripture and thus in a sense canonical; but they date from a period when, as will be argued below, there was not yet a canon of scripture properly speaking.

[3] See Gerald Sheppard, "Canon," *The Encyclopedia of Religion* (ed. Mircea Eliade; New York: Macmillan, 1987), 3:62–69, esp. 62–63; and H. W. Beyer, "*Kanōn*," *TDNT* 3:596–602.

[4] Bruce Metzger, *The Canon of the New Testament: Its Origin, Development, and Significance* (Oxford: Clarendon, 1987), v.

[5] Beyer, "*kanōn*," 596–602.

principally in Ezekiel (40:3, 5; 41:8; 42:16–19; see also Isa 46:6), in the derived meaning of measuring rod (six cubits), no biblical use of the word is attested in the extended meta-phorical sense of a moral measure, as, for example, *'nk* ("plumb line") is used in Amos 7:7–8. In the New Testament the only relevant occurrence of *kanōn* is in Gal 6:16, where it is used in the general sense of "measure of assessment," "norm of one's own action," "norm of true Christianity."[6] But precisely what Paul is referring to in his summary blessing "for those who will follow *tō kanoni toutō*" is not exactly clear; what is clear is that it does not refer to a set of books of scripture.[7] Thus, the term and discussion of it are absent from the Hebrew and Greek Bibles, suggesting that the term is postbiblical. If canon as such had been an important concept or reality in Judaism or nascent Christianity, one would expect that authors would discuss or at least mention it. Though that is admittedly an argument from silence, that silence is possibly significant. A further indication that the term is a postbiblical phenomenon is that it has no entry in *The Dictionary of Biblical Theology* and it does not figure in any meaningful way in the theologies of Walther Eichrodt and Gerhard von Rad.[8]

B. The Canon for Different Faith Communities

Clearly the contents of the canon are different for different faith communities, but the concept of canon is the same for each. Jews, Catholics, Protestants, and others will list different books in their canons, but the definition remains the same for all.

C. Mentalities

Some of the confusion arises from the different mentalities or approaches of those addressing the topic. It would seem that the proper stance of one using this book would be that of *the (religious) historian.* One looks at the realities in antiquity as neutrally as pos-sible and describes them as accurately as possible and with terminology appropriate for the period being described. A contrasting mentality would be that of *the pastoral apologist,* who starts with modern conceptions, categories, views, and conclusions (whether specific to one denomination or not) and imposes them upon, or at least sees them in, the evidence preserved in antiquity.[9] The stronger this mentality, the more one is tempted to find

---

[6] Ibid., 598, 600.

[7] That is, unless one could successfully prove both that Paul was referring to his full letter to the Galatians and that he was convinced that his letter was scripture.

[8] Xavier Léon-Dufour, ed., *Dictionary of Biblical Theology* (trans. P. J. Cahill et al.; 2d ed.: New York: Seabury, 1973). Walther Eichrodt has two brief, vague mentions of canon in *Theology of the Old Testament* (trans. J. A. Baker; 2 vols.; Philadelphia: Westminster, 1961, 1967), 2:66, 348. Gerhard von Rad, speaking almost at the end of his second volume of *Old Testament Theology* (trans. D. M. G. Stalker; 2 vols.; New York: Harper & Row, 1962, 1965) about the written publication of Deuter-onomy at the time of Josiah, does have the single sentence: "Thus the process of forming a canon began" (2:395). He has another mention of "canonical saving history"; it refers, however, not to the biblical canon but to a tradition used by Ezekiel that ends with the conquest, though it "was appar-ently not that of any of the source documents which form our Hexateuch" (2:227–28).

[9] For a similar critique of this mentality see Andrew E. Steinmann, *The Oracles of God: The Old Testament Canon* (St. Louis: Concordia, 1999), 183.

today's beliefs planted as far back as possible in yesterday's evidence. Yet another mentality is that of *the neophyte or generalist* who comes to the topic without the disciplined training in philosophy or theology required to enter the discussion with sufficient clarity. Thus, I suggest that the discussion should proceed using the historian's approach, trying to see sharply what antiquity holds, without affirming more than is actually there or minimizing what is there, and describing all in terminology that is accurate and appropriate for the period.

D. Historical Shifts

All would agree that at some distant point in the past there was no canon of scripture and that eventually a canon came into being in the Jewish and Christian communities. Along that trajectory, a number of concomitant developments were taking place, some of which influenced the canonical process. The following shifts influenced the canon of the Hebrew Bible, but analogous shifts may be highlighted for the canon of the New Testament.

First, there was a shift from the national literature of Israel to the sacred scripture of Judaism. Just as the Homeric poems had religious significance but were principally seen as national epics, so too the Yahwist's narrative originally would likely have been perceived more as a national epic than as "scripture." Similarly, an early prophetic booklet would perhaps have been seen as a work which *contained some elements* of revelation, but not as a *revealed book*. The Psalms, probably until quite late, were understood as human hymns to God, and only in the late Second Temple period were they seen as inspired words of God to humanity.[10] In the same way, the collection of Proverbs, starting with chapter 10, would have been seen as precisely a collection of proverbs, until the more theological chapters 1–9 were prefixed to it. Thus, just because the name of a book is mentioned in an ancient source, that does not necessarily mean it was in its final "biblical" edition or that it was even considered a book of scripture.

Second, after 70 C.E. there was a shift from a temple-based religion to a text-based religion in Judaism. This shift undoubtedly placed more importance and scrutiny on the scriptures than formerly. A reconsideration of the status of the Law and the Prophets and the other ancestral books was undoubtedly required, as well as more highly nuanced reflection and debate about which books would have, and which books would not have, been accorded supreme authority.

Third, there was a dramatic shift from the fluidity, pluriformity, and creativeness in composition of the text of the books of scripture to a "frozen" (not "standardized") single textual form for each book.[11] It is quite likely that some books which eventually came to be

---

[10] This is explicitly said in 11QPs[a] col. 27 line 11, where the text states that David composed all the Psalms through prophecy given to him from the Most High: *kwl 'lh dbr bnbw'h 'šr ntn lw mlpny h'lywn*. See also 1 Chron 25:1, where "David and the officers of the army also set apart for the service the sons of Asaph, and of Heman, and of Jeduthun, who should prophesy [*hnb'ym*] with lyres, harps, and cymbals" (NRSV).

[11] Eugene Ulrich, *The Dead Sea Scrolls and the Origins of the Bible* (Studies in the Dead Sea Scrolls and Related Literature 2; Grand Rapids: Eerdmans; Leiden: Brill, 1999), 12; see also note 34 below.

viewed as scripture became so only in—and due to the theological thrust of—a late, revised form or edition. An example might be the book of Esther, insofar as 9:18–32 was added to that book of "historical fiction" as the basis for the celebration of Purim.[12]

Fourth, there was a gradual shift from viewing revelation as dynamic and ongoing to viewing it as verbal and recorded from the distant past.[13] This is related (but not necessarily closely related) to the eventual conviction that prophecy had ceased sometime in the Second Temple period.

Fifth, the format of the books of the scriptures shifted from individual scrolls, usually containing one or two books, to the codex, which could contain many books. With scrolls, the table of contents of the scriptures was a *mental notion,* but it became a *physical object* when a codex contained those books included in that table of contents and no others. The shift from individual scrolls to collected codex had important ramifications on decisions regarding which books were recognized as belonging to the collection of scripture and which were not. Critical discussions of whether a book was officially or widely recognized as sacred scripture were more likely to arise when dealing with a single collection placed between a front and back cover than when dealing with separate scrolls.

2. The Definition of Canon

How has the term been used in the past, how is it used today, and how is it to be used in the future? In this age of the computer, the internet, and rapidly developing communications systems, the imaginative redesignation and use of old words for new realities is common, colorful, and often helpful within those worlds. But in a discussion that spans two millennia and includes writers from antiquity, thinkers from the Middle Ages, and theologians from the Enlightenment to the present and beyond, using many different languages and systems of thought it is imperative that terminology be understood and employed properly. Haphazard, or convenient, or ideological, or religiously defensive redesignation of terms is sure to bring confusion and muddy the argument—and this is indeed what has happened in the area of canon.

The discussion must proceed along several lines, dictated by (A) guidance from dictionaries; (B) distinctions between the concept of canon and closely associated but not identical concepts or realities; (C) essential elements of the concept of canon; and (D) examination of factors that tend to cause confusion in the discussion of canon.

A. Guidance from Dictionaries

It will be helpful to begin with the more general definitions of the word in broader areas. In general English usage, the relevant meanings of the word are rather close to the two used in theological discussion and in fact are probably derived from the theological uses: (1) a law, principle, body of law, or set of standards, enacted or endorsed by a competent

---

[12] See *The Access Bible* (ed. Gail R. O'Day and David Peterson; New York: Oxford University Press, 1999), Old Testament, p. 624.
[13] See James Sanders's contribution in this volume.

authority, "accepted as axiomatic and universally binding"; and (2) an officially recognized set of books; "any comprehensive list of books within a field"; "the works of an author which have been accepted as authentic."[14] The *Encyclopaedia Britannica* concurs with these two principal meanings:

> The general applications of the word fall mainly into two groups . . . , rule [and] . . . list or catalogue, *i.e.,* of books containing the rule. Of the first . . . the principal example is of the sum of the laws regulating the ecclesiastical body (see Canon Law). In the second group [is] . . . that of the authoritative body of scriptures. . . . [15]

Note that the general dictionaries prominently mention the two uses of the term canon when applied to the scriptures. In a discussion of the topic for world religions, Gerald Sheppard notes that the current uses of the term entail the same two aspects, with the Jewish and Christian scriptures establishing the patterns of usage for world religions in general.[16] With great clarity he speaks of "canon 1" and "canon 2" to denote the two aspects.

Theological dictionaries—Jewish, Catholic, and Protestant—provide yet more clarity for the definition:

1. Canon of Scripture: A technical term in theology designating the collection of inspired books that composes Holy Scripture and forms the rule of faith.[17]

2. The Greek word *kanōn* means both 'rule' and 'list,' and in the second capacity came to be used by the church at a rather late date . . . to designate those Scriptural books which were regarded as inspired. The Protestant canon and the Roman Catholic New Testament canon are identical, but Protestants follow the Old Testament canon of the Hebrew Bible. . . .[18]

3. The process by which the various books in the Bible were brought together and their value as sacred Scripture recognized is referred to as the history of the canon. . . . While the Old Testament canon had been formally closed. . . . The rise of heresy . . . was a powerful impulse towards the formation of a definite canon. A sifting process began in which valid Scripture distinguished itself from Christian literature in general on the basis of such criteria. . . . The canon was ultimately certified at the Council of Carthage (397).[19]

4. The term [canon] as applied to the Bible designates specifically the closed nature of the corpus of sacred literature accepted as authoritative because it is believed to be divinely inspired. . . . In the second century, *kanōn* had come to be used in Christian circles in the sense of 'rule of faith.' It was the church Fathers of the fourth century C.E. who first applied 'canon' to the sacred Scriptures. No exact equivalent of this term is to be found in Jewish sources although

---

[14] *The Random House Dictionary of the English Language* (ed. J. Stein; New York: Random House, 1969), 217.

[15] *The Encyclopaedia Britannica: A Dictionary of Arts, Sciences, Literature and General Information* (11th ed.; 29 vols.; Cambridge: Cambridge University Press, 1910), 5:190.

[16] Sheppard, "Canon," 62–63.

[17] Karl Rahner and Herbert Vorgrimler, *Theological Dictionary* (ed. C. Ernst; trans. R. Strachan; New York: Herder and Herder, 1965), 65.

[18] *The Westminster Dictionary of Church History* (ed. J. C. Brauer; Philadelphia: Westminster, 1971), 156.

[19] *Baker's Dictionary of Theology* (ed. E. F. Harrison; Grand Rapids: Baker, 1960), 94–95.

the phrase *Sefarim Ḥizonim* ('external books': Sanh. 10:1), i.e., uncanonical, is certainly its negative formulation. . . . The concept enshrined in the 'canon' is distinctively and character- istically Jewish. . . . In short, the development of the canon proved to be a revolutionary step in the history of religion, and the concept was consciously adopted by Christianity and Islam.[20]

5. Canon . . . [is a] term that came to be applied to the list of books that were considered a part of authoritative Scripture. The fixing of the canon of the Hebrew Bible was a long process about which we know little. . . . it is clear that certain books not in the present list were accepted by some communities; also, some in the present canon were evidently not univer- sally accepted.[21]

6. The term *canon* . . . was first used by the fourth-century Church fathers in reference to the definitive, authoritative nature of the body of sacred Scripture. Both Jews and Christians needed to define, out of the available literature, what should be regarded as divinely inspired and hence authoritative and worthy of preservation; the process was one of rejection rather than selection, a weeding out from among books commonly regarded as sacred.[22]

7. Canon: En grec: règle. (1) Toute décision solennelle. . . . (2) Nom donné . . . à la grande prière de la messe. . . . (3) Liste des ouvrages qui font partie du catalogue des livres sacrés, et sont reconnus comme d'inspiration divine et donc canoniques: 'canon des Ecritures'.[23]

8. At.licher Kanon . . . Vorstufen: Lange bevor die Schriften des AT . . . kanonisch wurden . . . , beanspruchten und erhielten viele ihrer Bestandteile eine Geltung, die der Kanonizität schon verwandt war und den Weg zu ihr hin nachträglich als logisch erscheinen lässt.

Es ist das Besondere der nt.lichen Kanonbildung, dass die Alte Kirche hist. unter deutlicher Beachtung apostolischer Verfasserschaft der Schriften den Kanon abschloss und begrenzte, [und] dass sie . . . in der Korrelation von Norm und Schrift herausstellte. . . . Die Kanonbildung selbst ist somit nur aus der Geschichte des Urchristentums, aus ihrem Weg in die Alte Kirche und aus den sie bestimmenden Motiven erklärbar.[24]

---

[20] *Encyclopaedia Judaica* (Jerusalem: Encyclopaedia Judaica Jerusalem/Macmillan, 1971), 4:817–18.

[21] *Dictionary of Judaism in the Biblical Period: 450 B.C.E. to 600 C.E.* (ed. J. Neusner and W. S. Green; New York: Simon & Schuster Macmillan, 1996; repr., Peabody, Mass.: Hendrickson, 1999), 1:112.

[22] Norman Solomon, *Historical Dictionary of Judaism* (Lanham, Md.: Scarecrow, 1998), 79.

[23] Paul Christophe, *Vocabulaire historique de culture chrétienne* (Paris: Desclée, 1991), 52: "Canon: In Greek: rule. (1) Every solemn decision. . . . (2) Name given . . . to the great prayer of the Mass. . . . (3) List of works which constitute part of the catalogue of sacred books and are recognized as of divine inspiration and thus canonical: 'canon of scriptures.'"

[24] Rudolf Smend and Otto Merk, "Bibelkanon," *Evangelisches Kirchenlexikon: Internationale theologische Enzyklopädie* (ed. Erwin Fahlbusch et al.; 5 vols.; Göttingen: Vandenhoeck & Ruprecht, 1986–1997), 1:468–74: "Old Testament canon . . . Preliminary Stages: Long before the writings of the OT . . . became canonical . . . , many of their constituent parts laid claim to and received a recog- nition that was already related to canonicity and that made the path toward canonization subse- quently appear as logical. It is the characteristic of NT canon formation that the early church historically closed and delimited the canon under the clear consideration of apostolic authorship of the writings, [and] that it . . . presented them in the correlation of rule and writing. . . . The canon formation itself is accordingly explainable only from the history of early Christianity, from its pro- cess through the early church, and from the motives that determined it."

9. Los griegos usan el vocablo *Canon* como sinónimo de *registro* o *catálogo;* y en este sentido lo oímos de los Libros de la Escritura. . . . no es canónico, si está fuera del catálogo. El *Canon Bíblico* es el catálogo de libros inspirados y reconocidos como inspirados.[25]

The sources above are unanimous in their general definition of canon, each including many of the essential aspects, although all omit some aspects important for the complete definition. This is not surprising, since there has not usually been such an acute need to clarify the definition so comprehensively. But it should be noticed that, though aspects may be missing, there is no hint of disagreement. From them we learn:

"Canon" is a technical term (1; 4?).

The term is late and Christian (2, 4, 6; 8?), though the idea is Jewish (4).

It means both "rule" and "list" (1, 2, 4, 8, 9).

"List" predominates in the discussions (2, 4, 5, 6, 7, 9; 3?, 8?).

The list involves books (1, 2, 3, 5, 6, 7, 9) not their textual form (not explicit).

The list is closed or delimited (3, 4, 5, 6, 7, 8, 9; 2?).

There was a lengthy process whose end was the canon (3, 5, 8; 4?).

The closed list is the result of a reflective judgment or series of reflective judgments, i.e., the books have been recognized and accepted through sifting or debate according to criteria (3, 4, 5, 6, 7, 8, 9).

The books were authoritative (4, 6) because (4) inspired (2, 4, 6, 7, 9).

The list of books was accepted or certified by a group or community (6, 8; 3?, 5?).

Thus, when used in biblical or theological discourse among Jews and Christians, the "canon of scripture" is a technical term with a long-since established meaning in the history of theology. It properly denotes one of two principal meanings:

1. The canon of scripture, i.e., the canon which scripture constitutes, the *rule* of faith articulated by the scriptures (= *norma normans*), the rule that determines faith, the authoritative principles and guiding spirit which govern belief and practice.

2. The canon of scripture, i.e., the canon which constitutes scripture, the *list* of books accepted as inspired scripture (= *norma normata*), the list that has been determined, the authoritative list of books which have been accepted as scripture.

Though the adjective "canonical" is used legitimately in both senses, the noun "canon [of scripture]" is predominantly used in the second sense, less in the first.[26] When

---

[25] Ricardo Rabanos, *Propedeutica biblica* (Madrid: Editorial la Milagrosa, 1960), 110: "The Greeks use the word canon as synonymous with 'register' or 'catalogue'; and in this sense we hear it of the books of Scripture. . . . it is not canonical if it is outside the catalogue. The biblical canon is the catalogue of books that are inspired and recognized as inspired."

[26] The phrase "canonical text," however, is usually used inappropriately; it is often a collapsed way of saying the text of a book that is canonical or the contents of a canonical book. But it should

the first meaning is being used, thought is seldom given to the distinction between books that are widely accepted as officially recognized scripture and books that are not; usually the former is simply vaguely assumed. Most religious groups and individuals are seldom influenced by the full range of canonical books while totally excluding noncanonical books, but are guided by a particular part of the canon (a canon within a canon). That is because there are conflicting theologies within the canon, and the discussion usually has a specific focus and therefore envisions a particular thrust or thematic within the canonical literature. Thus, the canon as rule of faith is used in theological discussion, but most frequently—especially in relation to the discovery of the scrolls—it is the second sense, the official corpus of books accepted as scripture, that is intended.

In such cases, the proper meaning of canon is the definitive list of inspired, authoritative books which constitute the recognized and accepted body of sacred scripture of a major religious group, that definitive list being the result of inclusive and exclusive decisions after serious deliberation.

In light of the definition given above, it is now encouraging to note that *The Access Bible* (1999) offers the following definition: "By the *biblical canon* is meant the official list of the books which make up the scriptures of the Old and New Testaments. Books which appear on this list are called *canonical* and all other books *non-canonical*."[27] Contributors to *The Access Bible* include Protestants, Catholics, and Jews; though it is unknown whether all were consulted on that particular definition and endorsed it, agreement on the concept's definition (if not on the contents) would be plausible in light of the definitions collected from dictionaries and encyclopedias from each tradition.

B. Distinctions between Canon and Related Concepts

It is essential to distinguish between a number of terms or realities that are closely associated with, but not identical to, the concept of canon:

An authoritative work is a writing which a group, secular or religious, recognizes and accepts as determinative for its conduct, and as of a higher order than can be overridden by the power or will of the group or any member. A constitution or law code would be an example.

A book of scripture is a sacred authoritative work believed to have God as its ultimate author, which the community, as a group and individually, recognizes and accepts as determinative for its belief and practice for all time and in all geographical areas.

---

not be used to designate the textual form of a book, because it is not the textual form but the book—regardless of textual form—that is canonical in antiquity. Later, in the case of those whose religious belief includes the canonical status, not only of the books of the canon, but also the wording as in the MT, the MT can be spoken of as "the canonical text." But does this then imply that readings from other textual traditions should not be used to correct the MT? Also, this would seem to be a religious conviction that crystallized after "the great divide"—textually (in Talmon's sense), but also religiously. That is, Christianity had already appropriated its Jewish scriptures, which were neither closed as a collection nor uniform in textual editions, before the Masoretic form of each book became the sole Hebrew form that survived.

[27] "The Nature of the Biblical Canon" (26), and similarly "Glossary" (424), in *The Access Bible* (emphasis in the original).

The textual form of most books of scripture was pluriform in antiquity. A book may have been widely and definitively considered scripture, but it may have been circulating in several textual forms and may have been still developing. It is the book, and not the textual form of the book, that is canonical (see below).

The canonical process is the journey of the many disparate works of literature within the ongoing community of Israel (including eventually both rabbinic Judaism and Christianity, each claiming to be the true Israel) from the early stages when they began to be considered as somehow authoritative for the broader community, through the collection and endorsement process, to the final judgment concerning their inspired character as the unified and defined collection of scripture—i.e., until the judgment of recognition that constituted the canon. The canonical process would not seem to reach back as far as the earliest sources (national religious epic, liturgical and priestly texts, folk wisdom) when they were simply literature and were not yet perceived as authoritative. Canon as such is a static concept, the result of a retrospective conclusion that something has come to be. If the focus is on a book or the collection of books while a historical, developmental trajectory is envisioned or is still in process, then the proper term is "process toward canon" or "canonical process."

A collection of authoritative scriptures was certainly in existence and taken to be fundamental to the Jewish religion from sometime in the first half of the Second Temple period. But it is necessary to keep in mind Bruce Metzger's distinction between "a collection of authoritative books" and "an authoritative collection of books."[28] One can designate the growing collection of authoritative books as "canonical" in the first sense of rule, but there is not yet a canon in the second sense of an authoritative list.

The Bible, in the singular, denotes a written form of the full collection of canonical books. Whereas the canon is the normative list of the books, the Bible is the material copy of that fixed collection of books, conceived of as a single anthology, and usually presented as such. In a sense, the term may seem anachronistic until the format of the collection of scriptural books was the codex (third century C.E.?). "The scriptures" may be an open collection, but the "Bible" would seem to indicate an already closed collection.

C. Essential Elements in the Concept of Canon

Eichhorn once said that "it would have been desirable if one had never even used the term canon,"[29] but the concept is rich and important, and perhaps it would be better to say that it would be desirable if everyone used the term properly. In fact, many major scholars of the latter twentieth century transmitted discussions concerning the correct usage. Here I can cite only a few examples for illustration; they and many others will be discussed more fully in this volume. James Barr maintained that the canon is a later concept and term, and that it is a technical term requiring precise definition and precise usage.[30] Bruce Metzger was strong on the reflective nature of the decisions regarding canon, pointing out that the process by which the canon was formed "was a task, not only of collecting, but also of sift-

---

[28] Metzger, *The Canon,* 283.
[29] Cited in B. S. Childs, *Introduction to the Old Testament as Scripture* (Philadelphia: Fortress, 1979), 36.
[30] J. Barr, *Holy Scripture: Canon, Authority, Criticism* (Philadelphia: Westminster, 1983), 50.

ing and rejecting."[31] Similarly, Julio Trebolle Barrera noted that use of "the Greek term 'canon' comes from New Testament studies . . . [and] belongs to a very late period in the history of the formation of the NT canon . . . [and that in the biblical period to] apply the term 'canon' to the Hebrew Bible, therefore, is quite unsuitable."[32] Sid Leiman provided a definition of a canonical book as "a book accepted by Jews as authoritative for religious practice and/or doctrine, and whose authority is binding upon the Jewish people for all generations. Furthermore, such books are to be studied and expounded in private and in public."[33] It is understandable that not every definition and discussion in the past has explicitly mentioned every essential aspect of the definition of canon. But the definitions given above all agree with each other in their explicit elements and show no sign of disagreement due to the elements missing or implicit.

Eichhorn notwithstanding, and in light of the related but distinct terms listed in section B above, there is a need for a definition of "the canon of scripture." There was and is a need for a term that denotes the final, fixed, and closed list of the books of scripture that are officially and permanently accepted as supremely authoritative by a faith tradition, in conscious contradistinction from those books that are not accepted. From the fourth century, "canon" is the term employed to denote that list. All the elements of that definition must be present, or the term will be used in a way that may cause confusion.

There are three elements in the definition of canon that perhaps need more discussion due to the new situation occasioned by the discovery of the biblical Dead Sea Scrolls and recent discussions involving varying understandings of canon. First, the canon involves books, not the textual form of the books; secondly, it requires reflective judgment; and thirdly, it denotes a closed list.

The book, not its textual form. Prior to the discovery of the scrolls, there was an assumption that the text of the Hebrew Bible was simply equated with the Masoretic Text. The Samaritan Pentateuch and the Septuagint were generally delegated to the sidelines and used primarily to "fix" the MT when there was a problem; the Targums and Peshitta also added overwhelming witness to the form of text as in the MT. But the scrolls have illuminated an unsuspected stage in the history of the biblical text: a period in which the text of the books of scripture was pluriform and still creatively developing, prior to the period of a single text for each book.[34] The composition and compilation of each book was a

---

[31] Metzger, *The Canon*, 7. Note Athanasius's directive (cited in Metzger, *The Canon*, 212): "Let no one add to these; let nothing be taken away from them."

[32] J. Trebolle Barrera, *The Jewish Bible and the Christian Bible* (tr. W. G. E. Watson; Leiden: Brill; Grand Rapids: Eerdmans, 1998), 148.

[33] Sid Z. Leiman, *The Canonization of Hebrew Scripture: The Talmudic and Midrashic Evidence* (Hamden, Conn.: Archon Books, 1976), 14.

[34] The latter period is often labeled the period of "stabilization"; but this appears to be a misnomer, since no evidence surfaces that the rabbis critically examined the various text forms in circulation and consciously selected a single text per book. They rather appear simply to have continued to use one of the several editions available for each book. Apparently they deliberately chose the Jewish ("square") script against the Palaeo-Hebrew script used by the Samaritans, and they deliberately chose the Hebrew language against the Greek texts increasingly used by the Christian Jews. But it is difficult to find evidence that they selected among the editions of a book or "stabilized" the text. Insofar as this is accurate, the text was more "frozen" than "stabilized"; though "single form" or "uniform" may be a more neutral term.

lengthy, diachronic development, from its earliest sources up through its latest literary editions. The process usually involved more than one major author (cf. J, E, D, P for the Pentateuch; the Deuteronomists and their sources for Deuteronomy to Kings; First, Second, and Third Isaiah; the many composers of Psalms and Proverbs; and so forth) in addition to a series of minor authors, redactors, and contributing scribes. Qumran demonstrates that the textual form of most books was still in that state of creative development until at least 70 C.E. and possibly as late as 132. Now, when considering the books of scripture in the period of the late Second Temple and the origins of Christianity and rabbinic Judaism, we must distinguish between the book or literary opus and the particular wording or literary edition of that opus which may still have been in the stage of creative development. It was the book, i.e., the scroll, not its particular wording or literary edition, which made the hands unclean, according to the rabbis.[35] Likewise for Christian theologians:

> Eusebius and Jerome, well aware of such variation in the witnesses, discussed which form of text was to be preferred. It is noteworthy, however, that neither Father suggested that one form was canonical and the other was not. Furthermore, the perception that the canon was basically closed did not lead to a slavish fixing of the text of the canonical books.

> Thus, the category of 'canonical' appears to have been broad enough to include all variant readings (as well as variant renderings in early versions). . . .

> In short, it appears that the question of canonicity pertains to the document *qua* document, and not to one particular form or version of that document.[36]

Reflective judgment. The fact of canon represents a conscious, retrospective, official judgment; it confirms that what has gradually come to be will now and must forever be.[37] In philosophical terms this is called a reflective judgment. It examines what has become the case and ratifies it. It looks back over a process and consciously affirms it as now a static, enduring situation. In this case, it considers the experienced fact that certain books have been functioning as authoritative for the faith community, weighs the situation, recognizes that the necessary criteria have been met, explicitly accepts and affirms the reality, and decides that this will ever be so:

> Thus, for a long while the community handed down sacred writings that increasingly functioned as authoritative books, but it was not until questions were raised and communal or official agreements made that there existed what we properly call a canon. The simple practice of living with the conviction that certain books are binding for our community is a matter of authoritativeness. The reflexive judgment when a group formally decides that it is a constituent requirement that these books which have been exercising authority are henceforth binding is a judgment concerning canon.[38]

Closed list. An essential part of the process toward the canon was the judging and sifting to determine which books were supremely authoritative and which not. As long as the list was open, there was a collection of authoritative books, a collection of scriptures, but there was not yet an authoritative collection of books, a canon. We have noted

---

[35] *M. Yad.* 3:5, 4:6.
[36] Metzger, *The Canon*, 269–70.
[37] See R. Funk's paper in Part Three for a different perspective on this matter.
[38] Ulrich, *Scrolls and Origins*, 57.

Metzger's insistence, echoing Athanasius, that the process by which the canon was formed "was a task, not only of collecting, but also of sifting and rejecting."[39]

Thus, the requirement of reflective judgment and an exclusively closed list of books (prescinding from the textual form of the books) are essential elements in the concept of canon. As long as those elements are missing, the community indeed has a collection of authoritative books of scripture, but it does not yet have a canon.

D. Sources of Confusion in Discussions of Canon

One of the most learned and sophisticated books on canon to appear recently is John Barton's *Holy Writings, Sacred Text*. One of the few moments in which I would disagree with him is when he says, "Modern scholars are of course perfectly entitled to use these terms as they wish. . . ." But he immediately exculpates himself when he continues: "but [they] need to recognize the danger of building the conclusions into the premises if they want to use them in discriminating among different historical reconstructions."[40] In fact, his statement results in part from the "sterility of the resulting discussion . . . [g]iven their diverse definitions of 'canon.' "[41]

I would like to make two points. Barton may agree with the first for purely utilitarian reasons; he would doubtless agree with the second, since I owe the idea to him. First, for future discussion to be useful and to escape from the confusion that now muddies the water, it is imperative to reach consensus on the definition of canon.[42] If the definition I have presented above is inaccurate or inadequate, appropriate revisions should be made and agreed upon, but continuing confusion has little to recommend itself.

Second, the definition of canon is a relatively minor matter. Much more important, interesting, and ripe for analysis is the canonical process—the historical development by which the oral and written literature of Israel, Judaism, and the early church was handed on, revised, and transformed into the scriptures that we have received, as well as the processes and criteria by which the various decisions were made. *Prophecy and Canon*, by Joseph Blenkinsopp, constitutes an excellent and promising bellwether which, unfortunately, few have followed.[43] John Barton also gives as one of his aims "to open up the question what people did with the 'canon' in the ancient world, and what kinds of meaning they looked for in it."[44] The chapters that follow will contribute to this second point. With regard to the first point, there is scope here for only a few concluding reflections.

---

[39] Metzger, *The Canon*, 7.

[40] John Barton, *Holy Writings, Sacred Text: The Canon in Early Christianity* (Louisville, Ky.: Westminster John Knox, 1997), 15. The book was originally published as *The Spirit and the Letter* (London: SPCK, 1997).

[41] Barton, *Holy Writings*, 14.

[42] Barton in fact later states that a "lack of agreement about the use of terms bedevils many areas of study. . . ." He defends Sundberg's distinction "between the 'Scripture' which results from the growth of writings perceived as holy, and the 'canon' which represents official decisions to exclude from Scripture works deemed unsuitable. In my view this distinction can greatly clarify our thinking about both the Old and the New Testament" (ibid., 157–58).

[43] Joseph Blenkinsopp, *Prophecy and Canon: A Contribution to the Study of Jewish Origins* (Notre Dame, Ind.: University of Notre Dame Press, 1977).

[44] Barton, *Holy Writings*, 159.

3. Conclusions

The canon of scripture, in the sense that that term has been used in the history of Christian theology and within Judaism after it borrowed the term from Christian usage, is the definitive, closed list of the books that constitute the authentic contents of scripture. It should not be confused either with stages in the canonical process or with simply books that are canonical, because books can be, and were, canonical (in the sense of canon 1) long before there was a canon of scripture. Although Lee McDonald is correct in general, he invites confusion when he says: "In a very real sense, Israel had a canon when the tradition of Moses receiving the Torah on Sinai was accepted into the community. Whatever functioned in the community of Israel as an authoritative guide was 'canon' in the sense of Sheppard's 'canon 1.' "[45] That statement is true, but is it helpful for discussions of the canon of the scriptures? Is the noun "canon" properly used in that sense? Is the term still meaningful when it denotes only a basic authoritative guide toward doing good? Did not Adam and Eve have a canon in this sense when God said " . . . but of the tree of the knowledge of good and evil you shall not eat" (Gen 2:17)? Neither consistently in antiquity, nor through the history of theological discourse, nor normally today is the noun "canon" used in the sense of canon 1. Scripture certainly functioned as authoritative guide, but seldom was it referred to as "a/the canon" in that sense. McDonald himself indicates this when he more prominently says: "Canon, in the general sense that we intend here, denotes a fixed standard or collection of writings that defines the faith and identity of a particular religious community."[46]

If the canon is by definition a closed list of books that have been considered, debated, sifted, and accepted, then talk of an open canon is confusing and counterproductive; it seems more appropriate to speak of a growing collection of books considered as sacred scripture. Andrew Steinmann's *The Oracles of God,* in the midst of many valid and helpful points, asserts that "The canon may be open. . . . The canon may be closed."[47] But this can only perpetuate the confusion in terminology. Steinmann considers the canon "the collection of holy, inspired, authoritative books in the Temple. The canon could be *assumed* to be known and acknowledged by most Jews because of this normative archive."[48] The problem here, however, is that there is no way of knowing which books were normative in that archive beyond the Law and the Prophets, or even knowing which books were included among the Prophets. It would seem likely that there were books beyond those that eventually formed the Masoretic collection, and unlikely that the *only* books preserved by the Jerusalem priests were those that eventually formed the Masoretic collection. Would it not have been more likely that the priests had Sirach and Jubilees and Enoch (if only as sources to confute) than that they had the Song of Songs? Steinmann is focusing on the collection of authoritative scriptures during the canonical process; they were canonical (in the sense of canon 1), but there was no canon of the scriptures yet.

---

[45] Lee M. McDonald, *The Formation of the Christian Biblical Canon* (rev. and enl. ed.; Peabody, Mass.: Hendrickson, 1995), 20.

[46] Ibid., 13.

[47] Steinmann, *Oracles of God,* 19, for both quotations.

[48] Steinmann, *Oracles of God,* 185; emphasis in the original.

Mere mention of the name of a book or even of a collection of books is occasionally equated with its canonical status, i.e., with wide-spread acceptance of that book as scripture or of that collection as the canon of the scriptures as we know them.[49] Such maximalist claims must inevitably yield to later, more balanced assessments. Just as it is a necessary corrective to reflect that the books of the New Testament were not in circulation at the time of Jesus and the first Christians, it is corrective to reflect that the books of the Law and the Prophets were not circulating in the form that we know them at the time of Ezra. The books that came to be the Bible did not start off as books of the Bible. In many passages that now constitute those books, the authors did not think that they were writing scripture. Other than for the book of Daniel, the letters of Paul, and the Gospels, usually a lengthy period stretched between the composition of a book and its general acceptance as a book of scripture.

Thus, with Plato, I urge that we formulate and agree upon a precise definition of the canon of scripture for the sake of clarity, consistency, and constructive dialogue. If the definition proposed above is inaccurate or insufficient, revisions in harmony with the history of theological discourse will be welcome.

---

[49] An example would be the interpretation of Luke 24:44 ("the Law of Moses and the Prophets and Psalms") as: "This saying suggests that 'the Law of Moses', 'the Prophets' and '(the) Psalms' are now established names for the three parts of the canon"; see Roger Beckwith, *The Old Testament Canon of the New Testament Church* (Grand Rapids: Eerdmans, 1985), 111. The book is rich in data but tends toward maximalist interpretation; see further the review of Beckwith by Albert C. Sundberg Jr. ("Reexamining the Formation of the Old Testament Canon," *Int* 42 [1988]: 78–82), and Andrew Steinmann's critique (*Oracles of God*, 71 n. 113).

3

The Jewish Scriptural Canon in Cultural Perspective

Philip R. Davies

Let me begin with two fundamental observations. One is that canon formation is a cultural phenomenon; the other is that canon formation is a natural process in any literate (and perhaps even nonliterate) society. The Jewish canon, to be understood culturally, needs to be seen in perspective.[1]

These statements imply, of course, a certain definition of canon. This volume is about particular canons, those of Judaism and Christianity, and a good deal of discussion about these canons assumes that "canon" is a religious phenomenon, and that its formation and effect are to be described in religious categories, namely in terms of what that society believed and/or what the theologians or authorities of that religion determined (e.g., "authority" and "inspiration"). But in the hellenized world of early Judaism and the New Testament, the most influential canon was that of the educated Greek speakers, and it included the works of Homer (preeminently), of Euripides, Menander, and Demosthenes, of Hesiod, Pindar, Sappho, Aeschylus, Sophocles, Aristophanes, Herodotus, Thucydides, and Aesop. The canon(s) of the Greeks and Greek-speakers, promoted in the schools and libraries, represented the best examples of the fundamental genres or the basic modes of cultural life: philosophy, epic, drama, poetry, and history. Greek literature did not form a religious canon at all, any more than the "Western canon" of such literary critics as Harold Bloom,[2] referring to the fundamental works of English literature, including Shakespeare, Milton, and Dickens.

The second statement with which I opened is that canon formation is a natural process. Again, books on the Jewish and Christian canons tend to focus on one particular (and not inevitable) process of canonizing: the drawing up of fixed lists. Now in the process of arguing about what is "the best," individual critics and aficionados often will draw up their own list. Institutions like schools and universities can also impose such lists on their entrants and members. And these lists can be called "canons." This was also the case in the Hellenistic world. But these various lists are not created ad hoc; such canons are in fact versions of what a wider group (a class, a nation, a civilization) holds to be its own canon. These individual canons are always derived from a collection of works that are already

---

[1] A more detailed account of such an approach to the canonizing of the Hebrew scriptures is given in my *Scribes and Schools: The Canonization of the Hebrew Scriptures* (Library of Ancient Israel; Louisville, Ky.: Westminster John Knox, 1998).

[2] Harold Bloom, *The Western Canon: The Books and School of the Age* (New York and London: Harcourt Brace, 1994).

canonized. One cannot simply declare a work canonical if it has no canonical pedigree; one can only affirm or deny that a work's canonical status is formally recognized by a particular group.

We do not, then, begin to understand the origin, nature and history of the Jewish and Christian canons if we confine ourselves to processes in which religious authorities drew up lists of inspired or authoritative religious texts. We have to ask not only why these works came to be considered at all, but also why they were preserved up to that point, and, most importantly, *where the idea of a canon came from*. As far as we can tell, the idea of a fixed number of religiously authoritative writings is a peculiarity of Judaism and Christianity; and, since the two canons are historically and culturally connected, we are probably talking about a single phenomenon. But despite the importance of the biblical canon in Christianity (and to a lesser extent in Judaism), these canons cannot be taken as representative examples of human canonization. They constitute an unusual and particular instance of a common human cultural process. To understand *why there are canons at all,* including these two canons, we have to look at canonizing as a common and natural activity of literate societies.

1. Literacy in Ancient Agrarian Societies

Cultural processes like canonizing are perhaps best understood by the widest possible form of comparison. In most cultural studies, where human behavior, whether individual or social, is being investigated, a small sample is not at all desirable. However, in a short chapter one cannot survey the entire range of human canonizing. Rather, we can look at the process in the great civilizations of the world in which Judaism and Christianity first developed, the world dominated politically and culturally first by Egypt and Mesopotamia, then by Persia, then Greece and Rome. Fortunately, the literatures of Egypt, Babylonia (understood in the cultural sense, including Assyria), Greece and Rome are well enough preserved for us to know their canons, and to understand why and how they came into being. We can assume that the inhabitants of Palestine were aware of the literatures of those civilizations that ruled and colonized them, and, certainly in the case of the Greek canon, that many Jews in the Diaspora were taught the works of the Greek canon. By looking at the canons of these civilizations, then, we are not only making a *comparative* study but a *historical* one. The Jewish (and Christian) canons did not originate in a vacuum, but out of a world of which canons were a natural part.

In the widest sense of the word, we can speak of oral canons, of works that form the core of a society's spoken literature.[3] For canonizing is not confined to literate societies. But writing, and the emergence of a literate class within a society, has decisive effects on the production of canons. These are (a) the representation of canons in written texts and (b) the formal education of a literate class. Written texts enable canons to be physically represented, and represented in historical forms. Writing makes explicit the process of editing, a process that in oral cultures is more elusive. The existence of writing makes possible the canonization of specific texts rather than of stories, tales, lore, rites, however

---

[3] On this see Susan Niditch, *Oral Word and Written Word* (Library of Ancient Israel; Nashville: Westminster John Knox, 1996).

much or little such things may change in oral societies. The restriction of writing to a particular group of people constitutes canonizing as a class process, for those who can read
and write learn to do so, and practice their skill, as distinct operations within the social
system: as clerks, administrators, diplomats. Writing accords control of public knowledge
to one layer of society, and represents one of the most obvious mechanisms by which complex societies are formed, by the differentiation of functions and by the creation of hierar-
chies. The creation of a literate class forming part of the state administration illustrates
both processes. And it is within these groups that the literary canons of the ancient Near
East originate; as repositories not of a *society*'s literature, but of the literature of a *class*.
(The case of ancient Greece is different; here the emergence of political rule by citizens and
the lack of political power exercised by temples created different conditions).

But literacy itself does not immediately generate a canon, for a canon is a collection
of *literature,* not merely *texts,* and the ability to write does not mean the ability to write *literature.* Indeed, the writing of *literary* texts, as distinct from administrative texts such as
tax receipts, records of gifts to a temple, or lists of personnel or names of classes of objects
(heavenly bodies, for example) does not come about as a matter of course. Writers on literacy in ancient Israel and Judah[4] sometimes obscure this fact. Nor does the ability to write
mean that existing oral compositions will necessarily begin to be written down. This is
another erroneous assumption that some scholarship on biblical literature has made.
Writing down folk tales, legends, or myths does not help preserve them. These texts are
quite satisfactorily preserved orally and do not need to be written. Indeed, writing them
down has the opposite effect. In an ancient agrarian society 95 percent (or more) of the
population cannot read, though they can hear; writing down *restricts communication to the
privileged class.* Writing is power, and no cultural analysis of writing, and thus of canonizing and canons, must pretend otherwise.

2. Early Uses of Literacy

The production of literature arises from various causes. We can identify two main
arenas for such activity: the state and the scribal community. Scribes (this is the most convenient term to use for the literate class) learned and practiced writing in the service of the
state, at least in the societies of the ancient Near East. In Greece, and in the Hellenized
world, this ceased to be the case as literacy spread further.[5] But in the beginning, literacy is
a function of the state and represents an important instrument of its control. In its service,
scribes perform the tasks of writing letters to and from king and palace: drafting military
reports such as the letters from Lachish, and conducting diplomatic correspondence
between states and among themselves, as at Arad.[6]

---

[4] E.g., André Lemaire, *Les écoles et la formation de la Bible dans l'ancien Israel* (OBO 39;
Fribourg: Editions universitaires, 1981); Alan Millard, "An Assessment of the Evidence for Writing
in Ancient Israel," in *Biblical Archaeology Today* (Jerusalem: Israel Exploration Society), 301–12.

[5] For Greek and Hellenistic cultures, the role of writing and canons is well covered by H. I.
Marrou, *A History of Education in Antiquity* (trans. G. Lamb; London: Sheed and Ward, 1956).

[6] For the texts referred to, see Graham I. Davies, ed., *Ancient Hebrew Inscriptions* (Cambridge:
Cambridge University Press, 1991).

Temple scribes also wrote divinations, lists of sacrifices, and records of cultic activity. Prophets, perceived as official messengers of the gods, and in the service of a temple or members of prophetic guilds, were consulted by kings, elders, and perhaps occasionally individuals. They sometimes—perhaps even quite often—wrote their oracles. At any rate we have not only the evidence of such texts at Mari,[7] but also the phenomenon of written Judean prophecy.[8] Priestly scribes wrote lists of omens and the text of hymns and prayers. Although these liturgical items could have been learned orally, writing them down could have served a number of purposes. Written texts are easier to keep secret from unauthorized access. The written form also protects more securely the precise wording, important in any religious ritual; inaccuracy could prevent efficacy. Changes in wording could also be effected authoritatively and efficiently by means of written texts. The point is that *writing permits control of data.* The written text has a sanctity that an oral recitation does not, even where oral recitation is the purpose for which the text is written (there is some evidence that silent reading was an art developed only in classical times).

In order to understand the mentality and culture of the scribal class, it is important to recognize that writing was regarded as a gift of the gods, not a mere convenience nor a human invention. And while this claim certainly helped to preserve the aura of the scribe and his craft (the "his" is deliberate here), it is probably true that even the scribes regarded writing as something of a miracle, or at least a kind of esoteric art, enabling what other people said to be reproduced verbally by someone who had never heard the original words spoken.[9]

Writing in the service of the scribal class involves us in the vexing question of the "scribal school." The existence of such schools, by which is meant here not merely groups with a common interest but a formal institution of instruction and study, is well-known in ancient Egypt and Babylonia. At some point there will have been a scribal school also in Jerusalem, perhaps even during the monarchic period. While the scribal art seems to have been largely hereditary, and thus passed on from father to son (the "father-son" language remained traditional for instruction, as for example in the book of Proverbs), the growth of the class would entail the training of non-hereditary members and the necessity for ensuring a common education. Increasing complexity and specialization also broadened the scope of scribal activity. Scribal education would involve in the first instance the knowledge of how to write the characters (and probably to write in more than one language and alphabet). Alphabetic script, with less than thirty signs, held clear advantages

---

[7] A. Malamat, "A Forerunner of Biblical Prophecy: The Mari Documents," in *Ancient Israelite Religion: Essays in Honor of Frank Moore Cross* (ed. P. D. Miller, P. D. Hanson, and S. D. McBride; Philadelphia: Westminster, 1987), 33–52. The relevant literature is published by J.-M. Durand in *Archives epistolaires de Mari I/1* (Archives royales de Mari 26; Paris: Editions Recherche sur les Civilisations, 1988).

[8] On the written origins of prophetic literature, see my " 'Pen of Iron, Point of Diamond' (Jer 17:1): Prophecy as Writing," in *Writings and Speech in Israelite and Ancient Near Eastern Prophecy* (ed. M. Floyd and E. Ben Zvi; Atlanta: Scholars, 2000), 65–81, and the volume generally.

[9] Some readers may recall the scene from the film *Black Robe* in which a word spoken by a native chief to one of the Europeans is conveyed by writing to another, who is then able to repeat, to the astonishment of the speaker, what was secretly said, without the benefit of any oral transmission.

over the syllabic cuneiform system, with hundreds of signs and some choice in the manner of transcription (since syllables can be divided in different ways).

Without the theory of scribal schools, the discipline of paleography is of course impossible, so we need to conclude that the controlled evolution of writing styles is due to the existence of some official schooling that guaranteed consistency.[10] The advent of large administrative empires in the ancient Near East—Assyrian, Babylonian, Persian—led to the establishment of common imperial languages, scripts, and styles. The Assyrians earn the credit for applying standards that were largely followed by their successors, including the use of Aramaic as the international language of correspondence in the Levant (replacing Akkadian, the language used in the Amarna correspondence between Egypt and Palestine in the Middle Bronze period).

With the emergence of the scribal school, the scribal community acquires an institution that formally represents it, much as the sanctuary represents the priesthood or the palace the king. Here not only scribal skills were passed on, but also scribal values. The skills comprised several levels. At the basic stage the scribe needed to be able to write accurately. He also needed to be able to write in the correct style and language. How do you phrase a treaty document, a legal contract (such as a loan or a marriage document), or a prayer of petition? This level corresponds to the skills one acquires nowadays at a secretarial college. The third level is a matter of worldview, of professional attitude. A scribe serves the king or temple, and here lies both a privilege and a danger. The scribe must, of course be trustworthy, since he will sometimes write in the name of a ruler, and that ruler will probably be illiterate. His words are the king's words. As an administrator, he will acquire knowledge that will often see him consulted by the ruler on matters within his expertise. On the other hand, he will also be in direct communication with scribes who serve other masters: other kings, who may be equal, superior, or inferior to his own ruler.

Diplomatic skills entail the cultivation of professional virtues: honesty, tact, prudence, restraint, rationality, and the careful acquisition of relevant knowledge. They can be acquired through formal training, and there need be little doubt that a good deal of the wisdom literature of the Hebrew Bible, in which such virtues are upheld (e.g., in the book of Proverbs), reflect the values of the scribal class who no doubt originated many of the wise sayings, and certainly were responsible for collecting them and writing them down (see Prov 25:1).

The scribal school thus generates, as well as preserves, traditions of writing, and in this preservation and cultivation of genres we can see the beginnings of the canonizing process. The school will both train its new scribes in writing the genres required for service to the king or temple, and generate forms that serve the education of the scribe as a member of the class, such as what we call the "wisdom literature," including not only proverbs and didactic speeches, but also narratives that demonstrate the perils and rewards, virtues and vices, that a scribe may need or encounter in his service at court. Of these scribal tales three in particular, Sinuhe, Wen-Amon, and Ahiqar, were widely known. Esther and the tales of Daniel are biblical examples.[11]

---

[10] However, it remains a possible flaw in paleographical analysis that schools may have developed slightly different writing traditions and their script may have evolved at different rates. The analogy with pottery typology is instructive.

[11] See L. M. Wills, *The Jew in the Court of the Foreign King* (Minneapolis: Fortress, 1990).

Another important dimension of the world of the scribe is that it includes relations with other states. The cosmopolitan aspect of scribal culture is due to specific factors: first, that the work of scribes brought them into communication with their counterparts in other societies, through their diplomatic activities: second that these activities required them to have a knowledge and understanding of other societies; third, that in their interest in the acquisition of knowledge they did not respect the boundaries of their own society but took a natural interest in the world beyond. Scribal stories like *Wen-Amon, Sinuhe,* and *Ahiqar* (or like Tobit and the Joseph story) all involve travel to other countries. Finally, as indeed with the middle-class intellectuals of our own day, the culture of the scribe is less geographically rooted; he belongs to a class that exists in every society that has evolved into a state, sharing with scribes everywhere the precious secret of writing and the arts and responsibilities that it affords. It is not difficult to see how loyalty to a profession and to the intellectual agenda of a class often overrides an affiliation with one particular society. The simplest illustration of this frame of mind is the biblical wisdom literature itself (Proverbs, Job, Ecclesiastes) in which the norms of behavior are individual and universal, in contrast to the chauvinistic theology of Israel and its national god who runs the world in accordance with a covenant with one chosen people. Let us not forget, though, that scribes are responsible for both literatures—their writings in the service of the state and in the interest of their own class do not necessarily cohere. Such is the nature of diplomats, who are never rulers themselves but always "servants of the state" (or the monarch).

3. Archives and Libraries

The modern reader can distinguish archives and libraries, though there is no universally accepted definition of that difference, and indeed it is not clear how far ancient literary collections represent such a distinction. For the purposes of analysis, archives preserve administrative texts and records, libraries literary works. Records are generally preserved as long as they remain pertinent to the affairs of the state, and are then discarded (ancient archives that have been excavated show that such texts were in fact thrown out after a certain period). A library contains writings collected for their intrinsic worth, reflecting the cultural interests of the individual ruler (Ashurbanipal, for example, or numerous individual book collectors in the classical world) or the temple or city, or the scribal school and class. The essential point is that the contents of archives are not the subjects of canonization, while those of libraries, generally speaking, are. The primary criterion for canonizing is not administrative usefulness, and documents that have a short shelf life obviously do not become canonized. They have no continuing value.

Both archives and libraries entail classification. The importance of archiving for our study of canonizing is that it illustrates the role of the scribe as an *accumulator and organizer of knowledge.* In their role as custodians of written documents, the scribes needed to develop or learn the habits of accurate classification, so that records could be consulted and retrieved. The excavation of many ancient libraries unfortunately took place before the importance of such things was appreciated, with the result that we cannot reconstruct as we would like the categories by which the ancient archivists classified their documents. However, there is sufficient evidence that this was done by means of boxes, shelves, rooms and buildings.

These archives represented to the scribe something quite wonderful and valuable: knowledge in a material and circumscribed form. And, being the (self-styled) intellectuals of their day (they not only called themselves in Hebrew *soferim*, "writers," but also *hakhamim*, "intelligentsia"), the scribes were fascinated by their ownership of knowledge that could be physically represented. They sought not only to organize the knowledge of their world of work, but to acquire and organize the knowledge of the entire world: lands, animals, stars—whatever could be named and listed. An entire science of *listing* developed early as part of scribal culture. Without being too fanciful, we could say that the scribe wished to archive the world, to embrace its secrets within the confines of a written archive—to which he and his class alone, of course, would have access! One example in the Bible of such accumulated knowledge of the natural world, and the pride taken in it, is found in Job 28, where already the limited extent of this knowledge is being recognized. But the scribal intellectual was interested also in the origins and ends of things: the beginnings of humanity, the causes of death and evil, the mysterious engines of history, the hidden rules of personal success (ethics) and the ideal structure of human society. All these concerns are clearly recognizable in the Hebrew Bible: the early stories of Genesis are highly intellectual despite their apparent simplicity, as they seek to explore the nature of humanity and the origin of evil; the prophetic books, and to an extent the "historical" books probe the meaning and destination of history, including the fate of Israel, Judah, and the nations. Political philosophy can also be found in the ideal societies sketched in Leviticus, Numbers, and Deuteronomy. And of course the organizing of laws falls within the scribal concern too, for scribes were closely associated with the administration of justice. In early Judaism, indeed, the "intellectual" and the judge were subsumed into a single institution, the rabbinate—and no doubt, even early, the scribe, regarded as wise and knowledgeable, would regularly serve as a judge or arbiter in disputes. Hence in the biblical story it is Solomon's wisdom, the property above all of the scribes, that enables him to exercise justice.

Archiving, then, is the practical aspect of the intellectual task of acquiring, storing, and classifying knowledge. And canons are, in a sense, the result of a *classification,* an organizing, of a certain kind of knowledge as well as of acts of discrimination. But that knowledge is not preserved in the Jewish canon in the scientific form of lists, nor contained in the genres of everyday commercial or political transactions. It is not the material of an archive, but of a library. Scribal knowledge moves, with the scribal art, beyond lists into literature.

4. Scribal Literature

We can now move from the first important topic in our study of canonizing, the scribe, the canonizer, to that which is canonized, the literature. What makes literature different from mere writing?

One obvious difference is that literature is designed to be read, or at least read in a different way. Literature is not merely information. It functions differently. It may be possible to define what literature is in a few paragraphs; but this is unnecessary, since all readers of this book will know that there is an essential difference between a timetable, a receipt, a contract, on the one hand, and a novel, a poem, a joke, on the other. This is not to say that a huge gulf bridges the two. Quite the opposite: the transition from one to the other is easy and the distinction sometimes blurred. A letter, for example, may be an official communication, couched in the required terminology and fulfilling little more than a formal acknowledgement. But a letter may also be a highly literary form, such as we find everywhere in the classical world, and in the New Testament. There is no sudden transition from writing to literature that requires an explanation. After all, stories, myths, proverbs and jokes are full-fledged genres of oral communication that do not require the invention of writing. Writing came into a world that was already full of (oral) literature.

Why should the gift of writing be employed for the preservation of literature? It is a real and serious question. Ancient societies like Israel and Judah had storytellers, poets, singers, messengers. In an oral recitation, large numbers of nonliterate people could hear. A text, on the other hand, can be read by only one, literate, person at a time. There is no obvious advantage in writing "literature" and we therefore need to look carefully to discover why the literature in the Hebrew Bible was indeed written at all, and who, if anyone, was supposed to read it.

A simple example of the problem is the royal inscription. For some reason, we have no ancient royal inscriptions from any kings of Judah or Israel,[12] so we shall take Mesha, the king of Moab. He had an inscription (the "Mesha stele" or "Moabite Inscription") written that celebrated what he had done during his reign, featuring his successful liberation of his people from the hegemony of Israel. Now, why did he have this written? I suggest two reasons, connected with the content and the author. As for the content: writing, as said earlier, was widely understood (and especially by nonpractitioners) as containing some peculiar virtue. What was written was *fixed* (and so Pilate was able to say "what I have written, I have written"). Whatever may have happened was past and recalled only by human memory, which could indeed change anything. But events fixed in writing were more real than events that happened. I mean this not in any metaphorical or exaggerated sense, but very seriously and very exactly, for writing is a challenge to collective memory, and, together with collective (and for a lifetime only, individual) memory, is the only sense in which "history" exists in the ancient Near East). "What happened" means *what is remembered* by the vast majority of the people (that is, told in story, myth, legend), *or what is written*, and thus understandable only by the literate, who are, of course, among the rulers. This is not, of course, to say that what is written is more *accurate*, for writers can lie as easily as speakers, and usually more deliberately. But *writing transfers public knowledge from the people to the state*.

So Mesha *fixes his history*. In the second place, he also fixes himself. There is a well-known ancient genre in which writers justify their deeds to the god (Nehemiah's memoir is the best biblical example). To some extent this is, of course, a fiction, since the gods do not need to be told anything in writing. The real audience is human. But while a victorious king can shout his triumph at the battlefield, he will soon have to leave, and eventually he will die. An inscription ensures that his word, his presence, remains forever (or until a successor effaces it).

So inscriptions are not placed in public places such as a public square, temple, or a throne room, so as to be read by any passer-by. No doubt the contents of the inscription

---

[12] The so-called Hezekiah inscription once found in the Siloam tunnel does not name him; its ascription to him is only traditional.

can quickly become public knowledge, but there is rarely anyone in the vicinity to read it. What matters is that *it is written,* and this regardless of whether it is read at all. In a related way, it is important for all official documents to be not only written but kept, for thus the knowledge remains, even if it is never consulted. So, even to this day, in the words of the letter to the Hebrews, Mesha, more literally than Abraham, "being dead, still speaks."

Let us now look at a different kind of reading. The book of Nehemiah contains a story of an assembly in Jerusalem at which the law was read out to the people (chapter 8). In Jer 36 is an account of how the prophet orders his scribe Baruch (Jeremiah apparently being illiterate) to write down all his prophecies in order that Baruch could read them out to the people. Whether or not we choose to believe that either of these events is an accurate account of a particular event, they do show that public recitations were one means of reading written texts.

The question for this category of reading is, why use a written text at all? It is an interesting question for Jer 36 whether Jeremiah should be understood to have spoken his prophecies earlier. But in any event, he can remember them all perfectly, and. presumably, had he been able to address the inhabitants of Jerusalem, he would have done so without the need for any written text. The reason the text is written is that Baruch cannot learn them by heart in a short space of time, and of course, they need to be reproduced exactly, because they are not really Jeremiah's words, but those of his god. We do not, then, have in this story any reason why prophetic books as a whole should have come into existence, merely a theological explanation that equates written prophecy with written law, and makes prophecy, through writing, an eternal and fixed word of the deity.

The case of the recital of law is presumably different. Although we know that in practice laws were generally applied in all ancient Near Eastern societies (including Israel and Judah) locally by elders, according to the local tradition, it was the habit of kings, in pursuit of their claim to have legitimate authority to rule others, to defend the rights of all and thus to proclaim laws that were in theory obeyed in their realm. Laws are among the earliest of literary texts. It is unlikely that they were intended to be learnt by heart by judges; more likely their function was closer to that of the royal inscriptions discussed earlier.[13]

But with the advent of large empires, in which as a result of deportation or voluntary migration populations were often distanced from their native society and lived in proximity to other populations, the administration of law became a more serious political, administrative issue; to the extent that local ethnic groups were able to practice their own customs, they would administer their own justice, according to their own legal traditions. However, the Persians, at any rate, seem to have promoted the notion of written laws that could be applied throughout the empire to different ethnic groups. Thus Ezra's law is not merely for Judah, but for anywhere within the satrapy of "Beyond the River" (Ezra 7:25). In more complex and variegated societies, such as empires generate, the value of writing as against speech is enhanced. Bigger empires, like bigger businesses, mean bigger bureaucracy, and bureaucracy means paperwork, and paperwork means *writing down.* Inevitably, written laws will tend to prevail over oral traditions, regardless of the fact that practice will

---

[13] On the function of such laws, see B. S. Jackson, "Ideas of Law and Legal Administration: A Semiotic Approach," in *The World of Ancient Israel* (ed. R. E. Clements; Cambridge: Cambridge University Press, 1989), 185–202.

always follow local customs as well—at least, such was universally the case until the rise of the modern nation-state.

Thus, some texts are written for public consumption, and "heard" rather than "read." However, it remains doubtful whether we can actually identify any piece of (Hebrew) biblical law that was written for the purpose of being read out; Deuteronomy is the most likely candidate, since that document itself calls for its recitation.[14] It is certainly unlikely that most of the contents of the Hebrew Bible were known to the largely illiterate population of Judah through recitation, any more than through reading. The point I wish to underline again is that the literary canon is not a popular phenomenon. It is a class phenomenon, the creation and property of the literate, mostly on their own behalf but partly on behalf of the state.

This observation brings us to a third category of reading: class reading. Here we focus particularly on those texts that were generated and used within the scribal school, which, as I said earlier, is the quintessential institution of the scribal class. It is also here, I suggest, that the process of canonization has its heart. The literary canon of ancient Judah, part of which comprised also the canon of the Samaritans, was hardly developed publicly in a society that was illiterate, apart from the small scribal class, and whose canon was oral. It was within the scribal school, and the scribal community, that certain writings achieved a classic status. Classic works are those that are continually copied (and copying usually meant editing; the notion of a fixed text is postcanonical) and retained as models of their kind, as points of reference for future literary composition, or as definitive accounts of an important theme or issue. The mechanisms by which this canonizing occurred were copying and teaching, and the criteria were *functional* (teaching how certain forms of writings were properly executed, teaching scribal values) and *aesthetic* (the most elegant, beautiful, valuable achievements of literary art). As a class whose profession was writing, and performing tasks that devolved from writing, notably archiving, scribes necessarily accumulated their own literary heritage. These classic works would form their canon; indeed, culturally a canon is nothing else than the classics, until or unless it becomes divorced from its culture, as with the Jewish and Christian canons, when it ceased to be a cultural heritage and became a religious one.

As examples of canonized literary works we can suggest collections of psalms (the book of Psalms is an agglomeration of several canonized lists) and proverbs. In both cases functionality and aesthetics play a role. Other examples include genealogies, legal stipulations, prophetic oracles of various forms, such as the accusation, the tirade against a foreign nation, and the letter from the deity, the so-called messenger-speech. But in the canon we have inherited these building blocks of scribal formation are overshadowed by more ambitious, complex structures. These are mostly narrative structures: historiographies, origin myths, ethnographies. They attest the deployment of the more simple forms in combination. The first eleven chapters of Genesis are an example of easily recognizable simple narratives rewritten and combined into a longer but unified narrative. The same is true of the stories of the ancestors. In some cases we can guess at intermediate

---

[14] See Deut 31:10–13. This part of Deuteronomy perhaps reflects the same social and political situation as do Ezra and Nehemiah: the production of an (imperially-sponsored) written legal code. It is an unlikely practice in a native monarchy, where the king is the law.

stages in the process by which these larger units were developed, but however little or much scholars agree on this, it is clear that the scribes of Judah, as far as the preserved evidence lets us conclude, went far beyond their Near Eastern counterparts in their development of historiographical and prophetic genres, and, I think, also in their intellectual ambition. For instance, in the final connected narrative of the origins and history of "Israel" they constructed an idealized past society, rooted in their one true god and descended from a single ancestor, a society created by divine rescue, the giving of divine law and the donation of a land subsequently lost and only partly regained. In some cases these more extensive works reflect the interest of colonial masters (the Chronicler is an obvious example). But on the whole they serve the scribal class, both as an intellectual class curious about the past, the future, the structures of history and society, and about their own and their society's place in the "scheme of things," and also as members of the leadership of a society that was wedded to a single deity and a single temple, and later as an *ethnos* comprising people scattered over the Near East and beyond.

Finally, a word needs to be said about private reading. Jeshua ben Sira, a scribe and teacher in Jerusalem at the beginning of the second century B.C.E., speaks of the activities of the scribe, who studies law, prophets, and wise sayings. The book of Ecclesiastes ends with an editor's warning that while the book is worthwhile reading, some books would be better not written and this one needs reading with care. Most dramatically of all, the book of Hosea ends with the statement; "Those who are wise understand these things, those who are discerning know them," identifying the readership of the prophetic books with the use of terminology with which the scribal class identified itself. While individuals do not create canons, we must nevertheless reckon that at some point individual scribes took the trouble to read *and study* the works of their canon. The reasons given in the verses just cited point clearly to a religious motivation. For ben Sira, torah is the highest expression of wisdom (the scribe's ambition) and is to be found in the canonized writings, though torah is not exactly equated with the literature. It would not be correct, then, to suggest that the scribal canon became a religious canon at some defined point when that canon was fixed; but at least in the Ptolemaic period (ca. 315–200 B.C.E.) it was identified as divine and as a repository of the essential values of the religion of Judeans. Perhaps it would be more accurate, and more far-reaching, to say that within Judea itself, the national culture was becoming a religious phenomenon. This conclusion is not so obvious as it may seem: most ancient canons were not religious, and the reason why the Jewish one is religious has to do with the fact that Judean culture was regarded, at least in Judea itself, as a matter of religion. That the Greeks could not see their culture in such a way exposes one of the fundamental causes of tension between them.

5. Nonscribal Writing

To conclude this review of cultural processes of canon formation it is necessary to look at a small number of books that may have originated *outside* the scribal class and which thus point to a wider circle of literacy at some stage. I include among these the books of Ruth, Song of Songs, Jonah, and Esther. Two of these are short novels, featuring women, with little evident religious content; Jonah is a satirical story about a prophet, and the Song of Songs a collection of love poems. Debates about the date and origin of all except Esther point to some ambiguity about them. We know that the scribes often wrote short stories, but usually about their own kind, and never about women. Esther, perhaps, is not really about Esther at all, but about Mordecai; but Ruth is undoubtedly about women. As for the Song of Songs, no doubt the scribes enjoyed erotic poetry, but would they have written *and canonized* it? Not impossible, and there are parallels to such collections in Egypt[15]—but, again, the Song has a strong female voice. Is the female presence in several of these works coincidental?

Whether or not these writings can be assigned to the scribal class, we do know that during the age when the center of ancient Western civilization was swinging from Asia to Europe (something that began, as far as the Levant was concerned, already under the Persians), the rather more rigid structures of the agrarian societies of the ancient Near East were being undermined. The enlargement of empires territorially, the spread of the use of the lingua franca of first Aramaic and then Greek, the (now largely voluntary) emigration of populations and mixing of *ethnē*, the introduction of coinage and expansion of trade, accelerated, among other things, the power and cultural ambition of a once tiny, but now rapidly growing, class that had wealth, knowledge of the world, and a certain impatience with backward chauvinism. Even the Jews of Judah, who were able to sustain the basic structures of their own religious culture, were outnumbered by Greek-speaking "Judeans" for whom the Greek way of life was manageable alongside the embrace of their Jewish religion. While most Judean farmers remained illiterate, many Jews from the cities of the Persian, Greek, and Roman empires could read and write, as their lifestyle required. So, perhaps, could their wives, whose household labor was usually delegated to slaves, and who were therefore free and keen to be educated, to read and to write.

In Jerusalem, both ben Sira and the author of Ecclesiastes taught private pupils. As scribes themselves, they filtered the typical scribal modes of understanding; ben Sira commended the scribal tradition, while Ecclesiastes challenged traditional wisdom with the common sense of the individual. Probably both authors spoke and read Greek, though only Ecclesiastes shows it.

But their pupils no doubt mostly spoke a good deal of Greek, and their world was not that of the scribal intellectual, the scholar, the diplomat. It was the world of the estate, the villa, the seaport, the merchant, the financier. What was the canon of this new, but still Jewish, class? In many cases it was already Greek, for the Greeks had their public schools and theaters and libraries, unlike the Jews. Greek literature contained, as the Jewish scribal canon did not, both romance and exotic locations, including the sea (in which only Jonah in the Hebrew Bible has any interest).

To what extent do the books of Ruth, Esther, the Song of Songs, and perhaps Jonah, reflect a different class of literature? If they do not, it remains a problem that they have all been edited in different ways so as to modify their radical implications. Ruth's women give way to a male genealogy; in the Greek version of Esther the presence of the deity is introduced; Jonah is embedded in a book of twelve prophets, its voice now a member of a chorus; while the Song, textually unedited, as far as we can tell, was quickly allegorized. The

---

[15] See M. V. Fox, *The Song of Songs and the Ancient Egyptian Love Songs* (Madison, Wis.: University of Wisconsin Press, 1985).

conundrum is that these books were canonized. By whom, and how, if their contents needed revising and their ideology bending?

This question brings us to the verge of the topic of canon-fixing. Before we engage that, some consideration of the cultural context of the Jewish canon in particular is required.

6. The Jewish Canon

The amendments to the books of Ecclesiastes and Hosea offer clues to an important stage in the development of the Jewish scriptural canon, namely its function increasingly as a religious resource. I have mentioned that for ben Sira, torah represented the essence of Jewish culture; Ps 1 also redefines the collection of Psalms as literature for the "wise" to enable them to live according to the divine will.

This development, I suggest, tells us less about the canon than about the culture itself. It is not that the canon is narrowly religious by a process of selection; rather that Judean culture (at least its urban, intellectual, literary culture) itself became more and more focussed on its deity and its cult. Intellectual questions became more and more, it seems, determined by Judah's monotheism and Jerusalem's cult. How and why this happened, how the religion of Judaism within Judah began to define itself is well beyond the scope of this essay and indeed constitutes a major agenda of contemporary research into early Judaism. But we can see the effects in its literary canon.

What has been said up to now implies that the Jewish scriptural canon is not a careful selection of ancient Hebrew literature but represents more or less all that there was. It thus became a religious canon not by exclusion of inappropriate works but, where necessary, by emendation. This is not to say that no other literary works existed, or that in fixing the canon (see below) exclusion was not deliberately practiced. Indeed, while I have been referring throughout this essay to a "Jewish canon" it would be more correct to speak of several canons: the Mosaic canon (the Pentateuch), the prophetic canon (four collections of books of oracles and stories), canons of psalms and proverbs (each of these two biblical books is a canonical collection of poems and wise sayings). This fact in part explains reference to "law, prophets, and writings" in sources from the Greco-Roman period such as the books of Maccabees, the New Testament, and Josephus—none of these speak of anything like a canon, but a list of collections of holy books, i.e., canons (plural).

There were other writings, possibly other canons that for some reason were abandoned. That is to say, other writings were, for some Jews, at one time, regarded as canonical, part of the classical literary repertoire. We have come to appreciate in recent decades that in the Greco-Roman period no single normative Judaism existed, but that numerous groups, not only Sadducee and Pharisee, but also the adherents of the Enochic calendar responsible for the Qumran scrolls, vied for the claim to be true servants of the god of Israel. The scribal class was involved in this division, naturally, but how far back do such divisions go: to the Hasmoneans? To the time of Nehemiah? Somewhere in between? We cannot tell. I have up to this point spoken deliberately of a single "scribal class." This remains a correct description, but differences of ideology between, say, the Deuteronomic and the priestly literature, suggest different scribal traditions, affiliations, or colleges. Yet these variants were obviously not seen as incompatible, and their views are amalgamated in the scriptural canon, often even in individual scrolls.

In the Greco-Roman period, the figure of Enoch was celebrated by many Jews in an Enochic canon, which possibly included the (five?) books of Enoch and the book of Jubilees, which promoted the merger of Enochic calendar and Mosaic traditions. But the Enochic canon was an Aramaic one, though Jubilees was written in Hebrew. Enoch himself is only minimally represented in the book of Genesis, Enochic myths being systematically rewritten (see Gen 6:1–4). At once we can see how and why: a different theory of the origin of sin was preferred, one that provided an anthropological and theological basis for the rule of Mosaic torah by originating sin in the human will, not in a fall from heaven.[16] Tobit, Sirach, and the first book of Maccabees (all originally in Hebrew) are also works not endorsed in the scriptural canon, but for reasons we cannot know. Yet despite these few cases, we can conclude that the Jewish scriptural canon represents, as far as we know, and in the light of the range of texts from Qumran, almost the totality of the Hebrew literary classics. That the canon as a whole was subject to some overall revision remains a possibility, indicated by the presence of a chronological system that points to the recapture of the temple by Judas Maccabee in 164 B.C.E.[17]

By contrast, we can point to much more extensive Jewish literature in Greek. Yet as far as we know, no Jewish Greek canon was born. For this there are cultural and social, rather than theological reasons. There was no class basis, no institution, and no function for a corpus of Jewish classics written in Greek: the Greek language, in any case, had its own classics.

7. Fixing the Canonical Lists

We turn finally to what many writers on the Hebrew canon regard as their central problem: the fixing of a canonical list. Again from a general cultural perspective we can draw attention to such lists among the scholars of the Greek libraries and schools. But the impetus behind their listings seems to have been concern for the preservation of genuine works, followed by a concern for a stable text (again, reflected in the selection of official Masoretic Text forms in Palestine). It is not clear that in the case of the Jewish scriptural canon such concerns came into play: though there are numerous examples of pseudepigrapha, these are not in Hebrew and were hardly perceived as seriously compromising the "genuine" writings of Moses or Isaiah or Jeremiah.

Who, then, set forth a Jewish biblical canon, and why was a Jewish canon fixed? Just as oral texts do not necessarily become written by some inevitable law, neither do canons become fixed. The modern "Western canon" of English literature contains broadly agreed members, but cannot be "fixed" except arbitrarily by an individual critic. There is no authority with the power to achieve this.

The "why" and the "who" in this case belong inextricably together. Such canons obviously entail a political authority: who was in a position to decree, as both Josephus and the writer of 4 Ezra assert, that the Jews have a *fixed number of holy books*, even if the arithmetic of the two authors does not exactly coincide? Even if, by some natural process

---

[16] See my "Women, Men, Gods, Sex and Power: The Birth of a Biblical Myth," in *A Feminist Companion to Genesis* (ed. A. Brenner; Sheffield: JSOT, 1993), 194–201.

[17] On this see J. Hughes, *Secrets of the Times: Myth and History in Biblical Chronology* (JSOTS 66; Sheffield: JSOT, 1990).

connected with the transformation of essentially literary into essentially religious classics, it was argued that the written Torah ended with Moses, psalms with David, wisdom with Solomon, and that prophecy was dead, leaving all religious authority to interpreters of texts, who had the power to insist on this, and indeed, to initiate the standardization of the Hebrew text?

With many other scholars, I conclude that the fixing of a canonical list was almost certainly the achievement of the Hasmonean dynasty. The presence of Daniel in this list suggests that the rise of this dynasty is the *terminus a quo*. One also sees the Hasmoneans struggling to maintain the unity of their realm by siding in turn with different parties and by engaging in external conquest and internal repression, promoting the use of Hebrew on their coins and very probably rekindling political messianism in the figure of the priest-king. More particularly, 2 Macc 2:13–14 reports that Judas "collected all the books that had been lost" in the same way that Nehemiah had once founded a library. The notice plausibly points at least to the existence of such a collection, presumably an official one in the temple, in the author's time. Given that the Hasmoneans, for all their later Hellenistic leanings, were brought to power by a coalition of reactionary parties opposed to what they saw as Hellenizing innovation, we could assume that they were interested in fixing some kind of norm, by way of defining what it was they stood for, as in the case of the calendar. Such definitive decisions may well have alienated the writers of the Qumran scrolls, for instance, accelerating the formation of sectarian groups. An officially sponsored system of Jewish schooling, modeled on the Greek but replacing Homer with Moses, Euripides with Isaiah, is also likely to have been a Hasmonean initiative; the rabbinic school system probably had a precursor. The endorsement of an approved "canon" for such schooling is more likely to have come from the Hasmoneans than from Herod or any of Herod's successors.

So to go with their geographically "Davidic" realm and their revived Israelite monarchy, the Hasmoneans (which of them we can only guess) are the prime candidates for having installed an official list of Jewish writings, a canon for all, a basis for devotion and for education, a cultural resource to define the newly-independent Jewish state, a response to the totalitarianism of Greek language, learning and literature. The Hebrew canon was fixed, if this supposition is correct, as a matter of political policy and not through any internal logic of the canonizing process itself leading to "completion."

But the story of the fixing of the canon is not complete, for the Hasmoneans had control of a Jewish state that soon dissolved and after two revolts against Rome disappeared. The most remarkable episode in the history of the Jewish scriptural canon is the creation of a Jewish religion built upon the language of Hebrew (never to be a Jewish vernacular until the twentieth century) and study of the Hebrew scriptures. It is also worth pointing out that a Greek Jewish scriptural canon was never fixed, so that Christianity did not inherit a definitive form of the "Old Testament," several versions of which exist in various denominations today.

8. Canon and Authority

The rabbis, then, though they occasionally picked over one or two cases (Ecclesiastes, Song of Songs), did not fix the scriptural canon; they inherited it. They may have formalized its tripartite division, for although both Torah and Prophets are well established as names for canonical collections before the rabbinic period, the name Writings for the remainder was apparently not established before the rabbinic period. Yet this canon did not entirely suit the purposes and program of the rabbis. For the rabbinic agenda was focussed on Torah, and in a real sense it was the Torah that was the rabbinic canon (as it had earlier been the canon of the Sadducees). While the scriptural canon of Torah remained closed, a larger canon of Torah was generated through the addition of the Mishnah and then the Talmud. Indeed, within Judaism torah itself remains in principle open-ended, ever subject to new interpretation and clarification, always generating new rulings and definitions. Here the contrast between Christian and Jewish understandings of canon is most evident. Although some texts from the Prophets and Writings were incorporated into synagogue liturgy, particularly the Five Scrolls (Song of Songs, Ruth, Lamentations, Ecclesiastes, and Esther), the exegesis of all these Jewish writings was directed towards the Torah, and it was the Torah that was read through in the annual synagogue liturgical cycle. Rabbinic Judaism is not a religion of the Hebrew Bible, but a religion of Torah. Theologically, the prophets have always been regarded as teachers of Torah, and rabbinic exegesis of the Writings always tends toward its assimilation to Torah also, as a reading of the Midrash Rabbah to the Five Scrolls will quickly illustrate. The juxtaposition of the five festival scrolls with the five books of Moses in this Midrash is also significant.

Because a fixed literary canon was something the rabbis inherited rather than created, they also found it necessary to integrate this collection into their religious system, and this they did by sanctifying the physical scrolls themselves. Unable or unwilling to find a way of separating the *content* of Torah from non-Torah, they separated scrolls that contained the scriptural writings from all others, which they called "outside scrolls." Thus, rabbinic discussion of the canon, such as it is, turns precisely on whether a particular scroll "defiles the hands" (i.e., is scriptural) or not. For, of course, since the Jews, unlike the Christians, did not use such a thing as a biblical codex, a single book containing all of scripture, there was no such thing as a "Bible." The earliest Jewish scriptural codex is medieval.

Finally, the rabbis also inherited a fixed biblical text. This, too, like the scroll that contained it, was treated as a physical entity; its letters were sacred. The Massoretes, the rabbinic textual scholars, proceeded to hedge around this text, fixing its pronunciation by marking vowels, noting its irregularities, counting, annotating, and in some rare cases replacing unacceptable readings (by annotating, not changing, the written text). The written words and letters themselves thus became holy objects and the writing of a Torah scroll was, and is, subject to certain stringent rules, the breaking of which makes the scroll profane and unusable. In a religion without a cult, the Torah scroll has become the most sacred object in Judaism.

9. Conclusion

By way of conclusion, some general reflections on the cultural effects of canon are in order. Canon and authority go hand in hand. Until or unless a canon is fixed, it operates as an arbiter, a definer, of *class* values. Its authority is enforced by the teacher and the group ethos. It is open, but it is also in the nature of canons to be self-referential: canonical works proclaim themselves as such by being quoted, rewritten, interpreted, and in the canon of the Jewish scriptures one can readily see how the parts refer to each other.[18]

Once a canon becomes a religious collection, the nature of its authority changes: divine sanction is invoked, even divine authorship can be claimed. This process does not of itself preclude the continuity of the canonizing process: ben Sira, for instance, seems to have thought his own words a deserving companion to the wisdom of the ancients (Sir 39:6–9). The *fixing* of a canon is a further step that both entails a political and religious authority capable of dictating and imposing uniformity, and also creates a dichotomy between canon and non-canon, making the canon itself a symbol of the distinction between human and divine knowledge. Thereafter the natural processes by which canons would grow are shut off, and the mode of interpretation takes over: the fixed text, the fixed collection are subject (as we have seen preeminently in the case of the Masoretic Text) to *commentary* that must remain formally outside. The meaning of the contents of the canon can, and will, forever change, but that change will not be reflected in the text, but in the framework of understanding that informs its reading.

Control of meaning lies with the reader as much as, perhaps more than, with the author. The latest phase in the conjunction of canon and authority is therefore control of the politics of *reading*. With or without a Reformation, the Latin text of the Bible would eventually have been accessible in translation anyway, and the authority of the church over the act of reading it would have waned. The invention of printing and the rise of the nation state ensured that. But Protestant Christianity, faced with a gap left by the removed authority of church, pope and priest, has allowed the Bible to fill much of that gap, and evangelic Protestant biblical scholarship still seeks to direct the reader to the "true" meaning of the scriptural text. Yet the Bible addresses a much wider constituency, and at the beginning of the twenty-first century the Western world, at least, faces the challenge and the dilemma of a canon which remains culturally one of its most precious resources but with its associated context of authoritative reading and confessional loyalty growing ever weaker. "Bible as literature" hermeneutics in a real sense is partly re-engaging an earlier stage of canon formation, when aesthetic and utilitarian considerations governed the perception of what was "classical," allowing freedom to criticize its contents on moral and cultural (as well as religious) grounds.

Indeed, there are signs that the canon itself can be remade. Thus, for example, the New Revised Standard Version does not contain any Christian or Jewish canon. At the time when Catholic biblical scholarship was tending to adopt the Protestant Old Testament canon, there began a move towards reintegration of the apocryphal books into that canon. In this age of individualism and high literacy rates, the authority of the autonomous reader is paramount and thus the role of the canon less and less aligned to any particular class or society. The study of human culture and of the Jewish scriptural canon shows us, in any case, that no authority is ever autonomous, and, indeed, no canon either.

---

[18] The classic exposition of this feature of the Hebrew scriptures is Michael Fishbane, *Biblical Interpretation in Ancient Israel* (Oxford: Clarendon, 1985), though this work remains essentially taxonomic and does not offer any plausible analysis of the cultural and social processes that generated the intertextual phenomena.

4

The Formation of the Hebrew Bible Canon: Isaiah as a Test Case

Joseph Blenkinsopp

The purpose of this contribution to the canon debate is to probe beneath the surface of the section of the canon comprising the four prophetic books (Isaiah, Jeremiah, Ezekiel, the Twelve), to pass from this inquiry to a closer examination of one of the four, i.e., Isaiah, and to ask in what ways the results of the investigation bear on our understanding of scriptural canons in general. Probing beneath the surface implies moving chronologically back from the point when something resembling a canon is recognizable. Starting from this admittedly ill-defined point and working backwards, I want to make some probes or soundings in familiar terrain with the purpose of testing a particular way of construing canonicity.

1. Four Moments in the Precanonical Process

Specifically, I propose to take as the point of departure a brief consideration of four "moments" in the precanonical process: Josephus, Ecclesiasticus (Sirach), Chronicles, and Deuteronomy, together with related writings.

A. Josephus

I begin with the oft-quoted passage from Josephus, *C. Ap.* 1.38–42:

It therefore naturally, or rather necessarily, follows (seeing that with us it is not open to every-body to write the records, and that there is no discrepancy in what is written; seeing that, on the contrary, the prophets alone had this privilege, obtaining their knowledge of the most remote and ancient history through the inspiration which they owed to God, and committing to writing a clear account of the events of their own time just as they occurred)—it follows, I say, that we do not possess myriads of inconsistent books, conflicting with each other. Our books, those which are justly accredited, are but two and twenty, and contain the record of all time. Of these five are the books of Moses, comprising the laws and the traditional history down to the death of the lawgiver. . . . From the death of Moses until Artaxerxes, who succeeded Xerxes as king of Persia, the prophets subsequent to Moses wrote the history of the events of their own times in thirteen books. The remaining four books contain hymns to God and precepts for the conduct of human life. From Artaxerxes to our own time the complete history has been written, but has not been deemed worthy of equal credit with the earlier records, because of the failure of the exact succession of the prophets.

Josephus here testifies to the existence of a *closed collection*, one which he disingenuously contrasts with Greek literature produced, as he implies, without quality control; a collection, moreover, limited not just quantitatively but chronologically, i.e., produced between the time of Moses and Artaxerxes I (465–425).[1] In his capacity as prophetic historian, Moses covered the three thousand years or so from creation to his own time, and the prophets who followed Moses recorded the history from Moses to Artaxerxes. At that point the prophetic *diadochē* came to an end. One fairly obvious implication is that true prophecy is essentially a thing of the past. The thirteen books covering the history after the death of the lawgiver must have included the four known much later as Former Prophets (Joshua, Judges with Ruth, Samuel, Kings) and the four prophetic compilations (Isaiah, Jeremiah, Ezekiel, the Twelve). The number would be filled out with Job, Daniel, Esther, Ezra-Nehemiah, and Chronicles.

Josephus is not the most disinterested and objective witness in matters religious, and we may be sure that, in spite of relegating prophecy to a circumscribed epoch in the past, he wrote in awareness of his own profession as historian and his own claims to prophetic inspiration, opportunely discovered or activated as he faced the prospect of an unpleasant death in the cave at Jotapata (*B.J.* 3.351–354). Nevertheless, the description of prophecy and the prophetic role that he presents here, though incomplete, is consistent with what he says or refrains from saying elsewhere in his writings.[2] Its major features are also congruent with rabbinic dicta on the subject, especially on the frequently attested topic of the end of prophecy (*sôp hannĕbû᾽â*).[3]

B. Ecclesiasticus

They are also in line with earlier statements bearing on the subject of biblical prophecy. Josephus wrote his treatise against Apion in the last decade of his life, towards the end of the first century C.E., and Jesus ben Sira wrote his book early in the second century B.C.E. Ben Sira treats of biblical prophets in an encomiastic review of national heroes which highlights the *res gestae* of rulers, warriors, counselors, sages, prophets, poets, and plutocrats (Sir 44–50). Since the survey is chronological, beginning with Enoch and ending with his contemporary, the high priest Simon son of Onias, prophets are named in the order in which they were presumed to have lived rather than in any "canonical" sequence. The prophetic continuum begins with Moses, followed by Joshua who succeeded Moses in the prophetic office (46:1, cf. *A.J.* 4.165), and ends with the Twelve (49:10). Following the proto-prophet and his successor, Jesus ben Sira's prophetic "canon" comprises Samuel, Nathan, Elijah, Elisha, Isaiah, Jeremiah, Ezekiel, and the Twelve. What is at once obvious is that the emphasis is on the biographical element rather than on the prophetic message of social regeneration that has featured so prominently in the study of prophecy in the mod-

---

[1] Josephus identified the Ahasuerus (Asueros) of Esth 1:1 and *passim* with Artaxerxes rather than with Xerxes, and according to his retelling of the biblical story Esther stands at the end of the biblical history (*A.J.* 11.184–296). The prophetic *diadochē* is therefore limited to the biblical period.

[2] On Josephus's understanding of prophecy and his own claims to prophetic status of a sort see J. Blenkinsopp, "Prophecy and Priesthood in Josephus," *JJS* 101 (1974): 245–55.

[3] The Holy Spirit (meaning the spirit of prophecy) departed from Israel after the destruction of Solomon's temple (*b. B.Bat.* 12a; *b. Yoma* 21b; *b. Soṭah* 48a) or after the death of the last biblical prophets (*b. Yoma* 9b; *b. Sanh.* 11a).

ern period. Beginning with Moses (45:3), these prophetic figures are ʾanšê maʿaśîm, "men of deeds," i.e., miracle workers, the miracles being designed to recall the people to repentance. This feature was easy to pick out with the biblical accounts of Elijah and Elisha (Sir 48:1–14), less so with Joshua near the beginning (46:1–6) and Isaiah near the end (48:23), both of whom worked a sun miracle. Samuel, too, produced a meteorological miracle, with reference to the preternatural thunderclap that discomfited the Philistines at Mizpah (46:16–17; cf. 1 Sam 7:9–11; cf. 12:18).

For Jesus ben Sira, then, the prophet is no longer the destabilizer of the ruling class, the stern critic of society, the demagogue and pamphleteer (Max Weber), the one who makes a unique and extraordinary claim to authority by reason of a direct divine revelation. The concept of prophecy has been generalized and diluted to the point where the author can characterize his own sometimes pedestrian teaching as a form of prophecy (24:33; 39:12; 50:27). Above all, the prophet is essentially an object of biographical interest, a "man of God" who stands apart by virtue of thaumaturgical and therapeutic powers and the gift of intercessory prayer.[4]

C. Chronicles

Somewhat similar views can be detected in the historical work written rather less than two centuries earlier and known simply as Chronicles (dibrê hayyāmîm). The author numbers prophets and seers so often among his sources as to leave little doubt that he takes the writing of history to be essentially a prophetic activity. These prophetic authors include figures well known from earlier biblical sources and some less well known: Samuel (1 Chron 29:29), Nathan (1 Chron 29:29; 2 Chron 9:29), Gad (1 Chron 29:29), Ahijah of Shiloh (2 Chron 9:29), Shemaiah (2 Chron 12:15), Iddo (2 Chron 12:15; 13:22), Jehu ben Hanani (2 Chron 20:34), and Isaiah the prophet (2 Chron 26:22; 32:32). This surprising expansion of Isaiah's range of competence will call for comment at a later point. The progressive institutionalization and scribalization of prophecy is apparent in other aspects of the author's work. If we are to speak of preaching as a biblical activity and the homily as a biblical genre, it is clear that both the activity and the *Gattung* must be associated not with priests but with prophets.[5] After the rebuilding of the Jerusalem temple in the Persian period the role of preacher devolved on Levites, and in Chronicles it is represented as carried out under divine, i.e., prophetic inspiration. Hence, we hear of the spirit of God (Yahweh) coming on the Levites Azariah ben Oded and Jahazael, urging kings and commoners to be faithful to their religious commitments or to stand firm in battle (2 Chron 15:1–7; 20:14–17).[6] Preaching is therefore also a form of prophecy (nebûʾâ, 2 Chron 15:8).

Another activity which comes to be redefined as prophetic in the author's work is the composition and rendition of liturgical music. Prophecy and poetry had always been

---

[4] I say "man of God" advisedly, since Jesus ben Sira mentions none of the female prophets in Israel, seven according to a rabbinic count (b. Meg. 14a), not even Huldah during the reign of Josiah (49:1–3). This is hardly surprising in view of the author's extremely jaundiced views on women.

[5] The closest term in Biblical Hebrew would be hēṭîp, literally, to drip, which apparently did not carry the unfortunate connotation then that it does now in the vernacular (Amos 7:16; Mic 2:6, 11; Ezek 21:2, 7). The substantive, "preacher," is maṭṭîp (Mic 2:11).

[6] We are not told that the former was a Levite, but Azariah is a common Levitical name (1 Chron 5:35, 39 [6:9, 13]; 6:21 [6:36]; 2 Chron 29:12; Neh 8:7).

closely associated in antiquity, and the use of music and percussion to induce states of mantic consciousness is well attested in Israel as elsewhere (e.g., 1 Sam 10:5–6, 9–13; 2 Kgs 3:15–16). Typically, however, the activity is now routinized and we hear no more of ecstatic states. The professional activities of the guilds of Levitical musicians named for Asaph, Heman, and Jeduthun are now categorized as prophecy (*nebû'â*, 1 Chron 25:1–8) and their practitioners as seers (*hōzîm*, 1 Chron 25:5; 2 Chron 29:30; 35:15). One of the Levitical leaders, a certain Chenaniah, is described as *śar hammaśśā'* (1 Chron 15:22, 27), generally translated "precentor" but which Mowinckel attached closely to prophetic status by translating more literally as "master of the oracle."[7] These prophetic liturgists perform under the leadership of David their founder, "the sweet singer of Israel" (2 Sam 23:1–7), who composed liturgical hymns as the poet and prophet *par excellence*. The Davidic tradition represented here will lead to the attribution of Psalms to David and the utilization of specific Psalms as prophetic texts (e.g., Acts 1:16; 2:25–31, 34). According to the Psalms scroll from the eleventh Qumran cave (11QPs[a]), David composed 4,050 hymns "by means of the prophetic gift *(hannĕbû'â)* given him by the Most High."

Summarizing what has been said so far: according to the tradition typified by these mainstream authors, prophecy is no longer a presence that makes claims of a peremptory nature in the religious sphere. It is essentially a thing of the past, the essential pastness of which is enshrined in *written* texts. The prophet has also become the object of biographical interest. Corresponding to these transformations, the language of prophecy (*nābî'*, *hitnabbē'*, *nibbā'*) has undergone a considerable semantic expansion to include such activities as preaching, liturgical psalmody, and the recording of the nation's past. Even before Chronicles, practically any significant figure in the religious tradition (e.g., Abraham, Moses) could be described as a *nābî'*.[8]

D. The (Deuteronomic) History

It now remains to demonstrate that these transformations can be traced back one stage further to Deuteronomy and writings closely related to it. Mindful of recent admonitions about inflationary usage and the dangers of pan-Deuteronomism,[9] it will be helpful to make some clarifications before taking this step. I assume, then, that Deuteronomy and the associated historical work come to us from the postdisaster period, whatever their origin and whatever previous compositional or editorial stages they may have undergone. I am concerned here neither with origins nor with the identification of an author or authors, and I have no problem with the term "Deuteronomic school"—by analogy with, say, the Antiochean or Alexandrian schools—in the sense of a plurality of savants sharing more or less the same ideology and active over more than one generation. I will avoid unnecessary terminological awkwardness by using the one adjective "Deuteronomic" and by referring to the historical work as "the History" *tout court*.

---

[7] S. Mowinckel, *The Psalms in Israel's Worship* (New York/Nashville: Abingdon, 1967), 2:56.

[8] The usage continues in rabbinic writings; for example, Job is considered a *nābî'* in addition to being a *hākām* according to *b.B. Bat.* 15b.

[9] I am thinking especially of articles by Richard Coggins, Norbert F. Lohfink, and Robert R. Wilson in *Those Elusive Deuteronomists: The Phenomenon of Pan-Deuteronomism* (ed. Linda S. Schearing and Steven L. McKenzie; Sheffield: Sheffield Academic Press, 1999), 22–82.

This being said, it will be convenient to take off from a remark by Richard Coggins in this connection about "ideological pressures at work to impose a particular view of Israel's past, of its relation with its God, of the meaning of the various events that had befallen it, culminating in the destruction of Jerusalem and the deportation of its leading citizens."[10] One effect of these pressures is that in the History the primary role of the prophet is to admonish rulers and the people in general to observe the laws, political disaster being the outcome in the event of nonobservance. This hardly needs demonstrating at length. It can be seen in the paradigm case of Samuel in relation to Saul (1 Sam 7:3–4; 8:8; 12:10, 14–15; 13:13–14; 15:10–31) replicated, with variations, in successive instantiations including Ahijah of Shiloh (1 Kgs 12:29–39; 14:6–16), Jehu ben Hanani (1 Kgs 16:1–4), Elijah (1 Kgs 18:18), and Huldah (2 Kgs 22:14–20). It comes through even more clearly where the Historian refers to prophets in general as "his (Yahweh's) servants the prophets" (ʾabādâv hannĕbîʾîm, 2 Kgs 17:13, 23; 21:10–15; 24:2–4). Reflecting on the fall of the Kingdom of Samaria, the author states that the role of prophets and seers is to warn or admonish (ʿôd, Hiphil) people to "turn," i.e., repent (šûb), and observe the commandments and statutes, in keeping with the law communicated through Yahweh's servants the prophets, beginning with Moses the protoprophet (2 Kgs 17:13; 18:12). The concern is to associate prophecy formally and professionally with the law and with Moses the lawgiver, to explain why the recent disasters had taken place, and to prescribe a remedy for the future.

These aspects of the prophetic role as laid out in the History conform to the description of the way prophecy is to function according to the Deuteronomic program (Deut 18:15–22). Prophecy, which originated as the specifically Israelite form of mediation at Horeb, continues the work of Moses as protoprophet and lawgiver. When the prophet speaks Yahweh's words,[11] the prophet commands obedience. Severe restrictions are placed on the exercise of the prophetic function. Those who serve as mouthpieces for gods other than Yahweh, or who make unauthorized pronouncements, are subject to the death penalty, and the prophet whose predictions are falsified by events can be safely disregarded.[12]

One notable feature of the History is that there is practically no overlap between prophets named by the Historian (Ahijah, Shemaiah, Jehu, Elijah, Elisha, Micaiah, Jonah, Isaiah, Huldah) and the canonical fifteen. The only question about Jonah is why the author of the book with this title gave his hero (or anti-hero) the name of a supportive and optimistic prophet active during the reign of Jeroboam II (2 Kgs 14:25). The Historian's Isaiah (2 Kgs 19:1–7, 20–34; 20:1–19) has, as we shall see, a very different prophetic profile from the Isaiah of the pronouncements, and is mentioned exclusively in connection with and as supportive of Hezekiah, one of the Historian's heroes. This *Prophetenschweigen* issue, which provides important clues to the Deuteronomic ideology, is in need of further study, but can be dealt with here only to the limited extent that it bears on these prescriptive

---

[10] Coggins, *Those Elusive Deuteronomists*, 34, n. 8.

[11] There is perhaps a studied ambiguity in the use of the term *debārîm*, meaning either legal stipulations or prophetic utterances, which becomes univocal only in the final verses (21–22), often taken to be an addition to this section.

[12] Hence the execution of the Baal prophets by Elijah (1 Kgs 18:40) and the pronouncement of the death penalty on Hananiah by Jeremiah (Jer 28:15–17). However, unfulfilled predictions by Amos (Amos 7:11) and Huldah (2 Kgs 22:20) seem to have gone unnoticed, and Micah's prophecy of the destruction of Jerusalem was subject to reinterpretation (Mic 3:12; Jer 26:18).

Deuteronomic ideas about prophecy.[13] The non-mention of Hosea is especially noticeable in view of the thematic and linguistic linkage with Deuteronomic writings.[14] One plausible explanation is that Hosea condemned the Jehu dynasty (Hos 1:4), in spite of its having been founded as the result of prophetic anointing (1 Kgs 9:1–13) and assured prophetically of a four-generation duration (1 Kgs 10:30 cf. 15:12). The remarkably positive evaluation of this dynasty by the Historian (1 Kgs 13:4–5, 22–25; 14:23–29) was no doubt due to its initial anti-Baalist fervor which, in the Historian's view, postponed the inevitable doom on the Kingdom of Samaria. If this is so, it illustrates how, in the Deuteronomic ideology, prophecy was subordinated to and had to be accommodated to a broader, schematic understanding of Israel's past. It is also worth noticing that in the History disaster is brought about not by the various forms of social injustice and inequality castigated by the classical prophets but exclusively on account of cultic aberrations.

Another absentee is Amos, active during the reign of Jeroboam II in the middle years of the eighth century B.C.E. The Historian's account of this ruler, the second-last of the Jehu dynasty, is quite positive (2 Kgs 14:23–29). After the routine negative judgment passed on all the kings of Israel, the Historian records his military successes abetted by the optimistic and supportive prophet Jonah ben Amittai, by virtue of which Jeroboam became the savior of his people. But then, out of nowhere, the author insists that "Yahweh had not spoken to the effect that he would blot out Israel's name from under the sky" (14:27). The statement is certainly polemical, and the way it is phrased (velo'-dibbēr YHWH . . .) indicates polemic against a *prophetic* pronouncement of doom, and the only prophet around at that time known to us who actually made such a pronouncement was Amos (Amos 8:2; 9:8a).[15] We therefore have a strong contrast between 2 Kgs 14:23–29 and the brief biographical passage in the book of Amos which pronounces doom on Jeroboam and the priest-in-charge at Bethel, a high state official (7:10–17). These could therefore be regarded as alternative accounts of the reign: one positive, featuring a supportive prophet but without Amos; the other decidedly negative, featuring Amos as prophet of doom. Only the former fitted the author's overall historical schema and the call to "turning" (repentance) and a new beginning after the collapse of the Judean state.[16] Amos did not have the right message for that time and was therefore omitted from the History.[17]

---

[13] One might consult K. Koch, "Das Profetenschweigen des deuteronomistischen Geschichtswerks," in *Die Botschaft und die Boten: Festschrift für Hans Walther Wolff* (ed. J. Jeremias and L. Perlitt; Neukirchen-Vluyn: Neukirchener Verlag, 1981), 115–28; and Christopher Begg, "The Non-Mention of Amos, Hosea and Micah in the Deuteronomistic History," *BN* 32 (1986): 41–53.

[14] R. A. Kugler, "The Deuteronomists and the Latter Prophets" in *Those Elusive Deuteronomists*, 138–39, lists some recent discussions of this connection.

[15] Frank Crüsemann, "Kritik an Amos im deuteronomistischen Geschichtswerk. Erwägungen zu 2. Könige 14:27," in *Probleme biblischer Theologie: Gerhard von Rad zum 70. Geburtstag* (ed. H. W. Wolff; Munich: Kaiser, 1971), 57–63.

[16] This view of the two passages as alternative versions of the reign is argued persuasively by Peter R. Ackroyd, "A Judgement Narrative between Kings and Chronicles? An Approach to Amos 7:9–17," in *Canon and Authority: Essays in Old Testament Religion and Theology* (ed. G. W. Coats and B. O. Long; Philadelphia: Fortress, 1977), 71–87, repr. in *Studies in the Religious Tradition of the Old Testament* (London: SCM, 1987), 195–208.

[17] The suggestion that the legend about the Judean "man of God" who condemned the Bethel cult under the first Jeroboam (1 Kgs 13) is a reworked version of Amos 7:10–17 is ingenious if

Another interesting test case is the unconditional prediction of disaster pronounced over Jerusalem by Micah: "Zion will be a ploughed field, Jerusalem will be a heap of ruins, and the temple mount will become wooded heights" (Mic 3:18–19). According to a narrative passage in Jeremiah, the Deuteronomic character of which is widely acknowledged, the prophet's life was saved by the timely citing of this pronouncement by the elders of the land at Jeremiah's trial (Jer 26:16–19).[18] This strategy could work only by reinterpreting an unconditional oracle of doom as in fact conditional, that is, as a call to repentance addressed to Hezekiah, one which we are told he accepted.

The prophet most conspicuously absent from the History is Jeremiah, this especially in view of the fact that the book of Jeremiah is rounded off with the last chapter of the History, even though Jeremiah himself is not mentioned in it (Jer 52 = 2 Kgs 24:18–25:30). This is a large issue that can be dealt with only in summary fashion here. While the formation and production of the book of Jeremiah is still in several respects a contentious issue, there is considerable, perhaps overwhelming, support for the thesis that the prophetic profile of Jeremiah has undergone a transformation at the hands of Deuteronomic editors. One of the most telling indicators of this transmutation is the occurrence of the phrase "his servants the prophets" (ʾabādâv hannĕbîʾîm: 7:25; 25:4; 26:5; 29:19; 35:15; 44:4), the standard Deuteronomic term for the prophetic office. It is generally the case that such editorial rewriting or overwriting is less than complete and thorough; indeed, if it were otherwise we would have no basis in the text for assuming an editorial strand with a distinctive interpretation. So, on the one hand, we have Jeremiah the proponent of law and covenant in accordance with Deuteronomic language and ideas (Jer 11:1–5); on the other, the Jeremiah who denounces "handlers of the law" and legal specialists for turning the law into a lie (Jer 2:8; 8:8). What seems to have happened is that certain members of the Deuteronomic school, perhaps with some distinctive though still recognizably Deuteronomic ideas of their own, set out to refashion a profile for Jeremiah closer to the "Mosaic" model, in keeping with the programmatic statement in Deut 18:15–20. The first of several indications throughout the book is the account of Jeremiah's commissioning for a forty-year long prophetic career (Jer 1:1–3 corresponding to the period 627–587 B.C.E.). A final suggestion: the range of Deuteronomic editing, much more extensive than in the other prophetic books, combined with this remodeling of the prophetic profile, may indicate that Jeremiah was taken by the Deuteronomic editors to be the last in the series of "his servants the prophets," as Moses was the first.

---

unprovable. Since the moral seems to be that countermanding an original revelation by a new one can have fatal consequences, it might however help to explain the Historian's opposition to Hosea and Amos, both of whom condemned the Jehu dynasty established by prophetic authority.

[18] This trial narrative is the sequel to the temple sermon (7:1–8:3), one of the clearer instances of Deuteronomic composition in the book, and the account of the trial itself contains such characteristic Deuteronomic expressions as "emend your ways and your doings" and "obey the voice of Yahweh your God." The death penalty for what was taken to be false prophesying by Jeremiah (Jer 26:8–9, 11) is also in accord with Deuteronomic guidelines on prophecy (Deut 18:20). See the detailed analysis of 7:1–8:3 in W. Thiel, *Die deuteronomistische Redaktion von Jeremia 1–25* (Neukirchen-Vluyn: Neukirchener Verlag, 1973), 105–19; also E. W. Nicholson, *Preaching to the Exiles* (New York: Schocken Books, 1970), 52–55; F. L. Hossfeld and I. Meyer, "Der Prophet vor dem Tribunal: Neuer Auslegungsversuch von Jer 26," *ZAW* 86 (1974): 30–50.

All of this is to say that the transformations in the understanding of prophecy noted in Chronicles, Sirach, and Josephus can be traced back to Deuteronomy and related writings. Deuteronomy itself has several of the key characteristics of a canonical work. It contains the standard prohibition against adding anything to it or subtracting anything from it (4:2; 12:32); in other words, it is a *closed* book. It is also an official document that must be deposited in the temple archives and read in public at stated intervals (31:10–13, 26). The ruler must have a copy by him and read from it, or have it read to him, at frequent intervals (17:18–20). It defines a normative epoch in the past, coterminous with the life of Moses, which provides the standard for all future developments and institutions, including prophecy (34:10–12).[19] It is, we may say, the first attempt to impose an orthodoxy and orthopraxy in matters civic and religious. Given this situation, it would be imperative for Deuteronomic authors to counteract prophetic claims to new revelations and the often destabilizing influence of institutionally unattached prophecy. Once a written law was available, sporadic prophetic revelations were both unnecessary and undesirable, and had to give way to the authority invested in the official interpreters of the law. And it goes without saying that the prerogative of issuing prescriptive interpretations of the laws translates into a great deal of social power. We have seen some of the ways in which these people went about offsetting prophetic influence: by redefinition and re-description, as in Deut 18:15–22; by simple omission, as in the History; by concentrating on biographical traits rather than the prophetic message, also in evidence in the History; and neutralizing by addition.[20] Of this last we have an example in the book of Isaiah, which now calls for discussion. But first, some preliminary remarks on Isaiah as a canonical book are in order.

2. Isaiah as a Canonical Book

The first stage in the history of the interpretation of any biblical book, including Isaiah, has to be recovered from indications in the book itself. The capacity to generate commentary is one sign of canonical status, but unfortunately we can have only a very approximate idea of the time when addenda of different kinds could no longer be incorporated in the text but had to take the form of commentary apart from the text. The earliest extant commentaries on Isaiah are the two or more Qumran *pešārîm* reconstructed from several fragments (4QpIsa[a–e] and 3QpIsa = 4Q161–5 and 3Q4), but the complete Isaiah scroll from the first Qumran cave (1QIsa[a]) indicates that the text was more or less fixed earlier, probably no later than the mid-second century B.C.E. The very paraphrastic Greek version (the Septuagint) is usually assigned the same date, though that is only an educated guess. In the early years of the same century Jesus ben Sira was familiar with material from both major sections of the book (1–39 and 40–66), since he tells us that the same Isaiah who worked the miracle of the sun and healed Hezekiah comforted the mourners in Zion

---

[19] Compare the Babylonian idea that all revealed knowledge had been handed down once and for all to the antediluvian ancestors as exemplified in the *Babyloniaka* of Berossus, on which see W. G. Lambert, "Ancestors, Authors, and Canonicity," *JCS* 11 (1957): 1–14; F. Rochberg-Halton, "Canonicity in Cuneiform Texts," *JCS* 36 (1984): 127–44.

[20] I have taken this expression from Samuel Sandmel, "The Haggada within Scripture," *JBL* 80 (1961): 105–22.

and revealed hidden things concerning the end of time (Sir 48:22–25). He therefore implicitly acknowledges that there was only one book of Isaiah, but it does not follow that the book had by that time reached the point of canonical closure.

More important in that regard is Jesus ben Sira's naming in sequence Isaiah, Jeremiah, Ezekiel, and the Twelve (48:23–25; 49:6–10). This suggests that the literary construct we call Latter Prophets was in existence *in some form* by the time he was writing. If we accept that structure is an important vehicle of meaning, especially in ancient texts, we will give due importance to the efforts that clearly had to be made to come up with twelve prophetic authors in the *dodekapropheton*, no doubt representative of twelve-tribal Israel. It would then be a short step to concluding that the 3 + 12 structure of Latter Prophets stands for the three ancestors and the twelve sons of Jacob/Israel; in other words, for the ingathered, reintegrated Israel of the end time to which the prophetic books in their finished form beckon. If this is so, the end-time perspective is encoded in the structure of the prophetic collection itself.[21]

Isaiah generally occupies the first place in Latter Prophets, but the classic rabbinic text (*b.B. Bat.* 14b–15a) places Isaiah after Jeremiah and Ezekiel and immediately before the Twelve, and Isaiah also adjoins the Twelve in the Septuagint. The critical study of the book in the modern period lends some plausibility to this arrangement. As a collection of miscellaneous pronouncements with numerous addenda attributed to a plurality of authors, Isaiah resembles the Twelve as a corpus more closely than it does either of the other two books. Then there is the question of authorship. There is reason to suspect a degree of fluidity and artificiality in assigning attributions in the *dodekapropheton*. Two anonymous sections (Zech 9–11 and 12–14) had to be assigned to Zechariah in order to maintain the important duodecimal symbolism, and Malachi may not be the only fictitious prophetic persona to whom material of unknown origin available to the compilers was assigned. While there is no reason to doubt that a prophet or man of God called Isaiah was known to have existed, and did in fact exist, and while prophetic books are not self-referential, attribution of the pronouncements to Isaiah must be considered weak on any showing. He is named as their author three times (Isa 1:1; 2:1; 13:1), but all three titles are acknowledged to be late, and one (13:1), introducing a pronouncement against Babylon, cannot be from Isaiah. All of the six other Isaiahs mentioned in biblical texts are from the postdestruction period (1 Chron 3:21; 26:25; Ezra 8:7,19; Neh 11:7), three of them are Levites, and one of these three is a Levitical musician who "prophesied" (1 Chron 25:3,15).[22] The titles (1:1; 2:1) also refer to "Judah and Jerusalem," the order generally found in later texts and the reverse of the order in passages generally taken to be early (3:1–8; 5:3; 22:21). It is beginning to look as if the book named for him can be assigned to Isaiah only in somewhat the same way that Psalms are assigned to David and sapiential compositions to Solomon.

---

[21] I argued this several years ago in *Prophecy and Canon: A Contribution to the Study of Jewish Origins* (Notre Dame, Ind., and London: University of Notre Dame Press, 1977), 120–23, and found a confirmation in the finale of the collection (Mal 3:23–24), which speaks of unification effected through *Elias redivivus* as a prelude to the final judgment, in which sense it seems to be understood in Sir 48:10.

[22] The name also occurs in the Elephantine papyri (AP 5:16; 8:33; 9:21); Abraham Cowley, *Aramaic Papyri of the Fifth Century B.C.* (Osnabrück: Otto Zeller, 1967 [1923]), 11, 23, 26, and on a seal, on which see Nahman Avigad, "The Seal of Yeshaʻyahu," *IEJ* 13 (1963): 324.

A. Narrative Insertions and Ideological Compromise

As the record of different voices enunciating different and often conflicting points of view, Isaiah reproduces on a smaller scale important features of the biblical canon as a whole. One of these, sometimes overlooked, is that characteristically a canon represents a resolution of ideological conflict either by imposition of a particular dominant ideology or orthodoxy by *force majeure* or as a compromise between different ideologies. Canon also represents closure in the sense of excluding further revelations, which generally involves the exercise of authoritative and binding interpretation of the textual deposit. It goes without saying, however, that this exercise of control is not always successful, for the texts are always there to be interpreted afresh after the authoritative and supposedly definitive interpretation has been issued. A study of the ideological lines of force and ideological tension and conflict running through the book of Isaiah and embedded or encoded in its final, canonical form would constitute a major work. All that is possible in the space permitted is to sketch out one or two illustrations that may be relevant to our understanding of the biblical canon as a whole.

Our first example takes us back to what was said earlier about the Deuteronomic understanding of the prophetic role and the relations between the Deuteronomic *oeuvre* and prophetic books. Opinions have been expressed both for and against Deuteronomic influence on pronouncements in both major sections of Isaiah.[23] This is an interesting and potentially important topic, but for the moment our concern is exclusively with the narrative content of Isa 1–39. The first narrative prose passage is the account of the meeting between Isaiah and Ahaz (7:1–17, omitting the "on that day" addenda in vv. 18–25) sandwiched between two first person narratives (6:1–13; 8:1–22). It opens with an introduction taken from 2 Kgs 16:5 which, however, substitutes "in the days of Ahaz son of Jotham son of Uzziah" (7:1) for the simple "then" (*ʾaz*) of 2 Kgs 16:5 in order to provide the appropriate historical context. It also omits the reference to a siege (*vayyāṣurû*), presumably because a siege would have ruled out a meeting at the location indicated (7:3). It is tempting to conclude that Isa 7:1–17 originated as one of several prophetic legends in the History. The Isaiah of this passage would fit the profile, the meeting takes place at the spot where the Rabshakeh called for the surrender of the city in a narrative originally part of the History (Isa 36:2 = 2 Kgs 18:17), and the parallel passage in the History breaks off suddenly and switches to Edom, suggesting that something has been omitted (2 Kgs 16:5). The hypothesis is possible but no more than that; at least we find here another link between the History and the prophetic books. We might think of it as a parallel to the case of Jeroboam II and Amos dealt with earlier; in other words, two versions of an important incident during the reign of Ahaz: one generally negative towards Ahaz from which Isaiah is absent (2 Kgs 16:5–9); one rather more positive featuring Isaiah (Isa 7:1–17).

The second prose account of an incident featuring Isaiah is the story of how the man of God simulates the humiliation of Egyptian and Ethiopian prisoners of war by parading

---

[23] No attempt will be made to document these discussions. Robert A. Kugler ("The Deuteronomists and the Latter Prophets" in *Those Elusive Deuteronomists*, 134–35) has some brief and generally negative remarks on the views of Kaiser and Vermeylen regarding chapter 1, but nothing on either Isa 40–66 or the prose passages which are discussed here.

naked in public (20:1–6). The occasion envisaged was the Philistine revolt against Sargon (713–711 B.C.E.), but our only concern here is to point out the close ties with the style and lexicon of the History. The annalistic formula for an account of a military campaign with which it opens occurs routinely in the History. It consists of a temporal indication, the name of the aggressor, approach to the target location, the aggressor's fight against it, and its capture.[24] Also indicative is the unobtrusive temporal phrase "at that time" (*bāʿēt hahîʾ*, 20:2) which occurs very frequently in the History but only here and in a prose addendum (18:7) in Isaiah.[25] Then again, divine communication *beyad yešaʿyāhû* (20:2) is a type of expression ("by the hand of prophet X") used frequently where prophetic interventions are mentioned in the History but unattested elsewhere in Isaiah.[26] The clearest marker is, however, the description of Isaiah as "my servant Isaiah" (*ʿabdî yešaʿyāhû*, 20:3). We have seen that the term *ʿebed* is standard for prophet in the History,[27] but this designation is otherwise absent from Isaiah.

The third and by far the longest narrative insertion in the book of Isaiah is the section 36–39, corresponding to 2 Kgs 18:13–20:19 with the addition of a psalm composed by Hezekiah (Isa 38:9–20). It contains four incidents featuring the prophet (he is actually identified as a *nābîʾ* only in this section: 37:2, 38:1, 39:3): (1) an intervention in the political crisis of 701 solicited by Hezekiah (36:21–37:7); (2) an unsolicited intervention in the same crisis (37:21–35), probably a variant of (1); (3) healing of the king, and the sun miracle (38:1–8,21–22); (4) prediction of exile in Babylon (39:1–8). That these incidents have been copied from the History into the book of Isaiah rather than the reverse seems fairly certain.[28] That is clearly the case with 7:1 and 20:1–6 as we saw earlier, and it is equally certain that Jer 52 has been transcribed from 2 Kgs 24:18–25:30. Another indication is that the fifteen additional years of life granted to Hezekiah in Isa 38:5 (= 2 Kgs 20:6) are calculated on the basis of annalistic data in the History, where we learn that Hezekiah reigned for twenty-nine years (2 Kgs 18:2) and the crisis took place in the fourteenth year of his reign (2 Kgs 18:13). The manner in which the ruler consults a prophet who announces good news for the short term and bad news further into the future (39:5–8) also follows the pattern in the History, the clearest example being the delegation sent to Huldah during Josiah's reign and her response to it (2 Kgs 22:11–20; see also 1 Kgs 11:31–36).

The issue of the relationship between the History and this section of the book of Isaiah is complicated by indications that the legendary account of the last-minute deliverance of Jerusalem in 2 Kgs 18:13, 17–37; 19:1–37 = Isa 36–37 (known as version B in modern

---

[24] 1 Kgs 14:25–26; 2 Kgs 12:18; 15:29; 16:5; 18:9, 13; 24:10; 25:1.

[25] 1 Kgs 8:65; 11:29; 14:1; 2 Kgs 8:22; 16:6; 18:16; 20:12; 24:10. Isa 39:1, where it occurs, is taken from 2 Kgs 20:12.

[26] 1 Kgs 8:53, 56; 12:15; 14:18; 15:29; 16:7, 12, 34; 17:16; 2 Kgs 9:36; 10:10; 14:25; 17:13, 23; 21:10; 24:2.

[27] 1 Kgs 14:18; 15:29 (Ahijah); 2 Kgs 9:36; 10:10 (Elijah); 2 Kgs 14:25 (Jonah); 2 Kgs 9:7; 17:13,23; 21:10; 24:2 (prophets collectively). Note, too, that in carrying out his sign-act Isaiah is to be *ʾôt ûmôpēt*, "a sign and a portent," a Deuteronomic expression also used in connection with prophetic activity (Deut 4:34; 6:22; 7:19; 13:2–3; 28:46; 29:2; 34:11).

[28] Two dissidents are Klaus A. D. Smelik, "Distortion of Old Testament Prophecy: The Purpose of Isaiah xxxvi and xxxvii," *OTS* 24 (1986): 70–93; J. Vermeylen, "Hypothèses sur l'Origine d'Isaïe 36–39," in *Studies in the Book of Isaiah* (ed. J. van Ruiten and M. Vervenne; Leuven: Leuven University Press & Peeters, 1997), 95–118.

scholarship), to which the first two episodes involving Isaiah belong, betrays familiarity with pronouncements of Isaiah recorded elsewhere in the book. One or two examples must suffice. The Rabshakeh's attempt at intimidation closely resembles Assyrian boasts recorded in Isa 10:8–14, even mentioning some of the same cities captured in previous campaigns. The same official's sarcastic query about the basis of Jerusalem's confidence and the nature of their plan of action echoes major themes in Isaian preaching.[29] What this suggests is a *deliberate* attempt to replace the intransigent prophetic opponent of the Judean *nomenklatura* with a very different profile of a "man of God" (*ʾîš hāʾelohîm*), one who, like others in the History, works miracles, heals, and provides religious support and legitimation for the ruler. As is the case with Amos vis-à-vis Jeroboam II, Isaiah must fit the Historian's broader historical schema. The Historian's heroes are Hezekiah and Josiah, and their portrayal in the best possible light results in an alternation of the wicked Ahaz with the righteous Hezekiah, and the very wicked Manasseh with the exemplary Josiah.[30] That other Isaiah, who condemned the Judean leadership inclusive of Hezekiah, though without naming him, and did so with quite exceptional acrimony during the rebellion against Sennacherib and its aftermath, had the wrong message for that situation.[31] Some representative of or sympathizer with the Deuteronomic school, therefore, chose another route and drew on other sources, and the result achieved permanence when the book of Isaiah reached the point of canonical fixity.

As a footnote to these observations on the Deuteronomic ideology at work in the book of Isaiah, a reading of the incident of Merodach-Baladan's delegation to the Judean court during Hezekiah's convalescence (2 Kgs 20:12–19; Isa 30:1–8) may afford a glimpse into the ideologizing process at work. As critical readers, we would have to note that, according to the historically reliable version A (2 Kgs 18:14–16), Hezekiah had just handed over all his gold and silver to the Assyrians, even stripping the gold from the doors of the temple in order to meet the conqueror's demands. This leaves us wondering what he would have had left to display before the Babylonian envoys. Moreover, we know that the revolt of Merodach-Baladan II (Marduk-apla-iddina) had been crushed by the Assyrians two years before the Palestinian punitive campaign; therefore such a visit after that date is histori- cally quite implausible. If, therefore, the visit took place, it would presumably have been in connection with overtures for another anti-Assyrian alliance, and Hezekiah's "show and tell" would have had the purpose of demonstrating that he was a credible coalition partner. If this is a plausible scenario, it would have the purpose of exonerating Hezekiah from the

---

[29] The verb *bṭḥ* occurs seven times in the Rabshakeh's first harangue, cf. Isa 12:2 and 26:4; on the *ʿēṣâ* of Yahweh contrasted with human machinations see Isa 5:19; 14:26; 19:17; 25:1; 28:29; 29:15–16; 30:1–2.

[30] Thus serving as an illustration of the Deuteronomic rejection of intergenerational moral accountability; Deut 24:16; 2 Kgs 14:6; cf. Ezek 18:5–20.

[31] Most commentators in the modern period read the dire threats and comminations in Isa 28–31 (or 28–33) against the background of the fateful events of 705–701 B.C.E. The civil and religious leadership of Judah is cynical, lacking in judgment, and idolatrous. Their plans will end in defeat and death. Hezekiah is not named but must be included among the Judean *môšlîm* (leaders, 28:14) of that time, and the bitterly denounced overtures to Egypt could not have been going on without his knowledge and consent (30:1–5; 31:1–3). The prophet also denounces an individual who vio- lated the treaty and despised the witnesses (33:8), which, in the context, could refer to Hezekiah's violation of his vassal oath to the Assyrian king, an oath witnessed by Yahweh (cf. Ezek 17:11–19).

charge of seeking an alliance with the detested Babylonians and putting the blame for the disasters to be inflicted in due course by the same Babylonians squarely on the shoulders of Manasseh (cf. 2 Kgs 21:10–15; 23:26–27; 24:3–4).

This process that I have called neutralizing by addition should not be dismissed because not in line with editorial procedures followed in our day. The urge to create one definitive reading of the past and, in so doing, to record prescriptive moral judgments, had to be balanced by a reverence for past prophetic revelations. The book of Isaiah has preserved both prophetic profiles which embody quite different ideological positions on the nature of prophecy and the understanding of the nation's past. Once the book achieved canonical status, both became available for interpretation and reinterpretation. The past is therefore seen, from this canonical point of view, as something quite other than an unassimilable and inert entity. The past can change in relation to a changing present, just as an object visible in the distance can assume different forms as one moves forward along a plane of observation. As representatives of what might be called central as opposed to peripheral religion, the author of Chronicles, Jesus ben Sira, and Josephus adopted the Deuteronomic line in their reading of prophetic texts inclusive of Isaiah. But Isaiah offered other options which survived alongside of and, in some cases, in spite of Deuteronomic editing. With this we come to our final precanonical probe into the book of Isaiah.

B. Eschatology and Canon Formation

One of the most striking features shared by the book of Isaiah and several of the Twelve is that they conclude by presenting a scenario of the future and final condition of Israel, in some instances coinciding with the consummation of history and the transformation of the cosmos. This complex scenario sometimes stays more or less within the bounds of historical plausibility, including such prospects as return from the Diaspora and a mission to foreign peoples, but more often than not it describes a "singularity" involving a universal meteorological catastrophe, warfare on a cosmic scale, new heaven and new earth, a final judgment by fire, and similar motifs.[32] While this apocalyptic mentality has been identified throughout the prophetic writings, and throughout the first part of Isaiah in particular,[33] the fact that it occurs so consistently at the end of individual books suggests that individuals or groups owing allegiance to the apocalyptic worldview were involved in the final stages of the composition and publication of these books, and perhaps also, as hinted earlier, of the 3 + 12 compilation as a whole. We therefore arrive by a somewhat different route at the same point as Otto Plöger. Plöger's examination of key prophetic passages (Joel 3, Zech 12–14, Isa 24–27) led him to conclude that the prophetic books were edited in the later Second Temple period by anonymous groups, the precursors of the Asidaioi (*ḥasîdîm*) of 1 Macc 2:42 and 7:13 and the author(s) of the book of Daniel, in the direction of an apocalyptic and sectarian worldview.[34] Several aspects of Plöger's thesis are admittedly debatable, not least the way in which he set up a rather too clear-cut contrast between theocracy and eschatology. His choice of texts also imposed certain limitations,

---

[32] See Isa 66 and *passim*; Joel 3:1–4:3; 4:9–21; Amos 9:11–15; Obad 15–21; Mic 7:8–20; Zeph 3:8–20; Zech 14:1–21; Mal 3:19–24.

[33] By no means confined to the misnamed "Isaian apocalypse," Isa 24–27.

[34] Otto Plöger, *Theocracy and Eschatology* (Richmond: John Knox, 1968).

and left the existence of the eschatological conventicles that he postulated more up in the air than was necessary. Yet the argument seems to be basically sound, and invites corroboration by taking a different route through the available texts. What follows is no more than a brief sketch of one direction this investigation might take.

Recent commentary on Isaiah has made much of the linguistic and thematic parallels between the first and the last chapter of the book. Some of the more obvious instances are: the condemnation of those who rebel against Yahweh (*pōšeʿîm bî*, 66:24, cf. 1:2, 28), new moon and Sabbath (66:23, cf. 1:13), transgressive cults carried out in gardens (66:17, cf. 1:29), and the final judgment on reprobates under the image of unextinguishable fire (66:24, cf. 1:31).[35] This structural feature of inclusio tells us that Isa 1–66 is one book; all of the different and heterogeneous parts converge in one way or another on this final event of salvation and judgment.

Chapter 66, and therefore the book as a whole, ends with three oracular pronouncements *(neʾum YHWH)* (vv. 17, 18–21, 22–23) that speak of the ingathering in Jerusalem at the end-time, a mission to the Gentiles preceding the final theophany, and the creation of new heavens and a new earth. These are rounded off with a finale (v. 24) so dark and menacing—the bodies of the dead consigned to fire unquenched and food for the worms—that in the synagogue liturgy the preceding verse of the *haftara* was stipulated to be repeated after it.[36] These last chapters of the book also provide incontrovertible evidence of intense internecine conflict occasioned by such apocalyptic beliefs. According to one pronouncement, which brings to mind the Beatitudes in Matt 5:2–12 = Luke 6:20–23, the "servants of Yahweh" will be the ones who will eat, drink, rejoice, and sing for joy in the final theophany, while their enemies *within the community* will go hungry and thirsty, and will suffer shame and anguish (65:13–14). This typically sectarian theme of eschatological reversal also comes to expression in the address of a seer to those who "tremble at his (Yahweh's) word" who, we learn, have been excommunicated by their brethren, i.e., their fellow-Jews, because of their belief in an imminent parousia, or at least on account of their exclusive claim to salvation when the great day dawns (66:5).[37] For the understanding of canonicity in general, it is of crucial importance that these protests of the socially dispossessed, nourished as they were on the interpretation and appropriation of older prophecy, were not expunged from the record.

3. Conclusion

The compilation of Latter Prophets may have gone through several phases, possibly including a Deuteronomic phase, before it reached its final configuration during the

---

[35] Other parallels have been noted by L. J. Liebreich, "The Compilation of the Book of Isaiah," *JQR* n.s. 46 (1955/1956): 276–77; R. Lack, *La Symbolique du Livre d'Isaïe* (Rome: Biblical Institute, 1973), 139–41; M. A. Sweeney, *Isaiah 1–4 and the Post-Exilic Understanding of the Isaiah Tradition* (Berlin: de Gruyter, 1988), 21–24.

[36] Note that the term *dērāʾôn*, "horror, abhorrence" (66:24), occurs elsewhere only at Dan 12:2.

[37] I took a closer look at this section of the book in "A Jewish Sect of the Persian Period," *CBQ* 52 (1990): 5–20, and "The Servant and the Servants in Isaiah and the Formation of the Book," in *Writing and Reading the Scroll of Isaiah: Studies in an Interpretive Tradition* I (ed. C. C. Broyles and C. A. Evans; Leiden: Brill, 1997), 155–75.

obscure century of Ptolemaic rule. It was at that time, the early Hellenistic period, that books began to be produced with explicit attributions and resembling more closely our concept of the book.[38] In the absence of external information on the circumstances under which this final form was produced, the only recourse is scrutiny of the prophetic books themselves. In this respect the book of Isaiah reflects the characteristics of the canon of the Hebrew-Aramaic Bible as a whole; it can be read as a canon *in nuce*. One of these characteristics is the juxtaposition within a canonical collection of different and ideologically incompatible points of view. We have seen that the inclusion of Deuteronomic narrative in Isaiah sets up an understanding of the prophetic office over against that of the prophet as the social conscience of the society and the preacher of social reform and moral regeneration. The Isaian biographical tradition in the later biblical period and postbiblical period, and rabbinic statements about prophecy in general, show to what degree this Deuteronomic element in Isaiah, and therefore in the prophetic canon as a whole, proved to be influential.[39] It was only in the early modern period that other aspects of the prophetic profile returned to the surface. On the other hand we see, already within the book of Isaiah, how the interpretation of prophecy by those excluded from power led to the "new prophecy" of apocalyptic and the revelation of truths of overwhelming relevance and transforming power for those who chose to live by them.

Canonicity is generally taken to imply normativity and, as such, to justify mandatory acquiescence in and obedience to a comprehensive and internally consistent statement of religious orthodoxy. But what we have seen about these conflicting views of prophecy in Isaiah, and about Isaiah, as reproducing some of the basic characteristics of the Hebrew-Aramaic canon as a whole, suggests that normativity is not at all a straightforward concept, and that there are tensions within what counts as normative which cannot be disregarded or set aside, which theological honesty requires us to take seriously. Acceptance of these tensions and antinomies would, one suspects, lead to a richer and more complex appreciation for the biblical canons by the faith communities within which they came into existence and still function.

---

[38] Within the biblical-Judaic tradition Jesus ben Sira is the first explicitly attested author of a book (Sir 50:27).

[39] I deal with this biographical tradition in "The Prophetic Biography of Isaiah," in *Mincha: Festgabe für Rolf Rendtorff* (ed. Erhard Blum; Neukirchen-Vluyn: Neukirchener, 2000), 13–26.

5

The Septuagint: The Bible of Hellenistic Judaism

Albert C. Sundberg Jr.

By "Hellenistic Judaism" we mean the Judaism that was deeply influenced by the spread of Hellenistic culture, initiated by Alexander the Great (356–323 B.C.E.) and carried out by his successors, the *diadochoi*.[1] Hellenization was so successful that Koine Greek became the lingua franca of the lands that had fallen under the conquests of Alexander. This Hellenization, however, was not so ubiquitous in Jewry. Even though Alexander had made Babylon his capital, the sizable Jewish colony there continued to maintain and cultivate its own culture and language, producing the Babylon Talmud in Hebrew and Aramaic in the sixth century C.E. In the West, however, centering in Alexandria and Egypt, Hellenization among Jews became so complete that Hebrew and Aramaic were forgotten and Greek became the mother tongue.[2]

Until recently the accepted line of division between Eastern and Western Jewry has been Jerusalem/Palestine and Alexandria/Egypt. Now, however, it has become evident that Hellenization became an inescapable factor in Jerusalem/Palestine as well. Therefore, a discussion of Hellenistic Judaism must include Jerusalem/Palestine as well.

1. Naming the Septuagint (LXX)

The Septuagint (LXX), from the Latin for *seventy (septuaginta)*, is the traditional name of the Greek translation of the Hebrew scriptures commonly held to be the Bible of the Hellenistic Jews. Some scholars believe that the name was derived from Exod 24:1, 9, where it is said that seventy elders of Israel accompanied Moses to the holy mountain where he received the law and the commandment.[3] It should be noted that the seventy elders were not the full complement of visitors to the mountain. Aaron also accompanied

---

[1] Josephus, *Ag. Ap.* 1.213; an unnoticed use of the term in 12.5. Cf. *Josephus* 1–9 (ed. R. Marcus; Cambridge, Mass.: Harvard University Press, 1961–65). For a discussion of Jewish settlements in the Diaspora, cf. Henry B. Swete, *An Introduction to the Old Testament in Greek* (rev. Richard R. Ottley; New York: KTAV, 1968), 309–10.

[2] Edward Lohse, *The New Testament Environment* (trans. John E. Steely; Nashville: Abingdon, 1976), 128. Cf. Swete, *O.T. in Greek,* 7–9.

[3] Erwin Nestle, "Seventy," in *A Dictionary of the Bible* (ed. James Hastings; New York: Scribners, 1898–1904), 4:438; John W. Wevers, "Septuagint," *IDB* 4:273; Bruce M. Metzger, "Seventy or Seventy-two Disciples?" *New Testament Studies* 5 (1959): 299–306.

Moses; Moses and Aaron frequently function as a unit (Exod 4:10–16, etc.). Moreover, Moses was instructed to include two other persons, Nadab and Abihu, the first two sons of Aaron (Exod 6:23). Thus, the full complement accompanying Moses, beside Aaron, totals seventy-two. Again, in the garbled verses Exod 24:13–14, we read, "So Moses rose with his servant Joshua [not previously mentioned], and Moses went up into the mountain of God. And he said to the elders, 'Tarry here for us until we come for you again; and, behold, Aaron and Hur [not previously mentioned] are with you' "⁴—also equaling seventy-two. There is no mention of tribes or the distribution of these men among them. Thus, the Exod 24:1–16 story can also suggest or support the number seventy-two.⁵ The so-called *Letter of Aristeas*⁶ is a fable of how the Jewish scriptures came to be translated from Hebrew into Greek. The facts which this story purports to relate are of great importance because they relate the origin of the Hellenistic Jewish Bible as well as the first translation of a significant piece of literature from one language into another. Aristeas also includes the first time in the history of Jewish apologetic that the allegorical method, for which Alexandria became famous, was used.⁷ An outline of the *Letter* is as follows:⁸

Preface (1–8)

The plan to have the Law translated (9–11)

The emancipation of all the Jewish slaves in Egypt (12–27)

The memorial drawn up by Demetrius regarding the translation request (28–33)

The exchange of letters between Ptolemy and the Jewish high priest, Eleazar (34–50)

A description of the royal presents (51–82)

A description of Jerusalem and its environs (83–120)

---

⁴Scriptural quotations are from *The Holy Bible: Revised Standard Bible* (Toronto: Thomas Nelson & Sons, 1952).
⁵Sidney Jellicoe, *The Septuagint and Modern Study* (Oxford: Clarendon, 1968), 58.
⁶Citations of the *Letter of Aristeas* in English are from: Herbert T. Andrews, trans., "The Letter of Aristeas," in Robert H. Charles, *Apocrypha and Pseudepigrapha of the Old Testament* (Oxford: Clarendon, 1968), 2:94–122; citations in Greek are from Henry St. J. Thackeray, ed., "The Letter of Pseudo-Aristeas," in Swete, *O.T. in Greek*, 551–606.
⁷Andrews, "Aristeas," 85.
⁸Texts: Paul Wendland, *Aristeae ad Philocratem epistula* (Leipzig: B. G. Teubner, 1900); Thackeray, "Pseudo-Aristeas," 551–606; Henry G. Meecham, *The Letter of Aristeas* (Manchester: Manchester University Press, 1935), reproduces Thackeray's revised text; Raffaele Tramontano, *La lettera di Aristea a Filocrate* (Naples: Ufficioi succursale della civiltà cattolica in Napoli, 1931); Moses Hadas, *Aristeas to Philocrates* (New York: Harper & Brothers, 1951), 91–227, reproduces Thackeray's revised text. Translations: Henry St. J. Thackeray, *The Letter of Aristeas* (London: S.P.C.K., 1917); Andrews, "Aristeas," 83–122; Henry G. Meecham, *The Oldest Version of the Bible: Aristeas and Its Traditional Origin* (London: Holborn, 1932); Paul Wendland, "Der Brief des Aristeas," in Emil Kautzsch, *Die Apokryphen und Pseudepigraphen des Alten Testaments* (Tübingen: J. C. B. Mohr [Paul Siebeck], 1900), 2:1–31; Paul Riessler, "Brief des Aristeas," in *Altjüdisches Schrifttum ausserhalb der Bibel* (Augsburg: B. Filser, 1928), 193–233; Tramontano, *La lettera di Aristea a Filocrate*; Hadas, *Aristeas to Philocrates*. Cf. Swete, *O.T. in Greek*, 10; Hadas, *Aristeas*, 85–87.

The qualities of the selected translators (121–27)

Eleazar propugns or defends the Jewish Law (128–71)

Arrival of the translators in Alexandria (172–81)

The seven welcoming banquets (182–300)

The place and work of translation (301–7)

Reception of the translation by the Jewish people and the king (308–17)

The departure of the translators and the conclusion of the Letter (318–27).[9]

It is to be noted that the translation included only the Law; no reference was made in Aristeas to other books of Jewish scriptures. While the *Letter of Aristeas* does not name the Greek translation of the Law that it describes, many think that it was from this letter, with its several references to the *seventy-two* translators,[10] that the name *Septuagint* was derived by the simple process of syncope.[11]

Josephus, the Jewish historian from Jerusalem and later Rome (37/38–ca. 100 C.E.), next draws attention regarding numbering and naming. In *Jewish Antiquities* 12.11–118, Josephus gives a close paraphrase of a large portion of the *Letter of Aristeas*.[12] Three times in his paraphrase, Josephus refers to seventy-two translators: 12.39, 46, and 56. Shortly thereafter, however, in 12.57, Josephus changes the number of translators from seventy-two to seventy. He writes, "But I have not thought it necessary to report the names of the seventy *(hebdomēkonta)* elders . . . who brought the Law," and, again, in 12.86, "and Ptolemy heard . . . of the coming of the seventy *(hebdomēkonta)* elders." Ralph Marcus thinks that Josephus has carelessly forgotten that there were six translators from each of the twelve tribes.[13] However, since Josephus's first use of *seventy* falls so close to his last reference to "six from each tribe," and since the number *seventy* is repeated in 12.86, it appears to this writer, that his use of the term *seventy* was more deliberate than Marcus suggests. In any case, Josephus does not use *seventy* as a name for the translation. Marcus believes that it was this use by Josephus that produced the name of the Greek translation, "Septuagint." Josephus calls the Letter simply, "the book of Aristeas" (*to Aristaiou biblion; Ant.* 12.100).

In his article, "Septuagint: B. Earliest Greek Versions," in the *I.D.B.* Supplementary Volume,[14] Robert A. Kraft tells us that, "As early as the second century A.D., *Septuagint* was

---

[9] Cf. Gunther Zuntz, "Aristeas Studies 2: Aristeas on the Translation of the Torah," *JSS* 4 (1959): 109–26.

[10] *Ep. Arist.* 39, "six elders from each tribe"; 49, "six elders from each tribe"; 50, "they were seventy-two in all" (*hoi pantes hebdomēkonta dyo*). Quoted texts of Josephus are from Henry St. J. Thackeray, *Josephus 1–9* (LCL; Cambridge, Mass.: Harvard University Press, 1926–1965).

[11] Jellicoe, *Septuagint and Modern Study,* 57; Hadas, *Aristeas,* 66; Lohse, *N.T. Environ.,* 129, etc.

[12] Josephus's spelling is *Aristaios, Ant.* 12.17, etc. Cf. Hadas, *Aristeas,* 3.

[13] Marcus, *Josephus,* vol. 7, p. 31, note b.; page 43, note b.

[14] Nashville: Abingdon, 1976, p. 811. Elias J. Bickerman, "Some Notes on the Transmission of the Septuagint," in *Alexander Marx: Jubilee Volume* (English section; New York: The Jewish Theological Seminary of America, 1950), 150 n. 2, says, "Justin (110–165 C.E., *Apol.* 1:31) is, probably, the first writer to ascribe the translation of the Prophets to the Seventy." However, in this passage, Justin's version of the Aristeas story, *prophets* does not refer to the *Prophets* collection of the Jewish canon; it

used as an umbrella term for the Christian collection(s) of Jewish scriptures in Greek translation." Kraft, however, gives no references to or illustrations of this use.[15] Josephus, as we have seen, does not use "seventy" as a name for the Jewish scriptures in Greek. Indeed, that naming of the Greek translation does not appear until relatively late. Christian writers do refer to the Aristeas story[16] but, in so far as this writer can determine, do not name the Greek translation until Eusebius of Caesarea (263–339 C.E.). Justin Martyr does come close. In his *Dialogue with Trypho* 68 we read, "your (Jewish) teachers . . . venture to assert that the explanation which your seventy elders *(hebdomēkonta presbyteroi)* that were with Ptolemy the king of the Egyptians gave is untrue in certain respects." A similar statement occurs in §72. However, it is evident that the "seventy elders" refers to the translators and not to the translation.[17] Justin does extend the scope of the "seventy translators" apparently to the whole Jewish scripture since the term is used of Isa 6:7 (*Dial.* 68:7).

In *Ecclesiastical History* 6.16.1, Eusebius writes, "Thus, too, he [Origen] traced the edition of the other translators of the sacred writings besides the seventy" *(para tous hebdomēkonta).*[18] Here for the first time the Greek translation of the Jewish scriptures is clearly named: "the seventy," the Greek equivalent of the Septuagint. This is confirmed by Eusebius's later statement in 6.16.4, where he writes, "He [Origen] made a further separate arrangement of the edition of Aquila and Symmachus and Theodotion together with the [translation] of the Seventy *(hama tē tōn hebdomēkonta)* in the Tetrapla." Here it is probable that "the [translation] of the Seventy" names the column in the Tetrapla, as do Aquila, Symmachus, and Theodotion.[19] Thus, it was not until the fourth century that the Greek translation of the scriptures was actually named. However, in his account of the *Letter of Aristeas* in the *Praeparatio evangelica* 8–9, where Eusebius has an epitome of about one-fourth of Aristeas,[20] he does not use a name for the Greek translation. Elsewhere Eusebius dubs the translators the *seventy:* "He was reckoned among the seventy who translated the sacred and divine scriptures for Ptolemy Philadelphus and his father" (*Hist. eccl.* 7.32.16). Here the *Seventy* are clearly the translators, not the translation (*hos en tois o′ kateilegmenos*).[21]

---

includes all of the Jewish scriptures. First, the Law is referred to as *prophets,* that is, the books Ptolemy requested from Herod *(sic)* to be translated for his library. Justin begins §32, "Moses then, who was the first of the prophets." Thereafter, Justin continues, "in the succession of generations prophets after prophets arose," referring, apparently, to the rest of the books of the Jewish collection. However, the *Prophets* collection is not named. Cf. Clement of Alexandria, *Strom.* 1:22 below.

[15] Cf. Jellicoe, *Septuagint and Modern Study,* 57: "How the number seventy, which attaches itself permanently to the Greek version as *Septuagint,* arose has not definitely been established."

[16] Swete, *O.T. in Greek,* 9 nn. 1, 13; Hadas, *Aristeas,* 70–73; Jellicoe, *Septuagint and Modern Study,* 41–44. Wendland, *Arist. ad Phil.,* 90–166) has logged over eighty testimonies to the *Letter of Aristeas,* to which more have been added by André Pelletier; see Pelletier, *Lettre d'Aristée à Philocrate* (Paris: 1962), 5ff., cited in Jellicoe, *Septuagint and Modern Study,* 33–35.

[17] In Pseudo-Justin, *Hortatory Address to the Greeks* 13, there is another summary of Aristeas.

[18] Quotations of Eusebius, *Hist. eccl.,* are from LCL 1, 2 (trans. Kirsopp Lake and H. J. Lawlor; Cambridge, Mass.: Harvard University Press, 1953).

[19] Cf. A. Speber, "New Testament and Septuagint," *JBL* 59 (1940): 193–205, on Origen's work.

[20] Cf. a similar précis in *Hist. eccl.* 6:16.

[21] On the use of omicron (used as a numeral for seventy) as a designation for the Septuagint, cf. Swete, *O.T. in Greek,* 9–10. This usage can hardly stem from Eusebius but was probably introduced into Eusebius's text by a later copyist. As we have seen, naming the Greek translation was not yet a settled matter in Eusebius's day, whereas, substituting the numeral *(hoi) o′*, as here, presupposes a

Epiphanius of Salamis (315–403 C.E.), in his *Weights and Measures* 2–20,[22] gives his digest of the Aristeas story, interspersed with sundry other items such as: that stars are still in the heavens even if obscured by clouds or the sun; an explanation of the diacritical markings of Origen's *Hexapla;* [23] how the Jewish canon is counted as twenty-two or twenty-seven books; the reason transliterations were made from Hebrew to Greek; that there were twenty-two canonical and seventy-two *(hebdomēkontadyo)* apocryphal books;[24] that Moses, even though commanded by God to take seventy men with him to the holy mountain (Exod 24), actually took seventy-two to avoid consternation among the tribes, etc. Epiphanius has the most elaborate embellishments to the Aristeas story. He argued that the Greek translation was actually better than the Hebrew text. The Greek left out words that were superfluous because repetitious; the seventy-two handed down a more accurate reading that could not be expressed as concisely in Hebrew; their additions gave clarity to the text. Epiphanius refers to "the seventy-two translators" *(hoi hebdo-mēkontadyo hermēneutai)* some nine times in paragraphs 2–20, and "by the translation of the seventy-two" *(hypo tōn hebdomēkontadyo hermēneias)* in §§2, 8, 11, 15. Ten times Epiphanius refers simply to the "seventy-two," usually with the article *(hoi hebdomēkontadyo).* Except for the occurrences in §§9–11, these appear to name the translation, as in Eusebius (above) and Augustine (below), except the number is seventy-two. John Chrysostom of Antioch (344–407 C.E.) says in his *Homilies on St. Matthew* 5.2, that the Seventy made their translation a century or more before the coming of Christ, naming the translators the *Seventy (hebdomēkonta).*

However, it was not until the time of Augustine of Hippo (354–430 C.E.) that the Greek translation of the Jewish scriptures came to be called by the Latin term *septuaginta.* In his *City of God* 18.42, while repeating the story of Aristeas with typical embellishments, Augustine adds the remark,[25] "It is their translation that it has now become traditional to call the Septuagint" *(quorum interpretatio ut Septuaginta vocetur iam obtinuit consuetudo).*[26] Augustine thus indicates that this name for the Greek translation of the scriptures was a recent development. But he offers no clue as to which of the possible antecedents led to this development: Exod 24:1–8, Josephus, or an elision. Far from having been a practice "from the early second century" C.E., this name *Septuagint* appears to have been a fourth- to fifth-century development. Despite its late date, scholars in general use the name "Septuagint" or "LXX" even when referring to the Greek translation of the scriptures as it existed prior to the fourth century.

---

general usage of "Septuagint" in naming the Greek translation. In this instance it is the translators who are dubbed oʹ. It is the only appearance of this usage in the Aristeas texts in Eusebius.

[22] English translation of Epiphanius is from *Epiphanius' Treatise on Weights and Measures* (ed. J. P. Dean; Chicago, Ill.: University of Chicago Press, 1935); Greek text, cf. n. 23 below.

[23] Cf. "Translations of the Canonical Bible," in Emil Schürer, *The History of the Jewish People in the Days of Jesus Christ* (ed. Geza Vermes, Fergus Millar, Martin Goodman; Edinburgh: T&T Clark, Ltd., 1986), 1:480–84.

[24] Hadas (*Aristeas,* 77) and Jellicoe (*Septuagint and Modern Study,* 45) render Epiphanius as saying "twenty-two apocryphal books" (Jellicoe, *Septuagint and Modern Study,* 45 n. 7, noting that the Syriac reads twenty-two). However, the Greek text in P. G. 43.236–94, Epiphanius, *Weights and Measures* 10, reads as per text above.

[25] William C. Greene, *Saint Augustine: City of God* (LCL; Cambridge, Mass.: Harvard University Press, 1960), vol. 6, 41–42.

[26] Swete, *O.T. in Greek,* 9 n. 1; Hadas, *Aristeas,* 78.

2. The Integrity of the *Letter of Aristeas*

The *Letter of Aristeas* appears to have been widely accepted in antiquity. However, witnesses from the Jewish community are few. Philo, the Jewish philosopher of Alexandria[27] (ca. 20 B.C.E.–ca. 50 C.E.) gives a short but enthusiastic synopsis of the Letter, adding some embellishments, in his *Life of Moses* (2.25–44). These include: the extraordinary stature of Ptolemy Philadelphus (§§28–29); that the high priest was also king of Judea (§31); the high priest thought Ptolemy's inquiry resulted from God's guiding care (§32); the translators were joyfully sent (§32); the translators chose the work-cite for themselves (§34); they worked in the presence of the elements of nature—earth, water, air, and heaven (§37); God assented to their prayers for success, they were inspired (§37); all seventy-two, though working individually, wrote the same translation, word for word, even though Greek abounds in terms (§37); they were prophets and priests of the mysteries (§40). There is no doubt of Philo's approval; he regarded the translation as identical in meaning with the Hebrew text of the Law; "the Greek words used corresponded literally with the Chaldean" (*onomasi ta Ellēnika tois Chaldaikois;* §38).[28] This was the Bible Philo used.[29]

Similarly Josephus warmly welcomes the Aristeas story. In his *Jewish Antiquities* 2.11–118, Josephus reproduces about one third of Aristeas in a paraphrase so like the Aristeas text that his account has been useful in establishing the text of Aristeas (*Ant.* 2.11–118).[30] Josephus writes, "Eleazar, who yielded in virtue to none of our high priests, did not scruple to grant the monarch the enjoyment of a benefit. . . . Accordingly, I thought that it became me also . . . to imitate the high priest's magnanimity" (*Ant.* 1.11–12). He tauntingly adds, "For he [Philadelphus] failed to obtain all our records *(oude gar pasan ekeinos ephthē labein tēn anagraphēn),* it was only the portion containing the Law which was delivered to him" (*Ant.* 1.12).[31] Josephus is the first ancient writer whom we know to have had a text of Aristeas before him.[32] The acceptance of the *Letter of Aristeas* by these two writers, Philo and Josephus, almost the only information we have, engendered the view that the Septuagint was widely accepted from its inception as the Bible of Hellenistic Jews. The authority it envisioned for the Law was readily extended to the other Jewish

---

[27] Quotations from Philo are from F. H. Colson and G. H. Whitaker, *Philo* (9 vols.; LCL; Cambridge, Mass.: Harvard University Press, 1954–60).

[28] Hadas (*Aristeas*, 25) and Jellicoe (*Septuagint and Modern Study*, 40) state that the annual feast on the Isle of Pharos to celebrate the Septuagint translation was added to the story by Philo. This, of course, is in error, since *Aristeas* 180 reads, "I [Ptolemy Philadelphus] have enacted that this day, on which you arrived, shall be kept as a great day and it will be celebrated annually *(kat' eniauton)* through my lifetime"; cf. Hadas, *Aristeas*, 168–71. Philo adds that the feast still continued in his day. In Philo the feast appears at the end of his account of the translation, whereas in *Aristeas* the feast day is declared on the day the translators arrived in Alexandria.

[29] Peter Katz, *Philo's Bible: The Aberrant Text of Bible Quotations in Some Philonic Writings and Its Place in the Textual History of the Greek Bible* (Cambridge: University Press, 1950); Schürer, *Hist. of Jewish People,* 1:479.

[30] Hadas, *Aristeas*, 18; Thackeray, "Pseudo-Aristeas," 533, 548, 549. Cf. Josephus, *Ag. Ap.* 2:45–47.

[31] Thackeray comments, "Josephus does not mention that the version of the Law was followed up by translations, which he freely used, of the rest of the Hebrew Scriptures" (*Josephus* 4:7 n. d.).

[32] Hadas, *Aristeas*, 18.

scriptures as they became translated into Greek;[33] this authority apparently extended to extracanonical Jewish religious writings as well.[34]

The *Letter of Aristeas*, however, proved to be a fiction.[35] Two early critiques appeared. Ludovicus de Vives (1492–1540 C.E.), a Spanish scholar, published the first critical evaluation of *Aristeas* in his commentary on Augustine's *City of God* (18.42) in 1522.[36] Another critique by Joseph J. Scaliger followed in 1606.[37] These were superseded by a thoroughgoing critique by Humphrey Hody (1659–1707) which completely destroyed any claim for the historicity of *Aristeas*.[38] The problems are numerous and vary from the gross to minutia and can only be illustrated here. They include the following:

1. Demetrius Phalereus is depicted as an intimate friend of the king and librarian of the Alexandrian library under Ptolemy Philadelphus (ca. 283 B.C.E.). However, he was patron of Ptolemy I Soter. He was sent into exile soon after Philadelphus's accession to the throne and died shortly thereafter, bitten by an asp, probably at the king's instigation. Demetrius never was chief of the Alexandrian library.[39]

2. The syntax and grammar used in Aristeas is not of the quality one would expect to emanate from the royal palace of Egypt. Swete illustrates: the Letter uses such barbarisms as *geiōras* (proselyte) rather than *prosēlytos* (proselyte); *sabbatha* (rest) rather than *anapausis* (rest), etc.[40]

3. The Greek of the Pentateuch and the rest of the LXX is Egyptian, not such as would be expected from Palestinian translators.[41] John P. Mahaffy has compared the vocabulary found in Egyptian papyri to that of the LXX and concluded, "in the vocabulary of the papyri we find a closer likeness to the Greek of the LXX than to any other book I could name."[42]

4. The Hellenist Demetrius used LXX Genesis before the reign of Philometor (182–46 B.C.E.).[43]

5. *Aristeas* itself uses the Septuagint. For example, in the description of the table sent by Ptolemy to Eleazar; the description uses and amplifies the description of the table of shew-bread (LXX Exod 25:23–30). Similarly, the description of the vestments worn by the Jewish high priest (§§96–99) uses many terms from the LXX (Exod 28–29). These and other parallels prove that the Septuagint existed before *Aristeas* was written. Such discrepancies led Zuntz to conclude

---

[33] Helmut Koester, *Introduction to the New Testament* (2 vols.; Philadelphia: Fortress, 1982), 1:106.

[34] Albert C. Sundberg Jr., *The Old Testament of the Early Church* (Harvard Theological Studies 20; Cambridge: Harvard University Press, 1964), 129–69.

[35] David W. Gooding, "Aristeas and Septuagint Origins: A Review of Recent Studies," *VT* 13 (1963): 359.

[36] Hadas, *Aristeas*, 78; Jellicoe, *Septuagint and Modern Study*, 31.

[37] Hadas, *Aristeas*, 78; Jellicoe, *Septuagint and Modern Study*, 32 and n. 1.

[38] "Contra historiam lxx. interpretum Aristeae nomine inscriptam" in *De biblioruum textibus originalibus* (Oxford: Stephens Bibliopolae Oxon., 1684). Cf. Swete, *O.T. in Greek*, 15; Hadas, *Aristeas*, 5 n. 1; Jellicoe, *Septuagint and Modern Study*, 31.

[39] Swete, *O.T. in Greek*, 18–19; Hadas, *Aristeas*, 6, 96 n. 9.

[40] Swete, *O.T. in Greek*, 18–19.

[41] Ibid., 20–21.

[42] "Notes of Recent Exposition," *ExpTim* 3 (1892): 290–92; John P. Mahaffy, *Greek Life and Thought, from the Death of Alexander to the Roman Conquest* (London: Macmillan, 1896), 198–99.

[43] Fragments preserved in Clement of Alexandria, *Strom.* 1:21; Eusebius, *Praep. ev.* 9:21, 29. Cf. Swete, *O.T. in Greek*, 117–18; Hadas, *Aristeas*, 67.

"that any historical reality or any relation to a specific point of the history of the Septuagint is sought in vain." However, Zuntz immediately follows this conclusion with "Philo's report about the annual feast celebrated on Pharos in commemoration of the translation seems genuine and points to an ancient tradition."[44]

I. Abrahams has suggested a more tempered approach to *Aristeas* than Hody's, citing works utilizing the vocabulary of the Greek papyri that showed Aristeas's substantial accuracy on many points.[45] He probably claims too much for *Aristeas*, but successfully tempers Hody's onslaught.

3. Purpose and Date of the *Letter of Aristeas*

The loss of historical integrity for *Aristeas* destroyed the mutual relationship between the *Letter* and the time of writing. It can no longer be dated simply by reference to the date of Ptolemy Philadelphus (285–167 B.C.E.) or Queen Arsinoe (288–270).[46] Since the *Letter of Aristeas* has proved to be a fiction, its evident purpose as a historical document announcing the translation of the Jewish Law into Greek is lost. The *Letter of Aristeas* is not what it purports to be. Even its form as a letter is a pretense. Rather than being from and to the persons indicated, it is a piece of propaganda intended for as wide an audience as possible and written by a Jew intending to glorify the Jewish people and the Jewish Law, the letter form being a recognized literary device.[47]

Aristeas twice notices previous translations of Jewish scriptures. Near the end, Demetrius is made to reply to the king's inquiry, that previous disuse of the Jewish scriptures has been "because the Law is sacred and of divine origin" (§§312–16). He goes on to cite two instances of dire results from previous attempted uses. Theopompus (a Greek historian and rhetorician, born ca. 380 B.C.E.) was driven out of his mind because he had intended to include some incidents "from the earlier and somewhat unreliable translations of the law" *(tina tōn proērmēneumenōn episphalesteron ek tou nomou)*. Also, Theodektes (ca. 380–34 B.C.E.), a tragic poet, when "about to adapt some incidents recorded in the book" *(ti tōn anagegrammenōn en tē biblō)* for a play, became afflicted with cataracts in both eyes. Both instances imply pre-Septuagint translations of the Law.[48] Similarly,

---

[44] Zuntz, "Aristeas Studies 2," 125.

[45] "Recent Criticism of the Letter of Aristeas," *JQR* 14 (1901/02), 321–42; Thackeray, "Pseudo-Aristeas," 502. Cf. Schürer, *Hist. of Jewish People*, 1:474–77.

[46] Hadas, *Aristeas*, 4–5; Zuntz, "Aristeas Studies 2," 125.

[47] Henry J. Cadbury, *The Making of Luke-Acts* (New York: Macmillan, 1927), 190–91, 194–209, esp. 202; Paul E. Kahle, *The Cairo Geniza* (New York: Frederick A. Praeger, 1960), 209–10; Jellicoe, *Septuagint and Modern Study*, 29–30.

[48] *Aristeas* §§ 30–31, sometimes regarded as referencing a pre-LXX translation, probably does not; the phrase, "having been carelessly translated," appears to be incorrect and should read, "have been carelessly written" *(sesēmantai)* and thus refers to Hebrew texts rather than to earlier Greek translations. Hadas (*Septuagint and Modern Study*, 110 n. 30) and Kahle (*Geniza*, 212–14) favor "translated"; Marcus (*Josephus*, 7:21 n. c. sic.), Bickerman ("The Colophon of the Greek Book of Esther," *JBL* 63 [1944]: 343), Jellicoe ("Aristeas, Philo, and the Septuagint Vorlage," *JTS*, n.s. 12 [1961]: 267), Zuntz ("Aristeas Studies 2," 117), D. W. Gooding ("Aristeas and LXX Origins," 358–78), and G. Howard ("The Letter of Aristeas and Diaspora Judaism," *JTS*, n.s. 22 [1971]: 337–48) argue conclusively for "written." Cf. also Kahle, *Geniza*, 213 and n. 1.

Aristobulus of Alexandria, a Jewish philosopher (of uncertain date) but described in 2 Macc 1:10 as "the teacher of King Ptolemy," is reported by Clement of Alexandria (*Strom.* 1.22, quoted by Eusebius, *Praep. ev.* 3.12) to have said that before Demetrius Phalereus and prior to Alexander and the Persians " . . . others . . . have translated both the narrative of the exodus of the Hebrews . . . from Egypt . . . and the conquest of the land, and the exposition of the whole Law . . ."[49] (note that this statement is independent of *Aristeas*). These prove that the Septuagint was already in existence before *Aristeas* was written.

There is evidence that the LXX Pentateuch itself was in circulation by the late third century B.C.E. Demetrius, an Hellenistic historian writing under Ptolemy IV Philopator (222–205 B.C.E.), used the LXX Pentateuch as the basis for his *On the Kings of Judaea (Peri tōn en tē Ioudaia basileōn)*.[50] Thus, the *Letter of Aristeas,* written, as we will see, about a century later, cannot have been written to introduce the Septuagint translation. Under these circumstances and with the integrity of Aristeas greatly diminished, scholars have been pursuing the question of why the Letter was written.

Many answers have been suggested. Swete and Thackeray suggested that, despite Hody's devastating critique of the *Letter of Aristeas*, there still remained a kernel of historical material. Allowing that the work was clearly written by a Jew with the obvious purpose to glorify the Jewish race, still it should not be inferred that it has no historical value.[51] Knowledge of the Alexandrian court shows that the letter was written under some Ptolemy.[52] LXX Genesis was in existence anterior to Philometor's reign (182–146 B.C.E.; cf. Demetrius, above). Since Demetrius's chronology continues only to the reign of Philopator I (222–208 B.C.E.), the author probably lived under that Ptolemy.[53] Hence, Swete concludes, the *Letter of Aristeas* probably was written under Ptolemy Philadelphus (285–247 B.C.E.).[54]

Moses Gaster proposed Jerusalem as the venue for the translation of the Greek Pentateuch.[55] The story of an Egyptian king requesting a copy of the Jewish Law for his library can only have been a legend. Only a Palestinian origin would have given a Greek translation sufficient prestige for it to have been accepted in the Diaspora. He rejected the view that the Jews of Alexandria had forgotten their language; nothing could take the place of Hebrew, the language of God. Rather, the translation of the Law was part of a general assertion by the Jews of their own superiority and antiquity. By translating the Law the Jews carried their struggle into the enemy's camp.[56]

Kahle proposed that the *Letter of Aristeas* was written to promote a recent revision of the Jewish scriptures to replace an old translation that had been carelessly transmitted.[57] Indeed, the old material was from a number of "unofficial" versions that appeared among

---

[49] Andrews, "Aristeas," in Charles, *Apoc. and Pseud.,* 2:98 n. 30.

[50] Swete, *O.T. in Greek,* 17–18; Hadas, *Aristeas,* 67. Josephus confused him with Demetrius Phalereus in *Ag. Ap.* 1:218.

[51] Swete, *O.T. in Greek,* 15.

[52] Ibid., 15–16, 53–54.

[53] Ibid., 18–19.

[54] Ibid., 18.

[55] Moses Gaster, *The Samaritans* (London: The British Academy, 1925), 112ff.

[56] Cf. Hadas, *Aristeas,* 67–68; Jellicoe, *Septuagint and Modern Study,* 63–64.

[57] Kahle, *Geniza,* 209–14; cf. idem, "Untersuchungen zur Geschichte des Pentateuchtextes," *TSK* 88 (1915): 399–439; ET in *Opera minora* (Leiden: E. J. Brill, 1956), 3–37; Albertus F. J. Klijn, "The Letter of Aristeas and the Greek Translation of the Pentateuch in Egypt," *NTS* 11 (1964–65): 156.

the Greek speaking Jewish communities in Egypt similar to the unofficial written Targums that followed the Aramaic translations of Hebrew readings of the text for the synagogue. Thus, a recent revision was made by Egyptian Jews to meet their needs for an official, standardized text. While it includes older material, the *Letter* must be placed ca. 127 or 100 B.C.E.; it refers, not to the original translation but to a recent revision called the standard translation, which Kahle wants to extend to the Prophets and the rest of the books. "We have to suppose," he says, "that at a certain period the need for an authorized Greek text of the Jewish Law arose among the influential Jewish circles in Alexandria."[58] A translation commission was formed, probably composed mainly of Jewish scholars from Egypt, while the Hebrew text was procured from Jerusalem. The annual festival, reported in the Letter and by Philo, would not have been instituted without a cause. Kahle's strongest case for such a revised translation is his oft-repeated comment regarding the *Letter*, "Nobody makes propaganda for something a hundred or more years old. Propaganda is made for something contemporary."[59]

However, Kahle's case for contemporaneity[60] is ill served by his dating to about the end of the second century B.C.E. in the face of evidence, as we have seen, of the use of the Septuagint Pentateuch already in the third century.[61] Until Kahle, the main stream of Septuagint studies has followed the lead of P. A. de Lagarde, who proposed that all extant manuscripts of the Septuagint be collected into three families that he called the "threefold truth" *(trifaria veritas)*;[62] behind these lay the original translation of the Hebrew scriptures which, by patient research, would be recoverable.[63] Now we have the publication by Dominique Barthélemy of a LXX manuscript of the Twelve Prophets obtained from Bedouin from a cave South of Murabbaᶜât, obtained in July 1952.[64] This manuscript, a lost, old Greek recension of the LXX from the third-second centuries B.C.E.,[65] has turned the tide in Septuagint studies in favor of Lagarde's approach.[66]

Klijn argues that *Aristeas* was written to steady faith in the Septuagint against a new revision or translation that has been produced.[67] He says that the way Aristeas indicates the import of the LXX translation is: (1) the translation was made by seventy-two elders, six from each Jewish tribe; (2) the translation was made with agreement among the translators; (3) the translation was made in seventy-two days—not accidental; (4) the Alexandrian Jews accepted the translation. These show that *Aristeas* was defending a particular translation of the Law. But there is no agreement about what this defense was against.

---

[58] Kahle, *Geniza*, 214.

[59] Ibid., 211.

[60] Hadas, *Aristeas*, 69.

[61] Cf. S. Jellicoe, "The Occasion and Purpose of the Letter of Aristeas," *NTS* 13 (1968–69): 149.

[62] But cf. Alexander Sperber, "The Problems of the Septuagint Recensions," *JBL* 54 (1935): 73–91.

[63] Swete, *O.T. in Greek,* 188; Howard, "Aristeas and Diaspora," 340–41.

[64] "Redécouverte d'un chaînon manquant de l'histoire de la Septante," *RB* 60 (1953): 18–29; and *Les devanciers d'Aquila* (Leiden: E. J. Brill, 1963), 272. Cf. Frank M. Cross, *The Ancient Library of Qumran* (3d ed.; Minneapolis: Fortress, 1995), 35 n. 1 for additional bibliography.

[65] Cross, *Ancient Library,* 34–35.

[66] Frank M. Cross, "The History of the Biblical Text in the Light of the Discoveries in the Judean Desert," *HTR* 57 (1964): 283.

[67] Klijn, "Aristeas and Greek Trans.," 154–58.

Kahle, as we have seen, attempted to show that it was against existing, carelessly written translations. Klijn, however, believes that it was against a new revision/translation. The accurate text(s) of the scriptures exist in Hebrew only in Jerusalem. However, Hebrew texts in Alexandria had been carelessly handled and corrupted. The LXX was a translation of the Jerusalem Hebrew texts whereas the new Greek revision derived from the Alexandrian Hebrew texts. The *Letter of Aristeas* was written to defend the LXX against this new, corrupted Greek translation. Klijn cites, "it is only right that it [the LXX] shall remain as it is and no revision *(diaskeuē)* shall be made" (§310), from which Klijn concludes that a new revision was implied.[68]

Apparently unaware that T. Lewis, Grabe's translator,[69] had preceded him, Jellicoe, substantially agreeing with Klijn, proposed that it was at the Jewish temple at Leontopolis, built in 154 B.C.E. after the pattern of the Jerusalem temple, that the new Greek translation was made. This translation centered the text on the Leontopolis temple,[70] as the Samaritan Pentateuch centered on Gerizim. Replying to Kahle's telling remark, "Nobody makes propaganda for something a hundred or more years old. Propaganda is made for something contemporary," Jellicoe says that propaganda for something a hundred years or more old "would be supremely apposite, if that 'something'—the original Greek version of the Torah—were placed in jeopardy by an incipient rival"; the issue of contemporaneity no longer is an issue.[71] Thus, since Aristeas can be construed as counter-propaganda to a new translation, he asks whether history provides an appropriate setting. Alexandria, with its rush to literary activity following the Septuagint, would be one possibility. However, that very rush to literary activity would tend to preclude Alexandria, since it was preoccupied with other matters. Another possibility would have been the new, fully equipped temple of Leontopolis, with all its ensuing activity. Any text produced there could hardly escape being judged "carelessly rendered" in Alexandria. Jellicoe puts forth this hypothesis "very tentatively," as it is without direct documentary evidence.

Date is also an almost insoluble problem: *Aristeas* has been dated from 200 B.C.E. to ca. 33 C.E.[72] We have noticed that Hadas's examination of external evidence for clues to purpose and date proved fruitless. Nevertheless, he suggests that cumulatively the external evidence "definitely points in the direction of a Ptolemaic and perhaps an early Ptolemaic period."[73] No linguistic evidence requires a date later than 150 B.C.E. If ben Sira's objection (Prologue 21–22) refers to the un-revised version, then a date shortly after 132 B.C.E. for the composition of *Aristeas* is likely.[74] Harry M. Orlinsky, however, is not so negative as Hadas. He suggests that had the Leontopolis temple been in existence, *Aristeas* would almost certainly have noticed it; it has no reference to the Seleucids and Antiochus Epiphanies; there is no reflection of the Jewish struggle between high priest and king. Orlinsky concurs with William F. Albright that the list of translators in *Aristeas* §§47–50 contains

---

[68] Ibid.

[69] In J. E. Grabe, *Vetus Testamentum juxta LXX interpretes* 1 (trans. T. Lewis; Oxford: E Theatro Sheldoniano, 1775).

[70] Jellicoe, "Purpose of the Letter," 144–50.

[71] Jellicoe, "Occasion of Aristeas," 145.

[72] Jellicoe, *Septuagint and Modern Study*, 48.

[73] Hadas, *Aristeas*, 54.

[74] Ibid., 54, 69.

authentic third-century names; the statement in §97 that the High Priest was wearing the 'oracle' on his breast suggests a pre-Pharisaic dating since the Pharisees abolished that practice; among the Zenon papyri, in P. Cairo Zenon 59003 and 59075, dealing with certain letters of a Tobias addressed to Apollonius and Philadelphus, the writer relates to the Egyptian monarch in terms reminiscent of Eleazar's reply to Philadelphus in *Aristeas* §§41–46. These give the letter verisimilitude for the general period of its purported date.[75]

There remains the evidence of language. Andrews makes the following observations: the omission of the pronoun in the formula *ean oun phainētai* ("if it please you," §32) appears in the papyri only from 163–70 B.C.E.;[76] Strach has shown that the plural, *tōn archisōmatophylakōn* ("chief of the bodyguards," §40) does not appear in the papyri until 145 B.C.E.;[77] "friends" (*philoi*; §45), as a court title, did not come into prominence until Ptolemy V (205–182 B.C.E.);[78] the use of *Koilan Syrian* (Coele-Syria) as a territorial designation, *Aristeas*'s usual name for Palestine, is not documented before the second century.[79] Abrahams, however, has raised points of caution with respect to each of these and concluded that "there is nothing so far discovered that militates against a pre-Maccabean date for the Letter."[80]

4. Alexandrian/Egyptian Bibles

We turn now to the question of Alexandrian/Egyptian Bibles. There is no need to enter again into a discussion of the now defunct Alexandrian (or Septuagint) canon.[81]

The earliest example we have of an Alexandrian/Egyptian Bible is in the *Letter of Aristeas*. That Bible includes only books of the Law, the five books of the Pentateuch that were translated into Greek. It has been noticed above that the direct attention given to the Law in the *Letter* is relatively limited. However, it is the tacit expectation of the writer that everything said in the *Letter* that is favorable about the Law would devolve upon the Greek translation. This expands the material related to the Law. Eleazar, the high priest, is said to have documents in his possession of highest value to the Jews of his country and to folk in foreign lands for the interpretation of the divine law (*tou theiou nomou*, §3), which is of divine origin (*hōs an ousan theian*, §31). The Law is called "sacred" (*semnos*, §5) and deserving a place in the royal library (§10). The God who gave the Jews their Law is the same God who maintains the Ptolemaic kingdom and is the Lord and Creator of the universe (§15). The Law is full of wisdom and free of blemish (§31). The power of God pervaded the whole of the Law (*dia pasas tēs nomothesias to tou theou dynaton endeiknymenos,*

---

[75] Cf. ibid., 45–47.

[76] Andrews, "Aristeas," 98 nn. 32, 86.

[77] Ibid., 99 nn. 40, 86.

[78] Ibid., 86; however, John P. Mahaffy points out that it is used in 1 Kgs 4:5; see *The History of Egyptians under the Ptolemaic Dynasty* (London: Methuen, 1899), 161; Andrews, "Aristeas," 100 n. 45.

[79] Hadas, *Aristeas*, 98.

[80] I. Abrahams, "Recent Criticism of the Letter of Aristeas," *JQR* 14 (1901/02): 373; Kahle, *Geniza*, 210–12.

[81] Cf. Sundberg, *O.T. of Early Church*; Peter Katz, "The Old Testament Canon in Palestine and Alexandria," *ZNW* 47 (1956): 191–217, esp. 203 n. 19a; Otto Eissfeldt, *Einleitung in das Alte Testament* (2d ed.; Tübingen: Mohr [Siebeck], 1956), 227; Frank M. Cross, *From Epic to Canon* (Baltimore: Johns Hopkins, 1998), 227.

§133). The Law was not delivered thoughtlessly but with reason (§§161, 168). Upon receiving the scrolls of the Law, Philadelphus thanks the Jewish envoys, Eleazar who sent them, "and especially God, whose oracles they are" (*megiston de tō theō houtinos esti ta logia tauta*, §177). A curse was set upon anyone who should alter the Greek translation in any way, whether by addition or subtraction, ensuring the preservation of the book unchanged for all future generations (§311). "The Law is sacred and of divine origin" (*ekeinos de ephē: Dia to semnēn einai tēn nomothesian kai dia theou gegonenai*, §313). It is evident that for the writer of *Aristeas* the Law was of supreme value and importance, and that importance was extended to the Septuagint Greek translation. It is fair to say that Alexandrian Jews came to regard the Septuagint as their Bible. This was probably a revised version of an Old Greek translation of the Law.[82]

The next witness to the Septuagint as the Bible of Alexandrian Jews is found in 2 Maccabees, a post-Maccabean writing said by the author to be an abridgment of a five-volume history by Jason of Cyrene (2 Macc 2:19–32). It covers the period of the Hasmonean rebellion from shortly before the accession of Antiochus Epiphanies (175 B.C.E.) to 160 B.C.E., paralleling 1 Macc 1–7, and is written in the inflated Greek of the Ptolemaic style.[83] Ostensibly these are letters written by Jerusalem Jews to their Jewish brethren in Egypt,[84] except for the two letters which commence the writing.[85]

Second Maccabees was written in Egypt in Greek. One passage sets forth the Hellenistic Bible at the time of writing. Maccabeus "encouraging them from the law and the prophets (*paramythoumenos autous ek tou nomou kai prophētōn*), . . . made them the more eager" (2 Macc 15:9). Here for the first time the Bible of Hellenistic Judaism is said to include the Law *and* the Prophets. The second introductory letter of 2 Maccabees dates to 124 B.C.E. and this epitome was probably written shortly thereafter.[86]

The Wisdom of ben Sira, Sirach, Ecclesiasticus are names given to a book of wisdom ascribed to Jesus (Heb., Joshua), son of Sirach,[87] a teacher of wisdom in Jerusalem during the first quarter of the second century B.C.E. It is the largest piece of Jewish wisdom literature extant, and of the ancient Jewish literature excluded from the canon this book came closest to canonization. Probably it was excluded because the author is named and known to have been post-Artaxerxes.[88] It has been suggested that the writer anticipated that his work would be included in the Hebrew canon.[89] Indeed, it was cited several times in the Talmud as canonical.[90] This book of wisdom was written in Hebrew in Jerusalem and,

---

[82] *Aristeas* §31 citing a quotation from Hecataeus of Abdera §313. Cf. Charles, *APOT*, 2:87.

[83] Charles C. Torrey, *The Apocryphal Literature* (New Haven: Yale University Press, 1945), 76–78; William W. Brownlee, "Books of Maccabees," *IDB* 3:206–10; Solomon Zeitlin, *The Second Book of Maccabees* (New York: Harpers, 1954), 240–41. Zeitlin places the writing in Antioch.

[84] Beckwith, *O.T. Canon of N.T. Church*, 142.

[85] These letters, 2 Macc. 1:1–9 and 1:10–2:18, apparently composed in Aramaic (or Hebrew) may be authentic (Torrey, *Apocryphal Literature*, 78). However, they do not pertain here.

[86] Torrey, *Apocryphal Literature*, 78.

[87] Swete, *O.T. in Greek*, 269–70. On text, cf. Jellicoe, *Septuagint and Modern Study*, 306–10.

[88] Josephus, *Ag. Ap.* 1:38–41; 4 Esd. 14:45–46 (Charles, *APOT*, 2:624); *B. Bat.* 14b–15a.

[89] 24:33; Robert H. Pfeiffer, *Introduction to the Old Testament* (New York: Harper & Brothers, 1941), 65; Torrey, *Apocryphal Literature*, 95.

[90] *m.'Abot* 4:4; *b. Pesaḥ.* 113b; *b. B. Meṣiʻa* 112a; *Tanḥ. Mikkeṣ* 10; *Shemoth Rabbah* 21:7; *B. Qam. 92b*. Cf. Arthur E. Cowley and A. Neubauer, *The Original Hebrew of a Portion of Ecclesiasticus*

consequently, as such has no relevance to this discussion of the Alexandrian Greek Bible. However, the grandson of the author visited Alexandria for some time, arriving there in the thirty-eighth year of Euergetes (II [Ptolemy Physkon]), i.e., 132 B.C.E. He remained there long enough to learn to write Egyptian Greek, [91] so it is more likely that his Bible was Egyptian than Palestinian. With a copy of his grandfather's work in hand, he determined to translate it into Greek and publish it "for those living abroad," i.e., in Egypt. The Prologue he wrote has proved to be important; [92] it contains significant information regarding the shape of the Greek Bible in his day (near the end of the second century B.C.E.). Three times this information is repeated in this short prologue. The first reads, "Many and great teachings have been given to us through the law and the prophets and others that followed them" (*dia tou nomou kai tōn prophētōn kai tōn allōn tōn kat' autous ēkolouthēkotōn;* 1).[93] In 7–10 we have, "My grandfather, Jesus, after devoting himself especially to the reading of the law and the prophets and the other books of our fathers" (*ho pappos mou Jēsous epi pleion heauton dous eis te tēn tou nomou kai tōn prophētōn kai tōn allōn patriōn bibliōn anagnōsin*). It should be noted that here the translator attributes the same Bible to his grandfather as he acknowledges for himself. However, this statement should not be pressed since it is a common misconception to regard the present circumstance as of long standing. Finally, in 23–26 we read. "Not only this work, but even the law itself, the prophecies, and the rest of the books (*ou monon de tauta, alla kai autos ho nomos kai hai prophēteiai kai ta loipa tōn bibliōn*) differ not a little as originally expressed."[94] Here, for the first time among Hellenistic Jews a wider Bible, including Law, Prophets, and additional books as well, is noted. [95] We can only guess what books he so included; probably the books later included in the "Writings," possibly others as well.[96]

We have noticed above Philo's warm support of the Law as the Bible of the *Letter of Aristeas*. Philo also mentions another Bible, that of the people he calls Therapeutae or Therapeutrides, a Jewish sect in Egypt[97] which he contrasts with the Essenes described elsewhere as inhabitants of Judaea and Palestine.[98] Philo says that the Therapeutae, whom

---

(Oxford: Clarendon, 1897), xix–xx; Lee M. McDonald, *The Formation of the Christian Biblical Canon* (rev. and enl. ed.; Peabody, Mass.: Hendrickson, 1995), 36 n. 36; Sid Z. Leiman, *The Canonization of Hebrew Scripture* (Hamden, Conn.: Archon, 1976), 90–102; "Sirach," *The Jewish Encyclopedia* (12 vols.; ed. Cyrus Alder; New York: Funk and Wagnalls, 1901–1906), 11:390–91.

[91] Swete, *O.T. in Greek*, 20–21, 300; Kahle, *Geniza*, 216.

[92] Usually dated 132 B.C.E., but sometimes as late as ca. 119. Cf. Jellicoe, *Septuagint and Modern Study*, 60. For a discussion of Peter Katz on the authenticity of the Prologue, cf. Kahle, *Geniza*, 215–18.

[93] Katz, "O.T. Canon," 191–217.

[94] Some take his statement as a possible or probable criticism of the *Letter of Aristeas* which fosters the exact correlation between the Greek translation and the Hebrews text (cf. §310). See Hadas, *Aristeas*, 65.

[95] James C. VanderKam, *The Dead Sea Scrolls Today* (Grand Rapids: Eerdmans, 1994), 35.

[96] Albert C. Sundberg Jr., " 'The Old Testament of the Early Church' Revisited," in *Festschrift in Honor of Charles Speel* (ed. Thomas J. Seinkewicz and James E. Betts; Monmouth, Ill.: Monmouth College, 1996), 90.

[97] Philo, "On the Contemplative Life or Suppliants," 1–90 (trans. Colson, *Philo* 9:112–69). Cf. Sundberg, *O.T. of Early Church*, 68 n. 38; Schürer, *History of the Jewish People*, 3:1.856–59. For a discussion of the authenticity of "On the Contemplative Life," cf. Colson, *Philo*, 9:106–8.

[98] *Hypothetica* 11.1–18; "Every Good Man Is Free," 75–91; Colson, *Philo* 9:436–43; 53–63.

he greatly admires, have in each house a consecrated room called a sanctuary or closet into which they take nothing "but laws and oracles delivered through the mouth of prophets, and psalms and anything else which fosters and perfects knowledge and piety" (*alla nomous kai logia thespisthenta dia prophētōn kai hymnous kai ta alla hois epistēmē kai eusebeia synauxontai kai teleiountai, Contempl.* 25, cf. 28–29). This is very similar to the Bible in the Prologue to Sirach except that Psalms is named. The "anything else which fosters and perfects knowledge and piety" is similar to Orlinsky's "et cetera" for Sirach's "the others that followed them," "the other books of our fathers," "and the rest of the books."[99] Harry Wolfson regarded the books cited in *De vita contemplativa* 25 as Philo's own canon.[100] He overstates the case, since Philo does not overtly endorse this canon. Nevertheless, neither does he criticize it.

Thus we have three Alexandrians witnessing to a Bible consisting of Law and Prophets with two of them noting other books of similar stature but apparently not formed into a named collection. These books probably included books later formed into the "Writings" collection and books later called apocrypha, pseudepigrapha, etc.

5. A Reflected Egyptian Bible

The foregoing is the extent of our primary evidence of the Jewish Bible in Egypt. When we come to Christian writings, however, we find considerable evidence of the use of Jewish religious literature: the Law, the Prophets, one instance of the Psalms (Luke 24:44),[101] and others extending beyond the bounds of the Hebrew canon. This evidence commences with the earliest Christian writings, the New Testament collection, and continues into the Apostolic Fathers, the fathers of the early church, and beyond. This evidence includes the use of the books now called the apocrypha or deuterocanonical books and the pseudepigrapha.[102] The following are reflected in the books of the New Testament: 1 Esdras (Matt), Tobit (Matt, Luke, John, Paul, Rev), Wisdom of Solomon (Matt, Mark, John, Acts, Paul, 2 Tim, Jas, Rev), Sirach (Matt, Mark, Luke, John, Acts, Paul, 2 Tim, Jas, 2 Pet), Baruch (John, Paul, 1 Tim), 1 Maccabees (John, Acts, 1 Tim), 2 Maccabees (Matt, Luke, Acts, Paul, 2 Tim, Rev), *4 Maccabees* (Matt, John, Acts, Paul, 1 Tim, 2 Tim), 4 Esdras (Matt, 2 Pet), *Psalms of Solomon* (Matt, Luke, John, Acts, Paul, Rev), *Assumption of Moses* (Matt), *Assumption of Isaiah* (Heb), Enoch (1 Pet, Jude).[103] The Apostolic Fathers reflect five books of the apocrypha: Tobit, Judith, Wisdom of Solomon, Sirach, and 2 Maccabees,

---

[99] Harry M. Orlinsky, "Some Terms in the Prologue to Ben Sira and the Hebrew Canon," *JBL* 110 (1991): 483–90.

[100] Harry Wolfson, *Philo* (2 vols.; Cambridge, Mass.: Harvard University Press, 1947), 1:117; Swete (*O.T. in Greek*, 217) suggests that a fourfold Bible may be reflected here, i.e., Law, Prophets, Psalms, and other books.

[101] Cf. also Luke 20:42; Acts 1:20; 13:33.

[102] It should be noted that the apocrypha and pseudepigrapha were not discrete collections in this period; our anachronistic use of these terms is for convenience. They did not become named collections until after the Jewish canon and the Christian Old Testament were closed.

[103] The particulars of these are in Sundberg, *O.T. of Early Church*, 53–55; Bruce M. Metzger, "New Testament Parallels and Allusions to the Apocrypha," in *An Introduction to the Apocrypha* (New York: Oxford, 1957), 158–204.

and also, 2 Esdras, *Enoch,* and the book of *Eldad and Modad.*[104] The Ante-Nicene Fathers reflect 2 Esdras, Tobit, Judith, Wisdom of Solomon, Sirach, Baruch, 1, 2, *4 Maccabees.*[105] Since Christians adopted this Jewish nonsectarian religious literature not included in the later Jewish canon from Egyptian Judaism, it is fair to assume that this Christian usage probably reflects Egyptian Jewish usage.[106]

6. Greek in Jerusalem/Palestine

A significant change that has come about during the second half of the past century is a growing awareness of the Hellenization of Jerusalem/Palestinian Jewry. The Greek section of Joseph A. Fitzmyer's presidential address to the Catholic Biblical Association entitled "The Languages of Palestine in the First Century A.D.,"[107] is the best summary of recent developments known to this author and will be followed here with some additions. Already, by about the middle of the second century B.C.E., the Septuagint was cited in Jerusalem: Eupolemus, a Jewish historian, usually identified with the ambassador sent to Rome by Judas Maccabeus (1 Macc 8:17; 2 Macc 4:11), based his history on the Septuagint version of Chronicles.[108] Among the Aramaic stories that form part of Daniel, the first clear instance of Greek invading a Palestinian Aramaic text is found; in Dan 3:5 the names of three musical instruments, the lyre, the harp, and the bagpipe, "are given in slightly Aramaicized forms of clearly Greek names" *(kitharas, psaltēriou, symphōnia).*[109] Daniel appears in Hebrew and Aramaic in its proto-canonical form, but its deuterocanonical form is in Greek.[110] Carsten Colpe has collocated a list of Jewish writers who wrote in Greek;[111] fragments of some of their writings are preserved in church fathers such as Clement of Alexandria[112] and Eusebius of Caesarea.[113] Only a few of these relate to first-century Palestine, the most important being Justus of Tiberius[114] and Flavius Josephus, both writing mainly historical works. Although Justus was Josephus's adversary, Josephus

---

[104] Cf. the marginal notes in *The Apostolic Fathers* (LCL; trans. Kirsopp Lake; Cambridge, Mass.: Harvard University Press, 1945–46), 1:51, 145; 2:23, 393, 396; *The Ante-Nicene Fathers* (10 vols.; ed. Alexander Roberts and James Donaldson; Peabody, Mass.: Hendrickson, 1994), 1:1–155; 9:235–36.

[105] *Ante-Nicene Fathers,* 9:235–36.

[106] Robert A. Kraft, "The Multiform Jewish Heritage of Early Christianity," in *Christianity, Judaism, and Other Greco-Roman Cults* (ed. Jacob Neusner; Leiden: E. J. Brill, 1975), 194–96.

[107] Joseph A. Fitzmyer, "The Languages of Palestine in the First Century A.D.," *The Catholic Biblical Quarterly* 32 (1970): 507–18.

[108] Swete, *O.T. in Greek,* 24; cf. Jacob Freudenthal, *Alexander Polyhistor und die von ihm erhaltenen Reste judaischer und samaritanischer Geschichtswerke* (Breslau: H. Skutsch, 1875), 119; Schürer, *History of Jewish People,* 3:1.477; Bickerman, "Notes on LXX," 164.

[109] Fitzmyer, "Languages of Palestine," 509.

[110] Ibid. Fitzmyer's unsupported claims that 1 Esdras, 2 Maccabees, and the additions to Esther were written in Greek and in Palestine are equivocal ("Languages of Palestine," 510); cf. Torrey, *Apocryphal Literature,* 44, 78, and 58–59, respectively; and *IDB* 1:141; 3:209; 2:152, respectively.

[111] "Jüdisch-hellenistiche Literatur," in *Der kleine Pauly: Lexikon der Antike 2* (Stuttgart: A. Darückenmüller, 1967), 1507–12.

[112] *Stromata* 1.21–23.

[113] *Praep. ev.* 9.22–28.

[114] Josephus, *Vita* 65, 88, 175–78, 279, 336–40, 341–43, 355–60, 390–93, 410; cf. Fitzmyer, "Languages of Palestine," 510 n. 31.

acknowledged his skill in Greek;[115] he wrote a history of the first Jewish revolt against Rome, parallel to that of Josephus, of which Joseph was highly critical.[116]

At the close of his *Antiquitates judaicae,* Josephus tells us about his experience with Greek.[117] On the one hand, Josephus says that he had labored hard, not only at Greek grammar but, also at Greek prose and poetry and was not unversed in Greek culture.[118] Few Jews attained skill in Greek; he himself had not gained proficiency in pronunciation because of his constant need to revert to his native tongue *(patrios . . . synētheia).* But such skill was readily achievable by freedmen and even slaves, if they wished. Besides, proficiency in "the speech of many nations" was not highly regarded among Jews. With them, knowledge of the Jewish law was all important and in this he excelled far beyond his fellow countrymen, so that even as a youth of fourteen the chief priests and leading men of Jerusalem constantly sought him out for the precise meaning of their ordinances.[119] During the latter part of the War he sometimes interpreted for Titus.[120] Josephus initially wrote *Bellum judaicum* in his native tongue (probably Aramaic) for Jewish consumption, but later translated it with help into Greek.[121] He wrote his Greek works, not in Palestine, but in Rome. His equivocal attitude toward Greek tells us little about the extent of the use of Greek in Palestine in his day.

Despite Josephus's indecisive testimony, as Fitzmyer says, "there are many other considerations that persuade us that Greek was widely used at this time" in Palestine.[122] A number of Hellenistic cities were founded in Palestine, including the Decapolis, Pella, and Didon. Similarly, older towns were turned into *poleis:* Acco became Ptolemais; Rabbat-Ammon became Philadelphia; Philoteria was established on the western shore of Lake Gennesaret; Joppa was hellenized; Beth Shan became Scythopolis; Strato's Tower became Caesarea Maritima, Samaria, Sabaste; and others. These spread Hellenistic culture into their surroundings.[123]

Epigraphic material testifies to the use of Greek. Shortly after the middle of the twentieth century, Erwin R. Goodenough published his monumental *Jewish Symbols in the Greco-Roman Period.* He found that Greek names were nearly as common as Hebrew and Aramaic names together on Jewish tombs in Palestine in the time of Christ. Approximately one-third of the names on ossuaries from 150 B.C.E. to 150 C.E., probably antedating the fall of Jerusalem, are Greek.[124] One Greek inscription from Jerusalem, dated pre-70, records the building and dedication of a synagogue "for the reading of the Law and the teaching of the Commandments." The inscription is in Greek; the name of the builder, Theodotos, son of Vettenos, is Greek. He was a Priest, and he, like his father and grandfather before him, was Archisynagogos (synagogue ruler). The dedication inscription is written in Greek, and

---

[115] Josephus, *Vita* 40, 87–88, 336–40, 355–60.

[116] Ibid., 34–41, 336–40, 341–43, 355–60; Eusebius, *Hist. eccl.* 3.10.8.

[117] *Ant.* 20:263–65.

[118] *Vita* 40.

[119] *Vita* 9; cf. Luke 2:41–51.

[120] *B.J.* 5:361.

[121] *B.J.* 1:3, 5–9; *Ant.* 1:6–8; *C. Ap.* 1:50; *Vita* 50.

[122] Fitzmyer, *Languages of Palestine,* 512.

[123] Ibid., 508.

[124] E. R. Goodenough, *Jewish Symbols in the Greco-Roman Period* (13 vols.; New York: Pantheon, 1953), 1:1; Fitzmyer, "Languages in Palestine," 513.

Goodenough thought that the Law was read in Greek in this synagogue.[125] Just as the Dead Sea Scrolls were breaking upon the world, how could Goodenough have been so prescient as to write of this dedicatory tablet:

> Even if we had only this inscription, we should be hereafter unwarranted in setting hellenized Judaism as Alexandrian, over against the Judaism of Palestine, that is in contrasting them as two distinct geographical entities each unified within itself.[126]

Other inscriptions include the "balustrade" inscriptions from Herod's temple in Jerusalem. Two copies have been found; they read, "No foreigner is to enter within the balustrade and enclosure around the temple. Whoever is caught will render himself liable to the consequent penalty of death" (cf. Acts 21:28–29).[127]

The saga of the Dead Sea Scrolls began in 1947 when Bedouin brought seven ancient scrolls to Jerusalem for sale.[128] Apocrypha (deuterocanonical books) and pseudepigrapha were found, including a number not previously known: the Genesis Apocryphon; Noah texts (1Q19; 4Q246?, 534); a Jacob text (4Q537); Joseph texts (4Q371–73); the Qahat (Kohath) text (4Q542); Amram (Exod 6:20) texts (4Q543–48); Moses texts (1Q22, 29; 2Q21; 4Q3674–75, 376[?], 377, 388a, 389, 390); Joshua texts (4Q378–79); a Samuel text (2Q22; see first Psalms scroll from Cave 11); Jeremiah texts (4Q383–84[?]; cf. 385b, 387b); Ezekiel texts (4Q384 [?]–390, 391); Daniel texts (4Q242 [243–45, 551?]); and an Esther text (4Q550?).[129] Other texts include commentaries on Biblical material, legal texts, writings for worship, poetic compositions, eschatological works, wisdom texts, and biographical notes.[130]

Some of the apocryphal literature was shared by both the Qumran Essenes and the early Christians. However, there was not a simple one-to-one ratio in this sharing. Essenes had books not used by Christians and Christians had books not shared by Essenes. Thus Christians did not simply adopt the extracanonical Jewish religious literature from the Essenes. Not all the apocryphal writings used by Christians have been found at Qumran; those not found there apparently did not circulate among the Essenes. Of the apocrypha in Christian use, only Ps 151, Tobit, Sirach (found in Hebrew also at Masada), and the *Letter of Jeremiah* (Bar 6) are extant at Qumran. Of the pseudepigrapha used by Christians the following were found: Enoch materials (11 MSS represented) were found but *Enoch* was not yet a finished book (chs. 37–71, the Similitudes, or Parables, are missing); *Jubilees* (fifteen or sixteen MSS represented); probable sources of the *Testaments of the Twelve Patriarchs*, such as *Testaments of Levi, Judah,* and *Napthali* were found but not the complete book.[131] Apocrypha and pseudepigrapha utilized by Christians but not found at Qumran

---

[125] Goodenough, *Jewish Symbols,* 1:179–80; Fitzmyer, "Languages of Palestine," 512–13.

[126] Goodenough, *Jewish Symbols,* 1:180.

[127] Ronald J. Williams, "Inscriptions," *IDB* 2:712; Fitzmyer, "Languages of Palestine," 512. Fitzmyer also lists inscriptions of a hymn inscribed in the necropolis of Marisa, the edict of Augustus (or some other first-century emperor) regarding the violation of tombs found at Nazareth.

[128] Goodenough, *Jewish Symbols,* 1:180.

[129] Cross, *Ancient Library,* 19–53; VanderKam, *DSS Today,* 1–70.

[130] VanderKam, *DSS Today,* 43–70. Cross, *Epic to Canon,* 225; James H. Charlesworth, ed., *The Pseudepigrapha of the Old Testament* (2 vols.; Garden City, N.Y.: Doubleday, 1983–85); Sundberg, "Revisited," 95.

[131] Jozef T. Milik, *Ten Years of Discovery in the Wilderness of Judea* (trans. John Strugnell; Naperville, Ill.: Alec R. Allenson, 1957), 31–36; VanderKam, *DSS Today,* 35–41.

include: *1–2 Esdras*, Additions to Esther, Wisdom of Solomon, Baruch, Prayer of Azariah, Song of the Three Young Men, Susanna, Bel and the Dragon, 1–2 Maccabees, *Letter of Aristeas*, the *Books of Adam and Eve*, the *Martyrdom and Assumption of Isaiah*, the *Sibylline Oracles*, the *Assumption of Moses*, the *Book of the Secrets of Enoch*, *2–3 Baruch*, *4 Esdras*, *Psalms of Solomon*, *4 Maccabees*, *'Abot*, and *Ahiqar*. This large number of non-sectarian writings peculiar to each group suggests a wider circulation of this literature in Judaism than simply among these two groups. The Pharisees appear to be the most likely source, since some of these books continued to circulate in Judaism even after the closing of the Jewish canon about the end of the first century C.E.[132]

An important feature of the apocryphal literature at Qumran is that some are cited in the sectarian literature in ways that are indistinguishable from the ways in which canonical writings (Law and Prophets) are cited. Bleddyn J. Roberts, noting abundant quotations from the apocryphal writings in sectarian writings at Qumran, observed, "we can visualize the Biblical literature of the New Covenanters as covering a far wider range than either the Hebrew or the Alexandrian Canon."[133] Jean Carmignac, studying the quotations and allusions in *The War of the Sons of Light Against the Sons of Darkness*, concluded that one cannot differentiate between the use of the books of the Hebrew canon and the extracanonical writings in this work.[134] After reviewing the *Zadokite Work*, H. L. Ginzberg remarked,

> But if in their own literary products these sectarians as we have seen, not only echo the terminology and ideology of the Book of Jubilees, First Enoch, and kindred works, but cite them as authorities, they must have had copies in their libraries, surely portions of some of these copies ought to be present. They are.[135]

There are very few statements reflecting the status of canon among the Dead Sea Scrolls. Occasional references to "the Law and the Prophets" occur. The *Manual of Discipline* reads, "in accordance with what He has commanded through Moses and His servants the Prophets" (I, 1). Again, in the same scroll, a portion of VIII, 1–10 reads, "The reference is to the study of the Law which God commanded through Moses to the end that, as occasion arises, all things may be done in accordance with what is revealed therein and with what the Prophets also have revealed through God's holy spirit." We find the following in *The Damascus Document*: "The expression, 'Sikkuth your king' refers to the Books of the Law . . . and the expression, 'Kiyyum your image,' refers to the books of the prophets whose words the House of Israel despised" (VII, 17–18).[136]

---

[132] Sundberg, "Revisited," 95–99; Philip R. Callaway, "The Temple Scroll and the Canonization of the Old Testament," *RB* 13 (1988): 239–43.

[133] B. J. Roberts, "The Dead Sea Scrolls and the Old Testament Scriptures," *BJRL* 36 (1953/54): 84.

[134] J. Carmignac, "Les citations de l'Ancien Testament dans 'La guerre des fils de lumière contre les fils de ténèbres,'" *RB* 63 (1956): 234–60.

[135] H. L. Ginzberg, "The Dead Sea Manuscript Finds: New Light on Eretz Yisrael in the Greco-Roman Period," in *Israel: Its Role in Civilization* (ed. M. Davis; New York: The Seminary Israel Institute of the Jewish Theological Seminary of America, 1956), 47.

[136] Translations are from Theodor H. Gaster, *The Scriptures of the Dead Sea* (London: Secker & Warburg, 1957).

The *Miqṣat Ma'aśe Ha-Torah* ("Some of the Works of the Torah," commonly called 4QMMT), has recently been published.[137] It contains fragments of six manuscripts, 4Q394–99, written over the period from 50 B.C.E. to 50 C.E., from which a composite text of some 114 lines was reconstructed.[138] One instance of "the Law and the Prophets" occurs at C line 17. It reads, "[It is written in the book] of Moses [and in the books of the Prophets]."[139] This name for the Hebrew scriptures thus far canonized is familiar from its appearance in the Prologue to *Sirach,* from instances above in Qumran texts, and from its frequent use in the New Testament and early church fathers. It is the name for the scriptures that Christians received from Judaism.

Another more interesting text, C lines 10–11, reads, "we have [written] to you so that you may study (carefully) the book of Moses and the books of the Prophets and (the writings of) David [and the] (11) [events of] ages past."[140] I take "(the writings of) David" to be the Psalms—the plain and simple meaning of the text, parallel to Luke 24:44, "the Law of Moses and the Prophets and (the) Psalms," and similar to the Therapeutae described by Philo (above), who took only the Laws, Prophets, Psalms, and other books into their oratories. Nehemiah's collected library in 2 Maccabees consists of "books about the kings and prophets and the writings of David, and letters of kings about votive offerings" (2:13). The consonance of the 4QMMT texts in their reading in this passage throughout their period of composition shows that no change in canon occurred that would cause a scribal variation. Beckwith, however, would have us believe that the "Psalms" in Luke 24:44 and "the writings of David" in this text should be understood as a kind of code standing for the whole of the Writings collection.[141] He argues that the Law, Prophets, and Psalms were then the three parts of the Jewish collection. At one time, he says, the title "Psalms" was used as a title for the Hagiographa, citing a tenth century C.E. Arabian writer, al-Masudi, who speaks of the Law, the Prophets, and the Psalms, which are the twenty-four books. Similarly, the phrase, "the Law, the Prophets, and the Psalms, which are the twenty-four books," used in the Tosefta, the Jerusalem Talmud, and certain minor tractates of the Talmud, should be understood in the same way. Beckwith's evidence, however, is centuries removed from the period of our discussion and hardly can be taken as definitive for the understanding of these texts.[142] Eybers holds that the Psalms were canonical at Qumran.[143]

---

[137] Elisha Qimron and John Strugnell, *Qumran Cave 4* (DJD 10; Oxford: Clarendon, 1994), 5; Sundberg, "Revisited," 97–98.

[138] Qimron, *4QMMT,* 43–63.

[139] Ibid., 60–61.

[140] Ibid., 58–59, 112.

[141] Beckwith, *O.T. Canon of N.T. Church,* 111–15.

[142] Sundberg, "Revisited," 98–99. Cf. Norman Golb, *Who Wrote the Dead Sea Scrolls* (New York: Scribners, 1995), 198. Qimron and Strugnell, *4QMMT,* 59 and 112, is equivocal, saying first that "Psalms" probably represents the Hagiographa, but later that it is not clear whether "David" denotes a *Ketubim* collection. Frank M. Cross Jr. says, "There is no evidence in Pharisaic Jewish circles before 70 A.D. of either a fixed canon or text" ("The Text Behind the Text of the Hebrew Bible," in *Understanding the Dead Sea Scrolls* [ed. Hershel Shanks; New York: Vintage Books, 1992], 152). This undermines the attempt to secure evidence for a pre-70 fixed tripartite Hebrew canon through the expedient of finding the "Writings" squirreled away under the name of "David" or "Psalms."

[143] I. H. Eybers, "Some Light on the Canon of the Qumran Sect," in *The Canon and the Masorah of the Hebrew Bible* (ed. S. Z. Leiman; Library of Biblical Studies; New York: Ktav, 1974), 23–36, at 24–25.

Thus we have from Alexandria/Egypt and from Palestine descriptions of Bibles that are very similar. The Law and the Prophets appear as fixed collections in each. In addition, in Egypt we find "other books," "other books of our fathers," "the rest of the books," "the writings of David" (probably the Psalms), and "psalms and anything else that fosters perfect knowledge and piety." From Palestine we have the Law, the Prophets, and the Law and the Prophets and "(the writings of) David." In both Egypt and Palestine we have evidence for the circulation and use of a large extracanonical literature that is not confined simply to the usage of Essenes and early Christians but probably among Pharisees as well.

There are evidences of continued use of this apocryphal literature in rabbinic literature of later times. *Sirach* is quoted as scripture three times in the Talmud. Twice it is cited with the introductory formula, "for so it is written in the Book of Ben Sira."[144] It is also cited as "Writings" when the rabbis are proof-texting, e.g., "This matter is written in the Pentateuch as written . . . , repeated in the Prophets, as written, . . . mentioned a third time in the Hagiographa, as written, (here *Sirach* 12:15 is cited), it was learned in the Mishnah."[145] Pfeiffer tells us that *Sirach* was still being copied as late as the twelfth century C.E. It is quoted by name in *Sanhedrin* 100b. According to L. Israel,[146] single verses appear in *Y. Berakot* 11b; *Y. Ḥagigah* 13a, 77c; *Y. Taʿanit* 66d; *Niddah* 16b; *Genesis Rabbah* 8, 10, 73; *Levitus Rabbah* 33; *Wayishlah* 8; *Tan. Mikkeṣ* 10; *Tan. Hukkat.* 1. Origen knew a Hebrew name for the books of Maccabees, "Sar beth Sabnaiel."[147] Jerome had Hebrew texts of Sirach, Tobit, Judith (in Aramaic, or "Chaldee"), 1 Maccabees, and *Jubilees*, presumably from Jews, translating them into Latin. Moses ben Nahaman (Nachmanides, ca. 1194–1270 C.E.) used an Aramaic text of Wisdom, citing 7:5–8, 17–21 in the "Introduction," and in 1:7, 8, 11 in his *Commentary on the Pentateuch;* he also indicated some acquaintance with Bel and the Dragon and Judith by Jews in Spain in the twelfth and thirteenth centuries.[148] These indications of circulation of many Jewish apocryphal writings among rabbis implies that this literature also circulated among pre-70 Pharisees, since the rabbis were the successors of the Pharisees. It is evident that this wider collection of apocryphal literature circulated among Pharisees, Essenes, and Christians. We have no information concerning other groups and unaligned Jews. However, it is evident that this wider circulation including Pharisees is the storehouse from which early Christianity received its scriptures from Judaism.

We turn now to the findings of Greek texts in the Judean Desert. Cave 4 at Qumran yielded fragments of some 575 manuscripts.[149] Greek fragments of Leviticus and Numbers were found. Cave 7 yielded fragments of about nineteen very fragmentary manuscripts, all in Greek, including the *Letter of Jeremiah* (Baruch 6).[150] In Cave 7 the legible manuscripts are all in Greek.

---

[144] *Ḥag.* 13a; *Yebam.* 63b; *ʿErub.* 54a.

[145] *B. Qam.* 92b.

[146] "The Wisdom of Jesus the son of Sirach," in *The Jewish Encyclopedia*, 11:388–97.

[147] In Eusebius, *Hist. eccl.* 6.25.2.

[148] A. Max, "An Aramaic Fragment of the Wisdom of Solomon," *JBL* 40 (1921): 57–69.

[149] Cross, *Ancient Library*, 41; VanderKam, *DSS Today*, 10–11; *Qumran Cave 4: Palaeo-Hebrew and Greek Biblical Manuscripts 4* (DJD 9; ed. Patrick W. Skehan, Eugene Ulrich, and Judith E. Sanderson; Oxford: Clarendon, 1992).

[150] VanderKam, *DSS Today*, 11, 36. *Les grottes de Murabbaʿât* (DJD 3; ed. Maurice Baillet, Jozef T. Milik, and Roland de Vaux; Oxford: Clarendon, 1962), 1, 2.

The Qumran caves provide a circumscribed offering of Greek texts that for this study only show the presence of Greek writings of Biblical and extrabiblical material.[151] In 1952 fragments of a Greek version of the Book of the Twelve were offered for sale at the *Ecole Biblique* in East Jerusalem. The Bedouin identified the sight from which they came as South of Wadi Murabbaʿât, later identified as the "Cave of Horror" in Nahal Ḥever. An expedition to this cave in 1961 recovered an additional thirteen fragments of this text, all dating from the Simon ben Kosiba revolt (132–135 C.E.).[152] Dominique Barthélemy was given this material to research and publish, resulting in his *Les devanciers d'Aquila: Première publication intégrale du texte des fragmentes du Dodécaprophéton.*[153]

Barthélemy provides a transcription and analysis of the scroll and locates its place within the development of the Greek Bible. He was able to determine several features distinguishing this text from the standard Septuagint text(s) current in Egypt. The Murabbaʿât Book of the Twelve text proved to be from the last half of the first century B.C.E. to (more likely) the last half of the first century C.E. It is a revision, not of the current Septuagint text in Egypt, but of an earlier old Greek translation and contains several distinguishing Hebraisms. Perhaps the most common is that Hebrew *gam* is translated *kaige*, which has come to be the name with which the recension is dubbed (pp. 31–32). These Hebraisms have resulted in the identification of other books belonging to this recension, including the long form of Daniel and Baruch.[154] Cross has cogently remarked that it is unlikely that the Pharisaic proto-rabbinate who produced this recension would have included the long form of Daniel and Baruch in it if a closed Hebrew canon had obtained at the time.[155] It appears to have been this form of the Book of the Twelve that Justin used in his quotations.[156] It closely parallels the fifth column of Origin's Hexapla.

In addition to the *kaige* recension of the Book of the Twelve, the Cave of Horrors produced other items of importance to this inquiry. There were coins of the first and second centuries C.E., including nine from the second revolt; Aramaic deeds dated in "the year 3 of Israel's Freedom" (134 C.E.); grain transactions; contracts of marriage and remarriage; fragments of philosophical and literary texts; texts written in a Greek shorthand. Two letters in Greek were found addressed by "Simeon ben Koseba, Prince of Israel" to a "Jeshua ben Galgola and the men of the front," and another, also in Greek, addressed to "Jeshua ben Galgola, commander of the camp." One letter from the Cave of Letters in Wadi Habra is of particular interest. It is written by one Soumaios. The editor of the letter, B. Lifshitz,

---

[151] Qumran Cave 7 is a special circumstance. In spite of the paucity of Greek texts at Qumran, all of the legible material in it is Greek. Norman Golb, in accord with his notion that the Qumran caves were repositories of individual libraries from Jerusalem, thought Cave 7 was such a library of Greek holdings (*Who Wrote the Dead Sea Scrolls?* [New York: Scribner, 1995], 100, 129, 147–48, 258, 367–68).

[152] Barthélemy, "Redécouverte d'un chaînon manquant," 18–29; B. Lifshitz, "The Greek Documents from the Cave of Horror," *IEJ* 12 (1962): 201–7; Barthélemy, *Devanciers d'Aquila*, 161–98.

[153] Leiden: E. J. Brill, 1963. Cf. Cross, "History of the Biblical," 281–99.

[154] Barthélemy, *Devanciers d'Aquila*, 32–44; Frank M. Cross Jr., "The Text Behind the Text," 300 n. 11; Peter Katz, "Septuagintal Studies in the Mid-Century," in *The Background of the New Testament and Its Eschatology* (ed. William D. Davies and David Daube; Cambridge: The University Press, 1956), 206–8.

[155] Cross, *Epic to Canon*, 222.

[156] Barthélemy, *Devanciers d'Aquila*, 203–12.

thinks *Soumaios* is a Greek form of *Simeon ben Kosibah,* the real name of Bar Kokhba, leader of the second revolt. If not Bar Kokhba, then someone closely associated with him writing to the same two lieutenants to whom Bar Kokhba wrote the other two letters and about the same matter. He writes, "No[w] (this) has been written in Greek because a [des]ire has not be[en] found to w[ri]te in Hebrew" *(Egraphē d[e] Elēnisti dia t[o hor]man mē eupēth[ē]nai Ebraesti g[ra]psasthai).* Here, at a time when nationalism must have been strong, Bar Kochba or someone close to him preferred to write in Greek rather than Hebrew.[157]

The last items take us to the very heart of first century C.E., Palestinian Judaism, and demonstrate its Hellenization. These include the Greek Book of the Twelve manuscript (leading to the definition of a probably late first century C.E., Palestinian, Pharisaic, Greek recension of the Hellenistic Jewish Bible, produced by the Jerusalem proto-rabbinate, that included the long form of Daniel and the book of Baruch), and other artifacts from the Cave of Horrors (especially the two letters composed in Greek by Simon bar Kosiba, the commander of the army in the second revolt of the Jews against the Romans). The Pharisaic *kaige* recension lies very close in time and place to the canonization of the Palestinian Jewish Bible; we find in it material that proved later to be extracanonical, similar in kind if not quantity to what we suppose to have been the situation in Hellenized, Jewish Egypt. The *kaige* recension is our best candidate for the Bible of Palestinian, Hellenized Jews. And we have the commander of the forces in the revolt, at the very heart of Palestinian Jewry, Hellenized, preferring to write in Greek to an officer in his troops! For these foregoing reasons it is evident that the area of Jewish Hellenization in the first century B.C.E. to the first century C.E. (to 70) included Palestine and extended eastward to the Jordan River and the Dead Sea.

[157] Ginsberg, "Dead Sea Manuscript Finds," 40–41; B. Lifshitz, "Papyrus grecs du désert de Juda," *Aegyptus* 42 (1962): 240–56; Fitzmyer, "Languages of Palestine," 513–15.

6

Questions of Canon Viewed through the
Dead Sea Scrolls

James C. VanderKam

As nearly as we can tell, there was no *canon* of scripture in Second Temple Judaism. That is, before 70 C.E. no authoritative body of which we know drew up a list of books that alone were regarded as supremely authoritative, a list from which none could be subtracted and to which none could be added. There is nothing new or surprising in a statement such as this. It was thought for a time, apparently a long time, that the finishing touches were put on such a canon only two decades or so after the end of the Second Temple period, when rabbinic scholars gathered in Yavneh are supposed to have closed the scriptural list by including the Writings and adding them to the already canonized Law and Prophets. That thesis has taken some heavy blows over the last thirty-five years, and it richly deserved them. Our evidence for what rabbis at Yavneh did and what authority they possessed is paltry indeed, and hardly bears the weight the theory imposed upon it. Moreover, that the Law and Prophets were *canonized* at earlier times goes beyond our data.[1]

In short, we do not know how, when, or by whom the list of books now found in the Hebrew Bible was drawn up. All we have are hints over a considerable historical span suggesting that some books were regarded by certain writers as sufficiently authoritative that they could be cited to settle a dispute, explain a situation, provide an example, or predict what would happen. In that limited sense there is evidence for a set or sets of authoritative works in Judaism from an early time. We would like to know more about which scrolls were involved and what sort of authority was attributed to them, but usually we have to settle for much less. It is evident that many of the books which now find a place in the Hebrew Bible enjoyed lofty status for Jewish writers and did so from early in the second

---

This paper bears some resemblance to an essay scheduled to appear in the volume of essays from the Hereford Conference of 2000, sponsored by the Scriptorium. The emphasis in that paper was on text-critical issues; here it has been modified considerably to focus on canonical matters.

[1] See, for example, J. P. Lewis, "What do we mean by Jabneh?" *JBR* 32 (1964): 125–32. The most detailed recent study of canonical development remains R. Beckwith, *The Old Testament Canon of the New Testament Church and its Background in Early Judaism* (Grand Rapids: Eerdmans, 1985). For a critique of his views, see my essay "Revealed Literature in the Second Temple Period," in VanderKam, *From Revelation to Canon: Studies in the Hebrew Bible and Second Temple Literature* (JSJSup 62; Leiden: Brill, 2000), 1–30.

temple period, but we are not justified in making such a claim about all of them. There are other scrolls not in the Hebrew Bible that were deemed authoritative by some individuals or groups. This is simply another way of saying that what we might call canonical boundaries were not definitively drawn in that time.

The thesis that I would like to defend regarding the second temple period is that while there were authoritative writings, and these were at times gathered into recognizable groupings (e.g., Law, Prophets, Others), the category of revealed literature was not considered a closed and fixed one, at least not for the type of Judaism for which we now have the most evidence—the people of the Dead Sea Scrolls (Essenes according to most scholars). This is in line with their documented belief that revelation was not confined to the distant past but continued in their time and fellowship. About the Teacher of Righteousness it is said that to him "God made known all the mysteries of the words of His servants the Prophets" (1QpHab VII, 4–5).[2] Regardless whether that gift extended to others, the text is clear that revelation continued at least in the Teacher's time. Whether others who did not belong to the Qumran community's persuasion would have agreed that divine disclosures occurred in the present we do not know—with the exception, of course, of the group of Jews who followed Jesus of Nazareth.

1. The Pentateuch at Qumran

It will be most convenient here to limit the topic to the first five books of the Hebrew Bible which we name variously the Books of Moses, the Torah, or the Pentateuch. I have selected these books not only because they raise some intriguing questions but also because with respect to them we now have a substantial body of evidence for addressing the issue of authoritative literature. It can be inferred from Josephus that the Pharisees, Sadducees, and Essenes agreed on the authority of Moses' Torah, and the other literature available to us bears that out. So, for example, several passages in the specifically sectarian scrolls from Qumran refer to normative groups of books such as the Law and the Prophets. 1QS I, 1–3 says of the *maskil* that he is to teach the community members to "seek God with a whole heart and soul, and to do what is good and right before Him, as He commanded by the hand of Moses and all His servants the prophets." Here, not surprisingly, God's authority stands behind the words of Moses just as it does for the prophetic message. Or 1QS VIII, 15–16 reads with reference to Isa 40:3: "This (path) is the study of the Law which He commanded by the hand of Moses, that they may do according to all that has been revealed from age to age, and as the Prophets have revealed by His Holy Spirit." For this writer again, the law and prophets are revealed. 4QMMT or the *Halakhic Letter* (4Q394–99) has made a familiar contribution to discussions of authoritative literature at Qumran. Although most of the work concerns itself with a series of legal disputes between the authors and others (a noteworthy contribution indeed), toward the end, in a more irenic tone, the writers address theological or theoretical concerns, including this sentence: "And we have [written] to

---

[2] Translations of Qumran texts are from G. Vermes, *The Complete Dead Sea Scrolls in English* (New York: Penguin, 1997), unless otherwise specified. For a survey of the issue in the Qumran texts, see VanderKam, "Authoritative Literature in the Dead Sea Scrolls," *DSD* 5 (1998), 382–402.

you *[ʾlykh]* so that you may study (carefully *[tbyn]*) the book of Moses *[bspr mwšh]* and the books of the Prophets and (the writings of) David [and the events of] ages past" (C 9–11).[3] Here the Mosaic corpus is conceived as one book. This survey of statements about authoritative literature in the Scrolls could be expanded; there is no question about the authority of the Torah for the covenanters of Qumran. But what was included in this Torah? Does the term *Torah* (or *Moses*) embrace just what we consider Genesis through Deuteronomy (in whatever textual form), or did the category encompass more?

All of our pentateuchal books are well represented in the Qumran caves and elsewhere in the Judean Desert. From Qumran alone, we have the following numbers of copies (copies combining two books are counted twice):[4]

Genesis	18
Exodus	17
Leviticus	13
Numbers	6
Deuteronomy	29

Besides actual copies of the pentateuchal works, passages from them are quoted and commented upon in other writings. So, for example, there are several commentaries on Genesis from cave 4 (4Q252–54), the Sinai revelation in Exodus surfaces elsewhere (e.g., the *Temple Scroll*), Leviticus and Numbers provide the basis for the festal calendar, Numbers contains the Balaam prophecy noted in several scrolls, and Deuteronomy also features in important ways (again the *Temple Scroll* is an example).

Given that at least these five books would have been accepted as revealed and hence authoritative by all Jewish groups, what may we infer from this fact regarding the questions mentioned at the beginning? Did the Qumran community consider them *biblical* in the sense of a closed, fixed list, that is, did they regard them as the *full and only* authoritative version of the material from creation to the death of Moses, or is the situation more complex? Do they stand apart from all other texts in that sense? I maintain that texts found at Qumran suggest that, at least for this one tradition in second temple Judaism, the matter was more complex. As a result, it is inappropriate to use the word *Bible* for our books Genesis through Deuteronomy, or to assume that *Torah* or *Moses* means just these five when talking about the Qumran group and its time. It seems that authoritative representations of pentateuchal material were not limited to these five compositions, and the text of none of them was, as it were, set in stone.

Let me first say a few words about the nature of the evidence we have for the five books of our Pentateuch and then turn to the series of texts offering us the fuller picture.

---

[3] The translation is from E. Qimron and J. Strugnell, *Qumran Cave 4*, V Miqṣat Maʿase Ha-Torah (DJD 10; Oxford: Clarendon, 1994), 59. See the commentary on 93–94, where they cite parallels for "the book of Moses" as "an alternative name for 'the Torah' "; and their brief canonical analysis on 111–12.

[4] The numbers are based on the list published by E. Tov, "A List of the Texts from the Judaean Desert," Appendix III in *The Dead Sea Scrolls After Fifty Years: A Comprehensive Assessment* (2 vols.; ed. P. Flint and J. VanderKam; Leiden: Brill, 1998–99), 2:669–717.

2. Evidence for Textual Fluidity

First, some pentateuchal manuscripts are unusual in a graphic way: they are among the few texts inscribed in a paleo-Hebrew script. Not all copies of Genesis, Exodus, Leviticus, Numbers, and Deuteronomy were, of course, written in that archaic script, but several were: two of Genesis (4Q12, 6Q1), one of Exodus (4Q22), a manuscript with both Genesis and Exodus (4Q11), four of Leviticus (1Q3 [Leviticus and Numbers], 2Q5, 6Q2, 11Q1), and two copies of Deuteronomy (4Q45–46). While the implications of this fact are not clear, it may mean that, for the copyists, these books were associated with Moses and the period of the ancestors. The editor of the paleo-Hebrew texts from cave 4, Eugene Ulrich, has concluded about them: "except for their script, the palaeo-Hebrew biblical manuscripts from Qumran Cave 4 do not appear to form a group distinguishable from the other biblical scrolls in either physical features, date, orthography, or textual character."[5] It should be added that there are four other cave 4 manuscripts copied in the same sort of script (4Q101, 123–25). They are designated as 4QpaleoJob[c], 4QpaleoParaJosh, 4Qpaleo-Unidentified (1), and 4QpaleoUnidentified (2).[6] The existence of these four apparently non-pentateuchal copies makes the use of paleo-Hebrew script for some manuscripts of Genesis, Exodus, Leviticus, Numbers, and Deuteronomy interesting but not a unique characteristic.

Second, Emanuel Tov has divided the entire corpus of the so-called Qumran biblical manuscripts and fragments into five categories: texts written with the special orthographic practices of Qumran scribes (ca. 25 percent); proto-Masoretic texts (ca. 40 percent), pre-Samaritan texts (ca. 5 percent), texts close to the Hebrew model for the Septuagint (ca. 5 percent); and nonaligned texts (ca. 25 percent).[7] Although there are some problems with these categories because not all of them are of the same kind (the first deals with copies written with a certain system of spelling, not with the nature of their text), they do give one extremely well informed scholar's overview of the situation. A sizable portion of the copies belong, to one degree or another, in the textual tradition that eventuated in the Masoretic Text. Yet how does one classify a fragmentary copy that agrees with both the MT and the Samaritan Pentateuch? In general the situation at the small site of Qumran was one of some textual diversity and fluidity. To step outside the Pentateuch, the pesharim or commentaries on biblical prophecies indicate that the commentators were aware of variant readings in biblical manuscripts, but no Qumran discussion of the phenomenon of variants and whether they bothered anyone has survived. The pesharists at times even

---

[5] "The Palaeo-Hebrew Biblical Manuscripts from Qumran Cave 4," in *Time to Prepare the Way in the Wilderness: Papers on the Qumran Scrolls by Fellows of the Institute for Advanced Studies of the Hebrew University, Jerusalem, 1989–1990* (STDJ 16; ed. D. Dimant and L. Schiffman; Leiden: Brill, 1995), 129; reprinted in Ulrich, *The Dead Sea Scrolls and the Origins of the Bible* (Studies in the Dead Sea Scrolls and Related Literature; Grand Rapids: Eerdmans, 1999), 147.

[6] These were published in *Qumran Cave 4 IV Palaeo-Hebrew and Greek Biblical Manuscripts* (DJD 9; ed. P. Skehan, E. Ulrich, and J. Sanderson; Oxford: Clarendon, 1992).

[7] Tov, *Textual Criticism of the Hebrew Bible* (Minneapolis: Fortress; Assen/Maastricht: van Gorcum, 1992), 114–17; the percentages are revisions from those given in the 1992 book, and were communicated privately by Tov (see VanderKam, *The Dead Sea Scrolls Today* [Grand Rapids: Eerdmans, 1994], 134, 158).

exploited variant readings by using both to argue their case. For our purposes, it should be noted that pentateuchal copies from the caves fall into all of Tov's five categories and therefore in this respect do not differ from the other parts of the corpus. So, for example, among the copies written in the Qumran practice are 1QDeut^a, 4QNum^b, 4QDeut^{h,j,k,m}, 11QLev^b. A proto-MT manuscript would be 4QLevNum^a; 4QpaleoExod^m and 4QNum^b have been identified as pre-Samaritan types, while pre-Septuagint examples are 4QLev^d, 4QDeut^q, and among the non-aligned manuscripts are 4QDeut^{j,n} and 5QDeut.

Third, Ulrich, has divided the sorts of variant readings we find in Qumran "biblical" manuscripts into three categories: 1. orthographic or spelling differences between copies—differences that seem unrelated to the textual type of a manuscript; 2. major individual textual variants such as the longer passage between 1 Sam 10 and 11 in 4QSam^a; and 3. variant literary editions (or multiple literary editions) of units "appearing in two or more parallel forms . . . , which one author, major redactor, or major editor completed and which a subsequent redactor or editor intentionally changed to a sufficient extent that the resultant form should be called a revised edition of that text."[8] Exodus is one example of a book appearing in a revised literary edition.

From this evidence it is clear that at Qumran, even for the pentateuchal books, there was some textual fluidity, not a single fixed text, and that they were treated no differently than other books, apart from the fact that a few copies were made using the paleo-Hebrew script. The so-called pre-Samaritan group of texts is especially interesting. As Tov describes it, "[t]he main feature characterizing these texts is the appearance of harmonizing additions within Exodus and of harmonizing additions in Exodus and Numbers taken from Deuteronomy. . . ."[9] These texts, which have nothing Samaritan about them other than that one of them presumably served as the textual base for the later Samaritan Pentateuch, will be especially significant as we look at other kinds of compositions.

These "biblical" manuscripts have all been published. As is the practice in the official DJD series, "biblical" manuscripts are placed first in any volume or have entire volumes devoted to them alone. That is, what are identified as "biblical" manuscripts are often treated separately by scrolls scholars, with some focusing all or almost all of their scholarly labors on them. It seems to me that this segregation of texts is not a valid procedure in that it does not reflect what comes to expression in the ancient works found at Qumran.

First, we have much more direct evidence of the wording of Genesis–Deuteronomy than lists such as Tov's suggest. We have not only the so-called "biblical" manuscripts, but also have targums, tefillin, and mezuzot which reproduce the text of these books. In other cases we have works that quote from them. These too should be considered in attempting to come to a fuller understanding of the textual situation at Qumran. Including them in Tov's statistics would alter his percentages, though perhaps not greatly.

---

[8] Ulrich, "The Canonical Process, Textual Criticism, and Latter Stages in the Composition of the Bible," in *"Sha°arei Talmon": Studies in the Bible, Qumran, and the Ancient Near East Presented to Shemaryahu Talmon* (ed. M. Fishbane and E. Tov, with W. Fields; Winona Lake, Ind.: Eisenbrauns, 1992), 278; see also his "Multiple Literary Editions: Reflections toward a Theory of the History of the Biblical Text," in *Current Research and Technological Developments on the Dead Sea Scrolls* (STDJ 20; ed. D. Parry and S. Ricks; Leiden: Brill, 1996), 78–105. Both of these essays are reprinted in *The Dead Sea Scrolls and the Origins of the Bible* (51–78 and 99–120).

[9] Tov, *Textual Criticism of the Hebrew Bible*, 98.

Second, a stronger warning against segregating "biblical" manuscripts comes from another set of works uncovered at Qumran. These are books that experts usually place under Geza Vermes's rubric, "Rewritten Bible," which might be better designated "reworked scriptures." They are: *Reworked Pentateuch*, the *Temple Scroll*, and *Jubilees* (one could also include the *Genesis Apocryphon*). These works, which contain evidence pertinent to our deliberations about canonical matters and also large amounts of textual information that is rarely exploited fully in text-critical publications, will be the focus in the remainder of this paper. The compositions in question all have to do with the text of parts of the Pentateuch, and all of them allow glimpses into the history of the scriptural texts in the Hebrew language during the late Second Temple period. As it turns out, they also present a range of possibilities and challenges in connection with our question about whether there was a Bible at the time.

3. Reworked Scriptures

In regard to the reworked scriptures listed above, two phenomena should be examined: the nature of the book in question (e.g., how the author presents the material, claims to authority, its relation to older texts, etc.), and the text-type of its scriptural citations. The nature of the text provides some idea of its relationship to older writings, and the character of the "biblical" material in it allows us to relate it to the types identified by Tov. These two phenomena should help us to understand the books and their significance for the issue of whether there was a Bible. It should be noted that other texts could have been included in this survey (e.g., 4Q252, 4Q368), but the ones selected give a good impression of the types of questions that arise.

A. Reworked Pentateuch

The *Reworked Pentateuch* (formerly called *Pentateuchal Paraphrase*, 4Q158, 364–67), present in either four or five fragmentary manuscripts from Qumran cave 4 and unknown before the Qumran discoveries, is virtually a copy of large stretches of the Torah. In fact, it may actually be a copy—that is the real question, as we shall see. Tov analyzed its literary type and concluded that "this composition contained a running text of the Pentateuch interlaced with exegetical elements. The greater part of the composition follows the biblical text closely, but many small exegetical elements are added, while other elements are changed or omitted and in other cases their sequence is altered."[10] The other editor of the work, Sidnie White Crawford, observes: "There are no scribal indications in any of the manuscripts of the *Reworked Pentateuch* to signal differences from the received text of the Pentateuch; to the casual reader, the scroll would have looked like any other manuscript of the Torah."[11] The only exception she notes is that the work apparently would have included

---

[10] "The Textual Status of 4Q364–367 (4QPP)," *The Madrid Qumran Congress* (2 vols.; ed. J. Trebolle Barrera and L. Vegas Montaner; STDJ 11; Leiden: Brill, 1992), 49. See also the edition of 4Q364–367 (in *Qumran Cave 4 VIII Parabiblical Texts, Part 1* [DJD 13; consulting ed. J. VanderKam; Oxford: Clarendon, 1994], 191) for virtually the same sentences.

[11] White Crawford, "Reworked Pentateuch," *Encyclopedia of the Dead Sea Scrolls* (2 vols.; ed. L. Schiffman and J. VanderKam; New York: Oxford University Press, 2000), 775.

the entire Torah (copy c has parts of all five books) in a single scroll estimated to be some 22–27 meters or 72–89 feet long; if true, this would be the longest scroll represented at Qumran. The other Qumran witnesses for pentateuchal texts have a single book or at most two of them on one scroll.

Though the work may indeed contain elements that justify calling it *Reworked* Pentateuch and excluding it from the list of "biblical" manuscripts found at Qumran, it nevertheless looks like the Pentateuch and it quotes (if that is the right word) sizable amounts of it. *Reworked Pentateuch* is thus another important witness to its Hebrew wording at a relatively early time. A comparison of its readings with those of other ancient witnesses has led Tov to describe its underlying scriptural text as "belonging to a group of texts recognized previously in research, namely, the so-called pre-Samaritan group."[12] Specifically, it agrees with the MT in twenty-seven cases and disagrees in thirty-five, while it agrees with the Samaritan Pentateuch forty times, disagreeing in seventeen readings; also it "agrees exclusively with [the MT] against [the Samaritan Pentateuch] in only two instances, while it agrees exclusively with [the Samaritan Pentateuch] against [the MT] (?) in seventeen instances."[13] Hence, *Reworked Pentateuch* consists mostly of a running text of the Pentateuch in a well-attested textual form.

As noted earlier, Tov assigns *Reworked Pentateuch* to the category Rewritten Bible,[14] but if that is its proper classification the accent would have to fall on the word *Bible,* not on *Rewritten.* It is not easy to see how the *Reworked Pentateuch* differs in character from, say, the Qumran witnesses to the pre-Samaritan form of the Pentateuch, and in some of his comments Tov acknowledges as much. As he discusses the relation between 4Q158 and 4Q364–67, he notes that 4Q158 and 4Q364 reflect the text of the Samaritan Pentateuch "in its major harmonizing characteristics in several small details and in its deviating sequence of biblical passages in frg. 6–8."[15] He attributes these readings to the "biblical" manuscript being used by the writer. So, for example, in 4Q158 Exodus passages in the Sinai pericope are supplemented with parallels drawn from Deuteronomy; this procedure of combining passages that are separated in other witnesses such as the MT and Septuagint is, of course, also characteristic of the pre-Samaritan manuscripts from Qumran and the Samaritan Pentateuch. An interesting example from another context is the pairing of the two passages about the daughters of Zelophehad (Num 27 and 36) in 4Q365 frg. 36, because 4QNum[b] may do the same.[16] In the Numbers manuscript, as reconstructed by N. Jastram, the two pericopes are combined, but not in exactly the same way: frg. 36 of 4Q365 presents four words from Num 27:11 before eight words from Num 36:1–2; according to Jastram's reconstruction of the Numbers copy, the order was: Num 36:1–2; 27:2'–11'; 36:3–4; 36:1'–2'; 36:5–13.[17] The procedure in 4QNum[b] has not caused the manuscript to be removed from the "biblical" category. Why should similar procedures lead one to classify *Reworked Pentateuch* as *reworked,* not as *Pentateuch?*

---

[12] DJD 13,196.

[13] DJD 13,195. The numbers here differ slightly from the earlier formulation in "The Textual Status," 78.

[14] "The Textual Status," 51–52.

[15] Ibid., 47.

[16] Ibid., 50.

[17] N. Jastram, "4QNum[b]," in *Qumran Cave 4 VII* (DJD 12; ed. E. Ulrich, F. M. Cross, et al.; Oxford: Clarendon, 1994), 262–64.

White Crawford distinguishes *Reworked Pentateuch* from the pre-Samaritan copies in that it *adds* new material not drawn from elsewhere in the Pentateuch.[18] Noteworthy among the examples of extra material in *Reworked Pentateuch* are a song of Miriam in Exod 15 (between vv. 21 and 22 [4Q365 6a ii and c]), a passage before Gen 28:6 in which Isaac consoles Rebekah (4Q364 3 II), and reference to the festivals of oil and wood after Lev 24:2 (4Q365 frg. 23). Why should such pluses relative to other copies of Genesis, Exodus, and Leviticus be thought to make *Reworked Pentateuch* less authoritative? To cite a parallel case: 4QSamª has, as we have seen, a longer text between 1 Sam 10 and 11. This plus has, to my knowledge, not led any scholar to dismiss 4QSamª from the ranks of "biblical" manuscripts. Why should one think a few modest pluses in *Reworked Pentateuch* remove it from the category into which we place copies of Genesis through Deuteronomy?

Recently M. Segal has phrased the point a bit differently: "In the (pre-)Samaritan Pentateuch, the additions and harmonizations are taken from other sections of the Pentateuch, and are not composed *ex nihilo* by the scribe responsible for those changes. In contrast, in 4Q364–5 the scribes have gone one step farther. They continue to preserve the biblical text as in the pre-Samaritan biblical texts, but they have now added their own material. . . . however, these additions and changes are made in biblical style and follow precedents of textual transmission found within the Hebrew Bible itself."[19] But as regards our concerns is it accurate to say "they have added their own material," and, if so, does it make any difference for questions of authority and status? Tov distinguishes rewritten scriptural texts from copies of the pre-Samaritan text in that while the former "insert several or many new elements into the biblical text, the SP group used existing biblical elements, mainly as *repetitions*."[20] But his formulation assumes that there was a Bible (note "biblical elements") consisting of the books in our Bibles today, although that is precisely the point in question. At Qumran, other books besides Genesis–Deuteronomy may have served as sources for these so-called "biblical elements."

One way of ascertaining whether a work was considered authoritative is to check how it is used in other compositions. The pentateuchal texts are often quoted as authorities in the Qumran works, but since *Reworked Pentateuch* consists almost entirely of text that we know from copies of Genesis–Deuteronomy, one cannot tell whether a citation of Torah material is taken from *Reworked Pentateuch* or some other text. Conversely, there are some candidates for use of *Reworked Pentateuch,* not of Genesis–Deuteronomy as we know them from many manuscripts. The Song of Miriam (in 4Q365) seems unique, but it appears to be fashioned, at least in part, from the language of the Song of Moses in Exod 15. The plus regarding Isaac and Rebekah is paralleled in *Jub.* 27:14, 17; the direction of influence, if there was one, is not known. The two additional festivals are treated in the

---

[18] S. W. Crawford, "The 'Rewritten' Bible at Qumran," *Frank Moore Cross Volume* (ErIsr 26; Jerusalem: IES and Hebrew Union College–Jewish Institute of Religion, 1999), 3*. Writers such as the author of *Jubilees,* may in this way signal a difference from the older text. But the case of *Jubilees* makes plain that the issue of form differs from the issue of authority.

[19] M. Segal, "4QReworked Pentateuch or 4QPentateuch?" in *The Dead Sea Scrolls Fifty Years after Their Discovery: Proceedings of the Jerusalem Congress, July 20–25, 1997* (ed. L. H. Schiffman, E. Tov, and J. C. VanderKam; Jerusalem: IES and the Shrine of the Book, 2000), 394.

[20] Tov, "Rewritten Bible Compositions and Biblical Manuscripts, with Special Attention to the Samaritan Pentateuch," *DSD* 5 (1998): 339.

Temple Scroll; again the direction of any possible influence is uncertain. In fact there has been debate whether 4Q365 frg. 23 (= Lev 23:42–24:2 + add.), the piece with the two extra festivals, is a part of the *Temple Scroll*. Yadin identified it as coming from another copy of the *Temple Scroll* with which it agrees not only for the two festivals but also for an unusual order of the tribes (cols. 21–24).[21] M. Wise deals with it in his analysis of what he calls "the Deuteronomy Source" of the *Temple Scroll* and writes: "I would suggest then that the fragment is a part of the original D source which the redactor rejected when he chose portions for the TS. He did not need it because he replaced the Deut 16 portion of the synopsis— which included the modification of Lev 23 contained in fragment 1 [= 4Q365 frg. 23]— with the Festival Calendar Source."[22] The editors Tov and White Crawford have kept the fragment with 4Q365, the third copy of *Reworked Pentateuch*, but some sort of relationship with the *Temple Scroll* is clear, and possibly with 4Q365a which may also be a copy of the *Temple Scroll*.

Reworked Pentateuch, then, is a difficult case. Should we designate it as a copy of the Pentateuch or is it an example of rewritten scripture? More important, how can we tell? It seems to be a borderline case falling at a point on a continuum very close to or even at the same place as the so-called pre-Samaritan texts (e.g., the earlier stratum in the Samaritan Pentateuch, 4QpaleoExod^m, 4QNum^b, 4QDeut^n, 4QTest). It shares the same sorts of traits and readings, e.g., harmonizations, grammatical adjustments. Since we lack the beginning of the work and any statement of purpose it may have contained, we can only guess about its purpose and the setting chosen by the author. The composition strains the adequacy of our terminology, as may be inferred from the use of such an unusual label as *Reworked Pentateuch*.[23] What is the dividing line between a scriptural text of the "pre-Samaritan" type and a supposedly rewritten scriptural text such as *Reworked Pentateuch*? As M. Bernstein puts it: "The Reworked Pentateuch (4Q364–367) texts stand on the unclearly marked border between biblical text and biblical interpretation."[24] One could add that 4Q158 and

---

[21] *The Temple Scroll* (3 vols; Jerusalem: IES, Instutute of Archaeology of the Hebrew University of Jerusalem, and the Shrine of the Book, 1983), 3, pl 40*, 1.

[22] M. O. Wise, *A Critical Study of the Temple Scroll from Qumran Cave 11* (SAOC 49; Chicago: University of Chicago, 1990), 50. He treats the fragment on 46–50 and points to the presence of several instances of deuteronomic language in it.

[23] Tov ("Biblical Texts as Reworked in Some Qumran Manuscripts with Special Attention to 4QRP and 4QparaGen-Exod," in *The Community of the Renewed Covenant: The Notre Dame Symposium on the Dead Sea Scrolls* [Christianity and Judaism in Antiquity 10; ed. E. Ulrich and J. VanderKam; Notre Dame, Ind.: University of Notre Dame Press, 1994], 111–34) distinguishes between "reworking/rewriting which involved a limited intervention in the biblical text, and rephrasing involving a major intervention, often in such a way that the underlying biblical text is hardly recognizable. Adding exegetical comments to the biblical text is a form of rewriting" (112).

[24] M. Bernstein, "Pentateuchal Interpretation at Qumran," in *The Dead Sea Scrolls after Fifty Years: A Comprehensive Assessment* (2 vols.; ed. P. Flint and J. VanderKam; Leiden: Brill, 1998–99), 1:134–35. Bernstein doubts that all of the *Reworked Pentateuch* texts are from the same composition, and does not think 4Q158 belongs with 4Q364–67. This point was argued by M. Segal ("Biblical Exegesis in 4Q158: Techniques and Genre," *Text* 19 [1998]: 45–62). Segal has more recently maintained that while 4Q158 is from a different work than 4Q364–67, even these latter four numbers are not copies of one composition: 4Q364–65 are copies of the Pentateuch, the fragmentary 4Q366 is also a copy of the Pentateuch, while the poorly preserved 4Q367 may be an excerpted text of Leviticus (Segal, "4QReworked Pentateuch or 4QPentateuch?" 391–99). E. Ulrich has written: "it is pos-

4Q364–67 may lie at slightly different points on that "unclearly marked border." So, what is it—scripture or rewritten scripture? On the basis of form, wording, and contents, there seem to be no strong reasons for denying *Reworked Pentateuch* the status that scrolls of Genesis to Deuteronomy had, although in the DJD series it was published in vol. 13, one of the parabiblical volumes.

B. Temple Scroll

The *Temple Scroll* (4Q365a?; 4Q524; 11Q19–20; 11Q21?) should be examined next because it resembles *Reworked Pentateuch* in some ways. As we have seen, some scholars have concluded that a fragment published as part of a copy of *Reworked Pentateuch* is actually from a copy of the *Temple Scroll* (4Q365 frg. 23). In fact, there is even more disputed material: there has been considerable debate about whether the fragments designated 4Q365a (they were copied by the scribe who wrote 4Q365) should be classified as part of *Reworked Pentateuch* or as coming from the *Temple Scroll*. Yadin thought that at least some of the five fragments (nos. 2 and 3) were from a copy of the *Temple Scroll*, while Wise disagreed, assigning frg. 2 to his Temple Source for the *Temple Scroll* and frg. 3, which overlaps with the *Temple Scroll*, he sees as showing that these fragments are from a proto-*Temple Scroll*. Strugnell assigned the fragments to 4Q365 and placed them after frg. 23; the editor, S. White Crawford, concluded that they do not belong to *Reworked Pentateuch*, and placed a question mark after the designation 4QTemple.[25] My purpose here is not to adjudicate the dispute but simply to say that, wherever they belong, the two texts show a similarity.

The *Temple Scroll* includes material from approximately Exod 24 through much of Deuteronomy, but Deuteronomy appears to be the central scriptural foundation. As Wise writes: "The TS mixes and matches portions from the latter four books with no real regard to the order of books in the Torah. The real basis for the scroll's redactional plan is quite different. Put simply, the redactor had in mind the production of a new Deut—that is, of the legal portions—but he chose to organize that material in terms of concentric circles of holiness. . . . The redactor has rearranged material from the D source in accordance with the circle to which it applies, and added his other sources according to the same plan. Always, however, he had in mind the production of a new Deut, so he accounted for every portion of the relevant laws."[26] The procedure of the editor makes it seem likely that he was working with and modifying an older text; possibly this has to be said about his sources. It would be difficult to argue that the topical centralization in the *Temple Scroll* is original, while the scattering and repetition in Exodus–Deuteronomy are editorial revisions. There is

---

sible that 4Q364–367 preserve yet a third variant literary edition of the Pentateuch, alongside the MT and the second Jewish variant edition that was at home in Second Temple Judaism and used by the Samaritans as the textual basis for their form of the Pentateuch" ("The Dead Sea Scrolls and the Biblical Text," *The Dead Sea Scrolls after Fifty Years*, 1:89).

[25] S. W. Crawford, "4Q365a. 4QTemple?" in DJD 13.319–33. There she discusses the various views advanced. Yigael Yadin includes the fragments in *The Temple Scroll* (Jerusalem: Israel Exploration Society, 1977–1983), vol. 3, supplementary pls. 38*, 40*, and handles them at the appropriate places in his multi-volume work on the text. For Wise's treatment, see *A Critical Study of the Temple Scroll*, 50–58.

[26] Wise, *A Critical Study of the Temple Scroll*, 178.

no evidence that the writer considered the *Temple Scroll* itself as a replacement for Exodus through Deuteronomy; rather it seems to be an authoritative, revealed reading of what we regard as the older text, making it a law for the last times. The author apparently presents it as a revelation given at the same time as the first one.

The *Temple Scroll* is available in one large copy (about 8 meters or 26 feet long, the longest stretch of preserved scroll from Qumran) and perhaps as many as four much more fragmentary ones. Compared to *Reworked Pentateuch*, it often stands at a greater remove textually from what we normally think of as "biblical" manuscripts. Furthermore, in it we can glimpse something of the new setting into which the author/redactor has placed all of the older scriptural sections—a direct revelation to Moses. As F. Garcia Martinez has written: "Although the beginning is lost, column ii suggests that the narrative framework, which integrates the body of concrete laws forming the work, was similar to that in *Jubilees* and in the Sinaitic covenant (as in *Ex.* 34 and *Dt.* 7)."[27] The first column of the text for which we have evidence is based on Exod 34:10–16.

The many parts of the text that may be called scriptural citations have been isolated and studied in detail by Tov.[28] He notes that in the *Temple Scroll* there are numerous deviations in wording relative to the MT, a number of which agree with the Septuagint, the Samaritan Pentateuch, or both. But there are two fundamentally different ways of assessing these variants: (1) they preserve ancient readings, or (2) they are due to the nature of the scriptural rewriting in the *Temple Scroll* which must first be considered in evaluating the citations in the scroll. If the latter is the case, the resulting differences from the MT and other witnesses would not constitute ancient readings but redactional touches.

Tov tests these two possibilities. First he examines whether variations between the scriptural material in the *Temple Scroll* and the MT are due to the author's having taken liberties with details of the "biblical" text (just as he demonstrably took liberties with its content). Tov finds evidence that this is the case: the writer not only substitutes first-person references to the deity for third-person references (though incompletely and inconsistently) but also makes similar changes in other passages, leaving the impression that he altered the base text in such cases. Some of these modifications reflect the linguistic situation of the author's time. Also the writer abbreviated scriptural passages worded awkwardly in the original, and inserted parallel verses that appear in different places—whether in the same chapter, a different chapter, or another book. Tov also notes possible omissions and harmonizations. He concludes that the better one comes to know the *Temple Scroll*'s system of combining sources and skipping over "irrelevant" details, the more one attributes differences between the *Temple Scroll* and the MT to this authorial tendency.[29]

As he goes on to explain, however, these types of readings must be balanced by many others in which the *Temple Scroll* differs with the MT and is supported in this disagreement by one or more of the ancient witnesses. Tov places some sixty-three readings in this category, and compares them with the Septuagint, the Samaritan Pentateuch, the Peshitta, the Vulgate, and targums *Onqelos* and *Pseudo-Jonathan*,[30] He attributes most of the scroll's dif-

---

[27] F. G. Martinez, "Temple Scroll," *Encyclopedia of the Dead Sea Scrolls*, 929.
[28] " *'mgylt h-mqdš' wbyqwrt nwsh h-mqr'*," *Orlinsky Volume* (ErIsr 16; Jerusalem: Israel Exploration Society, 1982), 100–111.
[29] Ibid., 100–103.
[30] Ibid., 104–8.

ferences to the author's method of rewriting, but he acknowledges that the work preserves some ancient pentateuchal readings. His statistics for agreements with the ancient versions are:

Temple Scroll = LXX SP ≠ MT   22
Temple Scroll = LXX ≠ SP ≠ MT   26
Temple Scroll = SP ≠ LXX   2
Temple Scroll = SP = MT   6[31]

The statistics suggest that the "biblical" material in the *Temple Scroll* is related most closely to the Hebrew text underlying the Septuagint and then to the Samaritan Pentateuch.

However, numbers of agreements taken in isolation must be evaluated in the light of two other types of readings: those where the *Temple Scroll* disagrees with the Septuagint and Samaritan Pentateuch and those for which the scroll has unique readings. When the text of the *Temple Scroll* is scoured for these categories of readings, the following figures result:

Temple Scroll ≠ LXX SP   33 (for these the LXX and SP usually agree)
Temple Scroll ≠ LXX   6
Temple Scroll ≠ SP   11

Moreover, when unique readings (which are difficult to isolate in such a text) are taken into account, it can be seen that the *Temple Scroll* deviates from, more than it agrees with, the versions. That is, the *Temple Scroll* is an independent witness to the text of the Torah. This supports Tov's familiar thesis that we should not speak of text types or recensions but simply of texts that are related with one another in a complicated pattern of agreements and disagreements.[32]

After Tov's comprehensive study was published, other treatments of parts of the biblical material in the *Temple Scroll* appeared. George Brooke analyzed the passages in it that "correspond in some measure with Exod 35–40 to discover whether the Hebrew text of Exodus reflected in some parts of 11QT[a] can be described as offering an example of what may have been akin to a Hebrew *Vorlage* for the translator of the Septuagint of these chapters."[33] Brooke mentions a few cases in which the compiler of the scroll seems to reflect a text like the MT, not the Septuagint, but finds considerably more evidence of agreement with the Septuagint, not with the MT. In cols. 3–10, which are poorly preserved, he locates and discusses nine passages. From them he concludes: "Whilst the interpretative skills of the Greek translator of Exod 35–40 should not be denied, nevertheless some of the Septuagint text's principal characteristics, discernible especially in the order and brevity of its *Vorlage*, are now vaguely recognizable in part of the *Temple Scroll*, particularly 11QT[a] 3 and 10."[34]

---

[31] Ibid., 109.

[32] Ibid., 110.

[33] Brooke, "The Temple Scroll and LXX Exodus 35–40," in *Septuagint, Scrolls, and Cognate Writings: Papers Presented to the International Symposium on the Septuagint and Its Relations to the Dead Sea Scrolls and Other Writings (Manchester, 1990)* (SBLSCS 33; ed. G. J. Brooke and B. Lindars; Atlanta: Scholars, 1992), 81.

[34] "The Temple Scroll and LXX Exodus 35–40," 100–101.

Lawrence Schiffman, in the same collection in which Brooke's essay appeared, contributed a study of what he calls "shared 'halakhic' variants" between the *Temple Scroll* and the Septuagint. He adduced nine passages in which the two agree on readings that both differ from what is present in the MT and also have legal significance—usually clarifying a law that was left ambiguous in the MT. He observes:

> In these cases, we cannot assume that the scroll has originated the particular reading, especially in passages which deal with halakhic matters known to have been debated in Second Temple times. In general, the examples we have examined are cases in which we must conclude that either the author/redactor of the scroll found these variants in his *Vorlage* or that he knew of the exegesis represented in the Septuagint and incorporated this interpretation into his scroll. In either case, it seems that the rulings of the shared halakhic variants cannot be considered to be original to the *Temple Scroll*.[35]

Brooke returned to the subject of the underlying scriptural text in his 1992 essay containing comparisons of the text of the *Temple Scroll* with that of the newly published Qumran manuscripts of the Pentateuch, especially 4QpaleoExod[m], 11QpaleoLev, Tefillin and Mezuzot, and 4QtgLev.[36] He notes the readings with mixed textual associations in all these witnesses but concludes that "[t]he treatment of the biblical text in the *Temple Scroll* and even the very text of the scriptural passages it interprets and supplements stands in the tradition of scribal activity to which these Qumran pentateuchal manuscripts witness in the last two or three centuries B.C.E."[37] Or, as he says in another place, "it is no longer so easy to distinguish between exegesis within biblical texts and exegesis of biblical texts."[38] For our purposes, that is an important point: the *Temple Scroll* or at least the scriptural text presupposed in it stands in the same tradition as the manuscripts with which he compared it—manuscripts whose "biblical" identity is not in dispute.

These studies have helped to clarify the nature of the scriptural readings in the *Temple Scroll*, while at the same time highlighting problems inherent in evaluating their significance for textual criticism and in assessing the nature of the work. The *Temple Scroll* poses another difficulty for our terminology because, though it does in fact rework a scriptural base and place it in a different setting, it does so in ways that are often found in the so-called biblical manuscripts from Qumran; moreover, it claims to be divinely inspired and thus supremely authoritative, the very words of God. So, it may fall into two categories, scripture and rewritten scripture, just as Deuteronomy and 1–2 Chronicles do. Its readings, when they can be separated from the author's method of rewriting, reveal the wording of a Hebrew text of the Torah in the Second Temple period.

Should we call the *Temple Scroll biblical?* Experts have debated how to characterize the composition. Yadin thought of it as a Torah and believed that it was the one sent by the Teacher of Righteousness to the Wicked Priest (the Torah mentioned in 4QpPs[a]).[39]

---

[35] "The Septuagint and the Temple Scroll: Shared 'Halakhic' Variants," *Septuagint, Scrolls and Cognate Writings*, 277–97, at 292.

[36] Brooke, "The Textual Tradition of the *Temple Scroll* and Recently Published Manuscripts of the Pentateuch," in *The Dead Sea Scrolls: Forty Years of Research* (STDJ 10; ed. D. Dimant and U. Rappaport; Leiden: Brill, 1992), 261–82.

[37] Ibid., 282.

[38] Ibid., 263.

[39] Yadin, *The Temple Scroll*, 1:390–92, 396–97.

H. Stegemann has maintained that it is a sixth book of the Torah which had originated about two centuries before the Qumran community and whose purpose was to complete the first five books of the Torah; B. Z. Wacholder argued that it was a new Torah, also revealed at Sinai, meant to replace the older temporary one; and Wise sees it as an eschatological law for the land written by the Teacher of Righteousness—an inspired individual who spoke, not pseudepigraphically as the old Moses, but as a new one.[40] In a recent study D. Swanson argued that it was intended to bring unity to the older texts, harmonizing them, and solving problems in them.[41]

These are positions adopted by modern scholars. To reflect the views of the people at Qumran, should we put the *Temple Scroll* in the same category as Genesis–Deuteronomy? It is difficult to imagine why we should not. True, it is even further removed from Genesis–Deuteronomy than *Reworked Pentateuch,* and shows more evidence of an editorial hand; its lengthy quotations of pentateuchal material come especially in the Deuteronomy section of the scroll, that is, in columns 51 and following, where Deut 12–26 are the basis, less so in the other sections. Yet even in the Deuteronomy section the editor's role is evident. As Wise puts it, "The redactor represented every single portion of Deut 12–26 in one of three ways: he either took it over complete, replaced it with a new formulation (or source), or deleted it—all in accordance with a discernible ideology."[42] But what does this signify? The text is still largely that of the Pentateuch, somewhat rearranged with expansions and abbreviations. Its readings align with known types, and it claims to be words spoken directly by God.

Was the *Temple Scroll* regarded as authoritative by the Qumran community? If a legal text claims to be the words of God, and if some five copies of it—an extremely long composition—were preserved in the caves, it seems reasonable to conclude that they considered it authoritative. Yadin wrote: " . . . it seems that, in light of the analysis of the content of the scroll and the method of its editing, it is difficult to avoid the conclusion that the author—and, *a fortiori,* the members of the sect—regarded it as a veritable Torah of the Lord."[43] Yet there are few if any references to it elsewhere in Qumran literature, although we have already seen some points where it is related somehow to other texts or fragments.[44] So, for example, we have noted the similarities with material that may belong to the *Reworked Pentateuch,* i.e., the festivals of oil and wood. The oil festival is also mentioned in the Qumran calendars, and, if Yadin is correct, the *Temple Scroll* is called a *Torah* in a Psalms pesher.

---

[40] For Stegemann, see, for example, "The Origins of the Temple Scroll," *Congress Volume Jerusalem* (VTSup 40; Leiden: Brill, 1986), 235–56; and "Is the Temple Scroll a Sixth Book of the Torah—Lost for 2,500 Years?" *BAR* 13 (1987): 28–35; for Wacholder, see *The Dawn of Qumran: The Sectarian Torah and the Teacher of Righteousness* (HUCM 8; Cincinnati: Hebrew Union College, 1983); and for Wise, see *A Critical Study of the Temple Scroll,* 188–89.

[41] D. Swanson, *The Temple Scroll and the Bible: The Methodology of 11QT* (STDJ 14; Leiden: Brill, 1995).

[42] Wise, *A Critical Study of the Temple Scroll,* 167.

[43] Yadin, *The Temple Scroll,* 1:392.

[44] Yadin (*The Temple Scroll,* 1:393–97) considered the possibility that it is the Book of Hagu/Hagi, the sealed book of the law in CD V, 1–5, and the book of the second law (4Q177 [4QCatena^a] 1–4.14; see 4Q171 [4QpPs^a] 3–10 IV, 8–9 for the law that the Teacher sent to the Wicked Priest). He seems to think it not unreasonable that all of these refer to the same book, the *Temple Scroll* (p. 397).

C. Jubilees

The Book of Jubilees (1Q17–18; 2Q19–20; 3Q5; 4Q176 frgs. 19–21; 4Q216, 218–24; 11Q12) is a work similar to the *Temple Scroll* in that it is a rewriting of earlier pentateuchal material which it places in a new setting (Sinai). It quotes extensively from a more ancient text of Genesis and Exodus. We have the beginning of the text, which identifies the setting: Moses is told to ascend Mount Sinai, there to receive the law and the testimony—terms that some have interpreted as referring to the Torah (that is, our Pentateuch) and to *Jubilees*. If so, the writer was claiming that both were revealed to Moses at Mount Sinai, with neither having precedence over the other or replacing it. The contents of *Jub.* 2–50, from creation to Sinai, are said to have been disclosed to Moses by an angel of the presence who was reading the words from the heavenly tablets. This angel of the presence seems to be modeled on the angel who went before the camp of Israel and who is virtually identified with the Lord himself in Exod 23:20–23 and 33:12–16. As a result, the claim to authority staked by the book is a powerful one indeed: God commands the angel of the presence to read the words to Moses from the celestial tablets. Clearly *Jubilees* presents itself as inspired and reliable.[45]

Jubilees, packaged as revelation from Sinai, follows the scriptural narrative thread from Gen 1 to Exod 24, while the *Temple Scroll* begins at that point (relying more heavily on Exod 34 than on the parallel in Exod 24) and then, in its own way as we have seen, carries through to the end of the Pentateuch. *Jubilees* explicitly refers to an older text. In *Jub.* 6.22 the angel says to Moses, about the festival of weeks: "For I have written (this) in the book of the first law in which I wrote for you that you should celebrate it at each of its times one day in a year."[46] Here we should recall the phrase *spr h-twrh šnyt* in 4Q177 1–4.14. In *Jub.* 30.24, where the subject is intermarriage with Gentiles, the angel says: "For this reason I have written for you in the words of the law everything that the Shechemites did to Dinah. . . ." Later in the verse he quotes from Gen 34:14. Just as *Reworked Pentateuch* and the *Temple Scroll* collect parallels and harmonize, so our writer brings together what he takes to be related passages separated in our Pentateuch. That is, through a kind of harmonizing, he introduces legal material into his text at points where he thinks the narrative implies it. So, for example, he situates legislation about the festival of weeks after the flood story because he associated covenants with the festival of the third month, the month when, on his view, Noah entered into the agreement of Gen 9 (see *Jub.* 6).

Jubilees exhibits throughout the transparent hand of an editor. A prominent way in which his work comes to expression is through the chronological framework which gives the book its name. The narratives from creation to Mount Sinai are encased in a chronology of fifty periods of forty-nine years each (= a jubilee period). The last of these periods will end as the freed Israelite slaves enter their patrimonial land that, in *Jubilees*, had been given

---

[45] H. Najman, "Interpretation as Primordial Writing: Jubilees and Its Authority Conferring Strategy," *JSJ* 30 (1999): 379–410. For the law and testimony in *Jubilees* 1, see C. Werman, "H-twrh w-h-tʿwdh h-ktwbh ʿl h-lwḥwt," *Tarbiz* 68 (1999): 473–92.

[46] The translation cited is VanderKam, *The Book of Jubilees* (2 vols.; CSCO 510–11, Scriptores Aethiopici 87–88; Leuven: Peeters, 1989), 2:40.

to them at the time of Noah.[47] Through his efforts at rooting pentateuchal legislation in the narratives of the ancestors, the author/editor shows that at least one of his goals was to demonstrate that the laws were not an innovation from Moses' time but had been practiced long before by the heroes of Genesis. He apparently wished to make this point to counter contemporary claims that there had been a much more law-free time before Moses came along and separated the Jewish people from other nations by means of narrow legislation.[48]

Unlike the other works considered to this point, we have explicit evidence that *Jubilees* was regarded as authoritative both in Jewish and Christian circles. In the Damascus Document it is cited as a source of precise information about the times of Israel's blindness. The context in which it is placed is suggestive: " . . . therefore a man shall bind himself by oath to return to the Law of Moses, for in it all things are strictly defined *[mdwqdq]*. As for the exact determination *[prwš]* of their times in which Israel turns a blind eye, behold it is strictly defined *[mdwqdq]* in the *Book of the Divisions . . ." (Jub.* 16.1–4). Here a point is first made from the Torah of Moses and then from *Jubilees* (called *The Book of the Divisions . . .* in Hebrew sources). It is not clear to me whether the author is here distinguishing two sources—the Torah and *Jubilees*—or referring to a specific text within the Torah. Another Qumran text that may base a teaching on *Jubilees* is 4Q228, but the text is too broken for certainty.[49] The Qumran community accepted the understanding of the festal calendar and of the weeks/covenant association given in *Jubilees,* as well as its reading of Lev 12 in association with the expulsion from Eden (see 4Q265). Later, whatever its fate in early Judaism, the work found a place in the Old Testament of the Abyssinian church.[50]

Jubilees was perhaps the first rewritten scriptural text to be exploited by modern scholars for its possible contribution to understanding the early history of the biblical text in Hebrew. A. Dillmann, who presented the first translation and edition of Ethiopic *Jubilees,* took up the question in his initial publication on the book in 1850–51. At that early stage, he concluded that its agreements with the Septuagint were due to a translator who had altered the original Semitic text toward the Septuagint as he rendered it into Greek.[51] Some thirty years later, armed with a more secure textual basis, he returned to the question in greater detail. In a weighty article,[52] he adduced eighty-nine readings in which *Jubilees* sided with the MT against the Septuagint; in a shorter list he specified cases of the reverse kind, that is, ones in which *Jubilees* supported the Septuagint against the MT. For this latter set he found three explanations: (1) most of the readings in agreement with the Septuagint were due to the person who translated *Jubilees* into Greek (or the Latin translator); (2) a smaller number of

---

[47] See VanderKam, "Das chronologische Konzept des Jubiläenbuches," *ZAW* 107 (1995): 80–100. An English translation of the article appeared in VanderKam, *From Revelation to Canon: Studies in the Hebrew Bible and Second Temple Literature* (JSJSup 62; Leiden: Brill, 1999), 522–44.

[48] See VanderKam, "The Origins and Purposes of the Book of Jubilees," *Studies in the Book of Jubilees* (TSAJ 65; ed. M. Albani, J. Frey, and A. Lange; Tübingen: Mohr [Siebeck], 1997), 3–24.

[49] The text, published by VanderKam and Milik, DJD 13.177–85 with pl. XII, is called "Text with a Citation of *Jubilees*."

[50] See R. Cowley, "The Biblical Canon of the Ethiopian Orthodox Church Today," *Ostkirchliche Studien* 23 (1974): 318–23.

[51] A. Dillmann, "Das Buch der Jubiläen oder die kleine Genesis," *Jahrbücher der Biblischen Wissenschaft* 3 (1851): 88–90.

[52] A. Dillmann, "Beiträge aus dem Buch der Jubiläen zur Kritik des Pentateuch-Textes," in SPAW 1 (Berlin: Verlag der königlichen Akademie der Wissenschaften, 1883), 323–40.

them were instances in which the author adopted exegetical traditions found in the Septuagint (especially in explaining rare expressions); and (3) others were actual variants and were to be traced back to the Hebrew scriptural text that the author used. For Dillmann, this last category proved that the Hebrew copies of the Pentateuch at the time when *Jubilees* was composed by no means agreed fully with the later official text. He thought that the differences relative to that official text were not as numerous as one finds in the Septuagint, and usually concerned only unimportant matters. The readings stemming from a variant *Vorlage* were often in agreement with the Septuagint or the Samaritan Pentateuch.[53] It is curious that Dillmann found more cases in which *Jubilees* agreed with the MT than with the Septuagint; as we shall see, the numbers actually point in the opposite direction.

I later compiled all of the "biblical" citations in *Jubilees* and compared all of them in detail with the ancient witnesses (MT, Samaritan Pentateuch, Peshitta, Septuagint, Old Latin, Ethiopic [since *Jubilees* survives fully only in Ethiopic], the targums, the Genesis Apocryphon, and Josephus).[54] There was no indication that citations from Genesis and Exodus had been altered toward Greek, Ethiopic, or Latin biblical versions as Jubilees was translated into those languages. Rather, the data favored the view that the scriptural material reproduced in Ethiopic *Jubilees* was a reliable reflection of a Hebrew copy of Genesis and Exodus. A comparison of Ethiopic *Jubilees* with the few Qumran Hebrew fragments of the book then available gave further grounds for considering the Ethiopic text to be a faithful rendition, via Greek, of the Hebrew base. Those data could be interpreted within the framework of F. M. Cross's theory of local texts as evidencing an early Palestinian text, or within the framework of E. Tov's "modern textual outlook" as another independent text of the Pentateuch, closer to the Hebrew base of the Septuagint and to the Samaritan Pentateuch than to the MT, but not identical with any of them. In other words, its underlying scriptural text is of a type familiar from the pre-Samaritan copies from Qumran.

How did the people of Qumran judge *Jubilees*? It seems to have been important: fourteen copies of it have been identified among the fragments from the caves, and it is quoted at least once as an authority. Yet we know of two instances in which its views were opposed: its rejection of a lunar calendar (6:36–37; some Qumran calendars have data for both solar and lunar calendars, just as *1 Enoch* 72–82 does), and a detail of its chronology of the flood (compare the simple statement in *Jub.* 5:27 with 4Q252 I, 7–10,[55] which adds two days while the ark rested on the mountain to make up the full total of five months). What do both kinds of evidence say about its authority?

4. Conclusions

We have glanced at three compositions which are of different literary types and which work with older texts in one way or another. What conclusions may we draw from the survey?

---

[53] Ibid., 324–34.

[54] VanderKam, *Textual and Historical Studies in the Book of Jubilees* (HSM 14; Missoula, Mont.: Scholars, 1977), 142–98; idem, "Jubilees and the Hebrew Texts of Genesis-Exodus," *Text* 14 (1988): 71–85 (= *From Revelation to Canon*, 448–61)

[55] G. Brooke, "4QCommentary on Genesis A," in *Qumran Cave 4 XVII Parabiblical Texts, Part 3* (ed. J. VanderKam; DJD 22; Oxford: Clarendon, 1996), 193–94.

1. These three texts are intimately related to the older compositions that we call Genesis–Deuteronomy, although they do not all stand in the same relation to them. *Reworked Pentateuch* is closest in wording and content to Genesis–Deuteronomy, the *Temple Scroll* is somewhat more distant, and *Jubilees* is perhaps still farther removed. For the material from Genesis–Deuteronomy that they reproduce or reflect, the three evidence textual forms that fall into patterns recognizable from the ancient versions of the Pentateuch in the MT, Septuagint, SP, and the Qumran copies.

2. It is not easy to define what might separate these works from Genesis–Deuteronomy, apart perhaps from age. There appears to be nothing in content or form that requires us to put the *Reworked Pentateuch* in a different category than Genesis–Deuteronomy, whatever we may call that category. Its contents are those of the Pentateuch, and its textual form is of a well-attested type. The same could be said about the *Temple Scroll,* which also reproduces pentateuchal material and generally has a known form of scriptural text. It does stand apart, at least as we have it, by adopting a different setting for some of the pentateuchal legislation (direct speech from God to Moses at Sinai) and rearranging texts more extensively. However, its claim to authority is more apparent than in Genesis–Deuteronomy and *Reworked Pentateuch. Jubilees* resembles the *Temple Scroll,* but concerns itself primarily with a different part of the Pentateuch. We know that it exercised a certain authority at Qumran and elsewhere. So, then, should we put the *Temple Scroll* and *Jubilees* in a different basket from the one that holds Genesis–Deuteronomy and *Reworked Pentateuch?* If it is charged that these books are different from Genesis–Deuteronomy because they rework these older texts, we can object that generous parts of Genesis–Deuteronomy are themselves rewritings of older pentateuchal sources. *Reworked Pentateuch, Temple Scroll,* and *Jubilees* could simply represent other points in the same continuum, before canonical decisions were made.

3. Evidence such as this suggests that we cannot be sure about the precise meaning of the term *Torah* when it appears in a Qumran text as a designation for a body of literature. Did it mean just our pentateuchal books or could it include the works we have surveyed? It seems reasonable to think some or all of them could have fallen under the rubric *Torah,* and that the term encompasses various renditions of the material from creation to the death of Moses.

4. The common practice, enshrined even in the official DJD series, of sorting manuscripts into biblical and parabiblical categories fails to address these issues satisfactorily, and merely reflects later canonical decisions. Perhaps more seriously, the scholars who draw up statistics and classifications of biblical manuscripts at Qumran are guilty of reading subsequent authoritative judgments back into earlier sources. The statistics for the types of copies of Genesis–Deuteronomy should include the evidence from the works we have studied, and others as well. Compilations of Qumran scriptural readings, such as in the recently published *The Dead Sea Scrolls Bible,* should include all of the evidence, not just what appears in the so-called biblical manuscripts.[56]

---

[56] M. Abegg, P. Flint, and E. Ulrich, trans., *The Dead Sea Scrolls Bible* (San Francisco: HarperSanFrancisco, 1999). Of course, it should be acknowledged that the translators had intended to include more texts, but constraints of space limited the contents.

5. In view of the evidence from Qumran, we should avoid using the words *Bible* and *biblical* for this period and this community. This is not to deny the group had authoritative writings; the difficulty is that we, at our remove of a couple of thousand years, cannot always be sure which of those writings were authoritative and which were not. We do not know which books the word *Torah* embraced. Therefore, we should follow the ancient practice of using more general, less suggestive terms such as *scriptures* and *rewritten scriptures,* instead of *Bible* and *rewritten Bible.*

7

Josephus and His Twenty-Two Book Canon

Steve Mason

For the study of scripture in early Judaism the writings of Josephus are a necessary reference point.[1] His extensive biblical paraphrase in *Jewish Antiquities* 1–11 has invited a massive amount of detailed study;[2] the main results of which are readily available in recent surveys.[3] Rather than revisiting his tendencies in handling the Bible, this essay will focus on one passage and one issue: the scope of Josephus's Bible or "canon" and his apparently programmatic statement on the question in *Against Apion* 1.37–43.

---

[1] This is a revised and updated version of my "Josephus on Canon and Scriptures," in *Hebrew Bible / Old Testament: The History of Its Interpretation, I/1: Antiquity* (ed. Magne Saebø; Göttingen: Vandenhoeck & Ruprecht, 1996), 217–35. I am grateful to Robert Kraft for having condensed that original essay for publication.

[2] Some of the important detailed studies are H. St. J. Thackeray, *Josephus: The Man and the Historian* (New York: Ktav, 1967 [1929]), 75–99; S. Rappaport, *Agada und Exegese bei Flavius Josephus* (Vienna: A. Kohut Memorial Foundation, 1930); M. Braun, *Griechischer Roman und hellenistische Geschichtsschreibung* (Frankfurt: V. Klostermann, 1934); B. Heller, "Grundzüge der Aggada des Flavius Josephus," *MGWJ* 80 (1936): 237–46; H. R. Moehring, "Novelistic Elements in the Writings of Flavius Josephus" (dissertation, University of Chicago, 1957); N. G. Cohen, "Josephus and Scripture: Is Josephus' Treatment of the Scriptural Narrative Similar Throughout *Antiquities* I–XI?" *JQR* 54 (1963–64): 311–32; H. W. Attridge, *The Interpretation of Biblical History in the Antiquitates Judaicae* (Missoula, Mont.: Scholars, 1976); T. W. Franxman, *Genesis and the Jewish Antiquities of Flavius Josephus* (Rome: Biblical Institute Press, 1979); L. H. Feldman, "Use, Authority, and Exegesis of Mikra in the Writings of Josephus," in *Mikra: Text, Translation, Reading and Interpretation of the Hebrew Bible in Ancient Judaism and Early Christianity* (ed. M. J. Mulder/H. Sysling; Minneapolis: Fortress, 1988); idem, *Josephus's Interpretation of the Bible* (Berkeley: University of California Press, 1998); idem, *Studies in Josephus's Rewritten Bible* (Leiden: Brill, 1998); G. E. Sterling, *Historiography and Self-Definition: Josephos, Luke–Acts and Apologetic Historiography* (NovTSup 44; Leiden: E.J. Brill 1992); C. T. Begg, *Josephus's Account of the Early Divided Monarchy (AJ 8.212–420): Rewriting the Bible* (Leuven: University Press, 1993); idem, *Josephus' Story of the Later Monarchy* (Leuven: Leven University Press, 2000).

[3] For summaries of the main results of the works in the previous note, see H. W. Attridge, "Josephus and his Works," in *Jewish Writings of the Second Temple Period: Apocrypha, Pseudepigrapha, Qumran Sectarian Writings, Philo, Josephus* (ed. Michael E. Stone; Philadelphia: Fortress, 1984), 210–227; P. Bilde, *Flavius Josephus between Jerusalem and Rome: His Life, His Works, and Their Importance* (Sheffield: JSOT, 1988), 80–104; L. H. Feldman, *Josephus and Modern Scholarship (1937–1980)* (Berlin: W. de Gruyter, 1984), 121–91; idem, "A Selective Critical Bibliography of Josephus," in *Josephus, the Bible, and History* (ed. L. H. Feldman and G. Hata; Detroit: Wayne State

In the ongoing debate over the shape of the first-century Jewish canon(s), this passage must be dealt with by those who argue for any of the positions on the table: whether the canon was closed or still open in the late first century, and whether it was in three divisions (tripartite)— corresponding to the later rabbinic scheme of Torah, Prophets, and Writings in twenty-four volumes[4]—or two (bipartite). Not surprisingly, Josephus tends to support the scholar who is making the argument. For example, S. Leiman avers: "From Josephus's statement, it is evident that he recognized a tripartite canon. . . ."[5] J. Barton, however, contends:

> At all events the primary idea to which Josephus is a witness is not that the books of Scripture were organized into a tripartite form, but that they derived from either of two sources: Moses and the prophets. . . . Such evidence as we have from Hellenistic Judaism thus confirms the essentially bipartite character of Scripture. . . .[6]

This debate provides an example of a more general problem. Scholarship on ancient Judaism and Christian origins needs Josephus, and what he says often appears to provide self-evident parallels for phenomena known from outside his texts. But closer examination, in the context of his writings and thought, occasionally weakens or even altogether dissolves those parallels.[7]

This essay attempts to contribute to the discussion of canons by examining the celebrated passage again, in context. I would caution the reader, however, that for the scholarly canon quest my analysis renders the passage even less useful than has been feared, though it may throw further light on Josephus.

University Press, 1989), 352–66; S. Mason, *Josephus and the New Testament* (Peabody, Mass.: Hendrickson, 1992), 64–73.

[4] How early this scheme was in place is the question at issue. The fifth-century Babylonian Talmud assumed the arrangement (*b. B. Bat.* 13b–14b) and the fourth/fifth-century Christian teacher Jerome knew it well: "for all scripture is divided by them [the Jews] into three parts: the Law, the Prophets, and the Hagiographa, which have respectively five, eight, and eleven books" (*Praef. Vulg. Dan.*).

[5] S. Z. Leiman, *The Canonization of Hebrew Scripture: the Talmudic and Midrashic Evidence* (Hamden, Conn.: Archon, 1976). This is the traditional position, proposed as early as J. G. Müller, *Des Flavius Josephus Schrift gegen den Apion* (Hildesheim: Georg Olms 1967 [1877]), 99–103; cf. P. R. Ackroyd and C. F. Evans, *From the Beginnings to Jerome* (Cambridge: Cambridge University Press, 1970), 117, 136–37; E. E. Ellis, *The Old Testament in Early Christianity* (Tübingen: Mohr [Siebeck], 1991), 7. In his later article, "Josephus and the Canon of the Bible" (in *Josephus, the Bible, and History,* 55), Leiman qualifies this position in deference to R. Beckwith's proposal. Beckwith (*The Old Testament Canon of the New Testament Church* [Grand Rapids: Eerdmans, 1985], 125) argues that Josephus has transferred, ad hoc, the narrative books of the third section of the rabbinic canon (Writings) to the Prophets. But Beckwith and Leiman ("Josephus," 53–54) still understand the resulting canon as tripartite.

[6] J. Barton, *Oracles of God: Perceptions of Ancient Prophecy in Israel after the Exile* (Oxford: Oxford University Press, 1986), 49.

[7] So already W. C. van Unnik, *Flavius Josephus als historischer Schriftsteller* (Heidelberg: Lambert Schneider 1978), 18. This is no searing criticism of Leiman and Barton, who are both admirably sensitive in principle to Josephus's context. The problem is one we all face when forced to use a wide range of ancient texts from Homer to Tacitus to the Talmud; it is a great challenge to interpret the passages we need in a way that does justice to the entire corpus.

1. Context and Purpose of *Against Apion* 1.37–43

Although there is little critical agreement about Josephus's larger aims in the *Against Apion* (i.e., concerning his audience, his reason for adopting a defensive-judicial mode of rhetoric in the heart of the book, and hence the performative or "illocutionary" force of the work),[8] there is widespread agreement about the "locutions," about what he actually says. That is because he takes the trouble to spell out, in essay-like format, the main transition points in the text.[9] His magnum opus, the *Antiquities,* has already treated Judean origins at length, he says, but there are still those who disbelieve his claims about his people's antiquity on the ground that Judeans do not appear in Greek literature (*C. Ap.* 1.1–5). So he devotes this more systematic study to the issue.

After extensive preliminary remarks on Judean and Greek historiography (1.6–59), Josephus takes up the ignored evidence for Judean antiquity (1.60–218). The central section of the book then deals with specific issues raised by literary adversaries of the Judeans (1.219–2.144), and the final section is an encomium on the peerless Judean constitution (2.145–296).

Josephus denies that Greek sources should be considered the final authority on historical matters. The argument within this lengthy digression (1.6–59) falls into three parts: the lateness of Greek culture (1.6–14), the many contradictions among Greek accounts of their past (1.15–18)—which Josephus attributes to both a lack of "official records" (*anagraphai,* 1.19–22) and the Greeks' preoccupation with rhetorical competitiveness (1.23–27)—and the superiority of Oriental (*barbaroi,* 1.58), especially Judean, record-keeping (1.28–59).

Within the subargument on Oriental record-keeping, Josephus tries to show that the Judeans' measures for maintaining official records are even more rigorous than those of their more famous Eastern neighbors, which are in turn qualitatively superior to Greek practices. Whereas the Egyptians and Babylonians entrusted their records to priests and Chaldeans, the Judeans assigned theirs to *chief* (or high) priests and—apparently improving upon the famous Chaldeans—prophets:[10]

> 1.29 But concerning our forebears, that they practiced . . . even greater (care) than those mentioned with respect to the official records, having assigned this matter to the chief priests and prophets, so that until our own times this charge has been cherished with all precision—and if it is not too bold to say, it will be (so) cherished (in the future also)—I shall attempt concisely to demonstrate.

Although Josephus does not explain in this passage the role that the Judean priests play in the keeping of records, it may be inferred from evidence elsewhere in his writings that he

---

[8] See the diversity of perspectives in *Josephus'* Contra Apionem: *Studies in its Character and Context with a Latin Concordance to the Portion Missing in Greek* (ed. J. H. Feldman and J. R. Levison; Leiden: Brill, 1996). A central issue in the debate is whether Josephus directly addresses opponents or writes for a benevolent audience (e.g., the same group that first received the *Antiquities*), and thus whether his purpose is really as apologetic as the form of the central part might suggest.

[9] Although the transition points are clear enough, the hierarchical order is not so obvious. For the first effort—remarkably—to order the parts, see Bilde, *Jerusalem and Rome,* 117–18.

[10] The following translations, unless otherwise noted, are mine.

sees the chief priests and their subordinates as preservers, executors, and philosophical ex-positors of the records, somewhat like the aforementioned Egyptian priests.[11] But he leaves no doubt that it was the prophets who actually wrote the records:

> 1.37 Accordingly . . . then, seeing that the writing (of the records) is not the personal preroga-tive of everyone, nor is there actual disagreement among any of the things written, but the prophets alone learned the highest and oldest matters by the inspiration of the God, and by themselves plainly recorded events as they occurred, 38 so among us there are not myriads of discordant and competing volumes, but only twenty-two volumes containing the record of all time, which are rightly trusted.

> 39 Now of these, five are those of Moses, which comprise both the laws and the tradition from human origins until his passing; this period falls little short of 3000 years. 40 From Moses' passing until the Artaxerxes who was king of the Persians after Xerxes, the prophets after Moses wrote up what happened in their times [or, as they saw things] in thirteen vol-umes. The remaining four (volumes) comprise hymns toward God and advice for living among humanity. 41 From Artaxerxes until our own time all sorts of things have been writ-ten, but they have not been considered of the same trustworthiness as those before them, because the exact succession of the prophets failed.

> 42 Now it is clear in practice how we approach our special texts: for although such an age has already passed [sc. since Artaxerxes], no one has dared either to add anything or to take away from them or to alter them. But it is innate among all Judeans from their very first moments of existence to consider them decrees of God, to stand by them, and for their sake, if neces-sary, cheerfully to die. 43 Thus already many of (our) prisoners of war have on many occa-sions been seen patiently enduring tortures and the ways of all sorts of deaths in theatres, without letting slip a single word against the laws and the related official records.

The main contribution of this section to the larger argument comes in the first sentence (1.37–38). Unlike the hopelessly competitive Greek situation (see 1.12–18), Josephus as-serts, among the Judeans only *prophets* could write official records. Divine inspiration en-abled them to learn things beyond the limits of human knowledge (in this case, the distant past; elsewhere, the future). In addition, they accurately recorded affairs of their own times. The result is a collection of twenty-two harmonious and wholly reliable volumes of national records (plural in 1.43), which are so consistent that Josephus can also designate them as a single record (*anagraphē;* 1.38). The practical corollary of having such an estab-lished and carefully preserved tradition (1.42–43) is that all Judeans know it well and are unswervingly committed to it.

The middle section (1.39–41), which is our chief interest, supports the claim that prophets wrote a unified national record by describing this material according to several criteria. Here we need to exercise care, because Josephus's language ("prophets") creates a false parallel with the second division of the later rabbinic canon (Prophets). The language here works on another level.

---

[11] *B.J.* 2.411; 3.352; *A.J.* 4.304; *C.Ap.* 2.185–185, 188. On the priestly bias of his biblical para-phrase, cf. S. Rappaport, *Agada;* Heller, "Grundzüge"; more generally, S. Mason, "Priesthood in Josephus and the Pharisaic Revolution," *JBL* 107 (1988): 657–61.

Leaving aside the question of "prophets" for the moment, Josephus's language might appear to suggest that the official Judean records are divided according to author and chronology—a division that would still support canonical analysis. But he does not adopt these criteria consistently. As for authorship: he mentions Moses and unnamed subsequent prophets. This authorial distinction is, therefore, not carried beyond the world-famous legislator. There is certainly also a chronological aspect to Josephus's discussion. Although the *Antiquities* (1.18–26) and the remainder of *Against Apion* (2.173 *et passim*) feature Moses as the Judean legislator *par excellence,* the distinction between him and the *other* prophets in this passage seems mainly intended to help mark the different periods of history covered by the records: "from Moses' passing until Artaxerxes. . . ." Yet the chronological criterion is not fully developed either, for Josephus does not specify when the last four books were written.

His most comprehensive criterion for classifying the Judean records here is that of *genre.* Moses' writings themselves—and this is critical—include *both* laws *and* tradition from a period of three thousand years. The other prophets continued the records until the time of Artaxerxes by writing about "what happened" in their days—and so also wrote history or tradition (i.e., not laws). Finally, the collection includes both hymnic and hortatory material. Of the four genres mentioned—laws, historical tradition, hymns to God, and practical advice—Josephus's interest here and in the *Antiquities,* as a historian, is primarily in the second group. But his classification is generic: Moses wrote in two genres; other prophets wrote historical tradition; and the final group (of prophets!) wrote both hymns to God and advice to mortals. Josephus thus describes the *kinds of material,* with some attention to date and chronology, that comprise the Judean records.

Contrary to virtually universal opinion,[12] then, Josephus does not arrange the Judean sacred texts in divisions, whether two or three. If he did, we should have to reckon with a five-part canon (Mosaic laws, Mosaic tradition, later history, hymns, and practical advice). Obviously, this is not his aim. He does not suggest that Moses composed two divisions, though the legislator wrote in two different genres, or that Moses' books may simply be called "the Law/Torah," or that the final four books represent two (small!) divisions: hymns and advice. Still less is there a division called "prophets" in this passage, for *all* of the authors—and this is basic to his entire argument—are prophets. The distinction of genres, along with the other two criteria (not consistently pursued) of authorship and chronology, seem intended to help the Gentile reader understand the scope, antiquity, and variety of material within the twenty-two volume official Judean record. Josephus does not here describe divisions within it.

Josephus mentions two authorial entities, so to speak, Moses and not-Moses, but that is more easily explained by his audience's background than by his effort to describe a bipartite canon; they would likely know the name of the Judean lawgiver (as of Lycurgus the Spartan or Solon the Athenian).[13] Similarly, Josephus describes the texts in three strokes: law and tradition from Moses' time, material describing the period to Artaxerxes, and non-historical material. But this does not a tripartite canon make.

Josephus's main points, then, seem clear. In contrast to the many Greek authors who aggressively contradict each other and deal with a relatively brief and recent period of time

---

[12] Ackroyd and Evans, *History,* 136; Leiman, *Canonization,* 31–34; Beckwith, *Canon,* 125; Barton, *Oracles,* 38, 49, in spite of many salutary qualifications; Ellis, *Old Testament,* 9.
[13] Cf., e.g., John Gager, *Moses in Greco-Roman Paganism* (Nashville: Abingdon, 1972).

(1.6–18), the record of the Judeans' national origins is completely harmonious, even though it covers a vast and remote period dating back as far as creation. The Judean authors had no rivals, partly because they simply told the truth, either witnessed or revealed by God. Further, this whole process was so ancient that it was already completed by the time of the Persian Artaxerxes (464–424 B.C.E.), successor of the renowned Xerxes who had captured Athens—thus, by a time when Greek historiography was barely beginning with Herodotus and Thucydides (ca. 460–400 B.C.E.). Although the Judeans, like the Greeks, possess writings from the period of Artaxerxes and later, *they* do not even recognize these recent texts.

2. Key Terms

The digression on Judean records is highly stylized, exhibiting a preference for formal balance over rigorous logic: the argument that truth is settled by agreement (or lack of competition), the use of the "myriad" (!) Greek historians as the Greek counterpart to the Judean constitution, and the identification of history with tradition are all intellectual short-circuits.[14] These meretricious arguments might, however, have won over an audience that was favorably predisposed toward Josephus, and therefore uncritical.

However that may be, the language appears deliberately generic: each nation is assumed to have its own official records *(anagraphai)* or tradition of communal lore *(paradosis)*, and Josephus can impose these universal categories to the Judeans' advantage over against counterparts among "the Greeks." His use of "tradition," for example, to describe what Moses taught in addition to the laws (1.39), parallels "the tradition" of the Phoenicians (1.28) and of the Orientals in general (1.8; cf. Also *A.J.* 20.259).[15] Similarly, he takes over the "accuracy" or "precision" *(akribeia)* word group from standard Hellenistic historiography, and applies it with vigor to all aspects of Judean culture—to the official records, to his own writings (*B.J.* 1.9, 17; 7.454; *A.J.* 20.263), or to the failure of others to achieve precision (*C.Ap.* 1.18).[16] Or again, when he says that the Judean records are rightly *trusted (dikaiōs pepisteumena)*, he is not reflecting the Judean community's unique language of "faith" or some such thing, but only providing a contrast to his earlier notice that the Greeks are loath to trust even their oldest works (1.14; cf. 1.161). For those who wish to learn about in-house Jewish phenomena and terminology, his argument is largely opaque.

The most important word in this section of the argument is *anagraphē*, "official record(s)": the Greeks lack ancient and stable records (1.7, 11, 20, 21, 23), and non-Greeks

---

[14] Cf. S. J. D. Cohen, "History and Historiography in the *Against Apion* of Josephus," in *Essays in Jewish Historiography* (ed. A. Rapoport-Albert; *History and Theory* 27 [1988]), 1–11; J. W. van Henten and Ra'anan Abusch, "The Depictions of the Jews as Typhonians and Josephus's Strategy of Refutation in Contra Apionem," in Feldman and Levison (*Josephus'* Contra Apionem, 271–309); J. M. G. Barclay, "Josephus v. Apion: Analysis of an Argument," in *Understanding Josephus: Seven Perspectives* (ed. S. Mason; Sheffield: Sheffield Academic Press, 1998), 195–221. Of course, the whole thrust of Greek historiography in Herodotus and particularly Thucydides was to undermine uncritical acceptance of tradition ("what was handed down").

[15] Josephus does use this term elsewhere to describe an internal Judean phenomenon: the special Pharisaic tradition (*A.J.* 13.297, 408). But the exception proves the rule, for he must carefully explain to his readers what the word means in that context (*A.J.* 13.297–298). Cf. S. Mason, *Flavius Josephus on the Pharisees: A Composition-Critical Study* (Leiden: Brill 1991), 233–235, 289–293.

[16] Cf. Mason, *Pharisees*, 64–66, 75–79, 89–96, 108–15.

are superior in maintaining their national records (1.58). More than half of the forty-two occurrences of this noun in his writings are in *Against Apion* 1. It is not a usage that Josephus has learned late in life, however, for his own speech in *Jewish War* 6.109, written a couple of decades earlier, already refers to "the official records of the ancient prophets." And both the introduction and conclusion to *Antiquities* designate the "sacred writings" by this term in the singular (1.12; 20.261). But ordinarily, when Josephus wishes to refer generically to a nation's traditional laws and customs he uses such phrases as *hoi patrioi nomoi, ta patria ethē, ta patria,* or *hoi nomoi* (e.g., *C.Ap.* 2.164; 2.237).[17] His preference for *anagraphai* in *C.Ap.* 1 evidently reflects his desire here to emphasize *written* records. Although the Greeks have ancient oral traditions, they possess only late and lacunose written records. He makes this point early, and later returns to an explicit contrast between Greeks and Judeans (2.155–156). Only Judeans and other Easterners have ancient, official, written (and therefore precise) *records.*

Given this emphasis, it is noteworthy that Josephus uses the same term, *anagraphai,* of his own major historical compositions (*B.J.* 7.455; *A.J.* 1.18). Does he, then, think of his writings as an authoritative—even prophetic—continuation of the ancient records? That question brings us to his famous observation that the Judeans do not esteem things written after Artaxerxes the same as the ancient records *because* "the exact succession of the prophets failed"—according to the usual translation.[18] The Greek says less prejudicially: "on account of the absence *(mē genesthai)* of the exact succession of the prophets." (1.41). This statement is a linchpin in discussions of the cessation of prophecy in Israel and the closure of the "canon."[19] So what does it mean?

Josephus's use of prophet terminology is a complex subject. With reference to scripture and canon, we have already noted that as early as *B.J.* 6.109 Josephus credited the prophets with the writing of the "records." Further, in the preface to the *B.J.* (1.19) he begins his account in the time of Antiochus IV because his literary predecessors, both Judean and Greek—"the historians . . . as well as our own *prophets*"—had left off at that point (1.17–18). The phrase "our own prophets" obviously refers to Judean prophets, in contrast to Greek historians, who derived information more or less accurately from the Judean records (see *C.Ap.* 1.218).[20] Thus, when Josephus in the *Against Apion* (in the 90s)

---

[17] Cf. ibid., 96–106.

[18] Cf. the LCL translation by H. St. J. Thackeray.

[19] Notably, J. Jeremias, *New Testament Theology,* vol. 1, *The Proclamation of Jesus* (New York: Charles Scribners Sons, 1971), 80 and n. 6; H. Krämer, "*Prophētēs*," *TDNT* 6:783–796; Ackroyd and Evans, *History,* 114–35; R. Meyer, "*Prophētēs*," *TDNT* 6:817; D. E. Aune, *Prophecy in Early Christianity and the Ancient Mediterranean World* (Grand Rapids: Eerdmans, 1983), 103–6; R. Gray, *Prophetic Figures in Late Second Temple Jewish Palestine: The Evidence from Josephus* (Oxford: Oxford University Press, 1992), 7–9.

[20] Barton (*Oracles,* 59) infers that the historians wrote only until the exile, since that is the last item mentioned in Josephus's list of things already documented (*B.J.* 1.17). Although this reading is possible, the list of items covered by others appears representative rather than exhaustive. Josephus plainly establishes the beginning point of his narrative at the time of Antiochus IV (1.19); this, not the exile, seems to be where the "historians" (dependent upon the Judean prophets) finished. This might imply that the prophets reached down to the Maccabean period; see the comments below on John Hyrcanus. It seems likely that Josephus misconstrues Judean authors as Greek. See the close parallel in *C.Ap.* 1.218, where the identical phrase, "without missing much of the truth," is used of Demetrius Phalereus, Philo the Elder, and Eupolemus, at least two of whom were probably Judeans.

characterized the ancient authors of the Judean records as prophets, it is no recent development in his thought; his understanding of the Judean *anagraphai* as a fixed corpus, closed long ago when prophets lived, must have been part of his basic outlook and training.

This hypothesis is supported by Josephus's instinctive lexical choices, for throughout his writings he reserves the "prophet" *(prophēt-)* word group for those who lived long before his own time.[21] Almost all such occurrences refer to the characters of the Hebrew Bible who play a role in *A.J.* 1–11, where Josephus underlines his interest in the subject by introducing prophetic vocabulary where the extant biblical texts lack it.[22] His prophets include those who wrote books, such as Moses and Joshua (*A.J.* 2.327; 3.60; 4.311, 420), along with many who did not, such as Jacob, Aaron, Phineas, and Nathan (*A.J.* 2.194; 3.192; 5.120; 6.57; 7.214). Although he does not advertise the fact—and this shows how deeply the concept runs in his thinking—study of the concordance shows that Josephus allows hardly any extrabiblical applications of prophet terminology.[23] The Hasmonean John Hyrcanus (high priest and ruler, 135–104 B.C.E.) is the last "prophet" recognized by Josephus (*B.J.* 1.68–69; *A.J.* 13.299). Hyrcanus's exceptionally late date, with no immediate predecessors and no sequels, may therefore account for the phrase "*exact* succession of the prophets": he was a prophet long after prophecy had otherwise ceased.

Josephus's consistency of usage is the more conspicuous when we realize that he refrains from using "prophet" language even of his most admired contemporaries, who nevertheless receive authentic revelations and make accurate predictions, namely the Essenes and himself.[24] Moreover, after discussing the roles of priests and prophets in maintaining the Judean records, he offers his own writings as an example of the Judeans' concern for historical truth: "But I myself have composed a truthful record" (*anagraphē;* 1.47). Given the context, in which "record(s)" is a key word, it is hard to avoid the conclusion that he means to insinuate himself into the company of the ancient prophets.[25] Yet, proud

---

[21] Cf. J. Blenkinsopp, "Prophecy and Priesthood in Josephus," *JJS* 25 (1974), 239–62, esp. 240–46; L. H. Feldman, "Prophets and Prophecy in Josephus," *JTS* 41 (1990), 386–422; Gray, *Prophetic Figures,* 23–26.

[22] Cf. van Unnik, *Schriftsteller,* 52–53; Blenkinsopp, "Prophecy," 239–62; and especially Feldman "Prophets," 392–93.

[23] Extrabiblical referents of prophet language in Josephus include: contemporary "false prophets," such as Theudas (*B.J.* 2.26; 6.286; *A.J.* 20.97, 169); an "Egyptian prophet" (sarcasm?) cited by Chaeremon *(C.Ap.)* 1.312, see 1.289; "Cleodemus the prophet," mentioned by Alexander Polyhistor (*A.J.* 1.240); the Hasmonean ruler and high priest John Hyrcanus (135–104 B.C.E.; *B.J.* 1.68–69; *A.J.* 13.299). As Gray has convincingly shown (*Prophetic Figures,* 20), for Josephus the shining of the high priest's "breastplate" was a prophetic phenomenon that had ceased at the time of John Hyrcanus (*A.J.* 3.218).

[24] Certainly, Josephus is not reluctant to claim perfect accuracy for his works (*B.J.* 1.1–16; 7.455; *A.J.* 1.17; 20.260–263); he everywhere stresses his priestly qualifications (*B.J.* 1.3; 3.352; *Vita* 1–6; *C.Ap.*1.54); and he models *Antiquities* on the much earlier Greek Septuagint (*A.J.* 1.10–13). But his argument that the Judean records had long been completed, and that no Judean would countenance an addition, would be invalidated if he seriously placed his own work on the same level. And even if he had done so, few other Judeans would have granted his writings such authority: there is no question of his works being "trusted" in this way (cf. 1.41).

[25] R. Mayer and C. Möller, "Josephus—Politiker und Prophet," in *Josephus-Studien: Untersuchungen zu Josephus, dem antiken Judentum, und dem Neuen Testament* (ed. O. Michel, et al.;

though he is of his own achievements (cf. *A.J.* 20.262–66), he cannot bring himself to use the word "prophet" of himself, much less of any contemporary, and this must be significant in view of his deep interest in the subject of prophecy.[26] If there were prophecy in his day, he would be a prophet, but of course there is not and he is not.

The ethnic criterion for prophets, which is seldom discussed, is as important as the chronological criterion.[27] Although "prophet" *(prophētēs)* and cognates were well established terms in the Greek world,[28] and although Josephus elsewhere uses generic vocabulary without hesitation, as we have seen, he reserves prophetic language for the ancient *Judean* tradition. Gentile and contemporary Judean prophet-like phenomena are designated instead by the "seer" *(mant-)* word group, along with a few other terms. Thus, the Gentile Balaam, the medium of Endor, and Egyptian seers are not "prophets" for Josephus.[29] In the few cases in which an ancient Gentile seer *is* called a prophet, and the term is not directly traceable to Josephus's source, it appears that he uses the language sarcastically, for his emphasis is on the ineffectiveness of these so-called "prophets" (*A.J.* 8.339; *C.Ap.* 1.312). His refusal even to use "prophet" for the renowned oracle at Delphi[30] confirms his tendency. That he considers prophecy the preserve of the Judeans perhaps explains why he compares Judean prophets to Chaldeans, not "Babylonian prophets" or the like, in our passage.[31]

Another key term that Josephus uses here consistently with his language elsewhere is *diadochē* ("succession"). In other passages, he speaks about successions of kings, high priests, and prophets, despite the near absence of this language from the Septuagint/Old Greek biblical tradition.[32] The succession of the prophets, of which he speaks in our pas-

---

Göttingen: Vandenhoeck & Ruprecht, 1974), 239–62; van Unnik, *Schriftsteller,* 42; Feldman, "Prophets," 421–22; Mason, *Pharisees,* 270; Gray, *Prophetic Figures,* 35–79.

[26] Correctly, Feldman, "Prophets," 405; *contra* the others mentioned in the preceding note.

[27] Feldman ("Prophets," 416–18), characteristically, observes this.

[28] See, e.g., Krämer, "*Prophētēs,*" *TDNT* 6:783–96.

[29] *A.J.* 2.241; 4.104, 112, 157; 6.330–331, 338.

[30] Cf. Feldman, "Prophets," 417.

[31] Barton (*Oracles,* 48) has suggested that Josephus's concern in *C.Ap.* 1 with the prophets' role as record writers does not match his preoccupation with predictive prophecy in the *Antiquities.* This apparent contrast has led Gray to argue that Josephus regarded "only one very limited type of prophecy"—the scripture-writing kind—as having ceased (Gray, *Prophetic Figures,* 9). But this conclusion cannot be wrung from his language, in which prophecy is a unified and venerable phenomenon belonging to the distant Judean past. While in the *Antiquities* Josephus seems genuinely impressed with various predictions (10.142, 276; 11.1–3, 331–335; 10.266), he adheres rigorously, there as here, to his goal of providing a historical account. He largely omits the major and minor prophets—Jeremiah and Daniel are his chief exemplars of predictive prophecy—except for their historical material (cf. Franxman, *Genesis,* 7). He pointedly excuses himself, *as a historian,* from elaborating on the predictions of Daniel (10.210), and he affirms the truth of Jonah's predictions about Nineveh without reporting them, so as not to seem "irksome" to his readers (9.242). Feldman ("Prophets," 394) plausibly suggests that a focus on predictions might have inspired ridicule. Thus, Josephus features predictive prophecy only to prove that a divine power authorized the Judean constitution (*A.J.* 1.14, 20; 10.276–81). He makes the same point here, but in the other direction: only prophets could have known what happened long before they lived (*C.Ap.* 1.37). He reserves prophet terminology almost uniformly for biblical figures.

[32] See Sir 46:1, 48:8; 2 Macc 4:29; 14:26; and in a different sense in 2 Chron 18:17, 26:11, 28:7. On his modification of biblical succession terminology for kings, see Mason, *Pharisees,* 235–39.

sage, is not featured in the *Antiquities* as the successions of high priests and kings are. Perhaps it would have been awkward to establish a prophetic "succession" in the proper sense because the office of prophet, in contrast to kingship and high priesthood, was not hereditary. Still, there are clues that this category was already in his thoughts as he wrote the *Antiquities*. Josephus summarized Moses' handing on of his role to Joshua (Num 27:15–23) by saying that he appointed Joshua "his successor *[diadochos], both in the prophetic functions and as commander*" (*A.J.* 4.165; compare Sir 46.1). Deuteronomy's claim that there was never again a prophet like Moses (Deut 34:9–10) is also reflected by Josephus (*A.J.* 4.329), but he says enough to hint at the beginnings of a prophetic "succession."

This incidental evidence tends to confirm that, although Josephus nowhere articulates for his readers a symmetrical, trilateral succession of prophets, kings, and high priests from Moses' time, he did conceive of it.[33] Of these three lines, only the high priestly succession has continued uninterrupted though two thousand years to the present, and this guarantees the preservation and proper exposition of the records. Both royal and prophetic successions, by contrast, lapsed after the return from exile.[34] When Josephus writes of the failure of the prophetic succession, therefore, and of the consequent lack of recent Judean "official records," he seems to be tapping a deep vein in his thinking, which he only fleetingly exposes to our view. In a society in which "old is good,"[35] he happily presents the Judean community as thriving on the interest of the ancient deposit, scrupulously preserved, and he is scandalized by newcomers (pseudo-prophets) who claim prophetic gifts.

Rather than regretting the absence of contemporary prophets, as the translation "failure" might seem to imply, Josephus plainly views the long ages since official Judean record-writing ceased as a great advantage over the Greeks, who were "born yesterday" (*C.Ap.* 1.7). He conveys no sense here of prophet-deprivation nor any feeling of "nostalgia" for the prophetic past.[36] Such sentiments would run directly counter to his purpose, which is to boast that the Judean records have been so long in place.

3. The Integrity of Josephus's Biblical "Record"

This broad coherence of Josephus's outlook and language should not blind us to rhetorical flourishes in the passage at hand. Most obviously: his insistence that no Judean

---

[33] Compare the eschatological hope for a return of anointed prophet, ruler, and priest at Qumran (1QS IX, 11; 4Q175). Eschatological urgency and the language of anointing are, however, wanting in Josephus.

[34] Josephus claims that a new royal line emerged with the later Hasmoneans, after Aristobulus I assumed the diadem. John Hyrcanus, who stopped short of becoming a king, was singularly privileged to revive and embody all three functions within himself (*B.J.* 1.68; *A.J.* 13.299). That royal line would falter again and, after John Hyrcanus, only the high priestly succession endured. Josephus cannot himself claim to be a king, a high priest, or a prophet. But his *diadochē* gives him a high priestly and royal heritage (*Vita* 1–6), while his accurate predictions and record-writing impart to him *something* of the old prophetic aura.

[35] Cf. Cicero (*Leg.* 2.10.27; *Nat. d.* 3.1.5–4.10); and L. H. Feldman, *Jew and Gentile in Antiquity: Attitudes and Interactions from Alexander to Justinian* (Princeton: Princeton University Press, 1993), 177–78.

[36] *Contra* Barton, *Oracles*, 60, 115; Gray, *Prophetic Figures*, 8.

has dared to alter the records (1.42) seems to conflict with his own practice in *A.J.* 1–11, which is a thoroughly tendentious interpretation of the records rather than a translation. He omits a great deal, adds significant portions, and casts the whole history into a frame that suits his literary purposes.

To be sure, his changes follow identifiable and fairly consistent criteria.[37] He sets out to prove the nobility of the Judean constitution, that it is highly philosophical, and that its divine author is active in human affairs, always rewarding virtue and punishing vice (*A.J.* 1.6, 14, 20). Although internally consistent, his biblical paraphrase does not consistently coincide with any known version of the text or rabbinic halakah or haggadah; he parallels all of these from time to time, but often goes his own way.

In view of his pointed contrast between the harmony of the Judean records and the discordant accounts of the Greeks (*C.Ap.* 1.37–38), it is noteworthy that Josephus achieves his narrative unity in *A.J.* 1–11 only with strenuous effort. He tacitly harmonizes biblical documents that in fact *overlap and compete* with each other, for example: Genesis/Numbers/Deuteronomy, Isaiah/Kings, Jeremiah/Kings, and Kings/Chronicles. While failing to tell the reader about his constant harmonizing activity, he parades examples of *apparent* conflict (e.g., between Jeremiah and Ezekiel; *A.J.* 10.106–107, 141) and conspicuously resolves them in order to reinforce the impression of actual harmony. He also introduces corroborating testimony from Greek and Oriental writers, and even quietly corrects the biblical sources (e.g., *A.J.* 10.229; 11.106, 120) to agree with the external evidence.

All of this makes it impossible to regard Josephus's Judean history in the *Antiquities* as anything like a translation along the lines of the Septuagint (contra *A.J.* 1.9–13); it is rather a *tour de force* in the service of his literary aims. Nevertheless, even here the conflict is not between his thematic statement in *Against Apion* and his practice in *Antiquities,* but between his editorial statements and his practice in general. For his strongest assurances about his treatment of the text are those that introduce and punctuate the history in the *Antiquities.* For example, he remarks on his carefully crafted summary of selected Mosaic laws, which we know to include many non-pentateuchal items:

> All is here written as he [Moses] left it; nothing have we added for the sake of embellishment, nothing which has not been bequeathed by Moses. Our one innovation has been to classify the several subjects; for he left what he wrote in a scattered condition, just as he received each several instruction from God (*A.J.* 4.196–197, trans. Thackeray; cf. 1.17; 10.218).

Although such statements provide ready material for those who see Josephus as an incurable liar, that facile option seems excluded by the immediate juxtaposition of these statements with the product itself. Consider also the sheer energy that was required for him to rework his material, while recognizing that some other Judean readers might accuse him of rearranging the texts (*A.J.* 4.197). Since he does not excuse the major alterations

---

[37] See notes 2 and 3 above. Josephus omits episodes that might be used to support current anti-Judean literary slanders (e.g., about alleged origins of misanthropy in the Judeans' leprosy); highlights and adds material that features Judean virtue; portrays Abraham, Moses, Solomon, Daniel and others as peerless philosophers; stresses divine providence and the fulfillment of prophecy; reflects editorially on universal philosophical issues; relentlessly moralizes; provides as much entertainment as possible; and accommodates the texts to his own times, priestly biases, and career.

that we have noted, we can only conclude that he was largely insensitive to what we post-Enlightenment readers expect in view of his promises.[38]

4. Scope and Arrangement of Josephus's Scripture

Let us consider, then, the extent to which Josephus's actual use of the ancient Judean record in *Antiquities* elucidates his statement in the *Apion* about the scope and order of the Judean records. An obvious problem is that, in spite of his avowed intention to translate the nation's official records (*A.J.* 1.6, 17), the *Antiquities* does not in fact end with the reign of Artaxerxes, coinciding with the Esther story (*A.J.* 11.184, 296),[39] as we should expect on the basis of *C.Ap.* 1.38. It is a well known but not insurmountable problem that Josephus at some point decided to continue through the eve of the great revolt.[40] The one possibility that we may exclude on the basis of *C.Ap.* 1.38 and antecedent probability, it seems to me, is that he considered the "canon" open-ended, such that the material he presents after the Bible (e.g., Aristeas, 1 Maccabees, Herod's career) is meant to have the same level of authority.[41]

---

[38] S. J. D. Cohen (*Josephus in Galilee and Rome: His Vita and His Development as a Historian* [Leiden: Brill, 1979], 27–29) suggests that this common historian's promise not to alter one's sources, was not taken seriously—in our sense—by any of those who made it. Van Unnik (*Schriftsteller*, 26–40) takes it to mean only that Josephus will not allow flattery or hatred to color his work; he will recast his sources faithfully. Cf. Feldman, "Mikra," 466–70.

[39] The identification of this Artaxerxes deserves comment. Many scholars assume with Barton that the remark "is probably to be understood as meaning that it [an official document] must not postdate the age of Ezra, because it was in that period that prophets existed" (*Oracles*, 60; see also Ackroyd and Evans [*History*, 115–16], who make much of the connection with Ezra). But although the biblical Ezra names Artaxerxes as king of the Persians (e.g., Ezra 4:7, 23), Josephus systematically corrects this to "Cambyses" and also replaces the Artaxerxes of Nehemiah with "Xerxes" (*A.J.* 11.21). The Artaxerxes who succeeded Xerxes appears in Josephus only in his rendition of the Esther story.

[40] Thackeray suggested that Josephus continued in order to imitate the twenty volumes of the *Roman Antiquities* by Dionysus of Halicarnassus (*Josephus*, 56–58). I would propose rather that he became so engrossed in his major themes—divine providence, reward and punishment—that he thought he could fruitfully rework the period already represented by the *Jewish War* along the same lines. His plentiful new information about the Septuagint translation, the Hasmoneans, the now dastardly Herod, the Roman emperors Gaius and Claudius, Mesopotamian Judeans, and the rebels against Rome would have invited such an extended portrayal of the themes begun in the biblical paraphrase. See my "Introduction to the *Judean Antiquities*," in *Judean Antiquities 1–4* (Brill Josephus Project 3; ed. Louis H. Feldman; general ed. Steve Mason; Leiden: E. J. Brill, 2000), ix–xxxvi.

[41] I say this both because the passage in *Against Apion* is so forthright and, since Josephus claims to speak for all Judeans, subject to immediate disproof, and because there is a noticeable seam in his narrative as soon as he is finished with the biblical narrative at the time of Artaxerxes (to *A.J.* 11.296). Immediately thereafter, Josephus briefly summarizes the high-priestly succession for the following century (11.297–303) and then jumps ahead to Alexander the Great (ca. 334 B.C.E.), who appeared "at about this time"—a century later (11.304)! The chronological gap papered over by this characteristic phrase (cf. *A.J.* 4.226; 5.352; 6.49, 213, 271, 292; 7.21; 9.239 *et passim*; D. R. Schwartz, "*Kata touton ton kairon*: Josephus's Source on Agrippa II," *JQR* 72 [1982], 241–68) and the chronological unevenness of the remainder of the *Antiquities* alert us to Josephus's personal knowledge that his continuously connected sources up to this point, the "records," are exhausted.

Josephus manipulates the biblical text so extensively that he prevents us from learning much about the internal arrangement of the Judean records that he used. The sequence of his biblical source material in *A.J.* 1–11 is roughly as follows:[42]

A.J. 1: Gen 1–35

A.J. 2: Gen 36–48; Exod 1–15

A.J. 3: Exod 16–40; Exod/Lev/Num conflated for the summary of laws

A.J. 4: Num 14–36; Deuteronomy, conflated with Exod/Lev/Num

A.J. 5: Joshua, Judges, Ruth, 1 Sam 1–4

A.J. 6: 1 Sam 5–31

A.J. 7: 2 Sam 1–24; 1 Kgs 1–2 conflated with 1 Chr 1–29; David is a singer and musician (7.305)

A.J. 8: 1 Kgs 2–22 conflated with 2 Chr 1–18; Solomon composed 1,005 volumes of odes/songs and 3,000 volumes of parables (8.44)

A.J. 9: 2 Chr 19–31 conflated with 2 Kgs 1–17, Jonah, Zech 14:5, and Nah 2

A.J. 10: 2 Kgs 18–24 conflated with 2 Chr 32–36, Isa 38–39, Ezek 1, 12, and some biographical passages (rearranged) from Jeremiah (a lament by Jeremiah is also mentioned; 10.78); Dan 1–8. Isaiah and Daniel wrote "books"—plural (10.35, 267)

A.J. 11: 1 Esdras, perhaps conflated with Ezra (though generally preferring 1 Esdras); Nehemiah; Haggai and Zechariah mentioned; Esther (including "Greek additions" B-E)

By the end of his biblical paraphrase, with the period of Ezra-Nehemiah and Esther, Josephus is apparently relying heavily on Greek biblical texts, in spite of his promise to provide a translation of the Hebrew records (1.17). The nature of his *Vorlage* is a large and still unsettled problem: some think that he used primarily Greek texts throughout; others find more evidence of a Semitic source in the early books, and so surmise that he only later opted for the Greek—perhaps through weariness of translation.[43] We cannot tackle the source-critical problem here. We might wonder, though, how Josephus would reconcile his use of the fuller Greek texts of Esdras and Esther with his clear statement about the limited number of official records. Perhaps he knew Hebrew editions of these texts that more closely approximated the Greek than do the ones known to us. In any case, he must have seen little material difference in using the Greek rather than the Hebrew. That these distinctions did not trouble him offends our sense of precision, but we can hardly hold him responsible for that.

---

[42] Cf. also Appendix B in S. Schwartz, *Josephus and Judaean Politics* (Leiden: Brill, 1990), 225–26.

[43] The problem is conveniently surveyed in Feldman, "Mikra," 455–66.

In view of Josephus's thorough editing of his material, it would be unwise to make deductions about the arrangement of his canon beyond the obvious: it starts with the Pentateuch, after which he follows the best chronology he can. No *divisions* are apparent in his biblical paraphrase. To be sure, Moses and his laws have an axiomatic supremacy throughout Josephus's works (e.g., *A.J.* 3.317–322). But the laws are the basis of the "constitution" by which Judean communities around the world govern themselves, and so are parallel to the national laws of other peoples.[44] Moses' laws, as we have seen, do not constitute a division of Josephus's Bible: they represent only one kind of composition by Moses. When he summarizes the laws in *A.J.* 3.223–286; 4.196–302, he even apologizes for digressing from the historical narrative, making it clear that the laws constitute only a small part of what Moses wrote (3.223; 4.196). This agrees with his language in *C.Ap.* 1.39.

Nor can his famous recognition of Daniel as "one of the greatest prophets" (*A.J.* 10.266), in contrast to the rabbinic scheme that left Daniel among the "Writings," serve as evidence of order within Josephus's Bible.[45] Rather, this designation is consistent with his claim in *C.Ap.* 1.37 that all of the record writers were prophets. Moses too was a prophet without equal (*A.J.* 2.327; 3.60; 4.320, 329). There is no *division* of "prophets" implied in the biblical paraphrase.

In *A.J.* 10.35, Josephus, commenting on a prediction by Isaiah, observes that "not only this prophet but also others, twelve in number, did the same [*sc.* wrote predictions]," further tantalizing the reader with the promise of information about Josephus's canon. But this passage also offers little help in identifying divisions. Some commentators have understandably wanted to identify these thirteen authors with the thirteen volumes of "the prophets after Moses" in *C.Ap.* 1.40,[46] thus proposing a tripartite internal arrangement: Moses, thirteen *predictive* prophets, and Writings.[47] Beckwith observes, however, that the twelve prophets in question are more likely the minor prophets[48] because Josephus stresses their predictive writing, whereas the rabbinic "prophets" from Joshua onward mainly wrote history. Moreover, Josephus speaks here of twelve authors, not books, but if the thirteen books mentioned in *C. Ap.* 1.40 are to comprise most of the Bible outside the

---

[44] Cf. Mason, *Pharisees,* 96–106.

[45] *Contra* Marcus, note *d* to this passage in the Loeb edition; Barton, *Oracles,* 36–38. Curiously, Barton elsewhere (*Oracles,* 19) concedes that Josephus considers all biblical writers prophets.

[46] See Leiman, "Canon," 55: it "can only be understood as a reference to the (total of) thirteen historical books by the prophets"; also Feldman, "Prophets," 409 n. 83, and note *c* of the Loeb translator, R. Marcus, at this passage: "there seems to be no other explanation. . . ."

[47] The narrative of *Antiquities* would suggest fifteen prophetic volumes: Joshua, Judges, Ruth, Samuel, Kings (as one), Chronicles (as one), Isaiah, Ezekiel, Jeremiah, Lamentations, Daniel, Ezra (or 1 Esdras), Nehemiah, Esther, and the twelve minor prophets as one text (since he mentions several of them). But several combinations are plausible to reach the figure of thirteen. The combinations Judges-Ruth, Jeremiah-Lamentations, and Ezra-Nehemiah are all attested in later Christian and Jewish lists (cf. Leiman, *Canonization,* 31–34; Beckwith, *Canon,* 235–73). If we accepted the common reading of "Isaiah plus twelve" as equivalent to the thirteen "prophets after Moses" of *C.Ap.* 1.40, we would have in Josephus an inkling of a tripartite canon, *but* the second and third parts would differ in content from those of the rabbinic canon.

[48] Beckwith, *Canon,* 99–100 n. 80. Beckwith notes: "One might add that Josephus's introduction of these twelve near the end of the biblical paraphrase, as if they were a novelty, and his promise to discuss them in the sequel, would suit the largely neglected minor prophets better than the more noted major authors."

Pentateuch, they must include the twelve "minor prophets" (therefore twelve authors) in just one of the thirteen scrolls. So the tantalizing parallel between the language here and that in our passage does not seem to bear scrutiny.

While Beckwith's theory is not without its own difficulties,[49] no other solution seems more satisfactory at this time. There are simply too many variables and insufficient evidence to reconstruct how Josephus understood the categorization of biblical materials.

5. The Bible in the *Jewish War*

Studies of Josephus's Bible generally ignore the *Jewish War*, for obvious reasons. His first composition, which begins long after the biblical period and deals with national history leading up to the great revolt, rarely mentions scripture. The only sustained discussion of the Bible comes in Josephus's speech before the walls of Jerusalem, in which he adduces examples from Israel's past in favor of the pacifist option (*B.J.* 5.379–93).

Moreover, an influential stream in Josephan scholarship sees the *War* as either a work of betrayal and pro-Roman propaganda or of postwar politicking among the surviving Judean elites.[50] Scholars of this persuasion tend to argue that Josephus only became interested in the religious aspects of Judean culture after he had completed the *War*. And even this interest is sometimes regarded as pretense to gain influence with the Yavnean Rabbis. Such views leave one hardly inclined to plumb the *War* for the possible impact of Jewish scriptures on Josephus's outlook.

S. Schwartz extends this approach with an examination of allusions and references to biblical materials in the *War*. He concludes: "there is little evidence that [when Josephus wrote *War*] he knew the biblical texts at all."[51] Schwartz argues that the *War*'s routine contradiction of biblical details—even where this does not appear to serve his rhetorical needs—and the priestly bias of his biblical interpretation indicate that he knew only selections from the scriptures; he acquired these nuggets via the oral culture of the priesthood rather than through firsthand study of the texts.

Coming from another perspective altogether, Helgo Lindner has found in the *War*'s view of history clear traces of influence from Jeremiah and Daniel. These influences appear not so much in direct reference as in Josephus's most basic views: that nations rise and fall under divine supervision, that Rome is the current choice as world power, and that God is using Rome to punish Israel for its transgressions.[52] These views, which constitute the fabric of the *War*, are also important themes in *Antiquities*, where they are presented as the main trend of Judean tradition, drawn from Jeremiah and Daniel.[53] In the *War*,

---

[49] In particular, Josephus will go on to parade the fulfilled predictions of Jeremiah, Ezekiel, and Daniel (*A.J.* 10.79, 107, 142, and 269), which suggests that they are among those who are like Isaiah.

[50] This stream is represented prominently by Laqueur (*Josephus*, 126–27), Thackeray (*Josephus*, 27–28), S. J. D. Cohen (*Galilee and Rome*, 84–90), and Schwartz (*Judaean Politics*, 13–17).

[51] Schwartz, *Judaean Politics*, 25.

[52] H. Lindner, *Die Geschichtauffassung des Flavius Josephus im Bellum Judaicum* (Leiden: Brill 1972), 42–48. See also Gray, *Prophetic Figures*, 70–79.

[53] Cf. S. Mason, "Daniel, and the Flavian House," in *Josephus and the History of the Greco-Roman Period: Essays in Memory of Morton Smith* (ed. F. Parente and J. Sievers; Leiden: Brill, 1994).

Josephus seems to depart from the biblical text frequently and significantly, but one might gain a similar impression from a proportionate sampling of *Antiquities,* where Josephus *has* the biblical texts at hand. In addition, Schwartz may underestimate the rhetorical ends served by some of the *War*'s departures from scripture.[54]

The question of the use of scripture in the *War* will doubtless remain a controversial issue for some time to come because it is closely tied to more basic issues of Josephus's literary and intellectual integrity, self understanding, and Judean identity. That Josephus publicly prides himself on the reputation that he had among his compatriots for traditional learning is not in doubt. Exactly what that might mean for a topic such as this requires further exploration.

6. Conclusions and Implications

Reading *Against Apion* 1.37–43 in context shows how little it has to do with our usual questions about a first-century Jewish "canon." In writing to persuade Greek speakers of the nobility and antiquity of Judean culture, Josephus simply wishes to stress the great age, small number, harmony, and prophetic authorship of the Judean records. He uses the generic language of his implied readers, not intramural Judean terminology—if indeed that was significantly different. His actual use of scriptural materials in *Antiquities* agrees by and large with the summary statement in *Against Apion:* he really did believe at some deep level that uniquely inspired "prophets" wrote the records in a bygone age. Although much is omitted from his biblical paraphrase, what we have represents the heart of both traditional Hebrew and Greek canons; he seems aware, without saying as much, that books like 1 and 2 Maccabees are later and separate.

So this effort to engage Josephus's world of thought and language says little directly about the shape of the Jewish Bible(s) in the first century. My goal has been to clarify what exactly Josephus says, which any broad historical hypothesis will need to take into account. We may now spell out in a preliminary way some direct implications of this study for the historical discussion.

1. Josephus boasts about the age of the Judean records. He does not convey any sense of either deprivation or nostalgia. In our passage he neither pines for a closed prophetic age nor hopes for its return. Thus he provides a very poor foil for claims that Jesus or Christianity fulfilled a Jewish dream in bringing the return of the "quenched spirit." Whether such a foil might be found in other literature is another issue.

2. Josephus claims his positions are held in common by all Judeans—women, children, prisoners of war—and he would presumably be vulnerable to refutation if he were

---

[54] See my review of Schwartz in *Ioudaios Review* 2.008 (April 1992) at *listserv.lehigh.edu/lists/ ioudaios-review,* especially 3.7. Note also that Josephus prides himself on the reputation that he had among his compatriots for traditional learning; accordingly, he claims that his education between *War* and *Antiquities* consisted mainly of *Greek* grammar, poetry, and prose (*A.J.* 20.263). If, as Schwartz proposes, this interim period was also devoted to acquiring a basic knowledge of the scriptures in Hebrew and Greek, along with Alexandrian and other Judean literature, then Josephus was most fortunate to discover so much in the Bible that happened to support his main emphases in the earlier *War!*

making this up or presenting idiosyncratic views. It would accordingly be hard to argue from Josephus for an open canon or for one that had been recently settled—at Yavneh in the 70s and 80s, for example.[55] Those who are convinced by other evidence of the fluidity of scriptural boundaries in the first century do better, perhaps, to isolate Josephus as idiosyncratic, in spite of his claim to speak on behalf of Judeans, than to try to enlist his statements in support.[56]

3. But isolating Josephus, too, would be hard to justify. Perhaps the most significant corollary of this study is its negative result regarding any appeal to circumstantial evidence in support of the argument for an open canon. Rudolf Meyer, for example, argues for an open canon on the grounds that: (a) other sources such as Sirach's "praise of the fathers" (44.1–50.24) and the Dead Sea Scrolls make no distinction between biblical, pre-Mosaic, and post-Artaxerxian texts (e.g., 1 Enoch and Tobit); (b) even within the Dead Sea Scrolls' versions of such biblical texts as the Psalms, there is rearrangement and non-biblical material; and (c) the texts of these documents often differ from the Massoretic text. This evident freedom to interpret, add to, and subtract from biblical texts leads Meyer to isolate Josephus's fixed notion of a canon as an inner-Pharisaic view that could only have gradually come to prominence with the emergence of the rabbinic coalition after 70; it cannot reflect a common first-century Jewish view.[57]

The problem with this reasoning will now be obvious, for all of the phenomena that Meyer finds in other sources are much more clearly and fully present in Josephus's own use of the scriptures in *Antiquities*. As we have seen, he also continues his narrative to the present, treating books such as Pseudo-Aristeas and 1 Maccabees the same way that he treats biblical material. For the biblical period itself, he splices in all sorts of oral and written traditions. He quite thoroughly alters the texts to suit his own needs. And in numerous ways he evokes a prophetic aura (though not the terminology) for his own accounts. In other words, if we lacked the *Against Apion*, Josephus himself would offer a clear case for an open canon. But we *do* have the *Against Apion*, in which this same Josephus emphatically, but also matter-of-factly, insists that the Judean records have long since been completed in twenty-two volumes.

Plainly, then, the circumstantial evidence of Josephus's own use of the Bible in the *Antiquities* does not mean what it might otherwise have seemed to mean: it does not, after all, imply an open canon. Indeed, once we know *Against Apion*, we can go back to *Antiquities* and discover that Josephus really does believe that the succession of prophets has ceased, and we can discern a seam after the "records" have been exhausted. *Against Apion* was written as a deliberate sequel to *Antiquities*, so it is unlikely that Josephus is aware of any substantial conflict between the two. This means that his willingness to alter the biblical

---

[55] Barton (*Oracles*, 59) strains Josephus's words beyond tolerance, I think, when he remarks (emphasis added): "In maintaining the small compass of Jewish Scripture he does not, as a matter of fact, say that no other book could conceivably be found that would meet the criterion of prophetic authorship, only that no more than twenty-two have *until now* been found to do."

[56] So A. C. Sundberg, "The Old Testament: A Christian Canon," *CBQ* 30 (1968): 143–55; R. Meyer, "Bemerkungen zum literargeschichtlichen Hintergrund der Kanontheorie des Josephus" (in *Josephus-Studien*, 285–99); Barton (*Oracles*, 59) says: "in setting limits to the canon at all Josephus is out of step with his contemporaries."

[57] R. Meyer, "Kanontheorie," 290.

text in manifold ways proves nothing about his formal view of canon. His example removes the force from appeals to circumstantial evidence as proof that the Dead Sea Scrolls' authors or Philo or Ben Sira had an open canon.

4. Josephus's remarks in *Against Apion* 1.37–43 cannot be made to specify divisions within the first-century canon. His language is on a different plane. His most consistent ordering criterion is that of genre: laws, tradition, hymns, and advice. These genres do not correlate to divisions of the Bible. They simply provide a means of elaborating for Gentile readers the various kinds of material to be found among the twenty-two volumes.

5. Because these genres confound all other categories, the phrase "the laws and the related official records" at *Against Apion* 1.43 cannot indicate a major canonical division.[58] Josephus operates in a public world of discourse, according to which any nation's laws are self-evidently basic to its tradition. The phrase "and the related official records" would thus include everything that Josephus has just mentioned, even Moses' nonlegal writings ("tradition").

6. What we have in Josephus is not inconsistent with the most traditional views of an early tripartite canon—or for that matter, with modified tripartite and bipartite theories. He simply says nothing about any of this. One may not conclude, either, that his canon differed from traditional canons, and that this supports a theory of canonical or scriptural pluralism. We presently have no way of recovering the internal shape of his Bible from *C.Ap.* 1 or from his actual use of scripture in *A.J.* 1–11.

7. The often overlooked *A.J.* 10.35 might say more about Josephus's Bible than the much discussed *C.Ap.* 1.37–43—if its twelve-plus-one prophets corresponded to the thirteen prophets of the latter passage. But the meaning of that remark is unclear, and Beckwith's hypothesis connecting it with the minor prophets faces fewer obstacles than any other theory.

---

[58] *Contra* Barton, *Oracles*, 48; Feldman, "Mikra," 470.

8

Origins of a Tripartite Old Testament Canon

Julio C. Trebolle Barrera

The problem of the origin of the tripartite canon of the Hebrew Bible can be broken down into two questions. The first concerns the expressions used by the ancient sources which seem to allude, with various formulae, to the whole bi- or tripartite canon: "Law and Prophets," "Law, Prophets, and Psalms," "Law, Prophets, and Writings." The second question concerns the origin and formative process of these two or three large divisions of the biblical canon. These questions contain a third concerning the concept of canon. This cannot be used univocally to refer equally, on the one hand, to the first stages of the formation of the collections of biblical books still in the process of being edited and, on the other hand, the final stage when certain collections went on to make up a canon or list of books held to be canonical, excluding others, considered apocryphal or "external" *(ḥiṣonîm)*. Nor can the adjective "canonical" be used univocally in reference to the three sections of the canon, since not all the books which entered the definitive canon enjoyed the same canonical authority.[1]

1. Expressions Used by the Ancient Sources

Expressions and references contained in ancient Jewish sources from *ca.* 200 B.C.E. to *ca.* 100 C.E. demonstrate an awareness of two or three large collections of biblical books which were granted the authority of scripture. Such expressions and references, however, do not spell out the bi- or tripartite origin of the canon nor specify the number and identity of the books that initially made up the collection of the Prophets and, above all, the Writings. For that it will be necessary to turn to other data drawn from the history of the formation, transmission, and interpretation of the books which ultimately made up the canon.

In about 190 B.C.E., the apocryphal book of Sirach or Ecclesiasticus speaks of "the law of the Most High," "the wisdom of all the ancients," and "prophecies": "How different the one who devotes himself to the study of the law of the Most High! He seeks out the wisdom of all the ancients, and is concerned with prophecies" (Sir 38:34–39:1). This passage already seems to point to a tripartite structure of the canon. Some have even wanted

---

[1] I thank Dr. Wilfred G. E. Watson for translating my Spanish text. The translation of the biblical texts is taken from *The New Revised Standard Version* (Oxford: Oxford University Press, 1995).

to see in the order of the terms "law . . . wisdom . . . prophecies" the sequence of the three sections of Law, Wisdom Writings, and Prophets in which the biblical books appear in Greek and Latin Bibles.[2] However, the expression "the wisdom of all the ancients" may refer not to the Writings, the third part of the canon, but to the wisdom literature of ancient Israel in general and even to ancient Near Eastern literature.[3]

In about 132 B.C.E., Ben Sira's grandson completed the Greek translation of his grandfather's work. In the prologue that he added, he refers three times to a tripartite division of the biblical books: "Many great teachings have been given to us through the Law and the Prophets and the others that followed them. . . . So my grandfather Jesus, who had devoted himself especially to the reading of the Law and the Prophets and the other books of our ancestors. . . . Not only this book, but even the Law itself, the Prophecies, and the rest of the books differ not a little when read in the original." However, the name for the third corpus of books is different in each case: "the Law and the Prophets and the others that followed them / and the other books of our ancestors / and the rest of the books." The expression "the others that followed them" *(katakolouthein)* could denote a secondary statute rather than a temporal sequence of "the other" books in respect of the Law and the Prophets. The "other" books have the merit of being "ancestral," but their worth is not comparable to that of the books of the Law and the Prophets, since law and prophecy were given to Moses and the prophets by God. The vagueness of the adjective "other" should not make one think that it could also include books that did not ultimately form part of the Writings, as Barton tends to think.[4] On the other hand, the definite article—"the other" or "the rest of"—is not enough to suggest a closed number of books which by the time of Ben Sira could already comprise the third section of the canon, as Beckwith concludes.[5]

In the same period or a little later, the first book of Maccabees reports that in the persecution by Antiochus "the books of the law that they found they tore to pieces and burned with fire" (1:50). The phrasing seems to restrict the sacred books to "the books of the law," but further on, in 2:50–60, there is a reference to "the law" and "the deeds of the ancestors" and, without mentioning any particular book, it alludes to the biblical traditions of Abraham, Joseph, Phinehas, Joshua, Caleb, David, Elijah, the three Israelites in the fiery furnace, and Daniel, which implies a reference to the Pentateuch, the historical books

---

[2] Patrick W. Skehan and Alexander A. Di Lella, *The Wisdom of Ben Sira* (AB 39; New York: Doubleday, 1987), 452.

[3] A. van der Kooij, "The Canonization of Ancient Books Kept in the Temple of Jerusalem," in *Canonization and Decanonization: Papers Presented to the International Conference of the Leiden Institute for the Study of Religions (LISOR) Held at Leiden 9–10 January 1997* (SHR 82; ed. A. van der Kooij and K. van der Toorn; Leiden: E. J. Brill, 1998), 17–40, 34–35.

[4] Barton argues that even "the Prophets did not yet form a closed canon in New Testament times" (J. Barton, "The Significance of a Fixed Canon of the Hebrew Bible," in *Hebrew Bible / Old Testament: The History of Its Interpretation* [vol. I/1; ed. Magne Saebo; Göttingen: Vandenhoeck & Ruprecht, 1996], 67–83, 29); idem, *Oracles of God: Perceptions of Ancient Prophecy in Israel after the Exile* (London: Longman and Todd, 1986), 35–95.

[5] "And not only does he (the grandson of Jesus ben Sira) state that in his own day there was this threefold canon, distinguished from all other writings, in which even the Hagiographa formed a closed collection of old books, but he implies that such was the case in his grandfather's time also," R. T. Beckwith, "Formation of the Hebrew Bible," in *Mikra: Text, Translation, Reading and Interpretation of the Hebrew Bible in Ancient Judaism and Early Christianity* (CRINT II/1; ed. M. J. Mulder; Assen/Maastricht: Van Gorcum; Philadelphia: Fortress, 1988), 39–86, 52.

or former prophets and to the book of Daniel. On the other hand, in 1 Macc 7:17, Ps 79:2b–3 is quoted with the formula "in accordance with the word that was written," which suggests that the book of Psalms was acknowledged as canonical.

Second Maccabees mentions "the law" in 2:2–3, but goes on in vv. 13–14 to speak of "books about the kings and the prophets" and "the writings of David and letters of kings": "The same things are reported in the records and in the memoirs of Nehemiah, and also that he founded a library and collected the books about the kings and prophets, and the writings of David, and letters of kings about votive offerings. In the same way Judas also collected all the books that had been lost on account of the war that had come upon us, and they are in our possession." The expression "the writings of David" in 2 Macc 2:13–14 probably refers to the book of Psalms, which here may or may not stand for the whole collection of the Writings. "The books about kings and the prophets" could be the books of Samuel and Kings, and perhaps also Chronicles, Ezra, and Nehemiah.[6] While this passage could be taken as evidence for a tripartite canon, it should be noted that in another passage the same book seems to reflect a bipartite division of the canon: "Encouraging them from the law and the prophets, and reminding them also of the struggles they had won, he made them the more eager" (15:9). However, here the reference to the law and the prophets could correspond to a global allusion to the ancient history of Israel, as contained in the Pentateuch and the prophets, especially in the "former" prophets or historical books. It certainly should not be taken as a precise reference to a division of the biblical books into laws and prophecies.

The *Halakhic Letter* or *Miqṣat maʿaśê ha-Torah* (4QMMT), from the mid-second century B.C.E., refers explicitly to "the book of Moses," an expression equivalent to "law of Moses" which also occurs in 2QJuridical Text (2Q25) and earlier in a doublet of 2 Kgs 14:6: "the book of the law of Moses." According to the reconstruction of the editors, 4QMMT also mentions explicitly "the words of his prophets" to which are added the words "of David": "to you we have wr[itten] that you must understand the book of Moses [and the words of the pro]phets and of David [and the annals] [of eac]h generation" (95–96). The editors see this as "a significant piece of evidence for the history of the tripartite division of the Canon."[7] However, the Psalms here seem to be considered prophetic words, and the mention of annals or chronicles may refer only to the historical books or former Prophets, or even to these books and the books of Chronicles together with Ezra and Nehemiah. At all events, this writing seems to indicate a third series of biblical books but does not give it a name. Nor does it seem to consider non-historical wisdom books, which later came to form part of the collection of the Writings. On the other hand, 4QMMT seems compatible with a bipartite division of the canon: "[It is written in the book] of Moses [and in the books of the prophets] that. . . ."[8]

[6] Jonathan A. Goldstein, *II Maccabees* (AB 41A; New York: Doubleday, 1983), 187.
[7] E. Qimron and J. Strugnell, *Qumran Cave 4.V: Miqṣat Maʿaśê ha-Torah* (DJD 10; Oxford: Clarendon Press), 59.
[8] "[And it is written in the book of] Moses and in [the words of the prop]hets that . . .", F. García Martínez, *The Dead Sea Scrolls Translated: The Qumran Texts in English* (trans. W. G. E. Watson; Leiden: E. J. Brill, 1994), 79; "[And it is written in the Book] of Moses and in Boo[ks of the prophet]s that . . . ", G. Vermes, *The Complete Dead Sea Scrolls in English* (Allen Lane: Penguin Press, 1997), 227.

In two passages the *Community Rule* seems to point to a bipartite canon: "as commanded by means of the hand of Moses and his servants the Prophets" (1QS I, 2–3), and "This is the study of the law which he commanded through the hand of Moses, in order to act in compliance with all that has been revealed from age to age, and according to what the prophets have revealed through his holy spirit" (1QS VIII, 15–16).[9]

The *Damascus Document* also speaks of "the books of the law" and "the books of the prophets": "The books of the law are the Sukkat of the King, as he said 'I will lift up the fallen Sukkat of David'. The King is the assembly; and the plinths of the images <and the Kiyyum of the images> are the books of the prophets" (VII, 15–16).[10]

Probably composed in about 40 C.E., *4 Maccabees* also speaks of "the law and the prophets": "While he was still with you, he taught you the law and the prophets" (18:10). In what follows this reference is made explicit in the allusion to the narratives in the Pentateuch and the books of Daniel, Isaiah, David "the psalmist," Proverbs, and Ezekiel. It is not possible to know whether David's Psalter and the book of Daniel are included among the prophets. The inclusion of Proverbs among the prophetical books is more surprising.

In the New Testament the expression "the law (of Moses) and the prophets" occurs very frequently: Matt 5:17; 7:12; 22:40; Luke 16:16, 29, 31 ("Moses and the prophets"); John 1:45; Acts 13:15; 28:23 and Rom 3:21. The Gospel of Luke includes the expression "Moses and all the prophets" in 24:27, but a little later on it knows another, longer expression: "the law of Moses, the prophets, and the psalms" (24:44). The reference to Psalms could be taken to include the whole collection of Writings, and would see in these terms a tripartite canon, but such a supposition is debatable. As we will see, the reference to Psalms or to "David" has to be understood, *sensu stricto,* only and exclusively in connection with the book of Psalms.

Matt 23:35 (Luke 11:50) has been taken to signify that in the time of Jesus the canon ended with the book of Chronicles, which describes the murder of Zechariah by Joash as the final assassination in a chain started by Cain's murder of Abel (Gen 4:1–6): "upon you may come all the righteous blood shed on earth, from the blood of righteous Abel to the blood of Zechariah son of Barachiah, whom you murdered between the sanctuary and the altar" (2 Chron 24:20–21). However, the text of Matthew and Luke may refer to the murder of Zechariah the son of Baris in Jerusalem during the first Jewish revolt, as related by Josephus (*J.W.* 4.335).[11] Or the passage simply points to the chronologically last murder in the Bible, without implying that Chronicles was the last book of the Bible, as is the case in the present sequence of books but not in other traditions known in the Talmudic period.[12]

Philo's work *On the Contemplative Life* lists "laws and oracles delivered through the mouth of Prophets, and hymns and anything else which fosters and perfects knowledge and piety" (25).[13] This could be a reference to the tripartite canon, in which the hymns or

---

[9] Martínez, *The Dead Sea Scrolls Translated,* 3, 12.

[10] Ibid., 38.

[11] *The Jewish War,* in *Josephus with an English Translation by H. St. J. Thackeray* (vol. 3; LCL; Cambridge Mass.: Harvard University Press; London: William Heinemann, 1961), 99; O. Eissfeldt, *The Old Testament: An Introduction* (trans. Peter R. Ackroyd; Oxford: Blackwell, 1966), 568.

[12] Van der Kooij, "The Canonization of Ancient Books," 22.

[13] *On the Contemplative Life,* in *Philo with an English Translation by F. H. Colson* (vol. 9; LCL; Cambridge Mass.: Harvard University Press; London: William Heinemann, 1960), 127.

Psalms represent the collection of Writings, but it does not seem that this was the canon of Philo. His works include quotations taken almost exclusively from the Pentateuch, but occasionally also from Ben Sira and Wisdom of Solomon, so going beyond the limits of the third part of the canon.[14]

The evidence from Josephus in *Against Apion* could be considered the most complete and explicit of those preserved, but its interpretation continues to bristle with difficulties: "Our books, those which are justly accredited, are but two and twenty, and contain the record of all time. Of these, five are the books of Moses, comprising the laws and the traditional history from the birth of man down to the death of the lawgiver. This period falls only a little short of three thousand years. From the death of Moses until Artaxerxes, who succeeded Xerxes as king of Persia, the prophets subsequent to Moses wrote the history of the events of their own times in thirteen books. The remaining four books contain hymns to God and precepts for the conduct of human life" (*C. Ap.* 1.38–40). Josephus lists twenty-two books, classified into three sections: the first comprises the five books of Moses; the second, the thirteen books written by the prophets and the third, "the remaining four books," which could be Psalms, Song of Songs, Proverbs and Qoheleth.[15] In *Antiquities* 10.35 Josephus mentions Isaiah and "also others, twelve in number," thirteen in all, which do not seem to correspond to the thirteen prophetical books to which allusion is made in *Against Apion* 1.38–40, but to the books of Isaiah and Twelve Prophets.[16] The passage from *Against Apion* is usually thought to indicate a tripartite conception of the canon at that time, possibly pharisaic, involving a specified number of books, although classified in a way different from that known from other Jewish sources. But Josephus could be speaking, not of divisions of the canon of his time, but of literary forms (laws, tradition, hymns, and advice) which do not correspond to canonical divisions.[17] Since the text indicates that the books derive from either of two sources, Moses or the prophets, Josephus may provide evidence for the essentially bipartite nature of scripture.[18]

Thus, several earlier witnesses can be produced in support of the opinion according to which, at the beginning of the second century B.C.E., there already existed a particular idea of a canon with a tripartite structure and, in the middle of the same century or in its second half, there was also a formula for referring to this tripartite canon, with variants for

---

[14] Folker Siegert, "Early Jewish Interpretation in a Hellenistic Style," in *Hebrew Bible/Old Testament*, 130–98, 176; Beckwith, "Formation of the Hebrew Bible," in *Mikra*, 54.

[15] Thackeray identifies the thirteen books written by the prophets as "Probably (1) Joshua, (2) Jd. + Ruth, (3) Sam., (4) Kings, (5) Chron., (6) Ezra + Neh., (7) Esther, (8) Job, (9) Isaiah, (10) Jeremiah + Lam., (11) Ezekiel, (12) Minor Prophets, (13) Daniel," *Against Apion or on the Antiquity of the Jews*, in *Josephus with an English Translation by H. St. J. Thackeray* (vol. 1; LCL; Cambridge Mass.: Harvard University Press; London: William Heinemann, 1926), 162–411, 179 n. *b*. Beckwith proposes a different identification: Job, Joshua, Judges (possibly with Ruth), Samuel, Kings, Isaiah, Jeremiah (possibly with Lamentations), Ezekiel, the Twelve prophets, Daniel, Chronicles, Ezra-Nehemiah, Esther. Cf. R. Beckwith, *The Old Testament Canon of the New Testament Church and Its Background in Early Judaism* (London: William Clowes Ltd, 1985), 119.

[16] *Jewish Antiquities* 10.35, in *Josephus with an English Translation by Ralph Marcus* (vol. 6; LCL; Cambridge Mass.: Harvard University Press; London: William Heinemann, 1958), 177. Cf. Beckwith, *Old Testament Canon*, 99–100.

[17] S. Mason, "Josephus on Canon and Scriptures," *Hebrew Bible / Old Testament*, 215–35, 234.

[18] J. Barton, *Oracles of God: Perceptions of Ancient Prophecy in Israel after the Exile* (London: Longman and Todd, 1986), 49.

the second and third parts respectively: The Prophets and the other/the rest of the books (Sirach); the words of the prophets and (the words) of David (4QMMT); the books about kings and prophets, and the writings of David and letters of kings (2 Macc); oracles delivered through the mouth of Prophets, and hymns (Philo); the prophets and the psalms (Luke); the prophets subsequent to Moses who wrote in thirteen books, and the remaining four books/hymns and precepts (Josephus). However, these sources do not specify how many books or which ones made up the second and third parts of a tripartite canon. It is not clear whether the references to David (4QMMT; 2 Macc), hymns (Philo), or Psalms (Luke) are equivalent to the "Writings," however long this last section might be. Nor is it possible to establish which Jewish groups held the idea of a canon, either open or closed, in which periods.

For all these reasons it is necessary to turn to other data derived from the history of the formation, transmission, and interpretation of the books which make up the two or three collections which formed the biblical canon. The book of Psalms becomes a key element in this discussion, because it is at the borderline between Prophets and Writings. In our opinion, the reference to "Psalms" in the expression "Law, Prophets, and Psalms" has to be interpreted *sensu stricto*, that is, only and exclusively in connection with the book of Psalms and not the Writings as a whole.

2. The History of the Formation of the Biblical Collections

The book of Psalms acquires special characteristics which make it very like the prophetical books, and in particular, the book of Isaiah and the Minor Prophets. The heading of the Psalms, with the references to David *(ldwd)* and to the events of David's life and the periods of the monarchy and the exile, certainly do not have historical value. Rather, they indicate that the first collections of Psalms were connected, at first, with the collection of Former Prophets, given that David was considered to be a prophet. In turn, the historical books also contain an occasional Psalm. David composed a total of four thousand and fifty songs: "He composed them all through the spirit of prophecy" (11QPsalms[a], 11Q5, col. XXVII 11). The *pešarîm* from Qumran only comment on prophetical books, Isaiah and the Minor Prophets; the fact that there are also *pešarîm* on the Psalms suggests that this book was also considered prophetic. First Maccabees 7:16–17 quotes the Psalms as predictive, using Ps 79:2–3, probably also cited in 4QTanhumim (4Q176) together with prophetic texts taken from Isaiah and Zechariah.[19] The New Testament also interprets the psalms in a prophetic sense. In any case, the dividing line between the prophetical books and the Writings was not defined, as shown by the different distribution of books in the Greek Bible. The book of Psalms lies on the borderline between Prophets and Writings. Placed initially at the end of the prophetical books, it ended up heading the set of Writings, although the books of Job or Ruth could precede them in later lists.

A *concatenatio* of three important biblical passages connects "the law, the prophets and psalms" or "psalms" with "the law and the prophets." Two appendices at the end of the

---

[19] Isa 40:1–5; 41:8–9; 43:1–2, 4–6; 49:7, 13–17; 51:22–23; 52:1–3; 54:4–10; Zech 13:9 (frag. 15), and probably Ps 79:2–3 (frag. 1–2 I, 1–4), J. M. Allegro, *Qumran Cave 4.I (4Q158–4Q186)* (DJD 5; Oxford: Clarendon Press, 1968), 60–67.

book of Malachi have a joint reference to "the Law and the Prophets," serving as the colophon of Minor Prophets as well as of the whole collection of Prophets and even of the canon of "Law and Prophets": "Remember the *torah* of my servant Moses. . . . I will send you the prophet Elijah . . ." (Mal 4:4–5).[20] By means of the expression "the Torah of my servant Moses," the close of Prophets refers to its beginning, that is, to the beginning of the book of Joshua, where the same expression occurs (Josh 1:7). The introduction of the book of Psalms, in the opening verses of Ps 1, also refers to the beginning of Joshua: "you shall make your way prosperous *(hiṣlîaḥ)*" (Josh 1:7 and 8)—"in all that they do, they prosper *(hiṣlîaḥ)*" (Ps 1:3b); "This book of the law shall not depart out of your mouth; you shall meditate *(hgh b-)* on it (the book) day and night *(yômām wâlaylâh)*" (Josh 1:8)—"and on his law they meditate *(hgh b-)* day and night *(yômām wâlaylâh)*" (Ps 1:2b). This *concatenatio,* which explains the addition of Ps 1:3b, makes clear that the final editors of these books were aware that Moses, Elijah and David, or "the law, the prophets, and psalms" formed an interrelated whole.[21]

All the books of the canon of "Law, Prophets, and Psalms" had their roots in preexilic situations and writings. Thus they link the ancient period of the Israelite monarchy with the new period of the Restoration, and so ensure the continuity of the ancient traditions and institutions of Israel.

Like the book of Psalms, the book of Isaiah and the Minor Prophets were all composed by the addition of previously independent books. Some of these originated before the exile, but were later revised; others originated after the exile. From the close of the eighth century there was in Jerusalem a scribal elite who knew the art of writing, as shown by the *bullae* found in that city and by many biblical references (Isa 8:1; 30:8; Jer 3:8; 17:1, 3; 32:10–16, 44; 36:18–23, 26; 52:25). The book of First Isaiah (Isa 1–39) and from the Minor Prophets the books Hosea, (Joel), Amos, Obadiah and Micah, as well as books 1–2/3 of Psalms, had their roots in the monarchic period. On the other hand, Second and Third Isaiah (Isa 40–55; 56–66), Haggai, Zechariah, Malachi, and the last third of the Psalter were composed during or after the Exile. The first set ultimately formed the first third or half of these books in their definitive form (Isaiah, Minor Prophets, and Psalms); the second set formed the final part.[22] The last third of Psalms is the section with the greatest textual fluidity, as shown by some of the Psalters found at Qumran.[23]

---

[20] B. S. Childs, "The Canonical Shape of the Prophetic Literature," *Int* 32 (1978): 46–55; J. Blenkinsopp, *Prophecy and Canon: A Contribution to the Study of Jewish Origins* (Notre Dame, Ind./London: University of Notre Dame Press, 1977), 122–23.

[21] Cf. B. Janowski, "Die 'Kleine Biblia': Zur Bedeutung der Psalmen für eine Theologie des Alten Testaments," in *Der Psalter in Judentum und Christentum* (Herder's Biblical Studies 18; ed. E. Zenger; Freiburg: Herder, 1998), 381–420, 406–10; R. G. Kratz, "Die Tora Davids: Psalm 1 und die doxologische Fünfteilung des Psalters," *ZTK* 93 (1996): 1–34.

[22] Cf. J. Nogalski, *Literary Precursors to the Book of the Twelve* (Berlin and New York: De Gruyter, 1993); idem, *Redactional Processes in the Book of the Twelve* (Berlin and New York: De Gruyter, 1993).

[23] P. W. Flint, *The Dead Sea Psalms Scrolls and the Book of Psalms* (STDJ 17; Leiden: E. J. Brill, 1997), 227; G. H. Wilson, *The Editing of the Hebrew Psalter* (SBLDS 76; Chico, Calif.: Scholars, 1985), 139–228. According to J. Sanders, the Qumran Psalter as represented by 11QPs[a] was regarded as "canonical," while M. H. Goshen-Gottstein and others considered it as a secondary liturgical compilation. New evidence from caves 4 and 11 supports the scriptural status of this Psalter, cf. J. A.

The books of the Pentateuch are also based on legal and narrative traditions from the monarchic period. Some literary theories assume the existence of a basic text, later rewritten and expanded with supplements of oral or written origin, a narrative which started from the creation and ended with the death of Moses (Van Seters, M. Rose, N. Wrybray).[24] Other hypotheses suppose the existence of parallel sources, of various lengths and from different periods and places, with differing styles and religious tendencies; these sources would also set out history from creation (or from Abraham) up to the death of Moses, to which one or more other sources were added until the present Pentateuch was formed (J + E → J + E + D → J + E + D + P). Instead of starting from modern hypotheses which attempt to reconstruct "accounts on a large scale" developed across the various biblical books, a method of study which starts with the biblical manuscripts from Qumran favors the study of each book of the Pentateuch separately, or at most in pairs such as Genesis-Exodus (4Q1), Exodus-Leviticus (4Q17), or Leviticus-Numbers (4Q23). The books of the present Pentateuch are probably based on writings or books already in existence in the preexilic period, each of which corresponds to one of the narrative cycles which focus on the patriarchs (Gen 12–50), on the events of the departure from Egypt and at Sinai (Exodus), or the crossing of the desert as far as the Transjordan (Numbers) (R. Rendtorff, E. Blum, R. Albertz),[25] as well as on collections of laws like those included in Leviticus and Deuteronomy. At all events, the Pentateuch incorporates traditions and texts rooted in the preexilic period, to which were added others from a later period.[26]

The historical books also originate from traditions and sources of the monarchic period, and are certainly based on writings such as the ones quoted in those books (*The Book of Jashar,* Josh 10:13; *The Book of the Acts of Solomon,* 1 Kgs 11:41; *The Book of the Annals of the Kings of Israel,* 1 Kgs 14:19; 2 Kgs 15:26, 31, and *The Book of the Annals of the Kings of Judah,* 1 Kgs 14:29; 2 Kgs 24:5). The historical books have been subjected to one or more Deuteronomistic redactions to form another "account on a large scale" which stretches from the death of Moses to the Exile. The book of Jeremiah and to a lesser extent the book of Ezekiel also underwent Deuteronomistic redaction.[27]

Sanders, *The Psalms Scroll of Qumran Cave 11 (11QPsᵃ)* (DJD 4; Oxford: Clarendon Press, 1965); M. H. Goshen-Gottstein, "The Psalms Scroll (11QPsᵃ): a Problem of Canon and Text," *Textus* 5 (1966): 22–33; P. W. Flint, *Dead Sea Psalms Scrolls,* 160–64; 258–59; idem, "The Contribution of the Cave 4 Psalms Scrolls to the Psalms Debate," *DSD* 5/3 (1998): 320–33; H.-J. Fabry, "Der Psalter in Qumran," *Der Psalter in Judentum und Christentum,* 137–63.

[24] J. Van Seters, *In Search of History: Historiography in the Ancient World and the Origins of Biblical History* (New Haven and London: Yale University Press, 1983); M. Rose, *Deuteronomist und Jahwist: Untersuchungen zu den Berührungspunkten beider Literarwerke* (ANANT 67; Zürich: Theologischer Verlag, 1981); R. N. Whybray, *The Making of the Pentateuch: A Methodological Study* (Sheffield: Sheffield Academic Press, 1987).

[25] R. Rendtorff, *Das überlieferungsgeschichtliche Problem des Pentateuch* (BZAW 147; Berlin: Walter de Gruyter, 1997); E. Blum, *Studien zur Komposition des Pentateuch* (BZAW 189; Berlin: Walter de Gruyter, 1990); R. Albertz, *Religionsgeschichte Israels in alttestamentlicher Zeit* (Teil 2; ATD.Erg 8/2); Göttingen: Vandenhoeck & Ruprecht, 1992), 495–535.

[26] David N. Freedman, "The Earliest Bible," in *Backgrounds for the Bible* (ed. M. P. O'Connor and D. N. Freedman; Winona Lake, Ind.: Eisenbrauns, 1987), 29–37.

[27] Deuteronomistic texts are to be found in Jer 7:1–8:3*; 11*; 18*; 21*; 25*; 32*; 33f.*; 44* and Ezek 11:18–20; 20:27–29, 41f.; 28:25f.; 34:23–24; 36:26–28, 31f.; 37:13b–14, 20–23, 24a; 38:17, W. Thiel, *Die deuteronomistische Redaktion von Jeremia 1–25* (WMANT 41; Neukirchen-Vluyn:

Among the Writings, the book with a history of formation most akin to those considered above is Proverbs. The oldest substratum of Proverbs is probably from a period before the Exile and is included in chapters 10–22:16 and 25–29. The origins of the *inscriptio* which heads this last collection, "(proverbs) that the officials of King Hezekiah of Judah copied/collected" (25:1), go back to the final years of the eighth century B.C.E. This could be factual, as the frame of reference fits the monarchic period well, although it was revised in a period after the Exile. The opening (1–9) and closing (30) sections of the work were formed after the Exile, and the final redaction of the book must have been concluded in the fourth or third century B.C.E. This book, which includes preexilic and postexilic writings, from the start features in an embryonic tripartite canon, and is an integral component of its third part. The other books of the collection of the Writings are postexilic creations.

Thus the authority granted to the books of "Law, Prophets, and Psalms" is based on the fact that they assure continuity between the ancient and recent history of Israel. Among the Prophets, the book of Isaiah and the Minor Prophets, as well as Psalms, were composed by the accretion of writings from before and after the Exile, whereas the historical books are distinguished for having been subjected to one or more Deuteronomistic redactions.

Moving on to the history of literary formation and textual transmission, it is clear that the text of the Pentateuch, Isaiah, Minor Prophets, and Psalms is relatively homogeneous, at least compared with the text of the historical books and of Jeremiah and Ezekiel. The variants in Genesis and Exodus seem to be better explained as textual types (Septuagint, MT and "proto-Samaritan") than as different editions, except perhaps for the final chapters of Exodus (35–40).[28] The text of Isaiah was known in a rather stable form and the Qumran text of Minor Prophets coincides substantially with that of the MT.[29] On the other hand, Jeremiah, Ezekiel, and the historical books were transmitted in various editions. 4QJosh[a], 4QJudg[a], 4QSam[a], 4QJer[bd] and the Old Greek of these books and of Kings and Ezekiel (LXX[967]) attest editions which differ from the MT.[30] As for the Psalms, this book shows a remarkable textual homogeneity, all the more surprising since the Qumran manuscripts of the Psalms emphasize the complexity of its editorial history. If the stability of the text of a book indicates its antiquity and its recognition as canonical,[31] the books of the Pentateuch, Isaiah, Minor Prophets, and Psalms comprise an older and recognized nucleus of the biblical canon.

Neukirchener Verlag, 1973); idem, *Die deuteronomistische Redaktion von Jeremia 26–45* (WMANT 52; Neukirchen-Vluyn: Neukirchener Verlag, 1981).

[28] J. Davila, DJD 12, 31–78; idem, "Text-Type and Terminology: Genesis and Exodus as Test Cases," *RevQ* 61 (1993): 3–37.

[29] R. Fuller, DJD 15, 221–71.

[30] E. Ulrich, "The Canonical Process, Textual Criticism, and Latter Stages in the Compositon of the Bible," in *"Sha'arei Talmon": Studies in the Bible, Qumran, and the Ancient Near East Presented to Shemaryahu Talmon* (ed. M. Fishbane and E. Tov with the Assistance of W. W. Fields; Winona Lake, Ind.: Eisenbrauns, 1992), 267–91; idem, "The Bible in the Making: The Scriptures at Qumran," in *The Community of the Renewed Covenant* (ed. E. Ulrich and J. VanderKam; Christianity and Judaism in Antiquity 10; Notre Dame, Ind.: University of Notre Dame Press, 1994), 77–93; idem, "Multiple Literary Editions: Reflections towards a Theory of the History of the Biblical Text," in *Current Research and Technological Developments on the Dead Sea Scrolls* (STDJ 20; ed. D. W. Parry and S. D. Ricks; Leiden: Brill, 1996), 78–105.

[31] "The stabilization of the Torah was apparently compressed into a remarkably short period of time, in contrast to the Prophets and Writings and even the New Testament literature. I have suggested that a new law seems to be emerging in textual study of both testaments: the older the texts or

The history of the versions may reflect some idea of a canon in the period of translation, although the known facts do not allow definite conclusions. The Pentateuch was first
to be translated into Greek, then the Prophets and Psalms. Finally, and less literally, the
Writings were translated. Similarly, the Prophets were translated into Aramaic less literally
than the Pentateuch and more literally than the Writings.[32] The Pentateuch, Isaiah, Minor
Prophets, and Psalms seem to have been the first books translated into Syriac in the first
and second centuries C.E. in connection with the Targum tradition, a version possibly
made at least in part by Jews. A Jewish influence or even a targumic origin has been proposed for the Pentateuch, Isaiah, Psalms, Minor Prophets, Job, and Proverbs. Isaiah, the
Minor Prophets, and Psalms present common characteristics of translation.[33] Jerome
began his translation according to the *veritas hebraica* precisely with the version of the
Psalter *iuxta Hebraeos,* following immediately with that of the prophetic books. As for the
character of the Greek translation, the Septuagint of the Pentateuch, Isaiah, Minor Prophets, and Psalms helps more as a source of data for the study of Jewish exegesis in the period
than for the critical reconstruction of the Hebrew text, while the main contribution of the
Greek version of the historical books, Jeremiah, and Ezekiel lies in the recognition of an
intensive editorial activity affecting the corresponding Hebrew books.[34]

The number of manuscripts preserved of each biblical book in the Qumran caves
and their state of conservation tell us a great deal about how highly they were regarded in
the Qumran period. According to C. Perrot, "The scrolls of the Pentateuch, Minor Prophets and Psalms found at Qumran stand out easily from the other scrolls by their height or
the carefulness of their script."[35] The book of Isaiah may be included among these. E. Tov
lists the Qumran scrolls with the largest writing block per column (34 lines or more):
1QapGen, 34 lines; 1QIsa[b], 35; 4QIsa[a], 35; 4QGen-Exod[a], *ca.* 36; 11QPs[c], 36; 4QJub[d], 38;
MurXII, 39; 4QDeut[i], *ca.* 39; 4QRP[b], 39–41; 4QGen[b], 40; 4QIsa[c], *ca.* 40; 4QIsa[g], 40;
4QEnAstr[b], 40; 4QLev[b], 41; 1QH[a], 41, 42; 11QpaleoLev[a], 42; 4QEzek[a], 42; MasEzek, 42;
4QIsa[b], 42; 8HevXIIgr, 42–45; 4QExod[c], *ca.* 43; 4QSam[a], 43–44; 4QRP[c] (4Q365), 43–47;
4QShirShabb[d], 50; 4QGen[e], *ca.* 50; 4QpapJub[h] (4Q223–4), 54; 4QpaleoGen-Exod[l], 55–60;
4QExod-Lev[f], *ca.* 60 lines.[36] While the books of Samuel and Ezekiel are also present in the
list above, the best represented books are those of the Pentateuch, Isaiah, Minor Prophets,
and Psalms, together with important sectarian writings as the book of *Jubilees* (4QJub[d]
and 4QpapJub[h]), *Genesis Apocryphon,* and *Hodayot,* well kept in the important cave 1
(1QapGen and 1QH[a]).

---

versions the less likely they were copied accurately"; James A. Sanders, *From Sacred Story to Sacred
Text* (Philadelphia: Fortress, 1987), 181.

[32] Cf. G. Dorival, M. Harl, O. Munnich, *La Bible grecque des Septante: Du judaïsme hellénis-
tique au christianisme ancien* (Initiations au christianisme ancien; Paris: Editions du Cerf/Editions
du C.N.R.S., 1988), 86–111.

[33] Peter B. Dirksen, "The Old Testament Peshitta," in *Mikra,* 289.

[34] E. Tov, *The Text-Critical Use of the Septuagint in Biblical Research* (Jerusalem Biblical Studies 8; 2d ed.; Jerusalem: Simor, 1997), 237–63.

[35] C. Perrot, "The Reading of the Bible in the Ancient Synagogue," in *Mikra,* 137–59, 155; *La
lecture de la Bible dans la synagogue: Les anciennes lectures palestiniennes du shabbat et des fêtes* (Coll.
Massorah 1/1; Hildesheim: Gerstenberg, 1973), 117–27.

[36] E. Tov, "The Dimensions of the Qumran Scrolls," *DSD* 5/1 (1998): 69–91, 85.

Among the biblical manuscripts from the Dead Sea, there are forty copies of Psalms, thirty-two (+ 3?) of Deuteronomy, twenty-two of Isaiah and ten (+ 1?) of Minor Prophets. Cave 1, where the scrolls were preserved in pottery jars, has provided two copies of Isaiah (1QIsa[ab]), three of Psalms (1QPs[abc]) and one copy each of Genesis, Exodus, Leviticus, and Deuteronomy, as well as of Judges and 1 Samuel. Cave 11 also preserved important scrolls, among them six copies of Psalms (11Q5–9; 11Q11), two of Leviticus, one of Deuteronomy, and only one copy of a book of the second series, namely Ezekiel (11Q4). Important scrolls were also entrusted to caves 2, 3, 5, and 6. Cave 2 provided twelve copies of books of the Pentateuch, one of Psalms, one of Job, as well as two of Ruth and one of Jeremiah; cave 3: one manuscript of Psalms, Ezekiel and Lamentations each; cave 5: one copy of Deuteronomy, Isaiah, Amos and Psalms each, as well as two of Lamentations and one of Kings; cave 6: three copies of books of the Pentateuch and one of Psalms (6Qpap6Q5), as well as one of Kings, Song of Songs and Daniel each.[37] The book of Minor Prophets was particularly valued in the Qumran period, until the Second Jewish Revolt.[38] This book had a special significance, obviously a messianic and eschatological one.

The number of copies and the form of preservation of the manuscripts indicate that the Pentateuch, Isaiah, Minor Prophets, and Psalms had particular importance, followed by Jeremiah, Ezekiel, and the historical books and, lagging far behind, the Writings.

3. Evidence from the History of Interpretation

The history of the interpretation of biblical books, and in particular the explicit quotations of biblical passages contained in the oldest Jewish literature, help to determine the limits of the canon of books which enjoyed enough authority to be cited in decisive issues, such as those concerning matters involving law or messianic legitimacy.[39] All the

---

[37] Cf. E. Tov, "A List of the Texts from the Judaean Desert," in *The Dead Sea Scrolls after Fifty Years: A Comprehensive Assessment* (2 vols; ed. P. W. Flint and J. C. VanderKam; Leiden: E. J. Brill, 1999), 2:669–717. An index of passages in the biblical Dead Sea manuscripts elaborated by E. Ulrich gives also an idea of which were the most represented books: Pentateuch, 494 entries (37.2%); books of the first series: Isaiah, 176 (13.2%); Minor Prophets, 133 (10%); Psalms, 216 (16.2%); Job, 13 (0.9%); Proverbs, 6 (0.4%); books of the second series: 1–2 Samuel, 56 (4.2%); Jeremiah, 43 (3.2%); Ezekiel, 15 (1.1%); Daniel, 25 (1.8%); Joshua-Judges-Kings, 27 (2%); cf. E. Ulrich, "An Index of the Passages in the Biblical Manuscripts From the Judean Desert (Genesis-Kings)," *DSD* 1/1 (1994): 113–29; idem, "An Index of the Passages in the Biblical Manuscripts From the Judean Desert (Part 2: Isaiah-Chronicles)," *DSD* 2/1 (1995): 86–107.

[38] The zealots of Naal destroyed by fire all their documents except a well used copy of this book (8ḤevXIIgr) that they buried with their dead in the innermost parts of the Cave of Horror; cf. B. W. R. Pearson, "The Book of the Twelve, Aqiba's Messianic Interpretations, and the Refuge Caves of the Second Jewish War," in *The Scrolls and the Scriptures: Qumran Fifty Years After* (JSPSup 26; ed. S. E. Porter and C. A. Evans; Sheffield: Sheffield Academic Press, 1997), 221–39, 234–35.

[39] Explicit quotations are those that are introduced with a *formula quotationis* ("as it is written," or "the scripture says") and aim at a *verbatim* reproduction of the biblical text or texts; G. Vermes, "Biblical Proof-Texts in Qumran Literature," *JSS* 34/2 (1989): 493–508; F. L. Horton, "Formulas of Introduction in the Qumran Literature," *RevQ* 7 (1969–71): 505–14; M. Bernstein, "Introductory Formulas for Citation and Re-Citation of Biblical Verses in the Qumran Pesharim: Observations on a Pesher Technique," *DSD* 1 (1994): 30–70.

inner-biblical quotations refer to the books of the Law. There are eight cases of literal or abbreviated quotations with introductory formulae such as *katûb* or *lēʾmor:* 1 Kgs 2:4 (Deut 29:8); 2 Kgs 14:6 (Deut 24:16); Neh 8:14 (Lev 23:42); Neh 13:1 (Deut 23:4–6); Jer 3:1 (Deut 24:1–4); Jer 17:21–22 (Deut 5:12–14); Hag 2:11–14 (Lev 6:20);[40] the only non-pentateuchal passage quoted with an introductory formula, *lēʾmor,* although not precisely *verbatim,* is 2 Sam 7:7–16, alluded in 1 Kgs 2:4.

The books of the Law, the Prophets, and Psalms make up the Bible quoted by Qumran legal and exegetical literature. Among the prophets, Isaiah and Minor Prophets are more highly regarded than Jeremiah, Ezekiel, the Former Prophets, or historical books.

A survey by J. C. VanderKam of introductory formulas and the number of times that biblical books are quoted in Qumran sectarian texts yields the following results: Pentateuch thirteen; Isaiah nine; Minor Prophets nine; Ezekiel four; Psalms two; Daniel two; 2 Samuel one; Jeremiah one; Proverbs one.[41] Among the Qumran legal writings the *Community Rule* has three quotations, one from Exodus (23:7) and two from Isaiah (2:22; 40:3). The *Damascus Document* introduces twenty quotations from the Pentateuch, eight from Isaiah, eleven from the Minor Prophets, two from Ezekiel, and one each from 1 Samuel and Proverbs. 4QSerek Damascus Rule (4Q265) adduces Lev 12:2; 12:4, Isa 54:1–2, and Mal 2:10. 4QDamascus Document[a] (4Q266) cites Lev 26:31 and Joel 2:12–13, and 4QTohorot A (4Q274) Lev 13:45. The *War Scroll* (1QM) quotes Deut 20:2–4; Num 10:9; 24:17–19 and Isa 31:8; and the *War Rule* (4Q285) Isa 10:34–11:1 and Ezek 19:3–4. *Miqṣat Maʿaśê ha-Torah* has one quotation each from Leviticus (7:13), Deuteronomy (30:1–2), and Jeremiah (2:3).[42]

The Qumran *pešarîm,* four of them kept in the important cave 1 (1QpHab, 1QpMic, 1QpZeph and 1QpPs), comment only on Isaiah, the Minor Prophets (Hosea, Micah, Nahum, Habakkuk, Zephaniah and Malachi), and Psalms (1Q16, 4Q171, 4Q173). As for the exegetical literature, the thematic midrashim with eschatological content also quote from the Torah, Prophets, and Psalms and, among the Prophets, mainly from Isaiah and

---

[40] M. Fishbane, *Biblical Interpretation in Ancient Israel* (Oxford: Clarendon Press, 1985), 144–62; D. Dimant, "Use and Interpretation of Mikra in the Apocrypha and Pseudepigrapha," in *Mikra,* 379–419, 385, and 386 n. 28.

[41] J. C. VanderKam, "Authoritative Literature in the Dead Sea Scrolls," *DSD* 5/3 (1998): 382–402.

[42] Cf. M. Fishbane, "Use, Authority and Interpretation of Mikra at Qumran," in *Mikra,* 339–77, 347-48; S. Metso, *The Textual Development of the Qumran Community Rule* (STDJ 21; Leiden: E. J. Brill, 1997); J. G. Campbell, *The Use of Scripture in the Damascus Document 1–8, 19–20* (Berlin and New York: De Gruyter, 1995); J. Baumgarten, "Scripture and Law in 4Q265," in *Biblical Perspectives: Early Use and Interpretation of the Bible in Light of the Dead Sea Scrolls. Proceedings of the First International Symposium of the Orion Center for the Study of the DSS and Associated Literature, 12–14 May, 1996* (ed. M. E. Stone and E. G. Chazon; Leiden: E. J. Brill, 1998), 25–33; J. Carmignac, "Les citations de l'Ancien Testament dans 'La guerre des fils de lumières contre les fils de ténèbres," *RB* 63 (1956): 234–60; 375–90. On "implicit exegesis" in the *War Scroll,* cf. D. O. Wenthe, "The Use of the Hebrew Scriptures in 1QM," *DSD* 5/3 (1998): 290–319; M. Bernstein, "The Employment and Interpretation of Scripture in 4QMMT: Preliminary Observations," in *Reading 4QMMT: New Perspectives in Qumran Law and History* (ed. J. Kampen and M. Bernstein; Atlanta: Scholars, 1996), 20–51; G. Brooke, "The Explicit Presentation of Scripture in 4QMMT," in *Legal Texts and Legal Issues: Proceedings of the Second Meeting of the International Organization for Qumran Studies. Cambridge 1995. Published in Honour of Joseph M. Baumgarten* (STDJ 23; ed. M. Bernstein, F. García Martínez, and J. Kampen; Leiden: E. J. Brill, 1997), 67–88.

Minor Prophets. 4QCatena^a (4Q177 = 4QMidrEschat^b) quotes from Isaiah to interpret some Psalms, and from Mic 2:10–11 to comment on Ps 11:1–2; Zech 3:9 on Ps 12:7; Ezek 25:8 on Ps 13:5; and Hos 5:8 on Ps 17:1. 4QFlorilegium (4Q174 = 4QMidrEschat^a) interprets 2 Sam 7:10–14 with the help of Exod 15:17–18 and Am 9:11; Ps 1:1 with that of Isa 8:11 and Ezek 37:23; and Ps 2:1–2 with Dan 12:10 and 11:32.[43] 4QCatena^b (4Q182 = 4QMidrEschat^c) draws upon Jer 5:7. 4QTestimonia (4Q175) cites only from the Pentateuch but ends with a quotation of Jos 6:26. 4QTanhumim (4Q176) quotes from Isaiah, Zechariah, and probably Ps 79:2–3.[44] 11QMelchizedek (11Q13) quotes Lev 25:9–13; Deut 15:2; Isa 52:7; 61:2–3, and Ps 7:8–9; 82:1–2.

The hymnic and apocalyptic genres do not attempt at explicit quotations, but their numerous implicit allusions to biblical sources point mainly to Psalms, Isaiah, the Minor Prophets, and the Pentateuch. *Hodayot* (1QH^a,b = 1Q35; 4Q^a-f = 4Q427–432) offers forty-eight clear allusions to the Psalms, sixty-eight to Isaiah, thirty-one to Minor Prophets and twenty-nine to the Pentateuch, plus ten to Job and eighteen to Jeremiah. 4QMessianic Apocalypse (4Q521), a wisdom text with apocalyptic character, alludes to Ps 146 and Isa 61:1 (frag. 2 II).[45]

Of the deuterocanonical or apocryphal books Tobit, Judith, 2 Maccabees, 3 Maccabees, 4 Maccabees, Susanna, and Baruch present a total of nineteen explicit biblical quotations: thirteen from the Pentateuch, one each from Amos and Isaiah, two from Psalms, and one each from Ezekiel and Proverbs.[46] At the end of the Second Temple period, Philo continued to quote almost exclusively from the Pentateuch: 2260 instances (97 percent of his quotations).[47] Towards 70 C.E. or shortly before, Pseudo-Philo rewrites the Pentateuch and continues the biblical history to the period of Saul's death. His *Biblical Antiquities* includes

---

[43] The citation of 2 Sam 7:10 does not coincide with any known text form, and the quotations from both Ezekiel and Daniel, although introduced by citation formulas, are paraphrases; cf. A. Steudel, *Der Midrasch zur Eschatologie aus der Qumrangemeinde (4QMidrEschat^a.b): Materielle Rekonstruktion, Textbestand, Gattung und traditionsgeschichtliche Einordnung des durch 4Q174 ("Florilegium") und 4Q177 ("Catena") repräsentierten Werkes aus den Qumranfunden* (STDS 13; Leiden: E. J. Brill, 1994), 135–51; M. J. Bernstein, "Introductory Formulas for Citation and Re-citation of Biblical Verses in the Qumran Pesharim: Observations on a Pesher Technique," *DSD* 1/1 (1994): 30–70, 53–54; G. J. Brooke, *Exegesis at Qumran: 4QFlorilegium in its Jewish Context* (JSOTSup 29; Sheffield: JSOT Press, 1985), 97–98.

[44] Isa 40:1–5; 41:8–9; 43:1–2; 43:4–6; 49:7; 49:13–17; 51:22–23; 52:1–3; 54:4–10; Zech 13:9 (frag. 15), and probably Ps 79:2–3 (frag. 1–2 I, 1–4), J. M. Allegro, *Qumran Cave 4: I (4Q158–4Q186)* (DJD 5; Oxford: Clarendon Press, 1968), 60–67.

[45] S. Holm-Nielsen, *Hodayot: Psalms from Qumran* (Acta Theologica Danica 2; Aarhus: Universitetsforlaget, 1960), 301–15; E. Puech, "Une apocalypse messianique (4Q521)," *RevQ* 15/60 (1992): 475–522; idem, *La croyance des esséniens en la vie future: immortalité, résurrection, vie éternelle? Histoire d'une croyance dans le Judaïsme ancien* (2 vols.; Etudes bibliques 21–22; Paris: J. Gabalda, 1993), 2:627–29.

[46] Tob 2:6 (Amos 8:10); 8:6 (Gen 2:18); Jdt 9:2 (Gen 34:7); Bar 2:2 (Lev 26:29); Sus 53 (Exod 23:7); 1 Macc 7:16–17 (Ps 79:2–3); 2 Macc 1:29 (Exod 15:17); 7:6 (Deut 32:36); 10:26 (Exod 23:22); 3 Macc 6:15 (Lev 26:44); 4 Macc 2:5 (Exod 20:17); 2:19 (Gen 49:7); 17:19 (Deut 33:3); 18:14 (Isa 43:2); 18:15 (Ps 34:20); 18:16 (Prov 3:18); 18:18 (Deut 32:39); 18:19 (Deut 30:20); 4 Macc 18:17 (Ezek 37:3); cf. D. Dimant, "Use and Interpretation of Mikra in the Apocrypha and Pseudepigrapha," in *Mikra*, 379–419, 385.

[47] Psalms, nineteen quotations; 1–4 Kgdms, sixteen; Proverbs, five; Isaiah, four; Minor Prophets, three; Ezekiel two, and one quotation from Joshua, Judges, and Job each. Cf. W. L. Knox, "A Note on Philo's Use of the Old Testament," *JTS* 41 (1940): 30–34.

twenty quotations introduced with the Latin *dicens, lē'mor* in Hebrew. All of these are taken from the Pentateuch except for one from Psalms (99:6).[48] Finally, the *Wisdom of Solomon* employs the books of Exodus, Deuteronomy, and Isaiah.[49]

The historical books as well as the books of Jeremiah and Ezekiel were not suitable for pesher-type commentaries or for explicit quotation. However, together with the Pentateuch, especially the first eleven chapters of Genesis, they provided the textual base for the creation of parabiblical developments in new writings now called "apocrypha," "pseudo-," "paraphrases," "psalms," or "visions": *Pseudo-Joshua* (4QPsalms of Joshua, 4Q378–379), *Pseudo-Samuel* (4QVision of Samuel, 4Q160; 6QApocryphon of Samuel-Kings, 6Q9), *Pseudo-Jeremiah* (4QApocryphon of Jeremiah, 4Q385b and 4Q387b), *Pseudo-Ezekiel* (4Q385), *Pseudo-Daniel* (4Q243–245), etc.[50]

The New Testament offers the best evidence for a canon comprising "the law and the prophets" or "the law of Moses, the prophets, and the psalms" (with Psalms understood as that book and no other). The Pentateuch, Isaiah, Minor Prophets, and Psalms are quoted almost exclusively. This is especially the case in the earliest Christian writings (Mark, the double or triple synoptic tradition, Acts, Romans, and Galatians) and, in particular, of the quotations attributed to Jesus, Peter, and Stephen, often resembling *pesher* interpretation. The problem of distinguishing direct quotations from allusions, references to Old Testament history, or use of biblical phraseology makes it difficult to establish the exact number of quotations in the New Testament. Without considering here combinations of two or more biblical texts, the numbers in Table 8-1 should be fairly accurate.[51]

---

[48] *L.A.B.* 51; cf. E. Reinmuth, *Pseudo-Philo und Lukas: Studien zum* Liber Antiquitatum Biblicarum *und seiner Bedeutung für die Interpretation des lukanischen Doppelwerks* (Tübingen: Mohr [Siebeck], 1994), 211–29.

[49] H. B. Swete, *An Introduction to the Old Testament in Greek: Revised by R. R. Ottley with an Appendix containing the Letter of Aristeas edited by H. St. J. Thackeray* (2d ed.; Cambridge: Cambridge University Press, 1914), 371ff.; J. Fichtner, "Der AT-Text der Sapientia Salomonis," *ZAW* 57 (1939): 155–92. Of the Jewish Hellenistic writers, Aristobulos alludes to Gen 1:3, 6, etc.; 2:2; Exod 3:9, 20; 13:9; 17:6; 19:11, 18, 20; 20:4; 24:16; Deut 4:11 etc., and Prov 8:22–31, with a reference to "one of our ancestors, Solomon" (frg. 5 n. 11).

[50] D. Dimant, "Apocalyptic Texts at Qumran," in *The Community of the Renewed Covenant: The Notre Dame Symposium on the Dead Sea Scrolls* (Christianity and Judaism in Antiquity Series 10; ed. E. Ulrich and J. C. VanderKam; Notre Dame, Ind.: University of Notre Dame Press, 1994), 175–91.

[51] J. A. Fitzmyer, "The Use of Explicit Old Testament Quotations in Qumran Literature and in the New Testament," *NTS* 7 (1960–61): 297–333; E. E. Ellis, "Old Testament Quotations in the New: A Brief History of the Research," in E. E. Ellis, *The Old Testament in Early Christianity: Canon and Interpretation in the Light of Modern Research* (Tübingen: Mohr [Siebeck], 1991), 51–74, with bibliography, 63–65; idem, "The Old Testament Canon in the Early Church," in *Mikra*, 653–90. According to D. A. Koch, Paul's letters contain twenty-five quotations from Isaiah, twenty from Psalms, thirteen from Deuteronomy, twelve from Genesis, five from Exodus, three from Hosea, two from Leviticus, three from Proverbs, two from 1 Kings, two from Job, one from Habakkuk, one from Malachi, one from Joel; four quotations cannot be identified with certainty. *Contra* Koch's opinion, Hübner asserts that 1 Cor 1:31 and 2 Cor 10:17 contain short quotations of Jer 9:22–23. See D. A. Koch, *Die Schrift als Zeuge des Evangeliums: Untersuchungen zur Verwendung und zum Verständnis der Schrift bei Paulus* (BHT 69; Tübingen: Mohr [Siebeck], 1986), 33; H. Hübner, "New Testament Interpretation of the Old Testament," in *Hebrew Bible / Old Testament*, 332–72, 340.

Table 8-1. Quotations of the Old Testament in the New Testament

	TOT.	Pent.	2 Sam	1 Kgs	Isa	Jer	12 Pr.	Pss	Prov	Job
Matt	37	17	—	—	9	—	6	5	—	—
Mark	9	5	—	—	1	—	1	2	—	—
Luke	16	9	—	—	3	—	1	3	—	—
John	7	—	—	—	2	—	2	3	—	—
Acts	23	7	—	—	5	—	4	7	—	—
Rom	45	16	—	2	14	—	4	9	—	—
1 Cor	15	4	—	—	6	1	—	3	—	1
2 Cor	7	3	—	—	1	1	—	2	—	—
Gal	10	8	—	—	1	—	1	—	—	—
Heb	38	11	1	—	2	3	2	18	1	—

Three quotations of Matthew (2:18; 21:13; 27:9–10) come from Jeremiah, although the second includes also a quotation of Isaiah and the third combines texts of Jeremiah and Zechariah. The important passage of Matt 11:10 (Luke 7:27) combines two texts that embrace the whole of prophetical tradition: Isa 40:3 (cited also in Qumran) and Mal 3:1: "He is the man of whom it is written: 'See, I sent my messenger before you, who will prepare *your* way before *you*.' "

The New Testament contains only two quotations from the historical books. Second Samuel 7:14 is quoted in Heb 1:5b, but its joining with Ps 2 into something of a messianic catena (as in 4QFlorilegium) makes this passage a special biblical source to be quoted only in relation with that Psalm or other passages from books of the first series. Romans 11:3–4 quotes 1 Kgs 19:14, 18 ("the scripture says of Elijah") with an eschatological application, "So too at the present time there is a remnant. . . ." However, the quotation seems to indicate more the messianic figure of Elijah than the book of Kings.

Two books, Psalms and Isaiah, and a third one provide the text for half of all biblical citations present in the New Testament. The third one corresponds to Minor Prophets in Jesus' quotations, Deuteronomy in those of the whole New Testament, or Genesis in those of Paul and the church fathers of the second century. The books of the Pentateuch, Psalms, and Isaiah are the most quoted by Clement of Rome. Justin also quotes mainly from these books and from Minor Prophets.[52] These three most quoted books derive from a canon of the Law, the Prophets, and Psalms, one book from each section. They account for more than half of all the Old Testament citations in early patristic sources. Until the third century the churches could not afford all the books of the Old Testament. Besides the New Testament, they had at their disposal the more frequently used Old Testament books such as Genesis, Isaiah, and Psalms and, varying according to circumstances and region, other books used particularly in baptismal instruction. In the third century (Origen, Clement of

---

[52] D. A. Hagner, *The Use of the Old and New Testaments in Clement of Rome* (*NTS* 34; Leiden: Brill, 1973); P. Katz, "Justin's Old Testament Quotations and the Greek Dodekapropheton Scroll," in *Studies in the Septuagint: Origins, Recensions, and Interpretation* (Library of Biblical Studies; ed. S. Jellicoe; New York: Ktav Publishing House, 1974), 530–40; P. Prigent, *Justin et l'Ancien Testament* (Etudes Bibliques; Paris: J. Gabalda, 1964).

Alexandria, Cyprian and the *Didaskalia*) the picture changes and the quotations do not concentrate so much on the books of Genesis, Isaiah, and Psalms.[53]

The lists of *haftarot* in the triennial circle indicate that Isaiah and Minor Prophets were the books used most. Some Psalms were evidently used in the temple, although the book of Psalms came into the synagogue service only slowly and to a relatively restricted degree. The Palestinian synagogues, small and numerous, could probably not afford all the scrolls, but most synagogues possessed the whole Pentateuch in its five volumes and some other scrolls, such as Isaiah and Minor Prophets and probably Psalms. These were the books most in use.[54]

As for the Writings, Job and Proverbs were especially important, and formed the nucleus of the collection of Writings. The book of Job is the only book, besides the Torah, of which a copy written in a formal Palaeo-Hebrew script has been found in Qumran (4Q101). In spite of its great difficulty, the text of Job has been transmitted in a rather stable form, like the Pentateuch, Isaiah, and Minor Prophets. The presence of a targum of Job among the Qumran manuscripts (4Q157, 11Q10) also demonstrates the special esteem that the book enjoyed. Certain rabbis considered Job a contemporary of the Queen of Sheba or of the patriarchs or Moses, and the book of Job was placed between the writings of David and Solomon.[55] The history of formation of the book of Proverbs resembles that of the books of the more nuclear canon in that it too has an older, probably preexilic, core. It is cited in the Qumran texts, in the Pseudepigraphal writings, and by Philo. The books of Job and Proverbs ("Solomon") were employed for authoritative quotations in the letters of Paul as well as the New Testament Jewish Christian tractates (Hebrews, James, and 1–2 Peter). Job is quoted in Rom 11:34–5; 1 Cor 3:19, and Proverbs in Rom 12:19–20; Heb 12:5; Jas 4:6; 1 Pet 4:18; 5:5; 2 Pet 2:22.

The books in the collection of Writings presuppose the written tradition of the Law and the Prophets, to which they frequently allude. The number of writings that make up this third collection was not fixed until the rabbinic period, or at least not all Jewish groups accepted the same collection of Writings. The Qumran Community seems to have granted at least a degree of canonical value to other books of which multiple copies have been found, such as *1 Enoch* and *Jubilees*.[56] The edited form of the Writings as well as the fixation of their text remained in a state of flux that gave rise to a multiplicity of editions and texts.

Certain expressions of the Hebrew Bible seem to indicate who the transmitters were who contributed to the formation of the canon in either its bipartite or tripartite from. Priests and prophets occur frequently, as parallel terms, representing law and prophecy: "The prophets prophesy falsely, and the priests teach as the prophets direct" (Jer 5:31).[57] Priests, prophets, and wise men may represent the future tripartite structure of the canon:

---

[53] Stuhlhofer, "Der Ertrag von Bibelstellenregistern für die Kanongeschichte," 259.

[54] C. Perrot, "The Reading of the Bible in the Ancient Synagogue," in *Mikra*, 137–59, 154–55; idem, *La lecture de la Bible dans la synagogue*, 117–27.

[55] Beckwith, *The Old Testament Canon of the New Testament Church*, 203, 209.

[56] VanderKam, "Authoritative Literature in the Dead Sea Scrolls," 396–402.

[57] MT *yirddû*, "rule," but BHS proposes *yôrû* or *hôrû*, "teach" (the law), which fits, in line with the frequent parallelism between priests and prophets, as representing the law and prophecy respectively.

"for instruction *(torah)* shall not perish from the priest, nor counsel from the wise, nor the word from the prophet" (Jer 18:18); "How can you say, 'We are wise, and the law of the Lord is with us.' . . . The wise shall be put to shame . . . from prophet to priest everyone deals falsely" (Jer 8:8–10). The wise man is connected with the law, like the priest, although it is not clear whether he forms a third group, separate from the priests. Ezekiel 7:26 also attests three functions: prophetic vision, priestly torah, and counsel of the elders or wise men, "they shall keep seeking a vision from the prophet; instruction (*torah* in Hebrew) shall perish from the priest, and counsel from the elders." The counsel of the wise men was certainly compared to the instruction of the priests and the words of the prophets. The temporary disappearance of the priesthood during the exile and the complete disappearance of prophecy later helped to give the wise man more independence. Consequently, "the sages took over the prophetic claim to mediate revelation, leading to the rabbinic statement that prophecy has been taken from the prophets and given to the sages. It was by virtue of such a claim that the biblical canon came to be expanded to cover a miscellaneous body of writings over and above the Law and the Prophets."[58]

Among the oldest biblical manuscripts found in Qumran, which predate the Community and were taken from Jerusalem and elsewhere, there are books from all three sections of the canon: 4QExod-Lev[f] (4Q17) *ca.* 250 B.C.E.,[59] 4QpaleoDeuteronomy[s] (4Q46) "in the second half of the third century,"[60] 4QpaleoJob[c] (4Q101) *ca.* 225–150,[61] 4QJer[a] (4Q70) *ca.* 200,[62] 4QJer[bd] (4Q71, 4Q71a) *ca.* 200–150,[63] 4QDeut[a] (4Q28) *ca.* 175–150,[64] 4QPs[a] (4Q83) *ca.* 150.[65] There is also a manuscript of the Septuagint, 4QLXXDeut (4Q122), *ca.* 175–150, "in the earlier or middle second century B.C.E."[66] At all events, these dates do not allow an excessively low chronology, as proposed by N. P. Lemche, for the books and collections that make up the Hebrew Bible.[67]

4. Conclusions

Possible conclusions from the above are as follows:

1. The tripartite canon is a further development of the canon of the Law and the Prophets, or rather, of the canon of "Law, Prophets, and Psalms." The books in these collections have features in common which make them the first biblical canon.[68]

---

[58] J. Blenkinsopp, *Wisdom and Law in the Old Testament: The Ordering of Life in Israel and Early Judaism* (Oxford: Oxford University Press, 1995), 5.

[59] F. M. Cross, *DJD* 12, 134.

[60] P. W. Skehan, E. Ulrich, and J. E. Sanderson, *DJD* 9, 153.

[61] Ibid., 154.

[62] E. Tov, *DJD* 15, 145–70.

[63] Ibid., 171–77 and 203–7.

[64] S. White Crawford, *DJD* 14, 7.

[65] P. W. Flint, and A. E. Alvarez, "The Oldest of All the Psalms Scrolls: The Text and Translation of 4QPs[a]," in *The Scrolls and the Scriptures,* 142–69.

[66] P. W. Skehan, E. Ulrich, and J. E. Sanderson, DJD 9, 195.

[67] N. P. Lemche, "The Old Testament—A Hellenistic Book?" *SJOT* 7 (1993): 163–93.

[68] "If a tripartite division of the canon was relatively early, however, the books assigned to the latter two divisions were in flux. . . . An older division into Law and Prophets, simply, may be

2. Within this first canon, the Pentateuch, Isaiah, Minor Prophets, and Psalms exhibit similar histories of literary formation, textual transmission, transmission of manuscripts, and of authorized interpretation which identify them as the nuclear components of the biblical canon. Particularly important is authorized interpretation as scripture through explicit quotations in matters concerning the Law, messianic hope or, in the New Testament, christological concepts.

3. Within the section of the Prophets, the historical books, Jeremiah, and Ezekiel, as well as Daniel in the tradition represented by the Septuagint, exhibit a history of literary redaction, editorial formation, and textual transmission which is less stable and more diverse than that of Isaiah and Minor Prophets; they are hardly used for explicit quotations, but they are the source of many parabiblical rewritings, especially of an apocalyptic or prophetic character.

4. The book of Psalms lies on the borderline between Prophets and Writings. In its history of composition, edition, and textual transmission it is also at the boundary between books with a more stable text and more frequent use as scripture (Pentateuch, Isaiah, and Minor Prophets) and books with multiple editions, less stable texts, less use as scripture and, in some cases, even doubts concerning their canonicity (in ascending order: historical books, Jeremiah, Ezekiel, Daniel, other Writings). Initially located at the end of the prophetical books or as an appendix to the Law and Prophets, it was ultimately moved to the beginning of the Writings. The book of Psalms also lies at the boundary between text and sacred rite, between the function of scripture and the liturgical use of its text.

5. Right from the beginning there was a tendency to grant some type or degree of authority to books later included among the Writings. The books of Job and Proverbs comprise the nucleus of what later would become the collection of Writings, to which the book of Psalms was transferred.

6. The expressions "Law and Prophets" and "Law, Prophets, and Psalms" refer primarily to the authority of these books as scripture, whereas the expression "Law, Prophets, and Writings," which dates much later, marks instead all the books which comprise the scriptures of Judaism. The concept of "canon" is not applied equally to the first collections of biblical books with established antiquity and recognized authority, although still being edited to some extent (Law, Prophets, and Psalms) and to the final collection or complete list of books held to be canonical, to the exclusion of others, considered "external" (ḥiṣonîm).

---

postulated, for in the canonical theory of the Pharisees all books were written under prophetic inspiration by an unbroken sequence of prophets" (F. M. Cross, "The Stabilization of the Canon of the Hebrew Bible," in F. M. Cross, *From Epic to Canon: History and Literature in Ancient Israel* [Baltimore and London: The Johns Hopkins University Press, 1998], 219–29, 228).

9

Jamnia Revisited

Jack P. Lewis

Ezra is said to have dictated ninety-four books of which seventy were stored up but twenty-four were for general reading.[1] Alternatively, the formation of the Hebrew Bible has been traced to Nehemiah's library.[2] Elias Levita proposed in 1538 C.E. that the canon of scripture was closed by the men of the Great Synagogue.[3] Not convinced by any of the above, Heinrich Graetz in 1871 proposed that the canon was closed by the synod of Jamnia about 90 C.E.[4] In his *History of the Jews,* Graetz surveyed the deposition of R. Gamaliel II and the choice of Eleazar ben Azariah as *nasi* and called the gathering at Jamnia "the college," "the college of the Synhedrion," "Synhedrion of Jabne," and "the College of Seventy-two."[5]

The status of Ecclesiastes and Song of Songs was by no means the only question discussed at Jamnia on which Bet Hillel and Bet Shammai differed. But about these matters scholars have been content with the terms "college"[6] and "school-house."[7] A Bat Qol declared, "The teachings of both schools are the words of the living God, but practically the laws of Hillel only are to carry weight."[8] R. Joshua only demurred that objectionable cases can be decided by the majority but that a miracle cannot decide such cases. Graetz calls the group the "Synhedrion of Jabne":

> The old contest was now taken up by the College of Seventy-two which had not approved of the decisions of Hillel, but it is not clearly known with what result. Later on these Halachas were included in the collection (Canon) of the Holy Writings, after which the Canon was completed and several writings in the Hebrew language were rejected as Apocrypha such as the proverbs of Sirach, the first book of the Maccabees, and several others.[9]

---

[1] 4 Ezra 14:37–38; *b. B. Bat.* 14b.
[2] 2 Macc 2:13.
[3] Elias Levita, *The Massoreth ha-Massoreth* (trans. C. D. Ginsburg: 1861; repr. New York: KTAV, 1968).
[4] H. Graetz, *Kohelet oder der solomonische Prediger,* Anhang I, "Der alttestamentliche Kanon und sein Abschluss" (Leipzig: C. F. Winter, 1871), 147–74.
[5] H. Graetz, *History of the Jews* (Philadelphia: The Jewish Publication Society, 1893; repr., 1956), 2:342, 344.
[6] Ibid., 337.
[7] Ibid.
[8] Ibid.
[9] Ibid., 344.

1. Elaboration of the Council of Jamnia Hypothesis

Graetz's case for a council/synod was expounded by Samuel Davidson, who spoke of a discussion about 65 C.E.; there the school of Shammai, in the majority, excluded Ecclesiastes. Davidson had the question emerge again at the Synod of Jamnia where, with the Hillelites in a majority, it was decided that Ecclesiastes and Song of Songs pollute the hands. Davidson summarized, "The canon was virtually settled at Jamnia," and speaking of the two episodes, he says, "Thus the question of canonicity of certain books was discussed at two synods."[10]

In 1891, Frants Buhl elaborated the Council of Jamnia idea:

It was not until 90 C.E. that the whole question was brought up for discussion before a Synod [*Synode*] at Jabne . . . , the very one at which Gamaliel II was deprived of his office of patriarch. At that Synod the canonicity of the whole of sacred writings was acknowledged. Special emphasis was laid on the affirmation of the canonicity, not only of Ecclesiastes, but also of Canticles, which affords clear evidence of the existence of an opposition against this latter book.[11]

G. Wildeboer examined all the rabbinic texts, finding only Ecclesiastes and Song of Songs discussed on the day of the deprivation of R. Gamaliel II. Rabbinic discussion of other books is either later or earlier than that event. Wildeboer concluded that Graetz's hypothesis was nothing but guesswork. He placed the *terminus ad quem* of the canonization of the Writings at the latest at the issuing of the Mishnah by R. Judah, 200 C.E.[12]

The Jamnia hypothesis was popularized further in the English speaking world by H. E. Ryle, who cites Buhl in two footnotes.[13] After surveying the texts for the existence of "the Third Canon," Ryle, without citing supporting texts, says in his survey,

Now we happen to know that a council of Jewish Rabbis was held at Jamnia (Jabne), not very far from Jaffa, about the year 90 A.D., and again, perhaps in 118 A.D. Rabbi Gamaliel II seems to have presided, and Rabbi Akiba was the prominent spirit. In the course of its deliberations the subject of the Canon was discussed. It was decided that the difficulties which had been felt about the book of Ecclesiastes and the Song of Songs could be fairly answered (*Eduyoth*, 5:3). The suggestion has been made, that we have in the Synod of Jamnia the official occasion, on which the limits of the Hebrew Canon were firmly determined by Jewish authorities.[14]

Confronted with such graphic description and with Ryle's "we happen to know," it is only natural that the reading public would assume that Ryle's assertions rested on definite texts (though he cites none). Scholars are perhaps to be excused for their overlooking the

---

[10] Samuel Davidson, *The Canon of the Bible* (London: C. Kegan Paul & Co., 1878), 56–57.

[11] Frants P. W. Buhl, *Kanon und Text des alten Testaments* (Leipzig: Academische Buchhandlung, 1891); ET *Canon and Text of the Old Testament* (trans. J. MacPherson: Edinburgh: T&T Clark, 1892), 24.

[12] G. Wildeboer, *The Origin of the Canon of the Old Testament* (trans. B. W. Bacon: London: Luzac & Co. 1895), 63–64, 148–49.

[13] H. E. Ryle, *The Canon of the Old Testament* (2d ed.; London: Macmillan and Co., 1892; repr. 1904), 196 n. 2, and 218 n. 2.

[14] Ibid., 182–83.

uncertainty expressed in Ryle's next paragraph with the words "may," "apparently," "conjecture," and "symbolize."

> It may, indeed, very well have happened at this, or at some similar, gathering about that time. In the absence of precise information—for the Rabbinic evidence is fragmentary and the reverse of precise—we can only say that, as [sic] the time at which the Synod of Jamnia was held, and apparently the subjects which occupied its discussions, are favourable to the conjecture, there is no reason for objecting to it. As a matter of fact, the Synod of Jamnia can be little else to us but a name; still, as it is a name connected with the ratified canonicity of certain books, it may symbolize the general attitude of the Jewish doctors, and their resolve to put an end to the doubts about the "disputed" books of the Hagiographa.[15]

Ryle saw a gradual process of canonization beginning at the era of the Maccabean ascendancy. "Two centuries and a half later the final results of that process received an official ratification at Jamnia or elsewhere."[16] When Ryle surveyed the crucial passage of *m. Yadayim* 3:5 later in his book, he spoke of "the school at Jamnia."[17]

K. Budde reflects the earlier discussion of Buhl and Ryle in citing *m. Yadayim* 3:5 and *m. Eduyoth* 5:3. He sees Jamnia as having dealt with the question of Qoheleth and the Song of Songs as holy scripture, but prefers a date of 100 C.E. Budde notes that the question is again being discussed some decades later but was settled by a confirmation of the decision at Jamnia.[18] F. H. Woods, also dependent on Buhl and Ryle, says, "The decisions of this school, if not considered absolutely binding, must at least have had a very strong and reaching influence on Jewish opinion. If it is an exaggeration to say that the canon of the O.T. was finally settled at the Council of Jamnia, it goes a long way towards the truth."[19]

Not only was "synod" used for the gatherings at Jamnia but also for those later at Usha.[20] Evidently not all had been persuaded. While T. K. Cheyne in his article on "Jabneel" in the *Encyclopaedia Biblica* notices that R. Yohanan formed a Sanhedrin at Jamnia,[21] neither he nor C. Warren in the Hastings *Dictionary* takes notice of any discussion of the canon at Jamnia.[22]

2. The Consensus

Based upon these earlier studies, the critical consensus in canon study at mid-century, with some dissenting voices, postulated a collection of Law closed by 400 B.C.E., of

---

[15] Ibid., 183.

[16] Ibid., 184.

[17] Ibid., 210.

[18] K. Budde, "Canon," in *Encyclopaedia Biblica* (London: Adam and Charles Black, 1899), 1:670–71; *Der Kanon des alten Testaments* (Giessen: J. Ricker'sche Verlagsbuchhandlung, 1900), 58–60.

[19] F. H. Woods, "Old Testament Canon," in *A Dictionary of the Bible* (ed. James Hastings; Edinburgh: T&T Clark, 1900), 3:607.

[20] S. Krauss, "Usha, Synod of," *Jewish Encyclopedia*, 11:645–46.

[21] T. K. Cheyne, "Jabneel," *Encyclopaedia Biblica* (London: Adam and Charles Black, 1901), 2:2303.

[22] C. Warren, "Jabneel," *A Dictionary of the Bible* (ed. James Hastings; Edinburgh: T&T Clark, 1899), 2:524–25.

Prophets closed by 200 B.C.E., and of Writings closed at the Council of Jamnia about 90 C.E. The Jamnia theory was affirmed in popular works with varying degrees of dogmatism. Robert Pfeiffer stated, "When the Jewish authorities assembled at Jamnia (*ca.* A.D. 90) defined the canon of Hebrew scriptures, they officially declared, 'The Gospel and the books of the heretics are not sacred Scripture.' "[23] Elsewhere Pfeiffer commented, " . . . the Council of Jamnia (*ca.* A.D. 90), under the leadership of Johanan ben Zakkai, fixed for all times the canon of scriptures."[24] W. O. E. Oesterley suggested that the canon was fixed "in one act, as it were," at Jamnia.[25] O. Eissfeldt spoke of "a synod held in about A.D. 100 in Jamnia (Jabne), some twelve miles south of Jaffa. . . . Now what had come into being as a result of gradual growth was formally declared binding and for this purpose was also undergirded with dogmatic theory."[26] Some extended the action of the Council to cover the exclusion of the apocrypha.[27]

Other students were more restrained than the champions of the consensus. A. Bentzen remarked, "The synod of Jamnia did not define the Canon, but it undertook a *revision*. The Canon in reality was finished before the time of the synod, but perhaps more in the character of a collection grown out of practical use. The synod of rabbis tries to account for the right of the *books* to be parts of the *Book*."[28] H. H. Rowley cautioned, however, "It is, indeed, doubtful how far it is correct to speak of the Council of Jamnia. We know of discussions that took place there amongst the Rabbis, but we know of no formal or binding decisions that were made, and it is probable that the discussions were informal, though none the less helping to crystallize and to fix more firmly the Jewish tradition."[29]

Albert Sundberg, in his very influential monograph on the canon, stated, "About A.D. 90, contemporary with the writing of Josephus, the Jewish canon of Holy Scriptures was closed by the rabbinical schools at Jamnia."[30] Sundberg played down the term "council," admitting that "The term 'Council of Jamnia' is . . . a loose term designating the decisions of the Pharisaic schools that gathered at Jamnia and gained the ascendancy in Judaism following the fall of Jerusalem and the destruction of the temple in A.D. 70."[31] He adds, "It is

---

[23] R. H. Pfeiffer, *Introduction to the Old Testament* (New York/London: Harper & Brothers, 1941), 75.

[24] Ibid., 64; idem, "Canon of the O.T.," *IDB* (New York/Nashville: Abingdon Press, 1962), 1:510.

[25] W. O. E. Oesterley, *An Introduction to the Books of the Apocrypha* (London: SPCK, 1925; repr. 1953), 4; B. W. Anderson, *Understanding the Old Testament* (Englewood Cliffs, N.J.: Prentice-Hall, 1957), 535–36. See also R. Gordis, *Koheleth: The Man and His World* (New York: The Jewish Theological Seminary of America, 1951), 41.

[26] O. Eissfeldt, *The Old Testament: An Introduction* (trans. P. Ackroyd; New York: Harper and Row, 1965), 568.

[27] C. T. Fritsch, "Apocrypha," *IDB* (New York/Nashville: Abingdon, 1962), 1:163; B. M. Metzger, *An Introduction to the Apocrypha* (New York: Oxford University Press, 1957), 8.

[28] A. Bentzen, *Introduction to the Old Testament* (4th ed.; Copenhagen: G. E. C. Gad, 1958), 1:31.

[29] H. H. Rowley, *The Growth of the Old Testament* (London: Hutchinson University Library, 1950; repr., 1960), 170.

[30] Albert C. Sundberg Jr., *The Old Testament of the Early Church* (Harvard Theological Studies 20; Cambridge: Harvard University Press, 1964), 72.

[31] Ibid., 113.

important to note that the actions of the schools of Jamnia were not official decisions."[32] But he also says, "A decision defining the canon in a school would be the act of canonization if commonly received in Judaism."[33] Sundberg assumed that the decisions gained influence and soon became accepted practice within Judaism.[34]

Sundberg bridged the gap between rabbinic sources and Josephus by assuming that the canonical position of the School of Hillel had been developing for some time and had gained some influence in Judaism even before the Jamnia declaration. Thus Josephus, also writing about 90 C.E., and *4 Ezra* slightly later,[35] show acquaintance with the limitation of the number of books and the rabbinic theory of canonization.[36] Sundberg later spoke of the "Jamnia canon," "post-Jamnia Judaism with a defined, closed Pharisaic canon,"[37] and "the Writings (defined as a collection at Jamnia)," and insisted that "in Judaism canonization did not occur until the end of the first century A.D."[38]

The consensus postulated canons of Law and Prophets which could not be traced to a specific date, action, or responsible body; but it felt it had found a date and body responsible for closing the Writings. However, the term "Writings" was not used until long after the proposed date of its closing.[39]

The vividness with which some described the action at Jamnia created the impression that specific ancient texts were being summarized. Walter Harrelson writes:

> In any case, the Jamnia gathering had to exclude much of the available Jewish literature which did not have an established place in the community. . . . The Jamnia convention, then, excluded all books which had no sound claim to antiquity (in their view). They fixed the limits of sacred scripture and declared all the remaining Jewish literature no part of the Holy Book. From this time forward, the canon of the Old Testament was settled for the Jewish community. We should point out, however, that the gathering at Jamnia was not analogous to a church council.[40]

It was customary to make room under the "Jamnia tent" for all books for which rabbinic literature records discussion, disregarding the date of the rabbis who are said to be in the discussion and the date of the preserving record. A further fallacy was the failure to distinguish adequately between the expression of an opinion by an individual rabbi and the announcement of a conciliar decree. A. Bentzen has Ezekiel, Proverbs, the Song of Songs,

---

[32] Ibid., 127.

[33] Ibid., 127 n. 71.

[34] Ibid., 128.

[35] B. M. Metzger dates *4 Ezra* between 100 and 120 C.E.; *The Old Testament Pseudepigrapha* (2 vols.; ed. J. H. Charlesworth; Garden City, N.Y.: Doubleday, 1983), 1:520.

[36] Sundberg, *The Old Testament,* 127.

[37] Albert C. Sundberg, "A Symposium on the Canon of Scripture; 2. The Protestant Old Testament Canon: Should it be Re-examined?" *CBQ* 28 (April 1966): 199, 201.

[38] Albert C. Sundberg, "The Old Testament: A Christian Canon," *CBQ* 30 (April 1968): 147, 148.

[39] Akiba speaks of "for all the Writings are holy" (*m. Yad.* 3:5), but one can argue whether a division of scripture distinct from Law and Prophets is intended, or all scripture. The threefold terminology is used by Gamaliel II as cited in the Talmud, *Sanh.* 90B.

[40] W. Harrelson, *Interpreting the Old Testament* (New York: Holt, Rinehart and Winston, Inc., 1964), 14–15.

Ecclesiastes, Esther, and perhaps Chronicles discussed.[41] G. Fohrer said, "The Canon was therefore completed between 100 B.C. and A.D. 100, and the so-called synod held at Jamnia . . . apparently made some contribution to the process. Later disputes about individual books made no change in the canon."[42]

3. Questioning the Consensus

The mid-twentieth-century consensus seems to have ignored completely the paper of W. M. Christie who, a quarter of a century earlier, found scant evidence for it in a survey of all the relevant rabbinic texts:

> Ben Azzai seems to declare that the canonicity of Canticles and Koheleth was decided in a full Sanhedrin at Jamnia, on the day of the deposition of Rabban Gamaliel, and that is frequently accepted as the date of the formal and authoritative closing of the Old Testament Canon. There is reason for serious doubt on that point. . . . No question of the canon was involved, for there would not be time for discussing it that day. . . . The most that could have reached the ears of Ben Azzai would be some incidental remark. Besides the question was not settled, for the discussions on Esther, Canticles, and Koheleth as between R. Akiba and his companions, as given above, clearly point to a later date, say A.D. 115 and further till the year A.D. 200 the matter was still being discussed.[43]

The present writer, an amateur, unpublished in either rabbinics or canon study, had assumed that such certainty as that represented by the critical consensus must rest on solid evidence. To my surprise, I discovered that the more I examined the relevant sources, the more ephemeral the evidence for such a gathering and for such action became. A consensus had formed by repetition of what was at first a tentative suggestion.

My work on the subject dates to a paper presented before the New Testament section of the Society of Biblical Literature at Union Theological Seminary in New York on December 28, 1962. This work, an appeal for clarity, provoked no questions from the audience. Privately, Henry Cadbury suggested that the paper should have been presented to the Old Testament section of the Society instead of the New. Krister Stendahl asked if the paper was part of a dissertation; it was not. Stendahl, as editor of the *Harvard Theological Review,* rejected the paper for publication. It appeared in the *Journal of Bible and Religion.*[44] Between the reading of this paper and its publication, the Jewish scholar Samuel Sandmel wrote,

> Jamnia and 90 represent a convenience, not an irrefutable conclusion. Many objections to Jamnia and 90 exist. Two are worth noting here. First, disputes over some books are known to have continued beyond 90, so that to speak of a settlement in 90 is an exaggeration. Second, to speak of Jamnia 90 creates the false impression that some convention along modern lines

---

[41] Bentzen, *Introduction,* 29.

[42] G. Fohrer, *Introduction to the Old Testament* (trans. D. E. Green; Nashville: Abingdon Press, 1968), 486.

[43] W. M. Christie, "The Jamnia Period in Jewish History," *JTS* 26 (July 1925): 356.

[44] Jack P. Lewis, "What Do We Mean by Jabneh?" *JBR* 32 (April 1964): 125–32.

was held, with delegates debating over the agenda and the coming to a vote and decision. Canon, however, was a matter of evolution of opinions which converged over a period of decades, 90 being a likely terminal date, but far from a definitive one.[45]

Raymond Brown then noted with regard to my paper that the Jamnia hypothesis "had been subjected to a much-needed criticism." He insightfully observed that the Jamnia gatherings were a school, that no list of books was drawn up, that specific discussion of books is attested only for Ecclesiastes and Song of Songs, that arguments persisted decades after the Jamnia period, and that we have no record of books excluded at Jamnia.[46]

Ten years after the first appearance of my paper, Sid Z. Leiman, who had made his own challenge of the hypothesis in a thesis at the University of Pennsylvania not published until later,[47] reprinted the paper in his book on the canon,[48] and it began to turn up in footnotes. Bit by bit, the consensus began to come apart.

Peter Schäfer, after a detailed consideration of *m. Yad.* 3:5 (whose narrative he considers historical) found the discussion at Jamnia not to be a final closing of the canon for Judaism but only a consideration of Song of Songs and Qoheleth. The discussion was an inner Jewish problem, not a Jewish-Christian one.[49] I. H. Eybers questioned the consensus, projecting instead a *de facto* Old Testament canon prior to Jamnia.[50] Lewis later wrote on the topic for the *Anchor Bible Dictionary.*[51] Günter Stemberger, remarking that a "Synode von Jamnia" is not supported in rabbinic sources and that an exact dating is impossible, pointed out that the Jamnia gathering did not terminate discussion of Qoheleth, Song of Songs, and Esther (*t. Yad.* 2:14). He saw Jamnia as only a step in the process of canonization.[52] J. Blenkinsopp declared the Jamnia hypothesis "a myth of Christian scholarship without documentary foundation."[53]

Robert Newman surveyed assertions about the Council of Jamnia in scholarly works.[54] He summarized the various ancient traditions on different questions connected

---

[45] Samuel Sandmel, *The Hebrew Scriptures* (New York: Knopf, 1963), 14 n. 6.

[46] Raymond E. Brown, in "Canon of the Old Testament," *JBC* (1968), 2:521–22. The article appears with only slight modification in *The New Jerome Bible Commentary* (1990), 1040.

[47] Sid Z. Leiman, *The Canonization of the Hebrew Scripture: The Talmudic and Midrashic Evidence* (Hamden, Conn.: Archon Books, 1976), 120–24.

[48] Sid Z. Leiman, *The Canon and Masorah of the Hebrew Bible* (New York: KTAV Publishing House, 1974), 254–61.

[49] Peter Schäfer, "Die sogenannte Synode von Jabne," *Judaism* 31 (1975): 110–24.

[50] I. H. Eybers, "The 'Canonization' of Song of Solomon, Ecclesiastes and Esther," in *Aspects of the Exegetical Process* (*OTWSA* 20; ed. W. C. van Wyk; Pretoria, South Africa: Dept. of Semitic Languages, University of Pretoria, 1977), 33–52.

[51] Jack P. Lewis, "Jamnia (Jabneh), Council of," *ABD* (1992), 3:634–37. Lewis also read a paper "Jamnia Revisited" at the SBL meeting in Chicago, November 21, 1988, which he did not publish. He further discussed issues in "Some Aspects of the Problem of Inclusion of the Apocrypha," in *The Apocrypha in Ecumenical Perspective* (ed. S. Meurer; New York: United Bible Societies, 1991), 161–207.

[52] Günter Stemberger, "Die sogenannte 'Synode von Jabne,'" *Kairos,* N.F. 19 (1977): 16, 19–21.

[53] J. Blenkinsopp, *Prophecy and Canon* (Notre Dame, Ind./London: University of Notre Dame Press, 1977), 3, 156 n. 3.

[54] Robert C. Newman, "The Council of Jamnia and the Old Testament Canon," *WTJ* 38 (Spring 1979): 319–49.

with Jamnia, including the canon question, and attempted to date the various persons in rabbinic texts who made statements about biblical books. About *M. Yadayim* 3:5 he concluded, "Yet the disagreement among these men on just what was disputed and what was decided in these previous discussions seems to belie any widely-publicized decision. . . . Thus Jamnia saw at least one discussion of canon in the Beth Din and, later, another in the Beth ha-Midrash."[55] Newman then summarized later discussion of Ecclesiastes, and also pointed to a discussion of Esther in the fourth century C.E.[56] He recognized that the texts affirm that books were discussed at Jamnia, but they were also discussed at least once a generation before and several times long after the Jamnia period. He saw the Jamnia rabbis testing a *status quo* which had existed beyond memory. "But no text of any specific decision has come down to us (nor, apparently, even to Akiba and his students)."[57]

Jack N. Lightstone further criticized the "Council of Jamnia theory," suggesting that the sources likely reflect views of the third- and fourth-century Amoraim rather than the actual historical situation of persons cited in the texts.[58]

Roger Beckwith observed that "the theory of the Synod of Jamnia has been thoughtfully sifted by J. P. Lewis, who questions whether it was a synod at all, or merely an academic discussion, and demonstrates that it had only limited influence on later rabbinical opinion."[59] He further declared, "Though others have lately expressed hesitations about the theory, its complete refutation has been the work of J. P. Lewis and S. Z. Leiman."[60] Beckwith noted the question of terminology, the problem of date, the limitation of books discussed, and the fact that discussion went on later.

4. The Sources

Neither Josephus nor ancient Christian literature knows anything of a Council of Jamnia or of a closing of the canon of scripture at its sessions. We are totally dependent on rabbinic sources, with only one early text (*m. Yadayim* 3:5) mentioning a discussion of biblical books there.

M. Yadayim 3:5 is not a contemporary report, nor does it resemble minutes kept at a meeting. It begins by discussing whether a scroll with erased letters, yet still having a minimum of eighty-five letters, renders the hands unclean—that is, still has holiness. The Mishnah affirms that all the holy scriptures render the hands unclean, but does not define their extent. That the Song of Songs and Ecclesiastes have this quality is affirmed without citing supporting authorities. R. Judah affirms that Song of Songs has this quality, but notes that there is dissension about Ecclesiastes. R. Jose claims that Ecclesiastes does not

---

[55] Ibid., 343.

[56] *B. Meg.* 7a.

[57] Newman, "The Council of Jamnia," 349.

[58] Jack N. Lightstone, "The Formation of the Biblical Canon in Judaism of Late Antiquity: Prolegomenon to a General Reassessment," *SR* 8 (1979): 141–42.

[59] Roger Beckwith, *The Old Testament Canon of the New Testament Church* (Grand Rapids: Eerdmans, 1985), 6.

[60] Ibid., 276.

render the hands unclean, but that there is dissension about Song of Songs. To this debate R. Simeon in another text adds that the School of Shammai adopted the more lenient ruling and the School of Hillel the more stringent.[61] R. Simeon b. Azzai claims to have heard a tradition from the seventy-two elders that on the day when they made R. Eliezer b. Azariah head of the college it was asserted that both the Song of Songs and Ecclesiastes render the hands unclean.[62]

In this discussion R. Akiba insisted that no man in Israel ever disputed about the Song of Songs that he should say that it does not render the hands unclean, for all the ages are not worth the day on which the Song of Songs was given to Israel. All the Writings are holy, but the Song of Songs is the Holy of Holies. Akiba affirmed that if aught was in dispute, the dispute was about Ecclesiastes alone. The Mishnah closes with R. Johanan b. Joshua, the son of Akiba's father-in-law, affirming that the scholars debated as Simeon ben Azzai had said and that the decision was as he had reported—-that is, that both Song of Songs and Ecclesiastes render the hands unclean.

A. Books Discussed

The two books that the Mishnah explicitly mentions being discussed at Jamnia are Ecclesiastes and the Song of Songs (*m. Yad.* 3:5). The relevant Mishnah begins with the affirmation that both books defile the hands, but then describes earlier differences of opinion among specific rabbis. According to the Talmud, shortly after 100 B.C.E., long before the time of Jamnia, Simeon ben-Shetach quoted Qoheleth 7:12 as scripture to Alexander Jannaeus.[63] The book was known also to the Qumran sect. The schools of Shammai and of Hillel are said to have differed over it, with the school of Hillel accepting it.[64] The sources do not report their differing over any other book.

But, as reported in the Talmud, Jamnia is by no means the end of the matter. R. Simeon b. Menasia, in the second half of the second century, opposes the accepted view and asserts that Qoheleth is Solomon's wisdom only.[65] The attitude of the sages is reported in Rab's name in the third century.[66] Further doubts are expressed in *Qoheleth Rabbah* 1:3; 11:9; *Vayyiqra Rabbah*, Sec. 23, and *Aboth of R. Nathan* 1. The Mishnah affirms that Song of Songs, another book previously known to the Qumran sect, renders the hands unclean. To this R. Judah concurs, while R. Jose demurs that there is dissension about Song of Songs. Akiba, who defends the Songs of Songs, does not claim to have been present or to have participated in the prior discussion and decision. The Mishnah closes with R. Johanan b. Joshua affirming that the words of Ben Azzai accurately describe the discussion and the decision.

A Tosefta text has Akiba saying that the one who trills his voice in chanting the Song of Songs in the banquet house and makes it a sort of song has no part in the world to

---

[61] *M. ʿEd.* 5:3; *t. ʿEd.* 2:7 [Zuck., 458].
[62] *M. Zebaḥ* 1:3; *m. Yad.* 4:1; *b. Ber.* 28a.
[63] *B. Ber.* 48a.
[64] *M. ʿEd.* 5:3; *m. Yad.* 3:5.
[65] *T. Yad.* 2:14 [Zuck., 683]; *b. Meg.* 7a.
[66] *B. Šabb.* 30b.

come.[67] An anonymous statement has one who pronounces a verse of Song of Songs in a banquet house not in its time brings evil into the world.[68]

B. Other Books Discussed in Rabbinic Sources

In the past, some in the Jamnia consensus tended to assume that all discussion of the place of biblical books in rabbinic sources reflected discussion at the "Council of Jamnia." This tendency is without supporting evidence. Account of discussion of the book of Ezekiel (a book alluded to in Sir 49:8, represented in Qumran fragments, and quoted in Qumran documents) is preserved in the Talmud but not earlier in Tannaitic sources. Some sought to store *(ganaz)* it up because of the conflict of some of its statements with the Law and because of fear that the chariot material would stimulate speculation, a fear increased by the unfortunate experience of the lad reading Ezekiel to whom the rabbi sought to explain the word *hashmal* (NRSV: "gleaming amber"; Ezek 1:4): Fire came from it and burned the lad.[69] The authorities who wanted to store up the book are not named. At this point the sages of the school of Shammai outnumbered the school of Hillel (*m. Shab.* 1:4). Hananiah ben Hezekiah, who was of the School of Shammai in the generation before the fall of Jerusalem, said of the effort to store up *(ganaz)* the book, "If this is wise, then all are sages." Hananiah spent three hundred jars of oil harmonizing the book of Ezekiel with the Pentateuch. Jerome reports that problems about the reading of Ezekiel (though considered canonical) continued unto his own times.[70] The discussion of this book is earlier than any gathering at Jamnia and has no connection with Jamnia.

Despite Brockington's assertion that the book of Esther was considered by the Jamnia scholars[71]—a book not represented in the Qumran scrolls, the New Testament, the list of Melito, of Origen, or of Jerome—there is no supporting evidence that it came to the attention of the Jamnia scholars at a fixed meeting. Early knowledge of Esther is attested by the allusion to the "day before Mordecai's Day" (2 Macc 15:36), the Greek subscript to the book of Esther (which attributes its translation to a man from Jerusalem, Lysimachus, son of Ptolemy, whom some have estimated to have lived 114–115 B.C.E.),[72] and the fact that the book in its Greek form was known to and used by Josephus.[73] The book circulated before the Jamnia period.

There is an entire tractate of the Mishnah (*m. Megilla*) devoted to the book of Esther. A person reading the Law must stand, but the person reading the Scroll of Esther could stand or sit. Where the custom was to say a Benediction (after it) they may say it; where

---

[67] *T. Sanh.* 12:10 [Zuck., 433].

[68] *B. Sanh.* 101a.

[69] *B. Šabb.* 13b; *b. Ḥag.* 13a; *b. Men.* 45a; cf. G. F. Moore, *Judaism in the First Centuries of the Christian Age: The Age of the Tannaim* (Cambridge: Harvard University Press, 1946), 1:247 n. 1.

[70] "The beginning and ending of Ezekiel . . . are involved in so great obscurity, that like the commencement of Genesis they are not studied by the Hebrews until they are thirty years old" (*Epist.* 53:8 [*NPNF*², 6:101]; *PL* 22:547).

[71] L. H. Brockington, *A Critical Introduction to the Apocrypha* (London: Gerald Duckworth & Company, 1961), 135.

[72] L. B. Paton, *The Book of Esther* (ICC; Edinburgh: T&T Clark, 1908), 30.

[73] *A. J.* 11.6.1–13 [184–296].

there is not the custom, they do not say it.[74] The Talmud reports that figures who had been present at Jamnia continued to discuss the book long after the Jamnia period. R. Simeon (ca. 150) asserts that the book of Esther defiles the hands.[75] R. Eliezer, R. Akiba, R. Meir, and R. Jose b. Durmaskith all assert that the book's composition was of the Holy Spirit, and each gives a proof text.[76] No opposition is cited, and no specific day or meeting for the opinions is given. Levi b. Samuel and R. Huna b. Chiyya, while arranging coverings of the books in the house of R. Judah, said, "This is Megillath Esther." Judah did not ask for a covering but said, "This too savors of irreverence *(aphqirotha)*."[77]

In the third century, Rab Judah (250–290 C.E.) in the name of R. Samuel (ca. 254) argues that the book of Esther does not defile the hands (is not canonical), but in apology for his attitude others explain that he meant that the material was intended to be recited by heart and not to be written.[78] On the other hand, in the same century Simeon b. Lachish exalted Esther by affirming that even in the days of the Messiah the scroll of Esther would not pass away.[79] The depiction of Esther, Ahasuerus, and Mordecai in panels of the Dura-Europas synagogue reflects the book's popularity.[80] These texts dealing with the book of Esther tell against the "Council of Jamnia" hypothesis.

One midrash passage listing biblical books speaks of "twelve (minor) prophets, excluding Jonah which is a book by itself."[81] But no authorities, time, or place are indicated. There is no compelling reason for assigning this opinion to a "Council at Jamnia." The term "a book by itself" occurs concerning Num 10:35–36, but no question about that book is raised.[82] Jonah deals with Gentiles, not with Israel.[83] Jon 3:10 is cited in *m. Taan.* 2:1, introduced with *ne'amar.* The book was read in the synagogue on the day of atonement.[84] Similar dating problems affect the midrash where scholars say in the name of Rab (*ca.* 250 C.E.) that Chronicles "was not given except as a Midrash."[85] A late text deals with Proverbs: "At first they suppressed Proverbs, Canticles, and Koheleth because they were mere parables as in Prov. 7:7–20. . . . The men of the Great Synagogue came and interpreted them."[86] In the tradition, the Great Synagogue was a collection of 120 elders who returned from the Exile and succeeded the prophets long before the Jamnia period.[87]

---

[74] *M. Meg.* 4:1.

[75] *B. Meg.* 7a.

[76] *B. Meg.* 7a.

[77] *B. Sanh.* 100a.

[78] *B. Meg.* 7a.

[79] *Y. Meg.* 1:1; 70d; cited in Moore, *Judaism,* 1:245.

[80] M. Avi-Yonah, "Goodenough's Evaluation of the Dura Paintings: A Critique," in *The Dura-Europas Synagogue: A Re-evaluation (1932–1972)* (ed. J. Gutman; Missoula, Mont.: American Academy of Religion, 1973), 123.

[81] *Num. R.* 18:21.

[82] *B. Šabb.* 116a.

[83] The twelve prophets (of which Jonah is one) appear as a unit in Sir 49:10. Jonah fragments in Greek were found at Nahal Ḥever (8ḤevXIIgr ii and iii). Jonah is echoed in the New Testament (Matt 12:39–41; 16:4; Luke 4:29–30), and is summarized by Josephus (*A. J.* 9.10.2).

[84] *B. Meg.* 31a.

[85] *Midr. Vayyik.* 1:3, cited by W. M. Christie, "The Jamnia Period in Jewish History," *JTS* 36 (July 1925): 355.

[86] *Abot R. Nat.* 1; *b. Šabb.* 30b.

[87] *M.'Abot* 1:1.

One Talmud passage cites R. Simeon as saying that Koheleth is of the light things of Bet Shammai but is of the weighty things of Bet Hillel, but Ruth, Canticles, and Esther defile the hands.[88] There is no further discussion of Ruth; its biblical status is not questioned anywhere in talmudic literature.[89] The texts dealing with these books do not support the once common assertion that the canon was fixed "once for all time" or "in one act" at the Council of Jamnia.

5. Terminology

The meanings of *ganaz* ("to store up") and of "defile the hands" are directly relevant to the "Council of Jamnia" question. Long ago Wildeboer pointed out that the books of the apocrypha are never called *sepharim genuzim* ("withdrawn books"). "The words *ganaz* and *ganuz* are used only of some of our well-known canonical books." A Torah scroll which has become dirty is also "hid away."[90] While G. F. Moore argued that *ganaz* did not mean to declare apocryphal,[91] Strack-Billerbeck translated the term in German as "für apokryph erklärt."[92] The consensus operated with a like assumption.

The consensus took the phrase "defile the hands" as the Jewish equivalent of the later Christian term "canonical," which does not itself occur in rabbinic sources.[93] The sources affirm that Ecclesiastes and Song of Songs "defile the hands."[94] A Talmud passage claims the same for Esther.[95] At the same time it is stated about scrolls, "They do not defile the hands unless they are written in Assyrian characters, on parchment, and in ink."[96] A *Jerusalem Talmud* passage asks, "Did they not decree that Scriptural books defile the hands because they are Sacred?"[97] R. Simeon b. Menasia states, "The Song of Songs defiles the hands because it was composed under divine inspiration. Ecclesiastes does not because it is only the wisdom of Solomon."[98] It is also stated that the Gospels and heretical books do not defile the hands.[99] The meaning of this term continues to be discussed.[100]

---

[88] *B. Meg.* 7a.

[89] Leiman, *The Canonization,* 190 n. 504; *Ruth R.* 2:14.

[90] Wildeboer, *The Origin of the Canon,* 92; *m. Šabb.* 16:1.

[91] Moore, *Judaism,* 1:247.

[92] H. L. Strack and P. Billerbeck, *Kommentar zum neuen Testament aus Talmud und Midrasch* (6 vols.; Munich: C. H. Beck, 1929), 4:426.

[93] S. Zeitlin, "An Historical Study of the Canonization of the Hebrew Scriptures," *PAAJR* 3 (1931–1932), 121; repr., *The Canon and Masorah of the Hebrew Bible* (ed. S. Z. Leiman; New York: KTAV, 1974), 164. The contrary view is given by Leiman, *The Canonization,* 113, 119–20.

[94] *M. Yad.* 3:5.

[95] *B. Meg.* 7a.

[96] *M. Yad.* 4:5, 6.

[97] *Y. Soṭah* 2:4, 18a.

[98] *T. Yad.* 2:14 [Zuck., 683].

[99] *T. Yad.* 2:13 [Zuck., 683].

[100] S. Friedman, "The Holy Scriptures Defile the Hands: The Transformation of a Biblical Concept in Rabbinic Theology," in *Biblical and Other Studies Presented to Nahum M. Sarna in Honor of His 70th Birthday* (JSOTSup 154; ed. M. Brettler and M. Fishbane; Sheffield: Sheffield Academic Press, 1993), 115–32; M. J. Broyde, "Defilement of the Hands, Canonization of the Bible, and the Special Status of Esther, Ecclesiastes, and Song of Songs," *Judaism* 44 (Winter 1995): 65–79.

6. Some Observations

Since there is no other ancient text (Christian or Jewish) that connects discussion of biblical books with Yavneh, some observations are in order. First, the texts call Yavneh "a college *(yeshiva)*" or "a gathering" (*m. Yadayim* 3:5), which does not at all suggest a "council." Next, seventy-two elders *(zekenim)* are said to have participated. Ryle's assertion that Gamaliel II presided is doubtful, unless one is willing to argue that the discussion took place before his deposition rather than after it. The preserved traditions concerning R. Gamaliel II reflect nothing of such a question.[101] Gamaliel II is quoted in a Talmud text as having answered the *minim's* question about where the resurrection was taught, "It is said in the Law, Prophets and Writings."[102] Whether he actually said it can neither be proved nor disproved. Whether he made the statement before or after the day of his deposition from headship of the academy is unknown. He does not define the content of any of the three categories. In Jewish sources one does not have a listing of books before *B. Baba Bathra* 14b–15a. This use of "Writings" *(kethubim)* in this context presupposed the formation of a corpus of that name. Whether Gamaliel thought of it as closed cannot be known.

Furthermore, *m. Yadayim* 3:5 represents Akiba as a later commentator on what happened, not as one of the seventy-two elders themselves or even as having been present at Yavneh. Firsthand knowledge is not claimed for him.

There seems to be no basis for Pfeiffer's attributing leadership in the matter to Johanan ben Zakkai. R. Gamaliel II had succeeded Johanan as leader, and the text speaks of the deposition of R. Gamaliel in favor of R. Eleazar b. Azariah on the day *m. Yadayim* reports discussion of Qoheleth and Song of Songs. The ancient texts do not attribute participation by Johanan's five disciples (R. Eliezer ben Hyrcanus, R. Joshua ben Hanania, R. Jose the priest, R. Simeon ben Nathaniel, and R. Eleazar ben Arakh) in discussion of books being in the canon. No ancient text specifically links Johanan to discussion of the canon.

No ancient text suggests a discussion or an exclusion of the apocrypha from the canon at Yavneh. While it is true that Akiba said that the one who reads "outside books" has no share in the world to come,[103] no time, place, or gathering is given for the statement. The books of the apocrypha, other than Sirach (Ecclesiasticus),[104] are not mentioned in rabbinic literature. Sirach is quoted three times as scripture.[105] The finding of the Qumran scrolls revealed a Judaism that copied and possessed books outside the twenty-two. Solomon Schechter identified a fragment of Sirach from the Cairo

---

[101] See the study of Shamai Kanter, *Rabban Gamaliel II: The Legal Traditions* (Brown Judaic Studies 8; Chico, Calif.: Scholars, 1980).

[102] *B. Sanh.* 90b. If the statement is genuine and is before the deposition of Gamaliel II, then there is a threefold canon before that even discussed in *m. Yadayim* 3:5. R. T. Herford (*Christianity in Talmud and Midrash* [London: Williams and Norgate, 1903; repr., Clifton, N.J.: Reference Book Publishers, 1966], 231–32) conjectured that the conversation took place in Rome about 95 C.E.

[103] *M. Sanh.* 10:1.

[104] *T. Yad.* 2:13 [Zuck., 683]; *b. Sanh.* 100b.

[105] *B. Ḥag.* 13a; *b. Yeb.* 63b; *B. Qam.* 92b.

Geniza.[106] Some fragments were found at Qumran,[107] and Y. Yadin found another at Masada,[108] but none of these discoveries establishes a discussion of such books at Yavneh.

D. E. Aune has shown that Spinoza in 1670 hypothesized the selection of sacred books by a "concilium Pharisaiorum" of the Second Temple period without assigning a time or place for the act. Spinoza did not mention Jamnia. Whether Graetz borrowed the idea of a synod from Spinoza cannot be known. Aune affirms, "There can be little doubt, however, that Spinoza, and Graetz after him, conceptualized the process whereby Judaism achieved a final definition of the extent of the Hebrew Scriptures based on the conciliar process used by the Christian Church to decide the extent of the Old and New Testament canon."[109] While not knowing in 1962 of Spinoza's use of "concilium" or of Graetz's use of "Synodal," which Aune has pointed out,[110] I still see my proposal of terminology as valid:

> In the sources the terms *beth din,*[111] *methivta,*[112] *yeshiva,*[113] and *beth ha-midrash*[114] are used to designate the meetings in addition to the phrase already noticed, "In the vineyards of Jabneh."[115] In discussions of the Jabneh gatherings where the canon is not concerned, these terms are commonly translated "academy," "court," or "school." When, however, canon is under consideration, the group suddenly becomes a "council" or "synod." Though these are legitimate renderings of these terms, sixteen hundred years of ecclesiastical usage and twenty-one ecumenical councils have given these latter words connotations of officially assembled authoritative bodies of delegates which rule and settle questions. These titles are not appropriate for Judaism. One's mind immediately thinks of gatherings like Nicea, Hippo, or Trent. It is a fallacy to superimpose such Christian concepts upon Judaism. It is proposed that the terms "court," "school," or "assembly" would more nearly convey the true nature of the body at Jabneh than would terms like "council" or "synod."[116]

7. Current Status

In the last forty years the "place" of the close of the canon has given way to "the venue" of the close. Much has happened in the meantime. In particular, the publishing of the Qumran scrolls has made known what books circulated in that community.

---

[106] Paul E. Kahle, *The Cairo Geniza* (2d ed.; Oxford: Basil Blackwell, 1959), 9.

[107] 2QSir and 11QPs^a.

[108] Y. Yadin, *The Ben Sira Scroll from Masada* (Jerusalem: Israel Exploration Fund, 1965); Pancratius C. Beentjes, *The Book of Ben Sira in Hebrew* (Leiden: E. J. Brill, 1997).

[109] D. E. Aune, "On the Origins of the 'Council of Javneh' Myth," *JBL* 110 (Fall 1991): 491–92.

[110] Ibid., 492.

[111] *T. Ber.* 2:6 [Zuck., 4]; *m. Roš Haš.* 4:1–2; *m. Sanh.* 11:4.

[112] *B. Ber.* 28a; see S. B. Hoenig, *The Great Sanhedrin* (Philadelphia: Dropsie College, 1953), 292 n. 4.

[113] *M. Zebah.* 1:3; *m. Yad.* 3:5; 4:2; *y. Ber.* 4:1, 7d; Hoenig, *The Great Sanhedrin,* 292 n. 5.

[114] *B. Ber.* 28a.

[115] *M. 'Ed.* 2:4; *m. Ketub.* 4:6.

[116] Lewis, "What Do We Mean by Jabneh?" 127–28.

Ruth,[117] Chronicles,[118] Proverbs,[119] Qoheleth,[120] Song of Songs,[121] Ezekiel,[122] Jonah,[123] and Daniel[124] are all attested at Qumran.

The studies of J. Neusner and his students have made more accessible to the nonspecialist the detailed concerns of the Yavneh scholars without turning up any new texts relevant to canon discussion. *M. Yadayim* 3:5 remains the only text dating within a hundred years of Jamnia which speaks of discussion of biblical books. The Talmud texts preserve traditions, but date more than three centuries after the events.

The "Council of Jamnia" hypothesis has from the start had difficulty accounting for Josephus. He knows nothing of such a gathering, and he had been in Rome approximately twenty years when, about 90 C.E., he writes of the Jews' twenty-two sacred books "justly accredited," claiming antiquity for this position. "For, although such long ages have now passed, no one has ventured either to add, or to remove, or to alter a syllable; and it is an instinct with every Jew, from the day of his birth, to regard them as decrees of God, to abide by them, and, if need be, cheerfully to die for them."[125] Thackeray grants that Josephus, claiming to be a Pharisee, was representing a Pharisaic viewpoint and implies that the canon had long been closed.[126] Sundberg insists, however, that Josephus was simply in error.[127]

As prestigious a work as the *Cambridge History of Judaism* was, without giving detailed evidence, still affirming in 1989 that the Synod of Jamnia carried out a purge of scripture and that Ecclesiasticus was excluded by that gathering.[128] It also stated that the acceptance of Chronicles into the canon was delayed until the Synod of Jamnia.[129] The *Anchor Bible* volume on Song of Songs was written at the height of the "Council of Jamnia" myth and uses the term "council," while stating that the issue was not whether the book was included in the canon, but whether it should be.[130] The volume on Ecclesiastes, published later, differs markedly.[131]

---

[117] 2QRuth[a]; 2QRuth[b].

[118] Cited in 4QFlor.

[119] 4QProv[a]; citation in *CD* XI, 20–21.

[120] 4QQoh[a].

[121] 6QCant.

[122] 1QEzek; 3QEzek; 4QEzek[a]; 4QEzek[b]; 11QEzek. Citations are in *CD* III, 20–42; XIX, 11–12.

[123] 4QXII[f]; 8HevXII gr ii; 8HevXII gr iii. MurXII is later than any Jamnia discussion.

[124] 1QDan[a]; 1QDan[b]; 4QDan[a]; 4QDan[b]; 4QDan[c]; 6QDan. Citation of 11:13–16; 12:10 is in 4QFlor.

[125] *C. Ap.* 1:8 [42].

[126] H. St. John Thackeray, *Josephus, The Man and the Historian* (New York: Jewish Institute of Religion Press, 1929), 79.

[127] Albert C. Sundberg Jr., " 'The Old Testament of the Early Church' Revisited," in *Festschrift in Honor of Charles Speel* (ed. T. J. Sienkewicz and J. E. Betts; Monmouth, Ill.: Monmouth College, 1996), 98.

[128] M. Delcor, "The Apocrypha and Pseudepigrapha of the Hellenistic Period," in *The Cambridge History of Judaism* (ed. W. D. Davies: Cambridge: Cambridge University Press, 1989), 2:416, 421.

[129] M. Delcor, "Jewish Literature in Hebrew and Aramaic in the Greek Era," in *The Cambridge History of Judaism* (ed. W. D. Davies: Cambridge: Cambridge University Press, 1989), 2:369.

[130] M. H. Pope, *Song of Songs* (AB 7C; Garden City, New York: Doubleday 1977), 19.

[131] C. L. Seow, *Ecclesiastes* (AB 18C; New York: Doubleday, 1997), 3–4.

James Sanders saw the closing of the Writings at Yavneh to be a consequence of the destruction of the temple:

> And despite the fact that we do not inherit from antiquity the agenda or minutes, there is strong evidence that the responsible Jews who survived the tragedy met not long thereafter in a Palestinian town called Jabneh or Jamnia, to face up to the existential question which had to be answered. The date traditionally assigned to the meeting is A.D. 90–100. It may have been earlier. . . . What of all the various writings from the later period of old Israel and the long stretch of early (pre-70) Judaism should be considered canonical, or, as they put it, "soiled the hands" (because of its tabu or sacred nature)? And thus did the third section of the Hebrew scriptures take shape, the Writings.[132]

Sanders later cautioned:

> It is prudent to be careful in speaking of the assemblies at Jamnia between 70 and 100 C.E. since a recent review of the literary evidence concerning those meetings indicates that the early biblical critics since Johannes Salomo Semler had gone beyond what the evidence indicates. We especially should not speak of a Council of Jamnia as introductions and handbooks on the O.T. still do. The early critics apparently read into the rabbinic evidence there is about Jamnia too much, in thinking of it in conciliar terms.[133]

Three years later, Sanders declared, "We now know that the Jabneh mentality cannot dominate the way we must now think about the canonical process up to the first centuries B.C.E. and C.E." But he also wrote:

> Despite the apparent lack of clear reference to Jabneh, there is abundant indirect evidence for the convening, at the end of the first century C.E., of a group of rabbis who felt constrained by the compelling events of the day, largely the threat of disintegration due to the loss of Jerusalem and her religious symbols, to make decisions regarding the contents of the Hagiographa. . . . The effectiveness of the conciliar decisions at Jabneh (or what we extrapolate from the plethora of evidence for a Jabneh council) points as does very little else to the enormity of the fall of Jerusalem in 69 C.E.[134]

Frank M. Cross designates the Council of Jamnia "a common and somewhat misleading designation of a particular session of the rabbinic academy (or court) at Yabneh." He adds, "Recent sifting of the rabbinic evidence makes clear that in the proceedings at the academy of Yabneh the Rabbis did *not* fix the canon, but at most discussed marginal books, notably Ecclesiastes (Qohelet) and the Song of Songs. . . . Moreover, it must be insisted that the proceedings at Yabneh were not a 'council,' certainly not in the late

---

[132] James A. Sanders, *Torah and Canon* (Philadelphia: Fortress, 1972), 94–95; cf. his "Adaptable For Life: The Nature and Function of Canon," in *Magnalia Dei: The Mighty Acts of God* (ed. F. M. Cross, W. E. Lemki, and P. D. Miller Jr.; Garden City: Doubleday, 1976), 532–33.

[133] James A. Sanders, *Canon and Community* (Philadelphia: Fortress, 1984), 10–11.

[134] James A. Sanders, *From Sacred Story to Sacred Text* (Philadelphia: Fortress, 1987), 12–13. Sanders further evaluates the Jamnia theory in his recent papers: " 'Spinning' the Bible," *Bible Review* 14 (June 1998): 29; "The Scrolls and the Canonical Process," in *The Dead Sea Scrolls after Fifty Years* (ed. P. E. Flint and J. C. VanderKam; Leiden: Brill, 1999), 7; and "Intertextuality and Canon," in *On the Way to Nineveh: Studies in Honor of George M. Landes* (ASOR Books vol. 4; ed. S. L. Cook and S. C. Winter; Atlanta: Scholars, 1999), 317.

ecclesiastical sense."[135] Cross sees Josephus, independent of any Jamnia proceedings, reflecting "a clear and coherent theological doctrine of canon that must stem, we believe, from canonical doctrine of Hillel and his school."[136]

Albert Sundberg recognizes that the "Council of Jamnia" hypothesis is dead.[137] At the same time, still contending that the Hebrew tripartite canon was probably fixed between 70 and 135 C.E., he suggests that my own view of the hypothesis may have been too quickly accepted. He asks, "What alternatives are there to Jamnia as the venue?"[138] Lee McDonald summarizes the case, "There is evidence that a discussion was held at Jamnia on the canonical status of Ecclesiastes and the Song of Songs, but this is not enough to suggest that any binding or official decisions were made regarding the scope of the biblical canon at Jamnia."[139]

---

[135] F. M. Cross, "The Text Behind the Text of the Hebrew Bible," in *Understanding the Dead Sea Scrolls* (ed. Hershel Shanks: New York: Random House, 1992), 152–53.

[136] Ibid., 153–54.

[137] Sundberg, " 'The Old Testament of the Early Church' Revisited," 100.

[138] Ibid., 103.

[139] Lee M. McDonald, *The Formation of the Christian Biblical Canon* (rev. and enl. ed.; Peabody, Mass.: Hendrickson, 1995), 49. Also rejecting the "Council of Jamnia" hypothesis are D. Barthélemy ("L'Etat de la Bible juive depuis le début de notre ère jusqu'à la deuxième révolte contre Rome [131–135]," in *Le canon de l'Ancien Testament: Sa formation et son histoire* [ed. Jean-Daniel Kaestli and Otto Wermelinger; Geneva: Labor et Fides, 1984], 25–30), S. Talmon ("Heiliges Schrifttum und kanonische Bücher aus jüdischer Sicht: Überlegungen zur Ausbildung der Grösse 'Die Schrift' in Judentum," in *Mitte der Schrift?* [ed. M. Klopfenstein; Bern: Peter Lang, 1987], 69–79), G. Maier ("Der Abschluss des jüdischen Kanons und das Lehrhaus von Jabne," in *Der Kanon der Bibel* [ed. G. Maier; Giessen/Basel: Brunnen Verlag, 1990], 1–3), A. van der Kooij ("The Canonization of Ancient Books Kept in the Temple of Jerusalem," in *Canonization and Decanonization* [eds. A. van der Kooij and K. van der Toorn; Leiden: Brill, 1998], 17), and Z. Zevit ("The Second-Third Century Canonization of the Hebrew Bible and Its Influence on Christian Canonizing," in *Canonization and Decanonization* [eds. A. van der Kooij and K. van der Toorn; Leiden: Brill, 1998], 139–40).

10

The Rabbis' Bible: The Canon of the Hebrew Bible and the Early Rabbinic Guild

Jack N. Lightstone

This chapter deals with the (alleged) "fixing" of the biblical canon of scriptures of rabbinic Judaism by "the rabbis" sometime in the first several centuries C.E. By "fixing" one usually means the authoritative, normative determination of the inner structure of the scriptural collection as well as the specification of what documents are included or excluded.

This subject has a long history in modern scholarship. Over the course of much of the nineteenth and twentieth centuries, scholars within the Christian and Judaic communities have dealt with the question of when and how the "rabbinic" collection of biblical scriptures assumed their "final," "fixed" form. Indeed, the question of what precisely constituted the Jewish biblical scriptures was important to early Christian communities in their struggle for legitimacy within the Roman world, since many Christians claimed to have succeeded Judaism. The question also bore upon quarrels and competition among different Christian communities throughout the church's history. The evidence for similar controversies within and among Judaic communities from antiquity through the medieval period is more difficult to interpret. That such controversies existed is undeniable.

In modern times, there has been an inevitable interplay between religiously interested and secular scholarship, for much is felt to be at stake on both sides. For the former, matters of religious authority, authenticity, and the legitimacy of sacred texts and traditions are at stake. For the latter, issues of the validity of evidence and methodological self-consciousness, free from premises dictated by religious authority, come to the fore. Not a few scholars in the modern period have had a foot in both camps. Consequently, assumptions about the validity of the evidence are not as easily separated from convictions about the authenticity of the ancient witnesses from which the evidence comes. When assumptions or convictions are informed, self-consciously or not, by *religious* commitment, whether traditional or liberal, the dangers of circular or tautological reasoning mount.

1. The Context of the Discussion

It is because of the foregoing that this chapter attempts carefully to contextualize and situate the topic at hand before plunging headlong into the assigned subject matter, namely, the ancient rabbis' role in "fixing" the biblical scriptures of Judaism. I suggest that the following elements are critical to situating the chapter's principal subject matter.

1. The assigned topic is replete with inherent assumptions; these need to be spelled out and (re-)considered.

2. Many readers of this book will need some brief introduction to the early rabbinic movement and guild (from the second through early seventh centuries C.E.). Many students of biblical literature are far more familiar with Ancient Judaism than with the Judaisms of the second century onward.

3. The establishment or promulgation of the rabbinic biblical canon in Judaism has a history in early medieval times subsequent to, and as result of, events in the rabbinic period. Moreover, the emergence of a Judaic canon of scriptures began well before the activities of the rabbis in the second and subsequent centuries C.E. As the early rabbis themselves claim, the phenomenon necessarily has important roots in antiquity. These provide an inescapable backdrop for what may have transpired in the rabbinic era. Hence, scholars must consider what precisely the rabbinic guild in the second and several subsequent centuries actually effected, and what margins of manoeuverability they had in setting the canon of Hebrew scriptures. Therefore, any discussion of the pertinent evidence from the rabbinic period will have to be framed by the "before" and the "after." This chapter tries briefly to describe these two historical bookends—to assume, as it were, a wider angle of vision—before focusing upon the early rabbinic period.

4. This leads us to the far more problematic and difficult middle period, the early rabbinic era. As we approach this, our principal subject matter, we shall distinguish worthwhile questions from fruitless ones. Much good scholarship has already shown the futility of certain queries, given the evidence at hand.

Let me forewarn the reader where we shall end up, for it is not where one might have expected or wanted. Simply put, we have not sufficient, reliable evidence to determine with any precision or confidence the "how," "when," "where," "who," or "why" of the "fixing" of the rabbis' Bible. On the matter at hand, the rabbinic guild from the second through early seventh centuries C.E. is somewhat of a "black box"—or at least an opaque one. We know what appears at the output end of the box, that is, in the Middle Ages, in Judaic communities under rabbinic authority. We also see hints that conflict about the shape of the Jewish canon of biblical scriptures continued outside and alongside our box. But to a large extent this evidence comes indirectly, from intra-Christian controversy about what constituted the Judaic Bible and, thus, the Christian Old Testament.

As to the input end of the box, there is much evidence at hand. However, it shows that while (1) some matters with respect to the Judaic collection of biblical scriptures were already the objects of firm consensus among the Judaic communities of antiquity, and (2) the notion of a biblical canon with a delimited number of constituent "books" (twenty-two or twenty-four) was accepted by at least some Judaic communities, nevertheless, a degree of fluidity or controversy about the shape and content of the biblical canon existed among the Judaic communities. The ultimate "triumph" of the rabbinic movement in the seventh and subsequent centuries C.E. brought this to an end. Hence, we can estimate what *"marges de manoeuvre"* did and did not exist for any Judaic community or group, including the early rabbis, in the second century C.E. But let us be careful; the preceding claim does not mean that any one Judaic community, including the rabbis, *believed* or *admitted* that they had any *"marges de manoeuvre."* Any one group may have taken the stance that what they had inherited was immutable. The fact that some other Judaic group's canon of biblical scriptures differed from their own may have been read as indication that the other group was, in this particular regard, misguided (or heretical). It is less likely that another community's differing scriptural collection would have been interpreted as indicating a continuing degree of flexibility regarding the canon.

Consequently, to return to the black or opaque box of the early rabbinic guild, our evidence is insufficient to determine whether they believed they were fixing what was still fluid, reaffirming and promulgating intact what they had inherited, or something in between. Indeed, to complicate matters more, it is a widespread tendency of religious communities to claim (and to believe) that they are doing the latter, even when they are engaged in the former.

Thus our conclusions will have more to do with the significance and meaning of the shape of the rabbis' Bible (as it emerged from the box) in light of how the rabbis constructed and imagined other aspects of their "world." We will demonstrate the tight "fit" between the rabbis' biblical canon and these other aspects.

2. Questioning Assumptions

The topic itself assumes much. It assumes a significant degree of particularity about the rabbis' canon versus others who laid claim to the same biblical tradition. The "others" would include non-rabbinic Jews. For many scholars of Christianity, "others" comprise especially the primitive, patristic churches and those forms of early Judaism from which early Christianity arose. Certainly the medieval Old Testament canons of the Roman Catholic and Eastern Orthodox churches differ in substantial ways from the Hebrew Bible of medieval rabbinic Judaism, and not just in language.

The second major assumption inherent in the chapter's topic is that specific action by "the rabbis" is largely responsible for the particularity of the canon of the Hebrew Bible. That is to say, the rabbis "fixed" something which was, as yet, not set, or changed what had been the case, or defined as appropriate one canon from among a host of alternatives. Be it one or the other, the early rabbinic guild of the second through sixth centuries C.E., it is assumed, effected something significant in establishing their canon of the Hebrew Bible.

For over a century both these assumptions—that the rabbis undertook significant action to define a particular and distinctive canon—were accepted as fact by most modern scholars. As regards the canonizing activity of the early rabbis, scholars believed that they had identified the very time, place, and persons responsible, as well as the substance of their decisions. Until early 1970s, it had become accepted fact that a rabbinic "council" met at Yavneh (Jamnia) in southwestern Roman Palestine about 90 C.E. under the leadership of Rabbi Eleazar ben Azariah, while Rabban Gamaliel II was temporarily deposed as the head of the (national) council (sic!), comprising, of course, rabbinic sages. Concerning the other assumption, scholars claimed that the emerging "sectarian" biblical canons—the sacred literature of the Essenes or Qumran covenanters, of the early church (with its Gospels and other texts), and, most important, of an "accommodationist" Hellenistic Judaism allegedly "headquartered" in Alexandria—provided the rabbis with points of comparison for, and indeed the impetus to produce, their particular canon.

For many scholars today, this edifice of alleged certainties has been demolished. Notable members of the demolition team included S. Z. Leiman, A. C. Sundberg, and more recently, R. T. Beckwith. Some attempts were made to build anew.[1] But I am no more convinced of the validity of any new edifice proposed so far, than of the older, now largely abandoned, one. My own reasons for opting for scholarly discretion (or outright avoidance) over valor on these specific questions were already detailed over twenty years ago.[2] At that time I pointed out a number of crucial conceptual and methodological flaws which pervaded the scholarly assessment and interpretation of extant, allegedly relevant, evidence. I need but summarize the principal points of the article at this juncture, and refer the reader to the complete text for a more comprehensive treatment:

(a) Scholars (including Leiman) wrongly presume that the tripartite Jewish canon (Torah, Prophets, and Hagiographa) developed in linear fashion, with each part being, for the most part irrevocably, "closed" in succession. Such historical "mono-linearity" is highly unlikely.

(b) Closely related to the first, scholars (again Leiman among them) seem to assume that once a book was generally recognized as edifying it was immediately and spontaneously a candidate for inclusion in that part of the tripartite canon which was not yet "closed." As a corollary, if such a book was not included in, let us say, part two of the canon (the Prophets), but came to be included in part three (the Hagiographa), then part two of the canon must have already been "closed" when the book in question was first promulgated. Both the first assumption and its corollary are false, by reason of both faulty logic and contrary evidence.

(c) In a related vein, Leiman and others assume that when such a book which is not obviously sectarian in origin comes to be included in one community's canon but not in another's, it is because the latter community knew the work in question but specifically rejected it. This assumption too is false by reason of logic and contrary evidence. Therefore, one may safely claim that a community rejected a book from its canon, only after one has convincingly argued that the book was well known to that community.

(d) Again related to the foregoing—scholars such as Leiman hold too strong a notion of a dominant normative Judaism in both prerabbinic and rabbinic times. This overstatement of normative Judaism in fact underlies the first three faulty assumptions. The existence of many normative elements common to most Jews in Hellenistic and Roman times, which can be demonstrated on evidentiary grounds and which I will talk about later in this chapter, does

---

[1] The more definitive works in this regard are still S. Z. Leiman, *The Canonization of the Hebrew Scriptures: The Talmudic and Midrashic Evidence* (Hamden, Conn.: Archon, 1976); A. C. Sundberg, *The Old Testament of the Early Church* (Cambridge, Mass.: Harvard University Press; London: Oxford, 1964); and more recently, R. T. Beckwith, "Formation of the Hebrew Bible," and E. E. Ellis, "The Old Testament Canon in the Early Church," both in *Mikra: Text Translation, Reading and Interpretation of the Hebrew Bible in Ancient and Early Christianity* (CRINT 2.1; ed. M. J. Mulder and H. Sysling; Assen/Maastricht: Van Gorcum and Philadelphia, Pa.: Fortress, 1988), 39–86 and 653–90 respectively. On our specific topic, Beckwith provides a concise and up-to-date tally of the relevant evidence.

[2] J. Lightstone, "The Formation of the Biblical Canon in Judaism of Late Antiquity: Prolegomenon to a General Reassessment," *Studies in Religion/Sciences religieuses* 8/2 (1979): 135–42.

not bespeak an institutionalized and organized normative Judaism (sectarians excepted). Indeed, much evidence suggests the reverse.

When I wrote that article, I did not speculate as to why these (in my view) false assumptions came to confound methodological and conceptual approaches to the study of the rabbinic canon. Nevertheless, I believed that the assumptions stemmed from some theological bias about which the scholars were insufficiently aware. Today, that explanation seems to me to be overly naive. We all have biases, some of which we come to recognize, others which we do not. But the recognition of such biases has as much to do with the quality and specificity of the evidence as with a priori commitments. Simply put, the weight of abundant and good evidence to the contrary is an important impetus to recognize and correct one's biases. When the evidence is incomplete, episodic, ambiguous, and indirect, it is all too easy and tempting to fit the evidence into some preconceived framework. Therefore, the root cause of scholarly misstepping regarding the subject of this chapter rests ultimately on the poverty of the evidence. There is simply no rabbinic evidence of the same reliability and specificity as that which exists for the early churches' establishment of their versions of the "Old Testament" canon.

Consequently, I herein attempt no alternative reconstruction of *precisely* how and when the rabbis' Bible came to be. Based on the evidence at hand, they may have done very little, because a fairly normative definition of the Judaic biblical canon of scriptures already obtained in Palestine before the advent of the rabbis. Or they may have done a great deal, because much was still a matter of dispute, or because the rabbis disagreed with what had already emerged as a dominant Judaic canon before the onset of the second century C.E. But now I am ahead of myself. At this point, I merely stress that understanding what we cannot know, and why we cannot know it, is a necessary prelude to discussing what we can know. Useful queries are those which will not frustrate our capacity to answer them because of the limitations of the evidence.

3. The Modern Scholarly Discovery of Rabbinic Judaism and the Rise and Triumph of the Rabbinic Guild

As already intimated, the official collection, the canon, of biblical scriptures in use in almost all Jewish communities from the high Middle Ages until today is the Hebrew Bible authorized by "the rabbis"—the Bible of "rabbinic Judaism." But what do we mean by "rabbinic Judaism," and how did "the rabbis" come to exercise authority over the shape of the canon?

A. Rabbinic Judaism

"Rabbinic Judaism" refers to all forms of Judaism which find their origins in the teachings, literature, and the claims to divinely sanctioned authority of a late antique *professional guild* of "masters" who addressed one another by the honorific "rabbi" (*rbby* = my master). By reason of their claim to mastery over a divinely sanctioned body of knowledge, and by their alliance to other traditional and emerging authoritative institutions, these "rabbis" came to function as teachers, court officials, and bureaucrats within the organized (sometimes semi-autonomous and self-administering) Jewish communities. This occurred, first, in Roman and Byzantine Palestine and environs in the second through fifth century C.E., second, in Sassanid-Persian Mesopotamia and Iran in the third through early seventh century C.E. and, finally, in all the lands of the Mediterranean basin and Europe in the Middle Ages. Almost all forms of Judaism for nearly the last millennium and a half are developments, reformations, or, in some cases, repudiations of that form of Judaism developed, promulgated, and enforced by the rabbinic guild of masters that had formed sometime in the last half of the second century C.E.

Back at the beginning of the nineteenth century, the designation "the rabbis" or "our rabbis" would have made sense to Christians and Jews, lay persons and scholars. The term "rabbinic Judaism" would have had less clarity. The religiously sanctioned way of life over which the rabbis exercised their mastery was simply "Judaism." A century and half of modern Judaic scholarship has taught both scholars of Christianity and of religion, on the one hand, and a goodly proportion of the lay Jewish community (particularly in North America), on the other, to refer to all of these developments and reformations from the late-Roman imperial period to the dawn of the twenty-first century by the rather differentiating *and* unifying term "rabbinic Judaism."

That is not to say that modern scholars of the history of Judaism do not see differentiation, change, schism, discontinuities, and accommodations, over the course of this millennium and a half. Quite the contrary. The invention of "rabbinic Judaism" by modern scholars was meant to telegraph two important claims particularly to Christian scholars, on the one hand, and to the increasingly secularized and "modernized" Jewish community, on the other. The two claims are corollaries. First, the development of Judaism(s) did not end or go into some arrested state following the destruction of the Second Jewish Commonwealth in the Land of Israel, or the advent of Christianity in the Middle East and the Mediterranean basin. Second, something very new and eventually cogent and successful, sociologically and historically, developed within and around that guild of Judaic virtuosi/literati/bureaucrats who called one another, and would have others come to call them, "my master" (rabbi).

To be sure, these claims served, and continue to serve, apologetic purposes, again twofold. First, modern scholars of Judaism proffered these claims to legitimate contemporary Jews' aspirations to social, religious, and legal acceptance within the largely Christian societies of Europe and North America. Jews thereby sought to rehabilitate early, medieval, and early modern Christianity's image of the Jew and of Judaism as the fossilized and degenerate remains of the nation and religion of the "Old" Testament, in contrast to Christianity as its true, living development. The history of rabbinic Judaism—equally alive, equally vibrant with change and development—was contemporaneous with, and parallel to, the history of Christianity. Rabbinic Judaism too was a postbiblical (that is, post–Old Testament) religion and cultural system.

The second apologetic purpose served by these claims concerned struggles within the Jewish communities themselves in nineteenth- and twentieth-century Europe and America. These relate to the disputes between traditionalists and liberals of various stripes along what was becoming an ever wider continuum of views concerning accommodation to, and living as Jewish "co-citizens" within, modern societies (largely Christian, but increasingly secular). Until the 1960s, modern scholars of Judaism, particularly in Europe and North America, overwhelmingly identified with liberalizing movements in Judaism, and were often leaders of such movements. These movements included the Liberal and Reform movements in Europe and England, and the Conservative, Reconstructionist, and Reform movements in North America. The nomenclature "rabbinic Judaism," a scholarly invention, concretized in everyday language the radical transformations effected by the early rabbinic guild of masters following the dissolution of their "traditional" society at the end of the first and beginning of the second centuries C.E. If "the rabbis" of late antiquity could be remembered as having saved, not destroyed, Judaism by effecting radical changes, then so too could the liberalizing Judaic movements of the nineteenth and twentieth centuries.

Alas, as is the case with so many apologetics, these claims primarily convinced the already "converted." On the one hand, Jewish Orthodoxy of the right wing remain unconvinced, and in some ways they are more influential today than they were fifty years ago. On the other hand, nearly a century of the systematic promulgation of anti-Judaic and anti-Semitic views, in secularized versions detached from earlier Christian anti-Judaism, led to the almost total destruction of European Jewish society in World War II. This hundred–year sowing of the fields which produced the Holocaust coincides almost exactly with the rapid rise and flowering of the modern scholarly "discovery" and study of "rabbinic Judaism."

But for the "convinced" in both the Jewish and non-Jewish communities, the new-found ability to differentiate clearly early rabbinic Judaism and/or the early rabbinic movement of the second and third centuries C.E. from that which preceded—and in particular from the communities and literatures of the so-called Old Testament and Inter-Testamental periods, to use the terms of Protestant biblical scholarship—produced entirely new bases for "categorizing" evidence for analysis and study, both in the seminary and in the university. And it is the placement of things in different categories which is the conceptual requisite of comparison, study, and analysis. This new categorization allows one to differentiate an early "rabbinic" Judaism from a "biblical" Judaism (about which we shall speak in section 5).

B. The Entrenchment of the Authority of the Rabbinic Guild

Let us now consider how "the rabbis" came to exercise authority over the shape of the canon. By the time of the Muslim conquest of the Persian Empire in the mid-seventh century C.E., the rabbinic movement had firm authority over the religious, civil, and commercial law (the *halakah*, "the way") of the Near Eastern Jewish communities. The shape and content of the Hebrew Bible was as much a matter of *halakah* as any other aspect of Jewish communal and personal life.

Sociologically and historically, the rabbis came to exercise this authority over the *halakah* by virtue of their positions on local community courts in Late Roman and Byzantine Palestine and in Persian Babylonia before and after the Muslim conquest. In addition, rabbis held posts within the trans-local bureaucracies of the Jewish Exilarch's administration in the Persian Empire from the late third until the mid-sixth century (when the powers of the Exilarchate were curtailed), and of the Jewish Patriarch's "government" in Roman Palestine in Southern Syria from the end of the second until the first quarter of the fifth century (at which time Rome abolished the Patriarchate).[3] In the first several centuries after the Muslim conquest, and largely in tandem with it, rabbinic authority spread throughout the Jewish communities of the Mediterranean basin and northward into west-central Europe.

By the Muslim period, Rabbinic literature, especially the Mishnah (Roman Palestine, ca. 200 C.E.) and the Babylonian Talmud (Persian Babylonia, ca. 550–600 C.E.), had become the most authoritative sources of the *halakah*. The Babylonian Talmud became the chief object of study of members of the rabbinic class, as had the Mishnah before it. Thus the principal rabbinic texts composed between 200 and 600 C.E. were canonical for the rabbinic movement in every meaningful sense of the word—ideologically, theologically, and sociologically. These texts, and "the rabbis" who claimed mastery of their meaning, interpreted and adjudicated God's will for the Jewish polity. Certainly by the dawn of the Muslim period, the rabbis claimed that the content of these texts as well as their own interpretive traditions ultimately stemmed from God's revelation to Moses at Mount Sinai, transmitted *orally* alongside the "written Torah" by generations of tradents down to the rabbis of Late Antiquity. And so the canonical status of the principal rabbinic texts (chiefly Mishnah and the Babylonian Talmud) found expression and legitimation in a sacred story, a mythic account of God's revelation in hoary antiquity. This, of course, invites the obvious question, What of the biblical scriptures in this early Muslim period?

Another set of canonical documents in hand within the triumphant rabbinic movement at the dawn of the Islamic era is its "authorized" collection of biblical literature, the Hebrew Bible which emerged at the output end of our aforementioned black or opaque box.

4. The "After": The Rabbis' Bible in the Medieval Period

As intimated, we know how the rabbis' Bible eventually turned out; it is the biblical canon which became almost universally accepted as authoritative by medieval Jewry. This medieval rabbinic Bible differed from Saint Jerome's canon of the Old Testament, and even more from Saint Augustine's. The medieval rabbinic Bible had three major divisions: the Torah/Pentateuch *(tôrâh);* the Prophets *(nĕbiʾîm);* and the Sacred Writings or Hagiographa *(kĕtûvîm).* Moreover, near the end of the first millennium, a group of Jewish scholars who were schooled in the new Islamic metier of comparative semitic philology and grammar, and who were affiliated with the rabbinic guild, "fixed" the orthography and vocalization of the Hebrew biblical text.[4] To fix the vowels of the written text together with the orthography is in essence to fix the grammatical and semantic meaning of the

---

[3] I have described the symbiotic relationship between the early rabbinic guild and the nascent Patriarchate in J. Lightstone, "Mishnah's Rhetoric: Other Material Artifacts of Late-Roman Galilee and the Social Formation of the Early Rabbinic Guild" in *Text and Artifact in the Religions of Mediterranean Antiquity: Essays in Honour of Peter Richardson* (Studies in Christianity and Judaism; ed. S. Wilson and M Desjardins; Waterloo, Ont.: WLU Press, 2000), 474–504.

[4] Like other Semitic languages, the earlier written forms of Hebrew were all consonantal. Only in the medieval period did standard forms of representing vowel sounds emerge.

scriptures. The results of these scholars' activities became known as the masoretic text of the Hebrew Bible (from the Hebrew word *mesorah,* meaning "[the] tradition").[5]

The ultimate shape of the tripartite rabbinic masoretic Bible of the medieval period is as follows:

(I) The Pentateuch (*Torah* [of Moses]): (1) Genesis, (2) Exodus, (3) Leviticus, (4) Numbers, (5) Deuteronomy

(II) The Prophets (*Nevi'im*): (A) The Former Prophets: (6) Joshua, (7) Judges, (8) 1 Samuel, (9) 2 Samuel, (10) 1 Kings, (11) 2 Kings; (B) The Latter Prophets: (12) Isaiah, (13) Jeremiah, (14) Ezekiel, and (15) "the Twelve" [minor prophets], i.e., Hosea, Joel, Amos, Obadiah, Jonah, Micah, Nahum, Habakkuk, Zephaniah, Haggai, Zechariah, Malachi;

(III) The Writings (*Ketuvim*): (16) Psalms, (17) Proverbs, (18) Job, (19) the "Five Scrolls," i.e., Song of Songs, Ruth, Lamentations, Ecclesiastes, Esther; (20) Daniel, (21) Ezra, (22) Nehemiah, (23) 1 Chronicles, (24) 2 Chronicles.

In order to put in context the significance of the medieval masoretic rabbinic Bible (acronym, TaNaK), let me turn to the church of the fourth century C.E., some half a millennium earlier.[6] Both Jerome's and Augustine's Old Testament canons coincide with the rabbinic masoretic collection as regards the first division (Torah). Beyond that Jerome and Augustine differ substantially, with the former's views closer to the end state of the masoretic rabbinic Bible, both as regards structure and content. Augustine, on the other hand, differs in two respects. First, the structure of his Old Testament canon more closely follows the early church's Septuagint tradition, in which the Law (*Torah*) is followed by all the "histories," "poetry" (Psalms and other books of the wisdom collection), and the "oracles" of the prophets (the great prophetic literary documents). Second, Augustine's Old Testament canon includes as an integral and indistinguishable part Septuagint additions, which Jerome relegates to the apocrypha and categorically excludes from his Old Testament canon.

It is not the purpose of this paper to discuss at length the early church's Old Testament canon and its development. I wish merely to situate our treatment of the emergence of the rabbinic Bible, by indicating that the fourth-century churches, while claiming that its Old Testament was nothing more or less than the scriptures of the Jews, disagreed about what that canonical tradition was. This discrepancy may be the result of several factors. First, the claim to have taken over "exactly" the Jews' scriptural canon also functions as an apologetic and polemical statement; and polemical needs often have priority in the perception of facts. Second, the church may indeed have taken over "a" or "the" Jewish

---

[5] Two seminal studies on the early masoretic scholars and their works are those by M. Goshen-Gottstein, "The Rise of the Tiberian Bible Text," first published in his *Biblical and other Studies* in 1963 and reprinted in *The Canon and Masorah of the Hebrew Bible* (ed. S. Z. Leiman; New York: Ktav, 1974), 666–709, and "The Authenticity of the Aleppo Codex," first printed in *Textus* in 1960 and reprinted in *Canon and Masorah,* 773–814.

[6] An excellent review of the evidence for the early church's Old Testament canon may be found in E. E. Ellis, "The Old Testament Canon in the Early Church," in M. J. Mulder, ed., *Miqra: Text, Translation, Reading and Interpretation of the Hebrew Bible in Ancient Judaism and Early Christianity* (CRINT 2.1; Assen/Maastricht: Van Gorcum and Philadelphia: Fortress, 1988), 653–90.

scriptural canon, but several centuries of Christian usage and tradition may have shaped or modified the canon "received" from the Jews. However, neither of these factors sufficiently account for the nature or the degree of the discrepancies observed. Rather, the divergence between the traditions reflected in Jerome and Augustine (and their respective predecessors), coupled with the ubiquitous claim that the Christian Old Testament was the Jews' scriptures, leads one strongly to suspect that as late as the fourth century C.E., the height of the "rabbinic period", Jewish communities in middle eastern and Mediterranean lands themselves had at least two quite different and well-established traditions concerning the structure and content of the canon. One tradition, an ancestor of the masoretic collection, resembled Jerome's; the other resembled Augustine's.

What enables me to make this assertion? In the fourth century C.E., major and influential Jewish communities were to be found in all of the larger urban centers of these lands. Up to and throughout the fourth century, intra-Christian controversies and disputes were rampant. The opportunity of a protagonist to attack an opponent on the grounds that the latter's Old Testament, which is supposed to be no more or less than the Jew's scriptures, differed substantially from the local Jewish community's biblical collection would have been a powerful weapon, had it been available.

Since Jerome's Old Testament and the eventual medieval masoretic Bible are of the same family, and since Jerome did his work in fourth-century Palestine, where the rabbinic guild was already powerful, can we conclude that the Judaic tradition reflected in Jerome's Old Testament was in fact the direct result of the efforts of the early rabbis to define and fix the structure and content of the Hebrew Bible? The answer is no, we cannot draw such a conclusion—not yet. We must first go to the "before" (section 5) and then review the early rabbinic evidence itself (section 6).

5. The "Before": Judaic Biblical Scripture(s) before the Rise of the Rabbinic Guild

The first constraint on the biblical canons of both early Christian and Judaic communities in the Roman period is the Judaic conception of canon itself. The notion that God not only reveals his will to the people bound to him by covenant, but also that his will is fully, irrevocably, and authoritatively contained in a written text, to which nothing can be added and from which nothing can be removed, is a basic premise expressed in Deuteronomy. Deuteronomy refers to that document as the Torah of Moses, and at many junctures in Deuteronomy the term is self-referential; that is to say, Deuteronomy *is* the Torah of Moses. The late sixth- and fifth-century B.C.E. community in Jerusalem that identified Ezra and Nehemiah as their heroes adopted and aggressively promulgated this notion and extended its reference to include the Pentateuch, which probably emerged in something like its final form in this era.[7] So successful was this community and its heirs that within a relatively short period (150 years at the most) they assimilated or swept away opposing views. The Samaritans seem to have stemmed from a group that assimilated to them for a

---

[7] I discuss this extensively in J. Lightstone, *Society, the Sacred, and Scripture in Ancient Judaism* (Waterloo, Ont.: Wilfrid Laurier University Press, 1988), ch. 2 and notes.

period and subsequently demurred, but not before they had succumbed to the "canonical principle" of the neo-Deuteronomic community in Jerusalem. Thus by the time of Alexander's conquest, and leaving aside the complex case of the Samaritans, we can identify no Judaic community that does not accept (a) the unassailable primacy of the Pentateuch as *the* Torah of Moses, and (b) the inherent canonical principle. These two "articles" become the litmus test of anyone claiming to share in Israel's covenantal relationship with Yahweh.

To say that the emergence and acceptance of this canonical principle is intimately tied to the production and promulgation of the Pentateuch as the Torah of Moses does not mean that other biblical texts like Samuel or Isaiah were produced *after* the Pentateuch, as later additions. That is much too linear a model for either the emergence of the biblical literature or the evolution of the biblical canon.[8] It is highly improbable that Joshua or 1 and 2 Samuel originated in, let us say, the last part of the fifth century B.C.E. The evidence is far more consistent with an earlier dating for most of the books ultimately grouped in the *nĕbî'îm*. Indeed, given the literary evidence, many of these "biblical" books may have assumed their more or less final form before the Pentateuchal books assumed theirs, and the texts in question could have been read and revered in the same community that produced the Pentateuch. However, that these books appear to have emerged virtually contemporaneously with the Pentateuchal books does not mean, as some unconvincingly argue, that the prophetic section of the canon was established at roughly the same time as the pentateuchal section.[9] The utter primacy and exclusivity of the Pentateuch as the Torah of Moses in all discourse from the fifth century B.C.E. on, coupled with the total absence of any notion that the Pentateuch constituted only one "section" of a more extensive canon of scriptures proves the point. In the same vein, I am struck that the myth, subsequently preserved in the *Letter to Aristeas,* of the translation into Greek of the sacred books of the Jews concerns only the Pentateuch. That myth's purpose is self-evidently to establish divine sanction for the Greek version of scriptures in use in the early Hellenistic Jewish community of Alexandria. For this community, the Pentateuch (in Greek), no more and no less, requires this sanction. That which is written about Moses' career or attributed to Moses' authorship defines what is truly canonical in the Judaisms of the last half of the first millennium B.C.E.

Nevertheless, as demonstrated in the Prologue of the Greek version of Ben Sirah, the notion of a tripartite division of the sacred writings into the Law, the Prophets, and the (other) Writings became coinage within Jewish communities sometime before the last third of the second century B.C.E. How did they square this with the exclusive primacy of the Torah of Moses as the core canonical principle, a principle which, in my view, distinguishes all forms of Judaism from ancient Israelite religion and society? I really cannot say. Barring some extraordinary discovery, the answer to this question will probably elude us. The tripartite notion is repeated by Philo (*Vita Contemplativa* 3.25) and Josephus (*Contra Apionem* 1.37–43) at the middle and end of the first century C.E. respectively. However, while all parties clearly meant the same thing when they referred to the first division, the Torah, the same may not be said about the distribution of books across the other two divisions. Josephus's distribution differed substantially from what became the masoretic

---

[8] See Lightstone, "The Formation of the Biblical Canon," 135–42.
[9] See Beckwith, "The Formation of the Hebrew Bible," in *Miqra,* 39–86.

TaNaK,[10] but does prefigure the Old Testament of some early Christian circles, including that reflected in Augustine's writings. However, Augustine writes of four divisions (Law, Histories, Poetry and Prophets) and includes substantially more books in the Old Testament canon than does either Josephus or Jerome.

This brings us to the question of "open-endedness." Inherent in the canonical principle which lies at the heart of the conception of the Torah is the dictum, "You shall add nothing . . . , nor shall you remove anything . . ." (see Deut 4:2). *In situ,* this dictum applies to Yahweh's teachings and commandments as revealed to Moses. It came to apply to all the Pentateuchal texts, understood to be the Torah of Moses. By some cultural, social, and political slight of hand, not only did the original pentateuchal canon give way to a larger tripartite one, in some sense in contravention of the dictum, but many Jewish communities came to apply the dictum to the expanded, tripartite scriptures. How so? *Fourth Ezra* 14:44 and Josephus (*Contra Apionem* 1.37–43) fix the total number of books at twenty-four and twenty-two respectively. The limitation to twenty-two or to twenty-four books appears regularly thereafter in rabbinic as well as Christian circles, although some Christian writers, like Augustine, include many more, resulting in the final, official Catholic and Orthodox Old Testaments. So we cannot conclude that the notion of a canon limited to twenty-two or twenty-four books was universally accepted either by the early churches or the Jewish communities whose Bible they had taken over. Finally, for those Jewish communities who ascribed to the twenty-two or twenty-four book limit, just how to distribute them among the three divisions seems to vary from one authority to another, as witness Josephus—except that no variation is in evidence concerning the Pentateuch.

As we come to the end of this section, there is one other development that should be noted: emerging notions of extracanonical revelation. Even before the advent of the rabbinic guild, several Judaic communities express the notion that in addition to the accepted biblical scriptures, a supplementary, parallel, or subsequent body of authoritative teachings was revealed by God. Only those who possess this supplementary material have God's complete revelation. Consequently, only they can live their lives truly in accordance with God's wishes. The notion is explicit in the *Community Rule* of the Qumran Covenanters. 1QS V, 8–9 has initiates to the community swear allegiance both to the precepts of the Torah of Moses and to "that which has been revealed to the Sons of Zadoq, the priests. . . ."[11]

Fourth Ezra 14:44ff. also provides clear prerabbinic evidence of the notion of a supplementary revelation, this time to Ezra. Over a period of forty days, God "re-reveals" to Ezra the twenty-four books of scripture, which he is told to commit to writing. In addition, over the course of the same forty days God reveals seventy other books, which Ezra is to transmit orally to the "wise" among Israel. Ezra here functions as a second Moses, reestablishing God's revelation to him. In my view, this text strongly implies that God's original revelation to Moses entailed all twenty-four books of scripture as well as the additional

---

[10] S. Z. Leiman, *The Canonization of the Hebrew Scripture: The Talmudic and Midrashic Evidence* (Hamden, Conn.: Archon), 32.

[11] In a doctoral dissertation submitted in the Fall of 2000 at Concordia University, Montreal, Maria Mamfredis convincingly argues that there are strong reasons to conclude that the Qumran Covenanters identified this supplementary revelation at least in part with the Temple Scroll. Mamfredis demonstrates the dependency of the specifically sectarian scrolls, like the *Community Rule* and the *Damascus Covenant,* on the Temple Scroll.

seventy transmitted orally. The additional seventy books were "*re*-revealed" just like the twenty-four, for it seems improbable that the author of *4 Ezra* would have regarded Ezra as a greater and more worthy vehicle of God's complete revelation than Moses himself.

The notion of a supplementary or complementary revelation in addition to scripture is interesting because of its implications. First, it clearly serves to justify one Judaic community's claim of superior authority and legitimacy versus other Judaic communities. In other words, it constitutes part of a community's "myth" in the service of social formation; "our" group's existence, as a distinct social formation, is divinely sanctioned, since we and only we are the keepers of God's complete revelation. Second, such notions of a supplementary or complementary revelation, in particular as expressed in *4 Ezra*, tell us something about the pervasiveness of the perception that (written) scripture comprised a "closed set" of "immutable" documents. I do not thereby claim that everyone agreed that scripture was limited to twenty-two or twenty-four books. As I have already argued, insofar as evidence from early Christianity sheds some light on contemporary Jewish communities in the Mediterranean basin, some Judaic communities seem to have had a biblical collection which included more volumes. Nor do I assert that everyone had to agree completely on what these documents were. But it does imply that nearly everyone thought that everyone *ought* to agree. That is an integral element of the canonical principle, pervasive in Judaism at the turn of the Christian Era. This key notion is central to the overall argument of this chapter. That one or another of the divisions of scripture was still open to additions was, in all probability, clearly and in principle rejected universally. Equally clear and central to our argument is the claim that by the turn of the Christian era, the foregoing pervasive canonical principle was counterbalanced in some communities by the notion that "true Israel" possessed a supplementary or complementary, extrascriptural body of revealed teachings. The latter were either vouchsafed to some post-Mosaic elite (e.g., Ezra or the Sons of Zadoq) or to Moses himself (as implied in *4 Ezra*).

As we shall see, the early rabbinic movement clearly stands within several already well established conceptual traditions—although, as stated, these traditions cannot have been universally held by all Judaic groups. First, biblical scripture consisted of a "closed" set of books organized in three divisions, in descending authority and sanctity: the Torah of Moses (= the Pentateuch), the Prophets, and the Writings. Second, this tripartite scripture does not exhaust the full body of revealed knowledge vouchsafed to Israel. Third, all divinely revealed teachings, scriptural and extrascriptural, trace their origins to Moses. I strongly suspect that this frame was set *for* the rabbinic guild, and not created *by* them—although this does not mean that they self-consciously adopted and advocated all of this schema *ab initio*. While it is a truism that the rabbis might in fact have radically rejected the shared belief system of the communities whence they sprang, with respect to these three notions about the nature of scripture and revealed teachings, there is no evidence that they differed. More likely, all three of these notions came to be adopted and perceived by the members of the earliest rabbinic guild as part of the framework within which one works.

6. The Evidence for "Canonical Activity" within the Early Rabbinic Guild

If the reader agrees with my argument thus far, the problem of interpreting the evidence from the early rabbinic guild becomes at one and the same time easier and more difficult. It is easier, because the *marges de manoeuvre* of the members of the guild to "fix" and to "shape" the canon was probably limited. Therefore, the paucity of any *explicit* evidence indicating or claiming that the early rabbis fixed and established the shape of the biblical canon is now rendered less problematic. We do not have to square this paucity by tortuous interpretations with the once widespread assertion that rabbis gathered at a council at Jamnia ca. 90 C.E. and fixed the canon. Matters are made more complex, because it leaves quite unresolved the meaning and significance of the rabbis' alleged canonical activity.

The *locus classicus* is found in the Mishnah, the earliest document authored by the nascent rabbinic guild (circa 200 C.E.). Since the passage (*Yadayim* 3:5b) is the source for several subsequent elaborations and explications in later documents of the early rabbinic guild, permit me to cite the pericope:[12]

1. All holy scriptures render the hands unclean.

2. [Among them] the Song of Songs and Ecclesiastes [which therefore also] render the hands unclean.

3. Rabbi Judah says: the Song of Songs renders the hands unclean, and [concerning] Ecclesiastes [there is] dispute.

4. Rabbi Yose says: Ecclesiastes does not render the hands unclean, and [concerning] the Song of Songs [there is] dispute.

5. Rabbi Simeon says: Ecclesiastes is [the subject of] a lenient [ruling] of the House of Shammai, and is [the subject of] a stringent [ruling] of the House of Hillel.

6. Said Rabbi Simeon ben Azzai: I have a tradition directly from the seventy-two elders on that day that they seated Rabbi Eleazar ben Azariah in the Academy [as its president]—

7. that [both] the Song of Songs and Ecclesiastes render the hands unclean.

8. Said Rabbi Aqiva: Heaven forbid! No one in Israel disputes that

9. the Song of Songs renders the hands unclean,

10. for the whole world is not equal [in value] to the day that the Song of Songs was delivered to Israel,

11. for all of the scriptures is [like] the Sanctuary *(qdš),* and the Song of Songs is [like] the Holy of Holies,

12. and if they disputed, they disputed only regarding Ecclesiastes.

13. Said Rabbi Yohanan ben Joshua, the son of the father-in-law of rabbi Aqiva: In accordance with [the teaching of] Ben Azzai—so they voted *(nhlqw)* and so they taught.

The volume of scholarly print on this and cognate passages is enormous, and the issues to which this passage has been linked by scholars are legion. Leiman provides a good

---

[12] The translation is my own.

sampling of those published before 1976 concerning the canonization of the Hebrew scriptures.[13] Permit some brief points.

First, all other traditions in early rabbinic literature on whether Song of Songs, Ecclesiastes, or any other named biblical book render the hands unclean seem ultimately generated by this mishnaic passage, directly or by second remove. Thus this passage is deemed to be the best evidence for any thesis that the rabbis fixed and shaped the canon of Hebrew scriptures circa 90 C.E. or at any other time until the sixth century C.E. Consequently, a great deal of evidentiary weight must be born by Mishnah Tractate *Yadayim* 3:5b.

Second, apart from the story element attributed to Ben Azzai at 6, and the exclamation attributed to Aqiva at 8, 10, and 11, most of the pericope displays the typical literary and rhetorical traits of Mishnah, which spins out legal cases and rulings, often highly hypothetical, by the repetition, inversion, and permutation of words and phrases. The resulting rulings are then attributed to named sages. The purpose of the enterprise, as I have argued extensively elsewhere, is to model and inculcate in the potential member of the rabbinic guild the capacity and natural tendency ever more finely to parse and differentiate matters. Thus the study of Mishnah functioned to help train the student of Mishnah in what was deemed the core expertise of the rabbinic guild.[14] Since the pericope evinces these typical mishnaic traits, it serves Mishnah's dominant function and place within the early rabbinic guild. Mishnah *Yadayim* 3:5b cannot bear the weight of the claim that the earliest rabbinic guild members fixed and shaped what eventually evolved into the masoretic Hebrew Bible. Moreover, none of the other passages which elaborate on this text are able to bear this weight either.

Third, what remains of the pericope, sections 6, 8, 10, and 11, are wholly insufficient grounds for supporting the contention that a "council" at Jamnia met to pronounce, among other things, on the shape, limits, and content of the rabbinic Bible. These elements have literary and rhetorical traits more typical of expository midrashic and aggadic documents of the rabbinic corpus, which only on occasion appear in Mishnah. Such literary elements are generally regarded as scoring low in historicity, for their function seems otherwise, namely, to edify and to model a certain ethos (rather than expertise) among the members of the rabbinic guild. So too, one cannot give any credence to other midrashic-aggadic passages, all in documents authored after the Mishnah, which elaborate this "historical" narrative about the alleged appointment of Eleazar ben Azariah in favor of Rabban Gamaliel II as head of the "council" (sic!) of rabbinic sages at Yavneh, and which marry to it other originally unrelated elements from disparate rabbinic documents and passages.[15]

Consequently, this passage offers flimsy evidence for any alleged activity by the early rabbinic guild to close, fix, or shape the canon of the Hebrew scriptures. Moreover, since this is the "best" and "earliest" evidence that one could adduce, the matter rests here due to

---

[13] Leiman, *Canonization*, 102–24.

[14] See J. Lightstone, "Whence the Rabbis?" *Studies in Religion/Sciences religieuses* 26.3 (1997): 275–95. My forthcoming book on these issues will be published in the series Studies in Christianity and Judaism, Wilfrid Laurier University Press.

[15] Again Leiman shares this view (*Canonization*, 120–24). The seminal literary and historical critique of the passages on the deposition of Gamaliel at the "council" of Jamnia is by Robert Goldenberg in "The Deposition of Gamaliel," in *Persons and Institutions in Early Rabbinic Judaism*, 1 (ed. W. S. Green; Missoula, Mont.: Scholars, 1977).

insufficient evidence. In any case, as argued earlier, a great deal would have been settled for the rabbis before the formation of the rabbinic guild in the second century C.E., leaving the rabbis with some, but limited, *marges des manoeuvre.*

All this being said, the early rabbinic guild did have a scriptural canon; perhaps one could even say, *its* scriptural canon. However, the rabbis probably stood firmly within one of a limited number of established traditions about its shape and content. And they probably inherited as well the notion that the canon was closed. As an authoritative ordered element in the early rabbis' world, how did the order and structuring of their scripture fit and reinforce that world? For it is in such fit that the social-psychological cogency of cultural worlds resides. These are issues about which we can say much, and for which we have abundant good evidence. The next section can but scratch the surface.

7. The Shape of the Rabbis' Bible and the Ideal World of Early Rabbinic Literature: Reinforcing Homologies

A. The Shape

Let me once again start at the end rather than the beginning. The only extensive canonical list from the early rabbinic guild is found in the relatively late Babylonian Talmud (ca. 550–600 C.E.), the first and only rabbinic text effectively to displace Mishnah as the quintessential object of study within the early rabbinic guild. The passage in question (*Baba Batra* 14b–15a) elaborates upon an allegedly earlier "Tannaitic" source, or *baraita.* But in fact the source is probably not earlier than the second half of the third century C.E., and may well be substantially later.[16] Permit me to cite the *baraita* at the passage's core.[17]

1. Our Rabbis taught:

2. The order of the Prophets [is]:

3. Joshua and Judges, Samuel and Kings, Jeremiah and Ezekiel, Isaiah and the Twelve [Minor Prophets]. . . .

6. The order of the Writings *(ketuvim)* is:

7. Ruth and the Book of Psalms and Job and Proverbs, Ecclesiastes, Song of Songs and Lamentations, Daniel and the Scroll of Esther, Ezra [which includes Nehemiah] and Chronicles. . . .

8. And who wrote them?

---

[16] Ancient, medieval, and many modern scholars date these *beraitot* to the second and late first centuries C.E. I do not share this view, because *beraitot* as a class share the literary traits of postmishnaic texts like Tosefta and the halakic Midrashim. The passages of these texts are often literarily dependent upon Mishnah. Indeed, many beraitot are literary developments of passages in the Tosefta (mid- to late-third century C.E.), halakic Midrashim (late-third century C.E. or later), and the still later Palestinian Talmud (mid-fifth century C.E. or later). Therefore although some could date from the second century C.E., I generally would not date *beraitot* any earlier than the second half of the third century, and many are probably later.

[17] The translation is my own.

9. Moses wrote his book [i.e., the Pentateuch], and the passage of Bil'am [in Num 22–24] Job;

10. Joshua wrote his book [i.e., Joshua], and [the final] eight verses which are in the Torah [which describe the death of Moses];

11. Samuel wrote his book [i.e., I and II Samuel], and Judges, and Ruth;

12. David wrote the Book of Psalms

13. by means of [also incorporating the work of] ten elders:

14. By means of [incorporating the work of] The First Man [Adam], by means of [incorporating the work of] Melchizedek, and by means of [incorporating the work of] Abraham, and by means of [incorporating the work of] Moses, and by means of [incorporating the work of] Heman, and by means of [incorporating the work of] Yeduthan, and by means of [incorporating the work of] Asaph, and by means of [incorporating the work of] the three sons of Korah.

15. Jeremiah wrote his book [i.e., Jeremiah], and the Book of Kings, and Lamentations.

16. Hezekiah and his attachés wrote Isaiah, Proverbs, Song of Songs, and Ecclesiastes.

17. The Men of the Great Assembly wrote Ezekiel, and the Twelve [Minor Prophets], Daniel and the Scroll of Esther.

18. Ezra wrote his book [i.e., Ezra and Nehemiah] and the genealogies of the Chronicles, until his own [time].

As Leiman correctly points out, the order and constituent books of the Pentateuch, the Torah of Moses, are assumed as given in *Baba Batra* 14b–15a and, therefore, warrant no attention at the beginning of the passage.[18] If the talmudic editor's source contained such a section, the editor wasted no ink reproducing it. The authorship of the Pentateuch presumably is of interest because of the anomalies presented by Num 22–24 and the last eight verses of Deuteronomy. The passage also appears to assume as commonplace the tripartite division of the biblical scriptures. Perhaps the passage also assumes, as Leiman maintains, a complement of twenty-four scriptural books: the nineteen dealt with explicitly, and the five books of the Pentateuch. Certainly, that these and only these books are scriptural seems not to be the point of the passage. So what does the author of the *baraita* wish to communicate which would not be commonplace or banal to his readership? What is the point?

In sections 1–5, the *baraita* seems to consider its didactic contribution to be the precise distribution of books across the second and third divisions of scripture and/or the order of books within the divisions. We can only speculate concerning why it was felt important to make this point, but clearly the writer felt it necessary. I suspect that the *baraita*'s creator was aware of other distributions of books across the divisions of the Prophets and Writings and/or other ways of ordering the books within these divisions. Such a didactic contribution would be relevant chiefly in one probable context: a "family"

---

[18] Leiman, *Canonization*, 53.

of communities which adhered to an already longstanding tradition that scriptures numbered twenty-four or twenty-two books distributed across three divisions, but with some variation as to what book belonged in which division and/or how the books were to be ordered in their respective divisions.

This does not mean that the tripartite division and the twenty-two or twenty-four book limit was by this author's time universally accepted; as already noted, the early church provides indirect evidence that some Judaic communities did not accept either the three-part structure or the limit of twenty-two or twenty-four constituent books. But this passage does not address these communities or acknowledge them. Rather, it serves to fix matters of distribution and order in the Prophets and Writings for a readership that does assume the tripartite division and the twenty-two or twenty-four book limit.

The remainder of the *baraita* deals with authorship. Of importance to us is the claim in sections 6 through 16 that the period of authorship starts with Moses and ends with Ezra. Anything outside these temporal bookends cannot be scripture.

Again, what is the problem or situation to which this point might be relevant? Perhaps the *baraita*'s author and audience are aware of communities which include among their scriptures books whose alleged authors lived after Ezra. For example, the *baraita* would address Judaic communities that accepted books like Sirach. But it also might address Christian communities, in which the New Testament has been taking shape as a canon of scriptures. Unfortunately, there is insufficient evidence to demonstrate either motive.

The early rabbinic corpus offers little that can add to this picture of the shape and structure of the Bible of the rabbinic guild. The tripartite division of scripture into Torah, Prophets, and Writings is already assumed by Mishnah (ca. 200 C.E.), the first Rabbinic document. To choose just one example, Mishnah Tractate *Rosh Hashanah* 4:6 prescribes the ritual recitation of biblical verses during the "additional" (i.e., *musaf*) service on the New Year. The passage is unintelligible without assuming the division of scripture into Pentateuch, Prophets, and Writings. Moreover, if serious disagreements existed among the intended readers concerning which scriptural book belonged in which division, they would have found the passage unclear without further explication. Yet no such explication appears. Nor is the matter of which book belongs where evoked in the corresponding chapter of Tosefta (*Rosh Hashanah* 2:12–14), even though Tosefta's principal *raison d'être* is to explicate Mishnah. Neither is distribution across the tripartite division of scripture a concern in the Palestinian Talmud (*Rosh Hashanah* 4:7, 59c), which again takes the Mishnah passage as its point of departure.

Numerous other passages from later documents *assume* nothing different: scripture has the same three divisions. Occasionally these passages indicate that some rabbis did not particularly like some of the biblical books listed in our *baraita,* and in various ways counseled restricting their use. But there is no indication that the early rabbinic guild believed that these books either could or should be excluded from their canon. Within the guild at least, the matter was settled by the time of the Mishnah. Similarly, some rabbinic sources show an affinity for Sirach, but no one suggests that there was enough leeway to include it in the canon.[19]

---

[19] These sources are exhaustively catalogued in Leiman (ibid., 51–124).

Like the authors of *4 Ezra* and the *Community Rule,* the early rabbinic guild maintained that there was a body of teachings revealed by God in addition to those contained in
scripture. At some point in late antiquity, this notion became formalized in a revised version of the myth of God's revelation of the Pentateuch to Moses: On Sinai, God revealed to
Moses the "whole Torah," some of which was written down in scripture, and the remainder
of which was transmitted orally from master to disciple in an unbroken chain down to the
founders of the rabbinic guild. Therefore, only the members of the rabbinic guild possess
this "whole Torah." The teachings and literature of the guild are grounded in this "whole
Torah," and give expression to it. Jacob Neusner has systematically analyzed the development of this rabbinic myth of God's revelation to Moses.[20] He demonstrates that the fully
articulated version is not present in Mishnah, although some elements of what became the
full version are found there: *Avot,* in my view a mid-third-century C.E. addition to the
Mishnah, provides in chapter 1 a chain of tradents beginning with Moses to whom was
passed "torah" (in a generic sense). The important corollary is that what the rabbinic guild
member teaches is, therefore, by definition torah. The Palestinian Talmud (ca. 450 C.E.)
gives the full myth (*Ḥagigah* 1:7; *Megillah* 4:1). Therefore, the elements from which the
myth was constructed must have come to be accepted within the rabbinic guild in the
Land of Israel from the mid-third century C.E. The convergence was completed sometime
before the mid-fifth century C.E., again in Palestine.

At least some of the myth's generative elements, e.g., as reflected in Mishnah *Avot* 1,
stand behind a foundational aspect of the social formation of the rabbinic guild at the end
of the second or the beginning of third century C.E. This foundational aspect is the promulgation of the Mishnah itself within the early rabbinic guild. Virtually from its appearance, the mastery and lifelong study of Mishnah, in addition to the mastery of scripture,
qualified one as a member of the guild. To be a rabbi, one had to master Mishnah. This
remained the case at least until the promulgation of the Babylonian Talmud (ca. 550–600),
which sometime thereafter (near the rise of Islam, perhaps) displaced Mishnah in this
regard. Beginning with the turn of the third century C.E., the biblical-scriptural collection
was becoming a canon within a larger canon, even before the emergence of the full-blown
myth of the "whole Torah."

Subsequent to Mishnah's promulgation, the list comprising this necessary or core
rabbinic curriculum of sacred teachings grew. Thus at nearly half a dozen junctures, *Avot
de Rabbi Nathan,* an exposition of Mishnah Tractate *Avot* and probably dating from the
fourth or fifth century C.E., exhorts members of the rabbinic guild to study "Scripture,
Mishnah, midrash, halakah, and aggadah."[21] Permit me to cite just one passage from *Avot
de Rabbi Nathan,* version A, chapter 8, to illustrate the formulation of this four-part curriculum of sacred teachings.[22]

---

[20] Jacob Neusner, *Torah: From Scroll to Symbol in Formative Judaism* (Philadelphia: Fortress,
1985), especially 74–79. See also Jacob Neusner, *The Oral Torah, The Sacred Books of Judaism: An
Introduction* (San Francisco: Harper and Row, 1986).

[21] Midrash is that rabbinic genre which seeks to induce proofs for rabbinic teaching from
scripture. Halakot refers to the corpus of rabbinic legal teachings, and discussions and elaborations
thereon. Aggadot are very short narratives/anecdotes of an aretalogical character either about biblical or rabbinic heroes; they often serve to communicate a certain ethos or set of values.

[22] The translation is my own; I have used the Schechter edition of the Hebrew.

1. "Appoint for yourself a master" (cited from *m. Avot* 1:6).

6. How so?

7. It teaches that he should make the appointment of a master permanent *(qv'),*

8. and he shall learn from him scripture, and Mishnah, midrash, halakot (pl.), and aggadot (pl.).

9. [When the student] proffers a reason [derived] in scripture, [by the] conclusion [of the exercise, the master] should tell him [one] in Mishnah.

10. [When the student proffers a reason derived in Mishnah, by the conclusion of the exercise, the master should tell him one in midrash.]

11. [When the student] proffers a reason [derived] in midrash, [by the] conclusion [of the exercise, the master] should tell him [one] in the halakot.

12. [When the student] proffers a reason [derived] in the halakot, [by the] conclusion [of the exercise, the master] should tell him [one] from the aggadot.

13. The outcome—this selfsame man dwells in his abode, filled with goodness and blessing.

Here then was the larger canon of sacred teachings of the rabbinic guild by the fourth or fifth century C.E. Only the first two elements refer to texts per se; the books of scripture and *the* Mishnah. The remainder refers to literary genres which are reflected in numerous texts produced in the last several centuries of the Roman Period. By the time of the editing of the Palestinian Talmud (ca. 450 C.E.), not only scripture, but also Mishnah and texts and teaching comprising "midrash, halakah and aggadah" were perceived as constituent elements of the "whole Torah," all of which rested on the authority of Moses.

B. The Fit

I need to begin by spelling out my use of the concept of fit. Berger and Luckmann have taught us that all humans live in socially constructed "worlds," since almost the totality of our lives are lived together in cultural constructs.[23] These worlds are made up of shared norms, perceptions, and beliefs that channel the pattern of our daily lives with others in an ordered manner. They determine the roles we play and how we play them. What we build—cities, houses, temples, etc.—are physical representations of these world-ordering norms and perceptions.

Most humans experience their socially constructed world as a given, and behave accordingly. In fact, this shared sense of givenness is necessary for the survival of societies and cultures. Were we to see our society or culture as constituted of mere convention, it would dissolve in short order, because it would have no authority over us. To say that for some ancients this sense of givenness resided in the belief that God had revealed matters to particular persons really does not take one very far theoretically; the cogency of that belief,

---

[23] Peter Berger and Thomas Luckmann, *The Social Construction of Reality* (New York: Penguin, 1966).

central as it might seem to a culture, is not *prima facie* any more or less self-evident than others within that society. Most human societies have lived near, and were aware of, other societies who differed with regard to which God had revealed what to whom. Clifford Geertz[24] and Mary Douglas[25] have both argued that the cogency of social cultural systems lies in the fit across the many ordered spheres that constitute a society and its culture. The pattern in one sphere is felt to be emotionally satisfying and appropriate because it replicates and is replicated by the pattern in many other spheres. Neither Geertz nor Douglas treat religious beliefs and practices as a sphere *sui generis*. They are interwoven among other social spheres, especially in premodern societies.

We can produce no detailed social description of the early rabbinic guild, especially in its formative period up to the end of the second century C.E. What we have for this period is Mishnah, their magnum opus, which remained their principle document until the promulgation of the Babylonian Talmud. To understand the cogency of the canonical tradition of the early rabbis, we must look to Mishnah for a homologous fit.

Mishnah concerns itself with an ideal, ordered world, still centered on the Jerusalem temple operating under the authority of the priestly caste.[26] That world was "ideal" in at least two senses. First, the temple had not physically existed since its destruction by the Romans in 70 C.E.; so Mishnah's temple is ideal in that it exists only in the mind. Second, Mishnah's treatment of that world is "ideal," because Mishnah seems less bent upon remembering what was than upon analyzing how such a world should "ideally" be constructed. For Mishnah, every item and discrete situation in that imaginary world could be perfectly classified, so that one can determine whether one rule or another applies to it. In this latter aspect, only two elements are authoritative: analytic logic or reason, and the dicta of scripture and in particular the legal content of the Pentateuch. Curiously, despite the fact that scriptural law is almost everywhere assumed by Mishnah, scripture is not routinely cited.

The formal pervasive literary and rhetorical traits of Mishnah serve to reinforce what I have said about its subject matter. The characteristic literary traits of Mishnah everywhere give the appearance of a systemic, systematic, and exhaustive treatment of the subject matter at hand, but in the most terse and economical language possible. Intermediate conceptual units (which, roughly speaking, became the numbered chapters in the medieval manuscripts) exhibit strong literary markers which indicate formally the unit's beginning and end, quite apart from substance. Constituent pericopes perform their exhaustive analytic exercise by using literary devises in order to parse with the highest possible definition the pericope's object of analysis. For example, a typical mishnaic pericope might take the form:

Condition *a* plus condition *b*, the rule is *x;*

condition *a* plus condition *not b*, the rule is *y;*

---

[24] Clifford Geertz, "Religion as a Cultural System," in *Anthropological Approaches to the Study of Religion* (ed. M. Banton; London: Tavistock, 1966).

[25] Mary Douglas, *Natural Symbols* (2d ed.; London: RKP, 1973); "Self-Evidence," in *Implicit Meanings* (ed. Mary Douglas; London: RKP, 1975).

[26] See Jacob Neusner, *Judaism: The Evidence of the Mishnah* (Chicago: University of Chicago Press, 1981); *The Mishnah: An Introduction* (Northvale, N.J.: Aronson, 1989).

condition *not a* plus condition *b,* the rule is *y;*

condition *not a* plus condition *not b,* the rule is *x;*

and rabbi *z* says, the rule is *y.*

The role of the student of Mishnah is not so much to learn these rules, many of which will define circumstances so hypothetical as to be improbable, but to figure out and internalize the "why" and the "how" of it.

Hence both in substance and in literary form Mishnah gives the impression of completeness, exhaustiveness, and closure. And the world which is its subject matter is the ideal temple world, not the temple world that stood in the decades preceding its destruction in 70 C.E. That is to say, Mishnah's world is the Temple world as enjoined in scripture, by the authority of Moses. Moreover, that "ideal" world existed in the rabbis' view at only several moments, between two "historical" bookends: the lifetime of Moses, when the scriptural narrative has Moses, not Aaron, build and inaugurate God's sanctuary and the ordered world around it; and the career of Ezra, when Ezra, "priest" and "scribe," "expert in the Torah of Moses" is portrayed as reestablishing that perfect Mosaic temple and temple-centered community. However, these same historical bookends define the limits of the rabbis' canon. In their view, no books authored outside of this frame are scriptural, and, therefore, scripture is closed by definition. It is a perfect whole, with every constituent book a necessary and sufficient element—just as Mishnah, in its subject matter and literary traits, strives to convey that its analysis of that ideal temple society is exhaustive and complete.

It should little surprise us that in postmishnaic rabbinic literature, Moses and Ezra are portrayed as the architects of the world defined in rabbinic teachings. It is an understatement to say that the members of the early rabbinic guild strongly identify with these two biblical figures. It is also a fact that the rabbis assimilate Moses and Ezra to themselves; thus Moses becomes "Moses, our rabbi" in rabbinic literature. But do they not thereby implicitly claim as well to be the embodiment of Moses and Ezra? Thus scripture is that which lies between the foundation of the ideal temple centered world in Moses' Torah, and its great reestablishment in Ezra's Mosaic reform. When the rabbis study Mishnah, they are imaginatively "living" in these two worlds of Moses and Ezra, claiming their authority for themselves.

Here, then, appears to be the basis for the rabbis' excluding from their canon of scriptures any documents that they deemed to be written subsequent to the career of Ezra—it simply does not fit in their ideal world that such writings could be scripture. Therefore, as much as they admired *Sirach,* it could not be part of their scriptures. Even though the commemoration of the Maccabean revolt formed the basis for a sacred festival, Hanukkah, neither 1 nor 2 Maccabees could be admitted to the canon. These books' inclusion would belie the fit between scripture and the world which was the object of contemplation of the rabbinic guild.

The Scriptures of Jesus and His Earliest Followers

Craig A. Evans

From the sources we possess, it is not possible to deduce the precise boundaries of the "canon" of Jesus. Of course, in his day the canon was not fixed, so in a pedantic sense it would be impossible to determine the canon of scripture for anyone in the early first century of the common era. However, one may infer which biblical books were important for Jesus and which books may also have given significant shape to his theology and self-understanding. The present study will attempt to do so.

1. The Evidence of the Synoptic Gospels

According to the Synoptic Gospels, Jesus quotes or alludes to twenty-three of the thirty-six books of the Hebrew Bible[1] (counting the books of Samuel, Kings, and Chronicles as three books, not six). Jesus alludes to or quotes all five books of Moses, the three major prophets (Isaiah, Jeremiah, and Ezekiel), eight of the twelve minor prophets,[2] and five of the Writings.[3] In other words, Jesus quotes or alludes to *all* of the books of the Law, *most* of the Prophets, and *some* of the Writings. Superficially, then, the "canon" of Jesus is pretty much what it was for most religiously observant Jews of his time.

This claim can be corroborated to some extent by the Dead Sea Scrolls. More than two hundred Bible manuscripts have been identified; only Habakkuk, Esther, and Nehemiah are missing. But Habakkuk was probably present at Qumran, for a lengthy commentary, or *pesher,* is devoted to it (1QpHab). The presence of a portion of Ezra argues for the presence of Nehemiah because the two books usually made up a single scroll. Only Esther seems to be truly missing, probably deliberately so.

The Scrolls include some eighty manuscripts of books of the Law, some seventy manuscripts of the Prophets, and about sixty-one manuscripts of the Writings[4] (of which

---

[1] See the helpful tabulation in R. T. France, *Jesus and the Old Testament* (London: Tyndale, 1971), 259–63.

[2] That is, Hosea, Joel, Amos, Jonah, Micah, Zephaniah, Zechariah, and Malachi. Omitted are Obadiah, Nahum, Habakkuk, and Haggai.

[3] That is, Psalms, Proverbs, Job, Daniel, and Chronicles. Omitted are Song of Solomon, Ruth, Lamentations, Ecclesiastes, Esther, Ezra, and Nehemiah.

[4] M. G. Abegg Jr., P. W. Flint, and E. Ulrich, *The Dead Sea Scrolls Bible: The Oldest Known Bible Translated for the First Time into English* (San Francisco: HarperCollins, 1999). The index provided

thirty-four manuscripts are from the Psalter, a collection apparently regarded at Qumran as prophetic). The proportion of quotations in the nonbiblical scrolls is roughly consistent: some seventy-five quotations of the Law, some eighty-one quotations of the Prophets, and some thirty-seven quotations of the Writings. Had it not been for the disproportionate number of quotations of Isaiah (about thirty-five), the correlation between manuscripts and quotations would have been closer.

However, it is this great interest in Isaiah and the Psalms that connects Jesus' use of scripture with the evidence from Qumran most closely. According to the Synoptic Gospels, Jesus quotes or alludes to Deuteronomy some fifteen or sixteen times, Isaiah some forty times, and the Psalms some thirteen times. These appear to be his favorite books, though Daniel and Zechariah seem to have been favorites also.

In the nonbiblical Scrolls[5] the book of Deuteronomy is quoted some twenty-two times, Isaiah some thirty-five times, and the Psalter some thirty-one times.[6] Moreover, just as Jesus and his first followers viewed the Psalms as prophetic, so also did the Qumran sectarians, devoting two or three prophetic *pesharim* to a few of them.

It seems, then, that Jesus' usage of scripture was pretty much in step with what we observe in similar circles, circles that took the Law very seriously, understood the Prophets eschatologically, and had some regard for the Writings, though this last division was very open-ended. Of the writings that make up the last division, the Psalter seems to have been of especial interest, both for personal worship and for additional prophetic insight, perhaps almost on a par with the Prophets.

We are left with two specific questions with regard to Jesus and the canon of scripture. First, did Jesus recognize a tripartite canon? If not, what sort of canon did he recognize? Second, did Jesus attach authoritative status to a particular version of scripture, e.g., the proto-Masoretic, another Hebrew version, the Septuagint, or the Aramaic? Although certainty cannot be obtained, we may speak with some confidence. Addressing these questions is useful, because they may shed light on the historical Jesus, and may help us appreciate better the early church's understanding of scripture.

2. Did Jesus Recognize a Tripartite Canon of Scripture?

The above review of biblical manuscripts and quotations of scripture in nonbiblical manuscripts was divided along the lines of the tripartite canon: the Law, the Prophets, and

---

by J. A. Fitzmyer (*The Dead Sea Scrolls: Major Publications and Tools for Study* [SBLRBS 20; Atlanta: Scholars, 1990], 205–37) combines the contents of the biblical scrolls with quotations of scripture in the nonbiblical scrolls. For further clarification of the "canon" of scripture at Qumran, as well as lists of manuscripts, see E. Ulrich, "The Canonical Process, Textual Criticism, and Latter Stages in the Composition of the Bible," in *"Shaʿarei Talmon": Studies in the Bible, Qumran, and the Ancient Near East Presented to Shemaryahu Talmon* (ed. M. Fishbane and E. Tov; Winona Lake: Eisenbrauns, 1992), 267–91; idem, "Index of Passages in the Biblical Scrolls," in *The Dead Sea Scrolls after Fifty Years: A Comprehensive Assessment* (2 vols.; ed. P. W. Flint and J. C. VanderKam; Leiden: Brill, 1998–99), 2:649–65.

[5] The *pesharim* are also excluded.

[6] J. C. VanderKam, "Authoritative Literature in the Dead Sea Scrolls," *DSD* 5 (1998): 382–402. I gratefully acknowledge the updated data supplied by my colleague Martin G. Abegg Jr.

the Writings. This was done for heuristic purposes only, and was not meant to imply that in the early first century a tripartite canon was recognized. We may now raise that question. Was a tripartite canon recognized during the time of Jesus and his earliest followers?[7]

Possibly the earliest hint of a tripartite form of the canon comes from the Wisdom of Yeshua (or Jesus) ben Sira (ca. 180 B.C.E.), whose book is also known as Ecclesiasticus: "He who devotes himself to the study of the law of the Most High will seek out wisdom of all the ancients, and will be concerned with prophecies" (Sir 39:1). The "law of the Most High" and the "prophecies" are unmistakable references to the first two divisions of the Hebrew Bible.[8] But is "wisdom" a reference to the third division of the canon of scripture? Probably not. The reference to wisdom is out of proper sequence ("wisdom" appears in second position, instead of third), and nowhere else is the third division of scripture called "wisdom." It has been suggested that Yeshua ben Sira referred to the third division of scripture in this way because of his concern with wisdom. But that is no more than a guess.

The next possible reference to the tripartite form of the canon is found in the recently published 4QMMT (ca. 150 B.C.E.): "We [have written] to you, so that you will understand the Book of Moses [and] the book[s of the Pr]ophets and of Davi[d, along with the chronicles of every] generation. In the Book it is written . . . [It is written in the Book] of Moses and in [the books of the Prophets] that [blessings and curses] will come [upon you . . ." (4Q397 14–21 ii 10–12).[9] The "Book of Moses," the "books of the Prophets," and "David" could refer to the three divisions of scripture. However, "David" may only refer to the Psalms, while the "chronicles of every generation" obscures a possible tripartite division. The first two divisions—"Book of Moses" and "books of the Prophets"— seem clear enough. We seem to have merely another undefined cluster of writings that fall outside of these two well recognized categories. Although the author of 4QMMT may presuppose a tripartite division of scripture, it is not obvious.[10]

The next possible reference to the tripartite form of scripture comes from Yeshua ben Sira's grandson,[11] who translated his grandfather's work into Greek and added a preface. In this preface (ca. 132 B.C.E.) the grandson states: "My grandfather Jesus (i.e., Yeshua) . . . very much gave himself to the reading of the Law, and the Prophets, and other books of our fathers . . . Not only this work, but even the Law itself, the Prophecies, and the rest of the books differ not a little as originally expressed." Not only is it clear that Yeshua's grandson understood the canon as consisting of three groupings of writings, it is also clear that the third grouping had no agreed upon name. The first group is called the "law" or

---

[7] The comments that follow are a mere summary; for a more detailed study, see the chapter above by Julio Trebolle Barrera, as well as L. M. McDonald, *The Formation of the Christian Biblical Canon* (rev. and enl. ed.; Peabody: Hendrickson, 1995), 34–49.

[8] In his praise of the fathers, ben Sira lauds the prophets Isaiah (48:22), Jeremiah (49:6), Ezekiel (49:8), and the Twelve (49:10).

[9] For reconstruction of this text, see E. Qimron and J. Strugnell, *Qumran Cave 4: V. Miqṣat Maʿaśe Ha-Torah* (DJD 10; Oxford: Clarendon, 1994), 58–61. They date 4QMMT to 159–152 B.C.E. (p. 121). The extant fragments themselves are dated to 75–50 B.C.E.

[10] *Pace* P. W. Flint (*The Dead Sea Psalms Scrolls and the Book of Psalms* [STD 17; Leiden: Brill, 1997], 219), who speaks of 4QMMT as providing "the first clear evidence of a tripartite division of the Hebrew scriptures that antedates Luke's similar description." It is indeed evidence of a sort, but it is going too far to call this evidence "clear."

[11] The authorship of the preface is disputed; cf. McDonald, *Formation,* 37e.

"Moses" (or "Book[s] of Moses," or "Law of Moses"), while the second group is called the "Prophets" (or "Prophecies," or "books of the Prophets"). But the third group has no particular name. Yeshua's grandson calls it the "other books" and the "rest of the books." The author of 4QMMT might have referred to this group as "David," but it is also possible that he meant only the Psalms. Yeshua himself, if he had a collective term for these writings, may have called them "wisdom."

The author of 2 Maccabees passes on an interesting tradition: "Nehemiah . . . founded a library and collected the books about the kings and prophets, and the writings of David, and letters of kings about votive offerings" (2:13). The "books about the kings" are probably Samuel and Kings (perhaps also Joshua and Judges), while the writings of David again probably mean primarily the Psalter. The "letters of kings about votive offerings" may refer to 1 Esd 4:61–63; 5:46–50. While there is no mention of the Law, the Prophets and David again seem to be recognized categories of scripture.

In all of the writings from Qumran, with the possible exception of 4QMMT, we have references only to the first two divisions of the canon of scripture. Only 4QMMT could perhaps refer to all three, but this is far from certain. The only other early, potential witness to the tripartite form of scripture comes from the grandson of Yeshua ben Sira. However, "David" in 4QMMT probably refers only to the Psalms,[12] which at Qumran may have been understood as somewhat related to the Prophets.[13] This possible connection between the Prophets and the Psalms may be relevant to the canon of Jesus, which will be considered below.

Even in the first century C.E. the third division of the canon is not clearly defined, for the order and contents of this division remain uncertain. However, the tripartite division of scripture may be attested in Philo of Alexandria, the Jewish exegete and philosopher (ca. 20 B.C.E.–45 C.E.). In describing the Therapeutae, a Jewish sect in Egypt, Philo tells us that they possessed "laws and oracles delivered through the mouths of prophets, and psalms and anything else which fosters and perfects knowledge and piety" (*Contempl.* 25). Some have suggested that we have here an adumbration of the tripartite form of the canon. However, others have argued that the language is too vague to draw conclusions.[14] The problem is that the "laws and oracles" are said to have been uttered by prophets. Therefore, the divisions of Law and Prophets may not be in view. Of course, Philo may well have regarded the great law-giver Moses as a prophet (cf. *Mut.* 125; *Mos.* 1.57; 2.2–7), in which case he is saying that "laws" have been given by Moses (the prophet) and "oracles" by (the other) prophets (cf. Matt 11:13, where the law is said to have "prophesied"). Thus, we have "laws," "(prophetic) oracles," and "psalms," along with "anything else."

The fairly consistent pattern, from the second century B.C.E. until well into the first century C.E., is that of two widely recognized and defined divisions of scripture (the Law and the Prophets) and a vaguer cluster of other writings, possibly designated "David" or

---

[12] So E. Ulrich, "Canon," in *Encyclopedia of the Dead Sea Scrolls* (2 vols.; ed. L. H. Schiffman and J. C. VanderKam; Oxford: Oxford University Press, 2000), 1:117–20, at 118.

[13] As is argued by E. Ulrich, "Pluriformity in the Biblical Text, Text Groups, and Questions of Canon," in *The Madrid Qumran Congress: Proceedings of the International Congress on the Dead Sea Scrolls Madrid 18–21 March, 1991* (2 vols., ed. J. Trebolle Barrera and L. Vegas Montaner; STDJ 11; Leiden: Brill, 1992), 1:23–41, at 34.

[14] As McDonald points out (*Formation,* 39).

the Psalms. A century or two later, the formal tripartite division of scripture was presupposed by the early rabbis, as the following discussion illustrates: "Our rabbis taught: 'It is permissible to fasten the Torah, the Prophets, and the Writings *[tôrâh, nĕbiʾîm, ûkĕtûbîm]* together.' This is the opinion of Rabbi Meir. Rabbi Judah, however, says that the Torah, the Prophets, and the Writings should each be in a separate scroll; while the Sages say that each book should be separate" (*b. B. Bat.* 13b).

Jesus' understanding of the Jewish canon of scripture is consistent with what has been observed. Recognized divisions of Law and Prophets are presupposed, with occasional allusions to a vaguer undefined grouping. Several utterances in the dominical tradition bear this out. From a critical point of view, one of the better attested statements is Jesus' remark that "all the prophets and the law prophesied until John" (Matt 11:13). This saying is probably derived from Q, whose Lukan parallel reads: "The law and the prophets were until John" (Luke 16:16). Luke's order ("law and prophets") is probably the original order of Q, while the Matthean order ("prophets and law") is probably due to the evangelist's prophetic emphasis.[15] Although the Matthean and Lukan evangelists appear to have understood this dominical utterance in different ways and edited and contextualized the material accordingly, there is no good reason for denying its authenticity.

The same twofold division of scripture is attested elsewhere in the dominical tradition. The so-called Golden Rule states, "So whatever you wish that men would do to you, do so to them; for this is the law and the prophets" (Matt 7:12). In the parable of the Rich Man and Lazarus, Abraham tells the suffering rich man: "They have Moses and the prophets; let them hear them" (Luke 16:29; cf. v. 31). In the Sermon on the Mount, Jesus declares, "Think not that I have come to abolish the law and the prophets; I have come not to abolish them but to fulfill them" (Matt 5:17). Although many suspect this is later Matthean addition, it is nevertheless clear that the categories "the law and the prophets" was understood in the first century to sum up the contents of scripture, or at least its legal and prophetic components. The same may be said in the Matthean version of the question of the greatest commandment: "On these two commandments depend all the law and the prophets" (Matt 22:40).[16]

The divisions of the Law and the Prophets may very well be reflected in the warning concerning judgment: "There you will weep and gnash your teeth, when you see Abraham and Isaac and Jacob and all the prophets in the kingdom of God" (Luke 13:28). "Abraham and Isaac and Jacob" may allude to the Law, for the narratives and oracles of the patriarchs are found in Genesis, the first book of Moses. Thus, the key persons of the Law and the Prophets may be in view. They will be in the kingdom of God, but those who reject Jesus' message will find themselves thrust out.

More complicated is the saying found in Luke 11:51: "from the blood of Abel to the blood of Zechariah, who perished between the altar and the sanctuary"; and its parallel in Matt 23:35: "from the blood of innocent Abel to the blood of Zechariah the son of Barachiah, whom you murdered between the sanctuary and the altar." The words and

---

[15] So W. D. Davies and D. C. Allison Jr., *A Critical and Exegetical Commentary on the Gospel according to Saint Matthew*, vol. 2, *Commentary on Matthew VIII–XVIII* (ICC; Edinburgh: T&T Clark, 1991), 2:256–57. The "all" of "all the prophets" is also Matthean.

[16] Although this is clearly Matthean redaction, it is quite possible that the evangelist's gloss is itself draw from authentic dominical tradition.

phrases "innocent," "son of Barachiah," and "whom you murdered" are probably Matthean additions designed to intensify and clarify the meaning of the utterance.[17] What does "from the blood of Abel to the blood of Zechariah" mean? Some have contended that it implies the whole of the Hebrew Bible, that is, from Genesis (in which Abel is murdered) to 2 Chronicles (in which Zechariah is murdered). But this argument assumes not only that in the time of Jesus 2 Chronicles was considered canonical, but that it had already been assigned the last place in the third division of scripture, as it is in the present Hebrew Bible. The assumption is in any case very doubtful.[18] For one thing, it does not seem to have this meaning in Matthew. By adding "son of Barachiah," the evangelist directs our attention away from the Zechariah murdered in 2 Chr 24:20–21, identified as "son of Jehoida the priest," alluding instead to the prophet Zechariah (cf. Zech 1:1, "Zechariah, son of Berechiah"), thus strengthening the prophetic testimony to which Jesus has appealed. Thus, Jesus' comment "from the blood of Abel to the blood of Zechariah" is probably meant to sum up Israel's history, not Israel's sacred scripture.

Consistent with his recognition of the authority and status of the Law and the Prophets, Jesus refers to what "Moses commanded" (e.g., Mark 1:44; 10:3; cf. 12:26) and to God's sending of "prophets" (e.g., Matt 23:34; 23:37 = Luke 13:34). Jesus refers to the "prophet Daniel" (Matt 24:15; cf. 4Q174 IV, 3; Josephus, *Ant.* 10.11.4 §249; 10.11.7 §266–267) and to the "prophet Jonah" (Matt 12:39), and says that "Isaiah prophesied" concerning Jesus' legalistic hypocrites (Mark 7:6). But for Jesus the office and function of prophet entailed more than producing and leaving scripture for posterity. It is the act of speaking the word of God and exhibiting the power of God that qualifies one as a prophet. For this reason Jesus refers to John as a prophet, indeed, as "more than a prophet" (Matt 11:9 = Luke 7:26), and even refers to himself as a prophet (Mark 6:4; cf. Mark 6:15; 8:28; Luke 7:16), which his opponents dispute (cf. Luke 7:39; Mark 11:27–28; 14:65). For Jesus, then, the "prophets" spoke, acted, and wrote, and in the case of himself and John, continue to speak and act. For Jesus the division of scripture called the prophets may or may not have been closed; in any case, he and many of his contemporaries believed that God still raised up true prophets.

Did Jesus recognize the third division of scripture? Some think he did—at least as he speaks as the Risen One. The risen Jesus explains to the two disciples on the road to Emmaus the things concerning himself in "Moses," in "all the prophets," and in "all the scriptures" (Luke 24:27). In the later appearance before all of the disciples, Jesus again explains how "all things written about" him "in the law of Moses and the prophets and the psalms must be fulfilled" (Luke 24:44). Here again we have a reference to the Psalter. And, as in the case of 4QMMT, we are not sure if the Lucan evangelist meant to refer to a third division of scripture, or if he simply meant the Psalter and nothing else. However, because of the close association of the Psalter to the Prophets, as seen in the Dead Sea Scrolls, and because in the New Testament David is viewed as a prophet (cf. Acts 1:16; 2:30; 4:25) and

---

[17] Either the Matthean evangelist added "son of Barachiah," thus identifying the martyr with the prophet Zechariah, or the Lukan evangelist deleted the familial epithet, because he realized that the person murdered "between the sanctuary and the altar" was another Zechariah. On balance, it is more likely that Matthew added the epithet to the Q tradition, for Jesus more typically refers simply to the given name, e.g., "Jonah" not "Jonah son of Amittai," or "Isaiah" not "Isaiah the son of Amoz."

[18] See the summary of problems in McDonald, *Formation,* 46–47.

the Psalms as prophecy (cf. Acts 1:20), "the prophets and the psalms" should probably be taken together.[19] That is, the things written about Jesus are found in the Law and the Prophets (including the Psalms), not in the Law, the Prophets, and the Writings. Indeed, the utterance in Luke 18:31 ("Behold, we are going up to Jerusalem, and everything that is written of the Son of man by the prophets will be accomplished") probably has the same meaning, in that the "prophets" refer to the Prophets and the Psalms.

In my opinion, both the Lucan evangelist and the author of 4QMMT appealed to the Law, the Prophets, and the Psalter, in order to muster the fullest scriptural support possible for their respective positions. The author of 4QMMT believed that consideration of the whole body of scripture would convince his readers of the truth of the position for which he has argued: "Think of the kings of Israel and contemplate their deeds: whoever among them feared [the To]rah was delivered from troubles; and these were the seekers of the Torah whose transgressions were forgiven" (4Q398 23–25).[20] Similarly, the risen Christ appeals to the whole of scripture as support of the gospel proclamation, which if heeded, will lead to forgiveness of sins. But the whole of the scriptures was probably understood as the Law and Prophets (including David or the Psalms), and possibly some other writings (as especially seen in 4QMMT), be they the Psalms or other writings. In any event, a third division of scripture is not clearly recognized.

3. Did Jesus Recognize a Specific Text of Scripture?

Did Jesus recognize a specific text form of scripture? It does not appear so, for his usage of scripture is allusive, paraphrastic, and—so far as it can be ascertained—eclectic. We find agreement with the proto-Masoretic text, with the Hebrew underlying the Septuagint (perhaps even the Septuagint itself), and with the Aramaic paraphrase. Several examples from each category will illustrate the phenomena. The examples that are chosen are the most obvious, in that they stand over against the readings in the other versions.

A. Agreements with the Proto-Masoretic Text

Some of Jesus' quotations and allusions to scripture agree with the proto-Masoretic text against the Septuagint.[21] In the parable of the Growing Seed (Mark 4:26–29) Jesus alludes to Joel 4:13 (ET 3:13): "he puts in the sickle, because the harvest has come." Mark's *therismos* ("harvest") renders literally the Hebrew *qsyr*, unlike the Septuagint's *trygētos* ("vintage"). In Matt 11:29 Jesus bids his hearers to take his yoke upon them: "and you will find rest *[anapausin]* for your souls." The saying alludes to Jer 6:16 in the Hebrew, where the Lord speaks through his prophet: "walk in (the good way), and find rest *[mrgw']* for your souls"; and not to the Septuagint, which renders the passage: "and you will find puri-

---

[19] *Pace* Flint, *The Dead Sea Psalms Scrolls*, 219.
[20] Qimron and Strugnell, *Qumran Cave 4*, 61, 63.
[21] Again I am indebted to France, *Jesus and the Old Testament*, 240–58.

fication *[hagnismon]* for your souls." In Mark 13:8 Jesus warns his disciples that in the tribulation that lies ahead "nation will rise against nation, and kingdom against kingdom." He alludes to Isa 19:2 in the Hebrew, which in part reads: "city against city, kingdom against kingdom"; the Septuagint, in contrast, reads: "city against city, province against province." In Luke 16:15 Jesus asserts that "what is exalted among humans is an abomination *[bdelygma]* in the sight of God." This alludes to Prov 16:5 in the Hebrew, where the wise man claims: "Every one who is arrogant is an abomination *[tw'bh]* to the LORD"; not to the Septuagint: "Every arrogant person is unclean *[akathartos]* before God." Finally, In the words of institution, Jesus speaks of his blood, "which is poured out *[ekchynnomenon]* for many" (Mark 14:24), which alludes to Isa 53:12 in the Hebrew: "he poured out *[h'rh]* his soul to death"; not in the Septuagint: "his soul was given over *[paredothē]* to death."

B. Agreements with the Septuagint

Jesus' scripture quotations and allusions sometime agree with the Septuagint against the proto-Masoretic Hebrew. Jesus' quotation of Isa 29:13 is quite septuagintal, both in form and meaning (cf. Mark 7:6–7). The identification of John the Baptist as Elijah who "restores" *(apokathistanei)* all things (Mark 9:12) seems dependent on the Septuagint form *(apokatastēsei)*, or at least a Septuagintal form of Hebrew, not the proto-Masoretic Hebrew, which reads *hshyb* ("return" or "turn back"). Curiously, both of these elements are found in Sir 48:10, in which the returning Elijah is expected "to turn [Septuagint: *epistrepsai;* Hebrew: *lhshyb]* the heart of the father to the son, and to restore [Septuagint: *katastēsai;* Hebrew: *lhkyn]* the tribes of Jacob." Both elements may well have been present in the original Hebrew version of Sirach.[22] The quotation of Ps 8:3 (ET 8:2) in Matt 21:16 follows the Septuagint. But this may be the work of the evangelist. Finally, the highly important allusions to phrases from Isa 35:5–6; 26:19; and 61:1 in Matt 11:5 = Luke 7:22 agree in places with the Septuagint. Of course, agreements with the Septuagint no longer require us to think that Jesus read or quoted the Septuagint.[23] Thanks to the Bible scrolls of the Dead Sea region, we now know that there were Hebrew *Vorlagen* underlying much of the Greek Old Testament. Indeed, there are examples where Jesus' quotations of and allusions to scripture agree with some Greek versions against others. Jesus' use of the Bible attests the diversity of the textual tradition that now, thanks to the Scrolls, is more fully documented.[24]

---

[22] For the Hebrew text (i.e., the collated fragments from the Genizah of the Ezra Synagogue in Cairo), see I. Lévi, *The Hebrew Text of the Book of Ecclesiasticus* (Leiden: Brill, 1904), 67. Our passage is not preserved in the Sirach scroll from Masada.

[23] Given the widespread use of Greek in first-century Palestine, and the presence of Greek biblical manuscripts at Qumran, we should not rule out the possibility that Jesus was familiar with the Greek Bible. On the question of Greek in Palestine, Jesus' possible ability to speak Greek, and the relevance of Greek for issues of authenticity and *ipsissima verba Jesu,* see S. E. Porter, *The Criteria for Authenticity in Historical-Jesus Research: Previous Discussion and New Proposals* (JSNTSup 191; Sheffield: Sheffield Academic Press, 2000).

[24] Another important question is the extent to which the transmission of the dominical tradition in Greek assimilated to the Septuagint (as seen clearly in Matthew's editing of Mark, and in scribal activity).

C. Agreements with the Aramaic

There are also several important examples of agreement with the Aramaic tradition, which arose in the synagogue and eventually assumed written form as the Targum. These examples will be treated in more detail.[25]

There are significant examples in which Jesus' language agrees with the Aramaic tradition. The paraphrase of Isa 6:9–10 in Mark 4:12 concludes with " . . . and *it be forgiven* them." Only the Isaiah Targum reads this way.[26] The Hebrew and the Septuagint read "heal." The criterion of dissimilarity argues for the authenticity of this strange saying, for the tendencies in both Jewish[27] and Christian[28] circles were to understand this Isaianic passage in a way significantly different from the way it appears to be understood in the Markan tradition. The saying, "All those grasping a sword by a sword will perish" (Matt 26:52), has dictional agreement with *Targum Isaiah* 50:11: "Behold, all you who kindle a fire, who grasp a sword! Go, fall in the fire which you kindled and on the sword which you grasped!" The items that the targum has added to the Hebrew text are the very items that lie behind Jesus' statement. Jesus' saying on Gehenna (Mark 9:47–48), where he quotes part of Isa 66:24, again reflects targumic diction. The Hebrew and the Septuagint say nothing about Gehenna, but the targum has: " . . . will not die and their fire shall not be quenched, and the wicked shall be judged in Gehenna. . . ." The verse is alluded to twice in the Apocrypha (Jdt 16:17; Sir 7:17), where, in contrast to Hebrew Isaiah, it seems to be looking beyond temporal punishment toward eschatological judgment. But the implicit association of Gehenna with Isa 66:24 is distinctly targumic. And, of course, the targumic paraphrase is explicitly eschatological, as is Jesus' saying. The distinctive reading found in *Targum Pseudo-Jonathan* Lev 22:28, "My people, children of Israel, as our Father is merciful in heaven, so shall you be merciful on earth," lies behind Jesus' statement in Luke 6:36: "Become merciful just as your Father is merciful." While it is unlikely that Jesus has quoted the Targum,[29] and even less plausible that the Targum has quoted him,[30] the parallel demands explanation. Most probably the Targum and Jesus both repeat a saying that circulated in first-century Palestine (cf. *y. Ber.* 5:3; *y. Meg.* 4:9).

There are other instances of thematic and exegetical coherence between Jesus' use of scripture and the Aramaic tradition. The parable of the Wicked Vineyard Tenants (Mark 12:1–12 par.) is based on Isaiah's Song of the Vineyard (Isa 5:1–7), as the dozen or so words in the opening lines of the Markan parable demonstrate. But Isaiah's parable was directed

---

[25] I am indebted to the works of B. Chilton, especially *A Galilean Rabbi and His Bible: Jesus' Use of the Interpreted Scripture of His Time* (GNS 8; Wilmington: Glazier, 1984).

[26] The Peshitta also reads this way, but it is dependent upon the Targum here; cf. C. A. Evans, *To See and Not Perceive: Isaiah 6.9–10 in Early Jewish and Christian Interpretation* (JSOTSup 64; Sheffield: JSOT Press, 1989), 77–80, 195 (for the notes).

[27] See *Mek.* on Exod 19:2; *b. Roš Haš.* 17b; *b. Meg.* 17b; *y. Ber.* 2:3; *Sed. Elij. Rab.* 16 (§82–83); *Gen. Rab.* 81.6 (on Gen 42:1).

[28] See Matt 13:11b–17; Luke 8:10; Acts 28:26–27; John 12:40. The latter is an exception, serving the Fourth Evangelist's distinctive scriptural apologetic.

[29] A. T. Olmstead, "Could an Aramaic Gospel be Written?" *JNES* 1 (1942): 41–75, esp. 64.

[30] See M. Black, *An Aramaic Approach to the Gospels and Acts* (3d ed., Oxford: Clarendon Press, 1967), 181.

against the "house of Israel" and the "men of Judah" (cf. Isa 5:7). In contrast, Jesus' parable is directed against the "ruling priests, scribes, and elders" (cf. Mark 11:27), who evidently readily perceived that the parable had been told "against them" and not against the general populace (cf. Mark 12:12). Why was this parable so understood, when it is obviously based on a prophetic parable that spoke to the nation as a whole? The answer is found once again in the Isaiah Targum, which in place of "tower" and "wine vat" reads "sanctuary" and "altar" (cf. Isa 5:2 and *Tg.* Isa 5:2),[31] institutions which will be destroyed (cf. Isa 5:5 and *Tg.* Isa 5:5). The Isaiah Targum has significantly shifted the thrust of the prophetic indictment against the priestly establishment. Jesus' parable seems to reflect this orientation: the problem does not lie with the vineyard; it lies with the caretakers of the vineyard. A few of these components appear outside of the New Testament and the Isaiah Targum. In *1 Enoch* 89:66–67 the temple is referred to as a "tower." Its first destruction is referred to, but without any apparent allusion to Isa 5. This Enochic tradition appears in *Barnabas* 16:1–5, where it is applied to the second destruction, but without reference to either Isa 5 or Mark 12. Thus the coherence between *Targum Isaiah* 5 and Mark 12 is distinctive, and probably cannot be explained away as coincidence. 4Q500, which dates to the first century B.C.E., alludes to Isaiah's parable of the Vineyard and applies it to the Temple, demonstrating the antiquity of the exegetical orientation presupposed later in Jesus and later still in the Targum.

Even the problematic quotation of Ps 118:22–23 may receive some clarification from the targum. Klyne Snodgrass has argued plausibly that its presence is due to a play on words between "the stone" *(h°bn)* and "the son" *(hbn)*, which probably explains the reading in *Targum* Ps 118:22: "The son which the builders rejected. . . ."[32] This kind of word play is old and is witnessed in the New Testament (cf. Matt 3:9 par.: "from these stones God is able to raise up children [which in Aramaic originally could have been "sons"] to Abraham"; cf. Luke 19:40) and in Josephus (*B.J.* 5.6.3 §272). The quotation was assimilated to the better known Greek version, since it was used by Christians for apologetic and christological purposes (cf. Acts 4:11; 1 Pet 2:4, 7), and possibly because second generation Christians were unaware of the original Aramaic word play.

Perhaps most important of all is Jesus' proclamation of the kingdom of God: "The time is fulfilled, and the kingdom of God has drawn near; repent, and believe in the good news" (Mark 1:15). Jesus' "good news" *(euangelion)* harks back to the "good news" *(bśr)* of Isaiah, but not in the Hebrew: "O Zion, you that bring good news . . . say, 'Behold, your God'" (40:9); or "who proclaims good news of good . . . who says to Zion, 'Your God reigns'" (52:7); rather, in the Aramaic: "prophets who proclaim good news to Zion . . . say, 'The kingdom of your God is revealed'" (*Tg. Isa.* 40:9); or "who proclaims good news . . . who says to . . . Zion, 'The kingdom of your God is revealed'" (*Tg. Isa.* 52:7).[33]

---

[31] This allegorizing interpretation appears also in the Tosefta (cf. *t. Me'il.* 1:16; *t. Sukk.* 3:15).

[32] K. R. Snodgrass, *The Parable of the Wicked Tenants: An Inquiry into Parable Interpretation* (WUNT 27; Tübingen: Mohr [Siebeck], 1983), 111; C. A. Evans, "On the Vineyard Parables of Isaiah 5 and Mark 12," *BZ* 28 (1984): 82–86, esp. 85.

[33] For technical discussion of the relationship between Aramaic Isaiah and Jesus' proclamation of the kingdom of God, see C. A. Evans, "From Gospel to Gospel: The Function of Isaiah in the New Testament," in *Writing and Reading the Scroll of Isaiah: Studies of an Interpretive Tradition* (VTSup 70.2; FIOTL 1.2; ed. C. C. Broyles and C. A. Evans; Leiden: Brill, 1997), 651–91.

D. Mixed Phenomena

This overview could be expanded by adding examples where one part of the quotation or allusion agrees with one textual tradition and another part agrees with another textual tradition. Sometimes the quotation or allusion agrees with two or more textual traditions, e.g., in instances where the Septuagint translates the Hebrew literally, or the Aramaic translates the Hebrew literally. In such cases it is not clear which text was in fact primary. Mixed phenomena confirm that Jesus' use of scripture was allusive, paraphrastic, pragmatic, and exegetically and theologically driven when it came to versional preferences. That is not to say that Jesus consciously and studiously compared three or more textual traditions, then made a selection. The evidence suggests that Jesus was not wedded to a particular text, but appealed to words, phrases, and sometimes whole passages—whatever their textual origin—in an ad hoc, experiential fashion.

4. Conclusion

We see in Jesus' use of the scripture of his day more or less what we have seen at Qumran and more generally in Judaism of this period. The first two divisions of scripture—the Law and the Prophets—are clearly recognized, though Jesus, and perhaps the sectarians of Qumran, may not have viewed the prophetic era as closed. There is awareness of additional authoritative writings, but the contours of a third division of scripture remain undefined. Jesus, like the sectarians at Qumran, evidently regarded the Psalms as inspired scripture, possibly because they were in some sense prophetic.

Jesus also seems to have quoted scripture freely, partly due to the pluriform nature of scripture in his day and partly because of his paraphrasing, allusive, and conflating style. Jesus' allusive quotation of scripture did not always distinguish text from interpretation; the two seem to blend together. What may in part account for this approach to scripture was Jesus' "spirit-filled" orientation, and his experience that the Spirit of God that had inspired scripture was again acting powerfully to fulfill scripture and adapt it, as it were, to the circumstances and effects of Jesus' ministry. The canon of scripture for Jesus, then, remained open, for God's revealing work was not yet complete.

12

The Old Testament Apocrypha in the Early Church and Today

Daniel J. Harrington, S.J.

The question now in the "canon debate" is not, in my opinion, whether the so-called apocrypha belong in the Christian Old Testament.[1] That has been settled for the present in one way or another—by the custom of including them in Eastern Orthodox Bibles; by the decree of the Council of Trent (in 1546) for their inclusion in Roman Catholic Bibles; by the practice, now current again, of including these books in most Protestant Bibles, but in special section apart from the undisputed canonical books; or by omitting them entirely in Jewish and Evangelical Protestant Bibles.[2] The question now is how Christians and Jews today might be encouraged to recognize the complex history of the topic, and might agree to read and study these books on their own merits as important witnesses to Second Temple Judaism (and as essential resources for appreciating the Jewishness of Jesus and of the early Christian movement).

After an examination of the early Jewish and Christian manuscripts and lists of the Old Testament apocrypha, this article surveys their use in the early church (in the New Testament and patristic writings), and sketches the history of their inclusion in and exclusion from Christian Bibles. Then it presents a case for taking these books seriously today—whether as scripture or not.

1. Early Jewish and Christian Manuscripts and Lists

A. Early Jewish Manuscripts and Lists

The earliest Jewish manuscripts of the Hebrew Bible and of some Old Testament apocrypha are from Qumran.[3] The discovery of the Dead Sea Scrolls in 1947 gave access to

---

[1] I am using the term "apocrypha" (and "deuterocanonical") in the neutral sense that it carries among biblical scholars today. As a Roman Catholic theologian, I follow the inclusive canon of the Council of Trent. I am pleased that the New Revised Standard Version in its Apocrypha section includes the "core" books (Tobit, Judith, Wisdom, Sirach, Baruch, and 1 and 2 Maccabees) as well as several others that are in the biblical canons of Eastern churches. The problem, of course, is how much to include.

[2] For the history of these developments, see the essays in *The Apocrypha in Ecumenical Perspective* (ed. S. Meurer; Reading, U.K./New York: United Bible Societies, 1991). Helpful treatments

biblical texts some thousand years older than the manuscripts on which the standard printed editions had been based. The Qumran biblical manuscripts range in age from the second century B.C.E. to the first century C.E. Every book of the modern Hebrew Bible is represented except Esther. Whether Esther was omitted because its Hebrew version contains no explicit mention of God, or simply by accident of preservation, or for some other reason cannot be determined. The Qumran manuscripts bear witness to a certain fluidity in the wording of the Hebrew textual tradition before the Masoretic text, which is only one of the several text-types represented at Qumran, began to assume a standardized form in the late first or early second century C.E.

What books were canonical at Qumran? It is probably anachronistic even to ask that question. At most we can talk about use. At Qumran the individual books tend to appear in individual manuscripts. There is nothing like the huge collection that came to be known as "the Bible." It is clear that some works were treated as having a certain degree of authority. The narratives and legal materials in the Pentateuch are often cited as authoritative precedents and rulings. The Prophets and Psalms are given verse-by-verse commentaries in the pesharim. These commentaries are concerned to show how the "mysteries" of the biblical text can be resolved by reflection on the life and history of the sect and its Teacher of Righteousness. The *Genesis Apocryphon,* a nonsectarian Aramaic text, provides an expanded paraphrase of parts of Genesis that solves problems that arise in exegesis—for example, Did Abram and Sarah concoct a lie in Gen 12?—and supplies related traditions. Here Genesis is clearly a text worthy of comment and clarification. And yet there seems to be no hesitation about reworking the Pentateuchal text in a free and sometimes fanciful way.

There is no list of canonical books at Qumran. From the use of books as seen in the manuscripts discovered at Qumran, it appears that the Pentateuch, the Former Prophets (the historical books), the Latter Prophets (including the Twelve), and the Psalms were often used in ways that suggest that they possessed a certain degree of authority. There are fragmentary manuscripts of other "biblical books" (Proverbs, Qohelet, etc.) and of some apocrypha (Sirach, Tobit, Letter of Jeremiah, Psalm 151). But there is no way of knowing which of these writings were regarded as authoritative or canonical in any sense. Indeed, it appears that some sectarian works, such as the *Rule of the Community,* the *Hodayot,* and even an apparently nonsectarian work like *1 Enoch,* had much greater use and influence than any of the apocrypha or Old Testament Writings apart from Psalms. There is no trace of Judith, Wisdom, Baruch, 1 and 2 Maccabees, 1 and 2 Esdras, Prayer of Manasseh, 3 and 4 Maccabees. Some of these we would not expect to find on grounds of their place of composition (Wisdom, 3 Maccabees), date (2 Esdras and 4 Maccabees), original language (Greek), and position within Jewish history (1 and 2 Maccabees). But the absence of Hebrew originals of Judith and Baruch is mildly puzzling.

The earliest Jewish reckonings of canonical books come from the late first and second century C.E. In *Contra Apionem* 1.37–43 Josephus claims that there are twenty-two "justly accredited books" and gives the time of "Artaxerxes who succeeded Xerxes as king

of the history of the canon include F. F. Bruce, *The Canon of Scripture* (Downers Grove, Ill.: InterVarsity, 1988); and L. M. McDonald, *The Formation of the Christian Biblical Canon* (rev. and enl. ed.; Peabody, Mass.: Hendrickson, 1995).

³ See E. Tov, *Textual Criticism of the Hebrew Bible* (Minneapolis: Fortress, 1992).

of Persia" as the cutoff point for inclusion. The idea behind this number (which equals the letters in the Hebrew alphabet) seems to be that all truth is contained in twenty-two books, written with the twenty-two letters of the Hebrew alphabet. The small number of books and the early cutoff date would not allow the inclusion of any of the apocrypha in this canon. It should be noted, however, that Josephus drew extensively on 1 Maccabees as a source for his account of events in the second century B.C.E. in his *Antiquitates judaicae.*

Fourth Ezra 14:45–46, a late first-century C.E. Jewish apocalypse, distinguishes between "the twenty-four books" that are to be made public and "the seventy that were written last" and reserved for "the wise." Neither *4 Ezra* nor Josephus provides a complete list of the titles of their twenty-four or twenty-two canonical books. But it is likely that they had the same core canon, and that the difference in numbers arose from Josephus's combining books in order to arrive at the number of letters in the Hebrew alphabet.[4] The mention of the seventy additional books in *4 Ezra* 14 is the basis of the idea of "apocrypha" or hidden books. Whereas for Josephus the major concern was antiquity, in *4 Ezra* the distinction between canonical and apocryphal books resided in the appropriate audience— the general public versus "the wise"—and presumably the appropriate content.

These passages from Josephus and *4 Ezra* represent the earliest evidence for including some books and excluding others from the authoritative collection or "canon" of Jewish scriptures. They suggest that such a movement was taking place in the very late first century C.E. as part of the effort at reconstructing Judaism after the destruction of the Jerusalem temple in 70 C.E.

A second-century C.E. *baraita* (an early Jewish tradition) preserved in the Babylonian Talmud (*b. B. Bat.* 14b–15a) treats the order and authorship of the Jewish scriptures. Without naming the individual books in the Pentateuch, whose authority is assumed, it lists the Prophets (Joshua, Judges, Samuel, Kings, Jeremiah, Ezekiel, Isaiah, and the Twelve Minor Prophets) and the Hagiographa (Ruth, Psalms, Job, Proverbs, Ecclesiastes, Song of Songs, Lamentations, Daniel, Esther, Ezra, and Chronicles). These amount to twenty-four books (as in *4 Ezra* 14:45–46). The list is divided into three parts: Torah, Prophets, and Writings—the origin of the Hebrew acronym TaNaK.

In the early rabbinic period there were disputes about whether certain books (Ezekiel, Proverbs, Ecclesiastes, Song of Songs, Esther) belonged in the authoritative collection or "canon." The existence of such debates and the rabbinic concept that the sacred books "defile the hands" provide still more evidence that the concept of a canon of Jewish scriptures and its content had become important issues at least by the post-70 C.E. period. The insistence on a twenty-two or twenty-four book canon left no room for the inclusion of the apocryphal books as part of the Jewish canon.

B. Early Christian Manuscripts and Lists

The three earliest and most important Christian manuscripts of the Greek Bible, from the late fourth and early fifth century C.E., show some openness to the Old Testament apocrypha.[5] Codex Vaticanus contains Wisdom, Sirach, Judith, and Tobit, along with

---

[4] Cf. *Jubilees* 2:23–24 for the importance of the number twenty-two.
[5] See A. C. Sundberg, *The Old Testament of the Early Church* (Cambridge, Mass.: Harvard University Press, 1964), 59; and McDonald, *The Formation of the Christian Biblical Canon*, 272–73.

Baruch and the Letter of Jeremiah. Codex Sinaiticus includes Tobit, Judith, 1 and 2 Maccabees, Wisdom, and Sirach. Codex Alexandrinus has Baruch and the Letter of Jeremiah, along with Tobit, Judith, 1 and 2 Maccabees, 3 and 4 Maccabees, Wisdom, Sirach, and the Psalms of Solomon. These books are interspersed among the "canonical" books and not placed in a separate section. The order of the books in each manuscript is different. These facts suggest that the edges of the Christian Old Testament canon were still fluid, and that the core apocrypha and then some were welcomed in biblical manuscripts.

There are many lists of canonical Old Testament books from various church fathers and councils.[6] The lists from the Eastern churches tend to support a restricted canon very much like that of the Hebrew tradition. In several cases (Origen, Athanasius, Cyril of Jerusalem, and Epiphanius) Baruch and the Letter of Jeremiah are included as parts of Jeremiah-Lamentations, with no other apocrypha mentioned. One of the two lists from Pseudo-Chrysostom contains Sirach, and a second list includes Tobit, Judith, Wisdom, and Sirach. The list from the Council of Laodicea allows only Baruch and the Letter of Jeremiah.

Among the Western fathers, Jerome and Rufinus agree with the traditional Hebrew canon, whereas Hilary adds Tobit and Judith, and includes the Letter of Jeremiah with Jeremiah. Augustine's list in *De doctrina christiana* includes Tobit, Judith, 1 and 2 Maccabees, Wisdom, and Sirach. The list from the Council of Rome contains Wisdom, Sirach, Tobit, Judith, and 1 and 2 Maccabees. The Council of Hippo has Sirach, Wisdom, Tobit, Judith, and 1 and 2 Maccabees. The Canon Muratori even includes the Wisdom of Solomon in its list of New Testament books.

In all these Christian manuscripts and lists there is no obvious fixed order of books. Where the apocrypha are present, they are interspersed among the nondisputed books, not relegated to a separate collection. The early Eastern churches seem to have been somewhat less open to including these books. In the Western witnesses, apart from Jerome's resistance, one can perceive the development toward the inclusive canon that became the Vulgate tradition, which in turn was officially affirmed by the Council of Trent in 1546.

Judaism's restrictive twenty-two or twenty-four book canon had repercussions among early Christians. In the late second century C.E., Melito the bishop of Sardis in western Asia Minor journeyed to Palestine in order to ascertain what books belonged in the Old Testament. That he felt obliged to make this journey suggests that there was confusion about the extent of the biblical canon not only among Christians but also among Diaspora Jews. He discovered that the Jews of Palestine observed a twenty-two book canon, and so his list of canonical books includes no apocrypha. Melito apparently regarded this finding to be significant for the debate about the scope of the Christian Bible.

Further Christian evidence for the twenty-two book canon appears in the writings of Origen, Athanasius, Cyril of Jerusalem, Gregory Nazianzus, and Epiphanius. While several of these writers recommended the reading of the apocrypha, their Old Testament lists reflect the tradition, first glimpsed in Josephus, that the number of biblical books equals the number of letters in the Hebrew alphabet. These lists also show some misgivings about the inclusion of Esther.

---

[6] See Sundberg, *Old Testament,* 58–59; and McDonald, *Formation,* 268–73.

In short, the evidence from the early Jewish and early Christian manuscripts and lists of Jewish scriptures shows a tendency among Jews to restrict their canon of sacred scripture to twenty-two or twenty-four books. It also shows a tendency among some early Christians especially, in the East to follow the Jewish practice, whereas in the West (except for Jerome) there is more openness to include some of the books that have come to be known as the apocrypha.

2. Possible Uses in the New Testament and Early Christian Writings

A. New Testament

Can one prove that Jesus or the New Testament writers knew and used the apocrypha? One way to begin to answer this question is to consult the list of *loci citati vel allegati* in the Nestle-Aland *Novum Testamentum Graece*. Both Sundberg and McDonald have culled this source for references to the apocrypha and pseudepigrapha, and have produced their own lists that are very impressive at first glance.[7] But what do such lists prove?

The first problem emerges with the Latin adjective *allegati*. How strong are these alleged references? This in turn raises the question whether we are dealing with verbal similarities, or background information, or conceptual parallels, or merely "will-o'-the-wisps" proposed by modern scholars. Each of these references must be weighed on its own merits. On closer examination many of the alleged sources or parallels disappear.

The second problem is that even if one could prove that Jesus or a New Testament writer did use one of the apocrypha, this alone would not prove that they regarded the text as sacred scripture or as canonical. After all, Acts 17:28 has Paul quoting the Greek poet Aratus, and no one regards Aratus as canonical. Also, Jude 14–15 contains a quotation from *1 Enoch* 1:9. In the rhetorical context of both passages, the quotations are presented as possessing some intrinsic authority but not necessarily as scriptural or canonical. Moreover, neither Jesus nor any New Testament author introduces a real or alleged quotation from the apocrypha with a fulfillment formula such as "all this took place to fulfill what had been spoken by the Lord through the prophet" (Matt 1:22).

The most that can be proved from the *loci citati vel allegati* is that Jesus and the New Testament writers may have used some of the apocrypha. Nothing can be inferred about the authority, canonicity, or sacred character that they may or may not have attributed to these books.

Rather than assessing the entire list, I will look at what are perhaps the three most promising cases that biblical scholars have proposed as positive evidence for New Testament dependence on the apocrypha. The goal is to sharpen awareness of the methodological problems involved in such arguments. The issue is whether one can *prove* that Jesus or one of the New Testament writers used a book of the apocrypha.

1. Matthew 11:25–30. Perhaps the most promising candidate for the direct dependence of the Synoptic tradition on a text from the apocrypha is Matt 11:25–30 and Sir 51. The two texts are said to share a common outline: thanksgiving to God (Sir 51:1–12 = Matt

---

[7] Sundberg, *Old Testament,* 58–59; and McDonald, *Formation,* 259–67.

11:25–26), the revelation of a mystery (Sir 51:13–22 = Matt 11:27), and an appeal to others (Sir 51:23–30 = Matt 11:28–30). The vocabulary and themes in Matt 11:28–30 and Sir 51:23–27 are especially similar: the invitation to come and learn, the image of the yoke, and the promises of an easy burden and of rest for the soul. But do these apparently impressive parallels really prove direct dependence? The problem is that each phrase and motif has a rich biblical background, and so it is hard to prove Matthew's (or Jesus') direct dependence on Sir 51. Having sifted through all the evidence, W. D. Davies and Dale C. Allison conclude that the case for direct dependence "falls to the ground" and that the two passages "exhibit certain similarities because they both incorporate Torah and Wisdom motifs."[8]

2. Romans 1:18–32. The most promising case for direct Pauline dependence on the apocrypha is Rom 1:18–32 and Wis 13–14. Both texts take ignorance or rejection of the true God (the God of Israel) as the starting point for the downward spiral of humankind into sinfulness. The worship of false gods has negative moral consequences that feed human vices, producing in turn a thoroughly sinful society. For the author of Wisdom, the remedy is the worship of the God of Israel, who is the source of true wisdom, from which will flow appropriate behavior and a wise society. For Paul, the argument demonstrates the need for Gentiles to recognize their hopelessly sinful condition before and apart from Christ. Joseph A. Fitzmyer observes cautiously that "Paul's argument about the inexcusable situation of pagan humanity has to be understood against the background of such pre-Christian Jewish thinking, especially that in the *(sic)* Wis 13:1–19 and 14:22–31."[9] Of course, "background" is not the same as dependence. While Wis 13–14 does provide a remarkably clear parallel to Paul's meditation on the condition of Gentiles before and apart from Christ in Rom 1, it is difficult to prove that Paul actually read Wis 13–14 and incorporated it in his own work.

3. Hebrews 1:3. Here Jesus is described as the Wisdom of God: "He [Christ] is the reflection of God's glory and the exact imprint of God's very being, and he sustains all things by his powerful word." The verse seems to be a quotation or adaptation of an early Christian confession of Jesus as the Wisdom of God (see also Col 1:15–20 and John 1:1–18), which in turn depends on the Jewish tradition of Wisdom personified (see Prov 8:22–31; Sir 24; Wis 7; *1 Enoch* 42:1–3). According to Wis 7:26, Wisdom is "a reflection of eternal life, a spotless mirror of the working of God, and an image of his goodness." While the concepts are similar, the one solid verbal link that might prove direct dependence is the Greek word *apaugasma* ("reflection"). Is this single word enough to establish the direct dependence of Hebrews (or its hymnic source) on Wis 7? Again the path of caution suggests that it is preferable to speak about parallels or background rather than direct dependence.

In his very positive essay entitled "The Significance of the Old Testament Apocrypha and Pseudepigrapha for the Understanding of Jesus and Christology," Peter Stuhlmacher concludes that the "so-called Septuagintal Apocrypha thus belongs *(sic)* inseparably to the Holy Scripture of early Christianity."[10] My own ecclesial identity as a

---

[8] W. D. Davies and D. C. Allison, *A Critical and Exegetical Commentary on the Gospel According to Saint Matthew* (3 vols.; Edinburgh: T&T Clark, 1988–1997), 2:293.

[9] Fitzmyer, *Romans* (New York: Doubleday, 1993), 272.

[10] Stuhlmacher in Meurer, *The Apocrypha in Ecumenical Perspective,* 12.

Roman Catholic, and my high esteem for Stuhlmacher as a biblical scholar, the examples that he gives, and the enthusiasm for these books that he displays would normally lead me to embrace his optimistic conclusion. But in too many cases his evidence is not completely convincing. Even less persuasive is the judgment that these books "belong inseparably to the Holy Scripture of early Christianity." The available evidence seems insufficient to support that claim.

B. Patristic Evidence

The evidence for the use of the Old Testament apocrypha by patristic authors is much stronger. Corresponding to the development witnessed in the biblical manuscripts and the lists of books, there seems to have been a growing tendency to treat these books as part of Christian scripture. As the Old Testament was translated into Latin, Coptic, Syriac, Ethiopic, Armenian, and Arabic, generally depending on the Septuagint tradition, many books of the apocrypha were taken as scripture into those church traditions. Early Christian writers frequently appealed to characters in these books as moral examples. They also used material in these books to confirm Christian (and Jewish) doctrines such as angels and resurrection. Again three examples must suffice to bring out the nature of the evidence and the methodological problems associated with it.[11]

1. Tobit. The book of Tobit features an interesting plot and many attractive characters. It also contains some curious details, and so it is not surprising that it attracted the attention of early Christian writers. The manuscripts found in Cave 4 at Qumran included some substantial fragments of the book of Tobit in its original Aramaic version. However, it was the Greek version of Tobit that became part of the Christian collection of Old Testament books and generally served as the basis for the early translations, Jerome's Vulgate being an exception.

Origen was especially interested in Tobit for its teachings about angels, in particular for the relationship between their names and their tasks (e.g., Raphael and healing), as well as their role in presenting the prayers of human beings to God. Cyprian of Carthage found in Tobit an example of patience and fidelity in the midst of suffering, of prayer combined with good works, and of the value of almsgiving. The dangerous marriage between Tobias and Sarah also attracted early Christian attention, and Raguel's blessing on the couple (Tob 8:15–17) was eventually incorporated into the wedding liturgy. Jerome's curious translation of Tob 8:4 ("when the third night is over, we will be in our wedlock") led to the even more curious custom of deferring the consummation of a marriage for three nights (called "Tobias nights").

2. 2 Maccabees. What in 2 Maccabees attracted the most attention in antiquity was the episode about the martyrdom of the seven sons and their mother, in chapter 7. The Jewish work known as *4 Maccabees* used the episode as the occasion to explore at length the mystery of the suffering of righteous persons and how they could overcome physical pain and even death. Its author freely mixed biblical and philosophical materials in producing a memorable portrait of the terrible sufferings and the courage of the Maccabean martyrs.

---

[11] See the information in *The International Bible Commentary* (ed. W. R. Farmer; Collegeville: Liturgical Press, 1998).

Early Christian authors such as Cyprian also invoked the good example of the Maccabean martyrs to encourage their Christian audiences. John Chrysostom and Gregory Nazianzus wrote homilies on them for the special feast day celebrated in their honor at Antioch in Syria. The frequent references to resurrection in the dialogue between them and the wicked king, in 2 Macc 7, naturally attracted the attention of early Christian writers. And the mother's comment about her sons in 2 Macc 7:28 ("God did not make them out of things that existed") became the dubious biblical basis for the doctrine of *creatio ex nihilo*.

3. *Sirach.* The book of Sirach, also known as Ecclesiasticus, was composed in Hebrew by Jesus ben Sira, a Jewish wisdom teacher of Jerusalem, around 180 B.C.E. His grandson translated the book into Greek around 117 B.C.E. Fragments of the Hebrew text have been found at Qumran and Masada. It was frequently quoted with respect in the Talmud and other rabbinic works. But it did not become part of the Hebrew canon of scripture, most likely because it was regarded as having been composed too late (see Josephus, *Against Apion* 1.37–43). Through the grandson's Greek version it became part of the Greek Bible tradition and the Christian Old Testament.

The earliest patristic evidence for the use of Sirach occurs in *Didache* 4.5 and *Barnabas* 19.9. Both works appear to cite Sir 4:31 as good advice, but without attribution and in a different Greek form. Many Greek writers (Clement of Alexandria, Origen, John Chrysostom, Cyril of Jerusalem) and Latin writers (Tertullian, Cyprian, Jerome, Augustine) quoted or adapted material from Sirach. For example, in his *Stromateis,* composed in the late second century C.E., Clement of Alexandria quoted Sir 1:1 ("all wisdom is from the Lord") to justify the study of Greek wisdom (1.4.27), and Sir 25:9 ("happy . . . is the one who speaks to attentive listeners") to emphasize the need for receptivity toward the gift of God's wisdom (2.4.15). Clement even suggested that Sirach, whom he identified as Solomon, inspired the pre-Socratic philosopher Heraclitus (2.5.17, 24).

3. Inclusion and Exclusion

From the ancient manuscripts and lists of authoritative books that were discussed above in Part One, two clear tendencies emerged: a movement within Judaism in the late first century C.E. toward a three-part canon composed of twenty-two or twenty-four books, depending on how one counts them; and the growing acceptance of a wider and more inclusive Old Testament canon among Christians in the late fourth and early fifth centuries.

To explain these developments, modern scholars have proposed that the Jewish canon was fixed and closed at the Council (or Synod) of Jamnia/Yavneh in the late first century C.E., and that early Christians were following the more inclusive canon current in the Jewish community of Alexandria. These two explanations suffer from lack of hard evidence. While there was surely a movement to reconstruct Jewish life after 70 C.E. that was based in Jamnia/Yavneh, the idea of a special meeting analogous to a church council or synod to determine authoritatively the limits of the Hebrew canon of scripture has no firm foundation.[12] The theory that the wider Christian canon was borrowed from the Jews of

---

[12] J. P. Lewis, "Some Aspects of the Problem of the Inclusion of the Apocrypha," in Meurer, *The Apocrypha in Ecumenical Perspective,* 161–207.

Alexandria also lacks any firm foundation.[13] The historical realities were undoubtedly more complex.

These scholarly theories of the past are regarded by scholars today as "myths." But myths often convey some important truths. The Jamnia myth seeks to explain the movement among Jews in the late first century C.E. to fix definitively the wording and the extent of the authoritative scriptures of Israel. The Alexandria myth seeks to explain why Christians gradually embraced certain Jewish books beyond those of the Hebrew Bible and serving, for the most part, little or no obvious Christian theological purposes.

The most influential exception was Jerome, the greatest biblical scholar of Christian antiquity. The mature Jerome wanted Christians to accept the Hebrew canon as authoritative and to relegate the other books to a collection with secondary (deuterocanonical) status. Jerome began his Latin translation on the basis of the Greek Septuagint. But as he progressed in his study of Hebrew, he saw the need to make his translation directly from the Hebrew. He also embraced the twenty-two/twenty-four book canon of the Hebrew scriptures, and concluded that "whatever falls outside these must be set apart among the apocrypha."[14] Jerome used the term "apocrypha" with respect, and held these books to be well worth reading. He perceived correctly that Sirach and 1 Maccabees were composed in Hebrew, and that Wisdom and 2 Maccabees were composed in Greek. He claims to have translated Tobit and Judith from "Aramaic." His theological principle—and this is most important for subsequent developments—was that these books can and should be read "for the edification of the people but not for establishing the authority of ecclesiastical doctrines." This is the principle that Luther and other Reformers would revive more than a thousand years later.

In his correspondence with Jerome, Augustine did not deny the value of the Hebrew text, but argued in favor of basing the new Latin version on the Septuagint because this would promote unity among the Greek-speaking churches of East and the Latin-speaking churches of the West. In his list of canonical books Augustine followed what had become the Western Christian tradition (forty-four books = twenty-two times two). He included the so-called apocrypha among the undisputed canonical books: Tobit, Judith, and 1 and 2 Maccabees among the historical books; Wisdom and Sirach/Ecclesiasticus among "the prophetical books, since they have won recognition as being authoritative"; and Baruch, as part of Jeremiah, among "the books which are strictly called the Prophets." In Augustine's list the apocrypha are interspersed among the undisputed books, without distinction.

As Jerome's Vulgate translation became authoritative in the Western church, it gradually came to include not only the core apocrypha, interspersed among the undisputed books, but also as a kind of appendix *3 Esdras* (the "Greek Ezra") and *4 Esdras* (the *Apocalypse of Ezra*, in chapters 3–14, along with the Christian sections, in 1–2 and 15–16), and the Prayer of Manasseh. There were still, however, some distinguished Christian proponents of the narrow Hebrew canon. For example, Hugh of St. Victor described the core apocrypha as "read [in church] but not inscribed in the body of the text or in the canon of authority." The early vernacular English translations included the apocrypha, since they were based on the Vulgate and followed its traditional contents.

When Luther enunciated the principle of *sola scriptura* in his theological debates, he was forced to delineate more exactly what constituted scripture. In general, Luther's crite-

[13] Sundberg, *Old Testament*, 51–79.
[14] Bruce, *Canon*, 90.

rion ("what promotes Christ") was theological rather than historical, and it led him into negative judgments even about some universally accepted canonical books—the most famous example being James, "the epistle of straw." With regard to the apocrypha, Luther's judgment was shaped to some extent by the theological controversy about the doctrines of purgatory and praying for the dead, which were traditionally based on 2 Macc 12:45–46. He appealed to Jerome's distinction between the (Hebrew) canonical books and the apocrypha, and to his principle that these books should not be used for establishing ecclesiastical doctrines. In his German translation Luther departed from the practice of the Vulgate and relegated the apocrypha to a separate section headed "Books which are not held to be equal to holy scripture, but are useful and good to read." The tradition of including the apocrypha but separating them from the undisputed books held firm in the early Protestant Bibles. Their gradual omission was apparently prompted first by practical considerations on the part of publishers, since they took up space and added to the cost of Bibles. Then in the nineteenth century the apocrypha began to be omitted on theological grounds, as extracanonical and not inspired, and so not to be used to establish church doctrines.[15]

In its fourth session (April 1546) the Council of Trent rejected the distinction of Luther, and ultimately Jerome, between canonical Old Testament books and the apocrypha. Its definitive list of canonical books was the first ever issued by an ecumenical council, since the pertinent councils of the patristic period were local. It included the core apocrypha and placed them among, not apart from, the undisputed books. And it issued an anathema upon those who might think otherwise. And so Bibles published under Roman Catholic auspices present the apocrypha as part of the Christian Old Testament without qualification. It should not be imagined, however, that these books receive disproportionate attention among Roman Catholic biblical scholars or theologians, or in the liturgy.

Most modern Bible versions, whether under Catholic or Protestant auspices, now include the apocrypha. Some place it in a separate section (the New Revised Standard Version, the Good News Bible, and the New [and Revised] English Bible). Others intersperse it among the other Old Testament books (the New American Bible and the Jerusalem Bible). The New International Version, published under Evangelical auspices, is exceptional in omitting it completely. The New Revised Standard Version has a very inclusive collection, divided into four sections: (a) books that are in the Roman Catholic, Greek, and Slavonic Bibles (Tobit, Judith, Additions to Esther, Wisdom of Solomon, Sirach, Baruch, Letter of Jeremiah, Additions to Daniel, 1 Maccabees, and 2 Maccabees); (b) books in the Greek and Slavonic Bibles but not in the Roman Catholic canon (1 Esdras, *Prayer of Manasseh*, Psalm 151, 3 Maccabees); (c) a book in the Slavonic Bible and in the Latin Vulgate appendix (2 Esdras); and (d) a book in an appendix to the Greek Bible (4 Maccabees).

4. Taking the Apocrypha Seriously Today

The history of the Old Testament apocrypha's inclusion in and exclusion from the Christian Old Testament is indeed complicated. The historical evidence is not adequate

---

[15] See the various essays in Meurer, *The Apocrypha in Ecumenical Perspective.*

to justify the conclusion that the apocrypha were always part of the Christian Old Testament. Neither does it prove that they were never part of the Christian canon. When the issue became a factor in the polemics between the Reformers of the sixteenth century and the fathers of the Council of Trent, the outer limit of the Christian Old Testament canon assumed more importance than ever before. To this day it remains an obstacle to Christian unity.

There are, of course, more obvious and difficult obstacles to Christian unity than the extent of the Old Testament canon. In any truly ecumenical council that might involve Roman Catholic, Protestant, and Orthodox Christians, it would probably not be high on the agenda. But to prepare for that blessed event, it might be beneficial if all Christians (and Jews) began to take these books more seriously in their own right.

Since the history of the canonical question yields no univocal conclusion, perhaps we should follow Luther's lead and adopt a theological criterion. Luther's criterion was expressed in his German formula *was treibt Christum* ("what promotes Christ"). I propose that we take Luther's criterion but define it differently. Whereas Luther had little patience for things Jewish (for example, he railed against Esther and 2 Maccabees for containing "too much Judaism and no little pagan vice"), I want to define his dictum to mean that whatever helps us better to appreciate Jesus in the context of Judaism best promotes Christ today. In this redefinition I am taking up what I regard to be one of the most important directions in recent biblical scholarship: the Jewishness of Jesus.[16]

Renewed attention to the Old Testament apocrypha, as well as to the works of Josephus and Philo, the Dead Sea scrolls, the Old Testament pseudepigrapha, and the rabbinic writings, can help all Christians (and Jews) better to understand the Jewishness of Jesus and of the earliest Christian movement. The apocrypha represent only one corpus in the much larger body of Second Temple Jewish literature. But since these books do appear in most Christian Bibles today, they are certainly the most convenient starting point for such an undertaking. In what follows I want to offer some examples to suggest how the apocrypha, here defined widely as the New Revised Standard Version does, might serve as a bridge between the Old Testament and the New Testament. I will proceed on three levels: literary, historical, and theological.[17]

A. Literary Contributions

The books of the apocrypha add considerably to the inventory of literary genres and techniques present in biblical literature. There are histories or historical novels (1 Esdras, 1–3 Maccabees), prayers (Prayer of Manasseh, Additions to Esther), detective stories (Additions to Daniel), and so forth. But for better understanding and appreciating the genres of the New Testament books, the most important apocrypha are those that take the form of narrative (Tobit and Judith), instruction (Sirach), discourse (Wisdom, 4 Maccabees), and apocalypse (4 Ezra).

---

[16] For surveys, see D. J. Harrington, "The Jewishness of Jesus: Facing Some Problems," *CBQ* 49 (1987): 1–13; and "Retrieving the Jewishness of Jesus: Recent Developments," *New Theology Review* 11.2 (1998): 5–19.

[17] For full discussions, see D. J. Harrington, *An Invitation to the Old Testament Apocrypha: Approaches to the Mystery of Suffering* (Grand Rapids: Eerdmans, 1999).

1. Narrative. The books of Tobit and Judith present good stories with edifying purposes. The plot of Tobit starts from the tribulations of two righteous persons: Tobit and Sarah (chs. 1–3). Their stories come together through the journey of Tobias and Raphael (chs. 4–6), which results in the wedding of Sarah and Tobias (chs. 7–9) and the healing of Tobit from his blindness (chs. 10–11). The story ends with Raphael's revelation and Tobit's hymn and last testament (chs. 12–14). The characters are attractive and memorable, and the plot tells the story of the classic quest: Tobias's journey to a far country and his return home. The plot moves along with a skillful shifting of scenes from one place to another.

Judith is a widow whom God uses to save Israel through her piety, beauty, and cleverness. The ironic message of the book is that God saves Israel from its enemies "by the hand of a woman." The narrator makes ample use of speeches and dialogues, and summarizes the whole story with a hymn (16:1–17). The two main parts of the narrative (2:14–7:32 and 8:1–16:25) proceed according to concentric outlines, and the shifts in place serve to move the plot along.

These two highly sophisticated narratives set the stage for the equally sophisticated narratives found in the Gospels and Acts. They can make us more sensitive to plot, character development, structure, and irony as essential components of the biblical narratives.

2. Instruction. The book of Sirach is a huge wisdom instruction, analogous in style to the five great discourses in Matthew's Gospel (chs. 5–7, 10, 13, 18, 24–25). Ben Sira's favorite mode of communication is through short sayings made up of two members in synonymous or antithetical parallelism. His major contribution to the Jewish wisdom tradition consists in his joining individual sayings by common words or themes, and using small units to develop a topic or argument in paragraph form.

Within the literary framework of instruction, Ben Sira used the devices typical of wisdom literature: numerical sayings ("I take pleasure in three things . . ."), beatitudes ("happy are those who . . ."), warnings or prohibitions ("do not . . ."), rhetorical questions, comparisons, and so forth. He also employed poetic devices (assonance, alliteration, rhyme), inclusions (beginning and ending a unit in the same way), chiasms, acrostics, and hymns. The book of Sirach is a rich resource for studying the instructional material in the Synoptic Gospels and James.

3. Discourse. Some of the New Testament Epistles, especially Paul's letters to the Galatians and the Romans, and Hebrews, are remarkable for their sophisticated rhetorical techniques in the service of theological argument. In this respect they have much in common with the book of Wisdom and 4 Maccabees.

The book of Wisdom is an exhortation to seek wisdom and to live by it. The author encourages Diaspora Jews to remain faithful to the Jewish tradition, and argues that Judaism is superior to other religions and philosophies. The three main parts concern righteousness and immortality (chs. 1–5), the nature and function of Wisdom (chs. 6–9), and Wisdom's role in the early history of Israel (chs. 10–19). While the basic structure is clear, the many connections, excurses, anticipations, and other rhetorical devices indicate an even more complex and sophisticated literary structure. The author knew some basic techniques of classical Greek rhetoric, as well as some basic concepts of Greek philosophy, and used them in the service of his theological argument.

The combination of Greek rhetoric and philosophy in the service of Jewish theology also appears in 4 Maccabees. The author has a clear and simple thesis: Devout reason is

sovereign over the emotions. In the first part (1:1–3:8) he adopts the persona of the philosophy professor with his thesis, definitions, and illustrations. Then in his greatly
expanded version of the martyrdoms of Eleazar, the seven brothers, and their mother in
3:19–18:24 (cf. 2 Macc 6–7), he narrates each confrontation between the wicked king and
the martyrs with the help of emotional dialogues, descriptions of gruesome tortures, and
defiant speeches.

   4. Apocalypse. The book of Revelation was composed around 95 C.E., about the same
time as *4 Ezra* (= 2 Esd 3–14). Both works are apocalypses, and both are concerned with
the sufferings of God's people in "this age" and their vindication in "the age to come." A
large part of *4 Ezra* is devoted to three dialogues (3:1–5:20; 5:21–6:34; 6:35–9:25) in which
Ezra raises theological questions about Israel's exile and the angel Uriel responds with
predictions about the future and the "signs" that will mark the end of this age and the
beginning of the age to come. The dialogues are followed by three dream visions and their
interpretations: the mourning woman (9:26–10:59), the eagle and the lion (11:1–12:51),
and the man from the sea (13:1–58). Within the dialogues and dream visions there are
addresses, questions and answers, lists, prayers, small apocalypses, and so forth. In content
and form *4 Ezra* greatly illumines Revelation.

B. Historical Contributions

   Many of the apocrypha are best interpreted as historical novels, especially Tobit,
Judith, Esther, and 3 Maccabees. While they may contain some historical information—as
historical novels do—it is generally futile to try to discover and defend the historical
details in these books. We are on somewhat firmer ground with 1 Esdras and 1 and
2 Maccabees. But here too we should not expect from these ancient writings an objective
chronicle of events.

   1. Return from Exile. First Esdras tells the story of Israel's exile to Babylon and its
return to Jerusalem. The book covers material found in the Hebrew Bible in 2 Chr 35–36,
almost the entire book of Ezra, and parts of Nehemiah (7:6–8:12). The main concern is the
rebuilding of God's people through their religious and social institutions: the renewal of
the sacrifices at the Jerusalem temple, the observance of the traditional festivals, the
rebuilding of the temple structures, the clarification of who really belongs to Israel, the
prohibition of marriages with non-Jews, and the public reading of the Torah as "the law of
the land." In the project of reconstructing God's people, the priest Joshua and the governor
Zerubbabel as well as the priest-scribe Ezra play pivotal roles. They stand in continuity
with King Josiah, whose reform based on the discovery of a law-book in the Jerusalem
temple led to the ideal observance of Passover, according to 1:1–22.

   2. The Maccabean Revolt. The first half of the second century B.C.E. was a very important period in Jewish history. In this time the people of Jerusalem and Judea faced a major
crisis when the Syrian King Antiochus IV Epiphanes, with the encouragement and support
of some local Jews, transformed the temple into what many other Jews regarded as a pagan
shrine. This crisis in turn provided the opportunity for Judas Maccabeus and his brothers
to gain back the temple for traditional worship, to position themselves as leaders of the
Jewish people, and to win national independence with the help of Rome as a patron.

First and Second Maccabees are the best sources for these decisive ever̶
begin with 2 Maccabees, since it starts in the reign of Seleucus IV (187–¹
ends with Judas Maccabeus's defeat of Nicanor in 161 B.C.E. The author, who in ᵢₐ~
condenser or epitomator of a five-volume work by Jason of Cyrene, set out to inform and
entertain. His work has been described as both "pathetic history" (since it appeals to the
emotions or *pathē* in Greek), and "temple propaganda" (since it focuses on the Jerusalem
temple). The work does, however, provide some important and generally reliable historical
information about the persons and events that led up to the Maccabean revolt and Judas's
subsequent efforts at exercising leadership.

The focus of 2 Maccabees is the Jerusalem temple. Its main part (chs. 3–15)
describes three attacks on the temple and its successful defense by God and the people of
Judea under the leadership of Judas Maccabeus. The first attack (3:1–40) takes place under
Seleucus IV, when Heliodorus tries to plunder the temple treasury. The second attack
(4:1–10:9), under Antiochus IV, results in the recapture and rededication of the temple
under Judas. The third attack (10:10–15:36), under Antiochus V, involves the defeat and
death of his general Nicanor as he tries to capture and kill Judas.

The main character in 2 Maccabees is Judas. The author is interested in Judas primarily as God's instrument in defending the temple. He also contrasts the pious high
priest Onias III with the scoundrels Jason, Menelaus, and Alcimus who succeeded him.
The most famous part of the book, however, is the dialogue between the wicked king and
the seven sons and their mother in chapter 7, with its many appeals to hope for the resurrection of the body in the face of present sufferings.

First Maccabees traces the history of the Maccabean family or dynasty through three
generations, from 167 to 134 B.C.E. After describing the crisis under Antiochus IV and the
resistance begun by the priest Mattathias (1:1–2:70), it narrates the military and political
achievements of Judas (3:1–9:22) and his brothers Jonathan (9:23–12:53) and Simon and
their nephew John Hyrcanus (13:1–16:24). The author explains how God used the
Maccabee family to throw off the yoke of Seleucid oppression, and how the Jewish high
priesthood came to reside in this family. The book's perspective is made explicit in its
account of the defeat of Joseph and Azariah because "they did not listen to Judas and his
brothers. But they did not belong to the family of those men through whom deliverance
was given to Israel" (1 Macc 5:61–62).

The persons and events described in 1 and 2 Maccabees transformed Judea from
being part of, successively, the Persian, Ptolemaic, and Seleucid empires to independent
statehood with a national identity based on the temple, the land, and the Torah. They also
brought the Romans into Jewish history, thus providing the context for Judea's incorporation into the Roman empire and setting the stage for the events described in the Gospels.

C. Theological Contributions

In this area the contributions of the apocrypha are so rich that I must be quite selective. I will focus on God, suffering, and Wisdom.

1. God. The apocrypha contribute much to theology proper, the "doctrine of God."
They emphasize God's love for and protection of Israel (Judith, 3 Maccabees), care for
righteous persons (Tobit), use of weak instruments (Judith), and defense of the Jerusalem

temple (2 Maccabees). Because there is only one true God, the worship of other gods (idolatry) is the worst folly, and brings about many evil effects (Wisdom, Letter of Jeremiah, Bel and the Dragon).

2. Suffering. All of the apocrypha in one way or another deal with the problem of suffering, either in the case of individuals (as in Tobit) or in the collective sufferings of Israel as God's people (Judith, 1–3 Maccabees, etc.). They all agree that the God of Israel is omnipotent and just, though *4 Ezra* raises some questions about this. They all admit that Israel has sinned, and that its sufferings are just punishments for its sins.

From this starting point, the books of the apocrypha approach the problem of suffering in different ways, ways that derive for the most part from the Hebrew Bible and appear in another theological context in the New Testament. In some cases (as in 2 Maccabees) the present sufferings of Israel are viewed as a divine discipline by which the merciful God educates and purifies his people. In many instances (Tobit, Judith, Esther, Daniel, Judas Maccabeus, etc.) the fidelity of key figures moves God to act on behalf of his people and rescue them from danger. In other cases (Letter of Jeremiah, Baruch, 1 and 2 Esdras) Israel's present sufferings, especially the destruction of Jerusalem and the exile, serve as a warning for Israel to return to the way of the Torah.

Several books (Wisdom, 2 and 4 Maccabees, 4 Ezra) present life after death or the full coming of God's kingdom as the time when God's sovereignty and justice will be fully manifest, and when the wicked will be punished and the righteous will be rewarded. Four Maccabees develops the idea, raised in Isa 53 and 2 Macc 7, of the expiatory or atoning value of the martyrs' deaths on behalf of God's people. Their sacrifice makes possible a renewed Israel in which God's sovereignty and justice are manifest, and God's Torah can be observed.

3. Wisdom. Several of the apocrypha give special attention to how God works in the world through the figure of personified Wisdom (cf. Prov 8:22–31). According to Sir 24, Wisdom makes her dwelling place in the Jerusalem temple ("in the holy tent . . . in Zion") and is the Torah ("the covenant of the Most High God, the law that Moses commanded us"). In the book of Wisdom, Wisdom fills the world and "holds all things together" (1:7). Functioning as the world soul, Wisdom animates all creation with "a spirit that is intelligent, holy, unique, manifold, subtle, mobile, clear, unpolluted, distinct, invulnerable, loving the good, keen, irresistible" (7:22). According to the book of Baruch, the task for Israel, and for all human beings, is to "learn where there is wisdom" (3:14) and search for her, for to find Wisdom is to find God. Baruch goes on to state: "Afterward she [Wisdom] appeared on earth and lived with humankind" (3:37). For Jews, as for the author of Baruch, Wisdom is the Torah (cf. 4:1). For Christians, this passage is a prophecy of Jesus, the Wisdom of God (cf. John 1:1–18; Col 1:15–20; and Heb 1:3–4).

13

The Pseudepigrapha in the Early Church

William Adler

great read !

In the early church, "pseudepigrapha" referred to religious compositions falsely attributed to a revered figure of the past. In its earliest attested use, the word was assigned to books making what were deemed to be spurious claims of apostolic authorship. A work might earn the designation "pseudepigraphic" if it was not widely known or contained questionable doctrines apt to promote heresy. This is the way, for example, that Serapion, the second-century bishop of Antioch, describes the *Gospel of Peter*. Concerned that members of the church of Rhossus were being led into heresy by this work, Serapion admonishes them about "pseudepigrapha" passing under the name of Peter and the other apostles. "We reject these works as men of experience," he writes, "knowing that such were not handed down to us."[1] Amphilochius, the fourth-century bishop of Iconium, describes pseudepigrapha in much the same way. Under the heading "pseudepigrapha in use among the heretics," he speaks of sectarian groups who paraded "compositions of demons" as genuine works of the apostles.[2]

1. "Pseudepigrapha" and "Apocrypha" in Early Christianity

Only at a later date was the word associated with certain noncanonical compositions attributed to prominent figures in early Judaism or the Old Testament. A work entitled the *Synopsis of Sacred Scripture,* attributed to Athanasius but probably composed in the sixth century, refers to the "pseudepigrapha" of prominent biblical prophets and patriarchs, among them Daniel, Habakkuk, Baruch, and Elijah. Along with the *Book of Enoch, The Testaments of the Twelve Patriarchs,* the *Prayer of Joseph,* and the *Testament* and *Assumption of Moses,* the *Synopsis* classifies these pseudepigrapha as "apocrypha of the Old Testament."[3] The modern classification of "Old Testament pseudepigrapha" originates in a distinction introduced by the Protestant Reformation. Protestant scholars reserved the term "apocrypha" for books that were included in the Vulgate and the Septuagint, but were lacking in the Hebrew Bible. Thus, books that the early church had designated

---

[1] Cited in Eusebius, *Hist. eccl.* 6.12.3.

[2] C. Datema, ed., *Amphilochii Iconiensis opera* (CC Series Graeca 3; Turnholt: Brepols, 1978), 235 frg. 10.

[3] (Ps.-) Athanasius, *Synopsis of Sacred Scripture* 75 (*PG* 28.432B).

"Old Testament apocrypha" came to be known as "Old Testament pseudepigrapha."[4] R. H. Charles's edition of the Old Testament apocrypha and pseudepigrapha in English translation exemplifies the distinction. His volume of "apocrypha" consists of those books that in his words "constitute the excess of the Vulgate over the Hebrew, and (that) this excess is borrowed from the Septuagint." What was left over, namely "(a)ll the . . . extant non-Canonical Jewish books written between 200 B.C. and A.D. 100 with possibly one or two exceptions," were assigned to the pseudepigrapha.[5]

Although most of the better-known works included in early Christian lists of "Old Testament apocrypha" now make up the nucleus of modern editions of the pseudepigrapha, the two terms are not entirely coterminous. Early Christian writers and canon lists mention several Old Testament apocrypha that no longer survive. And because modern scholarly conventions differ in places from the criteria of selection employed in the early church, documents that were never known in the early church as "apocrypha" are now likely to be found in recent collections of Old Testament "pseudepigrapha." The discussion of the Old Testament pseudepigrapha that follows is necessarily confined to those works that came to compose what the early church knew as "Old Testament apocrypha." When did early Christian writers first identify certain works in this way? What did they mean by the term? And how did they conceive of the relationship of these documents to the canonical books of the Old Testament?

2. Early Christian Classification of Old Testament Pseudepigrapha as Apocrypha

Once Christian scholars began concentrated comparison of the two Testaments, they soon discovered citations and references in the New Testament to Jewish writings and traditions that could not be readily authenticated in the recognized books of the Old Testament. Debates in the third and fourth centuries over canon and authority sparked increased interest in the pseudepigraphic sources of these references. Christian biblical critics on both sides of the issue rightly understood that the use of these works in the New Testament represented a powerful argument for their authority.[6] Locating the precise origin of these references often proved difficult, however. In only one instance was the pseudepigraphic origin of a citation unmistakable. This was Jude's much-discussed quotation from the book of *Enoch* (Jude 14). Prefaced with the words "Enoch prophesied," Jude's citation provided apologists for *Enoch* with ample evidence that the author regarded the work as a genuine composition of the antediluvian patriarch. In other cases, the evidence was less secure. New Testament writers occasionally quote as scripture passages that are

---

[4] Jerome also used the word apocrypha in the modern sense, that is, as a description of works found in the Septuagint but absent from the Hebrew Bible. See his *Preface to the Books of Samuel and Malachi* (*PL* 28.601A–603A). The word "pseudepigrapha" to describe religious literature found in neither the Greek nor the Hebrew Bibles first appears in J. Fabricius, *Codex pseudepigraphus Veteris Testamenti* (Hamburg, Leipzig: 1713).

[5] R. H. Charles, ed., *Apocrypha and Pseudepigrapha of the Old Testament* (2 vols.; Oxford: Clarendon, 1913), 2:iv.

[6] See below, 219–20, 225–27.

unknown in the Old Testament. They also know extrabiblical legends attested in Jewish pseudepigrapha. But since they do not mention specific Jewish books as the source of these quotations or legends, it required the learning and resourcefulness of later interpreters to locate them.[7]

The other problem was one of classification. When Origen first began investigating the pseudepigraphic sources of certain quotations and references in the New Testament, he had a fairly definite idea of the books that were formally recognized by both the church and the synagogue. Books that lacked this standing he classified collectively as "apocrypha." After Origen, this nomenclature became commonplace. But by applying it in regard to New Testament allusions to these works, Origen and his successors ran the risk of anachronism. The admittedly few New Testament authors and apostolic fathers who quote from Jewish pseudepigrapha do not differentiate between "apocryphal" and "recognized" books of the Old Testament, nor do they ever broach the question of the authority of the pseudepigraphic sources from which they quote. In fact, the formulaic expressions used by (ps.-)Barnabas in citing from the book of *Enoch*—for example, "Enoch says," "as it is written," and "scripture says"—suggest that at least in certain circles *Enoch* continued to command the same esteem extended to it by the epistle of Jude.[8]

The situation is not substantially different in the rather copious citations from Jewish pseudepigrapha in the writings of Origen's predecessor, Clement of Alexandria. Clement uses no generic term of classification to identify this literature; generally, he does not even identify his pseudepigraphic sources as written works. References from the book of *Enoch*, for example, are either unidentified or ascribed simply to Enoch.[9] The same practice extends to his quotations from pseudepigraphic works circulating in the name of the "prophets" Ezra, Ham, Ezekiel, or Zephaniah.[10] This is hardly surprising, given Clement's

---

[7] Among the citations and references in the New Testament that later Christian authors variously ascribed to Jewish pseudepigrapha were the following: (a) Matt 27:9 ("Then was fulfilled what had been spoken through the prophet Jeremiah, 'And they took the thirty pieces of silver . . .'"), from the *Apocryphon of Jeremiah;* (b) 1 Cor 2:9 ("What no eye has seen, nor ear heard, . . ."), from the *Apocalypse of Elijah* and the *Ascension of Isaiah;* (c) Gal 6:15 ("For neither circumcision nor uncircumcision is anything but a new creation is everything"), from an apocryphal book of Moses; (d) Eph 5:14 ("Therefore it says, 'Sleeper, awake! Rise from the dead, and Christ will shine on you'"), from apocryphal books of Elijah and Jeremiah; (e) 2 Tim 3:8 (the opposition of Jannes and Jambres to Moses) from the *Book of the Penitence of Jannes and Mambres;* (f) Jude 9 (the contest between Satan and the archangel Michael for the body of Moses) from the *Assumption* or *Ascension of Moses.* The Christian writers who proposed these various attributions are discussed later in this essay.

[8] *Barn.* 4.3, *peri hou gegraphai, hōs Enōch legei* . . . ; 16.5, *legei . . . hē graphē;* 16.6, *gegraptai.* On the book of *Enoch* in *Barnabas* and other Christian sources, see James C. VanderKam, "1 Enoch, Enochic Motifs, and Enoch in Early Christian Literature," in *The Jewish Apocalyptic Heritage in Early Christianity* (CRINT 3.4; ed. J. VanderKam and W. Adler; Assen: Van Gorcum, 1996), 33–101.

[9] See, for example, Clement, *Eclogae propheticae* 2.1.1 (GCS 17; ed. O. Stählin et al.; Berlin: Akademie Verlag, 1970): "This is what Daniel says, agreeing with Enoch, who has said, 'And I beheld all matter'" (based on *1 Enoch* 19:3); 53.4.3: "Now Enoch also says that the transgressing angels taught humankind astronomy, divination and other arts."

[10] As examples, see the following citations from pseudepigrapha in Clement's works: (a) *Paed.* 1.9.84.2–4; 10.91.2 (SC 70; ed. M. Harl; Paris: Cerf, 1960), *Apocryphon of Ezekiel,* cited simply as "Ezekiel"; (b) *Strom.* 3.16.100.4 (GCS 52; ed. O. Stählin and L. Früchtel; 2d ed.; Berlin: Akademie

own lax understanding of the sources of religious authority. As R.P.C. Hanson has observed, Clement has "almost no conception of what we mean by the Canon of Scripture, in the sense of a list of books guaranteed as authentic tradition in contrast to others whose genuineness is not certain."[11] Indeed, Clement's understanding of the sources of higher wisdom is not even confined to written documents; it is, he says in one place, a living tradition of "ineffable teachings, entrusted to logos, not to writing."[12]

On the two occasions when Clement does use the word "apocrypha" as a designation for written documents, it is in connection with dubious secret works in the possession of heretical or gnostic groups.[13] To this extent, Clement's use of the term conforms to the practice of other Christian writers of the late second and early third centuries. This period witnessed the proliferation of secret books, often attributed to some ancient worthy and promising access to esoteric higher wisdom. Groups in possession of these documents sometimes described them as "apocrypha," that is, works both concealed from and incomprehensible to the masses. To undermine these claims, Christian heresiologists invested the word "apocrypha" with a completely opposite sense. In their hands, it became a term of censure, implying falsehood or corruption. This pejorative use of the term may date as early as the mid-second century. According to Eusebius, the Jewish Christian writer Hegesippus proved that "some of the 'so-called apocrypha' *(tōn legomenōn . . . apokryphōn)*" were fabricated by certain heretics in his time.[14] Irenaeus's subsequent description of the secret books of the Marcosians is typical of the Christian heresiologist. These heretics, Irenaeus writes, "smuggle in an untold number of apocryphal and corrupt writings *(apokryphōn kai nothōn graphōn)*, which they themselves have fabricated, for the amazement of the ignorant, who do not understand the writings of the truth."[15]

The earlier linguistic history of the word "apocrypha" thus makes Origen's use of the term all the more remarkable. Only rarely does he apply the term to heretical Christian works.[16] Instead, he restricts its use chiefly to what modern scholarship now calls "Old Testament pseudepigrapha," that is, Jewish sources which, as he acknowledges, were not formally recognized by either the church or the synagogue. Nor is the word "apocrypha"

Verlag, 1960), *4 Ezra* 5:35, cited as the "prophet Ezra"; (c) *Strom.* 5.11.77.2, *Apocalypse of Zephaniah*, cited as "Zephaniah the prophet"; (d) *Strom.* 6.6.53.5 (from Isidore's *Expositions of the Prophet Parchor*), citing the "prophecy of Ham."

[11] R. P. C. Hanson, *Origen's Doctrine of Tradition* (London: SPCK, 1954), 133.

[12] Clement, *Strom.* 1.1.13.2–3.

[13] Ibid., 1.15.69.6, on the possession of "apocryphal books *(biblous apokryphous)*" in the name of Zoroaster by the followers of Prodicus; 3.4.29.1, on a libertine gnostic group who took their teachings from "a certain apocryphon *(ek tinos apokryphou)*."

[14] Eusebius, *Hist. eccl.* 4.22.9.

[15] Irenaeus, *Haer.* 1.12.1. The contrasting connotations of the word apocrypha are drawn clearly in the later heresiologists. See, for example, Theodoret's description of the works of the Quartodecimans (*Compendium haereticorum fabularum* [*PG* 83.405B]); the Quartodecimans, he writes, used works misleadingly called Acts of the Apostles, "as well as other corrupt works *(allois nothois)*, which they call 'apocrypha.'"

[16] See below, 221 n. 52. For Origen's views on Old Testament pseudepigrapha, see A. von Harnack, *Die kirchengeschichtliche Ertrag der exegetischen Arbeiten der Origenes* (*TU* 42.4; Leipzig: Hinrichs, 1919), 42–50; J. Ruwet, "Les 'Antilegomena' dans les oeuvres d'Origène," *Biblica* 24 (1943): 18–58; idem, "Les apocryphes dans le oeuvres d'Origène," *Biblica* 25 (1944): 143–66.

uniformly a term of disparagement. For Origen, "apocrypha" is mainly a neutral term of classification, intended to distinguish certain Jewish sources from those circulating more widely in the public domain. In his *Commentary on Matthew,* for example, Origen writes that Jesus' teachings about the slaying of the prophets are not found "in a work circulating among the public and popularly known books *(graphē ou pheromenē . . . en tois koinois kai dedēmeumenois bibliois)*"; Jesus must, therefore, have known this tradition from a work "in circulation among the apocrypha *(en apokryphois pheromenē)*."[17] He draws the same contrast between "apocryphal" and "known" books in his *Epistula ad Africanum.* Although the story recorded in the epistle to the Hebrews about the martyrdom of Isaiah is attested in none of the "public books *(tōn phanerōn bibliōn),*" attestation for it, he writes, is found "among the apocrypha *(en apokryphois)*."[18]

How can we account for Origen's departure from the conventional understanding of the term "apocrypha" among Christian writers of his time? There is reason to conclude from Origen's own testimony that between the time of Clement and Origen a controversy had developed in the Alexandrian church about the authority of the pseudepigrapha. The features of this controversy did not differ substantially from disputes generated by the many other books that the church came to designate as "apocrypha." That is, were those books literary fabrications, or sources of higher hidden wisdom? In his own deliberately neutral system of classification, Origen navigated a middle course between the two extremes. As Origen would say in another context, the pseudepigrapha were "mixed works," neither entirely spurious nor entirely genuine.[19] Because, in Origen's view, the classification of works as "apocrypha" denoted in itself little more than the fact that these works were "hidden," the assessment of the worth of individual works in this corpus had to extend beyond a sweeping prejudgment based on their failure to gain formal recognition in the church and synagogue.

3. Origen and Early Christian Controversies over the Pseudepigrapha

In *Contra Celsum,* Origen refers to a class of Christians who, in his words, know "deeper principles *(logōn . . . baryterōn)* and as a Greek might say both esoteric and intended for the initiated *(esōterikōn kai epoptikōn)*."[20] His predecessor Clement speaks at even greater length of an inner circle of Christians known for their grasp of these mysteries. In his *Stromateis,* he characterizes them as the "initiated," that is, those in the possession of what he variously describes as "gnosis," "gnostic tradition *(paradosis),*" or "hidden

---

[17] Origen, *Comm. Matt.* (GCS 40; ed. E. Klostermann; Leipzig: Hinrichs, 1935–37), 10.18.60 (on Matt 13:57).

[18] Origen, *Ep. Afr.* (SC 302; ed. N. de Lange; Paris: Cerf, 1983), 13. Cf. also Origen, *Comm. ser. Matt.* (GCS 38; ed. E. Klostermann; Leipzig: Hinrichs, 1933), 46 (on Matt 24:23–28), 94.18–21; 117 (on Matt 27:3–10), 250.7–9. In this anonymous Latin translation of Origen's commentary on Matthew, the contrast is typically drawn between "secretae scripturae (= *apokrypha biblia*)" on the one hand, and "vulgatae scripturae *(dedēmeumena biblia* or *koina biblia),*" "publicae scripturae *(phanera biblia),*" or "regulare librum," on the other.

[19] This threefold classification of "genuine *(gnēsion),*" "spurious *(nothon),*" and "mixed *(mikton)*" appears in Origen's *Comm. Jo.* 13.17 (GCS 10; ed. E. Preuschen; Leipzig: Hinrichs, 1903). There, he uses the category of "mixed" in connection with the *Kerygmata Petrou.*

[20] Origen, *Cels.* 3.37 (GCS; ed. P. Koetschau; Leipzig: Hinrichs, 1899).

traditions of true gnosis."[21] Among the assorted sources of Clement's secret wisdom, Jewish pseudepigrapha figure prominently.

A. Jewish Pseudepigrapha and Alexandrian Gnosis

Like many of the secret works that circulated under the name of some ancient worthy in the second and third centuries, certain Jewish pseudepigrapha, especially the apocalypses, posed as stores of revealed wisdom that might complete or even surpass more public sources of religious knowledge. *Fourth Ezra,* a Jewish apocalypse familiar to both Clement and Origen, communicates this idea explicitly. Ezra, the only one "worthy to learn this secret of the Most High," is told to "write all these things that you have seen in a book, and put it in a hidden place; and you shall teach them to the wise among your people, whose hearts you know are able to comprehend and keep the secret."[22] Ezra is commanded to take five men to a field, where he receives wisdom and understanding. For forty days, the men in his company recorded ninety-four books "in characters which they did not know." Ezra is then commissioned to "make public the twenty-four books that you wrote first and let the worthy and the unworthy read them." But the seventy others that were written last were to be kept secret and revealed only to the wise. "For in them are the springs of understanding, the fountains of wisdom, and the river of knowledge."[23]

It would be easy to conclude from this narrative that, for those possessing the capacity to understand them, the secret books of the Jews offered a valuable resource of hidden wisdom. This is in fact the way Clement appropriates much of this literature. In his *Stromateis,* he embellishes upon his description of secret wisdom with certain legends from Jewish pseudepigrapha. From *Enoch's* story of the fallen angels, Clement derives an explanation of the origin of the many erroneous ideas of Greek philosophers; these ideas, he writes, are rooted in the illicit teachings of the fallen angels, who "told to the women the secrets which had come to their knowledge."[24] The story of Joshua's vision of Moses' two bodies represents for him an allegory about the ability of only a select few to penetrate beyond the "body" of sacred scriptures. "In my opinion," he writes, "the narrative shows that knowledge is not the privilege of all." Only the initiated can see through to the underlying thoughts and what is signified by the names in scripture, "seeking the Moses that is with the angels."[25] At another place in the *Stromateis,* Clement recalls a Jewish tradition about the heavenly name of Moses ("Melchi") after his ascension into heaven. Although the ultimate source of both of these references was probably the *Assumption of Moses* or a related work, Clement names as his informants a circle of religious savants whom he characterizes only as the "initiated *(hoi mystai).*"[26] By the end of the second century, elites

---

[21] For Clement's various characterizations, see, for example, *Strom.* 1.1.15.2; 5.10.62.1, 63.2; 6.16.146.3.

[22] *4 Ezra* 12:36–38, *Fourth Ezra: A Commentary on the Book of Fourth Ezra* (trans. M. E. Stone; Minneapolis: Fortress, 1990).

[23] Ibid., 14:37–47.

[24] Clement, *Strom.* 5.1.10.

[25] Ibid., 6.15.132.2–3.

[26] Ibid., 1.23.153.1. For the relationship of these Moses traditions to the incompletely preserved *Assumption of Moses,* see J. Tromp, *The Assumption of Moses: A Critical Edition with Commentary*

within the early church had evidently come to value these pseudepigraphic legends about Moses as a conduit for hidden higher wisdom.

If the actual number of citations from this literature accurately reflects interest, Origen was an equally avid student of the pseudepigrapha. Here too, the attraction was fueled by the promise of insights inaccessible to the broader public. Origen praises the "many secrets and mysteries *(secreta . . . et arcana)* in the little books that are called 'Enochic.' "[27] Like Clement, he understands the story of Moses' two bodies (originating, he writes, in a "little book" not included in the canon) as a mystery referring symbolically to the superiority of spiritual to literal interpretation of the Bible.[28] On several occasions Origen even alleges that elites in Jewish society owed their superior knowledge to little-known Jewish sources. In his *Commentary on Matthew,* for example, Origen allows that the questions about heavenly mysteries that the Jewish high priests and elders posed to Jesus might have come either from "traditions or else from apocrypha."[29] And in his *Commentary on John,* he suggests that those who speculated about whether Jesus was a prophet or John *redivivus* probably derived this and "tens of thousands of other things" from "tradition or apocrypha"; access to these sources had given them a knowledge far exceeding that of the masses.[30]

The chief difference between the two writers is one of attitude. In his rather wide-ranging appeal to the pseudepigrapha, Clement betrays barely a hint of uncertainty about the standing of the pseudepigrapha in the Alexandrian church.[31] By contrast, Origen usually restricts himself to those parts of this literature bearing directly on the meaning of the biblical text. And even as he commends these works as a rich asset for the biblical critic, Origen repeatedly cautions his readers against consulting the pseudepigrapha uncritically. The discernment and judgment required to sift the wheat from the chaff makes them unfit, he writes, for wider and more public consumption. Origen's familiarity with the books that comprised the traditional Jewish Bible partially explains his increased awareness of the contested authority of the pseudepigrapha. There was, however, another more

---

(SVTP 10; Leiden: Brill, 1993), 283–85. In *Strom.* 1.23.154.1, Clement attributes to "the initiated" the claim that Moses killed the Egyptian by his word alone.

[27] Origen, *Hom. Num.* 28.2 (GCS 30; ed. W. Baehrens; Leipzig: Hinrichs, 1921).

[28] Origen, *Homilies on Joshua* (GCS 30; ed. W. A. Baehrens; Leipzig: Hinrichs, 1921), 2.1: "Finally also there is a certain little book, in which, although it is not included in the canon, a figure of this mystery is also described. In it, there is a report that two Moses were seen: one living in the spirit and another dead in the body. What is represented there is indisputable: that if you look at the letter of the law which is dead and empty of all things we have mentioned above, this is the Moses dead in his body. But if you are able to remove the veil of the law and understand that the law is spiritual, this is the Moses who lives in the spirit."

[29] Origen, *Comm. Matt.* 17.2 (on Matt 21:23).

[30] Origen, *Comm. Jo.* 19.15.97.

[31] A possible exception to this statement is a fragment from Clement's commentary on the epistle of Jude. Here he states that Jude 9, describing the dispute between Michael and Satan over the body of Moses, "confirmat assumptionem Moysi" (*Adumbrationes in Ep. Jud.* 9 [GCS 17; ed. O. Stählin and L. Früchtel; Leipzig: Hinrichs, 1909] 207). If this is a reference to the *Assumption of Moses,* it would suggest that Clement sought to validate the work by appealing to the same tradition in Jude. However, as Tromp points out (*The Assumption of Moses,* 273), the Latin may simply mean that Jude "confirms that Moses was taken up."

immediate catalyst behind his more guarded treatment of these sources. Especially in his later writings, Origen acknowledges growing skepticism in the early church about their authority.[32]

B. Origen's Prescriptions on Selective Reading of the Pseudepigrapha

A statement that Origen makes in his *Commentary on Matthew* conveys some sense of the dimensions of the controversy. Origen alludes here to certain interpreters who had rejected 2 Timothy on the grounds that it included the story of Jannes and Jambres (2 Tim 3:8)—a story, Origen concedes, not found in "known books *(publicis libris)*, but rather in an apocryphal book *(libro secreto)* entitled the *Book of Jannes and Jambres.*"[33] Although this was probably not the only reason why 2 Timothy was subject to criticism, Origen's report demonstrates that reservations about the pseudepigrapha had spilled over into discussions about the standing of certain New Testament books that allegedly cited from them.

Origen disdains this criticism of 2 Timothy, challenging the epistle's detractors to weigh the wider implications of their own reasoning. First Corinthians also cites from the apocryphal *Apocalypse of Elijah,* he notes, yet "it has never come to my attention that someone opposed (it) . . . as not genuine for this reason."[34] But Origen was not unaffected by controversies about their authority. His references to the pseudepigrapha are frequently hedged with qualifications (e.g., "if someone accepts this work"). After issuing this warning about the *Prayer of Joseph* in his *Commentary on John,* he comments at length about that work's discourse on angels, then adds somewhat defensively: "We have made something of a digression in introducing this story about Jacob and appealing to a writing which we cannot well treat with contempt."[35]

In the case of the book of *Enoch,* to which he refers five times, Origen's own mounting uncertainty can be readily documented. In *De principiis,* one of his early and more speculative works (ca. 225), he quotes from "Enoch, in his book" without qualification.[36] Elsewhere, however, he turns more cautious. In his *Commentary on John,* begun about the same time, a reference to *Enoch* is accompanied by the words, "if one wants to accept this book as sacred scripture."[37] Later, in his *Homilies on Numbers* (ca. 246–255), he mitigates his praise of this work with an observation that the book of *Enoch* does "not seem to be authoritative among the Hebrews."[38] And in *Contra Celsum,* the exclusion of *Enoch* from the books that "circulate in the churches as divine" could count as a decisive argument against it. Calling *Enoch* "some book or other," Origen chides his adversary for citing a tradition from *Enoch* that is "neither mentioned nor heard of in the churches of God."[39]

---

[32] On Origen's evolving views on the authority of the pseudepigrapha, see Ruwet, "Les 'Antilegomena,'" 57–58.

[33] Origen, *Comm. ser. Matt.* 117 (on Matt 27:11), 250.7–9.

[34] Ibid., 250.10–12. See also *Comm. ser. Matt.* 28 (on Matt 23:37–39), 51.2–7.

[35] Origen, *Comm. Jo.* 2.31.188.

[36] Origen, *De principiis* 4.35 (ed. H. Karpp; Darmstadt: Wissenschaftliche Buchgesellschaft, 1976).

[37] Origen, *Comm. Jo.* 6.217.

[38] Origen, *Hom. Num.* 28.2.

[39] Origen, *Cels.* 5.54–55.

Origen made this last remark in hopes of exposing Celsus's shallow understanding of Christianity. Therefore, we need not assume that he had now disowned a work that he had quoted favorably on several other occasions.[40] What is in any case clear is that for Origen, unlike Clement, the Jewish pseudepigrapha had to be carefully examined for their reliability and truthfulness. Origen sets out his own guidelines for profitable use of this literature in his *Commentary on Matthew,* written in Caesarea towards the end of his life (ca. 246). There he strikes a defensive posture, in one instance urging his readers not to stray into the "outside wilderness" of "hidden and unknown writings (secretas et non vulgatas scripturas)" that cannot be confirmed by ecclesiastical tradition.[41] After quoting copiously from Jewish pseudepigrapha (*Jannes and Jambres, Apocalypse of Elijah,* and an Isaiah apocryphon), he acknowledges his own grave misgivings. Some of the pseudepigrapha, he writes, may have been fabricated by Jews determined to dismantle Christian teachings. For the sake of those unable to discern the true words from the false words contained in them, works "outside of canonized scriptures (extra canonizatas scripturas)" should not be used to verify Christian doctrine. Nevertheless, he sees no reason to abjure those parts of Jewish pseudepigrapha found useful in confirming the truth of Christian scriptures. The right approach when reading this literature is to heed the words of Paul: "test all things, and hold to that which is good" (1 Thess 5:21).[42]

As works that were not widely known or recognized, the pseudepigrapha were, by definition, "apocrypha." But this alone was not automatically disqualifying. Nowhere in this cautiously worded defense of the pseudepigrapha does Origen plead for popular or broader recognition of books that he understood perfectly well were not widely known or read. He was entirely content to continue screening these writings from readers who are unable to distinguish "whether their words are true or false."[43] Origen's chief purpose in defending the pseudepigrapha was only to ensure that discriminating readers could continue to consult these works selectively.

This principle of "selective reading" underlies many of Origen's statements on the benefits of Jewish pseudepigrapha. In his letter to Africanus, he allows that Jewish authorities might have deliberately suppressed or corrupted apocryphal works that slighted them in some way. One such work, an Isaiah apocryphon, suffered "manifestly incorrect" interpolations meant to undermine the entire work. But even if it was neither read publicly nor entirely free of corruption, this in no way discredited the work altogether. The authenticity of other portions of the book could be checked and guaranteed by the New Testament itself. In particular, the account of the martyrdom of the prophet Isaiah found there was authenticated by a similar report of the death of the prophets in the epistle to the Hebrews.[44]

---

[40] Oepke ("*Kryptō*," *TDNT,* 3:995, n. 162) may be correct in describing Origen's comment on *Enoch* as "tactical." On Origen's wavering opinions on *Enoch,* see Hanson, *Origen's Doctrine of Tradition,* 136; Ruwet, "Les 'Antilegomena,'" 48–50.

[41] Origen, *Comm. ser. Matt.* 46 (on Matt 24:23–28), 94.17–30. See also *Comm. on Matt.* 17.35, where Origen warns against seeking the meaning of Jesus' words against the Sadducees (Matt 22:29–33) by fleeing to apocryphal books that are in conflict with accepted doctrine.

[42] Origen, *Comm. ser. Matt.* 28 (on Matt 23:37), 51.8–22.

[43] Ibid., 51.17–19.

[44] Origen, *Ep. Afr.* 13. See also *Comm. Matt.* 10.18 (on Matt 13:57): "And Isaiah is reported to have been sawn asunder. And if someone does not accept the statement because of its being found in an apocryphal book (*ex apokryphou*), let him believe what is written in the epistle to the

If Hebrews and other books of the New Testament quoted or appealed to traditions from the pseudepigrapha, why, Origen asks, should uncertainties about their authority be allowed to threaten the important work of biblical interpretation? Jesus himself, he suggests, sometimes drew upon the apocryphal books and secret traditions of the Jews. In several places, Origen points out to his readers that Jesus' condemnation of the Pharisees contained charges difficult to corroborate from the officially sanctioned books of Jewish scripture. His teachings about the murder of the prophets (Matt 23:31) and the martyrdom of Zechariah (Matt 23:35) must, therefore, have come from a work circulating among the "apocryphal books."[45] Certain pseudepigrapha also had proven value in the interpretation of Jesus' teachings. The narrative about the angel Jacob/Israel recorded in the *Prayer of Joseph,* one of the "apocryphal books in circulation," both illuminated and made "more credible *(pistikōteros)*" the meaning of Jesus' words in John. For that reason, he writes, we do well not to treat it with contempt.[46] Denying Christian interpreters access to these sources would thus mean depriving them of important supplementary materials, invaluable in the elucidation of otherwise incomprehensible or unsubstantiated passages in the Bible.

Origen's treatment of the "secret" content in the pseudepigrapha served much the same purpose. As we have seen, Origen valued some of the pseudepigrapha as sources of hidden knowledge. In addition to his customary designation of these sources as *ta apokrypha,* there are also occasions in which he describes hidden books or traditions as *ta aporrēta.* This is not uncommon usage among early Christian writers, who often understood both words as connoting overlapping ideas of esoteric and ineffable wisdom. But in Origen, these categories constitute a much more mixed selection of written sources and traditions. Like *apokrypha biblia, ta aporrēta* might include erroneous or misleading speculation circulating in secret among the Jews.[47] Nor, according to Origen, did the Jews place a work among *ta aporrēta* only because its esoteric content made it unfit for wider circulation. There were political motives as well. For example, in his *Epistle to Africanus,* Origen claims that the Hebrew version of Susannah existed "for a long time *en aporrētois,* preserved only by the more learned and more honest."[48] Here, Origen only means to suggest that Jewish authorities excluded Susannah from scriptures publicly read in the synagogue because they disliked its unflattering representation of the two Jewish elders; it has nothing

---

Hebrews." For the story of Isaiah's death in this way, see the *Ascension of Isaiah* 5:1–14, *New Testament Apocrypha* (2 vols.; ed. W. Schneemelcher; ET; Louisville, Ky.; Westminster John Knox, 1992), 2:603–20.

[45] Origen, *Comm. Matt.* 10.18.60 (on Matt 13:57). See also *Ep. Afr.* 14; *Comm. ser. Matt.* 28 (on Matt 23:37–39), 49.19–51.7, where Origen notes that Jesus' condemnation of Jerusalem for "killing the prophets and stoning those who are sent to you," found nowhere in the Old Testament, might have originated in "more hidden books (ex libris secretioribus)."

[46] Origen, *Comm. Jo.* 2.31.192.

[47] For the expression *ta aporrēta* in connection with the secret traditions of the Jews, see Origen, *Comm. Jo.* 6.73, 76, 83. For false speculation contained in apocryphal books, see Origen, *Comm. ser. Matt.* 55 (on Matt 24:36), 124.10–20. In the latter, Origen writes that Paul probably issued his warning against eschatological speculation in 2 Thess 2 as a counterblast against Jews in his day who claimed to have received "knowledge about the time of the end either from scriptures or from apocrypha (secretis = *apokryphois*). For other examples, see Ruwet, "Les apocryphes," 146–51.

[48] Origen, *Ep. Afr.* 18. It is not clear why Origen includes Susannah among the Jewish *aporrēta* and in the same letter categorizes other non-canonical Jewish works as *apokrypha.*

to do with esoteric teachings in that work. For Origen, the only shared feature of all these hidden books and traditions is that they are not widely known or accessible.

In those cases in which Origen does intend to express a consistent idea of concealed higher truths, he normally confines the use of these same words to the concealed meaning of passages of the Bible.[49] This practice is entirely consistent with Origen's views on secret tradition. As Hanson has demonstrated, Origen feels that hidden, higher wisdom originates entirely from the Bible, derived from it by means of allegorical exegesis, an interpretative method restricted to an intellectual elite within the church.[50] In a curious way, then, Origen inverts the relationship of the apocrypha to the recognized books of the Old Testament. Although these works might assist the interpreter in disclosing the veiled meanings of the biblical text, they had no autonomous role as sources of esoteric higher truths.

C. Origen, the Pseudepigrapha, and the Bible of the Jews

In his analysis of Origen's use of the word *apokrypha*, Oepke argued that Origen's terminology was not an original formulation on his part; it was rather a formulation of the early church in its struggles against gnosticism. In response to gnostic claims about secret books, the church applied this same designation to the hidden books of the Jews:

> In time . . . the Church itself comes to use *biblioi apokryphoi* for Jewish apocalypses which were much loved and almost canonized. It is doubtful whether the synagogue itself used the designation. It could only do so by borrowing from the Gnostic usage, not by a technical use of *gnz*. This use of *apokryphos* is first found in Origen. But he finds it so natural that he can hardly be its inventor. The Church probably liked to be able to oppose to the secret books of the Gnostics its own secret books, and it is striking that it took these exclusively from the Synagogue. Because of the position of the Jewish people in salvation history, these seemed to guarantee the genuineness of prophecy in so far as later generations of Jews had not falsified the books. This view made its way all the more easily because the Jews themselves had already weeded out and rejected their own apocrypha.[51]

Oepke is probably correct in asserting that Origen's designation of Jewish pseudepigrapha as apocrypha was not his own invention; his casual use of this term seems to presuppose his readers' familiarity with this system of classification. It is also likely that in restricting the word apocrypha to Jewish pseudepigrapha, Origen hoped to dissociate these sources from works of low repute. Extending the word apocrypha to include the many secret books of the gnostics that the church had condemned as fabrications would have undermined his own efforts both to rehabilitate the word apocrypha and promote his own defense of the pseudepigrapha.[52] But Oepke's assertion that Origen's distinction

---

[49] See, for example, *Frag. Prov.* (*PG* 13.25B), where he adduces Jotham's parable (Judg 9:8) as an illustration of "something ineffable in secret *(en apokryphē ti aporrēton)."*

[50] Hanson, *Origen's Doctrine of Tradition*, 74. For example, in speaking of the many names found in the book of Joshua, Origen observes that the only way one can understand the meaning of these names is to realize that "unspeakable mysteries are implied in these names, mysteries which are greater than human speech can pronounce" (*Hom. Jes. Nav.* 23.4). See also Origen, *Comm. Matt.* 17.2.

[51] Oepke, "*Kryptō,*" 998.

[52] For a notable exception, however, see *Comm. ser. Matt.* 28 (on Matt 23:37–39), 51.8–14. Here, after referring extensively to Jewish pseudepigrapha, Origen issues one of his strongest warn-

between "apocryphal" and "publicly recognized" books owes nothing to Jewish usage flies in the face of Origen's own statements to the contrary.[53] Commenting on the absence of the words "Let us go out to the field" in the Hebrew version of Gen 4:8, Origen notes that "the Hebrews say" that the missing words could be found *en tō apokryphō*.[54] Here the words *en tō apokryphō* refer to a reading lacking in the Hebrew text of Genesis read and used by the Jews in their synagogue service. On several occasions Origen calls attention to the absence of the "apocrypha" from the Jewish canon, stating in his *Epistula ad Africanum* that the Jews knew these works by a formal category. Despite the circulation of Tobit and Judith in the Christian canon, he writes, the Jews "use *(chrōntai)* neither Tobit nor Judith, nor do they have them among the 'apocrypha in Hebrew *(en apokryphois hebraïsti)*.'"[55]

Statements like these raise the possibility, first proposed by Zahn, that Origen's classification of the apocryphal books as works not publicly recognized by the Jews has some connection with the treatment of "hidden books" in the synagogue of his time. Zahn argued that in the early synagogue, the designation of books as "hidden" was not meant as a "dogmatic or historical judgment." Books might be removed because they were considered corrupt or inaccurate, because their contents were deemed somehow unsuitable, or because they were deemed too elevated for general understanding. Although the removal of a work might understandably plant suspicions about it, the characterization of a book as hidden was only a "statement about the factual relationship of a book" to a religious community.[56] Origen's neutral categorization of books as "apocryphal" (that is, "hidden" as opposed to "public") simply reflected a conventional Jewish distinction.[57]

---

ings against indiscriminate use of pseudepigrapha, even likening these works to the secret books of gnostics: "(W)e are not unaware that a great deal of the hidden books (multa secretorum = *polla tōn apokryphōn*) have been made up by the impious . . . , and indeed the Hypthiani (?) use certain fabrications, and the followers of Basilides use others. It is therefore necessary to examine them (i.e., Jewish pseudepigrapha) cautiously, so that we might not embrace all the hidden books (omnia secreta = *panta apokrypha*) that circulate in the name of holy men—this is because of the Jews who in confirming false doctrines have fabricated certain things (quaedam) to destroy the truth of our scriptures." As already noted (218–19), in this commentary, Origen is more defensive about his use of Jewish pseudepigrapha than in his previous writings, acknowledging mounting disquiet about this literature.

[53] See also Oepke, "*Kryptō*," 997, where, discussing the meaning of the word "*apokryphos*" in Origen, Oepke states: "No one disputes the actual connection between the Church and the Synagogue. A mutual interaction of usage may thus be accepted. The only point is that the root of the usage is not to be found in the Synagogue but in pagan Gnosticism." It is unclear how Oepke reconciles "a mutual interaction of usage" with his statement that "the root of the usage" is gnostic.

[54] Origen, *Selecta in Genesim* (*PG* 12.101C).

[55] Origen, *Ep. Afr.* 19. But cf. Jerome, *Praef. in Judith* (*PL* 26.39B): "Apud Hebraeos Judith inter apocrypha legitur. . . ."

[56] T. Zahn, *Geschichte des neutestamentlichen Kanons* (Erlangen: Deichert, 1888), 1.123, 127. Zahn further held (131–32) that Origen's system of classification was shaped by the Semitic word *gnwz*, a word that can mean "hidden or removed from official and general usage." On the relationship of *gnwz* to *apokryphos*, see also G. Hölscher, *Kanonisch und Apokryph* (Naumburg: Lippert, 1905), 59–64; R. Meyer, "*Kryptō*," *TDNT*, 3:983–84; Ruwet, "Les apocryphes," 146–51.

[57] Zahn, *Geschichte*, 131–32. Zahn overstates the case, however, in further suggesting that Origen's use of the term "apocrypha" also reflected the prevailing understanding of the word in the early church. As he writes (*Geschichte*, 135), "church teachers before Origen did not have a different concept of the apocrypha and its opposite; this is self-evident *since this concept is the original one and it cannot be assumed that the thinking of Irenaeus and his contemporaries was more modern than*

Origen himself is not clear as to the significance of the Jewish "removal" of the pseudepigrapha. As we have seen, Origen recognized that the exclusion of the pseudepigrapha from recognized Jewish scriptures was a legitimate cause for concern. Yet elsewhere he insists that the Bible of the Jews was of little consequence for the church. In response to Africanus's suggestion that Susanna's absence from Jewish scriptures militated decisively against its authority, Origen accused him of subjecting the church to the bidding of the synagogue.[58] The inclusion of Susanna in the church's version of Daniel shored up Origen's position, and yet Origen knew that the underlying problem was not essentially different. Thus in the same letter, Origen defended Jewish pseudepigrapha with the same battery of arguments that he used to support Susanna. As with Susannah, Jewish authorities removed other books from public circulation and sometimes even deliberately tampered with their contents.[59]

Origen's claims about Jewish corruptions of the pseudepigrapha did serve tactical purposes. Questionable teachings in these sources could readily be attributed to later corruption. Since the average reader lacked the ability to discriminate between the original content and subsequent corruptions, it was best to keep these works out of popular circulation. Most importantly, Origen's usage established a connection, not at all self-evident, between a "hidden" book and a "corrupt" book. That is, the removal and corruption of the pseudepigrapha were part of the same process by which Jewish authorities undermined works that they knew contained material damaging to their reputation.

But by severing the church from the constraints of Jewish scriptures, Origen's argument set a dangerous precedent. If the pseudepigrapha had been unfairly stigmatized by deliberate corruption and removal from public reading in the synagogue, would this then mean that these works, apart from their later corruptions, were otherwise genuine? Although Oepke might be correct that this was the logical corollary of Origen's thinking,[60] Origen himself refused to allow the argument to proceed that far. Nowhere, for example, does Origen undertake to identify these alleged corruptions. He never even produces an example of one of them. As his discussions with Africanus about the authenticity of Susanna demonstrate, Origen was fully conversant with philological analysis in the study and identification of forgery and textual corruption. But Susanna, part of the text of Daniel widely read and accepted by the church, required this rigorous defense. The pseudepigrapha were a different story. For Origen, the claim of Jewish tampering was only a blunt instrument that he could wield in defense of his own views about the selective value of the

<hr>

Origen" (italics mine). Zahn's statement begs the question. It is based on the undemonstrated assumption that the early church from its very inception understood by "apocrypha" the Jewish conception of books "hidden" or "removed" from public reading. Origen is in fact the first Christian writer to treat the term apocrypha as a formal category for Jewish works removed from public reading. The fact that Origen departs from the strictly negative understanding of the word "apocrypha" in Irenaeus and others implies that Origen was directly influenced by Jewish usage, and did not conform to the accepted understanding of the word in the early church.

[58] See *Ep. Afr.* 8: "When we notice such things (that is, differences between the Septuagint and the Hebrew Bible), we are forthwith to reject as spurious *(athetein)* the copies in use in our churches, and enjoin the brotherhood to put away the sacred books current among them, and to coax the Jews and persuade them to give up copies which shall be untampered with and free from forgery!"

[59] See above, 219.

[60] Oepke, "*Kryptō*," 998.

pseudepigrapha. Anything more would have required an additional step in their legitimation that Origen was unwilling to take. So in spite of his own professed suspicions about the motives behind the removal of the pseudepigrapha from the synagogue, Origen continued to hedge his citations from these books with the warning that they were not found among the public scriptures of the Jews.

4. The Defense of the Pseudepigrapha after Origen

Tertullian, roughly contemporary with Origen, did take the next step. In his *De cultu feminarum,* he reports that some Christians did not receive the book of *Enoch* because it was not admitted into the Jewish canon (armarium judaicum). But this for him has little consequence. Like Origen, Tertullian ascribes to the Jews nefarious motives. The Jews, he writes, might have rejected *Enoch* "just as they also rejected other things which proclaim Christ (sicut et caetera fere quae Christum sonant). . . . Nor is it remarkable if they have not received other scriptures which speak of him, just as they would not receive him when he spoke openly." For that reason, the true worth of *Enoch* and other books like it should be measured by their proclamation of Christ, not by the opinion of the Jews: "Since this same writing of Enoch also proclaimed about Christ, nothing at all should be rejected by us, which pertains to us. And we read: 'all scripture is inspired by God which is useful for teaching'" (2 Tim 3:16).[61] The consequences of removing the constraints of Jewish scriptures were now becoming clear.

It is not surprising that in the reaction against Tertullian's special pleading, the validity of the Jewish canon was again reaffirmed. In his *City of God,* Augustine grants the view previously put forth by Origen, namely that "some truth is found" in apocrypha. And like Tertullian he considers it certain that some things were written under divine inspiration by Enoch; this is so because "the apostle Jude says this in a canonical letter." But where he differs from his two predecessors is in his appraisal of the prescriptive authority of the Jewish Bible. Jude's citation from *Enoch,* Augustine writes, is not probative for the rest of the works attributed to Enoch. The reason for this is that Enoch's writings lacked the care in preservation required to ensure their accuracy. The Jews did not reject these books out of self-interest. To the contrary, *Enoch* and other apocrypha are with "good reason not included in the canon of Scripture which was carefully kept in the temple of the Hebrew people by a succession of priests." They were impossible to validate "because of their age," and in the case of *Enoch,* "it was impossible to ascertain whether they were what Enoch had written since they were not presented by men who were found to have kept them with proper ceremony through successive generations." For this reason, *Enoch* and works like it belonged in the same class as all of the other works which circulated under the name of prophets and apostles but whose authenticity was impossible to confirm: all of them go under the name of "apocrypha."[62]

---

[61] Tertullian, *Cult. fem.* 3 (SC 173; ed. M. Turcan; Paris: Cerf, 1971).

[62] Augustine, *Civ.* 15.23. On the question of the validation of the book of *Enoch* by Jude's citation, see also Jerome, *Comm. Tit.* (PL 26.608C); Jerome argues that just as Paul occasionally quotes Greek poets, Jude's citation of one verse from *Enoch* in no way guarantees the worth of the entire book.

✗ Because of validation from the DSS (Enoch),
  Augustine's conclusion must be rejected.

As we have seen, Origen's case for the pseudepigrapha relied heavily on their presumed benefits for the study and confirmation of the New Testament. Later apologists for this literature, among them the fourth-century Spanish monk Priscillian of Avila, enthusiastically embraced aspects of the same argument. Certain nit-pickers, Priscillian writes, "who esteem slander more than honesty," will say: "you should examine nothing further; it is enough for you to read what is written in the canon."[63] In response, Priscillian points to the many New Testament allusions to prophets whose words and writings are not recorded in the Old Testament. Who is this Enoch, he asks, whom the apostle adduces in the testimony of his prophecy? And what was Jesus referring to when in the Gospel according to Luke (11:50–51) he describes the death of the prophets "since the foundation of the world, from the blood of Abel to the blood of Zechariah, who was killed between the altar and the sanctuary"?[64] Without recourse to apocryphal writings, the words of Jesus and Jude would be lacking any independent attestation. If, Priscillian asks, only statements in canonical books are subject to investigation and "it is a sin to read anything else," then Christians will be forced to conclude that the deaths of the prophets cannot be demonstrated from these same books. "If no book outside of the canon should be taken up or possessed, we cannot put our faith simply in fables, nor can we hold fast to the history of scripture by confirmation of the facts."[65]

Recognizing that the putative New Testament usage of the pseudepigrapha made the most persuasive argument in their defense, advocates intensified their efforts to locate the pseudepigraphic origin of previously contested references and citations in the New Testament. Origen, the first to pursue this line of investigation, was not always confident that a New Testament citation lacking in the Old required the supposition of an apocryphal source. While acknowledging that Matthew's quotation from Jeremiah (Matt 27:3–10) was not found "anywhere in books that are either read in the churches or recorded by the Jews," Origen only holds out the possibility that the citation might have originated in a secret work of Jeremiah. But until and unless someone actually located this secret book, Origen grants that it is equally plausible that "there was an error in writing and Jeremiah was put there instead of Zechariah."[66] Origen also vacillates in his position on the source of Paul's problematic quotation in 1 Cor 2:9, "What no eye has seen, nor ear heard, nor the human hear conceived, what God has prepared for those who love him." Although inclining to the belief that this quotation originated in the *Apocalypse of Elijah*, Origen suggests in at least one place that the formulaic words *kathōs gegraptai* did not mean that Paul was quoting the Old Testament verbatim. He might simply have been paraphrasing Isa 64:4, expressing the same idea as Isaiah, but in different words.[67]

---

[63] Priscillian, *Tract.* 3.68, in *Priscilliani quae supersunt* (CSEL 18; ed. G. Schepss; Vienna: Tempsky, 1889), 53.3–5.

[64] Ibid., *Tract.* 3.56 (44.19–20); 3.60 (47.3–12).

[65] Ibid., *Tract.* 3.60 (47.13–18). On Priscillian's interest in the pseudepigrapha, see H. Chadwick, *Priscillian of Avila: The Occult and the Charismatic in the Early Church* (Oxford: Clarendon, 1976), 74, 80–83; A. A. Jacobs, "The Disorder of Books: Priscillian's Canonical Defense of Apocrypha," *HTR* 93 (2000): 135–59.

[66] Origen, *Comm. ser. Matt.* 117 (on Matt 27:3–10), 249.16–250.2.

[67] In J. A. Cramer, *Catenae Graecorum Patrum in Novum Testamentum* (Oxford, 1841; repr. Hildesheim: G. Olds, 1967), 5.442.

yikes! ✱

Fourth-century opponents of the pseudepigrapha, Jerome in particular, found the latter approach more agreeable than postulating a noncanonical source. In his *Commentary on Isaiah,* for example, he denies that 1 Cor 2:9 originated in the *Apocalypse of Elijah.* Although Paul was not quoting quotation word for word, he expressed the "sensuum . . . veritatem" of Isa 64:4.[68] Quite predictably, champions of the pseudepigrapha held differing views on the subject. The fourth and fifth centuries witnessed an explosion in discoveries of passages in the pseudepigrapha supposedly shedding new light on the sources of certain contested quotations in the New Testament. Jerome himself was diligent in chasing down reports about the apocryphal sources of contested citations in the New Testament. Despite his own doubts about the use of a Jeremiah apocryphon in Matt 27, Jerome reports of a "Hebrew of the Nazarene sect" who informed him of the existence of the disputed quotation in Matthew in a Jeremiah apocryphon; in that work, Jerome writes, "I discovered this passage written word for word *(ad verbum).*"[69] He also discovered two apocryphal sources of 1 Cor 2:9: the *Apocalypse of Elijah,* and the *Ascension of Isaiah.*[70] Jerome's suspicions about these findings were not entirely misplaced. The Latin version of the *Ascension of Isaiah* does in fact contain the passage in question. But since it is lacking in the other recensions, there are good reasons to suspect that the passage was not original to it.[71] Here, as elsewhere, we may suspect that the motive behind these interpolations was to legitimize these works by demonstrating their influence on books of uncontested authority.

The same may be said about many of the other new discoveries of the sources of Pauline citations. In the third century, Hippolytus of Rome traced Paul's quotation in Eph 5:14, prefaced with the formula "it says," to the book of Isaiah.[72] Epiphanius now proposed that the source of this quotation was actually an Elijah apocryphon.[73] In a learned study of the origin of extrabiblical witnesses cited in the epistles of Paul, the fifth-century Alexandrian deacon Euthalius found another source for the same citation: an apocryphal book of Jeremiah. He also claimed that in Gal 6:15 Paul cited from an apocryphal book of Moses.[74] If the purpose of these discoveries was to advance the cause of the pseudepigrapha, the campaign succeeded. In the ninth century, the Byzantine chronicler George Syncellus justified his own extensive use of *Enoch* and *Jubilees* by citing the same passages from Paul's epistles earlier offered by Euthalius. Syncellus's other arguments are a précis of Origen's.

---

[68] Jerome, *Comm. Isa.* 17 (on Isa 64:4,5) (CC Series Latina 73A; ed. M. Adriaen; Turnholt: Brepols, 1963), 735.8–13. See also Jerome's *Epistle to Pammachius* 57.9 (CSEL 54; ed. I. Hilberg; rev. ed.; Vienna: Verlag der Österreichischen Akademie der Wissenschaften, 1996). Here Jerome denounces commentators who "betake themselves to the ravings of apocryphal books." He claims that in this verse, the apostle did not quote Isaiah word for word, but rather "expressed the same sense with other words through paraphrase."

[69] Jerome, *Comm. Matt.* 4 (Matt 27:9,10) (CC Series Latina 77; ed. D. Hurst and M. Adriaen; Turnholt: Brepols, 1969).

[70] Jerome, *Comm. Isa.* (on Is 64:4,5), 735.15–19, ed. Adriaen.

[71] See E. Schürer, *A History of the Jewish People in the Time of Jesus Christ* (ET; Edinburgh: T&T Clark, 1890), 3:145.

[72] Hippolytus, *Comm. Dan.* 4.56.4 (SC 14; ed. M. Lefèvre; Paris: Cerf, 1947). Hippolytus may have considered the passage a paraphrase of Isa 60:1.

[73] Epiphanius (*Pan.* 42.12.3 [GCS 31; ed. K. Holl; Leipzig: Hinrichs, 1922]), perhaps in reference to the *Apocalypse of Elijah.* Epiphanius's statement is confusing, because in the same passage he states that the Ephesians citation originated in the Old Testament.

[74] Euthalius, *Editio Epistolarum Pauli* (*PG* 85.721BC).

✱ 1 Enoch lost after Jerome, until found again in Ethiopia circa late 17th Century

Paul's occasional quotations from pseudepigrapha are not a carte blanche, Syncellus warns, for indiscriminate use of these works; because the pseudepigrapha have been "corrupted by Jews and heretics," and contain material at odds with ecclesiastical teachings, less sophisticated Christians should avoid reading them altogether. But there is no reason why better informed Christians cannot consult these sources, however cautiously, to amplify and explain the biblical narrative.[75]

5. The Revival of the Pseudepigrapha after the Fourth Century

Champions of the pseudepigrapha after Origen do not, as a rule, urge that the canon of recognized scriptures be altered to suit their own reading preferences. Priscillian, for example, is entirely comfortable with the distinction between "apocryphal" and "canonical" books; his main concern is only to establish the point that inspiration is not bounded by the canon. Tertullian himself, the most ardent apologist for the book of *Enoch* in the Latin West, wavered on the issue of its canonical authority. There is no doubt that Tertullian and some of his North African contemporaries accepted *Enoch* as genuine, possibly canonical.[76] In answer to doubts about how *Enoch* could have survived the flood, Tertullian suggests that Noah might have preserved the work; or if that explanation fails to convince, then the work could have been divinely reconstituted after the flood, in much the same way that Ezra restored Jewish scriptures after the Babylonian conquest of Jerusalem. This argument, he writes, should meet the objections of those who do not "receive (recipi)" the work. It might thus appear that Tertullian was pleading a case for formal recognition of *Enoch*.[77] But even here his defense falls short of an outright campaign for universal acceptance. As Campenhausen notes, Tertullian is less interested in reforming the canon than in justifying his own continued appeal to a work that he finds personally edifying.[78]

Certain pseudepigrapha, notably *Enoch* and *4 Ezra*, did in fact gain canonical status in certain circles. *Fourth Ezra* (also known as *2 Esdras*) is included in most modern editions of the Vulgate. Canon lists of the Ethiopian Orthodox church include *Enoch* and *4 Ezra*.[79] The formal recognition of these two works probably has more to do with their longstanding use and popularity than to the efforts of specific writers. But these were the exceptions. Were it not for passing references in canon lists or quotations from early Christian writers, many pseudepigraphic works would now be entirely unknown.

---

[75] George Syncellus, *Ecloga Chronographica* (ed. A. A. Mosshammer; Leipzig: Teubner, 1983), 27.12–18. See also Photius, *Ad Amphilochium Quaestiones* 151 (*PG* 101.813C).

[76] See Tertullian, *Res.* 32 (CSEL 47.3; ed. A. Kroymann; Vienna: Tempsky, 1906). Although not identifying the book by name, Tertullian prefaces a rather loose paraphrase from *1 En.* 61:5 with the words "habes scriptum."

[77] "Recipi," as Zahn rightly notes (*Geschichte*, 1.120–21), is a form of the same word that Tertullian uses elsewhere in his discussions of the books of the Christian canon. For discussion of Tertullian's views on the canonical authority of *Enoch*, see also A. D'Alès, *Theologie de Tertullien* (Paris: Beauchesne, 1905), 225–26.

[78] H. von Campenhausen, *The Formation of the Christian Bible* (ET; Philadelphia: Fortress, 1972), 276.

[79] See R. W. Cowley, "The Biblical Canon of the Ethiopian Orthodox Church Today," *Ostkirchliche Studien* 27 (1974): 318–23.

We should not assume, however, that official condemnation of the pseudepigrapha led invariably to a diminished use of this literature. Especially in the Christian East, the opposite is true. R. A. Kraft has plausibly suggested that the monastic preservation of exotic literature, and the rise of hagiography and martyrology, may have had something to do with a revival of interest in the pseudepigrapha.[80] Quite often, the perceived value of these sources was enough to overcome residual doubts about their authority. This is certainly the case with *Jubilees*, a work whose exegetical value was already acknowledged by the titles by which the work known in Greek: the "Details of Genesis *(ta lepta Geneseōs),*" or "Little Genesis *(leptē Genesis)."* *Jubilees* was not especially well known in the early church before the fourth century. After that time time, however, it seems to have come into its own. A measure of the popularity of this work is the matter-of-fact way in which some later Christian commentators quote from the work. In Christian catenae on Genesis, material from *Jubilees* appears regularly alongside other respected commentators on Genesis, for example, John Chrysostom and Basil of Caesarea.[81] As late as the thirteenth century, the Byzantine chronicler George Cedrenus unapologetically names *Jubilees* along with "ecclesiastical historians" and "other books" as sources from which he has extracted not a little bit *(ouk oliga)* of material.[82]

Paradoxically, the sharpening of the boundaries between "canonical" and "apocryphal" in the fourth century may have even relieved misgivings about the pseudepigrapha previously generated by its uncertain status. In a letter to John of Litarba, the seventh-century Syriac polymath Jacob of Edessa goes so far as to suggest that the official condemnation of certain pseudepigrapha in the fourth century, however justified by the circumstances of that time, should not be determinative for all ages. Because of the threat of heresies in the fourth century, Jacob argues, Athanasius might have felt obligated to anathematize works in their possession. But it also led him to unfairly condemn a work, the book of *Enoch*, whose authenticity had been confirmed by Jude. The very fact that copies of some of the pseudepigrapha continue up to his day whereas others have perished, he writes, attests to the care that God had taken to provide for the survival of those that he considered useful. Now that the threat of heresy had lifted, Jacob saw no danger in consulting the pseudepigrapha that still survived, provided one exercised discernment.[83]

---

[80] R. A. Kraft, "The Pseudepigrapha in Christianity," in *Tracing the Threads: Studies in the Vitality of Jewish Pseudepigrapha* (SBLEJL 6; ed. J. C. Reeves; Atlanta: Scholars, 1994), 68–70. On the preservation of Jewish pseudepigrapha in Egyptian monasticism, see also D. Frankfurter, "The Legacy of Jewish Apocalypses in Early Christianity," in *The Jewish Apocalyptic Heritage in Early Christianity*, 185–95; and H. J. Lawlor, "The *Book of Enoch* in the Egyptian Church," *Hermathena* 30 (1904): 178–83.

[81] For *Jubilees* citations in Greek catenae on Genesis, see *La Chaîne sur la Genèse* (Traditio Exegetica Graeca; ed. F. Petit; Louvain: Peeters, 1991–1996) #551, #553, #585, #590, #833, #857, #861, #867, #2270. It is striking that in #867, the expression *kathōs gegraptai en tō Iōbēlaiō* accompanies a tradition from *Jub.* 12:12. The formulaic words *kathōs gegraptai* usually refer to passages from the Bible.

[82] George Cedrenus, *Historiarum Compendium* (CSHB; ed. I Bekker; Bonn: Weber, 1838), 6.2–3.

[83] Jacob of Edessa, *Epistle* 13.15, in W. Wright, "Two Epistles of Mar Jacob, Bishop of Edessa," *Journal of Sacred Literature and Biblical Record*, n.s. 10 (1867): 430ff. For French translation, see F. Nau, "Traduction des lettres XII et XIII de Jacques d'Edessa," *Revue de l'orient chrétien* 10 (1905): 198–208; 258–82.

14

The Codex and Canon Consciousness

Robert A. Kraft

For many years now, I have wondered whether the technological change from the scroll format to the large-scale codex influenced, at least in some situations, perceptions about "the Bible," and especially the extent to which the classical Christian concept of a closed or exclusive "canon" of scripture depended on that development.[1]

For the emerging Christian movements in the first century, or at least those that produced or laid claim to written materials, it is probably not irresponsible to assume that "in the beginning was the scroll." This seems to have been the prevalent format for Jewish as well as non-Jewish literature in the mid-first-century Greco-Roman world. Scrolls contained various kinds of writings intended for repeated use within a "literary" context—not ephemeral in nature. The codex format was far from unknown, especially for more workaday purposes, e.g., note taking, rough drafts, record keeping. Martial, in Rome in the late first century C.E., mentions experimentation with it in literary and publishing circles as well.[2] But there is little evidence of its psychological impact, either in surviving literary sources or in discoveries dating from that period.[3]

---

[1] This essay is merely a probe, the possible beginnings of a more thorough study. It attempts to explore issues in late antiquity that in some ways resemble the major shifts in technology that are now raising questions about how our perceptions concerning "text," "books," "reading," and the like are being affected. For example, Elli Mylonas, in an electronic announcement at a conference on the form of the book in October 2000, claims: "As the form of the book undergoes the profound transformations of the digital age, the knowledge, practices and values associated with it are also rapidly shifting ground. Electronic resources are already introducing changes in the way cultural offerings—literature, the arts, information, popular entertainment—are produced and accessed, and by whom."

[2] Martial, *Apophoreta* 1.2, and especially 14.184–192. For a careful, recent discussion of this material, see Roberts and Skeat, *The Birth of the Codex* (Oxford: Oxford University Press, 1983 [reissued 1987]), ch. 5. A fragment of a Latin parchment codex of an otherwise unknown historical text dating to about 100 C.E. was also found at Oxyrhynchus (P.Oxy. 30; see Roberts and Skeat, *Birth of the Codex*, 28). Papyrus fragments of a "Treatise of the Empirical School" (so R. A. Pack, *The Greek and Latin Literary Texts from Greco-Roman Egypt* [2d ed.; Ann Arbor: University of Michigan Press, 1965], # 2355), dated by its editor to the centuries 1–2 C.E., is also attested in the Berlin collection (inv. # 9015); E. G. Turner, *The Typology of the Early Codex* (Philadelphia: University of Pennsylvania Press, 1977), # 389, and Roberts and Skeat, *Birth of the Codex*, 71, call it a "medical manual."

[3] An interesting question in this regard might be how the Jewish authors and copyists who concerned themselves with the "heavenly tablets" (not scrolls) visualized that material in relation to their contemporary bookmaking techniques. For some discussion of the relevant literature, see my "Scripture and Canon in Jewish Apocrypha and Pseudepigrapha," in *Hebrew Bible / Old Testament:*

When Christianity erupted into the light of Roman respectability and imperial favor in the first half of the fourth century, a radical change in literary format is evident throughout the Greco-Roman world, but especially in emerging classical Christian circles. We are told that more than half of the surviving "pagan" texts from that period are in codex format, and the codex is almost universal for the identifiable Christian texts.[4] More important for my present purposes is the fact that from this period we get references to officially sponsored large-scale codices of "sacred scriptures"—in essence, *the* Bible as a single book, with roughly the same contents as would be found in classical Greek and Latin Christianity.[5] Although this practice of collecting the entire "Bible" in a single codex did not prevail during the following millennium,[6] I suspect that the new possibility (and concept) effected a major paradigm shift in how Christians henceforth thought about their "Bible" and its canonical cohesiveness. That is, "biblical canon" took on a very concrete meaning in the shadow of the appearance of the Bible as a single book in codex form.

In the intervening three hundred years of development, from the mid-first to the mid-fourth century, the "Christian" codex also had its significant developments, from simple single-quire productions of papyrus, usually containing a single writing, to multiple quire on papyrus and parchment, sometimes containing multiple works.[7] To some extent, this could be done with scroll technology as well, since we have examples of scrolls containing multiple works.[8] But in these circumstances, to speak of a "Bible" in the sense

---

The History of its Interpretation, vol. 1: From the Beginnings to the Middle Ages (Until 1300), part 1: Antiquity (ed. Magne Saebø; Goettingen: Vandenhoeck and Ruprecht, 1996), 199–216; also available electronically in a more expansive form on my web page http://ccat.sas.upenn.edu/rs/rak/kraft.html (electronic publications). It should be noted that "tablets" were widely used in the Greco-Roman world as well—see Roberts and Skeat, *Birth of the Codex,* chs. 3–4 (and on Jewish rabbinic evidence, 59).

[4] Roberts and Skeat, *Birth of the Codex,* chs. 7 and 8; of course, some of these "pagan" texts may have been produced by Christian copyists, and possibly also vice versa. Confessional or theological stance (or lack of such) may not always have been coterminous with publication procedures.

[5] Constantine is said to have commissioned fifty Bibles (Eusebius, *Vit. Const.* 4.36, cited in T. C. Skeat, "The Codex Sinaiticus, the Codex Vaticanus, and Constantine," *JTS* 50 [1999]: 604; dated 330–335); Athanasius refers to Bibles supplied for the emperor Constans ca. 338 (*Apologia ad Constantium* 4; see Skeat, "Codex," 591).

[6] The following list of more or less complete Bible manuscripts is adapted from H. B. Swete's *Introduction to the Old Testament in Greek* (Cambridge: Cambridge University Press, 1914 [1900]), 123: Vaticanus, Sinaiticus, Alexandrinus (includes a list of the contents by a later hand), Ephrem Rescriptus; MSS N+V (8th–9th cent.), 64 (10th–11th cent.), 68 (15th cent.), 106 (14th cent.), 122 (15th cent.), 131 (10th–11th cent.); note also MS 44 (15th cent., historical books + New Testament). Compared with the hundreds of extant manuscripts of portions of Jewish and Christian scriptures, this is a startlingly thin list.

[7] In the examples listed by Roberts and Skeat (*Birth of the Codex,* 40–41), we find early codices containing Exodus and Deuteronomy (P.Bad. 56); Numbers and Deuteronomy (P.Beatty 6); and Matthew and Luke (P[4] + P[64] + P[67]). The fragmentary nature of the remains makes it difficult to be sure whether multiple works were contained in a single codex, or whether the same copyist produced two similar codices. Conversely, it is virtually impossible to determine whether in some instances two different copyists may have worked on different sections of the same codex; such fragments would appear to us to be two different codices. Examples of all these possibilities can be found in later manuscripts.

[8] See, for example, the Minor Prophets scroll from Naḥal Ḥever published by Emanuel Tov, DJD 8 (Oxford: Clarendon, 1990).

of the entire canon was to speak of a physical collection of different ob[
scrolls or codices or a mixture of both, perhaps with their own special sp
pouch or box or shelf or cabinet or series of cubicles), but also held togethc.
of implied or expressed list of "scriptural books."[9] The primary example of a li..
together contemporaneous with the development of the "mega-codex" is the Paschal letter
of Athanasius in 367, often seen as the climactic event in the early definition of the New
Testament canon. Athanasius was well aware of the single-codex Bible, having been involved
in the production of such for the emperor Constans around the year 338 (see n. 5 above).

It is possible that the conceptual changes that I associate with the emergence of the
single-codex Bible had a more gradual evolution in Christian circles, perhaps with smaller
collections of, say, "the Gospel" or "the Apostle" already in the second century. Some have
even argued that the main event that sparked codex development in Christian communities may have been the early publication of some of Paul's epistles in codex form,[10]
although clear evidence is lacking at present. A similar case has been offered for Mark's
Gospel, or John's,[11] which might have led to the collecting into a codex of "the gospel" in

---

[9] Ancient images of scroll containers include the Pompeii wall painting reproduced in E. G. Turner, *Greek Manuscripts of the Ancient World* (Princeton: Princeton University Press, 1971; 2d ed.; rev. and enl. P. J. Parsons; Bulletin Supplement 46; London Institute of Classical Studies, 1987) plate 9, and the Domitilla catacomb picture from Rome, featured on the "folio" web page by Julia Bolton Holloway—http://www.umilta.net/folio.html (note also what seems to be a codex hovering above the scroll container!). Illustrations of codices in a cabinet are also preserved: see the famous frontis-piece to Codex Amiatinus, perhaps reflecting the situation of Cassiodorus in the sixth century (http://ccat. sas.upenn.edu/jod/Picts/Ezra2.gif; see also the jacket of *The SBL Handbook of Style* [Peabody, Mass.: Hendrickson, 1999]) or the early fifth-century Ravenna representation of the gospel codices (http://ccat.sas.upenn.edu/jod/Picts/bookcase.large.gif [from the tomb of Galla Placidia]; for a black and white reproduction see John Beckwith, *Early Christian and Byzantine Art* [New York: Penguin, 1979], 36). Early Christian lists of scriptural books include Melito (in Eusebius, *Hist. eccl.* 4.26.14), Origen (in Eusebius, *Hist. eccl.* 6.25.2), and the list in the Bryennios codex (see J.-P. Audet, "A Hebrew-Aramaic List of Books of the Old Testament in Greek Transcrip-tion," *JTS* 1 [1950]: 135–54).

[10] See the suggestions by Harry Y. Gamble, "The Pauline Corpus and the Early Christian Book," in *Paul and the Legacies of Paul* (ed. William S. Babcock; Dallas: SMU Press, 1990), 265–80, and in *Books and Readers in the Early Church: A History of Early Christian Texts* (New Haven: Yale University Press, 1995), 58ff.; also David Trobisch, *Paul's Letter Collection: Tracing the Origins* (Min-neapolis: Fortress, 1994), and his *Die Endredaktion des Neuen Testaments: Eine Untersuchung zur Entstehung der christlichen Bibel* (NTOA 31; Göttingen: Vandenhoeck & Ruprecht, 1996). Note also the critical comments by Eldon J. Epp, "The Codex and Literacy in Early Christianity and at Oxyrhynchus: Issues Raised by Harry Y. Gamble's *Books and Readers in the Early Church*," *CR* 10 (1997): 15–37. See also E. Epp's and H. Gamble's contributions to this volume.

[11] On the role of Mark, see C. H. Roberts, "The Codex," *Proceedings of the British Academy* 40 (1954): 187–91; Roberts and Skeat, *Birth of the Codex*, 54–57. But note that Skeat, who is responsible for the revisions of Roberts's earlier work, subsequently favored the theory that the Christian papy-rus codex, along with the *nomina sacra* codings, emanated from Jewish-Christian influences by way of Jerusalem and/or Syrian Antioch, perhaps to record Jesus' "oral law" as a sort of proto-gospel (*Birth of the Codex*, 57–61): "To sum up, although neither of the two hypotheses discussed above is capable of proof, the second [Jerusalem-Antioch] is decidedly the more plausible" (61). Even more recently, Skeat ("The Origin of the Christian Codex," *ZPE* 102 [1994]: 263–68, and "The Oldest Manu-script of the Four Gospels?" *NTS* 43 [1997]: 1–34) has posited an early four-gospel codex (emulat-ing the earlier codex of John) as the main impetus. See also Epp, "Codex and Literacy," 17, for a critical summary of these developments. More likely, in my estimation, is the sort of explanation

its various versions (according to Matthew, according to Mark, etc.).[12] Similarly, portions of what had been Jewish scriptures were issued as smaller collections in codices, sometimes reflecting a step already taken in scroll form (see nn. 7–8 above). Perhaps for someone such as Marcion, the accepted writings of Paul might have been joined together with Marcion's Gospel to form a unified "Bible," possibly in codex form, but evidence is lacking.

Whatever actually happened in any given case, is it possible that early Christians (or at least some of them) came to reserve the codex form for what they considered to be "scriptural" writings, both from their own recent past and from their increasingly more remote Jewish heritage?[13] Did they go through a stage in which it was argued that this is how "scriptures" should look, perhaps in contradistinction to the emerging classical Jewish focus on scriptural scrolls?[14] As we look back on the preserved remnants of those centuries, can we tell what format was being used by such authors as Justin, Irenaeus, Tertullian, Clement, Origen, Cyprian, and the rest? I have usually assumed that multi-"volumed" works such as Irenaeus's *Adversus haereses* or Tertullian's *Adversus Marcionem*, both in "five volumes," or the two volumes of Luke–Acts, reflected the use of multiple scrolls. If so, isn't it peculiar that our earliest examples of what came to be "biblical" Christian texts, apparently including the adopted Jewish scriptures, are predominantly papyrus codices?

But the exceptions are also noteworthy:[15] writings that might have been considered scriptural by some users are found in early codex fragments (the Egerton gospel [vH 586, T NTApoc7], *Gospel of Mary* [vH 1065], *Acts of Paul* [vH 605, see also 608]), as is some other literature less likely to have been viewed as scripture (notably Philo [vH 696, includes several tractates] and a hitherto unknown gospel commentary perhaps by Origen [vH 691]). The *Shepherd of Hermas* is found in both codex format (vH 665 parchment, 668 papyrus) and scroll (vH 662; see also 657 on back of a roll), as is the sayings *Gospel of Thomas* (P.Oxy. 1 [vH 594], codex; P.Oxy. 655 [vH 595] roll; P.Oxy. 654 [vH 593] is on the

---

offered by M. McCormick ("The Birth of the Codex and the Apostolic Life-Style," *Scriptorium* 39 [1985]: 150–58) and developed further by Epp, that itinerant early Christian representatives rather spontaneously recognized the value of the codex format for their purposes; I would add that such needs as instruction, excerpting (e.g., testimonia), and note-taking ("memoirs")—all associated with codex usage in the Greco-Roman world—may also have contributed to this development.

[12] Skeat ("Oldest Manuscript") argues that P[4], P[64], and P[67] are fragments of a single papyrus codex such as may have contained the four gospels, from the late second century. For details on early New Testament fragments, including codices that contained more than one work (especially Gospels, Paul), see Epp, "Codex and Literacy," *passim.*

[13] See E. Ferguson's contribution to this volume.

[14] For this theory, see Peter Katz, "The Early Christians' Use of Codices Instead of Rolls," *JTS* 46 (1945): 63–65, cited with approval by Irven M. Resnick, "The Codex in Early Jewish and Christian Communities," *JRH* 17 (1992): 7. Roberts and Skeat (*Birth of the Codex,* 45, 57 and 60) also note this as a possible factor (especially in the context of the Jerusalem-Antioch theory of origins, n. 11 above) as well as a significant result. It is difficult to assess the extent to which the codex format may have been used in non-Christian Jewish circles apart from emerging rabbinic Judaism. See n. 16 below for some of the evidence.

[15] The following information is garnered largely from the catalogue of Joseph van Haelst, *Catalogue des papyrus littéraires juifs et chrétiens* (Paris: Sorbonne, 1976) [= vH in the in-text references in this paragraph], Turner's *Typology* [= T], and Roberts and Skeat, *Birth of the Codex,* ch. 8. Only materials dated through the early third century have been selected. Epp, "Codex and Literacy," *passim*, gives further details on some of these fragments.

back of a survey list, which gives it the appearance of being a scroll as well). Scroll format is also attested in the "Naasene Hymn" of P.Fay. 2 (vH 1066), in a fragment of Aḥikar (vH 583, not necessarily "Christian"), the Fayum gospel fragment (vH 589, unless it is an isolated page), an Oxyrhynchos gospel fragmentary column (P.Oxy. 2949 = vH 592, from a roll?), *Sibylline Oracles* 5 (vH 581, not necessarily "Christian"), *Jannes and Jambres* (vH 1068, "Christian"?; see also 1069 on the verso) and in early fragments of Irenaeus (P.Oxy. 405 = vH 671) and of Julius Africanus (P.Oxy. 412 = vH 674). On the basis of such relatively slim evidence, no pattern is apparent. On the Jewish scriptures (Septuagint/Old Greek) side of matters, the situation is similarly complex.[16]

During this three hundred years of transition from Jesus to Eusebius, from Paul to Athanasius, evidence of how people thought about what we so unreflectively call "the Bible" is scarce. Probably the most frequently used term is "scriptures," or collectively "scripture," which doubtless gradually lost any plural significance (and any implied open-endedness?) as ideas of scriptural canon tightened.[17] We have glimpses of some relevant events and situations:

Marcion's mini-canon (ten letters of Paul and a shorter Luke);

Melito's distinction of "old" and "new" covenant writings (see n. 9 above);

Origen's list (see n. 9 above) and voluminous output, including the Hexaplaric tool that presumably had to be in codex format in order to be effective;[18]

Eusebius mentioning various disputed works, copying mega-codices for Constantine, and probably writing in scroll format himself.

But once it was possible to produce and view (or visualize) "the Bible" under one set of physical covers, the concept of "canon" became concretized in a new way that shapes our thinking to the present day and makes it very difficult for us to recapture the perspectives of earlier times. "The canon" in this sense is the product of fourth-century technological developments. Before that, it seems to me, things were less "fixed," and perceptions, accordingly, less concrete.[19]

---

[16] For the beginnings of a treatment of these materials, see my forthcoming article on "The 'Textual Mechanics' of Early Jewish LXX/OG Papyri and Fragments," in the collection of essays from the May 1998 conference on "The Bible as Book: The Transmission of the Greek Text" sponsored by the Van Kampen Foundation and The Scriptorium: Center for Christian Antiquities, which is a summary version of the more detailed electronic publication found at http://ccat.sas.upenn.edu/rs/rak/jewishpap.html.

[17] For discussions of relevant Greek terminology, such as *biblion, biblos, hē graphē*, and *hai graphai*, see the standard lexica such as Bauer-Arndt-Gingrich[-Danker], *A Greek-English Lexicon of the New Testament and Other Early Christian Literature* (Chicago: University of Chicago Press, 1979 [2000]). The use of "the scripture" in the singular as a collective from the earliest Christian period is certainly a step in the direction of viewing "the Bible" as a whole, although the precise limits of "scripture" are not always specified. On the terms used for "scroll," "tablet," "codex," etc., see Gamble, *Books*, ch. 2, and the literature cited there, especially Roberts and Skeat, *Birth of the Codex, passim*.

[18] Eusebius describes Origen's Hexaplaric labors in *Hist. eccl.* 6.16, but without commenting explicitly on the format. It is difficult to imagine the *Hexapla* as scrolls, if each "opening" (panel?) displayed the six (or more) columns; see the lengthy discussion in Swete, *Introduction*, ch. 3, esp. 74ff.

[19] See J. Sanders's discussion in this volume.

15

The Status of the Masoretic Text in Modern Text Editions of the Hebrew Bible: The Relevance of Canon

Emanuel Tov

In this study we turn to a theoretical analysis of the nature and status of the Masoretic Text (MT) and offer some thoughts about the practical problems posed by modern text editions of the Hebrew Bible. Our view about the ideal text edition will be determined by a close look at canonical issues (section IV).

At the beginning of the third millennium of the common era, we often pride ourselves in thinking that we have a good knowledge of the biblical text. After all, we have thousands of manuscripts of the MT, fragments of some two hundred texts from Qumran, many early papyri and codices of the Septuagint, and various additional ancient sources. These texts, however, constitute but a small portion of the sources that once existed; we shall never know how many Bible texts existed in the last three centuries before the common era, what percentage of these sources has survived, or how many texts existed in the three preceding centuries.

We scholars act, however, as if we know the biblical text well and, to some extent, we have no alternative, since each generation shapes its views based on the existing evidence. In the meantime, introductions to the Hebrew Bible and commentaries to the individual books are written as if the text of these books is known. But on which sources do we base our analysis of "the Bible"? When we speak about "the Bible" in general, do we mean the printed editions of the Masoretic Text? This problem is presented here because the more I consult the Qumran biblical manuscripts and the evidence of the Greek Septuagint in my own work, the less I feel drawn to consider the MT the central text. Other scholars who consult the Qumran and Septuagint texts less often may agree with the doubts voiced here, but in practice they still treat the MT as the central text more than they ought to. Perhaps because religious attention focuses on MT, this text still has a magical attraction for scholars.

1. The Masoretic Text and Other Witnesses

The vocalization of the MT provides evidence that one should not identify it with that abstract unit called "the Hebrew Bible." The vowels of the MT merely display one of several vocalization systems, namely the system finalized by Aharon ben Moshe Ben Asher in Tiberias in the tenth century. Though the consonantal text of the MT was transmitted with additional vocalization systems, in time Judaism accepted the Ben Asher system as the central system. Realizing the complexity of this situation, Goshen-Gottstein distinguished between the most commonly used form of MT, namely the Ben Asher tradition, which he named the Tiberian MT (TMT), and the other forms of MT.[1] The differences between the Tiberian MT and other vocalization systems are negligible at the content level, but important for grammarians and textual critics.

The differences in content, however, between the consonantal text of the MT and that of the other textual witnesses are significant. In spite of these other textual traditions, authoritative at the time, the MT eventually became the central text and then the sole authoritative text in Judaism. As a result, the MT has been copied many times and subsequently many printed editions of it have been produced, so that these editions are now being considered by many as the sole text of "the Bible," even by exegetes. Scholars think of the *Biblia Hebraica (Stuttgartensia)* as an objective tool that combines information from all textual sources. That edition, however, does *not* represent a *Biblia Hebraica* but rather a *Biblia Masoretica*, so to speak, since it presents the Masoretic text of the Bible rather than the Bible as a whole (unless one takes the details in the apparatus as representing the complete texts behind them).

Mainstream Judaism and Christianity adhere to the MT as the sole form of the Hebrew Bible. Surprisingly, even critical scholars use the MT almost exclusively as a base, an issue which has not been tackled in the literature. Even when analyzing the Hebrew Bible critically, scholars tend to consult mainly the printed editions of the MT. These printed editions, however, perpetuate the medieval MT and so continue a *single* textual tradition based on proto-Masoretic or proto-rabbinic texts such as those found at Qumran and Masada (before 68 and 73 C.E., respectively) and in additional sites in the Judean Desert (before 136 C.E.).

Detailed comparisons of the medieval manuscripts with texts from Murabbaʿat, Naḥal Ḥever, Sdeir, Ṣeʾelim, and Masada show that the medieval texts, though adding layers of vowels, accents, and Masoretic notes, preserved the ancient proto-rabbinic texts very well. They are actually identical since the ancient scrolls do not differ more from the medieval manuscripts than the latter differ among themselves.

That the modern printed editions and translations reflect these proto-rabbinic texts from the Judaean Desert results from the nature of these printed editions. Modern editions, based on one or more medieval manuscripts of the MT, thus display the same textual family as the texts left behind in the Judean Desert. However, when the proto-rabbinic texts were left behind in the Judean Desert, they represented one out of many textual traditions, while today we have only one form of the printed Bible. Just as a *textus receptus* was formed of the hand-written biblical texts from the first century C.E. onwards, so the second *Biblia Rabbinica*, edited by Jacob Ben-Hayyim (Venice 1524–1525, on the basis of now-lost manuscripts), has developed into a printed *textus receptus* of the MT from the sixteenth century onwards. While removing some of its printing errors, adding new ones, and changing several editorial parameters, all subsequent editions of the Hebrew Bible, with

---

[1] *Mikraot gedolot* (alternate title: *Biblia rabbinica: A Reprint of the 1525 Venice Edition*) (with introduction by M. H. Goshen-Gottstein; Jerusalem: Makor, 1972), 5–16.

the exclusion of a few diplomatic editions based on single manuscripts such as *BH(S)*, re-produce the text of the second *Biblia Rabbinica*. These changes pertain to such details as the vocalization, the *ga'ayot* (secondary stress), the presentation of two words as either one or two units (e.g., Kedor La'omer / Kedorla'omer in Gen 14), the division into chapters and verses, the numbering of verses, the amount of Masoretic notes included, and the layout of poetic sections.

2. The Use of the Masoretic Text in Modern Critical Scholarship

The printed editions of the MT gained an important status, not only in the believing communities, Jewish and Christian, but also in the scholarly world. In the wake of the prominent position of the Rabbinic Bibles and the Polyglots in the sixteenth and seven-teenth centuries, one could not imagine a printed edition based on anything other than the MT. The commentaries in these Rabbinic Bibles referred to the MT, but they were and are conceived of as commentaries on the Bible per se. Even the Targumim were conceived of as translations of the MT, included in the Rabbinic Bibles on facing pages.

Although critical scholars, as opposed to the public at large, know that the MT does not constitute *the* Bible, they nevertheless approach it in this way.[2] They base many *critical* commentaries and introductions on the MT; occasional remarks on other textual witnesses pay lip service to the notion that other texts exist.

Thus S. R. Driver's *Introduction to the Literature of the Old Testament*[3] is mainly an introduction to the MT. This influential work contains no section devoted to the textual witnesses, even though Driver used them extensively in his commentary on Samuel.[4] For example, he makes no mention of the different text sequence of the MT and Septuagint in Proverbs, although the sequence of the Septuagint differs recensionally from that of the MT. He mentions the evidence of the Septuagint in Jeremiah but, preferring the MT (p. 270), disregards it. He makes a few references to the Septuagint in the analysis of 1–2 Kings and mentions the shorter version of the story of David and Goliath in the Sep-tuagint version of Samuel.

Although the much-used introduction of E. Zenger and others, *Einleitung in das Alte Testament*,[5] has an extensive section on the text and versions (by H.-J. Fabri, 37–65), the analyses of the biblical books and the literary genres make few references to these versions. Likewise, Eissfeldt's *Einleitung* has a long introduction to the textual witnesses, but the analysis itself makes few references to texts other than the MT; though referring to the

---

[2] Commentaries based on the MT only are limited, but are not necessarily substandard. Very good commentaries have been written on the basis of MT alone, such as the commentaries of Luzatto and those of U. Cassuto, *A Commentary on the Book of Genesis* (in Hebrew) (2 vols.; 4th ed.; Jerusalem: Magnes Press, 1965); *A Commentary on the Book of Exodus* (Jerusalem: Magnes Press, 1967).

[3] S. R. Driver, *An Introduction to the Literature of the Old Testament* (New York: Charles Scribner, 1946).

[4] S. R. Driver, *Notes on the Hebrew Text and the Topography of the Books of Samuel, with an Introduction on Hebrew Palaeography and the Ancient Versions* (2d ed.; Oxford: Clarendon Press, 1913).

[5] E. Zenger, *Einleitung in das Alte Testament* (3d ed.; Stuttgart: W. Kohlhammer, 1998).

sequence differences in Proverbs, Eissfeldt does not even mention the important differences between the Septuagint and the MT of Ezekiel.[6]

Many critical scholars mainly practise exegesis on the MT. Thus H. Gunkel's thorough and critical commentary, *Genesis,* seldom referred to the evidence of the versions, since "we can really improve the transmitted text of Genesis only in relatively few places."[7]

The translation and commentary in M. Dahood's *Anchor Bible* volume of Psalms, based on the consonantal framework of the MT, disregards the ancient versions, "because they have relatively little to offer toward a better understanding of the difficult texts." At the same time however, Dahood changes the vocalization in accordance with what he considers valid parallels from the Ugaritic literature.[8]

Noth's commentaries pay little attention to textual variants and, in their English versions, rely on the RSV (i.e., mainly on the MT).[9] As Noth's main interest is source criticism, he marks the various sources in the translation with different typefaces and, without any reference to textual witnesses other than the MT, reconstructs the "original" text by bracketing words, parts of verses, verses, and complete sections that do not belong to that text. None of Noth's commentaries contains a section devoted to textual criticism, with the exception of a brief statement in the Introduction to Joshua: "The Hebrew text of Joshua is generally good, although it has preserved, as Baldi has observed, a number of traditional errors. . . ."[10] By stating that the MT of Joshua is "good," Noth implies that there is no need to consult any other text; this assertion, however, does not take the Septuagint adequately into account. The Kings commentary does make a few references to this version.[11]

C. Westermann's more than 1300 pages of introduction and commentary in *Genesis*[12] includes no section at all on textual criticism, and its exegesis of the MT includes only a few notes on the versions. With the exception of the commentaries by H. J. Kraus on Psalms[13] and W. Zimmerli on Ezekiel,[14] none of the prefaces to the volumes in the *Biblischer Kommentar* have a section on textual criticism.

J. Milgrom's thorough commentary on Leviticus is based on the MT alone, with occasional notes on the versions, and the introduction to this commentary of 2714 pages devotes six lines to the textual condition of the book.[15]

---

[6] O. Eissfeldt, *Einleitung in das Alte Testament, unter Einschluss der Apokryphen und Pseudepigraphen sowie der Apokryphen und Pseudepigraphenartigen Qumran-Schriften* (Tübingen: Mohr [Siebeck], 1964).

[7] H. Gunkel, *Genesis* (HAT; Göttingen: Vandenhoeck & Ruprecht, 1902), vii: "der überlieferte Text von Genesis kann von uns nur an verhältnissmässig wenigen Stellen wirklich verbessert werden."

[8] M. Dahood, S.J., *Psalms I, 1–50* (AB; Garden City, N.Y.: Doubleday, 1965), xxiv.

[9] M. Noth, *Exodus* (OTL; London 1966); *Leviticus* (OTL; London: SCM, 1965); *Deuteronomy* (OTL; London: SCM, 1966); *Joshua* (OTL; London: SCM, 1972).

[10] Noth, *Joshua,* 18.

[11] M. Noth, *Könige* (BK; Neukirchen-Vluyn: Neukirchener Verlag des Erziehungsvereins, 1968).

[12] C. Westermann, *Genesis* (BK; Neukirchen-Vluyn: Neukirchener Verlag des Erziehungsvereins, 1974).

[13] H. J. Kraus, *Psalmen* (BK; Neukirchen-Vluyn: Neukirchener Verlag des Erziehungsvereins, 1960).

[14] W. Zimmerli, *Ezechiel* (BK; Neukirchen-Vluyn: Neukirchener Verlag des Erziehungsvereins, 1969).

[15] J. Milgrom, *Leviticus 1–16, Leviticus 17–22, Leviticus 23–27* (AB; New York: Doubleday, 1991, 2000, 2001).

Andersen and Freedman defend the use of the MT, and in their thorough commentary of Amos claim: "The study of MT as it stands is a straightforward and intrinsically legitimate activity. If more justification is needed, then the MT is self-vindicating to the extent that it can be shown to make sense. Sometimes it is not possible to do so ... We keep the MT in the first place of interest and with first claim to be Amos' text."[16]

The terminology used by B. A. Levine in his commentary on Num 1–20 shows to what extent he employs the MT: "Taken as a whole, the variants exhibited by the Qumran scrolls cannot be said to *undermine* the Masoretic text of Numbers, and they seldom indicate that the Qumran scribes had before them, to start with, texts different from those underlying the Masoretic version."[17] The use of the term "undermine" indicates the central place ascribed to the MT.

On the other hand, having accounted for all the translational deviations, some scholars claim that the Septuagint more often than the MT reflects the original text of the Hebrew Bible. Therefore one could make the Septuagint the base for commentaries, since that version has as much importance for biblical scholarship as the MT. In antiquity the church fathers wrote commentaries on the Septuagint, but one may question whether the reconstructed Hebrew *Vorlage* of the Septuagint will ever form the basis of a modern critical commentary. For partial commentaries, see, for example, my own commentary on the *Vorlage* of Jer 27, and a study by Stulman on the prose sections in that book.[18]

One notes considerable and ongoing interest in the Septuagint and the scrolls. McCarter's commentary on Samuel makes much use of the Qumran scrolls.[19] Likewise, several commentaries, such as Cooke's insightful commentary on Joshua,[20] give much attention to the Septuagint; while the MT forms the basis of that commentary (in the Revised Version), Cooke focuses more than other commentators on readings of the Septuagint. Not only textual commentaries, such as Driver's monograph on Samuel (see n. 4 above), but also several general commentaries on Samuel, pay attention to the Septuagint.[21] Likewise, in his commentary, *Jeremiah*,[22] J. Bright created in translation his own biblical text which, by omitting some sections and rearranging others on the basis of the Septuagint, reflects both that version and the MT.[23]

---

[16] F. I. Andersen and D. N. Freedman, *Amos: a New Translation with Notes and Commentary* (AB; New York: Doubleday, 1989), 140–41.

[17] B. Levine, *Numbers 1–20* (AB; New York: Doubleday, 1993), 86; italics added.

[18] E. Tov, "Exegetical Notes on the Hebrew Vorlage of the LXX of Jeremiah 27 (34)," *ZAW* 91 (1979): 73–93; L. Stulman, *The Other Text of Jeremiah: A Reconstruction of the Hebrew Text Underlying the Greek Version of the Prose Sections of Jeremiah with English Translation* (Lanham, Md.: University Press of America, 1985).

[19] P. K. McCarter, *I Samuel, II Samuel: A New Translation with Introduction and Commentary* (AB; Garden City, N.Y.: Doubleday, 1980, 1984).

[20] G. A. Cooke, *The Book of Joshua in the Revised Version* (CB; Cambridge: Cambridge University Press, 1918).

[21] O. Thenius, *Die Bücher Samuels erklärt* (KEH; 3d ed.; ed. M. Löhr; Leipzig: S. Hirzel, 1898); J. Wellhausen, *Der Text der Bücher Samuelis* (Göttingen: Vandenhoeck & Ruprecht, 1871).

[22] J. Bright, *Jeremiah* (AB; Garden City: Doubleday, 1965).

[23] For example, Bright created the following sequence in translation: 24:1–19, 24, 20–23; 21:1–10 followed by 34:1–7; 34:8–22; 37:1–10; etc. In order to find a certain section, one has to turn to the list of contents.

On the theoretical level, several scholars also emphasized the importance of the Septuagint. In some periods a tendency toward extreme reliance upon the Septuagint coincided with a negative judgment of the value of the MT. In the seventeenth century, Cappellus in his *Critica sacra* (Paris, 1650) and Vossius, *De LXX interpretibus* (The Hague, 1661),[24] *inter alia*, represented this approach. For the nineteenth century, we may quote the instruction with which F. Hitzig opened his lectures on the exegesis of the Bible: "Sirs, do you have a Septuagint? If not, sell everything that you own and buy yourself a Septuagint!"[25] Jahn, Hitzig's contemporary, reconstructed the parent text of the Septuagint;[26] in the introduction to his commentary to Ezekiel (p. iii), he condemned the *soferim* as the creators of the MT and stated that, in his view, exegetical work on Ezekiel should focus on the Septuagint. But while some scholars have always much appreciated the Septuagint, the MT remains the primary basis of commentaries.

While the language barrier of Greek will remain a stumbling block for the perusal of the Septuagint in commentaries, in certain books it should in principle be possible to base a commentary on the Septuagint and also on 4QSam^a[27] or 1QIsa^a.

The following analysis shows that our emphasis on the MT in modern critical study of the Bible causes problems.

A. *The Proto-Masoretic Texts versus Other Textual Traditions*

Since the discovery of the Qumran scrolls, it has become clear that a unified text tradition before the turn of the eras never existed. In the last centuries B.C.E., a large number of copies of the biblical text, attesting to a large number of different texts, circulated in ancient Israel. Each manuscript constituted an independent entity, since scribes allowed themselves much freedom. Within this textual multiplicity, two distinct groups stand out: the proto-Masoretic or proto-rabbinic family of texts, and the so-called pre-Samaritan

---

[24] For a thorough discussion of the evaluation of the Septuagint in this period, see J. C. H. Lebram, "Ein Streit um die hebräische Bibel und die Septuaginta" in *Leiden University in the Seventeenth Century* (ed. Th. H. Lunsingh Scheurleer and G. H. M. Posthumus Meyjes; Leiden: Brill, 1975), 21–63; L. Diestel, *Geschichte des Alten Testaments in der christlichen Kirche* (Jena: Mauke, 1869).

[25] "Meine Herren, haben Sie eine Septuaginta? wenn nicht, so verkaufen Sie Alles, was Sie haben und kaufen sich eine Septuaginta!" See *F. Hitzig's Vorlesungen über biblische Theologie . . . des Alten Testaments* (ed. J. J. Kneucker; Karlsruhe: H. Reuther, 1880), 19, n. 1. I owe the reference to I. L. Seeligmann, "Problemen en perspectieven in het moderne Septuaginta Onderzoek," *Jaarbericht van het Voorziatisch-Egyptisch Gezelschap "Ex Oriente Lux"* 7 (1940): 381. Hitzig's approach is also reflected in his commentaries on the books of the Bible.

[26] G. Jahn, *Das Buch Esther nach der Septuaginta hergestellt, übersetzt und kritisch erklärt* (Leiden: E. J. Brill, 1901); idem, *Das Buch Ezechiel auf Grund der Septuaginta hergestellt, übersetzt und kritisch erklärt* (Leipzig; Eduard Pfeiffer, 1905); idem, *Die Bücher Esra (A und B) und Nehemja* (Leiden: E. J. Brill, 1909). On Jahn's reconstruction of Esther, see J. Wellhausen, *GGA* 164 (1902), 127–47 and J. Hoschander, *The Book of Esther in the Light of History* (Philadelphia: Dropsie College for Hebrew and Cognate Learning, 1923), 2, n. 2 ("an amateurish biblical parody"). Jahn replied in his *Beiträge zur Beurtheilung der Septuaginta: Eine Würdigung Wellhauenscher Textkritik* (Kirchhain, N.-L.: Max Schmersow, 1902).

[27] Such an analysis would be distinct from a textual commentary such as produced by E. D. Herbert, *Reconstructing Biblical Dead Sea Scrolls—A New Method Applied to the Reconstruction of 4QSam^a* (STDJ 22; Leiden: Köln; New York: Brill, 1997).

texts (especially 4QpaleoExod[m] and 4QNum[b]) which form a typological group together with the Samaritan Pentateuch known from much later sources.[28]

All these texts reflect textual multiplicity at Qumran and in ancient Israel as a whole. When the Qumran scrolls were written at Qumran and elsewhere, scribes created and consulted without distinction different texts of the Bible, all of which reflected the "Bible" and were authoritative, though not to the same extent.[29] While most groups did not insist upon a single text, temple circles, and later the Pharisees, embraced a single textual tradition (proto-MT).[30] According to van der Woude, the religious circles around the Jerusalem temple always had a relatively uniform textual tradition, but one suspects that textual diversity could have existed within those circles before the third century B.C.E.

The notion of textual uniformity was later perpetuated in the Judaism of the first century C.E. onward, together with the understanding that only the MT represents the Hebrew Bible.

B. Origins of the Notion of the Centrality of the Proto-Masoretic Text

After the first century C.E., when the views of rabbinic Judaism determined those for *all* of ancient Israel, the notion of a single central text became the only accepted view. This notion, of the MT as the only accepted Hebrew text in Judaism and in Christianity, persists even today. True, the Christian Old Testament, starting with the Greek Septuagint, through the Latin Vulgate, to modern translations, took different shapes during the course of the centuries; but during that time the point of reference for the *Hebrew* text remained the MT for most, but not for all, Christians. The Septuagint remains until today the only authoritative text for the Eastern churches, which still translate it into modern languages. In modern times Müller attempted to revive the centrality of the Septuagint in the western world, because it is closer to the text used by the early Christians.[31] Müller argued that the final form of the MT was fixed after the beginning of Christianity, and should therefore not be used in a church environment.[32]

---

[28] Another important witness of the biblical text is reflected in the Hebrew *Vorlage* of the Septuagint, also recognizable in a few Hebrew Qumran texts (especially 4QJer[b,d]). Furthermore, several independent manuscripts from Qumran are not close to either the MT, Samaritan Pentateuch, or the Septuagint.

[29] Thus also A. S. van der Woude, "Pluriformity and Uniformity—Reflections on the Transmission of the Text of the Old Testament," in *Sacred History and Sacred Texts in Early Judaism: A Symposium in Honour of A. S. van der Woude* (Contributions to Biblical Exegesis and Theology 5; ed. J. N. Bremmer and F. García Martínez; Kampen, The Netherlands: Kok Pharos, 1992), 151–69.

[30] It is hard to know what perception the temple circles had of their own text. It is often suggested that attempts were made to create a single text artificially, but real evidence is lacking. Three abstract models may be devised explaining the creation of a single text: (1) An attempt was made to discard all but one of the existing texts. (2) An attempt was made to correct all existing texts to a single one. (3) The central source of religious authority in ancient Israel, the temple circles, declared its own text as being central.

[31] M. Müller, *The First Bible of the Church: A Plea for the Septuagint* (JSOTSup 206; Copenhagen International Seminar 1; Sheffield: Sheffield Academic Press, 1996). However, the quotations from the Septuagint in the New Testament often differ from the known manuscripts of the Septuagint, so that Müller's suggestion is not without problems.

[32] This view is also shared by B. S. Childs (*Introduction to the Old Testament as Scripture* [Philadelphia: Fortress, 1979], 89): "Why should the Christian church be committed in any way to

After abandoning the Septuagint and the Vulgate and turning to the *Hebrew* Bible, Protestants had no alternative but to choose the MT. Thus, all Protestant translations are based on it. In recent years Catholic and ecumenical translations follow the same approach. Throughout the centuries, the Vulgate always had more authority than the MT for Catholicism, but following the papal encyclical *Divino Afflante Spiritu,* this no longer applies.[33] This encyclical reinstated the central position to the MT. Jerome had set the stage for the placing of authority in the MT, but his own translation, the Vulgate, had paradoxically replaced it.

After the Jewish and Christian world had made the MT its central text, the scholarly world also adopted it as its point of reference. This coincided with the appearance of the Rabbinic Bibles and the Polyglots in the sixteenth century. In spite of the new textual data, the MT has become more, rather than less, central.

C. Modern Translations and the Central Status of the Printed Editions of the Masoretic Text

Scholars may talk about the Bible in general, but they hold the printed editions of the MT in their hands and refer to them as "the Bible." One wonders whether our approach to modern translations enhances this practice. Christians, and to a lesser extent Jews, call the modern translations of whatever nature "the Bible." This terminology is justifiable, for what else should one call these translations? Most modern translations are eclectic, but only mildly so, containing merely a handful of readings from extra-Masoretic sources, and only rarely, if at all, emendations. As a result, one may call these modern translations Masoretic as well.

The following process seems to take place. Mildly eclectic modern translations centered on the MT are presented to us as the best form of the Bible. Since these translations are central in modern society, their use in turn reinforces the status of the MT itself.

Scholars do not, at a theoretical level, assent to the dominance of the MT, and seem to give equal weight to all ancient witnesses of the Bible. In principle, therefore, scholarly translations should differ from the MT and some do, for example some of the translations presented in the ICC, Anchor Bible, and Biblischer Kommentar. To some extent, however, this limited eclecticism pays mere lip service. While on occasion consulting additional sources, most scholars practice exegesis on the MT, which remains for them the central text of the Bible.

D. The Masoretic Text Not the "Original Text" of the Biblical Books

Mainstream Judaism believes that the MT reflects the original text of the Hebrew Bible, and Christianity shares this view with regard to the *Hebrew* shape of the Bible. But the Jewish-Christian tradition that the medieval text of the MT contains the original text of the

---

the authority of the Masoretic text when its development extended long after the inception of the church and was carried on within a rabbinic tradition?"

[33] See paragraphs 20–21 of this Encyclical in *The Papal Encyclicals,* vol. 4, 1939–1958 (compiled by Claudia Carlen; Wilmington, N.C.: McGrath, 1981), 65–79.

Bible implies that the text always included the vowels. When scholars realized the problematical nature of this understanding, a tradition developed to the effect that the written form
of the vocalization reflects an originally oral transmission. Not until the sixteenth century
did a scholar refute the Jewish-Christian belief in the divine origin of the vocalization.[34]

On the other hand, biblical research postulates that the text preserved in the various
manuscripts and editions of the MT does not reflect the "original text" of the biblical
books. Even if we were to grant that the MT does reflect the "original" form of the Bible, we
would still have to determine *which* representative of the MT does so. The MT does not reflect a uniform textual unit but rather is represented by many witnesses ranging from the
third century B.C.E. to the Middle Ages.

While Judaism and Christianity largely adhere to the MT with regard to the shape of
the Hebrew Bible, Christianity developed a more liberal approach toward the New Testament. Traditionally Christianity turns to the eclectic New Testament text of Erasmus,
while the accepted text is constantly changing in modern times with the appearance of
new critical editions. By the same token, Christianity allows room for changing modern
translations of the Old and New Testament based on an ever-changing textual basis. It
even allows room for changing attitudes concerning the inspiration of the ancient versions. Christianity thus *has* accepted the search for an original text of the New Testament
and, to a lesser extent, the Old Testament, both of which change all the time with our improved understanding of the textual sources. On the other hand, mainstream Judaism allows no room for such liberal views regarding the Hebrew Bible.

E. The Merits of the Masoretic Text versus Other Textual Traditions

Textual critics look for the representatives of a composition that best enable them to
analyze the textual condition of that composition. The MT does *not* provide such a choice
text. Compared to the incomplete Qumran fragments, the Greek Septuagint, and the less
trustworthy Samaritan Pentateuch, it represents the best available complete text of the Hebrew Bible. While it is a very good text, the MT does not reflect the original text, and in
many details, small and large, scholars prefer other witnesses.

The MT was not selected in antiquity because of its textual superiority. In fact, it was
probably not selected at all. From a certain point onwards it simply was used in temple circles. We do not know the prehistory of this text; in any event, no one created this text artificially, as some scholars believe. From a socio-religious point of view, the MT forms the
central text in Judaism, but from a textual point of view, it represents just another text. The
selection of the scrolls of the individual books in the archetype of the MT determined the
textual nature of the books included in this collection. To a great extent, chance played a
role in the choice of these scrolls. Thus, the specific copy of Samuel that was selected as the
archetype of the MT accounts for the somewhat corrupt nature of this book in MT. Accord-

---

[34] See Elias Levita, *Massoret ha-Massoret* (Venice, 1538; ed. C. D. Ginsburg, London 1867, repr.
New York: Ktav, 1968). The various discussions in the wake of this treatise were summarized by C.
Steuernagel, *Lehrbuch der Einleitung in das Alte Testament mit einem Anhang über die Apokryphen
und Pseudepigraphen* (Tübingen: Mohr [Siebeck], 1912), 84ff., and B. J. Roberts, *The Old Testament
Text and Versions: The Hebrew Text in Transmission and the History of the Ancient Versions* (Cardiff:
University of Wales Press, 1951), 68–69.

ingly, the special nature of Samuel does not reveal anything of the history of the book's transmission or the approach of early copyists toward it. Various small details, such as the whimsical nature and unequal distribution in the biblical books of the *Qere* notes, of the *puncta extraordinaria* (deletion dots), the sense divisions,[35] and of the idiosyncrasies of the orthography of several books and parts of books, indicate the chance element involved in the choice of scrolls. Similarly, only by chance did scholars discover in Qumran important data on the development of Jeremiah, and only by chance were such elements preserved in the Septuagint.[36]

The MT represents a good text; after a certain period, the scribes preserved it well. Before that time, however, it was copied like any other text, with less care. Consequently, the MT contains many early errors which the later scribes preserved with great care. They even transmitted the scribal marks in the archetype very carefully. Early scribes used *puncta extraordinaria* above and below letters, to delete those letters, but did not intend these marks to be transmitted from one manuscript to the next one. By an act of misplaced precision, however, they were nevertheless perpetuated. The inverted *nunim* in Num 10:35–36 represent scribal signs denoting misplaced sections in the text, and they, too, were meticulously transmitted.

F. Errors in the Masoretic Text

Although the recognition of errors remains subjective, all manuscripts of all texts from antiquity contain errors, including the MT. The very choice in antiquity of the MT as the basis for the biblical text entailed the inclusion of errors in that text.[37]

The fact that the MT contains mistakes does not cause a problem. One can either remove such mistakes in an eclectic edition or translation, or mark them in a multi-column edition. But the existence of mistakes does imply that focusing on the MT is not conducive to a good understanding of the Hebrew Bible as a whole.

3. Residual Preferential Use of the Masoretic Text by Scholars

The aforementioned problems regarding the central status of the MT relate to all who use it. Although scholars know that it does not represent the original text of the Bible and that other texts should be consulted as well, the MT still influences them by its prominent position. The following examples illustrate this point.

A. Preference for the Masoretic Text in the Evaluation of Readings

Most scholars evaluate individual readings found in the textual sources. They make judgments on the comparative value of such readings and attempt to determine either the

---

[35] There are no sense divisions in the MT of Ruth except for 4:17/18; the medieval manuscripts of Genesis have no sense divisions at all between Gen 28:10 and 32:14, nor between 41:1 and 44:18; and the long first discourse of Moses in Deut 1–4 has very few sense divisions.

[36] For some examples, see E. Tov, *Textual Criticism of the Hebrew Bible* (2d rev. ed.; Minneapolis: Fortress; Assen/Maastricht: Van Gorcum, 2001), 325–27.

[37] For some examples, see Tov, *Textual Criticism*, 8–11.

one reading from which all others developed or the so-called original reading. In the course of this procedure, scholars use arguments in favor of or against various readings, often preferring the MT. They have canonized this procedure in the form of textual rules, some of which assign a preferential status to the MT.

Thus many scholars make statements such as, "all other things being equal, the reading of the MT should be preferred." For example, Würthwein states in his handbook to textual criticism:[38] "As a general rule MT is to be preferred over all other traditions whenever it cannot be faulted either linguistically or for its material content, unless in particular instances there is good reason for favoring another tradition."[39]

The readings of the MT are indeed often preferable to those found in some texts, but not to the Septuagint, 4QSam[a], or other Qumran texts.[40] Furthermore, this statistical information should not influence decisions in individual instances, because one cannot predict exceptions. Concerning such judgments, statistical information has less relevance, though it does still influence scholars. The preference for the MT seems to go counter to accepted scholarly procedures.

B. The Centrality of the Masoretic Text in the Evaluation of the Septuagint

The MT does not represent the Hebrew *Vorlage* of the Septuagint. The Septuagint was based on a different text, which has not been found. To locate it, one should perhaps search the ruins of Alexandria or the sands of Pharos. But according to the *Letter of Aristeas,* the translators used a Torah scroll imported from ancient Israel, so that one could also search for similar scrolls in that country. Indeed several such texts and individual readings, often wrongly named "Septuagintal," were found at Qumran.

Because of this similarity between the Septuagint and some Qumran manuscripts, it would make sense to compare the Septuagint with some of the Qumran scrolls rather than with the more remote MT. When dust still covered the Qumran manuscripts, however, the principle was developed within the text-critical analysis of the Septuagint to compare it with the MT. In this procedure, one assumes that the Septuagint translators had in front of them a text like the MT, as long as one cannot prove that they possessed an underlying variant; the burden of proof rests on those who suggest the variant reading. However, we should now entertain the possibility that a translator sometimes used a Hebrew manuscript close to a Qumran manuscript. For example, harmonizing additions in the Septuagint of

[38] E. Würthwein, *Der Text des Alten Testaments: Eine Einführung in die Biblia Hebraica von Rudolf Kittel* (5th ed.; Stuttgart: Wurttembergische Bibelanstalt, 1988), 131. The translation is from the English edition (Grand Rapids: Eerdmans, 1979), 114.

[39] For a similar argument, see O. Thenius, *Die Bücher Samuels erklärt* (ed. M. Löhr; 3d ed.; Leipzig: S. Hirzel, 1898), xci; J. Méritan, *La version grecque des livres de Samuel, précédée d'une introduction sur la critique textuelle* (Paris, 1898), 58; M. Noth, *The Old Testament World* (trans. V. I. Gruhn; Philadelphia: Fortress, 1966), 359; J. A. Thompson, "Textual Criticism, Old Testament," *IDBSup,* 888–91, esp. 888; M. Z. Segal, *Mbw' hmqr',* vol. IV (Jerusalem: Kiryat Sefer, 1960), 883; H. Barth and O. H. Steck, *Exegese des Alten Testaments: Leitfaden der Methodik: Ein Arbeitsbuch für Proseminare* (2d ed.; Neukirchen-Vluyn: Neukirchener Verlag, 1976), 20–26, esp. 23.

[40] This situation makes generalizations even more difficult and, at the same time, may give rise to reverse generalizations amounting to a preference for the Septuagint or 4QSam[a] in the exegesis of Samuel, or for the Septuagint and 4QJer[b,d] in Jeremiah, which are equally problematic.

Numbers identical with similar additions in 4QNum[b] seem to come from such secondary Hebrew readings.[41] Though the traditional text-critical procedure of comparing the Septuagint with the MT will not change soon (because of the convenience of the printed editions of MT), we should now be more readily inclined to posit a Qumran reading at the base of the Septuagint.

C. The Central Position of the Masoretic Text in Critical Editions of the Hebrew Bible

Few critical editions of the Hebrew Bible, diplomatic *(BHS, HUBP)* or eclectic, exist. The eclectic editions, not numerous, cover only some individual books of the Bible.[42] Of the diplomatic editions, the edition of the *HUBP* covering only Isaiah and Jeremiah is still incomplete,[43] so that our attention turns to *BHS*. This edition presents codex Leningrad, a representative of the *medieval* MT, as the main text, while a critical apparatus presents the variants. A critical edition should either present the best available manuscript as the central text, while recording variants and emendations in its apparatus, or create an eclectic text,[44] but in view of what we said earlier, the choice of the MT as the best manuscript involves problems and perpetuates its assumed centrality.

D. Possible Prejudices

As Christian or Jewish believers, scholars may give in to their often unconscious prejudices. Some of the aforementioned commentaries and introductions which focus on the MT may result from such prejudices.[45]

---

[41] This especially pertains when the Greek wording of the two occurrences differs, so that no internal Greek harmonizing should be assumed. See my article "The Nature and Background of Harmonizations in Biblical MSS," *JSOT* 31 (1985): 3–29. On the whole, the Septuagint reflects many harmonizing readings based on Hebrew variants, as was pointed out by R. S. Hendel, *The Text of Genesis 1–11: Textual Studies and Critical Edition* (New York: Oxford University Press, 1998) and Kyung-Rae Kim, "Studies in the Relationship between the Samaritan Pentateuch and the Septuagint" (dissertation, Hebrew University, Jerusalem, 1994).

[42] Probably the best known eclectic edition is that by C. H. Cornill, *Das Buch des Propheten Ezechiel* (Leipzig: J. C. Hinrichs, 1886). The most recent ones are P. G. Borbone, *Il libro del profeta Osea: Edizione critica del testo ebraico* (Quaderni di Henoch 2; Turin: Silvio Zamorani, 1990), and Hendel, *Genesis.*

[43] M. H. Goshen-Gottstein, *The Hebrew University Bible, The Book of Isaiah* (Jerusalem: Magnes, 1995); C. Rabin, S. Talmon, and E. Tov, *The Hebrew University Bible, The Book of Jeremiah* (Jerusalem: Magnes, 1997).

[44] Thus for the Septuagint, the editions of Cambridge and Swete present codex B, the best single manuscript of the Septuagint, while the Göttingen Septuagint presents an eclectic Greek text.

[45] In yet another instance, in the introduction to his Anchor Bible commentary of Ezekiel, my friend and colleague Moshe Greenberg accepts the search for the original text of Homer as legitimate, because there are many manuscripts in which one can expect to find original readings, but not of Ezekiel or "most of the Hebrew Scriptures," since "for Ezekiel there is but one complete text, the so-called Masoretic Text" (M. Greenberg, *Ezekiel 1–20* [AB; Garden City, N.Y.: Doubleday, 1983], 19–20). Greenberg realizes that the text must have been changed and corrupted between the time of the prophet and the emergence of what he names the "standard text" of the Bible, but according to him we cannot penetrate behind this standard text. The evidence of the versions is problematic, and therefore we must base ourselves mainly on the MT. Greenberg discredits the evidence of the Septuagint,

4. Practical Options

Where do these deliberations lead us? They point to a theoretical analysis of the nature of the MT, and a practical discussion of the nature of the editions of the Hebrew Bible. We now turn to the practical issue.

A. Eclectic Editions

Because of the problems inherent with the MT, the analysis of modern editions suggests that we should focus less on that text.[46] But we have found no alternative solution for a diplomatic edition of the Hebrew Bible, because each procedure creates problems for different reasons. As a result, would an eclectic edition not serve the purpose of text-critical and exegetical analysis better? An eclectic edition does not focus on a single source, such as the MT or the Septuagint, but creates its own "original" text of the Hebrew Bible by selecting readings from all available sources. In practice, when creating an eclectic edition, editors take the MT as their point of departure and replace details of it with other readings. Thus an eclectic edition amounts to an edition like *BHS* but with the editor's preferences embedded in the text itself rather than in the apparatus. The editor thus presents to the readers a personal view of the original text of the book of Genesis or Kings. Needless to say, the reconstruction of such an *Urtext* requires subjective decisions, and if textual scholars indulged their textual acumen, each scholar would create a different *Urtext*.[47] If I were to follow this procedure myself, the *Urtext* I would create this year would differ from one five years hence. If we follow this approach, many different eclectic editions are bound to inundate us. Upon whose edition, or whose Bible, will scholars then focus their exegetical activity? If committees prepared such editions, the situation would not improve, because the judgment of a committee is not necessarily better than that of an experienced individual.

The creation of an eclectic edition involves the finding of solutions to all issues, including many which one would otherwise delegate to an apparatus. It requires solutions to small and large problems, many of which perhaps cannot be solved. Who can determine whether the text sequence of the Septuagint of Proverbs is preferable to that of the MT? Which chronology, that of the MT, the Samaritan Pentateuch, or the Septuagint, should one prefer in Genesis? In Kings, should one prefer the chronology of the Lucianic text to that of MT? Should we present as original the earlier Septuagint edition of Joshua–Judges, which combines these two books while omitting Judg 1:1–3:11?

---

claiming that we cannot reconstruct its Hebrew *Vorlage*. It seems, however, that Ezekiel is not a good example for such a claim, since its Greek translation is rather literal. Its shorter text needs constantly to be taken into consideration in exegesis, as was indeed done by W. Zimmerli, *Ezekiel 1, 2* (Hermeneia; Philadelphia: Fortress, 1979, 1983). See further Greenberg's programmatic article "The Use of the Ancient Versions for Interpreting the Hebrew Text," *VTSup* 29 (1978): 131–48.

[46] Even a scholar who is actively involved in the preparation of *BHQ* considers a diplomatic edition "ideal": A. van der Kooij, "United Bible Societies' Policies for the New Edition of the Hebrew Bible," *JNWSL* 19 (1993): 1–11, esp. 5. At the same time, this scholar recognizes the "uncertainties and complications" of such an edition, and he still prefers the eclectic procedure.

[47] Borbone's theoretical introduction to his eclectic edition of Hosea conveniently presents the various difficulties involved.

B. Canon and Presumed Urtext

Since the eclectic system does not offer a practical solution in the case of the Hebrew Bible, we return to our theoretical analysis. We based all our deliberations on the assumption that we have the so-called original text as our constant point of reference. E. J. Epp suggests moving away from the term "original text," and we may have to make such a move with regard to the Hebrew Bible.[48] In the case of the Hebrew Bible, the text-critical *Weltanschauung* basic to all critical editions, except the *HUBP,* assumes an original text.

Because of our focus on the canonical status of the MT, I used to defend the assumption of a single *Urtext,*[49] and expanded this definition by referring to the major differences between the textual sources at the literary level.[50] In this analysis I linked the definition of the original text with the canonical status of MT.

I now have second thoughts on this linkage. In my earlier description, I considered the long and secondary edition of Jeremiah (the MT) the *Urtext,* because it appears in the canonical text and represents the final literary shape of the book of Jeremiah. I represented the short edition of Jeremiah, found in the Septuagint and 4QJer[b,d], as a draft which preceded the canonical edition of Jeremiah. In the same way, the pre-Deuteronomistic forms of Joshua and Judges—which have not been preserved, but which must have existed—although earlier than the MT version, were not represented as the *Urtext.* Nor should we consider several original text sequences or the shorter text editions of Joshua and Ezekiel in the Septuagint to represent the original text of the biblical books; I described them as mere drafts, since they preceded the literary edition of the MT.

The textual and literary judgments expressed in these statements still hold true, I submit, but we need to reconsider the linkage between canon and *Urtext.* The longer texts

---

[48] E. J. Epp, "The Multivalence of the Term 'Original Text' in New Testament Textual Criticism," *HTR* (1999): 245–81. "Very recently the tasks of New Testament criticism have become more intriguing and more challenging as the discipline turns its attention, for example, away from the search for merely one 'original text' to an understanding of earlier stages of composition and to earlier texts—earlier 'originals'—that lie behind what textual critics have become accustomed to consider *the* 'original.' Which 'original' or 'originals' ought we to seek? Or to anticipate a more radical question, ought textual critics to seek or emphasize the search for an 'original' at all?" (p. 263).

[49] Tov, *Textual Criticism* (1st ed.; 1992), 177. I defined this *Urtext* as follows: "At the end of the process of the composition of a biblical book stood one textual entity (a single copy or tradition) which was considered finished at the literary level, even if only by a limited group of people, and which at the same time stood at the beginning of a process of copying and textual transmission. During the textual transmission many complicated changes occurred, making it now almost impossible for us to reconstruct the original form of the text. These difficulties, however, do not refute the correctness of the assumption. All the textual witnesses—except for those that are based on an earlier literary stage of the book (see remark 1 below)—developed from that textual entity (single copy or tradition) which it is the object of textual criticism to reconstruct, even if only in isolated details."

[50] Tov, *Textual Criticism,* 178, remark 1: "The preceding description is based on the assumption that the copying and textual transmission did not begin with the completion of the process of the literary composition of the biblical books, but rather, that at an even earlier stage parts of books and earlier editions were copied, and that some of them have been preserved. However, such textual evidence, which is mainly from 𝕲 (such as the short text of Jeremiah), is not taken into consideration in the reconstruction of elements of the original text, since it belongs to the layers of literary growth preceding the final composition."

of Joshua, Jeremiah, and Ezekiel developed from the shorter ones in a more or less linear way. In other books scribes likewise added and sometimes deleted sections, and only rarely should we assume large scale replacements of texts. In most cases we can thus point to a linear development and only rarely early parallel texts are recognized. By dissolving the linkage between the assumption of an *Urtext* and the canon of Jewish scripture, we thus assume a sequence of authoritative literary strata of a biblical book. We suggest that we should single out no stage as the presumed *Urtext*. As far as we can ascertain, all these early stages were equally authoritative, probably in different centers and at different times. That is, at first the short edition of the Septuagint and 4QJer[b,d] was authoritative, because otherwise it would not have been made the basis for the Septuagint translation at a later period, and would not have found its way to Qumran.[51] By the same token, the early text of Joshua that was at the base of the Septuagint was considered authoritative because otherwise that text would not have been brought to Egypt for translation into Greek. At a later time, or possibly at the same time, the editions that are now contained in the MT became authoritative as well. Possibly two texts were authoritative to the same extent, but in different milieus, or in different periods.[52] Upon the completion of each literary stage it was distributed and became authoritative. When the next stage was created and circulated, the previous one could not be eradicated any more, so that even at a late period such as the time of the Septuagint translation or in the Qumran period, both literary forms circulated. Therefore we found at Qumran both 4QJer[a,c] (= MT), which probably had the *imprimatur* of the Jerusalem spiritual center, and 4QJer[b,d] (= Septuagint), which lacked such an *imprimatur* when it was brought to Qumran, even though it must have been authoritative at an earlier period.

If these arguments are acceptable, what should the textual critic do? We should not express a textual judgment on these earlier texts, because the differences are not textual. Nor should we brush some variants aside as mere drafts. For our purposes, all these literary stages were equally original, or alternatively, none of these stages should be thought to constitute "the original text." Jeremiah presents a relatively uncomplicated case, but in the case of medium-sized or small recensional differences[53] we cannot well determine to which stratum each detail belonged, and should probably refrain from textual judgment. This difficulty may make textual evaluation often irrelevant and even somewhat anarchistic.

While the position developed here is abstract and theoretical, influenced especially by Epp's model for the New Testament, in retrospect it comes close to the views expressed in the *Preliminary and Interim Report on the Hebrew Old Testament Text Project* by Barthélemy and others[54] and to the views of J. A. Sanders, who participated in the same

---

[51] Other stages must have preceded this edition, but they are not documented, and none of them should be considered the *Urtext* either. Of course, linear development must have started from a kernel of some kind, but the complicated growth of the book does not warrant any one stage to be named "the *Urtext*."

[52] A similar development was described by T. Abusch for the long and short versions of the Akkadian *Maqlû* corpus: "An Early Form of the Witchcraft Ritual *Maqlû* and the Origin of a Babylonian Magical Ceremony," in *Lingering over Words: Studies in Ancient Near Eastern Literature in Honour of William L. Moran* (ed. T. Abusch et al.; Atlanta: Scholars, 1990), 1–57, esp. 6.

[53] E.g., the omission of 1 Kgs 16:34 in the Lucianic manuscripts of the Septuagint.

[54] D. Barthélemy and others formulated their position in the introduction to the *Preliminary and Interim Report on the Hebrew OT Text Project*, vols. 1–5 (2d ed.; New York: United Bible

project. As early as 1991 Sanders discussed the relation between text and canon and its relevance to the evaluation of variants. According to Sanders, the search for an original text is unrealistic since this stage (the "First Phase") cannot be obtained any more.[55] Our analysis also comes close to the views expressed by E. Ulrich, who reacted to my earlier position.[56] Even if doubting significant elements in the analysis of Ulrich,[57] we do agree with his challenge of earlier assumptions that textual critics must aim at a single original text.

If our suggestion that an original text never existed holds true, we deprive ourselves of a valid basis for eclectic editions. We also remove a solid point of reference for many, though not for all, textual comparisons. When evaluating suspected textual corruption, theological correction, glosses, or linguistic corrections, one still needs to decide on the originality of the transmitted readings.

These theoretical considerations show the difficulties in assessing textual evidence. Insurmountable problems confront the evaluation of sets of variations reflecting different

---

Societies, 1979–1980), esp. vi–vii. The authors of this report try to reach back to what they call a "Second Phase, consisting of the earliest form or forms of the text which can be determined by the application of techniques of textual analysis to existing textual evidence. This stage may be called the 'earliest attested text.'" On the other hand, the "First Phase" needs to be analyzed with the tools of literary analysis. These texts are named "original text," but the nature of these original texts has not been clarified. The authoritative status of these texts has not been dealt with in this analysis, nor has the relation between text and canon.

[55] See J. A. Sanders, "Stability and Fluidity in Text and Canon," in *Tradition of the Text: Studies Offered to Dominique Barthélemy in Celebration of His 70th Birthday* (OBO 109; ed. G. J. Norton and S. Pisano; Freiburg: Universitätsverlag; Göttingen: Vandenhoeck & Ruprecht, 1991), 203–17, esp. 214–17; idem, "The Judaean Desert Scrolls and the History of the Text of the Hebrew Bible," in *Caves of Enlightenment* (ed. J. Charlesworth; North Richland Hills, Texas, 1998), 1–17, esp. 15–17; idem, "The Task of Text Criticism," in *Problems in Biblical Theology, Essays in Honor of Rolf Knierim* (ed. H. T. C. Sun et al.; Grand Rapids: Eerdmans, 1997), 315–27, 325–27. Sanders does not deny the existence of an original text or original texts; he argues that these stages are beyond our reach, and he therefore contents himself with the reconstruction of the "Second Phase." We now argue that the whole concept of an original text or the "First Phase" as described in the *Preliminary and Interim Report* is irrelevant for the Hebrew Bible. Sanders's concern seems to be more the nature of the translated text for "believing communities" than the text editions of the Hebrew/Aramaic Bible (see "Stability," 214, 216; "Task," 326).

[56] E. Ulrich, "The Community of Israel and the Composition of the Scriptures," in *The Dead Sea Scrolls and the Origins of the Bible* (Studies in the Dead Sea Scrolls and Related Literature [1]; Grand Rapids: Eerdmans; Leiden: Brill, 1999), 3–16, esp. 12–16 (previously published in 1997); idem, "Multiple Literary Editions: Reflections toward a Theory of the History of the Biblical Text," 99–120, esp. 114–15 (previously published in 1996). Ulrich, "The Community of Israel," 14: "There would normally have been, at any time, not one but two or possibly more editions of many of the biblical books in circulation. Was there really an 'end of the process of the composition of a biblical book' that was anything more than the abrupt interruption of the composition process for external, hostile reasons (the Roman threat or the Rabbinic-Christian debates)? And clearly for some books two variant editions "stood at the beginning of a process of copying and textual transmission." See further Ulrich, "The Qumran Biblical Scrolls: The Scriptures of Late Second Temple Judaism," in *The Dead Sea Scrolls in Their Historical Context* (ed. T. H. Lim; Edinburgh: T&T Clark, 2000), 67–87.

[57] Ulrich's claim that the different literary editions had each a textual transmission of their own is debatable, since all known stages of the literary development of biblical books seem to reflect a linear development of an earlier stage. There seems to be little, if any, evidence for the parallel existence of early literary editions, such as is claimed, for example, by Ulrich ("The Community of Israel," p. 15) for 11QPs[a] as compared with the other textual witnesses.

stages in the development of literary compositions in an apparatus of a textual edition, diplomatic or eclectic. In my view, the data compel us to discontinue such evaluations and to record these variants without evaluation in *parallel columns* so as to facilitate our understanding of these texts and to enable an egalitarian approach to them.

An unbiased edition of the Bible will present the reader with all the textual evidence that has an equal claim of representing the Bible. Perhaps we have to think about a new type of textual edition that presents *all* the relevant information on the text of the Bible at the same level rather than in an apparatus to one of the texts, such as the MT. While such an edition may create more problems than it will solve, it will present a challenge for scholarship. Believing communities do not require such a parallel edition, since they adhere to the MT. Such an edition will, however, prepare the next generation of scholars to write less biased commentaries on the books of the Bible. This text edition should present the MT, the Septuagint, the Qumran evidence, and the Samaritan Pentateuch in parallel columns. Readings from the Peshitta, Vulgate, and Targumim can be recorded in an apparatus to the MT.[58]

Summarizing this aspect of our paper, the existing options for editions are:

1. MT only: all extant *noncritical editions* of the Hebrew Bible present the MT.

2. MT + variants (and emendations) in an apparatus: all extant *critical editions* present the MT (i.e., the TMT) and list deviations (and emendations) in one or more apparatuses. These editions (except for the HUBP) require the users to replace details of the MT in their minds.

3. MT + variants and emendations in the text *(eclectic editions):* Eclectic editions make a choice on the reader's behalf; such editions have much to be recommended, since not all users are experts in textual criticism and decision making. But the goal of such an edition, a single *Urtext*, is not realistic in view of the prehistory of the biblical books, and some might claim that it never existed.

4. A multi-column edition: such an edition would present the MT, Septuagint, the Samaritan Pentateuch, and some Qumran texts, on an equal base in parallel columns, with notes on the reconstructed parent text of the Septuagint, and perhaps with English translations of all the data. Such an edition would educate the reader toward an egalitarian and possibly eclectic approach to the textual witnesses—something the present tools cannot achieve. Only by this means can one hope that the next generations of scholars will have less bias in favor of the MT. The earliest example of such a multi-column edition, Origen's Hexapla, served a similar purpose in its day. In modern times, scholars sometimes present similar editions, when the complexity of the original shape of the composition makes other alternatives less viable.[59]

---

[58] I am not the first to present this idea. J. A. Sanders suggested a "pluriform edition" that would assign equal importance to pairs of parallel readings and textual traditions and record them in parallel columns; see his articles ("Stability," 216, and "Judaean Desert Scrolls," 15). Sanders speaks mainly about the parallel presentation of individual pericopes, and not of complete texts, as suggested here. H. Lichtenberger and A. Lange have also been considering the preparation of a multi-column edition of the Qumran texts and parallel biblical sources.

[59] P. Schafer and J. Becker, *Synopse zum Talmud Yerushalmi* (Tübingen: Mohr [Siebeck], 1991); idem, and others, *Synopse zur Hekhalot-Literatur* (Texte und Studien zum antiken Judentum 2; Tübingen: Mohr [Siebeck], 1981).

In sum, the text of the Bible is represented by the totality of its textual witnesses, and not primarily by one of them. Each Hebrew manuscript and ancient version represents a segment of the abstract entity that we call "the text of the Bible." One finds the "text of the Bible" everywhere and nowhere. I say "everywhere," because all manuscripts, from the ancient Qumran scrolls to the medieval Masoretic manuscripts, attest to it. I say "nowhere," because we cannot call a single source, extant or reconstructed, "*the* text of the Bible." For scholarly purposes we should go back, 2200 years or more, beyond the incongruities created by the domination of the Masoretic Text; only in this way can we understand "the Hebrew Bible."

16

The Issue of Closure in the Canonical Process

James A. Sanders

The recovery of ancient biblical manuscripts in the middle of the twentieth century has prompted critical scholarship to reconsider what it means when it applies the word "canon" to Jewish and Christian scriptures. Following the lead of Johann Salomo Semler, in the eighteenth century, and Heinrich Graetz, Samuel Davidson, Frants Buhl, H. E. Ryle, and others in the nineteenth century, a general consensus formed: A council of rabbis, meeting at Yavneh or Jamnia on the Palestinian coast within a decade or two of the disastrous failure of the Jewish Revolt against Rome of 66 to 73 C.E., had decided the content and extent of the Jewish canon.[1] The historical outline of the development a closed canon of Early Jewish literature was fairly clear: the Pentateuch was canonized by 400 B.C.E., the Prophets by 200 B.C.E., and the Hagiographa, the third and final section of the Jewish canon, was determined by the Council at Jamnia around 90 C.E. Well into the late twentieth century, until the Judaean Desert Scrolls were absorbed and evaluated in this regard, the major textbooks of colleges and seminaries throughout most of the Western world reflected this consensus and equated "canon" with closure.

This schematic view depended largely on two points: the concept of canonization, and the authority of extrabiblical data. The term "canonized" implies something officially or authoritatively imposed upon certain literature. Even those who spoke of a gradual process (Otto Eissfeldt, A. Bentzen, and H. H. Rowley) still saw closure as imposed upon select literature by an authoritative body for all Judaism.[2] The quest for closure spawned a corresponding quest for lists, or what could be construed as lists, in ancient Jewish literature outside the Tanak: Sirach, Second Maccabees, Jubilees, Philo, Josephus, and Luke. Similarly, work on the New Testament canonization process looked to "lists" in Tertullian, Eusebius, the Muratorian Fragment, Athanasius's Easter Letter, etc.[3] Such lists were taken

---

[1] Semler's attachment to biblical theology, based on the developing historical-critical method at mid-eighteenth century, led him to limit the concept of canon to the final stage of the formation of biblical literature; see Hornig Gottfried, *Die Anfänge der historisch-kritischen Theologie: Johann Salomo Semlers Schriftverständnis und seine Stellung zu Luther* (Göttingen: Vandenhoeck & Ruprecht, 1961). The pertinent references to Graetz, Davidson, Buhl and Ryle can be found in the chapter by Jack P. Lewis elsewhere in this volume.

[2] See the references in Lewis's article, "Jamnia Revisited" (ch. 9 above). Even Albert Sundberg, who denied that there was a canon of the Septuagint, still reflected the Jamnia view of the Ketuvim; see n. 31 below.

[3] See the critical discussion of them in Lee M. McDonald, *The Formation of the Christian Biblical Canon* (rev. and enl. ed.; Peabody, Mass.: Hendrickson, 1995), esp. 268–76.

to indicate closure for all of Judaism, or all of Christianity, instead of reflecting the distinctive purposes of a particular school or faction at a specific time. Ancient lists, or perceived lists, that contradicted or failed to support eventual official canons could be ignored as uninformed or irrelevant to the quest. Even after the discovery of the Nag Hammadi documents, the Judaean Desert Scrolls, and many New Testament Greek papyri, the consensus tended to hold on despite questions raised by the new discoveries.[4] Some scholars attempted to superimpose the old view on the new evidence. A blatant example was an attempt to read a reference to the whole of the Ketuvim (Hagiographa) in a vague phrase about "the writings of David" in 4QMMT (if that is indeed the correct reading of a very fragmentary witness).[5]

1. History of Formation

The recovery of hundreds of actual biblical manuscripts in Hebrew, albeit mostly fragmentary, a thousand years older than any known previously has necessitated a thorough review of the consensus. The discussion of the New Testament canon is undergoing similar changes.[6] One result has been a closer look at the significance of Jamnia for the canonical process. Shedding the "Jamnia" mentality has not been easy for the Western mind, which looks for decisions imposed by authorities, and often finds them where they do not exist.[7] In early efforts to come to grips with the impact of the Scrolls on the concept of canon the present writer still assumed the importance of Jamnia.[8] But an article by Jack P. Lewis, "What do we mean by Jabneh?" forced me to drop Jamnia from my thinking about "canonization."[9] Sid Leiman questioned the importance of Jamnia in his dissertation at Hebrew University, but he viewed the significance of Lewis's work differently from the way I did.[10] Leiman took it to mean that the Tanak had already been canonized by the second

---

[4] See Peter Flint, *The Dead Sea Psalms Scrolls and the Book of Psalms* [Leiden: Brill, 1997], for an excellent discussion of the new evidence; see also the writer's review of Flint in *Dead Sea Discoveries* 6/1 (1999), 84–89, as well as the review of Shemaryahu Talmon in *JBL* 118/3 (1999): 545–47.

[5] See *Miqsat Ma'ase ha-Torah* (DJD 10; Oxford: Clarendon, 1994), 59 n. 10; and the discussion of it in McDonald, *The Formation*, 41–43.

[6] In this same volume see the masterful articles by Eldon Epp and Daryl Schmidt, who reach the same conclusion.

[7] In *Scribes and Schools: the Canonization of the Hebrew Scriptures* (Louisville, Ky.: Westminster John Knox, 1998), Philip R. Davies belittles the role of communities in "canonization." He, like most Western thinkers, focuses on individual scribes and leaders. But leaders need followers as much as followers need leaders, and without continuing community support leaders have no effect in the canonical process.

[8] J. A. Sanders, *Torah and Canon* (Philadelphia: Fortress, 1972), and idem, "Adaptable for Life: The Nature and Function of Canon" in *Magnalia Dei: The Mighty Acts of God* (ed. Frank Moore Cross, Werner Lemke, and Patrick D. Miller; Garden City, N.Y.: Doubleday, 1976), 531–60; both were written before 1972.

[9] J. P. Lewis, "What Do We Mean by Jabneh?" *JBR* 32 (1964): 125–32; reprinted in *The Canon and Masorah of the Hebrew Bible: An Introductory Reader* (ed. Sid Z. Leiman; New York: KTAV, 1974), 254–61.

[10] S. Z. Leiman, *The Canonization of Hebrew Scripture: The Talmudic Evidence* (Hamden, Conn.: Archon Books, 1976), 131–32. The dissertation had been written a few years earlier.

century B.C.E., whereas I took it to mean that the Ketuvim were not stabilized until later.[11] In fact, if one means by "canonized" that the content and order of the Ketuvim were rigidly set, then this occurred only recently; note that the great Tiberian codices of the Hebrew Bible place Chronicles first among the Ketuvim, whereas Baba Bathra 14b and printed rabbinic Bibles place Chronicles last. The Biblia Hebraica series used the Second Rabbinic Bible as its base text in its first two editions (1902 and 1927) but retained the rabbinic order even after it adopted the Masoretic Leningradensis, the oldest Hebrew Bible in the world, as base text in the third and fourth editions (1937/1977). While one may argue that the difference did not affect the text of the Ketuvim, it certainly affected its hermeneutic structure.[12] Consequently, I prefer the terms "stabilization" and "canonical process" to "canonization."

Since it was now clear that Graetz, Buhl, Ryle, and other nineteenth-century scholars had read too much Western thinking into the various references to Yavneh/Jamnia, the terms of the debate shifted to what Lewis's work really implied. The field was divided between those who took it to mean that "canonization" of the Ketuvim predated Jamnia, and those who took it to mean that the canonical process was not yet complete at that time.[13] The former still looked for confirmation primarily from external references, while the latter examined the plethora of manuscripts now available for both testaments, and considered their implications for the history of the transmission of the text.[14] Most scholars took Lewis's work to mean that release from the Jamnia mentality signified release from the neat three-stage scheme of the canonization of the Hebrew Bible as well. The terms of the debate were re-formulated, as it were.

2. History of Transmission

Prior to the discovery of the Scrolls the history of transmission of the text of the Hebrew Bible was largely formulated in terms of *Vorlagen* underlying variant texts. The text critic explained the significant differences between the MT and the Septuagint primarily in

---

[11] Leiman's view is shared by Roger Beckwith (*The Old Testament Canon of the New Testament Church* [Grand Rapids: Eerdmans, 1985]), Philip Davies *(Scribes and Schools),* and Andrew Steinmann (*The Oracles of God: The Old Testament Canon* [St. Louis: Concordia, 1999]).

[12] See Sanders, "Intertextuality and Canon," in *On the Way to Nineveh: Studies in Honor of George M. Landes* (ed. Stephen Cook and Sara Winter; Atlanta: Scholars, 1999), 316–33, and "Spinning the Bible," *BR* 14/3 (1998): 22–29, 44–45; see also Sanders, "Stabilization of the Tanak" forthcoming in Eerdman's *History of Biblical Interpretation,* ed. by A. Hauser, et al.

[13] See Shaye J. D. Cohen, "The Signficance of Yavneh: Pharisees, Rabbis, and the End of Jewish Sectarianism," *Hebrew Union College Annual* 55 (1984): 27–53. For Cohen, Yavneh meant the creation of a (Rabbinic Jewish) society which tolerated disputes; challenges to reigning ideas did not have to come from sects and heresies. Such openness contrasted with Early Judaism before Yavneh, and, one assumes, Christianity thereafter. Sometimes, of course, Rabbinic Judaism has not tolerated dissent.

[14] In his contribution to this volume, François Bovon argues against the importance of outside forces in the canonical process, and Everett Ferguson, in his contribution, asserts that councils did little more than ratify, as it were, what was already customary in believing communities. See also Frank M. Cross, "The Stabilization of the Canon of the Hebrew Bible," in his *From Epic to Canon* (Baltimore: Johns Hopkins, 1998), 219–29.

terms of there having been a different Hebrew text lying back of the Septuagint. When in the seventeenth century the Samaritan Pentateuch apparently showed yet a third kind of text lying back of it, a theory about three families of texts arose. This theory was well stated by William F. Albright and given prominence by his student, Frank Moore Cross, after the discovery of the Scrolls.[15] The MT would have derived from Babylonian Jewish communities, the Samaritan from Palestinian, and the *Vorlage* of the Septuagint from the highly hellenized Egyptian Jewish communities around Alexandria that produced the Septuagint. Debates then centered on whether there had been a pristine "original" text out of which the three streams flowed, or numerous texts developed in many isolated communities which then gradually developed into the proto-MT, which became dominant by the beginning of the second century of the common era.[16]

The Qumran Scrolls, despite their relatively fluid texts, clearly showed the validity and high antiquity of the MT. Some of them, however, witnessed to texts underlying the variant readings in the Septuagint. Support for Samaritan readings in the Pentateuch was minimal. But where the Septuagint and the MT have the greatest diversity of readings, as in Samuel and Jeremiah, Qumran fragments of varying sizes indicated that there may have indeed been distinct Hebrew *Vorlagen* lying back of some of the Septuagint. In some cases, where there are lengthy pluses as in Septuagint Samuel, or lengthy minuses as in Septuagint Jeremiah, the Scrolls have provided similar ancient Hebrew texts. Other Septuagint variants also find some support in the Scrolls. The Qumran caves, thus seemed to confirm the existence of families of biblical texts deriving from pristine "originals."

But the general fluidity of biblical texts from Qumran gave rise to a different view as well. At the same time that Frank Cross was developing the three-family theory of texts of the Hebrew Bible out of his work on the Scrolls, especially the early fragments of Samuel, Dominique Barthélemy was working on the Greek Minor Prophets Scroll from Nahal Ḥever.[17] Barthélemy's work brought unprecedented clarity to the early history of transmission of the text.[18] What Barthélemy saw in the Ḥever Minor Prophets Scroll was a missing link in the history of transmission of the text of the Hebrew Bible. The Scroll, which dates to the late first century B.C.E. or to the early first century C.E., clearly shows that the early, rather fluid Greek translations were being brought closer to a text of the Hebrew Bible that was moving toward the Masoretic Text. The Ḥever Minor Prophets Scroll came at a historical midpoint, so to speak, between the older, more dynamic Greek translations, character-

---

[15] See the essays by Albright and Cross conveniently reprinted in *Qumran and the History of the Biblical Text* (ed. Frank Moore Cross and Shemaryahu Talmon; Cambridge: Harvard University Press, 1975). The essay by Talmon (on 321–400) presented a quite different theory and formally opposed the creation of an eclectic text of the Hebrew Bible such as the forthcoming *Oxford Hebrew Bible* will embody. See the writer's response to Ronald Hendel's call for creation of an eclectic text in *BR* 16/4 (August 2000): 40–49, 58.

[16] See the lucid discussion of the opposing theories of P. A. de Lagarde and Paul Kahle in this regard by Emanuel Tov in his *Textual Criticism of the Hebrew Bible* (Minneapolis: Fortress, 1992), 181–97.

[17] See again *Qumran and the History* (n. 15 above). Also, more recently, Frank Moore Cross, *From Epic to Canon: History and Literature in Ancient Israel* (Baltimore: Johns Hopkins University Press, 1998).

[18] Barthélemy, *Les devanciers d'Aquila* (VTSup 10; Leiden: Brill, 1963), and *The Greek Minor Prophets Scroll from Nahal Ḥever* (DJD 8; ed. E. Tov et al.; Oxford: Clarendon, 1990).

istic of much of the so-called Septuagint, and the very literal Greek translations of the second century C.E. known as Aquila, Theodotion, and Symmachus.

The history of Greek translations ran parallel to the history of early Hebrew texts from Qumran, on the one hand, and the later more stable Hebrew biblical texts, also from Qumran, dating from the late first century to early second century C.E. The Hever Scroll provided evidence of a gradual movement toward a more stable, proto-Masoretic text in the course of the first centuries B.C.E. and C.E. Barthélemy identified three stages in the history of the transmission of the text: the pre-Masoretic, which was relatively fluid, extending to the late first century; the proto-Masoretic, which exhibited a stage of stabilization of the text, dating from the late first century on; and the Masoretic, which we have in the great, classical, Tiberian codices, like Aleppensis and Leningradensis, dating from the early ninth to the early tenth centuries C.E. His understanding of the history of transmission is now widely accepted.[19]

The MT should thus be seen as an advanced stage in the stabilization process which had begun in the first centuries B.C.E. and C.E.[20] The MT is itself a system of preservation and interpretation of five interrelated elements: the consonants, vowels, accent markings, spacings, and marginal notes designed to keep scribes from altering the text either intentionally or unintentionally. There is no other literature in the world quite like it, designed so guardedly to guarantee accurate transmission and interpretation.

What this means is that the Jewish understanding of the authority of scripture gradually but firmly shifted from a kind of shamanistic or dynamic view of inspiration (the message of scripture), to verbal inspiration (the words), and then literal inspiration (the letters). One can witness this shift in the progression from Hillel's seven *middôt* (hermeneutic rules) at the end of the first century B.C.E., to the thirteen *middôt* of Nahum of Gamzu by the end of the first century C.E., to the thirty-two rabbinic *middôt* in use by 200 C.E. The *middôt* clearly apply to a stabilized text, and render it relevant to new situations.

3. Stability and Adaptability

The major characteristic of scripture as canon is its relevance to the ongoing life of the community that passes it on from generation to generation; second to this is the characteristic of stability.[21] In the early history of transmission tradents of the text, both scribes and translators, could focus on the need(s) of the community to understand the messages of the text, even to the extent of modestly altering or clarifying archaic or out-moded

[19] See S. Talmon, "Aspects of the Textual Transmission of the Bible in the Light of Qumran Manuscripts," *Textus* 4 (1964): 95–103; Moshe Goshen-Gottstein, *The Book of Isaiah: Sample Edition* (Jerusalem: Magnes, 1965), 12–13; and Barthélemy's own statement in *Interpreter's Dicitonary of the Bible, Supplementary Volume* (Nashville: Abingdon, 1976), 878–84.

[20] See the writer's "Stability and Fluidity in Text and Canon," in *Tradition of the Text: Studies Offered to Dominique Barthélemy in Celebration of His 70th Birthday* (ed. G. Norton and S. Pisano; Göttingen: Vandenhoeck & Ruprecht, 1991), 203–17.

[21] See the writer's *Canon and Community: A Guide to Canonical Criticism* (Philadelphia: Fortress, 1984), 21–45, and idem, "Canonical Criticism: An Introduction," in *Le canon de l'Ancien Testament: Sa formation et son histoire* (ed. Jean-Daniel Kaestli and Otto Wermelinger; Genève: Editions Labor et Fides, 1984), 341–62.

expressions so that their community could understand what it might mean to them.[22] This is not significantly different from what went on in the earlier period of the formation of the text. Clearly they could not alter either the tradition or the text to the point that the community being served did not recognize what the tradition was. The need for community recognition of the tradition led to constraint in the handling of the text, and helped keep it stable at all stages of formation and transmission. As the stabilization process intensified, the basic Jewish hermeneutic of the biblical text changed from divine inspiration of the messages in the text to verbal inspiration of the text itself, precisely during the course of the first century of the common era. The change also appears in citations and echoes of the First Testament (largely Septuagint) in the Second; in early New Testament literature such citations exhibit all the traits of textual fluidity one sees in early Jewish literature generally, but later New Testament citations appear to have been rectified or edited to reflect a more stable Septuagint text (as in the long citations in Matthew and Luke).[23]

All biblical tradents had and have two responsibilities: the past and the present, i.e., the *Vorlage* being copied or translated, and the community being served thereby. But as Jews were forced more and more to live in the strangely European, Greco-Roman world, the old laws and wisdom simply were not enough to help them address the new problems and issues that arose in such a very different cultural environment. The *peshat* or plain meaning of the old texts was often inadequate to new situations, no matter how relevant one tried to make them read or sound. This gave rise both to the dramatic shift in hermeneutic of the biblical text, and to the concept of Oral Torah in Pharisaic/Rabbinic forms of Judaism. Oral Torah, resulting eventually in Mishnah and Talmud, was also eventually believed to derive its authority from Moses' encounter with God on Mt. Sinai. The relation between Written Torah and Oral Torah was embedded in the shift from dynamic to verbal understandings of inspiration.[24] Where Oral Torah roots its wisdom in the Tanak it follows hermeneutic principals and rules that in effect make the text of scripture say what *peshat* or critical readings of it cannot support. A new kind of "exegesis" of scripture was needed. This was part of the genius of Rabbinic Judaism that Qumran Judaism resisted. The latter, like the Sadducees, rejected the concept of Oral Torah and insisted that all new legislation addressing new problems in the Greco-Roman world had to be derived from traditional exegesis of the biblical text. But it was Rabbinic Judaism that survived as Judaism, not the others.

The hellenization process forced Jews to decide what to do with the increasing irrelevance of much of the old Bronze and Iron Age wisdom and laws in the Tanak. Acceptable modifications of the text, as in the early period of relative textual fluidity, no longer sufficed. The Judaisms of the first century of the common era addressed the hellenization problem in various ways, ranging from attempts such as that at Qumran to live apart in a closed community, designed to look and act like the desert community that had gathered at the foot of Mt. Sinai, all the way to highly hellenized or "modernized" communities, such as first-century Christianity, which more and more simply dropped the old laws and

---

[22] See Elias Bickerman's penetrating observations in this regard of in his *Studies in Jewish and Christian History* (3 vols.; Leiden: Brill, 1976), 1:196.

[23] See Craig Evans and J. A. Sanders, *Luke and Scripture: The Function of Sacred Tradition in Luke–Acts* (Minneapolis: Fortress, 1993).

[24] See the writer's "Text and Canon: Concepts and Method," in *From Sacred Story to Sacred Text* (Philadelphia: Fortress, 1987), 125–51.

customs (as in Paul's letters) and created new ones, reading the old texts in other ways, allegorizing, spiritualizing, or eschatologizing them, so as to support new ideas. The shift from the pre-Masoretic period of textual fluidity to the proto-Masoretic period of a more stabilized text (accurately copied and passed on), together with the shift in understanding the nature of the biblical text, heightened the need for a stabilized or closed canon by the late first century of the common era.

4. Closures

Accompanying the hermeneutic shift from dynamic to verbal understandings of inspiration was Rabbinic Judaism's belief that revelation or prophecy had ceased at the time of Ezra-Nehemiah. Very clearly not all the Judaisms of the time held the belief; on the contrary, both the Qumran and the Christian forms of Judaism based their whole belief systems on God's continuing involvement in history. And Rabbi Akiba's support of Bar Kochba as the Messiah who would save Israel from Roman oppression, in 132–35 C.E., raises serious questions as to when Rabbinic Judaism itself embraced the belief in the cessation of divine revelation. Arguably, the belief took hold seriously only after the disastrous failure of the Bar Kochba revolt. Given that the Ketuvim of the Jewish canon, excepting only the book of Daniel, have as a major common trait reflection on God's past involvements in Israel's history, or on wisdom, but not on any further or future divine intervention in history, the closing of the Jewish canon would make most sense after the Bar Kochba debacle. Most of the Ketuvim reflect on God's involvement in Israel's past history, but only Daniel anticipates God's involvement in future battles or historical struggles; but Daniel is precisely in the Ketuvim and not in the Prophetic Corpus in the Jewish canon, and can therefore be read as dealing with God's interventions in history in the Babylonian period, and not, as in Christian hermeneutics, predicting future divine involvement in the affairs of later nations. The disaster of the Bar Kochba Revolt soon brought about the departure of Israel from history, concomitant with the increasingly widespread belief that God had already become more and more transcendent, distant, and remote.[25]

Rabbinic Judaism would henceforth live in stasis, in closed communities, in the Greco-Roman world.[26] In those communities the calendar, even the clock, revolved around the rituals of the temple that no longer stood, but still continued to exist in the hearts and worship of rabbinic Jews wherever they might live. Apart and to themselves, Jews could live lives of obedience, as they understood obedience to Torah written and oral, in, but not of, Greco-Roman culture, thereafter in, but not of, the Christian world around them. As David Hartman of the Shalom Hartman Institute in Jerusalem rightly observes, the founding of the State of Israel in the mid-twentieth century was possible only after the reentry of modern Jews into common-cultural history, beginning with the Jüdische Wissenschaft Movement in mid-nineteenth-century Germany.

---

[25] See the work of Lou Silberman in this regard, reviewed by the writer in "Identity, Apocalyptic, and Dialogue," in *The Echoes of Many Texts: Reflections on Jewish and Christian Traditions, Essays in Honor of Lou H. Silberman* (ed. William Dever and Edward Wright; Atlanta: Scholars, 1997), 159–70, esp. 165–66.

[26] See the work of Jacob Neusner in this regard in many of his writings, e.g., *Judaism in the Matrix of Christianity* (Philadelphia: Fortress, 1986).

The new understanding of the history of transmission of the text is important, therefore, to understanding the canonical process. While the history of transmission of the text of the New Testament has its own contours, it is similar to that of the First Testament. The early period of New Testament textual transmission was also one of relative fluidity, but by the fourth century C.E., with the emergence of Christianity as a state religion, it evolved into the desire for accurate transmission of the text and verbal stability.[27] Even so, the primary character of canon was still its relevance to the communities it served. Once the text could no longer be modified to show relevance, hermeneutic rules were devised to break open the frozen text, as it were, and make it applicable again to the needs of believing communities.[28] When new stories could no longer be added to the old, or new songs to the old hymns, the stabilized canon was subjected to new ways of reading what was there so that it could continue to guide the ever-changing communities.

5. Relevance

Relevance or adaptability has always been the primary trait of a canon, early and late. When one speaks of canon, in fact, one has to ask which canon of which community is meant, whether in antiquity or today. The Protestant canon is the smallest and the Ethiopian Orthodox canon the largest. While canons differ, all believing communities agree that their canon is relevant to their ongoing life. The concept of canon cannot be limited to a final stage in the history of the formation of a Bible, as it has been until recently. It must, on the contrary, be understood as part of the history of transmission of the text. Even the issue of its closure must be so understood. Clearly neither Qumran nor Christian Jews believed "the canon" was closed, since both added to it, and claimed canonical status for their contributions.[29] Peter Flint has shown that the Psalter was not yet closed for all Judaism in the first century;[30] and it is clear to many that for the Qumran community the Temple or Torah Scroll was as canonical as the Five Books of Moses. Other works found at Qumran were also functionally canonical for the community. Christians added the Gospels and Acts to whatever Jewish canon they had at the time, and eventually created a second testament to argue the claim that Christ's New Israel had superseded the Old. In response to Marcion they insisted on keeping a double-testament Bible. But the Christian Second Testament was not added to an already closed Jewish canon. The Jewish Bible that Christians worked with was in Greek translation, and, as Albert Sundberg asserted forty years ago, the so-called Septuagint was not in itself formally closed.[31] Jewish use of the Septuagint ceased

---

[27] See the writer's "Text and Canon: Old Testament and New," in *Mélanges Dominique Barthélemy* (Fribourg: Editions universitaires, 1981), 373–94.

[28] See the writer's "Adaptable for Life: The Nature and Function of Canon" (n. 8 above); see also the discussion above of the rabbinic hermeneutic *middôt*.

[29] See Daniel Harrington's contribution to this volume ("The Old Testament Apocrypha in the Early Church and Today"), which discusses the early church's uncertainty as to whether to follow the Jewish canon or the more open Septuagint.

[30] See n. 4 above.

[31] See the pivotal study of Albert Sundberg, his dissertation at Harvard, *The Old Testament of the Early Church* (Cambridge: Harvard University Press, 1964); also Martin Hengel, *The Septuagint as Christian Scripture: Its Prehistory and the Problem of Its Canon* (trans. M. E. Biddle; Edinburgh: T&T Clark, 2002).

after the Jewish revolts against Rome, and the Septuagint survived only as the Christian First Testament. But, as Septuagint manuscripts show, it was not stabilized or closed until it became the Christian First Testament, and then only gradually.

Just as there were many forms of Judaism in the Second Temple period so, as David Carr has demonstrated, there were numerous tracks in the canonical process.[32] The case of the Psalter illustrates the point. As Flint has shown, there were perhaps three forms of the book of Psalms at Qumran, just as there were two forms of the book of Jeremiah in Hebrew there. Focusing on the manuscript evidence now available, instead of on "lists" in external literature, brings a measure of realism to the present discussion of canon, just as the old historian's pursuit of "economy of explanation" has given way to the more realistic quest for the "ambiguity of reality." About the only unifying principle among the varieties of Judaism before the Bar Kochba Revolt, or indeed among the various forms of Judaism through the ages, was and is Torah. Even Sabbath observance and circumcision were not unifying factors for all forms of Judaism, especially in the Hellenistic era. As my teacher, Samuel Sandmel, often said, "Judaism is Torah, and Torah is Judaism; and until one understands that, one can never understand Judaism." By Torah, of course, he meant not only the Pentateuch but all tradition that has derived from it. But once one has grasped that fact, the varieties of interpretation of Torah and tradition begin. And so it is with canon. Even after a canon became completely stable for a community, interpretations and understandings of it continue the canonical process of adapting the old to the new.

In contrast to the Qur'an, which claims to be the record of divine revelation to an individual, the most that can be claimed for Jewish and Christian Bibles is that they are made up of records of various human responses to divine revelations over a period of some twelve hundred years. The Bible is pluralistic in a number of ways, intrinsically containing its own contradictions and discrepancies. In addition, the language of the Bible is inherently multivalent. That is, in order for a literature to get onto a tenure track toward canon it had to have been couched in multivalent language. All good poetry is multivalent, but so is good prose. It must be able to speak to many different communities in many different circumstances to get into a canon, and to function in it. The *raison d'être* of new translations is largely to make the Bible understandable and relevant to ever-changing situations. A canon's adaptability is its primary characteristic, stability its second.

6. Diversity

Because the Bible, Jewish and/or Christian, grew over such a long period in antiquity, it includes a number of sources, and different points of view of the same events. The Bible harbors a number of doublets, even triplets, conveying the same story or account from different periods, composed for different purposes. The most obvious are the history that ranges from Genesis to Kings, retold in a totally different way in Chronicles, and the four gospels. In a remarkable, recent book, Donald Harmon Akenson, an expert

---

[32] D. Carr, "Canonization in the Context of Community: An Outline of the Formation of the Tanakh and the Christian Bible," in *A Gift of God in Due Season* (ed. Richard Weis and David Carr; Sheffield: Sheffield Academic Press, 1996), 22–64.

in Irish history and literature, looks upon the compiler of the history that runs from Genesis through Kings as the world's first true historian, a genius who pulled the sources of preexilic Israelite history into a coherent story, without trying to harmonize them.[33] This history, which scholars call the Deuteronomistic history (DtH), Akenson sees as having given the surviving Judahites in exile a way to understand the disaster that occurred to them, and hence sufficient reason to form a remnant to continue that history in a transformed manner. This editor-inventor thus provided, according to Akenson, a model for later biblical historians to do the same in their time, including the gospel writers, especially Luke–Acts. Their respect for their sources was such that they did not attempt to harmonize them, but used them in order to address the particular problems of their time.

Akenson, an expert in an entirely different field, is well read in biblical scholarship but does a remarkable job not getting bogged down in it. He provides an excitingly fresh way of looking at the history of the formation of the various parts of the Bible, Jewish and Christian, and the Talmuds. The editor-inventors took accounts already accepted and respected in their communities and, instead of editing them into a harmonious whole, added their own perspective in order to make the older stories and accounts pertinent to and relevant for the problems and issues of their own time. The new thus was rooted in the old. "New ideas are given legitimacy by their being burnished with the patina of history: the newer an idea or practice is, the more it is claimed to be old."[34] That statement recurs many times in many ways throughout the book. If the editors-inventors had harmonized the old accounts too thoroughly to make their points, those accounts would no longer have been recognized by the communities as their old, old stories, and would have lost the authority sought in using them. But as vehicles for the new points being made they were powerful instruments for the change-in-continuity needed in the new situations addressed. The old was resignified or reconceived to address the new, honored but not harmonized. Thus the contradictions and discrepancies inherently embedded in biblical literature testify in powerful ways to the canonical process itself, and can serve as its own self-corrective apparatus. Add to that observation the Masoretic tradition (masorah) of jealously guarding the variants and discrepancies in the various doublets and triplets in the First Testament, and one is moved, indeed, to surpassing wonder at the whole canonical process that has issued in current canons.

7. Canonical Process

Several chapters in the present symposium in various ways also illumine the canonical process. Joseph Blenkinsopp's study on the changing meanings of prophecy within the Bible, with Isaiah as a showcase for the changes, illustrates the point. The meaning of

---

[33] D. H. Akenson, *Surpassing Wonder: The Invention of the Bible and the Talmuds* (New York: Harcourt Brace & Company, 1998). While I would dispute several points, I commend Akenson to anyone who would like to read an overview of the formation of the Bible, including the New Testament, and the Talmuds, in beautiful, engaging English.

[34] Ibid., 94.

prophecy underwent several transformations, including critical readings of the prophetic literature itself, the understanding of prophecy in Deuteronomy, Chronicles, Ben Sira, and then in Josephus. The prophet, once understood as "the social conscience of society and the preacher of social reform," eventually becomes a miracle worker who predicts the outcome of history. The older view was not eliminated when the newer was added; on the contrary the new was built on the old, and the divergent understandings were thus sustained together in the same canonical context. Consequently, Blenkinsopp rightly observes that a canon's "normativity is not at all a straightforward concept, and that there are tensions within what counts as normative which cannot be disregarded or set aside, which theological honesty requires us to take seriously. Acceptance of these tensions and antinomies would, one suspects, lead to a richer and more complex appreciation for the biblical canons by the faith communities within which they came into existence and still function." Shaye Cohen's view that "the sages of Yavneh . . . created a society based on the doctrine that conflicting disputants may each be advancing the words of the living God" is a brilliant reflection on the canonical process as it evolved in the Bible on into the Mishnah and the Talmud.[35] But it is an apt way also of reflecting on the process that issued in the highly diverse, even contradictory, expressions in the four gospels of what Christians have believed God was doing in Christ. The difference is that Judaism's stress on the corporate nature of covenant, within which individual worth and responsibility can be fully expressed, even in contradictory ways, keeps it from appearing as splintered as Christianity with its many denominations.[36]

8. Canonical Closures

The Bible is a dialogical literature that in turn gave rise to two dialogical religions based on it. The issue of the date of closure of the various canons of the two religions, the Tanak and the Talmud, and the double-testament Christian Bible, is elusive and difficult to pinpoint, now that we are freed of the Yavneh/Jamnia or conciliar mentality. Is it so important after all? Whatever a church council has done to declare its canon closed served to recognize and ratify what had come to be practiced in the majority of believing communities, as well as to curb the intra-canonical dialogue. Any such effort within Rabbinic Judaism would simply have become part of further debate. The closures enveloped enough internal dialogue for the process of repetition/recitation, which had started it all, to continue unabated in the communities that find their embracing identity in their canon. No closure can curb the dialogue that is inherent in a canon of scripture, which, over against the *magisteria* and *regulae fidei* that developed after closure in all churches, mandates dialogue about its continuing relevance and authority. A canon is basically a community's paradigm for how to continue the dialogue in ever changing socio-political contexts. Leaders within a community, the scribes, the translators, the teachers, the preachers, the

---

[35] See Cohen's "The Significance of Yavneh: Pharisees, Rabbis, and the End of Jewish Sectarianism," in *HUCA* 55 (1984): 27–53.

[36] See L. McDonald's, R. Wall's, and J. Dunn's contributions in this volume, which also warn against seeking a canon within the canon; but as Wall says, let "a full chorus of their voices" sing— an apt metaphor if "modern" dissonance is allowed as well as "classical" harmony.

midrashists and the commentators, precisely those convinced of its continuing relevance, have been and are tradents of the text, those who bring the text's past into the present in the contemporary terms of their ongoing community.[37]

Akenson concludes his engaging study thus, "One of the great vanities of human beings is that they have ideas. Little ideas maybe, but when it comes to big ideas, it is the ideas that have people."[38] Indeed.

---

[37] See the writer's "Scripture as Canon in the Church," pp. 121–43 in *L'interpretazione della Bibbia nella Chiesa: Atti del Simposio promosso dalla Congregazione per la dottrina della fede, Roma, settembre 1999* (Vatican City: Libreria editrice Vaticana, 2001). The argument in the paper was that Enlightenment reading of scripture was a gift of God in due season, and mandates dialogue between critical understandings of scripture and the magisteria that developed after closure of scripture in all churches. The 1943 encyclical, *Divino Afflante Spiritu,* with its support of biblical criticism, mandates such dialogue within the Roman Catholic Church as well; the paper was a celebration of the encyclical, over fifty years after its promulgation, for all Christian communities.

[38] Akenson, *Surpassing Wonder,* 413.

Part Three

The New/Second Testament Canon

17

The New Testament Canon: Recent Research and the Status Quaestionis

Harry Y. Gamble

Hans Lietzmann once remarked that the history of the canon is "one of the most complicated aspects of the study of church history."[1] Few who have broached this subject would disagree. The problem gained greatly in complexity throughout the twentieth century, and although measurable progress has been made, scholarship on the history of the canon is as lively today as it has ever been: new evidence continues to be identified, problems of interpretation persist, and fresh perspectives are being brought into play. The aim of this essay is to furnish an overview of research, especially in the last two decades, by way of identifying the main issues and providing a context in which to consider recent developments and to look ahead.[2]

1. General Conceptions of the History of the Canon

The twentieth century sponsored two largely distinct conceptions of the history of the New Testament canon, and it is helpful to begin with these. The last century began with the famous and fertile debate between two contemporaries of Lietzmann, Theodor Zahn and Adolf von Harnack, from which there is still something to learn.[3] Zahn's massive study of the history of the canon,[4] the most thorough ever undertaken, and his summary of conclusions,[5] argued that there was already a canon of Christian scriptures by about the end of the first century (80–110), not in the sense, of course, that all twenty-seven books of the historic canon were already known and shaped into an authoritative collection, but to the extent that there had arisen a body of Christian documents read in public worship and

---

[1] H. Lietzmann, "Wie wurden die Bücher des Neuen Testaments Heilige Schrift?" in H. Lietzmann, *Kleine Schriften,* vol. 2 (TU 68; ed. K. Aland; Berlin: Akademie, 1958), 15–98, at 3.

[2] For an earlier summary of the state of the discussion, see H. A. Gamble, "The Canon of the New Testament," in *The New Testament and Its Modern Interpreters* (ed. E. J. Epp and G. W. MacRae; Atlanta: Scholars Press, 1989), 201–43.

[3] U. Swarat, *Alte Kirche und Neues Testament: Theodor Zahn als Patristiker* (Wuppertal: Brockhaus, 1991), 331–52.

[4] Theodore Zahn, *Geschichte des neutestamentlichen Kanons* (2 vols.; Erlangen: Deichert, 1888–1892).

[5] Zahn, *Grundriss der Geschichte des neutestamentlichen Kanons* (Leipzig: A. Deichert: 1904).

broadly recognized and cited as normative. They consisted of the fourfold Gospel and a corpus of thirteen Pauline letters, as well as some other writings. Zahn believed that this was adequately documented by the fact that the church fathers, especially the early second-century Apostolic Fathers, were fully aware of these texts, which they clearly took to be fundamental resources of the church at large. This conception, which had in a measure been anticipated by B. F. Westcott, carried for Zahn an important corollary, namely that the New Testament was not self-consciously created by the church, either as a response to external stimuli or as a means to some end, but arose naturally and spontaneously from the inner life of early Christianity, above all in the contexts of worship and instruction. Thus the history of the canon, for most of the second and subsequent centuries, consisted mainly in ironing out small but inevitable variations in local usages.

This conception of the emergence of the canon was roundly repudiated by Harnack.[6] He did not challenge Zahn's data but his interpretation of it, claiming that Zahn failed to provide a *history* of the canon, not only because he located its existence at so early a time and did not bring it into any connection with the theological controversies of the second century, but also because he rested too much on public reading, as though public reading and canonical standing were the same thing. Hence most of Zahn's evidence Harnack found to be irrelevant for the real issue. Crucial for Harnack was not public reading, although that may have been a prerequisite to canonical status, but whether and when Christian writings were set on a par with Jewish scripture, the Old Testament. To Harnack, this did not appear to have occurred until appreciably later, namely toward the end of the second century. Hence he regarded the second century as the crucible of the formation of the New Testament canon. Moreover, Harnack brought its formation into the closest connection with the theological history of second-century Christianity, and discovered its origin in a reaction by the great church against heterodox movements, especially Marcionism and gnosticism. Thus, in sharp contrast to Zahn, Harnack regarded the New Testament canon as a deliberate creation of the church that was meant to secure it against these antagonistic forces, and located the formation of the canon in the latter half of the second century.[7]

Harnack's view came to dominate scholarship for most of the twentieth century. It found its most comprehensive and influential elaboration in the masterful book of Hans von Campenhausen,[8] and it has continued to be advocated, though not always with the same emphases, in many recent works. Von Campenhausen not only adopted the thesis that the late second century was the critical period in the history of the canon but, like Harnack, found that both its principal impetus and its fundamental structure were furnished by Marcion. Like Harnack too, von Campenhausen considered that the process was to all practical purposes complete by the end of the second century, as indicated, for example, by the Muratorian list, although von Campenhausen emphasized the influence of Montanism in prompting the church to define the limits of the canon.

Several developments during the late twentieth century conspired to draw this broad conception into question. Two seminal essays by Albert Sundberg had a large role in this.

---

[6] Adolf von Harnack, *The Origin of the New Testament and the Most Important Consequences of the New Creation* (2d ed.; London: Williams and Norgate, 1925).

[7] Harnack, *Marcion: Das Evangelium vom fremden Gott* (2d ed.; Leipzig: Hinrichs, 1924).

[8] Hans von Campenhausen, *The Formation of the Christian Bible* (trans. J. A. Baker; Philadelphia: Fortress, 1972).

In the first, Sundberg proposed a far sharper distinction than had previously been made between scripture and canon.[9] The relatively inexact and indiscriminate use of these terms was an underlying issue in the dispute between Harnack and Zahn, and Harnack was certainly right to insist against Zahn that the mere use of documents, even their authoritative use, is not an indication of canonical status. Yet Harnack's own view, that canonical status is signified when Christian writings gained an authority equivalent to that of Jewish scripture, is not adequate either. Sundberg sought to bring greater clarity to the whole question by taking a more phenomenological approach. He reserved the term "scripture" for religiously authoritative writings, without regard for the scope of such literature. "Canon," on the other hand, is precisely a matter of scope: the formation of a canon is the determination of a fixed and closed list or collection of scriptures held to be exclusively authoritative.[10] Thus the use of certain writings as authoritative, or reference to them by early Christian writers as scripture *(graphē)* or by means of a scripture citation formula *(gegraptai,* etc.)— the sort of evidence to which Zahn had appealed—says nothing about their canonical status. From the outset Christianity certainly regarded a large number of documents as religiously authoritative, first Jewish writings, and increasingly some Christian ones as well, but their scriptural status is not to be confused with their canonical status, though the recognition of documents as scriptural is a preliminary and prerequisite condition for the question of which and precisely how many such documents are exclusively authoritative, that is, belong to a canon. Hence for the formation of the canon what is decisive is not citation as scripture, but the existence of a definitive and closed collection of scriptural documents that cleanly distinguishes which are authoritative from which are not, as in the production of fixed lists. This terminological rigor means, however, that the period of canon formation proper can be located only with the appearance of such lists. Since, according to Sundberg, a canon is by definition fixed and closed, it obscures categories and misconstrues issues to speak of an "open canon," a "core canon," or a "developing canon."

But when did such lists begin to appear? The view that the New Testament canon came into being toward the end of the second century has usually depended heavily on the Muratorian fragment, a canon list traditionally dated to the late second or early third century and believed to have a Roman origin. As such, it has often served as the pivot-point in the history of the canon. Sundberg's second major contribution[11] was to challenge this date and provenance by arguing that the evidence favored rather a fourth-century date and an eastern origin for the Muratorian fragment. This would place it in the chronological context of other known lists, and thus locate the period of canon-formation in the fourth and fifth centuries. This revisionist claim initially met with a cool reception and had only limited influence on the discussion.[12] Two decades later, however, Sundberg's thesis was

---

[9] A. C. Sundberg Jr., "Toward a Revised History of the New Testament Canon," *SE* 4 (1968): 452–61.

[10] The distinction is elaborated by W. A. Graham, "Scripture," in *Encyclopaedia of Religion* (ed. Mircea Eliade; New York: Macmillan, 1987), 13:133–45, and in his *Beyond the Written Word: Oral Aspects of Scripture in the History of Religion* (New York: Cambridge, 1987). See also E. Ulrich's paper in this volume.

[11] A. C. Sundberg Jr., "Canon Muratori: A Fourth Century List," *HTR* 66 (1973): 1–41.

[12] Everett Ferguson, "Canon Muratori: Date and Provenance," *Studia Patristica* 18 (1982): 677–83.

n up and worked out in systematic detail by G. Hahneman,[13] who not only provided tne most thorough study of the Muratorian fragment to date, adding new arguments in support of its late date and eastern setting, but he also sketched out the whole history of the canon on these terms. While the claims of Sundberg and Hahneman have been persuasive to many,[14] many recent studies continue either to ignore[15] or flatly to reject them and reaffirm the traditional view.[16] Though recent opinion has inclined toward the traditional date and provenance, the issue has hardly been decided. The evidence is largely circumstantial, and the arguments are delicately balanced. It is hard to imagine what more could be said on either side to resolve the debate. Yet one question that still requires attention is the precise nature of the Muratorian fragment, specifically whether it ought to be regarded as a "list" readily comparable to fourth-century canon lists (which are simply lists), or whether, given its discursive and argumentative character, it should be seen as a kind of "preface" or "introduction" aimed at providing historical and hermeneutical perspectives on authoritative Christian documents and groups of documents.[17]

If recent scholarship has arrived at something of an impasse in evaluating the Muratorian fragment, it is important to recognize that our knowledge of the history of the canon is little affected by this document, or at any rate by its date. Those who would place it in the late second or early third century certainly recognize that the fragment was hardly the last word: various documents that became canonical are not so much as mentioned in it (Hebrews, 1 and 2 Peter, 3 John, James), while others that did not become canonical are

---

[13] G. M. Hahneman, *The Muratorian Fragment and the Development of the Canon* (Oxford Theological Monographs; Oxford: Clarendon, 1992).

[14] See G. A. Robbins, "*Peri tōn endiathēkōn graphōn:* Eusebius and the Formation of the Christian Bible" (Ph.D. diss., Duke University, 1986); R. M. Grant, *Heresy and Criticism: The Search for Authenticity in Early Christian Literature* (Louisville, Ky.: Westminster John Knox, 1993); Helmut Koester, *Ancient Christian Gospels: Their History and Development* (Philadelphia: Trinity, 1990), 243; Everett Kalin, "Re-examining New Testament Canon History: 1. The Canon of Origen," *Currents in Theology and Missions* 17 (1990): 274–82; H. Gamble, "Canon, New Testament," *ABD*, 1:852–61; L. M. McDonald, *The Formation of the Christian Biblical Canon* (rev. and enl. ed.; Peabody, Mass.: Hendrickson, 1995), 209–20; and J. Barton, *Holy Writings, Sacred Text: The Canon in Early Christianity* (Louisville, Ky.: Westminster John Knox, 1997), 10, among others.

[15] A. F. J. Klijn, "Die Entstehungsgeschichte des Neuen Testaments," *ANRW* 2.26.1 (1992): 64–97, at 80.

[16] See, for instance, B. M. Metzger, *The Canon of the New Testament: Its Origin, Development, and Significance* (Oxford: Clarendon, 1987), 193–94; E. Ferguson, review of G. Hahneman, "More on Redating the Muratorian Fragment," *Studia Patristica* 19–23 (1988); G. Hahneman, *The Muratorian Canon and the Development of the Canon* (Oxford Theological Monographs; Oxford: Clarendon, 1992); P. Henne, "La datation du Canon de Muratori," *RB* 100 (1993): 54–75; W. Horbury, "The Wisdom of Solomon in the Muratorian Fragment," *JTS* 45 (1994): 149–59; J. D. Kaestli, "La place du Fragment de Muratori dans l'histoire du canon," *Cristianesimo nella storia* 15 (1995): 609–34; C. E. Hill, "What Papias Said about John (and Luke): A 'New' Papian Fragment," *JTS* 49 (1998): 582–629; G. Lüdemann, *Heretics: The Other Side of Early Christianity* (Louisville, Ky.: Westminster John Knox, 1996), 314; G. N. Stanton, "The Fourfold Gospel," *NTS* 43 (1997): 317–46, at 322–25; Th. Heckel, *Vom Evangelium des Markus zum viergestaltigen Evangelium* (WUNT 120; Tübingen: Mohr [Siebeck], 1999), 340–42; M. Hengel, *The Four Gospels and the One Gospel of Jesus Christ* (Harrisburg, Pa.: Trinity, 2000), 21–17.

[17] D. Trobisch, *Die Entstehung des Paulusbriefsammlung: Studien zu den Anfangen christlicher Publizistik* (NTOA 10; Göttingen: Vandenhoeck & Ruprecht, 1989), 42; and E. Ferguson, review of G. Hahneman, *The Muratorian Canon and the Development of the Canon*, *JTS* (1993): 691–97, at 696.

favorably mentioned (*Apocalypse of Peter,* Wisdom of Solomon), and in any case through-out the third and well into the fourth century uncertainties about the scope of authorita-tive literature are well attested. Conversely, those who would place the Muratorian fragment in the fourth century do not doubt that by the late second century the four gos-pels, Paul's letters, and perhaps a few other documents, had already acquired commanding authority and broad use.

Nevertheless, an appreciation of the evidence that takes full account of Sundberg's contributions, and thus takes canonization to be a matter of arriving at fixed lists that draw a sharp boundary, has the effect of throwing the decisive period of canon-formation forward from the late second century to the fourth and fifth centuries. This at once pro-tracts the whole process that led up to the formation of the New Testament canon, and foreshortens the period of canonization proper. Further, an emphasis on the sharp distinc-tions furnished by lists tends to represent canonization more as a process of exclusion than of inclusion, thus emphasizing polemical and apologetical motives. This view also stresses the role of ecclesiastical authorities—bishops, synods, and councils—and downplays the importance of second-century controversies with heterodox movements.

Against this view, it is frequently objected by those who see the second century as crucial, if not decisive (however they may date the Muratorian fragment), that such a nar-rowly formal definition of canon and canonization underestimates the extent to which some writings had attained by the end of the second century such an indefectible author-ity and universal use in the church that there could be no question about them, nor any possibility of their absence from a fixed and final canon. Moreover, it underestimates the significance of this fact, which appears to signal the presence of the "idea" or "concept" of a theoretically determinate body of writings, even if a fixed list of them had yet to be finally determined. For these reasons many think it is appropriate to speak of an "open" or "devel-oping" canon (or, we might say, an implicit or functional canon), even in the absence of lists, by the end of the second century.

However distinct these two conceptions of the canon and its history may appear, they are differentiated in large measure simply by broader or narrower definitions of the terms "canon" and "canonical,"[18] while the evidence itself is not much in dispute. It is rec-ognized by all that (1) by the end of the second century the four gospels, the letters of Paul, and 1 Peter and 1 John had acquired very broad use and high authority in almost all re-gions of early Christianity, (2) that the status and use of other writings continued to be variable through the third and well into the fourth century, and (3) that lists that strictly delimit the scope of authoritative writings clearly belong mainly, perhaps exclusively, to the fourth and fifth centuries. The question, rather, is how the evidence is to be interpreted and integrated into a comprehensive explanatory scheme that attends to all the relevant considerations and properly places the emphases.

---

[18] H. Gamble, "The Canon of the New Testament," in *The New Testament and Its Modern In-terpreters* (ed. E. J. Epp and G. W. MacRae; Atlanta: Scholars Press, 1989), 201–43, at 204–5; McDon-ald, *The Formation,* 15–21; idem, "The Integrity of the Biblical Canon in Light of Its Historical Development," *BBR* 6 (1996): 95–132; Barton, *Holy Writings, Sacred Text,* 11–14; Metzger, *Canon,* 2; cf. G. T. Sheppard, "Canon," in *Encyclopedia of Religion* (New York: Macmillan, 1987), 3:62–9; and K. W. Folkert, "The 'Canons' of Scripture" in *Rethinking Scripture: Essays from a Comparative Per-spective* (ed. M. Levering; Albany, N.Y.: SUNY Press, 1989), 170–79.

A very important contribution to the debate has come from the unexpected direc-
،.on of statistical studies. Stuhlhofer has analyzed the actual use of early Christian writings
by measuring the frequency of their citation during the second through the fourth centuries, controlling for the size of the writings in question.[19] The illuminating result of his
study is to show that the evidence does not fall neatly into two distinct categories but
rather into three, with limited fluidity among them. Thus there are writings cited rather
more often than might be expected, others cited less often than might be expected, and
others cited very little. This *Dreiklassigkeit* (threefold classification) in the use of early
Christian literature by later writers holds good throughout the period, and is not resolved
until the fourth and fifth centuries into the *Zweiklassigkeit* (twofold classification) of canonical and noncanonical. At the same time, relatively few documents experienced a
movement from one class to another. This forthright statistical survey offers a healthy control on theoretical constructions of the history of the canon. The continuities of usage
charted by Stuhlhofer should check the persistent tendencies of scholarship toward assuming that writings were *either* authoritative or not, toward dividing the history of the
canon into sharply distinct periods, and toward emphasizing the significance of one period over against others. Moreover, just as Harnack[20] once imagined the various sorts of
"New Testaments" that could conceivably have arisen, Stuhlhofer has helpfully pointed out
the hazard of teleological presuppositions in the study of the canon, noting that the history of the canon is usually viewed too much in the light of its known outcome, and hence
on the presumptions of purpose and linear progress through stages to a preconceived result. His is an important reminder that this is an unhistorical approach which too readily
forecloses the vagaries and contingencies of an open-ended process.

Making good use of Stuhlhofer's work, Barton has lucidly pointed the way forward
by showing that, despite real and important differences, all of the major construals of the
history of the canon (namely of Zahn, of Harnack/von Campenhausen, and of Sundberg)
are both right and wrong, and suggesting that, once the stumbling block of differing definitions has been stepped over, the history of the canon can be grasped clearly and coher-
ently as a process comprising three somewhat overlapping stages.[21] The first stage,
belonging to the late first and the second centuries, marks the rise of certain early Christian writings to prominent use and authority—above all the Synoptic Gospels, the Gospel
of John, and the letters of Paul. In the second stage, belonging to the late second and third
centuries but extending also into the early fourth century, additional documents come increasingly into the picture and are cited and used alongside these, so that there is still no
idea of a "closed" group. The third stage, occurring in the fourth century, is characterized
by efforts to fix precisely the boundary between authoritative books and non-authoritative
books. This scheme is fairly common.[22] However, Barton rightly emphasizes that a double
dynamic ran across these stages, one toward the growth of Christian scripture, and an-

[19] F. Stuhlhofer, *Der Gebrauch der Bibel von Jesus bis Euseb: Eine statistische Untersuchung zur
Kanonゲeschichte* (Wuppertal: R. Brockhaus, 1988).
A. von Harnack, *The Origin of the New Testament and the Most Important Consequences of
Creation* (London: Williams and Norgate, 1925), 169–83.
arton, *Holy Writings, Sacred Text,* 14–27.
. A. Sundberg, "Toward a Revised History of the New Testament Canon," *SE* 4 (1968):
\59–60.

other toward its limitation. He notes that these tendencies were not simply linear and successive, but overlapped and interacted.[23] Interest in limitation did not arise only at the end of the whole process. With this integrative perspective, Barton points a way beyond old debates.

2. New Approaches and Perspectives

Recent years have seen new evidence being brought to bear on old problems, and new perspectives on the ways in which those problems have been, are, or might be construed. Several of these developments need to be noted here.

The second half of the twentieth century witnessed a strong renewal of interest in and research on the so-called New Testament Apocrypha. This interest is signaled by a new edition of Hennecke-Schneemelcher's *New Testament Apocrypha*,[24] by the launching of the new *Series Apocryphorum* of the *Corpus Christianorum* in 1981,[25] and by the multitude of special studies that have been devoted to individual items of apocryphal literature.[26] The attention given to this material has increased awareness of the scope and variety of early Christian literature, and of the breadth of its circulation and use in the ancient church. The ongoing production and use of this type of literature throughout the second and well into the third century requires to be correlated with the history of the canon. It does not comport easily with the view that the formation of the New Testament canon was practically complete by the late second century, or with the assumption that the literature available to the church was found fully sufficient. Supply corresponds to demand, and if there was a prospect of reception and use, the scope of putatively authoritative literature can hardly have been decided. At the same time, the continuing generation and circulation of additional literature in similar genres—gospels, letters, acts, and apocalypses—no doubt increasingly precipitated hard questions about what might or should be used, and thus brought the issue of limitation into view. The heightened modern appreciation of literature that would ultimately prove extracanonical furnishes a fuller, if also more complex, context in which to chart the history of the canon.

The history of the canon has traditionally been written mainly on the basis of patristic evidence as to the documents known, used, and valued by different writers in different periods and places. This is relatively easy to determine. Yet mere citation, regardless of the citation formulae employed, provides very little useful information. It is more and more widely recognized that what we need is a more thorough understanding of how documents were used. This is not a question simply of how often, to what purposes, or in what

---

[23] Barton, *Holy Writings, Sacred Text*, 24–71.

[24] Edgar Hennecke and Wilhelm Schneemelcher, *New Testament Apocrypha* (trans. and ed. R. McL. Wilson; 2 vols.; Philadelphia: Westminster, 1963; rev. ed. 1987; ET 1991–92). A still newer and reconceived edition is now in the making.

[25] For a discussion of this, see F. Bovon, "Vers une nouvelle édition de la littérature apocryphe chrétienne," *Aug* 23:373–78.

[26] See J. H. Charlesworth, *The New Testament Apocrypha and Pseudepigrapha: A Guide to Publications with Excurses on Apocalypses* (ATLA Bibliography Series 17; Meteuchen and London: Scarecrow, 1987).

contexts various documents were cited, but also of how they were interpreted and understood, that is, of the hermeneutical assumptions, intentions, and implications of their use. What is at issue here is the relationship of the history of the canon to the history of interpretation. That there is a strong relationship can hardly be denied, but its nature has only begun to be adequately described.

From an entirely different angle, the history of the canon now stands to profit from attention being given to the bibliographical and textual realia of early Christian literature.[27] The modern recovery of many early manuscripts provides a rich trove of new evidence. On the one hand, this material offers important empirical evidence about the production, copying, transmission, circulation, use, and collection of books in early Christianity.[28] While historians of the canon have always had a legitimate interest in manuscripts, especially their contents, arrangements, and such lists, prologues, tables and other aids as may be found in them,[29] the papyrus manuscripts now in hand both bring into prominence early Christian methods and conventions in the production of texts (the codex format, the *nomina sacra*) and shed new light on the dissemination, provenances, and uses of those texts. On the other hand, these new manuscript acquisitions are also bringing about a rapprochement between the history of the canon and textual criticism. There was a time when the history of the canon and the history of the text dwelt together under the rubric of "lower criticism," but the growing technical specialization of textual criticism effectively divorced them, to the disadvantage of both disciplines. Now, however, problems in the history of the canon are being addressed more and more with the aid not only of manuscripts but of their texts, and paleography, codicology, and textual criticism are rapidly becoming not only relevant but foundational concerns to students of the canon. What manuscripts and their textual traditions reveal about the actual use of texts and about early attitudes toward them are suddenly primary considerations for the history of the canon.[30] The importance of this change will become clear as we consider particular issues.

---

[27] For other discussions of this issue, see the contributions of Tov, Sanders, Schmidt, and Epp in this volume.

[28] C. H. Roberts, *Manuscript, Society and Belief in Early Christian Egypt* (London: Oxford University Press, 1979); C. H. Roberts and T. C. Skeat, *The Birth of the Codex* (London: The British Academy/Oxford University Press, 1983); and H. Gamble, *Books and Readers in the Early Church: A History of Early Christian Texts* (New Haven: Yale, 1995).

[29] J. K. Elliott, "Manuscripts, the Codex and the Canon," *JSNT* 63 (1996): 105–23.

[30] H. Koester, "The Text of the Synoptic Gospels in the Second Century," in *Gospel Traditions in the Second Century: Origins, Recensions, Text and Transmission* (ed. W. L. Petersen; Notre Dame: University of Notre Dame Press, 1989), 19–37; idem, *Ancient Christian Gospels: Their History and Development* (Philadelphia: Trinity, 1990); E. J. Epp, "The Significance of the Papyri for Determining the Nature of the New Testament Text in the Second Century: A Dynamic View of Textual Transmission," in *Gospel Traditions in the Second Century*, 71–103; idem, "Textual Criticism in the Exegesis of the New Testament, with an Excursus on Canon," in *Handbook to Exegesis of the New Testament* (NTTS 25; ed. S. E. Porter; Leiden: Brill, 1997), 45–97; idem, "The Multivalence of the Term 'Original Text' in New Testament Textual Criticism," *HTR* 92 (1999): 245–81; B. Ehrman, *The Orthodox Corruption of Scripture: The Effect of Early Christological Controversies on the Text of the New Testament* (Oxford: Oxford University Press, 1993); idem, "The Text as Window: New Testament Manuscripts and the Social History of Early Christianity," in *The Text of the New Testament in Contemporary Research: Essays on the Status Quaestionis* (SD 46; ed. B. D. Ehrman and M. W. Holmes; Grand Rapids: Eerdmans, 1995), 361–79; idem, "The Text of the Gospels at the End of the

In addition, a new interest is being shown to the relation of texts and their transmission to the social settings in which they were used, and to the sociological correlatives and functions of texts.[31] This emphasis is important by way of firmly grounding the history of the canon in the actual life of early Christian communities and preventing it from being considered too abstractly, whether in literary or theological terms. In this connection, the very concept of a canon is also at issue. The study of the New Testament canon has commonly worked with a very singular and narrow idea, largely Protestant, of what a canon is, how it is constituted, how it functions, and what authority belongs to it. But comparative studies are enlarging and diversifying our perceptions, and opening up new ways of thinking about different types of canons and the sorts of roles they play in religious communities.[32]

All of these approaches and perspectives enrich but also complicate the study of the New Testament canon. Clearly the day is past when the history of the canon can be narrowly construed or easily charted.

3. The History of the Smaller Collections

The New Testament canon is comprised of three smaller collections: the four gospels, the letters of Paul, and the catholic (or general) epistles. Together these account for all but two documents in the canon: Acts and the Apocalypse. Each of these collections had its own discrete history, prior to and independent of the history of the canon as a whole. The importance of this, often overlooked, is that the history of the canon is not a single and undifferentiated process in which individual documents were separately in play, nor is it to be understood as a selection of some documents from a larger pool. Rather, the canon is in the main a collection of collections, indeed of rather disparate collections that arose at different times and places under the force of different motives and agents. The history of

Second Century," in *Codex Bezae: Studies from the Lunel Colloquium, June 1994* (NTTS 22; ed. D. C. Parker and C.-B. Amphoux; Leiden: Brill, 1996), 95–122. See also the papers by Tov, Schmidt, and Epp in the present volume.

[31] E. Pagels, "Visions, Appearances and Apostolic Authority: Gnostic and Orthodox Traditions," in *Gnosis: Festschrift für Hans Jonas* (ed. B. Aland; Göttingen: Vandenhoeck & Ruprecht, 1978), 415–30; H. Koester, "Writings and the Spirit: Authority and Politics in Ancient Christianity," *HTR* 84 (1991): 353–72; D. Brakke, "Canon Formation and Social Conflict in Fourth-Century Egypt: Athanasius of Alexandria's Thirty-Ninth Festal Letter," *HTR* 87 (1994): 395–419; B. D. Ehrman, "The Text as Window: New Testament Manuscripts and the Social History of Early Christianity," in *The Text of the New Testament in Contemporary Research: Essays on the Status Quaestionis* (SD 46; ed. B. D. Ehrman and M. W. Holmes; Grand Rapids: Eerdmans, 1995), 361–79.

[32] J. Z. Smith, "Sacred Persistence: Toward a Redescription of Canon," in idem, *Imagining Religion: From Babylon to Jonestown* (Chicago: University of Chicago Press, 1982), 36–52; A. and J. Assmann, *Kanon und Zensur* (Beiträge zur Archäologie der literarischen Kommunikation 2; Munich: Fink, 1987); K. W. Folkert, "The 'Canons' of Scripture," 170–79; G. T. Sheppard, "Canon," in *Encyclopedia of Religion* 3:62–69; J. Gorak, *The Making of the Modern Canon: Genesis and Crisis of a Literary Idea* (London: Athlone, 1991); P. Baehr and M. O'Brien, "Founders, Classics and the Concept of a Canon," *Current Sociology* 42 (1994): 1–149; and A. van der Kooij and K. van der Toorn, eds., *Canonization and Decanonization: Papers presented to the International Conference of the Leiden Institute for the Study of Religions* (Leiden: Brill, 1998).

the canon therefore consists in large part in the histories of these smaller groups, and these histories are more difficult to trace than the larger and later process that forged them into one. It is to these smaller collections that we now turn.

A. The Gospels

The emergence of written gospels in the second half of the first century posed two important problems for the early church. The first was owing to early Christian use of the term gospel, which from the beginning had been used to designate the fundamental message of salvation, emphatically understood to be single and unified.[33] When this term came to be applied, secondarily and with some hesitation, to written accounts about Jesus, it was problematic in principle to think or to speak of "gospels" in the plural. The second problem arose from the availability of multiple gospel documents: a plurality of gospels raised the question of the adequacy of any single one of them. More particularly, the fact that these documents diverged from each other in noticeable ways posed thorny theological and exegetical problems that would be discussed for centuries.[34] All of these issues were at work in the history of Gospel literature in the early church.

A collection of the four gospels was assumed to have existed early in the second century by both Zahn, who placed it between 100 and 120, and Harnack, who preferred 120–140, so that both of them saw it as something subsequently repudiated by Marcion. This view was soon displaced, however, by other considerations. Coupled with the demonstration[35] that the Apostolic Fathers' citations of gospel-type traditions more likely represent oral tradition than free quotations of written gospels (to which no explicit appeals are made), form criticism's emphasis upon the vitality and persistence of oral tradition made it appear that written gospels did not quickly or easily gain authority or wide use. In addition, the discovery of the *Gospel of Thomas* in 1945 and a renewed attention to many other gospel-type documents that, judging from patristic and papyrological evidence, enjoyed early currency,[36] pointed to an ongoing production and use of a great diversity of gospels in the second century. This seemed to rule out the early or exclusive preeminence of the gospels that finally found their way into the New Testament. Hence, in contrast to Zahn and Harnack, von Campenhausen claimed that the fourfold Gospel did

---

[33] See H. Koester, "From the Kerygma-Gospel to Written Gospels," *NTS* 35 (1989): 361–81; idem, *Ancient Christian Gospels,* 1–48; cf. R. Gundry, "Euangelion: How Soon a Book?" *JBL* 115 (1996): 321–25.

[34] See O. Cullmann, "The Plurality of the Gospels as a Theological Problem in Antiquity," in *The Early Church* (ed. A. J. B. Higgins; Philadelphia: Westminster, 1956), 39–54; H. Merkel, *Die Widersprüche zwischen den Evangelien: Ihre polemische und apologetische Behandlung in der alten Kirche bis zu Augustin* (WUNT 13; Tübingen: Mohr [Siebeck], 1971); idem, *Die Pluralität der Evangelien als theologisches und exegetisches Problem in der alten Kirche* (Bern: Lang, 1978); and T. Baarda, "Diaphonia—Symphonia: Factors in the Harmonization of the Gospels, Especially in the Diatessaron of Tatian," in *Gospel Traditions in the Second Century: Origins, Recensions, Text, and Transmission* (ed. W. L. Petersen; Notre Dame: University of Notre Dame Press, 1989), 133–54.

[35] H. Koester, *Synoptische Überlieferung bei den apostolischen Vätern* (TU 65; Berlin: Akademie, 1957).

[36] H. Koester, "Apocryphal and Canonical Gospels," *HTR* 73 (1980): 105–30, and idem, *Ancient Christian Gospels.*

not originate until after the time of Marcion and indeed as a response to him, regarded it as already "an established entity" by the time of Irenaeus.[37] Other too, noting the ingenuity of the arguments adduced in its favor by Iren 3.11.8–9), have thought that the fourfold Gospel must have been a relativ ꜱꜱꜱꜱꜱ ꜱ Irenaeus's time, arising only late in the late second century. In any event, the Chester Beatty codex of the four gospels and Acts (P[45], dated to the first half of the third century) has commonly been regarded as the first manuscript witness for a collection of four gospels.

In an explosion of recent studies on the emergence of the four-gospel collection, this consensus is being called into question. Many are now arguing in favor of a considerably earlier creation and currency of an exclusive collection of our four gospels.

T. C. Skeat, appealing mainly to codicological evidence, claims that the early Christian predilection for the codex is owing to its suitability for a collection of four gospels, the combined texts of which could not be accommodated in a roll. Further, he suggests that the Bodmer codex of Luke and John (P[75]), usually dated 175–225, should be regarded as the second half of what was originally a four-gospel codex.[38] He also argues that the papyrus manuscripts designated P[4], containing fragments of Luke, and P[64] and P[67], containing fragments of Matthew, all come from the same manuscript, and that this manuscript too was a four-gospel codex.[39] If so, it was written not later than ca. 200, and thus would be our oldest extant manuscript of four gospels, though it would also have had appreciably earlier ancestors. Indeed, Skeat goes so far as to suggest that all the earliest papyrus gospel fragments, which appear to come from single gospel codices, actually derive from codices containing the four gospels, or at least presuppose such codices.[40]

Furthermore, Skeat argues that Irenaeus, in his apologia for the fourfold Gospel, was not inventing arguments but deriving them from an earlier source which appealed to Ezek 1:1–21 as well as the Apocalypse. Skeat thinks that this source, and the four-gospel collection it discussed, goes back at least to 170, and probably earlier.[41] He urges, moreover, that the idea of a collection of four gospels and their transcription together in a codex was precipitated by the publication of the Gospel of John, and hence occurred early in the second century, by about 125.

G. Stanton, relying on Skeat's work, likewise finds early roots of a four-gospel collection, dating it to a time shortly before 150, though he acknowledges that the universal adoption of a four-gospel canon took much longer, and that there were strong currents running in the other direction. Stanton associates the four-gospel collection especially with the Christian adoption of the codex, but specifies no particular agent or precipitating cause for such a collection.[42]

A still earlier origin of the four-gospel collection has been proposed, but on different grounds, by T. K. Heckel, who adduces strong theological motives for its creation. Heckel develops a complex argument that the collection of the four gospels was created by a part of the Johannine school which, under the necessity of combating docetic christological

---

[37] Von Campenhausen, *The Formation of the Christian Bible,* 171–74.
[38] T. C. Skeat, "The Origins of the Christian Codex," *ZPE* 102 (1994): 263–68.
[39] T. C. Skeat, "The Oldest Manuscript of the Four Gospels," *NTS* 43 (1997): 1–34.
[40] Skeat, "Origins of the Christian Codex," 264.
[41] T. C. Skeat, "Irenaeus and the Four-Gospel Canon," *NovT* 34 (1992): 194–99.
[42] G. N. Stanton, "The Fourfold Gospel," *NTS* 43 (1997): 317–46.

tendencies within Johannine circles (cf. 1 John), sought to open the Johannine tradition to other (i.e., synoptic) traditions in order to underscore the historical anchoring of the witness to Jesus. It did this, according to Heckel, by appending chapter 21 to the Johannine Gospel, by bringing John together with the Synoptics, and by fashioning the standard superscriptions of the gospels to emphasize that there is but one Gospel.[43] Thus Heckel would place the origin of the fourfold Gospel in Asia Minor between 110 and 120.

The dating of the emergence of a four-gospel collection has often taken its bearings from the peculiar form of the superscriptions or titles of the gospels: "the Gospel according to X." Martin Hengel argued from this that the titles must have originated, quite early, from the practical necessity of distinguishing among such documents when multiple gospels were at hand in the archives or liturgical libraries of particular communities.[44] Hence the titles are not late additions, but belonged to the gospels in their earliest period of circulation, and had historical tradition behind them. Accordingly, Hengel considers that the form of the titles had nothing to do with a formal collection or with the transcription of these gospels in a single codex, still less with the formation of a fourfold Gospel canon, which he regards as a gradual development culminating only late in the second century. In a recent study,[45] Hengel reiterates these points, laying out in more detail a conception of the gradual development of a collection of four gospels. He believes that the gospels originally circulated individually yet rapidly, so that by the early second century they were present together in church libraries of major centers; that in consequence of liturgical reading they came, by the middle of the second century, to be valued as much as, or even more than, Jewish scriptures; and that subsequently they began to be transcribed in small groups of two or three and finally four in a single codex. The fourfold Gospel, however, is seen by Hengel to emerge only late in the second century, and to be a product of the Roman church.

Even if it were granted that P[75] or P[4, 64, 67] represent codices of the four gospels, that alone would not push the emergence of such a collection back much before the late second century. Any claim that the collection of four gospels arose in the first half of the second century must be carefully measured against other evidence for that period, much of which suggests that such a collection did not immediately take hold or win through everywhere, but only slowly made its way toward general recognition. Certainly not all four received equal attention: Mark, for example, was little used, whereas Matthew early gained a very strong following.[46]

The famous testimony of Papias preserved by Eusebius is ever more finely parsed.[47] Among other things, it can now be seen that Papias's interest in "the living and abiding voice" does not signify that he was wholly committed to oral tradition and ill-disposed to

---

[43] Th. Heckel, *Vom Evangelium des Markus zum viergestaltigen Evangelium* (WUNT 120; Tübingen: Mohr [Siebeck], 1999).

[44] M. Hengel, "The Titles of the Gospels and the Gospel of Mark," in idem, *Studies in the Gospel of Mark* (trans. J. Bowden; London: SCM, 1985), 64–84.

[45] Hengel, *The Four Gospels and the One Gospel of Jesus Christ* (Harrisburg: Trinity, 2000).

[46] W.-D. Kohler, *Die Rezeption des Matthäusevangeliums in der Zeit vor Irenäus* (WUNT 2.24; Tübingen: Mohr [Siebeck], 1987).

[47] Eusebius, *Hist. eccl.* 3.39.15–16; see J. Kurtzinger, *Papias von Hierapolis und die Evangelien des Neuen Testaments* (Regensberg: Pustet, 1983); U. H. J. Kortner, *Papias von Hierapolis: Ein Beitrag zur Geschichte des frühen Christentums* (FRLANT 133; Göttingen: Vandenhoeck und Ruprecht, 1983); W. R. Schoedel, "Papias," *ANRW* 2.27.1 (1998): 235–70.

written materials,[48] but rather, in accordance with a widespread *topos,* that he preferred firsthand information.[49] Indeed, he should be understood to invoke oral tradition precisely to legitimize written Jesus tradition.[50] Papias was well acquainted with books, both as reader and writer, but the question of what gospels he knew and used is as problematical as ever. While most have been reluctant to read out of the Papias fragment more than knowledge of Mark and perhaps Matthew, others think he knew John.[51] Still others claim that Papias was already familiar with all four gospels and even a four-gospel collection.[52] Here, however, much depends upon how many of the subsequent ecclesiastical traditions about the gospels are thought to go back to Papias. Hill, who considers the patristic evidence in detail and traces most of it (including, importantly, Eusebius, *Hist. eccl.* 3.24.5–13) to Papias, surmises that a collection (or "canon") of four gospels arose in Asia Minor in the third or fourth decade of the second century.

The evidence provided by Justin also continues to be debated. It is generally conceded that Justin was acquainted with Matthew and Luke,[53] but his knowledge of Mark and John is far less certain. It can be cogently argued, if only on the basis of *Dialogus cum Tryphone* 106.3 (cf. also 103.8), that he knew Mark.[54] It is far more difficult to establish that he knew John.[55] If he did know John, which many doubt,[56] why did he make such scant use of it? Moreover, it is well known that Justin's citations of Jesus-tradition take peculiar forms. Many reveal harmonizations of Matthew and Luke, while others appear not to be derived from any known gospels. This suggests that even if Justin was acquainted with the texts of individual gospels, he commonly cited them very freely and inexactly, or, what is far more likely, did not appeal to them directly but relied upon a harmony of the Synoptic Gospels, or at least of Matthew and Luke, that had been or was being worked up, perhaps for catechetical or apologetic purposes.[57] The creator of this harmony, whether

---

[48] So von Campenhausen, *The Formation of the Christian Bible,* 130.

[49] L. Alexander, "The Living Voice: Skepticism toward the Written Word in Early Christian and in Graeco-Roman Texts," in *The Bible in Three Dimensions* (ed. D. J. A. Clines; Sheffield: JSOT Press, 1990), 221–47.

[50] W. A. Lohr, "Kanonsgeschichtliche Beobachtungen zum Verhältnis von mundlicher und schriftlicher Tradition im zweiten Jahrhundert," *ZNW* 85 (1994): 234–58; A. D. Baum, "Papias, der Vorzug der *Viva Vox* und die Evangelienschriften," *NTS* 44 (1998): 144–51.

[51] Hengel, "The Titles of the Gospels"; idem, *The Four Gospels,* 65–68; R. J. Bauckham, "Papias and Polycrates on the Origin of the Fourth Gospel," *JTS* 44 (1993): 24–69; C. E. Hill, "What Papias Said."

[52] Heckel, *Vom Evangelium,* 219–65; and Hill, "What Papias Said."

[53] Koester, *Ancient Christian Gospels,* 360–402; W.-D. Kohler, *Die Rezeption des Matthäusevangeliums in der Zeit vor Irenaeus.*

[54] C. J. Thornton, *Der Zeuge des Zeugen: Lukas als Historiker der Paulusreisen* (WUNT 56; Tübingen: Mohr [Siebeck], 1991); G. N. Stanton, "The Fourfold Gospel," 330–31; Hengel, *Die johanneische Frage: Ein Lösungsversuch* (WUNT 67; Tübingen: Mohr [Siebeck], 1993), 63–67.

[55] Metzger, *Canon,* 146–47; Stanton, "The Fourfold Gospel," 330; Hengel, *Die johanneische Frage,* 63–67; Heckel, *Vom Evangelium,* 320–24.

[56] M. R. Hillmer, "The Gospel of John in the Second Century" (Ph.D. diss., Harvard, 1966), 51–73; A. J. Bellinzoni, *The Sayings of Jesus in the Writings of Justin Martyr* (NovTSup 17; Leiden: Brill, 1967), 134–40; Koester, *Ancient Christian Gospels,* 258, 360.

[57] W. L. Petersen, "Textual Evidence of Tatian's Dependence upon Justin's 'Apomnemoneumata," *NTS* 36 (1990): 512–34; idem, *Tatian's Diatessaron: Its Creation, Dissemination, Significance and History in Scholarship* (Leiden: Brill, 1994).

Justin or someone else, would thus have anticipated and laid the groundwork for his student, Tatian. It is also still a question whether and to what extent Justin still drew upon free, perhaps oral tradition, or made use of "apocryphal" gospels, or both.[58] A good case can be made that the harmony he employed incorporated extracanonical traditions derived from a Jewish-Christian gospel, probably the *Gospel according to the Hebrews/Ebionites*.[59] Although considerable progress has been made, there is still no compelling explanation of the complex problem of Justin's use of gospel materials.

Irenaeus, writing about 180, manifestly possessed and promoted an exclusive collection of four gospels. Even if his comments depend upon an earlier source, it seems clear that he was not merely concerned to rationalize and recommend it, but felt the need to give it a vigorous defense. He apparently could not take for granted that it was or would be everywhere recognized. Indeed, Irenaeus acknowledges (*Haer.* 3.11.7) that many Christian groups, though heterodox in his opinion, are accustomed to using, or at least preferring, only one gospel, and that others employ more than four (*Haer.* 3.11.9). Incidentally, it cannot be assumed that Irenaeus himself always depended directly or exclusively on the written texts of the gospels. Blanchard argues that the relative freedom of some of his citations and the way he refers to *logia Jesu* as distinct from gospel reports reveal that Irenaeus shows similarities with Justin, and that he too may still have depended on oral traditions.[60]

In Irenaeus's time or even a little earlier, Tatian created his *Diatessaron,* combining Matthew, Mark, Luke and John, together with some additional materials drawn from other sources, into a unified and continuous narrative.[61] Tatian is thus our first incontestable witness to the common availability and use of four gospels, but at the same time, his handling of them shows both that these texts had not attained an inviolate or exclusive status and that the multiplicity of gospel documents was still felt to be problematic.[62] Tatian's was surely not the first harmony of written gospels,[63] but it was easily the most important. That it was able to secure a great breadth of distribution and use, especially in the East, and a surprising longevity and influence, is a powerful indication that the fourfold Gospel contemporaneously sponsored by Irenaeus was not broadly, let alone universally, recognized.

Also in the late second century we have evidence of the circulation and use of the *Gospel of Peter.* Serapion, the bishop of Antioch, initially had no objection to its use in the church at Rhossus. He later banned it (Eusebius, *Hist. eccl.* 6.12.2), not because he objected in principle to gospels other than Matthew, Mark, Luke or John—we know nothing about his acquaintance with or regard for them—but simply because he found theological fault

---

[58] O. Skarsaune, *The Proof from Prophecy: A Study in Justin Martyr's Proof-Text Tradition: Text-Type, Provenance, Theological Profile* (NovTSup 56; Leiden: Brill, 1987).

[59] See Petersen, "Textual Evidence", and idem, *Tatian's Diatessaron*. P. Pilhofer, "Justin und das Petrusevangelium," *ZNW* 81 [1990]: 60–78, argues that he used the *Gospel of Peter;* cf. Heckel, *Vom Evangelium,* 326–27.

[60] Y.-M. Blanchard, *Aux sources du canon: Le témoignage d'Irénée* (Paris: Cerf: 1993), *passim*.

[61] Petersen, "Textual Evidence," 512–34; idem, *Tatian's Diatessaron,* 9–83; idem, "The Diatessaron of Tatian," in *The Text of the New Testament in Recent Research* (ed. B. Ehrman and M. W. Holmes; Grand Rapids: Eerdmans, 1995), 512–34; C. D. Allert, "The State of the New Testament Canon in the Second Century," *BBR* 9 (1999): 1–18; T. Baarda, "Diaphonia."

[62] On Tatian's motives and aims, see Baarda, "Diaphonia," 143–54; and Petersen, *Tatian's Diatessaron,* 26.

[63] Petersen, *Tatian's Diatessaron,* 26–34.

with its contents. In addition, Irenaeus's contemporary, Clement of Alexandria, knew, valued, and used all four of our gospels, but took a latitudinarian approach to gospel literature: he repeatedly makes use of other gospels (the *Gospel of the Egyptians*, the *Gospel of the Hebrews*, the *Protevangelium of James*, and apparently also a *Secret Gospel of Mark*),[64] and he also attests a large number of *agrapha*.[65] Clement did not value such documents as highly as "the four gospels that have been handed down to us" (*Strom.* 3.13.93), yet it is equally clear that he did not take the collection of four gospels to be entirely exclusive. Finally, in the late second or early third century the Gospel of John met with stiff opposition in Rome by the anti-Montanist presbyter Gaius and the "Alogoi," who repudiated both the Gospel of John and the Apocalypse, attributing their authorship to the heterodox teacher, Cerinthus.[66] These various and widespread bits of evidence indicate that a collection of four gospels, though well-known near the end of the second century, had not by then secured unique or exclusive authority.

If an early origin of a four-gospel collection is to be claimed, allowance must be made for the great variation in the history of gospel literature throughout the second century. Much of this evidence tells against the use, or certainly against the exclusive use, of such a collection. Dismissing or minimizing indications of other practices, or subsuming them as mere exceptions to a rule, can only distort historical perception. For example, the proposal to regard all papyrus fragments of the gospels as derivative from four-gospel codices[67] unjustly minimizes evidence of the early circulation of individual gospels; insisting on Justin's knowledge of the Fourth Gospel exceeds what he actually says; or again, making Marcion reject the four gospels in fashioning his own scriptures unjustifiably assumes that he must have known them.

Beyond the acknowledgement of divergent usages of gospel literature, the history of this literature and its collection must also take account of important textual evidence. It is unarguable that during the second century the texts of the gospels were subject to a very free, dynamic, and largely uncontrolled process of transmission that was heavily affected by a variety of bibliographical, scribal, social, liturgical, linguistic and theological influences.[68] They were liable, on the one hand, to intentional changes, including interpolations

---

[64] M. Smith, *Clement of Alexandria and a Secret Gospel of Mark* (Cambridge: Harvard University Press, 1973).

[65] J. Ruwet, "Clement d'Alexandrie: Canon des écritures et apocryphes," *Bib* 29 (1948): 77–99, 240–68, 391–408; J. A. Brooks, "Clement of Alexandria as a Witness to the Development of the New Testament Canon," *SC* 9 (1992): 41–55.

[66] Irenaeus, *Haer.* 3.11.9; Epiphanius, *Pan.* 51.4.5–12.6; Dionysius Bar Salibi, *In Apoc.* 1. See also B. H. Streeter, *The Four Gospels: A Study of Origins Treating of the Manuscript Tradition, Sources, Authorship and Date* (London: MacMillan, 1924), 436–42; J. D. Smith, "Gaius and the Controversy over the Johannine Literature." Diss., Yale University; R. E. Heine, "The Role of the Gospel of John in the Montanist Controversy," *SC* 6 (1987): 1–19; and M. Hengel, *Die johanneische Frage*, 26–28.

[67] Skeat, "The Origins of the Christian Codex," 263–68.

[68] Koester, "The Text of the Synoptic Gospels," 19–37; K. Aland and B. Aland, *The Text of the New Testament* (trans. E. F. Rhodes; Grand Rapids: Eerdmans, 1987), 48–64; E. J. Epp, "The Significance of the Papyri"; B. D. Ehrman, "The Text of the Gospels at the End of the Second Century" in *Codex Bezae: Studies from the Lunel Colloquium, June 1994* (NTTS 22; ed. D. C. Parker and C.-B. Amphoux; Leiden: Brill, 1996), 95–122; idem, *The Orthodox Corruption of Scripture*; D. C. Parker, *Codex Bezae: An Early Christian Manuscript and Its Text* (Cambridge: Cambridge University Press, 1992); and idem, *The Living Text of the Gospels* (Cambridge: Cambridge University Press, 1997).

or additions of various kinds (e.g., the longer endings of Mark, John 21, and the pericope of the adulteress [John 7:53–8:11], to mention only the most obvious) and extensive harmonizations aimed at resolving inconsistencies among them and eliminating redundancies within them. On the other hand, they were also subject to many accidental changes: omissions, transpositions, and repetitions, etc. The result was a great wealth of textual corruption and diversification by the end of the second century. The distinctive text-types that can be identified in later periods (Alexandrian, Western, Neutral, etc.) all appear to have their roots deep in the turbid textual morass of the second century. This amply documented situation raises interesting and important issues for the history of gospel literature and for the history of the canon more generally. Such variations not only in individual readings but also in the broader complexions of texts comport poorly with the idea that any particular collection, edition, or recension of gospels played a controlling role in the second century. It also evokes the startling, even paradoxical, question what it may have meant to value *documents* as authoritative apart from the availability of established, more or less standardized *texts* of those documents. As Parker puts it, "while early Christianity may have come to make lists of authoritative books, there were no authoritative copies of them."[69] Here we have an example of the disorienting yet potentially valuable intersections between textual criticism and the history of the canon.[70]

B. The Letters of Paul

In recent years there has been rather less attention given to the emergence of the corpus of Pauline letters, yet here too there have been significant developments. Theories about the development of this corpus have been many and varied, but they can be generally sorted into two types: gradual development versus decisive moment.[71] Recent work suggests that these may be false alternatives, although a clear way between them has not yet appeared.

Paul's letters are the earliest extant Christian writings, and also the earliest documents to be circulated and collected. Already by the end of the first century one or more collections of them had come into being: 1 Clement, Ignatius, Polycarp, and the author of 2 Peter were acquainted with multiple letters of Paul, presumably in collections, though their precise scope cannot be determined.[72] They may have arisen during the early circulation of the apostle's letters among the individual churches to which he had written, a process intelligible enough in itself, but possibly owing something to Paul (cf. Col 4:16).

---

[69] Parker, *The Living Text of the Gospels*, 188.

[70] Epp, "The Significance of the Papyri"; and idem, "The Multivalence of the Term 'Original Text' in New Testament Textual Criticism," *HTR* 92 (1999): 245–81.

[71] See the surveys in Gamble, *The New Testament Canon: Its Making and Meaning* (Minneapolis: Augsburg/Fortress, 1985), 36–41; E. H. Lovering, "The Collection, Redaction, and Early Circulation of the Corpus Paulinum" (Ph.D. diss.; Southern Methodist University, 1988), 283–345; R. M. Price, "The Evolution of the Pauline Canon," *Hervormde teologiese studies* 53 (1997): 36–67; E. R. Richards, "The Codex and the Early Collection of Paul's Letters," *BBR* 8 (1998): 151–66.

[72] A. Lindemann, *Paulus im ältesten Christentum: Das Bild des Apostels und die Rezeption der ?n Theologie in der frühchristlichen Literatur bis Markion* (BHT 58; Tübingen: Mohr 1979), 91–97.

The manuscript evidence that bears on the history of the Pauline corpus, its contents, and arrangement, is almost overwhelmingly complex and yields no definitive conclusions on many issues.[73] Nevertheless, it is possible to make out at least two very early forms of the Pauline letter collection. The first witness to a full-blown edition of Paul's letters is Marcion, about 140 C.E. It consisted of ten letters, in the order: Galatians, 1 and 2 Corinthians, Romans, 1 and 2 Thessalonians, Laodiceans (= Ephesians), Colossians (with Philemon?), and Philippians. Harnack (1924) and von Campenhausen (1972) held the opinion that, if Marcion was not the collector of these letters, he was the first to elevate them to exclusively normative status, along with a version of the Gospel of Luke. They also maintained that the configuration of the collection with Galatians at the head reflected Marcion's distinctive theological outlook, and that he extensively revised the texts of the letters.

More recent studies have shown, however, that Marcion's Pauline corpus is derivative in both content and structure from another early edition of the letters.[74] With the exception of Galatians, Marcion's arrangement of the letters follows the principle of decreasing length, with letters to the same communities being counted together. Since this principle was not maintained by Marcion and apparently had no importance for him, his edition must have depended on another for which this principle was fully constitutive. We may infer that the pre-Marcionite edition was consistently ordered by decreasing length, counted letters to the same community together, and also had ten letters, but in the order: 1 and 2 Corinthians, Romans, Ephesians, 1 and 2 Thessalonians, Galatians, Philippians, Colossians, and Philemon. Such an edition emphasized by its arrangement the number of communities to which Paul had written, namely precisely seven churches. An edition of Paul's correspondence as "letters to seven churches" addressed a problem that Paul's letters posed for the early church, namely their particularity.[75] Because the apostle wrote to individual communities about issues of immediate and local concern, it was a question how such letters could be relevant, useful, and appropriate to other churches. It can be seen from the manuscript tradition that at an early time attempts were made to solve this problem by simply generalizing the addresses of some letters (Rom 1:1, 7; 1 Cor 1:2, Eph 1:2) and omitting other highly specific matter.[76] An edition presenting Paul's letters as written to exactly seven churches (seven symbolizing universality) addressed the same issue but in a more satisfactory way. It may be in consequence of such an edition of Paul's letters that we have two other groups of early Christian letters similarly addressed to seven churches: the letters of the Apocalypse (2:1–3:22), and of Ignatius. In any event, such an edition must go back to the late first or very early second century. The edition attested by Marcion,

---

[73] H.-J. Frede, *Altlateinische Paulus-Handschriften* (Vetus Latina 4; Freiburg: Herder 1964); K. Aland, "Die Entstehung des Corpus Paulinum," in idem, *Neutestamenliche Entwurfe* (TB 63; Munich: Kaiser, 1979), 302–50.

[74] Frede, *Altlateinische Paulus-Handschriften*, 295–97; N. A. Dahl, "The Origin of the Earliest Prologues to the Pauline Letters," in *The Poetics of Faith: Essays Offered to A. N. Wilder* (*Sem* 12; ed. W. Beardslee; Missoula, Mont.: Scholars Press, 1978), 233–77.

[75] N. A Dahl, "The Particularity of the Pauline Epistles as a Problem in the Ancient Church," in *Neotestamentica et Patristica: Freundesgabe O. Cullmann* (NovTSup 6; Leiden: Brill, 1962), 261–71.

[76] Dahl, "The Particularity of the Pauline Epistles," and H. Y. Gamble, *The Textual History of the Letter to the Romans* (SD 42; Grand Rapids: Eerdmans, 1977).

with Galatians at the head, arose soon after, probably from an effort to adapt the parent edition to chronological considerations, Galatians being taken as the earliest of the letters.[77] This arrangement of the letters is presupposed by the old prologues to the Pauline letters. While they have long been regarded as Marcionite, it is now clear that they are catholic products,[78] and thus the edition itself must be catholic.

Marcion's edition was not only substantively and structurally derivative from an earlier one, but also textually derivative. While Marcion undoubtedly revised the texts of the letters in accordance with his own theological viewpoint, Harnack (1924) vastly overestimated the character and extent of his textual revisions.[79] The studies of Clabeaux and (more fully) Schmid, which are devoted mainly to the nature of the Marcionite text, have amply demonstrated that Marcion's emendations were in fact quite limited, consisting mainly in omissions, and that the large majority of peculiar readings attested for Marcion can otherwise be closely paralleled in the larger textual tradition of Paul's letters, especially the so-called Western text and some parts of the Syrian tradition.[80] This means that Marcion is not to be credited with extensive tendentious emendations, and that his text of the epistles belonged to a common pre-Marcionite form of the Pauline text that was already current around the beginning of the second century. It was thus appreciably older than the text represented in P[46]. Consequently, Marcion's importance for the history of Pauline texts has been substantially diminished.

Besides the seven churches edition that was taken over by Marcion in altered form, other forms of the Pauline corpus arose during the second century. By far the most prevalent contained the same ten letters, but ordered them individually by decreasing length, and so had the order: Romans, 1 Corinthians, 2 Corinthians, Ephesians, Galatians, Philippians, Colossians, 1 Thessalonians, 2 Thessalonians, and Philemon, which closely approximates the standard canonical order. The earliest manuscript witness for this edition is P[46], dated to ca. 200,[81] which, however, includes Hebrews immediately after Romans.

P[46] points up two specific questions: What place, if any, did either Hebrews or the Pastoral Epistles have in early editions of the Pauline corpus? The relation of Hebrews to Paul and his letters is an old chestnut. Clement of Rome apparently knew and used Hebrews, but it subsequently commanded little interest or comment in the western church. Tertullian knew it and attributed it to Barnabas, but it was otherwise neglected until the fourth century. In the East, however, it was well known: Clement of Alexandria fully ac-

[77] Freda, *Altlateinische Paulus-Handschriften*, 165–66; U. Schmid, *Marcion und sein Apostolos: Rekonstruktion und historische Einordnung der marcionitischen Paulusbriefausgabe* (ANTT 25; Berlin: de Gruyter, 1995), 294–96.

[78] N. A. Dahl, "The Origin of the Earliest Prologues to the Pauline Letters."

[79] A. Harnack, *Marcion: Das Evangelium vom fremden Gott* (2d ed.; Leipzig: Hinrichs, 1924).

[80] See John J. Clabeaux, *A Lost Edition of the Letters of Paul: A Reassessment of the Text of the Pauline Corpus Attested by Marcion* (CBQMS 21; Washington: Catholic Biblical Association, 1989), 1–4; Ulrich Schmid, *Marcion und sein Apostolos: Rekonstruktion und historische Einordnung der marcionitischen Paulusbriefausgabe* (ANTF 25; Berlin/New York: de Gruyter, 1995). See also G. Quispel, "Marcion and the Text of the New Testament," *VC* 52 (1998): 349–60.

[81] On the date, see Y. K. Kim, "Paleographical Dating of P[46] to the Later First Century," *Bib* 69 (1988): 248–57, and S. R. Pickering, "The Dating of the Chester Beatty-Michigan Codex of the Pauline Epistles (P[46])," in *Ancient History in a Modern University*, vol. 2 of *Early Christianity, Late Antiquity and Beyond* (ed. T. W. Hilliard, et al.; Grand Rapids: Eerdmans, 1998), 216–27.

knowledged it as a letter of Paul, and Origen, though famously uncertain about its authorship, clearly regarded it as an authoritative document. Its inclusion in P[46] shows its close
eastern association with Paul. Most think that Hebrews did not originally belong to any
early collection of Paul's letters, but there are dissenting opinions.[82] It has similarly been
thought that the Pastorals, commonly regarded as deutero-Pauline and late, belonged to
no original or even especially early Pauline collection. Their absence from P[46] is often
taken to confirm this opinion, but the end of the codex is defective, and it can be cogently
argued that the Pastorals did have a place in it.[83] It can also be argued, somewhat less persuasively, that the Pastorals were part of at least some Pauline collections by the early second century.[84] The last word has hardly been said on either question.

The three editions so far mentioned—Marcion's edition, a seven-churches edition,
and a ten-letter edition (or thirteen-letter edition if it contained the Pastorals)—were all
available early in the second century. But the many other forms of the collection attested in
the manuscript tradition and the wide variations among them greatly complicate the
question of the ultimate origins of the Pauline corpus, including whether there was any
single, original collection of the letters. This problem has been freshly tackled by Trobisch,
who works backward from nine distinct forms of the Pauline corpus attested in the manuscript tradition to identify the earliest collections, and argues that all nine are ultimately
derivative from only two: (1) a thirteen-letter collection, corresponding closely to the present canonical corpus, which arranged and identified the letters by their specific addressees,
and (2) a four-letter collection consisting of Romans, Hebrews, 1 Corinthians, and Ephesians, in that order, and which omitted addresses and other particular matter so as to produce a catholic edition for the church at large.[85] He proposes that the interaction of these
two collections gave rise to all others. The most novel and valuable elements of Trobisch's
study are its emphasis on letter collections as an ancient *Gattung,* its discussion of the typical ways in which they were created and subsequently developed, and its comparison of the
Pauline collection with others of the period. He is led by these considerations to the surprising conclusion that the origins of both collections are to be traced to Paul's own lifetime and his personal auspices. Trobisch's disregard for other well-attested forms of the
collection and the complex transmission history he proposes diminish the appeal of his
conclusions, but he has shown the value of new methods. From another angle, Richards's
study study of Paul's use of secretaries[86] also suggests that the origins of the collection may
perhaps be sought in Paul's lifetime, since it was common in antiquity for authors or
their secretaries to retain copies of what they wrote, and editions of collected letters were

---

[82] K. Aland, "Die Entstehung des Corpus Paulinum," 302–50 (at 335); D. Trobisch, *Die
Entstehung des Paulusbriefsammlung: Studien zu den Anfangen christlicher Publizistik* (NTOA 10;
Göttingen: Vandenhoeck & Ruprecht, 1989), 61, 82–83, 106–8.

[83] D. Trobisch, *Die Entstehung des Paulusbriefsammlung,* 27–28, and J. Duff, "P[46] and the Pastorals: A Misleading Consensus?" *NTS* 44 (1998): 578–90.

[84] Frede, *Altlateinische Paulus-Handschriften,* 291; Trobisch, *Die Entstehung des Paulusbriefsammlung,* 108–10.

[85] Trobisch, *Die Entstehung des Paulusbriefsammlung,* and his more recent *Paul's Letter Collection* (Minneapolis: Fortress, 1994).

[86] See E. R. Richards, *The Secretary in the Letters of Paul* (WUNT 2/42; Tübingen: Mohr
[Siebeck], 1991), and especially his "The Codex and the Early Collection of Paul's Letters," *BBR* 8
(1998): 151–66.

commonly produced by their author or at their author's behest, often from copies belonging to the author. A dossier of Paul's letters would surely have been useful both to Paul and to his coworkers.[87] Hence more attention should be given to the possibility that second-century and later collections of Paul's letters may, at least in part, reach back ultimately to copies that were retained as a group during his lifetime.[88]

Nevertheless, *collections* of Paul's letters need to be differentiated from *editions* of Paul's letters. The former may well have arisen gradually and in various forms in different churches or regions, presumably mainly within the Pauline mission field. Yet it is hard to imagine that the attested early editions of the Pauline corpus arose through happenstance or merely by agglomeration. Their clearly methodical features betray deliberate activity informed by particular motives, conceptions, and aims. Taking into account that the corpus as we know it contains pseudonymous as well as authentic letters and retains signs of editorial activity, there is perhaps no better place to locate such effort than in the context of a Pauline school[89] that had its ultimate roots in the circle of Paul's historical associates and coworkers, and that labored to perpetuate, interpret, and elaborate Paul's legacy in the latter half of the first century. Conceptions of a Pauline school are admittedly vague and indeterminate, and need to be worked out in better detail, but that Paul had such successors is a certainty.

In this area, however, all hypotheses are tenuous. The evidence for the history of the Pauline corpus is so complex and multifaceted that no single theory seems capable of accounting for it all. It is very difficult to get behind editions attested for the second century and to chart with any confidence the prior history of Paul's letters or their formation into a collection. Lovering concludes his thorough survey of the theories advanced during the twentieth century by suggesting that it is misguided to attempt to trace the origins of the Pauline corpus to any single source, datable event, specific locale, or particular agency.[90] He proposes, rather, a period of gradual and unsystematic growth under the influence of many hands, resulting in multiple, early, partial, and local collections of Paul's letters. This may very well have been the case. Yet the early availability of smaller collections does not preclude subsequent deliberate efforts to shape such collections into more complete and definitive editions, even as the production of such editions led to later, modified, and expanded forms.

Contrary to older views that Paul's letters were long ignored on account of their appropriation and use by heterodox groups,[91] it is widely recognized today that Paul's letters

---

[87] A. Sand, "Überlieferung und Sammlung der Paulusbriefe" in *Paulus in den neutestamentlichen Spätschriften* (QD 89; ed. K. Kertelge; Freiburg: Herder, 1981), 11–24.

[88] Gamble, *Books and Readers in the Early Church: A History of Early Christian Text* (New Haven: Yale, 1995), 99–101.

[89] So argues H.-M. Schenke, "Das Weiterwirken des Paulus und die Pflege seines Erbes durch die Paulusschule," *NTS* 21 (1975): 505–18.

[90] Lovering, "The Collection". This proposal was made earlier by K. Aland, "Die Entstehung des Corpus Paulinum."

[91] W. A. Bienert, "The Picture of the Apostle in Early Christian Tradition," in *New Testament Apocrypha* (rev. ed.; ed. W. Schneemelcher; trans. R. McL. Wilson; Louisville, Ky.: Westminster John Knox/Cambridge: James Clarke, 1992), 2:5–27, at 22; W. Bauer, *Orthodoxy and Heresy in Earliest Christianity* (ed. R. A. Kraft and G. Krodel; Philadelphia: Fortress, 1971), 226–28; von Campenhausen, *The Formation of the Christian Bible*, 144–45.

were consistently known and used throughout the second century,[92] and by the late s
century had become fully and universally established as apostolic scriptures.

C. The Catholic Epistles

If both the Gospels and the Pauline Letters were shaped into firm collections during
the second century, this was not true of the third major component of the canon, the
Catholic Epistles. Although the description "catholic" was sometimes used for individual
letters in the second century (Eusebius, *Hist. eccl.* 5.18.5, in reference to a letter written by
the Montanist Themiso; and *Hist. eccl.* 7.25.7–10 [Origen, *Comm. Joh.*], referring to
1 John), we do not see this term applied to a *group* of letters until the fourth century, when
Eusebius speaks of "the seven [letters] called catholic" (*Hist. eccl.* 2.23.25). Nevertheless,
Eusebius himself placed all of these except 1 Peter and 1 John in the category of "disputed"
(*Hist. eccl.* 2.25.3). Thus even in the early fourth century a collection of Catholic Epistles
was hardly well established.

Of the seven letters in question, only 1 Peter and 1 John appear to have been much
known or used in the second and third centuries. According to Eusebius (*Hist. eccl.* 3.39.17),
Papias appealed to both 1 Peter and 1 John, Polycarp used 1 Peter (*Hist. eccl.* 4.14.9, cf.
Polycarp, *Phil.* 7), and "the ancient presbyters often employed 1 Peter" (*Hist. eccl.* 3.3.1).
1 Peter was known but seldom cited by Irenaeus (*Haer.* 4.9.2), Clement of Alexandria
(*Strom.* 3.18.10, 4.20.129, cf. 4.7.6), Tertullian (*Scorp.* 12), and Origen (Eusebius, *Hist. eccl.*
6.25.8). 1 John was known, beyond Papias, to Irenaeus (*Haer.* 3.16.5, 8), Clement of
Alexandria (*Strom.* 2.15.66) and Tertullian (*Pud.* 19.10, *Scorp.* 12.4, *Idol.* 2.3).

The earliest use of Jude is found in 2 Peter, written between 125 and 140 (2 Pet
2:1–22 incorporating much of Jude 4–16). Later, Jude was known but very sparingly cited
by Clement of Alexandria (*Paed.* 3.8.44, cf. Eusebius, *Hist. eccl.* 6.14.1), Tertullian (*Cult.
fem.* 1.3), and Origen (*Comm. Matt.* 10.17), but otherwise there is no evidence for its early
or widespread use. Nothing whatever is heard of 2 Peter until the third century when
Origen mentions it while also noting its disputed status (*Hom. Joh.* 5.3; Eusebius, *Hist. eccl.*
6.25.8). The letter of James is also rarely mentioned: not cited by Clement, James is quoted
by Origen (*Comm. Matt.* 19.61), who refers to it as "the epistle of James that is in circulation," thus suggesting some doubt about it.

The two small letters, 2 and 3 John, had an erratic history of reception.[93] They were
very little known in the first two centuries. Clement of Alexandria, referring to 1 John,
speaks of it as [John's] "larger epistle" (*Strom.* 2.15.66), implying a knowledge of 2 John,
but shows no awareness of 3 John. Irenaeus quotes from both 1 and 2 John (*Haer.* 3.16.5,
8), oddly as though from a single letter. Tertullian and Cyprian reveal no knowledge of 2 or
3 John. Origen, however, was aware of all three Johannine letters, speaking of "an epistle of

---

[92] A. Lindemann, *Paulus im ältesten Christentum: Das Bild des Apostels und die Rezeption der
paulinischen Theologie in der frühchristlichen Literatur bis Markion* (BHT 58; Tübingen: Mohr-
Siebeck, 1979); D. Rensberger, "As the Apostle Teaches: The Development of the Use of Paul's Letters
in Second Century Christianity" (Diss., Yale, 1981); E. Dassmann, *Der Stachel im Fleisch: Paulus in
frühchristlichen Literatur bis Irenaeus* (Munster: Aschendorff, 1979).

[93] See esp. J. Lieu, *The Second and Third Epistles of John: History and Background* (Edinburgh:
T&T Clark, 1986), 5–36.

a very few lines [=1 John], and it may also be a second and a third, for not everyone says these are genuine" (Eusebius, *Hist. eccl.* 6.25.10). Presumably Origen shared such doubts, since he nowhere cites 2 and 3 John. Soon after, Dionysius of Alexandria also shows some knowledge of 2 and 3 John, but is hesitant in using them (Eusebius, *Hist. eccl.* 7.25.11). In the same vein, Eusebius himself places 2 and 3 John among the disputed books (*Hist. eccl.* 3.25.3). Were the Muratorian fragment taken to be as early as the end of the second century, it should be noted that only two Johannine letters are mentioned there, no doubt 1 and 2 John, and that the only other Catholic Epistle mentioned is Jude.

From this checkered evidence it is apparent that the formation of a corpus of Catholic Epistles occurred quite late, probably not before the end of the third century, and that even when such a collection arose, particular items in it remained subject to dispute, as did the collection as a whole. Note, for example, that it did not belong to the oldest Syrian tradition. Moreover, the motives behind it are obscure. It was possibly shaped in order to document teaching that had come to be associated with primitive apostolic figures, perhaps especially the "pillar apostles": James, Peter, and John (Gal 2:9),[94] and to provide a broader and more balanced literary representation of the apostolic witness than the letters of Paul furnished by themselves.

The history of the Catholic Epistles holds significance for larger conceptions of the history of the canon. Since they found inclusion in the canon not individually but precisely as a group, since that collection did not take shape until late in the third century at the earliest, and since that collection came to constitute, along with the Gospels and the Pauline Letters, one of the three major sub-units of the canon, it is very difficult to speak of a New Testament canon having taken any clear shape, whether in conception or in substance, prior to the appearance of this particular collection, and therefore prior to the fourth century.

4. Other Writings

In addition to the three collections whose histories have so far been discussed, a considerable variety of early Christian writings were individually in circulation and use during the early centuries of the church. Some of these ultimately came to be included in the canon, while others did not, and a fair appraisal should take account of the whole range of these documents. Only three documents eventually included in the New Testament canon were not closely associated with the three constituent collections, namely Acts, the letter to the Hebrews, and the Apocalypse of John.

It is unclear when Acts was separated from its companion piece, the Gospel of Luke, but Acts had a completely distinct history of transmission and use. The early history of Acts[95] is largely obscure and needs further investigation. It seems to have been known by Justin about the middle of the second century (*1 Apol.* 50.12, cf. *2 Apol.* 10.6), but it is first clearly and extensively used only in the late second century, by Irenaeus (*Haer.* 3.12.1–15). Thereafter it is generally known. Apart from a strong tradition of authorship, its peculiar

---

[94] D. Luhrmann, "Gal. 2.9 und die katholischen Briefe," *ZNW* 72 (1981): 65–87.
[95] E. Haenchen, *The Acts of the Apostles* (Oxford: Blackwell, 1971), 3–14; D. W. Kuck, "The Use and Canonization of Acts in the Early Church" (S.T.M. thesis, Yale University, 1975).

value probably lay in its representation of the unity of the early apostles and their teaching, which made it a natural court of appeal against heterodox groups.

Hebrews, as noted earlier, was early associated with the Pauline epistles in the East, but its fate in the West was very different. There it was almost wholly neglected until the fourth century. There were probably two reasons: Hebrews had no strong tradition of authorship, even in the East (Origen, in Eusebius, *Hist. eccl.* 6.25.11–14), and in the West this was more problematic (*Hist. eccl.* 6.20.30). Also, the rigorism of Hebrews' teaching against a second repentance ran counter to the developing penitential theology and practice of the western churches. It's late acknowledgment in the West, achieved under the auspices of such authorities as Hilary, Ambrose, and Rufinus, yet without any general recognition of Pauline authorship, is reflected in the traditional placement of Hebrews not among the community letters but at the end of the Pauline corpus, after the letters to individuals. It is also to be seen in early western manuscripts, where the textual tradition of Hebrews differs from that of the other Pauline letters.[96]

The Apocalypse had a geographically opposite reception history. Although the chiliast Papias may well have known it, Justin (*Dial.* 81.15) is the first direct witness to it. Later it was well known and heavily used in Gaul (Irenaeus, *Haer.* 5.26.1, 5.30.3, etc., and Eusebius, *Hist. eccl.* 5.1), while Tertullian attests it in North Africa (*Marc.* 4.5, *Fug.* 1, *Pud.* 20). It was also known and used in the East in the second century (Eusebius, *Hist. eccl.* 4.26.2, 4.24.1, Clement of Alexandria, *Strom.* 6.13.106, *Paed.* 2.10.108), but the attack upon its authorship by Dionysius (Eusebius, *Hist. eccl.* 7.25) in reaction against chiliastic views severely undercut its standing, and thereafter it was little used in the Eastern churches until its partial rehabilitation in the later fourth century, clearly on the condition of its allegorical interpretation. The Apocalypse furnishes perhaps the clearest instance of the interplay between the authority and use of writings and problems of interpretation, and the history of its reception in the early church needs to be freshly studied in this light.

However, many writings other than these were highly esteemed, and often even more widely used. The letter known as *1 Clement* was prominent among them. Irenaeus (*Haer.* 3.3.3) spoke highly of it, Clement of Alexandria called it "a writing of the apostle Clement" (*Strom.* 4.17), and Eusebius underscores its long-standing use, probably in liturgical reading, from the earliest days up to his own time (*Hist. eccl.* 3.16). Similarly, *Barnabas* gained an early authority, especially in the East, and Clement of Alexandria (*Strom.* 2.6, 7.5) considered it, too, an apostolic letter. More widely popular than either of these, however, was the *Shepherd of Hermas*, which was fully acknowledged as scripture by Irenaeus (*Haer.* 4.20.2), Clement of Alexandria (*Strom.* 1.17.29, 2.1.9, 12), and Tertullian (*Or.* 16). Its strong representation among early Christian papyri discovered in Egypt probably reflects its popularity.[97] One could go on to mention a far greater number of writings—the *Apocalypse of Peter*, the *Didache*, the *Gospel of the Hebrews*, the *Gospel of Peter*, the *Gospel of Thomas*, and the *Acts of Paul*, among others, that were current in and valued by early

---

[96] See R. F. Schlossnikel, *Der Brief an die Hebräer und das Corpus Paulinum: Eine linguistische 'Bruchstelle' im Codex Claromontanus (Paris, Bibliothèque Nationale grec 107 + 107A + 107B) und ihre Bedeutung im Rahmen von Text- und Kanongeschichte* (VL 20; Freiburg: Herder, 1991), where he discusses Codex Claromontanus.

[97] C. H. Roberts, *Manuscript, Society and Belief in Early Christian Egypt* (London: Oxford University Press, 1979).

Christian communities. What needs to be emphasized in respect of many of these documents, especially *1 Clement, Barnabas,* the *Shepherd* and the *Didache,* is that the esteem and use attaching to them was appreciably earlier, more continuous, and more widespread than to many of the writings that were finally accepted in the canon, including Hebrews, 2 Peter, James, and 2 and 3 John. Some of them, indeed, continue to appear in canon lists and manuscripts of the fourth century. If the scope of the canon had been determined in the second century, it seems likely that they would have found a place in it. The attention that is properly paid to these writings and their impressive histories of reception serve to check the unwarranted assumption that the ultimate contents of the canon were somehow foreordained.

5. A Distinctive Proposal

Having reviewed the histories of the several smaller collections that, taken together, make up the vast bulk of the New Testament, we must now turn to the recent study of Trobisch.[98] His book questions fundamental assumptions that are almost universally made by historians of the canon: that each of these component collections had its own lengthy history, and that the large collection we call the New Testament, which comprises all three of these smaller collections, was fashioned over a long period. Because his approach is so distinctive, it is difficult to integrate Trobisch's thesis into any traditional scheme. In what is almost certainly the boldest proposal ever ventured on the history of the canon, Trobisch argues that the New Testament, more or less as we know it, far from being the end product of a centuries-long evolutionary process of development, was deliberately and carefully produced as a single book, a "canonical edition," about the middle of the second century, and was promptly received and used in Asia Minor and Rome. In this way he effectively inverts the ordinary perception of the history of the canon: the New Testament stands at the beginning of it as the basic datum, and what is called the history of the canon is no more or less than the subsequent, progressive recognition and use of it. Thus Trobisch wishes to distinguish his inquiry from the history of the *canon* to the extent that he conceives this as an aspect of the history of doctrine *(Dogmengeschichte).* He aims instead to account for the formation of the New Testament principally in literary and bibliographical terms. Accordingly, he has relatively little interest in the patristic testimony normally invoked, but attends to other sorts of evidence. Early manuscripts furnish evidence of two sorts: first, their consistency in regard to scope of contents, sequence of documents, and titles used, would be difficult to explain apart from the influence of an early canonical edition; second, the pervasiveness of the codex format and the system of *nomina sacra* point toward an early uniformity of practice in book production and editing. In addition, Trobisch centers on information internal to the New Testament documents concerning the authors to whom the various writings are attributed (especially the key figures, Paul, Peter, James, and John, but also other authors variously associated with them), and suggests that the collection was designed as a whole in such a way as to legitimize itself and to furnish the reader with sufficient cross-references to draw conclusions about the collection's origins and authority.

---

[98] David Trobisch, *Die Endredaktion des Neuen Testaments: Eine Untersuchung zur Entstehung der christlichen Bibel* (NTOA 31; Göttingen: Vandenhoeck & Ruprecht, 1996); ET *The First Edition of the New Testament* (Oxford: Oxford University Press, 2000).

Moreover, the editorial structure of the whole both encourages its use as a collection, and provides a hermeneutical context for its use and interpretation.

This is an ingenious, novel, and complex hypothesis, but it is set out in very sketchy form. The evidence adduced and the arguments developed will require close testing. If even all the phenomena Trobisch notes are correctly perceived and evaluated, which is arguable, it is yet another question whether they should all be taken together and traced to a single cause.

6. The Canonization of a New Testament

Although all the developments so far traced belong to the process that eventuated in the New Testament canon, the period of formal canonization belongs to the fourth and fifth centuries. It was then that specific lists began to be drawn up clearly distinguishing between those documents that might be regarded as authoritative and read in the churches, and those that might not. It is unnecessary here to review the evidence of these various lists, drawn up by bishops, synods, and councils.[99] The first such list that corresponds exactly to the New Testament as we know it is furnished by Athanasius of Alexandria in 367 (*Ep.* 39), who, probably not accidentally, seems also to be the first to use the term "canon" for a fixed list of authoritative documents (though Athanasius's list was not decisive even for Egypt).[100] Subsequent lists vary in some particulars, mainly in excluding or questioning certain writings (the Apocalypse, Hebrews, some of the catholic epistles), until in the fifth century a more or less final consensus was reached and shared by East and West. It is worth noting that no ecumenical council in the ancient church ever ruled for the church as a whole on the question of the contents of the canon.

The establishment of the canon in the fourth and fifth centuries elicits an observation, which in turn provokes a question. During the period from the late second through to the fourth century, the usages of the church appear to have changed very little, and underwent no major or decisive developments.[101] The collection of the four gospels continued to be valued and used (though the *Diatessaron* was a persistent exception in the East) as did Acts and the collected letters of Paul, but regard for most other writings continued to be fluid and variable with region, even locality, and with different social institutions, constituencies, and practices in the church.[102] The question of strict limitation did not arise. This observation raises the question when and why the issue of systematic limitation did arise.

So long as the second century has been taken to be the decisive period in the history of the canon, it has been natural to seek the primary stimuli in the heterodox movements of that time. A particularly prominent role has been assigned to Marcion, since he was, to our knowledge, the first to fix a collection of Christian writings as exclusively normative,

---

[99] Metzger, *Canon of the New Testament,* 305–15; McDonald, *Formation of the Christian Biblical Canon,* 191–227.

[100] So argue B. Ehrman, "The New Testament Canon of Didymus the Blind," *VC* 37 (1983): 1–21, and D. Brakke, "Canon Formation and Social Conflict in Fourth-Century Egypt: Athanasius of Alexandria's Thirty-Ninth Festal Letter," *HTR* 87 (1994): 395–419.

[101] F. Stuhlhofer, *Der Gebrauch der Bibel von Jesus bis Euseb: Eine statistische Untersuchung zur Kanongeschichte* (Wuppertal: R. Brockhaus, 1988).

[102] Brakke, "Canon Formation and Social Conflict."

namely ten letters of Paul and a form of the Gospel of Luke. Both Harnack and von Campenhausen[103] thus looked to Marcion as the first to conceive and to actualize a canon of Christian scripture, and as the one who furnished the structural model of Gospel-Apostle that was followed by the great church as it set about to create a larger, more representative canon in opposition to Marcion. Hoffmann attributes an even more radical importance to Marcion in the creation of the canon,[104] and Kinzig argues that Marcion introduced the name "New Testament," applying it to his own canon.[105] Such views of Marcion's creative role are still occasionally echoed,[106] but most recent studies offer more moderate estimates of his influence, suggesting that he prompted the church to become more self-consciously reflective about the scope of its scriptures and the basis of their authority, or that he only accelerated a development that was already underway.[107] Even this, however, may concede too much. It is quite uncertain, for example, that Marcion considered his canon to be closed and exclusive; his followers, in any case, apparently did not.[108] Furthermore, many of Marcion's special concerns (e.g., critical judgments about content, rejection of Jewish scripture) found no resonance in the church, and conversely there are many features of the church's scriptures, and of its regard for them, which Marcion clearly did not anticipate.[109] The Gospel-Apostle framework of Marcion's canon was certainly not his creation.[110] Hence Marcion is better viewed as a conservative or traditionalist than as an innovator,[111] and his collection of Christian scriptures as a case of arrested development.[112] Beyond Marcion, the church's conflict with gnosticism is often likewise seen as a crucial factor in heightening the church's canon-consciousness: by their emphasis upon esoteric apostolic traditions and their use of many books, gnostics provoked the church to determine more clearly which books conveyed true and authentic teaching.[113] Yet it was

---

[103] Harnack, *Marcion*, 210–15, 441–44; idem, *The Origin of the New Testament and the Most Important Consequences of the New Creation* (London: Williams and Norgate, 1925), 30–35, 57–60; and von Campenhausen, *Formation*, 148.

[104] R. J. Hoffmann, *Marcion: On the Restitution of Christianity* (Chico, Calif.: Scholars Press, 1984).

[105] W. Kinzig, "Kainē Diathekē: The Title of the New Testament in the Second and Third Centuries," *JTS* 45 (1994): 519–44.

[106] Lüdemann, *Heretics*, 199–201, 206.

[107] D. L. Balás, "Marcion Revisited: A 'Post-Harnack' Perspective" in *Texts and Testaments* (ed. W. E. March; San Antonio: Trinity University Press, 1980), 95–108; Metzger, *Canon of the New Testament*, 97–99; A. M. Ritter, "Die Entstehung des neutestamentlichen Kanons: Selbstdurchsetzung oder autoritative Entscheidung?" in *Kanon und Zensur: Beiträge zur Archäologie der literarischen Kommunikation II* (ed. A. and J. Assmann; Munich: Fink, 1987), 93–99; A. F. J. Klijn, "Die Entstehungsgeschichte des Neuen Testaments," *ANRW* 2.26.1 (1992): 64–97, at 82; U. Schnelle, *The History and Theology of the New Testament Writings* (Minneapolis: Fortress, 1998), 359–60.

[108] G. M. Hahneman, *The Muratorian Fragment and the Development of the Canon* (Oxford Theological Monographs; Oxford: Clarendon, 1992), 90–93.

[109] Stuhlhofer, *Der Gebrauch der Bibel von Jesus bis Euseb*, 73–76.

[110] Bovon, "La structure canonique de l'Evangile et de l'Apotre." *Cristianesimo nella storia* 15 (1994): 559–76.

[111] Barton, *Holy Writings, Sacred Text*, 42–62.

[112] Gamble, "Canon, New Testament," *ABD* 1:852–61.

[113] Metzger, *The Canon of the New Testament*, 75–90; Schnelle, *The History and Theology of the New Testament Writings*, 359; J.-D. DuBois, "L'exégèse gnostique et l'histoire du canon des Ecritures," in *Les regles de l'intepretation* (ed. M. Tardieu; Paris: Cerf, 1987), 89–97.

not to a fixed collection of certified books that the church appealed: Irenaeus (e.g., *Haer.* 1.9.4, 2.27.1) located the bastion against the gnostics in the apostolic tradition, and specifically in the *regula fidei*, which furnished the *skopos* or *hypothesis* by which the scriptures were to be understood.[114] This means that what was at stake between gnostic and non-gnostic Christians was not principally which books were authoritative, but rather how the scriptures were to be rightly interpreted. In point of fact, gnostic Christians employed virtually all the books that were used in the church at large.[115] The difference lay not in the documents, but in different hermeneutical programs.[116]

Von Campenhausen, again following Harnack,[117] laid an especially heavy emphasis on the importance of Montanism for the history of the canon, claiming that its conviction of continuing inspiration and new revelation provided the decisive impetus toward limitation, a movement precisely opposite the one attributed to Marcion. This view is still very much current.[118] It may be granted that scriptures played a role in the Montanist controversy, but not in a way that impinged directly on the canon, for it does not appear that the Montanists either rejected writings that were generally recognized and used in the church, or opposed their own oracles or writings to them.[119] The issue was not the scope or authority of scripture as such, but whether the church's tradition was normative and whether, therefore, it excluded new revelation. The response to Montanism was to confine authoritative revelation to the past.[120] This had consequences for the church's view of scripture as a dimension of tradition, but did not directly bring about any closure of the canon.

None of the heterodox movements of the second century can be shown to have had any strong, let alone decisive, effect on the history of the canon.[121] Nevertheless, they need to be kept in view because the history of the canon cannot be fully understood independently of church history, including the history of theology. On the other hand, the history of the canon is sure to be misconceived if it is regarded strictly or even mainly as a dogmatic construct, that is, as a function of the history of doctrine. It has as much or more to do with the liturgical life of the ancient church, which was the primary context of the use and interpretation of scripture.

---

[114] R. A. Norris, "Theology and Language in Irenaeus of Lyons," *ATR* 76 (1994): 285–95.

[115] C. A. Evans, *Nag Hammadi Texts and the Bible: A Synopsis and Index* (NTTS 18; ed. C. A. Evans, R. L. Webb, and R. Wiebe; Leiden: Brill, 1993).

[116] So argue W. A. Lohr, "Kanonsgeschichtliche Beobachtungen zum Verhältnis von mundlicher und schriftlicher Tradition im zweiten Jahrhundert," *ZNW* 85 (1994): 234–58, at 243–48; P. C. Miller, "Words with an Alien Voice: Gnostics, Scripture and Canon," *JAAR* 57 (1989): 459–83; P. Perkins, "Spirit and Letter: Poking Holes in the Canon," *JR* 76 (1996): 307–27; L. Painchaud, "The Use of Scripture in Gnostic Literature," *JECS* 4 (1996): 129–47; and J. A. Williams, *Biblical Interpretation in the Gnostic Gospel of Truth from Nag Hammadi* (SBLDS 79; Atlanta: Scholars Press, 1988).

[117] Von Campenhausen, *Formation*, 221–32; Harnack, *The Origin of the New Testament*, 35–39.

[118] Metzger, *The Canon of the New Testament*, 99–106.

[119] H. Paulsen, "Die Bedeutung des Montanismus fur die Herausbildung des Kanons," *VC* 32 (1978): 19–52.

[120] So argue Paulsen, "Die Bedeutung," and Heine, "The Role of the Gospel of John in the Montanist Controversy," *SecCent* 6 (1987):1–19.

[121] See now I. P. van Tonder, "An Assessment of the Impact of Second Century Heretical Christian Movements on the Formation of the Catholic Christian Canon of Scripture" (Ph.D. diss.; University of Cambridge, 2000).

While impulses toward the limitation of the scope of scripture were never absent, they did not take full effect until the fourth century, when definitive canon lists became the order of the day. Various factors may be cited to account for this, none of them mutually exclusive. Early in the fourth century the church, under the sponsorship of Constantine, finally attained to the status of the official religion of the Roman Empire. Whatever his motives, Constantine clearly sought to promote the consolidation and unity of the church, even as he sought to consolidate and unify the Empire. Agreement about the scope of authoritative scripture was hardly less important than theological agreement, since doctrine could scarcely be separated from its resources and authorities in scripture and tradition. The great theological issue of the day, Arianism, required mediation between the distinctive traditions of the eastern and western churches, which, despite much common ground, differed also in the scriptural resources to which they appealed. The focused interaction of eastern and western theological and scriptural traditions that began in the fourth century, and in which Athanasius was a prominent figure, furnished a strong impetus toward standardization of usages. Constantine's concern to build churches and to furnish them with copies of the scriptures is famously documented by his request to Eusebius to manufacture "fifty copies of the divine scriptures" (*Vit. Const.* 4.36). It is not altogether clear whether the Emperor had in mind the production of codices of the Gospels only,[122] of the Christian scriptures ("New Testament") only, or, as traditionally thought, of whole Bibles.[123] If the latter, a good case can be made that two extant codices, Sinaiticus and Vaticanus, were written in the scriptorium of the library at Caesarea, and indeed as part of the effort there to meet the imperial request.[124] However that may be, the appearance in the fourth century of very large, multiple quire codices finally capable of containing the whole of Christian scriptures suggests that the technology of book production played a role in the delimitation of the canon, even as it did in the creation of early smaller collections.[125] The aim of transcribing all scriptural documents in a single codex forced, in the most practical and unavoidable way, the question of precisely which books ought to be included, though it must be noted that whole Bibles, or pandects, were a relative rarity in the ancient church. Thus in the fourth century a variety of factors, political, theological and technological, all pointed to the issue of the scope of authoritative writings.

The history of the New Testament canon will not be adequately grasped until all of its dimensions have been comprehended. I have sought to suggest that these dimensions are far more numerous than is customarily thought. They include the social history of the early church, the history of theology and doctrine, the liturgical life of early Christian communities, the history of interpretation, the bibliographical practices of the church, and the textual history of particular documents and collections of documents. It is a daunting task.

---

[122] G. A. Robbins, "*Peri tōn endiathēkōn graphōn:* Eusebius and the Formation of the Christian Bible" (Ph.D. diss., Duke University, 1986).

[123] T. C. Skeat, "The Codex Sinaiticus, the Codex Vaticanus and Constantine," *JTS* 50 (1999): 583–625, at 605–9.

[124] Ibid., 583–609.

[125] Gamble, "The Canon of the New Testament," 222; J. K. Elliott, "Manuscripts, the Codex and the Canon," *JSNT* 63 (1996): 105–23.

18

Factors Leading to the Selection and Closure of the New Testament Canon: A Survey of Some Recent Studies

Everett Ferguson

The early followers of Jesus began with a set of scriptures, the sacred writings of the Hebrew Bible, but known to most in their Greek translation. The recognition of the Jewish scriptures may have been a barrier to Christians creating their own scriptures, but it may just as well have served as a pattern for that development. The recognition of a canon of New Testament writings placed alongside the scriptures of Judaism resulted primarily from internal dynamics of the Christian faith. The conviction of a new saving work of God in Christ, its proclamation by apostles and evangelists, and the revelation of its meaning and application by prophets and teachers, led naturally to the writing of these messages and their acceptance as authoritative in parallel with the books already regarded as divine. External factors did not determine that there would be a New Testament canon nor dictate its contents. However, external factors influenced the process of definition and likely hastened that process. But, first, let us consider what those on the inside of the church thought about the situation.

1. The Internal Dynamics

The first Christian writers to comment on which books were regarded as authoritative described them as having been "handed down" or "received." This standard language for tradition was used about the canonical books. In reference to the Gospels, for instance, Irenaeus spoke of "The gospels handed down to us from the apostles" (*Haer.* 3.11.9), and, "The gospel handed down to us by the will of God in scriptures" (ibid., 3.1.1). Clement of Alexandria specified "The four gospels that have been handed down to us" (*Strom.* 3.13.93). Serapion of Antioch rejected the *Gospel of Peter* as "pseudepigrapha," "knowing that we [orthodox Christians] did not receive such writings" (Eusebius, *Hist. eccl.* 6.12.3). The early ecclesiastical writers did not regard themselves as deciding which books to accept or to reject. Rather, they saw themselves as acknowledging which books had been handed down to them.[1] While they could have been self-deceived, or might have written to

---

[1] This was still the usage of Athanasius (*Ep. fest.* 39), "handed down to our ancestors."

deceive others, the first task of the historian is to determine what the participants understood about the circumstances. The consistency of usage across a broad spectrum of the early church is noteworthy.

A. Authority, Memory, and Scripture

Several internal needs of the new community favored the special recognition of certain books. The collecting and preserving of certain writings was a natural result of remembering and transmitting the testimony of the apostles and other eyewitnesses to Jesus and the stories about the early activities of his disciples. Authoritative materials were needed for various purposes.

As early communities developed, there was a need for guidance in the moral life of members. The *Didache* 1–6 shows a compilation built around the theme of the "Two Ways" used in the instruction of candidates for baptism. The teachings of Jesus on various questions were collected, preserved, and incorporated in the Gospels, and considerable sections of the letters of Paul and others address such topics.

What did it mean to believe in Jesus? Confessional materials used on many occasions, notably at baptism and codified in what was later called the "Apostles' Creed," required and led to the fixing of a consistent narrative framework for the life of Jesus. Accounts of conversion and the growth in the number of disciples, during and after the personal ministry of Jesus, served to strengthen faith and steadfastness in Jesus' followers.

Distinctive Christian worship practices also served as preconditions for a canon of scripture. The eucharist involved the remembrance of the passion of Christ and particularly the institution narrative. Prayers and confessional statements were grounded in the teachings of Jesus and the proclamation of his apostles. Christian materials were read in the assemblies from quite early (Mark 13:14; Rev 1:3; and see below on Paul's letters). The church did not have to wait until the end of the second century (and certainly not the fourth century) to know what books to read in church. Necessarily, the shift from oral message to writings took some time.

Material accepted as divine revelation would have been authoritative from its reception. This is evident in the book of Revelation. It presents itself as a "revelation" and a written "prophecy" (Rev 1:1–3). As divinely inspired, its words could neither be added to nor taken away (Rev 22:18–19). This principle applied to other revelations (e.g., Eph 3:5).

Authoritative materials were not transmitted exclusively in scripture. Baptismal instructions, confessions of faith, liturgical formulae, and similar materials were means of communicating Christian beliefs and practices. But writings were part of this transmitted material that from the beginning had a quasi-canonical status in Christian communities. The increasing passage of time decreased direct contact with living witnesses and put more premium on written records as aids to memory and a standard by which to evaluate teachings.

Papias lived toward the end of the time when the appeal to eyewitnesses was still possible. His words have commonly been taken as reflecting the decided preference for the oral tradition over written scriptures. The ancient world did value the oral word over the written word, but modern interpreters may read more into Papias's statement than he intended.

I will not hesitate to take into account along with my interpretations whatever I learned well and remember well from the presbyters, confirming the truth by them. For I did not rejoice, as many do, in those who talk a lot but in those who teach the truth, nor in those who recall alien commandments but in those who recall what was given in faith by the Lord and was derived from the truth itself. If ever someone who had accompanied the presbyters should come, I examined carefully the words of the presbyters, [to learn] what Andrew, Peter, Philip, Thomas, James, John, Matthew, or any other of the disciples of the Lord said and what things Aristion and the presbyter John, disciples of the Lord, are saying. For I did not suppose the contents of books would profit me so much as the words of the present and living voice. (Quoted by Eusebius, *Hist. eccl.* 3.39.1, 3–4, from Papias, *Interpretation of the Lord's Oracles*)

It is not at all clear that Papias is juxtaposing oral reports of apostolic teaching and apostolic writings. In fact it may be written documents that he was interpreting in his *Logiōn kyriakōn exēgēsis*, for "oracles" *(logia)* could be used of books.[2] Matthew and Mark certainly, and perhaps Luke and John,[3] had canonical status for him (Eusebius, *Hist. eccl.* 3.39.14–16). His concern was arriving at the truth, so his preference was for a primary over a secondary source.[4] Truth was found in apostolicity, so the contrast is between the teachings derived from the Lord and his disciples by way of the presbyters who had direct contact with them and the writings of heretical teachers.[5]

There are many early indications of the recognition of authoritative Christian writings. The acknowledgement of the scripture principle, although not yet a "canon," implicitly contained the idea of canon.[6] Paul expected his written instructions as well as his oral teaching to be received as authoritative (1 Cor 14:37; 2 Thess 2:15; 3:14). One of the documents accepted into the New Testament canon, 2 Peter, places Paul's letters on a level with the Old Testament scriptures (2 Pet 3:15–16). We find that Clement of Rome, Ignatius, and Polycarp made extensive use of Paul's letters and drew on them as authoritative. If the Latin version is reliable, Polycarp quoted Eph 4:26 as "scripture" (*Phil.* 12.1).[7] More significant overall is the overwhelming use Polycarp and others made of New Testament writings. Polycarp wove the phraseology of Paul's letters together with 1 Peter and 1–2 John for his own letter to the Philippians. The *Didache* several times appeals to "the gospel" as authoritative (8.2; 11.3; 15.3 and 4). It is debated whether he means only the message or also has a written document

---

[2] So of the Jewish scriptures: Josephus, *B.J.* 6.311 and *1 Clem.* 53.1; 62.3.

[3] Charles E. Hill, "What Papias Said about John (and Luke): A 'New' Papian Fragment," *JTS* n.s. 49 (1998): 582–629.

[4] Armin Daniel Baum, "Papias, der Vorzug der Viva Vox, und die Evangelienschriften," *NTS* 44 (1998): 144–51.

[5] A. F. Walls, "Papias and Oral Tradition," *VC* 21 (1967): 137–40; repr. in *Orthodoxy, Heresy, and Schism in Early Christianity* (Studies in Early Christianity 4; ed. E. Ferguson; New York: Garland, 1993), 107–10.

[6] See my comments in the "Introduction," to *The Bible in the Early Church* (Studies in Early Christianity 3; ed. E. Ferguson; New York: Garland, 1993), xi–xii.

[7] Affirmed by Charles Merritt Nielsen, "Polycarp, Paul, and the Scriptures," *AThR* 47 (1965): 199–216; so also B. Dehandschutter, "Polycarp's Epistle to the Philippians: An Early Example of 'Reception,'" in J.-M. Sevrin, *The New Testament in Early Christianity* (Leuven: University Press and Peeters, 1989), 275–91, at 281–83. J. B. Bauer (*Die Polykarpbriefe* [Göttingen: Vandenhoeck & Ruprecht, 1995], 69–71) understands the first part of *Phil.* 12.1 as saying that he has no authority to command as scripture does; he then surveys various interpretations of the quotation and suggests it is a combination of Ps 4:5 and Deut 24:14–15, and not an ascription of "scripture" status to Ephesians.

in mind; in each case the material referred to is found in Matthew.[8] Ignatius puts together the "Prophecies, the Law of Moses, and the Gospel" (*Smyrn.* 5.1); since the first two are written, the presumption is that the third is also, but his addition of "our own individual sufferings" may weaken the connection.[9] Both *Barnabas* (4.14) and *2 Clement* (2.4) quote Matthew, the former introducing Matt 22:14 as "it is written," and the latter quoting Matt 9:13 as "another scripture." It may be argued that the authority is the Lord and not a written document, but his words are found in a writing, and they are quoted from this writing in a manner that puts it on the same level with the Old Testament.[10]

Although second-century Christian authors accepted the Old Testament as scripture, they used the New Testament writings, in relation to their quantity, much more than the Old Testament.[11] Citation as "scripture" appears to be less significant than the overwhelming use and importance attached to the writings that form the core of our New Testament. It may claim too much "to say that the canon was fixed" already at the end of the first century,[12] "since its edges were still quite fuzzy; yet it would be equally mistaken to say that 'there was no Christian scripture other than the Old Testament'" at this time, "for much of the core [of the New Testament] already had as high a status as it would ever have."[13] In terms of the significance of scriptural status, there is no time when Christians did not treat the writings that would become the New Testament as scripture.[14]

It may be urged that the inexactitude in quotations by second-century authors indicates either that they were not quoting New Testament documents or, if they were, that they did not hold them in high regard. But there are several problems with this rea-

---

[8] C. M. Tuckett ("Synoptic Tradition in the Didache," in *The New Testament in Early Christianity* [ed. J.-M. Sevrin; Leuven: University Press and Peeters, 1989], 197–230) concludes that the *Didache* presupposes the finished gospels of Matthew and Luke. For further bibliography see my "Love of Enemies and Nonretaliation in the Second Century," in *The Contentious Triangle: Church, State, and University: A Festschrift in Honor of Professor George Huntston Williams* (ed. Rodney L. Petersen and Calvin Augustine Pater; Kirksville: Thomas Jefferson University Press, 1999), 81–95, at 84–85, nn. 12–13.

[9] Michael D. Goulder ("Ignatius' 'Docetists,'" *VChr* 53 [1999]: 16–17, n. 4) argues from this verse, from the possible quotation of John 3:8 in *Phld.* 7.1, and from the juxtaposition of the Prophets and the Gospel in *Phld.* 9.2 that the "Gospel" in *Phld.* 8.2 is written, as were the "archives" (Old Testament?). C. E. Hill ("Ignatius and the Apostolate: The Witness of Ignatius to the Emergence of Christian Scripture," *StPatr* 36 [2001]: 226–48) sees Ignatius's view of the apostles as testimony to the regard in which their writings were held.

[10] P. F. Beatrice ("Une citation de l'Evangile de Matthieu dans l'Epître de Barnabé," in *The New Testament in Early Christianity* [ed. J.-M. Sevrin; Leuven: University Press and Peeters, 1989], 231–45, at 232–34) argues that the identical theological and ecclesiological contexts confirms that *Barnabas* is indeed quoting the Gospel of Matthew.

[11] John Barton, *The Spirit and the Letter: Studies in the Biblical Canon* (London: SPCK, 1997), reprinted as *Holy Writings, Sacred Text: The Canon in Early Christianity* (Louisville, Ky.: Westminster John Knox, 1997), 18–19, with reference to the statistics gathered by Franz Stuhlhofer, *Der Gebrauch der Bibel von Jesus bis Eusebios: Eine statistische Untersuchung zur Kanongeschichte* (Wuppertal: R. Brockhaus, 1988).

[12] Cf. Theodor Zahn, *Geschichte des neutestamentlichen Kanons* (2 vols.; Erlangen: Deichert, 1888–1892); supported by U. Swarat, "Das Werden des neutestamentlichen Kanons," in *Der Kanon der Bibel* (ed. G. Maier; Giessen: Brunnen, 1990), 25–51.

[13] Barton, *The Spirit and the Letter,* 19.

[14] Ibid., 134–45.

soning.[15] Quotations may take various forms: in addition to verbatim quotations, there are interpretive quotations, intentional changes to affect the meaning, paraphrastic quotations, quotations accommodated to sentence structure, and simply loose quotations when the point does not depend on exact words. None of these need imply a lack of respect for the quoted text. If respect were lacking, there would be no quotation or allusion. Indeed, the greater the respect for the text, the more need for deliberate changes to make it appear to say what one wants it to say. Comparable variations are found in second-century authors' quotations from the Old Testament, and there is no question that its text was fixed in writing (even though there were different forms of the text) and was considered authoritative scripture. Quoting from memory is not the same as quoting from oral tradition.

Mary Carruthers's findings in regard to memory in medieval culture also apply to ancient culture, whose understanding and practices it followed, as her references to Cicero and Quintillian demonstrate.[16] For the ancients a book was a support for memory, and more confidence was placed in the memory than in books. Authoritative texts were often not quoted verbatim, for "memory for things" was preferred to "rote iteration" (memory of words), even when the speaker had accurate command of the original words.[17]

Another perspective to be considered is that a written text actually gives a speaker or writer more freedom in quotation than an oral message does. Something preserved only orally must be quoted, if not verbatim, with great faithfulness. There is not the same need for exactitude in regard to written materials, for the writer can assume that the reader knows the text and only needs to be reminded of it, or can always consult the original text. The presence of a written text provides a standard of reference that permits the one quoting to play with variations.

Other indications of the acceptance of some New Testament writings as scripture may be briefly indicated and their significance noted. Papyrus fragments from Egypt, notably the John Rylands fragment of John (P[52]), show an early circulation of the Gospels that may indicate their authority, certainly their use. Apocryphal writings from the second century tend to fall into the same literary genres as the canonical books: gospels *(Gospel of Peter, Protevangelium of James)*, acts *(Acts of Peter, Acts of Paul, Acts of John)*, letters *(Epistle of the Apostles)*, and apocalypses *(Apocalypse of Peter)*. This phenomenon may be indicative that certain forms of writing had already imprinted themselves on the Christian consciousness as the way Christian books were to be written if they were to have authority. The writings that came to make up the New Testament began to be translated into other languages quite early—Latin and Syriac before the end of the second century, and Coptic not much later. The language in which Tatian undertook his harmony of the gospels (the *Diatessaron*) is debatable, but in his time or shortly thereafter Syriac translations of some New Testament books were available.[18] The same had happened in Latin. There may not have been a "canon"

---

[15] Various ramifications of orality and textuality are brought out by Barton (*The Spirit and the Letter,* 87–104, 123–30).

[16] Mary Carruthers, *The Book of Memory: A Study of Memory in Medieval Culture* (Cambridge: Cambridge University Press, 1990), note esp. 26–27, 31–32, 160, 189–94.

[17] Martin Jaffee in a review, "Oral Culture in Scriptural Religion: Some Exploratory Studies," *Religious Studies Review* (1998): 223–30, at 227–28.

[18] The canon of the Syriac church is a special problem, because it later did not include the General Epistles and Revelation. J. S. Siker ("The Canonical Status of the Catholic Epistles in the Syriac

to determine which books to translate, but there certainly was a felt need and widespread use to justify such undertakings. A literary confirmation of the Latin translation is found in the *Acts of the Scillitan Martyrs* from North Africa in 180. One of the martyrs, Speratus, carried a case containing "books and letters of a just man named Paul" (12). The "books" is probably a reference to gospels, although the text may mean, "books, that is letters of Paul."[19]

Wherever Paul and his associates labored, there were those who were interested in his letters and respected them as authoritative. As part of his apostolic mission, Paul wrote letters as more than occasional correspondence. The letters of Paul were read and reread in the churches to which they were addressed, and he expected them to be read by others (1 Thess 5:27; Col 4:16), a practice that continued or was resumed quite early. Evidently he and others had copies from the beginning.[20] It is probable that several collections were made.[21] Paul's letters were collected by the end of the first century at the latest.[22] This is evident from their use by authors as geographically separated as Clement of Rome, Ignatius of Antioch, and Polycarp of Smyrna. The only question is the extent of the collection. Marcion's edition of the letters of Paul did not contain the Pastoral epistles, but Polycarp clearly used them, so much so that Campenhausen thought Polycarp wrote them, a view that did not gain much favor.[23] Hebrews was a special case, and its varying position among the letters of Paul reflects hesitation about accepting it as Pauline.[24]

Harry Gamble suggests that the collection of Paul's letters was the impetus for the Christian adoption of the codex.[25] The collection and preservation of Paul's writings obvi-

---

New Testament," *JTS* n.s. 38 [1987]: 311–40) points out that these letters were in the Philoxenian and Harclean versions; they were not included in the Syriac canon because of their absence from the Peshitta, which increasingly became the authoritative version of the Syriac New Testament.

[19] Gerald Bonner ("The Scillitan Saints and the Pauline Epistles," *JEH* 7 [1956]: 141–46) takes the books as gospels; but J. den Boeft and J. Bremmer ("Notiunculae martyrologicae IV," *VC* 45 [1991]: 116–17) translate "books of epistles."

[20] Lars Hartman, "On Reading Others' Letters," *HTR* 79 (1986): 137–46.

[21] Harry Y. Gamble (*Books and Readers in the Early Church: A History of Early Christian Texts* [New Haven: Yale University Press, 1995], 59–62) cites evidence for three different orders in which the letters were collected: (1) Marcion's collection that begins with Galatians and ends with Philemon; (2) Papyrus 46, dated about 200, that follows the order that became established except for reversing Ephesians and Galatians; and (3) the letters to seven churches, treating those to the same church as one letter and basing the order on length, so that Corinthians is first and Colossians (perhaps including Philemon) is last.

[22] Lewis Foster ("The Earliest Collection of Paul's Epistles," *Bulletin of the Evangelical Theological Society* 10 [1967]: 44–55; repr. in *The Bible in the Early Church* [Studies in Early Christianity 3; ed. E. Ferguson; New York: Garland, 1993], 150–61) suggests that Luke made the earliest collection of Paul's letters as a third volume to go with his Gospel and Acts. G. Zuntz (*The Text of the Epistles: A Disquisition upon the Corpus Paulinum* [London: British Academy, 1953]), drawing on textual criticism (working from P[46]), concluded that "the archetypal *Corpus* [*Paulinum*] was produced about A.D. 100" (279).

[23] Hans von Campenhausen, *Polykarp von Smyrna und die Pastoralbriefe* (Heidelberg: C. Winter, 1951).

[24] William H. P. Hatch ("The Position of Hebrews in the Canon of the New Testament," *HTR* 29 [1936]: 133–51) surveys the different positions of Hebrews in the manuscripts and canon lists; C. P. Anderson ("The Epistle to the Hebrews and the Pauline Letter Collection," *HTR* [1966]: 429–38) argues that it is more plausible that Hebrews was included among the letters of Paul before the formation of the corpus as a whole than that it was added to an existing Pauline corpus.

[25] Gamble, *Books and Readers in the Early Church*, 58–66.

ously occurred in the Pauline circle and thus near the lifetime of the apostle. May it go back even earlier? E. Randolph Richards has carried Gamble's proposal a step further. He suggests that Paul, like other letter writers of his time, kept a copy of his letters in codex form, as was common for an author's notebooks. Paul had this personal set of copies with him in Rome (cf. the *membranas* of 2 Tim 4:13), and they passed at his death to his disciples, who saw to their copying and distribution in the same form.[26] The theory is unprovable, but offers an explanation for the early knowledge of Paul's letters and the early use of the codex by Christians.

B. Early Regard for the Gospels

An earlier explanation of Christians' adoption of the codex appealed to the authority of the Gospels.[27] The words of Jesus carried authority from the beginning (1 Cor 7:10, 12; Acts 20:35),[28] and the passion narrative was the core of the apostolic preaching (1 Cor 15:1–8). A four-gospel canon was in place by the time of Irenaeus.

> It is not possible that the Gospels can be either more or fewer in number than they are. For since there are four zones of the world in which we live, and four principal winds, while the church is scattered throughout the world, and the "pillar and ground" [1 Tim 3:15] of the church is the Gospel and the Spirit of life; it is fitting that she should have four pillars. . . . The Word . . . who was manifested to humanity has given us the Gospel under four aspects but bound together by one Spirit. (Irenaeus, *Haer.* 3.11.8)

Irenaeus continues with other instances of the number four: the four living creatures of Revelation "among whom Christ is seated,"[29] and the four principal covenants made by God (the Noachic, the Abrahamic, the law by Moses, and the gospel through Christ). He names the four gospels as John, Luke, Matthew, and Mark. It is often stated that Irenaeus was arguing for something new and had quite weak arguments for his position. This approach misunderstands the importance of number symbolism in the ancient world and Irenaeus's use of it. He does not argue for four gospels because there are four winds or four corners of the universe. He appeals to this symbolism because he has four gospels. If he had three, five, or some other number, he would have found an appropriately fitting analogy. Irenaeus does not see himself as an innovator, but as champion of a traditional position in the church over against the Marcionite narrowing and Valentinian expansion of the Gospel canon.

---

[26] E. Randolph Richards, "The Codex and the Early Collection of Paul's Letters," *BBR* 8 (1998): 151–66.

[27] C. H. Roberts and T. C. Skeat, *The Birth of the Codex* (Oxford: British Academy, 1983), 57–61.

[28] David L. Dungan, *The Sayings of Jesus in the Churches of Paul: The Use of the Synoptic Tradition in the Regulation of Early Church Life* (Philadelphia: Fortress, 1971).

[29] T. C. Skeat ("Irenaeus and the Four Gospel Canon," *NovT* 34 [1992]: 194–99) explains the anomalies in Irenaeus's remarks (like the unusual order of the four gospels) as deriving from an earlier source that had interpreted the four creatures of Ezekiel and Revelation. The remarks presuppose a four-gospel canon and a four-gospel codex, and since earlier than Irenaeus, point to a date of 170 at the latest. Y.-M. Blanchard (*Aux sources du canon: Le témoignage d'Irénée* [Paris: Cerf, 1993]), on the other hand, argues that the gospels had not acquired normative status.

The significance of Tatian's *Diatessaron* (c. 170 ?) has been argued both ways.[30] It is commonly said that if the four gospels were regarded as sacred scripture, he would not have treated them so freely as to weave them together into a separate narrative (it is worth noting that the Gospel of John serves as the chronological framework). On the other hand, why would he have bothered unless the works were considered important? Because they were authoritative, Tatian was concerned enough to do the study involved in reducing the four authorities to one unified account.

Tatian may have inherited the idea and indeed the basis for his project from his teacher Justin. Several scholars find the best explanation for the wording of Justin's gospel quotations to be a harmony of the teachings of Jesus that he produced in his school.[31] Justin mentions the "Memoirs of the Apostles," a title his pagan readers would have understood from works like the *Memoirs of Socrates*. He testifies that Christians call them "gospels" (*1 Apol.* 66.3) and read them in their Sunday assemblies on a par with the Old Testament (*1 Apol.* 67.3). Many think these were only the Synoptic Gospels and profess to find no evidence that Justin knew the Fourth Gospel, but this reflects a curious scholarly blindness.[32] If we may press the exact words of Justin, "the memoirs, which I say were composed by his apostles [plural] and their followers [plural]" (*Dial.* 103.8), he knew at least two gospels by apostles and two by their associates. Quotations drawn from Matthew and Luke are frequent; there is a quotation from Mark 3:16–17 ascribed to the "Memoirs of Peter" (*Dial.* 106.3).[33] Moreover, one passage may put John among the Memoirs: "For I

---

[30] The most comprehensive study is W. L. Petersen, *Tatian's Diatessaron: Its Creation, Dissemination, Significance, and History in Scholarship* (Leiden: Brill, 1994), whose interests are textual and not canonical. Petersen calls attention to reports of two other harmonies near the time of Tatian, or a little later: "Theophilus [bishop of Antioch] . . . put together into one work the words of the four Gospels" (Jerome, *Ep.* 121.6), and "Ammonius the Alexandrine has left us the gospel as a diatessaron," in which he placed alongside the Gospel of Matthew the parallel pericopes of the other three gospels (Eusebius, *Ep. Carp.* 1) (32–33). These undertakings would seem to presuppose the special authority of the four gospels.

[31] Notably A. J. Bellinzoni, *The Sayings of Jesus in the Writings of Justin Martyr* (Leiden: Brill, 1967); idem, "The Gospel of Matthew in the Second Century," *SecCent* 9 (1992): 197–258, esp. 239–42, which accepts Koester's further elaboration: Helmut Koester, *Ancient Christian Gospels: Their History and Development* (Philadelphia: Trinity Press International, 1990), 360–402; also, Eric Osborn, *Justin Martyr* (Tübingen: Mohr [Siebeck], 1973), 123–24. Others think a compilation for catechetical purposes (and not a harmony) sufficiently accounts for the passages cited by Justin: Donald Hagner, "The Sayings of Jesus in the Apostolic Fathers and Justin Martyr," in *Gospel Perspectives* (ed. D. Wenham; Sheffield: JSOT, 1985), 5:249; Georg Strecker, "Eine Evangelienharmonie bei Justin und Pseudoklemens?" *NTS* 24 (1977–78): 297–316.

[32] In a nuanced study, J. W. Pryor ("Justin Martyr and the Fourth Gospel," *SecCent* 9 [1992]: 153–69) discounts some of the evidence adduced for Justin's use of the Fourth Gospel, concluding that Justin knew the work, but not as scripture or the work of an apostle. C. H. Cosgrove ("Justin Martyr and the Emerging Christian Canon: Observations on the Purpose and Destination of the Dialogue with Trypho," *VC* 36 [1982]: 209–32) sees Justin as devaluing the canonical authority of the New Testament, including the Gospels; Charles E. Hill ("Justin and the New Testament Writings," *StPatr* 30 [1997]: 42–48) counters by referring to Justin's apologetic purpose and high evaluation of apostolic authority (note especially *Dial.* 119.6, "God's voice spoken by the apostles").

[33] The whole context of this passage (*Dial.* 97–106) is a dialogue between the Old Testament and the New Testament (primarily the Gospels, but there are parallels to Paul and Hebrews) in interpreting Ps 22.

have already proved that he was the only begotten of the Father of all things, being begotten in a peculiar manner as Word and Power by him, and having afterwards become man through the Virgin, as we have learned from the Memoirs" (*Dial.* 105.1). The virgin birth comes from Matthew and Luke, but the language of "only begotten" (*monogenēs*) and designation as "Word" are found only in John.[34]

Contemporary with Justin, the *Martyrdom of Polycarp* by his church in Smyrna emphasized martyrdom "according to the gospel" (1.1; 19.1; cf. 4.1) in such a way as at least to include the teachings of written gospels.[35]

Recent study is pushing the collection of a four-gospel canon back to the early second century.[36] Irenaeus could have been familiar with four-gospel codices. P[45], from the first half of the third century, is the earliest codex of the four gospels and Acts.[37] P[75], from around 200, contains Luke and John, a combination that suggests it may have originally been combined with a codex of Matthew and Mark.[38] The fragments of P[4], P[64], and P[67] are from the same codex, dated late second century, and contain Matthew and Luke, making it possibly our earliest four-gospel codex.[39] Since these three codices are independent of one another, they are evidence for the four-gospel canon at the end of the second century, and unless the idea was independently arrived at by different compilers, there must have been predecessors. This consideration takes us back at the latest to the mid-second century.

Moody Smith's 1999 presidential address to the annual meeting of the Society of Biblical Literature in Boston carries us back to the very composition of the gospels.[40] Accepting the distinction between scripture and canon, Smith examined the gospels for indications that the authors understood themselves to be writing scripture. He finds appreciable evidence in Matthew and Luke that they were continuing the Old Testament story, were imitating it, and were writing a definitive account of the coming of Jesus and his place in the history of salvation. The intent of Mark and John in this regard was less obvious, but there is evidence that they too were functioning as scripture from quite early. This is implicit, according to Smith, in the commonly accepted view that Matthew and Luke used Mark, and in the way that 1 John presupposes the Fourth Gospel and was engaged in exegetical controversy over its meaning. The continuity of these gospels with the Old Testament story contrasts with the apocryphal gospels, notably the *Gospel of Thomas*. This finding coincides with the fact that there is no time in Christian history after the writing of the four gospels when one can find evidence of their not being accepted as scripture.

---

[34] The absence of an exact reference earlier in the *Dialogue* where Justin has done this does not carry much weight in view of Justin's rambling style, and he may be substituting Johannine language here to express the claims he has made for another being besides the Supreme God in the creation account and in the theophanies of the Old Testament.

[35] Gerd Buschmann, *Das Martyrium des Polykarp* (Göttingen: Vandenhoeck & Ruprecht, 1998), esp. 49–58.

[36] Graham Stanton, "The Fourfold Gospel," *NTS* 43 (1997): 317–46; repr. in *Norms of Faith and Life* (Recent Studies in Early Christianity 3; ed. E. Ferguson; New York: Garland, 1999), 1–30; Theo K. Heckel (*Vom Evangelium des Markus zum viergestaltigen Evangelium* [Tübingen: Mohr (Siebeck), 1999]) dates the formation of the fourfold collection ca. 110–120.

[37] F. G. Kenyon, *The Chester Beatty Biblical Papyri* (London: Emery Walker, 1933).

[38] T. C. Skeat, "The Origin of the Christian Codex," *ZPE* 102 (1994): 263–68.

[39] T. C. Skeat, "The Oldest Manuscript of the Four Gospels?" *NTS* 43 (1997): 1–34.

[40] Moody Smith, "When Did the Gospels Become Scripture?" *JBL* 119 (2000): 3–20.

Supportive of this claim is Richard Bauckham's contention that the gospels were written not just for one community but for any and every church that they might reach.[41] The early Christian movement was a network of communities in close communication with one another, their leaders traveled widely, Christianity was viewed as a worldwide movement, and early Christian literature circulated rapidly—indeed, the purpose of writing was to reach people beyond those with whom one had personal contact. All these factors support the contention that the gospels were written for all Christians. Such broader audiences and purposes are consistent with, but do not necessarily require, the writing of authoritative "scripture." Their early acceptance by Christians is presupposed by their later preeminence.

The evidence of textual criticism is against the four canonical gospels having undergone a long period of development involving several stages of composition. Positively stated, the history of the text shows that the gospels were composed in the form in which they exist today.[42] This situation in turn allows the time for them to be accepted and brought together in a collection by the early second century.

Codices P[66] and P[75] from about 200 give the titles of the gospels, "The Gospel [singular] according to . . . ," that is, the one gospel in multiple written forms. These titles imply a period of time during which the individual gospels were circulated together. They belong to an early stage of transmission, likely going back to the early second century.[43]

An indirect testimony to the four-gospel collection is the separation of Luke from Acts. These books were two volumes of one work, but there is no point in the transmission history of the two volumes where they are joined. If they were written on two scrolls, their separation would have been easy to effect, but when the codex came into use, why were they not put in the same codex? The most plausible explanation is that the two works were separated in order for Luke to become part of a Gospel collection. And this separation presumably occurred before Marcion, for he accepts Luke but not Acts.[44]

If other gospels such as the *Gospel of Thomas* and the *Gospel of Peter* were as early as the canonical gospels, then the need for differentiation between what was authentic and correct and what was not was equally early; if those works are later, they represent alternatives produced in part under the influence of the canonical gospels.

C. Early Christian Terminology for the Authoritative Writings

Early Christian writers made frequent reference to a threefold expression of authority: "the Prophets, the Lord, and the Apostles."[45] The pattern is already reflected in

---

[41] Richard Bauckham, "Introduction" and "For Whom Were Gospels Written," in *The Gospels for All Christians: Rethinking the Gospel Audiences* (ed. idem; Grand Rapids: Eerdmans, 1998), 1–7, 9–48.

[42] U. Victor, "Was ein Texthistoriker zur Entstehung der Evangelien sagen kann," *Bib* 79 (1998): 499–514.

[43] Martin Hengel, "The Titles of the Gospels and the Gospel of Mark," *Studies in the Gospel of Mark* (London: SCM, 1985), 64–84. Helmut Koester disagrees and puts the use of these titles at the end of the second century ("From Kerygma-Gospel to Written Gospels," *NTS* 35 [1989]: 361–81, esp. p. 373, n. 2).

[44] William R. Farmer and Denis M. Farkasfalvy (*The Formation of the New Testament Canon* [New York: Paulist, 1983], 64 and 73) suggest that Marcion's Gospel and Apostle (the letters of Paul) were modeled on and a substitute for Luke and Acts.

[45] Damien van den Eynde, *Les normes de l'enseignement chrétien dans la littérature patristique des trois premiers siècles* (Gembloux–Paris: J. Duculot, 1933). Robert B. Eno, SS (*Teaching Authority*

Clement of Rome, whose exhortation against schism includes examples and quotations ("it is written") from the Old Testament, along with, "Remember the words of the Lord Jesus," and, "Take up the epistle of the blessed Paul the Apostle" (*1 Clem.* 45–47).[46] One of the earliest explicit statements is from Polycarp: "As [Christ] himself commanded us and the apostles who preached the gospel to us and the prophets who announced beforehand the coming of our Lord" (*Phil.* 6.3). Ignatius made a similar combination of "apostles, prophets, and the church," but the distinctive feature of the gospel is the "coming of the Savior, our Lord Jesus Christ" (*Phld.* 9.1–2; cf. 5.1–2). Both Ignatius and Polycarp had persons in mind, but the messages of these authorities were found in books (see n. 9 above on Ignatius's other formulations). The same goes for Irenaeus: "The utterances of the prophets, of the Lord, and of the apostles" (*Haer.* 2.2.5) or more fully, "The preaching of the church, which the prophets proclaimed . . . but which Christ brought to perfection, and the apostles have handed down, from whom the church received [it]" (ibid., 5.pref.).[47] Irenaeus certainly implied books, as other statements, to which we shall come, make clear.[48] Clement of Alexandria explicitly refers to books. In a discussion of the scriptures as the demonstration of truth, "giving a complete exhibition of the scriptures from the scriptures themselves," Clement declares: "We have as the source of teaching the Lord, both by the Prophets, the Gospel, and the blessed Apostles" (*Strom.* 7.16.95, 97).[49] The Lord was the authority, but he made his teaching known in a threefold collection of writings: Prophets, Gospel, and Apostles. Prophets were taken by Christians as a comprehensive designation of their Old Testament, so that Moses and David were cited as "prophets." Elsewhere Clement exhorts, "Let one believe the Prophecies, Gospels, and Apostolic Words" (*Quis div.* 42.17). Origen began his *De principiis* by affirming that Christ is the truth, whose words include not only what he spoke while in the flesh but also what he spoke through Moses and the prophets and through the apostles (*Princ.* 1 *praef.* 1).[50] This threefold summary of authority was a natural expression of the Christian periodization of the history of salvation. But it is worth raising the question if the Jewish three-part canon of Law, Prophets, and Writings influenced Christians to posit their own authorities in a three-fold form. This threefold summary continued in use at a time when only by an extension of meaning

---

in the Early Church [Message of the Fathers of the Church 14; Wilmington: Michael Glazier, 1984]) concerns more the offices from which teaching was given.

[46] A similar "history of salvation" view appears in *Barnabas* 6.5–9: "The prophets prophesied" of Christ, and while teaching and doing miracles "he chose out his own apostles who were to preach his gospel."

[47] Almost identical wording in *Epid.* 98. Cf. *Haer.* 3.9.1, "Neither the prophets, the apostles, nor the Lord Christ in his own person"; 3.17.4, "The Lord testifies, as the apostles confess, and as the prophets announce"; and 1.8.1 quoted below.

[48] His contemporary Theophilus of Antioch certainly had books in mind: "Concerning the righteousness that the law enjoined, confirmatory utterances are found both with the prophets and in the Gospels, because they all spoke inspired by one Spirit of God"; and he quotes 1 Tim 2:12 and Rom 13:7–8 as "the divine word gives instructions" (*Autol.* 3.12, 14).

[49] *Strom.* 6.15 refers to the scriptures containing "the teaching of the Lord by his apostles" and what was announced by "prophecy and the Savior himself."

[50] Cf. "Gospels, Apostles, and Prophets" (*Comm. Jo.* 1.23). It may be noted that the Pseudo-Cyprian, *De aleatoribus* 10 cites its authorities in the order, "the prophet" (1 Kings), "the blessed apostle" (Paul), "the Lord in his gospel" (Matthew), and "the apostle John" (1 John).

could the terms cover the contents of scripture.[51] It shows how terminology from an early time remained in use with an altered or accommodated meaning. It is not evidence for the limitation of the canon to the books properly so named.

There was from early times another, fourfold formulation of the Christian authorities that more obviously referred to writings. This formulation balanced two collections from the Old Testament and two from the New: the Law, Prophets, Gospels, and Apostles. The "Law and the Prophets" often stood for the scriptures that would become the Old Testament (e.g., Matt 22:40; John 1:45; Acts 24:14; 28:23; Rom 3:21, and frequently later). Christians soon paralleled this with the Gospels and Apostles. Thus, Irenaeus could put the "writings of the Evangelists and the Apostles" alongside "the Law and the Prophets" (*Haer.* 1.3.6).[52] The *Epistle to Diognetus* 11.6 states, "The fear of the Law is sung, the grace of the Prophets is known, the faith of the Gospels is established, the tradition of the Apostles is kept, and the grace of the church exults." Clement of Alexandria, in a context discussing "reading the scriptures of the Lord," speaks of his four part Bible as "the ecclesiastical harmony of the Law and the Prophets together, and the Apostles also along with the Gospel" (*Strom.* 6.11.88.5). Tertullian writes of the church at Rome that "She combines the Law and the Prophets with the writings of Evangelists and Apostles, from which she drinks in her faith" (*Praescr.* 36).[53] This fourfold summary of scripture finds frequent expression in Origen. Note his listing, "Law, Prophets . . . Gospel Writings, and Apostles' letters" (*Comm. Cant.* 2.3).[54] He affirms the agreement "of the Old Scriptures with the New, of the Law with the Prophets, of the Gospels with the Apostolic Scriptures, and of the Apostolic Scriptures with each other" (*Comm. Matt.* 2). The scriptures "inspired by the Holy Spirit" were "the Gospels and Apostolic writings, and the Law and the Prophets" (*Princ.* 1.3.1).[55] He also spoke of "the Scriptures of the Law and Prophets and Apostles and Gospels" (*Hom. Exod.* 12.4). This traditional grouping continued at a later time, as by Cyril of Jerusalem, "Law and Prophets, and Gospels and Apostles" (*Catech.* 17.5).

A shorthand expression for the authorities recognized by Christians was "prophets and apostles," it being understood that the Lord's authority stood behind both. This appears already in 2 Pet 3:2, "Remember the words spoken in the past by the holy proph-

---

[51] The formulation continued in use as late as the early fifth century, e.g., "Prophets, Gospels, and Apostolic Writings" in Nicetas, *Utility of Hymn Singing* 3.

[52] Cf. "The preaching of the apostles, the authoritative teaching of the Lord, the announcements of the prophets, the writings [dictated words] of the apostles, and the ministration of the law" (*Haer.* 2.35.4). Irenaeus had various twofold formulations: "Law and Prophets" for the Old Testament (*Haer.* e.g., 3.9.2; 4.5.1; 4.64); "the entire scriptures, the Prophets and the Gospels" (2.27.2); "The Mosaic law and the grace of the new covenant" (3.12.11); "Law" and "Gospel" as two covenants (4.9.1; cf. 4.12.3–4). Threefold formulations: "the prophets, the apostles, and the Spirit himself" (3.19.2) "prophets, apostles, and all the disciples" (3.24.1); prophets, Christ, and the law (4.2.1).

[53] For the latter pair, cf. *Praescr.* 4, "the sayings of the Lord and the letters of the apostles." Tertullian more often makes a twofold classification, as "Law and Gospel": *Marc.* 1.19 (where they are described as "two documents"); 4.1; 4.11; 5.2, 13; this classification is frequently expressed as a distinction of the Old and New Testaments, for which see below.

[54] In the *Comm. Cant.*, as elsewhere, "Law and Prophets" stands for the Old Testament. Cf. 3.12 for "Old Testament Scriptures" and "Gospels."

[55] Cf. *Princ.* pref. 4: "God . . . gave the Law, the Prophets, and the Gospels, being also the God of the apostles and of the Old and New Testaments."

ets, and the commandment of the Lord and Savior spoken through your apostles." It serves as a summary of the scriptures read in church, according to Justin, *1 Apol.* 67.3 (cf. *Dial.*119.6). In the *Muratorian Fragment*, lines 77–78, the *Shepherd* was excluded from public reading because it did not belong to either of these categories. Compare the "prophetic and apostolic meadow," Clement of Alexandria's summary of the sources of knowledge (*Strom.* 1.1). This terminology may be seen as sketching a theology of the "pre-Canon" or "proto-Canon."[56] The two-part Christian Bible may also be anticipated in the reference to "the books and the apostles" in *2 Clem.* 14.2.

The terminology, however, that came to prevail was that of Old Covenant (Testament) and New Covenant (Testament). This usage began before the end of the second century.[57] Melito of Sardis reported going to Palestine where he "learned accurately the books of the Old Covenant" (Eusebius, *Hist. eccl.* 4.26.3), wording that might imply there were also books of a New Covenant but not necessarily with this title. An anonymous opponent of Montanism spoke of "the word of the new covenant of the gospel" (Eusebius, *Hist. eccl.* 5.16.3) but apparently with reference to the message more than to a collection of books (see further below). Irenaeus made frequent use of the terminology of old and new covenants, but it is not clear that he used "New Covenant" as a designation for a collection of books, although some statements approximate this.[58] "The old would be that previous giving of the law; and the new points out that manner of life according to the gospel" (*Haer.* 4.9.1). The two covenants came from the same God, a thrust against Marcion and some gnostics, and contained the highest and best laws in common (ibid. 4.12.3). In other passages Irenaeus makes more of a contrast between the covenants (ibid. 4.11.3; 4.13.1–2), and in some of these he comes closer to an identification of the new covenant with books. Thus, after quoting from 1 Cor 7, Irenaeus says the apostles "granted certain precepts in the new covenant" similar to what God did in the old covenant (ibid. 4.15.2). In speaking of the scriptures and the "difference of the covenants," he puts the "Mosaic law and the grace of the new covenant" together as both suited to their respective times (ibid. 3.12.11–12). However, even if we could be sure that Irenaeus was associating books with the new covenant, that does not make New Covenant a title for the books.

No uncertainty attaches to the use by writers after Irenaeus of Old and New Covenants as titles for collections of books. Clement of Alexandria says, "In both Covenants mention is made of the righteous" (*Strom.* 5.6.38), and "It is preached and spoken by the Old and New Covenant" (ibid. 5.13.85). He quotes Matt 5:27–28 as "the voice of the Lord in the New Covenant" (ibid. 3.11.71). The "ecclesiastical rule," as stated by Clement, is "the concord and harmony of the Law and the Prophets with the Covenant delivered at the

---

[56] Denis Farkasfalvy, " 'Prophets and Apostles': The Conjunction of the Two Terms before Irenaeus," in *Texts and Testaments: Critical Essays on the Bible and Early Church Fathers* (ed. W. Eugene March; San Antonio: Trinity University Press, 1980), 109–34, at 120.

[57] Wolfram Kinzig ("*Kainē diathēkē*: The Title of the New Testament in the Second and Third Centuries," *JTS* n.s. 45 [1994]: 519–44; repr. in *Norms of Faith and Life* [Recent Studies in Early Christianity 3; ed. E. Ferguson; New York: Garland, 1999], 59–84) provides more references. See note 87 for the use of the terminology in the Montanist controversy.

[58] See E. Ferguson, "The Covenant Idea in the Second Century," in *Texts and Testaments: Critical Essays on the Bible and Early Church Fathers* (ed. W. Eugene March; San Antonio: Trinity University Press, 1980), 144–48 (on Irenaeus), and 150–51 (on Covenant as a title for books).

coming of the Lord" (ibid. 6.15).[59] Tertullian's Latin gave "testament" *(testamentum)* as the equivalent to covenant in western European languages. His usual word for the scriptures was *instrumentum,*[60] and he used this word also for "covenant," but he recognized that "testament" was the common Christian term: "each Instrument, or Testament, as it is more usual to call it" (*Marc.* 4.1).[61] He referred to written passages in the Old Testament and New Testament in confirmation of his views on the Trinity (*Prax.* 15), and quotes prohibitions issued by Paul and Jesus in the "New Testament" (*Pud.* 6.5).[62] These passages make it likely that Tertullian, in the context of discussing the two dispensations of the Law and the Gospel, is using New Testament of a collection of books when he writes, "The New Testament is made very concise and is disentangled from the intricate burdens of the Law" (*Marc.* 4.1).

Hippolytus, likening the church to a ship, compared its tillers to "the two testaments" (*Antichr.* 59). The statement is not unambiguous between "agreements" or "written records" of the agreements, but the latter is more likely, especially in view of the usage of his predecessors and contemporaries. For him "holy scriptures" included books that we know as Old Testament and New Testament.[63] Cyprian a few years later used the terminology of "old and new," without the word "covenant," in reference to the scriptures: "As you examine more fully the scriptures, old and new, and read through the complete volumes of the spiritual books" (*Test.* pref.).

Origen followed common Christian usage by designating the two parts of scripture as "Old and New Covenants," but his philological training made him recognize the novelty of this usage, so he spoke of "the divine scriptures of the so-called Old and New Covenant" (*Princ.* 4.1.1).[64] When Eusebius spoke of "covenantal" writings (*Hist. eccl.* 3.3.3), he was not coining a new term for what was not yet called the canon, but making an adjective of the title that had been in use for at least a century for those books that we now call the canon. If there was a name for a collection of books as the New Covenant (Testament),

---

[59] For Clement's use of "covenant" language see Ferguson, "The Covenant Idea," 151, 152–54, and Kinzig, "The Title of the New Testament," 529.

[60] E.g., *Apol.* 21.1; *Res.* 21.1; 33.1; 39.8; 40.1; *Herm.* 19; 20; *Praescr.* 38.8; *Marc.* 4.2; 4.6.7. Especially notable is *Pud.* 10 where he notes that the *Shepherd* had failed to find a place in the *divino instrumento* ("divine Instrument"), the scriptures.

[61] Ferguson, "The Covenant Idea," 148–50, and Kinzig, "The Title of the New Testament," 529–30, 536–41. Kinzig suggests that it was Marcion who usually called his Bible *testamentum* (539–40).

[62] *Pud.* 1.5 refers to the judgments in "each Testament" and *Jejun.* 15 contrasts the teachings of the "Old Testament" and "New."

[63] "Whatever things, then, the holy scriptures declare, at these let us look" (*Noet.* 9), and in the following exposition he quotes not only from the Prophets and Psalms but also from Acts (specifically identified as scripture: 13, 14), John, Matthew, and Revelation.

[64] The same qualification occurs in *Comm. Jo.* 5.8; also for the Old Testament in *Or.* 22.1, and even for covenant in reference to God's agreements (*Mart.* 12). Kinzig ("The Title of the New Testament," 530–32, 543) attributes the reluctance to the Marcionite origin of the terminology (I understand "unaware of [the title's] origin" in his statement to be a misprint for "aware"), but Origen's qualification "so-called" even for "agreements" may reflect the common Hellenistic usage for "last will and testament." For Origen's distinction between the Old and New Testaments see also *Princ.* 3.1.16; *Comm. Jo.* 1.4–5 (where he includes Acts and the Epistles in "Gospel"); *Comm. Matt.* 10.12 ("Old and New Scriptures").

there must have been some recognizable entity to which this name referred, and it must have been set over against another body of writings known as "Old Testament."[65]

Whatever internal factors provided the motive for the recognition of a canon, what external factors hastened the process and sharpened the definition of the canon?

2. External Influences

Many of the debates in the postapostolic church were over the question of where to find the authentic voice of revelation and authentic Christianity. The church's struggle with false teaching and the consequent definition of the boundaries of right belief carried with them the recognition of certain books as the source of authentic teaching.

A. Marcion

The conflict with Marcion takes pride of place in the history of the formation of a canon of scriptures. Marcion had the first collection of authoritative Christian writings of which we are aware. Because of this, many ascribe the idea of a New Testament canon to him,[66] but others doubt this claim.[67] This claim is possible only by not recognizing the authority that New Testament books already had in the church. The letters of Paul were already collected by Marcion's time; the four gospels were written, in circulation, and perhaps already being brought together. The new contribution of Marcion, as far as available evidence goes, was to bring a gospel (Luke) and the letters of Paul into one collection. His introduction to this collection, the *Antitheses,* set forth the contrast between the Old Testament and the Gospel, a contrast that makes plausible the suggestion that Marcion was the one who first gave the designation Old Covenant and New Covenant to bodies of writings.[68] However, his explicit rejection of the Old Testament as Christian scripture raises doubts about this suggestion.

Marcion's combination of the Gospel and the Apostle is often seen as the impetus for his opponents to begin the process of bringing together more gospels and other writings, notably the Acts and perhaps some of the General Epistles, as a counterweight to his exclusive Paulinism. This was not the way his opponents saw the situation. Perhaps, writing from a later time, they saw the situation from the perspective of that later time, but the historian should allow for the possibility that they recorded what had been the reaction from an earlier time. What the early church remembered about Marcion, and repeatedly criticized him for, was his rejection of the God of the Old Testament, not a putative role in

---

[65] Kinzig, "The Title of the New Testament," 536.

[66] Adolf von Harnack, *The Origin of the New Testament and the Most Important Consequences of the New Creation* (London: Williams and Norgate, 1925); John Knox, *Marcion and the New Testament* (Chicago: University of Chicago Press, 1942).

[67] Barton (*The Letter and the Spirit,* 35–62) refutes Harnack's thesis that Marcion created the idea of the Christian canon and also its more plausible modified version, that Marcion expedited the process of canonization.

[68] See notes 57 and 64. Tertullian said, "The whole aim . . . of his *Antitheses* centers in establishing a diversity between the Old and New Testaments" (*Marc.* 4.6).

creating the New Testament.[69] Memories are not always accurate or complete, but the collective consciousness shows what was thought to be important.

The criticism of Marcion included his limiting the Gospel to Luke alone and revising the letters of Paul. Irenaeus had this to say on the subject:

> Marcion [besides abolishing the prophets and the law] mutilates the Gospel that is according to Luke. . . . He likewise persuaded his disciples that he himself was more worthy of credit than are those apostles who have handed down the Gospel to us, furnishing his followers not with the Gospel but merely a fragment of it. In like manner, too, he dismembered the letters of Paul. (*Haer.* 1.27.2)

Most of our detailed knowledge of Marcion's position comes from Tertullian's refutation.

> Marcion ought to be called to a strict account concerning these other Gospels [he has mentioned John, Matthew, and Mark] also, for having omitted them, and insisted in preference on Luke; as if they, too, had not had free course in the churches as well as Luke's Gospel from the beginning. (*Marc.* 4.5)

He elsewhere says:

> Since Marcion separated the New Testament from the Old, he is necessarily subsequent to that which he separated, inasmuch as it was only in his power to separate what was previously united. Having been united previous to its separation, the fact of its subsequent separation proves the subsequence also of the man who effected the separation. (*Praescr.* 30)

With reference to Paul, Tertullian criticizes Marcion for giving the title of Laodiceans to Ephesians, against the church's true tradition. He then dismisses the significance of all such titles with a statement that clearly reflects a longstanding "canonical" authority for Paul's letters: "In writing to a certain church the apostle did in fact write to all" (*Marc.* 5.17.1),[70] since he was a divine spokesman.

In the context of his statement about the four gospels, quoted earlier, Irenaeus noted the preference of various false teachers for one gospel:

> So firm is the ground upon which these Gospels rest that the very heretics themselves bear witness to them, and starting from them, each endeavors to establish his own peculiar doctrine. For the Ebionites . . . use Matthew's Gospel . . . ; Marcion mutilates that according to Luke . . . ; those who separate Jesus from Christ [Docetists] . . . prefer the Gospel by Mark . . . ; those who follow Valentinus make copious use of that according to John. . . . (*Haer.* 3.11.7)

The idea of having only one, or one principal, gospel had great appeal. That may have been behind Tatian's production of the *Diatessaron,* to retain the material from each of the four gospels, but to make explicit that they tell one story.

Justin Martyr tells us that he wrote against Marcion and other heretics (*1 Apol.* 26; cf. 58). The treatise was not preserved, whether from accident, from limitations in its argument, or from the taking up of what was of value in later refutations. If the last, may the argument against a narrowing down of the apostolic witness have also been affirmed by Justin? Was

---

[69] Barton, *The Spirit and the Letter,* 56. Irenaeus, *Haer.* 1.27.2; 4.38.1–5; Tertullian, *Praescr.* 30; 38.
[70] Cf. *Mur. Frg.* lines 41–59.

Marcion's use of only Luke a factor in Justin compiling collections of the teachings of Jesus from both Luke and Matthew? At any rate, it is clear that Tertullian was not the first to realize that there was a problem with Marcion's Bible and try to answer his claims. The classic statements of a position and (negatively) the classic responses usually come a generation or two later as an outgrowth of preliminary debates. Tertullian was a highly original thinker and writer, but the main issues were defined well before him by such as Justin and Irenaeus.

At any rate, the four-gospel canon, for whatever difficulties it may give theologians, was seen as a defense against heresy.[71] Moreover, it is a great boon to the historian to have multiple witnesses to the life of Jesus and to the Christian story. Not only the four-gospel canon and the addition of some of the other non-Pauline writings but the whole New Testament as a unified collection of writings may go back to the Marcionite crisis; so argues a significant new study by David Trobisch.[72]

Instead of taking the usual history of theology approach of tracing the development by examining literary sources, Trobisch argues that the proper approach is to examine the history of the Christian Bible as a book. The four oldest manuscripts of the New Testament—Sinaiticus, Vaticanus, Alexandrinus, and Ephraemi Rescriptus—are from the fourth and fifth centuries. Each manuscript is independent of the others, but their agreement in extent and order of contents means we must assume a common archetype.[73] The external identifying characteristics of the witnesses to the text of the Christian Bible—the types of abbreviation of the *nomina sacra,* use of the codex, a common pattern of names for the individual books ("Gospel according to . . . "; "General Epistle of . . . "; "Epistle of Paul to . . ."), and a uniform name for the two parts of the whole collection ("New Testament" and "Old Testament")—all go back to the earliest stage of transmission. They show the work of a single redactor who produced the canonical edition of the New Testament as part of a total Christian scripture.[74] The internal contents show an interest in unity and a harmonizing feature, between Paul and Peter and between Paul and the Jerusalem apostles. These features fit the time of the Marcionite conflict, and the inclusion of the Synoptic Gospels together with the Gospel of John suggest the context of the Easter controversy, when differences in custom were accepted as not inconsistent with the one faith. These considerations point to the middle of the second century at the latest for the production of the canonical edition of the Bible.[75] Trobisch does not venture a specific place, person, or circle where this edition originated, but its widespread acceptance in the Christian world at the end of the second century and beginning of the third attests its success in

---

[71] Oscar Cullmann, "Die Pluralität der Evangelien als theologisches Problem im Altertum: Eine dogmengeschichtliche Studie," *TZ* 1 (1945): 23–42, repr. as "The Plurality of the Gospels As a Theological Problem in Antiquity: A Study in the History of Dogma," in *The Early Church* (ed. Oscar Cullmann; London: SCM, 1956), 39–54; Helmut Merkel, *Die Pluralität der Evangelien als theologisches und exegetisches Problem in der Alten Kirche* (Bern: Lang, 1978), has a collection of texts.

[72] David Trobisch, *Die Endredaktion des Neuen Testaments: Eine Untersuchung zur Entstehung der christlichen Bibel* (Freiburg: Universitätsverlag; Göttingen: Vandenhoeck & Ruprecht, 1996), 122–23, 158. See also the recently published English version of this volume in idem, *The First Edition of the New Testament* (Oxford: Oxford University Press, 2000).

[73] Trobisch, *Endredaktion,* 35–39, 54, 58.

[74] Ibid., 16–35, 58–71.

[75] Ibid., 124, 158–99.

orthodox circles. The independent literary attestation for the use of some General Epistles is not as strong as for the other writings by the mid-second century, and the degree of uniformity in the order of books in the manuscript tradition may be exaggerated by Trobisch; but the uniform manuscript features and the way in which Trobisch ties the contents of the collection together support his overall thesis of a discrete circle that brought the individual writings together in a literary unity.[76] He asks if the early church's discussion about the authenticity of individual writings does not indicate a reaction to a completed book, rather than stages on the way to the collecting of a book.[77]

B. Gnostic Teachers

By the time of Marcion some of the early "gnostic" teachers were active. The charge was lodged against some gnostics of enlarging the canon to include more books than the great church recognized. Irenaeus contrasted the approach of Marcion and the Valentinians:

> Marcion, rejecting the entire Gospel, yea rather, cutting himself off from the Gospel, boasts that he has part in the Gospel. . . . Those who are from Valentinus, being, on the other hand, altogether reckless, while they put forth their own compositions, boast that they possess more Gospels than there really are. Indeed, they have arrived at such a pitch of audacity as to entitle their comparatively recent writing "the Gospel of Truth," though it agrees in nothing with the Gospels of the apostles. (*Haer.* 3.11.9)

He mentions the *Gospel of Truth,* which he contrasts with the gospels "handed down from the apostles" that he classifies as "scriptures." In more summary fashion, however, he says that apart from Marcion and his followers, who mutilate the scriptures, "all the rest, inflated with the false name of 'knowledge,' do certainly recognize the scriptures, but they pervert the interpretations" (*Haer.* 3.12.12). Tertullian too contrasted Marcion's reductionism with what he considered Valentinus's expansion of the gospel material:

> Of the scriptures we have our being before there was any other way, before they were interpolated by [heretics]. . . . One man perverts the scriptures with his hand, another their meaning by his exposition. For although Valentinus seems to use the entire volume, he has nonetheless laid violent hands on the truth only with a more cunning mind and skill than Marcion. Marcion expressly and openly used the knife, not the pen, since he made such an excision of the scriptures as suited his own subject-matter. Valentinus, however, abstained from such excision, because he did not invent scriptures to square with his own subject-matter . . . and yet he took away more, and added more, by removing the proper meaning of every particular word. . . . (*Praescr.* 38)

Tertullian's argument presupposes an entity that he calls the "Christian scriptures" (37) and "our scriptures" (38). The Old Testament is not the subject of this discussion. In

---

[76] Ibid., 11–16.

[77] Ibid., 57. The situation may be parallel to the discussions of the Jewish rabbis concerning Ecclesiastes, Song of Solomon (*Yadaim* 3.5) and Esther (*b. Meg.* 7a). They were not considering whether certain books should be admitted to the collection of holy writings, but why they had these books. Cf. Barton, *The Spirit and the Letter,* 108–31, for a plausible explanation of the rabbinic discussions. See also Barton's and Gamble's contributions to this volume for alternative explanations of the influence of Marcion on the origins of the New Testament canon.

passing, we note that Valentinus was using "the whole volume," so there must have been an identifiable body of Christian writings that could be treated as a single book *(integro instrumento)*. Valentinus achieved his purposes by the pen, by reinterpretation, but Marcion by the knife, by excision.

The gnostics provide some of the earliest testimony to the authority of New Testament writings. Some of them employ terminology in their titles from the usage of other Christians *(Gospel of Truth, Gospel of Philip)*, but the significant element to be noted is the wide acquaintance with and use of documents now considered canonical. The way in which the *Gospel of Truth*, for example, draws on language and gives a "gnosticizing" interpretation seems to imply a recognition of authoritative scripture.[78] The somewhat later *Gospel of Philip* uses citation formulas to introduce quotations from New Testament books.[79] Early gnostic teachers offered their own interpretations of New Testament books. Basilides (c. 117–138) quotes the gospels of Matthew, Luke, and John, and Paul's letters (Romans, 1 and 2 Corinthians, and Ephesians) as scripture, and wrote exegeses of the Gospel.[80] He is our earliest full witness to the New Testament as scripture, but the offhand way he speaks shows that he was not the first to do this and was reflecting common usage. Lloyd Patterson has concluded that the unity of scripture that Irenaeus found in the history of salvation was not his discovery but was expressed by the Valentinians. Irenaeus took over the pattern of the Valentinian interpretation but gave it a different content.[81] It seems possible to push the argument further back: The Valentinians could not have cited and used scripture the way they did unless the scriptures read and honored in the church had already won recognition as Christian scriptures. The use of the scriptures in a different way from that of the church forced an examination of scripture as a whole, as is done by Irenaeus (see further below). The first commentary on a New Testament book was by the Valentinian Heracleon, on the Gospel of John. Since gnostics had their own writings, presumably they would not have used New Testament books unless a consensus of earlier usage constrained them.

This constraint, of course, was not felt by those groups further removed from catholic Christianity, but for those closer to the orthodox, such as the Valentinians, the issue was not so much one of which scripture as of the interpretation of scripture, as the quotations from Irenaeus and Tertullian above indicate. Is there a plan within scripture (the rule of truth)[82] by which scripture is to be interpreted, or does one bring a plan from outside

---

[78] W. C. Van Unnik ("The 'Gospel of Truth' and the New Testament," in *The Jung Codex: A Newly Recovered Gnostic Papyrus* [ed. F. L. Cross; London: A. R. Mowbray, 1955], 81–129, esp. 108–26) finds acquaintance with the Gospels, Pauline Epistles, Hebrews, and Revelation, and traces of Acts, 1 Peter, and 1 John, used in such a manner that proves they had authority for the author and had enjoyed that authority for a considerable time.

[79] William J. Stroud, "New Testament Quotations in the Nag Hammadi Gospel of Philip," in *SBLSP* (Atlanta: Scholars Press, 1990), 68–81.

[80] Robert M. Grant, *The Formation of the New Testament* (New York: Harper & Row, 1965), 121–24.

[81] L. G. Patterson, "Irenaeus and the Valentinians: The Emergence of the Christian Scriptures," *StPatr* 18.3 (1989): 189–20.

[82] Valdemar Ammundsen, "The Rule of Truth in Irenaeus," *JTS* 13 (1912): 574–80; repr. in *Orthodoxy, Heresy, and Schism in Early Christianity* (Studies in Early Christianity 4; ed. E. Ferguson; New York: Garland, 1993), 138–44.

scripture and rearrange its contents to fit that plan? Irenaeus and the orthodox said there was a plan or plot within scripture itself. It is all the more significant that this plot derived from placing the Christian sources of authority alongside the Old Testament. Irenaeus, after identifying the triple authority of prophets, Lord, and apostles as "scriptures," used a graphic illustration from mosaic art to describe the situation:

> Such, then, is their [disciples of Ptolemaeus] system, which neither the prophets announced, nor the Lord taught, nor the apostles delivered, but . . . they gather their views from reading non-scriptural writings . . . , while they endeavor to adapt with an air of probability to their own peculiar assertions the parables of the Lord, the sayings of the prophets, and the words of the apostles in order that their scheme may not seem altogether without support. In doing so, however, they disregard the order and the connection *[taxis kai heimon]* of the scriptures, and so far as in them lies, dismember and destroy the truth. . . . Their manner of acting is just as if one, when a beautiful image of a king has been constructed by some skillful artist out of precious jewels, should then take this likeness of the man all to pieces, should rearrange the gems and so fit them together as to make them into the form of a dog or of a fox and even that but poorly executed; and should then maintain and declare that this was the beautiful image of the king that the skillful artist constructed pointing to the jewels that had been admirably fitted together by the first artist to form the image of the king but have been with bad effect transferred by the latter one to the shape of a dog, and by thus exhibiting the jewels should deceive the ignorant who had no conception what a king's form was like and persuade them that the miserable likeness of the fox was in fact the beautiful image of the king. (*Haer.* 1.8.1)

The scriptures must have been regarded as a sacred book for these gnostics to have used them in this way or have felt that they had to find their doctrine in them. Moreover, for Irenaeus there was already an established "order and connection" that was violated by the Valentinian interpretation.

Tertullian in his *Prescription against Heretics* disagrees concerning who has the right to interpret the scriptures.

> They [heretics] treat of the scriptures and recommend their opinions out of the scriptures. To be sure, they do. From what other source could they derive arguments concerning the things of the faith, except from the records of the faith? (ch. 14).

He denies this right to the heretics because the scriptures belong to the catholic Christians (ch. 15; 19). He charged Valentinus with tampering with the scriptures "by his different expositions and acknowledged emendations" (*Praescr.* 30).

The gnostic controversy made imperative a clarification of what writings accurately expressed apostolic teaching and apostolic authority. Against the secret tradition claimed by certain gnostic Christians, Irenaeus appealed to the public teaching of the churches. This included the teaching of the scriptures, as can be seen by Irenaeus's refutation in Books 3–5 of *Adversus haereses*. Irenaeus is recognized as the first orthodox Christian author whose works argue from scripture as a whole. After setting forth the views of the heretics (book 1) and giving a rational refutation (book 2), he declares that he will devote a special book to the "scriptures of the Lord" (2.35.4), referring to the immediately mentioned preaching and teaching of the apostles, Lord, prophets, and law. As he begins to adduce "proofs from the scriptures" (3 *praef.*), he appeals to the gospel first proclaimed in public and "at a later period by the will of God handed down to us in the scriptures to be the ground and pillar of our faith" (3.1).[83] He starts with the Old Testament (3.6) but then quickly turns to the gospels of Matthew (3.9), Luke (3.10.1–4), Mark (3.10.5), and John (3.11.1–6). He finds the doctrine of the "other apostles" in the book of Acts: Peter (3.12.1–7), Philip (3.12.8), Paul (3.12.9), Stephen (3.12.10), the letter of the apostles in Acts 15 (3.12.14), and Paul again (3.13–15). From the witness of the apostles in book 3, Irenaeus turns in book 4 primarily to "the words of the Lord," supplemented from the prophets and Paul.[84] The eschatological treatment in book 5 makes much use of Revelation (esp. 5.34–36).

C. Montanism

The principal criticism of Montanism concerned its manner of ecstatic prophesying.[85] The church affirmed in principle that prophecy continued in the church but found examples lacking as time went on. In regard to the Montanists, the church felt their claims did not measure up to scriptural standards. The standard by which to judge authentic prophesy was found in scripture, the New Testament as well as the Old Testament. We could wish to be able to identify the source used by Epiphanius in his description of Montanism, which critical opinion puts in the second or third century.[86] The author judges Montanist prophecy false when compared with "the prophecies which exist in truth and came to be in truth in the Old and New Testaments."[87] The earliest evidence is not unambiguous on how the Montanists related their prophecies to the New Testament. Did they supplement or interpret it? Their opponent Apollonius at the end of the second century says of a Montanist confessor named Themiso that he "composed a general epistle [katholikēn epistolēn] in imitation of the apostle," but there seems no claim of "scriptural" authority intended.[88] Another opponent of about the same time, Gaius in Rome, is described by Eusebius as "curbing the rashness and daring of [the Montanists] in composing new scriptures" (Hist. eccl. 6.20.3), but how much does this wording depend on Eusebius? The question may turn on what was acknowledged theoretically and what functioned practically in regard to authority. In the early third century Hippolytus characterized the Montanists as saying that "They have learned something more through them [Montanus, Priscilla, Maximilla] than from the Law and the Prophets and the Gospels"

---

[83] Bernard Sesboüé ("La preuve par les Ecritures chez S. Irénée: A propos d'un texte difficile du Livre III de l'Adversus haereses," NRTh 103 [1981]: 872–87), in examining Haer. 3.5.1 concludes that by "scriptures" Irenaeus primarily means the Old Testament, although he did regard the New Testament as scripture.

[84] For the unity of book 4 see Philippe Bacq, De l'ancienne à la nouvelle alliance selon S. Irénée: Unité du livre IV de l'Adversus haereses (Paris: Lethielleux, 1978), usefully summarized by Mary Ann Donovan, "Irenaeus in Recent Scholarship," SecCent 4 (1984): 219–41, at 221–23.

[85] Ronald E. Heine, The Montanist Oracles and Testimonia (Macon: Mercer University Press, 1989).

[86] See the comments on earlier study by Heine, Montanist Oracles, x.

[87] Epiphanius, Pan. 48.3.2. Cf. the Anonymous quoted by Eusebius, "They will not be able to prove that any prophet either of those in the Old Testament or the New was inspired in this [ecstatic] way" (Hist. eccl. 5.17.3).

[88] Quoted by Eusebius, Hist. eccl. 5.18.5.

(*Haer.* 8.19).[89] And so the Montanists came to be criticized also for expanding the realm of revelation beyond the apostolic age. The Pseudo-Tertullian charges, "They say that the Paraclete said more in Montanus than Christ revealed in the Gospel, and they say he has said not only more, but things that are better and greater" (*Adv. omn. haer.* 7).

The opponents of Montanism, therefore, expressed the conviction that the period of revelation had ended. There may be a question about referring the statements to written records, but they seem to be included in what the anonymous author quoted by Eusebius said.

> For a very long and considerable time, dear Avircius Marcellus, you have enjoined me to compose a treatise against the heresy of those who follow Miltiades. I was rather hesitant until now, not because I lacked the ability to refute the lie and bear testimony to the truth, but from fear and concern lest in any way I appear to some to add a new writing or add to the word of the new covenant of the gospel to which one who has chosen to live according to the gospel itself can neither add nor subtract. (*Hist. eccl.* 5.16.3)

The unknown author's profession of modesty is a conceit, but he may have chosen to express the literary convention of modesty in the way that he did because the Montanist oracles were adding "to the new covenant" and were being collected in writing. Van Unnik was correct to withdraw this passage as a witness to a completed New Testament to which nothing could be added or taken away, but he was right to see in it a connection of the new covenant with writings that recorded it.[90] Such is implicit in the Anonymous's professed reason for his reluctance to write, and the wording is pointless unless the "new covenant of the gospel" was now to be found in writings. Elsewhere, he speaks of "Old and New Testaments,"[91] possibly eras of time but also possibly collections of writings.

The Montanist controversy brought to the surface a consciousness that the time of revelation had ended and that there was a qualitative difference between the era of church's origins and the present. These developments had definite implications for the recognition of a canon of scripture. Henning Paulsen has argued that the aspects of "normativity, exclusiveness, and fixed interpretation," which emerged in the Montanist controversy, "when taken together mark the meaning of Montanism for the formation of the New Testament canon."[92] One could understand this as making explicit what was latent in the tradition and faith of the church.

D. Persecution and Martyrdom

Marcionites, Montanists, and mainstream Christians knew the experience of martyrdom. Little attention has been paid to the factor of persecution in the history of the

---

[89] Cf. *Haer.* 10.25, "They go astray by paying more attention to their [Montanus, Priscilla, and Maximilla] words than to the Gospels when they appoint new and unusual fasts."

[90] He argued for this passage as a witness to a fixed corpus of writings in "De la règle *mēte prostheinai mēte aphelein* dans l'histoire du canon," *VC* 3 (1949): 1–36; in "*Hē kainē diathēkē:* A Problem in the Early History of the Canon," *StPatr* 4 (1961): 212–27, he concludes that it refers rather to the total message, but he does suggest that the Anonymous was the first to link the name "New Testament" with a collection of books.

[91] See n. 87 above.

[92] "Die Bedeutung des Montanismus für die Herausbildung des Kanons," *VC* 32 (1978): 19–52, esp. 43 and 52.

canon, but William R. Farmer has called attention to how suitable the New Testament canon was for strengthening Christians facing martyrdom.[93] The four canonical gospels witnessed to the real flesh and blood martyrdom of the Son of God; the letters of Paul witnessed to the same gospel, told of Paul's sufferings, and set the cross of Jesus as a norm for Christian conduct; the Acts of the Apostles told of the triumphant sufferings of the early church; Revelation held out the hope of victory in the face of suffering and martyrdom; and other letters (especially 1 Peter and 1 John) set the humanity and sufferings of Jesus at the center of faith.

By the time of the Diocletianic persecution in 303 Roman authorities, in their campaign to confiscate Christian property, included the requirement that Christian books be handed in and burned. In the words of Eusebius, "We saw with our very eyes . . . the inspired and sacred scriptures committed to the flames in the marketplaces" in response to the imperial letter "ordering the destruction by fire of the scriptures" (*Hist. eccl.* 8.2.1 and 4). The requirement showed that the authorities knew Christians had an identifiable set of holy writings and knew their importance to the Christian communities.[94] Hierocles, governor of Bithynia and the chief promoter of the persecution, knew the Christian Bible, and had already attempted in two books against the Christians "to prove the falsehood of sacred scripture," by which was meant Christian sacred writings, as the reference to Paul and Peter makes clear.[95] Christians themselves thought they had an identifiable set of scriptures, for they immediately experienced a moral dilemma over giving up documents to the authorities, an issue that became the occasion for the Donatist schism. Christians might hide writings, try to pass off apocryphal and heretical texts, or in some cases debate what to hand over and what not to, but for the most part they knew what books the soldiers were looking for.

Particularly impressive is the size of the library of the church in Cirta, capital of Numidia in North Africa. The chief official asked that the "writings of the law [the Christian 'law'?] and anything else you have here" be brought out. The subdeacon Catullinus surrendered "one very large codex" (a text of the Gospels?) but explained that the lectors possessed most of the books. The authorities then searched the homes of seven lectors with the command to give up the "scriptures" and found thirty-six more books of varying size.[96] We are not told the contents of these volumes. However, it may be noted that according to Augustine, the Donatist schismatics, who arose out of conflicts resulting from different responses to the command to hand over scriptures, had no different canon from the Catholic churches of North Africa.[97]

---

[93] William R. Farmer and Denis M. Farkasfalvy, *The Formation of the New Testament Canon* (New York: Paulist, 1983), 22–26, 31–43, 55–56; on the canon of the Martyrs of Gaul (Eusebius, *Hist. eccl.* 5.1–2), see further Denis M. Farkasfalvy, "Christological Content and Its Biblical Basis in the Letter of the Martyrs of Gaul," *SecCent* 9 (1992): 5–25; repr. in *Christianity in Relation to Jews, Greeks, and Romans* (Recent Studies in Early Christianity 2; ed. E. Ferguson; New York: Garland, 1999), 279–99.

[94] Gamble, *Books and Readers,* 144–50.

[95] Lactantius, *Inst.* 5.2.

[96] *Gesta apud Zenophilum* (ET in O. R. Vassall-Philipps, *The Work of St. Optatus against the Donatists* [London: Longmans, Green, 1917]), 353, 355–58, for this information.

[97] *Cresc.* 1.37; cf. the definition of these in *Unit. eccles.* 19.51: "The canonical scriptures of the Law and the Prophets to which are added the Gospels, the Apostolic Epistles, the Acts of the Apostles, and the Apocalypse of John."

E. After Constantine

When the situation reversed under Constantine, the Roman government financed the multiplication of copies of scriptures instead of destroying them. Constantine directed Eusebius to have prepared for the churches in Constantinople fifty copies "of the sacred scriptures which you know to be especially necessary for the restoration and use in the instruction of the church."[98] Eusebius says his prompt fulfillment of the request was acknowledged by letter from Constantine (*Vit. Const.* 4.37). Constantine knew there was such an entity as the Christian scriptures, required for public reading in the new churches being built in Constantinople, and certain books were copied and others left out. Constantine's commission did not require that Christians decide what the contents of scripture were; it was intended to replace those copies of the scriptures destroyed in the persecution. In complying with Constantine's request, Eusebius was not allowed the nuance of his historical groupings; books were either copied or not.

What did Eusebius include? From his *Church History* 3.25.1–7 we learn what Eusebius concluded to be the "acknowledged" *(homologoumenai)* or "covenantal" *(endia-thēkai)* writings (the two terms are used synonymously) in the churches. These were twenty-two books, lacking James, 2 Peter, 2–3 John, and Jude from the present canon. Following the literary criticism of the time, Eusebius had three categories: acknowledged, disputed, and spurious books.[99] Within the "disputed" books *(antilegomenai)* he distinguished those that met the criteria of deriving from apostolic times and authorship by apostles or apostolic men from other works that, although not being "spurious" *(nothoi)*, did not. Eusebius's own canon (his word for what we call the canon was "covenantal"[100]) included the church's acknowledged books, with the exception of Revelation,[101] plus the writings from the "disputed" group that he accepted as apostolic.[102] Eusebius's canon was essentially what he found in Origen.[103] Origen while at Alexandria had doubted 2 Peter,

---

[98] Eusebius, *Vit. Const.* 4.36; cf. 4.34, "providing copies of the sacred oracles."

[99] Armin D. Baum, "Der neutestamentliche Kanon bei Eusebios (*Hist. eccl.* III, 25, 1–7) im Kontext seiner literaturgeschichtlichen Arbeit," *ETL* 73 (1997): 307–48. His thesis is that these categories employed by Eusebius were taken over from Greek criticism of authenticity (321). The latter two terms were not equivalent (337–38). For Eusebius genuine apostolic writings were "canonical" (315), but the list of candidates for canonicity included also writings from the apostolic epoch (316, 326–27). Eusebius had three criteria for grading the church's reception of writings, and all three had to be met for a writing to be "covenantal": use by church writers, evaluation by church writers, and public reading in church (328–33). Writings were classified as spurious on the basis of style and content (335–37).

[100] A. D. Baum, "Der neutestamentliche Kanon bei Eusebios," 333–34.

[101] Clementina Mazzucco ("Eusèbe de Césarée et l'*Apocalypse de Jean*," *StPatr* 17.1 [1982]: 317–24) refers to Eusebius's abundant use of Revelation outside the *Church History* and argues that Eusebius objected to an apocalyptic/eschatological interpretation of the book, not an allegorical or historical use of it. He applied its apocalyptic elements to the coming of Christ, the destruction of Jerusalem, and the persecutions of Diocletian and Galerius. His political understanding of the Roman empire precluded an apocalyptic interpretation of a millennial reign on earth after Jesus came again.

[102] Baum, "Der neutestamentliche Kanon bei Eusebios," 333–34 (for the church's canon); 341–42 (for Eusebius's canon).

[103] *Hist. eccl.* 6.25.3–14; Origen, *Comm. Jo.* 1.4–6; 5.3; Eusebius also cites the *Comm. Matt.* and the *Fr. Heb.* Baum, "Der neutestamentliche Kanon bei Eusebios," 322.

2–3 John, James, and Jude, the same books Eusebius listed as "disputed." Apparently during his stay in Caesarea these doubts were removed, for his writings from this later time include these books in the "scriptures."[104] Moreover, Origen believed the writing of scripture had ceased, and regarded its contents as "complete."[105] Presumably Eusebius would have had copied his twenty-six book New Testament in addition to the Septuagint.[106] That may help account for the numerous Greek lists of the scriptures that correspond to our New Testament but lack Revelation.

Our investigation has uncovered much information without reference to the Muratorian Canon. Trobisch quotes Hans Lietzmann to the effect that the document is "a kind of introduction to the New Testament."[107] As a corollary of that perspective, it presupposes a canon rather than seeking to establish one.

David Brakke studies external factors in Athanasius's famous *Festal Letter* 39 for the year 367, which first uses "canonized" *(kanonizomena)* for the scriptures and lists an explicitly closed New Testament canon of twenty-seven books.[108] He argues that Athanasius's disputes with Arians and Melitians reflected "fundamental conflicts between competing modes of Christian authority, spirituality, and social organization."[109] The bishop of Alexandria was not trying to impose a canon where one was lacking, or to close a canon that others preferred to leave open. Rather the conflict was "between two competing and distinct canon types."[110] Athanasius contends for an authoritative canon that functions in connection with an episcopally organized Christianity in order to restrain and control both an "academic" Christianity based on the authority of independent teachers, whose canon was not precise, and an "enthusiastic," "martyr" Christianity that drew inspiration from "apocryphal" books. Such may accurately describe the social context that prompted Athanasius to provide his list of canonical books for the Egyptian churches without depriving Athanasius of a significant place as a witness to a consensus that had long been emerging in the churches.

The councils of the church played little part in the canonization of scripture. When councils did speak on the subject, their voice was a ratification of what had already become

---

[104] William Gary Oliver, "Origen and the New Testament Canon," *ResQ* 31 (1989): 13–26, citing Origen, *Hom. Exod.* 13.2 and *Hom. Josh.* 7.1. For Origen's New Testament canon, see also Otto Bardenhewer, *Geschichte der altkirchlichen Literatur* (Freiburg: Herder, 1914), 2:152–56, who defends the reliability of Rufinus's translation of Origen's passages on the canon. Everett R. Kalin, "Re-examining New Testament Canon History: 1. The Canon of Origen," *CurTM* 17 (1990): 274–82, by defining canon as a closed list, denies that Origen had a New Testament canon list. He asserts rightly that Eusebius has compiled a list from Origen's writings, but his position on Origen's "canon" depends on discrediting Rufinus's translation of *Hom. Josh.* 7.1 and not considering the sequence of Origen's writings and the possibility that Origen changed his views.

[105] *Hom. Jes. Nav.* 7.1 and *Comm. Matt.* 10.12. Cf. the end of his Prologue to the *Comm. Cant.*, where Prov. 22:28, "Do not remove the ancient landmark that your ancestors set up," is quoted in support of not giving a place to apocryphal writings.

[106] Baum, "Der neutestamentliche Kanon bei Eusebios," 342–44.

[107] Trobisch, *Endredaktion*, 57, n. 149, citing H. Lietzmann, *Wie wurden die Bücher des Neuen Testaments heilige Schrift? Fünf Vorträge* (Tübingen: Mohr [Siebeck], 1907), 53.

[108] David Brakke, "Canon Formation and Social Conflict in Fourth-Century Egypt: Athanasius of Alexandria's Thirty-Ninth *Festal Letter*," *HTR* 87 (1994): 395–419.

[109] Ibid., 399.

[110] Ibid., 409.

the mind of the church.[111] Canon 60 of the Council of Laodicea (c. 363 C.E.) is likely a later insertion into the decrees of the council; it lists a twenty-six book New Testament, lacking Revelation. The first councils certainly to speak on the subject of the canon were in North Africa: Hippo (393) and Carthage (397 and 419). They were under the influence of Augustine, who regarded the canon as closed: "For the canon of the sacred writings, which is properly closed" (*Civ.* 22.8).[112]

---

[111] Bruce Metzger, *The Canon of the New Testament: Its Origin, Development, and Significance* (Oxford: Clarendon, 1987), 237–38; F. F. Bruce, *The Canon of Scripture* (Downers Grove, Ill.: InterVarsity, 1988), 97.

[112] His New Testament list, our twenty-seven, is in *Doctr. chr.* 2.8.13.

19

Reflections on Jesus and the New Testament Canon

William R. Farmer

These reflections are occasioned by the fact that on this side of the Atlantic, within certain circles of those interested in the problem of the "historical Jesus," a call for reconsidering which books to include in the "canon" has been raised. I have in mind specifically the proposal that certain books now included in the New Testament canon be excluded (for example, the book of Revelation) and that certain books not now included in the canon be included (for example, the *Gospel of Thomas*).

While one can disagree with these specific proposals, I rejoice that there are well-trained New Testament scholars like Professor Robert Funk who have the courage to make such daring proposals, because a serious consideration of these concrete recommendations provides an opportunity to reflect on how our New Testament canon came into being and what purpose it serves. In the long run, only good can come from such reflection. I am convinced that the specific proposals to eliminate the book of Revelation and add the *Gospel of Thomas* to the New Testament canon represent a comprehensive misunderstanding of what "canon" means and how canon functions among those who accept it. However, the opportunity to "reason together," as Isaiah encourages us to do, is to me irresistible, especially when we are dealing with serious proposals made by highly competent New Testament scholars. The following reflections represent my openness to engage in a critical dialogue with Robert Funk, though they are intended to be more than that. They are intended to expedite an overall discussion of canon by enlarging on what has already been written on what I term the archaic phase, the beginnings of the canon.

1. The Question in Context

My discussion of the archaic phase of the development of the New Testament canon may be found in largely the same words in *Jesus and the Gospel: Tradition, Scripture, and*

A few days after receiving Professor Farmer's chapter for this volume, the editors received news that Dr. Farmer ("Bill") had passed away. His death leaves a significant gap in New Testament scholarship and therefore we appreciate all the more this chapter as his final contribution to biblical scholarship. —The Editors

[1] William R. Farmer, *Jesus and the Gospel: Tradition, Scripture and Canon* (Philadelphia: Fortress, 1982), 227–37; William R. Farmer and Denis Farkasfalvy, O. Cist., *The Formation of the New Testament Canon: An Ecumenical Approach* (ed. with preface by Harold W. Attridge; intr. by Albert C. Outler; New York: Paulist, 1983), 48–56.

Canon and in *The Formation of the New Testament Canon: An Ecumenical Approach.*[1] In the latter version, in the opening paragraph of what is entitled "The Fundamentals of the Christian Canon" (changed from "The Protology of the Christian Canon" in the original version), I asked: "What are the underlying factors which led to the developed textual appearance of the New Testament?" I went on to say: "We ask not about the deeper and wider theological matters like faith in the God of Israel and belief in the saving benefits of the death of Jesus Christ. We focus rather on the earliest relation of 'Scripture' to these primal matters of faith and belief." Today, seventeen years later, I find it necessary to go beyond what I have previously written, and to begin to reflect exactly on "the deeper and wider theological matters like faith in the God of Israel" and *especially* on "belief in the saving benefits of the death of Jesus Christ."

It is not that I wish to make fundamental changes in what I wrote seventeen years ago. I simply recognize now the need to supplement and complement what I then wrote, for what I wrote then does not probe deeply enough into the "fundamentals" of the matter. My earlier writing did not do full justice to the history of Christian origins, and I have since learned much about biblical interpretation, or the discipline of hermeneutics.

Some historical problems are so complicated that a great deal of imagination is required even to sort out where to begin and how to organize the material. The topic of canon is such a problem.

The literary genre of "reflection" tolerates a fuller use of our powers of imagination, so long as these are disciplined by history and verifiable by experience. Hence the title of this essay. This allows me to bring before historians all kinds of new and interesting information that I think can fruitfully be brought to bear as we embark on this effort to reorient the discussion of canon in our time. We seek to reorient it in a way that will do more justice to the facts at hand and will stimulate us to work together to advance the discussion.[2]

We can begin by noting that there is a great deal of talking past one another at present in the field of New Testament criticism as it is practiced in the English-speaking part of the North Atlantic community. This follows quite naturally from the fact that the present discussion of canon is still in its infancy. We have not yet reached agreement on such fundamental matters as the meaning of terms. Different scholars use the word "canon" with different meanings.

Under these circumstances, where we cannot even presuppose that we all accept the same definition of the word "canon," the best way to proceed, in my opinion, is to help the reader understand why the topic of "canon" is so diffuse and charged with potential misunderstanding, especially when we begin to discuss concrete proposals like adding or dropping books from the New Testament.

Scholarship sometimes obscures the origins and meaning of the New Testament canon by failing to draw appropriate lines of contact between the church's New Testament

---

[2] As an example of a book that I believe could benefit from the kind of reorientation called for in this essay, I would like to mention Lee M. McDonald's valuable textbook, *The Formation of the Christian Biblical Canon* (rev. and enl. ed.; foreword by Helmut Koester; Peabody, Mass.: Hendrickson. 1995). Professor Koester points us in the right direction when he asks: "Why were these twenty-seven writings included and others excluded? How did these writings function in nourishing and building Christian communities, and why were other writings found lacking? What were the competing forces in the formation of the early Christian churches, and what roles did various writings claiming 'apostolicity' play in these controversies?" (xii).

and what the church believes God has done in the life, ministry, death, and resurrection of Jesus. Undoubtedly, the story of Jesus—what he did and said, the church's understanding of his fate, and who they believed he was—was at the heart of what was normative for early Christianity. If this is so, we should expect to uncover relevant connections between Jesus and the church's New Testament canon.

In my reflections, however, I do not intend to deal with specific questions concerning particular books, like the question of why the book of Revelation must remain in the canon or why the *Gospel of Thomas* is not to be introduced into it. Rather I would like to outline some basic presuppositions which must form the basis for any such decision, basic criteria which determined the concept of canon in the formative period of Christianity. I propose to reflect on the following three topics:

Paul's use of *kanōn*. What can we learn from reflection on the earliest use of *kanōn* in Christian literature, Gal 6:16, where the apostle Paul focuses on that "new creation" which flows from "the cross of our Lord Jesus Christ"? And what is the relation of this *kanōn* to the rule that Paul refers to in Gal 2:5 as "the truth of the gospel"? We note that Paul appeals to this norm in both his dispute with the false brethren who secretly slipped into the meeting he had with Peter, James, and John fourteen years after his meeting with Peter referred to in Gal 1:18, and in his dispute with Barnabas and the other Jews who acted insincerely following Peter's withdrawal from table fellowship with Gentile Christians in Antioch (Gal 2:14).

Num 25:1–13. What can we learn about "canon" from reflecting on this passage in Numbers that will help us understand the pre-Christian Paul who persecuted the church of God and ravished its "faith"? This pre-Pauline "faith" is the faith that Paul ended up preaching. This is important because it was "practice" *in accord with* this "faith" that was at issue in Paul's controversy with the false brethren over the "truth of the gospel," and likewise later in Antioch when Barnabas and the "rest of the Jews" acted insincerely in their failure to walk in a straightforward manner *(orthopodousin)* in face of Peter's withdrawal from table fellowship with Gentile Christians.

Jesus of Nazareth. What can we learn about canon from reflection on certain well-attested words and actions of Jesus within the context of his life situation, as illumined by our best historical sources?

2. Paul's Use of *Kanōn*

Near the conclusion of his letter to the Galatians Paul wrote as follows:

> See with what large letters I am writing to you with my own hand. It is those who want to make a good showing in the flesh that would compel you to be circumcised, and only in order that they may not be persecuted for the cross of Christ. For even those who receive circumcision do not themselves keep the law, but they desire to have you circumcised that they may glory in your flesh. But far be it from me to glory except in the cross of our Lord Jesus Christ, by which the world has been crucified to me, and I to the world. For neither circumcision counts for anything, nor uncircumcision, but a new creation. Peace and mercy be upon all who walk by this rule *(kanōn),* upon the Israel of God. (Gal 6:11–16)

The immediate context of Paul's use of *kanōn* makes it clear that the *kanōn* of which he writes is a particular rule by which those who belong to the "Israel of God" walk. The implication would seem to be that those who do not walk in accordance with this rule, walk by some other rule, or by no rule at all. The only other rule Paul mentions in this context is the rule of "keeping the law." Paul's point is that those who are troubling the Galatians are acting hypocritically, for while they compel the Galatians to be circumcised in accordance with the rule of keeping the law, they themselves do not follow this rule.

Earlier in chapter six Paul exhorts the Galatians to "Bear one another's burdens, and so fulfill the 'law of Christ' " (v. 2). In context it is clear that "the law of Christ" is the law of love. By way of contrast those who are troubling the Galatians are seeking to fulfill the law of Moses in a manner that, in the situation of the Galatians, works against the law of love. In truth, asserts Paul, they seek to glory in "the flesh" of those they compel to be circumcised. Paul, by way of contrast, writes: "But far be it from me to glory except in the cross of our Lord Jesus Christ, by which the world has been crucified to me, and I to the world. For neither circumcision counts for anything, nor uncircumcision, but a new creation" (vv. 14–15).

The immediate antecedent of *kanōn* in v. 16 is "a new creation." In context, however, it is a new creation which flows from "the cross of our Lord Jesus Christ," by which the world has been crucified to Paul, and Paul to the world (v. 14).

In context it is clear that the rule which the Israel of God is expected to observe is a rule that connects with the redemptive death of Christ on the cross. This "cross of Christ" is not something that is empty of meaning or power. It is the life-changing cross by which the world was crucified to Paul, and Paul to the world (v. 14).

Earlier in his letter to the Galatians, Paul recounted what happened at Antioch. Peter had drawn back from table fellowship and separated himself from the Gentile Christians; and the rest of the Jews present, including even Paul's close associate Barnabas, were not straightforward about the "truth of the gospel." Paul reports his response to Peter in the presence of everyone:

> We ourselves, who are Jews by birth and not Gentile sinners, yet who know that a man is not justified by works of the law but through faith in Jesus Christ, even we have believed in Christ Jesus, in order to be justified by faith in Christ, and not by works of the law, because by works of the law shall no one be justified. I have been crucified with Christ; it is no longer I who live, but Christ who lives in me; and the life I now live in the flesh I live by faith in the Son of God, who loved me and gave himself for me. (Gal 2:15–20)

This faith in the Son of God of which Paul speaks—as he makes his confession before Peter and everyone present, at the meeting in Antioch where the truth of the gospel was at stake—is grounded in his belief in the redemptive death of Christ for the sins of all, including Paul. Christ "loved me and gave himself for me"—"and for you too, Peter," he might have added. This much is clear from what Paul nails to the masthead of his greetings to the church of Galatia: "Grace to you and peace from God the Father and our Lord Jesus Christ, *who gave himself for our sins...*" (Gal 1:3).

From whence, it must be asked, did Paul draw the conclusion, or from whom did Paul accept as true, that Jesus Christ "gave himself for our sins"? If we can trace this confession to its original source we will not be far from identifying the norm of Christian faith, i.e., what later Christian writers like Irenaeus, Clement of Alexandria, Tertullian, and Origen had in mind when they spoke of the "rule of faith" or the "rule of the church" or the

---

[3] Cf. William R. Farmer, "Galatians and the Second Century Development of the *Regula Fidei*," *SecCent* 4, 3 (Fall 1984): 143–70. The research undergirding this article is basic to the reorientation recommended in this essay.

"rule of truth."[3] Western theologians, Protestant and Catholics alike, use the term "regula." But this is simply the Latin translation of the Greek term *kanōn*.

We started our reflection on "Paul's use of *kanōn*" by asking what we can learn from the earliest use of *kanōn* in Christian literature, found in Gal 6:16. Step by step we have been led to the conclusion that, as used by Paul, *kanōn* is bound up with a set of pregnant concepts that are all central to our understanding of Christian faith.

This set of theological concepts includes: "the new creation," "the cross of our Lord Jesus Christ," "the truth of the gospel," "the law of Christ," and, not least important, the confession that "Jesus Christ gave himself for our sins."

There is no simple or direct way to synthesize all these powerful concepts. But the congruence of the concept "the cross of our Lord Jesus Christ" with the confession that "Jesus Christ gave himself for our sins" is an obvious place to begin seeking for theological convergence between the various members of this family of theological concepts, and to continue our search for an answer to our question: "From whence did Paul or some theological predecessor(s) draw the conclusion that Jesus Christ 'gave himself for our sins'?"

Are there other texts in Paul's letters that throw light on this question and may help explain the meaning of *kanōn* for Paul? The answer is yes, there are at least two additional texts that invite further reflection. The first is found in Paul's Epistle to the Romans:

> Therefore, since we are justified by faith, we have peace with God through our Lord Jesus Christ. Through him we have obtained access to this grace in which we stand, and we rejoice in our hope of sharing the glory of God. More than that, we rejoice in our sufferings, knowing that suffering produces endurance, and endurance produces character, and character produces hope and hope does not disappoint us, because God's love has been poured into our hearts through the Holy Spirit which has been given to us.

> While we were still weak, at the right time Christ died for the ungodly. Why, one will hardly die for a righteous man—though perhaps for a good man one will dare even to die. But God shows his love for us in that while we were yet sinners Christ died for us. (Rom 5:1–8)

The first point to note is that the love of the Son of God which led him to give himself for Paul in Gal 2:20 is grounded in the love of God which reaches us through the redemptive death of Christ for our sins in Rom 5:8. And the Lord Jesus Christ who gave himself for our sins in Gal 2:4 is the same Christ who died for us while we were yet sinners in Rom 5:8.

The second point to note is that Christ's death for us "while we were yet sinners" gives to his death a meaning that can be distinguished from the heroic death of pagan martyrs who sacrificially laid down their lives out of love for their city or for some other noble reason. As Paul says: "perhaps for a good man one will dare even to die." But Christ died in the place of those who, because of their transgressions, were the least worthy of such a sacrifice. Such a death cries out for some explanation. What is the source of such astonishing love?

In answer to this question we turn to the second text that calls for further reflection. This is found in Paul's First Letter to the Corinthians.

> Now I would remind you, brethren, in what terms I preached to you the gospel, which you received, in which you stand, by which you are saved, if you hold it fast—unless you believed in vain.

For I delivered to you as of first importance what I also received, that Christ died for our sins in accordance with the scriptures, that he was buried, that he was raised on the third day in accordance with the scriptures, and that he appeared to Cephas, then to the twelve. Then he appeared to more than five hundred brethren at one time, most of whom are still alive, though some have fallen asleep. Then he appeared to James, then to all the apostles. Last of all, as to one untimely born, he appeared also to me. For I am the least of the apostles, unfit to be called an apostle, because I persecuted the church of God. But by the grace of God I am what I am, and his grace toward me was not in vain. On the contrary, I worked harder than any of them, though it was not I, but the grace of God which is with me. Whether then it was I or they, so we preached and so you believed. (1 Cor 15:1–11)

First we should note that when Paul writes: "Now I would remind you, brethren, in what terms I preached to you the gospel . . . by which you are saved—provided of course you hold it fast," he is saying in effect that *the gospel* the Corinthians received from Paul, if they hold it fast—i.e., abide by it as their rule *(kanōn)*—is *the gospel* by which they are saved. Within this context we can see that for Paul *the gospel*, in effect, *functions as a norm* for those who believe (15:2). This is to say that *the gospel* is the believer's rule *(kanōn)*. The apostle Paul insists that what is of first importance is the message he received and has delivered to the Corinthians, that *"Christ died for our sins* in accordance with the scriptures." To say that something is "of first importance" in this context is tantamount to saying that it is "normative," i.e., "canonical."

In the light of this exegesis, we can see the connection between *kanōn* as the "new creation" flowing from the "cross of Christ" (Gal 6:14–16) and the gospel Paul preached (1 Cor 15:1). The connection is the "good news" that "Christ died for our sins" (1 Cor 15:1–3; see also Rom 5:8, Gal 1:4).

But once again we ask the question: "What is the source of this astonishing teaching that 'Christ died for our sins'?" What Paul has written suggests that we search the *scriptures, not*, it must be noted, *Hellenistic literature*, which records the heroic sacrificial deaths of brave men who laid down their lives in defense of noble causes. Paul writes: "For I delivered to you as of first importance what I also received, that Christ died for our sins *in accordance with the scriptures*."

Note also that Paul does not say that we can find the teaching that "Christ died for our sins" *in* the scriptures. He puts the matter differently, he states that: "Christ died for our sins *in accordance with* the scriptures" (15:3).[4] To what scriptures could Paul have been referring? Presumably he has in mind certain of those time-honored sacred writings which were studied and read in the temple and in the synagogues.

But Paul is writing to the church in Corinth, to Hellenistic believers who read their scriptures in the Septuagint, i.e., in Greek translation. It happens that there is a certain scripture in the Septuagint not found in Hebrew, which Paul knows well. It is the Wisdom of Solomon, generally believed to have been composed in Alexandria in the first century before the birth of Christ. Paul appears to know this book. In the Wisdom of Solomon we read:

[4] Failure to make this distinction can lead to confusion. For example, one might conclude that because Isaiah does not say explicitly that the Servant of the Lord "died for our sins," Isa 53 was not one of the scriptures Paul had in mind in 1 Cor 15:3, or that because Jesus nowhere in the Gospels directly cites Isa 53:10, it must have had no importance for his ministry.

Let us lay a trap for the righteous man,
because he is inconvenient to us, and opposes our action;
he reproaches us for sins against the law . . .
He professes to have knowledge of God,
and calls himself a servant of the Lord . . .
He calls the final end of the righteous blessed,
and boasts that God is his father.
Let us see if his words are true,
let us test what will happen at the end of his life;
for if the righteous man is God's son, He will help him,
and will deliver him from the hand of his adversaries.
Let us test him with insult and torture,
that we may find our how gentle he is,
and make trial of his forbearance.
Let us condemn him to a shameful death,
for according to what he says, he will be protected. (Wis 2:12–20)

No doubt Paul read this text with great interest, for there is much in it that accords with what we otherwise know about Jesus. Certainly the words "let us condemn him to a *shameful* death" would have caught Paul's attention, as they catch our attention, for to die by crucifixion was certainly a shameful death. So Paul may have had this text in mind as one of the scriptures to which he refers in 1 Cor 15:3. And yet the Wisdom of Solomon lacks explicit reference to the death of this righteous Son of God as redemptive, as being a death for us, least of all a death for our sins.

Another scripture Paul may have had in mind is Ps 22. There a faithful son of Israel cries out to God in words that we might expect from a faithful Israelite who was undergoing maltreatment at the hands of his enemies. It is more than possible, though by no means certain, that the Apostle Paul would have read this text christologically. And in the light of his having formerly persecuted the church of God violently, we are permitted to imagine that if Paul read these words of the psalmist as the words of Jesus Christ spoken from the cross, they could have elicited tears of remorse. And yet, as with the text from the Wisdom of Solomon, nowhere in the text of this psalm is there any reference to redemptive suffering. There is not the slightest suggestion of the afflicted Israelite undergoing his afflictions on our behalf, for our sins.

But with our third text the situation is different. Here we draw near to the scriptural source of the gospel that saves us: the good news that Christ died for our sins.

How beautiful upon the mountain
are the feet of him who brings *good news,*
who publishes peace, who brings *good news* of good.
who publishes salvation,
who says to Zion, "Your God has become King." . . .
Behold, my servant shall prosper,[5]
he shall be exalted and lifted up,
and shall be very high. . . .
Who has believed what we have heard?

---

[5] Or "shall understand."

And to whom has the arm of the Lord been revealed?
For he grew up before the Lord like a young plant,
and like a root out of dry ground;
he had no form or comeliness that
we should look at him,
and no beauty that we should desire him.
He was despised and rejected by men;
a man of sorrows, and acquainted with grief;
and as one from whom men hide their faces
he was despised, and we esteemed him not.
Surely he has borne our griefs
and carried our sorrows;
Yet we accounted him stricken
smitten by God, and afflicted.
But he was wounded for our transgressions,
he was bruised for our iniquities;
upon him was the chastisement that made us whole,
and with his blood drawn by the whip we are healed.
All we like lost sheep have gone astray;
we have turned everyone to his own way;
and the Lord has laid on him the iniquity of us all.
He was oppressed, and he was afflicted,
yet he opened not his mouth;
like a lamb that is led to the slaughter,
and like a sheep that before its shearers is dumb,
so he opened not his mouth.
By oppression and judgment he was taken away;
and as for his generation, who considered that
he was cut off *out of the land of the living,*
stricken for the transgression of my people?
And they made his grave with the wicked,
his tomb with evil doers;
although he had done no violence,
and there was no deceit in his mouth.
Yet it was the will of the Lord to crush him with pain;
he was put to grief;
So that, *although he makes himself a guilt-offering* [or *an offering for sin* (ʾāšām)],
he shall see his offspring, he shall prolong his life;
the will of the *Lord shall prosper in his hand.*
The fruit of his suffering shall he see.
In knowing himself to be *righteous he shall be satisfied;*
My servant shall bring righteousness to many,
and *he himself shall bear their guilt.*
Therefore I will divide him a portion with the great,
and with the strong shall he share the spoil;
Because *he poured out his life blood to the utmost,*
and was numbered with the transgressors,
Yet *he himself bore the sins of many,*
and made intercession for the transgressors. (Isa 52:7–53:12)

Once we focus our attention on the italicized portions of this most remarkable text it becomes clear that no other text comes so readily and so deservedly to mind when we ask: "What scriptures are in Paul's mind when he writes: 'I delivered to you as of first importance what I also received, that Christ died for our sins in accordance with the scriptures'"? Clearly in v. 10 we have the vocabulary of sacrifice used, "an offering for sin" (*ʾāšām* in Hebrew).

Any reasonable doubt that this text from Isaiah was of importance to Paul is removed by thoughtful examination of what Paul writes in Rom 4:25.[6] Romans 3 is an even more important text grounding Paul's christology in Isa 53:

> Now we know that whatever the law says it speaks to those who are under the law, so that every mouth may be stopped, and the whole world may be held accountable to God. For no human being will be justified in his sight by works of the law, since through the law comes knowledge of sin.

> But now the righteousness of God has been manifested apart from the law, although the law and the prophets bear witness to it, the righteousness of God through faith in Jesus Christ for all who believe. For there is no distinction; since all have sinned and fall short of the glory of God, they are justified by his grace as a gift, through the redemption which is in Christ Jesus. For God showed him publicly dying as a *sacrifice of reconciliation* [or *as an expiation by his blood, hilastērion*], to be received by faith. This was to show God's righteousness, because in his divine forbearance he had passed over former sins; it was to prove at the present time that he himself is righteous and that he justifies him who has faith in Jesus. (Rom 3:19–26)

The only place in scripture where a messianic figure is set forth as a sacrifice of reconciliation, propitiation, or atonement in close relation to God's divine forbearance in passing over former sins (*hilastērion*, Rom 3:25), is Isa 53:10–12. It should not surprise us, therefore, that Paul writes: "But now the righteousness of God has been manifested apart from the law—and the law and the *prophets* bear witness to it. . . ." For Isaiah is certainly among the prophets that bear witness to this theological manifesto of Paul, and Isa 53:10–12 provides the linchpin for the theological norm that undergirds Paul's argument.[7]

3. Phinehas and Baal of Peor (Num 25:1–18)

In order to understand the basic theological argument presupposed in the "faith" Paul preached, we need to have a firm grasp of the theological tradition which undergirded his resolute and sometimes violent persecution of the church, motivating him to attack the "faith" of the apostles that gave birth to and inspired this church. To this end we

---

[6] So concludes Morna Hooker in her discussion of this passage in her essay, "Did the Use of Isaiah 53 to Interpret His Mission Begin with Jesus?" in *Jesus and the Suffering Servant: Isaiah 53 and Christian Origins* (ed. William H. Bellinger Jr. and William R. Farmer; Trinity Press International, 1998), 101–3. The fact that in 1 Cor 15:1–3 Paul makes it clear that the tradition he had *delivered* to the Corinthians was a tradition he had *received*, calls into question the suggestion of Professor Hooker that the use of Isa 53 to interpret the Mission of Jesus may have begun "with Paul" (103). This possibility appears to be ruled out by the fact that the tradition Paul received that "Christ died for our sins in accordance with the scriptures" was a *pre*-Pauline tradition. We must at least go behind Paul, the persecutor of the church, to the apostolic "faith" of that church to account for this pre-Pauline doctrine (Gal 2:23).

[7] "He makes himself an offering for sin" (53:10); "he himself bore the sins of many" (53:12).

need to focus our attention on a much neglected text: Num 25:1–18. We need to know what happened at Baal Peor that could lead the Jewish historian, Jacob Milgrom, to give this event in Israel's history such a prominent place. Milgrom has written: "Baal Peor came to be etched into the collective memory [of Israel] as a nadir in Israel's history."[8]

It is important to follow this story carefully as it is told by the author of Numbers, for while this text has been excised from the collective memory of the church, it remains the unexpressed premise of Paul's pre-Christian faith and therefore is quite essential for understanding Paul's *kanōn* of the "*new* creation." Numbers 25 provided the *kanōn* of Paul's pre-Christian faith. On the other hand, the opposite theological paradigm found in Isa 53, was the *kanōn* of the truly revolutionary faith of the church which at first Paul persecuted violently, but subsequently began to preach. As we read this text of Numbers we are being initiated into the mystery of how the New Testament canon came into being and why such proposals as those of Funk to omit Revelation and add *Thomas* are comprehensively "wide of the mark."

> While Israel dwelt in Shittim the people began to play the harlot with the daughters of Moab. They invited the people to the sacrifices of their gods, and the people ate, and bowed down to their gods. Thus Israel yoked himself to Baal of Peor, and the anger [and jealousy] of the Lord was kindled against Israel; and the Lord said to Moses, "Take all the chiefs of the people, and hang them in the sun before the Lord, that the fierce anger of the Lord may turn away from Israel." And Moses said to the judges of Israel, "Everyone of you slay his men who have yoked themselves to Baal of Peor."

> And behold, one of the people of Israel came and brought a Midianite woman to [the tent of] his family, in the sight of Moses and in the sight of the whole congregation of the people of Israel, while they were weeping at the door of the tent of meeting. When Phinehas the son of Eleazar, son of Aaron the priest saw it, he rose and left the congregation and took a spear in his hand and went after the man of Israel into the inner room [of his family tent], and pierced both of them, the man of Israel and the woman, through her body. Thus the plague was stayed from the people of Israel. . . .

> And the Lord said to Moses, "Phinehas the son of Eleazar, son of Aaron the priest, has turned back my wrath from the people of Israel, in that he was jealous with my jealousy among them, so that I did not consume the people of Israel in my jealousy. Therefore, say, 'Behold, I give to him my covenant of peace; and it shall be with him, and to his descendants after him, the covenant of a perpetual priesthood, because he was jealous for his God, and made atonement for the people of Israel.'"

The Hebrew text of Numbers at the point where we read "and made atonement" reads *wayĕkappēr*. The noun concerned is transliterated *kippur*. Phinehas's *kippur*-execution carried out in behalf of Israel (Num. 25:12) is directly connected with the laudation: he "turned back my wrath from the Israelites."[9]

In the Septuagint version of this text, verse 13 can be translated: "It shall be for him [i.e., Phinehas] and his descendants after him, a covenant of priesthood for all time, because he took impassioned action [was jealous] for his God, thus making expiation or atonement [*hilastērion*] for the Israelites."

---

[8] As evidence for this judgment, Milgrom provides three additional references: Deut 4:3, Hos 9:10, and Ps 106:28; *The JPS Torah Commentary* (Philadelphia/New York: Jewish Publication Society, 1990), 480.

[9] Ibid. See Milgrom, *JPS Torah Commentary,* 370.

The point is that God is propitiated or appeased by action that demonstrates respect for his dignity and honor. When anyone is shown disrespect, propitiation is in order. Otherwise human relations will spiral downward and lead to acrimony and even murder. There is nothing unnatural or unworthy of God in this understanding of the text. When propitiation appears *not* to be required, e.g., when faith in God's grace alone is believed to be sufficient to restore a right relationship between the sinner and God, *that* is what seems unnatural, *that* is what is offensive in the light of God's eternal covenant with Phinehas in response to Phinehas's jealous action of propitiation.

In taking action against the church, Paul put himself in God's place and executed God's wrath against the transgressors. This propitiated or appeased God and turned away his anger against Israel. In this way of looking at his persecution of the church of the apostles we can see that in Paul's own eyes he saw himself as making atonement for the people of Israel. How utterly wrong he came to see he was, on this point, comes to expression in his subsequent confession: "I am the least of the apostles, unfit to be called an apostle, because I persecuted the church of God" (1 Cor 15:9). This helps us understand how it was possible that Paul, a Pharisee of the Pharisees, out of zeal for God's jealousy, could persecute the church and attack its "faith." It also helps explain how he could later, through the redemptive death of Christ, be so radically changed that his victims "glorified God" in him (Gal 1:24) and the Jerusalem apostles extended to him the right hand of fellowship and agreed to entrust the apostolic mission to the Gentiles into his hands.

The heart of the matter is this: the atonement wrought by Phinehas came through the shedding of the blood of the transgressor by the righteous, whereas the atonement wrought by Christ came through the shedding of the blood of the righteous by the transgressors.

Josephus tells the story of some zealous Jews who caught a Roman soldier off guard and forcibly circumcised him. Why? They believed they were following the example of Phinehas, i.e., living in accord with the eternal covenant God gave to Phinehas. The message was: obey the law of Moses or get out of the holy land God has promised to Israel. The later rabbis laid down increasingly restrictive conditions under which "zealots" could appeal to the example of Phinehas for their "atoning" acts. Eventually in rabbinic Judaism the watchword of "shalom" replaced "zeal for the law."

But Paul and Jesus lived in the prerabbinic period, when "zeal for the law" was normative in the land of Israel, at least in the eyes of those we might call "right-wing" Pharisees.[10]

Into this world of conflict between the imperial power of Rome, and varied messianic hopes of Israel, Jesus of Nazareth was born. There was no norm in the scriptures by which God could fulfill his universal promise to save the nations, spoken of by the prophet Isaiah, except that set forth in Isa 53. If the nations were to be saved, it would not be by the sword, in contrast both to the Roman gospel of peace and prosperity and the competing message of hope grounded in the eternal covenant of Phinehas, but by the atoning sacrifice of God's servant people led by his Anointed.

---

[10] For the basic research that undergirds what is said about "zeal for the law," and Jewish history in general in this essay, see: William R. Farmer, "The Patriarch Phineas," *Anglican Theological Review* (January 1952): 26–30; idem, "The Palm Branches in John 12:13," *JTS* (April 1952): 62–66; idem, *Maccabees, Zealots and Josephus: An Inquiry into Jewish Nationalism in the Greco-Roman Period* (New York: Columbia University Press, 1956, repr. Westport, Conn.: Greenwood Press, 1973).

For Israel the example of Phinehas needed to be replaced by another no less passionate model, and that is exactly what happened. But it did not happen without an atoning sacrifice of infinitely greater power. The story continues.

4. Jesus of Nazareth

Jesus grew up in Nazareth, a small village roughly four miles south of Sepphoris which in his own day was being rebuilt as the capital city of the Roman principality ruled by Herod Antipas. Within the living memory of the parents of children with whom Jesus grew up, countless young Jewish men had been crucified in suppressions of uprisings against Roman hegemony in that very region. One of these suppressions took place *while* Jesus was growing up!

In Wales in the nineteenth century boys were often given the names of earlier Welsh patriots who had risen up against the oppressive rule of the "British empire." So it has often been. This explains why, according to the histories of the Jews written by the Jewish historian Flavius Josephus, so many of those young men who rose up against the authorities following the Roman general Pompey's takeover of the temple in Jerusalem in 63 B.C.E. bear names of earlier patriots who rose up against Seleucid oppressors in the days of the Maccabees. Mattathias, who led the revolt against the Seleucids, had five sons, Judas, Eleazar, Simon, John and Jonathan. These are the names of the Maccabees. Miriam, the name Jesus' mother bore, was that of a much-admired Maccabean princess.

At first the Maccabees had the Romans as their allies in a common struggle against the Seleucids. In a period of national expansion while allied with Rome, the Maccabees (or Hasmoneans, as the descendants of the Maccabees came to be called) protected their expanding northern borders by sending patriotic Jewish families from Judea to settle at strategic places in Galilee. These Galilean families of Judean origin never forgot their ties to the glorious days of the Maccabees.

So after Pompey and his successors took over control of Palestine, the hatred their Maccabean forefathers had borne against the oppressive Seleucids was easily transferred to the new oppressors: the Romans. And so, as the rule of the Romans became more oppressive, young men revolted against their neo-Philistine oppressors, just as young men had revolted against Seleucid rule in the days of the Maccabees.

More often than not the leaders of these Jewish revolts against Roman rule bore Maccabean names.[11] These were not the only popular names at the time. Joshua and Joseph were popular as well. Still, it is striking how many of those close to Jesus bore Maccabean names: his mother Miriam, his cousin John, his disciples Matthew, John, Judas, Simon called Peter, and Simon the Cananaean.

Why are we laboring this point? This data indicates a close cultural connection between the social circles in which Jesus moved with ease and effectiveness and a particular tradition of Judean history going back several generations to the days of the Maccabees.

What can we say about this heritage? Fortunately, a court historian of the Hasmoneans composed a history of the circumstances surrounding the Maccabean revolt against

---

[11] See the evidence as set forth by William R. Farmer in "Judas, Simon and Athronger," *New Testament Studies* (January 1958): 147–55.

the Seleucids. His remarkable account, which is found in 1 Macc 1–2, documents the essential respects in which the socioreligious situation of Israel in Judea in the time of the Maccabees resembled the time of the infamous apostasy of Israelites at Baal Peor in Moab. It also shows that the example of Phinehas (mentioned by name in 1 Macc 1:26, where Mattathias strikes down an Israelite who comes forward to sacrifice in accordance with the command of Antiochus, and again along with other biblical heroes in the last words of Mattathias in 2:54) was recognized as normative.

This provides an important scriptural connection between the zeal for the law of God that motivated Paul to ravish the "faith" of the church of God in his day and the zeal for the jealousy of God that motivated Phinehas to slay a fellow member of the covenant of Moses along with his Moabite consort at Baal Peor. The main difference is that between the time of the composition of Numbers and the Hasmonean account of what happened at Modin in Judea, Ezra and Nehemiah had promulgated the law as the *written norm*, i.e., the written canon, for Israel. From the time of the Maccabees forward to the days of Jesus and Paul a central issue for Israel was what governing authority to accord to this written account of the law of Moses. Some Jews were more strict in insisting on adherence to the jot and tittle of the law than were others. But what united all Jews was some measure of adherence to the law of God as embodied in the Mosaic written law. For many righteous Jews it was the *Pharisees* who sat in Moses' seat. So when Paul describes himself as a Pharisee of the Pharisees, he was confessing that he was, as a persecutor of the church, enforcing a very strict interpretation of the law. This required him to make painful and severe public judgments. This was part of what it meant to sit in Moses' seat.

On the other hand, while Jesus taught his disciples that not a jot or a tittle of the law would pass away, he excoriated those who judged others. Just how far removed Jesus is from the world of legal discourse that justified Paul in persecuting the church can in part be measured by the relatively infrequent reference to the law in Jesus' parables.[12] The exception that proves the rule is the parable of the two men who went up into the temple to pray.[13]

These parables have been referred to by Robert Funk as absolute metaphors for God. They are indeed powerful controlling images that are serving to shape a different future for the whole human family.[14] However, one may ask whether it is necessary to juxtapose the Jesus of the parables with the Jesus of the creeds as Funk does.[15]

---

[12] The fact that references to the law occur in other traditions coming from Jesus helps to balance any conclusions that might be drawn from the fact that such references are absent from all but one of his surviving parables.

[13] Luke 18:10–14a. Even here there is no explicit reference to the Law as such.

[14] In the reconstruction that follows I have drawn from earlier studies. For a fuller account of my thinking about the historical Jesus, see: "Quest for the Historical Jesus" in *Maccabees, Zealots, and Josephus*, 186–202; "An Historical Essay on the Humanity of Jesus Christ," *Christian History and Interpretation: Studies Presented to John Knox* (ed. W. R. Farmer, C. F. D. Moule, and R. R. Niebuhr; Cambridge: Cambridge University Press, 1967), 101–26; "The Historic Jesus: God's Call to Freedom through Love," in *The International Bible Commentary* (ed. William R. Farmer, Sean McEvenue, Armando J. Levoratti, and David L. Dungan; Collegeville, Minn.: The Liturgical Press, 1998, 242–53); "Reflections upon 'The Historical Perimeters for Understanding the Aims of Jesus'," *Authenticating the Activities of Jesus* (ed. Bruce Chilton and Craig A. Evans; Leiden: Brill, 1999, 59–81).

[15] See Robert Funk, *Honest to Jesus: Jesus for a New Millenium* (San Francisco: HarperSanFrancisco, 1996), 162. On our reading, the Jesus of the parables lends theological depth and

5. Jesus and John the Baptist

Jesus saw himself in prophetic continuity with John in his commitment to the call for covenantal repentance in the face of the imminent coming of the reign of God (Matt 11:7b–19). But Jesus was in radical discontinuity with John with regard to the basis for admission into that kingdom (Matt 11:18–19). John preached righteousness according to the law (Matt 21:28–32). The ostensible cause for his death was his denunciation of immorality in high places. Jesus came to save sinners, not to condemn them. They were to love their enemies even as God does (Matt 5:43–48 // Luke 6:27–28, 32–36). They were admonished to forgive freely, from the heart (Matt 18:21–35 // Luke 17:4).

The fellowship of such a community of forgiven and forgiving sinners was poignant and joyful: "There will be more joy in heaven over one sinner who repents, than over ninety-nine righteous persons who need no repentance" (Luke 15:7 // Matt 18:13).

6. The Heart of Jesus' Message

When certain parables of Jesus are interpreted within the context of his gracious call for repentance, they serve as mirrors in which it is possible to delineate the mind of Jesus. How was one to understand the delay in the coming of the kingdom that John had pronounced to be at hand? And if one were to continue to proclaim the coming of the kingdom how should one perceive this ministry? Was the work of God to be carried out during an extension of the period of grace in the face of the coming judgment? If so, was it not reasonable to expect that, failing fruits of repentance, this period of grace would come to a sudden and just end (Luke 13:6–9)?

Certainly parables that illustrate the folly of postponing repentance (Matt 22:1–10; 25:1–12; Luke 13:6–9) and teach the wisdom of living in ready expectation of God's gracious judgment (Luke 12:35–38) probably originated in situations where such expectations had been heightened, that is, in the period of Jesus' active ministry following his baptism into the movement of John, and his own continued proclamation of the imminence of the kingdom, following the arrest and death of John.

Jesus was not intimidated by what the authorities did to John. Jesus continued to preach: "No one can serve two masters. . . . Repent, and engage in the service of God . . . for the kingdom of heaven is at hand." For Jesus to say "take up your cross and follow me" or for him to say "let the dead bury their own dead" (Matt 8:22 // Luke 9:60) was to take upon himself the full measure of messianic leadership. In such startling statements Jesus challenged others to free themselves from a paralyzing fear of human authorities. In the first saying Jesus unobtrusively clarified the question whether he was calling his disciples into a course of action where the sacrifices being risked might be greater than he himself was prepared to bear. "What will it profit [any] to gain the whole world if they lose their soul?"

---

precision to the Jesus of the creeds, and the creedal statement "suffered under Pontius Pilate" provides the Jesus of the parables a place in history, without which we will certainly fail to understand him no matter how much attention we give his parables. Jesus *is* the one who spoke the parables. But he is more than that, much much more.

(Matt 16:26). And again, "Those who would save their souls must be prepared to give their lives" (Matt 16:25 // Luke 9:24 // Mark 8:35). Such brave words staved off the disintegrating effects of news of John's imprisonment and death. Even so, such sayings do not carry one to the heart of Jesus' message.

Some scribes and Pharisees objected to Jesus' practice of eating with tax-collectors and sinners; this led to a major crisis for Jesus. Succumbing to pressure to abandon this practice would possibly have brought Jesus favor. Instead he struck at the root of the problem, that is, the self-righteousness of a scrupulous religious establishment. When legal authorities neglected justice, mercy, and faith and emphasized the minutiae of the law, Jesus represented this as the council of "blind guides" (Matt 23:23–24). Jesus himself came from a background so akin to Pharisaism as to command the respect of the Pharisees. Their anxiety over what he was doing was rooted in a perception that one of their own kind was endangering the interests of "the righteous." Jesus openly said that he did not come to call the righteous (Matt 13:9–13 // Mark 2:13–17 // Luke 5:27–32) and although he himself was known as a righteous man, in eating with sinners Jesus was using forgiveness to break down the barriers by which many of his righteous contemporaries maintained the inner group strength necessary to withstand the external pressures to compromise religious scruples.

Jesus' table fellowship with repentant tax collectors and sinners provided the nucleus of a new community. If someone has a hundred sheep and one goes astray, does that shepherd "not leave the ninety-nine in the wilderness and go after the one that is lost?" (Luke 15:3–6; cf. Matt 18:10–14). How much more will our heavenly Father rejoice over the return of one of his lost children (Luke 15:11–24), and therefore how appropriate that we celebrate the repentance of those lost children of Abraham who, once dead in trespasses, are now alive through God's merciful judgment (Luke 15:25–32; 19:1–10).

By such forceful imagery as this Jesus defended his practice of table fellowship with tax collectors and sinners. Such parables as the lost son and his elder brother (Luke 15:11–32) and the laborers in the vineyard (Matt 20:1–15) were first created in response to this crisis in Jesus' ministry. They were used to defend the gospel of God's unmerited and unconditional acceptance of the repentant sinner. Similarly the parable of the great banquet" (Matt 22:1–10; Luke 14:16–24) reminds the righteous that they have no ground for complaint over the eschatological acceptance of sinners, since they themselves have turned their back on the kingdom (cf. Matt 23:13 // Luke 11:52). God's love, so abundant for the sinner, is not lacking for the righteous. "All that is mine is yours," says the father to his elder son, "but we had to celebrate and rejoice, because this brother of yours was dead and has come to life; he was lost and has been found" (Luke 15:32).

7. The Opposition to Jesus

In spite of the cogency of Jesus' defense of the gospel of God's mercy toward repentant sinners, opposition from the religious establishment stiffened. It was in this period that Jesus formulated his woes against the "scribes and Pharisees." These utterances are uncompromising. Israel was at the crossroads. Either it followed those whom Jesus characterized as "blind guides," who hypocritically held in their hands the keys of the kingdom but neither entered themselves nor allowed others to enter (Matt 23:13), or it could follow him. Irony turns to bitter sarcasm in the judgment: "Woe to you, scribes and Pharisees, hypocrites! For you build the tombs of the prophets and decorate the graves of the righteous, and you say, 'If we had lived in the days of our ancestors, we would not have taken part with them in shedding the blood of the prophets.' Thus you testify against yourselves that you are descendants of those who murdered the prophets" (Matt 23:29–31).

A parable like the Pharisee and the tax collector in the temple (Luke 18:9–14) was designed to heal. That particular Pharisee does not represent all Pharisees, and certainly not the ideal Pharisee. But in order to make his point that goodness can become demonic and destructive when it leads good people to place themselves above others, Jesus chose a man from one of the most pious circles of Jewish society. Such people, no matter how moral, if they place their trust in their own righteousness and look down on others, go from the house of God in a wrong relationship with God, whereas sinners who place their trust in the mercy of God return home in a right relationship to God.

8. The Outcome of Opposition to Jesus

Jesus certainly challenged Pharisaic norms. As for Roman order, it too was to be challenged, if not replaced, by God's reign. Consequently the authorities eagerly sought some charge on which to get rid of Jesus. The compliance of high-priestly circles and the rest of the Jerusalem oligarchy was assured once Jesus made it clear that he called for changes not only in people's hearts but in the institutions of Zion, specifically within the temple itself (Matt 21:12–13 // Luke 19:45–46; cf. Mark 11:15–17). With the Pharisees, the high priests, and the elders of the people in concert, the Roman authorities, had they insisted on due process, could have done so only at the risk of at least a small tear in a delicately woven fabric of political collaboration. Ostensibly in the interest of maintaining Jewish law and Roman order, Jesus was executed.

Jesus taught his disciples that unless their righteousness exceeded that of the scribes and Pharisees they would never enter the kingdom of heaven (Matt 5:20), yet it can hardly be doubted that in fulfilling the "Law and the Prophets" Jesus ran afoul of the scribes and Pharisees, not only when he ate with tax collectors and sinners but in other matters as well, as for example Sabbath observance (Matt 12:1–8 // Mark 2:23–28 // Luke 6:1–5). So the die had been cast well in advance, and while by the standard of the kingdom of heaven Jesus died a righteous man, he did not go to his cross innocent of breaking the law as represented by the mores of the local populace. In the end he was crucified by the Romans as a political criminal. We can imagine the mixed feelings of anguish and relief on the part of responsible Jewish authorities. We are not in a position to know with certainty the motives of the principals who were involved in Jesus' death. Even less are we in a position to apportion guilt.

9. The Character of Jesus

In retrospect, is it possible to say something about the character of Jesus on the basis of historical inquiry? Confining our inquiry to that nucleus of sayings and actions that can be accepted as authentic, we can draw certain conclusions.

In rebuking self-righteousness and chiding those who resented God's mercy toward sinners, Jesus disclosed something about the kind of person he was. His contemporaries could understand his concern for others, and many were moved by it. They saw his friendship for tax collectors and sinners and his concern for community. This compassionate but disconcerting and revolutionary stance of Jesus was a dynamic source of redemptive power that worked against the attempt of the established world of Jewish piety to structure human existence on the exclusivistic ground of the Mosaic covenant. This source of redemptive power also provided the basis for a distinctive style of life characterized by reaching out and touching the lepers of society with love instead of judgment. It was this stance, this personal structuring and restructuring of their historical existence, this shaping of the realities of their human environment, and the faith, love, compassion, and joy associated with this creative stance that sustained and gave theological depth and direction to their community. There is more to Jesus than this, but this understanding of his public career and character carries the investigator to the heart of what is essential and enduring in Jesus. The character of Jesus is the mark he "engraved" upon his disciples, including the tax collectors and sinners admitted to his fellowship. The members of this community heard Jesus gladly and remembered his words and actions, and from their number came forth those who took responsibility for formulating and handing on such authentic sayings of Jesus as have been preserved in the Gospels.

10. The Character of Jesus' Community

The character of the community that emerged following the death and resurrection of Jesus was theologically preformed by conflicts that beset Jesus. In situations where his disciples had different degrees of success and failure, and where praise and blame based on results had led to invidious comparisons and dissension, Jesus encouraged them to think of their work as that of a sower who sows indiscriminately. Those who sow will neither be elated because of good results nor discouraged because of poor results. The results are not in their hands. The one who does the work of God is not responsible for the response others make to that work. A disciple of Jesus is responsible only for how faithfully this work is done (Matt 13:3–9).

No amount of success, either for Jesus or for his disciples, could completely overcome the anxiety of some of the faithful as the weeks and months passed and the full restoration of God's sovereign reign over Israel continued to be delayed. To meet the uncertainty that this delay caused, Jesus compared the reign of God to mustard seed and leaven to remind the disciples that great things come from small beginnings (Matt 13:31–33 // Luke 13:18–21 // Mark 4:30–32), the corollary of which would be that what is impressive and grand can be deceptive (cf. Matt 24:1–2). Jesus argued repeatedly from everyday examples that it is reasonable to be hopeful and to believe that the inbreaking of God's sovereign love into the lives of the disciples would be followed by the coming of God's kingdom. Therefore we are not to give up petitioning God; what God holds for the faithful in promise will be fulfilled, and what God has begun, God will complete (cf. Luke 18:1–8; 11:5–13; 14:28–33). Pray expectantly, believing in your hearts: "Your kingdom come. Your will be done, on earth as it is in heaven" (Matt 6:10). We are encouraged to imagine, from the way Jesus' parables can be understood within the context of his earthly career, that in ways such as these he was able to reason with the disciples over the delay in the kingdom's coming.

It appears likely that there was an additional factor compounding uncertainty over the delay of the kingdom. We ought not think that all the disciples of Jesus were equally reassured that it was correct for Jesus to eat with tax collectors and sinners. If some of them wondered whether the scribes and Pharisees might be right to insist that Jesus was making them vulnerable by his openness to the unrighteous, then it is not difficult to imagine that uncertainty among the disciples would have been compounded by this disturbing criticism from the pillars of Jewish piety. It is understandable that some of Jesus' disciples would have expressed concern over the presence of persons of questionable character within their fellowship. Jesus' parable of the wheat and the weeds (Matt 13:24–30) expresses a response to this kind of concern. This parable may be viewed as a Magna Carta for the church, for in it Jesus teaches his disciples that *God* will separate the just from the unjust (see also Matt 13:47–52). This self-understanding within Jesus' community—that is, that its members should not judge one another—is an essential mark of the church and means that the community of the church, if it is faithful to this understanding, will be inclusive of sinners as well as saints.[16] We should note that the example of Phinehas was simply *not normative* for Jesus.

This does not mean that this community will have no ethical norms. Jesus' ethical teachings must have left a deep impression on his disciples, for the church has carefully preserved these sayings among the earliest Jesus tradition alongside his parables. Later the evangelists gave these ethical teachings a prominent place in their gospels. Jesus' teaching on love of enemies (Matt 5:43–48 // Luke 6:27–28, 32–36) carries the hearer to the central core of the gospel. It has no other ground than the character of God. Because God loves God's enemies, we should love our enemies. If one takes to heart the compassionate movement of the good Samaritan to the side of the injured stranger, and the corresponding compassionate movement of the father toward his penitent son, then the great liberating power of the gospel can begin to work among us.

Jesus *did* teach his disciples to love their enemies. Any reconstruction that stumbles on that fact will not stand up to criticism. God is love, and this love should be the source of a movement of compassion, of servanthood, of risk-taking for the sake of the other—a divine movement from the privileged position of strength and power to the side of the weak and excluded.

The historian, as historian, can only recapture fragments of the real Jesus, but as this fragment shows, the real Jesus was not a different Jesus from the one proclaimed by the church. Nor is the real Jesus simply a powerful moral forerunner of just any political martyr. The real Jesus is a Savior whose redemptive death has turned human history completely around, from death to life, and prefigures a glorious future for the human family as children of God.

---

[16] This does not preclude the right of the church, like any other community, to exclude from its membership those who refuse to listen to the church even under circumstances where the accused member is being accorded due process. The point is that disciples of Jesus do not follow the example of Phinehas and take upon themselves the role of judge and jury. They listen to the sinner as well as to those who bring charges against the sinner.

It is in this context that the historian can most fruitfully focus on the tradition that the apostle Paul passed on to his readers in the church of Corinth:

> The Lord Jesus on the night when he was betrayed took a loaf of bread, and when he had given thanks, he broke it and said, "This is my body that is [broken] for you. Do this in remembrance of me." In the same way he took the cup also, after supper, saying, "This cup is the new covenant in my blood. Do this, as often as you drink it, in remembrance of me." (1 Cor 11:23b–25)

This is the earliest tradition we have concerning the "Lord's Supper." Jesus' associating his body with the bread and his blood with the cup is strongly supported in the parallel traditions preserved in the gospels of Matthew, Mark, and Luke. This evidence indicates that Jesus consciously intended his death to be understood as a giving of himself on behalf of others. This is the essence of love. It is the kind of love that makes us free.

For Jesus to be seen as one who "gives himself for others" connects his ministry to that of the Servant of the Lord in Isa 53. We are not, of course, to expect that Jesus himself is directly responsible for the striking formal correspondence between the life and ministry of the Servant in Isaiah and the outline of Jesus' ministry in the church's gospels: birth, development, suffering, death, burial, vindication, and exaltation (resurrection). But it helps the historian in exploring the connection between Jesus and the canon of the New Testament to know that on the night he was handed over, Jesus *did,* at a kairotic moment in his relationship with his disciples, do and say certain things that connected his ministry indelibly with God's plan of salvation as it comes to expression in the book of Isaiah.

11. Implications for Understanding "Canon"

It is clear that Jesus did *not* read the Law and the Prophets through the eyes of Num 25. Our hypothesis is that the canon of the New Testament originated with Jesus, i.e., with the way in which his ministry was formed (or *normed*) by his reading and reflecting upon the Law and the Prophets. We have concluded that the historical evidence indicates that Jesus consciously intended his death to be understood as a giving of himself on behalf of others, and that this "giving of himself for others" connects his ministry to that of the Servant of the Lord in Isa 53.

This is about as far as we can go as historians. How Jesus understood his relationship to God the Father in Trinitarian terms carries us beyond an historical investigation of Jesus of Nazareth into the realm of the history of doctrine. But one thing should be clear to historians, the moment we recognize that Jesus consciously and intentionally decided to convey to his disciples that he wanted them to understand his death as a "giving of himself for others," and that this was done in relation to the text of Isaiah, especially Isa 53:4–6 and 8–12, such a powerful interpretive move would have affected how Jesus read the Law and the Prophets *as a whole.* What we have in the New Testament canon, then, reflects how Jesus read the Law and the Prophets as a whole, to the extent that he communicated this reading to his disciples through his teaching and actions. However, the New Testament further reflects the way in which this reading was subsequently received and developed by apostles and evangelists in the light of the actual death, burial, and resurrection of their leader and Lord, especially as this is worked out in the letters of Paul and in the Gospels, but also in the other books of the New Testament, notably Hebrews, the Pastoral Epistles, 1 Peter, 1 John, and Revelation.

Of course, the idea that the canon of the New Testament originated with the way Jesus read the Law and the Prophets is only a hypothesis. However, it is a hypothesis that has the possibility of being developed into a credible theory that will serve to clarify the connections between Jesus of Nazareth and the New Testament canon. Only when historians have achieved a studied understanding of these connections will they be in a position to consider whether to recommend expunging or adding books to the canon of the church. Meanwhile, the whole question remains open for further reflection and informed historical investigation.

20

Marcion Revisited

John Barton

In the patristic period Marcion, who died about 160, was described in highly negative terms.[1] He was, of course, a "heretic." His errors had been twofold, and both had to do
with the Bible. First, he had rejected the Old Testament as having any authority for Christians, arguing that the God of whom it spoke, the God of the Jews, was entirely different
from the Christian God who had revealed himself in Jesus as the Savior of the world;
indeed, it was from the evil creator-god of the Old Testament that Jesus had delivered his
followers. Second, Marcion had reduced even Christian scripture by deciding that there
should be only one gospel, Luke, and no epistles except those of Paul; and even these texts
he had expurgated and diminished, removing from them all references to the Old Testament and all mention of the true God, the Father of Jesus, as the creator of the world.
Marcion's version of the gospel was thus, in the eyes of the orthodox, a reduction of the
contents of the true "catholic" gospel to a message of salvation alone, shorn of any concern
with creation. And his effect on scripture was also reductionist, cutting away much that
the church valued, and constructing a sort of Bible through his own misguided efforts
instead of accepting the scriptures that had always been regarded as sacred in the church.

1. The Question of Marcion's Influence

Marcion's reputation survives today in the use of the term "Marcionite," which theologians sometimes use of other theologians if they suspect them of being hostile to the Old
Testament or of concentrating on salvation to the detriment of a creation theology.
Bultmann was often accused of "Marcionism" in this sense. And modern theology did
indeed produce one clear "Marcionite" in the person of Adolf von Harnack, with his
famous dictum, "To reject the Old Testament in the second century was a mistake which

---

[1] For an excellent brief guide to Marcion's thought, see S. G. Hall, "Marcion," in *A Dictionary
of Biblical Interpretation* (ed. R. J. Coggins and J. L. Houlden; London: SCM, 1990), 422–24. The
fragments that remain of Marcion's writings, together with patristic quotations and allusions, can
be found in A. von Harnack, *Marcion: Das Evangelium vom fremden Gott* (TU 45; Leipzig: J. G.
Hinrichs, 1921; 2d ed., 1924). See also E. Evans, ed., *Tertullian: Adversus Marcionem* (Oxford: Clarendon, 1972), and my own discussion of Marcion in *Holy Writings, Sacred Text* (Louisville: Westminster John Knox, 1998, 35–62). The British edition of this book is called *The Spirit and the Letter:
Studies in the Biblical Canon* (London: SPCK, 1997).

the Church rightly repudiated; to retain it in the sixteenth century was a fate which the Reformation could not yet avoid; but to continue to keep it as a canonical document after the nineteenth century is the consequence of religious and ecclesiastical paralysis."[2]

But detailed study of what Marcion actually taught, which in modern times takes its rise from the work of Harnack, has shifted the emphasis in our understanding of this maligned figure. It is not that anyone denies that Marcion tried to abolish the Old Testament and to truncate the New, but that his work has come to be seen as far less an opposition to an already prevailing understanding of scripture, and far more creative in prompting the church to make up its mind about the character of its scriptures, than the church fathers realized. Especially where the New Testament is concerned, modern scholars have argued that the church had not yet "canonized" (at least in the sense that term would come to bear) the New Testament by the time of Marcion, and that it was largely through the need to react to him that the standard Christian canon of the New Testament came to be established. Thus Harnack argued that "the Catholic New Testament beat the Marcionite Bible; but this New Testament is an anti-Marcionite creation on a Marcionite basis."[3] Campenhausen argued similarly: "The idea and reality of a Christian Bible were the work of Marcion, and the Church which rejected his work, so far from being ahead of him in this field, from a formal point of view simply followed his example."[4] And John Knox wrote, "The structural principle of Marcion's canon became the organizing idea of the catholic New Testament. Here is the fundamental fact in the relation of Marcion and the canon . . . Marcion is primarily responsible for the idea of the New Testament."[5]

More recent scholarship has been less sure of Marcion's influence on the formation of the canon, but still regards him as important. Metzger, in his definitive guide to the canonization of the New Testament, writes:

> It is nearer to the truth to regard Marcion's canon as accelerating the process of fixing the Church's canon, a process that had already begun in the first half of the second century. It was in opposition to Marcion's criticism that the Church first became fully conscious of its inheritance of apostolic writings. As Grant aptly puts it, "Marcion forced more orthodox Christians to examine their own presuppositions and to state more clearly what they already believed."[6]

Thus the impression persists that without Marcion the church might well not have developed a "New Testament," even though he may not have been the only or the dominant influence, as Harnack thought.

There are however two reasons why this position is harder to defend than it seems. First, Marcion's concern was to *exclude* books that he disapproved of from his "canon." He was not assembling a collection of Christian books, but making a (very restricted) selection from the corpus of texts which already existed and which must already have been rec-

---

[2] Harnack, *Marcion*, 248–49; translations from this work are my own.

[3] Ibid., 357.

[4] Hans von Campenhausen, *The Formation of the Christian Bible* (Philadelphia: Fortress, 1972), 148.

[5] John Knox, *Marcion and the New Testament* (Chicago: University of Chicago Press, 1942), 31.

[6] Bruce M. Metzger, *The Canon of the New Testament: Its Origin, Development, and Significance* (Oxford: Oxford University Press, 1987), 99, referring to Robert M. Grant, *The Formation of the New Testament* (New York: Harper and Row, 1965), 126.

ognized as sacred by many in the church—otherwise he would not have needed to insist on abolishing them. To have imitated Marcion, other Christian thinkers would have had to make their own selection (no doubt a larger one) and try to enforce its limits. Now there is little evidence of canonization in the sense of restricting accepted Christian writings to a limited compass as early as the second century. Setting bounds to what may be read as Christian scripture is essentially an activity of the fourth century, reaching its culmination in Athanasius's *Festal Letter 39* of 367.

There is really only one possible piece of evidence for the desire to *limit* the canon as early as the second century: the Muratorian Fragment. But the recent detailed study by Geoffrey Hahneman, following A. C. Sundberg, seems to have shown convincingly that this is a fourth-century text, and does not reflect the situation in the age of Marcion.[7] If this evidence is excluded, then there is little reason to suppose that the church at large followed Marcion's attempt to restrict the compass of acceptable Christian texts. Rather, their concern was to reject Marcion not by imitating but by contradicting him, and insisting that far more books had authority in the church than he was prepared to allow. In principle, what Christian writers of the second century defend is the variety and profusion of Christian texts, just as they also defend the continued acceptance and use of the Old Testament. As we shall see, Marcion did have successors who thought that scripture should be reconstructed in a minimalist way: Tatian's *Diatessaron* is one example. What was to become the mainstream of Christian thought, however, did not follow this example but insisted on accepting what had come down from the past, even if this resulted in the problem of inconsistencies, for example, as between the different gospels.[8]

Second, if Marcion caused the church to have a "New Testament," we should see an increase in the use of New Testament texts from the mid-second century onwards, as the church in general became more aware of its own scriptures as distinct from the Old Testament. Christians should have become, for polemical reasons, more self-conscious in using the texts that would eventually form the New Testament. But in fact this is not the case. The New Testament books, or at any rate the central "core" of the Gospels and the Pauline and Catholic Epistles, were already used very widely in the time before Marcion, and continued to be so used after him. Franz Stuhlhofer has shown by a detailed statistical analysis that, proportionately to their length, the New Testament scriptures were already cited considerably more intensively than the Old by the early second century, and no difference in their use can be established following Marcion.[9] He cites Overbeck's characterization of "the deep silence, for observers from later generations, in which the canon [of the New Testament] came into existence."[10]

---

[7] See Geoffrey M. Hahneman, *The Muratorian Fragment and the Development of the Canon* (Oxford: Clarendon, 1992); A. C. Sundberg, "Muratorian Fragment," in *IDBSup,* 609–10. [Within the present volume, see especially the contributions of H. Gamble (ch. 17), P. Balla (ch. 22), E. Kalin (ch. 23), and G. Hahneman (ch.24).]

[8] On this problem see Oscar Cullmann, "Die Pluralität der Evangelien als theologisches Problem im Altertum," *TZ* 1 (1945): 23–42; ET in Oscar Cullmann, *The Early Church* (London: SCM, 1956), 37–54; Helmut Merkel, *Die Widersprüche zwischen den Evangelien* (WUNT 13; Tübingen: Mohr [Siebeck], 1971).

[9] Franz Stuhlhofer, *Der Gebrauch der Bibel von Jesus bis Euseb: Eine statistische Untersuchung zur Kanongeschichte* (Wuppertal: Brockhaus, 1988).

[10] Ibid., 75, quoting Franz Overbeck, *Zur Geschichte des Kanons* (Chemnitz: E. Schmeitzner, 1980, repr. Darmstadt: Wissenschaftliche Buchgesellschaft, 1965).

Thus Marcion seems to have had far less influence on the development of the New Testament canon than he is still given credit for, despite modifications to Harnack's rather extreme proposal. He was rejected and anathematized, but not paid the compliment of being imitated, not even in the sense that the church felt constrained to produce a rival "New Testament" as a response to his truncated one. The development of the New Testament followed its own logic, and Marcion did not influence it one way or the other. But if this is so, in what does his importance really consist? Is there a stream of tradition within Christianity which is indeed indebted to him, or to which he belongs, or is he simply the outsider that the church fathers regarded him as being?

My tentative answer to this question is that Marcion was in all essentials a conservative thinker who did not realize that the tide of Christian opinion was moving beyond the attitudes for which he stood; but that he did have certain followers in his conservatism who eventually became, as those do who try to prevent the development of Christian thought, "heretics." We can see the importance of Marcion by surveying four topics: his attitude towards the Old and New Testaments respectively; his rejection of allegorical interpretation; his bipartite canon (Gospel plus Paul); and his writing of the work called *Antitheses* to be a companion to his reduced "Bible."

2. Marcion's Attitude toward the Bible

In what follows I shall refer to the "Old Testament" and the "New Testament," meaning by these terms those texts that are now so described, but with no implication that their limits were defined or that they were already established as "canonical" in Marcion's day—as we shall see, the term "canonical" is somewhat anachronistic for this period. My purpose is to describe, on the basis of such evidence as we have, how Marcion regarded the Old and New Testament books, and to show that his attitude is indeed more conservative than radical.

It is usually said that Marcion "rejected" the Old Testament and accepted in its place only his own canon of Luke plus Pauline Epistles, edited to remove all allusions to the Old Testament. This, however, obscures two important points. First, Marcion's rejection of the Old Testament was indeed total, in that he regarded it as completely alien to the revelation of salvation brought by Jesus and recorded in the New Testament documents he accepted. But this was not because he did not believe that the God of the Old Testament actually existed, or thought that the Old Testament itself was a purely human invention, pseudo-oracles of an imaginary god. On the contrary, Marcion firmly believed that the Old Testament God did exist, and that he was the Creator of the world. The problem was that his creation was evil, and he himself therefore a malign being; it was precisely the role of Jesus, and of the Unknown God now revealed in him, to deliver humankind from the malice of the evil Creator.

Furthermore, the creator-god really had spoken the words attributed to him in the Old Testament: these were fully true and accurate oracles, not a human invention. They truly expressed the thoughts of the maker of the universe, and there could be no question of suggesting that they had been falsified in any way or contaminated by human intervention. "The Jewish Scriptures represent a true revelation of the Creator, but they do not speak of or for the God whom alone Christians ought to worship."[11] Marcion's "rejection" of the Old

---

[11] Knox, *Marcion*, 7.

Testament thus needs to be qualified. He believed that when read properly (as we shall see, that meant without the help of allegorizing interpretation) it would at once be seen that it was incompatible with the New Testament. But that did not undermine its claim to a "divine" origin; it simply meant that the "divinity" who inspired it was an evil one.

Marcion's attitude to the New Testament, however, was not simply the mirror image of his attitude to the Old, as though the New Testament was equally divinely inspired only in this case by a good God. He appears not to have thought of the New Testament as "scriptural" in the sense in which the Old Testament was scriptural, but to have thought of it as a collection of generally reliable historical documents which, however, needed editing to remove errors and slips. The Gospels (or in Marcion's case the one true gospel, Luke) were not revealed scripture; they were a historical record of the doings and, especially, of the sayings of Jesus. He had no hesitation in reworking the book or books which he had received as the gospel of his own community, any more than he had in rewriting Paul: the important thing was to establish the truth about Jesus, and to remove from the texts those errors which, because he himself knew this truth, he could identify and correct. This is quite unlike his attitude to the Old Testament, which for him was not a record of independently existing tradition but the direct utterances of the (evil) creator-god. In an important sense, therefore, Marcion was not abolishing the Old Testament and putting the New in its place—as though he was substituting one "canon" for another. He was recognizing the continuing existence of "scripture" (the Old Testament), but announcing that "the gospel"—the good news of Jesus and the salvation brought by him—showed this scripture up for what it was, the utterances of an evil being.

Now—and this is my point—these attitudes, once we remove the negative *evaluation* of the Old Testament, are simply a mirror-image of the attitudes of most Christian writers in the second century. "Scripture" for them meant what we call the Old Testament, though exactly what were its contents is another question, which we cannot enter into here.[12] The life and teachings of Jesus, and the apostolic witness to them, were not "scripture," but "gospel," fresh divine revelation, but not inherently encoded in books and documents. The Christian books were merely memory-joggers, not independently existing scriptural oracles. Christians knew about Jesus from the tradition, not essentially from books. Even though in practice it might be from a book that a given Christian learned something about Jesus, it was not a book considered as "scripture," a kind of Torah, but a book considered as a historical record.

As Ellen Flesseman-van Leer puts it, "People knew what the gospel message was, and no one asked *how* they knew. The Church as a whole knew what had happened, and also knew its meaning, because it was constantly recounted and proclaimed."[13] Or, to quote Campenhausen, " 'The Gospel' to which appeal is normally made, remains an elastic concept, designating the preaching of Jesus as a whole in the form in which it lives on in

---

[12] See my discussions in J. Barton, *Oracles of God: Perceptions of Ancient Prophecy in Israel after the Exile* (London: Darton, Longman, and Todd, 1986; New York: Oxford University Press, 1988), and "The Significance of a Fixed Canon of the Hebrew Bible," in *Hebrew Bible/Old Testament: The History of Its Interpretation* (ed. Magne Sæbø; Göttingen: Vandenhoeck & Ruprecht, 1996), 1.1.67–83.

[13] Ellen Flesseman-van Leer, "Prinzipien der Sammlung und Ausscheidung bei der Bildung des Kanons," *ZThK* 61 (1964): 404–20, at 405.

church tradition. The normative significance of the Lord's words, which is the most important point, . . . is not transferred to the documents which record them."[14] Helmut Koester summarizes the matter well:

> In the first one and one-half centuries, "scripture," i.e., authoritative writing, comprised exclusively what was later called the Old Testament. Any additional authority referred to in order to underline the legitimacy of the Christian message and the teaching of the church was present in a variety of traditions which were still undefined. Sometimes these were transmitted orally, sometimes in written form. Such authority could be called "the sayings of the Lord," usually transmitted orally. But even the quotations of Jesus' sayings in 2 Clement, although drawn from a written source, are still introduced as words of the Lord, just as Justin (1 Apology 15–17) introduces the teachings of the gospels as "what Jesus said" and not as quotations from a book.[15]

Two features of early Christian manuscripts of the gospels help to confirm this impression. One is the well-known fact that Christians from early times preferred the codex to the scroll for recording their own texts (and in due course for all books, including the Old Testament). There has been much speculation on the reasons for this. C. H. Roberts, the main contributor to the debate, has emphasized the status of the codex in the ancient world as an essentially informal method of recording information, roughly corresponding to a note-pad.[16] His suggestion is that the gospels were not regarded as finished texts—the kind of thing one would write on a scroll—but as notes from which to develop oral proclamation or teaching. Like the Oral Law in Judaism, such material could legitimately be written down, but its essentially oral character was safeguarded by avoiding the use of a formal scroll. According to rabbinic conventions, the Oral Law may likewise be noted down to aid memory, but not enshrined in a scroll. To quote what I have written elsewhere,

> the first Christian codices, if Roberts is right, were used because the works they carried were not really "books." However the evangelists may have perceived their own work, their early readers saw it merely as a convenient repository of the kind of oral Jesus-tradition that they already knew, and were accustomed to pass on in teaching and preaching; and so they wrote them on sheets loosely sewn together, rather than on formal scrolls.[17]

A second point about the early manuscript tradition of the gospels is made by David Parker.[18] He argues that the early textual tradition of the sayings of Jesus is often flexible

---

[14] Campenhausen, Formation, 129.

[15] Helmut Koester, Ancient Christian Gospels: Their History and Development (London: SCM, 1990), 31. Cf. also Knox, Marcion, 30: "Harnack accounts for the very occasional use of gegraptai in introducing a quotation from a Gospel in the period before the New Testament had taken form by the practice of public lection. . . . This may well be true, especially for the several cases in Justin. Since in earlier cases, however, it is the words of Jesus which are always quoted, is not reverence for these words—a reverence which placed them on a par with or even beyond the Scriptures in importance—a more likely explanation?"

[16] C. H. Roberts, "The Codex," in Proceedings of the British Academy 40 (1954): 169–204; C. H. Roberts and T. C. Skeat, The Birth of the Codex (London: Oxford University Press, 1987).

[17] Barton, Holy Writings, 88.

[18] David Parker, The Living Text of the Gospels (New York: Cambridge University Press, 1997); idem, "The Early Traditions of Jesus' Sayings on Divorce," Theology 96 (1993): 372–83; idem, "Scripture Is Tradition," Theology 94 (1991): 11–17.

not merely in practice but in principle: the sayings were not treated in the church of the first two or three centuries as holy writ in the same way as the Old Testament, but were seen as enshrining basic ideas which could be developed flexibly in different situations. The flexibility was not infinite, but its bounds were not exactly defined, and they certainly were not so tight that we can confidently reconstruct, from the words a given writer cites as Jesus', precisely what he found in the manuscript of the gospels he habitually used. Against this background the existence of four varying versions of the life and teachings of Jesus, and perhaps even of other texts such as the putative Q and the *Gospel of Thomas,* was not the problem it has been for later, more "literalistic" readers. The existence of variant versions of what Jesus said or did on any particular occasion may have helped to authorize the preacher's freedom to tell the story in a new way, not corresponding exactly to any of the written accounts.

Along these lines one might argue that diversity, even inconsistency, in the handling of gospel materials was seen at least by some in the early church as having a distinctive value, rather than being simply a problem. Where the Old Testament was concerned, there was of course no corresponding sense of a freely adaptable text; these books had been written scripture from time immemorial, and inconsistencies within them could hardly be handled in the same way. In time Christians, like Jews, developed imaginative ways of resolving these, among which allegorical interpretation was important.

Marcion seems to fit well within this way of handling Old and New Testament materials. He differed from his "orthodox" contemporaries in thinking the Old Testament bad rather than good, but he agreed with them that it was a divinely inspired text, which could not be changed or edited. Like them he thought of the gospels as corrigible in the light of further information, and as forming a collection of archive material that Christians could develop further. Indeed, Marcion's successors seem to have felt free to modify his own work, apparently supplementing his "Luke" from Matthew and Mark.[19] There was no sense that he had established a kind of "scripture" in editing Luke, and in that sense Marcion's rival to the gospels was not "canonical," any more than the gospels then were for the larger church.

In a sense we may say that by dismissing the Old Testament as no longer having authority for Christians, Marcion abolished "scripture" altogether instead of substituting a "New Testament" for it. But paradoxically, as we have seen, his "abolition" of Old Testament scripture did not lead him to lose interest in it or to regard it as false. It remained a true revelation, but a revelation from an evil deity. Thus Marcion was in important respects a traditionalist who did not create any new way of looking at what would become the New Testament. He was much more radical than most contemporary Christians in regarding so much Jesus-tradition as erroneous; but he did not create the new category of Christian scripture. He remained firmly attached to the usual contemporary paradigm, in which gospel books were convenient but corrigible records—important for their reusability in telling the story of Jesus and reminding people of his words, rather than because they were "scripture" after the manner of the Old Testament.

The creation of "critical" versions of the gospels soon ceased in the patristic church, with the firm establishment of the four-gospel canon from the time of Irenaeus onwards.

---

[19] Cf. Barton, *Holy Writings,* 46.

There are two broad possibilities for dealing with the discrepancies within the gospels. One is to argue that the differences are only apparent, and to show that the texts really harmonize perfectly; this is the line taken by patristic treatises on the "consensus of the evangelists," and it remains popular today in circles where the Bible is not read critically. Eusebius's suggestion that the incidents in John fit into the "silent" period in the Synoptics between Jesus' temptations and the death of John the Baptist belongs to this approach.[20] The other possibility is to alter the texts so that they harmonize better. This approach rests on a clear perception that they are *not* harmonious as they stand. Marcion represents an extreme version of this tendency, actually deleting all the other gospels except Luke (not that we know for sure how many of them he was familiar with), and even then editing out passages he found objectionable. Tatian's *Diatessaron* is the logical successor to this attitude of Marcion's, producing as it were a single gospel by weaving together the existing four and eliminating contradictions, not showing that the gospels are harmonious but forcing them to be so. It is a pity that the term "harmonization" tends to do duty for both of these diametrically opposed operations.

But was Marcion innovating here? The very gospel he took as his base text, Luke, is surely an example of the same tendency, if we are to believe its prologue. "Luke" examined existing gospels and other traditions and wrote a definitive version of the events they narrated, correcting what was in error in earlier works. Marcion did (to his own mind) nothing different from this. Indeed, it seems plausible to think that each of the gospels represents an attempt to provide an authoritative answer to the question of what Jesus did and said. It is hard to imagine that any of the redactors of the gospels wrote with the intention that his version should stand alongside others in a multi-gospel canon. Rather, each is an attempt to supersede its predecessors. Marcion was, in effect, an evangelist, who unfortunately for him lived too late for this to be an acceptable profession. It was far from being an innovative role. On the contrary, it was one that had now gone greatly out of fashion. His idea was a simple and "primitive" one: to tell the story of Jesus in one straightforward account. But by his day the church at large had rejected this ideal in favor of the vastly more complicated task of coping with four alternative, and incompatible, gospels.

3. Marcion's Rejection of Allegory

Marcion refused to read the Old Testament allegorically. Now allegorical interpretation was one very important way in which the early church managed to hold on to the Old Testament as its own scripture rather than declaring it to be part of the older and superseded Jewish dispensation. For Marcion, the Old Testament was not a holy text but the revelation of an evil deity, and as such it did not qualify for the allegorical treatment which other Christians regularly practised. He insisted on its literal meaning, arguing, for example, that the Messiah predicted in the prophets was a royal, purely human figure who had not yet arrived but was still to come, just as the prophets had said. Other allegedly "messianic" texts were not interpreted messianically at all but were said to refer to ancient

---

[20] Eusebius, *Eccl. hist.* 3:24; see the quotation in Barton, *Holy Writings*, 85.

Jewish kings: Marcion anticipated the "historical-critical" reading of Isa 7:14 as referring to the birth of Hezekiah.

It is not easy to say which came first, Marcion's rejection of the Old Testament as authoritative or his insistence on nonallegorical reading. Common sense suggests that he noticed the literal meaning of the text, concluded that it contradicted the Christian revelation, and so "decanonized" it. However, I have suggested elsewhere[21] that the process may have worked in the opposite direction; being convinced that the Old Testament was not holy because it was the revelation of a non-Christian god, Marcion denied that it was a suitable candidate for allegorical interpretation, which in the ancient world generally was regarded as the most appropriate way of handling a sacred text. Thus Origen can write "Not even Celsus asserts that only vulgar people have been converted by the gospel to follow the religion of Jesus; for he admits that among them are some moderate, reasonable, and intelligent people who readily interpret allegorically."[22] It is true that there developed in Christianity an antiallegorical school of thought, the Antiochene school, but even some of their "literal" interpretations strike the modern reader as fairly allegorical in tone. The majority tradition in the church certainly operated with allegorization as the best way of reconciling Old and New Testaments.

Whichever of these suggestions is true, it is at any rate agreed that Marcion refused to allegorize the Old Testament, and that this fits well with his insistence on its lack of concord with the New. His contemporaries spent a lot of effort interpreting the Old Testament in such a way that it would appear to be in harmony with the new revelation in Christ. Justin's *Dialogue with Trypho* is a case in point: at every turn he tries to convince his opponent of the nonliteral meaning of Old Testament texts, and so to show that Jesus can be seen as their fulfillment. But this reminds us of a point that can easily be missed. Marcion was, of course, strongly anti-Jewish in his theology, believing Judaism to be the worship of the evil creator-god whom Jesus had come to defeat. Yet his literal reading of the Old Testament is often quite close to a Jewish reading. Jewish interpreters, like Marcion, argued that the messianic texts in the prophets were either yet to be fulfilled or were in fact simply concerned with actual earthly kings who had already existed. This means that the arguments attributed to Trypho in the *Dialogue* are often quite close to *Marcion's* arguments. Jewish and anti-Jewish readings are strangely united by their shared opposition to "mainstream" Christian allegorization. This is readily comprehensible once one realizes that Marcion shared the Jewish view that the Old Testament texts belonged to Judaism, not to Christianity.

This has led Charles Cosgrove to argue that the *Dialogue* is not really about Christian-Jewish discussion at all, but that the rabbi Trypho is instead a cipher for Marcion, whom Justin opposed with all his force. As in much early Christian polemic against the Jews, what may in reality be going on is a conflict with "judaizers" or those suspected of being such *within* the church. As Cosgrove writes,

> The apology draws the outer world into its own inner circle for judgment as a way for the group to make sure of itself. The ostensibly centrifugal cast of apologetic literature may

---

[21] Barton, *Holy Writings,* 53–55.
[22] Origen, *Cels.* 1:23.

function as a mere foil for this more pressing internal process of self-identification; the dialogue with the outsider may represent no more than internal monologue.[23]

According to Justin, the problem with Judaism is that by insisting on a literal observance of what is laid down in the Old Testament it encourages those Christians who want to understand the Law literally *so that they can be justified in rejecting it* as unworthy of the God revealed in Jesus. In other words, a literal Jewish reading ultimately gives comfort to Marcionism. To "judaize" is to read the Old Testament in a non-Christian way, and that has the consequence of making its lack of fit with the new revelation apparent, and therefore of leading to its rejection. And that in turn means that the one great truth for which the Old Testament is valued, namely that it teaches that there is a good creator, will be bound to fall by the wayside, and the way will be open to heresies such as Marcion's.

Modern biblical theology has often argued that the Old Testament, read in its own terms and with an eye to its literal meaning, is entirely compatible with Christian faith. "Pan-biblical" theologies[24] bear especial witness to this belief, but it is implicit in most if not all of the great theologies of the Old Testament written by Christian Old Testament scholars. The early church, on the other hand, did not in general think that a literal reading of the Old Testament would prove its compatibility with Christian faith. Some Christians went down the road of correcting the Old Testament to bring it into line with Christianity. This line of approach is represented by the *Clementine Homilies,* with their theory of "false pericopes," inserted in the Old Testament by the Jews, which Christians must remove. Even Justin makes occasional accusations of this kind, as in his discussion of Ps 96:10, which he, followed by later Christian tradition, claimed had been corrupted by the Jews to remove a reference to God reigning "from the tree."[25] But the majority did not adopt this radical approach to the text, but preferred to apply allegorical or other nonliteral reading strategies.

What was Marcion's effect on Christian attitudes to the Old Testament? If Justin is correctly interpreted along the lines proposed by Cosgrove, then the need to confute his rejection of the God of the Old Testament was one factor in promoting allegorical reading and deterring Christians from reading the Old Testament along the same lines as their Jewish contemporaries. He was also, of course, a factor in persuading the church that the Old Testament should continue to be honored, since its rejection was so strongly tied up with the Marcionite distinction between the Creator and the God and Father of Jesus Christ. To put it in a somewhat exaggerated form, Marcion was not responsible for Christians' adopting a New Testament; he was responsible for their retaining an Old Testament.

---

[23] C. H. Cosgrove, "Justin Martyr and the Emerging Christian Canon: Observations on the Purpose and Destination of the Dialogue with Trypho," *VC* 36 (1982): 209–32, at 219. Cf. Miriam Taylor, *Anti-Judaism and Early Christian Identity: A Critique of the Scholarly Consensus* (Studia postbiblica 46; Leiden: Brill, 1995); and P. F. Beatrice, "Une citation de l'Evangile de Matthieu dans l'Epître de Barnabé," in *The New Testament in Early Christianity/La réception des écrits néotestamentaires dans le christianisme primitif* (BETL 86; Leuven: Leuven University Press, 1989), 231–45. Campenhausen (*Formation,* 59) argues a similar case for 'the Jews' in John's Gospel.

[24] See especially M. Oeming, *Gesamtbiblische Theologien der Gegenwart* (Stuttgart: Kohlhammer, 1987), and the general discussion in James Barr, *The Concept of Biblical Theology* (Minneapolis: Fortress, 1999).

[25] Justin, *Dial.* 73.

Interestingly enough, Stuhlhofer's statistics indicate an *increase* in the citation of Old Testament texts by Christian writers from about the time of Marcion onwards.[26] The early tendency to feel that the gospel was so new that it hardly needed expounding in terms of the older scriptures gave way to a more even use of both testaments.

In his attitude to the Old Testament Marcion really does look more like an innovator than he was in his "canonization" of the New Testament. Nevertheless it is unlikely that his theology seemed so new to him. Rather, he regarded it as the continuation of a central theme in Paul: the supersession of the law by the gospel. Paul "spoiled" the novelty of this theme by continuing to quote the Old Testament as though it were authoritative for Christians, and Marcion accordingly had to expurgate even the Pauline letters that he retained. But Paul in any case refers much less to Old Testament texts than later Christian writers were to do, and there are whole epistles with very little Old Testament material in them, while his description of worship in Corinth, for example, does not suggest that much use was made there of the Old Testament (cf. 1 Cor 14). It was plausible, even though to a modern reader not convincing, to argue that Paul regarded the Old Testament as having been superannuated by the fresh revelation in Christ—the line sometimes developed by modern theologians accused of "Marcionism," such as Bultmann. Of course, in believing that the creator-god who had inspired the Old Testament was an evil being, Marcion departed very far from Pauline theology, but it is quite conceivable that he was not aware of doing so. Other people in the early church found Paul hard to understand (cf. 2 Pet 3:16), and the argument of James makes it likely that he was widely interpreted as antinomian, that is, as having taught that the Jewish law was now superseded and need not be observed at all.

Marcion's "low" reading of the Old Testament, which highlighted its lack of concord with the Christian gospel, was not an unknown position in the early church. As we have argued, following Cosgrove, what Justin combated in his *Dialogue* may well have been the view that Christians need no longer bother with the Old Testament. Ostensibly, he is trying to show *Jews* that, correctly interpreted, it points to Christ: that is, he is assuming that it is a valid revelation of the true God and then showing that it prophesies the life, death, and resurrection of Jesus. But the true line of argument probably runs in the opposite direction. Because the Old Testament can be shown (through allegorization and similar methods) to point to Christ, it is therefore not to be discarded by *Christians*. Marcion was probably not the only thinker in the early church to believe that it should be discarded, though he is the most prominent one known to us. The seeds of such a position are there in Paul. Whatever Paul himself meant by "Christ is the end of the law" (Rom 10:4), people could easily perceive it as a rejection of the Old Testament, as Marcion evidently did.

In respect of his antiallegorical stance, then, Marcion was quite innovative. I suspect that his main originality lies here. At the same time, this stance was connected with certain ideas about the way the Old Testament had been superseded in Christ which were definitely not new, but correspond to one facet of the many-sided Pauline gospel, divorced from other, complementary insights in Paul. A "Pauline" rejection of the Old Testament certainly seems to have been one option that some early Christians were drawn to: Irenaeus still has to argue at length for the identity of the Creator God, revealed in the Old

---

[26] See the discussion in Barton, *Holy Writings*, 64–65.

Testament, with the the Redeemer God, revealed in Jesus. Those he opposed were regarded by him, and naturally by later Christians, as "heretics," but at the time it was a question which party would eventually triumph.

4. Marcion's Bipartite "New Testament"

One of the ways in which Marcion is said to have influenced the development of a New Testament is in his bipartite "canon" of Gospel plus Epistles *(Apostolikon)*. Harnack argued that this was the foundation on which the church later developed its slightly more complicated New Testament, in which the Epistles are headed by Acts, and Revelation, a late arrival in many churches, and disputed by some even in the fourth century, is added at the end.

Now it is true that there is no evidence before Marcion for a dual collection of documents in this form. Obviously both the Gospels and the Epistles already existed, and there is some evidence that Paul's letters had already been collected into a *corpus Paulinum*, but we do not know when they were added to the Gospels to form a bipartite collection. Nevertheless the derivation of authority from two sources, "the Lord" and "the Apostle(s)," is well attested in the early church, and it seems to be essentially this model with which Marcion was working. It may be that writers who spoke in such terms were thinking primarily of oral tradition, though this is more plausible in the case of Jesus than of Paul, who after all was known only through his writings. As we have seen, early Christians often seem to have regarded Christian teaching as somehow inherently oral, even though in practice they may have encountered it through written texts. At all events all Christians seem to have been aware of the twofold source of Christian teaching, and it may well have existed in written form.[27]

Indeed, one example of this tendency can be identified: the *Didache*. I repeat here some observations from my *Holy Writings, Sacred Text:*

> The date of the *Didache* is still disputed, with English-speaking scholars tending to favour a mid- to late-second-century date, and continental [European] scholarship continuing to defend the late first century and so placing it before the writing of some of the later books of the New Testament. In either case, however, we may see it as a significant parallel to Marcion's *Apostolikon*. The final authority for the author of the *Didache* is the words of Jesus: the Lord's Prayer, for example, is to be recited *hōs ekeleusen ho kyrios en tō euangeliō autou* (as the Lord commanded in his gospel) (8:2), where *euangelion* could well mean a written gospel (perhaps Matthew); 9:5 cites a word of Jesus with the formula *hōs errethē*. There is no doubt that the *Didache* was intended to be the authoritative handbook for Christian practice in the churches for which it was written, probably in Syria, and most likely it was meant to stand alongside a gospel (Matthew?) as the official apostolic commentary on the words of the Lord himself.[28]

Matthew plus *Didache* would thus correspond to Marcion's Luke plus *Apostolikon*. The *Epistle of the Apostles* may well represent another experiment in this genre. If the *Didache* is

---

[27] [Within the present volume, see F. Bovon's argument (ch. 29) that the Gospel-Apostle structure was essential to Christian thought from the beginning.]

[28] Ibid., 49.

as early as some continental European scholars think, then Marcion would stand in a tradition that predates him.

5. Marcion's Antitheses

To accompany his "Bible" of Gospel and *Apostolikon,* Marcion also compiled a work called the *Antitheses.* Harnack argued that this text had a quasi-creedal character for Marcion's followers, providing a guide to the correct exegesis of the authoritative text. Apparently it contained an introductory section giving an account of the essential gospel message of deliverance through Christ from the evil creator-god, followed by a pericope-by-pericope exegesis of the Gospel and *Apostolikon,* showing how these exemplified the gospel message and also (vital for Marcion) how they differed from the Old Testament, read literally. The Old Testament is thus present in a shadowy form in Marcion's collection of texts: one needs to know it in order to recognize how wrong it is, and how fortunate Christians are to have been delivered from the god of whom it speaks.

The content of the *Antitheses* will thus have differed radically from anything else we know in the early church. Indeed, it must have argued for the very opposite of most doctrinal and exegetical positions espoused by "orthodox" Christians. Obviously we could argue that it marks Marcion out as a highly original writer. But things look rather different if we think more formally about the kind of "kit" which Marcion's various works provided for his followers. It consisted of (a) a gospel; (b) a collection of apostolic epistles; (c) a doctrinal handbook, containing a short creedal section followed by an exegetical guide to the "New Testament" and an account of how it differs from the Old; and (d) the Old Testament itself, of whose (literal) contents the reader needed enough knowledge to understand why it was to be rejected.

Seen in this light, the Marcionite "kit" looks not unlike that provided by other Christian teachers for their readers. For example, anyone who, some years later, would study with Irenaeus would have become familiar with (a) the Gospels; (b) various apostolic epistles; (c) the *Demonstration of the Apostolic Preaching,* giving guidance on the "canon of truth" or rule of faith, together with illustrations of it through exegesis of various parts of the "New Testament"; and (d) the Old Testament, which the reader had to understand allegorically in order to see how it conformed with the other three elements. This might suggest a broad agreement on the kind of documents a church needed to possess. *The Antitheses* in particular, though highly distinctive in the way it described the Christian faith, was similar to a text like Irenaeus's *Demonstration* in the sort of guidance it provided, combining creedal and exegetical material. Of course it showed the alleged lack of concord between Christianity and the Old Testament, whereas Irenaeus's work argues for a positive correlation, but formally speaking the task was much the same.

Irenaeus worked a little later than Marcion, so that it might be felt unreasonable to cite him as evidence against Marcion's originality—though I suppose few would argue that he borrowed the pattern of his work from Marcion! In any case, there are earlier parallels to the *Antitheses.* The *Epistle of Barnabas* and Melito's *Paschal Homily* are also examples of the genre; both take Old Testament passages and show how they are fulfilled in Christ through an allegorical or typological reading, just as Marcion showed how such passages were *not* thus fulfilled. And Justin's *Dialogue* seems quite close to the kind of thing the *Antitheses* must have been, with its extensive quotations of biblical material and its detailed attempts to demonstrate their concord with the gospel message. Harnack himself proposed various possible "canons" of texts that might have emerged in the early church instead of the Bible that in the end was accepted; and one of these is "A book of the synthesis or concordance of prophecy and fulfillment in reference to Jesus Christ, the Apostles, and the Church, standing side by side with the Old Testament."[29] This is more or less what Justin, Barnabas, Melito, and Irenaeus provided; and Marcion produced its exact opposite or mirror-image, a book of the *discord* of prophecy and fulfillment in relation to Jesus Christ, the Apostle, and the church, standing in contrast with the Old Testament. At the formal level, therefore, Marcion was not an innovator but a traditionalist. It was his doctrine that was novel, not the literary forms in which it was expressed.

6. Conclusion

My argument in this paper has been that in many respects Marcion should be seen as a conservative rather than as an innovator. In particular, his alleged importance in the development of a "New Testament" seems to have been much exaggerated. The documents which Christians accumulated and transmitted as the literary part of their religious heritage seem on the whole to have developed independently of Marcion, and his own writings, together with his editions of Gospel and Epistle texts, seem to have followed a pattern known to have been widespread in the second-century church. Like his contemporaries and predecessors, he tended not to see the Gospels or the Epistles as sacred texts, after the model of the Old Testament, but more as reliable documents which could be made even more reliable by those with special knowledge. He was not compiling a "New Testament," but a set of valuable historical and doctrinal texts, and in any case his chosen categories, "the Lord" and "the Apostle," correspond to the sources of authority normally cited by writers of his age. In thinking that the compass of Christian writings should be limited to a minimum he was not influential in his own time, for Christian teachers reacted rather by insisting on the authority of more texts than he allowed, and refusing to "close" the "canon" (both terms are rather anachronistic in any case for this period, as I have tried to show elsewhere).[30] And when the church did come to draw boundaries around the New Testament, it was a couple of centuries later, when his influence could not have been at work.

Marcion, we may conclude, was important for two reasons. He rejected the Old Testament as the document of an alien religion; and he taught that Jesus had come to save humankind from the control of the evil Creator to whom the Old Testament witnesses. These are precisely the two aspects of his work on which patristic condemnations, from Tertullian onwards, focus. In the process he denied the validity of allegorical interpretation of the Old Testament, which he saw as a means of accommodating it to Christian belief; this too is picked up by Tertullian. In short, Marcion was not a major influence on the formation of the New Testament; he was simply a Marcionite.

---

[29] Adolf von Harnack, *The Origin of the New Testament and the Most Important Consequences of the New Creation* (trans. J. R. Wilkinson; London: Williams and Norgate, 1925), 170.

[30] Barton, *Holy Writings*, 1–14.

21

Gnosticism and the Christian Bible

Pheme Perkins

What can be appropriately called a "Christian Bible" during the second century C.E., when the mythic-theological systems typical of the teachers of hidden gnosis and Valentinianism emerged?[1] Campenhausen's magisterial study of "canon" in this period rightly distinguishes references to Jewish writings in works which later became part of the New Testament from the Jewish scriptures as interpreted by Christian writers. Only the latter should be considered evidence of a "canon" or "Christian Bible" for this period.[2] To speak of the Christian Bible as "Jewish scriptures interpreted" masks the difference between Jews, for whom the canonical text remained the Hebrew Bible,[3] and Christians, for whom "scripture" is its Greek translation (Septuagint). However, elements of Genesis exegesis preserved in gnostic texts include puns and wordplays based on Hebrew or Aramaic texts.[4] Such puns, whether formulated by the gnostic author, or, more probably, inherited from Jewish tradition,[5] indicate that early Christians knew that the scripture used in their worship, teaching, and preaching did not retain its original language. Language or textual accuracy plays no role in the definition of canon as proposed by Trebolle Barrera. Texts can be said to be canonical when they are cited as authorities in religious teaching and practice.[6] They also serve as models for later apocryphal or parabiblical writing.[7]

---

[1] Since the ancient sources do not use the category "gnosticism," scholars are increasingly hesitant to apply it to the variety of sects and teachers who uncovered esoteric truths in the Jewish and Christian scriptures. The groups under consideration all employ a mythic system which distinguishes the material creation of the "Lord" from the impassible, precreation world which emanated from the incomprehensible divinity. See the discussion in Michael A. Williams, *Rethinking "Gnosticism": An Argument for Dismantling a Dubious Category* (Princeton: Princeton University Press, 1996), 7–53.

[2] Hans von Campenhausen, *The Formation of the Christian Bible* (trans. J. A. Baker; Philadelphia: Fortress, 1972), 103.

[3] First-century C.E. revisions of the Septuagint to bring it closer to the Hebrew show that the Hebrew Bible retained its authority among Greek-speaking Jews. See Julio Trebolle Barrera, *The Jewish Bible and the Christian Bible* (Grand Rapids: Eerdmans, 1998), 164–67.

[4] Birger A. Pearson, *Gnosticism, Judaism, and Egyptian Christianity* (Minneapolis: Fortress, 1990), 39–51, 88–94.

[5] Gedaliahu A. G. Stroumsa, *Another Seed: Studies in Gnostic Mythology* (NHS XXIV; Leiden: Brill, 1984), 46–49. The same tradition found in *Hyp. Arch.* 89:31–32 which connects Eve with the serpent, who is the father of Cain, also appears in the polemic of John 8:44 (p. 46).

[6] Trebolle Barrera, *Jewish Bible,* 153.

[7] Ibid., 170.

1. The Christian Supplement to Scripture

When texts composed by Christians came to be accepted as scripture, analogous to
the inherited Jewish writings, they did not replace but supplemented that heritage. Stroumsa
has compared this process of secondary canonization to the emergence of the Mishnah.
Each community embedded its understanding of the primary scripture in a secondary
text; these secondary texts not only fix the way in which the primary text is read, they make
the Jewish scriptures and Christian "Old Testament" into deeply different works.[8] Campenhausen has shown that early Christians saw their own compositions as reflecting the
oral traditions, words of the Lord, and the teachings of the apostles. "Books" or "texts"
refer to the Old Testament. When Dionysius of Corinth complains that heretics change the
writings of the Lord, he means the Old Testament (Eusebius, *Hist. eccl.* 4.23.12).[9] Their
misuse of Christian tradition is described as distorting or forging sayings of Jesus.[10]

Gamble's study of books in early Christian culture provides further evidence of the
early Christian distinction between the Old Testament as written scripture and the fundamentally oral embodiment of its Christian supplement.[11] Ignatius of Antioch complains
that some people will not believe in the gospel what is not to be found in the archives
(archeia). He responds by applying the term "archives" to the faith which results from the
cross, death, and resurrection of Jesus. This dispute appears to center on the christological
interpretation of the Old Testament, the archival records of the church.[12] Interrogated
about the contents of their book container, the Scillitan martyrs (d. 180 C.E.) replied, *libri
et epistulae Pauli viri iusti.* The "books" *(libri)* probably refers to the Old Testament as in
the expression *ta biblia kai hoi apostoloi* ("the books and the apostles") found in *2 Clem.*
4.2.[13] The teaching or letters of the apostles enunciate the message of salvation achieved in
Jesus Christ, which is the hermeneutical key to understanding the scripture. Neither the
words of Jesus nor the letters of Paul replace or correct the inherited canon. Nor could the
kerygma be proclaimed without appeal to the Old Testament.[14]

Christianity forged an astonishingly close relationship with books, perhaps as a consequence of its original engagement with the sacred Jewish texts. The production, circulation, and interpretation of books were essential to early Christian communities (e.g.,
1 Tim 3:13; Justin, *1 Apol.* 1.67).[15] This preoccupation was evident to the cultured oppo-

---

[8] Guy G. Stroumsa, *Hidden Wisdom: Esoteric Traditions and the Roots of Christian Mysticism*
(SHR LXX; Leiden: Brill, 1996), 88–90.

[9] Campenhausen, *Formation,* 170 n. 107.

[10] Ibid., 170 n. 108; also see Polycarp, *Phil.* 7.1; Irenaeus, *Haer.* 1 *praef.* Campenhausen notes a
shift in Justin Martyr's usage between the *First Apology,* which never refers to sayings of the Lord
with the formula "it is written," and the *Dialogue with Trypho,* which does (*Dial.* 49; 100; 105). This
change may reflect a shift among second-century Roman Christians toward viewing the gospels as
written records of dominical teachings.

[11] Harry Y. Gamble, *Books and Readers in the Early Church: A History of Early Christian Texts*
(New Haven: Yale, 1995), 150–52.

[12] Ignatius, *Phld.* 8.2; Gamble, *Books,* 152–53.

[13] Gamble, *Books,* 150–51.

[14] Ibid., 24.

[15] Ibid., 8–9. "The force of Christian dependence on Jewish scriptures for the question of the
literary culture of early Christianity is not much appreciated, and its implications have been
neglected under the influence of form criticism's preoccupation with oral tradition" (p. 9).

nents of Christianity, as Lucian's satirical picture of Peregrinus's career as a Christian bishop indicates (*Peregr.* 11).[16] Gamble has shown that early Christian literature was disseminated over a wider area and much more quickly than non-Christian works in the same period. From this perspective, the various gnostic and Valentinian teachers differ from other Christian counterparts in the particular version of the salvation story which is presented as the true meaning of scripture, and in their conviction that the apostles transmitted an esoteric teaching (Irenaeus, *Haer.* 1 *praef.*). But they do not possess a different understanding of canon, oral tradition, or the use of texts in Christian religious experience.[17]

2. Second-Century Crises and the Christian Bible

The conventional versions of canon history attach crucial importance to Marcion's having replaced the Old Testament and apostolic writings with a new canon consisting of a "theologically corrected" version of Luke and the Pauline letter collection. No form of allegory, typology, or prophecy could rescue the traditional Christian Bible, he felt.[18] To what extent is gnostic or Valentinian speculation responsible for this innovation? As an originating cause, not at all. Campenhausen speculates that Ptolemy may have formulated his theory of the levels of revelation in the Old Testament to distinguish himself from the teaching of Marcion as well as from that of orthodox Christians.[19] Ptolemy situates himself between those who treat the whole as decreed by God, on the one hand, and those who consider it the work of the devil who created the world, on the other.[20] He invokes words of the Savior as well as the teaching of Paul to defend his method of reading the Old Testament. But his "words of the Savior" are derived from Matthew and John—not Luke, as one might expect if he was familiar with Marcion's views. Hoffmann suggests that gnostic myth and speculation provided the material for followers like Apelles to systematize Marcion's theological views.[21]

---

[16] "He interpreted and explained some of their books, and even composed many, and they revered him as a god and made use of him as a lawgiver and regarded him as a protector," (quoted in Gamble, *Books,* 141). Gamble points out that in the later period Porphyry's attack on Christianity was devoted to a close criticism of Christian scriptures, and that Diocletian's first edict (303 C.E.) demanded the confiscation and destruction of Christian books (Eusebius, *Hist. eccl.* 8.2.4).

[17] Campenhausen's assertion (*Formation,* 87) that a gnostic canon is impossible because canon disintegrates on the basis of their principles of interpretation imposes the later image of a bounded canon of Christian writings on the early second century. He rightly recognizes that gnostic teachers were concerned with the question of how to interpret the Old Testament, not with generating a replacement scripture (80–86).

[18] Campenhausen, *Formation,* 77–79; 148–51; Alain le Boulluec, "The Bible in Use among the Marginally Orthodox in the Second and Third Centuries," in *The Bible in Greek Christian Antiquity* (ed. and trans. Paul M. Blowers; Notre Dame: University of Notre Dame, 1997), 197–205; Bruce M. Metzger, *The Canon of the New Testament: Its Origin, Development, and Significance* (Oxford: Clarendon, 1987), 77–90.

[19] Campenhausen, *Formation,* 165.

[20] Ptolemy, *Epistula ad Floram;* Epiphanius, *Pan.* 33.3, 2–3.

[21] R. Joseph Hoffmann, *Marcion: On the Restitution of Christianity: An Essay on the Development of Radical Pauline Theology in the Second Century* (Chico, Calif.: Scholars Press, 1984), 164–74.

The severe reductionism of Marcion's canon runs counter to the religious and literary culture of other Christians, gnostic and Valentinian as well as orthodox. However, his emphasis on correcting the texts of Luke and Paul reflects common issues in ancient literary production. What constituted publication is unclear. Authors complain that their unfinished texts have been copied and are circulated without approval. Such problems could be dealt with by correcting editions by removing accretions, or making the earlier versions outdated by releasing an expanded edition.[22]

The Apocryphon of James begins as a letter from James, the brother of the Lord,[23] to an individual who is a Christian teacher or apostle ("servant of salvation of the saints," 1.19–20; cf. 1 Cor 4:1; Luke 1:2).[24] It introduces what follows as a revelation not intended for general publication, since the Lord gave it to James and Peter alone,[25] not to the Twelve as a group (1.10–25). The reference to "Hebrew characters" (1.16) may be a detail intended to support the authenticity of the revelation, its sacredness, or further protection of its esoteric teaching.[26] The epistolary introduction concludes with a fragmentary reference to another apocryphon sent ten months earlier. The recipient is to contrast the earlier work revealed to James with the attached volume (1.29–2.7). The nature of the contrast between the two has been lost in the lacuna. The double revelation may be an affirmation of the author's status as the mediator of saving revelation,[27] but it may also be an example of authorial recall, correction, or addition to a work earlier parts of which have already been dispatched.[28] If taken as a correction or supplement, then the association of James with Peter goes beyond asserting the superior insight of James and those Christians who have faith in his teaching (1.26–28).[29] It confirms the validity of this revelation because it was also given to Peter, though not taught publically to the Twelve.[30] The issue of its "Hebrew characters" and textual correction reflects the same concern for establishing the correct

---

[22] Gamble, *Books*, 118–19. Gamble suggests that the text of a work only became relatively fixed when there were a large number of copies in circulation.

[23] Perhaps no longer clearly distinguished from the son of Zebedee, given his importance as leader in the Jerusalem church (Gal 1:18–19; 2:6–12) and as a witness to the risen Lord (1 Cor 15:7); see Francis E. Williams, "The Apocryphon of James," in *Nag Hammadi Codex I (The Jung Codex): Introductions, Texts, Translations, Indices* (NHS 22; ed. Harold W. Attridge; Leiden: Brill, 1985), 20–21.

[24] The lacuna at 1.2 contained either the name of the addressee or a designation ending in -*thos*; see Donald Rouleau, "L'Epître apocryphe de Jacques," in Donald Rouleau and Louise Roy, *L'Epître apocryphe de Jacques [NH I,2]: L'Acte de Pierre (BG 4)* (Bibliothèque copte de Nag Hammadi, section "textes" 18; Quebec: Les Presses de l'Université Laval, 1987), 92–95.

[25] As recipients of separate postresurrection visions of the Lord (1 Cor 15:5a and 7a; Eusebius, *Hist. eccl.* 2.1, 4).

[26] Rouleau ("L'Epître," 97) also points to the magical use of Hebrew sounding words and phrases in Marcosian rituals (Irenaeus, *Haer.* 1.21.3).

[27] So Rouleau, "L'Epître," 97.

[28] Gamble, *Books*, 118–26. Irenaeus had previously dispatched the first two books of *Adversus haereses* when he sent the third (*Haer.* 3 *praef.*).

[29] See the discussion in Rouleau, "L'Epître," 15–16.

[30] In *Gos. Mary* 10.1–13 Peter challenges the validity of a private revelation to Mary that was not given to the Twelve. Anne Pasquier has noted the relationship between these two texts; *L'Evangile selon Marie (BG 1)* (Bibliothèque copte de Nag Hammadi, section "textes" 10; Québec: Les Presses de l'Université Laval, 1983), 70.

text of an apostolic revelation that was evident in Marcion's project.[31] But the question of whether apostolic tradition rests in individual apostles, in the Twelve corporately, or must be confirmed by its coherence with other apostolic witnesses points toward the other crisis of the late second century: establishing a gospel canon.

We need not rehearse Campenhausen's detailed account of how Irenaeus appealed to the historical evidence of a four-gospel canon and Acts against his Valentinian opponents.[32] He observes that in so doing Irenaeus shifted the criteria of theological argument from the interpretation of the Old Testament to the sayings of the Lord and the writings which testify to apostolic tradition: the letters of Paul, and the Gospels and Acts, seen as teaching of the apostles. The Gospels and Acts supplement the older Christian tradition of appeals to the sayings of the Lord and Paul.[33] He opposes the Valentinian use of parables and riddle-like sayings to defend the distinction between exoteric and esoteric teaching (*Haer.* 3.5.1).[34] Irenaeus used the empiricist tradition of ancient medical writers to place strictures on theological inquiry and cut off the Valentinian quest for deeper wisdom about the divine world prior to the acts of creation recorded in Genesis (*Haer.* 2.25–28).[35] The four-gospel canon alone cannot serve as defense against the esoteric tradition; this esotericism is grounded in the oral tradition of Christian teaching and in the established cultural tradition among intellectuals that revered myths and sacred texts encoding higher philosophical truths. Stroumsa points out that Celsus rejected the allegorical interpretation of the Bible on the grounds that it was not mythological but the historical and legal material of a nation. Such writings are to be read according to their straightforward, plain meaning.[36] In short, the hermeneutical principle required to exclude esoteric interpretations of the four-gospel canon detracts from their cultural value as repositories of religious wisdom.

Stroumsa may be right in saying that "more than any other single cause, it is the gnostic challenge which is responsible for Patristic Christianity eventually 'opting out' of esoteric conceptions."[37] This radical departure from viewing the Christian writings as pluriform in meaning weakens the religious profundity in the texts. Marcion had made two conceptual shifts necessary to Irenaeus's project as well: denial of allegorical reading of the scripture, and the assertion that apostolic preaching, in his case Paul's gospel, is

---

[31] Gamble, *Books*, 126: "What is too little recognized is that in antiquity the conscientious reader was always interested in the correction of textual corruptions since, given the conditions of the production and transmission of texts, the accuracy of a text was necessarily an open question. The irony is that the attribution of authority to a document did not necessarily confirm the received text and ensure its careful preservation but, by heightening interest in its accuracy, opened the way for critical emendation."

[32] Campenhausen, *Formation*, 171–90.

[33] Ibid., 190–93.

[34] On the importance of riddle, enigma, and parable to ancient esotericism and early Christian interpretation of the Hebrew Bible see Stroumsa, *Hidden Wisdom*, 92–108.

[35] See the detailed argument in William Schoedel, "Theological Method in Irenaeus (*Adversus Haereses* 2.25–28)," *JTS* NS 35 (1984): 31–49.

[36] Stroumsa, *Hidden Wisdom*, 101–2. Origen attempts to defend a common style by which "our prophets, Jesus and his apostles" provided teaching that could win over the masses without excluding the need for esoteric interpretation required to attain the higher truths (*Cels.* 6.2).

[37] Stroumsa, *Hidden Wisdom*, 106.

resident in a book.[38] These developments may facilitate the transition to viewing a collection of Christian writings as equivalent to the Old Testament as sacred canon.

Gnostic teachers may have exploited these developments to advance their case for such sources of esoteric teaching as *The Apocryphon of James*. The author opens his account with the Twelve gathered as a group recording the Savior's teaching to each one, both exoteric and esoteric (2.8–15). Further, an allusion to Acts 1:10–11 in lines 17–18 attaches this new revelation to Jesus' promised return in Acts. The Twelve are witnesses to the Lord's additional teaching, which itself fulfills a promise indicated in the exoteric revelation. At the same time, the 550 days appears to reflect the tradition found in *The Ascension of Isaiah* 9.16 and gnostic writings (*Haer.* 1.3.2; 30.14) that the final postresurrection revelation occurred 18 months after Easter.[39] Acts traditions are also employed in the introduction to *The Letter of Peter to Philip* (NHC VIII 132.10–133.13).[40] Peter must summon Philip to join the other apostles from whom he is separated in order to receive the Lord's commandment to preach the gospel throughout the world. In this instance, the revelation is more closely linked to the gospel text than in *The Apocryphon of James*, since it occurs during the vision reported in Matt 28:16–20.[41] The revelation dialogue between Jesus and the disciples concludes with echoes of Luke 24:51–53 (138.3–10). Unlike *The Apocryphon of James*, which makes James rather than Peter the central figure in understanding and transmitting the Lord's teaching,[42] *The Letter of Peter to Philip* retains the emphasis on Peter as leader of the apostolic group found in the Synoptics and Acts.[43] Both writings might be said to attest to the growing importance of the narrative accounts of Jesus and the apostles in the four gospels and Acts advocated by Irenaeus. They might even be described as examples of "rewritten scripture" in Trebolle Barrera's terms.[44] No claim to apostolic teaching could be credible without evoking the authoritative, publicly available text.

Evidence that esoteric gnostic teaching has been cast in literary forms which presume general agreement concerning the authority of the "four gospels and Acts" supports the view that a major shift in Christian usage was underway in the later part of the second

---

[38] Eusebius, *Hist. eccl.* 3, 4. See John Barton, *Holy Writings, Sacred Text: The Canon in Early Christianity* (Louisville, Ky.: Westminster John Knox, 1997), 42–54.

[39] Rouleau, "L'Epître," 99.

[40] See the notes of Marvin Meyer in Frederik Wisse and Marvin Meyer, "The Letter of Peter to Philip," in *Nag Hammadi Codex VIII* (ed. John H. Sieber; NHS 31; Leiden: Brill, 1991), 235–37.

[41] See the echoes of Matt 28:16–17 (133,13–20) and 28:20 (134,17–18).

[42] Rouleau, "L'Epître," 100. The question of suffering discipleship and reward posed by Peter in Matt 19:27–30 has been shifted to James (4,22–31; ibid., 105–6).

[43] See the discussion of Peter in gnostic sources in Pheme Perkins, *Peter: Apostle for the Whole Church* (Columbia: University of South Carolina, 1994), 159–63, and Christian Grappe, *Images de Pierre aux deux premiers siècles* (Paris: Presses Universitaires de France, 1995), 170–76.

[44] See Trebolle Barrera, *Jewish Bible*, 184–91; an expression adopted by Grappe, *Images*, 171–72. This terminology has also been applied to gnostic rewriting of Genesis in such treatises as *Ap. John*, *Hyp. Arch.*, *Orig. World* and the sources reported in *Haer.* 1:29 and 30. On the question of "rewriting" and adaptation of non-Christian material to a framework acceptable to Christian readers, see Louis Painchaud, "La classification des textes de Nag Hammadi et le phénomène des Réécritures," in Louis Painchaud and Anne Pasquier, *Les textes de Nag Hammadi et le problème de leur classification: Actes du colloque tenu à Québec du 15 au 19 Septembre 1993* (Bibliothèque copte de Nag Hammadi, section 'Etudes' 3; Quebec: Les Presses de l'Université Laval, 1995), 76–85.

century C.E. In view of this shift, are we justified in speaking of Irenaeus's anti-gnostic polemics as the originating point of a four-gospel canon? Many scholars have challenged the historical plausibility of that view.[45] Trebolle Barrera suggests that reactions to hetero-dox forms of Christianity may have made important contributions to the evolution of the new Christian canon of the fourth century C.E. but were not capable of generating such developments. He suggests that other social and cultural factors must be considered: exhaustion of the oral tradition; the need to transmit authority; the ecumenical growth of the church, with Rome as crossroads between eastern and western traditions; and the fourth-century councils combined with the cultural interest in lists of classical authors.[46] Patricia Cox Miller, using a postmodernist hermeneutic to analyze the interplay of lan-guage, metaphor, allusion, and expression in *The Gospel of Truth* and *The Testimony of Truth,* concludes that what separates gnostic from orthodox teachers like Irenaeus is not the deliberate creation of a canon in opposition to the gnostics. Rather a major shift in understanding of text and language has occurred. For *The Gospel of Truth* the received text is discovered and uncovered in searching out truth through multiple meanings and over-lapping (and even conflicting) significations. What appears to Irenaeus as deceitful obfus-cation of true teaching is itself the truth of searching.[47] But this very process has been shaped by the move of religious traditions into the public arena of books during the Helle-nistic period.[48] The peculiar constellation of Old Testament exegesis, pagan mythology, philosophical *topoi,* and gnostic Christian materials found in a writing like *On the Origin of the World* is evidence of the strange bedfellows created by the literary culture of the Greco-Roman period.[49]

3. Did Gnostics Create a Scripture?

The view that a Christian Bible incorporating the four gospels and Acts is a reaction to gnostic and Valentinian teaching has often led to the image of dueling canons. Use of designations familiar from the later New Testament canon (gospel, epistle, acts, apoca-lypse) for writings found at Nag Hammadi has generated the popular misperception that gnostics had their own scriptures. The Nag Hammadi Library provides little evidence for such a conclusion. Gamble has pointed out that survival for any ancient text required that a number of copies be in circulation.[50] A number of the Nag Hammadi codices are multiple-copy survivors, though in some cases the additional witnesses are only fragmen-

---

[45] Earlier studies have confused canonicity with the authority obtained by widely used texts (see Barton, *Holy Writings,* 8–19). One should also beware of assuming that all books of the Bible were available in all Christian communities (ibid., 24).

[46] Trebolle Barrera, *Jewish Bible,* 239–40, 251–52.

[47] Patricia Cox Miller, "Words with an Alien Voice: Gnostics, Scripture and Canon," *JAAR* 57 (1989): 459–83.

[48] See Paul Veyne, *Did the Greeks Believe in Their Myths? An Essay on the Constitutive Imagina-tion* (Chicago: University of Chicago Press, 1984), 46.

[49] On the mythic background to *On the Origins of the World,* see M. Tardieu, *Trois Mythes Gnostiques: Adam, Eros et les animaux d'Egypte dans un écrit de Nag Hammadi (II,5)* (Paris: Etudes Augustiniennes, 1974).

[50] Gamble, *Books,* 126.

tary (*Gospel of Truth, Apocryphon of John, Gospel of Thomas, On the Origin of the World, Gospel of the Egyptians, Eugnostos, Sophia of Jesus Christ*). Some have titles and content which suggest that they are versions of works known to nongnostic authors (*Gospel of Truth* in *Haer.* 3.11.9 [?]; *Apocryphon of John* and source of *Haer.* 1.29; *Paraphrase of Shem* is related to a much more explicitly Christian *Paraphrase of Seth* in Hippolytus, *Haer.* 5.19–22; regarding *Second Treatise of the Great Seth*, Epiphanius refers to a number of works concerning Seth in *Pan.* 40.7.4; *Zostrianos* and *Allogenes* in Porphyry, *Vit. Plot.* 16).

Source analyses have suggested incorporation of material from one tract into another or a source common to both. The relationships between sayings collections are most complex, since both *The Gospel of Thomas* and Q have undergone several redactions.[51] *The Gospel of Thomas* underlies sayings found in *The Dialogue of the Savior*.[52] The evidence of the Greek fragments and patristic citations suggests that there was no stable tradition of these sayings until the early fourth century C.E.[53] *The Sophia of Jesus Christ* has incorporated most of *Eugnostos* into a revelation dialogue.[54] Somewhat more remote parallels in phrasing and rhetorical structure have been noted between *Eugnostos* and sections of *On the Origin of the World*.[55] The latter has also incorporated and rewritten a tradition concerning the exaltation of Sabaoth paralleled in *Hypostasis of the Archons* and incorporated elements of the revelation discourse, *Thunder: Perfect Mind*, into its presentation of Eve.[56] Often the incorporation of blocks of exegetical material or such parallels to other gnostic writings serve as indicators of more complex stages of redaction that have produced the Greek text whose Coptic translation we actually possess.[57] Use, revision, and rewriting demonstrate the ongoing significance of these traditions to a group of devotees. However, lack of stable text forms makes it difficult to see these texts as products of an effort to generate a gnostic substitute for the Christian Bible. Michael Williams has proposed that such a move dictated the order of tracts in Nag Hammadi Codex II. By treating *The Apocryphon of John* as rewritten Genesis, the codex begins with ancient tradition. *The*

---

[51] See James M. Robinson, John S. Kloppenborg, and Paul Hoffmann, *Critical Edition of Q* (Minneapolis: Fortress, 2000); Thomas Zöckler, *Jesu Lehren im Thomasevangelium* (NHMS 47; Leiden: Brill, 1999), 9–98.

[52] April D. de Conick, "The Dialogue of the Savior and the Mystical Sayings of Jesus," *VC* 50 (1996): 178–99.

[53] Zöckler, *Jesu Lehren*, 25–28.

[54] See the parallels edition by Douglas M. Parrott, *Nag Hammadi Codices V, 2–5 and VI with Papyrus Berolinensis 8502, 1 and 4* (NHS 11; Leiden: Brill, 1979).

[55] Louis Painchaud, *L'Ecrit sans titre: Traité sur l'origine du monde (NH II, 5 et XIII, 2 et Brit. Lib. Or. 4926 [1])* (Bibliothèque copte de Nag Hammadi, section "textes" 21; Quebec: Les Presses de l'Université Laval, 1995), 98–101.

[56] Painchaud (*L'Ecrit sans titre*, 254–89) attributes the Sabaoth material to the first or possibly second revision of *Orig. World*. The parallel to *Thund.* belongs to a second stage of revision (394–95).

[57] So far scholars have not reached any consensus on such analyses. For examples of detailed and thoughtful efforts see Alastair H. B. Logan (*Gnostic Truth and Christian Heresy: A Study in the History of Gnosticism* [Edinburgh: T&T Clark; Peabody: Hendrickson, 1996], 44–51) on *Ap. John*, and Painchaud (*L'Ecrit sans titre*, 117–43) on *Orig. World*. In both instances, the version(s) translated into Coptic may not have reached their final form before the last quarter of the third century C.E. even though the core text may have originated a century earlier, as the parallels between *Haer.* 1.29 and the opening sections of *Ap. John* indicate.

Gospel of Thomas, the ancient sayings gospel, represents the gospel tradition, while the *Gospel of Philip* offers an apostolic meditation on the teachings of the gospel. *The Apocryphon of John* opens two other codices (III and IV), and an expansion of the Pronoia hymn which concludes the long recension of *The Apocryphon of John* is related to the opening tract in Codex XIII *(Trimorphic Protennoia)* as well. *The Paraphrase of Shem,* the opening tract in Codex VII, is a Genesis substitute derived from a different exegetical tradition.[58] At best, Williams has shown that in the fourth-century codices of the Christian Bible which begin with Genesis and conclude with apostolic letters or Revelation could have influenced the order of tracts in these codices. This observation provides an important bit of evidence about the influence of the Christian Bible. Not only are certain Christian writings to be included with the Old Testament, but the books of this canon are to be grouped in a certain order.[59]

4. The Christian Bible in the Nag Hammadi Library

If gnostic and Valentinian teachers did not propose an alternative Bible, what can the gnostic codices from Nag Hammadi[60] suggest about the Christian Bible as used? The most obvious divergence between gnostics and other early Christian literature is the scarcity of citation formulae. Two conventional examples occur in *Orig. World:* "as it is written in the Holy Book" (110.30), and "as it is written concerning this" (122.28). The first introduces a general discussion of the tree of knowledge (Gen 3:6–7). Since its content is closer to *1 En.* 32:5, Painchaud opts for Genesis as read through the latter as the book in question.[61] The phrase "it is written in the holy book" recurs in *On the Origin of the World* 122.12–13 followed only by the phrase, "they eat it," in conjunction with the exegesis of the appearance of three phoenixes. The closest possible biblical references suggest a combination of the permission to eat of the trees of paradise in Gen 2:16 LXX and the only use of *phoinikes,* the fruit of the date palm, in 2 Sam 16:1–2 LXX. An elaborate word play on the two senses of the Greek word *phoinix* is presumed by this reference.[62] Finally, the phrase "it is written" introduces a quotation of Ps 91:13 LXX in 122.28. All three exegetical notes appear to be redactional additions to the original text.

On the Origin of the World contains a string of book titles directing the reader to further information concerning topics the author is not going to treat in detail. Some appear to be Old Testament apocrypha (102.8, "The Archangelic [Book] of the Prophet Moses"; 102.24, "The First Book of Norea"; 107.2–3). The others may be magical or cosmological speculation, though "The Configuration of the Fate of Heaven That Is beneath the Twelve"

---

[58] Michael A. Williams, "Interpreting the Nag Hammadi Library as 'Collection(s)' in the History of 'Gnosticism(s)'," in Painchaud and Pasquier, *Textes de Nag Hammadi,* 17–28.

[59] On canon lists and codex order see Williams, "Interpreting," 14–15.

[60] This survey omits *Plato Rep.,* the Hermetic texts *(Disc. 8–9; Pr. Thanks.; Asclepius)* and the wisdom collections *(Teach. Silv.* and *Sent. Sextus),* since they are generally agreed to be nongnostic compositions. Other writings whose gnostic provenance is sometimes questioned have been retained.

[61] Painchaud, *L'Ecrit sans titre,* 374.

[62] Ibid., 468–70.

(107.14–17) is matched with the "Book of Solomon." It describes the effects of beneficent androgynous powers, whereas the Solomon apocryphon deals with demons. "The Twelfth Cosmos of the Prophet Hieralias" (112.23–24) could be a deformed name taken from Greek: *hieros Elias* ("holy Elijah"), an account of the prophet's ascent into heaven (2 Kgs 2:1–11).[63] Like the Old Testament citation formulae, these notes also belong to later redaction of the text.

An exegetical tradition which cited and interpreted problematic biblical passages shows up in passages in which the gnostic authors of *The Apocryphon of John* and *The Testimony of Truth* undermine the ordinary Christian reading of Torah. *The Apocryphon of John* introduces a series of Genesis references with the expression, "not as Moses said" (NHC II 13.19–20, Gen 1:2; 22.22–24, Gen 2:21b;[64] 23.3, Gen 2:21c; 29.6–7, Gen 6:18 LXX). The correct interpretation of Gen 2:21b, the sleep which falls on Adam, follows from Isa 6:10 (22.26–27). Thus it is incorrect to treat this material as though gnostic exegetes simply rejected the authority of Genesis or even Moses.[65] The Isaiah text is introduced with the formula, "for he said through the prophet" (22.25–26). The "he" must be the subject of the actions performed on Adam, the creator. Despite his own intentions to deceive humanity, the creator has told the truth about his actions in scripture. Although cast in antithetical formulae, each item in the list involved problematic anthropomorphisms which might call for reinterpretation among the learned. The long version contains an interesting variant on "not as Moses said" in 22.22–23: "it is not as Moses wrote and you heard," a formula that depicts the way in which most persons experienced texts in antiquity. Such hearing carries with it a particular hermeneutic which the gnostic teacher must correct.

The Testimony of Truth uses citations in a midrash on the serpent of Gen 3 which incorporates references to Exod 4 and 7 and Num 21 (NHC IX 45.23–49.7).[66] Though this material shares exegetical interpretations with *The Hypostasis of the Archons* and *On the Origin of the World,* the citation formulae sometimes identify the book in question ("the Law," 45.23; "other book called Exodus," 48.19–20; "book of the generation of Adam" [= Gen 5], 50.5–6). Unlike the formulae in *The Apocryphon of John* and *On the Origin of the World,* which introduced brief phrases or even single words, most of the midrash in *The Testimony of Truth* consists of quotations from the Septuagint. Its function in the polemic against orthodox Christians and other gnostic teachers is difficult to discern since the bottom half of page 49 is lost. However details from the midrash turn up in the polemic

---

[63] Ibid., 386.

[64] The long version in codex II expands the formula "as Moses said" to identify the book, "in his first book," 1.24; perhaps a scribal expansion.

[65] *Pace* Nils Dahl, "The Arrogant Archon and the Lewd Sophia," in *The Rediscovery of Gnosticism Volume 2: Sethian Gnosticism* (ed. B. Layton; Leiden: Brill, 1981), 698; for a general critique of the view that gnosticism is born out of a radical reversal of Genesis see Michael Williams, *Rethinking,* 54–79; especially the chart of values attached to various elements in the Genesis narrative, 61–62.

[66] See Birger A. Pearson, "Gnostic Interpretation of the Old Testament in the *Testimony of Truth* (NHC IX,3)," *HTR* 73 (1980): 311–19; idem, *Nag Hammadi Codices IX and X* (NHS 15; Leiden: Brill, 1981), 106–13. The beginning of the midrash is marked by a paragraph sign in the margin between lines 22 and 23 (Pearson, *NHC IX and X,* 158).

against Christians in Julian the Apostate (*Against the Galileans* 75B–94A).[67] It may have already been a set piece of polemic when it was incorporated into *The Testimony of Truth*, apparently in defense of the claim to provide the true, Christian, spiritual reading of scripture. Orthodox Christians are identified with those for whom Moses wrote the Law (50.1–8).

The redactional character of the citation formulae passages suggests a secondary development that has adopted exegetical traditions from other Christian opponents.[68] There are even fewer citation formulae attached to New Testament texts—a further indication that the "New Testament" only came to be considered equivalent to the Old Testament in the third and fourth centuries C.E.? The "great apostle" warned of conflict with the powers (*Hypostasis of the Archons* 86.20–27; Col 1:13; Eph 6:12). The addressee may remember "reading in the gospel that Elijah appeared," citing the Transfiguration in defense of the author's teaching about resurrection (*Treatise on the Resurrection* 48.8–11).[69] "The scripture" introduces a conflation of Johannine sayings (*Second Treatise of the Great Seth* 49.29–35, John 17:21–23 with references to Spirit and water, 3:5, 4:14 and 7:38–39). The phrase "in the gospel" introduces an exegetical question about referring to the Savior as Man and Son of Man, in the Genesis story of *Sophia of Jesus Christ* (NHC III 103.22–104.4; BG 98.7–13).

Lack of citation formulae hardly signals lack of interest. Central to the enterprise is the subtle introduction of single words or phrases whose provenance and context the reader must recognize in order to understand the argument of a particular text.[70] Such facility presumes an audience that can hear such allusions easily. It requires reading of the Christian Bible independently of the instruction provided by the gnostic treatises. Study of the biblical allusions in the Nag Hammadi Library provides a glimpse into the operative collection of sacred texts in the their circles. However, the distinctions between citation, allusion, and construct in the mind of the reader are not always easy to determine. Scholars come to vastly different conclusions even in the case of works like *The Gospel of Truth* that have been the subject of extensive analysis.

The accompanying tables represent only a preliminary survey based largely on the biblical index of Evans, Webb, and Wiebe.[71] The codices have been grouped according to

---

[67] Pearson, *NHC IX and X*, 106.

[68] *The Exegesis of the Soul* adopts a set of explicit citations and quotations from the prophets (Jeremiah, Hosea, Ezekiel in 129.5–130.20; Isaiah in 136.3 and 9), the apostle Paul in 1 Corinthians and Ephesians (130.28–131.9), Genesis (attributed to "the prophet" [= Moses]; 133.1, 28–29); the prophet speaking in the Psalms (133.16; 134.16; 137.15), as well as "the Savior" (John, 134.35; Matt, 135.16) and Acts (135.22), to call the soul to repentance and return to its heavenly home. Citations from Homer are also included. This homiletic use of biblical citations is very different from the other gnostic texts; the work does not appear to reflect specifically gnostic use of scripture.

[69] M. J. Edwards ("The *Epistle to Rheginus:* Valentinianism in the Fourth Century," *NovT* 37 [1995]: 76–91) argues that this is a fourth-century C.E. interpretation of Paul's teaching on resurrection.

[70] See the demonstration of this point in the case of *On the Origin of the World* by Louis Painchaud ("The Use of Scripture in Gnostic Literature," *JECS* 4 [1996]: 129–47) and in the interpretation of *The Gospel of Philip* by Einar Thomassen ("How Valentinian is *The Gospel of Philip*?" in Turner and McGuire, *Nag Hammadi Library*, 251–79).

[71] Craig A. Evans, Robert L. Webb, and Richard A. Wiebe, eds. *Nag Hammadi Texts and the Bible* (NTTS 18; Leiden: Brill, 1993).

the scribal characteristics which link some of them together rather than in numerical order.[72] In Tables 21-1 through 21-4, Hebrews has been classified as "other" since the Nag Hammadi Library does not indicate whether or not its authors considered it Pauline.[73] Acts is also included as "other." Not surprisingly, almost all of the texts listed under "Torah" are taken from Genesis, particularly Gen 1–9. A rough breakdown of allusions to individual Pauline letters (Table 21-5) suggests a collection similar to that generally assumed for this period. Similarly, the citations of the gospels and Acts (Table 21-6) show a strong preference for Matthew and John. Mark hardly occurs at all. Once the unusually high figures for Luke in *The Gospel of Thomas* are recognized not as allusions to the finished gospel but as evidence that *The Gospel of Thomas* reflects the pregospel sayings traditions of the first century,[74] Luke is also considerably less prominent than Matthew. Marcion's choice of the latter cannot be attributed to the influence of early gnostic speculation.

Table 21-1: Biblical References in Nag Hammadi Codices I, XI, and VII

	Old Testament			New Testament		
	Torah	*Prophets*	*Other*	*Gospels*	*Paul*	*Other*
Codex I						
Ap. Jas.	—	—	1	14	1	—
Gos. Truth	5	1	—	26	17	3
Treat. Res	—	1	—	2	11	1
Tri. Trac.	7	—	—	8	10	3
Codex XI						
Interp. Know.	1	—	—	11	24	2
Val. Exp.	5	1	2	26	5	5
Allogenes	—	—	—	—	—	—
Codex VII						
Paraph. Shem	15	—	—	—	—	—
Treat. Seth	5	1	2	26	5	5
Apoc. Pet	—	—	—	13	2	1
Steles Seth	—	—	—	5	1	—

---

[72] See Williams, *Rethinking*, 243.

[73] On the disputed canonicity of Hebrews in the West, see Campenhausen, *Formation*, 232–33.

[74] Early origins for many of the *Gos. Thom.* logia does not preclude the accretion of later sayings that do reflect knowledge of the canonical gospel traditions or gnostic theology. Each case has to be argued on its own merits. See Charles W. Hedrick, "Thomas and the Synoptics: Aiming at a Consensus," *SecCent* 7 (1989/90): 39–56.

Table 21-2: Biblical References in Nag Hammadi Codices VIII, V, VI, and IX

	Old Testament			New Testament		
	Torah	*Prophets*	*Other*	*Gospels*	*Paul*	*Other*
Codex VIII						
Zost.	3	—	—	—	—	—
Ep. Pet. Phil.	1	—	—	11	5	20
Codex V						
Apoc. Paul	—	—	1	—	7	1
1 Apoc. Jas.	1	—	—	—	—	—
2 Apoc. Jas.	1	—	—	14	—	4
Apoc. Adam	20	—	1	—	—	3
Codex VI						
Acts Pet. 12 Apos.	—	—	2	4	—	1
Thund.	—	—	—	—	—	—
Auth. Teach.	—	—	—	—	—	—
Great Pow.	15	—	—	15	—	7
Codex IX						
Melch.	6	1	—	8	1	10
Norea	—	—	—	—	—	—
Testim. Truth	16	1	6	41	11	6

Table 21-3: Biblical References in Nag Hammadi Codices II and XIII

	Old Testament			New Testament		
	Torah	*Prophets*	*Other*	*Gospels*	*Paul*	*Other*
Codex II						
Ap. John	37	3	—	4	15	5
Gos. Thom.	5	1	2	150	12	6
Gos. Phil.	11	—	—	43	31	5
Hyp. Arch.	29	1	1	3	1	1
Orig. World	60	11	3	12	2	10
Exeg. Soul	4	7	2	3	6	1
Thom. Cont.	—	1	1	4	—	2
Codex XIII						
Trim. Prot.	2	1	—	25	11	1

Table 21-4: Biblical References in Nag Hammadi Codices III and X

| | Old Testament | | | New Testament | | |
	Torah	Prophets	Other	Gospels	Paul	Other
Codex III						
Gos. Eg.	2	1	—	4	2	—
Eugnostos	—	—	—	—	—	—
Soph. Jes. Chr.	6	—	—	9	—	1
Dial. Sav.	2	—	—	15	2	—
Codex X						
Marsanes	—	—	—	1	—	—

Table 21-5: References to Pauline Epistles in the Nag Hammadi Library

	Rom	1 Cor	2 Cor	Gal	Eph	Phil	Col	1–2 Thess	1–2 Tim
Codex I									
Ap. Jas.	—	—	—	1	—	—	—	—	—
Gos. Tr.	2	2	2	—	2	—	7	—	2
Treat. Res.	2	3	1	—	—	—	—	—	—
Tri. Trac.	3	3	—	1	1	—	2	—	—
Codex II									
Ap. John	2	2	1	—	3	2	3	—	2
Gos. Thom.	5	3	1	1	—	—	—	—	2
Gos. Phil.	4	10	3	3	1	2	2	1	—
Hyp. Arch.	—	—	—	—	1	—	—	—	—
Orig. World	—	1	—	—	1	—	—	—	—
Codex III									
Gos. Eg.	—	—	—	—	—	—	—	2	—
Dial. Sav.	—	1	—	—	—	—	—	—	1
Codex VII									
Treat. Seth.	—	3	1	—	—	—	1	—	—
Apoc. Pet.	—	—	1	—	—	—	—	—	—
Steles Seth	1	—	—	—	—	—	—	—	—
Codex VIII									
Pet. Phil.	1	—	—	—	5	—	—	—	—
Codex IX									
Melch.	—	—	—	—	1	—	—	—	—
Testim. Truth	—	1	2	2	6	—	—	—	—
Codex XI									
Interp. Know.	5	10	—	—	1	—	—	1	1
Val. Exp.	—	3	—	—	—	—	2	—	—
Codex XIII									
Trim. Prot.	1	3	—	1	—	1	6	—	—

Table 21-6: References to the Gospels and Acts in the Nag Hammadi Library

	Matt	John	Luke	Mark	Acts
Codex I					
Ap. Jas.	7	5	2	—	—
Gos. Truth	7	17	—	—	1
Treat. Res.	2	—	—	—	—
Tri. Trac.	2	5	—	—	—
Codex II					
Ap. John	2	2	—	—	—
Gos. Thom.	74	35	39	—	1
Gos. Phil.	22	17	4	—	—
Hyp. Arch.	—	2	—	—	—
Orig. World	10	2	—	—	—
Exeg. Soul	1	2	—	—	1
Thom. Cont.	2	—	2	—	1
Codex III					
Gos. Eg.	—	—	4	—	—
Soph. Jes. Chr.	4	2	2	1	—
Dial. Sav.	9	3	2	—	—
Codex V					
2 Apoc. Jas.	6	7	1	—	—
Codex VI					
Acts Pet. 12 Apos.	3	1	—	—	—
Great Pow.	8	2	4	1	1
Codex VII					
Treat. Seth	8	16	—	—	2
Apoc. Pet.	11	—	2	—	1
Steles Seth	—	5	—	—	—
Codex VIII					
Ep. Pet. Phil.	6	4	3	1	20
Codex IX					
Melch.	8	—	—	—	—
Testim. Truth	13	18	—	1	—
Codex X					
Marsanes	1	—	—	—	—
Codex XI					
Interp. Know.	7	2	—	—	1
Val. Exp.	—	6	1	—	—
Codex XII					
Trim. Prot.	6	15	3	—	—

5. Conclusion

One cannot press the data in this preliminary survey. The identification of references and allusions remains hotly contested. It is rendered more difficult by the fact that we are dealing with translations. Given the indirect style of gnostic treatment of the biblical tradition, the translators may even miss the reference and create further confusion in the text. Tuckett's observation that the use of Matthew in *The Gospel of Truth* suggests a text composed in the period before the four gospel canon had taken hold does seem to apply to the gnostic and Valentinian writings in the Nag Hammadi Library as a whole.[75] The most striking difference between gnostics and other Christians lies in their appropriation of the Old Testament, which, as we have argued, was the Christian Bible in the earliest centuries. While there is some evidence for gnostic use of other Old Testament texts, particularly the affirmations of divine sovereignty and the polemic against idols in second Isaiah,[76] Genesis (with Jewish apocryphal traditions developed around its opening chapters) is the only Old Testament book which is widely used and foundational to understanding key features in gnostic and Valentinian speculation about the origins of the world.[77] The Christian Bible, as we have noted above, was the inherited Jewish scripture read through a hermeneutic lens that was heavily dependent upon the prophets and psalms. The citation index to NA[27] has approximately 5 columns devoted to Genesis, 9 to the psalms, and 22 to the prophets, for example. Are gnostic authors simply unfamiliar with the prophetic canon? Hardly. *Ptolemy to Flora* recognizes that Jesus cited Isaiah in Matt 15:4–9 (4.13). *Tri. Trac.* 113.5–34 discusses the prophets' oracles concerning the Savior. They are not rejected, but each prophet can only speak of what he has seen. The true nature of the Savior has not been revealed to any of the prophets so their revelations are only partial.[78] Further the numerological scheme by which each prophet is assigned to one of the lower archons as his mouthpiece in *Haer.* 1.30.10–11 produces a list of twenty-two, the number of books in the Jewish scripture according to Josephus (*C. Ap.* 1.8.38–41).[79]

If gnostic and Valentinian authors are aware of the larger Old Testament canon and of the importance of prophetic texts in early Christian reading of that canon as the ex-

---

[75] C. M. Tuckett, "Synoptic Tradition in the Gospel of Truth and the Testimony of Truth," *JTS* ns. 35 (1984): 133–40.

[76] Painchaud, "Use," 134–44; see the discussion of Isa 41:24–29 LXX in *Orig. World* 103.25 (idem, *L'Ecrit sans titre*, 298).

[77] While I agree that one would never come up with the mythological scenario or its gnostic interpretation based solely on apocryphal Jewish traditions of Gen interpretation, Luttikhuizen's attempt to argue that this material is secondary to what was an essentially pagan myth fails to account for the attention to details in the Genesis material that are crucial to the shape of the gnostic and Valentinian myth (Gerard P. Luttikhuizen, "The Thought Patterns of Gnostic Mythologizers and Their Use of Biblical Traditions," in Turner and McGuire, *Nag Hammadi Library*, 89–101).

[78] Similar views of prophetic inspiration appear in *Haer.* 1.7.2 and *Exc. Theod.* 59.2, the prophets only knew the psychic Christ or in *Tri. Trac.* they could only perceive the bodily manifestation of the Savior (see Einar Thomassen in Louis Painchaud and Einar Thomassen, *Le Traité tripartite [NH I,5]* [Bibliothèque copte de Nag Hammadi, section "textes" 19; Quebec: Les Presses de l'Université Laval, 1989], 420–21).

[79] See Francis T. Fallon, "The Prophets of the Old Testament and the Gnostics: A Note on Irenaeus, *Adversus haereses*, 1.30.10–11," *VC* 32 (1978): 191–94.

amples above suggest they are, why so little engagement with these works? The only text which is consistently "rewritten" is Gen 1–11. This focus suggests that gnostic exegetes were only interested in elaborating their mythic and theological speculations concerning the origins of the universe, not in appropriating a received canonical tradition. They may even have concurred with Celsus's judgment that most of the Old Testament contains historical and legal materials which do not provide keys to a deeper wisdom. The Christian Bible originates in a hermeneutical framing of Jewish scriptures so that they retain their canonical authority and yet serve as witnesses to the Christ-centered experience of salvation. Gnostic and Valentinian exegesis adapts hermeneutics of esotericism to enlist parts of the emerging Christian Bible and the oral traditions about the words of the Savior to frame a different experience of self, world, and salvation. Within the larger culture, any myth or text that enjoyed public acceptance was expected to convey deeper philosophical and religious truth. Hermeneutics, not canon formation, is the central point at issue between Irenaeus and his Valentinian opponents.

22

Evidence for an Early Christian Canon
(Second and Third Century)

Peter Balla

Due to the scarcity of evidence, one cannot firmly conclude when exactly and as a result of what development the early church came to possess a twenty-seven-book collection called the New Testament and a two-part collection that comprises our Bible of Old and New Testaments.

Other chapters in the present volume discuss what we know of the factors that led to the canon and which criteria were decisive in its formation. This chapter surveys mainly two kinds of evidence: ancient lists which summarizes the view on the canon in certain regions, and manuscripts that may shed light on the status of the canon in a specific century in different areas. The first part of the chapter will also draw on some other kinds of evidence. I shall discuss the use of "biblical" books in the early church, and I shall ask what view of scriptural authority can be reconstructed from the New Testament itself. In this regard we shall not only discuss the second and third centuries, but the first three centuries of the common era.

1. Evidence, Hypotheses, Definitions

The problematic nature of the evidence can be summarized as follows: First, we have different uses of the term "canon" in the period under discussion. That is why a separate chapter in this volume is devoted to the notion and definition of the canon.[1] Second, we have little evidence from the period, and even our extant sources are open to different interpretations. Third, in some cases, the dating of the evidence is disputed.

There are two major hypotheses: First, it may be argued that the "orthodox" church, from an early time on, collected books it regarded as sacred. Although the boundaries were not clear (and not the same) in different regions, a main body of scripture reached "canonical" status perhaps by the second century. The church did not decide on the content of the canon; rather, it recognized as canonical those books (in an ever-widening circle) which

I thank the Alexander von Humboldt Foundation for enabling me to carry out research at the University of Heidelberg (1999–2000), in the course of which this chapter was written. I also thank Professor Pieter F. Craffert (Pretoria), Professor John C. O'Neill (Edinburgh), and Professor Gerd Theissen (Heidelberg) for their helpful comments on an earlier draft.
[1] See E. Ulrich, "The Notion and Definition of Canon" (ch. 2 of the present volume).

were used as authoritative writings from early times on. Second, it is also possible to argue that since we have clear evidence of the twenty-seven-book collection of the New Testament only from the fourth century, we can only speak of a biblical canon from this period onward.[2]

As regards the definition of canon, I follow those who distinguish between a book being "canonical" if it is mentioned in a standardized list, and a writing being "sacred," or "authoritative," which usually means that it was read in worship services as a guide in matters of belief and praxis. For example, James A. Sanders summarizes the two basic uses of the term "canon" in this way: "the one refers to the shape of a limited body of sacred literature; the other refers to its function."[3] However, I also suggest the use of the term "canonical development" in the sense of a process that had the standardized list as its end product. Chapter 24 will say more about the end product. In the first part we collect evidence on the state of the canon prior to the fourth century. The thesis of this section is as follows: the process that led to the end product started early; the majority of the books that later belonged to standardized lists were authoritative, sacred writings for at least some parts of the early church, and the use of these writings in worship services naturally led to their appearance on standardized lists. In other words, the New Testament canon is a recognition and acknowledgment of books that were authoritative from earlier periods on, not a creation of the fourth-century church.

2. Claims of Authority in the New Testament Writings

We begin the discussion with evidence from the New Testament itself. This decision is controversial, as many scholars do not think that the authors of the New Testament could write with a "canonical awareness." For example, Lee McDonald argues that "with the exception of the author of the book of Revelation, no conscious or clear effort was made by these authors to produce Christian scriptures."[4] I argue that the later use of the term "canonical" should not prevent us from seeing an awareness in the authors of the New Testament of a connection between the writings of the "Old Testament" and their own writings. Some passages in the New Testament imply that certain New Testament writings are accorded the same level of authority as the Old Testament writings. The key passages are as follows.

The apostle Paul can be seen as reporting events foretold by prophets in the Old Testament. He clearly says that the words of the prophets were reported in sacred writings. He does not say explicitly, but we may argue with probability, that his own reports, when put in writing, share the authority of the prophetic writings that foretold the same events. In Rom 1:1–5 Paul writes (RSV):

---

[2] This view will be argued in ch. 24 of the present volume by Geoffrey Hahneman.

[3] J. A. Sanders, "Canon, Hebrew Bible," *ABD* 1:839. See also his earlier article, "Adaptable for Life: the Nature and Function of Canon," in *Magnalia Dei: The Mighty Acts of God: Essays on the Bible and Archaeology in Memory of G. E. Wright* (New York: Doubleday, 1976), 531–60. Lee M. McDonald, *The Formation of the Christian Biblical Canon* (rev. and enl. ed.; Peabody, Mass.: Hendrickson, 1995), 106–7.

[4] McDonald, *Formation*, 142. Significantly, on the same page McDonald concedes that "to some extent the value of written sources was also recognized by their own authors in the first century (for example, Rom 15:15; the whole of Gal, 2 Cor 1:13; Col 4:16; John 20:30, 31; 1 John 2:1, 7, 8, *passim*)."

Paul, a servant of Jesus Christ, called to be an apostle, set apart for the gospel of God which he promised beforehand through his prophets in the holy scriptures, the gospel concerning his Son, who was descended from David according to the flesh and designated Son of God in power according to the Spirit of holiness by his resurrection from the dead, Jesus Christ our Lord, through whom we have received grace and apostleship to bring about the obedience of faith for the sake of his name among all the nations, . . .

Paul's apostleship (vv. 1 and 5) involves the spreading of the news that had been promised beforehand. These promises were recorded in sacred writings (v. 2), so we may infer that a report about the arrival of the promised Son of God has authority. Similarly, toward the end of the same letter, Paul claims that his writing activity is grounded in the grace of God that sends him to preach the gospel (Rom 15:15–16): "But on some points I have written to you very boldly by way of reminder, because of the grace given me by God to be a minister of Christ Jesus to the Gentiles in the priestly service of the gospel of God, so that the offering of the Gentiles may be acceptable, sanctified by the Holy Spirit."

The closing doxology of Romans (16:25–27) is missing in some manuscripts and it is located after chapter 14 or chapter 15 in others. It is possible that Paul added it to his own letter at some later stage; some scholars argue that it was added by someone other than Paul. In either case it is a witness of how the apostles' ministry was viewed by himself or by somebody else in the early church. In vv. 25–26 we read: "Now to him who is able to strengthen you according to my gospel and the preaching of Jesus Christ, according to the revelation of the mystery which was kept secret for long ages but is now disclosed and through the prophetic writings is made known to all nations . . . ." Prophetic writings of earlier centuries were regarded as sacred by Paul and the early Christians. Those Christians who spread the gospel by their preaching participated in that prophetic ministry. It is, therefore, plausible to suppose that the written form of that prophetic preaching was held to be authoritative.

We have some evidence that the apostolic letters were read not only by the original addressees, but were circulated in other congregations as well. Some scholars hold that the Letter to the Colossians was written by Paul; others hold that it was written by someone else, but in Paul's lifetime. Many think that it was written perhaps decades after Paul's death. However, it is generally agreed that it originates in the first century; thus it is a significant witness, whoever wrote it. In Col 4:16 we find a command to the house church in Colossae: "And when this letter has been read among you, have it read also in the church of the Laodiceans; and see that you read also the letter from Laodicea."

At some time in the first century Paul's letters were collected. We do not know when and who collected them first, but it is possible that at least some of them were collected and edited for publication by Paul himself.[5] Perhaps the collecting occurred decades later, we do not know. It is known, however, that either in the first century, or in the second (when many scholars argue 2 Peter was written), the collection was held to be authoritative as it was put alongside other "scriptures," i.e., sacred writings of the Old Testament. In

---

[5] This conclusion is reached for the earliest form of Romans, 1–2 Corinthians, Philippians, and 1 Thessalonians by David Trobisch, *Die Entstehung der Paulusbriefsammlung: Studien zu den Anfängen christlicher Publizistik* (NTOA 10; Freiburg: Universitätsverlag, Göttingen: Vandenhoeck & Ruprecht, 1989), 119. He calls the phenomenon, that has numerous parallels in the case of published correspondence around that era, an "Autorenrezension."

2 Pet 3:15–16 we read: "So also our beloved brother Paul wrote to you according to the wisdom given him, speaking of this as he does in all his letters. There are some things in them hard to understand, which the ignorant and unstable twist to their own destruction, as they do the other scriptures."

Paul clearly distinguishes between Jesus' authority and his own. However, through that very distinction we can see not only that he regarded Jesus' message as authoritative, but that he claimed authority for himself as well. In 1 Cor 7, this distinction appears repeatedly. In 1 Cor 7:12 we read: "To the rest I say, not the Lord, . . ." but in verse 17 we learn that Paul himself had the authority to give instructions for the congregations: "This is my rule in all the churches." Even when Paul does not give rulings, just advice, he expects that because of God's grace and Spirit given to him the congregation will obey him. Verses 25 and 40 can be cited as examples: "Now concerning the unmarried, I have no command of the Lord, but I give my opinion as one who by the Lord's mercy is trustworthy . . . and I think that I have the Spirit of God."

We can suppose that similar authority was claimed for all the epistles that were circulated as written by apostles. The authority of apostles stood behind those gospels which the early church held were written by apostles (Matthew and John) or by companions of apostles (Mark as Peter's companion, and Luke as Paul's). The Gospels were accorded authority not only because of their supposed authorship, but because of their content: they claimed to have reported events related to the coming of the Messiah, and his words and deeds.[6] We have to bear in mind that the coming of the Messiah was related to end-time expectations for some Jews (and Jewish Christians), so these traditions were very special to them. One can expect that these traditions were transmitted with care. Indeed, it can be argued that the warning at the end of the book of Revelation was a general rule for those who transmitted these traditions. As Revelation stood always as the last book in codices that held New Testament writings (even if a certain codex did not have all of the twenty-seven books), one might argue that its rule applied to the other books in the codices, i.e., to other authoritative ("canonical") writings as well (Rev 22:18–19): "I warn every one who hears the words of the prophecy of this book: if any one adds to them, God will add to him the plagues described in this book, and if any one takes away from the words of the book of this prophecy, God will take away his share in the tree of life and in the holy city, which are described in this book."[7]

3. The Manuscript Evidence

Unfortunately, we have few manuscripts that can be dated to the second and third centuries, and even these manuscripts are fragmentary.[8] It is not possible to ascertain

---

[6] For the possibility that at least the gospels of Matthew and Luke (perhaps Mark and John as well) were intended to be "scripture" already by their authors, see D. Moody Smith, "When Did the Gospels Become Scripture?" *JBL* 119 (2000): 3–20.

[7] This argument is applied to the Gospels by John C. O'Neill, "The Lost Written Records of Jesus' Words and Deeds behind Our Records," *JTS* 42 (1991): 483–504; see esp. 484.

[8] We probably do not have any manuscript from the first century. For arguments in favor of the view that P[4], P[64], and P[67] are papyri fragments of the oldest manuscript of the four gospels (to be

which books they had contained in the parts now missing. We shall see later that even in the fourth century it is difficult to infer what authority was attributed to the books contained in a codex. Nevertheless, the very act of collecting books in codices points to the likelihood that those writings were meant to be published; they were probably used by congregations. It is, therefore, significant to note the emergence of the codex for the purpose of transmitting authoritative writings in early Christianity.

We have already seen that it is possible to argue that Paul was responsible for editing at least some of his own letters. Similarly, it is plausible to hold that the four gospels were published together in the first half of the second century. The codex was a convenient means of preserving books together that would be too long to be copied on a single roll. Although the individual gospels do not contain the names of their authors, it is probable that the inscriptions naming them (for example, "According to Mark") were attached as soon as people knew about more than one gospel, or at latest when they were published together in a codex. T. C. Skeat has suggested that Christians adopted the codex in order that they could copy the four gospels together.[9] The consistent system of abbreviating certain words (*nomina sacra*, fifteen in total) in Christian biblical codices points to the likelihood of recensions, i.e., editions of the New Testament that aimed at a standardized text for Christian worship. This may have happened in the second century, and at latest in the third century.[10]

The few extant manuscripts from the second and third centuries seem to affirm this overall picture, although again results are not conclusive.

Appendix I of *The Novum Testamentum Graece*, twenty-seventh edition, lists ninety-eight papyri of the Greek New Testament. Among them only two papyri, P[52] (John 18:31–33, 37–38) and P[90] (John 18:36–19:1; 19:2–7), are dated to the second century (P[98] with a question mark; Acts 1:13–20), and a few others "around 200": P[32] (Titus 1:11–15; 2:3–8), P[46] (long parts of Pauline letters), P[64] (a few verses from various chapters of Matthew; P[67] belongs to it; we have seen that T. C. Skeat argues that together with P[4] they should be dated to the second century), and P[66] (several chapters of John). One papyrus is dated to the "second/third centuries" (P[77], Matt 23:30–9), and twenty-eight papyri are dated to the third century. Seven further papyri are dated to the "third/fourth centuries," and one "around 300." As far as we can tell, the majority of them come from codices.[11]

---

dated "late second century"), see T. C. Skeat, "The Oldest Manuscript of the Four Gospels?" *NTS* 43 (1997): 1–34, at p. 30.

[9] Skeat, "Oldest Manuscript," 31.

[10] For a discussion of the *nomina sacra* and other pointers to an editorial work on the New Testament, see David Trobisch, *Die Endredaktion des Neuen Testaments: Eine Untersuchung zur Entstehung der christlichen Bibel* (NTOA 31; Freiburg: Universitätsverlag, Göttingen: Vandenhoeck & Ruprecht, 1996), esp. 16–71. He cautiously suggests the second century as the date of the "canonical edition" of the New Testament (123–24).

[11] Kurt Aland and Barbara Aland affirm that P[12], P[13], P[18], and P[22] come from a scroll (*Der Text des Neuen Testaments: Einführung in die wissenschaftlichen Ausgaben sowie in Theorie und Praxis der modernen Textkritik* [2d ed., rev. and enl.; Stuttgart: Deutsche Bibelgesellschaft, 1989], at 111). For an argument for the significance of the early papyri, see 97–106. (The English translation of the 1981 first German edition, *The Text of the New Testament* [Grand Rapids: Eerdmans, 1987] has these data on 102 and 85–96 respectively.) Trobisch (*Endredaktion*, 33, 43) points out that in the case of some very small fragments it cannot be decided whether they are from a codex or from a scroll (e.g.,

None of them contains the entire New Testament. It is significant that some of the uncial parchment codices are also dated prior to the fourth century, but they, too, are fragmentary; it is only from the fourth century onward that we have entire New Testaments on parchment. Codex 0189 (Acts 5:3–21) is dated to the second/third centuries, codices 0212 (a *Diatessaron* text) and 0220 to the third century, codex 0171 "around 300," and codex 0162 to the third/fourth centuries.

Due to the fragmentary character of the extant manuscripts, it is impossible to state with certainty which books they contained. Papyrus 46 is an exception: it seems certain that it was a collection of Pauline letters, although it is disputed whether the three Pastoral Epistles were also included. Since the end of the codex is missing, and the letters are smaller in the latter part of the codex, the copyist may have been concerned about running out of space. This may indicate that even if he did not copy the Pastorals, he intended to do so.[12] This codex proves the existence of a Pauline collection in the late second century.

While the manuscript evidence does not prove canonicity, it confirms that the writings of the later "New Testament" were copied repeatedly. The late date of the papyri does not rule out a canonical process already in the second century, because what we have is purely accidental; note that only nine papyri were known before the end of the nineteenth century. More significant is the order of the books in the codices. On the one hand, it is often emphasized that the earliest manuscripts follow no fixed order.[13] On the other hand, it has been shown that the full editions of the New Testament from the fourth and fifth centuries suppose an archetype based on earlier collections; the four main types are the Gospels, Acts with the Catholic Epistles, the Pauline Corpus, and Revelation (the unique representative of this genre in the New Testament).[14] Although this archetype cannot be dated exactly, the "precursors" of the full editions may bear witness to this collection.[15] Thus, the manuscript evidence suggests that a "canonical process" was at work prior to the fourth century.

4. References to "Canonical" Books: From *1 Clement* to Irenaeus

In the sections that follow we survey references of the apostolic fathers and some of the early church fathers to books that later became part of the New Testament. In the title of this section we put quotation marks around the term canonical not only because of the problematic nature of the term "canon" discussed above, but also because some of the references listed here are controversial: it is not always certain that a reference to a passage or

---

P[31], P[43]), whereas there are also some talisman-like little text-pieces (P[50], P[78]) or "personal excerpts" (P[43], P[62]).

[12] See Trobisch, *Entstehung,* 27–28.

[13] Aland and Aland, *Der Text,* 91–92. They argue that the variations in the order of the four gospels are due to the fact that originally the gospels circulated one by one (p. 92). Similarly, the Pauline Corpus grew from smaller collections.

[14] Trobisch, *Endredaktion,* 38–42. Trobisch (43) points out that P[66] contained only one gospel (since the pagination of the codex begins with John 1), nevertheless it is clear that this gospel is regarded as part of a "canonical edition," since it is given a title: The Gospel According to John.

[15] Trobisch, *Endredaktion,* 46–47. He points out that the extant parts of the following papyri have the books (whichever are present) in the present "canonical" order: P[30], P[61], P[74], and P[75].

name of a book of the (later) New Testament really means that the author knew the same book we now have in our canon.

As regards the canonical gospels, there are a few quotations of Jesus traditions in the apostolic fathers that may derive from written gospels, or from traditions apart from our gospels.[16] For example, some scholars affirm that *1 Clement* (ca. 96 C.E.) alludes to Matthew, Mark, and Luke, while others regard this as "improbable."[17] Whatever view one adopts, it is significant that Jesus' sayings are referred to as an authoritative guide in ethical conduct in *1 Clem.* 13.1–4 and 46.7–8.

Several sources from the first half of the second century do not list books regarded as authoritative, yet refer to some New Testament texts or to the authority of Jesus. It is significant that, although vague as regards the number of authoritative books, they testify to New Testament traditions being held on the same level of authority as the "Old Testament." Lee McDonald has conveniently summarized the works that belong to this category:[18] the *Epistle of Barnabas* (ca. 90–130; see 4.14), the letters of Ignatius, especially his *Letter to the Philadelphians* (ca. 110–117; see 8.2), *2 Clement* (ca. 120–140, but no later than 170; see 2.4; 14.2), Polycarp's *Letter to the Philippians* (ca. 140–155; see 2.2–3; 7.1–2; 6.3; 8.2; 12.1). We have already seen that within the canonical New Testament some date 2 Peter to the second century. If this dating is accepted then 2 Pet 3:15–16 belongs to this circle as well as a witness to the letters of Paul being read as scripture.

Another controversial source is Papias of Hierapolis (writing between 110 and 140 C.E.). He does not use the term *gospel* but refers to Mark and to Matthew as people who wrote down the words of Jesus. Papias's work is no longer extant, but Eusebius quotes a few sentences (*Hist. eccl.* 3.39.15–16). Recently, Denis Farkasfalvy has argued that Papias's source is "significantly earlier" than his own time of writing.[19] He asserts that "in the fragments of Papias, Mark is judged by the same criteria which Luke held and that these reflect a gospel model developed in the early church under the influence of Matthew's gospel." He lists the following elements of an established gospel model shared by Luke and the presbyter referred to by Papias as his source: the gospel is (a) "based on eyewitness accounts. (b) It contains both deeds and words of Jesus. (c) It covers all information available. (d) It is an ordered composition."[20] Farkasfalvy points out that although many modern scholars do

---

[16] For the latter view, see Helmut Koester's doctoral thesis, *Synoptische Überlieferung bei den apostolischen Vätern* (Berlin: Akademie-Verlag, 1957); for a criticism of this thesis (arguing that the apostolic fathers may have known our Synoptic Gospels), see Peter Balla, *Challenges to New Testament Theology: An Attempt to Justify the Enterprise* (WUNT 2/95; Tübingen: Mohr [Siebeck], 1997; repr. Peabody, Mass.: Hendrickson, 1998), 57–65.

[17] For the former view, see McDonald, *Formation*, 143–44; for the latter, see Wilhelm Schneemelcher (ed.), *New Testament Apocrypha* (2 vols.; ET ed. R. McL. Wilson; Louisville, Ky.: Westminster John Knox, 1991–1992), the expression "improbable" at 1:19.

[18] McDonald, *Formation*, 146–50. McDonald emphasizes that Ptolemy's *Letter to Flora* 3.5–8 is a further significant witness, since it comes from an author who did not belong to the "orthodox" part of early Christianity.

[19] Denis Farkasfalvy, "The Papias Fragments on Mark and Matthew and Their Relationship to Luke's Prologue: An Essay on the Pre-History of the Synoptic Problem," in *The Early Church in Its Context* (ed. A. J. Malherbe et al.; Leiden: Brill, 1998), 92–106; this and the following quotation at p. 92.

[20] Farkasfalvy, *Papias Fragments*, 102–3.

not think that Matthew's Gospel is a translation from Aramaic, it is probable that the early church knew of some gospels that claimed to be translations of Matthew's Gospel.[21] Papias's fragment on this gospel may be a warning that the Greek-speaking Christians have Matthew's Gospel only in translation (indeed, several translations); the presbyter defends Mark's Gospel (though not written by an apostle) as corresponding to what was expected from a gospel. Whether or not the early church was right in holding that Matthew's Gospel was the first, the Papias fragment may witness to the "canonical process" going on not only at the time of Papias, but already at the time of the Prologue of Luke, and of Papias's source (the presbyter), i.e., toward the end of the first century.

We touch upon one further problematic source only briefly, as the factors leading to canonization are discussed in a separate chapter in this volume. Campenhausen's theory that the orthodox "great church" (or "main church"; German *Grosskirche*) created its canon as an answer to Marcion's canon has gained reasonable support.[22] It is true that the earliest clear evidence for the great church having four "canonical" gospels, no less and no more, is Irenaeus around 180 C.E. However, the early church may already have had four gospels by the time of Marcion (ca. 140 C.E.). In that case, Marcion's decision to have only an abbreviated Luke did not provoke the church to choose its own gospels. It may be that Marcion created his own gospel "canon" (without using this term) against that of the mainstream church.[23] Graham Stanton, examining the evidence in Irenaeus afresh, concludes that "Irenaeus is not defending an innovation, but explaining why, unlike the heretics, the church has four gospels, no more, no less: she has received four written accounts of the one Gospel from the apostles and their immediate followers."[24] He also claims that Justin Martyr "does not have Irenaeus's clear conception of the fourfold Gospel, but the references in his extant writings to written gospels suggest that he may well have had a four-gospel codex in his catechetical school in Rome by about 150 AD."[25] Thus, Stanton does not hold that the "fourfold Gospel" is the answer of the main church to Marcion. He rightly observes that four gospels would hardly have contributed to the struggle against Marcion's one.[26] One could as well argue that Tatian's one gospel put together from four, the *Diatessaron,* challenged the church to reaffirm its "canonical" gospels. But in fact Tatian's attempt presupposes the existence of four gospels in the main church.

As we have already mentioned, Stanton offers a fresh exposition of the two other main sources of the second century: Justin Martyr and Irenaeus. Concerning the former,

---

[21] Ibid., 100.

[22] Hans F. von Campenhausen, "Die Entstehung des Neuen Testaments," in *Das Neue Testament als Kanon: Dokumentation und kritische Analyse zur gegenwärtigen Diskussion* (ed. E. Käsemann; Göttingen: Vandenhoeck & Ruprecht, 1970), 109–23, at p. 116. See also H. von Campenhausen, *The Formation of the Christian Bible* (trans. J. A. Baker; London: Adam & Charles Black, 1972). McDonald holds that Irenaeus's four-gospel canon was probably a response to the teachings of Marcion (*Formation,* 159; see his detailed discussion of Marcion at 154–61).

[23] For an argument against attributing too much influence to Marcion in the "canonical process," see Schneemelcher (*Apocrypha,* 1:23–24); though he holds that "Marcion probably found no collection of the four Gospels in existence, but only individual Gospels" (23). He also affirms that Marcion "was certainly not the first to collect the Pauline letters, but found them already together."

[24] Graham N. Stanton, "The Fourfold Gospel," *NTS* 43 (1997): 317–46, at p. 322.

[25] Ibid., 331.

[26] Ibid., 336.

he points to a significant passage, often ignored in the literature, which shows that Justin must have reckoned with at least four gospels. In *Dialogue* 103.8 he refers to "memoirs" composed by Jesus' apostles and by those who followed them.[27] As noted above, this remark corresponds to the evidence that the early church thought that two gospels were written by apostles (Matthew and John), and two by followers of apostles (Mark as the interpreter of Peter, as per the Papias fragment, and Luke as the companion of Paul). Stanton also argues that *1 Apol.* 61.4 and *Dial.* 88.7 show that, apart from the Synoptics, Justin also knew John's Gospel, because the former draws on John 3:3–5 and the latter on John 1:19–20.

One particular problem of the evidence in Justin is worth mentioning. Although he does refer to the "gospel" in the singular (*Dial.* 10.2; 100.1), and in the plural (*1 Apol.* 66), he more often uses the term "the memoirs of the apostles." It is possible that this phrase is a reference to our canonical gospels, but it may be argued that it is a title, and refers to another collection of gospel material which subsequently ceased to be transmitted. In any case, it remains probable that by the time of Justin the church had several gospels available, possibly our canonical four. However, this must remain a hypothesis.

The first author who clearly asserts that the church has no more and no less than four authoritative gospels is Irenaeus. Some scholars argue that even in his time the number "four" must have been debated since he has to defend this number on theological grounds. This argument should not be stressed unduly since in the writing in which Irenaeus's views on the gospels have been preserved, generally referred to as *Against Heresies,* Irenaeus is not simply expressing his own views but is trying to counter heresies by referring to traditions of the main church that predate his own time.

Graham Stanton has rightly argued that it is a good method to point to the source that is most explicit, and "to work back from the full flowering of a concept or a development to its earlier roots."[28] If we find no sign of a major change in the view of the great church reflected in the previous sources, it can be argued that the situation clearly expressed around 180 C.E. by Irenaeus applies to earlier decades as well.[29] Irenaeus employs analogies from both nature and scripture (e.g., the four winds and the four-faced cherubim of Ezek 1; *Haer.* 3.11.8) to show that the church has to have no more and no less than four gospels. Additionally, "he reckons to 'scripture' . . . Acts and the thirteen letters of Paul. 1 Peter and the two Johannine letters (1 and 2) are appraised like the Pauline letters, while James and Hebrews are probably not so highly esteemed" (see, e.g., *Haer.* 1.9.4; 2.26.1–2; 3.1.1).[30] Schneemelcher's summary of Irenaeus's views on what was authoritative in the early church serves as an example for the remainder of our discussion: we shall see

---

[27] Ibid., 329–32.

[28] Ibid., 318. See also Stanton's discussion of Irenaeus's key passages with the result that by his time "the fourfold Gospel was very well established" (319–22; quotation at p. 322).

[29] This method was proposed by Theodor Zahn more than a century ago. See Balla, *Challenges,* 91–92.

[30] Schneemelcher (*Apocrypha,* 1:26). Schneemelcher's summary of the situation in the second and third centuries (26–33) serves as a basis also for the following discussion. Note his view that even our main source from the fourth century, Eusebius, probably reflects traditions originating in the third century (p. 31). Eusebius claims to be writing "according to ecclesiastical tradition" when he presents his own catalogue of recognized books (*Hist. eccl.* 3.25).

that most of the later "New Testament" was received as authoritative in various regions from early on; only the limits of the canon were fluid. The open boundaries of the canon must be acknowledged, but should not be overemphasized; the *Grundstock* (to use Zahn's term) or main bulk of the later canon was regarded as having "canonical" authority in the orthodox mainstream of early Christianity.[31] As McDonald puts it: "The major sections (the Gospels and Paul) of what was later called the New Testament literature were generally (though not completely) acknowledged by the end of the second century as scripture."[32]

5. References to Authoritative Writings in "Lists"

We have put the term "list" in quotation marks to indicate that we do not refer to phenomena like the fourth-century canonical lists, Athanasius's for example, but to reasonably short passages that discuss which books are accepted or rejected in certain parts of the church. This distinction must be emphasized, because it has been argued that lists in the sense of a catalogue appear only in the fourth century. Thus some scholars hold that the Canon Muratori originated in the fourth century, since it lists accepted books. However, if we distinguish between catalogues proper and works that not only list but also briefly discuss what is accepted as authoritative, then we can affirm that the latter category may have originated at the end of the second century.[33]

A. The Western Church

Until a few decades ago, the Muratorian Fragment (Canon Muratori) was held to have originated at the end of the second century. Recently, a growing number of scholars argue for a fourth-century date.[34] While the arguments for a fourth-century date are cogent, the issue does not seem to be settled yet. In my opinion, a second-century date can be maintained, though neither argument seems to be conclusive.[35] As the fourth-century case will be set out later, it is sufficient here to point to some recent arguments for a second-century date.

---

[31] Theodor Zahn, *Geschichte des Neutestamentlichen Kanons* (2 vols.; Erlangen: Verlag von Andreas Deichert, 1888–1892), 1:430–32. For a similar view, see Wilhelm Schneemelcher, "Bibel III: Die Entstehung des Kanons des Neuen Testaments und der christlichen Bibel," *TRE* 6:22–48. He affirms: "Der Kanon ist um die Wende vom 2. zum 3. Jh. grundsätzlich vorhanden" (46).

[32] McDonald, *Formation*, 190.

[33] The difference between the forms of the text of the Canon Muratori and the catalogue in the Codex Claromontanus can be conveniently seen in Schneemelcher, *Apocrypha*, 1:34–37.

[34] A fourth-century date has been argued by A. C. Sundberg and G. M. Hahneman, and more recently by Gregory A. Robbins ("Muratorian Fragment," *ABD* 4:928–29), and McDonald (*Formation*, 213–20). See also Geoffrey Hahneman's article in this volume (ch. 24). The proponents of a fourth-century date argue for an origin in the Eastern church, whereas the supporters of a second-century date hold that the Fragment reflects views in the Western church, centered in Rome.

[35] For a recent re-affirmation of a second-century date, see Theo K. Heckel, *Vom Evangelium des Markus zum viergestaltigen Evangelium* (WUNT 120; Tübingen: Mohr [Siebeck], 1999), 339–45.

.tical dialogue with the key arguments for a fourth-century date, Graham
.s reaffirmed the case for a second-century origin of the Muratorian Fragment.[36]
.s to phenomena that fit the second-century setting but are conspicuously absent
,urth-century sources. First, like Irenaeus, the Muratorian Fragment uses both the
title-like reference to an individual gospel (e.g., "Gospel according to Luke") and the plural
phrase (e.g., "fourth of the gospels"). Second, the Fragment devotes its most detailed discussion to the Fourth Gospel. Such a defense was needed in the second century, when the
Alogi voiced doubts about its Johannine authorship, but would not have been needed in
the fourth century. Third, the Fragment refers to two parousias of Christ as found in all
four gospels. The two-parousias schema is prominent in Justin's writings and is found in
Irenaeus and Tertullian (ca. 160–225) but plays no role in fourth-century sources. Fourth,
both Irenaeus and the Muratorian Fragment assert that there is one Gospel in fourfold
form, held together by one Spirit. To sum up, Stanton rightly points to the difference
between the Fragment and the fourth-century catalogues by affirming that the genre of
the former is "*Einleitung*" or introductory comments about the origin and authority of
early Christian writings.[37]

Tertullian, the "Father of Latin Theology" (ca. 160–225), witnesses to the authority
of writings in the Western church. He stressed the criterion of apostolicity. For example, in
his writing *Against Marcion* he clearly distinguishes gospels of apostolic origin and gospels
written by disciples of apostles. He writes: "Of the apostles, therefore, John and Matthew
first instill faith into us; whilst of apostolic men, Luke and Mark renew it afterwards."[38]
Tertullian did not produce a list of what was in his Old Testament and New Testament, but
it is significant that he refers to the two parts of the Christian Bible in a collective way as
totum instrumentum utriusque testamenti.[39] It seems that what we may call his "New Testament canon" included the four gospels, thirteen Pauline letters, Acts, 1 John, 1 Peter, Jude,
and Revelation. He referred to these writings in an authoritative manner, and called them
an "entire volume."[40] He names the main parts of the New Testament "Gospels" and "the
Apostles," the latter phrase probably denoting the apostolic letters.[41] Once again, we note
that the boundaries of the apostolic letters are not defined with certainty, but this should
not prevent us from seeing that for Tertullian the Bible was a "fixed entity."[42]

B. The Eastern Church

When discussing the witnesses of "canonical" authority in the Eastern church, we
face a difficulty in that our main source is Eusebius, the church historian, writing in the
fourth century. Some scholars hold that Eusebius's references to Origen shed little light
upon Origen's understanding of the origin and authority of New Testament writings.
Rather they reflect Eusebius's own interests by presenting other people's views in the form

---

[36] Stanton, *Fourfold Gospel*, 322–25.
[37] Ibid., 323.
[38] Tertullian, *Adv. Marc.* 4.2.2.
[39] Tertullian, *Prax.* 20.
[40] Tertullian, *Praescr.* 32.
[41] Tertullian, *Prax.* 15.
[42] Schneemelcher, *Apocrypha*, 1:27. See further McDonald, *Formation*, 205–6.

of "lists."[43] When a later writer refers to earlier sources it is often the case that the source has been altered according to the writer's own interests. However, it is also possible that Eusebius made a largely reliable attempt to summarize what was available to him. In the following, the latter view is adopted.[44]

As the head of the catechetical school in Alexandria and also as a refugee settling in Cappadocia, Clement of Alexandria (ca. 150–215) represents the views of the Eastern church. His New Testament included the four gospels of our canon (*Stromata* 3.93.1). Significantly, he did not accept as authoritative other writings of that genre: the *Gospel of the Hebrews* and the *Gospel of the Egyptians*. He also referred to or cited as scripture Acts, fourteen Pauline letters (attributing Hebrews to Paul), 1–2 John, 1 Peter, Jude, and Revelation, but not James, 2 Peter, or 3 John. He also quoted writings that are not in our canon, e.g., the *Shepherd of Hermas* and the *Didache*. Eusebius reports some traditions of "elders" taken over by Clement (we recall that Papias referred to an elder as his source as well). In this way he claims to cite traditions even earlier than Clement. For example, in *Hist. eccl.* 6.14.5–7 Eusebius writes:

> Clement has inserted a tradition of the primitive elders with regard to the order of the Gospels, as follows. He said that those Gospels were first written which include the genealogies. . . . When Peter had publicly preached the word at Rome, . . . those present . . . exhorted Mark . . . to make a record of what was said. . . . John, last of all, conscious that the outward facts had been set forth in the Gospels, was urged on by his disciples, and, divinely moved by the Spirit, composed a spiritual Gospel. This is Clement's account.

Clement does not provide us with a clearly defined New Testament "canon," though he, too, attests to the authoritative character of the main part of it. Clement draws on a wide range of traditions, some of which are unknown to us from elsewhere. Some of these traditions are so unexpected that it is unlikely that Eusebius thoroughly reworked his source at this point.

Our last third-century source is Origen (ca. 185–254). Since he travelled widely, he knew many traditions in different geographical areas—Egypt, Asia Minor, and Palestine—including traditions about what was recognized as authoritative scripture. Origen distinguished three categories of writings: (1) *homologoumena* (generally acknowledged writings); (2) *amphiballomena* (writings doubted by some parts of the church); and (3) *pseudē* (false writings forged by heretics). Since Eusebius is our main source concerning this categorization, it may be his doing. However, Eusebius himself uses other categories, so it is equally plausible that he took over the idea of classification from Origen and adapted it to his own views. If this is the case, then Origen is another independent source for the process that led to the twenty-seven-book New Testament canon by the fourth century. According to Eusebius, Origen was familiar with traditions (i.e., he did not simply summarize his own view) concerning the temporal sequence of the four gospels: they were written in the order as they appear in our canonical editions today.[45] Origen accepted an unspecified

---

[43] For a recent presentation of this view, shared by Sundberg, Hahneman, and Everett Kalin, see McDonald, *Formation*, 202–5. He urges caution regarding the reliability of Rufinus's translation of Eusebius's *Hist. eccl.* 6.25.3–14 as a source for reconstructing Origen's views on the "canon."

[44] See, e.g., Schneemelcher, *Apocrypha*, 1:27–31.

[45] Eusebius, *Hist. eccl.* 6.25.3–14.

number of Pauline epistles, plus a letter of Peter, adding: "it may be, a second, though it is doubted" (i.e., it belongs to the second category above). He held that John, the author of the Fourth Gospel, wrote the Apocalypse (Revelation) and a short letter, and "it may be, a second and a third, for not all say that these are genuine." It seems that Hebrews and Acts belonged to the "acknowledged" category. Origen held that only "God knows" who wrote Hebrews; and that Luke, the author of the Gospel, wrote Acts.

Origen does not have our twenty-seven-book New Testament canon, yet he knows that the larger part of it is acknowledged by the church. Some books in our canon today were disputed then, while once again we meet the phenomenon that writings outside our canon (e.g., *Barnabas* and the *Shepherd of Hermas*) were cited in support of an argument in the same way as scriptural writings, on occasion even introduced by an introductory formula, like "it is written."[46]

6. Conclusion

In conclusion, it is appropriate to emphasize some of the observations made in this chapter. It seems that recent scholarship is divided upon the issue whether the New Testament canon originates in the fourth century, i.e., the period from which we have clear evidence of all the twenty-seven books that comprise our present New Testament, or in the first two Christian centuries, from which we have only fragmentary evidence. The fact that church councils only made decisions in the latter part of the fourth century can be evaluated in two ways. It may bear witness to the creation of the canon at that time; however, it can also be argued that there was no need of decisions in the preceding centuries, because the "canonical process" was well on its way. Perhaps the situation in the fourth century— for example, in the time of Eusebius—differed so greatly from that of earlier centuries that it is not a good starting point for a reconstruction of the history of the canon.[47]

It remains plausible that from a very early time, indeed, from the production of apostolic writings claiming high authority, there was a process involving the writings, attributed to Jesus' apostles, that were being read and re-read in the congregations of the mainstream church. These writings guided the early Christian community in their everyday life and in their beliefs just as did the Septuagint ("Old Testament").

A separate chapter in this volume discusses the criteria later used to standardize lists of scripture. Without going into detail, we note that our discussion has shown the following factors to be significant: the conviction that the Messiah had arrived in Jesus' person; the apostolic summary of Jesus-traditions; apostolic advice on congregational matters; and repeated reading of early Christian books. Establishing the doctrine *(regula fidei)* of the mainstream church must have been a significant factor in the debates with heretical groups.[48] It is likely that, in the process that led to standardization, different criteria proved decisive in the case of different writings.

---

[46] Origen, *Princ.* 2.1.5.

[47] Heckel supports this conclusion, and criticizes the "deductive method" that starts from a definition of the notion of the "canon," and from Eusebius, *Evangelium*, 6–12.

[48] See, e.g., Irenaeus's *Adversus haereses.* Gerd Theissen argues that certain "religious axioms" shared by the mainstream early Christian church played a role in determining which writings

What was read in the congregation was probably a key factor in most cases, but even this phenomenon needs differentiation. We have seen that books not in our canon today were widely read by early Christians. However, this does not necessarily mean that they too were regarded as authoritative. The Muratorian Fragment shows that the *Shepherd of Hermas* was suggested as reading-matter, yet it was accorded a lesser authority and was not to be read "publicly in the church," because it had been written more recently (lines 77–78). Even the Festal Letter of Athanasius (from 367 C.E., containing a clear acknowledgment of the New Testament canon of twenty-seven books) permits the reading of other literature, including the *Shepherd of Hermas*. The early church possessed literature edifying as reading matter as well as writings with a higher authority.

The early church's use of writings not later accepted should not prevent us from seeing that the larger part of the present New Testament canon was undisputably held to have the authority of scripture, the same authority as the writings of the "Old Testament." The fact that writings attributed to the apostles were copied repeatedly, as per the manuscript evidence, and that they were published in codices, points to their widespread usage in the congregations, probably in worship from an early date, though we do not know exactly when. Yet, it must be acknowledged that a given book may have been accepted at different times in different regions. It is likely that the "canons" of the different regions influenced one another. The boundaries of the canon were fluid in the second and the third centuries.

To sum up, the church recognized as scripture in the fourth century those writings that had guided its life, at least in some regions, in the preceding centuries.

---

belonged to their canon, and as a "natural consequence" led to the "exclusion of Gnostic texts and groups from canon and church" (*A Theory of Primitive Christian Religion* [London: SCM Press, 1999], 271–85, at p. 282). He summarizes his view in the following way: "the consensus of primitive Christianity is governed by two basic axioms, monotheism and belief in the redeemer. In addition there are eleven basic motifs: the motifs of creation, wisdom and miracle; of renewal, representation and indwelling; of faith, agape and a change of position; and finally the motif of judgment" (282).

23

The New Testament Canon of Eusebius

Everett R. Kalin

This essay seeks to contribute to the ongoing discussion of New Testament canon history by analyzing one key text, Eusebius, *Hist. eccl.* 3.25.1–7. A context for this analysis will be provided by reference to, and brief excerpts from, an article of mine published a decade ago in *Currents in Theology and Mission:* "Re-examining New Testament Canon History: 1. The Canon of Origen."[1] That article's title presupposed that New Testament canon history needed reexamination and that analyses of individual texts (specifically two key texts from Origen) could further that reexamination. The "1" in the title implied that the article on Origen would have a sequel, which I hoped would be: "a similar presentation of text and analysis from Eusebius."[2] This Eusebius chapter is that sequel. Both it and the earlier Origen article utilize and update material from my doctoral dissertation, "Argument from Inspiration in the Canonization of the New Testament."[3]

1. Earlier Discussion

The simplest way to provide a context for this chapter on Eusebius is to summarize from the Origen article (1) the consensus on New Testament canon history; (2) an important challenge to that consensus; and (3) what was asserted about the Origen texts. The first and third items will be summarized briefly, the second in more detail.

A. The Consensus, Ten Years Ago and Now

In opposition to Marcion and to the Montanists the New Testament canon emerged swiftly and suddenly late in the second century under the influence of the church of Rome. This is the view espoused by Adolf von Harnack[4] and supported, with modification of

---

[1] E. R. Kalin, "Re-examining New Testament Canon History: 1. The Canon of Origen," *CurTM* 17 (1990): 274–82.

[2] Ibid., 274.

[3] E. R. Kalin, "Argument from Inspiration in the Canonization of the New Testament" (Th.D. diss., Harvard, 1967).

[4] A. von Harnack, *Das Neue Testament um das Jahr 200* (Freiburg: Mohr [Siebeck], 1889), and idem, *The Origin of the New Testament and the Most Important Consequences of the New Creation* (trans. J. R. Wilkinson; New York: Macmillan, 1925).

details, by many subsequent writers on the subject. Consider, for example, these words from Hans von Campenhausen: "It is undisputed that both the Old and the New Testaments had in essence already reached their final form and significance around the year 200."[5] Campenhausen says elsewhere about the production and collection of New Testament writings, "The open questions concern almost only *quisquilien* [little, insignificant details], of no interest to the non-specialist."[6] That certainly is one way of stating that, in Campenhausen's opinion at least, there seems to be a consensus.

B. The Challenge to the Consensus?

The Origen article noted that the most urgent calls for a reexamination of the consensus have come from Albert C. Sundberg Jr., who "believes that the decisive period in New Testament canon history is not the late second century but the fourth and fifth centuries, when there appeared a profusion of New Testament and Old Testament canon lists. . . ."[7] Important for Sundberg's view is his distinction between canon and scripture. He asserts

> that it is possible for a religious community to have scriptures, that is, authoritative sacred writings, without having a canon of scripture, that is, a closed collection of scripture to which nothing can be added, from which nothing can be taken away. Christians began to regard various writings of the New Testament era as scripture in the second century (at first primarily various gospels), but it is quite possible that they first got a canon of the New Testament . . . only in the fourth century.[8]

Key to the consensus that the New Testament canon was essentially in place in the late second century was the assumption that the Muratorian fragment or Muratorian Canon, a list of New Testament writings, came from Rome in the late second century. List number one in *Some Early Lists of the Books of the New Testament,* edited by F. W. Grosheide,[9] is the Canon Muratorianus. Grosheide says, "The canon was written at Rome or in its neighborhood, dates from the last part of the second century, and is perhaps the work of Hippolytus."[10] Sundberg challenged this interpretation in an article published in 1966. He tried to show that the Muratorian Canon came not from Rome but from the East and, even more significantly, not from the second century but from the fourth.[11]

Not unexpectedly, Sundberg's revision of the date of the Muratorian fragment, and thus of canon history, has gotten mixed reactions. Supporters include Robert Gnuse, who

---

[5] H. von Campenhausen, *The Formation of the Christian Bible* (trans. J. A. Baker; Philadelphia: Fortress, 1972), 327.

[6] H. von Campenhausen, "Die Entstehung des Neuen Testaments," a 1962 lecture of Campenhausen's quoted from Ernst Käsemann, ed., *Das Neue Testament als Kanon* (Göttingen: Vandenhoeck & Ruprecht, 1970), 109 [The translation of von Campenhausen's remark is my own, as are the translations of all German works cited in this article].

[7] Kalin, "Canon of Origen," 275. See Albert C. Sundberg Jr., "Canon of the New Testament," *IDBSup*, 136–40.

[8] Sundberg, "Canon," 137. See Kalin, "Canon of Origen," 276.

[9] F. W. Grosheide, ed., *Some Early Lists of the Books of the New Testament* (Textus Minores 1; Leiden: Brill, 1948).

[10] Ibid., 5.

[11] A. C. Sundberg Jr., "Canon Muratori: A Fourth Century List," *HTR* 66 (1973): 1–41.

says "the Muratorian Fragment . . . is viewed now as a fourth-century list,"[12] and Lee McDonald, whose account of Old and New Testament canon history, *The Formation of the Christian Biblical Canon*, accepts Sundberg's late dating of the fragment and in general follows his views of the history quite closely.[13] Brevard Childs rejects Sundberg's views: "I disagree with Sundberg's revisionist theory and I think that his redating of the Muratorian canon to the fourth century as a crucial support for his hypothesis is tendentious and unproven."[14] Similarly, Bruce Metzger writes, "The arguments used recently by Sundberg to prove the list to be of eastern provenance (Syria-Palestine) and from the mid-fourth century have been sufficiently refuted (not to say demolished!) by Ferguson and need not be rehearsed here."[15] Harry Y. Gamble appears to have modified his views over time. In his canon history, he says that the list "seems to have been composed in the very late second or early third century"[16] and asserts that Sundberg's "arguments, though interesting, are not convincing."[17] Yet not too many years later Gamble writes,

> The date and provenance of this list are in debate. For a long time the Muratorian Canon was taken to be a Roman (or at least Italian) product of the late 2d or early 3d century, but it would be unique at such an early time, and there are good reasons to consider it an Eastern list of the 4th century (Sundberg 1973; cf. Ferguson 1982).[18]

An important development in the debate is the appearance of Geoffrey Mark Hahneman's *The Muratorian Fragment and the Development of the Canon*,[19] a revision of his Oxford dissertation testing Sundberg's views. In Hahneman's view the evidence seems "to confirm that the Muratorian Fragment is not a Western late second-century document, but is instead a late fourth-century Eastern catalogue, probably deriving from Western Syria or Palestine."[20] For Hahneman, as for Sundberg, the fourth century becomes the decisive period in New Testament canon history.[21] Of course Hahneman's work also met with divided opinions. Ferguson begins his review of the book by saying that "a better case is made for the fourth-century eastern provenance of the Muratorian Canon than was made by A. C. Sundberg. . . . the number of converts to the later dating will no doubt grow," and then proceeds to question Hahneman's treatment of the issues at key points.[22]

---

[12] Robert Gnuse, *The Authority of the Bible: Theories of Inspiration, Revelation and the Canon of Scripture* (New York: Paulist, 1985), 108.

[13] L. M. McDonald, *The Formation of the Christian Biblical Canon* (rev. and enl. ed.; Peabody, Mass.: Hendrickson, 1995).

[14] Brevard Childs, *The New Testament as Canon* (Philadelphia: Fortress, 1984), 238.

[15] Bruce M. Metzger, *The Canon of the New Testament: Its Origin, Development, and Significance* (Oxford: Clarendon, 1987), 193; the critique of Sundberg's position to which Metzger refers is Everett Ferguson, "Canon Muratori: Date and Provenance," *StPatr* 18 (1982): 677–83.

[16] Harry Y. Gamble, *The New Testament Canon: Its Making and Meaning* (Guides to Biblical Scholarship, NT Series; Philadelphia: Fortress, 1985), 32.

[17] Ibid., n. 25, where he also notes Ferguson's critique (cf. n. 15 above).

[18] Gamble, "Canon. New Testament," 856.

[19] G. M. Hahneman, *The Muratorian Fragment and the Development of the Canon* (Oxford: Clarendon, 1992).

[20] Ibid., 217.

[21] Ibid., 218 and *passim*.

[22] Everett Ferguson, review of Geoffrey Mark Hahneman, *The Muratorian Fragment and the Development of the Canon*, *JTS* 44 (1993): 691–97.

For Robert M. Grant, "the Sundberg-Hahneman theory is eminently convincing, and the Muratorian fragment, like the 'anti-Marcionite gospel prologues' and the 'Marcionite epistle prologues' should be permanently removed from the second century."[23]

C. The Origen Article

The Origen article from a decade ago analyzed Eusebius, *Hist. eccl.* 6.25.3–14, which is usually seen as Origen's New Testament canon list. This text is called "The Canon of Origenes" and given as list number two in Grosheide's *Some Early Lists of the Books of the New Testament.*[24] The article also examined a list of New Testament writings found in Origen's *Homilies on Joshua,* 7.1. I argued that the list from Eusebius was not Origen's New Testament canon list at all, but a clever compilation by Eusebius, meant to parallel what he offers in *Hist. eccl.* 6.25.1–2 as Origen's twenty-two book "catalogue of the sacred scriptures of the Old Testament"; what Eusebius there represents as Origen's, and the church's, twenty-two book Old Testament canon was for Origen himself a list of the twenty-two books of scripture recognized by the Jews. Origen accepted as scriptural more Old Testament books than these. With respect to *Homilies on Joshua,* 7.1, I argued that the list owes less to Origen than to Rufinus, who translated it into Latin (the Greek original is lost). Rufinus's tendency to update canon history to his own time can be seen by comparing his translation of Eusebius, *Hist. eccl.* 6.25.3–14 with the Greek. We have no evidence that Origen ever gave us a New Testament canon list comparable to the many that appear in the fourth century.

Before proceeding to the analysis of the canon of Eusebius, a further observation is needed: The presence or absence of canon lists is by no means the only criterion for determining how far the canon process might have developed at any given period. Recently David Trobisch proposed that a second-century editing process produced and published the twenty-seven-book New Testament we have today, in the order: Gospels; Acts and the Catholic Epistles; fourteen letters of Paul, with Hebrews located between 2 Thessalonians and 1 Timothy; and Revelation.[25] Evidence is found in the choice of authors to whom New Testament books are ascribed, in editorial remarks in the New Testament writings themselves (including in Acts, 2 Timothy, 2 Peter, and John 21), in the widespread use of the *nomina sacra* in early manuscripts of the New Testament, and in the codex form. I mention Trobisch's proposal here, as I mentioned above the consensus view that the New Testament canon was in place in the late second century, only to ask how what we discover in Eusebius a century and a half later might challenge or support such views.

---

[23] Robert M. Grant, review of Geoffrey Mark Hahneman, *The Muratorian Fragment and the Development of the Canon, CH* 64 (1995): 639.

[24] Grosheide, *Lists,* 12–13.

[25] David Trobisch, *Die Endredaktion des Neuen Testaments: Eine Untersuchung zur Entstehung der christlichen Bibel* (NTOA 31; Freiburg: Universitätsverlag; Göttingen: Vandenhoeck & Ruprecht, 1996). Trobisch finds still earlier editorial work in the New Testament, making Paul responsible for the first edition of his own writings, a collection that included 1 and 2 Corinthians, Galatians and Romans, sent with a cover letter (Rom 16) to Ephesus: *Die Entstehung der Paulusbriefsammlung: Studien zu den Anfängen christlicher Publizistik* (NTOA 10; Freiburg: Universitätsverlag; Göttingen: Vandenhoeck & Ruprecht, 1989); a popular edition of the work's principal conclusions is *Paul's Letter Collection: Tracing the Origins* (Minneapolis: Fortress, 1994).

2. Eusebius's New Testament Canon

This essay, which updates and revises my previous work on Eusebius's New Testament canon,[26] draws upon and interacts with recent articles by Armin Daniel Baum[27] and Gregory Allen Robbins,[28] as well as Robbins's dissertation.[29] I begin the analysis of Eusebius, *Hist. eccl.* 3.25.1–7, by providing a translation of the text:

> It is reasonable to sum up here the writings of the New Testament that have been mentioned. First place must be given to the holy tetrad of the Gospels, followed by the Acts of the Apostles. (2) Next one must list the epistles of Paul; after them the so-called first epistle of John must be recognized, as well as the epistle of Peter. Following these, if it should seem appropriate, one must put the Revelation of John; we shall set forth the opinions about this book in due time.
>
> (3) These then belong to the accepted writings. Among the disputed writings that are, nevertheless, familiar to the majority there is extant the epistle said to be by James, that of Jude, the second epistle of Peter and the so-called second and third epistles of John, whether these are by the evangelist or by someone else with the same name. (4) Among the spurious writings must also be counted the Acts of Paul, the so-called Shepherd, the Revelation of Peter, and, in addition, the so-called Epistle of Barnabas and the work known as the Teachings of the Apostles and, moreover, as I said, the Revelation of John, if this should seem to be the right place for it. For some, as I said, reject it as spurious, while others reckon it among the accepted writings. (5) Now some have also counted among these writings the Gospel according to the Hebrews, which is especially favored by the Hebrews who have accepted Christ.
>
> (6) These would all be among the disputed writings, but we have been obliged to make a list of them also, thereby distinguishing the writings that according to the ecclesiastical tradition are true, genuine, and accepted and those that, in contrast to these, are not in the [New] Testament[30] *(ouk endiathēkous)* but disputed and yet known to most people in the church. We have done this in order that we might be able to know these writings as well as those published by the heretics under the names of the apostles, on the pretense that they comprise the gospels of Peter and Thomas and Mathias or even some others besides these, or the Acts of Andrew and of John and of the other apostles. Not a single one of the ecclesiastical writers down through the years has thought any of these worth mentioning. (7) Moreover, the type of language is different from apostolic usage and the thought and purpose of these writings is totally at odds with true orthodoxy, showing clearly that they are the work of heretics. For this reason, then, these must not even be classified among the spurious writings but instead shunned as totally absurd and ungodly.[31]

---

[26] Cf. Kalin, "Argument from Inspiration," 141–68, and idem, "Reexamining New Testament Canon History: The Canon of Eusebius," paper presented at the annual meeting of the SBL, Anaheim, California, November 1985.

[27] A. D. Baum, "Der neutestamentliche Kanon bei Eusebius (*Historia ecclesiastica* 3.25.1–7) im Kontext seiner literaturgeschichtlichen Arbeit," *ETL* 73 (1997): 307–48, and idem, "Literarische Echtheit als Kanonkriterium in der alten Kirche," *ZNW* 88 (1997): 97–110.

[28] G. A. Robbins, "Eusebius' Lexicon of Canonicity," *StPatr* 25 (1993): 134–41.

[29] G. A. Robbins, "*Peri tōn endiathēkōn graphōn:* Eusebius and the Formation of the Christian Bible" (Ph.D. diss., Duke University, 1986).

[30] This translation will be discussed below.

[31] This and all the translations of Eusebius in this article are my own unless otherwise noted. These translations were done several years ago in collaboration with Peter Krentz, now of Davidson College (any infelicities in the translations are, of course, my responsibility).

In this passage Eusebius divides various writings of the New Testament period into three categories, the *homologoumena* (accepted, acknowledged), the *antilegomena* (disputed, spoken against), and the heretical writings, here designated as *atopa pantē kai dyssebē* (totally absurd and ungodly). It is often claimed that the passage divides the writings not into three but four groups: the *homologoumena,* the *antilegomena,* the *notha* (spurious), and the heretical writings. Adding to the confusion is the fact that some writers speak of three groups when they really mean four (not including the heretical writings in the numbering; Bruce Metzger is an example; cf. n. 41 below). My division will be explained and defended below, in the discussion of the *antilegomena.*

In vv. 1–2 Eusebius lists the first group, the *homologoumena:* the four gospels, Acts, the letters of Paul, 1 John and 1 Peter and, provisionally ("if it should seem appropriate"), the Revelation of John. It is almost certain that Eusebius is including Hebrews among the letters of Paul. Otherwise it goes unmentioned in any of the three categories. And consider what he says in 3.3.4 about the *fourteen* letters of Paul:

> But the fourteen epistles of Paul are clear and evident; however, it is not proper to ignore the fact that some have rejected the Epistle to the Hebrews as spurious *(ēthetēkasi),* saying that it is rejected *(antilegesthai)* by the church of Rome as not being Paul's. And I shall cite at the proper time the things said about the book by our predecessors.

Thus this first group of writings from the apostolic period consists of twenty-one or twenty-two books (depending on the presence or absence of Revelation). The significance of the limiting of category number one will become clear below. Of this group, by way of summary, Eusebius says in v. 3a, "These then belong to the accepted writings" *(tauta ... en homologoumenois).* The passive of *homologeō* (agree) generally means agreed upon or granted by common consent. And what is agreed on by the common consent of the ancient church, of the tradition, is that *only* the writings ascribed to apostles—or, in the case of Mark and Luke, writings that are not ascribed to apostles but come from the apostolic period[32]—are "the writings that according to the ecclesiastical tradition are true *(alētheis),* genuine *(aplastous),* and accepted" *(anōmologēmenas;* 3.25.6). These parallel terms show that authenticity is key in determining the category to which a writing is assigned. Robbins, after defining these and other parallel terms and noting where they occur, adds, "It is clear from such terminology that Eusebius is concerned not only with ecclesiastical acceptance, but also with genuine *authorship.*"[33] Baum compares Eusebius, *Hist. eccl.* 3.25.1–7 to parallel discussions of authenticity among the ancient Greeks, especially in Alexandria.[34] The importance of authenticity will become increasingly evident as we proceed to the second and third categories or, rather, to the third and second. The middle category,

---

[32] Cf. the remark of Baum, "Literarische Echtheit," 109: "In the ancient church *anonymous writings* were regarded as admissible into the canon even if they were not classified as (direct) works of apostles. This is shown, for example, by the evaluation of the Gospels of Mark and Luke. . . ." In "Der neutestamentlichen Kanon bei Eusebius" (316 and elsewhere), he speaks both of "biobibliographischen" concerns (concerns about authorship by a given apostle) and of "chronobibliographischen" concerns (concerns about whether or not the work comes from the apostolic period).

[33] Robbins, "Lexicon of 'Canonicity,'" 135.

[34] Baum, "Der neutestamentliche Kanon bei Eusebius," 308–13.

the *antilegomena,* presents by far the biggest challenge, and so we defer discussion of it and proceed to the third category, the heretical writings, discussed in 3.25.6–7.

This third category consists of those writings that have been

> published by the heretics under the names of the apostles, on the pretense that they comprise the gospels of Peter and Thomas and Mathias or even some others besides these, or the Acts of Andrew and of John and of the other apostles. Not a single one of the ecclesiastical writers down through the years has thought any of these worth mentioning. Moreover, the type of language is different from apostolic usage and the thought and purpose of these writings is totally at odds with true orthodoxy, showing clearly that they are the work of heretics. For this reason, then, these must not even be classified among the spurious writings *(notha)* but instead shunned as totally absurd and ungodly.

Authenticity, or, in this case, the lack of it, is important here as throughout the catalogue: "published by the heretics under the names of the apostles, on the pretense that they comprise" works by Peter, Thomas, and other apostles. The inauthenticity of these writings is as important for Eusebius as was the authenticity of the *homologoumena,* and the issue also plays an important role in the discussion of the *antilegomena,* where Eusebius introduces the term *notha,* "spurious." But lack of authenticity is not the *essential* characteristic in the third category, the heretical writings, since these writings are *not* to be classified with the writings that Eusebius calls spurious *(notha)* when discussing the *antilegomena.* In the third and last category it is *heretics* who have done the forging, and the style, content, and purpose of the writings reveal them to be "totally absurd and ungodly," in other words "heretical." This, of course, is the reason Eusebius cannot imagine any ecclesiastical writer mentioning them (favorably, that is).[35]

Now to the middle group. Eusebius begins his discussion of the second group of writings, the *antilegomena,* with the words, "Among the disputed writings *(tōn d' antilegomenōn)*[36] that are, nevertheless, familiar to the majority . . ." (3.25.3b), and ends the category with the words: "These would all be among the disputed writings . . ." (3.25.6). In the middle of the section, after mentioning the epistles of James, Jude, 2 Peter, and 2 and 3 John, Eusebius continues: "Among the spurious writings *(en tois nothois)* must also be counted" the *Acts of Paul,* the *Shepherd of Hermas,* the *Revelation of Peter, Barnabas,* the *Didache* and "as I said, the Revelation of John, if this should seem to be the right place for it. For some, as I said, reject it as spurious *(athetousin)* while others reckon it among the accepted writings" *(tois homologoumenois,* 3.25.4). Some, he notes finally, would also assign the *Gospel according to the Hebrews* to this category.

3. The Nature of the *Antilegomena*

A basic question is the exact nature of this second category, the *antilegomena.* Many interpreters assume that this group is itself divided by Eusebius into two distinct parts, the *antilegomena* and the *notha,* yielding a fourfold division of the text: the *homologoumena,*

---

[35] Eusebius's extensive quotation of Serapion's discussion of the *Gospel of Peter (Hist. eccl.* 6:12) shows the grain of salt with which we need to take the statement that the writings in group three receive no notice from ecclesiastical writers.

[36] The idea is that their authenticity has been challenged, spoken against.

the *antilegomena,* the *notha* (spurious), and the heretical writings. However, those who make this distinction differ as to the nature of the division. The majority of scholars say that the difference relates to Eusebius's own opinion of the writings in question. For instance, Ellen Flesseman-van Leer understands the two groups as "1. those about whose authenticity he is in doubt and 2. those he regards as spurious *(notha). . . ."*[37] Goodspeed maintains that the division of the *antilegomena* is into "those that [Eusebius] accepted and those that he rejected."[38] According to Theodor Zahn, Eusebius distinguishes "those anti- legomena whose acceptance he desires from those he calls spurious *(notha)* and therefore wants excluded."[39] Johannes Leipoldt, on the other hand, considers the division to be based on the degree of acceptance a writing has received in the church. He thinks that Eusebius distinguishes between "those that are held in esteem by the majority and . . . [those that are] 'less widely accepted.' . . ."[40] For Metzger also it is the church's views Eusebius is cata- loguing: Eusebius counts

> the votes of his witnesses, and . . . classif[ies] all apostolic or pretended apostolic writings into three categories: (1) Those on whose authority and authenticity all the churches and all the authors he had consulted were agreed [the *homologoumena*]; (2) those which the witnesses were equally agreed in rejecting [the *notha*]; and (3) an intermediate class regarding which the votes were divided [the *antilegomena*].[41]

But in my opinion the task of deciding the basis of Eusebius's distinction between the *antilegomena* in the narrower sense and the *notha* is fruitless, for I do not think that he divides between the two groups *in any substantial way.* They are simply two different words for the same category.

Two things require clarification: (1) the importance of the issue of whether *antilego- mena* and *notha* are two distinct groups or simply two different ways of speaking of the same group, and (2) how the writings of both Robbins and Baum with respect to this issue are leading me to embrace a somewhat different position from that of my dissertation and my SBL presentation.

With regard to the latter point, in my statement above, "I do not think that he di- vides between the two groups *in any substantial way,"* the emphasized words represent a qualification of my more unequivocal assertions in the dissertation and at the SBL. It hap- pens that both Robbins and Baum agree that *antilegomena* and *notha* are not two distinct groups, and yet they distinguish the two, as subgroups, in strikingly different ways. Robbins says "that *antilegomena* and *notha* are, for Eusebius, simply two different words for the same

---

[37] Ellen Flesseman-van Leer, "Prinzipien der Sammlung und Ausscheidung bei der Bildung des Kanons," *ZTK* 61 (1964): 414 n. 36.

[38] E. J. Goodspeed, "The Canon of the New Testament," *Interpreter's Bible* (12 vols.; ed. George A. Buttrick; New York and Nashville: Abingdon, 1952–1957), 1:66.

[39] Theodor Zahn, *Grundriss der Geschichte des Neutestamentlichen Kanons* (2d ed.; Leipzig: A. Deichert, 1904), 56.

[40] Johannes Leipoldt, *Geschichte des neutestamentlichen Kanons* (2 vols.; Leipzig: Hinrichs, 1907), 1:72. Leipoldt maintains here that "less widely accepted" is what Eusebius means by *notha* (which is thus, in Leipoldt's opinion, an unfortunate choice of words); the meaning "inauthentic" also plays a role in Eusebius's use of *notha,* Leipoldt affirms.

[41] Metzger, *Canon,* 203. Note that Metzger here is dividing *Hist. eccl.* 3.25.1–7 into *four,* not *three,* categories, since he goes on to discuss the heretical writings after the section quoted here.

category," namely "orthodox Christian writings which were counterfeits."[42] Thus, according to Robbins, Eusebius considered *all* the *antilegomena* to be spurious. While Robbins adds that this category "was further sub-divided to delineate between those counterfeits many presumed to be genuine [the *antilegomena*] and those which were widely recognized to be spurious [the *notha*],"[43] he insists that Eusebius minimizes this distinction in the text itself (in ways we shall indicate below) so as to show that the whole group is to be distinguished clearly from the *homologoumena*. Baum's view is much more complex. On the one hand, he rejects the view of those who divide 3.25.1–7 into four groups by making the *notha* a distinct group.[44] On the other hand, he insists: "The thesis that Eusebius used the expressions *antilegomenos* and *nothos* synonymously is untenable."[45] What then is the difference for Baum? "Eusebius distinguished between those antilegomena that he considered inauthentic *(nothoi)* and those that he thereby implicitly classified as *gnēsios* [genuine]."[46] So for Robbins the difference between the two groups is the degree of doubt in the church about a writing's authenticity, and Eusebius is intent on minimizing the difference, since for him they are *all spurious* and must be carefully distinguished from the *homologoumena*. Baum, by contrast, finds the difference to be Eusebius's own opinion that the writings in the one group are spurious and those in the other group genuine. In Baum's view Eusebius is intent on magnifying, not minimizing that distinction, for reasons that can only be discussed after we have moved to the other preliminary item, the *importance* of whether the groups are or are not distinct.

If, as Robbins and Baum assert, the *antilegomena* and *notha* are not two clearly distinct groups, and yet there are some differences between them, why not leave it at that and say they are in one respect the same and in some other respect different? My insistence that, if there is a difference, it is not substantial is in part a response to those who magnify the difference and usually end up joining the *antilegomena* that are not called *notha* with the *homologoumena* when they identify the canon of Eusebius, something that in my view is contrary to his own explicit statement.

4. The Equivalence of *Antilegomena* and *Notha*

Now it is time for the evidence that the *antilegomena* and *notha* do not differ in any substantial way and that these are essentially two different terms for the same category, as noted by both J. Salaverri[47] and, almost two hundred years earlier, G. C. F. Lücke.[48]

---

[42] Robbins, "*Peri tōn endiathēkōn graphōn*," 138.

[43] Ibid. On p. 122, Robbins expresses the distinction thus: "those orthodox and widely-read writings which are very likely forgeries but which are *presumed* by many to be genuine (3.25.3). . . . [and] those orthodox and well-known writings, bearing the names of apostles, which are widely regarded to be spurious (*notha*—3.25.4–5)."

[44] Baum, "Der neutestamentliche Kanon bei Eusebius," 325.

[45] Ibid., 337.

[46] Ibid., 338.

[47] J. Salaverri, "El origen de la revelación y los garantes de su conservación en la Iglesia según Eusebio de Cesarea," *Greg* 16 (1935): 359–61. Max Mueller ("Die Überlieferung des Eusebius in seiner Kirchengeschichte über die Schriften des Neuen Testaments und deren Verfasser," *TSK* 105 [1933]: 429) seems to share this view when he describes the second class as "the *antilegomena*, synonymous with *notha*," but on the next page he still divides these (rather vaguely) into two subgroups, (1) "those with relatively greater similarity to the *homologoumena* . . . [and (2)] those without that."

[48] G. C. F. Lücke, *Über den neutestamentlichen Kanon des Eusebius von Cäsarea* (Berlin: F. Dumler, 1816), 11–14.

Although the listing of several writings, followed by the words *en tois nothois* and the listing of several more writings, could be taken to indicate a distinction between *antilegomena* and *notha,* the following considerations lead me to see here only a variation in names for one group:

1. The category summary in section 6, "These would all be among the disputed writings *(tōn antilegomenōn)*" follows the whole group, including the *notha.* It includes all the writings discussed in 3.25.3–5 just as the summary at the beginning of v. 3, "These then belong to the accepted writings," includes all those mentioned in 3.25.1–2.

2. The summary statement continues by distinguishing between the *homologoumena* (here described in other terms) and those that are *antilegomena* and yet known to most people in the church, and by specifically separating both of these from the third major category, heretical works. In this summary statement, then, the three categories are *homologoumena, antilegomena,* and the heretical works; if *notha* is a separate category, it goes unmentioned here. Baum emphasizes that in this summary Eusebius expressly states that he thus far distinguishes only two categories, the unanimously acknowledged and the disputed. On grammatical grounds Baum rejects the attempts of others to use this summary to distinguish the *notha* from the acknowledged and the disputed writings.[49]

3. The *kai* (also) at the beginning of section 4, *en tois nothois katatetachthō kai. . . .* ("Among the spurious writings must *also* be counted. . . .") is most easily explained by saying that with *The Acts of Paul* Eusebius is *continuing* a category under discussion, namely the *antilegomena,* even though he here uses a different word for it, a word that shows how large a role authenticity issues play in his discussion of all the writings mentioned in 3.25.1–7. Most translations and discussions of the passage ignore the *kai,* but Lücke stressed its importance[50] and Robbins used both the *kai* and the summary statement I discussed in points 1 and 2 above to demonstrate that Eusebius was here purposely *minimizing* whatever differences there might have been between the *antilegomena* and the *notha.*[51]

4. The discussion about the Revelation of John would be much more logical if the *antilegomena–notha* were one class instead of two; Revelation was mentioned provisionally at the end of the *homologoumena* (v. 2), and it is now also mentioned provisionally at the end of the *antilegomena–notha* (v. 4): "if this should be the right place for it. For some, as I said, reject it as spurious *(hēn . . . athetousin),* while others reckon it among the accepted writings." He had, in fact, said this very thing in 3.24.17–18, the section that immediately precedes our text:

> Of John's writings, besides the gospel, the first of the epistles has also been accepted as his without question, both by our contemporaries and by the ancients, but the other two are disputed. With respect to the Revelation there have been many advocates of either opinion up to the present.

Here the Gospel and the First Epistle of John are put in a category equivalent to the *homologoumena,* the other two epistles are *antilegomena;* opinion is divided as to whether Revelation belongs in the one class or the other.

---

[49] Baum, "Der neutestamentliche Kanon bei Eusebius," 324.
[50] Lücke, *Kanon des Eusebius,* 12–14.
[51] Robbins, "*Peri tōn endiathēkōn graphōn,*" 138.

̣ are three rather than four categories in a parallel summary statement in
.6:

> pages we have treated the facts that have come to our knowledge regarding the
> apostles and the apostolic period; the sacred writings they have left us [= the *homolo-
> goumena*]; the disputed writings which are nevertheless read publicly by many in most
> churches [= the *antilegomena–notha*]; and those writings that are totally spurious and for-
> eign to apostolic orthodoxy [= the heretical writings].

The threefold character of this summary supports my contention that there are three categories in 3.25.1–7; the *antilegomena* are not divided. Paradoxically, Eusebius designates the
heretical writings in 3.31.6 as *pantelōs nothōn* ("totally spurious"), despite the fact that in
3.25.7 he expressly said that the heretical writings are not even to be classed among the
notha, that is, the *antilegomena–notha*, when these orthodox writings are viewed from the
perspective of their possible or probable lack of authenticity.

6. What is said about James and Jude in *Hist. eccl.* 2.23.24–25 would place these letters among the *notha* rather than the *antilegomena*, if these groups were indeed divided:

> Such is the account about James. The first of the so-called Catholic Epistles is said to be his.
> But it should be noted that it is considered spurious *(notheuetai)*—at any rate, not many of
> the ancient writers mention it, as is true also of the epistle said to be Jude's, itself one of the
> seven so-called Catholic Epistles. Nevertheless, we know that these have been read publicly
> along with the remaining epistles in most churches.

The Epistle of James is said to be considered spurious (*notheuetai*, the verbal form of
notha is used) and that it had scant mention among the church's ancient writers. The same
is said of the Epistle of Jude. "The same" would have to mean "*notheuetai*" and/or "scant
mention among the ancient writers." The Epistle of Jude is mentioned twice more in the
Historia ecclesiastica. In 6.13.6 Eusebius notes that in the *Stromata* Clement of Alexandria
made use of testimonies from the disputed writings, giving as examples the Wisdom of
Solomon, Sirach, Hebrews, *Barnabas*, *Clement*, and Jude. In 6.14 it is said that in giving
concise interpretations of the scripture in the *Hypotyposes* Clement did not omit the disputed writings, including Jude and the other catholic epistles, *Barnabas*, the *Revelation of
Peter*, and Hebrews. In these two references to Clement's use of the *antilegomena*, the writings common to the *antilegomena-notha* listed in 3.25.3–5 are Jude, the other catholic
epistles (presumably James, 2 Peter, 2 and 3 John), *Barnabas*, and the *Revelation of Peter*.
There is certainly no indication in these references to Clement of Alexandria that *Barnabas*
and the *Revelation of Peter* (the two from the *notha* if that is a separate group) are in a category distinct from the rest, and the *notheuetai* used of James (and Jude) in 2.23.24–25 certainly confirms that perception.

7. Finally, neither alleged basis for the division is compelling. That the two groups
are divided by greater or less attestation in the church is contradicted by the summary
statement that follows the listing of the *notha*, that they are "known to most people in the
church" (v. 6). That the division represents Eusebius's own opinion contradicts his practice
in matters of canon, which is to catalog the tradition of the church rather than express his
own views. Thus, in my opinion, Eusebius did not have two groups of *antilegomena*,
but one.

His language here may be ambiguous enough to permit many to find two distinct groups, *antilegomena* and *notha*. But a *clear* statement of his—namely, that the only books that belong in the New Testament, that are canonical, are the homologoumena—is widely ignored. First, I shall discuss the statement and then offer examples of ways in which it is ignored.

5. *Endiathēkoi:* "In the New Testament"

After giving his list of disputed writings, beginning with James and ending with *The Teaching of the Apostles,* adding to the list Revelation, if it belongs here rather than in the *homologoumena,* and, according to some, *The Gospel of the Hebrews,* he says of them all:

> These would all be among the disputed writings *(tōn antilegomenōn),* but we have been obliged to make a list of them also, thereby distinguishing the writings that according to the ecclesiastical tradition are true *(alētheis),* genuine *(aplastous)* and accepted *(anōmologē-menas)* [= the *homologoumena,* described in slightly different terms] and those that, in contrast to these, are not in the [New] Testament *(ouk endiathēkous)* but disputed *(antilego-menas)* and yet known to most people in the church (3.25.6).

First I need to explain my translation of *ouk endiathēkous* as "not in the [New] Testament." Usually these words are translated "not canonical," but Gregory Robbins argues that Eusebius does not use *kanōn* (canon) or its cognates to designate a list of the books of scripture[52] (this use of the term *kanōn,* in fact, occurs for the first time in the second half of the fourth century with Athanasius, the council of Laodicea and Amphilochius of Iconium[53]). Instead, says Robbins, Eusebius uses the word "catalogue"[54] and "he refers to the Church's accepted Scriptures, the *homologoumena,* by the neologism: *endiathēkos* ('covenantal', 'encovenanted')."[55] Robbins asserts that "One cannot simply equate 'covenantal' with 'canonical'"[56] and calls it "misleading" to use "canonical" as a translation for *endiathēkos.*[57] I find myself caught between agreeing with Baum, who calls it unnecessary to evaluate this translation as "misleading"[58] and trying to take Robbins's distinction seriously. But since, in the context of the passage I am examining, I do not find that "covenantal" and "encovenanted" convey an easily understood meaning, I am using a phrase that in my view does convey Eusebius's meaning in words we can understand: "in the [New] Testament" (an equivalent would be "part of the [New] Testament"). The phrase in 3.25.1, *tas . . . tēs kainēs diathēkēs graphas* ("the writings of the New Testament") has as its exact opposite in 3.25.6 *tas . . . ouk endiathēkous [graphas]* ("those [writings] that . . . are not in the [New] Testament"). In some of the occurrences of *endiathēkos* in

---

[52] Robbins, "Eusebius' Lexicon," 136–39.

[53] Metzger gives the references in "Appendix I. History of the Word *Kanōn,*" *Canon,* 292.

[54] Robbins, "Eusebius' Lexicon," 139; cf. *Hist. eccl.* 3.25.6, "we have been obliged to make a list (or "catalogue"—*katalogon*) of them [the *antilegomena*] also, . . ." and 3.25.2, "Next one must list (or "catalogue"—*katalekteon*) the epistles of Paul; . . ."

[55] Robbins, "Eusebius' Lexicon," 135–36.

[56] Robbins, "*Peri tōn endiathēkōn graphōn,*" 259.

[57] Robbins, "Eusebius' Lexicon," 136.

[58] Baum, "Der neutestamentliche Kanon bei Eusebius," 334.

the *Historia ecclesiastica* "in the [New] Testament" is not an appropriate translation, and there one may need to use "canonical" or one of Robbins's counter proposals (though I am not quite sure what "covenantal" or "encovenanted" would denote in those contexts either).[59]

Enough about terminology and on to the substance. For Eusebius, *homologoumena* and *endiathēkoi* are parallel and virtually synonymous terms (cf. *Hist. eccl.* 3.3.3, *tōn endiathēkōn kai homologoumenōn graphōn* ["concerning the writings that are generally acknowledged and in the [New] Testament"]) and *antilegomena* and *endiathēkoi* are contrasting and mutually exclusive terms. In 3.25.6, the *antilegomena* are said to be *ouk endiathēkous:* "not in the [New] Testament," (or "not encovenanted," "not canonical"). All this is confirmed by what Eusebius says about the letters ascribed to Peter in 3.3.1:

> One epistle of Peter, his so-called first, is accepted, and the ancient elders made ample use of it as undisputed in their own writings. But we have received that the second epistle that is extant is not in the [New] Testament *(ouk endiathēkon);* nevertheless, since it has appeared useful to many, it has been studied with the other writings.

The only writings discussed in *Hist. eccl.* 3.25.1–7 that are, according to Eusebius, *endiathēkoi,* "in the [church's New] Testament" ("entestamented," "canonical") are the *homologoumena* cataloged in 3.25.1–2: the four gospels, Acts, the (14) letters of Paul, 1 John, 1 Peter and, perhaps, the Revelation of John—a collection of 21/22 writings. This is the way in which Eusebius is also understood both by Baum[60] and by Robbins.[61]

Since Eusebius says clearly that the *antilegomena* are not in the [New] Testament, or, to use the terminology of most commentators on the text, not canonical, it seems strange (to say the least) that Eusebius's canon is widely considered to be the *homologoumena* in 3.25.1–2 plus the "better" group of *antilegomena.* For example, Zahn writes: "Apart from Revelation, the New Testament according to Eusebius is the one we have; . . .";[62] Westcott: "Eusebius received as 'Divine Scriptures' the Acknowledged books, adding to them the other books in our present Canon, and no others, . . . with this single exception, that he was undecided as to the authorship of the Apocalypse.";[63] Goodspeed: "In order to find [Eusebius's] own New Testament list, therefore, we must take his 'acknowledged' list and add to it the books in his 'disputed' list which he did not call 'rejected.' ";[64] and finally, Metzger, who argues, "The orthodox books embrace the *homologoumena* and the *antilegomena,* which are canonical, and the *notha,* which are uncanonical."[65]

---

[59] The term *endiathēkos* occurs in *Hist. eccl.* 3.3.1; 3.3.3; 3.9.5; 3.25.6; 5.8.1; 6.14.1; 6.25.1.

[60] "In the eyes of Eusebius, the New Testament canon of the church comprises twenty-one writings, or, if the Revelation of John is included, twenty-two" ("Der neutestamentliche Kanon bei Eusebius," 334).

[61] "Eusebius has in mind a 22–book New Testament . . . [a] 22–book list of Christian scriptures, 'covenantal writings,' . . ." which, in Robbins's view parallels Eusebius's understanding of the church's Old Testament collection (*"Peri tōn endiathēkōn graphōn,"* 141–42).

[62] Zahn, *Grundriss,* 57.

[63] B. F. Westcott, *A General Survey of the History of the Canon of the New Testament* (6th ed.; Cambridge: Macmillan, 1898; repr. Grand Rapids: Baker, 1980), 423.

[64] Goodspeed, "Canon of the New Testament," 66.

[65] Metzger, *Canon,* 204. The same thing is said in chart form on the next page.

Baum explicitly rejects Metzger's assertion that in addition to the *homologoumena* Eusebius also classifies as canonical the *antilegomena* that are not designated *nothoi.*[66] With respect to the issue of which books were canonical in Eusebius's time, he asserts (1) that the concepts *endiathēkous* and *homologoumenos* are repeatedly equated and (2) that Eusebius believes the church's canon to consist of twenty-one or twenty-two books.[67]

Thus far it seemed that Baum had in the main agreed with my assessment of Eusebius, *Hist. eccl.* 3.25.1–7. But in the section that followed, "III. The Canon-critical Judgment of Eusebius" (334–344), the left hand seemed forcibly to reclaim what the right hand had conceded, for Baum claims that Eusebius overlays his discussion of *the church's* canon with *his own* canon-critical judgments. Here is the result:

> Apart from the Apocalypse of John, the boundaries of the New Testament canon Eusebius regards as correct agree with those drawn in A.D. 367 in the 39th Easter Letter of Athanasius and the borders of the canon today. The judgment that Eusebius did not acknowledge more ... than twenty-two books as canonical does not stand up.[68]

So, according to Baum, Eusebius accepts what has been handed on in the church both about the universally acknowledged works and the heretical works not worthy of mention. He does not comment about the former, while with respect to the latter his observations about style, content, and intention underscore the heretical nature of the documents and serve to shore up the border between orthodox and heretical writings.[69] Baum finds Eusebius's own judgments most apparent in his remarks about the *antilegomena,* several of which he declares to be spurious *(nothoi),* implicitly showing that he classifies the others (James, Jude, 2 Peter, and 2 and 3 John) as genuine.[70] In Baum's view Eusebius treats the Apocalypse of John as he does because, for reasons of content, *he* does not want it to be accorded authoritative status.[71]

Why does Eusebius plead for a twenty-six book canon in the middle of his narrative about the church's canon of twenty-one or twenty-two books? Baum's answer is that if Eusebius believed it desirable for the whole church to have a canon with definite borders, without giving up all the documents which had been questioned in even a minimal way, he had to make distinctions among the *antilegomena* on the basis of his own critical judgment.[72] Baum even speculates that the fifty copies of the sacred scriptures Eusebius supplied in fulfillment of Constantine's request, mentioned in Eusebius, *Vita Constantini* 4.34, 36–37, contained twenty-six New Testament books, materially influencing canon history in the East.[73]

6. Evaluating Baum's Proposals

I shall now comment on these proposals by Baum, more or less in reverse order. While it is true that many Eastern canon lists that appear after Eusebius's *Hist. eccl.* omit

---

[66] Baum, "Der neutestamentliche Kanon bei Eusebius," 334.
[67] Ibid. The latter point is explicitly quoted in n. 60 above.
[68] Ibid., 342.
[69] Ibid., 334–37.
[70] Ibid., 338.
[71] Ibid., 340.
[72] Ibid., 339.
[73] Ibid., 342–43.

the book of Revelation and have a twenty-six book New Testament,[74] it is by no means certain what books were included in the fifty copies Eusebius supplied at Constantine's request. Robbins, in his extensive discussion of the many puzzling issues about these
volumes,[75] speculates that Eusebius produced for the emperor fifty copies of the fourfold
Gospel collection.[76] That Eusebius would have wanted the whole church to have a canon
with definite borders seems on the face of it quite likely. I have elsewhere reported Martin
Elze's suggestion that in the Constantinian era, when canon lists begin and proliferate,
there would have been a desire to promote unity in the church and in the empire through a
specific collection of books.[77] But it is by no means self-evident to me that this list, *Hist.
eccl.* 3.25.1–7, constitutes a plea for the church to abandon what Eusebius admits in the list
itself is *the church's* twenty-two or twenty-one book canon for *his* twenty-six book canon.
That trumpet call for change would surely be issuing a far too uncertain sound! Take what
Eusebius says in 3.25.1–7 about the Revelation of John. It should either be in the *homologoumena*, "if it should seem appropriate" (v. 2), or the *antilegomena–notha* (by my reck-
oning, or the *notha*, by Baum's), "For some, as I said, reject it as spurious, while others
reckon it among the accepted writings" (v. 4). None of this, nor any of Baum's arguments
about Revelation in the rest of the *Historia ecclesiastica*, makes me see in 3.25.1–7 a plea to
reject Revelation, which, according to Baum, the church, on the basis of its tradition,
should accept.[78] And while Baum is absolutely correct that Eusebius wants *The Acts of Paul,
The Shepherd, The Revelation of Peter, Barnabas, The Didache*, perhaps the Revelation of
John, and, for some, *The Gospel of the Hebrews* to be catalogued among the spurious writings, this does *not* seem to me an implicit statement about the *genuineness* of James, Jude,
2 Peter, 2 and 3 John. Recall that 3.25.4 begins "Among the spurious writings must *also
(kai)* be counted the Acts of Paul, . . ." Baum takes no notice of the *kai*. The statement
about the *notha* is followed by statements that put *all* these documents (2 Peter as well
as *The Revelation of Peter*) among the *antilegomena* and assert that *all* of them are to be
distinguished from the *homologoumena*, which alone are *endiathēkoi* ("in the [New] Testament," "canonical," "entestamented" or whatever translation is deemed most apt). Therefore I do not find Baum convincing that in 3.25.1–7 Eusebius makes *his* own case for 26
instead of 22 canonical books by superimposing on the canon of the church, statistically

---

[74] This is true of Cyril of Jerusalem, *Catechetical Lectures* 4.36, Canon 60 of the Synod of
Laodicea, and the canon of Gregory of Nazianzus; Amphilochius of Iconium seems to wish Revelation omitted, but leaves open whether there should be three or seven catholic epistles.

[75] Robbins, "*Peri tōn endiathēkōn graphōn*," 160–216.

[76] Ibid., 191. See also Robbins's article " 'Fifty Copies of Sacred Writings' (VC 4.36): Entire
Bibles or Gospel Books?" *StPatr* 19 (1989): 91–98.

[77] Kalin, "The Canon of Origen," 282.

[78] By way of comparison Amphilochius of Iconium makes a somewhat clearer case for the
rejection of Revelation in a similar context: "And again the Revelation of John, / Some approve, but
the most / Say it is spurious." Amphilochius states his *own view* of another writing in dispute,
Hebrews, more forcefully: "Paul . . . [wrote] / Twice seven epistles: . . . But some say the one to the
Hebrews is spurious, not saying well, for the grace is genuine." But even his statement on Revelation
is a much clearer downgrading of that book than what Eusebius offers in our text. The best analogy
to Eusebius on Revelation is Amphilochius on the Catholic Epistles: "Some say we must receive
seven, but others say / Only three [James, 1 Peter, 1 John] should be received . . ." (the quotations use
the translations in Metzger [*Canon*, 314]).

established, and described in terms of reception (*homologoumenos, antilegomenos* [and *amnēmonoumenos*—not mentioned here]) and canonicity (*endiathēkos* and *ouk endiathēkos*), his own critical judgment about authenticity ([*gnēsios;* genuine and] *nothos*).[79]

While Baum is correct that *homologoumena* and *endiathēkos*, on the one hand, refer properly to ecclesiastical reception and being in the church's New Testament (or canon), respectively, and *nothos* and *gnēsios* (genuine), on the other hand, constitute critical assertions about authenticity (by Eusebius or whomever), in point of fact all these terms can apply to reception/authority *or* authenticity. *Homologoumenos* and related terms mean generally (or universally) accepted or agreed upon as authoritative, in the New Testament, or canonical because they mean accepted *as authentically apostolic* (or, in rare cases, authentically from the apostolic period). And what is disputed about a writing is not only whether it belongs in the church's authoritative collection but whether a given apostle wrote it or not. A few quotes from *Hist. eccl.* 3.3.1–7 can illustrate this. With respect to Peter's writings it is said:

> One epistle of Peter, his so-called first, is agreed upon *(anōmologētai)*, and the ancient elders made full use of it as undisputed *(anamphilektō)* in their own writings. But we have received that the second epistle that is extant is not in the [New] Testament *(ouk endiathēkon)*; nevertheless, since it has appeared useful to many, it has been studied with the other writings. . . . But I know that of the writings bearing Peter's name only the one epistle is genuine *(gnēsian)* and accepted *(homologoumenēn)* by the ancient elders (3.3.1, 4).

If in 3.25 *homologoumena* (especially in parallel to *endiathēkoi*) relates in first instance to general acceptance into the church's collection of authoritative documents, the text just cited shows how the term and its parallels relate to authenticity. It is clear that issues of acceptance/being in the New Testament/canonicity and authenticity are fully overlapping categories very difficult to untangle from one another; however much one today might *want* or *need* to do such untangling, neither Eusebius nor the traditions he cites had such an interest. And the statement in 3.3.4 that of Peter's writings only 1 Peter "is genuine and accepted by the ancient elders" not only makes dividing acceptance and authenticity difficult; it makes even more difficult Baum's attempt to find in 3.25.3–6 an implicit indication that Eusebius considered 2 Peter genuine.

Like *homologoumena*, the term *antilegomena* moves in a twofold direction. First, the *antilegomena* are contrasted to a class called fully accepted and in the New Testament (3.25.6). Thus the primary characteristic here is that the *antilegomena* are not accepted in the New Testament, even though some (or many) ecclesiastical writers used them and though they are read in various churches in Eusebius's day. But in 3.3.5 what is spoken against (*antilegesthai*, the indicative form related to *antilegomena* is used) by some is *Paul's authorship* of Hebrews.

At this point I would like to make an observation about terminology, using the text we are currently considering, 3.3.1–7. *Antilegomena* and the indicative of the verb *antilegesthai* (speak against) can and do surely mean "disputed," and in several places I have translated them this way. But if interpreters bore in mind that this verb can also mean

---

[79] Baum summarizes his views in a helpful chart, "Der neutestamentliche Kanon bei Eusebius," 346.

"rejected," it would become more difficult to *minimize* the line between the *homologoumena* and the "better" examples of *antilegomena*. Kirsopp Lake's translation of portions of 3.3.1–7 makes the point:

> And the fourteen letters of Paul are obvious and plain, yet it is not right to ignore that some dispute [*ēthetēkasi*—"have rejected as spurious"] the Epistle to the Hebrews, saying that it was *rejected [antilegesthai]* by the church of Rome as not being by Paul, . . . it should also be known that . . . [the *Shepherd of Hermas*] also is *rejected [antilelektai]* by some, . . . (3.3.4–6, emphases added).[80]

Here, at least, Lake seems to me to convey the meaning of the verb *antilegesthai* (speak against) more adequately with "reject" than with "dispute." And what Eusebius says about the Johannine writings in 3.24.18 (the immediate predecessor to 3.25.1–7) would seem to make better sense if we tried the translation "are rejected" rather than "are disputed" for *antilegontai*, in respect to 2 and 3 John:

> Of John's writings besides the Gospel, the first of the epistles has also been acknowledged as undisputed both by our contemporaries and by the ancients, but the other two are rejected *(antilegontai)*, and with respect to the Revelation public opinion is still evenly divided.

Thus, what is *disputed* about the Revelation of John is whether it belongs in category one (agreed upon or accepted) or category two (spoken against or rejected). Isn't that precisely what Eusebius says about Revelation in 3.25.4? "For some, as I said, reject it as spurious (*athetousin*, thus possibly placing it among the *antilegomena*), while others reckon it among the accepted writings."

What are the criteria by which Eusebius determined which writings belonged in each category? Basically there is only one, the tradition of the church, that is, that which *has been handed down* to him about each writing. Eusebius says in 3.25.6, after he has listed the *homologoumena* and the *antilegomena*, that he has distinguished between those writings that "*according to the ecclesiastical tradition* are true, genuine, and accepted and those that, in contrast to these, are not in the [New] Testament but disputed." To both of these groups he then contrasts the heretical forgeries, about which he says, "Not a single one of the ecclesiastical writers down through the years has thought any of these worth mentioning." What he says of the Petrine writings in 3.3.1–2 illustrates the same principle: "the ancient elders made full use of [1 Peter] as undisputed in their own writings. But *we have received* that the second epistle that is extant is not in the [New] Testament . . ." (even though he says that it is known and used by many). By contrast, works like the *Acts, Gospel, Kerygma,* and *Revelation* ascribed to Peter "*have by no means been handed down* among the catholic writings, because no ecclesiastical writer, past or present, used the testimonies from them."[81]

---

[80] K. Lake, *Eusebius: The Ecclesiastical History* (LCL; 2 vols.; Cambridge: Harvard University Press, 1959), 1:193.

[81] The last phrase, from *Hist. eccl.* 3.3.2, reminds us of what Eusebius says in 3.25.6 about the heretical writings ("Not a single one of the ecclesiastical writers down through the years has thought any of these worth mentioning"), and it is interesting to compare the Petrine writings listed in the two texts. In 3.3.2 the (heretical) Petrine works not getting any mention by orthodox writers are Peter's *Gospel, Acts, Preaching,* and *Revelation.* Among the heretical Petrine works listed in 3.25.6 we

The testimony of the writers of the ancient church interests Eusebius more than current practice. He would have approved of Origen's quotation of Prov 22:28 in a canon history context: "Do not remove the ancient landmark that your ancestors set up."[82] And the reason that the testimony of the ancient writers is important is that Eusebius is convinced that they were transmitting in written form "the traditions *that had come down to them* (presumably from the apostles) concerning the canonical (or entestamented) writings" (*peri tōn endiathēkōn graphōn, Hist. eccl. 5.8.1*). For instance, Eusebius says of the church's use of the Septuagint, "That it is to be used, our Savior's apostles and disciples have delivered from the beginning."[83]

As far as Eusebius is concerned, what is required for canonicity is that a writing come from apostolic times and itself be apostolic, either in the sense that it was written by an apostle or handed down by the apostles. In *Hist. eccl.* 3.31.6 he summarizes all we have been saying:

> Since we have treated in these pages the facts that have come to our knowledge regarding the apostles and the apostolic times, the sacred writings *which they have left us* [the *homologoumena*, which alone are "in the (New) Testament"], the writings which are disputed and yet used publicly by many in most churches [the *antilegomena-notha*] and those that are totally spurious and foreign to apostolic orthodoxy [the heretical writings], let us now proceed to the account of what followed.

7. Conclusion

In the early fourth century Eusebius, *Hist. eccl.* 3.25.1–7 provides us with a catalogue of the New Testament writings already mentioned in the history. Eusebius divides the writings he has been discussing into three categories, the *homologoumena* (the universally acknowledged writings), the *antilegomena* (the writings that have been spoken against and are thus disputed—or, in a certain sense, rejected, even though in wide use) and the heretical writings. Only the twenty-one or twenty-two books in the first category are in the church's New Testament (are canonical).[84] It is the ancient church's tradition of what the apostles wrote and handed on that is *the criterion* for evaluating these writings from the apostolic era, and only these twenty-one or twenty-two pass the test. In important recent contributions on this passage both Robbins and Baum agree that for Eusebius the church's canon consists of these twenty-one or twenty-two books. But Baum also claims that Eusebius here is overlaying this canon with his own critical canon of twenty-six books.

---

have the *Gospel* and (by inference) the *Acts*. But *The Revelation of Peter,* while among the writings explicitly called spurious is 3.25.4, is not among the heretical writings but among the *antilegomena*, which, as a group, are "known to most people in the church" (3.25.6). *The Preaching of Peter* goes totally unmentioned in 3.25.1–7.

[82] Origen, *Ep. Afr.* 5.

[83] *Chron.* 45.

[84] I take seriously Robbins's caution that Eusebius does not in this context use the term *kanōn*. But would we not say that the list of New Testament writings found in Cyril of Jerusalem's *Catechetical Lectures* 4.36 is no less a canonical list than the one found in Amphilochius of Iconium's *Iambics for Seleucus*, lines 289–319, though the former does not use the term *kanōn* while the latter does? (The texts can be compared in Metzger [*Canon*, 311, 314].)

To me Baum has not made this case, though his reading of the text is far superior to that of the many interpreters who find here the canon *of Eusebius and of the church* that consists of twenty-six or, more often, "our" twenty-seven books.

The first datable list of the church's New Testament comes to us from the early fourth century in Eusebius, *Hist. eccl.* 3.25.1–7; it is a canon of twenty-one or twenty-two books. On this key issue Robbins, Baum, and I agree, whether or not Baum is right in seeing Eusebius trying to push the church to a broader list. If we are correct, it is quite likely that Albert C. Sundberg Jr.'s perspective on New Testament canon history is preferable to the commonly accepted view.[85] Given what we see in Eusebius in the early fourth century it is virtually impossible to imagine that the church had settled upon a twenty-seven book collection, or even one that approximated that, in the late second century. Moreover, whatever the merits of David Trobisch's intriguing and important proposal that a twenty-seven book edition of the New Testament was produced in the second century,[86] that notion seems hard to reconcile with what we have found in Eusebius regarding the church's acceptance of apostolic writings in earlier centuries.

In the fourth century there were many New Testament lists; the issue of which books were in the church's authoritative and normative collection had clearly become important in the Constantinian era. Had it perhaps not become an urgent issue sooner because the church already had a canon, a canon of truth, a canon of faith that consisted in the church's confession about the work of God throughout history, with Israel and centering on Jesus Christ? From the first the church's use of the term *kanōn* centered on God's work in Christ. In Gal 6:14–16 Paul uses the term *kanōn* for the rule or norm according to which believers were to live.[87] This *kanōn* was the new creation called into being by the cross of Jesus Christ, which put to death in a believer's existence the power of the world in its hostility to God.

The many canon lists that followed Eusebius in the fourth and fifth centuries did eventually move out from the twenty-one- or twenty-two-book collection Eusebius documents to the twenty-seven-book collection for which Athanasius's thirty-ninth *Easter Letter* in 367 C.E. is the earliest evidence. In a sense the church did what Baum sees Eusebius urging it to do: it included more of the ancient documents that, though questioned by some, were being used in liturgy and life. One could say that when the church's New Testament canon finally was closed, it was "closed openly or inclusively." The decisions that had been made much earlier (by many, not by all) about the Gospels had the same kind of "open-closedness"; the *four* accounts were authorized, not the *one* gospel that had been favored in this or that region, and not Tatian's harmony. And the Pauline collection, it had been decided, was not to be Marcion's ten (omitting the Pastoral Epistles) but the two times seven, the fourteen (including Hebrews). And when, into the fourth and fifth centuries, many in the East rejected Revelation and accepted Hebrews and many in the West rejected (or ignored) Hebrews and accepted Revelation, the ultimate solution was not "either" or "neither" but "both." But now we have moved past Eusebius to what would have to be another study.

---

[85] Material on the consensus and Sundberg's counter views are presented above, nn. 4–23.

[86] See above, n. 25.

[87] The only other occurrences of the term *kanōn* in the New Testament are in 2 Cor 10:13, 15, 16, where the term concerns the sphere of ministry God had assigned to Paul (the NRSV translates *kanōn* as "field" in 10:13 and "sphere of action" in 10:15 and 16).

24

The Muratorian Fragment and the Origins of the New Testament Canon

Geoffrey Mark Hahneman

To speak of a Christian canon of scriptures at the beginning of the fourth century is an anachronism. Yet to speak of a Christian canon of scriptures at the end of the fourth century is commonplace. Thus the fourth century can easily be seen as the period when the church developed its book of holy scriptures, or Bible. That the Christian canon had its origin in the first three centuries of the common era is without dispute. In the earlier centuries, the various scriptures that later came to make up the canon were inherited or written, deemed authoritative, copied, circulated, quoted, and popularized. That the initial formation of the Christian biblical collection took place in the postapostolic second century is also likely, as evidenced by a collection of Pauline Epistles and the circulation of a Gospel collection. Yet it was not until the fourth century that a conceptual change in the mind of the church occurred which resulted in the creation of the Christian canon.

1. Origins of the Christian Canon of Scriptures

Albert Sundberg's important distinction between "scripture" and "canon" remains essential in understanding the formation of the Christian Bible in the midst of the fourth century.[1] "Scripture" is understood as literature that is appealed to for religious authority, and the early church writers did indeed appeal to a variety of scriptures, some of which did and some of which did not eventually make it into the canon.[2] "Canon," on the other hand, implies a closed set of "scriptures," to which nothing can be added and from which nothing can be subtracted. Whereas the concept of canon presupposes the existence of scriptures, the concept of scripture does not necessarily imply the notion of a canon. Thus it is entirely possible to possess scriptures without having a canon, and this was in fact the situation in the first few centuries of the Christian church.

---

[1] Albert C. Sundberg Jr., "Towards a Revised History of the New Testament Canon," *SE* 4/1 (1968): 453–54.
[2] Lee M. McDonald (*The Formation of the Christian Biblical Canon* [rev. and enl. ed.; Peabody, Mass.: Hendrickson, 1995], Appendix I, 259–67) gives New Testament citations and allusions to apocryphal and pseudepigraphal writings. E. Schürer (*A History of the Jewish People* [rev. G. Vermes, F. Millar, and M. Goodman; Edinburgh: T&T Clark, 1987], 3:2) give patristic citations for each book from what was later called apocrypha and pseudepigrapha.

To speak of a Christian "canon" of scriptures is an anachronism before the second half of the fourth century because it is only after that time that Christian writers begin to employ the word, either the Greek *kanōn* or the Latin *canon,* for a list of books counted as accepted scriptures. Prior to the fourth century, the word "canon" had a long history of being applied both to metaphorical standards and fixed lists in both the East and the West.[3] From the time of Irenaeus, the church leaders employed the word "canon" in a variety of ways to depict the normative ideals of Christian teachings, in phrases such as the "canon of truth," the "canon of faith," or the "ecclesiastical canon." In a similar way, the word "canon" was also used for a "list" or "table" in astronomical, mathematical, and chronological writings of Christians, but not for a list of accepted scriptures. After the Council of Nicaea (325), the word "canon" began to be employed for other kinds of lists, such as the resolutions of church synods or official lists of clergy. Soon thereafter, the word "canon" was extended to lists of accepted Christian writings. The adoption of this word suggests a conceptual transition in the mind of the church. Something new was happening and a new word was needed to express the shift in the understanding of Christian scriptures during the fourth century.

Eusebius is the first to use the term *kanōn* or its cognate (*Hist. eccl.* 6.25.3) for a list of Christian scriptures, but in reference only to the fourfold Gospel collection. Athanasius (c. 350) provided the earliest extant use of *kanōn* in reference to Christian scriptures in general, when he wrote that the *Shepherd of Hermas* was not "part of the canon" (*De decretis* 18.3). Somewhat later (367), Athanasius provided a catalogue of accepted Christian writings and described them as "canonical" (*kanonizomena, Ep. fest.* 39). At about the same time, the Council of Laodicea (c. 360) referred to the "canonical" *(kanonika)* and "uncanonical" *(akanonista)* books of the old and new covenants (canon 59). The use of the Latin word *canon* for a list of scriptures was soon employed by Western writers as well, occurring in the Mommsen Catalogue (c. 360), and later in Priscillian, Filaster, Rufinus, and Augustine. The Latin adjective "canonical" *(canonicus)* appears in Rufinus's translations of Origen, but it is probable that their presence there is due to Rufinus, and not Origen, since Rufinus frequently introduced the Latin word into his translation of Eusebius's *Historia ecclesiastica* where it was not present in the Greek.

Thus after the middle of the fourth century, the word "canon" was regularly used in both the East and the West for an accepted collection of scriptures. In Latin *canon* came to be used synonymously with *biblia.* This usage suggests the need to clarify a new concept in the thinking of the church. While the usage may be dependent upon the earlier sense of a metaphorical norm, the evidence suggests that here "canon" primarily had the sense of a "list," and thus it is not surprising that its appearance in this sense in the fourth century coincided with the proliferation of Christian catalogues. The introduction of the word "canon" at the same time as the sudden appearance of catalogues confirms the fourth century as the time of the formation of the Christian Bible.

2. The Muratorian Fragment: Dating, Provenance, and Importance

While the above information is generally acknowledged, the dating of the origins of the Christian canon is a matter of considerable dispute. Lying at the center of the debate

[3] H. W. Beyer, *"Kanōn," TDNT,* 3:596–602.

on the origins of the New Testament canon is a well-known document commonly called the Muratorian Fragment. Reconsideration of the date of this fragment began at the Third International Congress on New Testament Studies in Oxford in 1965, when Albert C. Sundberg Jr. argued for a redating of the Muratorian Fragment, publishing his argument in full a few years later.[4] The Muratorian Fragment, traditionally dated at the end of the second century, was believed to be the earliest extant list of a Christian New Testament and proof of New Testament canonization before the fourth century. Responses to Sundberg's argument were generally relegated to footnotes, and his thesis was usually ignored or dismissed.[5] Everett Ferguson published the only substantial rebuttal to Sundberg,[6] and a few years later Philippe Henne published a closer look at the arguments of the two, siding ultimately with Ferguson.[7] In 1992, I published a lengthy defense of Sundberg's proposal, having summarized my position at the Oxford conference in 1987.[8] Ferguson again refuted the claims, assisted principally this time by Charles Hill.[9] Despite some allegations of sloppy scholarship, circumstantial or tendentious evidence, special pleading, and arguments *ad hominem*, one can now say with some confidence that an earnest debate about the date of the Muratorian Fragment and the development of Christian canon has moved from footnotes to the center of the page.[10]

Many aspects of the question are generally agreed upon. The so-called Muratorian Fragment was first published in 1740 as a striking example of the barbarism of some scribal transcriptions, and a substantial portion of its poor Latin may be credited to the scribe of the so-called Codex Muratorianus. Missing folios in the Codex may account for the mutilated beginning of the Fragment, but not the abrupt ending. Excerpts of the Fragment found in certain Benedictine texts confirm that the poor Latin of the Fragment is not that of the archetype. Moreover, the Latin of the Fragment has now been dated to the early fifth century, based upon vocabulary and upon grammatical and philological analysis.[11] Thus if the Fragment was originally composed in Latin, it would have to be dated late fourth or

---

[4] Sundberg, "Towards a Revised History," 452–61; and idem, "Canon Muratori: A Fourth-Century List," *HTR* 66 (1973): 1–41.

[5] E.g., J. D. Quinn, "P⁴⁶—The Pauline Canon,?" *CBQ* 36 (1974): 379–85, at 382 n. 21; W. G. Kummel, *Introduction to the New Testament* (trans. H. C. Kee; London: SCM, 1975), 492 n. 69; John A. T. Robinson, *Redating the New Testament* (London: SCM, 1976), 319 n. 41; C. F. D. Moule, *The Birth of the New Testament* (London: A. & C. Black, 1981), 260 n. 1; R. E. Brown, *The Epistles of John* (AB 30; Garden City, N.Y.: Doubleday, 1982), 10 n. 14; W. R. Farmer and D. M. Farkasfalvy, *The Formation of the New Testament Canon* (New York: Paulist, 1983), 60; H. Y. Gamble, *The New Testament Canon: Its Making and Meaning* (Philadelphia: Fortress, 1985), 32 n. 25; D. M. Farkasfalvy, "The Ecclesial Setting of the Pseudepigraphy in Second Peter and Its Role in the Formation of the Canon," *SecCent* 5 (1985–1986), 3–29, at 29 n. 50.

[6] E. Ferguson, "Canon Muratori: Date and Provenance," *SP* 17/2 (1982): 677–83.

[7] P. Henne, "La datation du *Canon* de Muratori," *RB* 100 (1993): 54–75.

[8] G. M. Hahneman, *The Muratorian Fragment and the Development of the Canon* (Oxford: Clarendon, 1992); idem, "More on Redating the Muratorian Fragment," *SP* 19 (1989): 359–65.

[9] E. Ferguson, "Review of Geoffrey Mark Hahneman, *The Muratorian Fragment and the Development of the Canon,*" *JTS* 44 (1993): 696; C. Hill, "The Debate over the Muratorian Fragment and the Development of the Canon," *WTJ* 57 (1995): 437–52.

[10] For an excellent summary of the current debate, see McDonald, *Formation*, 209–20.

[11] J. Campos, "Epoca del Fragmento Muratoriano," *Helmantica, Revista de humanidades clasicas*, 2 (1960): 485–96.

early fifth century. The Fragment is therefore usually presumed to be a translation from Greek, and several of the difficult and confusing passages have been explained as poor translations or simple transliterations of a supposed Greek original.[12] Finally all the datable contents in the so-called Codex Muratorianus belong to the fourth and fifth century, the majority of them being clearly late fourth century, and almost two-thirds of the pages of the Codex contain Latin translations of known Eastern works. The dates of the other contents of the Codex argue for a fourth-century date for the archetype and not just the Latin translation as suggested by some, since the other works are fourth and fifth century in origin, not in translation.

According to Hill the "single greatest difficulty" in redating the Fragment is its references to the *Shepherd of Hermas.*[13] The traditional late second- or early third-century date for the Fragment has been fundamentally based upon the statements:

> Pastorem uero
> nuperrim e(t) temporibus nostris In urbe
> roma herma conscripsit sedente cathe
> tra urbis romae aeclesiae Pio eps fratre(r)
> eius et ideo legi eum quide Oportet se pu
> plicare uero In eclesia populo Neque inter
> profe(*)tas conpletum numero Neque Inter
> apostolos In fine temporum potest. (lines 73–80)[14]

> But Hermas wrote the *Shepherd* very recently, in our times, in the city of Rome, while bishop Pius, his brother, was occupying the [episcopal] chair of the church of the city of Rome. And therefore it ought indeed to be read; but it cannot be read publicly to the people in the church either among the prophets, whose number is complete, or among the apostles, for it is after [their] time. (lines 73–80)[15]

Given the episcopacy of Pius (I) as circa 140 to circa 154, these statements would seem to date the Fragment to the middle of the second century, in strict keeping with the words "very recently, in our times," but no one I know has so literally interpreted the Latin phrase. References to Marcion in the Fragment may require that these words not be too strictly interpreted; scholars have traditionally dated the Fragment from 170 (B. F. Westcott) to 220 (C. Erbes).[16] Much of the debate thus hangs upon the Latin phrase *nuperrime temporibus nostris,* "very recently, in our times."

It is at least questionable to date such a cornerstone in the development of the Christian canon on the basis of a three-word Latin phrase in a document first published as a striking example of scribal barbarism. We know that the Fragment was poorly transcribed

---

[12] S. P. Tregelles, *Canon Muratorianus: The Earliest Catalogue of the Books of the New Testament* (Oxford: Oxford University Press, 1867), 50–53; P. Katz, "The Johannine Epistles in the Muratorian Fragment," *JTS* 8 (1957): 273–74.

[13] Hill, "Debate," 438.

[14] Hahneman, *Muratorian Fragment*, 7.

[15] English translation of B. Metzger, *The Canon of the New Testament* (Oxford: Clarendon, 1987), 307.

[16] B. F. Westcott, *A General Survey of the History of the Canon of the New Testament* (4th ed.; London: Macmillan, 1875), 209; C. Erbes, "Die Zeit des Muratorischen Fragments," *ZKG* 35 (1914): 331–62 at 362; Hahneman, *Muratorian Fragment*, 27–30.

by a hand that has clearly shown itself, in the words of Westcott, "either unable or unwilling to understand the work which he was copying, and yet given to arbitrary alteration of the text before him from regard simply to the supposed form of words."[17] Additionally, it is generally agreed that Latin is not the language of the archetype, and that the translation itself was flawed and sloppy. Moreover, with the discovery of the Benedictine texts, we know that the Latin of the Fragment has gone through several editions. Finally, it is possible to translate the Latin phrase in a way that does not require dating the Fragment in reference to Pius's episcopacy.[18] Sundberg suggests that *nuperrime* be translated as an absolute superlative, meaning "most recently," in reference to the preceding books in the list, meaning that the *Shepherd* was the most recently written of the books mentioned. In addition, Sundberg suggests that the phrase *temporibus nostris* be understood as meaning in "our time" as opposed to the apostolic age, again emphasizing that the *Shepherd* is too late to be included in a collection of apostolic writings. Sundberg's interpretation is at least plausible, as even Ferguson conceded, and it may have a precedent in Irenaeus.[19]

These curious lines from the Fragment about the *Shepherd of Hermas* make several different assertions. For instance, they clearly suggest that Hermas, the author of the *Shepherd,* was the brother of Pius (I), bishop of Rome. However, it seems unlikely that Hermas was the brother of Pius. Hermas, who is clearly and repeatedly identified as the autobiographical author of the *Shepherd,* never mentions a brother in that work although he frequently refers to the leaders of the church in Rome and to the members of his family. Moreover his reference to "the elders who stand at the head of the church" (8.3) suggests a time before a monarchical episcopacy was even established in Rome. Hermas speaks of "officials of the church" *(proēgoumenois tēs ekklēsias),* "elders" *(tois presbyterois* and *presbyterous),* and "bishops" *(episkopoi).* Seven times he refers to the leadership of the church in Rome within the *Shepherd,* always in the plural.[20] Moreover, Hermas appears to have been a foundling slave (1.1) and would be unlikely to know who his parents or who his siblings were. Interestingly "Hermas" is a Greek name, while "Pius" is Latin. Finally the association of Hermas and Pius is not found elsewhere until the mid-fourth century, when it is repeated in the Liberian Catalogue (354) and the pseudo-Tertullian *Carmen adversus Marcionitas* (354+).[21] I am not suggesting the Fragment has taken on a position of pseudonymity here, as Ferguson and Hill misunderstand.[22] I am simply suggesting that the Fragment is mistaken, that it is repeating a false tradition associating Hermas and Pius. In a similar way, there is another tradition that the Hermas of the *Shepherd* was the same as the Hermas mentioned by Paul in Rom 10:14. This apostolic Hermas tradition cannot be attested before Origen, though the apparent insistence in the Fragment that the *Shepherd* was *not* apostolic might suggest a knowledge of this tradition of the apostolic Hermas.[23] Nonetheless, both traditions appear to be simply wrong.

---

[17] Westcott, *A General Survey,* 523.
[18] Sundberg, "Canon Muratori," 11.
[19] Ferguson, "Canon Muratori," 678.
[20] Cf. 6.6, 8.2, 9.8, 13.1, 17.7, 43.1, 104.2.
[21] Hahneman, *Muratorian Fragment,* 51–61.
[22] Ferguson, "Review," 692; Hill, "Debate," 439.
[23] Origen, *Commentary on Romans,* 10.31.

Second, these lines from the Fragment suggest that the *Shepherd* was written no sooner than the middle of the second century when Pius (I) assumed the episcopacy in Rome. However, the internal evidence for dating the *Shepherd* all suggests a date around the turn of the first century, 40–50 years before the beginning of Pius's episcopacy, and perhaps even before Pius was born, and 70–120 years before the traditional date of the Fragment. Even assuming different editions of the *Shepherd,* there is no internal evidence to suggest such a late date. For instance, there is no mention or influence of the later prominent teachers at Rome, e.g., Valentinus (c. 136), Cerdo (c. 140), Marcion (c. 140), or Justin (c. 148). Nor does there appear mention of any of the early documents to or from Rome, e.g., Paul's Romans (c. 58), the Gospel of Mark, (c. 65), or 1 Peter (c. 65). A date at the turn of the first century agrees with the *Shepherd*'s mention of Clement of Rome, the death of the apostles, and a persecution under Domitian or Trajan, as well as the lack of a monarchical episcopacy.[24] In addition, a conference of classical scholars meeting in Dublin in 1984 concluded that two existing fragments of the *Shepherd* themselves date from the second century. Bruce Metzger mentions in a footnote that "other paleographers present agreed on earlier second century rather than later second century" for one of the two.[25] With the dating of this particular fragment of the *Shepherd of Hermas,* it seems clear that the Muratorian Fragment is simply mistaken in its claim that the *Shepherd* was written while Pius was bishop of Rome. B. H. Streeter noted that "scholars of the sharpest critical acumen have allowed themselves to be terrorised, so to speak, into the acceptance of a date (for the *Shepherd*) which brings to confusion the history of the Church in Rome, on the evidence of an authority no better than the Muratorianum."[26]

Third, this crucial passage in the Fragment includes the encouragement that the *Shepherd* be read in private, but notes that it cannot be read publicly in church. Here different scholars, reading the same patristic evidence, come to quite different conclusions. The oldest extant testimony to the *Shepherd* is found in Irenaeus of Lyons (c. 130–c. 200), who simply quoted a passage from the work with the words, "Well said the scripture."[27] Clement of Alexandria quotes from the *Shepherd* about a dozen times, never questioning the reality and divine character of the revelations made to Hermas.[28] Tertullian also appears initially to have accepted the work, though twenty years later, after his conversion to Montanism, he came to utterly reject the *Shepherd* as "the book that loves adulterers," and declares that "all the church synods" have placed the work "among apocrypha and false (writings)."[29] Ferguson and Hill clearly accept the Fragment's statements about the *Shepherd* as fitting into this *milieu.* Ferguson suggested that "The approval which Irenaeus gave the work and Clement of Alexandria's regard for it as inspired could be the very use against which the *Canon Muratori* was protesting, or alternatively the very kind of private use which the author approved."[30] Yet it cannot be both, and Ferguson's inability to choose

---

[24] Hahneman, *Muratorian Fragment,* 37–43.

[25] Metzger, *Canon,* 63 n. 36.

[26] B. H. Streeter, *The Primitive Church* (London: Macmillan, 1929), 205.

[27] Irenaeus, *Haer.* 4.20.2; cf. Eusebius, *Hist. eccl.* 5.8.7.

[28] Clement, *Strom.* 1.1.1 (*Shepherd* 25.5), 1.85.4 (43.3), 1.181.1 (12.3), 2.3.5 (11.4), 2.43.5–44.4 (93.5–7), 2.55.3–4 (16.3–5, 7; cf. 30.2; 31); 4.74.4 (23.5); 6.46.5 (93.6); 6.131.2 (5.3–4).

[29] Tertullian, *De oratione* 16; *De pudicitia* 10; cf. Hahneman, *Muratorian Fragment,* 61–63.

[30] Ferguson, "Canon Muratori," 679.

suggests that the Fragment's comments do not fit this time period. For it is hard to correlate the Fragment's refusal to allow the public reading of the *Shepherd* with the evidence of Irenaeus, Clement of Alexandria, or Tertullian's early approval of the work. And it is also hard to correlate the Fragment's encouragement of the private reading of the *Shepherd* with Tertullian's later complete rejection of it or the church councils he mentions placing the work among apocryphal and false writings.

Clearly the Fragment assigns the *Shepherd of Hermas* to a secondary class of books that is neither completely rejected nor completely approved of; private reading is encouraged, but public reading in church is not allowed. We know that the *Shepherd* was reported to have been read in the churches only in the fourth century through references by Eusebius (*Hist. eccl.* 3.3.6), Jerome (*Vir. ill.* 10), and Rufinus (*Commentarias in Symbolum apostolorum*), references primarily derived from the East. Throughout the fourth century in the East, the *Shepherd* is also found in just such a secondary class, neither completely rejected nor accepted. Eusebius, for instance, includes the *Shepherd* among spurious works which he clearly distinguished from both the accepted ones, the *homologoumena,* and from the disputed works, the *antilegomena,* which included James, Jude, 2 Peter, and 2 and 3 John.[31] A similar hesitation with regard to the *Shepherd* is reflected in scribal markings in the list of the Codex Claromontanus.[32] Athanasius, in his famous paschal letter of 367, clearly places the *Shepherd* among a secondary class of works that are "not indeed in the list" but were none the less useful for catechetical instruction.[33] Jerome also notes that the *Shepherd* is not in the canon, but declares that it is a "useful" book and that many of the ancient writers quoted from it as authoritative.[34] Rufinus also noted that the *Shepherd* was not part of the canon, but included it among what he called the "ecclesiastical" writings, which were not authoritative, but *could* be read in church.[35] Thus the Fragment's statements about the reception of the *Shepherd,* encouraging the private use, but not the public reading in church, can be easily correlated with fourth-century Eastern traditions, but not with late second- or early third-century references.

Fourth and finally, the traditional dating of the Fragment at the end of the second century is derived from these same disputed lines that suggest that Hermas wrote the *Shepherd* quite recently while his brother Pius was bishop of Rome, at a time when the *Shepherd* ought to be read privately, but not publicly. However, it appears that (1) the Hermas of the *Shepherd* is probably not the brother of Pius (I), bishop of Rome, and (2) the *Shepherd* was probably not written during or shortly after the time of Pius (I) in Rome, and (3) the Fragment's encouragement to read the book in private but not in church does not correlate with the testimonies of the late second and early third century. Therefore, the statement in the Fragment that dates the work itself to the second century does not bear the weight previously given it; it is like these other statements, simply confused or mistaken. Those who would accept the portions of these disputed lines that date the Fragment at the end of the second century must also be willing to defend the rest, i.e., the parts that relate Hermas to

---

[31] Eusebius, *Hist. eccl.* 3.3.6, cf. 5.8.7; 3.3.7; 3.25.1–7.

[32] Hahneman, *Muratorian Fragment,* 67.

[33] Athanasius, *Ep. fest.* 39.7.

[34] Jerome, *Prologus Galestus; Vir. ill.* 10.

[35] Rufinus, *Symb.* 38.

Pius, that date the *Shepherd* to the middle of the second century, and that encourage private, but not public reading of the *Shepherd* at that time.

Excluding the Fragment, it is generally agreed that there are no known catalogues of the Christian canon until the fourth century, when there is a sudden and widespread appearance of fifteen undisputed lists and four complete codices, listed below.[36] Even Ferguson acknowledges the strength of Sundberg's observation that there are no clear parallels with the Fragment until this time. He argues, however, that the Fragment shares "none of the characteristics" of fourth-century lists: (1) "fourth-century lists associate a New Testament catalogue with the Old Testament," (2) "the Gospels are numbered and often not named," (3) "Hebrews is nearly always included in the *Corpus Paulinum*," and (4) that the Fragment, unlike the other catalogues of the fourth century, is more than a "bare list" of accepted books.[37] Each of these contentions, however, is misleading. To begin with, the beginning of the Fragment is missing. Therefore one cannot conclude whether a list of Old Testament books was originally present or not; in keeping with the other known lists it is likely. Second, the gospels are still named in two-thirds of the fourth-century lists, ten out of the fifteen, so that the Fragment's naming of the gospels would not be remarkable here. Third, Hebrews is missing or noted as disputed in more than a third of the fourth-century lists, six out of the fifteen. Thus the absence of Hebrews is not necessarily remarkable, and may simply be accidental.[38] Finally, that the Fragment is not a "bare list" may be conceded, for there is some narrative included among the listing of books, but this too is not remarkable. Eusebius's list (*Hist. eccl.* 3.3.6–7) clearly has more commentary than the fragment. Jerome's listing is also quite elaborate at first, and Amphilochius too goes into some detail. The Fragment, in the final analysis, is not remarkable in its narrative, and the Muratorian Fragment can in fact find its place quite easily among the other catalogues of the Christian canon that suddenly appear in the fourth century.

3. Comments, Collections, and Catalogues

The important distinction between "Comments," "Collections," and "Catalogues" also remains essential in understanding the gradual formation of the Christian Bible. "Comments" are simply references in early Christian writings to certain works as being authoritative or as scripture. "Collections" are gatherings of such scriptures with distinct boundaries, but boundaries which are easily altered or enlarged. Both comments and collections imply accepted scriptures, but not necessarily a canon, where nothing can be added or nothing can be subtracted. "Catalogues," however, are lists of scriptures with defined and established limits. Oftentimes, writings that are excluded from catalogues are noted and dismissed, once the concept is understood and accepted. Thus the move from collections to catalogues implies a conceptual change, a change which led to the formation

---

[36] Hahneman, *Muratorian Fragment*, 132–82.

[37] Ferguson, "Review," 696.

[38] While Hebrews does not appear to have been much disputed in the East, there was a change in its status in the fourth and fifth centuries, suggesting perhaps a questioning of its Pauline authorship, and this change may account for its absence in the Fragment, cf. Hahneman, *Muratorian Fragment*, 120–25.

of the Christian canon of scriptures. The gradual formation of the Christian canon of scriptures is evidenced in the transition from early comments or references to Jewish scriptures, to the collections of Pauline materials, and in the establishment of the fourfold Gospel canon. Yet it is not until the fourth century that a *complete* canon of scriptures is envisioned for the church.

In the fourth century there is a sudden and widespread appearance of Christian catalogues of scriptures. The appearance of these lists confirms a conceptual change in the mind of the church. Whether there were any lists before this time is doubtful. The use of scriptures by earlier Christian writers was a recurrent theme in Eusebius. Yet Eusebius had to create lists or Catalogues of the New Testament for the writings of his predecessors, namely Irenaeus, Clement of Alexandria, and Origen. The absence of original New Testament catalogues in Eusebius's work, other than his own (*Hist. eccl.* 3.25.1–7), indicates reliably that no such catalogues were known to him. Thus the interest in defining the canon by the use of catalogues, widespread in the fourth century, can be traced back no further than Eusebius. But in the fourth and early fifth century, there are fifteen undisputed lists of the Christian canon.

1. Eusebius (*Ecclesiastical History* 3.25.1–7), 303–25

2. Catalogue in Codex Claromontanus, 303–67

3. Cyril of Jerusalem (*Catechetical Lectures* 4.33), c. 350

4. Athanasius (*Festal Epistle* 39), c. 367

5. Mommsen Catalogue, c. 365–90

6. Epiphanius (*Panarion* 76.5), c. 374–77

7. Apostolic Canons 85, c. 380

8. Gregory of Nazianzus (*Carmen de veris scripturae libris* 12.31), c. 383–90

9. African Canons, c. 393–419

10. Jerome (*Epistle* 53), c. 394

11. Augustine (*On Christian Doctrine* 2.8.12), c. 396–7

12. Amphilochius (*Iambics to Seleucus* 289–319), c. 396

13. Rufinus (*Commentary on the Apostle's Creed* 36), c. 400

14. Pope Innocent *(Letter to Exsuperius),* c. 405

15. Syrian Catalogue of St. Catherine's, c. 400

Another indication that the concept of a canon was just developing in the fourth century was the lack of an established vocabulary and definitive categories in Eusebius. In discussing the works of the Apostles (*Hist. eccl.* 3.3.1–7), for instance, Eusebius employed a variety of words or phrases to distinguish the scriptures which were universally acknowledged from those which were disputed. For the acknowledged books:

anōmologētai, anamphilektō, endiathēkon (*Hist. eccl.* 3.3.1)

tōn endiathēkōn and *homologoumenōn* (*Hist. eccl.* 3.3.3)

homologoumenēn (*Hist. eccl.* 3.3.4)

en anamphilektois (*Hist. eccl.* 3.3.5)

homologoumenois (*Hist. eccl.* 3.3.6)

homologoumenōn (*Hist. eccl.* 3.3.7)

For the disputed books:

ouk endiathēkon (*Hist. eccl.* 3.3.1)

oud' holōs en katholikois ismen paradedomena (*Hist. eccl.* 3.3.2)

antilegomenōn (*Hist. eccl.* 3.3.3)

antilelektai (*Hist. eccl.* 3.3.6)

tōn mē para pasin homologoumenōn theiōn grammatōn (*Hist. eccl.* 3.3.7)

Eusebius refined his language somewhat within his New Testament catalogue (*Hist. eccl.* 3.26.1–7). The universally "acknowledged" works are called the *homologoumena*. Other works were "disputed" *(antilegomena)* and still others were "spurious" *(notha)* or "fictions of heretics." The spurious works represented a secondary category of works that were not universally accepted but were known to most ecclesiastical writers. However even with this secondary category, which itself was subdivided, Eusebius was unsure where to place certain works, like Revelation and the *Gospel according to the Hebrews,* and perhaps also *1 Clement.* This confusion suggests that the categories themselves were only just beginning to play a role in the formation of the canon, and that their development was still in the creative stages.

The precise motivation behind the rise of catalogues is uncertain, but their sudden and widespread appearance in the second half of the fourth century is undeniable. Earlier struggles with heretical sects, groups such as the Marcionites, the Montanists, and the Gnostics, must have forced the churches to grapple with what writings it accepted as scripture, but apparently not as canon. For if the churches were interested in delineating the canon against such heresies, one would expect to find numerous lists of canonical literature, but that is precisely what is missing. Persecutions, especially the Diocletian persecutions, may have been a factor or another stimulus for a canon; Christians were often forced to hand over their sacred documents, necessitating clarity about which writings were sacred and which were not. In the same way, the official recognition and later sanction of the Christian church by Constantine and his successors may also have played a part in the development of the Christian Bible. In 331, Constantine commissioned Eusebius to prepare fifty copies of the sacred scriptures for the church at Constantinople. Around 340 Alexandrian scribes (in Rome?) prepared copies of the Christian scriptures for the Emperor Constans (Athanasius, *Apol. Const.* 4). Thus within the fourth century, the concept of a Christian canon, a collection to which nothing can be added, and from which nothing can be subtracted, became widely accepted. The next step for the church was agreement as to the exact contents of that canon.

Before any conclusions are drawn, one further piece of evidence needs to be cited. Just as there are no catalogues of the Christian canon until the fourth century, so there are no extant manuscripts which appear to have contained a complete Christian Bible before the fourth and early fifth century. Though the number of surviving manuscripts may be small, the appearance of codices and versions of the entire Christian Bible also reflects a conceptual transition from scriptures to canon in the fourth century. Consequently, the contents and order of these collections are relevant to the formation of the Christian Bible. There are four undisputed manuscripts:

1. Codex Vaticanus

2. Codex Sinaiticus

3. The Peshitta

4. Codex Alexandrinus

4. Conclusion

There appear to be fifteen undisputed catalogues and four complete collections of the Christian canon belonging to the fourth and early fifth century. None of these catalogues or collections seems to predate Eusebius. Eusebius's writings seem to confirm an absence of earlier lists: as he is forced to create catalogues for Irenaeus, Clement of Alexandria, and Origen, and in his use of terminology is ambiguous and inconsistent, especially regarding secondary classes of writings. The earliest extant catalogues derive from Caesarea and Alexandria, and may represent a natural development of the biblical scholarship inherited from the ancient Christian schools at Alexandria and Caesarea. From there, the concept of canon seems to have spread northward to Asia Minor and westward to North Africa, then to Eastern Syria and across the Mediterranean to Rome/Italy.

While from the third century onward many early churches may have agreed generally about a "core" New Testament collection which included the four gospels, Acts, thirteen Pauline epistles, 1 Peter, and 1 John, there was no unanimity. But the fourth century saw a movement from loose collection to closed canon, to which nothing can be added and from which nothing can be subtracted. Soon thereafter numerous catalogues appear throughout the church. The Muratorian Fragment, dated correctly, finds its place among these. But at no time has the whole church entirely agreed upon its canon of scripture. If the earliest churches intended their successors to have a canon of scripture, either Old Testament or New Testament, we have no clear tradition to that effect. It was not until the second half of the fourth century that the churches agreed in principle to the concept of canon, and then began finalizing the details or contents of their catalogue of scriptures. That process of agreement continues to this day.

25

Identifying Scripture and Canon in the Early Church: The Criteria Question

Lee Martin McDonald

1. In Search of a Process

The *process* of the canonization of the New Testament began in the first instance with the church's reception of the story of Jesus. It was the remarkable impact of his life, ministry, and death, and the church's belief in his resurrection that led the early church to preserve his memory and tell the implications of his story. To speak of the impact of Jesus' life and career on his followers presumes, of course, the transforming experience that came through the sharing of this story. Eugene Ulrich correctly states that the first level of scripture began with an experience. Citing his earlier work, he claims that

> the process of the development of scripture is dialectical—Scripture, which began as experience, was produced through a process of tradition(s) being formulated about that experience and being reformulated by interpreters in dialogue with the experience of their communities and with the larger culture.[1]

This story of Jesus and the experience his story evoked was preserved and proclaimed first in the church's oral traditions and subsequently in the literature that comprises the New Testament. Those who wrote and those who preserved, modified, and transmitted this sacred tradition, the biblical scribes or *tradents,* in many cases actively added to that tradition; see for example John 19:34–36 and 21:24–25. The process also included the recognition by many Christians of the value of those writings for use in the worship and ministry of the early church. What was written, preserved, and even modified to make the tradition relevant to the changing circumstances of the church was what became the Christian scriptures. To make them continually relevant and adaptable to the contemporary needs of the church, the scribes or tradents found ways to modify, alter, and interpret the sacred texts. This important step toward canonization assumed the continuing validity of the sacred texts for the growing and changing community

---

[1] Eugene Ulrich, *The Dead Sea Scrolls and the Origins of the Bible* (SDSSRL; Grand Rapids: Eerdmans, 1999), 73–74; citing E. Ulrich and W. G. Thompson, "The Tradition as a Resource in Theological Reflection: Scripture and the Minister," in *Method in Ministry: Theological Reflection and Christian Ministry* (ed. J. D. Whitehead and E. E. Whitehead; San Francisco: Harper & Row, 1980), 31–52, at 36.

of faith.[2] The New Testament scriptures of the church set forth its identity and mission as well as its understanding of God's activity in Jesus the Christ. The adaptability of this literature to the changing needs of the churches anticipated its selection for a fixed collection of New Testament scriptures.

The process of canonization, then, began with Jesus and his impact on his followers, and was passed on by the transmitters and modifiers (teachers and scribes or tradents) of that tradition. The process was largely complete by the end of the fourth century when the church began to discuss which books belonged in its New Testament scriptures. It is difficult to discern a clear pattern in this process that led to their eventual canonization. Franz Stuhlhofer maintains that the process simply happened as the church collected its sacred writings, without a clear plan or aim.[3] Currently it appears that at no time before the fourth century did the church consciously make decisions about what literature was "canonical" and what was not. At least, no record of such proceedings or deliberations has survived. It is true that Irenaeus spoke of a four-gospel canon, those four and no more (*Haer.* 3.11.8–9 and cf. 3.1.1), but he said nothing about the rest of the New Testament scriptures and spoke of no fixed collection of scriptures beyond that of the Gospels. His primary concern in regard to the Gospels was lending his support to the use of the Gospel of John in the churches, not establishing a fixed biblical canon. The church did not discuss such issues until well into the fourth century. Before then, the only "canon" mentioned in the church was a "canon of faith" that was passed on in the churches. This does not take away from the fact that use of many New Testament writings was widespread among the churches at that time (170–200) and several New Testament writings, including the Gospels and Paul, were beginning to be called "scripture" or were introduced with scriptural designations (e.g., "it is written").

Two major attempts to establish conformity in the empire in the early fourth century C.E. probably also affected the scope of the New Testament canon by causing the church to make conscious decisions about what literature it considered sacred. The first of these was an edict of Diocletian on February 23, 303, to promote religious uniformity. This edict, which remained in effect until 313, led to the persecution of the church and called for the burning of its sacred writings. Diocletian also compelled Christians to turn over their sacred books to the authorities to be burned. The Christians tried to salvage as much of their sacred literature as possible by turning over to them less important texts that were not considered sacred. Those who gave in to pressure and handed sacred scripture over to the authorities were called "traitors" *(traditores)*. On the other hand, those who refused and consequently were imprisoned or killed were called confessors and martyrs (*homologētai* and *martyres*). Such distinctions presume, of course, that by this time individual congregations had determined which literature was sacred and which was not, what was worth dying for and what was not.

Second, and just as compelling, was Constantine's push for religious unity and conformity within the Christian communities, threatening banishment for those who did not

---

[2] Ulrich, *Dead Sea Scrolls,* 73–75, discusses this in more detail than is possible here. He depends largely on James Sanders (*Canon and Community* [Philadelphia: Fortress, 1984]) for his basic understanding of scripture and canon.

[3] Franz Stuhlhofer, *Der Gebrauch der Bibel von Jesus bis Euseb: eine statistische Untersuchung zur Kanongeschichte* (Wuppertal: R. Brockhaus, 1988), 84.

conform. This call to unity is the context in which discussions of biblical canons begin to appear, first in the writings of Eusebius and subsequently in other lists, discussions, and church councils. What may well have triggered Eusebius's interest in defining or delimiting the scope of the Christian scriptures was Constantine's request that he produce fifty copies of the Christian scriptures for use in the churches in the new capital of the Roman empire, Constantinople. These two historical factors provide the social context that led to the closing of the biblical canon.[4]

The early church's interest in preserving various Christian writings for use as scripture in its life and worship raises obvious questions about its selection process. What were the basic characteristics of that literature and what criteria did the church employ to identify the scriptures that would eventually become its fixed sacred collection? It seems clear that the canonization process was a largely unconscious and also highly complex process. Nevertheless several factors enable us to understand why some of the New Testament literature was canonized. None of these features, however, nor the criteria that will be discussed below, can account for all of the literature that makes up the New Testament canon. The criteria employed were generally not explicitly stated in later discussions of canonicity. The process of recognition and selection was inexact and inconsistently carried out in the churches, but we can reasonably identify some of the distinguishing features of this literature and some of the criteria that were employed in the process.

Identifying scripture and canon in the ancient world is not easy, however, since the basic properties of scripture and canon are generally assumed rather than clearly stated. According to Edward Farley, "scripture" for prerabbinic Judaism and early Christianity, included at least four essential ingredients: (1) it was a written collection, (2) of divine origin (from Yahweh), (3) that communicated God's will and truth to the covenant people, and (4) functioned "as an enduring source of regulations for the corporate and individual life of the people."[5] Similarly, Bentley Layton defines "scripture" as a body of sacred literature that members of a religious group consider authoritative in matters such as belief, conduct, rhetoric, or the running of practical affairs.[6]

Most biblical scholars have concluded that the writings of the New Testament addressed the needs of specific communities and that the writers had the needs of those communities in mind while telling their story (gospels) or admonishing specific churches (letters). It is therefore amazing that these ad hoc writings were viewed early on as having value for the wider Christian community for all time. What is it about these writings that led the churches to preserve them as "sacred" literature? Moody Smith adds that a distinguishing feature of the New Testament writings is that they generally continue or presuppose the biblical story of salvation history for the people of God and they interpret history.[7] He contends that those who wrote the gospels initially did so with the idea of producing an authoritative guide to the Christian faith for the church and with the idea of continuing the biblical story.

---

[4] See McDonald, *The Formation of the Christian Biblical Canon* (rev. and enl. ed.; Peabody, Mass.: Hendrickson, 1995), chapter 7, for a more complete discussion of this subject.

[5] Edward Farley, *Ecclesial Reflection* (Philadelphia: Fortress, 1982), 58. See also David H. Kelsey, *The Uses of Scripture in Recent Theology* (Philadelphia: Fortress, 1975), 89–94.

[6] Bentley Layton, *The Gnostic Scriptures* (Garden City: Doubleday, 1987), 18.

[7] D. M. Smith, "When Did the Gospels Become Scripture?" *JBL* 119/1 (2000): 3–20, at 8–9.

When the gospels were written, apostolic authorship had not yet er the most significant features of Christian scripture, and that is likely why fore produced anonymously. Nearly all biblical literature was produc with some of it later becoming pseudepigraphic literature, that is, false apostle. Eventually Matthew and John (in its recension, 21:24–25) were acknowleagcu — apostolic in origin; by the end of the second century Tertullian accorded them more authority than Luke and Mark precisely because of their apostolic origin. For Smith, New Testament scripture generally continues the story of the biblical narrative (or presumes it), and interprets the history of God's activity among the people of faith.[8] This literature also interprets the significance of Jesus for communities of faith. Interpreting, presuming, or continuing the biblical story, and especially the story of Jesus, appears to be important though not an essential ingredient in sacred scripture whether in the Old Testament or the New Testament.[9]

Unlike the Qur'an, the Bible is not a collection of writings that simply posit the revelation of God; rather it sets forth a story in which the revelation of God is proclaimed and explained. On the other hand, the Qur'an *is* revelation with little or no attempt at narrative. Both Old Testament and New Testament literature have an important narrative to share, a story that gives a believing community identity, hope, and meaning, as well as guidelines for living. However, the lack of precision in the definition of scripture continues to pose problems, for no available definitions fit all of the biblical writings nor their contents.

Some works that were selected for inclusion in the Christian Bible, especially the gospels and Paul's letters, were recognized by the end of the first century and the early second century to have considerable value for the church in its life and ministry. These writings may have been produced consciously as sacred story (scripture) with a scriptural quality inherent in them, as Moody Smith suggests, because they continued the story and the hope of the earlier scriptures that the church had inherited, the Old Testament or First Testament. The value of these and other writings was soon recognized. Several New Testament books, as well as some noncanonical books, were functioning like scripture (authoritatively) in many churches in the early second century, and were probably circulating among the churches a few decades earlier. Some New Testament writings were first recognized as authoritative scriptures and sacred even by their writers (Rev

---

[8] Ibid., 11–14.

[9] On pages 17–18 Smith posits that some New Testament writings may have been written *as* scripture for the Christian community, especially Matthew and Luke (see Luke 1:1–4 and Acts 1:1–2), but perhaps also the Gospel of John in its final recension and possibly even the original composition. He recognizes that he has not proved his case but claims that it is likely from the beginning that three of the gospels (perhaps not Mark) possessed an inherent authority that commended them to the churches. It is clear that the redactor(s) of John's Gospel had this in mind in regard to that gospel (21:24–25). It is also clear that Paul's letters were intended to be read publicly in churches, and this implies that they were viewed as something like scripture. Notice, for example, the authoritative tone in many passages in his letters that suggests that Paul also viewed his writings as authoritative if not prophetic (1 Cor 5:3–5; 6:1–6; 7:10–11, 17–20, 40; 11:23–34, Gal 5:1–4, *passim*). Second Peter 3:15–16 (ca. 150–80 C.E.) acknowledges Paul's writings as scripture and may well have reflected what many churches believed about the letters of Paul at the end of the second century. Irenaeus, Tertullian, and others bear this out.

∠2:18–19; 1 Cor 7:39–40), and then by others by the end of the first century. They were only beginning to be called "scripture" by the end of the second century.

2. Identifying Scripture

Several factors indicate when Christians viewed certain writings as sacred scripture. First, of course, is the manner in which the New Testament writings are cited in the various communities of faith. When the citations or allusions recognize the authority of the writing to settle issues of faith, mission, and disciplinary matters, or when they are used in worship in a liturgical setting, we can be assured that they carried a sacred authority not found in other writings of the time. An example is Justin Martyr's description of a worship service around the middle of the second century. He describes how the prophets and the "memoirs of the apostles" were read as the community gathered together for worship on the first day of the week (*1 Apol.* 67). In *1 Apol.* 66, Justin actually identifies these "memoirs" as "gospels." Most scholars agree that the "memoirs of the apostles" are probably just the Synoptic Gospels. He does not specifically say, however, that the Gospels were read in worship services *alongside* the "Prophets" (a common reference for the Old Testament scriptures in the churches of his day), but rather that they were sometimes read *instead* of the Prophets! He writes that "on the day called Sunday there is a meeting in one place of those who live in cities or the country, and *the memoirs of the apostles or the writings of the prophets* are read as long as time permits."[10] This, of course, speaks of the stature that these writings had attained by that time. This may also refer to a longstanding practice in the church, namely, that of giving special attention to the "teaching of the apostles" (Acts 2:42).

A second indicator is holiness. When a church perceived a writing's holiness, it became scripture for that community of faith. John Barton cites an example from Origen in which he argued that if the reader did not understand what was read in these scriptures, nevertheless "those powers which are present with us do understand, and they delight to be with us as though summoned by the words of a charm, and to lend us their aid."[11] Barton shows several ways in which scripture was perceived as holy in the churches and treated as sacred. He points first to the *non-triviality* of the text. For instance, in 1 Cor 9:9 Paul regarded Deut 25:4, a relatively unimportant text in the Old Testament regarding the treatment of an ox that was treading out the grain, as a very important text for the life of the Christian community.[12] The text appears trivial, but because it is scripture, Paul defends its relevance. Second, Barton claims that the sacredness of a writing is seen in its *non-ephemerality*. In other words, a text is sacred if it is relevant to all ages, not merely to a particular time in history. Scripture was always read as relevant to one's own day and situation. Early Christian writers, he says, "seem to take it for granted that what Jesus said will always have a bearing on present problems, aspirations, conflicts, and hopes: these sayings are canonical."[13]

---

[10] *1 Apol.* 67, trans. *ANF*; italics added.
[11] John Barton, *Holy Writings, Sacred Text: The Canon in Early Christianity* (Louisville, Ky.: Westminster John Knox, 1997), 129.
[12] Ibid., 134–36.
[13] Ibid., 137–39.

Third, Barton maintains that if a writing was believed to be scripture, it also was believed to be *internally self-consistent* and not self-contradictory. For example, in Justin's famous *Dialogue with Trypho,* he admonishes that if Trypho had spoken ill of the scriptures in error or without ill intent, he would be forgiven, but

> if you have done so because you imagined that you could throw doubt on the passage, in order that I might say the scriptures contradicted one another, you have erred. But I shall not venture to suppose or to say such a thing, and if a scripture that appears to be of such a kind be brought forward, and if there be a pretext for saying that it is contrary to some other, since I am entirely convinced that no scripture contradicts another, I shall admit rather that I do not understand what is recorded, and shall strive to persuade those who imagine that the scriptures are contradictory to be rather of the same opinion as myself. (Adapted from *Trypho* 65.2, ANF)

The concern to maintain the *inward consistency* of a text is a clear signal of its perceived scriptural status. Eugene Ulrich, speaking about the canonical process of the Old Testament, draws attention to the creative work of scribes to harmonize scriptures.[14] He adds, "sometimes the presupposition behind harmonization is that this text can be juxtaposed to that text because God is the author of both. That presupposition is clearly behind some of the Qumran, New Testament, and rabbinic texts."[15] The harmonizing activity of scribes assumes the sacredness of both of the traditions that they are trying to reconcile.

Fourth, Barton contends that the early church believed scriptural texts had *an excess of meaning.* He cites as an example Gal 3:15–18 where Paul emphasizes the special meaning of the singular "seed" of Abraham in Gen 12:7, rather than plural "seeds," indicating that the promises to Abraham would find fulfillment in one man, Jesus. The multi-layered meanings of a biblical text, often discovered through allegorical exegesis, emphasized that the text had fluidity and adaptability to ever changing circumstances. Writings that were searched for deeper meanings by means of the various hermeneutical methodologies in antiquity, especially allegorical exegesis, were generally acknowledged as sacred texts.[16] Multiple interpretations of texts were often followed by more extended interpretations or commentaries such as those produced by Origen on biblical books.

Along with this, and roughly at the same time, many translations of texts were produced, an activity that also suggests that what was translated was viewed as sacred. Finally, Barton has observed that when *nomina sacra* (sacred names that are abbreviated or contracted in the ancient biblical manuscripts) appear in ancient manuscripts, those manuscripts were considered sacred. The *nomina sacra* included important names such as Jesus, Father, Son, Christ, Holy Spirit, Savior, and such like. The fact that early Christian scribes contracted special words from both the Old Testament and the New Testament suggests that they viewed both collections as sacred in the same sense.[17]

---

[14] E.g., Isa 2:2–4 // Mic 4:1–4; and Obad 1–10 // Jer 49:7–22. In a personal note, James Sanders reminded me that the Masoretes protected the differences and discrepancies in the Masorah; they appear to have abhorred harmonization!

[15] Ulrich, *The Dead Sea Scrolls,* 77.

[16] Barton, *Holy Writings,* 142–43, 160.

[17] Ibid., 122–23. Barton shows several other examples of this practice.

When a text was actually called "scripture" is a different matter than when or whether it became part of a fixed collection of sacred scriptures. Scriptural identity could and often did change over time before the final fixing of the New Testament canon. For example, Hermas called the ancient writing *Eldad and Modad* "scripture" when he wrote: "The Lord is near those that turn to him, as it is written *(hōs gegraptai)* in the Book of Eldad and Modat, *who prophesied* to the people in the wilderness."[18]

Although we may see specific writings recognized or identified as scripture by individual churches or ancient writers, it does not follow that all churches of the same time or even location acknowledged the same writings as scripture. The evidence is to the contrary. There was considerable variety in what the early churches considered authoritative or sacred writings, especially in the second century. For example, most churches did not accept *Eldad and Modad* as scripture so far as the available evidence shows. Consider also the recognition of the inspiration of *1 Enoch* in Jude 14. The Alogi, a sect of Christians in Asia Minor (ca. 170) who denied the divinity of the Spirit and the Logos (hence the name "Alogi") also rejected John's Gospel, Revelation, and the book of Hebrews. It is also clear that other writings that had earlier been regarded as sacred scripture by a large segment of the Christian community were later excluded from that category. For example, *1 Clement*, the letters of Ignatius, the *Shepherd of Hermas*, and *Barnabas* were all called scripture by certain writers and were even placed in various collections of scripture through the fourth and fifth centuries. Eventually these writings were dropped from the sacred collections.

After determining that certain Christian writings were sacred and functioned as scripture alongside the Old Testament scriptures (and at times in their place; see the example from Justin's *1 Apol.* 67 above), the final step of the canonization process was delimitation or selection. In other words, the process was complete when a clearly defined collection of Christian literature existed from which some writings were excluded and nothing else accepted as "canon" for the Christian community. At this stage, roughly the fourth and fifth centuries, the recognized adaptability of this literature to various contexts further recommended its selection and placement in the New Testament canon. But recognition of the sacredness of the book did not mean that the text was automatically fixed. The canonical process extended only to the books as such, not to the individual words in them and the various Christian communities took considerable liberty with the texts over the centuries.[19] There was as yet no invariable biblical *text* even if such a list of *books* emerged. This will be discussed below.

Finally, it appears that Christian writers of the second century did not cite the Old Testament as much as the New Testament. John Barton tabulates the frequency of citations in the late first- and early second-century church fathers: *Shepherd, 2 Clement,* Ignatius,

---

[18] Herm. *Vis.* 2.3.4, LCL, italics added. This apocalypse is possibly also alluded to in *2 Clement* 11:2. The two names are mentioned in Num 11:26.

[19] Eugene Ulrich (*The Dead Sea Scrolls,* 57–58) and B. M. Metzger (*The Canon of the New Testament: Its Origin, Development, and Significance* [Oxford: Clarendon, 1987], 269–70) make this argument for the Old Testament writings and the New Testament writings respectively. Metzger underscores that while Eusebius and Jerome both saw that there were differences in the text of various manuscripts and wondered which to follow, neither writer chose a particular text. He notes that in antiquity, "the question of canonicity pertains to the document *qua* document, and not to one particular form or version of that document" (ibid., 270).

Didache, Polycarp. He shows that the Christian scriptures were cited many times more often in this period than were the Old Testament scriptures, and that this was a common practice until the third century when the citations began to balance out. Barton concludes that this practice probably reflects a scarcity of Old Testament texts and a relative abundance of Christian texts in the churches. His findings lead him to question the appropriateness of appealing to citations in ancient literature to determine what was considered sacred in the early churches.[20]

3. What Criteria Did the Churches Employ?

What criteria were employed by the early churches to identify which writings would make up their biblical canon? It is generally acknowledged that the churches used several criteria, often unequally, in order to determine the contents of their New Testament. There is no way to determine whether all churches used the same criteria in selecting their sacred collection, nor whether each criterion, namely authorship, orthodoxy, use, and antiquity, weighed equally in their deliberations. The variety of scripture canons from the fourth to the sixth centuries suggests otherwise (see Appendix A). The most common criteria employed in the process include apostolicity, orthodoxy, antiquity, and use. We will also look at two other features of ancient scripture, namely its adaptability and inspiration.[21]

The New Testament itself contains exhortations to discern among those who call themselves prophets and claim to speak in the power of the Spirit. Paul, for example, says that some Christians were given the ability to discern the spirits (1 Cor 12:10) and John admonishes that "every spirit that does not confess that Jesus is come in the flesh, is not of God" (1 John 4:2). The presence of "false spirits" in early Christianity was the cause for many concerns. The author(s) of the *Didache* advised readers to test prophets not only in regard to their doctrine but also in their conduct. If, for example, a prophet or an apostle came and stayed with them more than one or two days, he was considered a false prophet. It was also required that the prophet must have the "behavior of the Lord" when he spoke,[22] and if the prophet "shall say in a spirit, 'Give me money, or something else', you

---

[20] Barton, *Holy Writings, Sacred Text,* 18–19 and 64–65. He follows Franz Stuhlhofer's arguments (*Der Gebrauch der Bibel,* 84).

[21] To avoid confusion in our discussion, I believe that it is best to follow the advice of Albert Sundberg Jr. and Eugene Ulrich and employ the term "canon" to refer to a delimited collection of Christian literature that makes up our current biblical canon. The term is reserved for selected literature only in the postbiblical era when such notions of a closed biblical canon were discussed. Sundberg distinguishes between the terms "scripture" and "canon" in that the latter presumes the former, but not the other way around. Scripture was perceived long before the notion of a closed biblical canon emerged. See his "Towards a Revised History of the New Testament Canon," *SE* 4 (TU 102; Berlin: Akademie, 1968), 452–61, and also his more extensive contributions to this subject listed in the Select Bibliography at the end of this volume. Ulrich concurs with Sundberg and adds that the notion of canon is present when three aspects of canon are present: (1) that canon represents *a reflexive judgment on the part of a religious community,* (2) it denotes *a closed list of biblical books,* and finally (3) it concerns biblical *books* rather than the specific *text* of those books. The text of the books continued to vary both in Judaism and Christianity for a considerable time after the books had been selected. See his helpful discussion of these aspects in *The Dead Sea Scrolls,* 53–61.

[22] *Did.* 11:3–10.

shall not listen to him; but if he tells you to give on behalf of others in want, let none judge him."[23] Other guidelines on how to deal with prophets who decided to settle among them[24] suggest that there were some who abused their office. Guidelines were necessary for the believing communities to maintain the proper roles and functions of their leaders. Similarly, guidelines were needed to determine which books were to be included in their scripture collections and which were not. Some writings were produced in the name of an apostle in order to secure wider acceptance of a position or stance that otherwise would probably not have received much of a hearing. In this sense, apostolicity insured acceptance. Early in the church's history the inappropriate use of well-known names to secure acceptance of a writing was common. Paul himself needed to affix his own peculiar signature to his letters to ensure that other writings circulating in his name would not be taken as genuine.[25] We will now examine four important criteria for canonization.

A. Apostolicity

If a writing was believed to have been produced by an apostle, it was eventually accepted as sacred scripture and included in the New Testament canon. Eusebius's argument against the apostolic authorship of the pseudepigraphal literature reflects the universally acknowledged authority of apostolic writings and the rejection of writings not believed to have come from an apostle. After listing the writings that were widely accepted (*homolegoumena*) or "canonical" (literally "encovenanted," Greek = *endiathēkous*), he spoke of those writings that were disputed and yet were known to most writers of the church, "in order that we might know them and the writings which are put forward by heretics under the name of the apostles containing gospels such as those of Peter, and Thomas, and Matthias, and some others besides, or Acts such as those of Andrew and John and the other apostles."[26]

From early times the church's most important weapon against gnostics and other "heretics" was its claim to apostolicity, which guaranteed that its oral and written traditions were genuine. "Apostolic succession" represented a claim that the faith received by the apostles from the Lord was passed on by successive leaders in the church. After listing the succession of leaders in the church, Irenaeus explains the implications of apostolic succession:

> The blessed apostles, then, having founded and built up the church committed into the hands of Linus the office of episcopate [he then lists twelve successive leaders] . . . In this order, and by this succession, the ecclesiastical tradition from the apostles and the preaching of the truth have come down to us. And this is the most abundant proof that there is one and the same vivifying faith, which has been preserved in the Church from the apostles until now, and handed down in truth.[27]

---

[23] *Did.* 11:12, LCL.
[24] Chapters 12–13.
[25] See 1 Cor 16:21; Gal 6:11; Col 4:18; 2 Thess 3:17; and Phlm 19. We can see from the list of pseudonymous literature in the table below that this problem was already widespread in the second century and that care was needed in the church. Considerable doubt persists regarding the authorship of Colossians and 2 Thessalonians.
[26] *Hist. eccl.* 3.25.6, LCL.
[27] *Haer.* 3.3.3, ANF.

Again he writes: "How should it be if the apostles themselves had not left us writings? Would it not be necessary in that case to follow the course of the tradition which they handed down to those to whom they handed over the leadership of the churches?"[28] The authoritative New Testament literature reflected the "apostolic deposit." The church upheld the apostolic witness in its sacred literature as a way of grounding its faith in Jesus, represented by the apostles' teaching, and insuring that the church's tradition was not severed from its historical roots and proximity to Jesus, the primary authority of the early church. Scholars differ, of course, on how successful this was.[29]

Tertullian (ca. 200), for example, indicated that the gospels were written either by the apostles or by "apostolic men" and gave the former priority over the latter. He writes: "John and Matthew first instill faith in us, but Luke and Mark, who are apostolic men, renew it afterwards."[30] Later he criticizes Marcion for choosing Luke over the other gospels. Luke, Tertullian writes, "was not an apostle, but only an apostolic man; not a master, but a disciple, and so inferior to a master."[31] Clearly, for him, apostolicity was so significant that scriptures written by an apostle were superior to those written by "apostolic" men. In contrast, apostolicity did not seem to be an important factor in the initial production of Christian literature, as apostolic names were not placed on the gospels until near the end of the second century.

The criterion of apostolicity poses several problems today. Many scholars question how much of the New Testament was actually written by apostles. For example, it is difficult to establish that John and Matthew wrote the gospels that bear their names. While some scholars argue strongly for the apostolicity of 1 Peter and 1 John, the arguments are not conclusive. Again, there are lingering doubts about Paul's authorship of Ephesians, Colossians, 2 Thessalonians, and especially the Pastoral Epistles, even if they may contain some authentic Pauline traditions.[32] For example, how Paul died may be accurately portrayed in 2 Tim 4:6–17, and the statement that all of the churches in Asia had turned against him in 2 Tim 1:15 is probably an accurate reflection of Paul's words and experience. Ernest Best rightly observes that the ancient church's judgments about the apostolic authorship of the New Testament writings will be evaluated very differently today.[33]

How was the criterion of apostolicity applied in antiquity? Eusebius's doubts about accepting 2 Peter focused on the issue of its apostolicity. He accepted 1 Peter because it was widely regarded as genuine, but 2 Peter was not: "Of Peter, one epistle, that which is called his first, is admitted, and the ancient presbyters used this in their own writings as unquestioned,

---

[28] *Haer.* 3.4.1, adapted from *ANF*.

[29] Robert Funk, for example, in his *Parables and Presence* (Philadelphia: Fortress, 1982), 182–86, discusses the success of the church's attempt to ground its faith (traditions) in Jesus through a closed apostolic canon. He acknowledges that the early churches' appeal to their apostolic roots aimed at supporting their traditions, but he questions the outcome of their efforts.

[30] *Adv. Marc.* 4.2.2.

[31] Ibid., 4.2.5.

[32] Several important recent works discuss the problems of Pauline authorship of the Pastorals. Among them are J. D. Quinn and W. Wacker, *The First and Second Letters to Timothy* (ECC; Grand Rapids, Mich: Eerdmans, 2000); I. H. Marshall, *The Pastoral Epistles* (ICC; Edinburgh: T&T Clark, 1999); James D. Miller, *The Pastoral Letters as Composite Documents* (SNRS Monograph Series 93; Cambridge: Cambridge University Press, 1997).

[33] Ernest Best, "Scripture, Tradition and the Canon of the New Testament," *JRB* 61:2 (1979): 279.

but the so-called second Epistle we have not received as canonical, but nevertheless it has appeared useful to many, and has been studied with other scriptures."[34] Eusebius probably accepted as canonical ("recognized") only twenty-one or twenty-two of the books of our current New Testament canon. Besides 2 Peter, he questioned the legitimacy of James, 2 and 3 John, Jude, Revelation, and may or may not have included Hebrews with the letters of Paul.

The gnostic Christians of the second century and the Donatists of the fourth century also claimed apostolic support for their teachings.[35] The gnostic *Gospel of Thomas* is the first gospel that specifically claims apostolic authorship, and while many reject that claim many scholars today acknowledge that some twenty or more of the sayings of Jesus in it are authentic.[36]

After lengthy debate the early church concluded that Paul wrote the book of Hebrews, something which modern scholarship for a variety of reasons (style, theology, vocabulary, etc.) universally rejects. Attributing it to Paul may have stemmed from the desire to get a cherished writing into the canon rather than the sincere belief that Paul actually wrote it. Origen, like many others in the ancient church, had serious doubts about who wrote the letter. Observing that the thoughts were Paul's but the style and composition belonged to someone else, he concludes "but who wrote the epistle, in truth God knows."[37] Attributing the work to Paul, however, secured its place in the Christian canon. This leads us to conclude that there may have been other criteria operating, probably subconsciously. At times apostolic authorship may have been attributed to a writing that was cherished and considered useful in segments of the Christian community in order to justify its use in the churches. We will return to the intrinsic value and use of the writings later.

In the early church, the concern for apostolicity essentially had to do with the proximity of the apostles to Jesus and their presumed first hand knowledge of him and his ministry. Since Jesus was the ultimate "canon" of the church, in the sense that he was the primary authority figure of the church, the opportunity to glean information from those closest to him was highly valued. This is why Tertullian relegated John and Matthew to higher positions of authority than Mark and Luke. When the apostolic authorship of ancient writings was doubted, typically their canonical status was also questioned.[38]

Another factor that points to the importance of apostolic authorship is the presence of pseudonymous literature circulating in the early church. There were many writings attributed to apostles that nonetheless failed to be included in the canon, largely because they were considered pseudonymous. Representatives of all the genres present in the New Testament (gospels, acts, epistles, and apocalypses) are attributed to well-known apostles.

---

[34] *Hist. eccl.* 3.3.1, LCL.

[35] See the many gnostic documents in the *NHLE,* which claim either implicitly or explicitly the apostolic tradition, for example, the *Acts of Peter,* in *NHLE* 265. Note how the *Apocryphon of John* (paragraphs 2 and 32) claims to be a report of what the savior revealed to the Apostle John (ibid., 99, 115).

[36] See especially the important collection of noncanonical sayings of Jesus in John Dominic Crossan, *Sayings Parallels: A Workbook for the Jesus Tradition* (Philadelphia: Fortress, 1986). Although Crossan has gained a reputation for finding authentic sayings of Jesus in the most unusual places (e.g., the *Gospel of Peter* and the Egerton Papyri), and probably more than exist, he raises important questions about the application of the apostolic criterion in early Christianity.

[37] Eusebius, *Hist. eccl.* 6.25.14.

[38] Bruce, *The Canon of Scripture* (Downers Grove, Ill.: InterVarsity, 1988), 259, makes this point.

This mostly sectarian literature was written in an apostle's name in order to find acceptance in the church. Most of these works are described in detail elsewhere;[39] for our purposes we simply list some of the most important examples.

1. Gospels: *Protoevangelium of James, Infancy Gospel of Thomas, Gospel of Peter, Gospel of Nicodemus, Gospel of the Nazoreans, Gospel of the Ebionites, Gospel of the Hebrews, Gospel of the Egyptians, Gospel of Thomas, Gospel of Philip, Gospel of Mary*

2. Acts: *Acts of John, Acts of Peter, Acts of Paul, Acts of Andrew, Acts of Thomas, Acts of Andrew and Matthias, Acts of Philip, Acts of Thaddaeus, Acts of Peter and Paul, Acts of Peter and Andrew, Martyrdom of Matthew, Slavonic Acts of Peter, Acts of Peter and the Twelve Apostles*[40]

3. Epistles: *Third Corinthians, Epistle to the Laodiceans, Letters of Paul and Seneca, Letters of Jesus and Abgar, Letter of Lentulus, Epistle of Titus* (some would include the Pastoral Epistles and 1 and 2 Peter)

4. Apocalypses: *Apocalypse of Peter, Coptic Apocalypse of Paul, First Apocalypse of James, Second Apocalypse of James, Apocryphon of John, Sophia of Jesus Christ, Letter of Peter to Philip, Apocalypse of Mary*

In several instances the apostolic authorship of these writings was questioned in antiquity, but some churches nevertheless received them and were reserved in their comments about their origins. From early on it appears that the question of pseudepigraphy was a controversial issue in the church. Discussing the literature that was considered sacred in the fourth-century church, see how Eusebius describes those who falsely publish their own writings in the name of an apostle:

> Some have also counted [as canonical or recognized] the Gospel according to the Hebrews in which those of the Hebrews who have accepted Christ take a special pleasure. These [including those listed above] would all belong to the disputed books, but we have nevertheless been obliged to make a list of them, distinguishing between those writings which, according to the tradition of the Church, are true, genuine, and recognized, and those which differ from them in that they are not canonical but disputed, yet nevertheless are known to most of the writers of the Church, in order that we might know them and the writings which are put forward by heretics under the name of the apostles containing gospels such as those of Peter, and Thomas, and Matthias, and some others besides, or Acts such as those of Andrew and John and the other apostles. To none of these has any who belonged to the succession of the orthodox ever thought it right to refer in his writings. Moreover, the type and phraseology differs from apostolic style, and the opinion and tendency of their contents is widely dissonant from true orthodoxy and clearly shows that they are the forgeries of heretics. They ought, therefore, to be reckoned not even among spurious books but shunned as altogether wicked and impious.[41]

If it was believed that an apostle wrote a particular book, that writing was accepted and treated as scripture. There is no doubt that several books of the New Testament were placed in the canon because the majority believed that they were written by apostles or members of the apostolic community.

---

[39] See especially Wilhelm Schneemelcher, ed., *New Testament Apocrypha* (rev. ed.; Louisville, Ky.: Westminster John Knox, 1991–1992) for detailed descriptions and translations.

[40] The first five of these, called the "Lucian Acts," were often circulated together.

[41] *Hist. eccl.* 3.25.6–7, LCL.

B. Orthodoxy

Theological issues were a significant concern to the early church, and played an important role in its development. Manlio Simonetti offers a fair assessment of the role of scripture in the church's theological inquiry:

> We might say that the whole life of the community was conditioned by the interpretation of Scripture. It has been said that the history of doctrine is the history of exegesis, in that the whole development of catholic doctrine is based on the interpretation of a certain number of passages in Scripture in the light of particular needs; but the same could be said of any other aspect of the Church's life: organization, discipline, worship, and so on. For this reason, the study of Holy Scripture was the real foundation of Christian culture in the Church of the earliest centuries.[42]

This theological concern led the early church to employ the "rule of faith" as the criterion of "orthodoxy" to determine which writings could be used in the church. Bishop Serapion (ca. 200) rejected the reading of the *Gospel of Peter* in church because of this criterion of truth. When asked by the church at Rhossus, under his jurisdiction, whether the *Gospel of Peter* could be read in their services, he at first agreed because it had an apostle's name attached. But later he reversed his decision saying, "since I have now learnt, from what has been told me, that their [the authors'] mind was lurking in some hole of heresy, I shall give diligence to come again to you; wherefore, brethren expect me quickly."[43] His rejection was based upon the book's divergence from what was generally accepted as true in the churches. It was not because of its questionable authorship, though that may have played a small role, but because the theology was considered out of step with the "rule of faith" operating in the church. Serapion's initial willingness to accept the reading of the *Gospel of Peter* in his churches is also instructive. Had there been a widely recognized and closed four-gospel canon at that time (ca. 200 C.E.), he might well have rejected the *Gospel of Peter* on such grounds. In this example, apostolicity and antiquity evidently took a back seat to the criterion of truth. If a writing was too far away from what was believed to be the core or central teaching that had been handed on in the churches, it was rejected.[44]

Several scholars have argued that one of the distinguishing features of the New Testament literature is the *truth,* or canon of faith, that it presents.[45] However, as one examines the New Testament literature carefully, it is difficult to reconcile many of its theological positions and practical guidelines for living. For example, the eschatology of

---

[42] Manlio Simonetti, *Biblical Interpretation in the Early Church: An Historical Introduction to Patristic Exegesis* (ed. A. Bergquist and M. Bockmuehl; trans. J. A. Hughes; Edinburgh: T&T Clark, 1994), 1–2.

[43] Eusebius, *Hist. eccl.* 6.12.4, LCL.

[44] See also Eusebius, *Hist. eccl.* 3.25.7.

[45] See, for example, David Ewert, *From Ancient Tablets to Modern Translations* (Grand Rapids: Zondervan, 1983), 131; see also Glenn W. Barker, William L. Lane, and J. Ramsey Michaels (*The New Testament Speaks* [New York: Harper & Row, 1969], 30–31), who ask, "was that which was written a genuine witness to Christ and from Christ? . . . The church was confident that if a document were genuinely inspired it would conform to the truth which God had revealed through tested witnesses." See also Everett F. Harrison, *Introduction to the New Testament* (Grand Rapids: Eerdmans, 1977), 11–12.

the Synoptic Gospels declares the arrival of the kingdom of God in the near future (e.g., Mk 1:15; 13:3–37 and parallels) as well as its presence in the ministry of Jesus (e.g., Lk 11:20; 17:21, and by implication, 7:18–23), while John emphasizes the present nature of eternal life (John 3:16, 10:10; 20:30–31). Does Paul's view of the death of Christ "for our sins" square with Luke's lack of interest in that matter?[46] Paul's argument in Rom 13:1–3 that Christians ought to be subject to and not resist the governing authorities because they were appointed by God is difficult to square with Acts 4:19; 5:28–29, which rejects the authority of governing officials in favor of obedience to God. Apart from relativizing the message of Paul to specific contexts, how can these texts be harmonized?[47] Compare also the baptismal formulas in the book of Acts (2:38; 10:48; 19:5) with that in Matt 28:19.[48] And what about the organizational structure of the early church in Acts, compared to that in Paul, John, the Pastorals, and Matt 16:18–19? Many other examples could be listed here to show that there is a fair amount of diversity in the New Testament literature. Ernst Käsemann argues that such theological variety in the early church is "so wide even in the New Testament that we are compelled to admit the existence not merely of significant tensions, but, not infrequently, of irreconcilable theological contradictions."[49] Krister Stendahl agrees that such differences cannot and should not be resolved through clever exegesis because "when they are overcome by harmonization, the very points intended by the writers are dulled and distorted."[50]

In the midst of the diversity in the New Testament, is there also a common core of beliefs typical of early Christianity and essential to the church? James Dunn contends that if the New Testament has a theological core everywhere acknowledged or reasonably assumed, it is simply this, "Jesus-the-man-now-exalted."[51] I would add to this that it is everywhere stated or presupposed that he is also worthy of faithful obedience, and that the promise of the blessing of God awaits all who follow him. This confession, however, is not confined to the New Testament literature, but is affirmed in numerous noncanonical Christian writings as well.[52] Nevertheless the church unquestionably *believed* that the New Testament writings reliably conveyed the essential message of and about Jesus the Christ. Apostolicity witnessed to this, but apostolicity was not a substitute for content.[53]

---

[46] See for example, the speeches in Acts where the death of Christ "for our sins" is nowhere in view (2:14–39; 3:11–26; and so on), but found frequently in Paul, especially 1 Cor 15:3, as well as his focus on the cross in 1 Cor 1:17–2:2; Rom 3:23–25, Gal 2:21, *passim.*

[47] Best cites several other examples of problems of harmonization in the New Testament literature ("Scripture," 272ff.).

[48] For a careful discussion of this matter, see Lars Hartman, *'Into the Name of the Lord Jesus': Baptism in the Early Church* (SNTIW; Edinburgh: T&T Clark, 1997).

[49] Ernst Käsemann, *Essays on New Testament Themes* (London: SCM, 1968), 100.

[50] Krister Stendahl, *Meanings: The Bible as Document and Guide* (Philadelphia: Fortress, 1984), 63.

[51] Dunn, *Unity and Diversity in the New Testament* (2d ed.; Philadelphia: Westminster, 1992), 377.

[52] All of the Apostolic Fathers—Clement of Rome, Ignatius, Polycarp, Hermas, Barnabas, and the Didachist—could or did agree to this. So also could Marcion and the Montanists for that matter.

[53] Hans von Campenhausen (*The Formation of the Christian Bible* [trans. J. A. Baker; Philadelphia: Fortress, 1972], 330) makes this observation. For a brief discussion of the orthodoxy and heresy controversy, see McDonald, *Formation,* 232–36, but especially Walter Bauer, *Orthodoxy and Heresy in Earliest Christianity* (2d ed.; ed. R. Kraft and G. Krodel; Philadelphia: Fortress, 1971).

While it may be somewhat in vogue to claim that all theologies of the Bible and all theologies outside of the Bible equally represent the proclamation of the earliest Christian community, and that there was no theological core, but rather considerable confusion, this is simply not the case. One scholar, for instance, contends that there were justifiable reasons why the ancient church rejected the gnostic esoteric and ahistorical interpretation of Christian faith.[54] Although the Christian proclamation of the first century is broader than the late second century orthodoxy of Rome that eventually obtained prominence in the churches, all ancient theologies were *not* equally representative of the faith. There was a typical understanding of God, Christ, scripture, and hope in the majority of the churches coming out of the second century. This understanding became more pronounced in subsequent generations. Gerd Theissen asserts that most Christian communities shared certain beliefs, and these beliefs had a role in determining which writings were welcomed into the biblical canon. Other writings and groups that did not measure up to this theological core, such as the *Gospel of Peter* (mentioned above) and the other gnostic texts, were excluded. He adds that primitive Christianity "is governed by two basic axioms, monotheism and belief in the redeemer. In addition there are eleven basic motifs: the motifs of creation, wisdom and miracle; of renewal, representation and indwelling; of faith, agape and a change of position; and finally the motif of judgment."[55] I would also add the belief in the activity of God in the life, death, and resurrection of the "redeemer," Jesus. Theissen correctly concludes that there were common beliefs among the Christian communities and that these views must have had some impact on the overall structure of the New Testament canon.[56]

C. Antiquity

The traditional understanding of canon formation is that the church at first recognized only the Old Testament writings as scripture. Later, as the Gospels and Epistles (at first only Paul's) began to circulate among the churches they too were accorded scriptural status. Barton, however, challenges the traditional view, noting that in the first two centuries Christians generally referred to their own writings more than to the Old Testament. They did not cite the Old Testament equally until it was becoming finalized for the church. He also notes that during the second century, "all but a very few Old Testament books (such as Isaiah or the Psalms) already play second fiddle to the Christians' own writings."[57] Nevertheless, he acknowledges that antiquity played a significant role in society in the ancient world; a religion's antiquity enhanced its credibility. A high value was placed upon the past, and what was old was generally considered more reliable and acceptable than what was new. This attitude continued in the church until the time of the Enlightenment.

---

[54] George W. MacRae, "Why the Church Rejected Gnosticism," in *Jewish and Christian Self-Definition: The Shaping of Christianity in the Second and Thrid Centuries* (ed. E. P. Sanders; Philadelphia: Fortress, 1980), 1:126–33.

[55] Gerd Theissen, *A Theory of Primitive Christian Religion* (London: SCM, 1999), 271–85, at 282.

[56] Ibid. William Farmer, in ch. 19 of the present volume, emphasizes the importance of this *regula fidei* for the life of the early church and in the formation of its canon.

[57] Barton, *Holy Writings, Sacred Text*, 64.

Nevertheless, the early Christians believed that with the advent of Jesus something new and very important had arrived, surpassing everything that had gone before it.[58] For the church, the ministry of Jesus had become the defining moment in history. Consequently, the church's most important authorities were those closest to this defining moment.[59] The early Christians believed that the books and writings that gave them their best access to the story of Jesus, and thus defined their identity and mission, were those that came from the apostolic era. Barton further makes the astonishing claim that these books, the Gospels and Epistles, were so important to the early church that they "were more important than 'Scripture', and to cite them as *graphē* [scripture] might have diminished rather than enhanced them."[60] With time, as prophecy declined, the church appealed more to antiquity and its roots in the Old Testament. But the church continued to give priority to the period of Jesus' ministry, as the defining moment for the church, and to the apostles, as those who were closest to him and were the best representatives of this crucial period.

The church excluded from the biblical canon any writings that it believed were written *after* the period of apostolic ministry. The tradition that came from the time of Jesus' ministry took priority over all other periods. That is certainly the perspective of the author of the Muratorian Fragment (ca. 350 C.E.), who spoke against accepting the *Shepherd of Hermas* as scripture because it was not written in the apostolic age but more recently, in his own age—that is, any time after the apostolic age.[61] He writes:

> (73) But Hermas wrote the *Shepherd* (74) very recently, in our times, in the city of Rome, (75) while bishop Pius, his brother, was occupying the [episcopal] chair (76) of the church of the city of Rome. (77) And therefore it ought indeed to be read; but (78) it cannot be read publicly to the people in church either among (79) the prophets, whose number is complete, or among (80) the apostles, for it is after [their] time. (*Muratorian Fragment* lines 73–74)[62]

Antiquity, perhaps linked with apostolicity and the "rule of faith," appears to have been an important criterion for canonicity for some of the churches. A problem with the application of this criterion, however, is that it is not easy to determine which Christian writings were the earliest in the church. Many biblical scholars argue convincingly that some of the literature of the New Testament—especially 2 Peter and probably the Pastorals—was written later than such noncanonical Christian books as the *Didache, 1 Clement*, perhaps the *Epistles* of Ignatius, *Barnabas, Hermas*, the *Martyrdom of Polycarp*, and possibly even *2 Clement*. A few scholars also argue that even some of the apocryphal gospels may make similar claims.[63] This should be enough to show that the criterion of antiquity was not applied with unfailing success in the patristic church. If antiquity alone were the chief criterion for canonicity, some rethinking regarding the present biblical canon would be in order. In any case, it is unwise to place too much emphasis on such a changing and

---

[58] Ibid., 64–65.

[59] Ibid., 64–67.

[60] Ibid., 68.

[61] For a more complete discussion of this matter, see Geoffrey Hahneman, *The Muratorian Fragment and the Development of the Canon* (OTM; Oxford: Clarendon, 1992), 34–72. See also his contribution to this volume. A summary of the discussion can be found in McDonald, *Formation*, 209–20.

[62] Translation from Metzger, *Canon*, 307.

[63] See Helmut Koester, "Apocryphal and Canonical Gospels," *HTR* 73 (1980): 105–30.

imprecise criterion, given the variety of opinion among New Testament scholars on the dating of the New Testament writings. Earlier writings cannot be considered ipso facto more reliable. However, the Christian church has always been concerned to recover the earliest and most reliable traditions about Jesus, and the attempt to do so cannot be an ill-informed quest. The grounding of Christian faith and doctrine in the life and teachings of Jesus, as well as his death and resurrection, has been a constant since the beginning of the church, and the use of the criterion of antiquity as well as apostolicity, with appropriate caution, continues to be an appropriate means of getting closer to the defining and funda-mental moment of the Christian faith.

D. Use

The regular use of writings in the ancient churches was also an important factor in their selection for the New Testament canon. This is what Eusebius had in mind when he mentioned that certain writings were "recognized" *(homolegoumena)* among the churches and became "encovenanted" *(endiathēkoi* = "testamented" or "canonical").[64] The wide-spread use of the New Testament writings in the churches may have been the most deter-minative factor in the canonical process. The fact that the authorship of Hebrews was strongly questioned, yet it made it into the New Testament canon, suggests that churches were reluctant to dismiss a useful and cherished document. An important factor was who was favorable toward the acceptance of a document and who was not. Athanasius and Epiphanius, for instance, would have had a greater influence on the church than many lesser known figures. Also, larger churches in the metropolitan centers such as Antioch, Alexandria, Rome, Ephesus, and the New Rome, Constantinople, were more likely to have a greater influence on which books were included than were the smaller churches in rural areas. While most New Testament writings were known and used by most of the churches in Eusebius's day, doubt lingered over others. These "disputed" *(antilegomena)* writings included James, 2 Peter, 2 and 3 John, Jude, probably Revelation, and possibly Hebrews. Notice for example, how Eusebius acknowledges wide acceptance of 1 John, but is reluc-tant to accept 2 and 3 John and Revelation. For him, the Gospel of John and 1 John have been "*accepted without controversy by ancients and moderns alike but the other two are dis-puted,* and as to the Revelation there have been many advocates of either opinion up to the present. This, too, shall be similarly illustrated by *quotations from the ancients* at the proper time."[65] This shows his considerable interest in what the majority of churches concluded about the matter of canon.

The writings eventually incorporated into the New Testament apparently met the worship and instructional needs of the churches, while the others did not. The writings that did not remain in the church's sacred collections were those that did not meet the needs of the greater church and had more difficulty being adapted to the churches' chang-ing needs. Ulrich adds that the "use of Scripture—whether homiletical or liturgical, whether ancient or contemporary—involves a tripolar dynamic of interaction between the traditional text, the contemporary cultural situation, and the experience of the minister

---

[64] See his *Hist. eccl.* 3.25.1–7.
[65] Ibid., 3.24.18, LCL, italics added.

within the community. This tripolar dynamic is a reflection of, and is in faithful continuity with, the process by which the Scriptures were composed."[66] I would only add that use was also a factor in the final canonization process—as Ulrich, along with James Sanders, also acknowledges.

It is not clear, however, that all of the New Testament writings were more extensively used in worship and church life than some other writings of the late first and early to middle second-century texts. For example, Philemon, 2 Peter, Jude, 2 and 3 John were not cited or used as often as such noncanonical sources as *1 Clement,* the *Shepherd of Hermas,* the *Didache, Barnabas,* and the *Epistles* of Ignatius, and possibly also the *Martyrdom of Polycarp.* If frequency of citation is a guide, there is considerable room for doubt. Realizing this, Raymond Collins concludes that not all of the New Testament teachings and writings are of equal value for Christian faith and ministry, nor are they necessarily more important or closer to that "canon of truth" than certain noncanonical Christian writings. While still acknowledging the strong influence of the present New Testament canon on Christian thought, he adds that "a concern for the truth of history calls for the admission that some books within the canon have had a more influential function in shaping the expression of the church's faith than have others within the canon." He adds that "some books outside of the canon have had a more striking impact on the formulation of the church's faith than have some individual books among the canonical twenty-seven."[67]

Another side of the criterion of use is what F. F. Bruce calls the criterion of "catholicity," by which he means the unwillingness of a church to be out of step with other churches in regard to which documents were recognized as authoritative.[68] Without question, the classic case for the relationship between church use and canonicity comes from Augustine who admonishes the reader of scripture to:

> prefer those [writings] that are received by all Catholic Churches to those which some of them do not receive. Among those, again, which are not received by all, let him prefer those which the more numerous and the weightier churches receive to those which fewer and less authoritative churches hold. But if, however, he finds some held by the more numerous, and some held by the churches of more authority (though this is not very likely to happen), I think that in such a case they ought to be regarded as of equal authority.[69]

The variety in the canonical lists of scriptures of the fourth century shows that the catholicity criterion was far from absolute. Probably other historical circumstances besides utilization by large numbers and influential churches helped determine which books were included in the church's authoritative list. The reaction against Montanism prompted a broad suspicion of prophetic literature, leading to its neglect in succeeding generations of the church, especially in the East. The *Apocalypse of Peter* was not cited as frequently after the Montanist controversies as before, and the Book of Revelation also had a stormy reception, especially through the fourth century.

---

[66] Ulrich, *The Dead Sea Scrolls,* 74.

[67] Raymond F. Collins, *Introduction to the New Testament* (Garden City: Doubleday, 1983), 39.

[68] F. F. Bruce, "Tradition and the Canon of Scripture," in *The Authoritative Word: Essays on the Nature of Scripture* (ed. D. K. McKim; Grand Rapids: Eerdmans, 1993), pages 59–84, at 74.

[69] *Doctr. chr.* 2.12. I have used Metzger's translation (*Canon,* 237) of this awkward but important passage.

The historical circumstances that led to the canonization of the New Testament literature are not completely clear today, since there is no surviving literature that identifies the canonical process. But it seems likely that all of the above criteria played some role in shaping the New Testament canon. Ultimately, it appears that the writings that were accorded scriptural status were the ones that best conveyed the earliest Christian proclamation and that also best met the growing needs of local churches in the third and fourth centuries. The most important criteria in the selection process were apparently those that we have mentioned above. Conversely, it appears that the literature that was no longer deemed relevant to the church's needs, even though it may have been considered pertinent at an earlier time, was eliminated from consideration. If that is true, it would not be the only time that the church has focused on literature that was most relevant to its own historical situation; New Testament scholars have long recognized that the social circumstances of the life of the church played a significant role in the selection, organization, and editing of the materials that form the New Testament gospels. The relevance of New Testament writings to the churches in subsequent generations must have played some role in their preservation, while other contenders that ceased to be useful to the church gradually disappeared. This explanation best accounts for the variety of books in the surviving Old Testament and New Testament collections in the ancient church. Although the leaders of the church in the fourth century and later pushed for unity in the recognition of which books were inspired, authoritative, and therefore canonical, unanimity proved unattainable due to diverse circumstances in the churches. Nevertheless, the key to understanding the preservation and canonization of the books which make up our current New Testament is probably usage, especially usage in the larger churches during the third through the fifth centuries.

4. Additional Features of Scripture

In addition to these criteria used by the early churches to determine canonicity, the writings that functioned as scripture in worship and provided adequate catechetical instruction displayed additional features.

A. *Adaptability*

In particular, they were *adaptable* to the changing circumstances of the church's life; these writings survived in the biblical canon. Some writings that functioned as scripture earlier in the church's history, such as *Barnabas, 1 Clement,* the *Epistles* of Ignatius, *Shepherd of Hermas,* and *Eldad and Modat,* did not survive the criterion of usefulness or adaptability. They fell into disuse and dropped from the scripture collections. This happened mostly while the notion of canon was still fluid in the churches, namely before the fourth century. Some noncanonical writings, however, occasionally appear in New Testament codices into the fourth and fifth centuries. For instance, *Barnabas* and the *Shepherd of Hermas* are in Codex Alexandrinus, and *1 and 2 Clement* are in Vaticanus.

James Sanders has focused considerable attention over the years on the adaptability of the Old Testament and New Testament scriptures to the continually changing circumstances of the communities of faith. The sacred writings that brought hope in a hopeless situation for the people of Israel told a story that could be applied to new circumstances. This story, significantly enhanced through the creative hermeneutics that were employed by the church, offered hope and life to the new people of faith.[70] This is, of course, the story of God's activity in Jesus, the proclaimed Christ. That story continues to be adaptable to the changing circumstances of life of a variety of persons in a variety of cultures. Through it persons of faith perceive that God continues to release from bondage, bring healing, and offer hope to the hopeless. That is what is adaptable and what continues to inspire persons in every generation, and that is what the church canonized.

B. Inspiration

To what extent did inspiration play a role in the canonization process? Traditionally many have argued that the biblical canon resulted from the church's recognition of the inspired status of certain writings. However, it is more accurate to say that inspiration was a corollary, rather than a criterion, of canonicity. That is, acceptance of a writing as scripture and its inclusion in the biblical canon demonstrated that the writing was inspired by God. The problem with adding inspiration to the above criteria is twofold. First is the difficulty of determining what is or is not inspired. This difficulty stems from the term's fluidity of meaning in ancient Christianity. In fact, the church has never presented a comprehensive and clear definition of inspiration. The resultant ambiguity is seen in the variety of ways the term has been used throughout the ages, including our own. Second, and more important, the early church never limited the concept of inspiration to its sacred writings, but rather extended it to everything considered theologically true, whether it was written, taught, or preached.

The ancient church fathers believed that their scriptures were inspired, but inspiration alone was not the basis for including those works in the New Testament canon. Several writers of sacred truth believed that they were inspired as they wrote. The author of the book of Revelation, for example, claims prophetic inspiration and warns:

> everyone who hears *the words of the prophecy of this book:* if any one adds to them, God will add to him the plagues described in this book, and if any one takes away from the words of *the book of this prophecy,* God will take away his share in the tree of life and in the holy city, which are described in this book.[71]

Clearly he believed that he had the voice of prophecy and was inspired when he wrote these words.

The ancient churches assumed the inspiration of their scriptures, but to what extent did inspiration play a part in the canonizing process? Irenaeus makes it clear that the scriptures, even when they are not clearly understood, "were spoken by the Word of God and by His Spirit."[72] Similarly, Origen maintained that "the Scriptures were written by the Spirit

---

[70] James A. Sanders (*From Sacred Story to Sacred Text* [Philadelphia: Fortress, 1987], 9–39) has dealt with the adaptability issue in detail. He makes the case that what holds true for ancient Israel in this regard is also true for the church, namely that the story that had sufficient adaptability to meet the ever changing needs of the church was preserved and canonized.

[71] Rev. 22:18–19, NRSV, italics added.

[72] *Haer.* 2.28.2, ANF.

of God, and have a meaning, not such only as is apparent at first sight, but also another which escapes the notice of most."[73] Seeking to discredit the *Doctrine of Peter,* he says that he can show that it was not written by Peter "or by any other person inspired by the Spirit of God."[74] The operating assumption here, of course, is that scripture is inspired, but heresy and falsehood are not.

Theophilus of Antioch (ca. 180) reflects his belief that the scriptures were inspired when he asserts that "the holy writings teach us, and all the spirit bearing [inspired] men . . . that at first God was alone, and the Word in Him."[75] His understanding of inspiration was that "men of God carrying in them a holy spirit [*pneumatophoroi* = "borne along by the spirit"] and becoming prophets, being inspired and made wise by God, became God-taught, and holy and righteous."[76] The author of *2 Clement* believed that *1 Clement* was an inspired document, and cites 23:3, 4 with the words: "For the prophetic word also says" (*legei gar kai ho prophētikos logos, 2 Clem.* 11:2), the usual words to designate inspired writings. Also, *Barnabas* 16:5 introduces a passage from *2 Enoch* with the words, "for the scripture says" (*legei gar hē graphē).* In a somewhat different light, Clement of Rome (ca. 95) told his readers that Paul's letter, 1 Corinthians, was written "with true inspiration" (*ep' alētheias pneumatikōs),*[77] but later he claimed the same inspiration for himself, saying that his own letter was written "through the Holy Spirit" (*gegrammenois dia tou hagiou pneumatos).*[78] Ignatius likewise expressed awareness of his own inspiration when he commented:

> I spoke with a great voice—with God's own voice. . . . But some suspected me of saying this because I had previous knowledge of the division of some persons: but he in whom I am bound is my witness that I had no knowledge of this from any human being, *but the Spirit was preaching and saying this (to de pneuma ekēryssen legon tade).*[79]

There are in fact many examples of noncanonical authors who either claimed, or were acknowledged by others, to have been filled or inspired by the Spirit in their speaking or writing.[80] The point here is that *the scriptures were not the only ancient writings that were believed to be inspired by God.* Generally speaking, in the early church the common word for "inspiration" (*theopneustos,* see 2 Tim 3:16) was used not only in reference to the scriptures (Old Testament or New Testament), but also of individuals who spoke or wrote the truth of God. Everett Kalin, for example, observes that Gregory of Nyssa (ca. 330–95), when describing Basil's (330–79) commentary on the creation story, claimed that the work

---

[73] *Princ.,* Preface 8, *ANF.* Bruce (*Canon,* 267–68) has noted that Irenaeus was the first Christian writer to allegorize the New Testament writings because he was among the first to treat the New Testament as unreservedly inspired. Thereafter Origen and others felt free to allegorize the scriptures *because* they were considered inspired of God.

[74] *Princ.,* Preface 8, *ANF.*

[75] *Autol.* 2.22, *ANF.*

[76] *Autol.* 2:9, *ANF.* This passage also clarifies what Theophilus means by inspiration and perhaps how it was understood by his and other communities.

[77] *1 Clem.* 47:3, LCL.

[78] *1 Clem.* 63:2, LCL.

[79] Ign. *Phld.,* 7:1b–2, LCL, italics added.

[80] A number of other examples are listed in Albert C. Sundberg, "The Bible Canon and the Christian Doctrine of Inspiration," *Int* 29 (October, 1975): 4:365ff. Everett R. Kalin gives an even longer list in "The Inspired Community: A Glance at Canon History," *CTM* 42 (1971): 541–49.

was inspired and that his words even surpassed those of Moses in terms of beauty, complexity, and form. He said that it was an "exposition given by inspiration of God . . . [admired] no less than the words composed by Moses himself." [81] Kalin also notes that the famous epitaph of Abercius from about the fourth century was called an "inspired inscription" *(theopneuston epigramma)*, and that a synodical epistle of the council of Ephesus (ca. 433), describing the council's condemnation of Nestorious (d. ca. 451), was termed "their inspired judgment" (or "decision") *(tēs autōn theopneustou kriseōs)*.[82]

From these and many other examples, we see that the ancient church did not limit inspiration to the scriptures, or even to literature alone. In his *Dialogue with Trypho*, Justin Martyr argues that "the prophetical gifts remain with us even to the present time. And hence you ought to understand that [the gifts] formerly among your nation [the Jewish nation] have been transferred to us."[83] Even in writings which dealt with the Montanist controversy[84] in the latter third of the second century, Kalin could find no evidence that the early church confined inspiration to an already past apostolic age, or even to a collection of sacred writings.[85] The traditional assumption that the early Christians believed that *only* the canonical writings were inspired is highly questionable. The rabbinic notion that "when the last prophets, Haggai, Zechariah and Malachi, died, the holy Spirit ceased out of Israel"[86] was simply not shared by the church.[87] From his own investigation of the church fathers up to 400 C.E., Kalin failed to turn up one example where an orthodox but noncanonical writing was ever called uninspired; such a designation was reserved for heretical authors. He concludes: "if the Scriptures were the *only* writings the church fathers considered inspired, one would expect them to say so, at least once in a while."[88] He adds that in the early church inspiration applied not only to all scripture, but also to the Christian community, as it bore "living witness of Jesus Christ." Only heresy was considered to be non-inspired, because it was contrary to this witness.[89] Campenhausen agrees,

---

[81] *Apologia hexaemeron*, PG 44.61, but also in the wider context of 44.61–64, cited by Everett R. Kalin in his unpublished Harvard thesis, "Argument from Inspiration in the Canonization of the New Testament," (1967), 170. The translation of this text is from Metzger, *Canon*, 256.

[82] *Vita Abercii* 76. The writing was apparently penned by Abercius Marcellus himself, who was bishop of Hieropolis in Phrygia of Asia minor in the late second century. He died ca. 200 C.E. Kalin gives several other examples of the ancient use of the term "inspired" *(theopneustos)* to show that it was not exclusively used of scriptures. See Kalin, "The Inspired Community," 169–73.

[83] *Dial.* 82, ANF. See other illustrations of this in *Dial.* 87–88.

[84] Eusebius, *Hist. eccl.* 5.14–19 is especially helpful on the background to this controversy.

[85] Kalin, "The Inspired Community," 543. He concluded from his study of Irenaeus, Origen, Eusebius, and other ancient fathers that only the work of the false prophets mentioned in the Old Testament, the heathen oracles and philosophy were non-inspired. See also Kalin, "Argument from Inspiration," 163, 168.

[86] *T. Sotah* 13:2.

[87] See Joseph Blenkinsopp's contribution in this volume, where he discusses this issue in rabbinic Judaism and cites as examples of the belief that "The Holy Spirit (meaning the spirit of prophecy) departed from Israel after the destruction of Solomon's temple (*b. B.Bat.* 12a; *b. Yoma* 21b; *b. Soṭah* 48a) or after the death of the last biblical prophets (*b. Yoma* 9b; *b. Sanh.* 11a)" (p. 54 n. 3 above). See also his "Prophecy and Priesthood in Josephus," *JJS* 101 (1974): 245–55, and J. A. Sanders, "Spinning the Bible," *BR* (June 1998): 22–29, 44–45, for a similar perspective.

[88] Kalin, "The Inspired Community," 544–45.

[89] Ibid., 547.

and adds that the presence of prophetic literature among the Montanists, literature believed by the Montanists to be born of or prompted by the Holy Spirit, shows that at the end of the second century inspiration was not believed to have been confined to first-century literature.[90]

Inspiration played no discernible role in the later discussion of the formation of the biblical canon. James Barr summarizes the traditional understanding of the role of inspiration and canon formation as follows: "If we take a really strict old-fashioned view of inspiration, all books within the canon are fully inspired by the Holy Spirit, and no books outside it, however good in other respects, are inspired."[91] As he later stressed, one of the difficulties in the whole notion of canon in the early church is the difficulty of distinguishing inspired and non-inspired writings.[92] The problem the early church had in deciding what literature was or was not inspired demonstrates a lack of agreement on the meaning of inspiration.[93] The ongoing prophetic ministry of the Spirit, which called individuals through the proclamation of the good news to faith in Jesus Christ, was believed by the church to be resident in *their* community of faith and in *their* ministry, just as it was in the first century. The Christian community believed that God continued to inspire individuals in their proclamation, just as God inspired the writers of the New Testament literature. They believed the Spirit was the gift of God to the whole church, not just its writers of sacred literature. Does this conclusion pose an affront to the uniqueness and authority of the biblical literature? That would be the case if its only unique characteristic were its inspiration. But inspiration was not the distinguishing factor that separated either the apostles from subsequent Christians or the Christian scriptures from all other Christian literature. Krister Stendahl summarizes the role that inspiration played in early Christianity and biblical tradition as follows: "Inspiration, to be sure, is the divine presupposition for the New Testament, but the twenty-seven books were never chosen because they, and only they, were recognized as inspired. Strange as it may sound, inspiration was not enough. Other standards had to be applied."[94] F. F. Bruce agrees, adding that "inspiration is no longer a criterion of canonicity: it is a corollary of canonicity."[95] Similarly, Metzger notes that the focus of inspiration was on the truth claims of what was written, not inspiration itself. He writes: "while it is true that the Biblical authors were inspired by God, this does not mean that inspiration is a criterion of canonicity. A writing is not canonical

---

[90] Campenhausen, *Formation*, 215–50.

[91] James Barr, *Holy Scripture: Canon Authority, Criticism* (Philadelphia: Westminster, 1983), 48. Similarly, Paul J. Achtemeier (*Inspiration and Authority* [Peabody, Mass.: Hendrickson, 1999], 104–5) says that the prevailing view is that "God inspired the canonical books with no exception, and no noncanonical books are inspired, with no exception."

[92] Barr, *Holy Scripture*, 57.

[93] Take, for example, Clement of Alexandria who cited the *Didache* as scripture (*Strom.* 1.100.4) and believed that *1 Clement, Barnabas, Shepherd of Hermas, Preaching of Peter,* and the *Apocalypse of Peter* were inspired literature. See also Robert M. Grant, "The New Testament Canon," *The Cambridge History of the Bible: From the Beginnings to Jerome* (ed. P. R. Ackroyd and C. F. Evans; Cambridge: Cambridge University Press, 1970), 1:284–308, at 302.

[94] K. Stendahl, "The Apocalypse of John and the Epistle of Paul in the Muratorian Fragment," in *Current Issues in New Testament Interpretation: Essays in Honor of Otto A. Piper* (ed. W. Klassen and G. T. Snyder; New York: Harper & Row, 1962), 245.

[95] Bruce, *Canon*, 268.

because the author was inspired, but rather an author is considered to be inspired because what he has written is recognized as canonical, that is, recognized as authoritative."[96] Inspiration was not a *criterion* by which a New Testament book was given the status of scripture and later placed into a fixed biblical canon, but rather a corollary to its recognized status.

In summary, it was important to the church that its writings were produced by apostles or those close to them, e.g., Mark and Luke. It was also important, especially in the second to the fourth centuries, that these writings conform to the church's broad core of beliefs. The significance of the New Testament writings to the churches is shown by their widespread use in the life, teaching, and worship of those churches, and such use also contributed to their canonization. The end product of the long and complex canonization process was an authoritative and inspired instrument that continued to be useful in the ministry and worship of a changing church. That instrument clarified the church's essential identity and mission as a community of Christ.

---

[96] Metzger, *Canon of Scripture*, 257.

26

The Problem of Pseudonymity in Biblical Literature and Its Implications for Canon Formation

Kent D. Clarke

At least part of the difficulty inherent to any discussion of pseudonymity arises from the problem of definition.[1] Even distinguishing between the terms "pseudonymity" (from the Greek *pseudōnymos* meaning "under a false name" or "falsely called") and "pseudepigraphy" (from the Greek *pseudepigraphos* meaning "false inscription" or "falsely inscribed") has proven to be complicated.[2]

1. Defining Pseudonymity and Its Correlatives

Over a century ago, A. Gudemann defined "pseudonymity" as the process whereby an author uses another person's name; while more recently, K. Koch has stated that a text is to be considered pseudonymous when the author is deliberately identified by a name other than his own.[3] Similarly, C. Gempf describes "pseudonymity" as the practice of writing a literary work under the pretense that someone else, usually someone more famous, wrote it.[4] W. Speyer defines "pseudepigrapha" as literature deriving from an author different from the one alleged by the work's title, content, or transmission.[5] The same term is defined by E. E. Ellis as documents written under a name other than the true author, and

---

[1] See D. G. Meade, *Pseudonymity and Canon: An Investigation into the Relationship of Authorship and Authority in Jewish and Earliest Christian Tradition* (WUNT 39; Tübingen: Mohr [Siebeck], 1986), 1.

[2] Liddell and Scott, *An Intermediate Greek-English Lexicon* (Oxford: Clarendon, 1889) ad loc; and W. Bauer, W. F. Arndt, and F. W. Gingrich, *A Greek-English Lexicon of the New Testament and Other Early Christian Literature* (2d ed.; Chicago: University of Chicago Press, 1979), ad loc. In seeking to define these and other key terms I take seriously the point that etymology is not definition, either for ancient or modern usage.

[3] A. Gudemann, "Literary Frauds among the Greeks," in *Classical Studies in Honor of Henry Drisler* (New York: Macmillan, 1894), 57–94; and K. Koch, "Pseudonymous Writing," in *The Interpreter's Dictionary of the Bible: Supplementary Volume* (ed. K. Crim; Nashville: Abingdon, 1982), 712.

[4] C. Gempf, "Pseudonymity and the New Testament," *Themelios* 17 (1992): 8.

[5] W. Speyer, "Religiöse Pseudepigraphie und literarische Fälschung im Altertum," *JAC* 8/9 (1965/66): 88–125, reprinted in *Pseudepigraphie in der heidnischen und jüdisch-christlichen Antike* (Wege der Forschung 484; ed. N. Brox; Darmstadt: Wissenschaftliche Buchgesellschaft, 1977), 195–263. Further citations of this work are from the Brox reprint.

more broadly by B. M. Metzger as works wrongly attributed. Most contemporary literature regards the terms as synonyms and uses them interchangeably; however, a possible distinction might be that "pseudonymity" and its cognates generally refer to the *author* as subject, whereas "pseudepigraphy" and its cognates emphasize the *literature* as subject. Both terms refer to the use of false titles—one being assumed by the author and the other being ascribed to the literature—and in this sense are equivalent. As Meade points out, the problem of pseudonymity is the problem of pseudepigraphy.[6] However, pseudonymous authors (that is, authors writing under assumed names) produce pseudepigraphal writings (that is, literature falsely ascribed).[7]

The problem of definition is further compounded by the association of the word "pseudepigraphy" with "pseudepigrapha," the latter term now being used to refer to the history of the biblical canon and a specific collection of extracanonical or postcanonical Jewish and Christian literature, as opposed to issues related solely to literary ascription. Despite the fact that a large amount of literature falling within the canonical categories of Old and New Testament pseudepigrapha may be falsely ascribed (for example, to Hebrew patriarchs such as Adam, Abraham, Moses, and Enoch; and to Christian apostles like Peter, James, John, and Paul), other considerations besides authorship played a role in this work's designation as such. The same point is made concerning the apocrypha (from the Greek *apokryphos,* meaning "hidden," "concealed," "obscure," or "hard to understand") when Metzger states that the question of false attribution played very little part in identifying the books traditionally assigned to this category.[8] Even the line between pseudepigrapha and apocrypha is blurred, as both terms apply to Jewish as well as Christian extracanonical literature.[9] There is some precedent for applying the term "apocrypha" to all extracanonical

---

[6] Meade, *Pseudonymity and Canon,* 2. See also M. Rist, "Pseudepigraphy and the Early Christians," in *Studies in New Testament and Early Christian Literature: Essays in Honor of Allen P. Wikgren* (NovTSup 33; ed. D. E. Aune; Leiden: E. J. Brill, 1972), 75, who equates the two terms.

[7] Like Meade, L. R. Donelson acknowledges that "pseudonymity" and "pseudepigraphy" are used interchangeably in much contemporary scholarship. He does distinguish between the two when he explains that pseudonymity focuses more upon the authorial act and pseudepigraphy upon the character of the literary product, but adds that this is an occasional distinction. See L. R. Donelson, *Pseudepigraphy and Ethical Argument in the Pastoral Epistles* (HUT 22; Tübingen: Mohr [Siebeck], 1986), 7 n. 1. Donelson generally employs the term pseudepigraphy unless specifically referring to the authorial act, in which case he uses the term pseudonymity. So as not to confuse, I will equate the two terms, generally preferring to use the word pseudonymity unless explicitly referring to the literature as subject or emphasizing the character of the literary product.

[8] Bruce M. Metzger, "Literary Forgeries and Canonical Pseudepigrapha," *JBL* 91 (1972): 4. For a full discussion of the term *apokrypha* see *New Testament Apocrypha* (2 vols.; rev. ed.; ed. W. Schneemelcher; trans. R. McL. Wilson; Louisville, Ky.: Westminster John Knox, 1991), 1:13–15, 50–75.

[9] In relation to the Jewish extracanonical literature, C. A. Evans notes that a number of writings found in the Old Testament apocrypha, including the *Prayer of Manasseh* and *4 Ezra* (contained within 2 Esdras), belong in the Old Testament pseudepigrapha; while three writings generally found in the Old Testament pseudepigrapha, 3 Maccabees, 4 Maccabees, and Psalm 151, appear in some canon lists as part of the Old Testament apocrypha. See C. A. Evans, *Noncanonical Writings and New Testament Interpretation* (Peabody, Mass.: Hendrickson, 1992), 22, 189. In relation to the Christian extracanonical literature, Schneemelcher places only four extant works—the *Gospel of Peter,* the *Epistle to the Laodiceans,* the *Epistles of Paul and Seneca,* and the *Epistle of Titus*—into what he calls the "Apostolic Pseudepigrapha." Much of the literature traditionally placed under the heading New Testament

writings, while reserving the term "pseudepigrapha" and its cognates as a literary category, whether a given book is regarded as canonical or apocryphal.[10]

The difference between what might be called invented and borrowed pseudonyms is another important distinction. Most modern authors who, for whatever reason, are concerned with hiding their true identity make use of an invented pseudonym; that is, the name chosen by the author is not intended to reflect a recognized historical figure or actual person but is more or less a fictitious fabrication. The *nom de plume* or pen name typifies this form of pseudonymity.[11] The vast majority of surviving ancient pseudonymous literature, however, makes use of borrowed pseudonyms; meaning that these works were deliberately attributed by their authors to recognized historical figures or actual persons.[12] Although the motives underlying the use of both invented and borrowed pseudonyms may be similar, the latter category, with its implicit use of deception or forgery, is usually deemed far more problematic—particularly when employed in religious literature that appeals to some notion of "truth" or makes high ethical claims.[13]

2. Pseudonymity as Forgery and the Notion of Deceit

While the connotations of forgery, deceit, and falsification are inherent to any derivative of the term "pseudo," the extent to which such elements played a role in the production of pseudonymous literature in antiquity is debated.[14] The difficulty here centers on

---

pseudepigrapha cannot properly be termed pseudepigraphy, states Schneemelcher, who instead employs the broader designation New Testament apocrypha. See Schneemelcher, *New Testament Apocrypha*, 1:28–33. *Contra* Evans (*Noncanonical Writings*, 149–50), and L. M. McDonald (*The Formation of the Christian Biblical Canon* [rev. and enl. ed.; Peabody, Mass.: Hendrickson, 1995], 285–86), who include a larger collection of literature under the category New Testament pseudepigrapha.

[10] See Metzger, "Literary Forgeries," 4, who supports this proposal by C. C. Torrey, *The Apocryphal Literature: A Brief Introduction* (New Haven: Yale University Press, 1946), 10–11.

[11] The various pseudonyms used by Søren Kierkegaard (1813–55) fall into this category, as do the pseudonyms Currer, Ellis, and Acton Bell used by Charlotte, Emily, and Anne Brontë for the purpose of deflecting possible prejudice against female authors. During their lifetime, the Brontë sisters pseudonymously published between them one volume of selected poems and six novels.

[12] Some possible exceptions to this from antiquity include the apocryphal work of Tobit, the *Letter of Aristeas*, and Salvian's letter "From Timothy to All the Church." See discussion of each below.

[13] For discussion of both ancient and modern pseudonymity in general, see A. Taylor and F. Mosher, *The Bibliographical History of Anonyma and Pseudonyma* (Chicago: University of Chicago Press, 1951); S. Halkett and J. Laing, *Dictionary of Anonymous and Pseudonymous English Literature* (9 vols.; Edinburgh: Oliver and Boyd, 1926–62); and J. A. Farrer, *Literary Forgeries* (London: Longmans and Green, 1907).

[14] The Greek *pseudo* had a much wider sense than our English "lie." Its various meanings included simply to lie or to cheat by lies, to deceive, to beguile, to belie or contradict, to misrepresent, to say that which is untrue, to speak falsely or to falsify, to perjure or foreswear, and was also used to refer to the breaking of one's word or a promise, and to disappoint. The term had a less overtly negative sense in that it could characterize error or one who may have been sincerely mistaken in or about a thing such as an opinion or position. The passive verb and related forms could mean to be bilked, cheated, deceived, or disappointed, etc. More broadly, the term could apply to words such as "fiction" or "fictitious" and covered any statement describing events that may not have factually taken place. In this sense the word was applied to works of imagination or other genres including myth and allegory, parables and fables, or poetry and romance.

divergent views regarding what constitutes a "forgery," or as Metzger states, a lack of agreement on what differentiates literary fraud from innocent pseudonymous impersonation.[15] "A literary forgery," explains Metzger, "is essentially a piece of work created or modified with the intention to deceive. . . . In the case of genuine forgery (if this oxymoron may be permitted) the attribution must be made with the calculated attempt to deceive."[16] J. D. Deniston argues that, "with a true forgery the attribution must be made by the real author himself and there must be intention to deceive."[17] One of the broadest definitions of pseudonymity comes from M. Rist who, like Metzger and Deniston, emphasizes willful deceit:

> Pseudepigraphy, equivalent to pseudonymity, is the *false ascription* of a writing by one means or another to some one other than the actual author. This attribution, *designed to deceive,* is usually to some noted person, as a rule of the past, in order to borrow the authority and prestige which the real author does not himself possess, or it may be to some one whom we might consider to be legendary, or possibly to a divinity [italics added].[18]

Countering this position is J. C. Fenton who states, "A forger is one who writes in the name of another for his own profit: they [pseudonymous writers] did not do so. Forgery involves deceit for gain; pseudonymity did not."[19] K. Aland asserts that the almost insurmountable difficulties encountered by an author attempting to circulate a pseudonymous work into the public sphere and into a place of authority precludes against the association of deception with pseudonymity. However, we have numerous examples of this very thing taking place. In fact, the entire phenomenon of pseudonymous literature argues against such thinking. Aland's claim that pseudonymous works were initially composed and promoted openly by the author to his own community (i.e., the congregation understood that the pseudonymous address was written by its own member) is awkward since there would be little need to employ pseudonymity; the author's goals could be equally well accomplished without the use of it.[20] Adversely, if pseudonymity is the only means by which the

---

[15] Metzger, "Literary Forgeries," 21.

[16] Ibid., 4. Metzger adds that, "Accordingly, not all pseudepigrapha (that is works wrongly attributed to authors) are to be regarded as forgeries." He then clarifies this statement by excluding from the category of literary forgeries what he calls, "the copy made in good faith for purposes of study and the large class of writings that, in the course of their decent from antiquity, have become associated with the name of some great classical author or Father of the Church." These two exceptions, it will be argued, should not be viewed as pseudonymous in the strictest sense of the term.

[17] J. D. Deniston, "Forgeries, Literary," in *The Oxford Classical Dictionary* (ed. M. Cary, et al.; Oxford: Clarendon, 1949), 36.

[18] Rist, "Pseudepigraphy and the Early Christians," 75. Rist further allies pseudepigraphy with the use of a pen name *(nom de plume),* whereby a writer, in order to cloak his own identity, may use a fictitious name or alias. Ghost writing, or the practice by which a more or less noted person engages a writer to compose a speech, autobiography, or some other writing which he himself will present under his own name, according to Rist, is a reversal of pseudepigraphy.

[19] J. C. Fenton, "Pseudonymity in the New Testament," *Theology* 58 (1955): 55. Fenton's position is problematic in that some of the primary motives involved in the production of pseudonymous literature were, indeed, hope for personal profit or gain, whether this be financial or otherwise. The successful pseudonymous writer conceivably stood to gain more than simply financial benefit or monetary rewards.

[20] K. Aland, "The Problem of Anonymity and Pseudonymity in Christian Literature of the First Two Centuries," *JTS* 12 (1961): 43–44.

author can gain his desired ends, it follows that the recipients must be unaware of the device, for otherwise he might just as well issue the work under his own name.[21] D. Farkasfalvy more cautiously argues against any summary identification of pseudonymity with forgery by claiming that the concept of "apostolic authority" was not simply literary and historical, but also theological. As such, it was applied analogously to different cases of authorship, thereby allowing for the possibility of pseudepigraphy done in good faith. "What might be 'pseudepigraphic' and thus 'apostolic by false attribution' from a literary or historical point of view," explains Farkasfalvy, "might have been deemed genuinely apostolic (Pauline and Petrine) from a theological point of view by those who believed they were in possession of an oral tradition that the Church needed to have in written form."[22] Attempting to mediate between deception and forgery, as applied to pseudonymity, D. G. Meade states:

> The greater part of our revulsion to pseudonymity lies in its association with forgery, and as we have seen, this is manifestly not the case with the documents that we have considered. The consciousness of standing within an inspired stream of tradition, an attitude that can be traced back into Judaism nearly a thousand years before the New Testament, has effected an approach to literary attribution that is entirely foreign and highly appropriate to the modern mind. For this reason the moral objection to the deception of the recipients of the apostolic pseudepigrapha is mitigated by the realization that the pseudepigrapher really felt that he was a spokesman for the apostle.[23]

A number of scholars, including N. Brox and L. R. Donelson, have sought to justify the deceptive element inherent to pseudonymity by incorporating Plato's (ca. 427–347 B.C.E.) idea of the "noble lie." Plato rejects what he calls the "true falsehood," but with the understanding that deception may at times be beneficial to both citizen and country, he not only condones but commends the lie which brings good.[24] Other writers from antiquity posit similar ideas.[25] It is often argued that, in like manner, Christian writers

---

[21] D. Guthrie, *New Testament Introduction* (4th rev. ed.; Downers Grove, Ill.: InterVarsity, 1990), 1014.

[22] D. Farkasfalvy, "The Ecclesial Setting of Pseudepigraphy in Second Peter and its Role in the Formation of the Canon," *SecCent* 5 (1985–86): 29.

[23] Meade, *Pseudonymity and Canon*, 198–99, cf. 197. Meade's actual position is somewhat more confusing than this citation implies. While attempting to exonerate those involved in the production of pseudonymous literature from the charge of deception, he appears to admit that the intended recipients of pseudonymous works would, in all likelihood, view such an act as deceptive, regardless of the author's belief that he felt he was a spokesman for the apostle. Since he concedes that, "There is an overwhelming likelihood, therefore, that there is an element of 'deception' with all the pseudepigrapha . . . ," his efforts to separate the notion of deception from pseudonymity particularly at the authorial level seem perplexing. If the intended recipients of a pseudonymous work viewed such conventions as deceptive, it seems unlikely that those who produced this literature would remain oblivious to their audiences' negative perceptions. Therefore, some notion of the deceptive nature of pseudonymous literature would be held not only by the intended recipients, but also by those producing it.

[24] Plato, *Republic* 2.376E–3.392C; 3.414C–414E; 5.459D.

[25] Cicero, *Brutus* 9.42; Clement of Alexandria, *Strom.* 7.9; and Origen, *Cels.* 4.18–19. See also Donelson, *Pseudepigraphy and Ethical Argument*, 19; and N. Brox, *Falsche Verfasserangaben: Zur Erklärung der frühchristlichen Pseudepigraphie* (SBS 79; Stuttgart: Katholisches Bibelwerk, 1975), 83–84.

may have employed a literary device that, although likely to be deemed unacceptable if recognized, could provide direct apostolic sanction for the various doctrinal positions being presented—whether they be "orthodox" or "heterodox"—long after the apostles had passed on.[26]

It seems difficult to dismiss completely the idea of deception and forgery from the production of pseudonymous literature. Despite possible high ideals, "frauds are still fraudulent, even when perpetrated from noble motives. . . ."[27] An author writing under the guise of a pseudonym may have done so for some noble purpose—e.g., the desire to preserve and contemporize a great Master's teachings, or build upon and extend an "inspired" stream of tradition—but deceptive it was, nevertheless. The noble lie is still a lie.[28] Also difficult to substantiate is the idea that the religious interest of the author producing a pseudonymous work so deeply pervaded him that he was prepared to resort to a questionable means in order to attain his commendable end.[29]

A. The Limits of Pseudonymity

Rist identifies three general techniques of pseudonymity: textual alterations consisting of both interpolation and deletion of material; false attribution of an existing work; and false ascription within the work itself. He goes on to assert that:

> [S]ince no book was finally accepted into our present twenty-seven book Canon unless it was thought to have been by an apostle, or by one of their disciples, possibly about two-thirds of them are actually pseudonymous. . . . Accordingly, nine of the books, at most, are authentic. In my opinion the ascription by one means or another of the other eighteen to apostolic

---

[26] This point is articulated well in Donelson, *Pseudepigraphy and Ethical Argument*, 20.

[27] J. I. Packer, "Dr. Hebert on Pseudonymity in Scripture," in *"Fundamentalism" and the Word of God: Some Evangelical Principles* (Grand Rapids: Eerdmans, 1958), 184. See also Ellis, "Pseudonymity and Canonicity," 223.

[28] S. E. Porter, "Pauline Authorship and the Pastoral Epistles: Implications for Canon," *BBR* 5 (1995): 122. Despite Donelson's emphasis upon the noble lie, he too concedes that despite motive, the charge of deception against the forger cannot be removed. To believe oneself to be in accord with apostolic doctrine, or to be saying what an apostle would say if still alive, does not constitute believing oneself to be Paul or Peter. Donelson admits that, in all likelihood, different forgers held different attitudes toward this issue, some even believing their deceptions to be above reproach. Whatever their rationalizations, they were still consciously employing a lie which they knew was potentially damaging if discovered. See Donelson, *Pseudepigraphy and Ethical Argument*, 20 n. 62; and 55, respectively.

[29] That religious history does not substantiate this idea is noted by Guthrie, *New Testament Introduction*, 1019, who points out that the opposite appears to be true, for where the principle that "the end justifies the means" has been widely applied, as for instance in the Middle Ages, it has resulted in spiritual deterioration. See especially F. Torm, "Die Psychologie der Pseudonymität im Hinblick auf die Literatur des Urchristentums," in *Pseudepigraphie*, 123, who suggests that pseudonymous literature was produced because the pseudepigrapher believed that the end justified the means. Torm's work first appeared as *Die Psychologie der Pseudonymität im Hinblick auf die Literatur des Urchristentums* (Studien der Luther-Akademie, Heft 2; Gütersloh: Bertelsmann, 1932), 7–55, but was later included in Brox's edited collection of fifteen articles previously published between 1891 and 1973. Further citations of this work will be from the Brox reprint.

p is indeed dubious at best. This, alone, shows the influence of pseudepigraphy in church.[30]

on also acknowledges that eighteen of the twenty-seven books of the New ⌐re pseudepigraphal, allowing for only nine genuine works. He likewise concludes, "Whatever one's count on a question like that, the influence of pseudepigraphy in early Christianity was obviously enormous."[31] While the practice of pseudonymity may have been common in the early church, Rist's definition of the phenomenon and his three categories are overly broad. He has confused the issue by including scribal alterations as primary components of pseudonymity; he has incautiously equated the mistaken attribution of later readers and editors with an author's false ascription; he has erred in associating anonymity with pseudonymity; and lastly, by rejecting the authenticity of most New Testament works, Rist has also dismissed much sound historical scholarship.[32] Such confusion is endemic in discussions of pseudonymity, and by way of clarification the following considerations are offered.

First, and where possible to determine, the designation "pseudonymous" should be reserved for works containing *clear authorial ascriptions*. This excludes from the discussion all anonymous works.[33] Of the twenty-seven New Testament books, only eighteen contain clear authorial ascriptions.[34] Of these, only Ephesians, Colossians, 2 Thessalonians, 1–2 Timothy, Titus, and 1–2 Peter have been regularly considered pseudonymous. Anonymous New Testament works, that is works lacking any authorial ascription, include all four gospels—with evidence of their traditional attributions dating from the time of Papias (60–130 C.E.) and later—and Acts, Hebrews, and 1–3 John. Authorship claims in the Old Testament are more difficult to determine clearly due to the age of the literature and the obscurity of its compositional history, but authorial ascriptions or superscriptions are

---

[30] Rist, "Pseudepigraphy and the Early Christians," 89; for Rist's three general techniques of pseudonymity, 76.

[31] Donelson, *Pseudepigraphy and Ethical Argument*, 16. Scepticism regarding the authenticity of a large number of canonical books caused by assertions of pseudonymous authorship can be traced back at least as far as the "father" of the Tübingen school, F. C. Baur (1792–1860). See discussion below.

[32] For support of these criticisms, see Meade, *Pseudonymity and Canon*, 1; and Porter, "Pauline Authorship," 118. The support of Rist by Donelson (*Pseudepigraphy and Ethical Argument*, 16) is confusing since he too admits that of Rist's three categories, only the last one, that is the false attribution by the work itself, is pertinent. See also D. E. Aune, *Prophecy in Early Christianity* [Grand Rapids: Eerdmans, 1983], 110; Aune's categories of early Christian pseudepigraphal literature are, like Rist's, overly broad.

[33] For support of this distinction between pseudonymity and anonymity, see McDonald, *Christian Biblical Canon*, 288; Porter, "Pauline Authorship," 113; T. D. Lea, "The Early Christian View of Pseudepigraphic Writings," *JETS* 27 (1984): 66; Packer, "Pseudonymity in Scripture," 182; and less so Aland, "Anonymity and Pseudonymity," 41–43. See also Metzger, "Literary Forgeries," 19–20, who makes this same distinction yet appears to contradict it when he states that books such as Ecclesiastes and the Wisdom of Solomon, "are also pseudonymous—for, despite the absence of the name of Solomon within the body of either book, the total representation of authorship in both is intended to convey to the reader the assurance of Solomonic authorship."

[34] Rom 1:1; 1 Cor 1:1–2; 16:21; 2 Cor 1:1; 10:1; Gal 1:1; Eph 1:1; 3:1; Phil 1:1; Col 1:1; 4:18; 1 Thess 1:1; 2:18; 2 Thess 1:1; 3:17; 1 Tim 1:1; 2 Tim 1:1; Tit 1:1; Phlm 1, 19; Jas 1:1; 1 Pet 1:1; 2 Pet 1:1; Jude 1; Rev 1:1, 4, 9; 22:8.

found in the Psalms *(multi),* Proverbs (1:1; 10:1; 25:1; *multi),* Song of Songs (1:1), Isaiah (1:1; 2:1; 13:1), Jeremiah (1:1–3), Ezekiel (1:1–3), Daniel (7:2, 4, 6, 28; 8:1, 15; 9:2; 10:2; cf. 12:4), and in the opening verses of all the Minor Prophets excluding Jonah, which is anonymous. Additional anonymous Old Testament writings include the five books of the Pentateuch, Joshua, Judges, Ruth, 1–2 Samuel, 1–2 Kings, 1–2 Chronicles, Ezra-Nehemiah, Esther, Job, Ecclesiastes, and Lamentations. Psalms, Proverbs, Ecclesiastes, Song of Songs, Isaiah, and Daniel have at times been labeled pseudonymous.[35]

Second, and where possible to determine, authorial ascriptions that are deemed to have been *intentionally or deliberately made by the producer of the literature* in question are to be preferred for designation as pseudonymous. Thus, for a work to be considered pseudonymous, its authorial ascription should ideally be regarded as original to the said text or literary "autograph" (primary pseudonymity), as opposed to a later scribal alteration, interpolation, or mistaken attribution (secondary pseudonymity).

Third, and where possible to determine, authorial ascriptions that are deemed to have been made by the actual author of the work in question with *the calculated attempt to conceal his true identity by deliberately endorsing a false author as the real author* are to be preferred for designation as pseudonymous.[36] This last category might be further broken into (a) *Malicious or Self-serving Motives* (where deception is paramount) such as financial

---

[35] Any discussion concerning Old Testament authorship and the issue of pseudonymity is complicated by the difficulty in determining if the authorial ascriptions or superscriptions are original to the text or later interpolations or misattributions. If considered original, are they third person or first person designations of authorship? See discussion below concerning scribal alteration and misattribution. Many psalm titles contain the names of specific individuals, including David (approximately seventy-three times), Asaph (twelve times), the sons of Korah (eleven times), Jeduthun (four times), Solomon (two times), and Heman, Etan, and Moses (one time each). There is considerable difficulty in determining if these titles are authentic and if their true purpose is to designate authorship. Despite the Solomonic ascriptions (1:1; 10:1; 25:1), the book of Proverbs is really an anthology of compositions that ascribes authorship to "the wise" (22:17, 24:23), Agur (30:1), and King Lemuel (31:1) as well. Only Prov 1:8–9:18 and 31:10–31 lack explicit authorial attribution. The book of Daniel has no introductory authorial ascription or superscription, but clear attribution is made to Daniel by use of the first person singular (7:2, 4, 6, 28; 8:1, 15; 9:2; 10:2). General internal allusions to Mosaic authorship occur within the Pentateuch, but strictly speaking, these works are anonymous. Likewise anonymous is the book of Ecclesiastes, however the title "Qohelet," meaning literally "assembler," is considered by some to be the actual author's pseudonym. See the discussion below concerning pseudonymity in Jewish antiquity.

[36] Despite the problems inherent in separating primary and secondary pseudonymity, and although not all will agree with such a distinction, it has been purposely emphasized here. While it is tenable to designate later textual alterations and misattributions as techniques of pseudonymity, such a move tends to confuse the issue by increasing to the point of banality the body of literature deemed pseudonymous. In view of modern scholarship's proclivity for applying a wide range of interpolative and composite theories to most ancient literature, much of this material could be technically but unhelpfully deemed pseudonymous. An overemphasis upon secondary pseudonymity turns attention away from the constructive discussion of authorial ascription to the more conjectural matter of compositional theory. For support of the distinction between pseudonymity and misattribution, see Metzger, "Literary Forgeries," 4, 19–20; Ellis, "Pseudonymity and Canonicity," 212; and T. D. Lea, "Pseudonymity and the New Testament," in *New Testament Criticism and Interpretation* (ed. D. A. Black and D. S. Dockery; Grand Rapids: Zondervan, 1991), 535, 553; *contra* Rist, "Pseudepigraphy and the Early Christians," 76.

interests, promotion of ideas, or the slander of one's enemies; and (b) *Pure or Pietistic Motives* (where deception may be secondary) such as personal modesty, or love and respect for the attributed personage.[37]

B. Motives for the Production of Pseudonymous Literature

Inquiries into an author's intentions and motives are fraught with hermeneutical and philosophical difficulties. Pseudonymous authorship complicates the issue even further, since those individuals involved in the production of such literature are generally more purposeful in their attempts to disguise their personal motivations. Since one benefit of writing is the personal recognition that comes with the circulation of a work, one wonders about an author's purpose for hiding his true identity. The possible motivations underlying false attribution, however, prove to be so diverse that the mere presence of the literary device tells us little about the particular author's motives.[38] Nevertheless, scholarly investigations into the problem of pseudonymity must concern themselves with motivation as much as with issues of deceit and forgery. The diversity of these documents cautions against any wholesale explanation of the literary device, and encourages the careful examination of each individual pseudonymous work.[39] While the reasons behind the production of pseudonymous literature are as numerous and diverse as the individual documents, the following list, not intended to be exhaustive, enumerates some of the most important motives.[40]

1. For financial gain.

2. To malign, discredit, or defame opponents or enemies.

---

[37] Scholars have suggested a further category for Neutral Motives (where deception is more or less irrelevant), such as artistic and dramatic expression, or educational, literary, and rhetorical exercise. Such works do involve intentional or deliberate ascription to a false author. However, having further defined pseudonymity as the author's calculated attempt to conceal his true identity by deliberately endorsing a false author as the real author, a quality that is at least philosophically absent from this type of literature, the designation of pseudonymity does not truly apply here, and validates distinctions between what might be called "innocent" and "deceptive" pseudonymity. See Ellis "Pseudonymity and Canonicity," 212; Metzger, "Literary Forgeries," 4; Speyer, "Religiöse Pseudepigraphie," 195–263; and idem, "Fälschung, pseudepigraphische freie Erfindung und 'echte religiöse Pseudepigraphie,'" in *Pseudepigrapha I: Pseudopythagorica—Letters de Platon, Litterature pseudépigraphe juive* (ed. K. von Fritz; Entretiens sur l'antiquité classique 18; Vandoeuvres-Genève: Fondation Hardt, 1972), 333–66.

[38] Donelson, *Pseudepigraphy and Ethical Argument*, 16.

[39] Metzger, "Literary Forgeries," 19; and Guthrie, *New Testament Introduction*, 1019, 1020–21; *contra* E. J. Goodspeed, *New Chapters in New Testament Study* (New York: Macmillan, 1937), 172, who cautions against the study of isolated works. Instead, he asserts, the texts in question must be studied together from the point of view of their pseudonymous character.

[40] See also Gudemann, "Literary Frauds," *passim*; J. A. Sint, *Pseudonymität im Altertum; Ihre Formen und ihre Gründe* (Innsbruck: Universitätsverlag Wagner, 1960), 25–67; W. Speyer, *Die literarische Fälschung im heidnischen und christlichen Altertum: Ein Versuch ihrer Deutung* (Handbuch der Altertumswissenschaft, vol. 1, pt. 2; Munich: C. H. Beck, 1971), *passim*; R. Syme, "Fraud and Imposture," in *Pseudepigrapha I*, 1–21; Torm, "Psychologie der Pseudonymität," 111–40; and Metzger, "Literary Forgeries," 5–12.

3. To guard or preserve traditions or doctrines.

4. To express admiration for attributed author.

5. To express author's belief that he is extending teachings of ascribed author.

6. To express author's belief that he has received visionary sanction or been filled with the Holy Spirit.

7. Out of personal modesty.

8. As an aspect of artistic or dramatic composition.

9. As an educational, literary, or rhetorical exercise.

10. To invoke the reputation of an important figure of antiquity for various reasons, including the desire to secure greater prestige and credence for teaching or doctrine.

11. To create distance from or hide true authorship for various reasons including fear and need to maintain anonymity.

12. To provide earlier attestation for contemporary requirements.

3. Pseudonymity in the Ancient World

Despite the commonly held assumption that Christian writers shared the same literary outlook as their non-Christian contemporaries, the actual influences leading to the production of Christian pseudepigrapha are hard to pin down.[41] Some scholars assert that Greco-Roman literary practice provided the primary background for the production of Christian pseudepigrapha, while others emphasize the influence of Jewish apocryphal and pseudepigraphic writings.[42] A further difficulty lies in the nature, scope, and interpretation of the external historical evidence.

---

[41] The assumption that Christian writers shared the same perspectives as their contemporaries is questioned by D. Guthrie, "The Development of the Idea of Canonical Pseudepigrapha in New Testament Criticism," in *The Authorship and Integrity of the New Testament* (SPCK Theological Collections 4; ed. K. Aland; London: SPCK, 1965), 26; originally published in *Vox Evangelica* 1 [1962]: 43–59. All following citations are from the Aland reprint. Other individuals such as Meade (*Pseudonymity and Canon*, 10); Lea ("Early Christian View," 67; idem, "Pseudonymity and the New Testament," 536–37), and again Guthrie (*New Testament Introduction*, 1017) are correct in cautioning against uncritically accepting the position that a Christian writer would be prone to adopt pseudonymity, or perhaps more precisely to view it as an acceptable literary device, simply because of the numerous examples found in the ancient world.

[42] Whereas Donelson (*Pseudepigraphy and Ethical Argument*, 13–15, n. 37, 25) and M. Kiley (*Colossians as Pseudepigraphy* [Sheffield: JSOT Press, 1986], 23, 25, 35) emphasize Greco-Roman influence upon the production of Christian pseudepigrapha, the importance of Jewish literary practice figures large in Guthrie, "Idea of Canonical Pseudepigrapha," 25; idem, *New Testament Introduction*, 1011–15; Meade, *Pseudonymity and Canon*, 15, 44, 194, 198–99, 201; Speyer, *Die literarische Fälschung*, 150–70; Brox, *Falsche Verfasserangaben*, 41–45; M. Smith, "Pseudepigraphy in the Israelite Literary Tradition," in *Pseudepigrapha I*, 191–215; and A. Meyer, "Religiöse Pseudepigraphie als ethisch-psychologisches Problem," in *Pseudepigraphie*, 90–110; originally published in *ZNW* 35 (1936): 262–79.

A. Pseudonymity in Greco-Roman Antiquity

Pseudonymity was a widespread literary practice in Greco-Roman antiquity, as attested by a voluminous body of surviving documentary evidence. Consider the celebrated Greek philosopher Pythagoras (ca. 582–507 B.C.E.) who was held in such high esteem that, despite not leaving behind any personal writings, many years after his death admiring disciples known as the Pythagoreans produced a large body of literature and attributed it to his name. Olympiodorus of Alexandria (sixth century C.E.) cites three motives leading to the production of pseudonymous literature, including the desire for renown of rulers, the goodwill of disciples, and the similarity of names. He attributes the production of the Pythagorean corpus to the goodwill of later disciples.[43] The Syrian mystic Iamblichus (ca. 250–325 C.E.) speaks well of this literature and commends the humility of the Pythagoreans, claiming that it was honorable and praiseworthy not to ascribe to themselves the glory of their works by publishing their philosophical treatises under the name of such a respected teacher.[44] Along with the Pythagoreans, other philosophical schools such as the Cynics, Platonists, and Aristotelians created similar pseudonymous canons, spurred on by admiration for their progenitors and the desire to preserve their memory and propagate their teachings.[45] In his *Lives of the Sophists,* Philostratus (ca. 170–245 C.E.) appeals to rhythm and style to counter those who wrongly ascribe to the rhetorician Dionysius (fl. ca. 25 B.C.E.) a work entitled "The Lover of Panthea," but he also cites writings ascribed to the Roman emperor Marcus Aurelius (121–180 C.E.) as leading examples of the rhetorical letter, appearing to commend the authentic and pseudonymous alike.[46]

In contrast, the Roman historian Livy (59 B.C.E.–17 C.E.) tells of the burning of a spurious collection of works attributed to the legendary king of Rome and successor of Romulus, Numa Pompilius, thus indicating that at least in some circles, pseudonymity was

---

[43] Olympiodorus, *Olympiodori Prolegomena et in Categorias commentarium* §1.13 (Commentaria in Aristotelem Graeca 12; ed. A. Busse; Berlin: Reimer, 1902), 13. Cited in Kiley (*Colossians as Pseudepigraphy,* 22–23); and C. Müller, "Die neuplatonischen Aristoteleskommentatoren über die Ursachen der Pseudepigraphie," in *Pseudepigraphie,* 266–68 and n. 9; originally published in *Rheinisches Museum für Philologie* 112 (1969), 120–26.

[44] Iamblichus, *De vita Pythagorica* §§158, 198 (ed. L. Deubner; Leipzig: B. G. Teubner, 1937), 108, 4–7. Cited in Metzger, "Literary Forgeries," 7, and Donelson, *Pseudepigraphy and Ethical Argument,* 10 and n. 9. For works dealing with the Pythagorean literature specifically, see H. Thesleff, "On the Problem of the Doric Pseudo-Pythagorica," in *Pseudepigrapha I,* 59–87.

[45] For discussions of authenticity in relation to this various literature, on the Cynics, see A. J. Malherbe, ed., *The Cynic Epistles* (SBLSBS 12; Missoula, Mont.: Scholars, 1977); on the Platonists, see J. Harward, *The Platonic Epistles* (Cambridge: Cambridge University Press, 1932); and N. Gulley, "The Authenticity of the Platonic Epistles," in *Pseudepigrapha I,* 105–30; and on the Aristotelians, see C. B. Schmitt and D. Knox, *Pseudo-Aristoteles Latinus: A Guide to Latin Works Falsely Attributed to Aristotle Before 1500* (Warburg Institute Surveys and Texts 12; London: Warburg Institute/University of London, 1985).

[46] On Dionysius, see Philostratus, *Lives of the Sophists* (LCL, rev. ed.; trans. W. C. Wright; Cambridge: Harvard University Press, 1952), 95. Cited by R. Hercher, *Epistolographi graeci, recensuit recognovit adnotatione critica et indicibus instruxit* (Scriptorum graecorum bibliotheca 47; Paris: Didot, 1873), 14; and Kiley, *Colossians as Pseudepigraphy,* 18.

[47] Livy, *Ab urbe condita* 40.29 (trans. J. C. Yardley; Oxford: Oxford University Press, 2000). Cited in Torm, "Psychologie der Pseudonymität," 118, n. 3; and Kiley, *Colossians as Pseudepigraphy,* 18.

met with disdain.[47] Pseudonymity could also be used to defame an opponent: Diotimus the Stoic produced fifty letters of obscene content under the name of Epicurus (341–270 B.C.E.), thus tarnishing his character.[48] Similarly, Anaximenes of Lampsacus successfully undermined the reputation of the historian and sophist Theopompus of Chios (b. ca. 380 B.C.E.) by composing under the latter's name a treatise slandering the three Greek cities of Athens, Thebes, and Sparta. Anaximenes then sent the work to each city, and hatred for Theopompus grew throughout Greece.[49] The financial remunerations offered to those who could provide the great libraries at Alexandria (founded by Ptolemy Philadelphus 283–46 B.C.E.) and Pergamum (founded by Eumenes II 197–159 B.C.E.) with the works of eminent authors provided more than enough incentive for an enterprising individual to produce pseudonymous literature, as the famous second-century physician Galen (ca. 129–199 C.E.) attests.[50] Galen disapprovingly commented upon the spurious production of Hippocratic texts, asserting that of the sixty or eighty works he knew of only thirteen were authentic. In order to counter the production and sale of writings falsely attributed to himself, Galen produced a work entitled *On His Own Books*.[51]

The minor poems entitled "Culex," "Dirae," "Lydia," "Moretum," "Copa," "Priapeia," and "Catalepton," subsumed under the title *Appendix Vergiliana*, are generally discredited as authentic works of the Roman poet Virgil (70–19 B.C.E.).[52] The *Sibylline Oracles*, a fourteen-book collection of assorted Greco-Roman and Jewish pseudepigrapha with clear Christian interpolations, dating from the second century B.C.E. to the seventh century C.E., are ascribed throughout to the legendary "sibyls," aged women who uttered divine prophesies.[53] Similar heterogeneous corpora of pseudonymous literature include the numerous poems ascribed to the legendary pre-Homeric poet Orpheus; the 148 epistles attributed to Phalaris, the sixth-century B.C.E. tyrant of Acragas; and many of the over one hundred works ascribed to the Syrian satirist Lucian of Samosata (ca. 115–200 C.E.).[54] While further examples could be

---

[48] See Diogenes Laertius (200–250 C.E.) *Lives of Eminent Philosophers* (LCL; 2 vols.; trans. R. D. Hicks; Cambridge: Harvard University Press, 1958) II, 531. Cited in Kiley, *Colossians as Pseudepigraphy*, 20.

[49] See Pausanias (ca. 115–180 C.E.), *Descriptions of Greece* 6.18.2ff. (LCL; trans. W. H. S. Jones; Cambridge: Harvard University Press, 1933) III, 109. Cf. Josephus *C. Ap.* 1.24 §221, who also refers to the incident but appears to be ignorant of Theopompus's innocence. Cited in Gudemann, "Literary Frauds," 67; Metzger, "Literary Forgeries," 6–7; and Kiley, *Colossians as Pseudepigraphy*, 20–21.

[50] Galen, *In Hippoc. de nat. hominis.* 1.42, (Medicorum graecorum opera quae exstant 15; ed. K. G. Kuhn; Leipzig: C. Cnobloch, 1828), col. 105. Cited in Speyer, *Die literarische Fälschung*, 133–34; Gudemann, "Literary Frauds," 56, 73–74; Metzger, "Literary Forgeries," 5–6 and n. 5; and Kiley, *Colossians as Pseudepigraphy*, 20.

[51] Galen, *On His Own Books* (Claudii Galeni Pergameni Scripta minora 2; ed. J. Marquardt, I. Müller, and G. Helmreich; Leipzig: B. G. Teubner, 1891), 91–124. Cited in Metzger, "Literary Forgeries," 6; and Kiley, *Colossians as Pseudepigraphy*, 18. See *Pseudepigraphic Writings: Hippocrates* (ed. W. D. Smith; Leiden: Brill, 1990).

[52] See *Appendix Vergiliana* (ed. W. V. Clausen et al.; Oxford: Clarendon, 1966).

[53] See J. J. Collins, *The Sibylline Oracles of Egyptian Judaism* (SBLDS 13; Missoula, Mont.: Scholars, 1974); and idem, "Sibylline Oracles," in *The Old Testament Pseudepigrapha* (2 vols.; ed. J. H. Charlesworth; Garden City, N.Y.: Doubleday, 1983–85), 1:317–472. For brief but helpful discussions pertaining to pseudonymity and the *Sibylline Oracles*, see Rist, "Pseudepigraphy and the Early Christians," 80–82; and Metzger, "Literary Forgeries," 12.

[54] See here Sint, *Pseudonymität im Altertum*, 25–67. On the epistles of Phalaris, see Richard Bentley's (1662–1742) famous study entitled *A Dissertation upon the Epistles of Phalaris: With an*

cited, these suffice to show the difficulty of devising a comprehensive hypothesis whereby all questions pertaining to the production of pseudonymous literature might be answered. What emerges clearly is the widespread use of pseudonymity in Greco-Roman antiquity, a literary practice well-regarded by some but held in contempt by others.[55]

B. Pseudonymity in Jewish Antiquity

Ancient Judaism, like Greco-Roman antiquity, gave birth to a considerable body of pseudonymous literature. As already discussed, among the canonical books of the Old Testament, works such as Psalms, Proverbs, Ecclesiastes, Song of Songs, Isaiah, and Daniel have at times been identified as pseudonymous.[56] The fifteen books that make up the Old Testament apocrypha include examples of historical, romantic, didactic, devotional, and apocalyptic literature. Authorial ascriptions occur in 2 Esdras (1:1–3), Tobit (1:1–2), Ecclesiasticus (50:27), and Baruch (1:1–2). Authorial ascriptions are less obvious in the Wisdom of Solomon, the Epistle of Jeremiah, and the Prayer of Manasseh. First Esdras, Judith, and 1–2 Maccabees are essentially anonymous.[57] The three principle additions to the book of Daniel, including the Prayer of Azariah and the Song of the Three Children, Susanna, and Bel and the Dragon, as well as the Additions to Esther, are fitting examples of secondary pseudonymity.[58] A number of these writings were produced by persons whose

---

Answer to the Objections of the Honourable Charles Boyle, Esquire (London: Printed by J. H. for Henry Mortlock and John Hartley, 1699), where the authenticity of these works is disproved.

[55] For more extensive surveys of pseudonymous Greco-Roman literature, see Metzger, "Literary Forgeries," *passim;* Kiley, *Colossians as Pseudepigraphy,* 17–35; and Speyer, *Die literarische Fälschung, passim.*

[56] Of these, Psalms, Proverbs, Song of Songs, and Daniel serve as possible examples of primary pseudonymity. A number of the Psalms directly ascribed to David (cf. Ps 30 and 69) appear to describe events occurring after his time. Many have rejected Solomonic authorship of both Proverbs (cf. Prov 1:1; 10:1; and 25:1) and the Song of Songs (cf. Song 1:1) appealing to language and other issues as proof of a later date. While Daniel is referred to as the author of the book of Daniel (cf. Dan 7:2, 4, 6, 28; 8:1, 15; 9:2; and 10:2, where the first person singular is used, and 12:4, where Daniel is told to "seal up the book"), it is often regarded as a second-century B.C.E. pseudonymous work that employs *vaticinium ex eventu.* Possible examples of secondary pseudonymity include Isaiah, on the grounds of its later additions, and Ecclesiastes, on the grounds of its later misattribution by Pharisaic Judaism. In fact, if one emphasizes secondary pseudonymity, most of the books of the Old Testament, or at least portions thereof, can be technically regarded as pseudonymous.

[57] B. M. Metzger, *An Introduction to the Apocrypha* (New York: Oxford University Press, 1957), 3–4. Some editions of the Bible place the Epistle of Jeremiah as the final chapter of Baruch, thus constituting fourteen rather than fifteen books of the apocrypha.

[58] The difficulty in distinguishing between primary and secondary pseudonymity is well illustrated when referring to works of the Old Testament apocrypha. While Solomon is indirectly referred to as the author of the Wisdom of Solomon (7:1–14; 8:17–9:18), no direct authorial ascription occurs in the text. Cf. Porter, "Pauline Authorship," 116 and n. 39, who denies that the work is pseudonymous; *contra* Metzger, "Literary Forgeries," 20. The superscription of the epistle to Jeremiah, which is evidently not original to the text, claims that the work was written by the prophet Jeremiah, but the prophet's name never occurs in the Epistle itself. Cf. W. O. E. Oesterley, *An Introduction to the Books of the Apocrypha* (London: SPCK, 1958), 268, who argues against its pseudonymity; *contra* Guthrie, *New Testament Introduction,* 1012–14. Similar considerations apply to the Prayer of Manasseh. On the distinction between primary and secondary pseudonymity in relation to authorial ascription and textual interpolation, see Porter, "Pauline Authorship," 116–17

real identity has long been lost, or who perhaps wrote under an invented pseudonym (e.g., Tobit). Others used the names of known figures from Israel's past (e.g., Baruch).

The nearly seventy writings of the Old Testament pseudepigrapha range in date from the seventh or sixth century B.C.E. (i.e., *Ahiqar*) to the ninth century C.E. (i.e., *Apocalypse of Daniel*), and were composed by both Jews and Christians. This variegated collection includes apocalyptic literature, testaments, Old Testament expansions, wisdom and philosophical literature, poetic literature including prayers, psalms, and odes, and lastly fragments.[59] Some of these diverse works are most likely ascribed to their actual authors: Philo the Epic Poet, Theodotus, Ezekiel the Tragedian, Eupolemus, Cleodemus Malchus, and the first fragment of Pseudo-Hecataeus. However, the traditional appellation "pseudepigrapha" accurately describes much of this corpus. In addition to the *Sibylline Oracles*, which have already been discussed, specific mention might also be made of a number of other works coming from this collection. The book of *Enoch*, also called the *Ethiopic Apocalypse of Enoch* to distinguish it from several other works bearing the same name, is clearly ascribed (1:1–3) to the Hebrew patriarch Enoch who was assumed bodily into heaven (Gen 5:24). It was written between 200 B.C.E. and 50 C.E., and exists in complete form only in Ethiopic.[60] The *Letter of Aristeas,* written in Greek and addressed to one "brother Philocrates," purports to be an eyewitness account of the translation of the Septuagint from an otherwise unknown court officer named Aristeas (§19, 40, 43) who served under Ptolemy II Philadelphus (285–245 B.C.E.). As such, it constitutes one of the few examples from antiquity of an invented rather than borrowed pseudonym. Several historical anomalies betray the author's attempt to situate it in a much earlier setting. While some core of historical truth may lie behind *Aristeas,* the work was likely produced between 130–70 B.C.E., with further interpolations as late as the first century C.E.[61] The name of the Greek gnomic poet and bard Phocylides is attached to a poetic treatise on wisdom consisting of 230 verses. Phocylides lived in Miletus in Ionia in the middle of the sixth century B.C.E., and was regarded as a great authority concerning ethical matters. The author, a Diaspora Jew, skillfully attempts to antiquate the poem by writing in the old Ionic dialect. But he occasionally betrays himself with Hellenistic or early Imperial period vocabulary, meter, and

---

and n. 39. On the pseudonymity of Susanna, see the letter of Julius Africanus (ca. 160–240 C.E.) to Origen *(Ep. Afr.)* which argues that the work is a "more modern forgery," and Origen's response *(Ep. Afr.* 1), which maintains its authenticity.

[59] Evans, *Noncanonical Writings,* 23–44, and J. H. Charlesworth, "Pseudepigrapha," in *Harper's Bible Dictionary* (ed. P. J. Achtemeier; San Francisco: Harper and Row, 1985), 836–40. With the discovery of the Qumran scrolls, close to fifty more apocryphal and pseudepigraphal writings have come to light.

[60] The standard English edition is R. H. Charles's translation with an introduction by W. O. E. Oesterley, *The Book of Enoch* (London: SPCK, 1917). See also Tertullian (160–220 C.E.) *Cult. fem.* 1.3; some had argued that the book of *Enoch* must be spurious, for an antediluvian work is unlikely to have survived the flood. Tertullian counters that Noah, as the great grandson of Enoch, would likely have preserved the tradition.

[61] Eusebius extracts about a quarter of the letter, and Josephus paraphrases about two-fifths of it; Eusebius, *Praep. ev.* 8.2–5, 9; 9.38; and Josephus, *Ant.* 12.2.1 §11–12.2.15. §118. For text and discussion of the Letter of Aristeas, see H. B. Swete, *An Introduction to the Old Testament in Greek* (rev. R. R. Ottley; Cambridge: Cambridge University Press, 1914), 531–606; H. Thackeray, *The Letter of Aristeas* (London: SPCK, 1917); and M. Hadas, *Aristeas to Philocrates* (JAL; New York: Harper, 1951).

syntax, and influences from the Old Testament, Septuagint, and Stoicism. Consequently, the date of compilation of Pseudo-Phocylides likely falls between 200 B.C.E. and 150 C.E.[62]

C. Pseudonymity in Christian Antiquity

Since there is little evidence to suggest that Christian writers of pseudepigrapha had motives significantly different from their Greco-Roman or Jewish counterparts, and since Greco-Roman, Jewish, and Christian antiquity could point to authoritative examples of the practice from the time-honored past, it is not surprising that the history of early Christian literature is full of examples of pseudonymity—both orthodox and heretical.[63] However, in the early church notions of orthodoxy and heresy color the issue; the question of *pseudonymity* frequently becomes the question of *pseudo-apostolicity*. In other words, discussions of pseudonymity in Christianity are to some extent unique in that they are regularly bound to concerns over apostolic authorship and orthodox content as *criteria* of literary authenticity.

One of the earliest known references to Christian pseudepigrapha may be 2 Thess 2:1–2 where, if this letter itself is regarded as authentic, Paul admonishes his readers "not to be quickly shaken in mind or alarmed, either by spirit or by word or by letter, as though from us, to the effect that the day of the Lord is already here." He then seemingly authenticates this work by taking pen in hand and applying his own distinctive signature (3:17).[64] One of the most frequently cited cases of pseudonymity in early Christianity comes from Tertullian (ca. 160–220 C.E.), who has harsh words for the Asiatic presbyter apparently caught trying to pass off his own work (entitled the *Acts of Paul,* which included the *Acts of Paul and Thecla*) as authentically Pauline. Despite the author's claim that he had done it "for the love of Paul," he was disposed of his office. Whether judgment fell upon the presbyter for his attempt at forgery or for his alleged audacity in allowing a woman to teach and baptize is a matter of debate.[65] However, Tertullian also states, "[The Gospel] which

---

[62] While only a few genuine lines of Phocylides's poetry survive, numerous individuals from antiquity mention him, including Plato, *Republic* 3.407A–407B; and Aristotle, *Polit.* 4.11.1295b34. On Pseudo-Phocylides in general, see B. S. Easton, "Pseudo-Phocylides," *ATR* 14 (1932): 222–28; P. W. van der Horst, *The Sentences of Pseudo-Phocylides* (SVTP 4; Leiden: Brill, 1978); idem, "Pseudo-Phocylides Revisited," *JSP* 3 (1988): 3–30; and J. J. Collins, *Jewish Wisdom in the Hellenistic Age* (Louisville, Ky.: Westminster John Knox, 1997), 158–77.

[63] Brox, *Falsche Verfasserangaben,* 107; and Rist, "Pseudepigraphy and the Early Christians," 91.

[64] Cf. 1 Cor 16:21, Gal 6:11, Col 4:18, 2 Thess 3:17, and Phlm 19. The actual meaning of the passage is somewhat unclear. The phrase *mēte di' epistolēs hōs di' hēmōn* could be taken to mean either a lost letter from Paul or a forged letter claiming to be by Paul. Meade (*Pseudonymity and Canon,* 205) asserts that Paul was condemning pseudonymity in the service of heresy; the passage does not necessarily condemn pseudonymity per se.

[65] Tertullian, *Bapt.* 17. Despite repeated claims that this work was published under Paul's name, Schneemelcher (*New Testament Apocrypha,* 2:30, 215) firmly asserts that the *Acts of Paul and Thecla* is actually an anonymous romance and therefore cannot be considered pseudonymous. Both F. F. Bruce (*The Canon of Scripture* [Glasgow: Chapter House, 1988], 261) and C. F. D. Moule (*The Birth of the New Testament* [3d ed.; London: Adam and Charles Black, 1981], 248–49) concur. If true, it would seem that the presbyter was chastised for advocating a questionable position regarding women in the church. Origen (*Comm. Joh.* 20.12) knows the work and appears to speak approvingly of it.

Mark published may be affirmed to be Peter's whose interpreter Mark was. For even Luke's form of the Gospel men usually ascribe to Paul. And it may well seem that the works which disciples publish belong to their masters."[66] His remarks echo the views of Iamblichus who, as we have already seen, commended the pseudonymous literature produced by the disciples of Pythagoras.

Of equal importance to the discussion of pseudonymity in early Christianity is the account of Serapion, Bishop of Antioch (d. 211 C.E.), cited by Eusebius (ca. 265–339 C.E.). The bishop initially approved the *Gospel of Peter* for use in the church at Rhossus (a small town in Cilicia), but subsequently discovered that it included a number of heretical docetic teachings. He therefore cautioned them and promised to visit them immediately to resolve the matter. Once again, it is unclear whether Serapion's concern was evoked by the gospel's false authorship or its heretical teachings.[67]

Light is shed upon the possible motives for the production of pseudonymous writings, and how early Christianity reacted towards them, by Salvian of Marseilles (ca. 400–480 C.E.). In his ninth epistle, he defends a certain work that circulated under the title "From Timothy to all the Church." Upon examining the document, Salvian's bishop Salonius deduced that the work had originated from him and called for an account of its production. Without acknowledging that he was the author of the letter, Salvian attempts to explain the "unknown" author's motives for writing under a pseudonym:

> First, there is the reason that derives from the mandate of God, by whom we are ordered to avoid the vanity of worldly glory in all things lest, while we seek a little breath of human praise, we lose a heavenly reward. Consequently, God wishes us to offer prayers and gifts to Him in secret. He orders us to commend in secret the fruit of good work, because there is no greater devotion to faith than that which avoids the knowledge of men and is content with God as its witness. Our Saviour says: Let not your left hand know what your right hand is doing, and your Father who sees in secret will reward you. . . . The writer must confess that he himself is humble in his own estimation. He thinks he is the least and the last, and what is more important, he thinks in this manner in pure faith, not by the means of an assumed humility, but by the truth of honest judgement.[68]

If the motive of humility is not enough to allay Salonius's reservations, Salvian tries a different tact:

> Indeed, so weak are the judgements of our day and almost so meaningless that they who read do not consider so much what they read as whom they read, nor so much the force and strength of what is said as the reputation of him who speaks. For this reason, the writer wished to be completely hidden and to keep out of the way, lest writings which contained

---

[66] *Marc.* 4.5. However, see Meade, *Pseudonymity and Canon*, 10; and Lea, "Pseudonymity and the New Testament," 535.

[67] Eusebius, *Hist. eccl.* 6.12.3–6. Those who claim that Serapion was concerned about the letter's heretical content rather than its non-apostolic authorship see his questioning of the gospel's false ascription as a secondary issue, tacked on to help justify the decision he had already reached on grounds of content. Contrariwise, advocates of authorship rather than content see Serapion's questioning of the gospel's non-apostolic origin as the primary reason for its rejection and downplay the work's heretical nature as secondary.

[68] J. O'Sullivan, *The Writings of Salvian the Presbyter* (New York: Cima, 1947), 260–61. See also A. E. Haefner, "A Unique Source for the Study of Ancient Pseudonymity," *ATR* 16 (1934): 8–15.

much helpfulness should lose their force through the name of the author. This is the reason for anyone who inquires why the author assumed another's name.[69]

In case Salonius should yet remain unsatisfied by this explanation, Salvian asserts that the name of "Timothy" was chosen simply because it meant "the honor of God," not for the purpose of invoking the authority of the apostolic namesake.[70]

The Muratorian Canon was named after its discovery by Lodovico Antonio Muratori in 1738–40. Only one certain conclusion can be drawn from it: antiquity was occasionally able to detect pseudonymous writings.[71] The Muratorianum has been used to support the church's rejection of known pseudonymous works (lines 64–66, *Epistle to the Laodiceans* and *Epistle to the Alexandrians*); its acceptance of known pseudonymous works (lines 69–72, book of Wisdom and *Apocalypse of Peter*); the importance of apostolicity (lines 73–80, *Shepherd of Hermas*); and the importance of orthodoxy (lines 65–67, heresy of Marcion, and gall mixed with honey).[72]

That Eusebius was well aware of pseudonymous works is evident from his list of acknowledged, disputed, and spurious writings.[73] Eusebius acknowledges the role of ecclesiastical tradition in the validation of Christian books, but he attaches more importance to orthodoxy, declaring that spurious works betray a style, thought, and purpose so at variance with apostolic usage that their heretical origins are obvious. It is difficult to take that Eusebius's use of the term "fictions" (or forgeries) in this context could mean anything other than unorthodox content. The spurious nature of these writings is due not to their non-apostolic authorship, but rather their heterodoxy.

The *Apostolic Constitutions,* although attributed to the apostles, is likely a third-century work. While itself pseudonymous, in a manner analogous to 2 Thessalonians, it

---

[69] O'Sullivan, *Salvian the Presbyter,* 261.

[70] This account has been variously used to emphasize the possible "nobility of purpose" in the production of pseudonymous works, the unsuitability and rejection of known pseudepigrapha, and the importance of authorship over content. The latter is seen in the phrase "they who read do not consider so much what they read as whom they read, nor so much the force and strength of what is said as the reputation of him who speaks." Note, however, that Salvian's personal view, if sincere, flies in the face of this. In addition, if Salvian's claims are accepted, this pseudonymous letter ascribed to an undefined "Timothy" would constitute one of the few examples from antiquity of an invented rather than borrowed pseudonym.

[71] Adversely, church fathers often mistakenly accepted pseudonymous works as authentic. Eusebius (*Hist. eccl.* 2.2.1–2), Tertullian (*Apol.* 5), and Justin (*I Apol.* 35 and 48) all held to the authenticity of a supposed letter from Pilate to Tiberius telling of Christ's resurrection and miracles. Both Jerome (*Vir. ill.* 12) and Augustine (*Epist.* 153) accepted the authenticity of the *Correspondence of Seneca and Paul.*

[72] We are following here B. M. Metzger, *The Canon of the New Testament: Its Origin, Development, and Significance* (Oxford: Clarendon, 1987), 307. For discussion and Latin facsimile, see S. P. Tregelles, *Canon Muratorianus: The Earliest Catalogue of the Books of the New Testament* (Oxford: Clarendon, 1867); and for contemporary discussion of its date, G. M. Hahneman, *The Muratorian Fragment and the Development of the Canon* (Oxford: Clarendon, 1992). The fragment has been variously interpreted in regard to pseudonymity; compare H. von Campenhausen, *The Formation of the Christian Bible* (London: Adam and Charles Black, 1972), 253–62; Guthrie, *New Testament Introduction,* 1019–20; and Kiley, *Colossians as Pseudepigraphy,* 17, 19. Note also that the reference to the book of Wisdom is confusing in that it could refer either to the Wisdom of Solomon or the book of Proverbs.

[73] Eusebius, *Hist. eccl.* 3.25.4–7.

admonishes its readers not to be deceived by those who have composed "poisonous" books. More pointedly, it esteems the content and thought of a work more highly than the name it bears.[74] Origen reveals at least some concern for apostolic authorship when, commenting on the work entitled *The Doctrine of Peter*, he declares that it "is not included among ecclesiastical books; for we can show that it was not composed either by Peter or by any other person inspired by the Spirit of God."[75] The short work *Epilogue to Pamphilus* written by Rufinus (ca. 345–410 C.E.) includes an extract from one of Origen's letters, claiming that "a certain promoter of heresy, after a discussion which had been held between us in the presence of many persons, and notes of it had been taken, procured the document from those who had written out the notes, and added or struck out whatever he chose, and changed things as he thought right, and published it abroad as if it were my [Origen's] work."[76]

Eustathius of Sebaste (d. ca. 337) composed a series of letters purporting to be from Basil the Great (ca. 325–79 C.E.) and the heretic Apollinaris of Laodicea (ca. 310–90 C.E.) in hopes of swaying opinion in the midst of the Arian debates.[77] Eusebius recounts how the pseudonymous *Acts of Pilate* was forged for the purpose of maligning the person of Christ, and how upon the work's completion copies were sent with the emperor's approval "round to every part of his dominions, with edicts that they should be exhibited openly for everyone to see in every place, both town and country, and that the primary teachers should give them to the children, instead of lessons, for study and committal to memory."[78]

Like Galen, Dionysius of Corinth (ca. 170) expressed irritation in his *Letter to the Romans* when it was revealed to him that "apostles of the devil" had taken a number of his writings and filled them "with tares, by leaving out some things and putting in others." He added that it is "no wonder that some have gone about falsifying even the scriptures of the Lord when they have plotted against writings so inferior."[79] The same predicament befell Jerome (ca. 345–410 C.E.), who uncovered a pseudonymous letter bearing his name in which he is made to confess that he "had been induced by Jewish influence to make false translations of the Scriptures."[80]

4. Contemporary Theories of Pseudonymity and Implications for Canon

In contemporary scholarship there are two general positions taken towards the issue of pseudonymity. Some assert that the practice was regarded in antiquity as an acceptable, honorable, and innocent literary convention (licit or permissible); others claim that in antiquity pseudonymity was viewed as an unacceptable, dishonorable, and deceptive

---

[74] *Const. ap.* 6.3.16.
[75] Origin, *Princ.* Preface 8.
[76] Rufinus, *Epilogue to Pamphilus.*
[77] G. Bardy, "Betrug und Fälschungen in der Literatur der Christlichen Antike," in *Pseudepigraphie*, 174; originally published as, "Faux et fraudes littéraires dans l'antiquité chrétienne," *RHE* 32 (1936): 5–23, 275–302.
[78] Eusebius, *Hist. eccl.* 9.5.1 (LCL; 2 vols.; trans. K. Lake and J. E. L. Oulton; Cambridge: Harvard University Press, 1926/1942), 2: 338–39.
[79] Cited by Eusebius, *Hist. eccl.* 4.23.12 (LCL 2: 382–83).
[80] Jerome, *Apol.* 3.25.

literary device (illicit or prohibited). When the issue is directly related to questions concerning the formation of the biblical canon, two further correlatives often emerge. Those who maintain that pseudonymity was acceptable (and that, therefore, the presence of such works in the biblical canon is not problematic) generally emphasize orthodox content as the preeminent criterion for canonicity. Those who assert that pseudonymity was unacceptable (and that, therefore, the presence of such works in the canon is problematic) appeal to apostolic authorship as the preeminent criterion of canonicity.[81]

A. Pseudonymity as Acceptable, Honorable, or Innocent: A Licit or Permissible Convention

Although resources existed in antiquity for the detection of pseudonymity, many pseudonymous works were not detected until recently.[82] Modern critical scholarship's emphasis upon the origin and background of a text no doubt played a role in this.[83] Many nineteenth-century critics argued for the presence of pseudepigrapha in the New Testament, but F. C. Baur (1792–1860) was certainly the most influential, both for his critical acumen and his decisiveness.[84] Baur, following the much earlier example of Eusebius, allocated the thirteen Pauline letters into three classes: Romans, 1–2 Corinthians, and Galatians were placed into the *homologoumena* (acknowledged writings); Ephesians, Philippians, Colossians, 1–2 Thessalonians, and Philemon into the *antilegomena* (disputed works); and the Pastoral Epistles into the *notha* (spurious writings).[85] In time, however, Baur would come to regard all but the first four Pauline letters as pseudonymous, along with the seven General Epistles.[86] Baur's defense of pseudonymity was just as novel as the extent of his pseudonymous declarations, for he was first to assert that antiquity regarded

---

[81] Meade, *Pseudonymity and Canon*, 2–3; Donelson, *Pseudepigraphy and Ethical Argument*, 9, 18; Lea, "Early Christian View," 66; and idem, "Pseudonymity and the New Testament," 551.

[82] See Speyer, *Die literarische Fälschung*, 181–86; and R. M. Grant, *Heresy and Criticism: The Search for Authenticity in Early Christian Literature* (Louisville, Ky.: Westminster John Knox, 1993), for discussion of early Christianity's use of literary criticism to detect authenticity.

[83] Guthrie, "Idea of Canonical Pseudepigrapha," 15–16; Rist, "Pseudepigraphy and the Early Christians," 91.

[84] For a detailed history of the numerous nineteenth-century critics who argued for the presence of pseudepigrapha in the New Testament, see W. G. Kümmel, *Introduction to the New Testament* (NTL; rev. ed.; trans. H. C. Kee; London: SCM, 1975 [German orig. 1963]), *passim*; idem, *The New Testament: The History of the Investigation of Its Problems* (NTL; trans. S. M. Gilmour and H. C. Kee; London: SCM, 1973 [German orig. 1970]), *passim*.

[85] F. C. Baur, *Paulus, der Apostel Jesu Christi: Sein Leben und Wirken, seine Briefe und Lehre Christi* (Stuttgart: Becher and Müller, 1845); ET *Paul, the Apostle of Jesus Christ: His Life and Work, His Epistles and His Doctrine* (2 vols.; 2d ed.; trans. A. Menzies; London: Williams and Norgate, 1876 [1875]); following citations are from the English translation. See also idem, *Die sogenannten Pastoralbriefe des Apostels Paulus aufs neue kritisch untersucht* (Stuttgart: J. G. Cotta, 1835) where Baur first rejects the authenticity of the Pastorals. For Eusebius's categories, see *Hist. eccl.* 3.25.1–7; cf. 3.3.1–2, 6.

[86] Guthrie ("Idea of Canonical Pseudepigrapha," 21) remarks, "The fact is that Baur's literary criticism was dominated by his dogmatic presuppositions and since these had to be maintained at all costs, it was no embarrassment that pseudepigraphic writings became more normal in the extant Pauline canon than genuine works."

pseudonymity as an acceptable literary convention not undertaken with the intent to deceive.[87] "With few exceptions," notes Ellis, speaking of Baur and the Tübingen school, "they are the root of all subsequent scholarship that assigned pseudepigraphal authorship to New Testament documents. . . . [T]he Baur hypothesis became the Baur tradition."[88]

Subsequent representative advocates of pseudonymity as an acceptable literary device and of the likelihood of pseudonymous works in the biblical canon include A. Jülicher, M. Kiley, B. S. Childs, and D. G. Meade.[89] A. Jülicher, like Baur, was able to minimize the notion of deceit inherent to pseudonymity by arguing that the idea of "intellectual property" was a modern construct all but absent from antiquity, and that Christian writers could, with the best intentions, place into the mouths of the apostles a contemporising message. Consequently, he contended that "truth" in the early church applied more to a literary work's theological content (substance) than apostolic authorship (form).[90]

M. Kiley, in rejecting the authenticity of Colossians, claims that antiquity offered a differing world view from today's, one in which the production of pseudepigraphy was regarded as a permissible and honored custom practiced by students and admirers of a revered figure. Their motives were not personal gain, but rather, the desire to produce a fresh formulation of what was thought to be the renowned individual's thought for a new situation. Kiley counters those who maintain the authenticity of a work based upon its ethical admonition to truth by stating:

---

[87] Baur, *Paul, the Apostle of Jesus Christ*, 2:110–11.

[88] Ellis, "Pseudonymity and Canonicity," 213. Baur's principles were later carried to their logical conclusion by such individuals as the radical German biblical critic Bruno Bauer (1809–82), and W. C. van Manen (1842–1905) of the Dutch skeptical school. In reference to the Pauline Epistles, van Manen states, "They are all, without exception, pseudepigrapha. . . . No distinction can any longer be allowed between 'principal epistles' and minor or deutero-Pauline ones. The separation is purely arbitrary, with no foundation in the nature of the things here dealt with. The group . . . bears obvious marks of a certain unity, of having originated in one circle, at one time, in one environment, but not of unity of authorship. . . ." See W. C. van Manen, in *Encyclopaedia Biblica: A Critical Dictionary of the Literary, Political and Religious History, the Archaeology, Geography, and Natural History of the Bible* (4 vols.; ed. T. K. Cheyne; London: Macmillan, 1899–1903), vol. 3, col. 3634; also cited by Guthrie, "Idea of Canonical Pseudepigrapha," 21 and n. 26. For critique and discussion of Baur and the Tübingen school, see H. Harris, *The Tübingen School: A Historical and Theological Investigation of the School of F. C. Baur* (Leicester: Apollos, 1990).

[89] For more extensive historical discussions of proponents of the acceptability of pseudonymity, see Guthrie, "Idea of Canonical Pseudepigrapha," 16–39; Ellis, "Pseudonymity and Canonicity," 213–17; Lea, "Early Christian View," 72–74; and idem, "Pseudonymity and the New Testament," 543–53.

[90] A. Jülicher, *Einleitung in das Neue Testament* (Freiburg: Mohr [Siebeck], 1894), 38–42; ET *An Introduction to the New Testament* (trans. J. P. Ward; London: Smith, Elder, and Company, 1904), 52–54. Arguments against the concept of intellectual property in antiquity have become common fair in discussions of pseudonymity, and can be found in more recent examples like A. T. Lincoln, *Ephesians* (WBC 42; Dallas: Word, 1990) lxxi; and less so in M. Hengel, "Anonymität, Pseudepigraphie und 'Literarische Fälschung' in der jüdisch-hellenistischen Literatur," in *Pseudepigrapha I*, 283. This theory has, however, been debunked by Speyer (*Die literarische Fälschung*, 175–76), who has clearly shown the presence of such a concept in antiquity. See also Brox, *Falsche Verfasserangaben*, 68–70; Metzger, "Literary Forgeries," 12–13 and n. 33; Guthrie, "Idea of Canonical Pseudepigrapha," 38; Ellis, "Pseudonymity and Canonicity," 217; and Torm, "Psychologie der Pseudonymität," 119.

[Such a view] seems to me a severely limited notion of truth. It ignores the variety of truth, including the 'goodwill of disciples' concerned for a true application of an admired person's thoughts in a new time and place, according to a recognized cultural practice of a period. Col[ossians], along with many examples of Pauline pseudepigraphy, simply did not see the pseudepigraphical exercise as inconsistent with the reiteration of the early Christian topos of truth.[91]

A more nuanced approach to the issue is offered by the canonical critic B. S. Childs. He denies that a book's theological validity depends upon the correct determination of its historical author.[92] Childs protests that theories of pseudonymity, like all critical interpretations, are concerned with the reconstruction of the historical author's "real" intentions and purposes, despite the fact that they have been purposely concealed, rather than with the kerygmatic witness of the text and the significance of the portrayed "canonical" author. The text is no longer interpreted according to its verbal sense, with Paul writing in the first person, but rather the apostles' role has been altered by pseudonymous assertions to function in the third person. "Paul is no longer the real subject of the letter, but its object. The letters are not from Paul, but about Paul (*ein Paulusbild!*). The crucial canonical shaping of the Pastorals has thus been seriously altered on the basis of an historical and literary critical judgement."[93] In other words, Childs finds the distinction between the historical author and the canonical author problematic since the primary issue is not whether, for example, Ephesians is Pauline. The canonical process has already incorporated it within the Pauline corpus. While Childs "accepts as helpful many of the interpretive options which stem from the model of pseudepigraphy," he has, in essence, downplayed pseudonymity as it relates to the biblical canon by focusing, not on historical authorship, but on the theological witness a canonical work—pseudonymous or authentic—has upon generations of Christians who regard it as scripture.[94]

D. G. Meade emphasizes the importance of ancient Jewish literary practice and its influence upon Christianity. Using the work of Childs as a starting point, he suggests that the process of *Vergegenwärtigung* (contemporization) provided the impetus for the production of canonical pseudepigrapha.[95] The desire to preserve, hear anew, and apply the

---

[91] Kiley, *Colossians as Pseudepigraphy,* 26.
[92] B. S. Childs, *The New Testament as Canon: An Introduction* (Valley Forge, Pa.: Trinity Press International, 1994 [1984]) 52.
[93] Childs, *New Testament as Canon,* 383. Childs explains that his reservations to classify certain letters such as the Pastorals as pseudepigraphal "do not arise from an attempt to defend the direct authorship by Paul. I am convinced that the relationship is an indirect one. There are many signs that the material stemmed from a period after Paul's death and that the addressee shared many features of a non-historical construct. The major problem is that the term pseudepigraphical arose within a context of historical referentiality and it does not as yet seem capable of functioning within another theological frame of reference. The material remains 'pseudo', and even when a fraudulent intention is removed, the interpretation is strongly affected by this initial judgement" (386).
[94] Childs, *New Testament as Canon,* 323; cf. R. W. Wall, "Pauline Authorship and the Pastoral Epistles: A Response to S. E. Porter," *BBR* 5 (1995): 125–28. For poignant criticism of such positions, see Porter, "Pauline Authorship," 121–22; and idem, "Pauline Authorship and the Pastoral Epistles: A Response to R. W. Wall's Response," *BBR* 6 [1996]: 136 and n. 9. Porter emphasizes that theological conclusions need to be grounded in historical inquiry.
[95] See Meade, *Pseudonymity and Canon,* 24–26, 212–13, and 216–17, for his strong affirmation of Childs and the canonical approach.

prophetic, sapiential, apocalyptic, and apostolic traditions to new situations resulted in the growth of this literature. With the closure of the canon, however, the ongoing process of *Vergegenwärtigung* came to an end, thereby guaranteeing that the biblical tradition could not be significantly expanded in any fashion, either anonymously or pseudonymously.[96] Meade, recognizing the correspondence between contemporization and canonization, says of the ancient canonical criteria that "in the context of the canonical process, authorship is not primarily a statement of literary origins, but of authoritative tradition. Taken from a modern literary perspective, authorship cannot determine canonicity, and canonicity cannot determine authorship."[97]

B. Pseudonymity as Unacceptable, Dishonorable, and Deceptive: An Illicit or Prohibited Convention

Advocates of this position do not deny the presence of pseudonymous literature—its abundance in Greco-Roman, Jewish, and Christian antiquity prevents any such conclusion—but rather they question its acceptability. Representatives of this position include J. S. Candlish, J. I. Packer, D. Guthrie, and more recently S. E. Porter.[98]

One of the most significant attacks upon the innocence of pseudonymity came from J. S. Candlish.[99] His 1891 essay marks the turning away from thoroughly dogmatic to more critical appeals against the acceptability of pseudonymity as a literary device. The historical data lead Candlish to conclude that no known pseudonymous writing was ever accepted as authoritative in the early church—a conclusion shared by virtually all who regard pseudonymity as an unacceptable practice. He comments:

> [I]n the early Christian centuries, when any work was given out as of ancient or venerable authorship, it was either received as genuine, which was done with very great facility of belief, or rejected as an imposture; that such fictions, though very common, were regarded, at least by the stricter Christian teachers, as morally blameworthy; and that the notion of dramatic personation as a legitimate literary device is never mentioned, and seems never to have been thought of as a defense of such compositions. If any author wrote a pseudonymous book in such a way, he must have been very unsuccessful in his purpose; for it was generally taken as a genuine work, or else rejected as feigned and worthless.[100]

Candlish further claimed that since pseudonymity employed an element of deception, such works could not be regarded as inspired or part of the canon of scripture—another affirmation made by many proponents of this position. Betraying a dogmatic sympathy,

---

[96] Ibid., 203.

[97] Ibid., 207. Drawing upon Childs's understanding of the Pentateuch, Meade succinctly states that authorship is not so much an historical, but a theological designation. It is not a statement of modern research ("Moses wrote this") but a statement of authority ("This is Mosaic").

[98] For extensive discussion of those who have rejected pseudonymity as an acceptable literary device, see Guthrie, "Idea of Canonical Pseudepigrapha," 16–39; Ellis, "Pseudonymity and Canonicity," 213–19; Lea, "Early Christian View," 72–74; and idem, "Pseudonymity and the New Testament," 543–53.

[99] J. S. Candlish, "On the Moral Character of Pseudonymous Books," *Exp* 4 (1891): 91–107, 262–79.

[100] Candlish, "Moral Character of Pseudonymous Books," 103.

Candlish added that any manifestly inspired work that makes a specific claim to author-ship renders critical considerations secondary.[101]

J. I. Packer categorized pseudonymous writings as forgeries because, motive not-withstanding, they were fraudulent imitations of another's work, circulated for the pur-pose of getting one's own product accepted as someone else's.[102] Despite the possibility of an author incorporating genuine Pauline fragments into his work or accurately represent-ing the mind of Paul, and regardless of the presence of pseudonymous writings in antiq-uity, Packer maintained that by pretending to be Paul the writer sought to secure for himself the apostle's authority. "On this view," he declares, "the Pastorals are in truth a forgery and a fraud. And frauds are still fraudulent even when perpetrated from noble motives. . . ."[103] While authentic authorship, as opposed to orthodox content, functions implicitly as a criterion for canonization in the proposals of Candlish, Shaw, and Torm, Packer makes it explicit by claiming that proponents of the acceptability of pseudonymous literature fail to understand two things:

> [F]irst, the unique personal authority and historical significance of the apostolate, and, sec-ond, the biblical concept of Scripture. For the first: if the Pastorals did not come from within the original apostolic circle, then they are no part of the authoritative exposition of the faith which Christ inspired His apostles to give for the guidance of the universal Church, and so they are not canonical. For the second: if the Pastorals are Scripture, then their claim to authorship, like all their other assertions, should be received as truth from God; and one who rejects this claim ought also to deny that they are Scripture, for what he is saying is that they have not the nature of Scripture, since they make false statements. . . . [The] position, that their canonicity cannot be affirmed if their authenticity is denied, thus seems to be the only one possible; and we may lay it down as a general principle that, when biblical books specify their own authorship, the affirmation of their canonicity involves a denial of their pseudo-nymity. Pseudonymity and canonicity are mutually exclusive.[104]

Packer concludes that if a New Testament book is not authentically apostolic, then its na-ture as scripture as well as its place in the canon must be refused. To deny apostolic authen-ticity is to deny canonicity as well.

D. Guthrie's influential work on pseudonymity, while more clement than the preced-ing positions, draws many of the same conclusions regarding the acceptability of pseudo-nymity and its presence in the canon. He too finds little historical evidence in Christian literature that would indicate an acceptable literary device whereby an author, as a matter of literary custom and with the full approbation of his circle of readers, could publish his own works in the name of another. There was always, Guthrie claims, an ulterior motive.[105] Else-where he adds that "everything depends on whether the pseudonymous means was in fact regarded by the author's contemporaries as questionable. What little evidence there is in the early Christian period on this matter points to the conclusion that it was."[106] Guthrie asserts

---

[101] Ibid., 278–79.

[102] Packer, "Pseudonymity in Scripture," 183.

[103] Ibid., 184.

[104] Ibid.

[105] Guthrie, "Idea of Canonical Pseudepigrapha," 38; see also idem, *New Testament Introduc-tion*, 1012, 1017.

[106] Guthrie, *New Testament Introduction*, 1019, cf. 1020 as well.

that Tertullian condemned the Asian presbyter who penned the *Acts of Paul*, not because of the work's heresy, but rather because of its pseudonymous literary form. The priority of authentic authorship over orthodox content is evident when Guthrie claims:

> Pseudepigraphic hypotheses must assume that the author's notion of the truth contained nothing inconsistent with a literary method which he must have known would deceive many if not all his readers. It cannot be maintained that 'truth' is here used for the formal contents of the gospel and would therefore not apply to literary conventions, for we have seen reason to doubt whether the method proposed was ever such an accepted literary convention.[107]

Guthrie concludes that psychological difficulties lie in the path of theories of pseudonymous authorship.

In a recent study S. E. Porter affirms that, despite many contrary claims, there does not seem to have been a convention among ancient writers of treating works not written by the purported author on the same level with the author's genuine works, where such knowledge was available. Based on the limited evidence in the early church, he asserts, no known pseudepigraph was knowingly accepted into the New Testament canon.[108] Echoing Packer's sentiments, Porter states that while a disciple's motives for writing may have been noble, including finding a way for Paul to speak to his community, they were nevertheless deceptive, for "the noble lie is still a lie."[109] Among those who believe that pseudonymity was not an acceptable literary device in antiquity, Porter's work is unique for its rebuttal of Childs, Wall, Meade, and others who advocate some type of canonical-theological construal whereby pseudonymity is exonerated of all deceptiveness. In referring to the Pastoral Epistles he explains that:

> In the light of theological development and possible pseudepigraphal authorship, the question must be asked to what degree—if at all—the Pastoral Epistles can be used in establishing Pauline theology. . . . If the Pastoral Epistles are not part of the genuine letters, I think this calls into question whether they can be used to create a Pauline theology in this sense. They may be part of a record of how some people responded to Paul, how others developed his thought, how some people applied his ideas to later situations, or even how some people wished Paul could have spoken, but they can never be more than only one interpretation among many others. The fact that they were included in the canon may in some sense have enhanced their authority and may mean that they represent the most influential or powerful followers of Paul, but it does not raise their level of authenticity and hence the quality of their witness. They are still not authentically Pauline and thus should not be used to formulate a Pauline theology.[110]

---

[107] Ibid., 1021.

[108] Porter, "A Response," 136; see also idem, "Pauline Authorship," 119, where Porter declares that the "apparently universal response by the early church to known pseudepigrapha," was, "they were rejected carte blanche."

[109] Porter, "Pauline Authorship," 122; cf. 119–20.

[110] Ibid., 121–22. In his response to Wall, a representative of Childs's canonical approach, Porter states more pointedly that historical referentiality is essential for the grounding of theological concerns, adding that this is the traditional approach of orthodox Christian theology. No matter how important theology may have been, and regardless of the role it may have played in canonical formation, the process of acceptance of the Pastorals is a historical one. Porter argues that the distinction between personal and canonical referentiality was created by modern scholars, and has

Porter concludes that if the church and its scholars are no longer willing to accept the Pastoral Epistles as written by Paul, perhaps it should eliminate them as forgeries that once deceived but will no longer, rather than creating strained theological justifications for their continued canonical presence.[111]

Besides noting the absence of any known pseudonymous work being accepted as authoritative by the early church, adherents of this position point to the ethical dilemma raised by pseudonymity. This concern is expressed in any number of ways: How can forged documents serve as inspired and sacred literature for the church? Is it possible for the church to urge its members to be truthful and at the same time condone pseudonymous writings? How could individuals of such deep religious convictions, whose writings contain such a "nobility of thought" and urge the highest moral standards, employ a deceptive literary device? Pseudonymity involves the authors of canonical works in intolerable moral difficulties. For example, if pseudonymous, the writer of Ephesians denounces the very deceit he is perpetrating (4:25); the author of 2 Thessalonians appears to condemn forgeries while at the same time creating one (2:2–3); the individual who penned the Pastoral Epistles produces an elaborate and complex fabrication of detailed *personalia* to create the impression of Pauline authorship (4:9–19); the originator of several deutero-Pauline letters furthers his deception by claiming to append a genuine signature (Col 4:18, 2 Thess 3:17); and in 1 Peter the pseudonymous writer hypocritically admonishes his readers to put away all malice, guile, insincerity, and envy (2:1), and to conduct themselves in a manner above reproach.[112]

L. R. Donelson's work on pseudonymity and ethical argument in relation to the Pastoral Epistles breaks the general pattern of approach to the issue. Convinced that there is sparse evidence to support the claim that pseudonymity was practiced innocently, openly, and without the intent to deceive, Donelson admits that in Christian circles pseudonymity was instead considered a dishonorable convention, and if discovered, such a document was rejected and the author, if known, excoriated.[113] Having come to such a conclusion, one would expect Donelson to stress the importance of apostolic authorship over orthodox content, but this he does not do. Instead, he asserts that the difficulty of discovering if a document was forged or not, and the need to refute heresies, led the church to place doctrinal correctness above authorship. This, in turn, led to the view that every apostolic document was orthodox, and that every orthodox document was apostolic.[114] In support he cites Tertullian's reaction to the forged *Acts of Paul* and Serapion's rejection of the *Gospel of*

---

little bearing on what actually happened in the early church. Although one is free to accept such a model, one must be careful in representing it as something that the ancients would have recognized. See Porter, "A Response," 133–34, 136–37.

[111] Porter, "A Response," 138; see also idem, "Pauline Authorship," 123.

[112] For other examples where pseudonymous assertions create ethical difficulties for the biblical writers, see Ellis, "Pseudonymity and Canonicity," 220–23; and Guthrie, *New Testament Introduction*, 1021–22. On the issue of *personalia*, false biographical detail, and use of a pseudo-author and pseudo-recipient, see Donelson, *Pseudepigraphy and Ethical Argument*, 54–66.

[113] Donelson, *Pseudepigraphy and Ethical Argument*, 10, 17; cf. 55, 199.

[114] Ibid., 17–18 and n. 50; cf. 45, 55 n. 186, and 62, where he goes so far as to claim that early Christians were quite eager to admit the genuineness of a document if it suited their sense of orthodoxy.

Peter, claiming that the only working criterion in both these instances was whether the document was orthodox or not.[115] In conclusion, Donelson states:

> The embarrassment of pseudepigraphy strikes at the heart of scriptural authority. The vehemence of conservative scholars who resist the whole notion of pseudepigrapha in the canon is well-founded, for to admit it would be to admit that the canon is not what they want it to be. However, if the canon is just another moment in tradition, the first among many attempts by Christians to debate their various versions of the religious life, then a pseudepigraphon could be an explicable and valid voice in the debate. Admittedly, in a pseudepigraphon the prejudices and weaknesses of the author and the humanness of the theology therein are displayed so openly that they cannot be ignored. But then all theology is human and prejudiced and flawed. It is just here, in the face of such duplicity, that we must admit it at the outset.[116]

Thus Donelson accepts the view that the New Testament canon contains pseudepigraphal literature, deceptively produced. But by stressing orthodoxy over apostolicity, he downplays the issue of authorship and appears unknowingly to undermine his conclusions regarding the deceptiveness of canonical pseudepigrapha.

5. Conclusion

We have applied the term pseudonymity to works containing a *clear authorial ascription* determined to have been made by the *actual author* of the literature in question with the *calculated attempt to conceal* his true identity by *deliberately endorsing* a false author as the real author. While it is tenable to regard later textual alterations and mis-attributions as techniques of pseudonymity—and particularly secondary pseudonymity—we suggest that this category often confuses the discussion of more critical issues relating to authorship and false attribution. Modern scholarship has split on the issue of pseudonymity and its function in antiquity: it has either been perceived as an acceptable (licit) literary convention innocent in its intent, or as a dishonorable (illicit) device practiced with guile and deception. When related to the biblical text, the question of pseudonymity becomes the question of both canonicity and criteria. To those who regard the practice as acceptable, the presence of such works in the canon is not problematic. These individuals often regard the criterion of orthodoxy as central to canonization.[117] Those, however, who regard

---

[115] Donelson's argument does not remove the charge of deception against the forger, as he himself states. However, his further claim that proper doctrine served only to protect a document from rigid scrutiny and did not redeem it once it was known as a forgery (i.e., authentic authorship was obviously still central) seems convoluted in light of his emphasis upon orthodoxy. See Donelson, *Pseudepigraphy and Ethical Argument,* 20 n. 62.

[116] Ibid., 201.

[117] For emphasis on orthodox content or some other criterion over authentic apostolic authorship, but not specifically in regard to pseudonymity, see A. C. Sundberg, "Towards a Revised History of the New Testament Canon," *Studia Evangelica* 4/1 [Texte und Untersuchungen; Berlin: Akademie-Verlag, 1968], 459–61); Campenhausen, *Formation of the Christian Bible,* 254–61; Moule, *The Birth of the New Testament,* 246–48, 250–53; R. M. Grant and D. Tracy, *A Short History of the Interpretation of the Bible* (2d ed.; Philadelphia: Fortress, 1984), 174–75; and H. Y. Gamble, *The New Testament Canon: Its Making and Meaning* (Guides to Biblical Scholarship; Philadelphia: Fortress, 1985), 68–72.

pseudonymity as an unacceptable device usually deny its presence in the biblical canon. They identify authentic apostolic authorship as the primary criterion of canonization.[118]

That pseudonymity was a common literary device in Greco-Roman, Jewish, and Christian antiquity is irrefutable. That it was, when discovered, looked upon contemptuously seems most probable—although several examples to the contrary do exist. That apostolic authorship in its stricter sense functioned as the singular predeterminate for canonicity is doubtful, even allowing for hermeneutical difficulties in interpreting the historical evidence. Depending upon context and situation, other criteria appear to have played a role in the canonization process as well. A careful survey of the literature clearly shows that the early church was not of one mind in this regard. "I need not set this out in detail here," states Aland, "if one wanted to sum up in a formula the external principles which played a part in the choice of the canonical Scriptures, one can only speak of the principle of 'having no principles.'"[119] Therefore, to make apostolic authorship the foremost criterion of canonicity, and reciprocally, to question a work's canonical status based upon authorship alone (pseudonymous or otherwise) is to invoke a standard not used exclusively or even consistently by the early church.[120] Also problematic is the insistence upon the preeminence of orthodoxy. The formulation of canonical criteria in the early church does not appear to have been construed as an either-or issue. It would be truer to history to view the early church as more flexible in the canon-making process. Is it appropriate, then, to look more stringently upon the issue of authorship than did the early church, or to adopt the spirit of freedom seen in the church?

Equally in need of reconsideration is the idea that the early church may have been "duped" into accepting pseudonymous works into the New Testament canon. Where the authorship of a particular work was uncertain, all evidence indicates that other criteria were employed to evaluate the canonical worthiness of a writing already found useful to

---

[118] For emphasis on authentic apostolic authorship over orthodox content, but not specifically in regard to pseudonymity, see W. Marxsen, *Introduction to the New Testament* (trans. G. Buswell; Oxford: Basil Blackwell, 1968), 280–82; R. L. Harris, *Inspiration and Canonicity of the Bible: An Historical and Exegetical Study* (Grand Rapids: Zondervan, 1969), 159, 284; Kümmel, *Introduction to the New Testament,* 493–94, 499, 509; G. A. Robbins, "Eusebius' Lexicon of 'Canonicity,'" *Studia Patristica* 25 (1993): 134–35; and Rist, "Pseudepigraphy and the Early Christians," 84, 89, 91 (though Rist appears to contradict himself).

[119] K. Aland, *The Problem of the New Testament Canon* (London: A.R. Mowbray and Co., 1962), 14–15; see also G. W. Anderson, "Canonical and Non-Canonical," in *The Cambridge History of the Bible: From the Beginnings to Jerome* (3 vols.; ed. P. R. Ackroyd and C. F. Evans; Cambridge: Cambridge University Press, 1970), 1:113; and McDonald (*Christian Biblical Canon,* 252).

[120] Canon scholars tacitly acknowledge this when they broaden the definition of "apostolicity" to include authorship by followers of apostles, or derivation from the general time of the apostles, or simply didactic or doctrinal agreement with an apostle. See H. Y. Gamble, "Canon," in *The Anchor Bible Dictionary* (6 vols.; ed. D. N. Freedman; London: Doubleday, 1992), 1:857–58; idem, *New Testament Canon,* 67–68; K.-H. Ohlig, *Die theologische Begründung des neutestamentlichen Kanons in der alten Kirche* (KBANT; Düsseldorf: Patmos-Verlag, 1972), 57–156; McDonald, *Christian Biblical Canon,* 229–32; and Bruce, *Canon of Scripture,* 255–59. See also E. Best, "Scripture, Tradition and the Canon of the New Testament," *BJRL* 61 [1979]: 279, who notes that, "Our views today of which writings are apostolic differ considerably from those of the early church, not merely because we would say that the Gospels were not written by apostles, but because even our understanding of the word 'apostle' is different. Therefore the argument is usually put in terms of earliness rather than strict apostolicity."

the community of faith. In such an instance, the issue of authorship apparently became secondary. Before the issue of a New Testament canon became paramount, the majority of the works that were to be later included in that canon were already deemed important to the formation of the church's faith and were, therefore, in use. By the time the authorship of a given work was questioned, the usefulness of that work had already been proven:

> We must never forget that many of the deliberations regarding the "authenticity" and "canonicity" of many NT canonical and apocryphal pseudepigrapha took place long after their origins were forgotten and their usage (or lack of it) had been established by the church. . . . [T]here is not only a "history of the canon," where the inclusion or exclusion of certain books are decided, but there is also a "canonical process" or growing "canon consciousness," where traditions and their literary expressions gain authoritative status in the communities they sustain. Before the history of the NT canon began, the canonical process was well developed, and it is this factor more than any other that explains the presence of canonical pseudepigrapha.[121]

When the canonization process applied its scrutiny to a work that had already proved useful, there would probably have been a desire to associate that work more closely to an apostolic figure (i.e., Hebrews with Paul). But this would have been conciliatory and in addendum to that work's already recognized value. Of interest here is the fact that the community of faith, rather than church authorities, were responsible for this process; what they determined to be edifying and useful later found a place in the canon. Church authorities only authorized or sanctioned what had already been in use:

> In establishing the Canon, the Church authorities of the second and succeeding centuries only *subsequently* ratified the decisions which had already been reached by the Christian communities, or more exactly, by the individual believers. The organized Church as such did not create the Canon; it recognized the Canon which had already been created. It is only from the second half of the fourth century onwards, in connexion with the closing of the Canon, that the Church authorities began to have an effect.[122]

Similarly, the community, and not the prophetically inspired individual, is the focus of canon formation. Therefore, it would appear that the dominant criterion for canonicity was to have been traditional usage. And yet it seems that there were instances where all criteria came into play, no single criterion taking precedence over another:

> [W]hen the Church came consciously to apply these tests, it was sometimes one of them, and sometimes another which was uppermost. The original apostolic contact was clearly a primary demand; but it was not always possible to test this as rigorously as might have been desired; and along side came the traditional test of usage: Had the book proved its worth? Had it survived the critical sense of the Christian tradition?—for it is possible that certain writings had already asserted themselves as eminently useful and sound before evidence for apostolic contact was discovered. In some few instances it may even be that the letter was a

---

[121] Meade, *Pseudonymity and Canon*, 206. Given such a profound statement, it is ironic that Meade does not build as forcefully upon this idea as he does upon considerations of orthodoxy and doctrinal congruence. He does enlist it, however, for the purpose of calling into question assertions of authorial preeminence in canonization.

[122] Aland, *New Testament Canon*, 18; Meade, *Pseudonymity and Canon*, 213, 214.

post hoc rationalization. But in such cases the *communis sensus fidelium* had already been so soundly informed by authentic tradition that its own imprimatur was in fact sufficient.[123]

One final point to consider is the discrepancy between ancient and modern views of authorship.[124] While the determination of authorship for certain canonical books seems to have been as fraught with difficulties in the early church as in modern scholarship, it appears that there was a somewhat more lenient view of the issue in Christian antiquity. Furthermore, if modern scholarship has such difficulty in reaching consensus, why should one expect to find unanimity in the ancient church—an age which, it has often been suggested, was much less "critical" than our own? Can those individuals concerned with the issue of pseudonymity as it relates to the Christian biblical canon not concede that in some instances the early church fathers simply did not know who the authors of particular works were? In their inability to resolve questions of authorship, instead of emphasizing apostolic authorship, they turned to other criteria. This interpretation appears to reflect more accurately the situation in the early church as regards literary authorship:

> [T]here exists a great deal of confusion over the precise attitude of the early church toward literary authenticity. Indeed, this confusion probably reflects the actual state of affairs of the church at the time. It is probably not legitimate to talk about "the" attitude of the church in some monolithic fashion. . . . [T]hings were in a state of flux, and if there was an "official" attitude, it had not yet filtered down to all the rank and file.[125]

There is no shame in siding with Origen when he claims of the book of Hebrews, "Who wrote this Epistle, in truth, only God knows." Are there "forged" documents in the New Testament canon? If we view authorship by modern standards, then one cannot help but answer affirmatively. However, if we consider the issue in its historical context, that is, by ancient standards of authorship (which appear to be anything but unanimous or consensual), it is more difficult to give such an unequivocal response. Perhaps it is better to ask if the authorial complexities of these documents diminished their value for the church. Or was a work's usefulness for faith and praxis unimpaired by questions of authorship?

---

[123] Moule, *The Birth of the New Testament*, 248.
[124] See Bruce, *Canon of Scripture*, 260; and Meade, *Pseudonymity and Canon*, 205–6.
[125] Meade, *Pseudonymity and Canon*, 205.

27

The Greek New Testament as a Codex

Daryl D. Schmidt

The number of Greek "manuscripts that contain the entire New Testament canon" has recently been set at sixty-one (including one duplicate).[1] This is one more than previously calculated. In *The Text of the New Testament* the Alands claimed that only three uncials and fifty-six minuscules (excluding the duplicate one) "contain the whole of the New Testament."[2] In the new edition of his *Text of the New Testament,* Bruce Metzger claims fifty-eight complete copies but provides no documentation.[3] The fluctuation in count indicates the uncertainty over the actual contents of many of the minuscules.[4] Even the three great uncials on the list require a disclaimer, because their contents are not limited to "the whole New Testament." Codex Sinaiticus (א, 01) also includes *Barnabas* and *Hermas*, while Codex Alexandrinus (A, 02) adds *1–2 Clement.* Codex Ephraemi (C, 04) has many lacunae, including all of 2 Thessalonians, 2 John, and the ending, so it could have contained other writings as well. Codex Vaticanus (B, 03) has to be excluded because it ends at Heb 9:13, with the rest of Hebrews and Revelation supplied by a minuscule manuscript from the fifteenth century. As a result, the portion originally located between Hebrews and Revelation in the sequence of many earlier manuscripts, the Pastoral Letters and Philemon, is lacking entirely in the present combination of the two manuscripts. With such variations in mind, these "complete New Testament manuscripts" are the ones assumed to have been "originally complete" or "written as complete New Testaments,"[5] so far as can be determined.

---

[1] J. K. Elliott, "The Distinctiveness of the Greek Manuscripts of the Book of Revelation," *JTS* 48 (1997): 116–24, with explanation of recent adjustments (116) and appended list (124). I thank Texas Christian University for the research leave that supported my pursuit of this matter during Spring 1998, and especially the Research Librarian at Duke University, John L. Sharpe, for graciously guiding me to many useful resources and sharing his insights about the study of ancient codices.

[2] Kurt Aland and Barbara Aland, *The Text of the New Testament: An Introduction to the Critical Editions and to Theory and Practice of Modern Textual Criticism* (2d ed.; trans. E. F. Rhodes; Grand Rapids: Eerdmans, 1989), 78. Their numbers are repeated, e.g., by Eldon J. Epp, "Textual Criticism in the Exegesis of the New Testament, with an Excursus on Canon," in *Handbook to Exegesis of the New Testament* (ed. Stanley E. Porter; Leiden: Brill, 1997), 45–97, at 76.

[3] Bruce M. Metzger, *The Text of the New Testament: Its Transmission, Corruption, and Restoration* (3d, enl. ed.; New York: Oxford University Press, 1992), 263.

[4] For the present state of scholarship on the minuscules, see Barbara Aland and Klaus Wachtel, "The Greek Minuscules," in *The Text of the New Testament in Contemporary Research: Essays on the Status Quaestionis* (ed. Bart Ehrman and Michael Holmes; Grand Rapids: Eerdmans, 1995), 43–60.

[5] These formulations are from Elliott, *A Survey of Manuscripts Used in Editions of the Greek New Testament* (NovTSup 57; Leiden: Brill, 1987), xiii, and idem, "Manuscripts, the Codex and the Canon" (*JSNT* 63 [1996]: 105–23), 110.

1. Information in Available Catalogues

The Alands do not provide information on their 56 (or 57) minuscules; it must be gleaned from Aland's *Kurzgefasste Liste*,[6] which Elliott has done.[7] These are the fifty-six minuscules whose content is traditionally labeled as "e a p r," that is, they contain all four canonical parts of the New Testament: e = evangelia, gospels; a = apostolos, Acts + seven catholic epistles (James, 1–2 Peter, 1–3 John, Jude); p = fourteen "Pauline" epistles (including Hebrews); r = Revelation. This standard designation reveals nothing about the actual sequence of writings in the manuscripts themselves, only their overall contents, because the convention established by Gregory, and followed ever since, has been to indicate the contents in canonical sequence, regardless of the actual order in the manuscripts.[8]

In his survey of New Testament manuscripts, J. K. Elliott marks each "complete New Testament" manuscript "C" in his tables and provides a list of them.[9] One of them (205) exists in a duplicate copy (205abs = *Abschrift*), and two others (180 and 209) are in fact manuscripts copied in two different centuries but bound together to make a single codex. In the new list, reflecting the new edition of Aland's *Kurzgefasste Liste*, one manuscript was removed (886), after ascertaining that it lacks the Catholic Epistles, and another one 1248 (Sinai 267) was added after confirming that it contains Revelation.[10] Elliott also adds 1040, which Aland indicates might be paired with a self-contained copy of Revelation (2041) that once made it a complete New Testament.[11] The new edition of Aland further indicates that 1384 lacks 2–3 John.

In addition to the two codices that Elliott notes as composites (in 180 the Gospels are from a different period, and in 209 Revelation is later), Aland's list also indicates that 1668 is a composite. On the other hand, Codex 1352 (Stavros 94) is not included on these lists, even though it is the only complete New Testament that Hatch found among fifty-five Jerusalem manuscripts, because he labeled Revelation as a separate manuscript bound in the same codex.[12] Aland lists 1352 as "e a p" = [1352a], and Revelation is treated separately

---

[6] Kurt Aland, *Kurzgefasste Liste der griechischen Handschriften des Neuen Testaments* (2d ed.; Berlin: de Gruyter, 1994).

[7] First in *Survey*, xiii, and now updated in "Distinctiveness," 124.

[8] H. F. von Soden (*Die Schriften des Neuen Testaments* [Göttingen: Vandenhoeck & Ruprecht, 1911–13]) had indicated only whether a manuscript was the whole NT (δ = *Diathēkē*, with or without Revelation!), or only the Four Gospels (ε = *Euangelia*), or other parts (α = *Apostolos*). C. R. Gregory (*Textkritik des Neuen Testaments* [3 vols.; Leipzig: J. C. Hinrichs, 1900–1909]) indicated separately the presence of Revelation (r) in a fourfold scheme, eapr, but left "a = Acts and Catholic Epistles.

[9] Elliott, *Survey*, xiii.

[10] V. Gardthhausen (*Catalogus codicum graecorum sinaiticorum* [Oxford: Oxford University Press, 1886], 54) had listed it as one of sixteen manuscripts containing *Apostolos-euangelion*, with no other notation. When these manuscripts were later microfilmed, Kenneth Clark listed eight of the sixteen as "New Testament," without noting whether Revelation was included (*Checklist of Manuscripts in St. Catherine's Monastery, Mount Sinai, Microfilmed for the Library of Congress, 1950* [Washington, D.C.: Library of Congress, 1952], 4).

[11] Aland, *Kurzgefasste Liste*, 108. Codex numbers, unless otherwise qualified, are the Gregory numbers.

[12] W. H. P. Hatch, *The Greek Manuscripts of the New Testament in Jerusalem: Facsimiles and Descriptions* (Paris: Paul Geuthner, 1934), Plates 41 and 45, with descriptions. Kenneth Clark listed

as [1352b] and given its own manuscript number (2824).[13] It is not clear what distinguishes this composite codex from others judged to be composite.

Aland's updated list marks a total of eighteen of these manuscripts as "defective," usually without indicating which portions are missing.[14] In some instances the missing folios include the beginning and/or ending of the manuscript, or entire shorter books within the codex. Thus, 218 is missing the end of Paul, including all of Titus and Philemon, and parts of Revelation, including the end; 498 is now lacking the beginning of Matthew, most of James, all of Jude and some of Paul. Elliott makes explicit the implication that these manuscripts were "originally complete" but have since suffered damage. The discovery that 1384 lacks 2–3 John suggests that "defective" can mean entire writings may be missing. In fact, the "defect" in codex 498 includes all of Jude, and in other codices no detailed description exists to allow for any precise assessment.

In order to be as comprehensive as possible, the list that we work with here includes those manuscripts that often appear on lists of "the complete New Testament," but now have some uncertainty about their original contents:

> 18 35 61 69 141 149 175 180* 201 205 (205 dup.) 209* 218 241 242 296 339 367 386 498 506 517 522 582 664 680 699 757 808 824 [886] 922 935 986 1040 1072 1075 1094 1248 1352* [1384] 1424 1503 1597 1617 1626 1637 1652 1668* 1678 1704 1780 1785 2136 2200 2201 2352 2494 2495 2554 (* = composite of 2 mss; [] = apparently never contained some New Testament writings)

The number of codices that actually contain "the complete New Testament" thus appears to be closer to fifty than sixty. Before we take a closer look at them, however, we must note that many minuscules have never been carefully studied and reliable information about their actual contents is often not available. For example, almost half of these are on Aland's list of "Byzantine type minuscules":

> 18 141 201 367 386 498 506 664 680 699 757 824 922 1072 1075 1094 1248 1503 1597 1617 1626 1637 1668 2352 2554.[15]

The label "Byzantine type" usually means these are not important enough to be collated individually for variant readings. Of the "complete New Testament" minuscules, the Aland descriptive list of "most important minuscules" includes only: 61 69 209 241 242 522 1424 1678 1704 2495.[16]

Many of the minuscules are not readily accessible for scholarly study, especially those in remote locations, such as Mt. Athos. Microfilm copies now exist of most minuscules,

---

three others as "New Testament," Taphos 37, 47, and Stavros 101 (= Gregory 1315, 1319, and 1354; *Checklist of Manuscripts in the Libraries of the Greek and Armenian Patriarchates in Jerusalem: Microfilmed for the Library of Congress, 1949–50* [Washington, D.C.: Library of Congress], 1953). Aland lists all three as "eap" and the first two as defective.

[13] Aland, *Kurzgefasste Liste*, 126.

[14] Aland's category simply denotes something missing from the manuscript, without indicating whether it was caused by damage, was never there, or had been supplied later; Aland (*Kurzgefasste Liste*, XIV): "luckenhaft oder von späterer Hand reganzt."

[15] Aland, *Text*, 138–40.

[16] Ibid., 129, 132–38.

but some of them are nearly illegible.[17] A few must now be labeled "lost," no longer available. These would include at least 241 (was in Dresden), 339 (was in Turin), and possibly 1785 (was in Sofia?). As a result, fewer than half of the sixty minuscules on our beginning list have been studied carefully enough to provide reasonably accurate information about their actual contents.[18]

The catalogue lists that exist are of limited help in this regard. The published lists from Mt. Athos, for example, rarely label a codex "New Testament" *(Kainē Diathēkē)*. Even then the contents vary considerably. Table 27-1 lists seven complete New Testament minuscules from Mt. Athos Laura, with four titled simply "Gospel" *(Euangelion)*, as was Jerusalem Codex Stavros 94.[19]

Table 27-1. "Complete New Testament" Minuscules from Mt. Athos Laura

Greg. #	Mt. Athos #	Catalogue title	Parts listed
1072	Laura Γ 80	*Hē Kainē Diathēkē*	e a + c + p r
1075	Laura Λ 195	*Euangelion*	e a r
1503	Laura A 99	*Euangelion*	e a + c + p r
1617	Laura E 157	*Kainē Diathēkē*	*Hapanta Kainē Diathēkē*
1626	Laura Ω 16	*Kainē Diathēkē*	*Hapanta Kainē Diathēkē*
1637	Laura Ω 141	*Euangelion*	e + a
1652	Laura Θ 152	*Euangelion*	a l(c + p) e

Table 27-2. Mt. Athos Laura "Complete New Testament" Minuscules Lacking Revelation

Greg. #	Mt. Athos #	Catalogue title	Parts listed
1505	Laura B 26	*Kainē Diathēkē*	e a + c + p (+ psalms & hymns)
1509	Laura B 53	*He Kainē Diathēkē*	e a p c (+ lectionary materials)
1618	Laura E 164	*Kainē Diathēkē*	eJ a c p [Gospel of John only]

The preference in these catalogues is to list the components in three parts. Two of these manuscripts spell out the second part as "Acts, Catholic Epistles, Paul," but elsewhere it is simply "Apostle" (1075) or "Acts" (1637). Two manuscripts do not even indicate that

---

[17] Frederick Wisse, *The Profile Method for the Classification and Evaluation of Manuscript Evidence, As Applied to the Continuous Greek Text of the Gospel of Luke* (SD 44; Grand Rapids: Eerdmans, 1982), 48, and confirmed by firsthand experience.

[18] For most manuscripts the available information is limited to citations in catalogues identified in *Repertoire des bibliothèques et des catalogues de manuscrits grecs de Marcel Richard* (ed. Jean-Marie Olivier; 13th ed.; Turnhout: Brepols, 1995).

[19] From the "eacpr" schema I have created the general category "l" for "letters" (= c + p). The information is taken from: S. Eustratiades, *Catalogue of the Greek Manuscripts in the Library of the Laura on Mount Athos* (HTS 12; Cambridge, Mass.: Harvard University Press, 1925; repr., New York: Kraus, 1969); P. Lambros, *Catalogue of the Greek Manuscripts on Mount Athos* (Cambridge: Cambridge University Press, 1895); Ernest W. Saunders, *A Descriptive Checklist of Selected Manuscripts in the Monasteries of Mount Athos: Microfilmed for the Library of Congress and the International Greek New Testament Project, 1952–53* (Washington, D.C.: Library of Congress, 1957).

they contain Revelation. In 1652 only a few verses of Revelation survive.[20] A more puzzling feature of this manuscript is the arrangement of the parts, with the gospels last. Codex 1637 does contain Revelation,[21] so the catalogue label, "The Four Gospels and the Acts of the Apostles," in effect meant, "The Four Gospels and Acts, etc.," similar to Sinai 267. Sinai 279 is titled *Praxapostolos* and contains all but the gospels (a c p r), so also Jerusalem Saba 665 (Gregory 1893), while other codices with that title also lack Revelation. In contrast, other codices at Mt. Athos are labeled *Kainē Diathēkē*, but lack Revelation, e.g., 1505 (Laura B 26) lists its third component as psalms and hymns, similar to other manuscripts noted below (18 and 242).

The official listing used by Aland, e a p r, adopted from Gregory, tells us nothing about the actual sequence of the books in the original manuscript, only whether all four major sections of the New Testament are included. The variety of actual arrangements is quite surprising, and rarely mentioned by current textual critics. After noting that the sequence varies within each group, the Alands state: "The only characteristic common to the whole manuscript tradition . . . is that the Gospels stand at the beginning and Revelation at the end," with "all variations of sequence to occur" in the middle sections.[22] As we will see, even these characteristics vary.

One of the more interesting examples is Codex 69. As described by an early collator, "the Pauline Epistles immediately follow the fourth gospel" and "between the Hebrews and Acts of the Apostles are five pages of foreign matter."[23] The sequence indicated here would then be: e p a c r. In a later study on this codex, J. Rendel Harris argued that the codex had originally been bound with the Gospels last, beginning with the thirteenth quire. The first seven quires were the Pauline Epistles, followed by Acts and the Catholic Epistles, missing the last leaf that contained most of Jude. In a later rebinding of the codex (after the first printed editions?), the Gospels were placed first.[24] Subsequently, the codex was badly damaged, now missing the beginning till Matt 18:15 and the ending after Rev 19:10.

Another unexpected surprise is the several manuscripts, described more fully below, that have Revelation elsewhere than at the end. The badly damaged Codex 517 now begins with parts of the Catholic Epistles, followed by Revelation and Paul, then the Gospels,

[20] For most of these minuscules the only citation in Elliott's *Bibliography* regards their text of Revelation, treated (often quite briefly) in H. C. Hoskier, *Concerning the Text of the Apocalypse: Collations of All Existing Available Greek Documents With the Standard Text of Stephen's Third Edition* (vol. 1; London: Quaritch, 1919); for this manuscript, 720. Ernst W. Saunders indicates that a number of these manuscripts of Revelation are on microfilm at Harvard University (*A Descriptive Checklist of Selected Manuscripts in the Monasteries of Mount Athos* [Washington, D.C.: Library of Congress, 1957], 24–27).

[21] Hoskier, *Concerning the Text of the Apocalypse,* 719; also included in Joseph Schmid, *Studien zur Geschichte des griechischen Apocalypse-Textes* (Munich: Karl Zink, 1956).

[22] Aland and Aland, *Text,* 79.

[23] F. H. A. Scrivener, *An Exact Transcript of the Codex Augiensis* (London: Bell & Daldy, 1859), xliii. The "foreign matter" is described as "an exposition of the Creed and statement of the errors condemned in the seven general Councils, ending with the second of Nicea" and "the ordinary Lives of the Apostles, followed by an exact description of the limits of the Five Patriarchates" (xliii).

[24] J. Rendel Harris, *The Origin of the Leicester Codex of the New Testament* (London: J. C. Clay, 1887). Harris provides the text for the "non-Biblical portions," calling them "patristic tracts" (62–65).

breaking off at Luke 6:42. Codex 1424 (described below), on the other hand, has the Pauline Letters last, after Revelation, as does 205, and the oldest Vatican manuscript on the list apparently has Revelation in the middle. Elliott is one of the few contemporary scholars to pay attention to the many permutations of arrangements of the sections, as well as of the writings within each section. He identifies nine different sequences for the Gospels and seven sequences for the Catholic Letters, and notes that the Latin tradition has the Pauline Letters in seventeen different sequences. The sequence of Acts, Pauline Letters, and Catholic Letters occurs in most every arrangement possible (except for the Catholic Epistles in front of Acts), and Revelation can be found in several different positions other than last.[25]

In the traditional designation, "a" (Apostolos) means Acts and the Catholic Epistles. Numerous manuscripts have only these writings, and this sequence is common in the Greek manuscripts of "the complete New Testament." In some lists, such as Elliott's, "c" is listed separately, to indicate more explicitly the presence of the Catholic Epistles. In Codex 1780 only James precedes Paul, the rest of the Catholic Epistles come after Paul.

The standard use of "e a p r" also fails to indicate what else a codex actually contains. Aland's official list indicates that 205 and 218 also contain the Old Testament. Aland's list sometimes indicates "commentary," such as 1424 and 1678, but fails to note it at 1780. There is no mention of the other kinds of material these codices contain. There are one hundred folios of Psalms and hymns added to codex 18, with eighty-nine such folios in 242. A number of codices, such as 35, 69, 506, 680, 1248, and 1424 have briefer treatises inserted to create varieties of "annotated" Bibles.

Scrivener calls this material "foreign matter." He also indicates that "apocryphal material" was included in at least two of the manuscripts that were composites, 180 and 339. The latter, now listed as missing, was reported by Hort to contain: four gospels, *Epistle of Pilate and Reply, On the Genealogy of the Virgin,* Revelation and *Synaxarion,* Acts, Catholic Epistles, Paul, *Lives of the Apostles,* and a Psalter. It is likely that Revelation and the *Synaxarion* were originally last, since they are in the same hand as the Psalter.[26] The label "complete New Testament" fails to convey the actual contents of such codices.

The discussion thus far has not mentioned the matter of the text itself. There are, of course, no two identical copies—until the printing press. The codices considered to be complete New Testaments contain some of the more important variations. Codex 69 is one of the nine minuscules of Family 13, where the Pericope of the Adulteress in found after Luke 21:38, rather than in John 8. In contrast, in codex 149 it does not appear in either place. Codex 209 (and 205?) is part of Family 1, which has sixty-six unique readings in the Gospels alone. Codex 61 has the famous insertion in 1 John 5:7b–8a, that there are three heavenly witnesses corresponding to the three earthly witnesses. Apparently these extra words were added to meet Erasmus's challenge that these words exist only in Latin. Erasmus published his first edition of the Greek New Testament (together with the Latin) in 1516. He based it on the minuscule manuscripts available to him in Basel, none

---

[25] J. K. Elliot, "Manuscripts, the Codex and the Canon," *JSNT* 63 (1996): 105–23, esp. 108–11. A century earlier Scrivener had noted various arrangements. See Scrivener, *A Plain Introduction to the Criticism of the New Testament for the Use of Biblical Students* (4th ed.; ed. Edward Miller; 2 vols.; London: George Bell, 1894), 72–73.

[26] Scrivener, *Plain Introduction,* 200; comment on Codex 180, p. 188.

of which contained the whole New Testament. In fact, none contained Revelation at all. Erasmus borrowed a damaged copy and supplied the missing Greek by translating from the Latin.[27]

A printed Greek text already existed by then, as part of the Complutensian Polyglot, prepared in Spain in 1514.[28] More importantly, "more than one hundred editions of the Latin Bible" had been published by then, since the mid-1450s.[29] The emergence of these printed texts, in both Latin and Greek, soon influenced the content of Greek manuscripts, with Codex 61 only the most famous example of the Latin text generating variant readings in Greek manuscripts. Since manuscripts from the sixteenth century and later were subject to the influence of printed texts, they may be "tainted" witnesses to the history of the manuscript tradition, and therefore are not usually included in manuscript comparisons.

2. Assessment

We can now begin to assess the minuscules that reputedly contain the whole New Testament. Given the lack of access to reliable microfilms for some of the manuscripts, this assessment cannot be comprehensive or definitive, and many manuscripts cannot be described in any detail. However, we can at least increase our general awareness of the overall status of these "complete New Testament" manuscripts. The appendix presents a summary of the data presently available.

Of the sixty possible "complete New Testament" minuscule codices, at least twelve have to be bracketed as either incomplete (for whatever reason), composite, or "lost" (codices 241, 339, 1785). The incomplete ones include 1384, which apparently never had 2–3 John; 886, lacking the Catholic Epistles; 218, now missing Titus and Philemon; 498, now missing Jude. The composite codices (180, 209, 517, and 1668) are those assembled from more than one original manuscript.[30] They typically also are defective or have "nonbiblical" material included.

Our appended list is in chronological order, in an attempt to determine when the first truly complete New Testament manuscript appears. Using a narrow definition, it would have to contain only the New Testament, and in canonical order. But this too is problematic. The sequence that became fixed in printed Bibles was taken from the Vulgate, not from Greek manuscripts. The notable differences are the Catholic Epistles appearing before the Pauline in most Greek manuscripts, and Hebrews before the Pastoral Epistles, rather than after. This sequence was followed in the printed editions of Westcott and Hort, because it is "preserved in a large proportion of Greek MSS of all ages, and corresponds to

---

[27] The oft-told story of Eramus is summarized in Metzger, *Text*, 101, with a later caveat (291 n. 2), suggesting there are apocryphal elements in this tale.

[28] See J. H. Bentley, "New Light on the Editing of the Complutensian New Testament," in *Bibliothèque d'humanisme et renaissance: Travaux et documents* (Geneva: Librairie Droz; 1980), 24:145–56; James P. R. Lyell, *Cardinal Ximenes: Statesman, Ecclesiastic, Soldier and Man of Letters with an Account of the Complutensian Polyglot Bible* (London: Grafton, 1917).

[29] Aland and Aland (*Text*, 3). For a sense of this tradition see T. H. Darlow and H. F. Moule, *Historical Catalogue of the Printed Editions of Holy Scripture in the Library of the British and Foreign Bible Society* (London: The Bible House, 1903).

[30] In this case Von Soden assigned each part a separate number.

marked affinities of textual history."[31] This is also the sequence of the famous list in Athanasius's letter of 367, which is usually cited as the oldest list of the twenty-seven books that became the canonical New Testament.[32]

Our search can thus be framed this way: When did Athanasius's list first become a table of contents for a complete Greek codex? When did a Greek codex first exhibit the sequence now considered canonical? These questions cannot be answered with any certainty, but they can provide a focus for our inquiry.

The earliest two "complete New Testament" codices on our list, ninth/tenth century and tenth/eleventh century, are both peculiar in having the Pauline Epistles last. The older of the two (1424) also has commentary in a later hand in most of the codex.[33] The commentary is mostly in a parallel column, but often runs under the text, and at times above the text, surrounding it on all three sides in the style of the Talmud. It is also clear that the unusual arrangement is not the result of a later rearrangement. The text of Revelation is written in complete continuity within the manuscript. It begins on the same page that Jude ends (f. 224a), and when Revelation ends, the Pauline material, with twelve pages of prolegomena, begins on the same page (f. 243a), whereas each gospel and Acts begins a new page. The manuscript thus ends with Hebrews. It may be a "complete New Testament," but a rather unique one—certainly not an Athanasian codex.

The next oldest codex (175) is a Vatican manuscript that has never been cited in any critical edition of a printed Greek New Testament and apparently never carefully studied.[34] It has the unique distinction of being the only codex with Revelation located between Acts and the Catholic Epistles, which von Soden attributed to the bookbinder.[35] The sequence of the Pauline Epistles ends with Hebrews, so this codex concludes the same way as the previous one. The manuscript is defective, lacking the opening folios, and contains marginal corrections.[36] The oddities here again rule out an Athanasian codex.

Of the six manuscripts dated eleventh century, we have already noted that one is incomplete (1384 lacks 2–3 John), one is composite (1668),[37] and one is lost (241 was at

---

[31] B. F. Westcott and F. J. A. Hort, *The New Testament in the Original Greek: Introduction and Appendix* (New York: Harper & Bros., 1882), Introduction, 321.

[32] Both the text and the translation are given in Alexander Souter, *The Text and Canon of the New Testament* (2d ed.; London: Duckworth, 1954), 197, 198. Athanasius's sequence: four gospels (Matthew, Mark, Luke, John), Acts, seven catholic letters (one of James, two of Peter, three of John, and one of Jude), fourteen letters of Paul (first to the Romans, two to the Corinthians, one to Galatians, to Ephesians, to Philippians, to Colossians, two to Thessalonians, then to Hebrews, "without a break" *(euthys)* two to Timothy, one to Titus and lastly to Philemon), and the Revelation of John.

[33] See description and plate in W. H. P. Hatch, *Facsimiles and Descriptions of Minuscule Manuscripts of the New Testament* (Cambridge: Harvard University Press, 1951), 86–87, and Kenneth W. Clark, *A Descriptive Catalogue of Greek New Testament Manuscripts in America* (Chicago: University of Chicago Press, 1937), 104–6, Plate 24. The complete microfilm is of good quality and readily available.

[34] Elliott, *Survey*, 175. Elliott, *Bibliography*, 96, mentions only its text of Revelation in Hoskier, who calls the codex "a very neat copy of the whole N.T." (38).

[35] Von Soden, *Schriften*, 104 (δ95).

[36] Gregory, *Textkritik*, 162–63; Scrivener, *Introduction*, 216.

[37] The beginning till Matt 25:31 and the ending after 1 Cor 6:5 were supplied in the sixteenth century on paper; von Soden, *Schriften* 109 (δ306); Gregory, *Textkritik*, 1169.

Dresden).[38] There are questions about the integrity of the others. Codex 35 is written in three different hands, with many corrections, and a tract attributed to Chrysostom precedes the book of Revelation.[39] Hoskier judged only the Gospels portion to be written in the eleventh century, with Revelation eleventh/twelfth and the rest twelfth century.[40] Codex 506 is badly defective, missing a number of folios in different sections, including most of James. It contains "much liturgical matter" and other "foreign matter and scholia," including numerous glosses. Revelation and the initial liturgical material are written in a different hand, which often suggests a composite codex.[41]

Codex 699 is now in two separated pieces, divided between Galatians and Ephesians. The first part is badly damaged at the end, lacking the transitions from Romans to 1 Corinthians and from 2 Corinthians to Galatians.[42] One of its distinctive features is the location of Hebrews before the Pastoral Letters, in what is otherwise a "Byzantine" style manuscript with the overall arrangement of an Athanasian codex.

Codex 517 (eleventh/twelfth cent.) is so badly damaged that it is difficult to reconstruct the extent of the original manuscript. In its present state it begins with one folio of Acts, which von Soden judged to be from a different manuscript.[43] The remaining manuscript begins with 2 Peter and surviving parts of the Catholic Epistles, followed by Revelation, then the Pauline Letters followed by the Gospels, breaking off after Luke 6:42. The unusual feature of placing the Gospels last is also found in several other manuscripts on our list. The most interesting is probably 209, with Revelation added later to make a "complete" New Testament.[44]

A manuscript dated 1116 at Mt. Athos (Greg. 922) is a purer example of a complete New Testament codex. It could prove to be the oldest noncomposite complete New Testament with an Athanasian arrangement, although no detailed description is available to confirm this. As one of Aland's "Byzantine" type minuscules, it has the typical sequence found in other such Athos manuscripts, with Paul after the Catholic Epistles, and Hebrews last.[45]

---

[38] The earlier descriptions indicated its sequence as "eapcr," which would have been the earliest "complete New Testament" minuscule in that sequence; von Soden (*Schriften*, 116 [δ507]); Gregory (*Textkritik*, 171). Hoskier described the codex as "a lovely ms. of the whole N.T." with "fine handwriting," and "probably copied from a very early cursive, and evidently that cursive was copied very carefully from an older uncial" (133).

[39] For a concise description and plate see Hatch, *Facsimiles*, 140. For the catalogue description, see Robert Devreesse, *Le fonds Coislin* (Catalogue des manuscrits grecs 2; Paris: Imprimerie nationale, 1945), 176–77; Devreesse refers to "marginal glosses and scholia" in Revelation, and the tract as a "catechetical sermon," following Hebrews. The scribal hands are identified as (1) Prologue and Gospels, (2) Acts and Letters, (3) Revelation and the preliminary liturgical material.

[40] Hoskier, *Text*, 32. He describes it as "beautifully written."

[41] F. H. A. Scrivener, *Adversaria critica sacra* (Cambridge: Cambridge University Press, 1893), xxxiv, lxxviii. Hatch (*Facsimiles*, 160) has a concise description, with plate. A full description is in Irmgard Hutter, *Corpus der byzantinischen Miniaturenhandschriften: 4.1 Oxford Christ Church* (Stuttgart: Anton Hiersemann, 1993).

[42] Its history is reconstructed by Scrivener (*Adversaria critica sacra*, lxxxiv–lxxxvi).

[43] Von Soden, *Schriften*, 225 (a214). For a concise description and plate, see Hatch, *Facsimiles*, 150.

[44] The contents are described in E. Mioni, *Bibliothecae Divi Marci Venetiarum: Codices graeci manuscripti* (Rome: Instituto poligrafico e zecca della stato, 1967), 1:14–15.

[45] Lambros (*Catalogue*, 44) indicates *Tetraeuangelion; Apostolōn Praxeis kai Epistolai; Apokalypsis*. Gregory spells it out as "eacpr" (*Textkritik*, 232). Kirsopp Lake described the text as "ordinary"

One other twelfth-century manuscript is catalogued as complete: Gr. 242 in Moscow. But it also has eighty-nine folios of Psalms and hymns, and much liturgical material. It has Hebrews after the Pastorals, in the final canonical position, and it lacks the Pericope of the Adulteress.[46]

When we come to the thirteenth century there are a handful of "Byzantine" type manuscripts that may be complete New Testament codices in the Athanasian sequence (141, 757, 1072, 1084, 1597), but no detailed information is readily available.[47] The only dated manuscript in the group is from Mount Athos, so again little is known about it. The catalogue only has "the whole (*holoklēron*) New Testament," apparently typically Byzantine in sequence: e a c p r with Hebrews after the Pastorals.[48] The only well-known thirteenth-century manuscript on the list is at Duke University. Its distinctive feature is that James alone precedes Paul, with the remaining catholic epistles in their later canonical position. The major sections (except Acts, James, and Revelation) include commentary on three sides of the text, in Talmudic fashion.[49]

Our preliminary conclusion is thus that Athanasius's list became a kind of table of contents possibly by the eleventh or at least the twelfth century, but apparently did not become at all widespread until the thirteenth, if surviving manuscripts are a reliable indication. Even then, the Athanasian sequence had not become fixed.

Only a few of the remaining manuscripts on our list have been catalogued in much detail. What information is available indicates the typical pattern of the Catholic Epistles before Paul. The exceptions are remarkable, however, with Paul preceding even Acts in several manuscripts (61, 69, 522, 582, and 2495, all fourteenth to sixteenth centuries). This is the sequence adopted in the Complutensian Polyglot in Spain, and earlier seen in Codex Sinaiticus.

Several manuscripts begin to reflect the final canonical tradition of Paul inserted between Acts and the Catholic Epistles, previously seen only in the now lost Dresden manuscript. The only other complete New Testament with this arrangement prior to Erasmus is codex 367, dated 1331, an otherwise typically Byzantine manuscript. The famous case of Erasmus's edition reflects the circumstances of the manuscripts available to him in Basel, which happened to have this unusual arrangement.[50] The printed editions probably began to influence the manuscripts at the time, possibly including even the only two Mount Athos manuscripts with this arrangement 1626 (fifteenth cent.) and 1704 (1541). The likelihood of influence increased later: 296 (sixteenth cent.) and 2136 (seventeenth cent.).[51]

It is equally surprising to note that the present printed tradition did not become fixed until the twentieth century. Wettstein (1751–52) has the sequence used in the Complu-

---

("Texts from Mount Athos" in *Studia biblica et ecclesiastica* [Oxford: Oxford University Press, 1903], 174).

[46] Kurk Treu, *Die griechischen Handschriften des Neuen Testaments in der UdSSR* (TU 91; Berlin: Akademie Verlag, 1966), 259–60.

[47] The sequence for 141 is catalogued in Robert Devreesse, *Le fonds grec de la Bibliothèque vaticane des origines à Paul V* (Studi e testi 244; Vatican: Biblioteca apostolica vaticana, 1965), 223.

[48] Eustratiades, *Catalogue*, 176; Gregory, *Textkritik*, 1162. The same characterization seems to apply also to the other Mount Athos manuscripts of the thirteenth century (1072, 1094).

[49] See description and plate in Clark, *Descriptive Catalogue*, 51–53.

[50] This arrangement is attributed to Basil A. N. IV.5, traditionally "Paul. 4," now codex 2816.

[51] Each of these appears to have the Byzantine sequence in the Pauline Letters, with Hebrews last.

tensian Polyglot, with Paul before Acts,[52] whereas the nineteenth-century tradition preserved the common Byzantine sequence reflected in over half of the manuscripts on our list, with Paul after the Catholic Epistles: Tregelles, Tischendorf, and Westcott and Hort.

If these provisional findings are sustained after further research, at least one major irony seems apparent: a century of textual criticism to replace Wescott-Hort has produced a dominant tradition in the Nestle-Aland Greek text whose sequence resembles merely a handful of existing ancient manuscripts. It nonetheless claims to be the reconstructed "original" New Testament text. In all likelihood, such an early codex never existed.

3. Conclusion

Many gaps remain in the information assembled here. Examination of additional microfilms could disclose surprises among manuscripts not otherwise studied for purposes of textual criticism. In the meantime, our provisional findings call to mind James Sanders's observations on the contents of the Psalter in various Hebrew manuscripts:

> It was becoming clear that there were probably as many canons as there were communities. . . . Focusing on the question of fluidity in the matter of inclusion/exclusion of different books in different communities in antiquity brought attention to the question of literature considered authoritative—that is, functionally canonical, by one Jewish or Christian community but not by another.[53]

Sanders says he developed a new sense of what *canon* meant through his "passion to see in extant manuscripts . . . what ancient and medieval believing communities actually had available to them and how they used what they had." He contrasts this with the approach of "neo-neo-orthodoxy that clearly is not vulnerable to historical inquiry."[54]

I want to endorse at least this part of Sanders's approach to the question of canon. The extant manuscripts surely tell us something about the "sense" of canon in believing communities. The preoccupation with reconstructing "the original text," even if there never was one, has shifted the scholarly attention away from what these manuscripts might tell us about the actual development of the canonical tradition.

Table 27-3: Minuscules of the "Complete New Testament" Arranged Chronologically

Date (Aland)	Gregory Von Soden	Location and catalogue # = Alternative/earlier designations CONT contents DEF missing passages NOTES condition of ms. and text BIB bibliography
9/10th c.	1424 δ30	Chicago: Jesuit-Krauss-McCormick Libr. Gruber Ms 152 = Kosinitza 124 (von Soden/Gregory) CONT e a c r p + Paul Prolog/Martyrdom (6 f.) NOTES Commentary by a later hand (except Rev). Film observations: some notes on Rev. BIB Kenneth W. Clark, *A Descriptive Catalogue of Greek New Testament Manuscripts in America* (Chicago: University of Chicago Press, 1937).

[52] For a reproduction see Jacobus Wettstein, *Novum Testamentum Graecum* (Graz, Austria: Academische Druck, 1962).
[53] James A. Sanders, "Scripture as Canon for Post-Modern Times," *BTB* 25 (1995): 56–63, here 58.
[54] Ibid., 58, 61.

Date (Aland)	Gregory Von Soden	Location and catalogue # = Alternative/earlier designations CONT contents DEF missing passages NOTES condition of ms. and text BIB bibliography
10/11th c.	175 δ95	Rome: Biblioteca Vaticana Gr. 2080 = Basiliani 119 CONT e a r c p DEF until Matt 4:17 NOTES scholia in Acts; marg. corr.; later notes (von Soden) BIB C. R. Gregory, *Textkritik des Neuen Testaments* (3 vols.; Leipzig: J. C. Hinrichs, 1900–1909]), 1:162–63; F. H. A. Scrivener, *A Plain Introduction to the Criticism of the New Testament for the Use of Biblical Students* (4th ed.; ed. Edward Miller; 2 vols.; London: George Bell, 1894), 216.
11th c.	35 δ303	Paris: Bibliothèque Nationale Coislin Gr. 199 = old list 44 CONT e a c p Chrysostom r NOTES diff. hand each for e & r from rest; "many corr." (Scrivener) BIB Robert Devreesse, *Le fonds Coislin* (Catalogue des manuscrits grecs 2; Paris: Imprimerie nationale, 1945).
11th c.	[241] δ507	Dresden: Königliche Bibliothek. A.172 = "k" in Matthaei: fr. Constantinople CONT e a p c r (Gregory & von Soden) NOTES "rare readings" (Scrivener); lost since WWII BIB Gregory, *Textkritik*, 1:171.
11th c.	506 δ101	Oxford: Christ Church, Wake 12 = "Codex Dionysii" (scribe) CONT e a c p r (r in diff. hand, same as front matter) DEF over half John & Acts, most Jas, some Paul NOTES "Byz"; much liturgical matter, "foreign matter and scholia" (F. H. A. Scrivener, *Adversaria Critica Sacra* [Cambridge: Cambridge University Press, 1893]) BIB Irmgard Hutter, *Corpus der Byzantinischen Miniaturen-handschriften. IV Oxford Christ Church* (Stuttgart: Anton Hiersemann, 1993).
11th c.	699 δ104	London: British Museum Additional Ms. 28815 CONT e a c p (Rom, Cor, Gal) cont'd in Burdett-Coutts II.4 (= Egerton 3145) p (Eph ff.) r (von Soden) DEF end of Rom–beg 1 Cor, end of 2 Cor–beg Gal NOTES "Byz"; Heb bef. Past. BIB Scrivener, *Introduction*; Gregory, *Textkritik*, 1:213.
11th c.	[1384] δ100	Andros: Panachrantu 13 CONT e a c p r; 2–3 Jn not indicated by Lambros (Gregory) DEF ending NOTES "Byz" BIB Gregory, *Textkritik*, 1:259.
11th c.	[1668] δ306	Athos: Panteleimonos 15 CONT e a c p r (Lambros: e a + letters) NOTES 16th c. paper to Mt 25:31, after 1 Cor 6:5; "Byz"; lacks Pericope Adult., has Travels of Paul BIB Spyridon P. Lambros, *Catalogue of the Greek Manuscripts on Mount Athos* 2 (Cambridge: Cambridge Univ. Pr., 1895).
11/12th c.	[517] ε167 α214	Oxford: Christ Church, Wake 34 CONT (a) c r p e [a = 1 (later?) folio Acts 17:24–18:13] DEF begins at 2 Pet, ends at Luke 6:42, missing 1 leaf 1 John, 2 of Heb, 1 of Luke (Scrivener, *Critica Sacra*) NOTES von Soden: two diff. mss. bound together (out of order) BIB W. H. P. Hatch, *Facsimiles and Descriptions of Minuscule Manuscripts of the New Testament* (Cambridge, Mass.: Harvard University Press, 1951).
1116	922 δ200	Athos: Grigoriu 3 CONT e a c p r (e a+letters r, Lambros) NOTES "Byz" BIB Lambros, *Catalogue*.
12th c.	[180] ε1498 α300	Rome: Biblioteca Vaticana Borgianus Gr.18 = Cong. Propaganda Fide L.VI.19 CONT e a c p r + liturgical material DEF ends at Rev 22:20a before ερχομαι ταχυ NOTES Gregory: a c r later (1273); von Soden: a c p r later BIB P. Franchi de' Cavalieri, *Bibliothecae Apostolicae Vaticanae codices manu scripti recensiti: Codices graeci Chisiani et Borgiani* (Rome: Typis Polyglottis Vaticanis, 1927); Alexander Turyn, *Codices graeci vaticani saeculis XIII et XIV scripti annorumque notis instructi* (Rome: Bibliotheca Apostolica Vaticana, 1964)
12th c.	242 δ206	Moscow: Hist. Mus. Gr. 25 = Synodalbibliothek. 407 (CCCLXXX) CONT e a c p r + 89 fol. Pss/Hymns NOTES much liturgical material; lacks John 8:3–11 BIB Kurt Treu, *Die griechischen Handschriften des Neuen Testaments in der UdSSR* (TU 91. Berlin: Akademie Verlag, 1966).

Date (Aland)	Gregory Von Soden	Location and catalogue # = Alternative/earlier designations CONT *contents* DEF *missing passages* NOTES *condition of ms. and text* BIB *bibliography*
1289	1597 δ308	Athos: Vatopediu 966 = old number 763 (129) CONT e a c p r (Gregory; "New Testament," Eustratiades) NOTES "Byz" BIB Sophronios Eustratiades, *Catalogue of the Greek Manuscripts in the Library of the Monastery of Vatopedi on Mount Athos* (HTS 11; Cambridge, Mass.: Harvard University Press, 1924; reprint, New York: Kraus, 1969).
13th c.	141 δ408	Rome: Biblioteca Vaticana Gr. 1160 CONT e a c p r NOTES "Byz" BIB Robert Devreesse, *Le fonds grec de la Bibliothèque vaticane des origines à Paul V* (Studi e testi 244;Vatican City: Biblioteca apostolica vaticana, 1965).
13th c.	[218] δ300	Vienna: Nationale Bibliothek. Theol. Gr. 23 CONT OT + e a c p (Heb bef. Past.) r DEF mid-Acts, 2 Ti 2:10–Titus–Phlm 14, end Rev 20:7 NOTES "many peculiar readings" (Scrivener) BIB H. Hunger and O. Kresten, *Katalog der griechischen Handschriften der Österreichischen Nationalbibliothek* (Vienna: G. Prachner, 1961–1994).
13th c.	[339] δ303	Turin: Biblioteca Nazionale Universitaria B V.8 = Pasini Gr. 302 CONT e a c p r + Ps, Ep. Pilate, Nativ. Virgin (Greg. 1900) (?Lives of Apostles) NOTES sequence not preserved; 3 hands; 1904 fire; "e questi in pessime condizioni" (Stampini); "nur Fragmente" (Aland, *Kurtzgefasste Liste*) BIB Ettore Stampini, *Inventario dei codici superstiti greci e latini antichi della Biblioteca nazionale di Torino* (Turin: E. Loescher, 1904).
13th c.	757 δ304	Athens: National Libr. 150 = theological ms. 12 CONT e a c p r DEF Eph 4:28–6:24 NOTES "Byz"; Mt 1:1–2:11, 27:60–28:14 from 16th c. BIB Gregory, *Textkritik*, 1.219.
13th c.	1072 d406	Athos: Laura Γ 80 = old number 320 CONT e a c p r NOTES "Byz" + lect. 2030 BIB Sophronios Eustratiades, *Catalogue of the Greek Manuscripts in the Library of the Laura on Mount Athos* (HTS 12; Cambridge, Mass.: Harvard University Press, 1925; reprint, New York: Kraus, 1969); Kirsopp Lake, "Texts from Mount Athos" in *Studia biblica et ecclesiastica* (Oxford: Oxford University Press, 1903).
13th c.	1094 δ307	Athos: Panteleimonos 29 CONT e a c p r DEF begins at Matt 9:34 NOTES "Byz" BIB Lambros, *Catalogue.*
13th c.	[1352] δ396	Jerusalem: S. Saba Stavros 94 CONT e a c p r (Heb bef. Past.) DEF Rev 1:1–2:10; "He[b] *fehlt*," Gregory. NOTES r in 3 diff. later hands (= Codex 2824 in Aland); 2 fol. of Heb. = 2163 (St. Petersburg: Russ. Nat. Libr. Gr. 319; cf. Treu); "Byz" BIB Hatch, *Facsimiles and Descriptions*; Treu, *Griechischen Handschriften.*
13th c.	1780 d412	Durham, N.C.: Duke Univ. Libr. Gr. 1 = Kosinitza 60 CONT e a Jas p c (Pet John Jude) r w/comm. NOTES only Jas before Paul; r cf. Codex 1424 (Gruber 152) BIB Clark, *Catalog.*
13/14th c.	[1785] δ405	[was in Sofia?] Kosinitza 208 CONT e a c p r NOTES now lost BIB Gregory, *Textkritik*, 3.1180; Kirsopp Lake, "Texts from Mount Athos."
1316	2494 —	Sinai: St. Catherine's Monastery Gr. 1991 CONT e a p r (Aland; "New Testament" Clark) BIB K. W. Clark, *Checklist of Manuscripts in the Libraries of the Greek and Armenian Patriarchates in Jerusalem: Microfilmed for the Library of Congress, 1949–50* (Washington, D.C.: Library of Congress, 1953).
1317	1503 δ413	Athos: Laura A 99 CONT e a c p r NOTES "Byz" BIB Eustratiades, *Catalogue.*
1328	1637 δ605	Athos: Laura Ω 141 = old number 796 CONT e a c p r NOTES "Byz" BIB Eustratiades, *Catalogue.*

Date (Aland)	Gregory Von Soden	Location and catalogue # = Alternative/earlier designations CONT contents DEF missing passages NOTES condition of ms. and text BIB bibliography
1331	367 δ400	Florence: Bibliothecae Medicea Laurentianae, Conventi Soppressi 53 = Abbazia Fiorentina 2708 (46) CONT e a p c r (Gregory) NOTES "Byz" BIB Angelo Maria Bandini, *Catalogus codicum manuscriptorum Bibliothecae Mediceae Laurentianae. Accendunt supplementa...*Vol. 2 (orig: Florence, 1768–1770; reprint with suppl: Leipzig: Zentral-Antiquariat der Deutschen Demokratischen Republik, 1961).
1334	582 δ410	Ferrara, Italy: Univ. (Bib. Comm.) Cl. II. 187,188 N.A.7 CONT e p a c r (= vol. 4 w/ 3.vols. OT) BIB Emidio Martini, *Catalogo dei manoscritti greci esistenti nelle Biblioteche Italiane* 1:2 (Milan: Ulrico Hoepli, 1902; repr.: Rome: Istituto poligrafico dello Stato, 1967).
1357	201 δ403	London: British Museum Additional Ms. 11837 = B. M. Butler 2 (from Florence) CONT e a c p r NOTES "Byz"; many corr. (esp. in Rev), "foreign mat." BIB Gregory, *Textkritik*, 1:166; F. H. A. Scrivener, *A Full and Exact Collation of about Twenty Greek Manuscripts of the Holy Gospels...*(Cambridge: Cambridge University Press, 1853).
1364	18 δ411	Paris: Bibliothèque Nationale Gr. 47 = Regius 47; fr. Constantinople CONT e a c p r + 100 fol. Pss/Hymns NOTES "Byz" BIB Gregory, *Textkritik*, 1:133.
14th c.	[209] δ457 α1581	Venice: Biblioteca San Marco Gr. 10 (394) = belonged to Bessarion CONT a c p e r NOTES r is 15th c. ms. (Gregory; von Soden) BIB Elpidius Mioni, *Bibliothecae Divi Marci Venetiarum codices graeci manuscripti*, vol. 1, *Thesaurus antiquus, codices 1–120* (Rome: Ministero della pubblica istruzione, 1967).
14th c.	386 δ401	Rome: Biblioteca Vaticana Ottoboniana Gr. 66 CONT e a c p r NOTES "Byz" BIB Ernesto Feron and Fabiano Battaglini, *Codices manuscripti graeci ottoboniani Bibliothecae Vaticanae* (Rome, 1893).
14th c.	[498] δ402	London: British Museum Additional Ms. 17469 CONT e a c p r DEF beg. Matt, beg. Acts, most Jas, all Jude, beg. Rom, end 2 Th, parts of Past. (esp. 1 Tim 3:16ff) NOTES "Byz" BIB Hatch, *Facsimiles and Descriptions*.
14th c.	680 δ103	New Haven: Yale Univ. Libr. Gr. 248 = Phillipps (Cheltenham) 7682 CONT e a c p r (Heb. bef. Past.) + 20f. theol. treatise NOTES "Byz" (5 scr.); e from 11th c. (Gregory) BIB B. A. Shailor, *Catalogue of Medieval and Renaissance Manuscripts in the Beinecke Rare Book and Manuscript Library, Yale University* (Binghamton, N.Y.: Medieval and Renaissance Texts and Studies, 1984–).
14th c.	808 δ203	Athens: National Libr. 2251 = Chatzidakes 3 (Mamouka) CONT e a c p r NOTES 12th c. (Gregory); "Byz" BIB V. Gardthhausen, *Catalogus codicum graecorum sinaiticorum* (Oxford: Oxford University Press, 1886); Lambros, *Catalogue*.
14th c.	824 δ404	Grottaferrata: Bibl. della Badia, Convento di S. Nilo A.α.1 CONT e a c p r NOTES "Byz" BIB D. Antonii Rocchi, *Codices Cryptenses seu Abbatiae Cryptae Ferratae in Tuscalano* (Tuscany, 1883).
14th c.	935 δ361	Athos: Dionysiu 141 = old number 27 CONT e a c p r (e a + letters, Lambros) NOTES Rev 22:16–end from 15th c. BIB Lambros, *Catalogue*.
14th c.	986 δ508	Athos: Esphigmenu 186 = old numbers 178, 28 CONT e a c p r DEF beg. Mt, end Mk BIB Lambros, *Catalogue*.
14th c.	1040 δ465	Athos: Karakallu 121 (268) = old number 60 CONT e a c p (ends at Heb 13:6, von Soden) + 2041 r London: British Museum Additional Ms. 39612 BIB F. H. A. Scrivener, *An Exact Transcript of the Codex Augiensis . . . [with] a Full Collation of Fifty Manuscripts* (Cambridge: Deighton, Bell, 1859).

Date (Aland)	Gregory Von Soden	Location and catalogue # = Alternative/earlier designations *CONT contents* DEF *missing passages* NOTES *condition of ms. and text* BIB *bibliography*
14th c.	1075 δ506	Athos: Laura Λ 195 = old number 1005 CONT e a c p r (Gregory) NOTES "Byz" BIB Eustratiades, *Catalogue.*
14th c.	1248 δ409	Sinai: St. Catherine's Monastery Gr. 267 CONT e a c p r NOTES "with comm." (Clark); "Byz" BIB Clark, Checklist; Hatch, *The Greek Manuscripts of the New Testament in Jerusalem: Facsimiles and Descriptions* (Paris: Paul Geuthner, 1934); Gardthhausen, *Catalogus codicum graecorum sinaiticorum.*
14th c.	[1678] *	Athos: Panteleimonos 770 CONT Commentary on: e a c p r NOTES *von Soden: Comm. Theophylact for e & p; Comm. Andreou for a & r BIB Lambros, *Catalogue.*
14th c.	2200 δ414	Elasson: Olympiotissis (2) 79 CONT e a c p r (von Soden) BIB Gregory, *Textkritik*, 3:1199.
1434	[2554] —	Bucharest: Rumänische Akademie 3/12610 CONT e a p r (Aland) NOTES ?lost
15th c.	69 δ505	Leicestershire: Town Lib. Codex 6D32/1 CONT p (5 fol. theol. mat.) a c r e (Gos. now bound first) DEF beg. Matt 18:15; Acts 10:45–14:17; end Rev 19:10 BIB J. Rendell Harris, *The Origin of the Leicester Codex of the New Testament* (London: J. C. Clay, 1887); Scrivener, *Exact Transcript.*
15th c.	149 δ503	Rome: Biblioteca Vaticana Palatina Gr. 171 CONT e a c p r NOTES "Byz"; lacks pericope adulterae BIB Hatch, *Facsimiles and Descriptions*; Henricus Stevenson, *Codices manuscripti palatini graeci Bibliothecae Vaticanae* (Rome: Vatican, 1885).
15th c.	205 δ500	Venice: S. Marco Gr. 5 (420) = belonged to Bessarion CONT OT + e a c r p NOTES "peculiar rdgs"; parts copied from 209; Dup: 205A (δ501) = copy of 205 = S. Marco Gr. 6 BIB Mioni, *Bibliothecae.*
15th c.	664 δ502	Zittau: Stadtbibliothek. A.1 CONT OT + e a c p r NOTES "Byz" BIB Gregory, *Textkritik*, 1:210.
15th c.	1617 δ407	Athos: Laura E 157 = old number 619 CONT e a c p r (Gregory) DEF at end NOTES "Byz" BIB Eustratiades, *Catalogue.*
15th c.	1626 δ305	Athos: Laura Ω 16 = old number 671 CONT e a p c r DEF ends at Rev 9:15 NOTES "Byz" BIB Eustratiades, *Catalogue.*
15th c.	[2201] δ374	Elasson: Olympiotissis (3) 6 CONT a c p e (Aland e a p r def.) BIB Gregory, *Textkritik*, 3.1199.
15th c.	2352 —	Meteora: Metamorphosis 237 CONT e a p r (Aland) NOTES "Byz"
15th c.	2495 —	Sinai: St. Catherine's Monastery Gr. 1992 CONT e p a c r (film) BIB Clark, *Checklist.*
1515/16	522 δ602	Oxford: Bodleian Canonici Gr. 34 = from Venice CONT e p a c r + 5p. on apostolic traditions. BIB H. O. Coxe, *Bodleian Library Quarto Catalogues*, vol. 1, *Greek Manuscripts* (Oxford: Bodleian Library, 1969; corr. repr. of 1853 ed.).
1541	[1704] ε1157 α277	Athos: Kutlumusiu 356 = old number 90α CONT e a p c r + Makarismoi BIB Lambros, *Catalogue.*
16th c.	[61] δ603	Dublin: Trinity College A.4.21 = Ms 30, "Codex Montfortianus" CONT e p a c r + 1 John 5:7b–8a (resp. to Erasmus) NOTES 3 or 4 hands BIB Orlando T. Dobbin, *The Codex Montfortianus* (London, 1854).

Date (Aland)	Gregory Von Soden	Location and catalogue # = Alternative/earlier designations CONT contents DEF missing passages NOTES condition of ms. and text BIB bibliography
16th c.	296 δ600	Paris: Bibliothèque Nationale Gr. 123 + 124 = Regius 61 CONT e a p c r NOTES calligrapher, poss. influenced by printed ed. BIB Gregory, *Textkritik*, 1:177.
16th c.	[1652] δ604	Athos: Laura Θ 152 = old number 1567 CONT a c p r e (Gregory) DEF Rev 1:3–end NOTES e in diff. hand BIB Eustratiades, *Catalogue*.
17th c.	2136 ε700	Moscow: Hist. Mus. Gr. 26 = Synodalbibliothek 472 (Greek & Slavonic) CONT e a p c r BIB Treu, *Griechischen Handschriften*.

Table 27-4: Uncials of the "Complete New Testament"

Date (Aland)	Gregory Von Soden	Location and catalogue # = Alternative/earlier designations CONT contents DEF missing passages
4th c.	ℵ = 01 δ2	London: British Museum Additional Ms. 43725 = Codex Sinaiticus CONT OT + e p a c r (Heb before Pastorals) + Barn., Herm.
5th c.	A = 02 δ4	London: British Museum, Royal 1 D VIII = Codex Alexandrinus CONT OT + e a c p r (Heb before Pastorals) + 1–2 Clem (PssSol in table of contents) DEF Matt 1:1–25:6; John 6:50–8:52; 2 Cor 4:13–12:6

Table 27-5. Ordering of Contents in Major Printed Editions of the New Testament

Date	Edition CONT contents NOTES
1514	Complutensian Polyglot (Spain) CONT e p a c r + scholia & glossary
1516	Erasmus (1st ed.) CONT e a p c r NOTES based on (1), 2, 2814, 2815, (2816), 2817
1546	Stephanus CONT e a p c r
1751–1752	Wettstein CONT e p a c r
1857–1872	Tregelles CONT e a c p r (Heb before Pastorals)
1869–1872	Tischendorf CONT e a c p r (Heb before Pastorals)
1881	Westcott/Hort CONT e a c p r (Heb before Pastorals)
1903	Nestle CONT e a p c r

28

Issues in the Interrelation of New Testament Textual Criticism and Canon

Eldon Jay Epp

The lengthy and complex process that brought about the final consensus on what writings would constitute the canon of the New Testament is the province of other contributions in the present volume. The task of this essay is different and twofold: first, to expose ways in which manuscripts that preserve those writings were factors in or reveal aspects of that process, but also, second, to explore "canonical" issues that arise from the very fact of textual variation in and among these "New Testament" manuscripts, whether they were transcribed before or after the canon (or segments thereof) had been resolved. Naturally, canonical issues involving variant readings are also concerned with authority, for that is what canon is all about.[1] We begin, however, by examining rather matter-of-fact features of our "New Testament" manuscripts that have implications for canon, broadly defined.

1. Manuscript Contents with Implications for Canon

The varying content of manuscripts carrying writings that were to become part of the New Testament contribute to our understanding of how the early church was dealing with the issue of authority or canon. For example, what does it mean when manuscripts contain books ultimately not retained in the New Testament, or when certain manuscripts do not carry writings normally expected there, or, finally, when books are found in various manuscripts in different groups or in differing sequences? And what role did the conventional groupings of early Christian writings play in the formation of the canon? These, of course, are all features extraneous to the actual texts of the manuscripts, yet they provide valuable raw data useful in exploring matters of canon, though inevitably they require critical analysis and interpretation. Moreover, the reasons for the inclusion or exclusion of

---

[1] An excursus on "The Intersection of Textual Criticism and Canon," published in 1997, provides the core for the present essay, which, however, is much revised and vastly expanded: E. J. Epp, "Textual Criticism in the Exegesis of the New Testament, with an Excursus on Canon," in *Handbook to Exegesis of the New Testament* (NTTS 25; ed. S. E. Porter; Leiden: Brill, 1997), 73–91. Part of this earlier work evolved into an extensive treatment of "The Multivalence of the Term 'Original Text' in New Testament Textual Criticism," in *HTR* 92 (1999): 245–81.

writings, or for the order or combination of writings in our manuscripts, are not always apparent, often leaving investigators with a fair measure of uncertainty if not a sense of mystery.

We will treat these issues under three headings: (a) the presence of unexpected books in "New Testament" manuscripts, (b) the absence of expected books in "New Testament" manuscripts, and (c) the varying order of books in "New Testament" manuscripts. Yet to speak, as we have, of *expected* or *unexpected* writings in *New Testament* manuscripts is, of course, to take a modern stance toward an ancient situation, which is one of the difficulties in this entire subject: the risk of imposing on early Christianity the results of a canon process not yet completed at the time. Therefore, considerable freedom is used when referring to manuscripts of the first several centuries of Christianity as "New Testament" manuscripts, or when characterizing certain writings as "expected" or "unexpected," "canonical" or "non-canonical," or "apocryphal." And anomalies persist—indeed, anomalies multiply—when certain conventional time frames are adopted for recognition of the authoritative status, for instance, of the Pauline Corpus (ten letters collected early in the second century, expanded by adding the Pastorals, and achieving scriptural status over a wide area by the end of the second century), the fourfold Gospel (collected in the late second century and broadly accepted by the mid-third century), the Catholic Epistles (collected perhaps in the third century, and debated into the fourth), or the twenty-seven book New Testament as we know it (listed first by Athanasius in 367 and authoritative at least in Alexandria, though much later in the East).[2]

First, however, a listing and analysis of the groups in which early Christian writings circulated will provide perspective for later discussion.

A. Grouping of Manuscripts in the Circulation Process

Manuscripts containing writings that would eventually be recognized as canonical were transmitted in fairly well-defined groups, but not consistently. The conventional groupings, with the approximate totals of Greek manuscripts of each, are as follows: the four gospels are found in 2,361 manuscripts; the Acts and the Catholic Epistles in 662; the Pauline Letters in 792; and the Revelation to John in 287.[3] However, when details about these various groups are tabulated, the situation is much more complex than these figures and groupings imply. Leaving out the even more problematic papyri for the moment, Kurt and Barbara Aland reported in 1989 the following array of *majuscule* and *minuscule*

---

[2] See Harry Y. Gamble, "Canon: New Testament," *ABD* 1:853–56; idem, "The Canon of the New Testament," *The New Testament and Its Modern Interpreters* (SBLBMI 3; ed. E. J. Epp and G. W. MacRae; Philadelphia: Fortress; Atlanta: Scholars, 1989), 205–12; Helmut Koester, *Introduction to the New Testament: History and Literature of Early Christianity* (2 vols.; 2d ed.; New York/Berlin: de Gruyter, 1995–2000), 2:6–12; cf. Lee M. McDonald, *The Formation of the Christian Biblical Canon* (rev. and enl. ed.; Peabody, Mass.: Hendrickson, 1995), 189–90; 250–54.

[3] These figures and the following data are taken from Kurt Aland and Barbara Aland, *The Text of the New Testament: An Introduction to the Critical Editions and to the Theory and Practice of Modern Textual Criticism* (2d ed.; trans. Erroll F. Rhodes; Grand Rapids: Eerdmans; Leiden: Brill, 1989), 78–79. Since then, nineteen new papyri and eleven majuscules have been published (see the following note), as well as fifty new minuscules. Note that the statistics presented here and in the following list do not add up, because the latter does not contain all actual combinations.

manuscript contents (with the majuscules updated to 1998),[4] though not all actual combinations are included in the list:

a. Entire New Testament (as finally defined in twenty-seven books): three majuscules (ℵ, A, C[5]), some fifty-six minuscules.

b. All books except Gospels: one majuscule (P^apr), seventy-five minuscules.

c. All books except Revelation: two majuscules (B,[6] Ψ), 147 minuscules.

d. Four Gospels: 193 majuscules (119 fragmentary), 1,896 minuscules (fifty-seven fragmentary).

e. Gospels + Acts + Catholic Epistles: one majuscule (D), eight minuscules.

f. Gospels + Acts + Catholic Epistles + Revelation: two minuscules.

g. Gospels + Pauline Letters: five minuscules.

h. Gospels + Revelation: eleven minuscules.

i. Acts + Catholic Epistles (= Apostolos): thirty majuscules (twenty-eight fragmentary), forty minuscules (five fragmentary).

j. Acts + Catholic Epistles + Pauline Letters: eight majuscules, 256 minuscules.

k. Acts + Catholic Epistles + Revelation: three minuscules.

l. Pauline Letters: fifty-eight majuscules (forty-six fragmentary), 138 minuscules (six fragmentary).

m. Pauline Letters + Revelation: six minuscules.

n. Revelation to John: eight majuscules (four fragmentary), 118 minuscules (one fragmentary).

Placing the New Testament papyri in these same categories would involve undue speculation as to the nature and size of the codices of which nearly all were a part, especially since only fourteen papyri presently contain more than one writing. Many more than these fourteen certainly contained books in addition to those they now preserve, and the approximate or even exact original size of some papyri can be calculated, especially those with substantial text, such as P[45], P[46] (see below), P[74], and P[75], and even some fragmentary

---

[4] For papyri numbers 97–99 and majuscules 0299–0306, see Kurt Aland (ed.), *Kurzgefasste Liste der griechischen Handschriften des Neuen Testaments* (ANTF 1; 2d ed., rev. and enl.; Berlin/New York: de Gruyter, 1994), 16, 44; and, for New Testament papyri P[100]–P[115] and majuscules 0307–0309, see *Bericht der Hermann Kunst-Stiftung zur Förderung der neutestamentlichen Textforschung für die Jahre 1995 bis 1998* (Münster/Westfalen, 1998), 14–16.

[5] Codex C, a palimpsest, which has portions of every book except 2 Thessalonians and 2 John, has many lacunae throughout its text, though there is no reason to doubt its original completeness. For the lacunae, see Scrivener, *Plain Introduction*, 1:121 n. 1.

[6] It is generally assumed that Codex B originally had all twenty-seven books, but actually the Pastorals, Philemon, and Revelation are not extant (see discussion below).

488

Eldon Jay Epp

papyri, such as P⁶⁴ + P⁶⁷ + P⁴ (see below). At other times, the size of a quire can be determined, for example, the recently published P¹¹⁵,[7] though it cannot be known in this case whether such a quire stood alone or had been bound with others. Also, the likely original contents can now and again be projected; for example, T. C. Skeat has suggested that P⁷⁵, which preserves extensive portions of Luke and John, was originally a volume made up of two single quires, or maybe P⁷⁵ was one of two separately bound single quire codices, one with Matthew and Mark, and the other (P⁷⁵) with Luke and John.[8] Skeat, on more solid grounds, argued persuasively that P⁶⁴ + P⁶⁷ + P⁴, demonstrated to be the same manuscript,[9] now containing portions of Matthew and Luke, was a single quire volume that can be shown to have contained all four gospels originally.[10] On the other hand, a papyrus text like P⁴⁶ defies certainty or even reasonable guesses as to its original content, even though its exact size can be determined (see below). Incidentally, as just noted regarding P⁶⁴ + P⁶⁷ + P⁴, some fragments of papyri have been identified as portions of the same manuscript; other instances are P¹⁴ + P¹¹ and P³³ + P⁵⁸. Additional such identifications among our 116 papyri are unlikely, though new fragments of some could well be found, as with the recent case of P.Oxy. LXIV.4405, which was identified as a new fragment of P⁷⁷ (P.Oxy. XXXIV.2683).[11]

The content of our 116 "New Testament" papyri, representing 112 different manuscripts (most of which are fragmentary), might be summarized as follows (with some duplications, and considering only writings in Greek[12]):

a. More than one writing: fourteen papyri.

(1) More than one gospel: five papyri: P⁴⁴ (Matthew + John); P⁴⁵ (four gospels + Acts); P⁶⁴ + P⁶⁷ + P⁴ (Matthew + Luke); P⁷⁵ (Luke + John); P⁸⁴ (Mark + John).

(2) One or two gospels + another writing: two papyri: P⁴⁵ (four gospels + Acts, see above); P⁵³ (Matthew + Acts).

(3) Acts + other writings: three papyri: P⁴⁵ (above); P⁵³ (above); P⁷⁴ (Acts + 1–2 Peter + 1–3 John + Jude).

(4) Two or more catholic epistles: two papyri: P⁷² (1–2 Peter + Jude); P⁷⁴ (above).

(5) Two or more Pauline letters: six papyri: P³⁰ (1–2 Thessalonians); P³⁴ (1–2 Corinthians); P⁴⁶ (Romans + Hebrews +1–2 Corinthians + Ephesians +

---

[7] P.Oxy. LXVI.4499 (1999).

[8] T. C. Skeat, "The Origin of the Christian Codex," *ZPE* 102 (1994): 264.

[9] T. C. Skeat, "The Oldest Manuscript of the Four Gospels?" *NTS* 43 (1997) esp. 1–9.

[10] Ibid., 9–19; see also Graham N. Stanton, "The Fourfold Gospel," *NTS* 43 (1997): 327–28.

[11] J. David Thomas observed that P¹⁰³ of Matthew (P.Oxy. LXIV.4403) and P.Oxy. LXIV.4405 (now P⁷⁷, with P.Oxy. 2683) might be from the same codex, but considered it safer to treat them as from different codices (P.Oxy. LXIV, p. 6).

[12] P² contains portions of Luke and John in Coptic, in addition to Greek parts of John; P⁶, with segments of John in Greek, also has Coptic portions of John and James; P⁴¹ has both Greek and Coptic portions of Acts; P⁴² likewise has portions of Luke in Greek and Coptic (and also some Coptic Old Testament odes); P⁶² has the same six verses of Matthew in Greek and Coptic; P⁹⁶ also has a few verses of Matthew in Greek and Coptic; and P⁹⁹ contains parts of Romans, 2 Corinthians, Galatians, and Ephesians in Greek and Latin. Though P² and P⁶ each has a single writing in Greek but additional writings in Coptic, they are not counted as papyri with more than one writing.

Galatians + Philippians + Colossians + 1 Thessalonians); P[61] (Romans + 1 Corinthians + Philippians + Colossians + 1 Thessalonians + Titus + Philemon); P[92] (Ephesians + 2 Thessalonians); P[99] (Romans + Galatians + Ephesians).

b. Portions of a single writing: ninety-eight papyri.

(1) Portions of one gospel only: fifty papyri: twenty-one with Matthew; one with Mark; seven with Luke; twenty-one with John.

(2) Portions of Acts only: eleven papyri (P[8]; P[29]; P[33] + P[58]; P[38]; P[41]; P[48]; P[50]; P[56]; P[57]; P[91]; P[112]).

(3) Portions of Hebrews only: seven papyri (P[12]; P[13]; P[17]; P[79]; P[89]; P[114]; P[116]).

(4) Portions of one Catholic Epistle only: seven papyri: James (P[20]; P[23]; P[54]; P[100]); 1 Peter (P[81]); 1 John (P[9]); Jude (P[78]).

(5) Portions of one Pauline Letter only: sixteen papyri: Romans (P[10]; P[26]; P[27]; P[31]; P[40]; P[94]; P[113]); 1 Corinthians (P[11] + P[14]; P[15]; P[68]); Galatians (P[51]); Ephesians (P[49]); Philippians (P[16]); 1 Thessalonians (P[65]); Titus (P[32]); Philemon (P[87]).

(6) Portions of Revelation to John only: seven papyri (P[18]; P[24]; P[43]; P[47]; P[85]; P[98]; P[115]).

These papyri, of course, include the numerous earliest witnesses to the text of the eventual New Testament, among them the sixty-one that date up to and around the turn of the third/fourth century. Obviously, the units in which the early manuscripts circulated have significance for canon; yet, it is only occasionally possible to offer strong evidence that fragmentary papyri containing, for example, portions only of Matthew and Luke (P[64] + P[67] + P[4]) or only of Luke and John (P[75]) came from codices containing the four gospels, as noted earlier. More often such conclusions are based upon assumptions, reflected in claims such as "a codex containing only Luke and John [P[75]] is unexpected," or "we have no other example [beside P[75]] of a two-gospel codex,"[13] or "a codex containing three Gospels is unthinkable" [P[64] + P[67] + P[4]];[14] hence, "the only possible conclusion is that the manuscript *originally contained all four Gospels.*"[15] As already noted, plausible arguments have been made that both P[67] + P[64] + P[4] and P[75] are parts of original fourfold Gospel manuscripts, but such claims for papyri (or fragmentary majuscules) now preserving only a portion of a single writing are more difficult to accredit. Sometimes the claim rests upon

---

[13] Stanton, "The Fourfold Gospel," 326, is describing Skeat's view of P[75], though in a footnote Stanton cites P[53] as presumably a two-gospel codex, based on K. Aland's description of that papyrus: it contains portions of Matthew and Acts, and it would be unlikely for the codex to have held four gospels plus Acts; see K. Aland, ed., *Repertorium der griechischen christlichen Papyri*, vol. 1, *Biblische Papyri: Altes Testament, Neues Testament, Varia, Apokryphen* (PTS 18; Berlin/New York: De Gruyter, 1976), 283.

[14] Skeat, "The Oldest Manuscript of the Four Gospels?" 15. This statement appears in the process of argumentation: a third gospel must have existed between Matthew and Luke, etc. In actuality, no papyri contain three gospels, only four (P[45]) or two in varying combinations: P[44]: Matthew and John; P[64] + P[67] + P[4]: Matthew and Luke; P[75]: Luke and John; P[84]: Mark and John. Nor are more than two gospels found in any of the majuscules until after the turn of the third/fourth century: 0162: John; 0171: Matthew and Luke.

[15] Ibid. (italics in original).

the mere fact that the fragment is from a codex (the format of all the papyri except four),[16] which is taken as an automatic indication of the existence of a larger unit: a gospel portion implies a fourfold Gospel codex, a Pauline fragment implies a codex with the Pauline corpus, etc. Undoubtedly this is often the case, yet caution may be advisable in citing statistics. For example, the Alands indicate that the "Four Gospels manuscripts" include forty-three papyri[17] [the comparable number now would be fifty-five], yet only one of these papyri has portions of all four gospels (P[45], which includes Acts also), and only four others have parts of two gospels in various combinations, while fifty have one gospel only.[18] Similarly, it is stated that "the Apostolos (i.e., Acts and the Catholic Letters) is found alone in eighteen papyri"[19] [the figure now would be twenty-one], but, while twelve of these papyri have portions of Acts, only one of them has Acts plus any of the Catholic Letters (P[74], with Acts, James, 1–2 Peter, 1–3 John, and Jude). Finally, the Pauline Letters (including Hebrews) are said to occur in twenty-six papyri [now thirty-two], and P[46] indeed has portions of nine Letters, P[61] has seven, and P[99] three, but of the rest three have two letters and sixteen have only one. The picture indeed differs significantly for the first three score or so majuscules, plus a half-score of others down the list, which are extensive and offer greater numbers of manuscripts with all four gospels, or with both the Acts and Catholic Epistles, or with the Pauline Letters; yet, the two hundred and more remaining majuscules mostly are fragmentary with parts of one or a few writings. We end, then, with a note of caution about claims for regular and consistent combinations or groupings of writings in manu-

---

[16] The exceptions are P[12], P[13], P[18], P[22]. As the Alands indicate, all four "are either opisthographs or written on reused materials" (Aland and Aland, *Text of the New Testament*, 102). An opisthograph is a roll with writing on both sides (an unusual occurrence), of which P[18] (P.Oxy. VIII.1079) is one example; it contains Exod 40:26–32 on the recto, and, on the verso—written in the reverse direction—is Rev 1:4–7. P[13] (P.Oxy. IV.657) contains extensive portions from five chapters of Hebrews on the verso of a roll with portions of a Latin epitome of a history of Rome by Livy on the recto. P[12] (P.Amh.I.IIIb, pp. 30–31) has part of Heb 1:1 on the recto in a third or early fourth-century hand, followed by a Christian letter which, however, is in an earlier hand; on the verso, which was blank when the writer of the Hebrews verse used it, is Gen 1:1–5. Thus, the scribe who placed Heb 1:1 at the top of the letter was employing an already used papyrus—and also may have written the Genesis verses on the reverse: see Kenneth W. Clark, *A Descriptive Catalogue of Greek New Testament Manuscripts in America* (Chicago: University of Chicago Press, 1937), 170.

By their nature, these papyri do not enter into the roll *versus* codex discussion, for the scribe of P[12] was reusing a papyrus letter, while P[13] and P[18] each utilized the verso of a roll whose recto had been used already; hence, a codex could not have been formed for the New Testament material. P[22] (P.Oxy. X.1228) may at first appear to be an exception, for the reverse of both of its small fragments of John (from two consecutive columns) are blank, but John is written on the verso, and the blank portions are the recto. Obviously, more of John than several verses from chs. 15 and 16 were written originally, and the other side of the roll elsewhere—and doubtless extensively—was occupied by text of some kind; if not, the scribe of John certainly would have used the customary and smoother recto of the roll. (For another explanation, see Aland, *Repertorium der griechischen christlichen Papyri: I*, 242). For details on Oxyrhynchus papyri, see the designated volume and text number in B. P. Grenfell and A. S. Hunt, et al., eds., *The Oxyrhynchus Papyri* (London: Egypt Exploration Society, 1898–), 66 vols. to date.

[17] Aland and Aland, *Text of the New Testament*, 78.

[18] See the lists above.

[19] Aland and Aland, *Text of the New Testament*, 78.

scripts, especially the earlier ones, for—as noted in the lists above—a vast array of groupings are present.[20]

B. The Presence of Unexpected Books in "New Testament" Manuscripts

It is commonplace that some of the manuscripts relevant to our considerations contain writings that did not become constituent parts of the New Testament. The codex containing P[72] is the most ancient example.

P[72] and 1–2 Peter and Jude. P[72] (third/fourth century) contains the oldest known copy of Jude and 1–2 Peter, but these Epistles are interspersed among an array of other Christian writings and two Psalms, all bound into a single codex, though each section was designated a separate Bodmer papyrus, as follows: the *Nativity of Mary* (or *Apocalypse of James*) [Bodmer V]; the Corinthian correspondence with Paul and *3 Corinthians* [Bodmer X]; the eleventh *Ode of Solomon* [Bodmer XI]; then Jude [Bodmer VII]; the *Homily on the Passover* by Melito (ca. 170) [Bodmer XIII]; a hymn fragment [Bodmer XII]; the *Apology of Phileas* [Bodmer XX]; Pss 33 and 34 [Bodmer IX]; and, finally, 1–2 Peter [Bodmer VIII]. These nine works are quite separate sections bound together into one codex in the fourth century, though not all were copied by the same scribe or at the same time. Even Jude and 1–2 Peter (which together constitute P[72] and were each copied around the turn of the third/fourth century) probably were not produced by the same scribe,[21] though they and the other writings still bear older page numbers showing that they may have been parts of four codices that were utilized to construct the present ninety-sheet composite Bodmer volume.[22] Notice that 1–2 Peter and Jude are separated in the present, larger codex by four

---

[20] Aspects of these issues are treated in the important, seminal book of Harry Y. Gamble, *Books and Readers in the Early Church: A History of Early Christian Texts* (New Haven/London: Yale University Press, 1995), especially chs. 2–3 on "The Early Christian Book" (42–81) and "The Publication and Circulation of Early Christian Literature" (82–143); cf. E. J. Epp, "The Codex and Literacy in Early Christianity and at Oxyrhynchus: Issues Raised by Harry Y. Gamble's *Books and Readers in the Early Church*," *Critical Review of Books in Religion* 10 (1997): 15–37.

[21] Judgments about the scribe(s) of Jude and 1–2 Peter are hampered by the lack of a full photographic reproduction of Jude, of which only a single plate is available in the *editio princeps*: Michel Testuz, *Papyrus Bodmer VII–IX* (Cologny-Genève: Bibliotheca Bodmeriana, 1959), 12. He argued that the same scribe copied both Jude and 1–2 Peter (8, 29), followed by Floyd V. Filson, "More Bodmer Papyri," *BA* 25 (1962): 51–54, and though tentatively—awaiting photographs—by (the now late) Kurt Aland, *Repertorium der griechischen christlichen Papyri*, vol. 2, *Kirchenväter-Papyri*, Teil 1, *Beschreibungen* (PTS 42; Berlin/New York: De Gruyter, 1995), 366–68, 377, n. 14; cf. 374, n. 2. Postulating different scribes are Francis W. Beare, *The First Epistle of Peter* (3d ed.; Oxford: Blackwell, 1970), 9, n. 1; Eric G. Turner, *The Typology of the Early Codex* (Haney Foundation Series 18; Philadelphia: University of Pennsylvania Press, 1977), 79–80; and Kim Haines-Eitzen, *Guardians of Letters: Literacy, Power, and the Transmitters of Early Christian Literature* (Oxford/New York: Oxford University Press, 2000), 97–99, 173, nn. 87–90, who presents the most extensive and formidable evidence.

[22] On paginations, Turner's scheme (*Typology of the Early Codex*, 80) is followed by K. Junack and W. Grünewald (*Das Neue Testament auf Papyrus*, vol. 1, *Die Katholischen Briefe* [ANTF 6; Berlin/New York: De Gruyter, 1986], 18) and Haines-Eitzen (*Guardians of Letters*, 100, 174, nn. 94–96), namely four pagination series: (1) *Nativity of Mary, 3 Corinthians, Ode,* and Jude; (2) Melito and hymn; (3) *Phileas* and Pss 33–34; and (4) 1–2 Peter. David Trobisch (*Die Endredaktion des*

writings, but also were separate in their predecessor codices. This odd arrangement causes one to wonder, with Floyd Filson, whether 1–2 Peter and Jude "were really considered to be fully canonical by the fourth-century Christian who made up this codex."[23]

As for the unit made up of the Corinthian correspondence with Paul and of *3 Corinthians,* the latter was written in the late second century and not only appears in Greek for the first time in the Bodmer papyrus but the latter is also its oldest copy. It is of interest that this (apocryphal) correspondence between the Corinthians and Paul was treated as canonical in the Syrian church by Aphraat (ca. 340) and Ephraem (d. 373), and also, through the Syriac, by the Armenian church at least by the fourth century and for several centuries thereafter.[24] Beyond this, it is difficult (a) to assess the significance for canon either of the later multisectioned codex with its variously dated, diverse contents, or (based on the continuous pagination that remains) of a similarly diverse codex that earlier contained the *Nativity of Mary, 3 Corinthians,* the eleventh *Ode of Solomon,* and Jude, or (b) to explain the order chosen for 1–2 Peter and for Jude by the later compiler, or (c) to account for the separation of 1–2 Peter from Jude. It will be obvious, however, that both the third/fourth-century copying of 1–2 Peter and of Jude and the fourth-century compilation and binding of the present codex place these events clearly within the period when considerations of canon were most active, especially regarding the shorter catholic epistles.

While the history of canon formation for the Catholic Epistles shows that only 1 Peter and 1 John were quite well established in the third century, and that James, Jude, 2 Peter, and 2–3 John were still striving for acceptance, the history of the text of these Epistles reveals that often they do not share a uniform textual character in a single manuscript, especially when such a document holds the conventional Apostolos group (Acts plus Catholic Epistles). Rather, each writing may have a text quite different in complexion from the others. This suggests that they had earlier circulated as independent writings and, therefore, that their differing textual character in a manuscript that brought them together stems from the earlier, most likely separate manuscripts from which they were copied.[25] Jude in P[72] exemplifies aspects of this phenomenon. Even though this is the earliest manuscript containing Jude, it already shows a complex textual history for that Epistle.[26] More-

---

Neuen Testaments: Eine Untersuchung zur Entstehung der christlichen Bibel [NTOA 31; Freiburg: Universitätsverlag; Göttingen: Vandenhoeck & Ruprecht, 1996], 49) appears to have a different scheme: (1) *Nativity;* (2) *3 Corinthians, Ode,* and Jude; (3) Melito and hymn, *Phileas,* and Psalms; and (4) 1–2 Peter.

[23] Floyd V. Filson, "More Bodmer Papyri," 57. Cf. Wolfgang Wiefel, "Kanongeschichtliche Erwägungen zu Papyrus Bodmer VII/VIII (P[72])," *APF* 22/23 (1974): 292–93.

[24] See Bruce M. Metzger, *The Canon of the New Testament: Its Origin, Development, and Significance* (Oxford: Clarendon Press, 1987), 219, 223; cf. 7, 176, 182; Wilhelm Schneemelcher, ed., *New Testament Apocrypha* (2 vols.; rev. ed. of Edgar Hennecke and Wilhelm Schneemelcher, *Neutestamentliche Apokryphen* [6th ed.; Tübingen: Mohr (Siebeck), 1989–1990]; ET, ed. R. McL. Wilson; Louisville, Ky.: Westminster John Knox, 1991–92), 2:217, 228–29, 254–57; and earlier, A. F. J. Klijn, "The Apocryphal Correspondence between Paul and the Corinthians," *VC* 17 (1963): 2–23, esp. 2–16.

[25] Aland and Aland, *Text of the New Testament,* 49–50. Cf. Beare, *First Epistle of Peter,* 8–9.

[26] Aland and Aland, *Text of the New Testament,* 50, where this general statement is made but without a rationale; for the latter, see Edouard Massaux, "Le texte de l'Epître de Jude du Papyrus Bodmer VII (P[72])," *ALBO* 3.24 (1961): 108–25, who concludes by characterizing the text as "wild" (125); J. Neville Birdsall ("The Text of Jude in P[72]," *JTS* 14 [1963]: 394–99) shows, however, that

over, as noted earlier, the larger Bodmer codex contains not only 1–2 Peter and Jude, but a half dozen other early "non-canonical" Christian writings or writings used liturgically by Christians. Thus, not only might a book's presence in a manuscript that contains "unexpected" writings reflect fluidity in canon formation, but fluidity can be inferred also from the varying textual complexions of books in a single grouping or collection, implying, for instance, that writings valued by some were copied and used as individual books until they were more broadly accredited by inclusion in a regular canonical grouping.[27]

Other manuscripts with "unexpected" writings. The venerable Codex Sinaiticus (ℵ, mid-fourth century) preserves the Old and New Testaments and, following the twenty-seven books of the latter, the *Epistle of Barnabas* and the *Shepherd of Hermas* (part of which is lost; it is not clear whether additional works were included originally in the volume). That the missing portions of Codex Vaticanus (B, mid-fourth century) also originally contained some Apostolic Fathers is speculation based on analogy with ℵ and A.[28] Codex Alexandrinus (A, fifth century) likewise has the Old and New Testaments (the latter beginning at Matt 25:6) plus *1–2 Clement* (though the last two leaves are missing). Originally, as indicated by a table of contents, the eighteen *Psalms of Solomon* followed *Clement*.[29] It is noteworthy that this table of contents, prefixed to the Old Testament portion and under the heading *hē kainē diathēkē*, includes the two epistles of *Clement* immediately after Revelation, as if part of the canon, though the *Psalms of Solomon* appear to be separated from the preceding writings, as if not part of the canon, by a notation of the number of books.[30] This treatment of *1–2 Clement* agrees with their place in the "Apostolic Canons" 85, where (since Revelation is not included) they follow Jude.[31]

A very late papyrus, P[42] (seventh/eighth century, though its editors[32] dated it in the sixth), contains tiny portions of Luke 1 and 2 in Greek and Coptic, which are part of an extensive series of odes or hymns taken from the Jewish Bible and apocrypha, fragments of which are extant for thirteen selections in addition to those from Luke. The codex was

---

these "wild" aspects of the text in P[72] are shared by other witnesses, and he asks then whether "variant exegetical traditions" are reflected in P[72]'s version of the text (398).

[27] Aland and Aland, *Text of the New Testament*, 49–50.

[28] Eberhard Nestle (*Introduction to the Textual Criticism of the Greek New Testament* [London: Williams and Norgate, 1901], 60) reports the view of Alfred Rahlfs that *Didache* and *Shepherd of Hermas* were included; Aland and Aland (*The Text of the New Testament*, 109) suggest that "texts of the Apostolic Fathers" were probably present "as in ℵ and A."

[29] Caspar René Gregory, *Canon and Text of the New Testament* (International Theological Library; Edinburgh: T&T Clark, 1907), 343.

[30] This is the interpretation of Scrivener-Miller, *Plain Introduction*, 1:99. The same view is found in Eberhard Nestle, *Introduction to the Textual Criticism of the Greek New Testament* (London: Williams and Norgate, 1901), 59; idem, *Einführung in das Griechische Neue Testament* (3d ed.; Göttingen: Vandenhoeck & Ruprecht, 1909), 67; cf. Trustees of the British Museum, *The Codex Alexandrinus (Royal MS. 1 D v–viii) in Reduced Photographic Facsimile: New Testament and Clementine Epistles* (London: British Museum, 1909 ["Introduction" by F. G. Kenyon]), 8.

[31] English text in Metzger, *Canon of the New Testament*, 313; see discussion on 225; Greek text in Brooke Foss Westcott, *A General Survey of the History of the Canon of the New Testament* (4th ed.; London: Macmillan, 1875), 534–35.

[32] Walter Till and Peter Sanz, *Eine griechisch-koptische Odenhandschrift (Papyrus Copt. Vindob. K 8706)* (Monumenta biblica et ecclesiastica, 5; Rome: Päpstliches Bibelinstitut, 1939), 16–17 ("second half of the 6th century").

designed for Christian liturgical purposes, and, since it is very late and not a continuous text manuscript, it is not significant for canon.

The still later Greek and Latin majuscule, Codex Boernerianus (G^p, ninth century) of the Pauline Epistles, originally contained the *Epistle to the Laodiceans*, though only the superscription remains ("The Epistle to Laodiceans begins"), not the text. Curiously, this obviously spurious letter also appears in more than a hundred Latin Vulgate manuscripts, beginning with the mid-sixth-century Fuldensis, and in Arabic and other manuscripts, as well as in all eighteen German Bibles prior to that of Luther, where it is found between Galatians and Ephesians.[33]

Another ninth-century majuscule, P^{apr} (or P$_2$, a palimpsest), has Acts, all Catholic and Pauline Epistles, and the Revelation to John, but also fragments of *4 Maccabees*. As a final example, a twelfth-century Harklean Syriac New Testament contains *1–2 Clement* and locates them between the Catholic Epistles and the Pauline, specifically between Jude and Romans.[34]

At certain times in certain places, as known from patristic sources and several canon lists, books like *1–2 Clement*, the *Epistle of Barnabas*, the *Epistle to the Laodiceans*, and many others, but especially the *Apocalypse of Peter* and the *Shepherd of Hermas*, were treated as authoritative (or "canonical").[35] It is well documented that the latter two apocalypses, along with the Revelation to John, vied over a long period of time for a place among the authoritative writings. All three were mentioned in the Muratorian Canon,[36] with doubt expressed about the *Apocalypse of Peter* and clear rejection assigned to *Hermas*. Oddly, the *Apocalypse of Peter* has not been found as part of a "New Testament" manuscript, though it is included in the canon list attached to Codex Claromontanus (D^p, sixth century, but the list is thought to be earlier); this canon, by the way, also includes the *Shepherd of Hermas*, as well as the *Epistle of Barnabas* and the *Acts of Paul*, though the scribe has placed a dash to the left of these three, as well as the *Apocalypse of Peter*, to indicate that they are in some sense exceptional.[37]

We come now to some obvious questions: To what extent do our "New Testament" manuscripts reflect the status of canon formation in their times? Did they influence that process? One may assume effects in both directions, though proof is elusive. In the first two centuries of Christianity, books like *1 Clement, Epistle of Barnabas, Apocalypse of Peter, Shepherd of Hermas,* and others were treated as authoritative by various patristic writers,

---

[33] Metzger, *Canon of the New Testament*, 183, 239–40. J. B. Lightfoot (*Saint Paul's Epistles to the Colossians and to Philemon* [9th ed.; London: Macmillan, 1890; originally 1875], 272–98, esp. 279–98) provides a full discussion of this Epistle, including a Latin critical edition and a history of its inclusion in Latin, Albigensian, Bohemian, German, and early English Bibles over a period from the sixth to the fifteenth centuries. In general, see Schneemelcher, *New Testament Apocrypha*, 2:42–46.

[34] Metzger, *Canon of the New Testament*, 222.

[35] See the summary in McDonald, *Formation*, 223–25. On the *Shepherd*, see Metzger, *Canon of the New Testament*, 65.

[36] The text in English translation may be found in Metzger, *Canon of the New Testament*, 305–7.

[37] For the text in English translation and discussion, see ibid., 230, 310–11. See also Geoffrey Hahneman, *The Muratorian Fragment and the Development of the Canon* (Oxford: Clarendon, 140–43.

especially Clement of Alexandria. In the third century, books like these were known, used, and valued by leaders such as Origen (185–254), Hippolytus (170–235), and Eusebius (ca. 265–340). At the same time, Origen is reported to have "doubted" 2 Peter and to have deemed 2–3 John questionable, while Eusebius, who placed *Barnabas, Apocalypse of Peter,* and *Hermas* in the "disputed books" category, also relegated to that same category James, Jude, 2 Peter, 2–3 John, and perhaps the Revelation to John. At the end of the third century, of course, P⁷² appeared with 1–2 Peter and Jude among the codex's mixed contents. Naturally, all of this attests to the fair measure of fluidity that remained on the fringes of the New Testament canon in the early and mid-fourth century, when Codex ℵ was produced, with its *Barnabas* and *Hermas.* Movement toward the twenty-seven book canon accelerated as the fourth century closed, but not in all localities, for certainly there was no uniformity across the entirety of Christendom on these matters, especially between East and West and especially on books like Hebrews, Revelation, and *Apocalypse of Peter.*[38] So mysteries remain when attempting to spell out the significance of "unexpected" books in "New Testament" manuscripts, including P⁷²'s *3 Corinthians,* given this writing's later history, which might be significant were it not for the apparently haphazard collection in which it appears. Then too, Codex ℵ's inclusion of *Barnabas* and *Hermas* in the mid-fourth century is a puzzle, but more so *1–2 Clement* in Codex A in the following century. Yet the greatest puzzle is the lengthy virulence of the *Epistle to the Laodiceans,* reinforced in the mid-sixth century with the Vulgate Fuldensis and carried by Gᵖ through the ninth and then until the Reformation as part of the canon in certain areas.

C. The Absence of Expected Books in "New Testament" Manuscripts

If some "New Testament" manuscripts held writings that did not end up in the New Testament, there were other manuscripts that lacked certain books that might have been expected in their particular groupings, as well as manuscripts whose exact contents are difficult to discern. The earliest instance merits a thorough assessment; other examples will be treated more briefly.

The disputed contents of P⁴⁶. Dating to ca. 200, this is the earliest example of an important manuscript whose contents are disputed. For that reason, it has also become highly controversial. It has been customary to say something like the following: P⁴⁶ originally had ten letters of Paul, including Hebrews, but not Philemon, and it never contained the Pastoral Letters, for there is no room for them in the single quire codex when its missing first and last sections are reconstructed. I have twice made such statements,[39] based on secondary sources, as have others. Recent studies of the matter, however, require that we be more cautious, and our caution should begin by stating *positively* what P⁴⁶ contains and not by reporting what it is variously assumed *not* to have contained. P⁴⁶ preserves, in this

---

[38] See Harry Y. Gamble, *The New Testament Canon: Its Making and Meaning* (GBS; Philadelphia: Fortress, 1985), 48–56.

[39] E. J. Epp, "The Papyrus Manuscripts of the New Testament," *The Text of the New Testament in Contemporary Research: Essays on the* Status Quaestionis (SD 46; ed. B. D. Ehrman and M. W. Holmes; Grand Rapids: Eerdmans, 1995), 37; idem, "Textual Criticism in the Exegesis of the New Testament, with an Excursus on Canon," *Handbook to Exegesis of the New Testament* (NTTS 25; ed. S. E. Porter; Leiden: Brill, 1997), 76.

order, Rom 5:17–6:14; 8:15–end; Hebrews; 1–2 Corinthians; Ephesians; Galatians; Philippians; Colossians; and 1 Thessalonians (with lacunae) through 5:28. Since most pages of this single quire codex are numbered, it is clear that seven leaves or fourteen pages from the beginning of the codex have not survived, and there is no dispute that Rom 1:1–5:17 would fit onto those pages and originally occupied them. This means, of course, that fourteen pages also are missing from the end, and the difficult question arises, what writing(s) followed 1 Thessalonians?

It may appear self-evident that 2 Thessalonians followed 1 Thessalonians, but the question at least should be raised. One relevant approach would be to ask whether the two letters ever circulated separately, either in the known papyri or majuscules. The papyri evidence is extremely limited, but 1 and 2 Thessalonians are together in P³⁰ (third century); it is, in fact, the only papyrus with portions of both Epistles. But three other papyri have one of the Thessalonian letters: P⁶¹ (ca. 700) has small fragments of seven Pauline letters, including parts of 1 Thess 1:2–3 on the verso of a leaf that has parts of Col 4:15 on the preceding recto, but no immediately following leaves have survived.⁴⁰ P⁶⁵ (third century) contains most of chapter 1 and half of chapter 2 of 1 Thessalonians, but nothing else, so (as with P⁶¹) it is inappropriate to assume that 2 Thessalonians followed,⁴¹ since there is no possibility of knowing. Finally, P⁹² (third/fourth century) has survived in two tiny fragments, one with a few verses of Eph 1 on either side, and the other leaf, *quite separate from the Ephesians fragment,* contains 2 Thess 1:4–5 on the recto and 2 Thess 1:11–12 on the verso.⁴² As to P⁶¹ and P⁶⁵, then, we have no evidence of what followed the fragments of 1 Thessalonians, and for P⁹² no evidence of what came before 2 Thessalonians, leading to the conclusion that 1 and 2 Thessalonians are together in the papyri wherever an appropriate test can be made (i.e., only in P³⁰). Moreover, twelve Pauline majuscules with Thessalonians contain both epistles: ℵ A B Dᵖ Fᵖ Gᵖ I Kᵃᵖ Lᵃᵖ Pᵃᵖʳ Ψ 0278. Seven others, however, contain only portions of one or the other, but all of these manuscripts are fragmentary, most highly so, and in every case there is no evidence of what came immediately after the fragment of 1 Thessalonians or, if a fragment of 2 Thessalonians is preserved, of what immediately preceded it: C Hᵖ 048, 0111, 0183, 0208, and 0226.⁴³ Hence, as in the case of the papyri, there is no instance where it can be demonstrated that 2 Thessalonians does not follow 1 Thessalonians. Therefore, it is fair to assume that 2 Thessalonians fol-

---

⁴⁰ See Lionel Casson and Ernest L. Hettich, *Excavations at Nessana,* vol. 2, *Literary Papyri* (Princeton: Princeton University Press, 1950), 118–19.

⁴¹ See PSI XIV.1373 (pp. 5–7).

⁴² See Claudio Gallazzi, "Frammenti di un codice con le Epistole di Paoli," *ZPE* 46 (1982): 117–22 + plates.

⁴³ Those that have only one are C (a palimpsest, with portions of every book except 2 John and 2 Thessalonians; after Colossians comes 1 Thess 1:1–2:9, but the next extant portion is Heb 2:4ff.); Hᵖ (its leaves are scattered in eight different archives; nothing is extant between Col 3:11 and 1 Thess 2:9–13, and nothing after 1 Thess 4:11 until 1 Tim 1:7); 048 (part of 1 Thess 1, then nothing until 1 Tim 5); 0111 (fragment: 2 Thess 1:1–2:2); 0183 (fragment: 1 Thess 3:6–9; 4:1–5); 0208 (fragment of Col 1–2, then 1 Thess 2:4–7, 12–17, then nothing); 0226 (fragment: 1 Thess 4:16–5:5). Incidentally, the Muratorian Canon (English text in Metzger, *Canon of the New Testament,* 306–7) speaks of Paul's letters to the seven churches, first to the Corinthians . . . sixth to the Thessalonians, as if there were one each, but then adds that Paul wrote once more to each "for admonition." There is here no reason to think that the two letters to Thessalonians did not circulate together.

lowed 1 Thessalonians in P[46], especially in view of the regular series of Pauline letters that there precede 1 Thessalonians.

In speculating about what P[46] contained after 1–2 Thessalonians, certain data must be taken into account. First, it is self-evident that, in a single quire manuscript, pages at the beginning and at the end will be wider and therefore capable of carrying more text than those in the center, where all the sheets have been folded and where pages then were trimmed to provide an even right-hand edge for the codex. Second, it is observable that the scribe of P[46] used smaller letters as the copying progressed beyond half of the codex and that the lines per page increased from twenty-six in the first half to twenty-eight, thirty, and finally to thirty-two lines per page at the end.[44] Third, the calculated space on the missing fourteen leaves following 1 Thessalonians is inadequate to accommodate the remaining writings of the Pauline corpus as we know it, namely, 1–2 Timothy, Titus, and Philemon (Hebrews, as already mentioned, is present earlier in P[46], between Romans and 1 Corinthians).[45]

Naturally, numerous possibilities have been offered as to how the approximately fourteen pages might have been filled, always allowing nearly five pages for 2 Thessalonians, and therefore leaving some nine pages with unknown contents. Without Philemon, 1 Timothy alone would fit with only a portion of a page left blank, but that has not been proposed; 2 Timothy with Philemon would fit; and 2 Timothy and Titus might be squeezed in, but these are unlikely combinations and have not been suggested, nor has the duo of 1 Timothy and Philemon, which would really require an additional page and is also an unlikely pair. It is clear, however, that 1–2 Timothy would require more than five extra pages, and with Titus a total of almost nine extra; if Philemon were included with the Pastorals, some ten extra pages would be needed.[46] On the other hand, if only Philemon were added after 2 Thessalonians, at least seven pages would be left blank.

Several scholars, however, have argued that P[46], by design, contained only letters of Paul addressed to church communities, not personal letters, a distinction evident in the Muratorian Canon, which separates church letters from personal ones.[47] This would

---

[44] See Henry A. Sanders, *A Third-Century Papyrus Codex of the Epistles of Paul* (University of Michigan Studies: Humanistic Series, 38; Ann Arbor: University of Michigan Press, 1935), 5–6; Frederic G. Kenyon, *The Chester Beatty Biblical Papyri: Descriptions and Texts of Twelve Manuscripts on Papyrus of the Greek Bible, Fasciculus III Supplement: Pauline Epistles, Text* (London: Walker, 1936), ix; Robert M. Grant, *A Historical Introduction to the New Testament* (Touchstone Book; New York: Simon and Schuster, 1972 [original, 1963]), 210; David Trobisch, *Paul's Letter Collection: Tracing the Origins* (Minneapolis: Fortress, 1994), 13–17.

[45] For various calculations, see Sanders, *A Third-Century Papyrus Codex*, 10–11, who suggests that, "if I and II Timothy were included, they were in an abbreviated form," and that all three Pastorals could be included with "more crowding than on the existing leaves and at least three extra pages added"; Kenyon, *The Chester Beatty Biblical Papyri . . . Pauline Epistles, Text*, x–xi; Grant, *Historical Introduction*, 209–11; and Jeremy Duff, "P[46] and the Pastorals: A Misleading Consensus?" *NTS* 44 (1998): 581–82 (to be discussed below).

[46] I use the figures of Duff when available, but consulting also those of Kenyon, *The Chester Beatty Biblical Papyri . . . Pauline Epistles, Text*, x; and Grant, *Historical Introduction*, 210; see preceding note. The assumption at this point is that the average of 1,050 letters per page in the last extant section of P[46] continued in the missing pages. This will be adjusted slightly in the ensuing discussion.

[47] See the references in Duff, "P[46] and the Pastorals," 582 n. 11, who, among others, refers to Jerome D. Quinn, "P[46]–The Pauline Canon?" *CBQ* 36 (1974): 379–85; see also Raymond E. Brown,

presume that P⁴⁶, in the missing end portions, contained 2 Thessalonians but no other letters beyond it. As noted earlier, however, about nine pages then would be left blank at the end of the codex. So a difficult problem remains.

A single quire codex, of course, places heavy demands on the ability of the scribe to estimate in advance the adequacy of space available for what is to be included, though—in the event of miscalculation—the options remain (a) to leave blank pages at the end or (b) to glue on one or more pages and complete the copying. No such additional pages for P⁴⁶ exist, nor is there any way to tell whether any were added.

Recently Jeremy Duff presented a review of these aspects of P⁴⁶, including fresh calculations of the space used but especially of that remaining in the (reconstructed) codex, and he argues that the scribe of P⁴⁶ "was always intending to include all fourteen Pauline epistles," though the attendant difficulties require Duff then to offer not one but two alternative hypotheses regarding the missing pages. The first hypothesis stipulates that the scribe intended to include the Pastoral Epistles but, due to lack of space, did not after all do so.[48] Duff's second hypothesis states that, after copying past the center of the single quire codex, it was clear that space was limited, and the scribe then gradually increased the amount of text on each page; yet, in Duff's view, even this good faith effort meant that only half of 2 Timothy would have been transcribed before the codex ended. At this point, Duff suggests, the scribe added about four[49] extra pages to accommodate the rest of 2 Timothy and Titus, or perhaps an additional small quire. Duff prefers the second alternative, though he insists that both options are viable and "point to a scribe who produced P⁴⁶ assuming that the Pastorals were a constituent part of the Pauline corpus."[50]

Duff bases his hypotheses primarily on the scribe's increased number of lines per page and letters per line as the copying proceeded once the middle of the quire had been passed. To be sure, Duff's obviously careful counting of the number of letters on each page of P⁴⁶ is both impressive and helpful, yet questions need to be raised on some crucial matters. For instance, he correctly observes that "not long after the scribe passed the half-way point in the codex, he started fitting more and more text on each page," but two sentences later Duff asserts that the final section of the codex has some 50 percent more letters per page than in the middle.[51] These are not inaccurate statements in themselves,

---

S.S., *An Introduction to the New Testament* (Anchor Bible Reference Library; New York: Doubleday, 1997), 664. Quinn raises the intriguing possibility, but it is only that, of a comparable collection of Paul's personal letters, asking whether P³² (ca. 200, the same date as P⁴⁶) could have been part of such a codex (380–82). Note that P⁸⁷ (early third century) contains only Philemon.

[48] Here Duff is quite unclear, for his hypothesis is that "P⁴⁶ did not contain the Pastorals but was intended to do so" ("P⁴⁶ and the Pastorals," 586), yet, he immediately goes on to say that "the scribe then left the codex full but, in his own eyes, incomplete" (ibid.). How can this codex be full and yet not contain (part of) the Pastorals? If he stopped after 2 Thessalonians, some eight to nine pages would be blank; if Philemon was added, there would be seven empty pages. Clear or not, this hypothesis is far from compelling.

[49] According to the figures we have been using and Duff's own letter count, the Pastorals would require 18,900 letters, or eighteen 1,050-letter pages; hence, at least *nine* additional pages would appear to be requisite at this point (assuming, as Duff does, that Philemon had been copied after 2 Thessalonians).

[50] Duff, "P⁴⁶ and the Pastorals," 585–89.

[51] Ibid., 584.

but have the proper comparisons been made? If we take the average number of letters per page by using Duff's graph[52] and compare the first half of the extant codex with the second half, we find that the first half averages around 755 letters per page, while the latter half averages about 870, for a 15 percent increase of letters per page in the second part over the first. A better comparison (due to the changing widths of pages in a single quire) would be quarter by quarter: the first fourth of P[46] averages 875 letters per page, the second 700 (for a decline of 20 percent); the third quarter, beginning at the center of the codex, averages 760 (an increase of 8.6 percent over the second), and the fourth quarter averages 1000 letters per page (an increase of 32 percent over the third quarter). However, even these comparisons are not particularly useful inasmuch as the central pages in a single quire codex, as noted earlier, will be more narrow than the earlier and later pages due to trimming, the more so the thicker the codex. P[46] originally contained fifty-two papyrus sheets folded in the middle to form 104 leaves, that is, 208 pages. Hence, for such a single quire codex, the most appropriate comparison would be between the later pages, and not the most narrow middle leaf, but the comparable leaves at the beginning of the codex. Such a comparison, again using Duff's graph of letters per page, would begin with the pages showing the sharpest increase in letters and lines over preceding portions of text (namely, the last thirty-seven or so extant pages, but including also the missing pages 188–91, for a total of some forty-four pages, i.e., roughly pages 150–93) and would compare them with the comparable extant portion at the beginning of the codex (consisting of some forty-five pages, i.e., pages 20–64). This exercise yields a more appropriate result, showing that when the scribe began to add lines and to compress more letters into the available space, the latter forty-four pages contained 24 percent more letters than their extant counterparts in the front of the codex. Hence, while technically accurate, it is at the same time misleading to refer to a 50 percent increase at the end of the codex as measured against the middle, when in actuality the relevant portions show an expansion of text around half of that percentage when pages of roughly the same width are compared. To be still more specific about the second half of the codex, Duff's graph shows that after passing the middle the scribe compressed 7.6 percent more text per page into pages 105–29 than in the very central pages of the volume (pages 104–5); that pages 130–49 had 9 percent more than the preceding twenty-five pages; but that the final pages (150–93, i.e., the fourth quarter of the codex) crammed in 26 percent more text than pages 130–49. For this last reason, I chose to compare pages 150–93, the most strikingly compressed section of text, with the comparable pages at the outset of the scribe's extant work (pages 20–64). To repeat, this appropriate comparison showed a 24 percent increase in letters per page.

What does this all mean for Duff's hypotheses about the missing fourteen pages? According to his count—which is not being questioned—1 Thessalonians (5:28–end) plus 2 Thessalonians and Philemon would consist of 5,750 letters; the last extant pages of P[46]

---

[52] Ibid., 583. My comparisons were made by enlarging Duff's graph and assigning the appropriate number of letters to each bar in the graph, using the graph's scale on the left. I then averaged the letters per page for each quarter of the graph. The fourth quarter happens to begin where the scribe's most dramatic compression of the text also begins. Comparisons, which I presume are reasonably accurate, were then made between and among the extant halves, quarters, and other sections of P[46].

average 1,050 letters each, and, arbitrarily allowing the scribe another 10 percent expansion in number of letters on the increasingly wider outer pages, five of the fourteen missing pages (each now with about 1,155 letters) would be required to accommodate the rest of the Thessalonian letters and Philemon. That would leave nine pages for whatever else the scribe had in mind, permitting writings totaling about 10,400 letters to be included. 1–2 Timothy and Titus, however, consist of 18,900 letters and would require sixteen and a half 1,155-letter pages, or seven and a half pages more than the single quire P[46] contained; stating it differently, only 55 percent of the Pastorals could be included on the nine available pages and seven or eight additional pages would have to be glued on to contain all three.[53] This assumes that Philemon was included, which (as noted above) some scholars have doubted; without Philemon, another page and a half would be available—still not enough to accommodate all the Pastorals. It is doubtful, however, that the personal letter, Philemon,[54] would have been excluded if the personal Timothy and Titus letters were included.

The addition of extra pages or a small additional quire is not unknown in the manuscript tradition,[55] but one wonders whether a scribe who, we might assume, had such an option in mind would undertake so seriously a program of compression of the text that is obvious in P[46]; why not continue in the fashion of the first portions knowing that a few or several pages might be added if required? On the other hand, one might suppose (since extra pages in manuscripts are not everyday experiences) that a scribe's pride might be at stake if calculations of space are excessively off the mark. The scribe of P[46] has received mixed reviews and is described by H. A Sanders as "well trained in his method" of producing blocks of writing with more or less the same margins;[56] by F. G. Kenyon as employing a script that, in contrast to P[45], is "more calligraphic in character . . . with some pretensions to style and elegance";[57] while Günther Zuntz, who extols the quality of the text in P[46], nonetheless speaks of "the very poor work of the scribe who penned it," for "P[46] abounds with scribal blunders, omissions, and also additions."[58] Whether praised or castigated,

---

[53] The discrepancies in pages required in this discussion and in our earlier assessment is due to the (perhaps overly generous) allowance of more letters per page as the pages widened nearer the end of the codex, i.e., when 1,050–letter pages are assumed for the Pastorals, eighteen pages would be required in P[46], but if 1,155–letter pages are in view, sixteen and a half would be required; hence, with Philemon taking one and a half pages of the nine available, in the first instance (1,050–letter pages) more than ten extra pages would be required for the Pastorals, while in the second case (1,155–letter pages) only seven or eight extra pages would be needed. After making these calculations, I rechecked Kenyon (*The Chester Beatty Biblical Papyri . . . Pauline Epistles, Text,* x), who had virtually the same projection: "The space required [for Philemon and the Pastorals] is therefore nearly twice as much as is available," i.e., eighteen pages. Similarly, Trobisch's calculation estimates the need for nine more pages (*Paul's Letter Collection,* 16).

[54] Trobisch (*Paul's Letter Collection,* 25), however, suggests that Philemon could be placed among letters to congregations because it "actually is addressed 'to Philemon our dear friend and fellow worker, to Apphia our sister, to Archippus our fellow soldier and to the church that meets in your home' (Phlm 1–2)."

[55] Duff, "P[46] and the Pastorals," 582, gives a number of examples.

[56] Sanders, *Third-Century Papyrus Codex of the Epistles of Paul,* 5–6.

[57] Kenyon, *The Chester Beatty Biblical Papyri . . . Pauline Epistles, Text,* xiii.

[58] Günther Zuntz, *The Text of the Epistles: A Disquisition upon the* Corpus Paulinum (Schweich Lectures, 1946; London: British Academy, 1953), 212.

however, the scribe appears to have miscalculated in grand style, at least as long as it is assumed that the Pastoral Epistles and possibly Philemon were intended for inclusion.

But what if the scribe of P[46] used the missing pages, following 2 Thessalonians, for some "non-canonical" writing(s)? After all (as already reported), the codex containing P[72] (turn of the third/fourth century) preserved 1–2 Peter and Jude surrounded by an array of such writings—a hundred years later than P[46]! Of course, the codex containing P[72] may be a special case (see above), but then codices ℵ and A included assorted writings of the Apostolic Fathers fifty years after P[72]. Hence, the possibility must be kept open. The P[72] codex, by the way, includes correspondence allegedly from Corinth to Paul, followed by an (apocryphal) Pauline *church* epistle, *3 Corinthians.* This Corinthian correspondence dates from the late second century and is now judged to have had an origin independent of the *Acts of Paul,* where it is most frequently preserved.[59] It would have been a relatively new work around 200 and would have fit with the other church letters in P[46]—if that was what the scribe intended for the codex. Yet, both pieces of the Corinthian correspondence would have filled fewer than four pages in P[46], rendering the scribe's obvious compression of text no more meaningful than if only Titus had been added. Another church letter that could be a candidate for a Pauline codex (especially one comprised of letters to churches) is the *Epistle to the Laodiceans,*[60] which was attached to the Pauline Codex G[P], but it would occupy only about a page and a half (the size of Philemon) in P[46], and even with the (apocryphal) Corinthian correspondence, some four and a half pages would remain unused. The Apostolic Fathers, of course, would be unlikely in an exclusively Pauline collection and, moreover, each would be too long: the *Didache,* for example, would fill the nine remaining pages and would require about four more added to the quire. So, we are left with the same situation that existed before Duff argued for the inclusion of the Pastoral Epistles: no reasonable combination of "canonical" or "non-canonical" writings fits the space remaining in the single quire codex P[46].

Has Duff made the case or at least made it more likely that the scribe of P[46] intended to include 1–2 Timothy and Titus? Not really, for the Pastorals do not fit the space available, nor does either of his hypotheses provide a more likely solution than our proposals above. If the Pastorals fit the space, it might be different, but both his hypotheses are arguments from silence and not compelling. To claim that a scribe intended to fill nine pages with eighteen pages of material with no evidence other than the compression of the text in the last quarter of the extant portion of the manuscript, at a rate of compression that by a very large measure could never succeed, is not credible. And to theorize that the scribe made a concerted effort to include "all fourteen Pauline epistles" by an increasing compression of the text, but walked away from the task without including the Pastorals when it became clear that space was insufficient is even less convincing. It may be more believable that the scribe glued on pages for the extensive remaining text, but it raises the unsettling question of why he compressed text as long and as intently as he did, when that enterprise was destined from the outset to fail, given the amount of space he needed. This clearly observable compression of text does not make sense if the scribe expected to insert Philemon and all three Pastoral letters. A glance at the plates of P[46] shows a scribe who is

---

[59] Schneemelcher, *New Testament Apocrypha,* 2:228–29.
[60] See ibid., 2:42–46.

both well trained and experienced in the technique of ink on papyrus, for the result is precise and uniform. So great a miscalculation regarding space, if the Pastorals were in mind, is unlikely except by a novice in the trade or a rank amateur.

Yet, for a scribe to compress the text and still leave some nine blank pages does not make sense either. Hence, it would be far more reasonable to suggest that the scribe had the task of including one or more shorter writings. Indeed, my proposals above were intended less to be taken seriously and more to show that as yet neither Duff nor anyone else has a feasible answer to what occupied the end of P[46], for it must be admitted that what has become the traditional view—that P[46] did not contain the Pastoral Epistles—is also based on an argument from silence. Duff's proposals are what he calls them: hypotheses. At the end, though reaffirming the viability of his hypotheses, he actually admits, "It may be wise to refuse to speculate as to what was on the missing pages."[61] This was also the judgment, for example, of Robert M. Grant[62] and more recently David Trobisch,[63] and our lengthy discussion here confirms the wisdom of that approach, at least until some new evidence appears.[64]

Finally, I am grateful to Duff for warning us about making less than careful statements about P[46] and for raising a series of pertinent questions about this important manuscript. Yet, after repeated readings, it appears to me that from the very outset Duff is intent on providing any framework possible that would include the Pastorals in the early Pauline corpus. In this connection, it must be stated that our understanding of the nature of the Pastoral Epistles and of their place in early collections of Pauline Letters and, consequently, their place in the early New Testament canon, is not dependent on whether P[46] did or did not contain them. Rather, the character and role of the Pastorals will be determined primarily by other external evidence and especially by the extensive internal evidence present, including (a) linguistic peculiarities shared with second-century Christianity, among them soteriological terminology parallel to that in Hellenistic religions and the emperor cult; (b) a lack of connection between the situations portrayed and what is known of Paul's life and ministry; (c) the adoption of a literary genre of Paul the martyr, providing "Paul's Testament" in defense of his heritage (especially 2 Timothy); and (d) the use of a church order and Christian conduct genre without an eschatological motivation (especially 1 Timothy and Titus), all reflecting an early to mid-second-century period for the Pastorals' composition.[65] We might all wish that P[46] provided the definitive answer to the presence or absence of the Pastorals in our earliest manuscript of the Pauline Letters, but so far it does not.

---

[61] Duff, "P[46] and the Pastorals," 589.

[62] Grant, *Historical Introduction*, 210–11: "we do not know that [P[46]] did not include the Pastorals."

[63] Trobisch, *Paul's Letter Collection*, 16.

[64] Though the common assumption, as noted at the outset, has been that P[46] does not contain the Pastorals, few scholars who have investigated more thoroughly have given a definite affirmative or negative answer. An exception is Quinn ("P[46]—The Pauline Canon?" 385), who says it did not have the Pastorals, based on his carefully argued proposals for three second-century collections of Pauline letters, concluding that "the scribe of P[46] intended a collection of Pauline letters to churches. His inclusion of Hebrews witnesses to this concern."

[65] See, e.g., Koester, *Introduction to the New Testament*, 2:300–308.

Codex Vaticanus and the Pastorals—an idle question? It may surprise many to suggest that the venerable Codex B presents a case analogous to P[46] and the Pastorals. It is universally assumed that B's "New Testament" section contained all of our twenty-seven books, based, I suppose, on the fact that the other great majuscules of this general period that have the entire Bible (ℵ and A) have our twenty-seven books (plus some Apostolic Fathers). Actually, B contains the four gospels, followed by Acts, the Catholic Epistles, the Pauline Letters from Romans through 2 Thessalonians, and then Hebrews, breaking off in the middle of Heb 9:14. A fifteenth-century supplement (designated minuscule 1957) fills in the missing portion of Hebrews and the Revelation of John, but this late substitute is of no significance. Although B has ancient page numbers—a rarity among Greek manuscripts—that permit a calculation of the number of pages lost at the beginning (some forty-six chapters of Genesis), there is no way of telling how many leaves were lost at the end since, of course, this is a multiquire volume.[66] Alfred Rahlfs in 1889 surmised that B, in addition to the "New Testament," may have contained the *Didache* and the *Shepherd of Hermas*,[67] and the Alands also think it probable that, like ℵ and A, Codex B contained writings of the Apostolic Fathers.[68] Books of our New Testament that are missing from B as it stands (in addition to the rest of Hebrews) are 1–2 Timothy, Titus, Philemon, and the Revelation to John. However, given the mid-fourth-century date of both B and ℵ, it is a fair assumption that these writings were indeed in B. Yet no one seems ever to have raised the question, and that is the reason I mention it here. Though any connection is implausible, it is curious that 1–2 Timothy, Titus, and Philemon are the same Pauline letters that are in dispute in P[46] where, as we have seen, the three Pastorals do not fit in the available space and are unlikely to have been in P[46]. In the case of B, we lack any comparable evidence about space so that any proposals are mere speculation, except that the date of B a century and a half after P[46] makes it reasonable to guess, as every one has, that the rest of our New Testament writings were there originally.[69]

Hebrews, Catholic Epistles, and Revelation. Finally, questions are raised also (a) by the lack of Hebrews in the ninth-century Codex G[p] (but see below), although Hebrews' place in the canon was firm by the end of the fourth century, and (b) by the lack of the Revelation to John in numerous manuscripts where it might be expected. The whole "New Testament" (i.e., our twenty-seven books) is preserved in three majuscules (ℵ, A, and C) and fifty-six minuscules, but two other majuscule manuscripts (B and Ψ) and 147 minuscules (including the notable 33 of the ninth century) have the entire collection *except* the Revelation.[70] All who are acquainted with the history of canon will recognize that these two writings, Hebrews and the Revelation to John, along with several others, are among those that faced the strongest barriers in their paths to full acceptance.

---

[66] Gregory, *Canon and Text*, 344–45.

[67] Reported in Nestle, *Introduction*, 60.

[68] Aland and Aland, *Text of the New Testament*, 109.

[69] T. C. Skeat ("The Codex Sinaiticus, the Codex Vaticanus and Constantine," *JTS* 50 [1999]: 600) asserts that "there can be no doubt that the Pastoral Epistles and the Apocalypse would have followed."

[70] See the statistics presented earlier and n. 3, above; on codices C and B, respectively, see also nn. 5 and 6, above.

1. Hebrews. Hebrews, though it became part of the Pauline collection, could not be linked to Paul or to any apostolic author, and it is not mentioned in the Muratorian Canon. While only *1 Clement* (36.2–5; 17.1) appears to quote Hebrews prior to its appearance in the oldest extant manuscript containing it, namely P[46] (ca. 200), Hebrews is nonetheless firmly a part of the Pauline collection in that papyrus manuscript, standing between Romans and 1 Corinthians. The unusual position of Hebrews in this very early manuscript may reflect a conviction of Pauline authorship and, in addition, may constitute a canonical claim contemporary with Clement of Alexandria (ca. 200), who quotes Hebrews authoritatively and thought that Paul was in some way responsible for its content.

Codex G[p], a Greek-Latin diglot, however, requires a brief comment, for, once again, it is stated routinely that "it contains the Epistles of Paul but not Hebrews,"[71] implying that Hebrews might have been expected. Three majuscules (the Greek-Latin D[p] [of which two extant copies, D[abs1] and D[abs2], ninth and tenth centuries, also exist], K[ap], and L[ap]) and at least 329 minuscules have Hebrews immediately after Philemon.[72] It is relevant that while D[p] is sixth century, both K[ap], and L[ap] are, like G[p], from the ninth century, possibly supporting the notion that G[p] contained Hebrews. F[p], another ninth-century Greek-Latin manuscript and doubtless stemming from the same archetype as G[p],[73] does have Hebrews, though in F[p], which has Latin in one column of each page and Greek in the other, Hebrews is only in Latin, employing both columns of each page and perhaps suggesting that a Greek text of Hebrews was not readily available. This anomaly undoubtedly dilutes the support of F[p] for any claim that Hebrews stood in G[p]. Actually, as noted earlier, after Philemon G[p] inscribes the title for the *Epistle to the Laodiceans,* but not its text; rather, what follows is a Latin explanation of portions of Matthew and a Greek treatise "On Spiritual Law" with interlinear Latin.[74] In fact, F[p] has no trace of *Laodiceans.*[75] Was the text of *Laodiceans* copied into G[p] but is now lost, and is it likely that Hebrews once stood after it? Or, as appears more likely, was the remaining space in G[p] left blank, in spite of the scribe's intention to insert *Laodiceans,* and then filled in subsequently with the additional material? From all of this, an argument might be made for the presence of Hebrews in G[p], though it would be anything but definitive.

2. Catholic Epistles. Though the manuscript transmission of the Catholic Epistles does not so readily or so often involve canon issues, Codex Vaticanus contains chapter divisions that are revealing. As C. R. Gregory noted, "An old division found in the [Catho-

---

[71] Caspar René Gregory, *Textkritik des Neuen Testamentes* (Leipzig: Hinrichs, 1909), 112; Gregory, *Canon and Text,* 367; cf. Metzger, *Canon of the New Testament,* 238.

[72] This figure is from William H. P. Hatch, "The Position of Hebrews in the Canon of the New Testament," *HTR* 29 (1936): 143 n. 43, and is doubtless much out of date.

[73] See William H. P. Hatch, "On the Relationship of Codex Augiensis and Codex Boernerianus of the Pauline Epistles," *HSCP* 60 (1951): 187–99, esp. 195–97. They may have been copied mediately or immediately from the common ancestor.

[74] Alexander Reichardt, *Der Codex Boernerianus der Briefe des Apostels Paulus (Msc. Dresd. A 145ᵇ) in Lichtdruck nachgebildet* (Leipzig: Hiersemann, 1909), 7; cf. Gregory, *Textkritik,* 112. Gregory says the additional material is later; Reichardt agrees that the comments on Matthew are later, but that the treatise could be by the same hand as the Pauline Letters.

[75] Hatch, "On the Relationship of Codex Augiensis and Codex Boernerianus," 192.

lic] Epistles . . . does not appear to take any notice of Second Peter, and seems therefore to be the work of someone who rejected that Epistle."[76]

3. Revelation. The Revelation to John, though widely used in both West and East during the second century, faced difficulties in the third in the East with respect to apostolic authorship and in the West because of its use by Montanists (though it still was used significantly in the West). It also had strong rivals in the *Shepherd of Hermas* and especially the *Apocalypse of Peter*. Consequently, the place of the Revelation to John in the canon of Eastern Christianity was not certain until the late fourth century, and even later in some areas.[77] The comparative paucity of extant Revelation manuscripts may reflect uncertainty about its authority and canonicity, though there could be other reasons for the phenomenon. There are only 287 manuscripts containing the Revelation to John over against 662 with Acts and Catholic Epistles, 792 with Paul, and 2,361 that contain gospels.[78]

Should one wish to claim that the comparatively small number of manuscripts transmitting Revelation is due to the fact that it was not a part of the conventional groupings discussed earlier, and so probably circulated alone, the actual figures show that 133 papyri,[79] majuscules, and minuscules have only Revelation, which is fewer than half of the 287 manuscripts preserving Revelation. Hence, the majority of extant copies of Revelation circulated with other, more widely disseminated "New Testament" writings, which should have enhanced Revelation's chances of use and recognition. So quantity of manuscripts in circulation may have been a factor in the canonical acceptance of Revelation, but not the only one; another factor is that Revelation was never a part of the official lectionary of the Greek Church,[80] though this in turn undoubtedly affected the number of manuscripts preserving it.

D. The Varying Order of Books in "New Testament" Manuscripts

The arrangement of "New Testament" writings in some manuscripts differs from the traditional order, as mentioned above, and these differences may have affected or may reflect canon considerations, though the degree to which they do so is not easy to determine. For example, the four gospels occur in twelve different sequences across the manuscript tradition.[81] While most follow the traditional order, the deviation that has attracted the greatest attention, the so-called "Western" order, occurs in codices D (late fourth century) and W (fifth century), where the order is Matthew, John, Luke, and Mark. Perhaps this order is intended to highlight the first two apostles, who then are followed by

---

[76] Gregory, *Canon and Text*, 344; idem, *Textkritik des Neuen Testamentes*, 33. Cf. Scrivener-Miller (*Plain Introduction,* 1:181); Frederic G. Kenyon, *Handbook to the Textual Criticism of the New Testament* (2d ed.; London: Macmillan, 1926), 104; Heinrich Joseph Vogels, *Handbuch der Textkritik des Neuen Testaments* (2d ed.; Bonn: Hanstein, 1955), 50; Aland and Aland, *Text of the New Testament*, 110.

[77] See Gamble, "Canon: New Testament," 1.853–56, and n. 2 above.

[78] Aland and Aland, *Text of the New Testament*, 78–79, 83.

[79] P[47] would appear to be a papyrus codex that contained only Revelation, though there is no certainty; the recently published P[115] is extensive, but its editors say it is not possible to know whether it contained only Revelation or also other writings (P.Oxy LXVI: 4499, esp. 11); the others are highly fragmentary and the full extent of their original contents cannot be determined.

[80] Metzger, *Canon of the New Testament*, 217.

[81] See the latest inventory in P.-M. Bogaert, "Ordres anciens des évangiles et tétraévangile en un seul codex," *RTL* 30 (1999): 298–307.

the two Evangelists who are associated with apostles.[82] Beyond these, three other arrangements begin with Matthew, two with John, and two with Mark, but Luke, the longest gospel, is never first.[83] This would rule out descending length as an ordering principle. Acts nearly always follows the Gospels, but in ℵ and the Latin Codex Fuldensis (F, sixth century) Acts follows the Pauline Letters. Hebrews is very frequently included among the Pauline Letters; Greek manuscripts commonly place it after Philemon (D L Ψ, other majuscules, most minuscules) or between 2 Thessalonians and the Pastorals, that is, between letters to churches and those to individuals (ℵ A B C H I K P and many others), though chapter numbers remaining in B show that Hebrews followed Galatians in the manuscript from which these section numbers were taken.[84] However, as already noted, P[46] (and some nine minuscules) put Hebrews after Romans. Altogether Hebrews is found in nine different sequences in our manuscripts.[85] P[46] also has Ephesians before Galatians; in fact, Greek and versional manuscripts and patristic sources have arranged the Pauline Letters in some twenty different sequences.[86] Finally, the Catholic Epistles, named for their presumed authors, are preserved in some seven sequences, though organizing principles are not often obvious, except that in the West Peter's primacy among the attributed authors may be reflected in four of the sequences, where 1–2 Peter stand first. Descending length does not work, for, when ancient *stichoi* are applied, 1 John is the longest, followed by James and 1 Peter; or, grouped by author, 1–2 Peter are the longest, followed by 1–2–3 John, then James, and then Jude. The latter order is found in the Council of Carthage list (397) and in Apostolic Canon 85 (sixth/seventh century).[87]

---

[82] Further, see Gregory, *Canon and Text,* 468.

[83] In a study of the length of the Gospels and Acts in P[45], Luke is the longest in all counts, except for T. C. Skeat's final figures, in which Matthew is shown to have occupied a page more than Luke: T. C. Skeat, "A Codicological Analysis of the Chester Beatty Papyrus Codex of Gospels and Acts (P[45])," *Hermathena* 155 (1993): 27–43.

[84] Gregory, *Textkritik,* 33; idem, *Canon and Text,* 344, whose statement is careful and does not say the section numbers are older than B; yet, most publications I have seen claim that "the scribe of codex Vaticanus copied" the chapter numbers from "an ancestor of codex Vaticanus" (Metzger, *Textual Commentary,* 591 n. 2) or from its "archetype" (Hatch, "Position of Hebrews," 135–36). However, Skeat ("Codex Sinaiticus, the Codex Vaticanus and Constantine," 601) states that his examination of the section numbers makes it "obvious that they are *not* the work of either of the two scribes of the manuscript" and that "these numbers were *not* added in the scriptorium but after the manuscript had left it" (601). He reports that Carlo M. Martini, in the introduction to the 1968 Vatican facsimile edition of B, already understood these numerals as "subsequent additions" (601, n. 23). Hence, we face two unknowns: exactly how long after B had been produced these section marks were inserted and, more critical, whether the source was a manuscript older or younger than B. These uncertainties preclude such tempting speculations as (a) B's section markers preserve an older placement of Hebrews than B and a position more centrally among the Pauline letters, and (b) they reveal both an earlier conviction of Pauline authorship and perhaps a stronger view of canonicity for Hebrews.

[85] Metzger, *Canon of the New Testament,* 295–300; Bruce M. Metzger (for the Editorial Committee), *A Textual Commentary on the Greek New Testament* (2d ed.; Stuttgart: Deutsche Bibelgesellschaft/United Bible Societies, 1994), 591–92. For a chart of all positions of Hebrews, see Hermann Josef Frede, ed., *Epistulae ad Philippenses et ad Colossenses* (Vetus Latina, 24:2; Freiburg: Herder, 1966–1971), 292–303; cf. Trobisch (*Paul's Letter Collection,* 20–21).

[86] Frede, *Epistulae ad Philippenses et ad Colossenses,* 292–303.

[87] Metzger, *Canon of the New Testament,* 299–300.

The relevance of these data to canon is more complex and with more subtle implications than some of the preceding issues. As just intimated it is often claimed that "New Testament" books frequently were arranged according to length, usually from the longest to the shortest in their groups (using the occasionally recorded *stichoi* in manuscripts). Sometimes the writings of one author are counted as one work, and nearly always the Pauline church letters are separated from those to individuals.[88] Ordering by descending length appears to be operative at times, for example, with respect to 1–2 Timothy, Titus, and Philemon, but not often enough elsewhere to be a satisfactory overall explanation. For example, as already noted, the Gospels never occur with the longest gospel, Luke, first; Galatians-Ephesians is a common order, yet Galatians is shorter than Ephesians; and, finally, the length of Hebrews should place it between 1–2 Corinthians, but it is never found there because, of course, 1–2 Corinthians would not be separated. If diminishing length is to be the criterion, Hebrews would likely follow immediately after 1–2 Corinthians, as in fact it does in several minuscules. David Trobisch claims, however, that P[46], with its two anomalies—Hebrews between Romans and 1 Corinthians, and Ephesians before Galatians—has arranged Paul's letters "strictly according to their length," asserting (questionably, I think) that placing Hebrews *before* 1–2 Corinthians was the appropriate way to deal with Hebrews' greater length than 2 Corinthians.[89] Alternatively, in the case of Hebrews in P[46], W. H. P. Hatch suggests that its placement immediately after Romans was "on grounds of doctrine."[90] Hence, interpreting the manuscript data on the order of books may be difficult.

It is also possible that fluctuating sequences of books may indicate canonical fluidity or uncertainty. It has been suggested above that placing Hebrews deep into the clearly Pauline letters (as in P[46]) may show a desire to accredit its Pauline authorship, and thereby perhaps its canonical authority. Or Hebrews' varying positions may reflect not only uncertainty about authorship, but also about its destination or addressees, revealing, in turn, uneasiness about its canonicity. Trobisch points to minuscule 794, which copies Hebrews twice, once after 2 Thessalonians and again after Philemon.[91] Placing Hebrews between the Pauline letters to churches and those to individuals, rather than *within* the former group, may have been prompted by the view, well established by the third/fourth centuries, that Paul wrote to seven churches, not eight.[92] In sum, this situation may have been a two-way street: on the one hand, questions about the canonicity of Hebrews may have motivated some to place it within the Paulines, and, on the other hand, its varying locations may themselves have raised the very same kinds of questions.

Finally, we note that Codex B's order of books is identical to that of Athanasius of Alexandria's famous list in 367, the first such list known to contain all and only our

---

[88] Ibid., 296–300.
[89] Trobisch, *Paul's Letter Collection*, 16–17. Cf. Quinn, "P[46]—The Pauline Canon?" 379: "The letters that had been chosen were ordered on a stichometric principle."
[90] See Hatch, "Position of Hebrews," 133–34.
[91] Trobisch, *Paul's Letter Collection*, 21–22.
[92] See Nils Alstrup Dahl, "The Particularity of the Pauline Epistles as a Problem in the Ancient Church," *Neotestamentica et Patristica: Eine Freundesgabe, Herrn Professor Dr. Oscar Cullmann zu seinem 60. Geburtstag überreicht* (ed. W. C. van Unnik; NovTSup 6; Leiden: Brill, 1962), 261–64.

twenty-seven New Testament writings. On the assumptions that B originated in Egypt (Kirsopp Lake[93]) or in Alexandria itself (J. Neville Birdsall[94]) and that it contained all twenty-seven books, B on occasion has been understood as supporting this fourth-century canon of Athanasius. B's provenance, however, is disputed, though Skeat's recent, elaborate re-defense of Caesarea[95] undoubtedly will carry the day. Therefore, rather than a more precise claim, it is safer to say that Codex B documents a fourth-century view of canon, but not likely that of Egypt.

As the Alands affirm regarding the sequence of writings, "[t]he only characteristic common to the whole manuscript tradition (extending also to canon lists, patristic references, and other sources which allude to the sequence of the writings) is that the Gospels stand at the beginning and Revelation at the end."[96]

2. Manuscript Aids to Readers with Implications for Canon

Aids to readers of manuscripts take numerous forms, including punctuation, chapter and book titles, chapter divisions; glosses (explaining words or phrases), scholia (instructive comments of a teacher), catenae ("chains" of remarks from other writers), onomastica (providing etymology of names), and other marginal notations or marks; copying a text in sense lines; lection notes (designating portions to be read in worship); the Eusebian canons (markings and a table developed by Eusebius to help find parallel gospel passages), the Euthalian apparatus (aids for the Acts and Epistles attributed to a certain Euthalius or Evagrius, including a sketch of Paul's life and martyrdom, a list of Old Testament citations, etc.),[97] the so-called Marcionite prologues, and, I would add, the codex format. Some of these are relevant to canon, others are not.

Earlier we have shown (a) how a table of contents in Codex A points to material now lost and suggests that some writings it contained were more authoritative than another; (b) how section divisions in Codex B in one place indicate a different position for Hebrews and in another imply that someone rejected 2 Peter; and (c) how a title in Codex G^p ("the Epistle to the Laodiceans begins") identifies content even when its text had not been copied there. Three other topics require brief treatment.

A. "Marcionite" Prologues

Some manuscripts possess what usually are called "Marcionite" prologues. A number of Latin Vulgate manuscripts (including the prominent Codex Fuldensis, F, sixth cen-

---

[93] For a thorough discussion of Lake's views, see Skeat, "Codex Sinaiticus, the Codex Vaticanus and Constantine," 586–92.

[94] J. N. Birdsall, "The New Testament Text," *The Cambridge History of the Bible, Volume 1: From the Beginnings to Jerome* (3 vols.; ed. P. R. Ackroyd and C. F. Evans; Cambridge/New York: Cambridge University Press, 1970), 359–60.

[95] Skeat, "Codex Sinaiticus, the Codex Vaticanus and Constantine," 598–604, esp. 603–4.

[96] Aland and Aland, *The Text of the New Testament,* 79.

[97] Summarized from Bruce M. Metzger, *The Text of the New Testament: Its Transmission, Corruption, and Restoration* (3d ed.; New York/Oxford: Oxford University Press, 1992), 21–31.

tury) contain them, and they provide, for the Pauline letters, short descriptions of the addressees and reasons for writing, with an emphasis on Paul's conflict with false apostles. Currently, however, these are viewed as not of Marcionite origin, but as written for a Pauline corpus to seven churches that was not connected with Marcion's canon and which later gave way to the fourteen-letter corpus; moreover, the prologues presuppose an earlier "seven church" corpus that began with Galatians, 1–2 Corinthians, and Romans, which, to be sure, is the same order found in Marcion's canon, though the order is no longer thought to be attributable to Marcion.[98]

These prologues are difficult to assess, but they can provide help in understanding some aspects of the canon process and some controversies involved, such as the elusive role of Marcion, whose differing text of Paul was most likely not a new creation but "the adaptation of an already existing Pauline Corpus that began with Galatians,"[99] and the development of various collections of Pauline Letters, as noted in the preceding paragraph.

The so-called anti-Marcionite prologues to the Gospels (Mark, Luke, and John only) are found in nearly forty Latin biblical manuscripts of the fifth to the tenth centuries; the prologue for Luke is extant also in Greek. They were independently composed, and date from the fourth century, though that for Luke perhaps dates from the second. Their relevance to canon is negligible, though the early Lucan portion does refer to Luke as a follower of Paul, and that relationship could or might have been a factor in the canon process.[100]

B. Indicators of Textual Problems within Manuscripts

Scribes on occasion obviously had reservations about portions of text present in or absent from their exemplars, especially when they were aware of other manuscripts or traditions that differed from what appeared before them. Thus, it is relevant to ask how our manuscripts reveal textual uncertainties, since, in turn, they very likely indicate uncertainty as to the authority of problematic passages. Such passages commonly were marked with various scribal sigla; or blank spaces were left to indicate a passage that stood in the exemplar but was omitted by the scribe, or that the scribe knew existed in another manuscript but not in the exemplar; or a questionable section of text might be placed in an alternate position or in the margin, or a marginal note might be added.

For instance, all of these indicators appear in connection with the Pericope of the Adulteress (John 7:53–8:11). Most striking are the multiple locations in which scribes placed this paragraph: after 7:52 (most manuscripts), after 7:36, after 7:44, after 21:25, or in Luke, after 21:38. Also, a scribal asterisk or obelus alongside the passage—customary signs of a questionable portion of text—was placed in scores of manuscripts, occasionally

---

[98] See John J. Clabeaux, *A Lost Edition of the Letters of Paul: A Reassessment of the Text of the Pauline Corpus Attested by Marcion* (CBQMS 21; Washington: Catholic Biblical Association, 1989), 1–4; Ulrich Schmid, *Marcion und sein Apostolos: Rekonstruktion und historische Einordnung der marcionitischen Paulusbriefausgabe* (ANTF 25; Berlin/New York: W. de Gruyter, 1995), 287–89; Metzger, *Canon of the New Testament*, 94–97.

[99] Clabeaux, *Lost Edition of the Letters of Paul*, 4.

[100] See Helmut Koester, *Ancient Christian Gospels: Their History and Development* (London: SCM; Philadelphia: Trinity Press International, 1990), 243, 335–36.

with additional marginal comments. A few scribes (e.g., of L and Δ) left a small blank space—too small for the passage but an obvious signal that a portion of questionable text was known to these scribes.[101] Likewise, in Codex B, contrary to the scribe's practice when coming to the end of a writing, an entire column has been left blank after Mark 16:8, "evidently because one or other of the two subsequent endings was known to him personally, while he found neither of them in the exemplar which he was copying."[102] But Scrivener-Miller[103] interprets the vacant column to mean that the scribe was "fully aware" of the existence of the last twelve verses "or even found them in the copy from which he wrote." Similarly, manuscripts with Mark 16:9–20 often contain such sigla or even comments that older Greek manuscripts do not have the passage (see, e.g., minuscule 1).[104]

C. The Codex Format

The preceding items involve notations, additional marks, or spaces in manuscripts that assist the reader, but the very form of the book—the codex, adopted extremely early in Christianity as the vehicle for its valued writings—may well be treated as an "aid to the reader," even allowing for the fact that the scroll, in the hands of a skilled copyist, reader, or scholar, afforded remarkable efficiency in finding and checking points of inquiry.[105] Yet, the codex format was more convenient in general and certainly traveled more easily. These matters, and the early Christian use of the codex, have been much in discussion in recent decades and an extensive literature has resulted.[106]

One of the major emphases in the relationship between codex and canon involves the early and thorough adoption by Christianity of the codex format for its writings and, therefore, its possible influence upon the canonization, particularly, of the Pauline Letters and the fourfold Gospel, and other portions of the "New Testament." To raise only the dominant issue, did the new codex form facilitate the collection of authoritative writings and the actualization of the canon? More specifically, what was it about the codex that initially appealed to the Christians who utilized it? Several answers have been offered recently, but no definitive solution is possible.[107] And were there perhaps common sizes of codices

---

[101] For details, see Metzger, *Textual Commentary,* 187–89; Scrivener-Miller, *Plain Introduction,* 2:364–68.

[102] Brooke Foss Westcott and Fenton John Anthony Hort, *The New Testament in the Original Greek* (2 vols.; London, Macmillan, 1881–1882 [vol. 2, 2d ed., 1896]), 1:29 [*Notes*]).

[103] Scrivener-Miller, *Plain Introduction,* 1:108. Scrivener and Miller, of course, advocated the authenticity of the "longer ending" of Mark (1:7; 2:337–44). Their claim that the blank space in some way authenticates that ending is highly suspect, for the space, on any view, still expresses scribal doubt about what might have occupied it elsewhere.

[104] Metzger, *Text of the New Testament,* 226; idem, *Textual Commentary,* 103.

[105] See T. C. Skeat, "Roll versus Codex—A New Approach?" *ZPE* 84 (1990): 297–98; and idem, "The Origin of the Christian Codex," *ZPE* 102 (1994): 265.

[106] For discussion and further references, see Gamble, *Books and Readers in the Early Church,* 42–81; Epp, "Codex and Literacy in Early Christianity and at Oxyrhynchus," 15–26. More recent discussions include E. Randolph Richards, "The Codex and the Early Collection of Paul's Letters," *BBR* 8 (1998): 151–66.

[107] For a summary of several recent views, as well as a new proposal, see Epp, "Codex and Literacy in Early Christianity and at Oxyrhynchus," 15–26.

that seemed to many to be the most efficient and convenient, and did those sizes perchance best accommodate a certain number of gospels (four), or the Gospels plus Acts, or a certain sized collection of Paul's letters (seven, or ten, or thirteen)? If so, the codex may well have had an effect upon canon.

The fragmentary nature of our early papyri makes answers difficult, but among the papyri up to and around the turn of the third/fourth century, P[45] has the four gospels and Acts, and P[53] has Matthew plus Acts (possibly suggesting that it, like P[45], contained the four gospels and Acts[108]), while P[64] + P[67] + P[4] and P[75] have portions of two gospels,[109] but the vast majority now preserve portions of only one gospel. And P[46] has portions of nine Pauline Letters, P[30] and P[92] have two Letters, and the rest only one. Finally, there is no early codex that contains more than one Catholic Epistle in sequence.[110] Hence, there is little ground on which to argue that codices up to the early fourth century held to any rigid pattern of contents, though the preservation of writings in categories such as Gospels, or Gospels and Acts, or Pauline Letters has some support. Harry Y. Gamble argues that only the codex format would allow for the collection of the Pauline Letters in one volume, because an eighty-foot roll would be required to contain them, which is twice the maximum length and three times the normal length of Greek rolls![111] Similarly, Graham Stanton, following the lead of T. C. Skeat, concluded that the emergence of the fourfold Gospel must be connected with the "Christian adoption of the codex, for no roll could contain four gospels,"[112] and J. K. Elliott adds the interesting point that no extant codices up to the third century exceed three hundred pages, indicating that this early codex format "helped to limit the number of Gospels to these four and no more!" He notes also that we have no manuscripts in which "apocryphal" gospels were bound with any one or more of the "canonical" four, and that the codex possessed an automatic limiting or "canon" factor, for (unlike a roll) it demands advance planning, especially if it consists of a single quire.[113]

Something more can be said about the general sizes of early "New Testament" papyri, a relevant factor in the use and collection of Christian writings and therefore in canon issues. Any who have studied the codex format will be aware of E. G. Turner's classification of codices. Though highly complex, it can be stated that eighteen of our earliest

---

[108] The small size of this codex militates against four gospels and Acts, for about 325 leaves would be required; H. A. Sanders judges this not impossible, but thinks Matthew plus Acts would be a reasonably sized codex, though no such combination of books exists elsewhere: "A Third Century Papyrus of Matthew and Acts," *Quantulacumque: Studies Presented to Kirsopp Lake* (ed. R. P. Casey, Silva Lake, and Agnes K. Lake; London: Christophers, 1937), 153.

[109] P[44] and P[84] also have two gospels each, but they date to the sixth century or later.

[110] P[72], with 1–2 Peter separated from Jude, cannot be considered a codex of the Catholic Epistles, nor can its predecessor codex (see above). P[74] contains Acts and the Catholic Epistles, though this is seventh century. P[6] does have John and James, but the latter is preserved in Coptic only.

[111] Gamble, *Books and Readers in the Early Church*, 62–63.

[112] Stanton, "Fourfold Gospel," 337; see 338–39; and Skeat, "Origin of the Christian Codex," 263–68. For more detailed discussion, see Epp, "Codex and Literacy in Early Christianity and at Oxyrhynchus," 19–26.

[113] J. Keith Elliott, "Manuscripts, the Codex and the Canon," *JSNT* 63 (1996): 110 and 107. As to size, codices developed so that by the mid-fourth century B consisted of some 1600 pages and א of about 1460; both have lost portions at the end (ibid., 110). On the evolution of the codex, see Gamble, *Books and Readers in the Early Church*, 63–66; Bogaert, "Ordres anciens des évangiles et tétraévangile," 313.

"New Testament" papyri appear in his lists; that, with one exception (P⁴⁵), all fall into the various "modest" size categories (Groups 5, 6, 7, 8, and 9: no more than about seven inches wide and either narrow and tall or narrow and "squarish"); and, most important, that eleven of these codices fall into the two categories (Groups 8 and 9) judged by Turner most likely to represent the earliest codex form.[114]

This suggests that the media commonly used by and most appealing to early Christians were codices in the earliest attested form and sizes, which, in turn, rated high in portability, a feature not only valuable to early Christian travelers in their mission, but also convenient and practical in the dissemination of the writings they carried and used. Complete clarity on these matters remains to be achieved. Our earliest papyrus manuscripts offer tantalizing clues, but their fragmentary nature is a continuing frustration.

3. Textual Variants and Canonicity

The manuscripts that carried and preserved the texts destined to be part of the "New" or Second Testament are relevant for canon through their groupings, their contents, and the apparatuses accompanying them, as well as their very format. Yet, the texts themselves offer the most creative and vibrant interrelationship with matters canonical. A simple question will introduce the issue: When two meaningful variants occur in an authoritative writing, which reading is canonical, or are both canonical? Though the factors in achieving "canonical" status for either an entire writing or for a single reading are elusive, the phenomenon is essentially the same for both: acceptance as authoritative by an individual or a group. To be sure, community acceptance is the more common path for writings, and perhaps a more secure one, though it may be easier for a variant reading to become authoritative as an individual scribe creates it and/or incorporates it into a community's scripture.

A fascinating issue, raised occasionally in the past and more intensely by several current scholars, might be described by invoking an old phrase in a new way: "A canon within the canon." Traditionally this refers to defining one's beliefs and practice by reliance mainly on certain selected books from an authoritative canon (e.g., Luther's reliance upon Romans and Galatians while virtually dismissing James, or Zwingli's rejection of Revelation), though it may refer also to dependence on selected ideas. When it is applied to the textual variants within a New Testament variation unit and to the selection of one variant over the others, suddenly numerous disquieting questions arise, as a few examples will show. Actually, almost any variation unit where there are at least two meaningful textual readings would be illustrative,[115] though some of the issues raised may be cleaner and simpler than others. For example, it may appear to be easy to decide whether any of the endings of Mark beyond *gar* in 16:8 are canonical, or whether the pericope of the adulteress woman (John 7:53–8:11) is canonical. In the Marcan instance, neither appended ending is

---

[114] This analysis and interpretation of Turner's data may be found in Epp, "Codex and Literacy in Early Christianity and at Oxyrhynchus," 19–20; see E. G. Turner, *The Typology of the Early Codex* (Haney Foundation Series 18; Philadelphia: University of Pennsylvania Press, 1977), 13–25.

[115] For further examples, see Epp, "Textual Criticism in the Exegesis of the New Testament, with an Excursus on Canon," 81–82.

likely to have been part of the early Gospel of Mark, yet one or another of the so-called "shorter" and "longer" endings, and the latter's further expansions, surely was part of the canonical Mark as far as some early churches were concerned, and widely so where the Byzantine text prevailed. Even the "shorter" ending, with its grandiose, obviously non-Marcan language, was used in Greek-speaking churches, as well as in churches using Latin, Syriac, Coptic, Armenian, and Ethiopian, judging from manuscripts containing it.[116] It is quite possible that the "longer" ending of Mark, with its postresurrection appearances, "could have functioned to bring Mark's Gospel into harmony with the fourfold collection," and in this fashion influenced the canonical process.[117]

On the other hand, resolution of some seemingly less significant variants actually may be quite difficult, such as the two small, similar readings in two letters of the Pauline collection: "in Rome" in Rom 1:7 (and 1:15) and "in Ephesus" in Eph 1:1. Both are lacking in a small number of manuscripts, though the latter is absent from the very old P[46], $\aleph$, and B. So, are these geographical designations canonical or not? In addition, a doxology appears in several different locations in various manuscripts of Romans, is absent in some, and occurs twice in others.[118] So, is the doxology in Romans canonical after 14:23, after 15:33, or after 16:23, or after both 14:23 and 16:23, where several manuscripts place it, or was it never part of Romans, as other manuscripts and patristic witnesses testify? The further issue is whether Romans originally had fourteen chapters, or fifteen, or sixteen, as demarcated by the various positions of the concluding doxology, and more importantly, what does this placement of the doxology tell us about the textual history of Romans and therefore its canonical form?[119] These three examples might appear to involve somewhat insignificant variations, yet all are significant in themselves and important for understanding the history of the Roman and Ephesian letters and of the Pauline collection process, which in turn are critical for explaining some major factors in canon formation.

We may expand upon our question: when there are competing variant readings is only the "original" reading canonical? And when decisions between variants are difficult or impossible, are two or more of the plausible readings canonical? Or, in what sense are readings canonical that are suspected of being theologically motivated—for example, when a variant with an "orthodox" bias can be shown to be secondary to one that might be described as "heterodox"? Undoubtedly the scribes introducing such secondary readings considered their replacements to be canonical, as did those who unwittingly used the resultant text in worship and practice. The reverse situation is no different, when an

---

[116] Metzger, *Canon of the New Testament*, 270.

[117] Brevard S. Childs, *The New Testament as Canon: An Introduction* (Philadelphia: Fortress, 1984), 51–52.

[118] See Metzger, *Textual Commentary*, 470–73.

[119] Tracing out the evolution and interrelation of these three forms of Romans is highly complex, to say the least, but, according to Gamble, *The Textual History of the Letter to the Romans: A Study in Textual and Literary History* (SD 42; Grand Rapids: Eerdmans, 1977), 15–35; 96–129, it leads to the conclusion that a fourteen-chapter version of Romans, secondary to the sixteen-chapter original, was pre-Marcionite and came into existence prior to the collection of a Pauline corpus. Cf. idem, *Books and Readers*, 58–65; Ulrich Schmid, *Marcion und sein Apostolos: Rekonstruktion und historische Einordnung der marcionitischen Paulusbriefausgabe* (ANTF 25; Berlin/New York: de Gruyter, 1995), 284–94. For a very brief summary, see Epp, "Multivalence of the Term 'Original Text,'" 262–63.

"orthodox" reading has been replaced by a "heretical" one. In all such cases, to what extent are variants canonical that now have been judged secondary by textual critics but once were authoritative scripture? Finally, to raise the question to its highest level and broadest range, what can "canonical" mean when each of our 5,300 Greek New Testament manuscripts and perhaps 9,000 versional manuscripts, as well as every one now lost, was considered authoritative—and therefore canonical—in worship and instruction in one or more of the thousands upon thousands of individual churches *when no two manuscripts are exactly alike?* A corollary heightens the force of the question: If no two manuscripts are alike, then no two collections of Gospels or Epistles are alike, and no two canons—no two "New Testaments"—are alike; therefore, are all canonical, or some, or only one? And if some or one, which?

If, as we have affirmed, a scribe effecting a theologically motivated textual alteration was making a canonical decision, the process of canon formation was operating at two quite different levels: first, at the level of church leaders of major Christian localities or regions, who were seeking broad consensus on which *books* were to be accepted as authoritative for the larger church, and, second, also at the level of individual scribes, perhaps, representing a monastic or some other small community, concerned about *individual variants* that properly express their theological or other understanding of the sentences and paragraphs within their already authoritative books.

But there are other dimensions of these issues as well, for it is necessary to ask when the term "canonical" might or should be applied to a writing that ended up in the New Testament canon: at the completion of the writing (unlikely), upon its delivery to or receipt by a church or church representative (somewhat more likely); upon the writing's first use in worship in some local congregation (quite likely, but "canonical" in a local or limited sense); upon a consensus acceptance as authoritative in wider circles (very likely); at the time of incorporation into a collection, as the fourfold Gospel, or the Pauline collection (almost certainly); or when a writing is one of the final twenty-seven books at the time when that corpus, or a major portion thereof, achieved wide acceptance (certainly)? Recognition of individual readings as "canonical" might coincide with the "more likely" of such moments, but also at points much farther along in the process of transmission, extending the possibilities not only forward in time (up to the invention of printing), but also increasing their quantity and breadth as the manuscript stream widened.

To cite one instructive instance, David C. Parker in 1997 analyzed the twenty variations in the marriage-divorce passages in the Synoptic Gospels that arose over an extended period. Some reflect, for example, mores of the Roman Empire rather than a Jewish setting; some define adultery as divorcing one's spouse and remarrying, another sees divorce itself as adultery for a man, while others understand the divorce of one's wife to be treating her as though she were an adulteress (even if it is not so), etc. Parker's conclusion is that the recovery of a single original reading here is "impossible," for we are presented with "a collection of interpretive rewritings of a tradition," which means that "the recovery of a definitive 'original' text that is consequently 'authoritative' cannot be presumed to be an attainable target."[120] Rather, Parker asserts, we are compelled to recognize, not one form of

---

[120] David C. Parker, *The Living Text of the Gospels* (Cambridge/New York: Cambridge University Press, 1997), 78–93.

a text, but all (meaningful) forms as "living" interpretations stemming from actual church situations, and "there is no authoritative text beyond the manuscripts which we may follow without further thought."[121] Though Parker is not explicit about the relationship of this manifold gospel tradition to canon, it is this multiplicity of competing variants with which we are left, along with the questions raised earlier: which variant or (more realistically) which variants are canonical?

The compelling answer is that most if not all such competing variants were held to be canonical, wittingly or not, at various times and places in real-life Christian contexts, requiring the perhaps disquieting conclusion that canonicity of readings has virtually the same degree of multiformity as do the meaningful competing variants in a variation unit. That is, in many, many instances the term "canonical" can no longer be applied only to one variant reading; hence, no longer only to a single form of a New Testament writing; hence, no longer only to a single form of the fourfold Gospels or the Pauline Letters; and, hence, no longer only to any single text of the New Testament as a whole. Indeed, when viewed in the context of textual variation, the terms "canon" and "canonical," perhaps quite unexpectedly for most, have exploded into notions that are now both polyvalent and multileveled.[122]

4. Conclusion

Textual criticism and canon have long been placed in juxtaposition in introductions to the New Testament and elsewhere, but not always with good reason. A clearer rationale for analyzing their interrelation has appeared in recent times, and the primary difference stems from the ever-increasing number and importance of the "New Testament" papyri over the past century. Should this be doubted, one need only witness their prominence in the preceding essay. During the period when the great parchment codices of the mid-fourth century and later constituted the bulk of raw material for both text-critical and canon investigations, scholars were limited to documents from the period when consensus already had been reached in major sectors of Christianity on the dominant canonical issues: the fourfold Gospel, the Pauline collection, and Acts. Lacking was second- and third-century evidence on the early codex, especially its Christian use, and on the contents and order of writings in these Christian books up to the turn of the third/fourth century. That lack has been remedied, providing previously unknown opportunities to explore both text and canon in that early period, even though definitive answers are far fewer than we would like, as our summaries show. Indeed, it has been the overriding purpose of our explorations to identify relevant raw materials for canon issues and then, wherever necessary, to analyze and to clarify the nature of those data, as we have attempted to do for such manuscripts as P[72] and P[46]. The implicit hope throughout this exercise is that others will employ these data, and perhaps also the interpretations offered, to lead us to new insights on the development of the New Testament canon in its early and significant formative period.

---

[121] Ibid., 212; cf. 209–11.

[122] For additional discussion, see Epp, "Multivalence of the Term 'Original Text,'" 271–75, and the references to earlier views.

29

The Canonical Structure of Gospel and Apostle

François Bovon

In the pages that follow I would like to illustrate a theological structure that proved decisive for early Christian faith, that of Gospel and Apostle.[1] An analysis of several New Testament passages reveals the contours of this structure, its importance and universality. Once detected and understood, this structure may explain the formation of a two-part canon in the second century without assigning priority to the role of outside forces in shaping it. Clearly there was interaction between the Christians, Jews, and pagans with regard to their sacred texts. The Christian communities on their way to orthodoxy and heresy were influenced by these changes. But I wish to challenge the prevailing thesis that credits Marcion with the beginnings of New Testament canonization.[2] In my opinion, while Marcion may have contributed to the process, he was responsible neither for the idea of a collection nor for its bipolar structure. A "New Testament" containing Gospels and Epistles is the logical outgrowth and materialization of a revelation that articulates an event and the proclamation that follows, i.e., Jesus and his disciples. Thus the need for a New Testament and its two-part configuration is inscribed in the very nature of the Christian faith, from the beginnings of Christianity.

1. Paul and the Pauline School

Embroiled in a controversy with his adversaries in Corinth, the Apostle Paul refers in his Second Epistle to the salvific plan of God, which he formulates in terms of reconciliation. Significantly, he carefully outlines not just one, but two acts: salvation consists of both reconciliation itself as event and the "ministry (or *service*, Greek *diakonia*) of reconciliation." In other words, the proclamation communicates the event.[3] For Paul, Jesus

---

[1] I advanced this thesis in my farewell lecture at the University of Geneva in 1993, a lecture that was published in a small book entitled *L'Evangile et l'Apôtre: Christ inséparable de ses témoins* (Aubonne: Editions du Moulin, 1993). I summarize it here with additional material. It was first published in French under the title "La structure canonique de l'Evangile et de l'Apotre," in *Cristianesimo nella storia* 15 (1994): 559–76. This paper was translated by Laura Beth Bugg.

[2] Cf. H. von Campenhausen, *Die Entstehung der christlichen Bibel* (Tübingen: Mohr [Siebeck], 1968); ET *The Formation of the Christian Bible* (Philadelphia: Fortress, 1972). [See also the contributions in the present volume by J. Barton (ch. 20), E. Kalin (23), and L. McDonald (ch. 25).]

[3] 2 Cor 5:18: "All this is from God, who reconciled us to himself through Christ, and has given us the ministry of reconciliation." Note the side-by-side placement of "Christ" and "us," that is to say, the apostles.

Christ is the very heart of the event. As an apostle, Paul himself is responsible for the proclamation of the gospel. God acts through a gift by sending and resurrecting his Son, who
needs human collaboration to proclaim God's program. The apostolic word becomes the
indispensable complement to the act of redemption. The gospel has two faces: one represented by Jesus and the other represented by the apostles.[4]

The Epistle to the Galatians contains direct evidence of this with respect to Christ
and the apostles. The functioning of each is seen in the central part of this autobiographical passage: "But when God, who had set me apart before I was born and called me
through his grace, was pleased to reveal his Son to me, so that I might proclaim him among
the Gentiles, I did not confer with any human being . . ." (Gal 1:15–16). The divine origin
of this endeavor is evident from this encounter: this is God's project. The salvific role of
this appearance of the Son to the apostle may also be seen. It takes place so that the Gentiles will be touched by the good news and thus come to faith and saving grace. While the
Son is revealed in his Easter glory, with an implicit reference to his origin and his divine
mission, Paul is shown at the same time as believer and messenger. The fate of one
becomes the other's object of proclamation.[5]

In spite of different tasks and responsibilities, a profound analogy stands between
the Lord and his apostle. In effect, the vocation of apostle aligns the fate of the one who
practices it to the one who is preached. The Pauline imitation nevertheless does not imply
a slavish copy, but the participation of one's entire being. The apostle urges the same imitation of himself in return. He says to the Corinthians, "Be imitators of me, as I am of
Christ" (1 Cor 11:1). In order to understand Christ, to truly hear the gospel, one must not
only listen to the apostle but also see and discover in him a model to imitate. The structure
of Gospel-Apostle has salvific value, because Christ, at the heart of the good news, is the
image of God (2 Cor 4:4; Rom 8:29, cf. Col 1:15). The gift of divine origin, therefore,
extends to Christians by means of both the Gospel and the Apostle.[6]

Early Christianity did not spread the idea of several messiahs but of a multi-faceted
Christ: the one Messiah was at the same time King, Priest, and Prophet, Savior and Lord,
Son of Man and Son of God, proclaimed by the witness of many servants and disciples.
The Apostle Paul did not attempt to diminish the importance of the Twelve and the other
witnesses. On the contrary, persuaded of the value of his direct and personal Christological experience, he nevertheless gave great recognition to the existence and authority of
"the apostles before me."

The Pauline school, as we see it in the deutero-Pauline and Lukan writings, seeks to
maintain and clarify the theological position of its teacher. In the prologue to his work,
Luke urges his readers to remember "the events that have been fulfilled among us" (Luke
1:1). For the evangelist (Luke) as for the apostle (Paul), Christianity does not rest on an
abstract revelation, nor on a mystical experience. It rests instead on a story, an intervention

---

[4] Cf. V. P. Furnish, *II Corinthians, Translated with Introduction, Notes, and Commentary* (AB;
New York: Doubleday, 1984), 305–37.

[5] Cf. H. D. Betz, *Galatians: A Commentary on Paul's Letter to the Churches in Galatia* (Philadelphia: Fortress, 1979), 64–74.

[6] On imitation in Paul, cf. H. D. Betz, *Nachfolge und Nachahmung Jesu Christi* (Tübingen: Mohr
[Siebeck], 1967); E. A. Castelli, *Imitating Paul: A Discourse of Power* (Louisville: Westminster/John Knox,
1991). Paul refers quite often to these other apostles in his epistles; cf. 1 Cor 9:5; 15:7–10; Gal 2:8–9.

by God in time and space. In order to be effective, this salvific event needs to be expressed and attested. This is why Luke is eager to add that the observers of these events became both "eyewitnesses and servants of the Word" (Luke 1:2). The two poles are inseparable, but they should not be confused. The first is bound to an event, the coming of Jesus Christ, and the second to the proclamation, the apostolic witness. The first pole, of which Luke is immediately aware, is also related to language, and the second is also related to action. Jesus Christ himself is also a witness to the Word of God, and the gospel preached is by flesh-and-blood apostles. The gospel has two faces: the gospel as Christological event and the gospel as apostolic proclamation. Each face, in turn, has two sides: a historic aspect and a linguistic aspect. These aspects and faces are not to be confused or separated.[7]

In the same way that Pauline faith articulates the reconciliation and the ministry of reconciliation, Luke records the memory of the apostles alongside those of the founding Messiah. The coexistence of the book of Acts and the Gospel is not an anomaly, but the concretization of a theological conviction shared by Paul and his disciples.[8]

The authors of the deutero-Pauline epistles essentially shared the views of their teacher and of Luke. The author of the Epistle to the Ephesians in particular sees the matter in foundational terms. While Paul himself considered Christ the sole foundation of Christianity (1 Cor 3:11), the author of Ephesians, remaining faithful to Pauline theology, demands a further foundation, that of the apostles and prophets (Eph 2:20). The point is not to have two juxtaposed or successive foundations, but one double foundation: the interweaving of the event and its meaning, of Christ and his attestation by the apostles.[9]

This articulation was not easy to develop, express, or maintain. It could be poorly received and poorly expressed. The foundational event could be eclipsed by the weight of the witnesses, and the apostolic witness could be adulterated. Such dangers appear on the horizon of the Pastoral Epistles. In order to defend his teacher, the author privileges the Pauline witness to the detriment of the other apostles, who are consigned to obscurity, and overestimates the apostolic function in comparison with the role of Christ himself.[10] But these moves provoked by a specific ecclesial situation have not obscured the presence of the structure being examined. In the heart of the theology of these epistles, the two-part structure of Gospel and Apostle is once again found.[11]

2. The Johannine Movement

A comparison of the prologues of the Fourth Gospel and the First Epistle of John reveals the same schema in another current of early Christianity, the Johannine move-

---

[7] Cf. F. Bovon, *L'Evangile selon saint Luc (1,1–9,50)* (Commentaire du Nouveau Testament 3a; Geneva: Labor et Fides, 1991), 32–44.

[8] Cf. F. Bovon, *Luc le théologien: Vingt-cinq ans de recherches (1950–1975)* (Le Monde de la Bible; 2d edition; Geneva: Labor et Fides, 1988), 83–84.

[9] Cf. M. Goguel, "Tu es Petrus (Mt 16,17–19)," in the *Bulletin de la Faculté libre de théologie protestante de Paris* 15 (1938): 1–13. On this passage from Ephesians, cf. M. Bouttier, *L'épître de saint Paul aux Ephésiens* (Commentaire du Nouveau Testament 9b; Geneva: Labor et Fides, 1991), 124–31.

[10] Cf. Y. Redalié, *Paul après Paul: Le temps, le salut, la morale selon les épîtres à Timothée et à Tite* (Geneva: Labor et Fides, 1994), 242, who is less affirmative than I am.

[11] Cf. 1 Tim 2:5–7; 2 Tim 1:8–12.

ment. The prologue of the Gospel proclaims the coming of the Word, while that of the Epistle, shaped by an interpretive element, adds the force of an indispensable complement: the apostolic witness. Alongside the incarnation of the Logos and the manifestation of his divine glory stands the physical presence of the apostolic witnesses.[12] In the same way that the Pauline school skillfully maneuvered to find the proper place for its hero in the choir of witnesses, the Johannine community exercised theological diplomacy to defend the legitimacy of its Beloved Disciple. For the purposes of this study, the main item of interest is that in the Johannine movement as well we find the role of Apostle next to that of Revealer. Through the force of metaphor, Johannine theology illustrates the initial course of the revelation: from the Father to the Son and from the Son to the Beloved Disciple. As the Word rests in the Father's bosom in knowing intimacy (John 1:18), in the Johannine hermeneutic the Beloved Disciple rests his head on Jesus' bosom (John 13:25). The revelation is a religious one, in that it comes from God, but it is also a historic and human one, since it passes through persons and their words. As expressions of witness, the Johannine Epistles are to the Gospel what the Acts of the Apostles is to Luke and what the Pauline words are to reconciliation in Christ.[13]

Doubtless being part of the sacred collection of writings in the Johannine community, the Gospel and the Epistles attest to the second-century tendency to concretize the theological structure of Gospel and Apostle in canonical form.[14] Responding to the same internal demands, Marcion draws on a similar arrangement, though using undeniably different methods.

3. The Markan and Matthean Traditions

The narrative tradition that collected, adapted, and conveyed the memories of Jesus until the time of the evangelists, in particular Mark and Matthew, also attests to a two-part structure, in spite of its focus on the Master. It also specifies how individual roles should be distributed within the arrangement.

In retaining the accounts of the institution of the Twelve (Mark 3:13–19 and par.), of their commissioning (Mark 6:7–13 and par.), and of the appearances of the Resurrected One (Matt 28:16–20; Luke 24:36–53; cf. Acts 1:1–8), the bearers of these traditions established this strong relationship of the Lord and his disciples. The apostles constitute a group of officials who, though they are weak, have been made strong by the power of Christ. Sent out two by two, they carry on the work of Jesus, preaching the gospel of the kingdom of God and restoring life through exorcisms and healings.

---

[12] Cf. H. Conzelmann, *"Was von Anfang war,"* in *Neutestamentliche Studien für R. Bultmann* (ed. W. Eltester; Berlin: A. Töpelmann, 1954), 194–201; repr. in *Theologie als Schriftauslegung: Aufsätze zum Neuen Testament* (Munich: Kaiser, 1967), 207–14; and R. E. Brown, *The Epistles of John: Translated with Introduction, Notes, and Commentary* (AB; New York: Doubleday, 1982), 149–88.

[13] Cf. F. Bovon, "The Gospel According to John, Access to God, at the Obscure Origins of Christianity," in *Diogenes* 146 (1989): 37–50.

[14] Cf. J.-D. Kaestli, J.-M. Poffet, and J. Zumstein, eds., *La communauté johannique et son histoire: La trajectoire de l' Evangile de Jean aux deux premiers siècles* (Geneva: Labor et Fides, 1990).

At the end of Matthew, on Easter day, the disciples receive from the risen Christ a mission founded on a promise: "Jesus came to them and said these words" (Matt 28:18a). If divine authority belongs to Christ ("All authority has been given to me in heaven and on earth," 28:18b), the act of witnessing belongs to the apostles ("Go, therefore and make disciples of all nations," 28:19). Thus there is a distinction of roles just as there is a distinction of periods. Because Christ will leave that place, the apostles will have to act. But, as in the prologue to the First Epistle of John (1 John 1:3), the communion of Christ and his disciples will not end in spite of their physical separation: "I am with you always, to the end of the age" (Matt 28:20).[15]

Therefore, for the bearers of these traditions, the apostles represented a living link to the Resurrected One. The Lukan account of Pentecost (Acts 2:1–41) and the Johannine Christ's farewell discourse (John 14:15–21, 26; 15:26; 16:7) give a name to the facilitator of this link: the Holy Spirit, or Paraclete. According to Luke, the risen Christ receives from the Father the power of communion and of life: "Being therefore exalted by the right hand of God, and having received from the Father the promise of the Holy Spirit, he has poured out this that you both see and hear" (Acts 2:33). Christ has passed it on to his disciples, and by it they are transformed. Formerly hesitant, Mary Magdalene goes to the disciples boldly to confess her faith (John 20:11–18); formerly a traitor, Peter proclaims a message of assurance (Luke 22:61–62; Acts 2:14–41). Though at one time a persecutor, Paul is made apostle to the nations (Gal 1:23; 2:7–8); once eager for reward, James wears the mantle of martyrdom (Mark 10:35–37 and Acts 12:1–2).

4. The Pre-Easter and Post-Easter Gospel Contexts

The gospels differ from ancient biographies on at least one point, that they must be read on two levels. On one level, the gospels are the recollection of the pre-Easter life of Jesus. On a second level, they are windows through which the post-Easter life of the apostles and churches can be seen. These two planes can take many forms. In a temporal schematic, the mission of Jesus who proclaims the gospel (Mark 1:14–15) precedes the apostolic proclamation to the nations (Mark 13:10). If the significance of this reality is broadened, the authority to forgive sins, which is in the first instance the prerogative of the Son of Man (Mark 2:10), is then handed on to humans (Matt 9:8). In other words, this authority is transferred to the church and its apostles, and its ministers (cf. Matt 16:19; 18:18; John 20:23). Because of a hermeneutic that demands relevancy for a new situation, the message of Jesus becomes the Christian proclamation. While Luke maintains the parable of the Lost Sheep in a historical context (Jesus defends his missionary efforts in the face of the Pharisees' criticism, Luke 15:1–7), Matthew appropriates the story and integrates it into a chapter he has constructed on the theme of communal life (Matt 18:10–14). Consequently, the parable illustrates no longer the seeking of sinners but the responsibility of ministers to claim those among their flock who are lost. The shepherd, who in Luke represents God or Christ, in Matthew has become the figure of apostle or pastor. Operating in

---

[15] On the ending of Matthew, cf. J. Zumstein, "Matthieu 28, 16–20," in *RTP,* 3d series, 22 (1972): 14–33; repr. in J. Zumstein, *Miettes exégétiques* (Geneva: Labor et Fides, 1991), 91–112.

both the realm of reference (to the former time of Jesus) and the realm of relevance (to the present work of the church), the gospels confirm the existence and importance of the Gospel-Apostle structure.[16]

5. Apostolic Acts

Another early Christian reality to consider is the emergence of narratives concerning the life, ministry, and destiny of the apostles. Protestant theology, which has always insisted on the unique role of Jesus Christ, has often refused to accord the apostles the place they have earned in the economy of salvation. Thus several Protestant exegetes of the nineteenth and twentieth centuries considered the book of Acts an anomaly, a theological mistake.[17] For them, Acts was unseemly and even sacrilegious, because it focused attention on the type of witnesses that ought to vanish behind the Christological message. This opinion, rooted in Protestant polemic against the Catholic doctrine of apostolic succession, ignored the two-part structure of Gospel and Apostle and tipped the scales to favor the spiritual and the divine.[18]

Luke is not alone, however, in his interest in the fate of the apostles. The Epistles and even the Gospels give them a place in the transmission of the good news. Paul understands the cult to be the social and ecclesial *Sitz im Leben* of the Christian "news." Joined in prayer, the first communities praised God for the work of Christ, but they also rejoiced in the universal spread of the gospel (cf. 1 Tim 3:16; Rom 1:8). And they pleaded with God to protect and accompany the apostles and the missionaries (cf. Acts 13:3; 20:36–38). The early communities also recounted the edifying narratives of the pilgrimages of the missionaries and apostles and their success (cf. 1 Thess 1:6–10). Thus we can explain the origin of the cycles of travel narratives reworked by Luke in the book of Acts,[19] such as the dealings of Philip in Samaria and his setbacks with Simon the Magician (Acts 8:4–40), the missionary work of Peter and the foundation of the Caesarean community at the time of Cornelius's conversion (Acts 9:32–11:18), and the missionary expedition of Paul and Barnabas from Antioch as an official delegation (Acts 13–14). The narrative is driven by allegiance to the faith and shaped by Christian affection both for Jesus Christ the Savior and for his apostles, heralds, and missionaries.[20]

---

[16] P. Bonnard, "Composition et signification historique de Matthieu 18," in *De Jésus aux évangiles: Tradition et rédaction dans les Evangiles synoptiques* (ed. Ignace de la Potterie; Gembloux: Duculot, 1967), 130–40; repr. in P. Bonnard, *Anamnesis: Recherches sur le Nouveau Testament* (Geneva: Revue de théologie et de philosophie, 1980), 111–20.

[17] Especially F. Overbeck, *Christentum und Kultur: Gedanken und Anmerkungen zur modernen Theologie* (ed. C. A. Bernoulli; Basel, 1919; repr. Darmstadt: Wissenschaftliche Buchgesellschaft, 1973), 78–80.

[18] Cf. F. Bovon, "L'origine des récits concernant les apôtres," in *RTP*, 3d ser., 3 (1967): 345–50; repr. in F. Bovon, *L'oeuvre de Luc: Etudes d'exégèse et de théologie* (Paris: Cerf, 1987), 155–62.

[19] J. Jervell, "Zur Frage der Traditionsgrundlage der Apostelgeschichte," in *ST* 16 (1962): 25–41; ET J. Jervell, *Luke and the People of God: A New Look at Luke-Acts* (Minneapolis: Augsburg, 1972), 19–39.

[20] On the cycle of traditions contained in the book of Acts, cf. G. Schneider, *Die Apostelgeschichte, I. Teil. Einleitung. Kommentar zu Kap. 1,1–8,40* (Freiburg i. B.: Herder, 1980), 82–94.

This interest in the apostles extended to the second century and explains the contin-
... ion of narratives concerning them. The often unorthodox or sectarian orientation of
authors of so-called "apocryphal" acts, with their avid asceticism and occasional docetic
tendencies, brought prejudice against these remembrances expanded by legendary imagination. The church, the emerging "great church" or "catholic church," was at first distrust-
ful of these apostolic traditions, but after it had established a system of apostolic authority,
it attempted to recover and harness them. The church succeeded, and these narratives,
though not integrated into the canonical scriptures, were nevertheless preserved as religious works. These works became integrated into hagiographic collections along with
remembrances of martyrs and saints.[21]

6. Apostolic Fathers and Apologists

Everyone agrees that a New Testament canon did not appear before the middle of
the second century and that there is no evidence before this date of a collected grouping of
the Gospels and Epistles.[22] In my opinion, the Gospel-Apostle structure, manifest from the
first generation of Christians, prepares the way for the formation of a new body of scriptures as a complement or counterpart to the holy scriptures (the Septuagint) inherited by
the church. The formation of a New Testament canon was therefore the logical materialization of this theological structure. The presence of the Gospel-Apostle pair during the
time of the Apostolic Fathers and the apologists assured the transition from the parameters set by Paul, Luke, and John to the witnesses to the New Testament from the time of
Irenaeus of Lyon and beyond.

The church which would become the "great church" of the second and third centuries simultaneously rejected idolatrous veneration of the apostles at the expense of Christ
and refused a revelation that omitted human mediation. It also opposed a privileged position for any one apostle. In effect, it recognized the importance of these two elements,
Gospel and Apostle, Christ and his disciples. The *First Epistle of Clement* of Rome (ca.
95–98) clearly defines this demarcated structure: "The apostles received the good news for
us from our Savior, Jesus Christ; Jesus, the Christ, was sent by God. Thus Christ comes
from God and the apostles come from Christ; the two were sent out in good order by the
will of God" (*1 Clement* 42:1–2).[23]

For his part, Ignatius of Antioch (ca. 115) encourages the Magnesians to remain
firm "in the teachings of the Savior and the apostles." He urges the presbyters and deacons
to support the bishop as their invaluable spiritual leader; as leader, the bishop in turn must
submit to the apostles of Christ.[24]

---

[21] F. Bovon et al., *Les Actes apocryphes des apôtres: Christianisme et monde païen* (Geneva:
Labor et Fides, 1981).

[22] Of the recent works on the New Testament canon, see particularly B. M. Metzger, *The
Canon of the New Testament: Its Origins, Development, and Significance* (Oxford: Oxford University
Press, 1987); and *Le Canon des écritures: Etudes historiques, exégétiques et systématiques* (ed. C.
Theobald; Paris: Cerf, 1990).

[23] Translated after the French of Annie Jaubert, *Epître aux Corinthiens* (SC 167; Paris: Cerf,
1971), 168–69.

[24] Ignatius of Antioch, *Magnesians* 13.1–2.

Some years later, between 110 and 130, Papias of Hierapolis insisted on an apostolic mediation that would bring the Christians of his time into contact with the early manifestation of truth in Jesus. He preferred an oral testimony, verified by persons deemed worthy of faith, over writings of uncertain validity. To that end he sought direct contact with ancients who had known the apostles. In his own way, Papias attests to the Gospel-Apostle by attaching validity both to "the commandments given by the Lord" and to "those who recall them."[25]

In his *Apology,* Aristides (ca. 140) inscribes the faith of Christians within the structure of Gospel and Apostle. After presenting Christ in rather confessional terms, he evokes the memory of the twelve disciples who were called to record Jesus' salvific work (his "dispensation") and to make it known to all the earth. (*Apol.* 15.1–2).[26]

Bipolarity is also decisive for Justin, who emphasizes both the biblical prophecies realized in Jesus and the teachings of Christ transmitted by the apostles. Thus in the *First Apology* he presents the institution of baptism as an act required by Jesus Christ and known from "the doctrine that we have learned from the apostles" (*1 Apol.* 61.9).[27]

Around 180 C.E., Irenaeus of Lyon definitively expressed the schema examined here. In the preface to *Adversus haereses,* he speaks of "the one true and living faith, which the church has received from the Apostles and transmitted to its children." He continues, "The Lord of all things has in effect given to his apostles the power to proclaim the gospel, and it is through them that we have known the truth, that is, the teaching of the Son of God. It is also to us that the Lord said, 'Who listens to you listens to me, and who rejects you rejects me and the one who sent me.'"[28]

In the East as well as the West, the structure of Gospel and Apostle henceforth became the unshakable foundation of the church. In the fourth century, when Christianity was imposed throughout the Roman Empire, Eusebius of Caesarea vigorously reaffirmed this structure in his *Ecclesiastical History* (1.1.1).[29] His continual reference to episcopal succession demonstrates the normative role of the bipolar organization of Gospel and Apostle. Apostolic succession was mediated through the didactic and governmental device of bishops. But the ecclesiastical hierarchy that was put in place in correlation with the Gospel and Apostle structure—with the bishops in the highest position, and the priests below and then the deacons—left out the prophets, healers, and women who, in the first century, had all been standard witnesses of the Christian message.[30]

---

[25] Cited by Eusebius, *Hist. eccl.* 3.39.3. On Papias, see U. H. J. Körtner, *Papias von Hierapolis: Ein Beitrag zur Geschichte des frühen Christentums* (Göttingen: Vandenhoeck & Ruprecht, 1983).

[26] Apol. 15.1–2; E. J. Goodspeed, *Die ältesten Apologeten: Texte mit kurzen Einleitungen* (repr. of the 1st ed. of 1914; Göttingen: Vandenhoeck & Ruprecht, 1984), 19–20. The Latin text is a modern version of the German restoration of the text by J. Geffcken, but this does not appear clear in Goodspeed's introduction. The Greek text appearing in the apparatus is that of the *Life of Barlaam and Joasaph* which often builds on the *Apology* of Aristides. It speaks here of "that which among themselves [the Christians] is called the holy and evangelical scripture."

[27] A. Wartelle, ed., Justin, *Apologies* (Paris: Etudes augustiniennes, 1987), 182–85, 289–91.

[28] After the French of A. Rousseau, *Contre les hérésies* (Paris: Cerf, 1984), 275–76.

[29] Cf. F. Bovon, "L'*Histoire ecclésiastique* d'Eusèbe de Césarée et l'histoire du salut," in F. Christ, ed., *Oikonomia: Heilsgeschichte als Thema der Theologie* (FS O. Cullmann; Hamburg-Bergstedt: Reich, 1967), 129–39; H. W. Attridge and G. Hata, *Eusebius, Christianity, and Judaism* (Leiden: Brill, 1992).

[30] On the growing marginalization of the prophets, cf. A. von Harnack, *Die Mission und Ausbreitung des Christentums in den ersten drei Jahrunderten,* vol. 1 (4th ed.; Leipzig: J. C. Hinrichs,

7. The Great Church

The theological structure of Gospel and Apostle that underlies the progressive organization of ministries promoted the birth of a New Testament canon with two distinct parts. This structure was doubtless formed imperceptibly, yet irresistibly. During the formation of the great church, everyone was pleased to see the confirmation of doctrine and of ecclesial organization. In my opinion, Marcion's choice of a gospel and some epistles as a source and standard of doctrine was no innovation.[31] Marcion's canon, alongside the others, testifies to the structuring force of Gospel and Apostle. Ecclesiastical authors around the year 200 knew such a juxtaposition of Gospels and Epistles as a sacred collection for a new economy. However, it must be said that the theological structure of Gospel and Apostle matters more to them, in general, than the formal outline of a canon. Nevertheless, when the proconsul demanded the surrender of Christian books during the reign of Commodus (July 180), it is the *libri*—probably the Gospels—and the Epistles of Paul that are handed over, according to the account of the Scillitan martyrs.[32] Moreover, the Muratorian canon, from the second century of our era, enumerates the Gospels, then the Epistles.[33]

It is not surprising that in the Christian liturgy, consequently, the system of biblical readings is based on the model of our theological structure. Since the time of Justin[34] and the *Acts of Peter*,[35] Christian worship has included, besides the Hebrew Bible, readings drawn from the Gospels and the Epistles. In the West it was usual to speak of the Gospel and Epistle, while in the East it was the Gospel and the Apostle, yet both refer to the same reality. As is seen from the title of this article, I find the usage of the Orthodox East especially helpful here.[36]

8. Other Christian Communities

Thus far we have followed the path that lead to the great church. At the same time, however, there is evidence of a parallel track traveled by other Christian communities and

---

1924), 332–79, esp. 362–64; E. Norelli, "L'Ascensione di Isaia nel quadro del profetismo cristiano," in *Il profetismo da Gesù di Nazareth al montanismo: Atti del IV Convegno di studi neotestamentari, Perugia, 12–14 Settembre 1991* (ed. Romano Penna, published as *Ricerche storico-bibliche* 5/1 (1993): 123–48, esp. 147–48.

[31] On Marcion's canon, cf. A. von Harnack, *Marcion: Das Evangelium vom fremden Gott: Eine Monographie zur Geschichte der Grundlegung der katholischen Kirche: Neue Studien zu Marcion* (Leipzig: J. C. Hinrichs, 1924; repr. Darmstadt: Wissenschaftliche Buchgesellschaft, 1985), 35–73 and 40–255; E. Norelli, "La funzione di Paolo nel pensiero di Marcione," in *Rivista biblica* 34 (1986): 543–97.

[32] *Passio sanctorum Scilitanorum* 12, in G. Krüger and G. Ruhbach, ed., *Ausgewählte Märtyrerakten: Neubearbeitung der Knopfschen Ausgabe* (Tübingen: Mohr [Siebeck], 1965), 29.

[33] On this list, cf. the article of J.-D. Kaestli, "La place du *Fragment de Muratori* dans l'histoire du canon: À propos de la thèse de Sundberg et Hahneman," *Cristianesimo nella storia* 15 (1994): 609–634, and the bibliography found there. Cf. also Hahneman's article in the present volume.

[34] *1 Apol.* 67.3; read the introduction and notes of A. Wartelle in Justin, *Apologies*, 45–48 and 297–98.

[35] *Acts of Peter*, 20; L. Vouaux, *Les Actes de Pierre* (Les apocryphes du Nouveau Testament; Paris: Letouzey et Ane, 1922), 339 n. 7.

[36] Cf. H. Leclercq, "Evangéliaire," *DACL* 5, 1 (1922): 775–845; G. Godu, "Evangiles," *DACL* 5, 1 (1922): 853–923; Godu, "Epîtres," *DACL* 5, 1 (1922): 245–344.

movements. What is striking about these other texts, be they gnostic, Jewish-Christian, or apocryphal, is that they are also aware of the bipolar structure of Gospel and Apostle, even if they occasionally order them in different ways.

Certain New Testament traditions focus upon a particular apostle as Christ's successor and counterpart. The Gospel of Matthew accords a special place to Peter (Matt 16:18) without diminishing the role of others. The Pastorals claim an almost exclusive connection with Paul. A diverse group of traditions that do not find a place in the New Testament canon tend to valorize other apostolic figures. Thomas and James, the brother of the Lord, become the lead figures of certain gnostic and Jewish-Christian movements, as we learn from Epiphanius of Salamis,[37] producing the apocryphal *Gospel of Thomas*,[38] the *Apocryphon of James*,[39] as well as the two works titled *Apocalypse of James*.[40] The *Letter of Peter to James*, the *Formal Agreement* and the *Letter of Clement to James* preserved at the beginning of the *Pseudo-Clementine Homilies* also bear witness to the presence of this structure.[41]

The pseudo-Clementine literature reveals another arrangement of Gospel and Apostle. Here the apostolic circle becomes broken. The good apostles, especially Peter, must confront a negative figure, Simon the Magician, who probably represents the apostle Paul. Here the system of pairs, of two people "yoked together" *(syzygoi),* takes the form not of Christ and his apostles, but a false messenger of God confronting the figure of a true apostle. For the authors, that is what happened in the apostolic age. In fact, this alternation between the apostate and the true believer is an ancestral opposition: it goes back to the rivalry between Cain and Abel.[42]

In certain circles, an apostle was invested with such power and deemed the beneficiary of such revelation that Christ himself was neglected. In the apocryphal *Acts of Andrew*, for example, Jesus is present only as one of the names of God.[43] He represents the spiritual divinity who invites the soul to reach a superior world. Here below, the entire earth is occupied by the apostle. It is he who possesses the words of life.[44] The memory of the ministry of Jesus, of his acts and of his speeches, is completely erased. It is in the presence of the apostle, not of Christ, that salvation blossoms and death retreats.[45]

By desiring to privilege a particular apostle or apostolic circle one may omit certain witnesses, as happened with the women apostles. We may begin with Mary Magdalene,

---

[37] *Panarion* 88.7.7–9.

[38] *Gospel of Thomas,* title and 12.

[39] Nag Hammadi Codex I,2.

[40] Nag Hammadi Codices V,3 and V,4.

[41] Cf. *Die Pseudo Klementinen,* vol. 1, *Homilien* (GCS; ed. B. Rehm and G. Strecker; 3d ed.; Berlin: Akademie-Verlag, 1992).

[42] G. Strecker, *Das Judenchristentum in den Pseudoklementinen* (Berlin: Akademie-Verlag, 1981), 188–91.

[43] J.-M. Prieur, *Acta Andreae: Praefatio-Commentarius* (Turnhout: Brepols, 1989), 344–67.

[44] F. Bovon, "Les paroles de vie dans les Actes de l'apôtre André," in *Apocrypha: Le champ des Apocryphes* 2 (1991): 99–117; repr. in F. Bovon, *Révélations et écritures: Nouveau Testament et littérature apocryphe chrétienne* (Geneva: Labor et Fides, 1993), 271–87.

[45] On the second-century image of the apostles, cf. W. A. Bienert, "Das Apostelbild in der altchristlichen Überlieferung," in W. Schneemelcher, ed., *Neutestamentliche Apokryphen in deutscher Übersetzung,* vol. 2, *Apostolisches, Apokalypsen, und Verwandtes* (5th ed.; Tübingen: Mohr [Siebeck], 1989), 6–28.

mentioned in the gospels of Matthew and John (Matt 28:1–10 and John 20:11–18).[46] But already Paul and many authors of the second century have erased her from memory. Mary Magdalene does not figure, for example, in the list of the appearances of the Resurrected One (1 Cor 15:5–8). At most, the apostle to the Gentiles knows of pairs of apostles made up of a man *and* a woman, for example, Priscilla and Aquila[47] and Andronicus and Junia.[48] The institutionalization of the circle of the twelve apostles coincides with the marginalization of the role of these women. However, some heterodox Christian circles venerated their memory.

9. The Apologetic Function of the Gospel-Apostle Structure

Having noted the enormous diffusion of the two-part structure of Gospel and Apostle, we turn to its function. This structure was not put in place during a period of religious calm, nor in a spiritual desert. Instead, it existed in a time when Christians were confronted with diverse propaganda accompanied by claims of authority. In this context, the Christians drew upon Jewish theology to present their new claims: a new instance of revelation, a kind of ultimate "deuteronomic" work, a new and final testament. Claiming authority, they hoped this structure would be normative and have polemical value.

In fact, the Gospel-Apostle pattern was confronted with contemporary religious expressions both polytheistic and pantheistic. It also spread during an age that the Christians, marked by apocalypticism, decried as a period of decay. The image was of a humanity marked by hate, division, and violence, a world passing away and reaching an end (1 Cor 7:31).

It is against this background that the first Christian communities framed a revelation that proclaimed Christ's victory over evil, a triumph that destroyed hate, demolishing it like a wall (Eph 2:14). These communities testified to this victory with conviction and efficacy through the voices of their apostles and messengers.

Without the interpretive voice, events remain brute facts that offer some evidence, but that need the persuasive influence of the message. But without the harshness of the facts—the scandal of the Cross, the enigma of the Word incarnate—the apostolic language is just another cheap form of spirituality in the religious "supermarket" of antiquity.

Although the event of Christ occurred in the past, in the course of the history of God and his people, the apostolic word is unfurled, fragile yet effective, in the present. Shaken by the voices of other religions and other philosophies, this word is also threatened by sectarian or heretical tendencies within the church. The structure of Gospel-Apostle thus

---

[46] Cf. F. Bovon, "Le privilège pascal de Marie-Madeleine," *NTS* 30 (1984): 50–62; repr. in Bovon, *Révélations et écritures*, 215–30.

[47] Rom 16:3–5; 1 Cor 16:19; 2 Tim 4:19; Acts 18:1–2:26.

[48] Rom 16:7. Contemporary feminist exegesis insists rightly on "Junia" as the true name, a woman's name; cf. B. Brooten, "Junia . . . hervorragend unter den Aposteln, Röm 16,7," in E. Moltmann-Wendell, ed., *Frauenbefreiung: Biblische und theologische Argumente* (3d ed.; Munich: Kaiser, 1982), 148–51. This view was earlier expressed by M.-J. Lagrange, *Saint Paul: Epître aux Romains* (Paris: Gabalda, 1916), 366.

allows for the communication of the message but also serves in a polemical fashion to defend the truth and to criticize other models.

Besides the kerygmatic and apologetic functions, there is a third one, useful inside the Christian community. Through its bipolarity, the normative structure of Gospel and Apostle allows the community to grow in faith. A free faith expresses itself through a practice of love. The Gospel and Apostle pattern call for the ethic required by God, expressed through the two-part love command or through the words of Zechariah's hymn, the *Benedictus*, "to serve him without fear in holiness and righteousness" (Luke 1:74–75).

The Christian consciousness is further enlightened by the joining of gesture and the word, thus echoing the events of the gospel and the message of the apostles. Believers can grow in faith when they remember, as Luke says, what Jesus has *done* and what he has *taught* (Acts 1:1). They must also arrange their ecclesial life according to this two-part principle. It finds expression in the diaconate of the word and the diaconate of the table, the founding of which is evoked by the author of Acts (Acts 6:2–4).

The language of "edification" recalls the metaphors of the house and its foundation. That the foundation of the church is in one place said to be Christ (1 Cor 3:11) and in another the apostles (Eph 2:20) suggests an indispensable complementarity.

10. Conclusion

The plurality of gospels might have posed a problem for Christians of the first centuries,[49] and the putting into writing of their opinions or remembrances might have had unsettling consequences.[50] But the formation of a two-pronged collection, made up of Gospels and Epistles, does not seem to have upset them. Clearly, the theological structure of Gospel and Apostle had prepared them. Various attempts had cleared the way: Paul has added his epistles to the oral gospel; Matthew, following Mark, compiled the memories of Jesus in the form of a book, stressing the foundational role of the apostles and of Peter in particular; Luke's narrative relates both the story of Jesus and the story of the witnesses of the resurrection; the Johannine community channeled the revelation addressed through the Son to the Beloved Disciple and added epistles to their gospel; following the same principles, the orthodox communities in the middle of the second century formed a collection of gospels and of numerous epistles. At the same time Marcion, too, honors the structure of Gospel and Apostle.

The New Testament canon, faithful to the underlying theological structure, binds revelation to history following a logic proper to Christianity; it closely associates the gospel as the foundational event and the gospel as good news. By so doing, it proclaims a historic beginning and claims an indispensable apostolic mediation.

---

[49] Cf. H. Merkel, *Die Pluralität der Evangelien als theologisches und exegetisches Problem in der Alten Kirche* (Berne: P. Lang, 1978).

[50] L. Vischer, "Die Rechtfertigung der Schriftstellerei in der Alten Kirche," *Theologische Zeitschrift* 12 (1956): 320–36.

30

The Significance of a Canonical Perspective
of the Church's Scripture

Robert W. Wall

While the previous chapters of this collection have focused on various historical issues that swirl about in recent studies on the formation of the biblical canon, this chapter exploits an enduring theological interest in the final literary product of the canonical process, the Christian scriptures.[1] The theological conception of a biblical canon should not be viewed as somehow detached from or incidental to its historical conceptions; in fact, important clues for a theological reading of Scripture are recovered from the canonical process and are impossible to discern fully apart from the careful historical studies reflected in this book.

The "canonical approach" to biblical studies centers the interpreter upon Scripture's privileged role in Christian formation rather than proposing a novel interpretive strategy; that is, the aim of biblical interpretation is theological understanding. Accordingly, various biblical writings, picked up time and again, preserved and then canonized by the faith community, were brought together in their final form to function in two formative ways: first, as a *rule* whose teaching regulates the church's theological understanding; and, second, as a *sacrament* whose use mediates God's salvific grace to those who actually use Scripture.[2] Even as the Word made flesh was "full of grace and truth" (John 1:14), so now in his absence, the word made text mediates the grace and truth of the Son to those who seek him in faith. From this vantage point, biblical interpretation is more a theological discipline than a technical skill.

Those who approach biblical texts as authorized to serve the church in all matters of Christian formation are joined together not only by this orienting presumption, which then provides the chief touchstone for interpretation, but because they share as well an ambivalent appraisal of the modern historical-critical enterprise (although to different degrees and with different concerns). The methodological interests of historical criticism, which seem preoccupied by those contingencies that shaped particular biblical writings at various points of origin in the ancient world "behind the text," tend to subvert that text's intended use as a means of grace and rule of faith by which current believers are initiated

---

[1] This work draws heavily from my earlier study, "Reading the New Testament in Canonical Context," in *Hearing the New Testament: Strategies for Interpretation* (ed. Joel B. Green; Grand Rapids: Eerdmans, 1995), 370–93.

[2] Cf. Robert W. Wall, "Toward a Wesleyan Hermeneutic of Scripture," *WTJ* 30 (1995): 58–60.

into their new life with the Holy Trinity. For all their exegetical utility, the tools of historical criticism can be used in such a manner as to misplace Scripture's theological reference point with a historical one, freezing its normative meaning in ancient worlds that do not bear upon today's church. The canonical approach to biblical interpretation is organized around this orienting conception and criticism. Thus, rather than approaching Scripture as an anthology of ancient literary art, a record of historical events, or a depository of universal wisdom, the interpreter should first of all approach a biblical text at its ecclesial address and in light of its canonical roles for Christian formation. The faith community orients itself toward its scriptures with the presumption that biblical teaching will bring believers to maturity in theological understanding and in their love for God and neighbor.

1. The Authority of Scripture: Canonical Roles for Christian Formation

Of primary concern for the interpreter is the Bible's function as scripture within the community of faith. The Bible has authority to mediate God's grace to and delineate the theological boundaries of the one holy catholic and apostolic church. That is, Scripture's authority is understood in functional terms (e.g., divine inspiration, revelatory word, apostolic witness, christological confession) rather than in epistemic and dogmatic terms.[3] Clearly, the Bible's authority within the church is imperiled whenever it fails to perform its intended roles, whether through unruly interpretation or simple lack of use. Believers tend not to use Scripture if they perceive that its teaching either lacks relevance for their contemporary situation or is simply incomprehensible to them. When such a situation persists, the functional illiteracy of the church will inevitably lead to a serious distortion of Christian faith as believers turn to other non-canonical authorities, typically secular, to rule their faith and guide their witness to Christ in the world.

The act of sound interpretation, when provoked by this theological crisis, intends to demonstrate the Bible's authority for a particular congregation of readers by first clarifying what the text actually says (text-centered exegesis) and then by recovering from the text that particular meaning which addresses their current theological confusion or moral dilemma in productive ways—that is, in ways that end theological confusion and resolve moral dilemma in a truly Christian manner. Of course, the legitimacy of any biblical interpretation as truly Christian is not determined by its practical importance for a single readership but by general agreement with the church's rule of faith, whose subject matter has been disclosed through the incarnate Word of God, Jesus Christ, witnessed to by his apostles, and preserved by the Holy Spirit in the canonical heritage of the one holy catholic and apostolic church. While the precise relationship between God's truth and grace, which is now mediated through the biblical canon, and God's truth and grace, which is incarnate in the glorified Son, remains contested, my point for biblical interpretation is this: The limits of a properly interpreted text are not determined by an interpreter's critical orthodoxy but by whether an interpretation's content and consequence agrees with the church's rule of faith.[4]

---

[3] See the convincing new study of this point by William J. Abraham, *Canon and Criterion in Christian Theology: From the Fathers to Feminism* (Oxford: Clarendon, 1998).

[4] On this topic, see also papers in this volume by Kalin and McDonald.

The actual performance of Scripture within diverse faith communities, where its interpretation must address diverse challenges to devotion to God, requires a text sufficiently elastic to mediate the truth and grace of God across time and place. The text's history of reception *(Wirkungsgeschichte)* demonstrates that the canonical text gathers to itself a community of interpretations, all theologically orthodox and socially relevant for the Christian formation of diverse congregations of readers. According to this history, the biblical text functions canonically whenever faithful and competent interpreters pick it up again and again to seek after its divinely inspired meaning either to "comfort the afflicted" or "afflict the comfortable." Multiple readings from the same biblical text are discovered, each one a word on target to congregations of God's people whose worship and witness, in turn, presage a new creation.

In this sense the canonical process settled on more than an agreed list of inspired writings (if this ever was the case) that might continue to function as a sanctioned sacrament of the church or as a textual norm for what is truly Christian. The process also evinced a hermeneutic that ever seeks to adapt the plain teaching of a biblical text to its current audience, especially when its life with God is undermined by a theological crisis analogous to that to which the biblical text responds. In fact, the final list of canonical writings was completed by selecting from among those that were picked up again and again and reread by subsequent generations of believers, who continually heard through them the empowering word of God. The trust the church now grants these sacred writings is deeply rooted in this canonical process, not as a knee-jerk response to a precedent set by the primitive church, but in confidence that these same writings would continue to mediate a word from God to subsequent generations of believers. In canonical context, original meanings are ever "contemporized" by the strong interpreter, as new meanings of Scripture are found that allow this sacred text to function effectively in the formation of a faithful people.

The "intended meaning" of a biblical text, then, is not the sole property of its author, but belongs also to the ongoing church that holds the text to be scripture. The hegemony of modern criticism in the scholarly guilds of biblical interpretation tends to hold Scripture captive to an academic rather than religious end. While such an end may well be legitimate for the secular academy, these same interests are then transferred to the citadels of theological education with the unfortunate result of reproducing a clergy no longer interested in the formative intent of Scripture. A pedagogy of Scripture that serves purely historical or literary critical interests subverts Scripture's authorized role, which is to point believers to God, rather than to the ancient world of its authors and first readers/auditors or to the design of the literary text, as the locus of normative meaning. If the ultimate aim of biblical interpretation is theological understanding and not historical reconstruction, the test of sound interpretation is whether it makes the biblical text come alive with meaning that empowers a life for God. Certainly, the penultimate means to this interpretive end is sound exegesis, regulated by the accepted rules of historical and literary critical analysis. Yet, the role of critical exegesis is to make the faithful interpreter more fully "wakeful" to the theological subject matter of biblical teaching, which then is conveyed to the current faith community.

Scripture's functional authority is given added depth by the presumed simultaneity of Scripture's theological meaning—that is, every sacred part of this sacred whole, Old Testament and New Testament, may be rendered coherent by the same Christian theological beliefs and moral values. Of course, I am not suggesting that every biblical writing envisages the very same theology or moral vision; rather, every biblical writing contributes in part to a common theological and moral understanding that is distinctively Christian. If the aim of biblical interpretation is theological understanding, then it is directed by the core convictions of a Christian orthodoxy rather than by the methodological rules of a particular critical orthodoxy. That is, the meaning sought by the faithful reader is a decisively Christian one that is relevant to that particular situation and community. If the ultimate purpose of the meanings found in Scripture is the theological formation of its particular readers, then those meanings should cohere around the core convictions about God that the whole church confesses to be true, and yet in ways that address a particular moment and place in time.

Following Scripture's own hermeneutic, the faithful interpreter approaches a biblical text as the medium of God's truth and saving grace, the canonical context wherein a word from God for a congregation of believers is sought and found. Thus, the "right" rendering of a text sought by biblical interpretation is not that fixed in the author's mind for all time, nor is it determined by the constantly shifting social locations of its present interpreters—although both meanings may well make us more fully "wakeful" to a text's value for the Christian formation of particular readers. Rather, Scripture is canonical precisely because believers recognize its power to convey *God's* intended meaning and transforming grace to them. If the Christian meaning of Scripture is divinely intended and mediated by the inspired text itself, then it is the task of every faithful interpreter to seek after it. The act of reinterpreting Scripture as the vehicle of God's truth and grace, however provisional and seemingly tentative, is the courageous act of finding God's intended meaning for a community who in faith seeks after a more mature life with Christ in the realm of his Spirit. The intertextual character of Scripture—the constant repetition of one text alluding to or citing an earlier text—reflects the simultaneity of its subject matter. Rather than signifying common meanings, the simultaneity of the biblical canon conveys a sense that its authors did not place a wedge between what their Scripture meant and what it now means; this critical construction is simply foreign to the hermeneutics of the biblical literature itself. The (Old Testament) text a biblical author receives as canonical and the (New Testament) intertext he writes that then becomes canonical are equally valued texts in the dynamic process that seeks to hear and then submit to the word of God—a word that Christians believe is incarnate in God's Son, and is made ever new by God's Spirit.

2. Literal-Sense Exegesis of Scripture

A theological reading of the Bible integrates two discrete tasks, biblical exegesis and theological interpretation. The penultimate task is text-centered exegesis, which aims at a coherent exposition of the plain or literal sense of the biblical text studied.[5] This is so not

---

[5] By "literal sense," I am referring to the sense an exegeted text plainly makes given the words used and their grammatical relations, its rhetorical role within a particular composition, and the composition's role within the wider biblical canon. That is, the literal sense of a biblical text is a literary-critical and not a historical-critical construction. As such, my use of "literal-sense exegesis" as a hermeneutical rubric is neither naive nor courageous. It seeks rather to exploit two important discussions of theological hermeneutics, one medieval and another modern, the first Jewish and the

because the interpreter posits the word of God in the text (rather than in its inspired author, the historical Jesus, or some other critical construction), but because of the interpreter's practical interest in Scripture's canonical roles for Christian formation. If Scripture's lack of clarity is a major cause of its dysfunction within the church, then exegesis must make clear what the text of Scripture actually says to enable its performance as sacrament and rule. An interest in what a biblical text says rather than in what it meant at its point of origin, whether in the mind of its author/editor(s), its first readers/auditors, or in any of its sub- or pretexts, however valuable these critical constructions might be, presumes the importance of the biblical text *qua* canonical text. The exegetical aim to describe what the biblical text actually says merely recognizes that the church's canonical heritage is central for Christian formation. What is at stake in biblical interpretation is the believer's transformed life with Christ.

This is not to say, then, that the primary purpose of exegesis is apologetic—to privilege one line of interpretation as "canonical" for all believers for all time. The exegetical task must be collaborative, shared by an inclusive community of interpreters, whose different social locations and methodological interests help to expose a text's full meaning. It is within and for this interpretive community that practitioners of canonical criticism champion the hermeneutical importance of what the biblical text literally says, as informed by the interpreter's common sense and critical attention to a composition's rhetorical design, linguistic content, canonical setting, theological conception, and the like. The postmodern quest of a text's literal sense does not mark a return to premodern biblicism, as some critics have complained; rather than proposing a more elegant biblicism, literal-sense exegesis seeks to recover the broad range of theological conceptions found within Scripture.[6] To do so, the interpreter initially pursues meaning with ideological blinders on and without

---

second Christian. The first source for defining "literal-sense exegesis" is the medieval rabbinate, whose commentaries on Scripture typically distinguished between *peshat* ("straightforward") and *derash* ("investigation") as two integral exegetical modes. If the aim of biblical exegesis is *peshat,* the interpreter engages in a closely reasoned and careful description of what the text actually says. In this first mode, the interpreter responds to the epistemic crisis of a text's lack of clarity for its canonical audience. If the aim is *derash,* the interpreter engages in an imaginative interpretation of why the plain teaching of the text has religious relevance for its canonical audience, often involving "reading in" a meaning not found in a text's "literal sense." This second task, integral with the first, responds to a different crisis in Scripture's authority, which is the audience's perception of its irrelevance for contemporary living. The first is not inherently superior to the second; both are necessary ways of seeking after God's word for the contemporary audience; cf. David Weiss Halivni, *Peshat and Derash: Plain and Applied Meaning in Rabbinic Exegesis* (Oxford: Oxford University Press, 1991). Raymond Brown has reintroduced the idea of Scripture's *sensus plenior* into the scholarly debate over biblical hermeneutics ("The History and Development of the Theory of a *Sensus Plenior,*" CBQ 15 [1953]: 141–62; *idem, The* Sensus Plenior *of Sacred Scripture* [New York: Paulist, 1960]). According to Brown's more modern definition, the *sensus plenior* or "plenary sense" of a biblical text agrees with the theological aspect of the entire biblical canon. Although Brown's understanding of the plenary sense of Scripture is a historical-critical construction, determined by authorial (rather than ecclesial) intent, my spin on "literal sense" includes this piece of Brown's understanding: Any interpretation of any biblical text must agree with the whole of Scripture's witness to God.

   [6] For a working definition of "premodern biblicism" and a noble attempt to reclaim its most salient features, see David Steinmetz, "The Superiority of Pre-critical Exegesis" *Theology Today* 37 (1980): 27–39.

regard for the integral wholeness of Scripture, seeking only to restore to full volume the voice of every biblical writer. The final destination is the recovery of the whole sense of Scripture, which can be vocalized only as a chorus of its various parts. To presume the simultaneity between every part of the whole, without also adequately discerning the literal sense of each in turn, undermines the integral nature of Scripture and even distorts its full witness to God. If the penultimate aim of critical exegesis is to expose and articulate the different theologies within Scripture, then its ultimate purpose is "to put the text back together in a way that makes it available in the present and in its (biblical) entirety—not merely in the past and in the form of historically contextualized fragments."[7] In this sense, then, exegesis of the literal or plain sense of Scripture is foundational for scriptural interpretation, but has value only in relationship to a more holistic end.[8]

Even though literal-sense exegesis works with a stable text in search of a standard, working description, the exegetical history of every biblical text is actually quite fluid, especially in view of the inherent elasticity of words and multiple functions of their grammatical relations. Further changes in the perception of a text's meaning may result from new evidence and different exegetical strategies and from interpreters shaped by diverse social and theological locations. In fact, the sort of neutrality toward biblical texts that critical exegesis envisages actually requires such changes. Our experience with texts tells us that the ideal of a standardized meaning cannot be absolutized, whether as the assured conclusion of the scholarly guild or as some meaning ordained by (and known only to) God. Thus, the fluid nature of exegesis resists the old dichotomy between past and present meanings, and between authorial and reader intentions.

As a practical discipline, literal-sense exegesis intends only to bring greater clarity to the subject matter of Scripture, which in turn supplies the raw material for theological reflection that is formative of Christian faith. The straightforward description of the variety of biblical writings, considered holistically, helps to delimit the range and determine the substance of the church's current understanding of what it means to believe and behave as it must. Yet, whenever biblical theology is executed, with few notable exceptions it remains exclusively an exegetical enterprise—as though a careful description of the Bible's theology is sufficient to perform its canonical roles. In response to this misconception I claim exegesis is the means but not the end of the hermeneutical enterprise. The literal sense of Scripture must have contemporary meaning for its current readers before it can function as their scripture.

3. Theological Reflection on Scripture

The interpreter's ultimate task is directed toward the possible relevance of the canonical text for its current audience. The task of theological reflection upon what Scripture says turns again on the orienting concern of the canonical approach. If the subject matter of Scripture aims at God, so must its interpretation. Biblical interpretation,

---

[7] Jon D. Levenson, *The Hebrew Bible, The Old Testament, and Historical Criticism* (Louisville, Ky.: Westminster John Knox, 1993), 79.

[8] See especially Brevard S. Childs, *Biblical Theology of Old and New Testaments* (Minneapolis: Fortress, 1992), 719–27.

properly "ruled," is formative both of Christian theological understanding and of a life with Christ in the realm of his Spirit. If Scripture's lack of perceived relevance is responsible for its lack of use by the church, then theological reflection seeks to address this problem by making meaningful what the text actually says about our relationship with God and neighbor.

Toward this end, a taxonomy of theological reflection on Scripture must translate exegesis into practical terms adaptable to the church's work of Christian formation. Exegetical conclusions are "ruled" by the church's rule of faith, that is, in the theological terms and narrative logic of a Christian grammar of fundamental beliefs.[9] No interpretation of Scripture can be truly Christian unless it coheres to this rule. No interpretation of Scripture can contribute to the church's theological formation unless it coheres to this rule. No interpretation of Scripture can mediate the transforming grace of God to its readers unless it coheres to this rule: no sacrament of the church is foolishly or falsely distributed. My point is simply this: The principal aim of theological reflection is not to norm once and for all what all true Christians must believe and how they must live, but to be formative of Christian faith, to construct a canonical context within which the Spirit of the risen Christ is allowed free rein to constitute or correct Christian understanding and living. Thus, the biblical interpreter translates the data supplied by literal-sense exegesis in order to describe how a particular biblical text, read as scripture, informs the manner of life and faith held to be truly Christian by that particular congregation of believers. I suspect this theological work is "critical" in the best sense in that it should have the practical result of leading them into a more mature life with Christ.

Theological reflection on Scripture targets the social contexts of the faith community where the word of God, mediated through Scripture, is ultimately heard and embodied. Biblical interpretation, as I understand it, is fully contextual from beginning to end; not only must the exegetical task be executed within canonical context but subsequent theological reflection upon the text aims at an imaginative (i.e., analogical) adaptation of biblical text to a new social context so that the faith community might know who it is and how to act as God's people. While literal-sense exegesis aims to restrict the subject matter of a studied text to a standard description (at least in theory), the interpretive task seeks to adapt what the text says to the contemporary life of a people of God whose faith and life are being challenged anew. Of course, the problem to be met by the interpreter is that the biblical writings are occasional literature, written by particular authors for particular audiences in response to crises of a particular time and place. No biblical writing was composed for the biblical canon nor for the universal readership it now enjoys.

In fact, my account of canonical criticism presumes that current readers will *not* draw from the text the very same meaning from a composition that might have been intended by its author or understood by its first readers. For example, it is doubtful that Acts was included in the New Testament canon for the same reasons that prompted Luke

---

[9] By defining the church's rule of faith as a "grammar of fundamental beliefs" I refer to those non-negotiable theological agreements about God and God's gospel that the church catholic received from Jesus and confess to be universally true. These theological agreements form a "grammar" that enables believers to use faith-full language that other believers recognize and share as members of a particular faith community. Scripture belongs to and helps to regulate the life of these faith communities.

to write it. If Acts was written, at least in large part, to defend Paul and his Gentile mission against his opponents within the Jewish church (and perhaps Diaspora Judaism, with whom some Jewish congregations were still attached), surely such a defense was no longer necessary for the largely Gentile church at the end of the second century, when the Pauline theological perspective had prevailed.[10] Times and places change the significance of texts for new readerships. Rather than decanonizing certain parts of Scripture as irrelevant for contemporary readers, a "canonical" interpretive strategy seeks to find the text's meaning for its current readers. In this sense, the crisis of biblical authority is the propriety of prior interpretations of Scripture—including those of the biblical writers'—for a new situation. This is ultimately a theological crisis: the subject matter of biblical revelation has failed to convey God's Word to a particular people with clarity and conviction, either because they cannot understand what Scripture says or because they cannot understand its immediate relevance for life and faith.[11] In this case, the interpreter must use imagination upon the inherent multivalency of biblical teaching in order to find new meanings for new worlds. Thus, the interpreter presumes the literal sense of a biblical text, carefully exegeted, embodies a community of analogical meanings, while at the same time recognizing that not all of these meanings hold equal significance either for a particular interpreter or for the interpreter's faith community.

4. Reading the Bible as Canonical

If the performance of Scripture within the faith community is regulated by attention to Scripture's authorized roles and the community's confession of faith, interpretation would consist of a sequence of three discrete but related tasks: (1) canonical context, (2) canonical content, and (3) canonical conversations. What follows is a brief description of each as it relates to a ruled reading of Scripture.

A. Canonical Context

The whole of Scripture, Old Testament and New Testament, when received and read as a textual deposit of the church's canonical heritage, aims at Christian formation rather than historical reconstruction. This presumes the interpreter's interest in Scripture's final literary form—in the text *qua* canonical text—and leads the interpreter to an initial set of hermeneutical clues derived from consideration of both the placement and titles of New Testament writings, which are properties of their canonization.

For example, quite apart from authorial intentions, the literary design of the New Testament canon suggests that its discrete units (Gospels, Acts, Letters, Apocalypse) have particular roles to perform within the whole. This consideration of the structure of the

---

[10] In fact, the triumph of Paul within catholicizing Christianity may well have occurred earlier in the second century, if the church's "effective canon," to use John Barton's phrase, included not only the four gospels but also a collection of Pauline Letters; see *Holy Writings, Sacred Text* (Louisville, Ky.: Westminster John Knox, 1997), 14–34.

[11] Michael Fishbane, *The Garments of Torah* (Bloomington: Indiana University Press, 1989), 16–18.

New Testament orients the interpreter to the subject matter found within each of those canonical units in terms of their theological function within Scripture. Often the title provided each unit by the canonizing community brings to clearer focus what particular contribution each unit makes in forming a truly Christian faith. In this regard, the sequence of these four units within the New Testament envisages an intentional rhetorical pattern—or "canon-logic" to use Outler's apt phrase[12]—that more effectively orients the readership to the New Testament's pluriform witness to God and to God's Christ. By the logic of the final literary form of the New Testament canon, each unit is assigned a specific role to perform within the whole, which in turn offers another explanation for the rich diversity of theology, literature, and language that casts Scripture's subject matter.

Thus, the literary conventions of the canonical process, such as the final arrangement of canonical writings and their titles, purpose to facilitate their use as scripture. For example, the fourfold Gospel is placed first in the New Testament to underscore the importance of the story of Jesus' earthly ministry as the subtext for all the writings that follow in the New Testament. Among the four gospels, Matthew (not Mark, in spite of its probable historical priority) comes first since its portrait of Jesus best clarifies his (and therefore the entire New Testament's) relationship with the Old Testament: "I did not come to abolish the law and prophets, but to fulfill them" (Matt 5:17). Consider also the title given to *The Acts of the Apostles,* which is another property of the canonical process. Surely this title does not reflect the intentions of the author, who claims to have authored a literary "narrative" (*diēgēsis;* Luke 1:1–4) rather than a literary "acts," and whose central character is the Spirit of God rather than the apostolic successors to Jesus. By calling this composition *The Acts of the Apostles,* the church uses it to introduce the apostolic Letters that follow and, in so doing, enhances its performance as scripture. What biblical reader can now deny the authority of Paul, whose powerful "acts" prove not only the importance of his work but also of his New Testament Letters for Christian formation?

Sometimes new titles were provided individual compositions, including the naming of anonymous authors (e.g., "According to St. Matthew," or "The Letter of St. Paul to the Hebrews" as in many early canon lists). Titles added by the church in the course of the canonizing process shed additional light on how these compositions and collections, written centuries earlier for congregations and religious crises long since settled, may continue to bear witness to God and God's Christ for a nameless and future readership. The importance of any one biblical voice for theological understanding or ethical praxis is focused or qualified by its relationship to the other voices that constitute the whole canonical chorus. Extending this metaphor, one may even suppose that these various voices, before heard only individually or in smaller groups, became more impressive, invigorating, and even "canonical" for faith only as other voices add their contrapuntal harmonies to the full chorus.

In its final literary form, Scripture consists of Old Testament and New Testament as integral and inspired parts of a canonical whole. The nature of their relationship is envisaged by the New Testament handling of Old Testament texts. The free and fluid interplay between biblical texts, one repeating another by echo or citation, is an inherent feature of

---

[12] Albert C. Outler, "The 'Logic' of Canon-making and the Tasks of Canon-criticism," in *Texts and Testaments: Critical Essays on the Bible and Early Church Fathers* (ed. W. Eugene March; San Antonio: Trinity University Press, 1980), 263–76.

its revelatory power. The reader of Matthew's Gospel, for example, cannot help but take note of how frequently Old Testament texts are cited, even alluded to, as "fulfilled" in the life of Matthew's Jesus. Of course one should expect this, since Jesus claims that his messianic mission does not abolish Scripture but rather confirms its promise of salvation (Matt 5:17–18). The intertextuality of biblical literature points to a hermeneutical model that enjoins Old Testament with New Testament as an interdependent (or intertextual) medium for the word of the Lord. The current reductionism of interpreting the Old Testament or New Testament in isolation from the other, thereby undermining the New Testament's relationship to the "Hebrew Bible," is subverted by the New Testament's appeal to and exegesis of the Old Testament. Sharply put, the scriptures of the New Testament writers are "neither superseded nor nullified but transformed into a witness of the gospel";[13] certainly on the level of canonical authority, this point informs the orienting concerns (rather than the exegetical methods per se) of a hermeneutical model for our ongoing consideration of the relationship between Old Testament and New Testament within the church's Christian Bible.

Reading the New Testament as an "intertext" of the Old Testament requires the interpreter to listen for echoes of or allusions to the writer's own scripture (Old Testament). Only by doing so is the reader able to gain the fullest possible sense of a text's Christian meaning. Several observations follow about the relationship between Old Testament and New Testament as integral parts of a scriptural whole. (1) The Old Testament contains meaning for Christians. The Old Testament is the medium of God's word that is now "brought near" to God's people in such a way as to elicit their confession that "Jesus is Lord" (cf. Rom 10:8–9). The theological authority of the Old Testament presumes its trustworthy witness to God's gospel, now disclosed in Jesus. (2) This same Jesus refuses to decanonize Jewish scriptures (the Old Testament);[14] rather, we have received the Old Testament with him as the normative context in which his people deepen their faith in him as Lord.[15] (3) Paul's claim that Christ is the *telos,* or "aim," of Torah (Rom 10:4; Gal 3:24) may provide another biblical analogue for relating New Testament (= "Christ") and Old Testament (= "Torah"). If both Christ and Torah are Pauline metaphors for particular patterns of salvation, then the Christ-event is the climax of God's redemptive purpose for Israel, promised in Torah. The Christ-event insinuates itself upon Paul's Torah to bear authoritative witness to God's intended meaning. In an analogous way, then, the New Testament is the *telos* of the Old Testament within the Christian Bible. (4) Because we view the Christian Bible as a complete narrative—the Old Testament incomplete without the New Testament and together forming an irreducible and self-sufficient whole—we expect no "third testament" beyond these two. The Christ event is the climax of a variegated history whose

---

[13] Richard Hays, *Echoes of Scripture in the Letters of Paul* (New Haven: Yale University Press, 1989), 157.

[14] I am well aware that using "Old Testament" to speak of Jesus' scriptures or the scriptures of the New Testament writers may seem anachronistic, since according to some (e.g., A. Sundberg) the church's Old Testament was not fully formed nor accepted into the Christian Bible until the fourth century. My observations about Jesus' and the New Testament writers' use of the "Old Testament" are meant to be read as "analogical," to help the present reader to negotiate between the Old Testament and New Testament of the current canon.

[15] Francis Watson, *Text and Truth: Redefining Biblical Theology* (Edinburgh: T&T Clark; Grand Rapids: Eerdmans, 1997), 181–85.

beginning is narrated by the Old Testament. Indeed, the Christian Bible climaxes with Jesus' messianic mission (New Testament), which in turn heralds the coming triumph of God that all Scripture anticipates. (5) Viewing the Christian Bible as a coherent theology, its witness to the Holy Trinity unfolds within this same narrative. The Old Testament tells the story of the First Person of the Holy Trinity, while the story of the Second Person is hidden in prophecies of Israel's restoration. The Old Testament story of the Third Person is less mysterious but is typically confined to a select few mediators of God's covenant with Israel. In any case, the New Testament completes and makes more clear their roles and personae in its stories of the incarnation of the Son and the coming of the Spirit.[16] (6) In a kerygmatic sense, the theological subtext of the New Testament proclamation is the Old Testament narrative of God's response to a fallen creation and to an elect people, Israel, whom God called out of this broken and sinful world as a light to all the nations. Every redemptive *typos* claimed by the Old Testament prophets (e.g., the Creator's restoration of the created order; God's promise to Sarah and Abraham; Israel's exodus from slavery) is embodied by Jesus, and every promise made by God through them is fulfilled through him. In this sense, then, the Old Testament narrative of God continues in the New Testament; every event of God's saving activity in Israel's history, as narrated and interpreted by the Old Testament, is logically related to every event of God's saving activity in Christ, as narrated and interpreted by the New Testament. (7) The Old Testament, while not "about" Jesus, must be understood entirely in relationship to the gospel story about him. That is, the "truth and grace" now disclosed in the messianic event, to which the New Testament bears normative witness, establishes a theological and historical continuity with the truth and grace disclosed in the Israel event, to which the Old Testament bears normative witness. (8) The intertextuality of Old Testament and New Testament, then, is this: The Old Testament supplies the New Testament with its normative theological and historical markers, while the New Testament witness to the risen Messiah supplies the subject matter for a Christian hermeneutic by which the Old Testament becomes Christian scripture. The "old" meaning of the Old Testament is now relativized and made "new" by this christological midrash (i.e., re-reading of the Old Testament) that determines its present meaning in light of Jesus' life and work.

B. Canonical Content

A biblical text, once placed within its distinctive canonical context, acquires a potential for enhanced meaning that should help to guide its exegesis. A canonical approach to exegesis first of all carefully and critically describes what the biblical text plainly says—what its grammar and words allow, with the role the text performs according to its wider rhetorical design, according to the writer's literary artistry and thematic/theological tendencies, and with the distinctive contribution each witness makes to the overall canonical project (see above under "Literal-Sense Exegesis"). This part of the canonical critical enterprise is the most traditional. The canonical approach to theological hermeneutics does not employ a

---

[16] For a stimulating discussion of this perspective, see John Goldingay, "Biblical Narrative and Systematic Theology" in *Between Two Horizons* (ed. J. B. Green and M. Turners; Grand Rapids: Eerdmans, 1999), 123–42.

new exegetical strategy; rather, it sponsors a particular orientation toward the biblical text whose principle interest is its literal sense—the biblical text *qua* canonical text.

C. Canonical Conversations

The intended role of the biblical canon is to adapt its ancient teaching to contemporary life; this is also the primary objective of biblical interpretation. Under this final rubric, the results of the first two tasks are now gathered together as the subject matter of two formative and integral "conversations" about the community's life of faith. The first conversation is *intercanonical* (i.e., conversations between different biblical traditions/writers) and the second is *interecclesial* (i.e., conversations between the Bible and different faith traditions); the first "norms" and guides the second.

Although a number of metaphors work well to express the Bible's theological plurality I prefer to describe the interpreter's practical task as *conversation*. Naturally, there are different kinds of conversations. A canonical approach to the New Testament's pluriform subject matter envisages a conversation that is more complementary than adversarial. In one sense, the inter-canonical conversation is very much like an intramural debate over the precise meaning of things generally agreed to be true and substantial. The purpose or outcome of debate is not to resolve firmly fixed disagreements between members of the same community or panel—as though a normative synthesis were possible. Rather, it is the sort of debate that clarifies the contested content of their common ground. Likewise, the biblical canon stabilizes and witnesses to the historic disagreements between the traditions of the church's first apostles, which were often creative and instructive (cf. Acts 15:1–21; Gal 2:1–15). Not only do these controversies acquire a permanent value within Scripture, but Scripture in turn commends these same controversies to its current readers, inviting them to engage in a similar act of what Karl Popper calls "mutual criticism"[17] in order to provide balance to parochial interests or clarify the theological confession of a particular faith tradition.

In fact, this sort of conversation sometimes works better than the kind that seeks agreement, in that it more readily exposes the potential weakness of any point made *to the exclusion* of its counterpoint. It holds out the potential for a more objective and functional meaning that is neither the conception of any one biblical writer—a canon *within* the canon—nor the presumption of any one expositor—a canon *outside* of the canon. Rather, the canonical interpreter seeks to relate the different ideas of particular biblical writers and canonical units together in contrapuntal yet complementary ways, to expose the self-correcting (or "prophetic") and mutually informing (or "priestly") whole of New Testament theology. In this way, the diversity of biblical theologies within the New Testament fashions a canon of mutual criticism, resulting in a more objective interpretation of Scripture. A New Testament theology thus relates the individual parts, whose total significance extends beyond their compiled meaning; the New Testament's diverse theologies, reconsidered holistically as complementary witnesses within the whole, actually "thicken" the meaning of each part in turn.

---

[17] For a helpful description of Popper's categories, see Mark Brett, *Biblical Criticism in Crisis? The Impact of the Canonical Approach on Old Testament Studies* (Cambridge: Cambridge University Press, 1991), 124–27.

Take, for example, the relationship between the two collections of New Testament letters, Pauline and Catholic. Each bears trustworthy witness to God, but in part, not in whole; the sum of their various theologies constitutes Scripture's whole epistolary witness to God. When different communions privilege different witnesses, they follow a "canon within the canon." For example, the dominant position of the Pauline collection among Protestants has led some to a Pauline reductionism, which either reinterprets the Catholic Epistles in Pauline terms or neglects them entirely. For example, the Letter of James, which Luther virtually decanonized because it communicated a contrary gospel to the one he found in Galatians and Romans, is often still read through a Pauline filter in order to preserve its authority. Theological coherence is maintained, but at a cost; when James is read as a Pauline book its distinctive message is distorted or denied.

The full canon of Letters, however, gathers diverse theologies to form a community of meaning both Pauline and Catholic. In a sense this epistolary whole is actually better focused, not in agreement, but in disagreement. The text's "objective" witness to the truth is better forged by the mutual criticism of its contributors. Thus, the whole is greater than the sum of its parts, more robust than merely adding the contributions of James to what Paul has already brought to the table. The full effect is more like the vibrant sound produced by a complement of different and sometimes dissonant voices, intoned in this case by both Pauline and Catholic collections. The relationship between these two collections, complementary and reflexive, is absolutely strategic in their interpretation; one cannot be read in isolation from the other without diminishing their canonical purpose. More specifically, the theological substance of the second collection actually extends and enhances the theological setting required for reading the first. The Catholic Epistles, whose names and sequence recall the faith of the "pillars" of the Jewish mission (Gal 2:7–9), provide an authorized apparatus of various checks-and-balances that prevent the distortion—and indeed "thicken"—the church's understanding of the Pauline Epistles and so of the full gospel. In doing so, the Catholic voices are neither those of a ventriloquist nor of adversaries, but of colleagues whose authoritative witness to God in conversation with Paul deepens our understanding.

The midrash-like character of this species of biblical interpretation compels the contemporizing of texts, so that "new" meanings are not the result of textual synthesis but arise from contextual significance. Thus, by reconstituting these inter-canonical disagreements into a hermeneutical apparatus of checks and balances, the interpreter may actually imagine a comparable dialogue that aids the church's awareness of how each part of the New Testament canon is important in delimiting and shaping a truly biblical religion. In fashioning a second conversation under the light of the first, the checks and balances are re-imagined as inter-ecclesial conversations that continue to guide the whole church in its various ecumenical conversations. How the inter-canonical conversations are arranged and then adapted to a particular faith tradition is largely intuitive and depends a great deal upon the interpreter's talent and location, both social and religious. Informed readings of biblical texts and ecclesial contexts can be linked together, particular communions with particular New Testament writers, in order to define the normative checks and balances of a complementary conversation that maintains and legitimizes traditional distinctives, on the one hand, while correcting a tendency toward triumphal sectarianism on the other.

31

The Once and Future New Testament

Robert W. Funk

Two factors have brought the canon back to the consciousness of Christian reflection. The first is the steady erosion of canonical claims by the advance of historical-critical scholarship on the Bible. The second is the collapse of the ancient mythical frame of reference for the Christian gospel and creeds. These factors combined have prompted scholars to reconsider the process by which the canon was developed in the first place, and the role it continues to play in theology and religion. The process will be the focus of the first section of this essay.

In the second section, we will examine the various factors that have contributed to the erosion of canonical authority. The forces that have contributed to the decline of canonical warrant have perhaps come to a head in the reports of the Jesus Seminar. In those reports, the historical figure of Jesus appears to be at odds in important ways with the orthodox icon of the creeds. This discrepancy has produced a crisis in canonical authority: Shall we continue to affirm the picture of Jesus provided by the four canonical gospels, or shall we heed the findings of historical research?

The crisis has produced various proposals to revise the canon, especially the New Testament. In the third section, I will suggest a new concept of canon, together with proposals to issue more than one new New Testament.

1. The Process of Canon Development

The production and identification of a canonical collection of scriptures was a process that began quite early but has not been consummated even at this late stage. Here it is possible only to indicate some of the factors of this complex process.[1]

A. Jewish Scriptures

The Jesus movement began at a very early date to search the "scriptures"—principally the prophets and Psalms—to look for evidence that Jesus was the expected Messiah

---

[1] I have reviewed the process at length in three earlier essays. The first, "The New Testament as Tradition and Canon," appeared in *Parables and Presence* (Philadelphia: Fortress, 1982), 151–86. The second appeared in two chapters in *Honest to Jesus* (San Francisco: HarperSanFrancisco, 1996), 77–120. The third was published as a contribution to *Christianity in the 21st Century* (FS John S. Spong; ed. Deborah A. Brown; New York: Crossroad, 2000), 24–46, under the title "The Incredible Canon." This essay is based, in part, on those earlier studies.

and had fulfilled ancient prophecies. It is unclear how widely Christian scribes cast their nets among ancient documents available to them, but it is certain that the texts they canvassed do not correspond to any form of the present Old Testament.

The scriptures they searched, moreover, were the Greek translation of the Hebrew Bible (the Septuagint), rather than the Hebrew Bible itself. Because modern scholars know that the original language of most of the books was Hebrew, we have blithely substituted the Hebrew text for the Greek in preparing translations of the Christian "Old Testament." The canon of most modern churches thus embraces a different set of texts in a different language than was the case for Jesus and the apostles. We seem ready enough to ignore the historical facts about the canon when it is convenient to do so.

To put the matter succinctly: The Christian movement purloined a set of scriptures not its own, in a secondary language, and then created a "canon" of proof texts within that "canon" to support its own claims. In view of the history of this process, and in view of Christian-Jewish relations over the centuries, I think it is time we return the Hebrew Bible to the Jews whose Bible it is and confine ourselves to scriptures that were historically employed by the first Christians. If we need a collection of ancient documents that function as "background" to the rise of Christianity, we should readopt the Greek Old Testament (Septuagint) and translate it into English as our "First Testament."

B. Letters: Particularity

When Christians began to define themselves over against Judaism and paganism, and deal with issues that arose in their daily and institutional lives, they wrote letters to each other. The primary letters in the church's canonical collection are the Letters of Paul. The authentic Letters of Paul were written to specific churches with reference to particular problems. The question that arises in this connection is this: Are the particular solutions proposed by Paul of Tarsus to particular problems of Christians living in the first century binding for all time on Christian communities? The answer nearly all theologians give to that question is negative. Paul's responses, they reason, were relative to his time and place and to the range and purity of his vision. His responses in several important respects have required modification as the years passed and circumstances changed.

In addition, there are many competing voices in the Letters of Paul: he does not always say the same thing. What are we to make of his manifold perspectives? This problem has led some scholars to attempt to find the real voice of Paul among that chorus of voices—again, to find a canon within the canon.

The "canonization" of the letters is thus an ongoing process—an effort to locate and articulate the "normative" witness they are assumed to represent and to adapt that witness to altered circumstance.

C. Gospels: Plurality

As we all know, the gospels were created in stages. The earliest narrative gospel, Mark, went through more than one edition, in all probability. And Mark served as the basis for both Matthew and Luke, who may have combined the Sayings Gospel Q with Mark. If you don't like that theory, then Mark may be an epitome of Matthew, and Luke may have combined Matthew and Mark into a single gospel. This is the two-gospel theory advocated by a minority of New Testament scholars. In any case, it is certain that the synoptic tradition grew in stages, one author making use of earlier work in creating new gospels.

The Fourth Gospel also went through editions. Chapter 21 was appended to an earlier version that originally ended with chapter 20. A number of scholars have theorized that there was an earlier edition of John now referred to as the Signs Gospel. Others have argued that John shared a miracles source with the Gospel of Mark, which both evangelists freely edited. The Gospel of John apparently went through three or four stages, perhaps even more.

Behind the written gospels stand two or more decades of oral tradition. The first storytellers repeated the words of Jesus they could remember and told anecdotes about him. These anecdotes take the form of pronouncement stories, exorcisms, cures, resuscitations, call and commissioning stories, nature wonders, legends, and myths—story forms known to all storytellers of that age. Since these stories were formulated and transmitted orally, their content varied from telling to telling. As folklore, much of this lore is wrapped in memories that edited, deleted, augmented, and combined elements many times over many years. As a consequence, it is very difficult to distinguish fact from fiction. What is clear, however, is that very few, if any, of the oral stories are derived, in their present form, from eyewitnesses.

When the author of Mark decided to compose the first narrative gospel, the author gathered sayings and anecdotes from the oral tradition and arranged them in a continuous narrative without knowledge of the actual order of events. We know this because Mark groups anecdotes and sayings by type of story, by form, or by content, often employing catchwords to join independent sayings. To make the narrative relatively cohesive, the author provided the story with framing events: John the Baptist and the baptism of Jesus as inaugural events; the transfiguration and predictions of the passion as the turning point; and the passion and empty tomb story as the climax. It was that narrative frame— how the Son of God was identified at his baptism, then was conspired against and eventually led to his death—that provided the basis for what eventually became the Apostles' Creed.

Four gospels are included in the New Testament. Why four? Irenaeus's speculation that there are four gospels because there are four winds and four cardinal directions is simply implausible, even as humor. A more likely explanation is that there is more than one gospel because a single witness would not satisfy the fundamental requirement of at least two witnesses to convict. In effect, the New Testament provides two witnesses: the Synoptics and John. In any case, the gospels attest the plurality of the tradition. And plurality, like particularity, became a problem for the authority of canonical writings. The way around that problem was to produce a gospel harmony in which the four stories were blended into one. The creed allegedly summarized that story.

D. Unity of the New Testament

Historical criticism has called the unity of the New Testament writings into question. The New Testament is now viewed as a babel of voices. Scholars specialize in distinguishing one document from another, interpolations from the body of the writing, the use editors make of earlier sources, and so on.

There is irony in this dilemma. If the tradition were not particular and plural, it would not be historical either. This is precisely what makes the creeds an anomaly in the history of Christianity: The creeds pretend to be universal in their validity, not subject to the time and place in which they were created. That makes them ahistorical. Similarly, to regard the New Testament writings as authoritative guides for Christian belief and practice in all times and places is to rob them of their particularity and plurality and hence their historicity. To retain the traditional New Testament and understand it as a canon is to condemn it to progressive irrelevance with each passing century. I will return to this point briefly below.

E. Tradition as Oral and Written

The Christian movement, contrary to popular opinion, was not a religion of the book from the beginning. It was in fact a movement of the spirit. Jesus is represented as asserting his freedom over against the law and the prophets and the religious practices of his day. He spoke with immediacy, directness, and spontaneity, as Amos Wilder used to say.[2] He did not mimic the scribes and the purity party in the close exegesis of the law or the strict interpretations of purity codes. He had a strong preference, perhaps an exclusive preference, for the oral word.

The aversion to writing persisted in the early movement well into the second century. Although Paul writes to his churches, he promises in letter after letter to assert his real authority when he comes to them in person. It has frequently been pointed out that several of the church fathers preferred oral tradition to written as late as the middle of the second century C.E.

But the New Testament authors tend to move in the direction of a written tradition. The shift to writing goes together with the tendency to create something that is stable, crystallized, and definitive, something that can be handed around and on with ease. The very notion of canon presupposes tradition that is written. The transition from oral to written goes together with the move away from the free expression of the spirit to the controlled expression of bishops in an institution. It marks the transition from word *of* God to word *about* God. As Gerhard Ebeling once remarked, a word about God is a human word; only a word from God is a divine word.[3] Lee McDonald is entirely correct in stating that a fixed canon imposes a limit on the intrusion of the spirit.[4]

It is in this light that we should understand usage in the ancient churches as a criterion for canonicity. The usage criterion tells us how the bishops began to understand their own tradition: if the tradition had passed into the public domain and could be considered the opinion of the average communicant, then it was canonical. That indicates that the

---

[2] For example in: Amos Wilder, *Early Christian Rhetoric: The Language of the Gospel* (Cambridge, Mass.: Harvard University Press, 1971; repr. Peabody, Mass: Hendrickson, 1999).

[3] He discusses the relation of kinds of words at length in *Word and Faith* (Philadelphia: Fortress, 1961).

[4] Lee M. McDonald, *The Formation of the Christian Biblical Canon* (rev. and enl. ed.; Peabody, Mass: Hendrickson, 1995).

tradition has now been leveled, flattened, as it were, so that it can be readily understood by the average believer. Canonization, in fact, was an integral part of the bureaucratization and politicization of the tradition.

The canonical process itself functioned to flatten and crystallize the tradition. It was for that reason that the institutional church insisted on the right to interpret the written text: by doing so, the church held open the possibility of a revision of what stood written. However, the institution was not willing as a rule to endorse deviant interpretive behavior, which means that Jesus of Nazareth would have been no more welcome among the church fathers than he was among members of the purity party in his own day. That possibility should warn us of the dangers of understanding canon in any rigid, legal, or literal sense.

F. The Canonical Writings as "Apostolic"

The early fathers of the church argued that the canonical writings were produced by the "apostles," who were presumed to be either among the first followers of the historical Jesus or amanuenses (secretaries) to those followers. We now know that most if not all of those claims are inaccurate. This is another point at which the tradition has become historically untrustworthy. More significantly, the claim to apostolicity was in fact a belated claim to legitimate succession and thus to the authority to speak for Jesus and his first followers.

This same deficiency applies to the claim that the New Testament documents are ancient, that they belong to the formative stages of the tradition, and not to its institutional and hardening phase. We now believe that much of the New Testament was not written until late in the first century or early in the second. We think that the reports of the gospels and Acts are often derivative and historically unreliable. The councils were thus in error in making the claims they did about the age of the documents they canonized.

G. The Canon as Orthodox and Inspired

To claim that the New Testament documents were both orthodox and inspired is to say the same thing. A book was thought to be inspired if it were orthodox, and orthodox if it were inspired. The employment of these two criteria is a tactical ploy: define as canonical what the bishops have decided is orthodox and declare it to be inspired at the same time; eliminate everything that does not fit the orthodox mold and you produce an impregnable circle.

The canon of the early Christian movement is a spectrum of tradition and interpretation. The only question is whether the ancient councils and bishops narrowed the spectrum too much. They certainly did not expand it prodigally; yet they were wise enough to include a variety of documents in their lists of works recommended to be read in the churches; it was not a monolithic collection. It now appears that they were so exercised about heresy—read: their own authority and power—that they narrowed the spectrum too much both laterally and vertically. With respect to the lateral dimension, they failed to include a fully representative spectrum of memory and interpretation in their definition of orthodoxy. As a consequence, the tradition soon became too incestuous and brittle to adapt itself to new contexts and problems. With regard to the vertical dimension: the tradition was cut off at an early date from some of its roots—the vision of Jesus was obscured by interpretive overlay and the authentic voice of Paul smothered by Pauline imitators. These deficiencies, unfortunately, cannot be entirely remedied since some of the founding documents have been destroyed. Yet the issue of a new canon or canons utilizing fragmentary and newly discovered documents may help remedy the deficiency.

H. Canonical Languages

When the Roman Catholic church got around to canonizing its scripture in the sixteenth century—8 April 1546, to be exact—it canonized the Latin Vulgate. The canonical gospels for that church are thus the Latin translations of Jerome and others. In the Fourth Gospel, the Latin text included the pericope of the woman caught in the act of adultery (usually versified as 7:53–8:11). As a consequence, commentaries on John by Catholic scholars must address that pericope. Protestant scholars, who prefer for the most part to think of the Greek text as canonical, skip that pericope in their commentaries because they think that it did not belong to the original text of John. This is a minor example of an unresolved canonical problem.

So far as I know, no one has ever canonized the Greek text of the New Testament; the United Bible Societies are claiming copyright of the Nestle-Aland version, but they have not canonized it. Both Protestant and Catholic scholars simply buy each new edition of Nestle-Aland critical edition of the Greek New Testament as it appears and use it as though it were the real New Testament. Which edition of the Nestle-Aland Greek New Testament with its catalogue of more than seventy thousand significant variants is canonical? No one has yet been willing to say.

The early Jesus movement made almost exclusive use of the Greek translation of the Torah, Prophets, and Psalms. Should Christians not regard the Greek scriptures as their canon?

The original language of the gospels, so far as we know, was Greek. However, many of our colleagues think Jesus spoke only Aramaic. Were we to discover a text of Jesus' teachings in Aramaic, would that displace the Greek translations we have in our Greek New Testament? Why not adopt a retrotranslation from Greek into Aramaic as the real gospel? By analogy, would a retrotranslation from Coptic into Greek be acceptable as an earlier version of the *Gospel of Thomas?* All sorts of intriguing questions cluster around the question of the languages of the canon.

2. The Erosion of Canonical Authority

Scientific and historical scholarship, including biblical scholarship, has eroded the credibility of the traditional claims embodied in the church's creeds. These developments call into question the canonical authority of the Bible as traditionally understood.

A. Historical-Critical Scholarship and the Canon

The progress of historical-critical scholarship has undermined the historical reliability and theological dependability of the traditional biblical canon. The renewed quest of the historical Jesus has raised the canonical issue to crisis level. It has done so by further divorcing the author of the faith, Jesus of Nazareth, from canonical representations of him. Whatever else may be said of the issues involved, it is clear that the gap between the historical figure and canonical pictures has grown rather than contracted. Vocal critics of the Jesus Seminar have made it abundantly clear that a defense of orthodoxy is also a defense of the historical trustworthiness of the New Testament gospels and an assault on the use of all extracanonical gospels in reconstructing Christian origins. What is at stake for our critics is that version of the faith "once for all delivered to the saints" in canon and creed. This issue is so crucial that I will return to it below.

B. Darwin and the Creation Story

Darwin's *Origin of Species* (1859) became the spearhead of the first frontal assault on the reliability of the canon in modern times. The creation story has been the focal point of the controversy for more than a century. The history of that controversy illustrates how tenacious has been the effort to preserve traditional views of the canon. That history also illustrates how inevitably conservative interpreters have been forced to retreat from the Genesis account. If there is a viable creation story in circulation today it is the big bang theory. The big bang is no less mythical than the Genesis story. Its virtue is that it corresponds to what we know about the physical universe today, in contrast to what biblical authors knew about it more than two millennia ago. In other words, it is at least marginally believable, while the Genesis story we now know to be an ancient myth informed by an archaic worldview.

C. Einstein's Theory of Relativity

The second major assault on the canon turned out to be Einstein's theory of relativity. That theory holds sway in the scientific and philosophical world, and in much of the theological world as well. Yet conservative theologians have assigned themselves the task of ignoring its implications for traditional notions of "revealed truth" and biblical authority. It is for that reason that the churches have become museums of traditional affirmations about God, the incarnation, the Trinity, and the canon, as Don Cupitt has put it.[5] Theologians representing those churches have accordingly become museum curators. It has almost become incumbent on theologians to quit the precincts of the church in order openly and honestly to face the root questions surrounding traditional affirmations. The relativity of every point of view will continue to haunt the orthodox tradition so long as it continues to insist on its perspective as definitive.

D. The Collapse of the Old Symbolic Universe

An additional storm has gathered against orthodoxy and the canon in the second half of the twentieth century. As the result of a tissue of complex developments, the symbolic universe that served as the matrix in which the orthodox myth was conceived

---

[5] Don Cupitt, *Taking Leave of God* (London: SCM Press Ltd., 1980), 154–55.

suddenly became untenable. It simply disintegrated, leaving the creedal, orthodox faith with a fractured matrix. With the mythic matrix in ruins, the question of whether the orthodox creed is a legitimate expression of the Jesus tradition has become moot.

By the collapse of the mythical matrix I mean that the myth that serves as the matrix for the orthodox creed is bound up with a worldview that is even now passing away. That myth is the story of a redeemer figure who drops in from another world, is identified by his miraculous birth, performs a few miracles, and then dies on the cross to absolve humankind of sin and guilt. After his death, his corpse is resuscitated and he ascends to the heavens, whence he came. The story concludes with the promise that he will return eventually and sit in cosmic judgment on the world.

The loss of credibility for the framing worldview means that elements of the creedal story have peeled away one by one until there is virtually nothing left. We are left with a creed that is no longer believable and, as a consequence, with a Christ that is incredible.

We no longer believe that Jesus was born of Mary without the benefit of male sperm. We no longer think of him literally as performing miracles like walking on the water or stilling the storm. We no longer believe he fed 5,000 (not counting women and children, according to Matthew) with five loaves and two fish. We are relatively certain that the first reports of his resurrection were luminous apparitions prompted by grief. We think the empty tomb stories are a late and fictional attempt to certify a bodily resurrection. The ascension of Jesus into heaven can only be a fiction. We doubt that Jesus died to atone for the sins of the world, resulting from Adam's original error. We are convinced that Jesus did not intend to establish a new religion, appoint clergy, or inaugurate celibacy. In sum, there is little of the orthodox story that remains tenable.

The essential dogmas of the television evangelists, Fundamentalists, and many Evangelicals are museum exhibits: the divinity of Jesus, the virgin birth, the blood atonement, the bodily resurrection, and the second coming. The decay of the old symbolic universe is so far advanced that many believers no longer find such dogmas interesting enough even to discuss.

E. The Demise of the Paper Pope

For many the Bible continues to function as a paper pope. For them the Bible corresponds to the infallible magisterium of the Roman Church. Neither can be regarded as the indispensable fountains of truth they once were. Nevertheless, various segments of the Christian community invoke the Bible selectively to sanction various practices and beliefs of their choosing. That the Bible functions as an authority only to a limited extent indicates the extent to which the erosion of the Bible as an authority has taken place.

The sanctity of the Bible has been protected, for the masses, by a high level of illiteracy. In survey after survey, it has been demonstrated that a majority of people who insist that the Bible is the word of God are unfamiliar with much of its content. More than half of those declaring their faith in the Bible as God's word cannot name the four gospels. Few are aware that the Bible and traditional forms of Christianity continue to endorse causes and standards that none of us should be willing to tolerate, much less endorse.

We have forgotten that the Bible was the authorization for New England's Puritans to put witches to death as late as the seventeenth century. The first recorded execution of a witch in North America took place in Massachusetts in 1647. The infection broke out again in 1692, when nineteen, mostly women, died as witches. In Europe, thousands of women were executed as witches under the Inquisition, which was inaugurated by Gregory IX in 1231. The justification for this holocaust was the statement in the book of Exodus (22:18; Deut 18:10; cf. Gal 5:20): "You shall not permit a witch (a female sorcerer) to live." The execution of witches did not cease until the end of the eighteenth century and then only under the influence of the Enlightenment.

In working on the Scholars Version of the Letters and Epistles, I read once again with horror the injunction in Col 3:22: "Slaves, obey your earthly masters, not just for the sake of appearances, to gain human approval, but with a sincere heart, because you fear the Lord."

This injunction is repeated again in Eph 6:5, where it is said to be the will of God, and in 1 Tim 6:1–2, Titus 2:9–10, and 1 Pet 2:18–21, where slaves are urged to take their beatings patiently in order to win God's approval. In the Torah, Israelites were not to enslave each other, but were permitted to own both male and female slaves if they were foreigners or aliens in the land; such slaves were regarded as property that could be inherited along with other real goods (Lev 25:44–46).

And what about the charming portrait of the place of women found in 1 Timothy? Let a woman learn in silence with full submissiveness. I do not permit women to teach or to have authority over men. They are to remain silent. Recall that Adam was created first, then Eve. Adam was not deceived; on the contrary, it was the woman who was deceived and is responsible for the transgression. The salvation of women lies in childbearing, if they persist in faith and love and holiness with all modesty (1 Tim 2:11–15). Women are enjoined to be submissive to their husbands in Eph 5:22, Col 3:18, Titus 2:5, 1 Pet 3:1, which is where, I suppose, the Southern Baptists get their dicta for relegating women to a secondary role in human society.

These particulars are nothing compared to the tribal code to put aliens to the sword in war, at times with the direct aid of Yahweh himself.[6] Consider also the persecution of Jews in the belief that they killed Jesus. Then there is the suppression of sex, sexuality, women, and homosexuals, although the church fathers are probably more to blame for jaundiced views of sex than the Bible. The Bible is not really to blame for the intransigence of a male-dominated, medieval-minded, self-serving clergy; we men have managed this atrocity all by ourselves—although we have justified it by adopting the patriarchal system presupposed by numerous biblical authors.

We have been betrayed by a biblical faith. We have heeded the Bible because we trust it, and it has often betrayed our better judgments, which have now risen up in holy protest. The wonder is that a biblical faith still survives. It does so only because people are largely ignorant of its contents or poorly informed about its history and development. The positive side of this ugly scene is that the authority of the Bible is eroding by leaps and bounds. The canon is shedding its canonicity. Yet there is nostalgia in that loss, not because of the evil in the Bible, but because of some of the profound insights it does contain.

Unless we rightly divide the word of truth and raise the literacy level, the Bible is destined for oblivion in the third millennium. My own solution to the problem is to issue a revised canon, a new New Testament, by both shrinking and expanding the texts to be included.

---

[6] Josh 10.

F. The Renewed Quest and the Canon

The renewed quest of the historical Jesus is taken to be a significant element in the continuing critical assault on orthodoxy and the canon, to judge by the ire the findings of the Jesus Seminar have aroused.

The quest of the historical Jesus is nothing more or less than a continuation of the line historians have pursued beginning already in the seventeenth century. Questers have increasingly made distinctions between fact and fiction within the gospels. By isolating sayings and anecdotes that purport to capture the image of the historical Jesus, in contrast to other material in the gospels, we appear to be reducing the boundaries of the canon. To be sure, that is only another version of isolating a canon within the canon. This canon within the canon, however, turns out to stand in tension with the orthodox narrative frame imposed on earlier materials by the evangelists. Put succinctly, the emerging profile of the historical figure does not appear to be entirely compatible with the surrounding mythical narrative frame.

On the one hand, our growing conviction that much of the narrative gospel tradition consists of fictions has been taken to challenge the theological validity of the canonical gospels: for many scholars and believers historical reliability and theological validity are inseparably linked. The argument goes: If Christian faith is faith in the representations of Jesus of Nazareth in the New Testament gospels and those gospels cannot be trusted with historical information about Jesus, then they cannot be a basis of faith. And the Jesus they portray cannot be the object of faith.

On the other, the parables, aphorisms, and dialogues of the historical Jesus do not lend themselves readily to either the narrative framework or the theological formulations of the fourth century.

Jesus was a wandering teacher of wisdom. His voice emanates from a compendium of parables, aphorisms, and dialogues that can be isolated from the mass of tradition that accrued to his name. In those sayings, and correlative acts, we can occasionally catch sight of Jesus' vision, a vision of something he called God's domain or kingdom.

Visions come in bits and pieces, in random stunning insights, never in continuous, articulated wholes. Yet from such fragments of insight one can begin to piece together some sense of the whole. Taken together these fragments provide us with glimpses of the historical sage. Since Jesus' vision of the kingdom was nothing more nor less than a glimpse, the best we can hope for is a glimpse of his glimpse.

Among the glimmers that emanate from the Gospels are certain features of his discourse. Jesus always talked about God's domain in everyday, mundane terms—dinner parties, travelers being mugged, truant sons, the hungry and tearful, toll collectors and prostitutes, a cache of coins. His language was concrete and specific. He seems never to have used abstract language. He made no theological statements. He would not have said "All human beings have sinned and fallen short of the glory of God," or "I think, therefore I am." Although perhaps congenial to his way of viewing things, he would not even have formulated such a simple assertion as "God is love." Jesus did not have a doctrine of God; he only had experience of God.

Although his language was drawn from the mundane world around him, he did not have ordinary reality in mind. His language is indirect; it is highly figurative or metaphorical. We know the parable of the leaven is not about baking bread. The mustard seed and the sower are not about gardening. His admonition to lend to those who are unable to pay us back is not relevant to banking practice.

Jesus exercised freedom over against the law and tradition. That freedom goes together with the novelty of his speech forms. He speaks with immediacy, directness, spontaneity. He does not appear to be consciously creating tradition in the manner of the scribes. His words are concentrated on the immediate situation, in direct encounter with the hearer. The Jesus tradition is thus to be contrasted with the formal oral tradition—handing the law and its interpretation around and on—as well as with the written text, which, in any case, probably did not play a central role in his rhetorical strategy. Jesus himself may well have been unable to read and write.

Jesus came as close as he could to inaugurating a tradition without closely defined contours; it was completely open to unforeseen futures. He refused to specify what he meant in particular. He preferred to point to the horizon of the kingdom. He did so by looking *through* the particulars of daily existence to some region that lay beyond the everyday—or, to alter the figure, within the everyday, right there in the interstices of existence. He infringed the everydayness of the everyday by introducing a new dimension, a dimension that cuts across the customary and opens onto a fabulous yonder of Samaritans who care for enemies, of prodigals who return home, of laborers who receive undeserved wages. Of enemies to be loved and families to be hated. Of bankers who lend only to those who can't pay them back. Of those who give something to every beggar who asks. Of those who have become careless about life itself, since to attempt to preserve life is to forfeit life.

It now seems clear that Jesus made no claims for himself as a Messiah, or the Son of Man (in the technical sense), or as the Son of God (also in the restricted sense). He would not have said something like, "The Father and I are one."[7] Nor would he have asserted that he is in the Father and the Father is in him.[8] There are good reasons to think the several predictions of the passion are fictions created by the evangelist and not the result of some alleged messianic self-consciousness of Jesus. Jesus did not think he was born of a virgin by some divine miracle, nor did he believe he was to die for the sins of humankind. He probably did not compare himself to Moses or the prophets, and he certainly never thought of himself as the second person of the Trinity. John Hick has put the matter pointedly: "The historical Jesus did not make the claim to deity that later Christian thought was to make for him."[9] He then asks, "How is it possible for the church to know something so important about Jesus that he did not know himself."[10] Ultimately, then, the question for Hick, as for the rest of us, is whether the church is a divinely ordained institution whose pronouncements on the significance of Jesus of Nazareth take precedence over all historical judgments.[11] That we can still ask this question with a straight face, without even asking which church, is an index to the extent to which theological discourse inside the precincts of the church has lost its self-transcendence. It will not do to assert that the church (the Roman Church, the Greek Orthodox Church, the Methodist Church?) has been under the

---

[7] John 10:15.
[8] John 10:38.
[9] John Hick, *The Metaphor of God Incarnate* (Louisville, Ky.: Westminster John Knox, 1993), 27.
[10] Ibid., 30.
[11] Ibid., 151.

guidance of the Holy Spirit and its judgments are therefore trustworthy, as Cardinal Ratzinger has the audacity to assert.[12] We have no way of determining whether the judgments of the church councils were correct without evaluating the content of their pronouncements. And we would have to conduct those evaluations in relation to our knowledge of the history of the tradition and what we otherwise know of the world we inhabit. An appeal to the church, to the Holy Spirit, to the canon as the arbiter of theological disputes is merely to prolong the deception and deepen the crisis. To put the matter pointedly, the canon is one crucial factor nourishing the continuing pretense.

Gospel scholarship has come to be the focal point of the current debate in large measure because the Jesus Seminar has taken the discussion public. That has altered the status of the current debate. The issue is now out there in the public domain. Biblical scholars and theologians of all persuasions must now stand up and be counted.

3. Needed: A New Concept and a New Canon

A. A New Concept of Canon

The profile of the historical figure of Jesus that has emerged from the work of the Jesus Seminar reminds me of Harold Bloom's definition of a "canonical" work of literature.[13] The twenty-six works he includes in his canon of great western prose and poetry consists entirely of strong poets, poets who appeared on the stage as intrusions into their time and place. In a canonical work, Bloom writes, "you encounter a stranger, an uncanny startlement rather than a fulfillment of expectations." Strong poets trade in a mode of originality that startles, even frightens, that seems weird at first meeting. In them, Bloom says, we encounter greatness directly. Their words cannot be assimilated to the received tradition; rather in time they so assimilate us to their strangeness that we no longer regard them as alien: their madness has become the norm of our sanity.

Bloom reminded me of what we learned about the parables and aphorisms of Jesus thirty years ago. When you encounter the authentic words of Jesus—when you free them from the surrounding flattening prosaic terrain—you are as surprised as the victim in the ditch in the parable of the Samaritan, as those hired at the eleventh hour when paid a denarius, as the street people escorted into the great banquet, as the prodigal upon returning home. Our surprise is triggered by their surprise.

The followers of Jesus began to forget their startlement almost immediately. It was difficult for them to transmit. In addition, they willed to forget what was not practical and useful in their struggle to conquer the empire. Nevertheless, that surprise is preserved in incidental traces here and there in the canonical gospels and in the vision of Paul, but everywhere else was almost immediately suppressed.

---

[12] J. Ratzinger, *Journey Toward Easter* (Slough, England: St. Paul Publications, 1987), 131 (cited by Hick, *The Metaphor of God*, 37).

[13] Harold Bloom, *The Western Canon: The Books and School of the Ages* (New York: Riverhead, 1994), 3.

Jesus and Paul are the only authoritative voices in the New Testament, and they have been silenced by an oppressive overlay of ordinary iconography and tables of received virtue. We may think of this process as occurring in three stages. First, the community made the transition from orality to scribalism as a way to fix and thus narrow the original unruly vision. (By way of reminder, the oral may be written and not lose its orality, which is to say that orality is here a metaphor.) Then the redactors, the evangelists, and editors of letters, came along and encased Jesus and Paul in suffocating prose enclosures. Finally, in the third stage, the startling expressions of Jesus and Paul are assimilated to what everybody already knows, to the received myth, to proverbial lore, and its genius thereby effaced. The canon is thereby reduced to what is read with approval at the behest of the bishop, who has decided what is safe for us to read.

That process has been repeated throughout the history of the Christian tradition— partial rediscovery, eruption of the spirit, suppression by the "creedal party" or by the "canon party." The "creedal party" prefers their own formulation of what Jesus and Paul were all about and are willing to suppress unruly views. The "canon party" consists of those who want to credit the ancient formulations but prefer to keep the original Jesus and Paul out of the equation. And, for the most part, modern critical scholarship has obediently followed suit in its recent manifestations.

First, form criticism was designed to go behind the written gospels to recover the Jesus tradition in its fluid state. Form criticism came under fire as the subversion of what stands written. We were admonished to study the Gospels and the Letters as they stand in our reconstructed Greek texts. Then came redaction criticism with its penchant for ignoring the underlying soul of the tradition and its call to concentrate on how the individual evangelists interpreted Jesus and Paul. Under its tutelage, Mark, Matthew, and Luke displaced Jesus as the source of the primary vision. Last of all, reader response criticism reared its egalitarian head to produce the final flattening: Jesus and Paul mean whatever readers take them to mean; as reader I am the final authority.

Whether we like it or not, the old New Testament has long since ceased to be a canon in the Bloomian sense: it lacks authority in our society, despite appearances to the contrary. Is it surprising that Luke Timothy Johnson writes a commentary on the Pastorals? The Pastorals have all but obscured the historical Paul; they have replaced Paul with a manual of church management. They have drained the last ounce of creativity out of the Pauline tradition.

Similarly, the creedal party much prefers the framework stories of the Gospel of Mark where the myth of the Apostles' Creed is vested. One can draw a straight line from those framework stories to the first versions of the Old Roman Creed, and thence to Nicea and the Apostles' Creed of the fourth century and later. These creeds constitute the final abstraction of the historical Jesus. It is perfectly clear that most members of the creedal party have no use for the Jesus of the aphorisms and parables: that Jesus cannot be managed by the creedal party. One of our critics summarizes in a recent interview: "Jesus says if you want to follow me, you must give up your life, take up your cross and give up all your possessions. This is a hard, demanding Jesus who says that unless you repent you will be lost."[14] That is the Jesus of

---

[14] "Dr. Luke Timothy Johnson: In Search of the Real Jesus" (interview conducted by Robert Becker), *Cathedral Age* 73, no. 1 (Spring 1997): 6–9, at p. 8.

a monastic order. That is a reduced version of the Jesus of the creedal party. It has very little to do with the Jesus of the parables.

The assimilation of the canonical texts to the orthodox creed has posed an even more acute problem: Can the original vision be recaptured and re-mythologized in a new matrix amenable to the modern understanding of the physical universe and the history of the rise of the tradition? These turn out to be inseparable problems for us. The erosion of the mythical matrix of the creed has left exposed that part of the gospel tradition that does not depend on the ancient mythical matrix. The historical figure of Jesus may offer us the possibility of a version of the gospel without the original framing myth, ready to be taken up into a new story—a new myth—suitable for the modern age.

This version of the problem clarifies the essential difference between what I have termed the renewed quest and the third quest. In the third quest, everything appears to depend on whether the original mythical matrix can be salvaged, for, we are told, that is the essence of the gospel. The third quest has no interest in the vision of Jesus—witness the lack of interest in the aphorisms and parables—but is focused in a defensive posture on the "apostolic" interpretation of Jesus in the narrative gospels and the creeds. The renewed quest, on the other hand, is willing to go wherever the data and the requirements of the times lead. It is of course the case that it has been the untenable character of the framing myth that has opened our eyes to other possibilities. Like everyone else, we are at the mercy of our time and place in the evolution of human culture.

The renewed quest, rather than the third quest, is thus ingredient to all the fundamental theological issues facing us today. On the one hand, the shift in worldviews has grown increasingly problematic for any orthodox statement of the faith. The discrepancy between the current scientific worldview and the orthodox creed has grown to such proportions that it can no longer be ignored. On the other hand, the modern history of gospel scholarship has undermined all orthodox affirmations of the traditional collection of Christian scriptures. The New Testament no longer satisfies any of the criteria employed to identify authoritative scriptures (ancient, apostolic, inspired). And the canonical gospels do not provide us with a portrait of Jesus of Nazareth without drastic critical surgery. We are left without either a serviceable canon or a functional statement of faith. To learn these two fundamental things about the Christian tradition may be the salvation of that tradition in the third millennium. I might have said in the twenty-first century, but I doubt that the crisis facing the churches will deepen sufficiently to awaken them to the problem in time to resolve it in the next one hundred years. The mills of the gods grind slowly, it seems.

The concept of canon in the Christian tradition hardened early on into a compendium of affirmations designed to fence off orthodoxy from unruly versions of the faith. Creeds and canon have always been employed to marginalize the deviants, the radicals, the spontaneous. In other words, to contain the spirit. In contrast, the broad, secular sense of canon refers to any collection of literature produced during the formative or golden age of a cultural tradition. The canon on this broad definition need not be concerned with either "orthodoxy" or "heresy," only with the quality and variety of the emerging tradition. Reference is frequently made to the classical canon or the canon of literature in English. Classical scholars do not talk about either orthodox or heretical works produced during the classical age of Greece; they speak only of works of higher or lesser quality, works that are more or less representative of the genius of the golden age of Greece. The twenty-six works

Harold Bloom includes in his canon of great Western prose and poetry has nothing to do with either orthodoxy or heresy in great literature.[15]

When used of the Christian Bible, canon has customarily been taken to identify a set of ancient documents that defines the parameters of "the faith once for all delivered to the saints." This definition presupposes what became the orthodox contours of that faith. A definition of canon that does not presuppose an orthodoxy and correlative heresies seems preferable for the simple reason that canon in that restrictive sense can isolate us from the genius of the tradition. Canon understood in the broad secular sense as any collection of documents that provides successors with access to the insights of inaugural precursors is ingredient to a tradition that wants to incorporate its own critical powers into its founding documents.

B. Proposals for New New Testaments

The development of biblical scholarship in the second half of the twentieth century and the cultural winds that have blown and are blowing over theology have opened the door to a reconsideration of what ancient documents the Christian scriptures ought to contain. It will be a great tragedy if we do not seize the opportunity to revamp and revise. The vitality of the Christian movement and the future of the churches may well depend on the courage we can muster to meet the challenge.

We require a new New Testament, indeed, a new Bible, that will find its way into bookstores and on the internet in a section clearly marked "Bibles." There readers will stumble across it and be surprised at its contents. They will make use of copies in private study and in discussion groups, and carry those copies into their churches, where pastors and teachers will finally have room and warrant to respond to the issues being raised by biblical scholars, theologians, and secular critics. The effect will be electric.

Let me amend the statement just made. We need not one new New Testament but several new New Testaments. First of all, we need one smaller than the current twenty-seven books to indicate that the quest is always searching for a canon within the canon. In the second place, we need at least one larger than the current New Testament because the church fathers unduly narrowed the scope of the founding documents in order to preserve their own definition of the faith and secure the foundation of their power. In the third place, we need a new New Testament that is differently ordered than the traditional canon, which after all reflects many mistaken judgments about the rise of the tradition, both chronologically and theologically. In practice, a combination of these forms is probably desirable. In any case, our ingenuity in revising and redefining the function of canon will probably determine the future, if any, of the Christian tradition.

The notion of a canon within a canon suggests that the canon also admits of a narrowing from time to time as it seeks to identify its authentic voice, its center. All expressions of the faith will contain disparate voices that give rise to a spectrum of interpretation. It will always be important to distinguish Matthew from Jesus, Paul from his imitators, and of course the Paul who writes to the Romans from the Paul who writes to the Corinthians.

---

[15] Bloom, *The Western Canon*, 1, 43-479.

On the other hand, the Christ-event gives rise to innumerable futures just because it is a historical event and is to be appropriated historically: the meaning of the Christ-event, as it is termed, is disclosed only in the faith to which it gives rise. Like the Christ-event, faith too is historical. It follows that the vision of Jesus can be appropriated only in relation to particular social contexts. A single, monolithic tradition would yield a timeless, ahistorical faith and a frozen, ahistorical Jesus. A historical Jesus and historical faith necessarily give rise to a multiplicity of traditions and interpretations.

The canon is thus subject to reduction, on one side, and to expansion, on the other. The limits of both its inner and outer expressions depend on faith's comprehension of itself—on what it takes to be its trajectory from Jesus of Nazareth to the time and place of its appropriation.

In view of this polarity, the church was correctly driven to settle on a spectrum of witnesses in which the two poles were held together: the single historical person, Jesus of Nazareth, as the one pole, and the particularity and hence plurality of the appropriation of the faith inspired by him as the other. The ground of faith determines the outside limits: Christian faith assigns itself the limit of being connected to Jesus of Nazareth in his historical particularity. In practice, it is of course often extremely difficult to determine the precise point at which faith becomes disconnected from Jesus of Nazareth. That difficulty is what makes historical reconstruction and theological debate lively and ongoing.

The particularity and plurality of appropriation determines the inside limits; two or more witnesses are required to the inaugural event—one will not do. That is where the creeds went astray. The quest of the historical Jesus is intended to create tension between Jesus as the ground of faith and the various interpretations of faith in him. If it does not create tension, it is in the service of apologetics—the legitimation of the status quo ante. That is the reason I distinguish the renewed quest from the third quest.

In principle, the limits of the canonical New Testament are entirely arbitrary. Because faith must always be open to its own ground, or fountainhead, it must also be open to other, extracanonical witnesses. To its authentic future, the tradition must always be open, and that means open to new and other witnesses. No body of tradition can be its final and complete expression. In recognition of that limit, the canon of scriptures should itself be given a plurality of forms.

My concrete proposals for creating a new New Testament fall into three categories corresponding to the guidelines just articulated.

In one version of a new New Testament we should include whatever traces of the original strangeness of Jesus and Paul we can isolate or reconstruct and eliminate everything else. As Bultmann once suggested, excavate to the foundations. Save nothing that does not preserve fragments of the initiating, unsettling, disruptive dreams of the founders. Admit that Jesus died for a few provocative witticisms and a handful of subversive short stories that leave us gasping for breath at every reading. Applaud Paul for the agonizing struggle with his own Pharisaic past, the Paul who caught sight of the boundless community where no barriers separate female from male, Gentile from Jew, slave from free, black from white, homosexual from heterosexual. Reinstate the prophetic insight that Satan has been cast out of heaven and the heavens cleared of demonic powers. Recover the shocking notion that access to the spirit does not require brokers, that life is to be celebrated, that trust is the nectar of the gods. These are the provocative features of those who once caught a glimpse of God's domain.

This new New Testament would satisfy the requirement to identify a canon within the canon—a canon within the variety of interpretations that have survived from Christian antiquity. It would also put scholars to the test to determine whether they could make reasonable decisions about the foundational formulations of the Jesus movement.

A second version of the new New Testament should contain the current twenty-seven books plus others, such the Sayings Gospel Q and the *Gospel of Thomas*, arranged in historical progression. First would come those documents that can, with some confidence, be dated prior to the fall of Jerusalem in 70 C.E. In a second section would be those documents representing the transitional stage of the Jesus movement, spanning roughly the years 70–90 C.E. Dating here becomes a difficult issue. We will have to employ content analysis to place documents in a stage that falls between the originating writings and those that belong to the derivative stage of development. Chronology need not be the decisive factor. In a third section we should include late derivative documents that represent the institutionalization and hardening of the tradition. These three sections should be clearly distinguished.

This version of a new New Testament should encapsulate the best of critical scholarship over the past two hundred years. It would make the results of that scholarship directly available to a wide public. Such a New Testament would help raise the literacy level of the general public.

A third New Testament might consist of an entire library of early Christian texts. The Jesus Seminar has begun this process by collecting all the gospels into *The Complete Gospels*. We are now working on *The Complete Letters*. Eventually we plan to publish *The Complete Acts* and *The Complete Apocalypses*. Along the way we will include a few other early Christian writings, such as the *Didache*, that do not fall into any of these categories.

This version of the Christian scriptures would represent the scholars' library of ancient Christian texts. As things now stand, it is difficult for the uninformed to have easy access to all ancient Christian texts. Indeed, it is even difficult for scholars, especially if they want to use the original languages. We could remedy these deficiencies by completing work on *The Complete New Testament*.

New collections of scriptures will of course require new critical original language editions to go with the translations.

If we produce new versions of the New Testament (and the First Testament by translating the Septuagint into English), we will have laid the foundations for the renewed vitality of Christian scriptures in the third millennium.

32

Has the Canon a Continuing Function?

James D. G. Dunn

In *Unity and Diversity in the New Testament*[1] my aim was to produce an advanced introduction to the New Testament, one which could assume the basic "who wrote what, when, why" issues of most first-level introductions and go on to take stock of a wider range of features and to ask more probing questions than are appropriate at the first level.[2] Such features and questions all bore on the central theme of *Unity and Diversity* and in turn posed issues and questions for the traditional concept of canon. I attempted to gather these up and to reflect on them in the Conclusion under the heading, "Has the Canon a Continuing Function?" Some of them were issues and questions I have not seen taken up elsewhere, though my reading may well be defective as I have focused my research energies in other directions. But as I read that final section again, the issues and questions still seem to me, by and large, relevant and important for any realistic theology of canon. Of course, my ideas and hopefully valid insights have developed in the interval, and the constraints of the 1990 revision (to retain the same pagination) did not permit a thorough reworking of the text. But after a further ten years it is perhaps appropriate to think through these issues and questions afresh. I am grateful to the editors for their encouragement to do so for the present volume.

The task proved unexpectedly difficult, since, naturally, so much in the conclusion depended on and derived directly from the body of the book. The simplest way to resolve the problem, I finally concluded, would be to reproduce more or less the text of the conclusion, with notes pointing back to the discussion earlier in the book and summarizing it sufficiently for present purposes, and to follow each section by my own critique of what I had written earlier. Think of it as a kind of book review of a book first written nearly quarter of a century ago. It's a kind of rhetorical trick, if you like, and designed, of course, to tweak the readers' interest and possibly even to persuade them, either of the earlier view or, preferably, of its critical refinement.

What posed the issue of the canon most pressingly was the sharply contrasting picture of a *tightly focused unity* and a *wide-ranging diversity* which seemed to emerge in view of the features examined in earlier chapters.[3] In the light of such unity and diversity, it

---

This essay is offered in memory of and continuing gratitude for Ernst Käsemann.

[1] J. D. G. Dunn, *Unity and Diversity in the New Testament* (London: SCM, 1977; 2d ed., 1990).

[2] Subsequent to its publication I realized that an important gap was the absence of a chapter on New Testament ethics; but there never has been an appropriate opportunity to remedy that defect.

[3] Part I: ch. 2, "Kerygma or kerygmata"; ch. 3, "Primitive confessional formulae"; ch. 4, "The role of tradition"; ch. 5, "The use of the Old Testament"; ch. 6, "Concepts of ministry"; ch. 7, "Patterns of worship"; ch. 8, "Sacraments"; ch. 9, "Spirit and experience"; ch. 10, "Christ and christol-

seemed necessary to ask, "What continuing value has the canon?" Since the New Testament is not a homogeneous collection of neatly complementary writings, can we any longer speak of "the New Testament teaching" on this or that? Is the phrase "the New Testament says" any longer meaningful except when speaking of the central unifying factor? Must we not rather talk in terms of "*Jesus'* teaching," "*Paul* says,"[4] and so on? Since the New Testament writings do not speak with a united voice, where does that leave the authority of the New Testament? The orthodoxy of later centuries tried to read catholic tradition, order, and liturgy back into the beginnings of Christianity; the sectarian response has been to pursue the vision of the purity of the primitive church unsullied by the postapostolic "fall." The New Testament justifies neither expedient but bears witness to a diversity and disagreement within Christianity more or less from the first. So how does the New Testament function as a "canon," as a criterion for orthodoxy, as a norm for Christians of later generations?[5] Such were the questions that motivated my reflections on the canon in 1977. But it was their ramifications that proved most interesting.

1. A Canon within the Canon (*Unity and Diversity* #76.1)

We must observe first the historical fact that no Christian church or group has treated the New Testament writings as uniformly canonical. Whatever the theory and theology of canonicity, the reality is that *all Christians have operated with a canon within the canon.* Any who use their New Testament a great deal will at once acknowledge that some pages are more grubby with finger marks than others; how many sermons has the average "person in the pew" heard on Heb 7, say, as against Matt 5–7 or Acts 2 or 1 Cor 13? All Christians no doubt operate on the principle of interpreting the unclear passages by means of the clear; but, of course, a passage which gives a clear meaning to one is precisely the unclear passage for another, and vice versa. This we should recall includes the first-century Christians themselves, who used the scriptural passages (Old Testament) which spoke most clearly to their own faith and experience of God through Jesus Christ to interpret others which provided the basis for emerging Judaism.[6]

It is not much of an oversimplification to say that until recently the effective New Testament canon for Roman Catholic ecclesiology has been Matt 16:17–19 and the Pastoral Epistles.[7] The canon for Protestant theology has clearly been the (earlier) letters of Paul;

---

ogy"; Part II: ch. 11, "Jewish Christianity"; ch. 12, "Hellenistic Christianity"; ch. 13, "Apocalyptic Christianity"; and ch. 14, "Early Catholicism."

[4] My most recent monograph, *The Theology of Paul the Apostle* (Grand Rapids: Eerdmans/ Edinburgh: T&T Clark, 1998) has been criticized for attempting to achieve a composite voice of Paul from his letters, though I would prefer to speak of the theology of Paul at the time he wrote his letter to Rome, with the elements of his fuller theology not dealt with in Romans filled in from his other Letters.

[5] Cf. H. Koester, "*Gnōmai diaphoroi:* The Origin and Nature of Diversification in the History of Early Christianity," in *Trajectories through Early Christianity* (ed. J. M. Robinson and H. Koester; Philadelphia: Fortress, 1971), 114–57: "The term *canonical* loses its normative relevance when the New Testament books themselves emerge as a deliberate collection of writings representing various divergent convictions which are not easily reconciled with each other" (115).

[6] Referring back to *Unity and Diversity* #24 ("Principles of Interpretation").

[7] Cf. H. Küng, *The Church* (1967, ET London: Burns & Oates, 1968), 179.

indeed, for many Lutherans "justification by faith" is the real canon within the canon.[8] Eastern Orthodoxy and the mystical tradition within Western Christianity could be said to draw their principal New Testament inspiration from the Johannine writings, while Pentecostalism looks to the Acts of the Apostles for its primary authentication. Or again, the canon for nineteenth-century Liberal Protestantism was the so-called historical Jesus, whereas after the first World War the focus of authority for many Christian theologians became "the kerygma," while more recently others have sought to orient themselves in relation to "the apostolic witness."[9] Perhaps most arresting of all, we must remind ourselves that since early catholicism was only one strand within the New Testament,[10] consequently *orthodoxy itself is based on a canon within the canon,* where the lack of clarity of a Paul or a John (cf. 2 Pet 3:15–16) has been interpreted into a conformity with that single strand.[11]

Like it or not, then, all Christians have operated and continue to operate with a canon within the New Testament canon. Since the New Testament in fact enshrines such a diversity of first-century Christianity, it cannot be otherwise. It is inevitable that one should find Paul most congenial, while another recoils from Paul and relaxes with John, while yet another turns in puzzlement from both to the clarity of the Sermon on the Mount, or the simplicities of Acts, or the orderliness of the Pastorals, or is caught up in the fascination which the Apocalypse of John has exercised throughout the history of Christianity. To recognize the reality that each does in fact operate with a canon within the canon should not cause embarrassment or shame; it simply means accepting that Christians today are no different from their fellow believers of the first century.

Granted then that each Christian operates with a different canon within the canon, is there no *one* canon within the canon that would serve as the norm for all, like the "historical Jesus" for the Liberal Protestants and "justification by faith" for so many Lutherans? Granted the diversity of the New Testament, does the unity within the New Testament not offer itself as *the* canon within the canon? *Unity and Diversity* itself pointed towards an

---

[8] See, e.g., I. Lönning, *"Kanon im Kanon"* (Oslo: Universitets Forlaget, 1972), 272; S. Schulz, *Die Mitte der Schrift* (Stuttgart: Kreuz, 1976), 429ff.; E. Käsemann, *Das Neue Testament als Kanon* (Göttingen: Vandenhoeck & Ruprecht, 1970), 405. But Käsemann goes on: "Every christology which is not oriented to the justification of the godless abstracts from the Nazarene and his cross. Every proclamation of justification which does not remain anchored christologically and continuously drawn back to the Lordship of Jesus Christ ends in an anthropology or ecclesiology, or possibly in religious doctrine which can be legitimated in other ways . . ." (405).

[9] W. Marxsen, *The New Testament as the Church's Book* (1966; ET Philadelphia: Fortress, 1972). "The locus of the canon . . . can only be the earliest traditions of Christian witness accessible to us today by historical-critical analysis of those writings. Specifically the canon of the church . . . must now be located in what form critics generally speak of as the earliest layer of the Synoptic tradition, or what Marxsen in particular refers to as 'the Jesus-kerygma' . . ." (S. M. Ogden, "The Authority of Scripture for Theology," *Interpretation* 30 [1976] 258). This becomes the hermeneutical basis of Ogden's *The Point of Christology* (London: SCM, 1982). The same logic provides a sort of theological underpinning for the neo-Liberal enterprise of the Jesus Seminar, as illustrated by R. W. Funk, *Honest to Jesus* (San Francisco: HarperSanFrancisco, 1996), and of G. Lüdemann, *The Great Deception and What Jesus Really Said and Did* (London: SCM, 1998), though in each case talk of "canon" would be far from their thought.

[10] One of the key points to emerge from *Unity and Diversity,* Part II.

[11] In #63 and #64 I reflected on the fact that both Paul and John held appeal for, and could be said to have given some degree of support to, the gnostic sects of the second century.

affirmative answer, Jesus Christ. The common faith in Jesus-the-man-now-exalted was the consistent focus of unity throughout Part I, and in Part II we came to realize that that nuclear faith served not only as the center of unity but also to mark out the circumference of acceptable diversity.

Certainly, if the New Testament serves *any* continuing usefulness for Christians today, *nothing less than that canon within the canon will do*. Christianity begins from and finally depends on the conviction that in Jesus we still have a paradigm for our relationship to God and to one another, that in Jesus' life, death, and life out of death we see the clearest and fullest embodiment of divine grace, of creative wisdom and power, that ever achieved historical actuality, and that Christians are accepted by God and enabled to love God and their neighbors by a grace which we recognize to have the character of that same Jesus. This conviction, whether in these or in alternative words,[12] would appear to be the irreducible minimum without which "Christianity" loses any distinctive definition and becomes an empty pot into which people pour whatever meaning they choose. But to require some particular elaboration of it as the norm, to insist that some further assertion or a particular form of words is also fundamental, would be to move beyond the unifying canon within the canon, to erect a canon on only one or two strands within the New Testament and no longer on the broad consensus of the New Testament writings as a whole. It would be divisive rather than unifying. It would draw the circumference of acceptable diversity far more tightly than the canonical writings themselves justify.[13]

In short, the canon of the New Testament still has a continuing function in that *the New Testament in all its diversity still bears consistent testimony to the unifying center*. Its unity canonizes Jesus-the-man-now-exalted as the canon within the canon. Its diversity prevents us from insisting on a larger or different canon within the canon.[14]

Further reflection

The discerning critic will note a slight but significant shift in the formulation of the proposed "canon within the canon" from "Jesus-the-man-now-exalted" to the more elaborate formulation of the penultimate paragraph. The shift was from a christological focus (solely in terms of the life, death and resurrection of Jesus) to one which includes also the incarnation—from a Good Friday and Easter focused Christology, to one which includes also Christmas within the focus. The earlier, narrower focus reflected my own earlier perception of where the initial impetus and fulcrum point is to be found in earliest Chris-

---

[12] Cf. e.g., Luther: "The proper touchstone by which to find out what may be wrong with all the books is whether they treat of Christ. Whatever does not touch Christ is not apostolic, even if Peter or Paul teaches it. On the other hand, whatever preaches Christ, that is apostolic, even if it is done by someone like Judas, Annas, Pilate or Herod"; Preface to James (1522), cited by W. G. Kümmel, *Introduction to the New Testament* (1973; ET London: SCM , 1975), 505. Cf. J. Denney, *Jesus and the Gospel* (4th ed.; London: Hodder & Stoughton, 1911), who suggested that the confession, "I believe in God through Jesus Christ his only Son, our Lord and Saviour" would "safeguard everything which is vital to New Testament Christianity . . . include everything which ought to have a place in a fundamental confession of faith, and . . . (provide) the only basis of union broad enough and solid enough for all Christians to meet upon" (398ff.).

[13] The Lutheran canon within the canon in effect decanonizes James (as Luther found).

[14] See further below #5.

tian theology. But I was glad that I had even then recognized the need to broaden out the intra-canon formulation, for since then the importance of the incarnation as a fundamental element within Christian theology, and already within the New Testament, has become steadily clearer to me.[15]

The point is that while Good Friday and Easter are the definitive moment for Christian soteriology, Christmas is the definitive moment for Christian theology (taking "theology" in the narrower sense of "understanding of God"). The Christian doctrine of the incarnation starts from the insight that Jesus shows us what God is like; or in more weighty terms, that God has revealed himself in and through Jesus in as final a way as is possible in human flesh. "Definitive" means "normative" means "canonical." There is some tension between the two christological moments (Christmas; Good Friday and Easter).[16] But that tension is the basic stuff of Christian theologizing. To keep the appropriate balance between them is difficult: the Orthodox have tended to put more weight on the former; Protestants on the latter. But better to experience the difficulty of maintaining the balance than to lose the balance altogether. It is the wholeness of the Christ-event which is the canon within the canon, the fundamental reference point for both the characteristic and the distinctive features of Christianity.

The importance of including the moment of incarnation is that it includes the implication of *continuity*—continuity with Jesus' own religious and cultural heritage (Jesus the Jew, not just Jesus the Messiah), and continuity with creation (Jesus, the Wisdom of God). Too great an emphasis on the moment of Good Friday and Easter overweights the element of discontinuity between Jesus and the first Christians on the one hand and their Jewish heritage on the other. There begins a long road which winds its way through Marcion and leads eventually to Auschwitz. In the last twenty years it has become increasingly important for me to recognize that Christianity cannot understand *itself* properly without understanding itself in terms of its Jewish heritage, as in some sense part of Israel (on the model of the olive tree of Rom 11:17–24).[17] Similarly, too great an emphasis on the moment of Good Friday and Easter inserts too sharp a discontinuity between salvation and creation, almost as though "new creation" obliterated "old creation" (and concern for old creation) completely. That way led to gnosticism, to the extremes of apocalyptic, millennial fanaticism, and to the current malaise of ecological irresponsibility. Above all, it is the continuity between Jesus and God that is at stake. Without that continuity—expressed particularly in "Word of God" and "Son of God" terms—Christianity loses, or loses sight of, its most fundamental distinctive.

In short, the whole Christ-event is Christianity's canon within the canon, simply because without it Christianity loses its right to existence, loses its core definition, loses its single *sine qua non* identity factor.

---

[15] It was the fuller formulation which provided the jumping-off point for my *Christology in the Making* (London: SCM, 1980; 2d ed. 1989), which was the immediate successor to *Unity and Diversity* (*Christology* 6).

[16] I am using the term "moment" to signify both an event in time (more than a "moment" in the temporal sense, of course) and its importance ("of great moment," "momentous").

[17] See, e.g., my "Two Covenants or One? The Interdependence of Jewish and Christian Identity," in *Geschichte—Tradition—Reflexion*, vol. 3, *Frühes Christentum* (FS M. Hengel; ed. H. Cancik et al.; Tübingen: Mohr [Siebeck], 1996), 97–122.

2. Unity in Diversity (*Unity and Diversity* #76.2)

The canon of the New Testament has a continuing function also in that *it recognizes the validity of diversity;* it canonizes very different expressions of Christianity. As Ernst Käsemann pointed out in a lecture which gave ecumenical thinking a massive jolt in the middle of the century of ecumenism: "the New Testament canon does not, as such, constitute the foundation of the unity of the church. On the contrary, as such (that is, in its accessibility to the historian) it provides the basis for the multiplicity of the confessions."[18]

In other words the canon is important not just because it canonizes the unity of Christianity, but also because *it canonizes the diversity* of Christianity—not only the liberalism of Jesus but also the conservatism of the first Jerusalem Christians, not only the theological sophistication of Paul but also the uncritical enthusiasm of Luke, not only the institutionalization of the Pastorals but also the individualism of John.[19] To put it another way: despite Ebionism, the letter of James gained a place in the canon; despite Marcion, the letters of Paul were accepted as canonical; despite Montanism, the book of Revelation was accorded canonical status.

If we take the canon of the New Testament seriously, therefore, we must take seriously the diversity of Christianity. We must *not* strive for an artificial unity—a unity based on our own particular canon within the canon, or on some intricate meshing of traditions, hoping that somehow we can cajole the others into line, whether by claiming a monopoly of the Spirit or by the expedients of ecclesiastical blackmail. There never was such a unity which could truly claim to be rooted in the New Testament. The unity of the great church in earlier centuries owed more to social factors than to theological insights and could be justified theologically only by ignoring or suppressing alternative but equally valid expressions of Christianity—valid, that is, in terms of the diverse forms of Christianity preserved in the New Testament. Such "orthodoxy" is usually the worst heresy of all, since its narrow rigidity and intolerant exclusiveness is a standing denial of the love of God in Christ.

To recognize the canon of the New Testament is to affirm the diversity of Christianity. We cannot claim to accept the authority of the New Testament unless we are willing to accept as valid *whatever* form of Christianity can justifiably claim to be rooted in one of the strands that make up the New Testament. To put it another way, we must take with renewed seriousness the famous precept of Peter Meiderlin, quoted so often in ecumenical circles:

In essentials, unity;
in nonessentials, liberty;
in all things, charity.[20]

---

[18] E. Käsemann, "The New Testament Canon and the Unity of the Church" (1951); repr. in *Essays on New Testament Themes* (London: SCM, 1964), 103. It was the reminder of how much *Unity and Diversity* owed to the stimulus provided by Käsemann (as a glance at the author index will indicate) which prompted me to dedicate this further reflection to his memory.

[19] These are all summaries of the earlier findings in *Unity and Diversity.*

[20] R. Rouse and S. C. Neill, *A History of the Ecumenical Movement 1517–1948* (London: SPCK, 1954; 2d ed. 1967), 82.

If the conclusions of this study are sound, the only way we can take Meiderlin's precept seriously is by recognizing how *few* the essentials are and how *wide* must be the range of acceptable liberty. We must recognize that the Rom 14 paradigm of "the weak" and "the strong," conservative and liberal,[21] is of wider application than merely to matters of conduct and tradition. That is to say, we must recognize that other theological claims and ecclesiastical forms which embody the unifying faith in Jesus the man now exalted, or which truly spring from the diversity of the New Testament, are authentic and valid expressions of Christianity, even when they cross and conflict with some of the cherished claims and forms which we also derive from the New Testament. "Conservatives" who want to draw firm lines of doctrine and practice out from the center in accordance with their particular tradition's interpretation of the New Testament, and "liberals" who want to sit loose to all but the central core, must both learn to *accept* the other as equally "in Christ," must learn to *respect* the other's faith and life as valid expressions of Christianity, must learn to *welcome* the other's attitude and style as maintaining the living diversity of the faith. The conservative must not condemn the liberal simply because the latter does not conform to the former's particular canon within the canon. And liberals must not despise conservatives simply because the latter tend to count some nonessentials among their own personal essentials (cf. Rom 14:3). If "canon" is to remain meaningful it must be the *whole* New Testament canon; each must avoid confusing their own tradition's interpretation of the New Testament with the New Testament itself, of confusing their own canon within the canon with the canon proper.[22] There are obvious corollaries that follow from all this for our understanding of "the visible unity of the church," but to explore them here would take us too far beyond the proper scope of this study.

In short, whoever accepts the authority of the New Testament cannot ask less than the New Testament's own unifying canon within the canon as the basis for unity; but neither can we ask more without failing to respect *the canonical diversity of Christianity.*[23]

Further Reflection

On the whole I am happy with what I wrote in this section. It was meant to jolt readers out of any undue complacency on the subject—and evidently succeeded in not a few cases. Such reputation as I had previously enjoyed for evangelical "soundness" took a large knock here—though, I should add, the downturn in that opinion poll was more than offset by those who found the theme here, or the book as a whole, liberating in a spiritually maturing sense.

The broad-brush treatment was not intended to call for reassessment of the christological controversies of the early church; more on that under #3. It was much more directed to the ecumenical discussions of the twentieth century. One of the delights of the past twenty years has been the extent to which *Unity and Diversity* has been recognized as a

---

[21] Alluded to earlier in *Unity and Diversity* 79.
[22] "One must not make the canon in the canon into the canon" (Lönning, *Kanon,* 271).
[23] Cf. Käsemann, "Is the Gospel Objective?" in *Essays on New Testament Themes:* "Those who seek to maintain the identification of the Gospel with the canon are delivering Christendom over to syncretism, or, on the other wing, to the hopeless conflict between the Confessions" (57).

positive contribution to the ecumenical debate.[24] And in the same spirit I would want to reassert the importance of the points being made in #2 for the *wider* ecumenism which is ever more necessary, not simply between the traditional denominations and expressions of Christianity, but also for the expressions of Christianity which have grown and flourish outside the traditional denominations—the parachurch organizations, home churches, the independent African churches, and so on. If the Acts of the Apostles teaches anything, it is that the church must follow the Spirit, not expect the Spirit to follow the church.

In the interval since *Unity and Diversity* I have also found that Paul's conception of the body of Christ and Rom 14:1–15:6 are powerful ecumenical texts. The body of Christ, as expounded in 1 Cor 12, is *the* scriptural model of unity in diversity, for relations *between* churches as well as *within* churches. And Paul's counsel to the weak and the strong, the conservative and liberal in Rom 14 has a continuing value which too few have realized in their own intra- and interchurch relationships and disagreements.[25]

3. The Limits of Acceptable Diversity (*Unity and Diversity* #76.3)

The New Testament also functions as canon in that *it marks out the limits of acceptable diversity.* As was noted in the chapters on "Jewish Christianity" and "Hellenistic Christianity,"[26] even within the first century there were those who recognized that not all expressions of Christianity were to be accepted as equally valid. Already within the New Testament writings themselves the limits of acceptable Jewish Christianity and Hellenistic Christianity were being firmly drawn: Jesus was more than a prophet; the reality of his death was central, not just his teaching.[27] So too the character and limits of Christian apocalypticism were being defined;[28] though, it was also important to note, and regret, that "early catholicism" had not also been seen to be capable of a heretical, exaggerated expression.[29] The criterion we saw in these chapters was basically twofold: diversity which abandons the unity of the faith in Jesus the man now exalted is unacceptable; diversity which abandons the unity of love for fellow believers is unacceptable. In other words, where the conviction had been abandoned that worship of God was determined by Jesus of Nazareth and his resurrection, was now "through" Jesus, then diversity had gone too far. Or where the conviction had been abandoned that the one encountered in worship now was not really fully one with, continuous with, Jesus the man, then diversity had gone too far. Or again, where diversity meant a breach in love towards those who also

---

[24] Giving rise, e.g., to my " 'Instruments of Koinonia' in the Early Church," *One in Christ* 25 (1989): 204–16.

[25] I have found myself returning repeatedly to these passages in subsequent lectures; see, e.g., "Unity and Diversity in the Church: A New Testament Perspective," *Gregorianum* 71 (1990): 629–56; "Liberty and Community," in *Christian Liberty: A New Testament Perspective* (Carlisle: Paternoster/ Grand Rapids:Eerdmans, 1993), ch. 4; "Living with fundamental disagreements," in *Theology of Paul,* 680–89.

[26] *Unity and Diversity,* chs. 11 and 12.

[27] Referring particularly to *Unity and Diversity* ##58.2 and 65.2.

[28] Its Christ-centeredness, the already/not yet tension, and the cautionary note (*Unity and Diversity* #69.2).

[29] *Unity and Diversity* #74.4.

called upon the name of this Jesus, then diversity had gone too far. *The center also determined the circumference.*

The New Testament thus shows not only how diverse was first-century Christianity but also where that diversity lost its hold on the center. In which case the New Testament can be said to function as canon by defining both the breadth and the boundaries of the word "Christian." Of course, to accept the New Testament as canon is not simply a matter of restricting the adjective "Christian" only to the actual Christianity witnessed to by the New Testament (see also below #4). But it does mean that any claimants to the title "Christian" who cannot demonstrate their substantial dependence on and continuity with the New Testament (in its unity as well as its diversity) thereby forfeit their claim.

That such judgments about acceptable and unacceptable diversity were not lightly or easily achieved may perhaps be indicated by the difficulty which both James and Hebrews—and in a different way Paul and John—experienced in achieving canonicity. That is to say, the great church, consciously drawing the lines of orthodoxy more strictly, was not wholly comfortable with precisely those writings which were exploring the frontiers of Christianity and drawing in boundaries in a day when the border area was much more of a no man's land. In effect we continue to explore this twofold criterion of acceptable diversity and the difficulty of its application in the following three paragraphs—the interaction between the unity and diversity of faith in Jesus in ##4 and 5, and the interaction between diversity and the unity of love in #6.

Further Reflection

An issue insufficiently addressed in *Unity and Diversity* was that of the New Testament canon itself. That is, why just these writings? Since the study had taken the New Testament as it now is as the parameters for its discussion, it was not a question which I needed or had occasion to pose. The logic was straightforward: if this is the New Testament, and if the New Testament counts as "canon," what then follows in regard to the New Testament's canonical function? The questions raised even from that limited question seemed to me sufficiently challenging without going into further questions on the what and the why of the canon.

That was a pity, since the question of the legitimacy and limits of the canon had been posed sharply to twentieth-century scholarship from a history-of-religions perspective by William Wrede, to whom I had referred at the beginning of the book.[30] And since then the work particularly of Helmut Koester did not permit late-twentieth-century scholarship to escape that question.[31] The issue is now more pressing than ever. In earlier discussion it could always be claimed that a mark of canonicity was earliness: the New Testament consists more or less of all the extant Christian documents from the first century. But now the claim is pushed with great vigour, by Koester and others, that there are other gospels and forms of very early tradition outside the canon, which should be given equal

---

[30] W. Wrede, "The Task and Methods of 'New Testament Theology'" (1897); ET in R. Morgan, *The Nature of New Testament Theology* (London: SCM, 1973), 68–116.
[31] See particularly H. Koester, *Ancient Christian Gospels* (London: SCM/Philadelphia: TPI, 1990).

weight with the canonical gospels—notably, the *Gospel of Thomas.*[32] This is a challenge that should not be ducked.

I bring up the issue now simply because it seems to me that the concept of canon and its function as developed in *Unity and Diversity* provides something of an answer to this challenge. My point is twofold. First, if the findings of *Unity and Diversity* are at all on track, then it follows that the gospel about Jesus, the one sent from God, who died and was raised "for our salvation" was canonical more or less from the first. It defined and identified the new "sect of the Nazarene." It gave canonical shape to the written expressions of the new faith, including, not least, the gospels. But it also determined, more or less from the start, what were *less than adequate* as expressions of that gospel. If there was a Q document, containing only sayings, then it was valued as a collection of Jesus' teaching among the early Christian churches, though not as an alternative to the gospel. The argument that it was so conceived, that there was a "Q community," which knew only this form of Jesus' teaching and nothing of the gospel of Good Friday and Easter, or even was hostile to that gospel, is a scholarly hypothesis which confuses speculation with fact and difference with antithesis. All we know with any confidence is (a) that the only way Q was retained was within the framework of the passion-directed Gospel of Mark; and (b) that Q-type material was subsequently used by those who *did* see their form of Christianity as an alternative to the canonically presented Jesus (the *Gospel of Thomas*). There is nothing, beyond scholarly imagination and contrivance, to indicate that first-century diversity stretched much further than what is indicated by the New Testament writings themselves. And if there were groups more "radical" than, say, the "disciples" of Acts 19:1–7, or the "spirituals" of 1 Cor 1–4, that only shows that already in the earliest years the gospel regarding Jesus' life, death, and resurrection was working to demonstrate the inadequacy of such presentations, the limits of acceptable diversity. What if Q was dug up from the sands of Egypt? Would it not have to be included within the New Testament canon? No! Not at all! The decision was already made within the first century that Q should *not* be retained as it stood, but only as incorporated within the gospel form as we find in Matthew and Luke. Nothing which has been discovered since—that is, nothing beyond certain ill-founded, speculative reconstructions—requires us to reconsider that decision.

Second, we should not forget the dynamic of the canon process.[33] It is still sometimes assumed or implied that the New Testament writings did not function as canon until the church declared them canonical. That is simply an inadequate way to conceive of the canon, or I might say, a manifestation of the heretical form of "early catholicism" whose danger was not adequately perceived. Rather we have to recognize that there were various writings which so impressed their first readers/hearers as church-creating and church-sustaining that they were retained by the recipients, reread, pondered, and circulated more widely. Something of this is already hinted at in the letters of Paul. In other words, they exercised a shaping, defining influence (a canonical authority) from the first. Not everything written by a Christian leader in the first century became canonical: some of Paul's letters,

---

[32] So, e.g., R. W. Funk, et al., *The Five Gospels* (New York: Macmillan/Polebridge, 1993).

[33] I have reflected further on this aspect particularly in "Levels of Canonical Authority," *HBT* 4 (1982): 13–60; repr. in *The Living Word* (London: SCM/Philadelphia: Fortress, 1987), 141–74, 186–92.

for example, were not retained; Q was not retained as Q. The fact that the New Testament writings *were* preserved is itself a testimony to the *de facto* canonical authority which they exercised more or less from the first. In short, the New Testament canon was not so much decreed as *acknowledged*. The New Testament writings were hailed as canonical in recognition of the authority they had been exercising from the first and in steadily widening circles since then. It is not the church that determines the gospel, but the gospel which determines the church.

4. On Development (*Unity and Diversity* #76.4)

The New Testament canon also canonizes the *development* of Christian faith and practice. That is, it canonizes both the *need* for faith in Jesus the man now exalted to take new forms in new situations, and the *way* in which the New Testament witness to Christ has continually to be brought into interaction with the changing world in which faith must be lived out. The New Testament shows Christianity always to have been a living and developing diversity, and provides some sort of norm for the ongoing process of interpretation and reinterpretation.

The *need* for development is plain. For example, faith's talk of Jesus as the Christ had in other circumstances to be supplemented, in effect superseded, by the confession of Jesus as the Son of God; while in still other circumstances it was the (new) confession that Jesus Christ came in the flesh that became the vital expression of living faith.[34] Again, those who framed the hymns used in Philippians and Colossians, etc., evidently found it important and necessary to develop an expression of worship which spoke meaningfully in the language and thought forms of contemporary speculation.[35] Later on it would appear that the Jewish Christianity which failed to be canonized by the New Testament was precisely that form of primitive Christianity which failed to develop.[36] Or to put the point the other way round, it was only Matthew's and Hebrews' more *developed* christologies which countered the *more primitive* christology retained by the Ebionites; just as it was 1 John's more developed confession of Jesus Christ come in the flesh which countered interpretations that could be drawn from the more ambiguous Son of God confession. The fact is that no New Testament document as such preserves or embodies Christianity as it actually was in the very beginning; rather each shows us Christianity in a different place and at a different time, and consequently in a different and developed form.

As to the *how* of such development, two points of clarification are necessary. When I talk here of development, I am not thinking of the developments within the New Testa-

---

[34] Referring to the discussion of "Primitive Confessional Formulae" (*Unity and Diversity*, ch. 2); in particular, the way in which Matthew and John supplement and define Jesus' messiahship in terms of his sonship to God (as in Matt 16:16 and John 20:31); and the developed confession of 1 John 4:1–3.

[35] Referring to "Patterns of Worship" (*Unity and Diversity*, ch. 7); in particular Phil 2:6–11 and Col 1:15–20.

[36] Referring to "Jewish Christianity" (*Unity and Diversity*, ch. 11), including one of the most provocative conclusions to emerge from the study: "One of the earliest heresies was conservatism" (266).

ment as a straight line, of one development growing out of another, of Newman's idea of evolutionary development, whereby doctrinal developments can be justified as an organic growth from New Testament shoots.[37] I am not arguing, for example, that the Johannine christology of the personal preexistence of the Son is simply the fuller apprehension of what had always been true, the making explicit of what had always been implicit in earlier formulations. Nor do I argue that the orthodox Trinitarianism of the councils was simply the inevitable progressive unfolding of what had always been integral to the whole of New Testament theology.[38] That would be to make John, or a particular doctrine of revelation, or a particular doctrinal formulation, the effective canon within the canon, rather than one deriving from historical critical exegesis (as above #1). For if the canon is the New Testament as such, then why should the earlier, less developed expressions of faith not be equally normative, normative in their very uncertainty or unwillingness or refusal to head in the direction John followed so boldly? To argue that only one development within the New Testament is canonical is to fail to recognize the diversity of development within the New Testament. Indeed to argue that only one development within the New Testament is canonical is in fact to *deny* canonicity to the New Testament, where the elimination of elements unacceptable to later orthodoxy is far from complete. Such a view would shift canonical authority to the great church's *interpretation* of the New Testament writings from the late second century onwards—no longer a canon within the canon, but a canon outside the canon. In the New Testament picture each development is less like another length of pipeline, and more like another radius of a sphere (or spheroid), formed by immediate interaction between the unifying center and the moving circumference. Alternatively, the diverse developments of the New Testament are somewhat like a series of branches (to be sure, often intertwined) growing out of the trunk of the unifying center, with *nothing in the New Testament* itself to justify the claim that only the branch of early catholicism should become the main, much less the normative, line of growth.

The second clarification is that the New Testament functions as canon at this point in that it shows us the *how* of development, but not the *what* of development. If the New Testament canon does not support the sole legitimacy of only one of the subsequent developments (catholic orthodoxy), neither does it restrict legitimacy only to the developments which are actually enshrined within its pages. We must not absolutize the particular forms which Christianity took in the New Testament documents; we must not make the New Testament into a "law of the Medes and Persians." The New Testament as canon demonstrates how the unifying center of Christian faith came to diverse expression in the diverse circumstances of the first century; it does not dictate what the expression of Christian faith should be in any and every circumstance.

The *how* of development can be characterized as the interaction between my or a church's faith in the Jesus of the New Testament and my or a church's perception of the diverse challenges and needs confronting that faith as it seeks contemporary expression. In short, it is a dialogue between the historical Christ-event and the present Spirit. Christianity cannot be Christianity unless it lives out and expresses in its daily life the creative

---

[37] J. H. Newman, *Essay on the Development of Christian Doctrine* (1845; repr. London: Penguin, 1974).

[38] See Further Reflection below.

tension between the givenness of the historical past of its founding era and the vitality of the present Spirit. The more we believe that the Spirit of God inspired the writers of the New Testament to speak the word of God to people of the 60s, 70s, 80s, or 90s of the first century C.E., reinterpreting faith and life-style diversely to diverse circumstances, the more acceptance of the New Testament canon requires us to be open to the Spirit to reinterpret the word of God in similar or equivalent ways in the twentieth century.

Consequently, to accept the New Testament as canon means wrestling with such questions as these: if Matthew is canonical, who went so far as he did in presenting Jesus' attitude to the law so conservatively, what does Matthew's canonicity say concerning those who want to remain in close dialogue with their own particular traditions? If John is canonical, who went so far as he did in open dialogue with emerging (proto-) gnosticism, what does John's canonicity say concerning those who seek dialogue with the equivalent ideologies and (quasi-)religious philosophies of the twentieth century? If Revelation is canonical, and retained apocalyptic eschatology as part of New Testament Christianity even when the *parousia* had already been long delayed, what does that say about the character and form of Christian hope in the twentieth century? If the Pastorals are canonical, and evince to us early catholicism already within the first century, what does that say about the necessity for form and structure in community, about the desirability or inevitability of a growing institutionalism and conservatism in church structure and community leadership?

I should perhaps underline the point that by dialogue I mean *dialogue*—neither side dictating to the other, past to present, or present to past, but a critical interaction between the New Testament in all its first-centuriness and me and the church(es) in all our twentieth-centuriness, using all the tools of historical-critical exegesis to enable us to hear the words of the New Testament writings as they were heard by their first readers, to catch the full meaning intended by the writers, but always with an ear cocked for the unexpected word of God through the witness of the New Testament challenging our twentieth-century presuppositions and perceptions.[39]

Further reflection

In the 1990 revision of *Unity and Diversity* I was already regretting that I had expressed myself quite as I did in the third paragraph of #4. For as I pointed out in the new note 42 of chapter 10 (*Unity and Diversity* 409), my appreciation of the subtlety and sophistication of the classic Trinitarian formulae had grown as my grasp of what was at stake in incarnation theology had deepened. And when confronted with the outworking of an *evolutionary* model of christological development, as offered by my former Nottingham colleague Maurice Casey, I found myself driven back more to the Newman model of

---

[39] See further my *Living Word*. Cf. Käsemann, "Canon," in *Essays:* "The canon is not the word of God *tout simple*. It can only become and be the Word of God so long as we do not seek to imprison God within it; for this would be to make it a substitute for the God who addresses us and makes claims upon us. . . . The Spirit does not contradict the 'It is written . . .' but manifests himself in Scripture. But Scripture itself can at any moment become 'the letter' and indeed does so as soon as it ceases to submit to the authorization of the Spirit and sets itself up as immediate Authority, seeking to replace the Spirit. The tension between Spirit and Scripture is constitutive . . ." (105–6).

organic growth.[40] What is of continuing validity, I believe, in the concerns thus expressed rather inadequately can be restated in two ways.

First, we must recognize the historical particularity and limitations of the creedal formulations that seek to encapsulate the significance of the Christ event. Of course, both the Christ event itself and the canonical descriptions and assessments of the Christ event share the same character (historical particularity and limitation). We will return to that below (#5). Here the point is that there has been a tendency to absolutize the creedal formulae, as though they were not only sufficient to make their theological claim, but also so finally definitive that no departure or variation from them could be permitted. If biblicism results in a form of bibliolatry, then creedalism results in a form of creedolatry. In each case it is important to recognize the inadequacy of human language to express the reality of the divine. If the words of New Testament or creed are best seen as icons, that is, as windows into the divine, then it is important not to make the icon into an idol. If no words are adequate to the task, that includes the particular words used in the creedal formulae of the New Testament and beyond. In each case there is a reality that is being expressed inadequately, the Word within the words. That is not to say (and here is the correction I want to make to my earlier formulation) that any or many alternative formulations could prove as adequate or as enduring as the classic New Testament or confessional formulae. On the contrary, as with the canon, these ways of speaking of God and of Christ have proved themselves to be the most adequate and enduring for Christianity, and that constitutes a large part of their authority. But they are enduring and authoritative as the best approximation to the divine reality that we have been able to come up with in words. They are not the thing itself! Only when we learn to acknowledge the historical particularity and provisionality of such statements will we be able to prize them properly.

I had tried to express something of this in the conclusion to chapter 2 of *Unity and Diversity*, on "Kerygma or Kerygmata?" And I rather wished I had made more of these conclusions in the overall Conclusion to the book. In summary, the points which came through there were (1) that the core kerygma is never to be found as such in the New Testament, but (2) only in the expanded forms made necessary as the particularity of different situations are addressed, that is, (3) in the different forms which the different situations made necessary, and (4) that the differences were integral to the proclamations in and to these different situations. From that I concluded that any attempt to find a single, once-for-all unifying kerygma (we could now add, creed) is bound to fail. For concrete situations always call forth fuller expressions, and it is in the fuller expressions that the diversity, including differences and disagreements, lie. This, in turn, means that a truly ecumenical approach to the issue will always need to recognize a certain "beyondness," an uncontrollability by any particular group or tradition of the core gospel, of the canon within the canon, of the Word within the word. It means also an acceptance of the inevitability of different preached, written, and ecclesial forms of the gospel. The final unifying factor here

---

[40] See what is in effect my retraction of the implications of the third paragraph of #4 in "The Making of Christology: Evolution or Unfolding?" in *Jesus of Nazareth, Lord and Christ: Essays on the Historical Jesus and New Testament Christology* (FS I. H. Marshall; ed. J. B. Green & M. Turner; Grand Rapids: Eerdmans, 1994), 437–52, reprinted in my *The Christ and the Spirit*, vol. 1, *Christology* (Grand Rapids: Eerdmans, 1998), 388–404, which refers in turn to the foreword to the second edition of *Christology in the Making*, reprinted in *The Christ and the Spirit Vol. 1*, at 291–93.

can only be submission before the intangible otherness of Spirit and gospel and a warm embrace of all who share that submission.

Second, another way of putting the point is to recognize the degree of openness which we find in the New Testament, the openness of the kerygma to ever fresh expressions, the openness of the canon within the canon to ever fresh formulations of what is definitive in order to address the particularity of ever new challenges. What I was reacting against in the earlier formulation, I would now rephrase as the danger of reading in the developed creedal formulations too quickly, the *danger of premature closure,* of closing down too quickly on the formulations which may emerge from the New Testament as though those which did emerge in the controversies of fourth and fifth centuries left no room for others. This line of reflection has been partly stimulated by the current hermeneutical debate and the degree to which meaning is realized (I would not say "created") in the encounter between hearer/reader and text. I stress that I do not retreat one inch from my insistence on the canonical force of the Christ-event as the determiner of meaning and limitation on the range of meaning which the *sensus fidelium* should recognize. But I do want to underline the fact that the canon encourages and requires ever fresh reformulation of kerygma and creed and stands ready to authenticate (or disauthenticate) them.

5. The Importance of the New Testament (*Unity and Diversity* #76.5)

In the second half of #4 I spoke of "a *dialogue* between the historical Christ-event and the present Spirit . . . between the givenness of the historical past of its founding era and the vitality of the present Spirit." In this dialogue the New Testament canon has an indispensable function, in that *only through the New Testament have we access to the past, to the other pole of the dialogue,* to Jesus as he was encountered in the hills and streets of Palestine, to the initial encounters with the risen Jesus which from the first have been recognized as definitive for faith in Jesus as the exalted one. Or, in other words, only through the New Testament canon do we have access to the historical actuality of the Jesus who himself constitutes the unifying center of Christianity, to the first and definitive witness to the wholeness of the Christ event.

Here we must revert to our earlier talk of canon *within* the canon (#1) and define the concept more carefully, for in fact Jesus-the-man-now-exalted is *the Jesus of the New Testament:* he is not separable from the New Testament; the diverse New Testament witness to him cannot be peeled away like a husk leaving an easily detachable Jesus-kernel. In other words, in Jesus as the center we have not so much a canon *within* the canon, as a canon *through* the canon, a canon embodied in and only accessible through the New Testament. *It is not possible to hold to Jesus the center without also holding to the New Testament witness to the center.* For so far as the Jesus of first-century history and faith is concerned we are always like Zacchaeus, standing behind the crowd of first-century disciples, dependent on what those in the crowd nearest to us report of this Jesus whom we too would see. It is not possible to hear Jesus of Nazareth except in the words of his followers. It is not possible to encounter the Jesus of history except in the words of the New Testament.

All this of course does not mean that the New Testament writings become themselves the Christ event. As we have already noted, they are themselves products of a dialogue between Christ event and present Spirit. But without the New Testament it is not possible to recognize him we now encounter as Jesus, not possible to recognize the God and Father of our Lord Jesus Christ to be such. In the New Testament the Christ event always meets us clothed in particular forms and language culturally and historically conditioned; that is why historical-critical exegesis is necessary, that is why it must be a dialogue rather than a fundamentalist subserviency. But without the New Testament we have no possible way of tying our faith into the Christ event, no possible way of carrying forward the dialogue of faith for ourselves.

Nor does what I say mean that God's word cannot and does not come to expression apart from these writings; otherwise Christian belief in the Spirit would be without meaning. Revelation takes place every time God encounters us. But if Jesus is determinative for Christian faith, then, I say again, the New Testament is indispensable, because only through the New Testament writings have we access to the historical events involving Jesus and the first faith in him as risen. If we do not recognize Jesus and the character of Christian faith here, then we have no standard or definition, no criterion by which to recognize Jesus and the character of Christianity anywhere.

That is of course why the traditions of the New Testament have a normative authority that cannot be accorded to later church traditions—contrary to Roman Catholic dogma. For the New Testament is the primary source for the original traditions whose interpretation and reinterpretation is the purpose of the dialogue. The New Testament is the initial statement, complex in itself, of the theme on which all that follows are but variations. Later traditions can and should play a part in the dialogue, of course, for they demonstrate how the dialogue has been carried forward in other ages and situations; they provide many an object lesson on the "hows" and "how nots" of that dialogue. But the primary dialogue must be with the original traditions, for only they can serve as a norm for the authenticity of what we call Christian, only they can fill the word "Jesus" with authoritative meaning. If I may put it thus: with *only* the New Testament, and without all the rest of Christian history and documentation, we should have more than enough to serve as chart and compass as Christianity presses into the unknown future. On the other hand, with *all* the confessions, dogmas, traditions, and liturgies of church history, but without the New Testament, we would be lost, with no clear idea of what Christianity should be or of where it should be going.

Further Reflection

Here again my evangelical regard for scripture and very Protestant suspicion of tradition came through rather strongly. I have no wish to retreat on the former, as I hope is fairly clear from the strong emphasis I have placed on the New Testament witness to Jesus Christ, *the* canon for all Christian faith, the New Testament as providing *the* definition of what Christianity is. But it is desirable to pull back a bit from the latter. For in the interval I have come to appreciate two factors more adequately.

One I have already mentioned. I refer to my growing appreciation of the sophistication and subtlety of so many of the great theologians, fathers, and teachers within the history of Christianity. It is all too easy to take some summary, and therefore necessarily simplified, description of what one or other said, and to criticize it without making the effort necessary to get inside the greater profundities of their thought—in other words, a rather cheap criticism. And anyone with even a superficial acquaintance with Catholic and Orthodox theology cannot but be impressed by the seriousness with which they take the church's/churches' tradition, and live out of it, liturgically and theologically. Moreover, Hans-Georg Gadamer has taught many theologians that the interpreter does not stand over against the tradition, but in one degree or other is caught in and already determined by the tradition in the hermeneutical task.[41] To ignore tradition is to increase the likelihood of misinterpretation. Although I have stressed that the New Testament was in the event self-authenticating as canon, I can hardly ignore the fact that it was the developing great church which gave definitive recognition of the canonical status of the New Testament writings, and that it is through this tradition, in teaching and liturgy, that the New Testament has come down to us.

The other is that the New Testament is itself tradition, the product of the living tradition which stemmed particularly from Jesus and the Christ event as the primary *fons et origo.* In one sense, indeed, the New Testament writings are a series of particular crystallizations of the flow of that living tradition. That recognition warns us once again not to absolutize these particular forms, as though, for example, what Paul wrote to Corinth was of valid application to all times and places thereafter, irrespective of their different circumstances. On the other hand, it does not diminish the authority of the New Testament, so long as the historical particularities of each writing are respected. We must remember that diversity is being canonized here as much as the unity of the canon within the canon. The point, then, is that when one sets scripture and tradition in straightforward antithesis, one is simply untrue to historical facts and unrealistic regarding the interpretative task.

All that being said, however, I still want to underline two points. One is the importance of the role of the New Testament as canon within the complex of scripture and tradition. If tradition is also in some degree or other normative, then it is still important for the New Testament to be seen to function as "the norm which norms the norm," *norma normans.*[42] Here we have to pay due credit to the historical criticism that has been an important feature of Western Christianity since the Renaissance. It is that which has prevented us from domesticating the New Testament, from hearing it only through the tradition. It is that which has enabled us to hear the New Testament critically, that is, to hear it as criticizing ourselves and our traditions, where criticism is called for. The great example of this in the last fifty years is the recognition that the New Testament historically understood ren-

---

[41] I refer to Gadamer's concept of *Wirkungsgeschichte,* the "history of effect" of a text, which is not to be reduced simply to the recognition that the interpreter stands within a history influenced by the text. The key term is actually the more elaborate phrase, *wirkungsgeschichtliches Bewusstsein,* "historically effected consciousness." That is to say, the interpreter's consciousness has in some measure been brought into being by the text; it is itself in some degree a product of the text; it is a consciousness of the text to be interpreted. See further H.-G. Gadamer, *Truth and Method* (2d ed.; New York: Crossroad, 1989), particularly 300–307.

[42] That this albeit "Protestant" point is recognized from the Catholic side is indicated by J. Ratzinger in *Commentary on the Documents of Vatican II* (ed. H. Vorgrimler; London: Burns & Oates/New York: Herder & Herder, 1968), 3:192–93.

ders every and any form of Christian anti-Semitism indefensible.[43] Without such distancing of oneself from the tradition, which the New Testament read historically makes possible, it is unlikely that any Reformation would have taken place—including the "Counter-Reformation." It is the role of the New Testament as canon within the tradition that makes self-criticism possible, since it serves as *the* norm against which we must always measure our profession.

The other is the continuing importance of historical study in regard to Jesus and the New Testament period. The particularity of the New Testament witness to Jesus Christ is a historical particularity. The theology of incarnation gives the historical particularity of Jesus a central importance, as the person and time and place in and through which God manifested himself and his saving purpose most clearly and definitively, a centrality which in Christian perspective no other person, time, and place can share. In consequence, the Christian theologian and interpreter of these foundational traditions has no other choice than to examine that historical particularity in as much detail as possible. The "quest of the historical Jesus," for Jesus the Jew, is not a luxury with which faith can dispense, but a necessity to inform faith and for faith's self-understanding.[44] It cannot be effectively pursued without recourse to the tools of historical criticism as they have been refined through the past four centuries.

So to argue is not to make the church(es) too dependent on New Testament scholars or to give theologians undue importance.[45] It is an ecclesial, not an individual responsibility that is here in view. Within that communal responsibility, scholars and theologians have a role to play, a contribution (charism) which they have been gifted and granted to exercise in, for, and through the church. It is when the church(es) appreciate the importance of hearing and grasping the gospel in—or better, through—its first-century terms that the role of New Testament teaching will be given its proper place within its/their ministries.

A second, but not unimportant, corollary is that through its trained teachers and scholars the church(es) are able to participate in the wider academic, theoretical, and practical discussions which help shape our national life. The church should not expect its scholars to serve simply as catechists. On the contrary, their task, here seen in terms of historical study, helps them maintain a certain critical distance, which in turn helps keep both them and the church honest and deserving of respect in the wider intellectual search for knowledge, truth, and wisdom.

6. The New Testament as Bridge (*Unity and Diversity* #76.6)

One final reason why the New Testament writings can continue to function as canon is suggested by the fuller appreciation which emerged from *Unity and Diversity* of the role

---

[43] Orthodoxy which lives within the tradition and hears the New Testament only through the church fathers has yet to demonstrate that it can achieve the self-criticism necessary to condemn the Christian tradition of anti-Semitism.

[44] *Not* to *prove* faith, as Bultmann in particular rightly insisted.

[45] As, classically, Martin Kähler feared in his famous 1896 monograph, *The So-called Historical Jesus and the Historic Biblical Christ* (ed. and trans. C. E. Braaten; Philadelphia: Fortress, 1964).

played by the New Testament writings themselves within the diversity of first-century Christianity. I had in mind particularly the observation that some at least of the New Testament documents served as *bridge builders* or *connecting links* between different strands within first-century Christianity.[46] That is to say, their canonicity is a recognition not that they served as a founding charter for one kind of Christianity over against another, but a recognition rather of their eirenical spirit, *that for all their diversity they served also* to *promote the unity of the first-century churches.* Thus Matthew and Hebrews served not so much as Jewish-Christian party statements, but rather as bridges between a more narrowly conceived Jewish Christianity and a Jewish Christianity much more influenced by Hellenistic thought.[47] Mark and Paul seem to be fulfilling a similar function, holding together Gentile Christianity and diaspora Jewish Christianity. To be sure, Galatians or 2 Cor 10–13 in particular can hardly be called eirenic. But the canonicity of Paul at this point is a function not so much of any one letter (though Romans would most nearly fill the bill) as of the whole Pauline corpus, particularly when the Pastorals are included. For here within these thirteen letters we have embraced the whole sweep of Christianity, from apocalyptic enthusiasm to early Catholicism, from deep Jewish self-understanding and sympathies to wholehearted commitment to the Gentiles, from fervent insistence on the immediacy of revelation to complete subserviency to the inherited tradition, etc. Again Acts and John in different ways serve as bridges between the origins of Christianity and the situations facing Christianity towards the end of the first century: Acts serving as Luke's attempt to hold together the initial enthusiasm of Christianity with the growing influence of early catholicism; and the Johannine writings serving as a bridge between the message given "from the beginning" and the challenge facing Jewish Christians within the wider oriental-Hellenistic syncretism of the time. Even Revelation can be seen as a bridge in the way it sought to internationalize Jewish apocalypticism, that it might serve as a vehicle for the hopes of all Christians. Perhaps most striking of all, particularly in view of the tensions of second-century Christianity, is the function fulfilled by 1 Peter, in so far as in its theology and traditional authorship it serves to bring Paul and Peter together.

To explore this thesis in adequate detail would take far longer than is appropriate here. But perhaps I should just point out that this bridge-building function of the New Testament writings should not in any way be taken as a denial of the diversity of first-century Christianity explored in *Unity and Diversity,* Part II, nor of the full sweep of diversity embodied in the New Testament writings themselves. Those who explore the vague boundary areas between Christianity and the competing religious claims and languages round about, and who seek to let the central faith in Jesus determine where in any one instance the boundary line should be drawn, also show their concern thereby to hold fast links with their fellow Christians who wish to remain much further back from the boundary areas. It is precisely because the New Testament documents as a whole both represent such a wide-ranging diversity and build bridges linking up and overlapping with each other that the *whole* New Testament canon can serve as canon for the *whole* church.

One further very tentative thought is perhaps worth outlining briefly. If bridge building is a central reason for the canonicity of many of the New Testament writings, then

---

[46] *Unity and Diversity,* 47–48.
[47] Ibid., 47–48, 263–64.

perhaps this explains more fully why it was Peter who became the focal point of unity in the great church. For *Peter was probably in fact and effect the bridge-man* (pontifex maximus!) *who did more than* any *other to hold together the diversity of first-century Christianity.* James the brother of Jesus and Paul, the two other most prominent leading figures in first-century Christianity, were too much identified with their respective "brands" of Christianity, at least in the eyes of Christians at the opposite ends of this particular spectrum. But Peter, as shown particularly by the Antioch episode in Gal 2, had both a care to hold firm to his Jewish heritage, which Paul lacked, and an openness to the demands of developing Christianity, which James lacked. John might have served as such a figure of the center holding together the extremes, but if the writings linked with his name are at all indicative of his own stance he was too much of an individualist to provide such a rallying point. Others could link the developing new religion more firmly to its founding events and to Jesus himself. But none of them, including the rest of the twelve, seem to have played any role of continuing significance for the whole sweep of Christianity—though James the brother of John might have proved an exception had he been spared.[48]

So it is Peter who becomes the focal point of unity for the whole church—Peter who was probably the most prominent among Jesus' disciples, Peter who according to early traditions was the first witness of the risen Jesus, Peter who was the leading figure in the earliest days of the new sect in Jerusalem, but Peter who also was concerned for mission, and who as Christianity broadened its outreach and character broadened with it, at the cost to be sure of losing his leading role in Jerusalem, but with the result that he became the most hopeful symbol of unity for that growing Christianity which more and more came to think of itself as the church catholic.

No "further reflection" paragraph seems necessary here. I intended this section as an eirenic reflection and am happy for it to stand as it is, without qualification or further elaboration (beyond n. 48). The final conclusion can also stand without further reflection.

7. Summing Up (*Unity and Diversity* #76.7)

To sum up then, how meaningful is the concept of a New Testament canon, and has the New Testament canon a continuing function? I have not tried to explain or defend the canon in the traditional terms of *apostolicity,* for I do not think it can be done.[49] We cannot ignore the overwhelming conclusions of New Testament scholarship that some at least of the New Testament writings were not composed by "apostles" and are second (or even third) generation in their origin. And it does not help much if "apostolicity" is broadened to a concept like "the apostolic faith," since it tends to cloak the fact that the apostles did not all preach precisely the same message and disagreed strongly on several important points in their elaboration of what they nonetheless thought of as the common gospel.

---

[48] The *Gospel of Thomas* has brought Thomas back into prominence, and the Mar Thoma church of South India is a reminder of the danger of assuming that because we know so little of the rest of the "twelve" they were of no significance. But neither observation changes the main point made in the text.

[49] Other than in Luther's terms, that is (n. 12 above).

Nor have I said—or would I want to say—that the New Testament writings are canonical because they were *more inspired* than other and later Christian writings. Almost every Christian who wrote in an authoritative way during the first two centuries of Christianity claimed the same sort of inspiration for their writing as Paul had for his.[50] And I would want to insist that in not a few compositions Martin Luther and Charles Wesley, for example, were at least as inspired as the author of 2 Peter.

Nor would I attempt to define New Testament canonicity in terms of some kind of *orthodoxy*, for the findings of *Unity and Diversity* are clear that no real concept of orthodoxy as yet existed in the first century and that in terms of later orthodoxy the New Testament writings themselves can hardly be called wholly "orthodox." Nor can I enter here into the question of the limits of the canon which all this inevitably raises—whether, for example, 2 Peter should have been excluded from the New Testament canon and the *Didache* or *1 Clement* included—for that would take us too far beyond the already extended limits of the present study.[51]

Nevertheless if the conclusions drawn in the last few pages are sound, then the New Testament does have a continuing function as canon.

1. It canonizes the *unity* of Christianity. It embodies, albeit in diverse expressions, the unifying center of Christianity. It shows how small and how basic that canon within the canon actually is. It is a striking fact that all the *diversity* of the New Testament can claim to be justifiable interpretations of the Christ-event—James as well as Paul, Revelation as well as the Pastorals.

2. It canonizes the *diversity* of Christianity. It shows just how diverse, sometimes dangerously diverse, the expressions of that unifying faith could be. It is a standing corrective to each individual's, each church's more limited, more narrowly circumscribed perception of Christianity. To all who would say of only one kind of New Testament Christianity, "This alone is Christianity," the New Testament replies, "And that, and that too is Christianity."

3. It canonizes the range of acceptable diversity but also the *limits* of acceptable diversity. It recognizes the Gospel of Matthew, but not the *Gospel of the Ebionites*, the Gospel of John but not the *Gospel of Thomas*, the Acts of the Apostles but not the *Acts of Paul*, the Apocalypse of John but not the *Apocalypse of Peter*. If the conviction that God meets us now through the one who was Jesus of Nazareth marks the beginning and heart of Christianity it also marks the limits and edge of Christianity.

4. It canonizes the *development* of Christianity and provides the norm for the "how" of development, for the way in which the unifying center should be brought into interaction with the moving circumference, particularly at the points of pressure or of possible expansion. It shows us how genuine and deeply penetrating the dialogue between past and present must be, neither permitting a mere clinging to forms or formulations that are not meaningful to the contemporary situation nor allowing the contemporary situation to dictate the message and perspectives of its faith.

---

[50] See A. C. Sundberg, "The Bible Canon and the Christian Doctrine of Inspiration," *Interpretation* 29 (1975): 364–71. Of course inspiration has not only to be *claimed* but also *recognized* and *acknowledged* by the churches (see also the foreword to the second edition of *Unity and Diversity*, xxxi).

[51] But see now the Further Reflection on #3 above.

5. It serves as canon in that through it *alone* we have *access* to the events which determined the character of Christianity. The portraits of Jesus and statements about Jesus which we find in the New Testament are normative, not in themselves but in the sense that only in and through these portraits can we see the man behind them, only in and through these statements can we encounter the historical reality of the Christ event.

6. It serves as a canon because of the *eirenic* character of so many of the New Testament writings themselves, each maintaining the twofold tension between the (common) past and the particular present, but also between the resultant form of Christianity and the diverse forms of others. The New Testament is canonical not because it contains a ragbag of writings documenting or defending the diverse developments of the first century, not because it contains a cross section of first-century "party manifestos," but because the interlocking character of so many of its component parts holds the whole together in the unity of a diversity which acknowledges a common loyalty.

The New Testament does not of course function in the same way in each of these different roles. For example, in statements 1 and 5, James and Jude do not add anything to the Gospels; but in statement 2 James and Revelation would be more important than Luke; while in statement 3 Hebrews could be more important than Matthew. Or again in statement 4 Galatians and John would probably in most circumstances be more important than the Pastorals; whereas in statement 6 Matthew could provide more guidelines than Galatians. The point is of course that only when we recognize the full *diversity of function* of the canon as well as the full diversity of the New Testament material—only then can the New Testament canon as a *whole* remain viable. Or, more concisely, only when we recognize the unity in diversity of the New Testament and the diversity in unity of the New Testament, and the ways they interact, can the New Testament continue to function as canon.

Appendix A

Primary Sources for the Study of the Old Testament/Hebrew Bible Canon

Lee Martin McDonald

The following ancient sources are those most often cited by modern scholars investigating the origins and development of the Old/First Testament or Hebrew Bible. This list is not exhaustive, but the items listed are centrally important; any conclusions regarding the origins and development of the Old Testament canon must take account of them.

1. Ezra 9–10 and Neh 8–9: the reading of the law of Moses, and writings that were authoritative in the fifth century B.C.E.

2. Sir 49:8–10: Ezekiel, Job, and the Twelve Prophets. See also the context in Sir 44:1–50:25, the "praise of famous men." Is the focus in this passage on sacred literature or holy men?

3. Prologue to Sirach: three groupings of sacred literature. The third group is imprecise, and none of the literature within the groupings is specifically identified.

4. 1 Macc 1:54–57: the destruction of the Jewish sacred writings under the Seleucid tyranny.

5. 2 Macc 2:13–15: Judas Maccabeus's recovery and collection of Jewish sacred writings. The identity of these writings is not clear.

6. 4QMMT: see 6ab–28b, but especially C 9–12 (perhaps ca. 150 B.C.E.). This is a very difficult text to discern because of its corruption, but it does describe three or four vague groupings of sacred writings.

7. *Ep. Arist.* §308–311 (ca. 110–100 B.C.E.): the origins of the LXX. Only the law of Moses is mentioned in this tradition.

8. Philo, *Contempl.* 3.25–28 and *Mos.* 2.37–40: three or four categories of sacred writings among the Therapeutae (probably Essenes) in Egypt roughly just before the ministry of Jesus.

9. Luke 11:49–51: Jesus' reference to the martyrs in the OT beginning with the first (Abel) and concluding with the last (Zechariah). Was 2 Chronicles the last book in the OT in Jesus' canon (see 2 Chr 24:2–24) or simply the last martyr mentioned in the OT scripture? Does this passage suggest a closed biblical canon in the time of Jesus that began with Genesis and closed with the last book in the Writings (Ketubim), namely, 2 Chronicles? This is highly unlikely due to the place of 2 Chronicles in several manuscripts, especially in the Aleppo texts, and due to the repetition of the closing verses of 2 Chronicles in Ezra 1 (which shows that Ezra was written after 2 Chronicles).

10. Luke 24:44: a reference by Jesus to the Law, Prophets, and "psalms." Does "psalms" refer to the whole of the Writings, or does it refer only to the book of Psalms, or simply to some of the psalms? Did the later term "fifths" (Heb. = *ḥomašin*), which was used by the rabbinic sages of the second century C.E. of the book of Psalms and also of all of the Writings, refer to the whole of the Writings in the time of Jesus? Were the "psalms" equal to the later designated Writings?

11. *Jub.* 2:23–24 as cited by Epiphanius, *Mens.* 22 (ca. 380 C.E.). Is this the original form of the text, or is it the Qumran or Ethiopic version of the text? Did the original form refer to a twenty-two book biblical canon?

12. Josephus, *C. Ap.* 1.37–43 (ca. 90 C.E.), mentions a three-part, twenty-two book biblical canon. Are the books in each of the three categories of his list identifiable and are they the same as the later and more clearly defined collection called the Tanak (an acronym for Torah, Nebi'im, Ketubim)? Also on prophecy, see *C. Ap.* 1.8.41; *Ant. 13,* 311–13; *B.J.* 6, 286; 6, 300–309. Did Josephus believe that all prophecy had ceased from the time of Artaxerxes and therefore all Scripture or prophetic writing ended by ca. 400 B.C.E.? Did he view his writings as "inspired"?

13. *4 Ezra* 14.22–48 (ca 90–100 C.E.), describes the divine translation of ninety-four holy books—twenty-four plus seventy others. This is probably a reference to the sacredness of the apocryphal and pseudepigraphal literature besides a twenty-four book collection of Hebrew Scriptures. Why would many of the early Christians include this book (4 Ezra) in their sacred collections?

14. *Mishnah,* completed under the direction of Rabbi Judah Ha-Nasi (ca. 200–210 C.E.). There is not much focus on a biblical canon and very few references to the Hebrew scriptures. See *m. Yad.* 3.2–5 and 4.6 on which books "defile the hands."

15. *b. B. Bat.* 14b–15a (ca. middle to late second century C.E.). This is the first reference in Judaism that specifically lists by name the twenty-four books of the Hebrew Bible in three distinct categories. It is not clear how representative this list was of mainstream Judaism at that time.

16. Several references in the rabbinic literature indicate a conflict over the place of some books in their sacred collection. On Song of Songs, see *m. Yad.* 3.5 and *b. Meg.* 7a; on Ecclesiastes see *m. Yad.* 3.5 and *b. Shabb.* 100a; on Ruth see *b. Meg.* 7a; on Esther see *b. San.* 100a and *b. Meg.* 7a; on Proverbs see *b. Shabb.* 30b; on Ezekiel see *b. Shabb.* 13b, *Hag.* 13a and *Men.* 45a.

17. The church fathers' references to the OT/FT Scriptures:

    a. Justin, *Dial.* 100.1ff.; *1 Apol.* 28.1 and 67.3; *Cohort. Graec.* 13 (pseudo-Justin?).
    b. Melito's list of OT scriptures, see Eusebius, *Hist. eccl.* 4.26.12–14.
    c. Irenaeus, *Haer.* 2.27.2; 3.3.3; 3.11.8; 3.12.15; 3.14.1–15.1; 3.21.3–4; 3.17.4. See also Eusebius' reference to the biblical canon of Irenaeus in *H. E.* 5.8.1.
    d. Clement of Alexandria, *Strom.* 7.20. In *Hist. eccl.* 6.13.4–8 and 6.14.5–7, Eusebius gives what he claims is Clement's scriptural canon.
    e. Origen, *Ep. Afr.* 13 (cf. Julius Africanus, *Hist. Sus.*). Eusebius, *Hist. eccl.* 6.25.3–14, indicates that Origen added the books of the Maccabees (as "outside books") to the Hebrew Bible that he knew from contacts with Jews in the third century C.E. On his NT, see Eusebius, *Hist. eccl.* 6.25.3–14.
    f. Tertullian, *Marc.* 4.2.2,5; *Prax.* 15; and *Praescr.* 32, 36. On Marcion's view of the law and what he did to Luke's Gospel, see *Marc.* 1.29; 4.2; and 5.18.1; *Praescr.* 38.7; *Cult. fem.* 1.3.

g. Eusebius, *Hist. eccl.* 3.3.1–5; 3.25.1–7, for his own biblical canon, and compare with 5.8.1; 6.14.; 6.24–25; 7.25.22–27.

h. Jerome, *Prologus in Jeremiam, In libros Salomonis (Chromatio et Heliodoro), In Danielem prophetam, In Ezram, In librum Tobiae, In librum Judith, Commentaria in Isaiae prophetiam* 3.6.

i. Other church fathers referring to the Old Testament Scriptures in the 4th–5th centuries include: Athanasius, *Ep. fest.* 39; Cyril, *Catech.* 4.33–36; Rufinus, *Symb.* 38; Epiphanius, *Pond.* 22–23, *Pan.* 8.6.1ff.; Hilary of Poitiers, *Prologus in libros Psalmorum* 15; Augustine, *Doct. chr.* 2.13.

18. Canonical lists of the fourth and fifth centuries from both the East and the West (scc lists below as well as those in Bruce, Hahneman, Metzger, and Sundberg).

19. Cairo Geniza. A careful reading of selected texts from this collection of recovered documents in Egypt indicates that several writings were deemed sacred among the Jews in Cairo in the eighth and ninth centuries C.E. and considerably earlier in some instances. Non-sacred writings were also included in this collection because they contained sacred names and therefore caution is needed in any evaluation of their status within that community.

20. Canonical "glue" texts, that is, texts that united portions of the OT literature together. Some of the more important texts include: Deut 34:1–12; 2 Chron 36:22–23; Ezra 1:1–4; and Mal. 4:4–6. When were these passages added to tie the larger sections of the OT together?

Appendix B

Primary Sources for the Study of the New Testament Canon

Lee Martin McDonald

The following ancient sources are those most often cited by modern scholars investigating the origins and development of the New/Second Testament. Again, this list is not exhaustive, but the items listed are centrally important; any conclusions regarding the origins and development of the New Testament canon must take account of them.

1. Apostolic Fathers (writers who, for the most part, followed the writers of the NT). Passages that show use of NT literature and in some cases recognition of the authority of those writings: (1) *1 Clem.* 13.1–3; (2) *Barn.* 4.14; (3) Ign. *Phld.* 5.1–2; 8:2; (4) Poly. *Phil.* 2.2–3; 3.2; 6.3; 7.1–2; 8.2; 12.1; (5) *2 Clem.* 2.4–6; 14.2.

2. Reference to the authority of Jesus' words in early gnostic teaching (Ptolemy, *Flor.* 3.5–8; 4.1, 4; 7.5, 10).

3. Justin's use of NT writings to support Christian teaching and worship (Justin, *Dial.* 28.1; 65.2; 84.4; 100.1–8; *1 Apol.* 66, 67).

4. Writings that mention Marcion's limited collection of NT scriptures Marcion (*Marcionite Gospel Prologues;* Tertullian, *Marc.* 4.2–5; Adamantius, *Dial.* 2.18; Eusebius, *Hist. eccl.* 6.12.3–6).

5. Irenaeus on heresies and the use of scripture (*Haer.* 1.26.2; 2.27.2; 2.28.2; 2.35.4; 3.2.2; 3.3.1–3; 3.4.1–2; 3.11.8–9; 3.14.1; 3.15.1; 3.17.4; 4.15.2; 4.29–34).

6. Origen's awareness of NT literature *(Comm. Matt.* 15.3, which shows a Marcionite use of Matthew, and *Hom. Jes. Nav.* 7; and see also *Princ.*).

7. Discussion of scripture, tradition, and authority in the church (Clement of Alexandria, *Strom.* 1.20, on the value of philosophy for understanding God's truth; see also 7.16).

8. Gnostic beliefs and errors (see Irenaeus, *Haer.*, all of book 1, but also 3.3.1).

9. Second-century reference to Paul's writings as scripture (2 Pet 3:15–16).

10. Reference to Paul in scripture-like manner to argue his case in Athenagoras, *Res.* 18 (see also 7–8), ca. 180 C.E.

11. Theophilus's calling on Autolycus to reverence the scriptures and then citing Rom 2:7, 1 Cor 2:9, and Rom 2:8–9 (*Autol.* 1.14 and 2.9, 14, 22).

12. Tertullian's discussion of Marcion's editing of Luke and Paul (*Marc.* 1.29; 4.2; 5.18.1; 5.21; and *Praescr.* 32, 36, 38.4–7; *Prax.* 15).

13. Sources that may refer to earlier collections of scriptures in the second century (Hippolytus, *Haer.* 8.19.1).

14. Discussion of the burning of sacred books during the Diocletianic persecution (303 C.E.) in *Gesta apud Zenophilum* and *Acta Saturnini* 18.

15. Passages in Eusebius that list or discuss Christian writings: (1) his own perspective (*Hist. eccl.* 3.3.1 5; 3.25.1–7); (2) Papias' preference for oral sources over written sources (3.39.4); (3) Martyrs of Lyons and Vienna (5.1.3–63); (4) the Montanists (5.14–19); (5) on persecution and burning of sacred books (8.5–6); (6) on Irenaeus's NT canon and LXX collection (5.8.1–15); (7) on Origen's OT and NT canon (6.24–25); see also Rufinus' translation of *Hom. Jes. Nav.* 7; (8) on Clement of Alexandria's collection of divine names (6.13.4–8; 6.14.1–24); (9) on why Serapion rejected the *Gospel of Peter* (6.12.1–6); (10) Dionysius's perspective on scripture (7.25.22–27); (11) on Constantine's role in the churches and his ordering of fifty copies of scriptures (*V.C.* 2.2–4, 34–3, 65, 68).

16. Other important primary references include:

   a. Epiphanius, *Haer.* 5 and 76; *Mens.*
   b. Filastrius, *Haer.* 40
   c. Council of Hippo, Canon 38
   d. Council of Carthage, Canon 47
   e. Council of Laodicea, Canons 59, 60
   f. Jerome: *Prologus galeatus; Epist.* 50 *ad Paulinum; Commentaria in Matthaeum; Epistola ad Dardanum* 2; *De viris illustribus* 5–10, 15, 17, 36, 41, 63, 81, 135.

17. The most important NT canonical lists are as follows:

   a. Eusebius, *Hist. eccl.* 3.25.1–7 (ca. 303–325) from Palestine/Western Syria.
   b. Catalogue in Codex Claramontanus (ca. 303–367) from Alexandria/Egypt.
   c. Cyril of Jerusalem, *Catechetical Lectures* 4.33 (ca. 350) from Palestine.
   d. Muratorian Catalogue (ca. 350–75) from the East.
   e. Athanasius, *Ep. fest.* 39 (367) from Alexandria, Egypt.
   f. Mommsen Catalogue (365–90) from Northern Africa.
   g. Epiphanius, *Pan.* 76.5 (374–77) from Palestine/Western Syria.
   h. *Apostolic Canons* (ca. 380) from Palestine/Western Syria.
   i. Gregory of Nazianzus, *Carmen de veris scripturae libris* 12.31 (383–90) from Asia Minor.
   j. African Canons (ca. 393–419) from Northern Africa.
   k. Jerome, *Epist. 53* (ca. 394) from Palestine.
   l. Augustine, *Doct. chr.* 2.8.12 (ca. 396–97) from Northern Africa (see also 2.3.1).
   m. Amphilochius, *Iambi ad Seleucum* 289–319 (ca. 396) from Asia Minor.
   n. Rufinus, *Commentary on the Apostles' Creed* 36 (ca. 400) from Rome/Italy.
   o. Pope Innocent, *Letter to Exsuperius*, Bishop of Toulouse (ca 405) from Rome/Italy.
   p. Syrian catalogue of St. Catherine's (ca. 400) from Eastern Syria.
   q. Also see the collections in the following important biblical manuscripts:
      Codex Vaticanus (ca. 331–350) from Alexandria/Egypt.
      Codex Sinaiticus (ca. 331–350) from Alexandria/Egypt.
      Codex Alexandrinus (ca. 425) from Asia Minor.
      Syriac Peshitta (ca. 400) from Eastern Syria.

Appendix C

Lists and Catalogues of Old Testament Collections

Lee Martin McDonald

Table C-1: Old Testament Lists from the Eastern Churches

Melito[1]	Origen[2]	Athanasius[3]	Cyril[4]
Gen	Gen	Gen	Gen
Exod	Exod	Exod	Exod
Num	Lev	Lev	Lev
Lev	Num	Num	Num
Deut	Deut	Deut	Deut
Josh	Josh	Josh	Josh
Judg	Judg/Ruth	Judg	Judg/Ruth
Ruth	1–2 Kgs	Ruth	1–2 Kgs
1–4 Kgs	3–4 Kgs	1–2 Kgs	3–4 Kgs
1–2 Chr	1–2 Chr	3–4 Kgs	1–2 Chr
Pss	1–2 Esd	1–2 Chr	1–2 Esd
Prov	Pss	1–2 Esd	Esth
Eccles	Prov	Pss	Job
Song	Eccles	Prov	Pss
Job	Song	Eccles	Prov
Isa	Isa	Song	Eccles
Jer	Jer/Lam/Ep	Job	Song
Dan	(Twelve omitted)	Twelve	Twelve
Esd	Dan	Isa	Isa
(Esth omitted)	Ezek	Jer/Bar/Lam/Ep	Jer/Lam/Ep/Bar
	Job	Ezek	Ezek
	Esth	Dan	Dan

[1] Eusebius, *Hist. eccl.* 4.26.14 (ca. 320–325, Caesarea, Palestine).
[2] Eusebius, *Hist. eccl.* 6.25.2 (ca. 320–325, Caesarea, Palestine).
[3] Athanasius, *Ep. fest.* 39.4 (ca. 367, Alexandria, Egypt).
[4] Cyril of Jerusalem, *Catech.* 4.35 (ca. 394, Bethlehem, Palestine).

(Table C-1, continued)

Epiphanius[5]	Epiphanius[6]	Epiphanius[7]	Gregory[8]	Amphilochius[9]
Gen	Gen	Gen	Gen	Gen
Exod	Exod	Exod	Exod	Exod
Lev	Lev	Lev	Lev	Lev
Num	Num	Num	Num	Num
Deut	Deut	Deut	Deut	Deut
Josh	Job	Josh	Josh	Josh
Judg	Pss	Job	Judg/Ruth	Judg
Ruth	Prov	Judg	1–4 Kgs	Ruth
Job	Eccles	Ruth	1–2 Chr	1–4 Kgs
Pss	Song	Pss	1–2 Esd	1–2 Chr
Prov	Josh	1 Chr	Job	1–2 Esd
Eccles	Judg/Ruth	2 Chr	Pss	Job
1 Kgs	1–2 Chr	1 Kgs	Eccles	Pss
2 Kgs	1–2 Kgs	2 Kgs	Song	Prov
3 Kgs	3–4 Kgs	3 Kgs	Prov	Eccles
4 Kgs	Twelve	4 Kgs	Twelve	Song
1 Chr	Isa	Prov	Isa	Twelve
2 Chr	Jer	Eccles	Jer	Isa
Twelve	Ezek	Song	Ezek	Jer
Isa	Dan	Twelve	Dan	Ezek
Jer/Lam/Ep/Bar	1–2 Esd	Isa		Dan
Ezek	Esth	Jer		Esth
Dan		Ezek		
1 Esd		Dan		
2 Esd		1 Esd		
		2 Esd		
		Esth		

[5] *Haer.* 1.1.8 (ca. 374–377, Salamis, Western Syria).
[6] *Mens.* 4 (ca. 374–377, Salamis, Western Syria).
[7] *Mens.* 23 (ca. 374–377, Salamis, Western Syria).
[8] Gregory of Nazianzus, *Carm.* 1.12.5 (ca. 390, Cappadocia, Asia Minor).
[9] Amphilochius, *Iambi ad Seleucum* 2.51–88 (ca. 396, Iconium, Asia Minor).

Table C-2: Old Testament Lists from the Western Churches

Hilary[1]	Jerome[2]	Jerome[3]	Rufinus[4]	Augustine[5]	Carthage[6]
Moses (5)	Gen	Gen	Gen	Gen	Gen
Josh	Exod	Exod	Exod	Exod	Exod
Jdgs/Ruth	Lev	Lev	Lev	Lev	Lev
1–2 Kgs	Num	Num	Num	Num	Num
3–4 Kgs	Deut	Deut	Deut	Deut	Deut
1–2 Chr	Job	Josh	Josh	Josh	Josh
1–2 Esd	Josh	Judg/Ruth	Judg/Ruth	Judg	Judg
Pss	Judg	1–2 Kgs	1–2 Kgs	Ruth	Ruth
Prov	Ruth	3–4 Kgs	3–4 Kgs	1–4 Kgs	1–4 Kgs
Eccles	Sam	Isa	1–2 Chr	1–2 Chr	1–2 Chr
Song	3–4 Kgs	Jer	1–2 Esd	Job	Job
Twelve	Twelve	Ezek	Esth	Tob	Pss
Isa	Isa	Twelve	Isa	Esth	1–5 Sol[7]
Jer/Lam/Ep	Jer	Job	Jer	Jdt	Twelve
Dan	Ezek	Pss	Ezek	1–2 Macc	Isa
Ezek	Dan	Prov	Dan	1–2 Esd	Jer
Job	Pss	Eccles	Twelve	Pss	Ezek
Esth	Song	Song	Job	Prov	Dan
(Tob)	Sol	Dan	Pss	Song	Tob
(Jdt)	Esth	1–2 Chr	Prov	Eccles	Jdt
	1–2 Chr	1–2 Esd	Eccles	Wis	Esth
	Ezra-Neh	Esth	Song	Sir	1–2 Esd
				Twelve	1–2 Macc
				Isa	
				Jer	
				Dan	
				Ezek	

[1] Hilary, *Prolog. in Lib. Ps.* 15 (ca. 350–365, Poitiers).
[2] Jerome, *Ep.* 53.8 (ca. 394, Bethlehem, Palestine).
[3] Jerome, *Praef. in Lib. Sam. et Mal.* (ca. 394, Bethlehem, Palestine).
[4] Rufinus, *Comm. in Symb. Apost.* 35 (ca. 404, Rome, Italy).
[5] Augustine, *Doct. chr.* 2.13 (ca. 395, Hippo Regius, North Africa).
[6] Council of Carthage (397 C.E.), canon 26.
[7] It is likely, but not definitely known, that 1–5 Sol is Prov, Eccl, Song, Sir, and Wis.

Table C-3: Old Testament Lists from Important Uncial Manuscripts

Vaticanus (B) (4th cent.)	Sinaiticus (ℵ) (4th cent.)	Alexandrinus (A) (5th cent.)
Gen	Gen . . .[1]	Gen
Exod	. . .	Exod
Lev	. . .	Lev
Deut	Num . . .	Num
Josh	. . .	Deut
Judg	. . .	Josh
Ruth	. . .	Judg
1–4 Kgs	. . .	Ruth
1–2 Chron	1 Chron . . .	1–4 Kgs
1–2 Esd	. . . 2 Esd	1–2 Chron
Ps . . .	Esth	Hos
Prov	Tob	Amos
Eccles	Jdt . . .	Mic
Song	1–4 Macc	Joel
Job	Isa	Obad
Wis	Jer	Jon
Sir	Lam . . .	Nah
Esth	Joel	Hab
Jdt	Obad	Zeph
Tob	Jon	Hag
Hos	Nah	Zech
Amos	Hab	Mal
Mic	Zeph	Isa
Joel	Hag	Jer
Obad	Zech	Bar
Jon	Mal	Lam
Nah	Ps	Ep Jer
Hab	Prov	Ezek
Zeph	Eccles	Dan
Hag	Song	Esth
Zech	Wis	Tob
Mal	Sir	Jdt
Isa	Job	1–2 Esd
Jer		1–4 Macc
Bar		Ps[2]
Lam		Ps 151[3]
Ep Jer		Job
Ezek		Prov
Dan		Song
		Wis
		Sir

[1] Ellipses (. . .) indicate losses or omissions in the manuscript.

[2] Before the Psalms there is a letter of Athanasius to Marcellinus about the Psalter and a summary of the contents of the Psalms by Eusebius.

[3] After the Psalms, there are a number of canticles (called Odes) extracted from other parts of the Bible.

Table C-4: Current Canons of the Hebrew Bible/Old Testament

Jewish[1]	Orthodox[2]	Roman Catholic[3]	Protestant
Torah:	*Historical Books:*	*Pentateuch:*	*Pentateuch:*
Genesis	Genesis	Genesis	Genesis
Exodus	Exodus	Exodus	Exodus
Leviticus	Leviticus	Leviticus	Leviticus
Numbers	Numbers	Numbers	Numbers
Deuteronomy	Deuteronomy	Deuteronomy	Deuteronomy
	Joshua		
Prophets:[4]	Judges	*Historical Books:*	*Historical Books:*
Joshua	Ruth	Joshua	Joshua
Judges	1 Kingdoms[5]	Judges	Judges
1–2 Samuel	2 Kingdoms	Ruth	Ruth
1–2 Kings	3 Kingdoms	1 Samuel	1 Samuel
	4 Kingdoms	2 Samuel	2 Samuel
Isaiah	1 Chronicles	1 Kings	1 Kings
Jeremiah	2 Chronicles	2 Kings	2 Kings
Ezekiel	1 Esdras[6]	1 Chronicles	1 Chronicles
The Twelve	2 Esdras	2 Chronicles	2 Chronicles
Hosea	Nehemiah	Ezra	Ezra
Joel	Tobit	Nehemiah	Nehemiah
Amos	Judith	Tobit	Esther
Obadiah	Esther[7]	Judith	
Jonah	1 Maccabees	Esther[8]	*Poetic Books:*
Micah	2 Maccabees	1 Maccabees	Job
Nahum	3 Maccabees	2 Maccabees	Psalms
Habakkuk			Proverbs

This table is based on Appendix D of *The SBL Handbook of Style* (Peabody: Hendrickson, 1999), 168–71.

[1] The traditional number of books in the Jewish canon is twenty-four.

[2] "Orthodox" here refers to the Greek and Russian Orthodox churches, the Slavonic Bible being the traditional text of the latter. In Orthodox Bibles, 4 Maccabees and the Prayer of Manasseh—and in Slavonic, 3 Esdras—are in an appendix.

[3] The traditional number of books in the Roman Catholic canon is forty-nine. The order of books in Roman Catholic Bibles varies. This order reflects current editions, such as the Jerusalem Bible and the New American Bible. The appendix of the Latin Vulgate contains 3 Esdras, 4 Esdras, and the Prayer of Manasseh.

[4] The two subgroupings of the Prophets are traditionally known as the Former Prophets and the Latter Prophets. The Book of the Twelve counts as one of the Latter Prophets.

[5] 1 and 2 Kingdoms are the books of Samuel; 3 and 4 Kingdoms are the books of Kings.

[6] This 1 Esdras is called 2 Esdras in Slavonic Bibles. The 2 Esdras in this canon is equivalent to the book of Ezra in the NRSV; in some Bibles it also includes Nehemiah.

[7] Includes six additions.

[8] Includes six additions.

(Table C-4, continued)

Jewish	Orthodox	Roman Catholic	Protestant
Zephaniah	*Poetic and Didactic Books:*	*Wisdom Books:*	Ecclesiastes
Haggai	Psalms[9]	Job	Song of Songs
Zechariah	Job	Psalms	
Malachi	Proverbs	Proverbs	*Prophetic Books:*
	Ecclesiastes	Ecclesiastes	Isaiah
Writings:	Song of Songs	Song of Songs	Jeremiah
Psalms	Wisdom of Solomon	Wisdom of Solomon	Lamentations
Proverbs	Wisdom of Sirach	Ecclesiasticus	Ezekiel
Job			Daniel
Song of Songs	*Prophetic Books:*	*Prophetic Books:*	Hosea
Ruth	Hosea	Isaiah	Joel
Lamentations	Amos	Jeremiah	Amos
Ecclesiastes	Micah	Lamentations	Obadiah
Esther	Joel	Baruch[10]	Jonah
Daniel	Obadiah	Ezekiel	Micah
Nehemiah	Jonah	Daniel[11]	Nahum
1–2 Chronicles	Nahum	Hosea	Habakkuk
	Habakkuk	Joel	Zephaniah
	Zephaniah	Amos	Haggai
	Haggai	Obadiah	Zechariah
	Zechariah	Jonah	Malachi
	Malachi	Micah	
	Isaiah	Nahum	
	Jeremiah	Habakkuk	
	Baruch	Zephaniah	
	Lamentations of Jeremiah	Haggai	
	Epistle of Jeremiah	Zechariah	
	Ezekiel	Malachi	
	Daniel[12]		

[9] Includes Psalm 151.

[10] Includes Epistle of Jeremiah.

[11] Includes Prayer of Azariah and Song of the Three Young Men, Susanna, and Bel and the Dragon.

[12] Includes Prayer of Azariah and Song of the Three Young Men, Susanna, and Bel and the Dragon.

Appendix D

Lists and Catalogues of New Testament Collections

Lee Martin McDonald

Table D-1: Three Early New Testament Lists Based on Eusebius[1]

Irenaeus[2]	Clement of Alexandria[3]	Origen[4]
Matt	Jude	Matt
Mark	Barn.	Mark
Luke	Apoc. Pet.	Luke
John	Heb	John
Rev	Acts	1 Pet
1 John	Paul (nothing listed)	2 Pet?
1 Pet		Rev
Herm.	*Gospels:*	1 John
Wis	Matt	2–3 John ?
Paul (mentioned but epistles	Luke	Heb
not listed)	Mark	Paul (mentioned but epistles
	John	not listed)

[1] The following collections are modified somewhat from the collections found in A. Souter, G. M. Hahneman, B. M. Metzger, and F. F. Bruce (see the Bibliography).

[2] Eusebius, *Hist. eccl.* 5.8.2–8 (ca. 320–330, Caesarea, Palestine). While Eusebius attributes this "canon" *(peri tōn endiathēkon graphōn)* collection to Irenaeus (170–180), it is probably nothing more than Eusebius's listing of the references made by Irenaeus.

[3] Eusebius, *Hist. eccl.* 6.14.1–7 (ca. 320–330, Caesarea, Palestine). While Eusebius attributes this "canon" *(pasēs tēs endiathēkou graphēs)* collection to Clement (170), it is probably nothing more than Eusebius's listing of the references made by Clement.

[4] Eusebius, *Hist. eccl.* 6.25.3–14. As we observed above, it is likely that this list is Eusebius's invention based on a compilation of references to literature that Origen (220–230) cited.

Table D-2: New Testament Lists from the Fourth Century

Eusebius[1]	Cyril of Jerusalem[2]	Athanasius[3]	Cheltenham[4]
Recognized:	Gospels (4)	*Gospels:*	*Gospels:*
Gospels (4)	Acts	Matt	Matt
Acts		Mark	Mark
Paul's epistles (14?)	*Catholic Epistles (7):*	Luke	Luke
1 John	Jas	John	John
1 Pet	1–2 Pet		
Rev (?)	1–3 John	Acts	Paul's epistles (13)
	Jude?		Acts
Doubtful:		*Catholic Epistles:*	Rev
Jas	Paul's epistles (14)	Jas	1–3 John
Jude		1–2 Pet	1–2 Pet
2 Pet	*Pseudepigrapha:*	1–3 John	(no Heb)
2, 3 John	Gos. Thom.	Jude	
Rejected:		*Paul's Epistles (14):*	
Acts Paul		Rom	
Herm.		1–2 Cor	
Apoc. Pet.		Gal	
Barn.		Eph	
Did.		Phil	
Rev (?)		Col	
Gos. Heb. (?)		1–2 Thess	
		Heb	
Cited by Heretics:		1–2 Tim	
Gos. Pet.		Titus	
Gos. Thom.		Phlm	
Gos. Matt.			
Acts Andr.		Rev	
Acts John			
		Catechetical:	
		Did.	
		Herm.	

[1] Eusebius, *Hist. eccl.* 3.25.1–7 (ca. 320–330, Caesarea, Palestine).
[2] Cyril of Jerusalem, *Catech.* 4.33 (ca. 350, Jerusalem).
[3] Athanasius, *Ep. fest.* 39 (ca. 367, Alexandria, Egypt).
[4] The Cheltenham Canon is also known as the Mommsen Catalogue (ca. 360–370, Northern Africa).

(Table D-2, continued)

Epiphanius[5]	Apostolic Canons[6]	Gregory of Nazianzus[7]	African Canons[8]	Jerome[9]
Gospels (4)	*Gospels (4):*	Matt	Gospels (4)	*"Lord's Four":*
Paul's epistles (13)	Matt	Mark	Acts	Matt
Acts	Mark	Luke	Paul's epistles (13)	Mark
	Luke	John	Heb	Luke
Catholic Epistles:	John	Acts	1–2 Pet.	John
Jas		Paul's epistles (14)	1–3 John	
Pet	Paul's epistles (14)[10]		Jas	*Paul's Epistles (14):*
1–3 John	Peter's epistles (2)	*Catholic Epistles (7):*	Jude	Rom
Jude	1–3 John	Jas	Rev	1–2 Cor
	Jas	1–2 Pet		Gal
Rev	Jude	1–3 John	*OK to Read:*	Eph
Wis	1–2 Clem.	Jude	Acts of martyrs	Phil
Sir	Apost. Const.			1–2 Thess
	Acts			Col
				1–2 Tim
				Titus
				Phlm
				Heb
				1–2 Pet
				1–3 John
				Jude
				Jas
				Acts
				Rev

---

[5] Epiphanius, *Pan.* 76.5 (ca. 374–377, Salamis, Western Syria).

[6] *Can. ap.* 85 (ca. 380, Western Syria).

[7] Gregory of Nazianzus, *Carm.* 12.31 (ca. 390, Cappadocia, Asia Minor) and later ratified by the Trullan Synod in 692.

[8] African Canons (ca. 393–419, Northern Africa).

[9] Jerome, *Ep.* 53, ca. 394 (Bethlehem, Palestine).

[10] The number 14 indicates that Hebrews was included as one of Paul's letters.

(Table D-2, continued)

Augustine[11]	Amphilochius[12]	Rufinus[13]	Innocent[14]	Syrian Catalogue[15]
Gospels (4):	Gospels (4):	Gospels (4):	Gospels (4)	Gospels (4):
Matt	Matt	Matt	Paul's epistles (13)[16]	Matt
Mark	Mark	Mark	1–3 John	Mark
Luke	Luke	Luke	1–2 Pet	Luke
John	John	John	Jude	John
			Jas	
Paul's Epistles (14):	Acts	Acts	Acts	Acts
Rom		Paul's epistles (14)	Rev	Gal
1–2 Cor	Paul's Epistles (14):	1–2 Pet		Rom
Gal	Rom	Jas	Repudiated:	Heb
Eph	1–2 Cor	Jude	Matthias/	Col
Phil	Gal	1,2,3 John	James the less	Eph
1–2 Thess	Eph	Rev	Peter + John =	Phil
Col	Phil		Leucian	1–2 Thess
1–2 Tim	Col	Ecclesiastical:	(Andrew =	1–2 Tim
Titus	1–2 Thess	Herm.	Xenocharides	Titus
Phlm	1–2 Tim	Two Ways	& Leonidas)	Phlm
Heb	Titus	Pre. Pet.	Gos. Thom.	
	Phlm			
1–2 Pet	Heb (?)			
1–3 John				
Jude	Catholic Epistles (7?):			
Jas	Jas			
Acts	Pet			
Rev	John			
	Jude (?)			
	Rev (?)			

---

[11] Augustine, *Doct. chr.* 2.8–9.12–14 (ca. 395–400, Hippo Regius, North Africa).

[12] Amphilochius, *Iambi ad Seleucum* 289–319 (ca. 396, Iconium, Asia Minor). The list concludes by acknowledging that some have questions about 2 Pet, 2–3 John, Heb, Jude and Rev.

[13] Rufinus, *Comm. in Symb. Apost.* 36 (ca. 394, Rome, Italy).

[14] Pope Innocent, *Ad Exsuper. Tol.* (ca. 405, Rome, Italy).

[15] Syrian catalogue of St. Catherine's (ca. 400, Eastern Syria).

[16] Some add Hebrews to this and make it 14. It is uncertain.

(Table D-2, continued)

Muratorian Fragment[17]	Laodicea Synod[18]	Carthage Synod[19]
Gospels:	*Gospels (4):*	Gospels (4)
. . .	Matt	Acts
. . .	Mark	Paul (13)
Luke ("third book")	Luke	Heb
John ("fourth book)	John	1–2 Pet
		1–3 John
John's epistles	Acts	Jas
Acts		Jude
	Catholic Epistles (7):	Rev (later added)
Paul's Epistles to Churches:	Jas	
Cor	1–2 Pet	
Eph	1,2,3 John	
Phil	Jude	
Col		
Gal	*Paul's Epistles (14):*	
Thess	Rom	
Rom	1–2 Cor	
	Gal	
Epistles to Individuals:	Eph	
Phlm	Phil	
Titus	Col	
1–2 Tim	1–2 Thess	
	Heb	
Jude	1–2 Tim	
1, 2 or 3 Jn (2 Eps.)	Titus	
Wis	Phlm	
Rev		
Apoc. Pet.	(Rev missing)	
Forged (rejected):		
Ep. Lao.		
Ep. Alex.		
Others (? rejected):		
Herm.		
Works of Arsinous		
Valentinus		
Miltiades		
Basilides		
. . .		

[17] The Muratorian Fragment. While many scholars contend that this was a late second-century C.E. fragment originating in or around Rome, a growing number hold that it was produced around the middle of the fourth century (ca. 350–375) and that it originated somewhere in the eastern part of the Roman Empire, possibly in Syria.

[18] Synod of Laodicea, Canon 60 (ca. 363, Asia Minor).

[19] Synod of Carthage, Canon 39 (397, North Africa). Revelation was added later in 419 at the subsequent synod at Carthage.

Table D-3: New Testament Lists from the Fifth and Sixth Centuries

Eucherius [1]	Gelasius [2]	Junilius [3]	Cassiodorus [4]	Isidore [5]
Matt	*Gospels:*	*Gospels:*	*Gospels:*	*Gospels:*
Mark	Matt	Matt	Matt	Matt
Luke	Mark	Mark	Mark	Mark
John	Luke	Luke	Luke	Luke
Rom	John	John	John	John
1 Cor				
2 Cor	Acts	Acts	Acts	*Paul's Epistles (14):*
(Gal missing)	Rev	Rev	1 Pet	Rom
Eph			Jas	1–2 Cor
1 Thess	*Paul's Epistles (14):*	*Paul's Epistles (14):*	1 John	Gal
(2 Thess missing)	Rom	Rom		Eph
Col	1–2 Cor	1–2 Cor	*Paul's Epistles (13):*	Phil
1 Tim	Eph	Gal	Rom	1–2 Thess
2 Tim	1–2 Thess	Eph	1 Cor	Col
(Titus missing)	Gal	Phil	2 Cor	1–2 Tim
(Phlm missing)	Phil	1–2 Thess	Gal	Titus
Heb	Col	Col	Phil	Phlm
Acts	1–2 Tim	1–2 Tim	Col	Heb
Jas	Titus	Titus	Eph	
1 John	Phlm	Phlm	1–2 Thess	1–3 John
(2–3 John missing)	Heb	Heb	1–2 Tim	1–2 Pet
(Jude missing)			Titus	Jude
Rev	Rev	Jas	Phlm	Jas
	1–2 Pet	1–2 Pet	Rev	Acts
	1 John	Jude		Rev
	2–3 John	1–2 John	*Omitted:*	
	Jude		(2 Pet)	
			(2–3 John)	
			(Jude)	
			(Heb)	

---

[1] Eucherius, *Instructiones* (ca. 424–55, Lyons).

[2] *Decretum gelasianum de libris recipiendis et non recipiendis* (ca. sixth cent.). This canon list is attributed to Pope Gelasius I (492–496), but it is more likely from the sixth century.

[3] Junilius, *Instituta regularia divinae legis,* book I (ca. 551, North Africa).

[4] Cassiodorus, *Institutiones divinarum et saecularium litterarum* (ca. 551–562, Rome).

[5] Isidore, bishop of Seville, *In libros Veteris ac Novi Testamenti prooemia* (ca. 600

Table D-4: New Testament Lists from Biblical Manuscripts of the Fourth and Fifth Centuries

Vaticanus (B)	Sinaiticus (ℵ)	Peshitta (Syr^P)	Alexandrinus (A)	Claromantanus (D)
Matt	Matt	Matt	Matt	Matt
Mark	Mark	Mark	Mark	John
Luke	Luke	Luke	Luke	Mark
John	John	John	John	Luke
Acts	Rom	Acts	Acts	Rom
Jas	1 Cor	Jas	Jas	1–2 Cor
I Pet	2 Cor	1 Pet	I Pet	Gal
2 Pet	Gal	1 John	2 Pet	Eph
1 John	Eph	Rom	1 John	1–2 Tim
2 John	Phil	1 Cor	2 John	Titus
3 John	Col	2 Cor	3 John	Col
Jude	1 Thess	Gal	Jude	Phlm
Rom	2 Thess	Eph	Rom	1–2 Pet
1 Cor	Heb	Phil	1 Cor	Jas
2 Cor	1 Tim	Col	2 Cor	1–3 John
Gal	2 Tim	1 Thess	Gal	Jude
Eph	Titus	2 Thess	Eph	Barn.
Phil	Phlm	Heb	Phil	Rev
Col	Acts	1 Tim	Col	Acts
1 Thess	Jas	2 Tim	1 Thess	
2 Thess	1 Pet	Titus	2 Thess	*Others:*
Heb	2 Pet	Phlm	Heb	Herm.
	1 John	Heb	1 Tim	Acts Paul
Omitted:	2 John		2 Tim	Apoc. Pet.
(1 Tim)	3 John		Titus	
(2 Tim)	Jude		Phlm	*Omitted:*
(Titus)	Rev		Rev	(Phil)
(Rev)	Barn.		1 Clem.	(1–2 Thess)
	Herm.		2 Clem.	(Heb)
	. . .		Pss. Sol.	

Select Bibliography

The following bibliography is a compilation of useful articles, reviews, and volumes on the origins and notion of canon, the development of the Bible, and various related issues. It is not an exhaustive collection but is representative of the most important studies available on the various subjects discussed in this volume. The contributors to this volume have helped with the bibliography by offering many helpful suggestions and contributions to it. Those seeking additional sources should consult the numerous references to other sources in the footnotes of the papers above.

Abraham, William J. *Canon and Criterion in Christian Theology: From Fathers to Feminism.* Oxford: Clarendon, 1998.

Achtemeier, Paul. *The Inspiration of Scripture: Problems and Proposals.* Philadelphia: Westminster, 1980.

Ackroyd, Peter R. "Original Text and Canonical Text." *Union Seminary Quarterly Review* 32 (1977): 166–73.

———. "The Open Canon." Pages 209–24 in *Studies in the Religious Tradition of the Old Testament.* Edited by P. R. Ackroyd. London: SCM, 1987.

Akenson, Donald H. *Surpassing Wonder: The Invention of the Bible and the Talmuds.* New York: Harcourt Brace, 1998.

Aland, Kurt. "Die Entstehung des Corpus Paulinum." Pages 302–50 in *Neutestamenliche Entwurfe.* Edited by Kurt Aland. Theologische Bücherei 63. Munich: Kaiser, 1979.

———. "The Problem of Anonymity and Pseudonymity in Christian Literature of the First Two Centuries." *Journal of Theological Studies* 12 (1961): 39–49.

Alexander, Archibald. *The Canon of the Old and New Testaments Ascertained.* New York: Princeton Press, 1826.

———. *The Problem of the New Testament Canon.* Oxford: Mowbray, 1962.

Alexander, L. "The Living Voice: Skepticism toward the Written Word in Early Christian and in Graeco-Roman Texts." Pages 221–47 in *The Bible in Three Dimensions.* Edited by D. J. A. Clines. Sheffield: JSOT Press, 1990.

Allert, Craig D. "The State of the New Testament Canon in the Second Century: Putting Tatian's *Diatessaron* in Perspective." *Bulletin for Biblical Research* 9 (1999): 1–18.

Anderson, G. W. "Canonical and Non-Canonical." Pages 113–58 in *The Cambridge History of the Bible.* Edited by P. R. Ackroyd and C. F. Evans. Cambridge: Cambridge University Press, 1976.

Attridge, Harold W. "Christianity from the Destruction of Jerusalem to Constantine's Adoption of the New Religion: 70–312 C.E." Pages 151–94 in *Christianity and Judaism: A Parallel History of Their Origins and Early Development.* Edited by Hershel Shanks. Washington, D.C.: Biblical Archaeology Society, 1992.

Aune, David E. "Charismatic Exegesis in Early Judaism and Early Christianity." Pages 125–50 in *The Pseudepigrapha and Early Biblical Interpretation.* Edited by J. H.

Charlesworth and C. A. Evans. Journal for the Study of the New Testament: Supplement Series 119. Sheffield: JSOT Press, 1993.

Baehr, P., and M. O'Brien. "Founders, Classics and the Concept of a Canon." *Current Sociology* 42 (1994): 1–149.

Balás, David L. "Marcion Revisited: A 'Post-Harnack' Perspective." Pages 95–108 in *Texts and Testaments: Critical Essays on the Bible and Early Church Fathers: A Volume in Honor of Stuart Dickson Currie.* Edited by W. Eugene March. San Antonio: Trinity University Press, 1980.

Balch, David L. "The Canon: Adaptable and Stable, Oral and Written. Critical Questions for Kelber and Riesner." *Forum* 7 (1991): 183–205.

Baldermann, I. "Didaktischer und 'kanonischer' Zugang: Der Unterricht vor dem Problem des biblischen Kanons." *Jahrbuch für biblische Theologie* 3 (1988): 97–111.

Balz, H. R. "Anonymität und Pseudepigraphie im Urchristentum. Überlengungen zum literarischen und theologischen Problem der urchristlichen und gemeinantiken Pseudepigraphie." *Zeitschrift für Theologie und Kirche* 66 (1969): 403–36.

Barr, James. *Holy Scripture: Canon, Authority, Criticsm.* Philadelphia: Westminster, 1983.

Barthélemy, Dominique. "La critique canonique." *Revue de l'Institut Catholique de Paris* 36 (1991): 191–220.

Barton, John. "Canon." Pages 101–5 in *A Dictionary of Biblical Interpretation.* Edited by R. J. Coggins and J. L. Houlden. London: SCM, 1990.

———. *Holy Writings, Sacred Text: The Canon in Early Christianity.* Louisville, Ky.: Westminster John Knox, 1997. (This the American printing of *The Spirit and the Letter* [see below].)

———. *People of the Book? The Authority of the Bible in Christianity.* Louisville, Ky.: Westminster John Knox, 1988.

———. "The Significance of a Fixed Canon of the Hebrew Bible." Pages 67–83 in vol. I/1 of *Hebrew Bible / Old Testament: The History of Its Interpretation.* Edited by Magne Saebo. Göttingen: Vandenhoeck & Ruprecht, 1996.

———. *The Spirit and the Letter: Studies in the Biblical Canon.* London: SPCK, 1997.

Bauer, Walter. *Orthodoxy and Heresy in Earliest Christianity.* 2d ed. Edited by Robert Kraft and Gerhard Krodel. Philadelphia: Fortress, 1971.

Baukham, R. J. "Papias and Polycrates on the Origin of the Fourth Gospel." *Journal of Theological Studies* 44 (1993): 24–69.

Baum, Armin D. "Der neutestamentliche Kanon bei Eusebius: (*Hist. eccl.* 3.25.1–7) im Kontext seiner literaturgeschichtlichen Arbeit." *Ephemerides theologicae lovanienses* 73 (1997): 307–48.

———. "Papias, der Vorzug der *Viva Vox* und die Evangelienschriften." *New Testament Studies* 44 (1998): 144–51.

Beare, G. W. "Canon of the NT." Pages 520–32 in vol. 1 of *Interpreter's Dictionary of the Bible.* New York: Abingdon, 1979.

Beckwith, Roger T. "Canon of the Hebrew Bible and the Old Testament." Pages 102–4 in *The Oxford Companion to the Bible.* Edited by Bruce M. Metzger and M. D. Coogan. New York: Oxford University Press, 1993.

———. "Formation of the Hebrew Bible." Pages 39–86 in *Mikra: Text, Translation, Reading and Interpretation of the Hebrew Bible in Ancient Judaism and Early Christianity.* Edited by M. J. Mulder. Minneapolis: Fortress, 1990.

————. *The Old Testament Canon of the New Testament Church.* Grand Rapids, Mich.: Eerdmans, 1985.

Bellinzoni, A. J. *The Sayings of Jesus in the Writings of Justin Martyr.* Novum Testamentum Supplements 17. Leiden: Brill, 1967.

Best, Ernest. "Scripture, Tradition and the Canon of the New Testament." *Bulletin of the John Rylands University Library of Manchester* 61 (1979): 258–89.

Betz, Otto. "Das Problem des 'Kanons' in den Texten von Qumran." Pages 70–101 in *Der Kanon der Bibel.* Edited by G. Maier. Giessen: Brunnen, 1990.

Beyer, Hermann Wolfgang. "*Kanōn.*" Pages 596–602 in vol. 3 of *Theological Dictionary of the New Testament.* Edited by G. Kittel and G. Friedrich. Translated by G. W. Bromiley. 10 vols. Grand Rapids, Mich.: Eerdmans, 1964–1976.

Bickerman, Elias J. "Some Notes on the Transmission of the Septuagint." Pages 149–78 in *Alexander Marx: Jubilee Volume on the Occasion of His Seventieth Birthday* (English Section). New York: The Jewish Theological Seminary of America, 1950.

Bienert, W. A. "The Picture of the Apostle in Early Christian Tradition." Pages 5–27 in vol. 2 of *New Testament Apocrypha.* Rev. ed. Edited by W. Schneemelcher. Translated by R. McL. Wilson. Louisville, Ky.: Westminster John Knox, 1992.

Birch, B. C. "Tradition, Canon and Biblical Theology." *Horizons in Biblical Theology* 2 (1980): 113–25.

Blackman, E. C. *Marcion and His Influence.* London: SPCK, 1948.

Blenkinsopp, Joseph. *Prophecy and Canon: A Contribution to the Study of Jewish Origins.* Notre Dame, Ind.: University of Notre Dame Press, 1977.

————. " 'We Pay Heed to Heavenly Voices': The 'End of Prophecy' and the Formation of the Canon." Pages 19–31 in *Biblical and Humane: A Festschrift for John F. Priest.* Edited by Linda Bennett Elder, David L. Barr, and Elizabeth Struthers Malbon. Atlanta: Scholars Press, 1996.

Bloom, Harold. *The Western Canon: The Books and Schools of the Age.* New York: Harcourt Brace, 1994.

Blowers, Paul M., ed. and trans. *The Bible in Greek Christian Antiquity.* Notre Dame, Ind.: University of Notre Dame Press, 1997.

Bossman, D. M. "Canon and Culture: Realistic Possibilities for the Biblical Canon." *Biblical Theology Bulletin* 23 (1993): 4–13.

Bovon, François. "Vers une nouvelle edition de la litterature apocryphe chrétienne." *Augustinianum* 23 (1983): 373–78.

————. "The Synoptic Gospels and the Non-Canonical Acts of the Apostles." *Harvard Theological Review* 81 (1988): 19–36.

————. "La structure canonique de l'Evangile et de l'Apotre." *Cristianesimo nella storia* 15 (1994): 559–76.

Bowman, A. K. "The Vindolanda Tablets and the Development of the Book Form." *Zeitschrift für Papyrologie und Epigraphik* 18 (1975): 237–52.

Brakke, David. "Canon Formation and Social Conflict in Fourth-Century Egypt: Athanasius of Alexandria's Thirty-Ninth *Festal Letter.*" *Harvard Theological Review* 87 (1994): 395–419.

Brooke, G. "The Explicit Presentation of Scripture in 4QMMT." Pages 67–88 in *Legal Texts and Legal Issues: Proceedings of the Second Meeting of the International Organization for Qumran Studies, Cambridge 1995: Published in Honour of Joseph M. Baumgarten.*

Edited by M. Bernstein, F. García Martínez, and J. Kampen. Studies on the Texts of the Desert of Judah 23. Leiden: Brill, 1997.

Brown, Raymond E. "Canonicity." Pages 515–34 in *Jerome Biblical Commentary.* Edited by R. E. Brown et al. Englewood Cliffs, N.J.: Prentice-Hall, 1968.

Brown, Raymond E., and R. F. Collins. "Canonicity." Pages 1034–54 in *The New Jerome Biblical Commentary.* Edited by R. E. Brown, J. A. Fitzmyer, and R. E. Murphy. London: Geoffrey Chapman, 1989.

Broyde, M. J. "Defilement of the Hands, Canonization of the Bible, and the Special Status of Esther, Ecclesiastes, and the Song of Songs." *Judaism* 44 (Winter 1995): 65–79.

Bruce, F. F. *The Canon of Scripture.* Downers Grove, Ill.: InterVarsity, 1988.

———. "Scripture and Tradition in the New Testament." Pages 68–93 in *Holy Book and Holy Tradition.* Edited by F. F. Bruce and E. G. Rupp. Manchester: Manchester University Press, 1968.

———. "Some Thoughts on the Beginning of the New Testament Canon." *Bulletin of the John Rylands University Library of Manchester* 65 (1983): 37–60.

———. "Tradition and the Canon of Scripture." Pages 59–84 in *The Authoritative Word: Essays on the Nature of Scripture.* Edited by Donald K. McKim. Grand Rapids, Mich.: Eerdmans, 1993.

Bruns, G. L. "Canon and Power in the Hebrew Scriptures." *Critical Inquiry* 10 (1984): 259–89.

Buchanan, E. S. "The Codex Muratorianus." *Journal of Theological Studies* 8 (1907): 537–39.

Budde, Karl. *Der Kanon des Alten Testaments: Ein Abriss.* Giessen: J. Ricker (Alfred Töpelmann), 1900.

Buhl, Frants P. W. *Kanon und Text des alten Testaments.* Leipzig: Academische Buchhandlung, 1891.

Callaway, Philip R. "The Temple Scroll and the Canonization of the Old Testament." *Revue biblique* 13 (1988): 239–43.

Campenhausen, Hans von. *The Formation of the Christian Bible.* Translated by J. A. Baker. Philadelphia: Fortress, 1972.

Carr, David. "Canonization in the Context of Community: An Outline for the Formation of the Tanakh and the Christian Bible." Pages 22–64 in *A Gift of God in Due Season: Essays on Scripture and Community in Honor of James A. Sanders.* Edited by R. Weis and D. Carr. Sheffield: Sheffield Academic Press, 1996.

Carson, D. A., and John Woodbridge, eds. *Hermeneutics, Authority, and Canon.* Grand Rapids, Mich.: Zondervan, 1986.

Carson, D. A., and H. G. M. Williamson, eds. *It Is Written: Scripture Citing Scripture: Essays in Honour of Barnabas Lindars, SSF.* Cambridge: Cambridge University Press, 1988.

Chapman, S. B. *The Law and the Prophets: A Study in Old Testament Canon Formation.* Forschungen zum Alten Testament 27. Tübingen: Mohr Siebeck, 2000.

———. " 'The Law and the Words' as a Canonical Formula within the Old Testament." Pages 26–74 in *The Interpretation of Scripture in Early Judaism and Christianity: Studies in Language and Traditions.* Edited by Craig A. Evans. Journal for the Study of the Pseudepigraphia: Supplement Series 33. Studies in Scripture in Early Judaism and Christianity 7. Sheffield: Sheffield Academic Press, 2000.

Charlesworth, James H. *The Old Testament Pseudepigrapha and the New Testament: Prolegomena for the Study of Christian Origins.* Society for New Testament Studies Monograph Series 54. Cambridge: Cambridge University Press, 1985.

Charteris, A. H. *Canonicity: A Collection of Early Testimonies to the Canonical Books of the New Testament.* Edinburgh: William Blackwood & Sons, 1880.

Childs, Brevard S. *Biblical Theology in Crisis.* Philadelphia: Westminster, 1970.

———. *Biblical Theology of the Old and New Testaments: Theological Reflection on the Christian Bible.* Minneapolis: Fortress, 1993.

———. "The Canonical Shape of the Prophetic Literature." *Interpretation* 32 (1978): 46–55.

———. "The Exegetical Significance of Canon for the Study of the Old Testament." Pages 66–80 in Vetus Testamentum Supplements 29. Leiden: Brill, 1978.

———. *Introduction to the Old Testament as Scripture.* Philadelphia: Fortress, 1979.

———. *The New Testament as Canon: An Introduction.* Philadelphia: Fortress, 1985.

Christensen, Duane L. "Josephus and the Twenty-Two-Book Canon of Sacred Scripture." *Journal of the Evangelical Theological Society* 29 (March 1986): 37–46.

———. "The Centre of the First Testament within the Canonical Process." *Biblical Theology Bulletin* 23 (1993): 48–53.

Clarke, Kent D. "Original Text or Canonical Text? Questioning the Shape of the New Testament We Translate." Pages 281–322 in *Issues in Biblical Translation: Responses to Eugene A. Nida.* Edited by S. E. Porter and R. Hess. Journal for the Study of the New Testament: Supplement Series 173. Sheffield: Sheffield Academic Press, 1998.

Coats, George W., and Burke O. Long. *Canon and Authority: Essays in Old Testament Religion and Authority.* Philadelphia: Fortress, 1977.

Collins, J. J. "Before the Canon: Scriptures in Second Temple Judaism." Pages 225–41 in *Old Testament Interpretation: Past, Present, and Future.* Edited by James Luther Mays, David L. Petersen, and Kent Harold Richards. Nashville: Abingdon, 1995.

Collins, Raymond F. *Introduction to the New Testament.* Garden City, N.Y.: Doubleday, 1983.

Comfort, Philip Wesley, ed. *The Origin of the Bible.* Wheaton, Ill.: Tyndale, 1992.

Conrad, J. "Zur Frage nach der Rolle des Gesetzes bei der Bildung des alttestamentlichen Kanons." *Theologia viatorum* 11 (1979): 11–19.

Cosgrove, Charles H. "Justin Martyr and the Emerging Christian Canon: Observations on the Purpose and Destination of the Dialogue with Trypho." *Vigiliae christianae* 36 (1982): 209–32.

Cowley, R. W. "The Biblical Canon of the Ethiopian Orthodox Church Today." *Ostkirchliche Studien* 23 (1974): 318–24.

Crawford, White. "The 'Rewritten' Bible at Qumran." *Frank Moore Cross Volume.* Eretz-Israel 26. Jerusalem: IES and Hebrew Union College—Jewish Institute of Religion, 1999.

Cribiore, Raffaella. *Writing, Teachers, and Students in Greco-Roman Egypt.* Atlanta: Scholars Press, 1996.

Cross, F. L. "History and Fiction in the African Canons." *Journal of Theological Studies* 12 (1961): 227–47.

Cross, F. M. *From Epic to Canon: History and Literature in Ancient Israel.* Baltimore: Johns Hopkins University Press, 1998.

———. "The History of the Biblical Text in the Light of the Discoveries in the Judean Desert." *Harvard Theological Review* 57 (1964): 281–99.

———. "The Text Behind the Text of the Hebrew Bible." Pages 139–55 in *Understanding the Dead Sea Scrolls*. Edited by Hershel Shanks. New York: Vintage, 1992.

Cruesemann, F. "Das 'portative Vaterland': Struktur und Genese des alttestamentlichen Kanons." Pages 63–79 in vol. 2 of *Kanon und Zensur: Beiträge zur Archäologie der literarischen Kommunikation*. Edited by A. Assmann and J. Assmann. Munich: Wilhelm Fink, 1987.

Cullmann, O. "The Plurality of the Gospels as a Theological Problem in Antiquity." Pages 39–54 in *The Early Church*. Edited by A. J. B. Higgins. Philadelphia: Westminster, 1956.

Cunningham, Philip J. *Exploring Scripture: How the Bible Came to Be*. New York: Paulist, 1992.

Dahl, N. A. "The Particularity of the Pauline Epistles as a Problem in the Ancient Church." Pages 261–71 in *Neotestamentica et Patristica: Freundesgabe O. Cullmann*. Novum Testamentum Supplement 6. Leiden: Brill, 1962.

———. "The Origin of the Earliest Prologues to the Pauline Letters." Pages 233–77 in *The Poetics of Faith: Essays Offered to A. N. Wilder*. Edited by W. Beardslee. Semeia 12. Missoula, Mont.: Scholars Press, 1978.

Dassmann, E. "Wer schuf den Kanon des Neuen Testaments?: Zum neuesten Buch von Bruce M. Metzger." *Jahrbuch für biblische Theologie* 3 (1988): 275–83.

Davidson, Samuel. *The Canon of the Bible: Its Formation, History, and Fluctuations*. London: Henry S. King, 1877.

Davies, Philip R. *Scribes and Schools: The Canonization of the Hebrew Scriptures*. Louisville, Ky.: Westminster John Knox, 1988.

———. " 'Pen of Iron, Point of Diamond' (Jer 17:1): Prophecy as Writing." Pages 65–81 in *Writings and Speech in Israelite and Ancient Near Eastern Prophecy*. Edited by M. Floyd and E. Ben Zvi. Atlanta: Scholars Press, 2000.

Davies, W. D. "Canon and Christology." Pages 19–36 in *The Glory of Christ in the New Testament: Studies in Christology in Memory of George Bradford Caird*. Edited by L. D. Hurst and N. T. Wright. Oxford: Clarendon, 1987.

Dempster, S. "An 'Extraordinary Fact': Torah and Temple and the Contours of the Hebrew Canon." *Tyndale Bulletin* 48 (1997): 23–56, 191–218.

Dobschütz, E. von. "The Abandonment of the Canonical Ideal." *American Journal of Theology* 19 (1915): 416–29.

Dohmen, C. "Der biblische Kanon in der Diskussion." *Theologische Revue* 91 (1995): 452–60.

Dohmen, C., and M. Oeming. *Biblischer Kanon, warum and wozu? Eine Kanontheologie*. Quaestiones disputatae 137. Freiburg: Herder, 1992.

Donelson, L. R. *Pseudepigraphy and Ethical Argument in the Pastoral Epistles*. Hermeneutische Untersuchungen zur Theologie 22. Tübingen: J. C. B. Mohr, 1986.

DuBois, J.-D. "L'exégese gnostique et l'histoire du canon des écritures." Pages 89–97 in *Les règles de l'inteprétation*. Edited by M. Tardieu. Paris: Cerf, 1987.

Duff, Jeremy. "P46 and the Pastorals: A Misleading Consensus?" *New Testament Studies* 44 (1998): 581–82.

Duncker, P. G. "The Canon of the Old Testament at the Council of Trent." *Catholic Biblical Quarterly* 15 (1953): 277–99.

Dungan, David L. "The New Testament Canon in Recent Study." *Interpretation* 29 (October 1975): 339–51.

Dulles, Avery. "The Authority of Scripture: A Catholic Perspective." Pages 14–40 in *Scripture in the Jewish and Christian Traditions.* Edited by F. E. Greenspahn. Nashville: Abingdon, 1982.

Dungan, David L. "The New Testament Canon in Recent Study." *Interpretation* 29 (1975): 339–51.

Dunn, James D. G. "Levels of Canonical Authority." *Horizons in Biblical Theology* 4 (1982): 13–60.

———. *The Living Word.* Philadelphia: Fortress, 1987.

———. *Unity and Diversity in the New Testament.* 2d ed. Philadelphia: Westminster, 1992.

Dyck, E. "What Do We Mean By Canon?" *Crux* 25 (1989): 17–22.

Edwards, M. J. "The *Epistle to Rheginus:* Valentinianism in the Fourth Century." *Novum Testamentem* 37 (1995): 76–91.

Ehrman, B. D. "The New Testament Canon of Didymus the Blind." *Vigiliae christianae* 37 (1983): 1–21.

———. *The Orthodox Corruption of Scripture: The Effect of Early Christological Controversies on the Text of the New Testament.* Oxford: Oxford University Press, 1993.

———. "The Text as Window: New Testament Manuscripts and the Social History of Early Christianity." Pages 361–79 in *The Text of the New Testament in Contemporary Research: Essays on the Status Quaestionis.* Edited by B. D. Ehrman and M. W. Holmes. Studies and Documents 46. Grand Rapids, Mich.: Eerdmans, 1995.

———. "The Text of the Gospels at the End of the Second Century." Pages 95–122 in *Codex Bezae: Studies from the Lunel Colloquium, June 1994.* Edited by D. C. Parker and C.-B. Amphoux. New Testament Tools and Studies 22. Leiden: Brill, 1996.

Elliott, J. K. "Manuscripts, the Codex, and the Canon." *Journal for the Study of the New Testament* 63 (1996): 105–23.

Ellis, Earle E. "The Old Testament Canon in the Early Church." Pages 653–90 in *Mikra: Text, Translation, Reading and Interpretation of the Hebrew Bible in Ancient Judaism and Early Christianity. Compendia Rerum Judaicarum ad Novum Testamentus.* Edited by M. J. Mulder and H. Sysling. Minneapolis: Fortress, 1990.

———. *The Old Testament in Early Christianity: Canon and Interpretation in the Light of Modern Research.* Grand Rapids, Mich.: Baker, 1992.

———. "Pseudonymity and Canonicity of New Testament Documents." Pages 212–24 in *Worship, Theology, and Ministry in the Early Church: Essays in Honor of Ralph P. Martin.* Edited by M. J. Wilkins and T. Paige. Journal for the Study of the New Testament: Supplement Series 87. Sheffield: JSOT Press, 1992.

Epp, E. J. "The Codex and Literacy in Early Christianity and at Oxyrhynchus: Issues Raised by Harry Y. Gamble's *Books and Readers in the Early Church.*" *Critical Review of Books in Religion* 10 (1997): 15–37.

———. "The Multivalence of the Term 'Original Text' in New Testament Textual Criticism." *Harvard Theological Review* 92 (1999): 245–81.

———. "The New Testament Papyri at Oxyrhynchus in Their Social and Intellectual Context." In *Sayings of Jesus: Canonical and Non-Canonical: Essays in Honor of Tjitze Baarda.* Edited by W. L. Petersen et al. Leiden: Brill, 1997.

———. "The Significance of the Papyri for Determining the Nature of the New Testament Text in the Second Century: A Dynamic View of Textual Transmission." Pages 71–103 in *Gospel Traditions in the Second Century*. Edited by W. L. Petersen. Notre Dame, Ind.: University of Notre Dame Press, 1989.

———. "Textual Criticism in the Exegesis of the New Testament, with an Excursus on Canon." Pages 73–91 in *Handbook to Exegesis of the New Testament*. Edited by S. E. Porter. New Testament Tools and Studies 25. Leiden: Brill, 1997.

Evans, Christopher F. *Is Holy Scripture Christian?* London: SCM Press, 1971.

Evans, Craig A. "The Dead Sea Scrolls and the Canon of Scripture in the Time of Jesus." Pages 67–79 in *The Bible at Qumran: Text, Shape, and Interpretation*. Edited by P. W. Flint. Grand Rapids, Mich.: Eerdmans, 2001.

———. "Luke and the Rewritten Bible: Aspects of Lukan Hagiography." Pages 170–201 in *The Pseudepigrapha and Early Biblical Interpretation*. Edited by J. H. Charlesworth and C. A. Evans. Journal for the Study of the New Testament: Supplement Series 119. Sheffield: JSOT Press, 1993.

———. *Noncanonical Writings and New Testament Interpretation*. Peabody, Mass.: Hendrickson, 1992.

Evans, Craig A., Robert L. Webb, and Richard A. Wiebe, eds. *Nag Hammadi Texts and the Bible*. New Testament Tools and Studies 18. Leiden: Brill, 1993.

Fallon, Francis T. "The Prophets of the Old Testament and the Gnostics. A Note on Irenaeus, *Adversus Haereses*, 1.30.10–11." *Vigiliae christianae* 32 (1978): 191–94.

Farkasfalvy, Denis. "The Early Development of the New Testament Canon." Pages 97–160 in *The Formation of the New Testament Canon*. Edited by Harold W. Attridge. New York: Paulist, 1983.

———. "The Ecclesial Setting of Pseudepigraphy in Second Peter and Its Role in the Formation of the Canon." *Second Century* 5 (1985–1986): 3–29.

Farley, Edward. *Ecclesial Reflection*. Philadelphia: Fortress, 1982.

Farmer, W. R. "The Church's Gospel Canon: Why Four and No More." Pages 1246–50 in *The International Bible Commentary*. Edited by W. R. Farmer. Collegeville, Minn.: The Liturgical Press, 1998.

———. "A Dismantling of the Church's Canon." Pages 35–55 in *The Gospel of Jesus: The Pastoral Relevance of the Synoptic Problem*. Edited by W. R. Farmer. Louisville, Ky.: Westminster John Knox, 1994.

———. "Further Reflections on the Fourfold Gospel Canon." Pages 107–13 in *The Early Church in Its Context: Essays in Honor of Everett Ferguson*. Edited by J. Malherbe, F. W. Norris, and J. W. Thompson. Leiden: Brill, 1998.

———. *Jesus and the Gospel: Tradition, Scripture and Canon*. Philadelphia: Fortress, 1982.

———. "Galatians and the Second Century Development of the *Regula Fidei*." *The Second Century: A Journal of Early Christian Studies* 4 (Fall 1984): 143–70.

———. "Matthew and the Bible: An Essay in Canonical Criticism." *Lexington Theological Quarterly* 11 (April 1976): 57–66.

———. "The Role of Isaiah in the Development of the Christian Canon." Pages 217–22 in *Uncovering Ancient Stones: Festschrift for H. Neil Richardson*. Winona, Ind.: Eisenbrauns, 1994.

Farmer, W. R., and Denis M. Farkasfalvy. *The Formation of the New Testament Canon*. Edited by H. W. Attridge. Introduction by A. C. Outler. New York: Paulist, 1983.

Feldman, Louis H. "Introduction." Pages 17–49 in *Josephus, the Bible, and History*. Edited by Louis H. Feldman and Gohei Hata. Detroit: Wayne State University Press, 1989.

Feldman, Louis H., and Gohei Hata, eds. *Josephus, the Bible, and History*. Detroit: Wayne State University Press, 1989.

Fenton, J. C. "Pseudonymity and the New Testament." *Theology* 58 (1955): 51–56.

Ferguson, Everett. "Canon Muratori: Date and Provenance." Pages 677–83 in *Studia Patristica* 17/2. Edited by E. A. Livingstone. Oxford: Pergamon, 1982.

———. "Introduction." Pages xi–xiii in *The Bible in the Early Church*. Studies in Early Christianity 3. Edited by E. Ferguson. New York: Garland, 1993.

———. Review of G. M. Hahneman, *The Muratorian Fragment and the Development of the Canon*. *Journal of Theological Studies* 44 (1993): 691–97.

Filson, Floyd V. *Which Books Belong in the Bible? A Study of the Canon*. Philadelphia: Westminster, 1957.

Fitzmyer, Joseph A. *The Dead Sea Scrolls and Christian Origins*. Studies in the Dead Sea Scrolls and Related Literature. Grand Rapids, Mich.: Eerdmans, 2000.

Flint, Peter. " 'Apocrypha,' Other Previously-known Writings, and 'Pseudepigrapha' in the Dead Sea Scrolls." Pages 24–66 in vol. 2 of *The Dead Sea Scrolls after Fifty Years: A Comprehensive Assessment*. Edited by Peter W. Flint and James C. VanderKam. Leiden: Brill, 1999.

———. *The Dead Sea Psalms Scrolls and the Book of Psalms*. Leiden: Brill, 1997.

———. "Noncanonical Writings in the Dead Sea Scrolls." Pages 80–126 in *The Bible at Qumran: Text, Shape, and Interpretation*. Edited by P. W. Flint. Grand Rapids, Mich.: Eerdmans, 2001.

Folkert, K. W. "The 'Canons' of Scripture." Pages 170–79 in *Rethinking Scripture: Essays from a Comparative Perspective*. Edited by M. Levering. Albany, N.Y.: SUNY Press, 1989.

Fowl, Stephen. "The Canonical Approach of Brevard Childs." *Expository Times* 96 (1985): 173–76.

Freedman, David Noel. "The Earliest Bible." Pages 29–37 in *Backgrounds for the Bible*. Edited by M. P. O'Connor and D. F. Freedman. Winona Lake, Ind.: Eisenbrauns, 1987.

———. "The Symmetry of the Hebrew Bible." *Studia Theologica* 46 (1992): 83–108.

———. *The Unity of the Hebrew Bible*. Ann Arbor: University of Michigan Press, 1991.

Frerichs, E. S. "The Torah Canon of Judaism and the Interpretation of Hebrew Scriptures." *Horizons in Biblical Theology* 9 (1987): 13–25.

Friedman, S. "The Holy Scriptures Defile the Hands: The Transformation of a Biblical Concept in Rabbinic Theology." Pages 115–32 in *Biblical and Other Studies Presented to Nahum M. Sarna in Honour of His 70th Birthday*. Edited by M. Bretler and M. Fishbane. Journal for the Study of the Old Testament: Supplement Series 154. Sheffield: Sheffield Academic Press, 1993.

Funk, Robert W. *Honest to Jesus*. San Francisco: HarperSanFrancisco, 1996 (see especially pages 77–120).

———. "The Incredible Canon." Pages 24–46 in *Christianity in the 21st Century*. Edited by D. A. Brown. New York: Crossroad, 2000.

———. "The New Testament as Tradition and Canon." Pages 151–86 in *Parables and Presence*. Philadelphia: Fortress, 1982.

Funk, Robert W., et al. *The Once and Future Jesus*. Santa Rosa, Calif.: Polebridge, 2000.

Fürst, Julius. *Der Kanon des Alten Testaments nach den Überlieferungen in Talmud und Midrasch.* Leipzig: Dörffling und Franke, 1868.

Gamble, Harry Y. *Books and Readers in the Early Church: A History of Early Christian Texts.* New Haven, Conn.: Yale University Press, 1995.

———. "Canon. New Testament." Pages 852–61 in vol. 1 of *Anchor Bible Dictionary.* Edited by D. N. Freedman. 6 vols. New York: Doubleday, 1992.

———. "The Canon of the New Testament." Pages 201–43 in *The New Testament and Its Modern Interpreters.* Edited by E. J. Epp and G. W. MacRae. Society of Biblical Literature The Bible and Its Modern Interpreters 3. Philadelphia: Fortress, 1989.

———. "Christianity: Scripture and Canon." Pages 36–62 in *The Holy Book in Comparative Perspective.* Edited by F. M. Denney and R. L. Taylor. Studies in Comparative Religion. Columbia: University of South Carolina Press, 1985.

———. *The New Testament Canon: Its Making and Meaning.* Guides to Biblical Scholarship. Philadelphia: Fortress, 1985.

———. "The Pauline Corpus and the Early Christian Book." Pages 265–80 in *Paul and the Legacies of Paul.* Edited by William S. Babcock. Dallas: SMU Press, 1990.

Gerstenberger, Erhard S. "Canon Criticism and the Meaning of *Sitz im Leben.*" Pages 20–31 in *Canon, Theology, and Old Testament Interpretation: Essays in Honor of Brevard S. Childs.* Edited by Gene M. Tucker, David L. Peterson, and Robert R. Wilson. Philadelphia: Fortress, 1988.

Gese, H. "Die dreifache Gestaltwerdung des Alten Testaments." Pages 299–328 in *Mitte der Schrift? Ein jüdisch-christliches Gespräch: Texte des Berner Symposions vom 6.-12. Januar 1985.* Edited by M. A. Klopfenstein et al. Judaica et Christiana 11. Bern: Peter Lang, 1987.

Gnuse, R. *The Authority of the Bible: Theories of Inspiration, Revelation, and the Canon of Scripture.* New York: Paulist, 1985.

Golb, Norman. *Who Wrote the Dead Sea Scrolls?* New York: Scribners, 1995.

Gooding, David W. "Aristeas and Septuagint Origins: A Review of Recent Studies." *Vetus Testamentum* 13 (1963): 357–78.

Goodspeed, Edgar J. *The Formation of the New Testament.* Chicago: University of Chicago Press, 1926.

Gorak, J. *The Making of the Modern Canon: Genesis and Crisis of a Literary Idea.* London: Athlone, 1991.

Graham, William A. *Beyond the Written Word: Oral Aspects of Scripture in the History of Religion.* Cambridge: Cambridge University Press, 1987.

———. "Scripture." Pages 133–45 in vol. 13 of *Encyclopaedia of Religion.* Edited by Mircea Eliade. New York: Macmillan, 1987.

Grant, Robert M. *The Formation of the New Testament.* New York: Harper & Row, 1965.

———. "From Tradition to Scripture and Back." Pages 18–36 in *Scripture and Tradition.* Edited by Joseph F. Kelley. Notre Dame, Ind.: Fides, 1976.

———. *Heresy and Criticism: The Search for Authenticity in Early Christian Literature.* Louisville, Ky.: Westminster John Knox, 1993.

———. "The New Testament Canon." Pages 284–308 in vol. 1 of *Cambridge History of the Bible.* Cambridge: Cambridge University Press, 1976.

———. Review of Geoffrey Mark Hahneman, *The Muratorian Fragment and the Development of the Canon. Church History* 64 (1995): 639.

Gregory, Caspar René. *Canon and Text of the New Testament.* International Theological Library. Edinburgh: T&T Clark, 1907.

Groh, Dennis E. "Hans von Campenhausen on Canon: Positions and Problems." *Interpretation* 28 (1974): 331–43.

Grosheide, F. W., ed. *Some Early Lists of the Books of the New Testament.* Vol. 1, *Textus Minores.* Leiden: Brill, 1948.

Gutwenger, Engelbert. "The Anti-Marcionite Prologues." *Theological Studies* 7 (1946): 393–408.

Hahn, Ferdinand. "Die Heilige Schrift als älteste christliche Tradition und als Kanon." *Evangelische Theologie* 40 (1980): 456–66.

Hahneman, Geoffrey Mark. "More on Redating the Muratorian Fragment." Pages 359–65 in *Studia Patristica* 19. Edited by E. A. Livingstone. Leuven: Peeters, 1988.

———. *The Muratorian Fragment and the Development of the Canon.* Oxford Theological Monographs. Oxford: Clarendon, 1992.

Haran, Menahem. "Archives, Libraries, and the Order of the Biblical Books." *Journal of the Ancient Near Eastern Society* 22 (1993): 51–61.

Harnack, Adolf von. *The Origin of the New Testament and the Most Important Consequences of the New Creation.* Translated by J. R. Wilkinson. New York: Macmillan, 1925. Translation of *Das Neue Testament um das Jahr 200.* Freiburg: J. C. B. Mohr, 1889.

———. *Marcion: Das Evangelium vom fremden Gott.* 2d ed. Leipzig: Hinrichs, 1924.

Harrington, Daniel J. "Introduction to the Canon." Pages 7–21 in vol. 1 of *The New Interpreter's Bible.* 12 Vols. Nashville: Abingdon, 1994.

Harris, J. Rendel. "Marcion and the Canon." *Expository Times* 18 (1906–1907): 392–94.

Harris, R. Laird. *Inspiration and Canonicity of the Bible: An Historical and Exegetical Study.* Grand Rapids, Mich.: Zondervan, 1969.

Harris, William. "Why Did the Codex Supplant the Book-Roll?" Pages 71–85 in *Renaissance Society and Culture: Essays in Honor of Eugene F. Rice, Jr.* Edited by John Monfasani and Ronald G. Musto. New York: Italica, 1991.

Hatch, W. H. P. "The Position of Hebrews in the Canon of the New Testament." *Harvard Theological Review* 29 (1936): 133–51.

Heckel, Th. *Vom Evangelium des Markus zum viergestaltigen Evangelium.* Wissenschaftliche Untersuchungen zum Neuen Testament 120. Tübingen: J. C. B. Mohr (Paul Siebeck), 1999.

Hedrick, Charles W. "Kingdom Sayings and Parables of Jesus in *The Apocryphon of James:* Tradition and Redaction." *New Testament Studies* 29 (1983): 1–24.

———. "Thomas and the Synoptics: Aiming at a Consensus." *Second Century* 7 (1989–1990): 39–56.

Heine, R. E. "The Role of the Gospel of John in the Montanist Controversy." *Second Century* 6 (1987): 1–19.

Hengel, Martin. *The Four Gospels and the One Gospel of Jesus Christ.* Harrisburg, Pa.: Trinity, 2000.

———. "The Titles of the Gospels and the Gospel of Mark." Pages 64–84 in *Studies in the Gospel of Mark.* Edited by M. Hengel. Translated by J. Bowden. London: SCM, 1985.

Henne, P. "La datation du Canon de Muratori." *Revue biblique* 100 (1993): 54–75.

Hennecke, Edgar, and Wilhelm Schneemelcher. *New Testament Apocrypha.* Translated and edited by R. McL. Wilson. 2 vols. Philadelphia: Westminster, 1963.

Herklots, H. G. G. *How Our Bible Came to Us.* London: Ernest Benn, 1957.

Hill, Charles E. "Justin and the New Testament Writings." Pages 42–48 in *Studia Patristica* 30. Edited by E. A. Livingstone. Leuven: Peeters, 1997.

———. "What Papias Said about John (and Luke). A 'New' Papian Fragment." *Journal of Theological Studies* 49 (1998): 582–629.

Hillmer, M. R. "The Gospel of John in the Second Century." Ph.D. diss., Harvard, 1966.

Hoffmann, R. Joseph. *Marcion, On the Restitution of Christianity: An Essay on the Development of Radical Paulinist Theology in the Second Century.* Chico, Calif.: Scholars Press, 1984.

Hoffman, Thomas A. "Inspiration, Normativeness, Canonicity, and the Unique Sacred Character of the Bible." *Catholic Biblical Quarterly* 44 (1982): 447– 69.

Hoover, R. W. "How the Books of the New Testament Were Chosen." *Bible Review* 9 (1993): 44–47.

Horbury, W. "The Wisdom of Solomon in the Muratorian Fragment." *Journal of Theological Studies* 45 (1994): 149–59.

Howorth, H. H. "The Origin and Authority of the Biblical Canon in the Anglican Church." *Journal of Theological Studies* 8 (1906–1907): 1–40.

Hübner, H. "Vetus Testamentum und Vetus Testamentum in Novo receptum: Die Frage nach dem Kanon des Alten Testaments aus neutestamentlicher Sicht." *Jahrbuch für biblische Theologie* 3 (1988): 147–62.

Hughes, J. *Secrets of the Times: Myth and History in Biblical Chronology.* Journal for the Study of the Old Testament: Supplement Series 66. Sheffield: JSOT Press, 1990.

Hunt, H. "An Examination of the Current Emphasis on the Canon in Old Testament Studies." *Southwestern Journal of Theology* 23 (1980): 55–70.

Jacob, E. "Principe canonique et formation de l'Ancien Testament." Pages 101–22 of *Congress Volume: Edinburgh 1974.* Vetus Testamentum Supplement 28 Leiden: Brill, 1975.

Jeffery, Arthur. "The Canon of the Old Testament." Pages 32–45 in vol. 1 of *The Interpreter's Bible.* Edited by G. A. Buttrick et al. 12 vols. New York: Abingdon, 1952.

Jepsen, A. "Kanon und Text des Alten Testaments." *Theologische Literaturzeitung* 74 (1949): 65–74.

———. "Zur Kanongeschichte des Alten Testaments." *Zeitschrift für die alttestamentliche Wissenschaft* 71 (1959): 114–36.

Johnson, Luke T. *The Writings of the New Testament.* Philadelphia: Fortress, 1986.

Kaestli, J.-D. "La place du Fragment de Muratori dans l'histoire du canon." *Cristianesimo nella storia* 15 (1995): 609–34.

Kaestli, J.-D., and Otto Wermelinger, eds. *Canon de l'Ancien Testament: Sa formation et son histoire.* Geneva: Labor et Fides, 1984.

Kahle, Paul E. *The Cairo Geniza.* Oxford: Basil Blackwell, 1959.

Kalin, Everett R. "Argument from Inspiration in the Canonization of the New Testament." Th.D. diss., Harvard University, 1967.

———. "A Book Worth Discussing: *Canon and Community: A Guide to Canonical Criticism.*" *Concordia Theological Monthly* 12 (1985): 310–12.

———. "Early Traditions about Mark's Gospel: Canonical Status Emerges, the Story Grows." *Concordia Theological Monthly* 2 (1975): 332–41.

———. "The Inspired Community: A Glance at Canon History." *Concordia Theological Monthly* 42 (1971): 541–49.

————. "Re-examining New Testament Canon History: 1. The Canon of Origen." *Concordia Theological Monthly* 17 (1990): 274–82.

Käsemann, Ernst. "The Canon of the New Testament and the Unity of the Church." Pages 95–107 in *Essays on New Testament Themes*. London: SCM Press, 1968.

————. *Das Neue Testament als Kanon: Dokumentation und kritische Analyse zur gegenwärtgen Discussion*. Göttingen: Vandenhoeck & Ruprecht, 1970.

Katz, Peter. "Justin's Old Testament Quotations and the Greek Dodekapropheten Scroll." Pages 343–53 in *Studia Patristica* 1. Edited by K. Aland and F. L. Cross. Berlin: Akademie-Verlag, 1957.

————. *Philo's Bible: The Aberrant Text of Bible Quotations in Some Philonic Writings and Its Place in the Textual History of the Greek Bible*. Cambridge: Cambridge University Press, 1950.

————. "The Old Testament Canon in Palestine and Alexandria." *Zeitschrift für die neutestamentliche Wissenschaft und die Kunde der älteren Kirche* 47 (1956): 191–217.

Keck, L. E. "Scripture and Canon." *Quarterly Review* 3 (1983): 8–26.

Kelly, Joseph F. *Why Is There a New Testament?* Background Books 5. Wilmington, Del.: Michael Glazier, 1986.

Kermode, F. "The Argument about Canons." Pages 78–96 in *The Bible and the Narrative Tradition*. Edited by F. McConnell. Oxford: Oxford University Press, 1986.

Kinzig, W. "*Kainē diathēkē:* The Title of the New Testament in the Second and Third Centuries." *Journal of Theological Studies* 45 (1994): 519–44.

Klijn, A. J. N. "Die Entstehungsgeschichte des Neuen Testaments." Pages 64–97 in *Aufstieg und Niedergang der römischen Welt: Geschichte und Kultur Roms im Spiegel der neueren Forschung* 2.26.1. Edited by H. Temporini and W. Hasse. Berlin: Walter de Gruyter, 1992.

Knight, D. A. "Canon and the History of Tradition: A Critique of Brevard Childs' *Introduction to the Old Testament as Scripture*." *Horizons in Biblical Theology* 2 (1980): 127–49.

Knox, John. *Marcion and the New Testament*. Chicago: University of Chicago Press, 1942.

Koester, Helmut. "Apocryphal and Canonical Gospels." *Harvard Theological Review* 73 (1980): 105–30.

————. "*Gnōmai diaphoroi:* The Origin and Nature of Diversification in the History of Early Christianity." Pages 114–57 in *Trajectories through Early Christianity*. Edited by James M. Robinson and Helmut Koester. Philadelphia: Fortress, 1971.

————. "The Intention and Scope of Trajectories." Pages 269–79 in *Trajectories through Early Christianity*. Edited by James M. Robinson and Helmut Koester. Philadelphia: Fortress, 1971.

————. *Synoptische Überlieferung bei den apostolischen Vätern*. Texte und Untersuchungen 65. Berlin: Akadamie Verlag, 1957.

————. "The Text of the Synoptic Gospels in the Second Century." Pages 19–37 in *Gospel Traditions in the Second Century: Origins, Recensions, Text, and Transmission*. Edited by W. L. Petersen. Notre Dame, Ind.: University of Notre Dame Press, 1989.

————. "Writings and the Spirit: Authority and Politics in Ancient Christianity." *Harvard Theological Review* 84 (1991): 353–72.

Kohler, W.-D. *Die Rezeption des Matthäusevangeliums in der Zeit vor Irenaeus*. Wissenschaftliche Untersuchungen zum Neuen Testament. Second series 24. Tübingen: Mohr/Siebeck, 1987.

Kooij, A. van der. "The Canonization of Ancient Books Kept in the Temple of Jerusalem." Pages 17–40 in *Canonization and Decanonization: Papers Presented to the International Conference of the Leiden Institute for the Study of Religions (LISOR) Held at Leiden 9–10 January 1997*. Edited by A. van der Kooij and K. van der Toorn. Leiden: Brill, 1998.

Kooij, A. van der, and K. van der Toorn. *Canonization and Decanonization: Papers Presented to the International Conference of the Leiden Institute for the Study of Religions (LISOR) Held at Leiden 9–10 January 1997*. Leiden: Brill, 1998.

Kortner, U. H. J. *Papias von Hierapolis: Ein Beitrag zur Geschichte des frühen Christentums*. Forschungen zur Religion und Literatur des Alten und Neuen Testaments 133. Göttingen: Vandenhoeck & Ruprecht, 1983.

Kraemer, David. "The Formation of the Rabbinic Canon: Authority and Boundaries." *Journal of Biblical Literature* 110 (1991): 613–30.

Kuck, D. W. "The Use and Canonization of Acts in the Early Church." Thesis, Yale University, 1975.

Kümmel, W. G. "The Formation of the Canon of the New Testament." Pages 475–510 in *Introduction to the New Testament*. Edited by W. G. Kümmel. Translated by H. C. Kee. London: SCM, 1975.

Kurtzinger, J. *Papias von Hierapolis und die Evangelien des Neuen Testaments*. Regensberg: Pustet, 1983.

Lake, Kirsopp. "The Sinaitic and Vaticanus Manuscripts and the Copies Sent by Eusebius to Constantine." *Harvard Theological Review* 11 (1918): 32–35.

Le Boulluec, Alain. "The Bible in Use among the Marginally Orthodox in the Second and Third Centuries." Pages 197–216 in *The Bible in Greek Christian Antiquity*. Edited by P. M. Blowers. Notre Dame, Ind.: University of Notre Dame Press, 1997.

Lea, T. D. "The Early Christian View of Pseudepigraphic Writings." *Journal of the Evangelical Theological Society* 27 (1984): 65–75.

Leiman, Sid Z. *The Canon and Masorah of the Hebrew Bible: An Introductory Reader*. New York: KTAV, 1974.

———. *The Canonization of the Hebrew Scripture: The Talmudic and Midrashic Evidence*. Hamden, Conn: Archon, 1976.

———. "Inspiration and Canonicity: Reflections on the Formation of the Biblical Canon." Pages 56–63 in vol. 2 of *Jewish and Christian Self-Definition*. Edited by E. P. Sanders, A. I. Baumgarten, and Alan Mendelson. Philadelphia: Fortress, 1981.

———. "Josephus and the Canon of the Bible." Pages in 50–58 in *Josephus, the Bible, and History*. Edited by Louis H. Feldman and Gohei Hata. Detroit: Wayne State University Press, 1989.

Lemcio, Eugene. "The Gospels and Canonical Criticism." *Biblical Theology Bulletin* 11 (1981): 114–22.

Lewis, Jack P. "What Do We Mean by Jabneh?" *Journal of Bible and Religion* 32 (1964): 125–32.

Lienhard, Joseph T. *The Bible, the Church, and Authority: The Canon of the Christian Bible in History and Theology*. Collegeville, Minn.: Liturgical Press/Michael Glazier, 1995.

Lietzmann, H. "Wie wurden die Bucher des Neuen Testaments Heilige Schrift?" Pages 15–98 in *Kleine Schriften*, vol. 2. Edited by K. Aland. Texte und Untersuchungen 68. Berlin: Akademie, 1907.

Lightstone, Jack N. "The Formation of the Biblical Canon in Judaism of Late Antiquity: Prolegomenon to a General Reassessment." *Studies in Religion* 8 (1979): 135–42.

———. "Mishnah's Rhetoric, Other Material Artifacts of Late-Roman Galilee, and the Social Formation of the Early Rabbinic Guild." Pages 474–504 in *Text and Artifact in the Religions of Mediterranean Antiquity: Essays in Honour of Peter Richardson.* Edited by S. Wilson and M. Desjardins. Studies in Christianity and Judaism. Waterloo: WLU Press, 2000.

———. *Society, the Sacred, and Scripture in Ancient Judaism: A Sociology of Knowledge.* Studies in Christianity and Judaism 3. Waterloo: WLU Press, 1988.

Lindemann, A. *Paulus im ältesten Christentum: Das Bild des Apostels und die Rezeption der paulinischen Theologie in der frühchristlichen Literatur bis Markion.* Beiträge zur historischen Theologie 58. Tübingen: Mohr/Siebeck, 1979.

Link, H.-G. "Der Kanon in ökumenischer Sicht." *Jahrbuch für biblische Theologie* 3 (1988): 83–96.

Logan, Alastair H. B. *Gnostic Truth and Christian Heresy: A Study in the History of Gnosticism.* Edinburgh: T&T Clark, 1996.

Lohr, W. A. "Kanonsgeschichtliche Beobachtungen zum Verhältnis von mundlicher und schriftlicher Tradition im zweiten Jahrhundert." *Zeitschrift für die neutestamentliche Wissenschaft und die Kunde der älteren Kirche* 85 (1994): 234–58.

Lovering, E. H. "The Collection, Redaction, and Early Circulation of the Corpus Paulinum." Ph.D. diss., Southern Methodist University, 1988.

Luhrmann, D. "Gal. 2.9 und die katholischen Briefe." *Zeitschrift für die neutestamentliche Wissenschaft und die Kunde der älteren Kirche* 72 (1981): 65–87.

Luttikhuizen, Gerard P. "The Thought Patterns of Gnostic Mythologizers and Their Use of Biblical Traditions." Pages 89–101 in *The Nag Hammadi Library after Fifty Years: Proceedings of the 1995 Society of Biblical Literature Commemoration.* Edited by J. D. Turner and A. McGuire. Leiden: Brill, 1997.

Maccoby, Hyam. *Early Rabbinic Writings.* Cambridge Commentaries on Writings of the Jewish & Christian World, 200 BC to AD 200. Cambridge: Cambridge University Press, 1988.

MacGregor, Geddes. *The Bible in the Making.* London: John Murray, 1961.

Maier, G., ed. *Der Kanon der Bibel.* Giessen: Brunnen, 1990.

Maier, J. "Zur Frage des biblischen Kanons im Frühjudentum im Licht der Qumranfunde." *Jahrbuch für biblische Theologie* 3 (1988): 135–46.

Malamat, A. "A Forerunner of Biblical Prophecy: The Mari Documents." Pages 33–52 in *Ancient Israelite Religion: Essays in Honor of Frank Moore Cross.* Edited by P. D. Miller, P. D. Hanson, and S. D. McBride. Philadelphia: Westminster, 1987.

Margolis, M. L. *The Hebrew Scriptures in the Making.* Philadelphia: Jewish Publication Society, 1922.

Marxen, Willi. *The New Testament as the Church's Book.* Translated by James E. Mignard. Philadelphia: Fortress, 1972.

Mason, Steve. "Josephus on Canon and Scriptures." Pages 217–35 in vol. 1, part 1 of *Hebrew Bible / Old Testament: The History of Its Interpretation.* Edited by Magne Saebo. Göttingen: Vandenhoeck & Ruprecht, 1996.

———. *Josephus and the New Testament.* Peabody, Mass.: Hendrickson, 1992.

McArthur, H. K. "The Eusebian Sections and Canons." *Catholic Biblical Quarterly* 27 (1965): 250–56.

McDonald, Lee M. "Canon (of Scripture)." Pages 169–73 in *Encyclopedia of Early Christianity*. Edited by E. Ferguson. New York: Garland, 1990.

———. "The First Testament: Its Origin, Adaptability, and Stability." Pages 287–326 in *The Quest for Context and Meaning: Studies in Biblical Intertextuality in Honor of James A Sanders*. Edited by C. A. Evans and S. Talmon. Biblical Interpretation Series 28. Leiden: Brill, 1997.

———. *The Formation of the Christian Biblical Canon*. 2d ed. Peabody, Mass.: Hendrickson, 1995.

———. "The Origins of the Christian Biblical Canon." *Bulletin for Biblical Research* 6 (1996): 95–132.

Meade, David G. *Pseudonymity and Canon: An Investigation into the Relationship of Authorship and Authority in Jewish and Earliest Christian Tradition*. Grand Rapids, Mich.: Eerdmans, 1986.

Meecham, Henry G. *The Letter of Aristeas*. Manchester: Manchester University Press, 1935.

———. *The Oldest Version of the Bible*. London: Holborn, 1932.

Metzger, Bruce M. "Canon of the New Testament." Pages 123–27 in *Hastings Dictionary of the Bible*. 2d ed. Edited by F. C. Grant and H. H. Rowley. Edinburgh: T&T Clark, 1963.

———. *The Canon of the New Testament: Its Origin, Development, and Significance*. Oxford: Clarendon, 1987.

———. "Literary Forgeries and Canonical Pseudepigrapha." *Journal of Biblical Literature* 91 (1972): 3–24.

———. "Seventy or Seventy-Two Disciples." *New Testament Studies* 5 (1959): 299–306.

Meuer, Siegfried, ed. *The Apocrypha in Ecumenical Perspective*. UBS Monograph Series 6. Translated by P. Ellingworth. New York: United Bible Societies, 1991.

Meyer, Rudolf. "Supplement on the Canon and the Apocrypha." Pages 978–87 in vol. 3 of *Theological Dictionary of the New Testament*. Edited by G. Kittel and G. Friedrich. Translated by G. W. Bromiley. 10 vols. Grand Rapids, Mich.: Eerdmans, 1964–1976.

———. "*Prophētēs, ktl.*" Pages 812–28 in vol. 6 of *Theological Dictionary of the New Testament*. Edited by G. Kittel and G. Friedrich. Translated by G. W. Bromiley. 10 vols. Grand Rapids, Mich.: Eerdmans, 1964–1976.

Miller, J. W. *The Origins of the Bible: Rethinking Canon History*. Theological Inquiries. New York: Paulist, 1994.

Miller, Patricia Cox. "Words with an Alien Voice: Gnostics, Scripture, and Canon." *Journal of the American Academy of Religion* 57 (1989): 459–83.

Miller, P. D. "Der Kanon in der gegenwärtigen amerikanischen Diskussion." *Jahrbuch für biblische Theologie* 3 (1988): 217–39.

Moore, George F. "The Definition of the Jewish Canon and the Repudiation of Christian Scriptures." Pages 99–125 in *The Canon and Masorah of the New Hebrew Bible*. Edited by Sid Z. Leiman. New York: KTAV, 1974.

Morgan, Don F. *Between Text and Community: The 'Writings' in Canonical Interpretation*. Minneapolis: Fortress, 1990.

———. "Canon and Criticism: Method or Madness?" *Australasian Theological Review* 68 (1986): 83–94.

Morgan, R. L. "Let's Be Honest about the Canon: A Plea to Reconsider a Question the Reformers Failed to Answer." *Christian Century* 84 (1967): 717–19.

Murphy, R. E. "A Symposium on the Canon of Scripture: 1. The Old Testament Canon in the Catholic Church." *Catholic Biblical Quarterly* 28 (1966): 189–93.

Murray, Robert. "How Did the Church Determine the Canon of the New Testament?" *Heythrop Journal* 11 (1970): 115–26.

Neusner, Jacob. "The Formation of Rabbinic Judaism: Yavneh (Jamnia) from A.D. 70–100." Pages 3–42 in *Aufstieg und Niedergang der Römischen Welt: Geschichte und Kultur Roms im Spiegel der Neueren Forschung* 2.2. Edited by Wolfgang Haase. Berlin: Walter de Gruyter, 1979.

———. *Judaism and Christianity in the Age of Constantine: History, Messiah, Israel, and the Initial Confrontation.* Chicago: University of Chicago Press, 1987.

———. "The Mishnah in Philosophical Context and out of Canonical Bounds." *Journal of Biblical Literature* 112 (1993): 291–304.

———. *The Oral Torah: The Sacred Books of Judaism: An Introduction.* San Francisco: Harper & Row, 1986.

———. "Rabbinic Judaism in Late Antiquity." Pages 72–84 in *Judaism: A People and Its History.* Edited by Robert M. Seltzer. New York: Macmillan, 1989.

———. *Torah: From Scroll to Symbol in Formative Judaism.* Philadelphia: Fortress, 1985.

Neusner, Jacob, and W. S. Green. *Writing with Scripture: The Authority and Uses of the Hebrew Bible in the Torah of Formative Judaism.* Minneapolis: Fortress, 1989.

Niditch, Susan. *Oral Word and Written Word.* Library of Ancient Israel. Nashville: Westminster John Knox, 1996.

Nordenfalk, Carl. "The Apostolic Canon Tables." *Gazette des beaux–arts* 62 (1963): 17–34.

Ohlig, K.-H. *Woher nimmt die Bibel ihre Autorität? Zum Verhältnis von Schriftkanon, Kirche und Jesus.* Düsseldorf: Patmos Verlag, 1970.

———. *Die theologische Begründung des neutestamentlichen Kanons in der alten Kirche.* Düsseldorf: Patmos Verlag, 1972.

Oliver, William G. "Origen and the New Testament Canon." *Restoration Quarterly* 31 (1989): 13–26.

O'Neill, J. C. "The Lost Written Records of Jesus' Words and Deeds Behind Our Records." *Journal of Theological Studies* 42 (1991): 483–503.

Orlinsky, Harry M. "Some Terms in the Prologue to Ben Sira and the Hebrew Canon." *Journal of Biblical Literature* 110 (1991): 483–90.

Osiek, C. "The Shepherd of Hermas: An Early Tale That Almost Made It into the New Testament." *Bible Review* 10 (1994): 48–54.

Outler, A. C. "The 'Logic' of Canon Making and the Tasks of Canon-Criticism." Pages 263–76 in *Texts and Testaments: Critical Essays on the Bible and the Early Church Fathers.* Edited by W. E. March. San Antonio: Trinity University Press, 1980.

Pagels, E. "Visions, Appearances and Apostolic Authority: Gnostic and Orthodox Traditions." Pages 415–30 in *Gnosis: Festschrift für Hans Jonas.* Edited by B. Aland. Göttingen: Vandenhoeck & Ruprecht, 1978.

Painchaud, Louis. "The Use of Scripture in Gnostic Literature." *Journal of Early Christian Studies* 4 (1996): 129–47.

Patterson, L. G. "Irenaeus and the Valentinians: The Emergence of the Christian Scriptures." Pages 189–220 in *Studia Patristica* 18.3. Edited by E. A. Livingstone. Leuven: Peeters, 1989.

Patzia, Arthur G. "Canon." Pages 85–92 in *Dictionary of Paul and His Letters*. Edited by G. F. Hawthorne and R. P. Martin. Downers Grove, Ill.: InterVarsity, 1993.

———. "The Deutero-Pauline Hypothesis: An Attempt at Clarification." *Evangelical Quarterly* 52 (1980): 27–42.

———. *The Making of the New Testament: Origin, Collection, Text and Canon*. Downers Grove, Ill.: InterVarsity, 1995.

Paulsen, Henning. "Die Bedeutung des Montanismus für die Herausbildung des Kanons." *Vigiliae christianae* 32 (1978): 19–52.

Pearson, Birger A. "Gnostic Interpretation of the Old Testament in the *Testimony of Truth* (NHC IX,3)." *Harvard Theological Review* 73 (1980): 311–19.

———. *Gnosticism, Judaism, and Egyptian Christianity*. Minneapolis: Fortress, 1990.

———. "Use, Authority and Exegesis of Miqra in Gnostic Literature." Pages 635–52 in *Mikra: Text, Translation, Reading and Interpretation of the Hebrew Bible*. Edited by Martin J. Mulder and Harry Sysling. Compendia rerum iudaicarum ad Novum Testamentum 2.1. Philadelphia: Fortress, 1988.

Perkins, Pheme. "Spirit and Letter: Poking Holes in the Canon." *Journal of Religion* 76 (1996): 307–27.

Petersen, W. L. "The Diatessaron of Tatian." Pages 512–34 in *The Text of the New Testament in Recent Research*. Edited by B. Ehrman and M. W. Holmes. Grand Rapids, Mich.: Eerdmans, 1995.

———. *Tatian's Diatessaron: Its Creation, Dissemination, Significance and History in Scholarship*. Leiden: Brill, 1994.

———. "Textual Evidence of Tatian's Dependence upon Justin's 'APOMNEMONEU-MATA.'" *New Testament Studies* 36 (1990): 512–34.

Pfeiffer, R. H. "Canon of the OT." Pages 498–520 in vol. 1 of *The Interpreter's Dictionary of the Bible*. Edited by G. A. Buttrick. New York: Abingdon, 1962.

Pilhofer, P. "Justin und das Petrusevangelium." *Zeitschrift für die neutestamentliche Wissenschaft und die Kunde der älteren Kirche* 81 (1990): 60–78.

Porter, S. E. "Pauline Authorship and the Pastoral Epistles: Implications for Canon." *Bulletin for Biblical Research* 5 (1995): 105–23.

Price, R. M. "The Evolution of the Pauline Canon." *Hervormde teologiese studies* 53 (1997): 36–67.

Quinn, J. D. "P[46]—The Pauline Canon?" *Catholic Biblical Quarterly* 36 (1974): 379–85.

Quispel, G. "Marcion and the Text of the New Testament." *Vigiliae christianae* 52 (1998): 349–60.

Rendtorff, Rolf. *Canon and Theology: Overtures to an Old Testament Theology*. Overture to Biblical Theology. Minneapolis: Fortress, 1993.

Resnick, Irven M. "The Codex in Early Jewish and Christian Communities." *Journal of Religious History* 17 (1992): 1–17.

Reuss, Edward W. *History of the Canon of the Holy Scriptures in the Christian Church*. Translated by David Hunter. Edinburgh: R. W. Hunter, 1891.

Richards, E. Randolph. "The Codex and the Early Collection of Paul's Letters." *Bulletin for Biblical Research* 8 (1998): 151–66.

———. *The Secretary in the Letters of Paul*. Wissenschaftliche Untersuchungen zum Neuen Testament. Second series 42. Tübingen: Mohr/Siebeck, 1991.

Rist, M. "Pseudepigraphy and the Early Christians." Pages 75–91 in *Studies in New Testament and Early Christian Literature: Essays in Honor of Allen P. Wikgren.* Edited by D. E. Aune. Novum Testamentum Supplement 33. Leiden: Brill, 1972.

Ritter, A. M. "Die Entstehung des neutestamentlichen Kanons: Selbstdurchsetzung oder autoritative Entscheidung?" Pages 93–99 in vol. 2 of *Kanon und Zensur: Beiträge zur Archäologie der literarischen Kommunikation.* Edited by A. Assman and J. Assmann. Munich: Fink, 1987.

Robbins, Gregory Allen. "Muratorian Fragment." Pages 928–29 in vol. 4 of *Anchor Bible Dictionary.* Edited by D. N. Freedman. 6 vols. New York: Doubleday, 1992.

―――. "Eusebius' Lexicon of 'Canonicity.'" Pages 134–41 in *Studia Patristica* 19. Edited by E. A. Livingstone. Leuven: Peeters, 1993.

―――. " 'Fifty Copies of Sacred Writings' (*VC* 4.36): Entire Bibles or Gospel Books?" Pages 91–98 in *Studia Patristica* 19. Edited by E. A. Livingstone. Leuven: Peeters, 1989.

―――. "*Peri tōn endiathēkōn graphōn:* Eusebius and the Formation of the Christian Bible" Ph.D. diss., Duke University, 1986.

Roberts, B. J. "The Old Testament Canon: A Suggestion." *Bulletin of the John Rylands University Library of Manchester* 46 (1963–1964): 164–78.

Roberts, C. H. "Books in the Greco-Roman World and in the New Testament." Pages 48–66 in vol. 1 of *Cambridge History of the Bible.* Edited by P. R. Ackroyd and C. F. Evans. Cambridge: Cambridge University Press, 1970.

―――. "The Christian Book and the Greek Papri." *Journal of Theological Studies* 50 (1949): 155–68.

―――. *Manuscript, Society, and Belief in Early Christian Egypt.* London: Oxford University Press, 1979.

Roberts, C. H., and T. C. Skeat. *The Birth of the Codex.* Oxford: Oxford University Press, 1983.

Ruwet, J. "Clement d'Alexandrie: Canon des écritures et apocryphes." *Biblica* 29 (1948): 77–99, 240–68, 391–408.

Ryle, H. E. *The Canon of the Old Testament.* 2d ed. London: Macmillan, 1904.

Saebo, Magne. *On the Way to Canon: Creative Tradition History in the OT.* Journal for the Study of the Old Testament: Supplement Series 191. Sheffield: Sheffield Academic Press, 1998.

Saldarini, Anthony. "Within Context: The Judaism Contemporary with Jesus." Pages 21–40 in *Within Context: Essays on Jews and Judaism in the New Testament.* Edited by D. P. Efroymson, E. J. Fisher, and L. Klenicki. Collegeville, Minn.: Liturgical, 1993.

Sand, A. "*Kanōn.*" Page 249 in vol. 2 of *Exegetical Dictionary of the New Testament.* Edited by H. Balz and G. Schneider. Grand Rapids, Mich.: Eerdmans, 1990–1993.

Sanders, James A. "Adaptable for Life: The Nature and Function of Canon." Pages 531–60 in *Magnalia Dei: The Mighty Acts of God: Essays on the Bible and Archaeology in Memory of G. E. Wright.* New York: Doubleday, 1976.

―――. "Biblical Criticism and the Bible as Canon." *Union Seminary Quarterly Review* 32 (1977): 157–65.

―――. *Canon and Community: A Guide to Canonical Criticism.* Philadelphia: Fortress, 1984.

———. "Canon. Hebrew Bible." Pages 837–52 in vol. 1 of *The Anchor Bible Dictionary.* Edited by D. N. Freedman. 6 vols. New York: Doubleday, 1992.

———. "Canonical Context and Canonical Criticism." *Horizons in Biblical Theology* 2 (1980): 173–97.

———. "Canon as Shape and Function." Pages 87–97 in *The Promise and Practice of Biblical Theology.* Edited by J. Reumann. Minneapolis: Fortress, 1991.

———. "Cave 11 Surprises and the Question of Canon." *McCormick Quarterly* 21 (1968): 284–317.

———. "Deuteronomy." Pages 89–102 in *The Books of the Bible.* Vol. 1 of *The Old Testament/The Hebrew Bible.* Edited by B. W. Anderson. New York: Scribner's, 1989.

———. *From Sacred Story to Sacred Text.* Philadelphia: Fortress, 1987.

———. "Intertexuality and Canon." Pages 316–33 in *On the Way to Nineveh: Studies in Honor of George M. Landes.* Edited by S. Cook and S. Winter. Atlanta: Scholars Press, 1999.

———. "Palestinian Manuscripts 1947–72." *Journal of Jewish Studies* 24 (1973): 74–83.

———. "Scripture as Canon for Post-Modern Times." *Biblical Theology Bulletin* 25 (1995): 56–63.

———. "Scripture as Canon in the Church." Pages 121–43 in *L'interpretazione della Bibbia nella chiesa: Atti del Simposio promosso dalla Congregazione per la dottrina della fede, Roma, Settembre 1999.* Città del Vaticano: Libreria editrice vaticana, 2001.

———. "The Scrolls and the Canonical Process." Pages 1–23 in vol. 2 of *The Dead Sea Scrolls after Fifty Years: A Comprehensive Assessment.* Edited by P. Flint and J. VanderKam. Leiden: Brill, 1999.

———. "Spinning the Bible." *Biblical Research* (June 1998): 22–29, 44–45.

———. "Stability and Fluidity in Text and Canon." Pages 203–17 in *Traditions of the Text: Studies Offered to Dominique Barthélemy in Celebration of His 70th Birthday.* Edited by G. Norton and S. Pisano. Göttingen: Vandenhoech & Ruprecht, 1991.

———. "Text and Canon: Concepts and Method." *Journal of Biblical Literature* 98 (1979): 1–20.

———. "Text and Canon: Old Testament and New." Pages 373–94 in *Melanges Dominique Barthelemy: Etudes bibliques.* Edited by Pierre Casetti, Othmar Keel, and Adrian Scheuber. Orbis biblicus et orientalis 38. Freiburg: Editions Universitaires, 1981.

———. *Torah and Canon.* Philadelphia: Fortress, 1972.

Sanders, James N. "The Literature and Canon of the New Testament." Pages 676–82 in *Peake's Commentary of the Bible.* Edited by M. Black and H. H. Rowley. London: Thomas Nelson and Sons, 1962.

Sandmel, Samuel. "A Symposium on the Canon of Scripture: 3. On Canon." *Catholic Biblical Quarterly* 28 (1966): 203–7.

Scanlin, Harold P. "What is the Canonical Shape of the Old Testament Text We Translate?" Pages 207–20 in *Issues in Bible Translation.* Edited by Philip C. Stine. UBS Monograph Series 3. London: United Bible Societies, 1988.

Schlossnikel, R. F. *Bedeutung im Rahmen von Text- und Kanongeschichte. Vetus Latina: Die Reste der altlateinischen Bibel 20.* Edited by E. Beuron. Freiburg: Herder, 1991.

———. *Der Brief an die Hebräer und das Corpus Paulinum: Eine linguistische 'Bruchstelle' im Codex Claromontanus.* Paris: Bibliothèque Nationale grec 107 + 107A + 107B, 1991.

Schmidt, H.-C. "Das Spätdeuteronomistische Geschichtswerk Genesis I–2. Regum XXV und seine theologische Intention." Pages 261–79 in *Congress Volume: Cambridge 1995*. Edited by J. A. Emerton. Vetus Testamentum Supplement 66. Leiden: Brill, 1997.

Schnabel, Eckhard. "History, Theology, and the Biblical Canon: An Introduction to Basic Issues." *Themelios* 20 (1995): 16–24.

Schneemelcher, W. "General Introduction." Pages 9–69 in *New Testament Apocrypha*. Revised Edition. Edited by Wilhelm Schneemelcher. Translated by R. McL. Wilson. Cambridge: James Clarke, 1991. Translated from *Neutestamentliche Apokryphen*. Tübingen: J.C.B. Mohr (Paul Siebeck), 1990.

———, ed. *New Testament Apocrypha*. Translated by R. McL. Wilson. 2d ed. 2 vols. Louisville, Ky.: Westminster John Knox, 1991–1992.

Schnelle, U. *The History and Theology of the New Testament Writings*. Minneapolis: Fortress, 1998.

Schoedel, William R. "Papias." Pages 235–70 in *Aufstieg und Niedergang der römischen Welt: Geschichte und Kultur Roms im Spiegel der neueren Forschung* 2.27.1. Edited by H. Temporini and W. Haase. Berlin: Walter de Gruyter, 1998.

———. "Scripture and the Seventy-two Heavens of the First Apocalypse of James." *Novum Testamentem* 12 (1970): 118–29.

Schrenk, Gottlob. "*Graphē*." Pages 742–73 in vol. 1 of *Theological Dictionary of the New Testament*. Edited by G. Kittel and G. Friedrich. Translated by G. W. Bromiley. 10 vols. Grand Rapids, Mich.: Eerdmans, 1964–1976.

Schweizer, Eduard. "Kanon?" *Evangelische Theologie* 31 (1971): 339–57.

Sheppard, Gerald T. "Canon." Pages 62–69 in vol. 3 of *The Encyclopedia of Religion*. Edited by Mircea Eliade. 16 vols. New York: Macmillan, 1987.

———. "Canonical Criticism." Pages 861–66 in vol. 1 of *Anochor Bible Dictionary*. Edited by D. N. Freedman. 6 vols. New York: Doubleday, 1992.

———. "Canonization: Hearing the Voice of the Same God through Historically Dissimilar Traditions." *Interpretation* 37 (1982): 21–33.

Shires, Henry M. *Finding the Old Testament in the New*. Philadelphia: Westminster, 1974.

Silberman, Lou H. "The Making of the Old Testament Canon." Pages 1209–15 in *The Interpreter's One-Volume Commentary on the Bible*. Edited by Charles M. Laymon. New York: Abingdon, 1971.

Silver, Daniel Jeremy. *The Story of Scripture: From Oral Tradition to the Written Word*. New York: Basic, 1990.

Skarsaune, O. *The Proof from Prophecy: A Study in Justin Martyr's Proof-Text Tradition: Text-Type, Provenance, Theological Profile*. Novum Testamentum Supplement 56. Leiden: Brill, 1987.

Skeat, T. C. "The Codex Sinaiticus, The Codex Vaticanus, and Constantine." *Journal of Theological Studies* 50 (1999): 583–625.

———. "A Codicological Analysis of the Chester Beatty Papyrus Codex of Gospels and Acts (P[45])." *Hermathena* 155 (1993): 27–43.

———. "Irenaeus and the Four-Gospel Canon." *Novum Testamentem* 34 (1992): 194–99.

———. "The Oldest Manuscript of the Four Gospels." *New Testament Studies* 43 (1997): 1–34.

———. "The Origin of the Christian Codex." *Zeitschrift für Papyrologie und Epigraphik* 102 (1994): 263–68.

Smend, Rudolf. "Questions about the Importance of Canon in the Old Testament Introduction." *Journal for the Study of the Old Testament* 16 (1980): 45–51.

Smith, D. Moody. "When Did the Gospels Become Scripture?" *Journal of Biblical Literature* 119 (2000): 3–20.

———. "Why Approaching the New Testament as Canon Matters." *Interpretation* 40 (1986): 407–11.

Souter, Alexander. *The Text and Canon of the New Testament*. New York: Charles Scribner's Sons, 1917.

Sparks, H. F. D. *The Formation of the New Testament*. London: SCM, 1952.

———. "Canon of the Old Testament." Pages 121–23 in *Hastings Dictionary of the Bible*. Edited by F. C. Grant and H. H. Rowley. 2d ed. Edinburgh: T&T Clark, 1963.

Spina, Frank A. "Canonical Criticism: Childs versus Sanders." Pages 165–94 in *Interpreting God's Word for Today: An Inquiry into Hermeneutics from a Biblical Theological Perspective*. Edited by W. McCown and J. E. Massey. Anderson, Ind.: Warner, 1982.

Steck, O. H. *Der Abschluss der Prophetie im Alten Testament: Ein Versuch zur Frage der Vorgeschichte des Kanons*. Biblisch-theologische Studien 17. Neukirchen-Vluyn: Neukirchener, 1991.

———. "Der Kanon des hebräischen Alten Testaments." Pages 231–52 in *Vernunft des Glaubens: Wissenschaftliche Theologie und kirchliche Lehre*. Edited by J. Rohls and G. Wenz. Göttingen: Vandenhoeck & Ruprecht, 1988.

Steinmann, Andrew E. *Oracles of God: The Old Testament Canon*. St. Louis, Mo.: Concordia, 1999.

Stendahl, Krister. "Ancient Scripture in the Modern World." Pages 201–14 in *Scripture in the Jewish and Christian Traditions*. Edited by F. E. Greenspahn. Nashville: Abingdon, 1982.

———. "The Apocalypse of John and the Epistles of Paul in the Muratorian Fragment." Pages 239–45 in *Current Issues in New Testament Interpretation*. Edited by W. Klassen and G. F. Snyder. New York: Harper & Row, 1962.

———. "The Formation of the Canon: The Apocalypse of John and the Epistles of Paul in the Muratorian Fragment." Pages 239–45 in *Current Issues in New Testament Interpretation: Essays in Honor of Otto A. Piper*. Edited by W. Klassen and G. F. Snyder. London: SCM, 1962.

———. *Meanings*. Philadelphia: Fortress, 1984.

Streeter, B. H. *The Four Gospels: A Study of Origins Treating of the Manuscript Tradition, Sources, Authorship and Date*. London: MacMillan, 1924.

Stuart, Moses. *A Critical History of the Old Testament Canon*. London: George Routledge, 1849.

Stuhlhofer, Franz. *Der Gebrauch der Bibel von Jesus bis Euseb: Eine statistische Untersuchung zur Kanongeschichte*. Wuppertal: R. Brockhaus, 1988.

Sundberg, Albert C., Jr. "The Bible Canon and the Christian Doctrine of Inspiration." *Interpretation* 29 (1975): 352–71.

———. "Canon Muratori: A Fourth-Century List." *Harvard Theological Review* 66 (1973): 1–41.

———. "Canon of the NT." Pages 136–40 in *Interpreter's Dictionary of the Bible: Supplementary Volume*. Edited by Keith Crim. Nashville: Abingdon, 1976.

———. "Dependent Canonicity in Irenaeus and Tertullian." Pages 403–9 in *Studia evangelica III*. Texte und Untersuchungen 88. Berlin: Akademie-Verlag, 1964.

―――. "The Making of the New Testament Canon." Pages 1216–24 in *The Interpreter's One-Volume Commentary on the Bible*. Edited by Charles M. Laymon. New York: Abingdon, 1971.

―――. "The Old Testament: A Christian Canon." *Catholic Biblical Quarterly* 30 (1968): 403–9.

―――. "The Old Testament of the Early Church." *Harvard Theological Review* 51 (1958): 205–26.

―――. *The Old Testament of the Early Church*. Cambridge: Harvard University Press, 1964.

―――. " 'The Old Testament of the Early Church' Revisited." *Festschrift in Honor of Charles Speel*. Edited by T. J. Seinkewicz and J. E. Betts. Monmouth, Ill.: Monmouth College Press, 1996.

―――. "A Symposium on the Canon of Scripture: 2. The Protestant Old Testament Canon: Should It Be Re-examined?" *Catholic Biblical Quarterly* 28 (1966): 194–203.

―――. "Toward a Revised History of the New Testament Canon." Pages 452–61 in *Studia evangelica IV*. Texte und Untersuchungen 89. Berlin: Akademie-Verlag, 1964.

Swanson, T. N. *The Closing of the Collection of Holy Scripture: A Study in the History of the Canonization of the Old Testament*. Ph.D. diss., Vanderbilt University, 1970.

Swarat, U. *Alte Kirche und Neues Testament: Theodor Zahn als Patristiker*. Wuppertal: Brockhaus, 1991.

Swete, H. B. *An Introduction to the Old Testament in Greek*. Revised by R. R. Ottley. Cambridge: Cambridge University Press, 1914. Repr., Peabody, Mass.: Hendrickson, 1989.

Talmon, S. "Heiliges Schrifttum und kanonische Bücher aus jüdischer Sicht: Überlegungen zur Ausbildung der Grösse 'Die Schrift' im Judentum." Pages 45–79 in *Mitte der Schrift? Ein jüdisch-christliches Gespräch: Texte des Berner Symposions vom 6.–12. January 1985*. Edited by M. Klopfenstein et al. Judaica et christiana 11. Bern: Peter Lang, 1987.

Theobald, C., ed. *Le canon des Ecritures: Etudes historiques, exégétiques et systématiques*. Lectio divina 140. Paris: Cerf, 1990.

Theron, Daniel J. *Evidence of Tradition*. Grand Rapids, Mich.: Baker, 1980.

Toit, Andrie B. du. "Canon: New Testament." Pages 102–4 in *The Oxford Companion to the Bible*. Edited by Bruce M. Metzger and M. D. Coogan. New York: Oxford University Press, 1993.

Topping, R. R. "The Canon and the Truth: Brevard Childs and James Barr on the Canon and the Historical Critical Method." *Toronto Journal of Theology* 8 (1992): 239–60.

Tov, Emanuel. *The Septuagint Translation of Jeremiah and Baruch*. Missoula, Mont.: Scholars Press, 1976.

―――. *Textual Criticism of the Hebrew Bible*. Minneapolis: Fortress, 1992.

Towner, W. Sibley. "Daniel 1 in the Context of Canon." Pages 285–98 in *Canon, Theology, and Old Testament Interpretation: Essays in Honor of Brevard S. Childs*. Edited by Gene M. Tucker, David L. Peterson, and Robert R. Wilson. Philadelphia: Fortress, 1988.

Trobisch, David. *Die Endredaktion des Neuen Testaments: Eine Untersuchung zur Entstehung der christlichen Bibel*. Novum Testamentum et Orbis Antiquus 31. Freiburg: Universitätsverlag, 1996.

―――. *Die Entstehung des Paulusbriefsammlung: Studien zu den Anfangen christlicher Publizistik*. Novum Testamentum et Orbis Antiquus 10. Göttingen: Vandenhoeck & Ruprecht, 1989.

———. *Paul's Letter Collection: Tracing the Origins.* Philadelphia: Fortress, 1994.

Tucker, Gene M. "Prophetic Superscriptions and the Growth of a Canon." Pages 56–70 in *Canon and Authority: Essays in Old Testament Religion and Theology.* Edited by G. W. Coats and B. O. Long. Philadelphia: Fortress, 1977.

Tuckett, C. M. "Synoptic Tradition in the Gospel of Truth and the Testimony of Truth." *Journal of Theological Studies* 35 (1984): 131–45.

Turner, C. H. "Appendix to W. Sanday's Article: 'The Cheltenham List of the Canonical Books, and the Writings of Cyprian.'" *Studia Biblica* 3 (1891): 304–25.

———. "Latin Lists of the Canonical Books: 3. From Pope Innocent's Epistle to Exsuperius of Toulouse (A.D. 405)." *Journal of Theological Studies* 13 (1911–1912): 77–82.

Ulrich, Ernst. "Inspiration, Normativeness, Canonicity, and the Unique Sacred Character of the Bible." *Catholic Biblical Quarterly* 44 (1982): 447–69.

Ulrich, Eugene. "The Bible in the Making: The Scriptures at Qumran." Pages 77–93 in *The Community of the Renewed Covenant.* Edited by E. Ulrich and J. VanderKam. Christianity and Judaism in Antiquity 10. Notre Dame, Ind.: University of Notre Dame Press, 1994.

———. "Canon." Pages 117–20 in vol. 1 of *Encyclopedia of the Dead Sea Scrolls.* Edited by L. H. Schiffman and J. C. VanderKam. Oxford: Oxford University Press, 2000.

———. "The Canonical Process, Textual Criticism, and Latter Stages in the Compositon of the Bible." Pages 267–91 in *'Sha'arei Talmon': Studies in the Bible, Qumran, and the Ancient Near East Presented to Shemaryahu Talmon.* Edited by M. Fishbane and E. Tov with the assistance of W. W. Fields. Winona Lake, Ind.: Eisenbrauns, 1992.

———. "The Community of Israel and the Composition of Scriptures." Pages 327–42 in *Studies in Biblical Intertextuality in Honor of James A. Sanders.* Edited by C. A. Evans and S. Talmon. Biblical Interpretation Series 18. Leiden: Brill, 1997.

———. "The Dead Sea Scrolls and the Biblical Text." Pages 79–100 in vol. 1 of *The Dead Sea Scrolls after Fifty Years: A Comprehensive Assessment.* Edited by P. Flint and J. VanderKam. Leiden: Brill, 1998.

———. *The Dead Sea Scrolls and the Origins of the Bible.* Studies in the Dead Sea Scrolls and Related Literature. Grand Rapids, Mich.: Eerdmans, 1999.

———. "Pluriformity in the Biblical Text, Text Groups, and Questions of Canon." Pages 23–41 in *The Madrid Qumran Congress: Proceedings of the International Congress on the Dead Sea Scrolls Madrid 18–21 March, 1991.* Edited by J. Trebolle Barrera and L. Vegas Montaner. 2 vols. Studies on the Texts of the Desert of Judah 11. Leiden: Brill, 1992.

Unnick, W. C. van. "*Hē kainē diathēkē:* A Problem in the Early History of the Canon." *Studia patavina* 4 (1961): 212–27.

Urbach, E. E. "Torah." Pages 85–100 in *Judaism: A People and Its History.* Edited by Robert M. Seltzer. New York: Macmillan, 1989.

VanderKam, J. C. "Authoritative Literature in the Dead Sea Scrolls." *Dead Sea Discoveries* 5 (1998): 382–402.

———. *From Revelation to Canon: Studies in the Hebrew Bible and Second Temple Literature.* Journal for the Study of Judaism Supplement 62. Leiden: Brill, 2000.

VanderKam, J. C., and J. T. Milik. "The First *Jubilees* Manuscript from Qumran Cave 4: A Preliminary Publication." *Journal of Biblical Literature* 110 (1991): 243–70.

Vermes, Geza. *The Dead Sea Scrolls: Qumran in Perspective.* Philadelphia: Fortress, 1981.

Vokes, F. E. "The Didache and the Canon of the New Testament." Pages 427–36 of *Studia evangelica III*. Texte und Untersuchungen 88. Berlin: Akademie-Verlag, 1964.

Wainwright, Geoffrey. "The New Testament as Canon." *Scottish Journal of Theology* 28 (1975): 551–71.

Wall, Robert W. "The Acts of the Apostles in Canonical Context." *Biblical Theology Bulletin* 18 (1986): 1–31.

——. "The Canon and Christian Preaching." *The Christian Ministry* 17/5 (1986): 13–17.

——. "The Canon of the NT." *New Testament Interpretation Today*. Edited by Joel Green. Grand Rapids, Mich.: Eerdmans, forthcoming.

——. "Reading the New Testament in Canonical Context." Pages 370–93 in *Hearing the New Testament: Strategies for Interpretation*. Edited by J. B. Green. Grand Rapids, Mich.: Eerdmans, 1995.

Wall, Robert W., and Eugene Lemcio. *The New Testament as Canon: A Reader in Canonical Criticism*. Sheffield: Sheffield Academic Press, 1992.

Westcott, B. F. *A General Survey of the History of the Canon of the New Testament*. 6th ed. Cambridge: Macmillan, 1898. Repr., Grand Rapids, Mich.: Baker, 1980.

Wildeboer, G. *The Origin of the Canon of the Old Testament*. Translated by B. W. Bacon. London: Luzac, 1895.

Williams, Michael A. *Rethinking "Gnosticism": An Argument for Dismantling a Dubious Category*. Princeton, N.J.: Princeton University Press, 1996.

Wise, Michael. "The Dead Sea Scrolls: Non Biblical Manuscripts, Part 2." *Biblical Archaeologist* (December 1986): 228–39.

Yoder, J. H. "The Authority of the Canon." Pages 265–90 in *Essays on Biblical Interpretation: Anabaptist-Mennonite Perspectives*. Edited by Willard Swartley. Text-Reader Series 1. Elkhart, Ind.: Institute of Mennonite Studies, 1984.

Zahn, Theodore. *Forschungen zur Geschichte des neutestamentlichen Kanons und der altkirchlichen Literatur*. 10 vols. Leipzig: A. Deichert, 1881–1929.

——. *Geschichte des neutestamentlichen Kanons*. 2 vols. Erlangen: A. Deichert, 1888–1892.

Zeitlin, Solomon. "An Historical Study of the Canonization of Hebrew Scriptures." Pages 164–201 in *Proceedings of the American Academy for Jewish Research* 3 (1931–1932). Repr. in *The Canon and Masorah of the Hebrew Bible*. Edited by Sid Z. Leiman. New York: KTAV, 1974.

Zenger, E., ed. *Die Tora als Kanon für Juden und Christen*. Herders biblische Studien 10. Freiburg: Herder, 1996.

Zevit, Z. "The Second–Third Century Canonization of the Hebrew Bible and Its Influence on Christian Canonizing." Pages 133–60 in *Canonization and Decanonization*. Edited by A. van der Kooij and K. van der Toorn. Leiden: Brill, 1998.

Zuntz, Günther. "Aristeas Studies 2: Aristeas on the Translation of the Torah." *Journal of Semitic Studies* 4 (1959): 109–26.

——. *The Text of the Epistles: A Disquisition upon the* Corpus Paulinum. Schweich Lectures, 1946. London: British Academy Press, 1953.

Subject Index

Index of Modern Authors

Delcor, M., 160
Deniston, J. D., 443
Denney, J., 561
Deubner, L., 450
Devreesse, Robert, 477–78, 480–81
Di Lella, Alexander A., 129
Diestel, L., 239
Dillmann, A., 106–7
Dimant, D., 139–41
Dirksen, Peter B., 137
Dobbin, Orlando T., 483
Donelson, L. R., 441, 444–46, 448–50, 458, 464–65
Donovan, Mary Ann, 315
Dorival, M. Harl, 137
Douglas, Mary, 183
Driver, S. R., 236, 238
DuBois, J.-D., 292
Duff, Jeremy, 285, 497–502
Dungan, David L., 301
Dunn, James D. G., 3, 17, 262, 429, 558–59, 562, 564–65, 567–68, 570–71, 576, 578
Durand, J.-M., 39

Easton, B. S., 454
Ebeling, Gerhard, 544
Edwards, M. J., 365
Ehrman, B. D., 274–75, 281, 291
Eichhorn, J. G., 30
Eichrodt, Walther, 23
Eissfeldt, Otto, 79, 131, 149, 236–37, 252
Elliott, J. Keith, 274, 294, 469–71, 473–74, 476, 511
Ellis, E. E., 111, 114, 141, 166, 171, 440, 445, 447–48, 459, 461, 464
Elze, Martin, 400
Eno, Robert B., 304–5
Epp, Eldon J., 231–32, 247–48, 253, 274, 281–82, 469, 485, 491, 495, 510–13, 515
Erbes, C., 408
Eustratiades, Sophronios, 472, 478, 481, 483–84
Evans, C. F., 111, 114, 116, 121
Evans, Craig A., 6, 193–94, 257, 293, 365, 441–42, 453
Evans, E., 341
Ewert, David, 428
Eybers, I. H., 87, 152
Eynde, Damien van den, 304

Fabricius, J., 212
Fabry, H.-J., 135, 236
Fallon, Francis T., 370
Farkasfalvy, Denis M., 304, 307, 317, 321, 378, 407, 444

Farley, Edward, 418
Farmer, William Reuben, 202, 304, 317, 321, 324, 331–33, 407, 430
Farrer, J. A., 442
Feldman, Louis H., 110–11, 117–19, 121–23, 127
Fenton, J. C., 443
Ferguson, Everett, 232, 254, 269, 270, 297–98, 307–8, 388, 407, 409–10, 412
Feron, Ernesto, 482
Fichtner, J., 141
Filson, Floyd V., 491–92
Fishbane, Michael, 52, 139, 535
Fitzmyer, Joseph A., 83–85, 90, 141, 186, 201
Flesseman-Van Leer, Ellen, 345, 393
Flint, Peter W., 108, 134–35, 144, 185, 187, 191, 253, 259–60
Fohrer, G., 151
Folkert, K. W., 271, 275
Foster, Lewis, 300
Fox, Michael V., 47
France, R. T., 185, 191
Franchi de' Cavalieri, P. , 480
Frankfurter, D., 228
Franxman, T. W., 110, 118
Frede, Hermann Josef, 283–85, 506
Freedman, David N., 135, 238
Freudenthal, Jacob, 83
Friedman, S., 157
Fritsch, C. T., 149
Fuller, R., 136
Funk, Robert W., 3, 11, 321, 330, 333, 425, 541, 560, 567
Furnish, V. P., 517

Gadamer, Hans-Georg, 574
Gager, John, 114
Gallazzi, Claudio, 496
Gamble, Harry Y., 231, 233, 267, 270–71, 274, 282–83, 286, 292, 294, 300–301, 312, 317, 356–59, 361, 388, 407, 465–66, 486, 491, 495, 505, 510–11, 513
García Martínez, F., 101, 130–31
Gardthhausen, V., 470, 482–83
Gaster, Moses, 76
Gaster, Theodor H., 86
Geertz, Clifford, 183
Geffcken, J., 523
Gempf, C., 440
Ginzberg, H. L., 86, 90
Gnuse, Robert, 387–88
Godu, G., 524
Goguel, M., 518
Golb, Norman, 87, 89

Jaffee, Martin, 299
Jahn, G., 239
Janowski, B., 134
Jastram, N., 97
Jaubert, Annie, 522
Jellicoe, Sidney, 69–78, 80–81
Jeremias, Joachim, 5, 116
Jervell, J., 521
Johnson, Luke Timothy, 553
Jones, W. H. S., 451
Jülicher, A., 459
Junack, K., 491

Kaestli, J. D., 270, 519, 524
Kahle, Paul E., 75–79, 81, 159, 255
Kähler, Martin, 575
Kalin, Everett R., 270, 319, 383, 386–87, 390, 400, 436–37
Kanter, Shamai, 158
Käsemann, Ernst, 3, 387, 429, 560, 563–64, 570
Katz, Peter, 73, 79, 81, 89, 142, 232, 408
Kautzsch, Emil, 69
Kelsey, David H., 418
Kenyon, Frederic G., 303, 497, 500, 505
Kiley, M., 449–52, 456, 459–60
Kim, Kyung-Rae, 245
Kim, Y. K., 284
Kinzig, Wolfram, 292, 307–9
Klijn, Albertus F. J., 76–78, 270, 292, 492
Kloppenborg, John S., 362
Knox, D., 450
Knox, John, 309, 342, 344, 346
Knox, W. L., 140
Koch, D. A., 141
Koch, K., 58, 440
Koester, Helmut, 74, 270, 274–76, 279, 281, 302, 304, 322, 346, 378, 431, 486, 502, 509, 559, 566
Kohler, W.-D., 278–79
Kooij, A. van der, 129, 131, 162, 246, 275
Körtner, U. H. J., 278, 523
Kraft, Robert A., 70–71, 83, 228–30, 233
Krämer, H., 116, 118
Kratz, R. G., 134
Kraus, H. J., 237
Krauss, S., 148
Krentz, Peter, 390
Kresten, O., 481
Krüger, G., 524
Kuck, D. W., 288
Kugler, Robert A., 58, 62
Kuhn, K. G., 451
Kümmel, Werner Georg, 14, 407, 458, 466, 561
Küng, H., 559
Kurtzinger, J., 278

Lack, R., 66
Lagarde, P. A. de, 77, 255
Lagrange, M.-J., 526
Laing, J., 442
Lake, Kirsopp, 71, 83, 402, 457, 477, 481, 508
Lambert, W. G., 60
Lambros, Spyridon P., 472, 477, 480–83
Lampe, G. W. H., 12
Lane, William L., 428
Lange, A., 250
Laqueur, Richard, 124
Lawlor, H. J., 71, 228
Layton, Bentley, 418
Lea, T. D., 446–47, 449, 455, 458–59, 461
Le Boulluec, Alain, 357
Lebram, J. C. H., 239
Leclercq, H., 524
Leiman, Sid Z., 31, 81, 111, 114, 123, 152–53, 157, 166, 174, 176–77, 179–80, 253–54
Leipoldt, Johannes, 393
Lemaire, André, 38
Lemche, N. P., 144
Levenson, Jon D., 533
Lévi, I., 192
Levine, B. A., 238
Levita, Elias, 146, 242
Lewis, Jack P., 91, 151–53, 159, 203, 252–54
Lewis, T., 78
Lichtenberger, H., 250
Liebreich, L. J., 66
Lietzmann, Hans, 267, 319
Lieu, J., 287
Lifshitz, B., 89–90
Lightfoot, J. B., 494
Lightstone, Jack N., 153, 166, 170, 172–73, 177
Lincoln, A. T., 459
Lindemann, A., 282, 287
Lindner, Helgo, 124
Logan, Alastair H. B., 362
Lohfink, Norbert F., 56
Lohr, W. A., 279, 293
Lohse, Edward, 68, 70
Lönning, I., 560, 564
Lovering, E. H., 282, 286
Lücke, G. C. F., 394–95
Luckmann, Thomas, 182
Lüdemann, G., 270, 292, 560
Luhrmann, D., 288
Luther, Martin, 561
Luttikhuizen, Gerard P., 370
Lyell, James P. R., 475

MacRae, George W., 430
Mahaffy, John P., 74, 79

Index of Ancient and Medieval Sources

4. PSEUDEPIGRAPHA OF THE OLD TESTAMENT